process, any event on the timeline could be placed in more than one category. Some scholars claim that globalization has been happening for a long time, and others say it has only been happening for a relatively short time. As you read through this timeline, think about how current events happening in your social world are part of this larger process of global change.

1989 Fall of the Berlin Wall
1991 End of the USSR

1940–1945 WWII
1932 Saudi Arabia is established
1973 Oil crisis follows the 1973 Yom Kippur War

1945
Start of
the Cold War
1954 Racial segregation in U.S. schools outlawed by Supreme Court
1992 Creation of the European Union (EU)
1993 UN establishes High Commissioner for Human Rights

1919
League of Nations
established
1961
Soviet cosmonaut Yuri Gagarin is the first human to orbit the earth
1997 UK returns Hong Kong to China
2000 Supreme Court decides U.S. presidential election

Early 1930s
Great
Depression
1995 Foundation of the World Trade Organization (WTO)
1996 NATO forces deployed to the former Yugoslavia

1947
General Agreement on Tariffs and Trade (GATT) signed
1987
Stock market crash
Rapid growth of Chinese and Indian economies

1960 Creation of the Organization of the Petroleum Exporting Countries (OPEC)
2005
Chinese bid for Unocal

1929
Discovery of penicillin
1961
First live televised political news conference (John F. Kennedy) broadcasts
1976 First direct broadcast satellite
1977 First commercial use of fiber-optic cables

1930
World's population reaches 2 billion
1955
First McDonald's restaurant opens
1973 First mobile phone
2005
Pope John Paul II dies

1969 World's first global media event: U.S. astronauts land on the moon

1950
World's urban population reaches 30%
1971 Invention of the microchip by Intel
1969 Construction of the Concorde

1901 Nobel Prizes established
1966 Anti-Vietnam War protests
1997 Bird flu in humans
2002
Severe acute respiratory syndrome (SARS) is recognized
2005–2006
Danish cartoons of Mohammed spark fury

1962 Concept of the "Galactic Network"
1999 Seattle Anti-Globalization Movement

1918 Spanish flu kills between 20 and 40 million people
1960 Marshall McLuhan coins the term "global village"

1945
First atomic bombs dropped on Hiroshima and Nagasaki
1961 Bay of Pigs invasion
1962 First communications satellite launched
1957 Advent of the intercontinental ballistic missile
2005
London Transport bombings

1962 Cuban Missile Crisis
1998
India and Pakistan test nuclear weapons
2003
Iraq War

1954–1975
Second Indochina War, the Vietnam War
2006
Iran demands right to develop nuclear power

1967
World Health Organization (WHO) launches global smallpox eradication program
1986 Chernobyl nuclear accident
1980 HIV/AIDS identified in the United States

1944–1947
Bretton Woods and foundation of the United Nations, International Monetary Fund, and the World Bank
2004
Colin Powell declares genocide in Sudan

1949
North Atlantic Treaty Organization (NATO)
2001
September 11
Attack on the World Trade Center and launch of the War on Terror
2006
North Korea tests a nuclear weapon

1950–1953
Korean War
1967 Six Day War

1942–1946 Manhattan Project, the development of a nuclear bomb and the U.S. Atomic Energy Commission
2000 Human Genome Project completed

1946
First digital computer
1969 First Boeing 747
1996 First sucessful cloning of a mammal, Dolly the Sheep

1969 ARPANET, precursor to the Internet
1999 First hybrid car in United States

1942 Invention of the computer
1979 Three Mile Island nuclear power accident

1927 Development of the television
1973 Global positioning system (GPS)

1934–1937
Dust Bowl in the United States
1971
Greenpeace is founded
1987 Hole in the ozone layer is discovered

1972
Publication of *The Limits to Growth* for the Club of Rome
1979 1st World Climate Conference of the World Meteorological Organization
2004 Asian tsunami

1972
First UN Global Conference on the Environment
1992 Earth Summit in Rio de Janeiro
2005
Hurricane Katrina devastates Gulf Coast

1962
Rachel Carson writes *Silent Spring*, which helps start the environmental movement
1970 First Earth Day
1997 Kyoto Protocol to the UN

| 1950 | 1960 | 1970 | 1980 | 1990 | 2000 | 2001 | 2002 | 2003 | 2004 | 2005 | 2006 |

MODERN ERA

OUR SOCIAL WORLD
Introduction to Sociology

Jeanne H. Ballantine
Keith A. Roberts

Finally, here is a text that engages students. **Our Social World** develops sociological skills of analysis rather than emphasizing memorization of vocabulary. Key concepts and terms are introduced, but only in the service of a larger focus on the sociological imagination. The text is both personal and global; it speaks to sociology as a science as well as its applications; it has a theme that lends the course integration as it introduces the discipline. Unlike most introductory textbooks, **Our Social World** is a coherent analytical essay, not a disconnected encyclopedia.

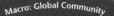

Macro: Global Community

Macro: National Society

Meso: National Institutions and Organizations; Subcultures and Minority Groups

Micro: Local Organizations and Community

Micro: You and Your Family

Micro: Local reference groups; deliberate exclusion of ethnic group members

Meso: Laws that intentionally or unintentionally discriminate; educational-testing biases

Macro: Laws or court rulings that set policy for state and local levels

Macro: Racial and ethnic hostilities at the national and global levels result in wars, genocide, or ethnic cleansing

Introduces the "Social World Model"

The model illustrates both the level of analysis of each topic, moving from micro to meso and from meso to macro, and how each topic is related. Each chapter is organized around this simple and effective model of the social world.

Incorporates a *Global Perspective*: Students are Citizens of the World

Our Social World is unique because the global perspective is woven into every part of the book and asks students to consider themselves citizens of the world, not just North Americans who look out at the world.

Encourages an *Active Engagement in Sociology*

In the "Contributing to Your Social World" feature, the authors suggest work and volunteer jobs where students can apply their sociological knowledge right away. In the "The Applied Sociologist at Work" feature, students are introduced to people who have built their careers in sociology and to what they can do with sociological knowledge using their own sociological imagination.

CONTRIBUTING TO YOUR SOCIAL WORLD

At the Local Level: *Big Brothers Big Sisters* helps a child with few resources and little cultural capital get a broader picture of society. By becoming a mentor, you could provide advice, support, and know-how to help develop skills that could make for success.

Commission on human relations: Most communities have organization(s) working for positive ethnic relations. Contact them to ask how you can become involved.

At the Organizational or Institutional Level: *Teaching Tolerance* (www.splcenter.org/center/tt/teach.jsp) is a program of the Southern Poverty Law Center that has curriculum materials for teaching about diversity and a program for enhancing cross-ethnic cooperation and dialogue in schools. Consider using their ideas and materials to enhance ethnic relations on a campus.

AmeriCorps (www.americorps.org) is a network of national service programs involving over 70,000 people in education, public safety, health, the environment. . . . Members are selected by and serve with local and national organizations such as Habitat for Humanity, the American Red Cross, and Big Brothers Big Sisters.

At the National and Global Levels: *Free the Slaves* (http://www.freetheslaves.net) fights slavery worldwide by helping people to freedom and helps to abolish slavery around the world.

Sociologists without Borders (http://www.sociologistswithoutborders.org) promotes human rights globally. Advocates that sociologists participate, democratically, with others to set standards for human well-being and devote energies to understanding how to achieve these standards.

Amnesty International (www.amnestyusa.org or www.amnesty.org) is a worldwide movement of people who campaign for internationally recognized human rights.

Kids with Cameras (www.kids-with-cameras.org) can be successful in fulfilling its mission of empowering children through the art of photography only when people are involved and excited about the work! Assist Kids with Cameras gain momentum and strength; donate, volunteer, buy a print, email the kids, and join the email list.

THE APPLIED SOCIOLOGIST AT WORK

[Re]ducing Racism in a Racial Tinderbox

[In] April 2001, Cincinnati, Ohio, received national and [int]ernational attention as the shooting death of an [un]armed black teenager by a white city police officer [spa]rked three days of civil unrest, during which pre[do]minantly African American crowds broke windows, [lo]oted stores, and challenged police practices. Rachel [ex]plains her role:

My community work in Cincinnati began several [m]onths after the unrest, when as a fresh college graduate [I] joined an AmeriCorps program called Public Allies in [or]der to apply my undergraduate sociology degree to [c]ommunity development. Although almost six months [h]ad passed, the issue of race relations within the [C]incinnati community still touched upon fresh wounds [a]nd unanswered questions. My work with the National [C]onference for Community and Justice (NCCJ) con[n]ected me with students and adults seeking racial healing [i]n their communities, and I spent much of my time facil[it]ating interracial dialogues and coordinating high school [p]rograms on topics such as stereotyping, social justice, and local and international human relations.

My sociological background provided me with a conceptual foundation as I engaged participants in exploring the complex dynamics of inequality and power. I utilized the sociological imagination in challenging misconceptions of white students with limited experience outside of suburbia, who stated, "Racism doesn't really exist anymore." My understanding of micro, meso, and macro facets of power and privilege enabled me to address the hidden dimensions of contemporary racism and to illustrate the powerful role that poverty played in fueling April's "race riots."

As I worked with community members, I soon realized that my greatest contribution toward racial healing was in acting as an ally and activist within the white

[chal]lenges to . . . discrimination and prej[udice] . . . obstacles to justice and equity reflect pa[tterns] within the white community—denial that racism and inequalities persist, denial of white privilege, and denial that the Civil Rights laws only partially addressed the legacies of slavery. Sociology teaches me to explore the roots of this denial and to view the world through a theoretical lens. As a white individual I have incredible influence within my own community when I move beyond my own privilege and share with others the tools for understanding social dynamics. As a student of sociology I explored the systems—at various levels—behind poverty and racism. Racism is much larger than prejudice and discrimination—it is manifest in systems of segregation, poverty, and institutionalized inequality and disadvantage compounded over generations.

In Cincinnati, the April 2001 unrest prompted dozens of community efforts, including dialogue series, ballot initiatives on police profiling, prejudice-reduction programs, and changes in city governance. However, in a town where whites consider themselves free from blame if they do not wear KKK robes, efforts that do not address power dynamics and historical discriminatory practices fail to truly tackle the underlying issues. Combining this sociological knowledge with my passion for justice within my hometown allowed me to dive deeper into the complexities of racism, white privilege, and civil unrest to fight for change at several levels of the social system.

Rachel Ernst graduated in 2001 from Hanover College in Indiana with a Bachelor of Arts degree in Sociology. She has now enrolled in a doctoral program in Sociology at Indiana University.

Develops and Promotes *Critical Thinking and Deep Learning*

"Thinking Sociologically" activities and "So What" summary sections encourage students to think critically and reflect on why the material is relevant, important, and applicable to their own lives.

THINKING SOCIOLOGICALLY

Should colleges consider an applicant's state of origin, urban or rural background, ethnicity, musical or athletic ability, alumni parent, or other factors in admitting students if it helps the college achieve its goals? Should men with lower scores be admitted because the college wants to have balanced gender enrollment? Is ethnic diversity so important to in-and-out-of-classroom learning to be considered an admissions criterion? Why or why not?

SO WHAT?

Why are minority group members in most countries poorer than dominant group members? This and other chapter opening questions can be answered in part by considering individual causes of prejudice and racism; physical and cultural differences that distinguish groups of people; and the fact that human beings have a tendency to create "we" and "they" categories and to treat those who are different as somehow less human. The categories can be based on physical appearance, cultural differences, religious differences, or anything the community or society defines as

important. Once people notice differenc[es] . . . inclined to hurt "them" or to harbor adv[antage] . . . there is competition over resources that b[. . .] Even within a nation, where people are su[. . .] there can be sharp differences and intense [. . .]

Indeed, "we" and "they" thinking can i[nfect] most intimate settings. Inequality is not limited to social classes, race or ethnic groups, or religious communities; it can infect relations between human males and females in everything from the home to the boardroom and from the governance of nations to the decisions of global agencies. More on this in the next chapter: "Gender Stratification."

Ancillaries

Instructor's Resource Manual (on CD-ROM)

The manual contains a number of helpful teaching aids, from goals and objectives for chapters to classroom lecture ideas, active learning projects, collaborative learning suggestions, and options for evaluating students. Suggestions for the use of visual materials—videos, transparencies, and multimedia—are also included. A listing of helpful Internet sources on teaching, including American Sociological Association Teaching Resources Center publications, is part of the manual.

Test Bank

The computerized test bank (compatible with both PC and Mac computers) allows for easy question sorting and exam creation. Available in both Microsoft Word and as a computerized program, the test bank includes multiple choice, short answer, and essay/discussion questions with the page number(s) or section of the book from which the question is taken. In keeping with the deep learning thrust of this book, however, the test questions will have more emphasis on application skills rather than rote memorization questions—the latter a too-common characteristic of test banks.

 PINE FORGE PRESS
An Imprint of Sage Publications, Inc.
Thousand Oaks • London • New Delhi

PowerPoint® Slides

Because visuals are an important addition to class lectures, and recognizing the varying learning styles of students, PowerPoint® slides that include lecture outlines and relevant tables, maps, diagrams, photos, and short quotes are included on the Instructor's Resource Manual CD-ROM for instructors to use in the classroom.

Companion Study Site

To further enhance students' understanding of and interest in the material, we have created a student website to accompany the text. This website will include the following:

- An additional chapter on institutions for those wanting to cover politics—Political Systems: Penetrating Power;

- Flash cards that allow for easy reviewing of key terms and concepts;

- Self-quizzes that can be used to check their understanding of the material or can be sent in to the professor for a grade;

- Web exercises that direct students to various sites on the Web and ask them to apply their knowledge to a particular topic;

- NPR's *This American Life* radio segments that illustrate each chapter's concepts;

- *Learning from Journal Articles* includes original research from SAGE journal articles, and teaches students how to read and analyze a journal article;

- A list of recommended websites that students can explore for research or their own edification; and

- Information on how to create photo essays.

About the Authors

Jeanne H. Ballantine (bottom center) is Professor of Sociology at Wright State University, a state university of about 17,000 students in Ohio.
She has also taught at several four-year colleges, including an "alternative" college and a traditionally black college. Jeanne has been teaching introductory sociology for over 30 years with a mission to introduce the "uninitiated" to the field and to help students see the usefulness and value in sociology. Jeanne has been active in the teaching movement, shaping curriculum, writing and presenting research on teaching, and offering workshops and consulting in regional, national, and international forums. She is a Fulbright Senior Scholar and serves as a Departmental Resources Group consultant and evaluator.

Jeanne has written several textbooks, all with the goal of reaching the student audience. As the original director of the Center for Teaching and Learning at Wright State University, she scoured the literature on student learning and served as a mentor to teachers in a wide variety of disciplines. She has been honored for her teaching and for her contributions to helping others become effective teachers by local, regional, and national organizations. In 1986, the American Sociological Association's Section on Undergraduate Education (now called the Section on Teaching and Learning) recognized her with the Hans O. Mauksch Award for Distinguished Contributions to Teaching of Sociology. In 2004, she was recognized for her contributions with the ASA Distinguished Contributions to Teaching Award.

Keith A. Roberts (center) is Professor of Sociology at Hanover College, a private liberal arts college of about 1,100 students in Indiana.
He has been teaching introductory sociology for over 30 years with a passion for active learning strategies and a focus on "deep learning" by students that transforms the way students see the world. Prior to teaching at Hanover, he taught at a two-year regional campus of a large university. Between them, these authors have taught many types of students at different types of schools.

Keith has been active in the teaching movement, writing on teaching and serving as a consultant to sociology departments across the country in his capacity as a member of the ASA Departmental Resources Group. He has written a very popular textbook in the sociology of religion, has co-authored a book on writing in the undergraduate curriculum, and annually runs workshops for high school sociology teachers. He has been honored for his teaching and teaching-related work at local, state, regional, and national levels. The American Sociological Association's Section on Teaching and Learning awarded him the Hans O. Mauksch Award for Distinguished Contributions to Teaching of Sociology in 2000.

2004 AMERICAN SOCIOLOGICAL ASSOCIATION

DISTINGUISHED CONTRIBUTIONS TO TEACHING AWARD

2000 AMERICAN SOCIOLOGICAL ASSOCIATION
Teaching and Learning Section:

HANS O. MAUKSCH AWARD FOR DISTINGUISHED CONTRIBUTIONS TO TEACHING SOCIOLOGY

OUR SOCIAL WORLD
Introduction to Sociology

Jeanne H. Ballantine
Wright State University

Keith A. Roberts
Hanover College

PINE FORGE PRESS
An Imprint of Sage Publications, Inc.
Thousand Oaks • London • New Delhi

For information:

Pine Forge Press
An imprint of Sage Publications, Inc.
2455 Teller Road
Thousand Oaks, California 91320
E-mail: order@sagepub.com

Sage Publications Ltd.
1 Oliver's Yard
55 City Road
London EC1Y 1SP
United Kingdom

Sage Publications India Pvt. Ltd.
B-42, Panchsheel Enclave
Post Box 4109
New Delhi 110 017 India

Printed in Canada

Library of Congress Cataloging-in-Publication Data

Ballantine, Jeanne H.
Our social world : introduction to sociology / Jeanne H. Ballantine, Keith A. Roberts.
    p. cm.
Includes bibliographical references and index.
ISBN 1-4129-3706-X or 978-1-4129-3706-1 (pbk.)
   1. Sociology. 2. Sociology—Cross-cultural studies. I. Roberts, Keith A. II. Title.
HM586.B35 2007
301—dc22

2006033727

07 08 09 10 11   10 9 8 7 6 5 4 3 2

Acquiring Editor:	Benjamin Penner
Editorial Assistant:	Camille Herrera
Associate Editor:	Deya Saoud
Production Editor:	Sanford Robinson
Copy Editor:	Ani L. Ayvazian
Proofreaders:	Jennifer Su-Lan Ang, Carole Quandt
Typesetter:	C&M Digitals (P) Ltd.
Indexer:	Kathy Paparchontis
Cover Designer:	Ravi Balasuriya
Photo Research:	Karen Wiley

DETAILED CONTENTS

Chapter 6 • Deviance and Social Control: Sickos, Perverts, Freaks, and Folks Like Us 154

PART III: Inequality 189

Chapter 7 • Stratification: Rich and Famous—or Rags and Famine? 190

Chapter 11 • Education:
What Are We Learning? 322

Additional "Institutions" chapter is available on the website. Go to:

www.pineforge.com/ballantinestudy

Chapter P • Political Systems: Penetrating Power

*Writing this book has been a labor of love for we are
both passionate about sociology and about teaching sociology.
Still, this labor of love has sometimes come at a steep price to others we love.
Thus, we dedicate this book to two saints of patience, support, and understanding,*

Hardy Ballantine

and

Judy Roberts,

our supportive and beloved spouses,

*and to our children who have shared their
educational trials and triumphs, giving us food for thought as we wrote.*

To Our Readers

This book asks you to think "outside the box." Why? Because the best way to become a more interesting person; to grow beyond the old familiar scenes, thoughts, and behaviors; and to make life exciting is to think about exciting things and new ideas. The world in which we live is intensely personal and individual in nature, with much of our social interaction occurring in intimate groups of friends and family. Our most intense emotions and most meaningful links to others are at this "micro" level of social life.

However, our lives are also influenced by larger social structures and global trends. At the beginning of the twenty-first century, technological advances make it possible to connect with the farthest corners of the world. Multinational corporations cross national boundaries, form new economic and political unions, and change job opportunities of people everywhere. Some groups embrace the changes, while others try to protect their members from the rapid changes that threaten to disrupt their traditional lives. Even our most personal relationships are shaped by events on the other side of the continent or the globe. From the news headlines to family and peer interactions, we confront sociological issues daily. The task of this book and of your instructor is to help you see world events and your personal lives from a sociological perspective. Unless you learn how to look at our social world with an analytical lens, many of its most intriguing features will be missed.

The social world you face in the job markets of the twenty-first century is influenced by changes and forces that are easy to miss. Like the wind that can do damage even if the air is unseen, social structures have effects that can be readily identified; but those structures are themselves so taken for granted that it is easy to miss seeing them. No wonder increasing numbers of undergraduate students are taking introductory sociology classes each year, courses that provide a framework for understanding the social environment that shapes our lives. Sociology provides new perspectives, helping students to understand their families, their work lives, their leisure, and their place in a diverse and changing world.

A few of you will probably become sociology majors. Others of you will find the subject matter of this course relevant to your personal and professional lives. Some of the reasons the authors of this book and your own professor chose to study sociology many years ago are the factors that inspire undergraduates today to choose a major in sociology: learning about the social world from a new perspective; working with people and groups; developing knowledge, inquiry, and interpersonal skills; and learning the broad and interesting subject matter of sociology, from small groups to global social systems. As the broadest of the social sciences, sociology has a never-ending array of fascinating subject matters to study. This book only touches the surface of what the field has to offer and the exciting things you can do with this knowledge. These same considerations motivated us and gave us direction in writing this introductory book.

WHERE THIS BOOK IS HEADED

Like an effective essay, a well-constructed course needs to be organized around a central question, one that spawns other subsidiary questions and intrigues the participants. The problem with introductory courses in many disciplines is that there is no central question and thus no coherence to the course. They have more of a flavor-of-the-week approach (a different topic each week), with no attempt at integration. We have tried to correct that problem in this text.

The Social World Model

For you to understand sociology as an integrated whole rather than a set of separate chapters in a book, we have organized the chapters in this book around the *social world model:* a conceptual model that demonstrates the relationships between individuals (micro level), groups and organizations (meso level), and societies (macro levels of analysis). At the beginning of each chapter, a visual diagram of the model will illustrate this idea as it relates to the topic of that chapter, including how issues related to the topic have implications at various levels of analysis in the social world. For example, the family chapter is pictured as a part of the whole social world, interrelating to other parts of society. No part exists in a vacuum. On the other hand, this model does not assume that everyone always gets along or that relationships are always harmonious or supportive. Sometimes, different parts of the society are in competition for resources, and intense conflict and hostility may be generated.

This micro- to macro-level analysis is a central concept in the discipline of sociology. Many instructors seek first and foremost to help students develop a *sociological imagination*, an ability to see the complex links between various levels of the social system; this is a key goal of your book. Within a few months, you may not remember all of the specific concepts or terms that have been introduced, but if the way you see the world has been transformed during this course, a key element of deep learning has been accomplished. Learning to see things from alternative perspectives is a precondition for critical thinking. This entire book attempts to help you recognize connections between your personal experiences and problems and larger social forces of society. You will be learning to take a new perspective on the social world in which you live.

A key element of that social world is diversity. We live in societies in which there are people who differ in a host of ways: ethnicity, socioeconomic status, religious background, political persuasion, gender, sexual orientation, and so forth. Diversity is a blessing in many ways to a society because the most productive and creative organizations and societies are those that are highly diverse. Why? People with different backgrounds solve problems in very different ways. When people with such divergences come together, it can create new solutions to vexing problems. However, diversity often creates challenges as well; misunderstanding and "we" versus "they" thinking can divide people. These issues will be explored throughout this book. We now live in a global village, and in this book, you will learn something about how people on the other side of the village live and view the world.

We hope you enjoy the book and get as enthralled with sociology as we are. It genuinely is a fascinating field of study.

Jeanne H. Ballantine *Keith A. Roberts*
Wright State University *Hanover College*

Special features woven throughout each chapter support the theme of the book. These will help students comprehend and apply the material and make the material more understandable and interesting. These features are also designed to facilitate deep learning, to help students move beyond rote memorization and increase their ability to analyze and evaluate information.

"WHAT TO EXPECT . . ." AND "THINK ABOUT IT . . ."

So that students know what to expect in each chapter, an outline of major topics provides an overview of the chapter contents. In addition, questions that we hope are relevant to everyday life are posed at the outset of each chapter. The purpose is to transform students from passive readers who run their eyes across the words into curious active readers who read to answer a question and to be reflective. Active reading is key to comprehension and retention of reading material. Instructors can also use this feature to encourage students to think critically about the implications of what they have read. Instructors might want to ask students to write a paragraph about one of these questions before coming to class each day. These questions might also provide the basis for in-class discussions.

Students should be encouraged to start each chapter by reading and thinking about these questions, looking at the "What to Expect . . ." topics, and asking some questions of their own. This will mean they are more likely to stay focused, remember the material long-term, and be able to apply it to their own lives.

A GLOBAL PERSPECTIVE AND THE SOCIAL WORLD MODEL

We are part of an ever-shrinking world, a global village. What happens in distant countries is not only news the same day but also affects relatives living in other countries, the cost of goods, work and travel possibilities, and the balance of power in the world. Instead of simply including cross-cultural examples of strange and different peoples, this book incorporates a global perspective throughout, both so students can see how others live different but rewarding lives and also see the connections between others' lives and their own. Students will need to think and relate to the world globally in future roles as workers, travelers, and global citizens. Our analysis illustrates the interconnections of the world's societies and their political and economic systems and demonstrates that what happens in one part of the world affects others. For instance, if a major company in the area moves much of its operations to another country with cheaper labor, jobs are lost and the local economy is hurt.

This approach attempts to instill interest, understanding, and respect for different groups of people and their lifestyles. Race, class, and gender are an integral part of understanding the diverse social world, and these features of social life have global implications. The comparative global theme is carried throughout the book in headings and written text, in examples, and in boxes and selection of photos. As students read this book, they should continually think about how the experiences in their private world are influenced by and may influence events at other levels: the community, organizations, the nation, and the world.

For students to understand both the comparative global theme and sociology as an integrated whole rather than a set of separate chapters in a book, we have organized the chapters in this book around the *social world model:* a conceptual model that demonstrates the relationships between individuals (micro level), groups and organizations (meso level), and societies (macro levels of analysis). At the beginning of each chapter, a visual diagram of the model will illustrate this idea as it relates to the topic of that chapter, including how issues related to the topic have implications at various levels of analysis in the social world.

OPENING VIGNETTES

Chapters typically open with an illustration relevant to the chapter content. For instance, in Chapter 2, "Examining the Social World," the case of Hector, a Brazilian teenager living in poverty in a *favela*, is used to illustrate research methods and theory throughout the chapter. Chapter 3, Culture and Society," begins with scenarios of mealtime scenes from around the world to illustrate the variations in human cultures. In Chapter 4, "Socialization," the case of an immigrant child attending school in his new society and facing a new learning environment is discussed. These vignettes are meant to interest the student in the upcoming subject matter by helping them relate to a personalized story; in several cases, they serve as illustrations throughout the chapters.

"THINKING SOCIOLOGICALLY" QUESTIONS

Following major topics, students will find questions that ask them to think critically and apply the material just read to some aspect of their lives or the social world. The purpose of this feature is to encourage students to actually use the material by applying the ideas and concepts to their lives. These questions can be the basis for in-class discussions and can be assigned as questions to start interesting conversations with friends and families to learn how the topics relate to their own lives.

KEY CONCEPTS, EXAMPLES, AND WRITING STYLE

Key terms that are defined and illustrated within the running narrative appear in bold. Other terms that are defined but are of less significance are italicized. The text is rich in examples that bring sociological concepts to life for student readers. Each chapter has been student tested for readability. Both students and reviewers describe the writing style as reader friendly, interesting, and accessible, but not watered down.

BOXES

Although there are numerous examples throughout the book, boxed inserts provide more in-depth illustrations of the usefulness of the sociological perspective to understand world situations or events with direct relevance to a student's life. There are four kinds of boxed material. "Sociology in Your Social World" boxes focus on a sociological issue or story, often with policy implications. In "Sociology around the World" boxes, we vicariously take readers to another part of the globe to explore how things are different (or how they are the same) from what they might experience in their own lives. "The Applied Sociologist at Work" boxes feature profiles of contemporary sociologists who are working in the field so that students can learn what sociologists actually study and do. "How Do We Know?" boxes describe well-known sociological studies and are included to help students learn how sociologists know what they know. These summaries are a way to reinforce the point that sociology is a social science rooted in empirical methods of gathering data and testing theories.

TECHNOLOGY AND SOCIETY

Nearly every chapter examines issues of technology as they would be relevant to that chapter. We have especially sought out materials that have to do with the Internet and with communications technology.

SOCIAL POLICY AND BECOMING AN ACTIVE CITIZEN

Most chapters include discussion of some social policy issues: an effort to address the concerns about public sociology and the relevance of sociological findings to current social debates. Finally, because students sometimes feel helpless to know what to do about social issues that concern them at macro and meso levels, we have concluded each chapter with a few ideas about how they might become involved as active citizens, even as undergraduate students. Suggestions in the "Contributing to Your Social World" section may be assigned as service learning or term projects or simply used as suggestions for ways students can get involved on their own time.

A LITTLE (TEACHING) HELP FROM OUR FRIENDS

Whether the instructor is new to teaching or an experienced professor, there are some valuable ideas that can help invigorate and energize the classroom. A substantial literature on teaching methodology tells us that student involvement is key to the learning process. Built into this book are discussion questions and projects that students can report on in class. In addition, there are a number of suggestions in the supplements and teaching aids for active learning in large or small classes.

THE INSTRUCTOR'S RESOURCE MANUAL (ON CD-ROM)

The manual contains a number of helpful teaching aids, from goals and objectives for chapters to classroom lecture ideas, active learning projects, collaborative learning suggestions, and options for evaluating students. Suggestions for the use of visual materials—videos, transparencies, and multimedia—are also included. A listing of helpful sources on teaching, including American Sociological Association Teaching Resources Center publications, is part of the manual.

TEST BANKS

Available in both Microsoft Word and as a computerized program, test banks include multiple-choice, short answer, and essay-discussion questions with the page number(s) or section of the book from which the question is taken. In keeping with the deep learning thrust of this book, however, the test questions will have more emphasis on application skills rather than rote memorization questions—the latter a too-common characteristic of test banks.

The computerized test bank (compatible with both PC and Mac computers) allows for easy question sorting and exam creation.

POWERPOINT® SLIDES

Because visuals are an important addition to classroom lectures, recognizing the varying learning styles of students, PowerPoint® slides that include lecture outlines and relevant tables, maps, diagrams, pictures, and short quotes are included in the Instructor's Resource Manual CD-ROM for instructors to use in the classroom.

COMPANION STUDY SITE

To further enhance students' understanding of and interest in the material, we have created a student website to accompany the text. This website will include the following:

- **An additional chapter** on institutions for those wanting to cover politics—Political Systems: Penetrating Power;
- **Flash cards** that allow for easy reviewing of key terms and concepts;
- **Self-quizzes** that can be used to check their understanding of the material or can be sent in to the professor for a grade;
- **Web exercises** that direct students to various sites on the Web and ask them to apply their knowledge to a particular topic;
- *This American Life* radio segments that illustrate each chapter's concepts;
- *Learning from Journal Articles* that include original research from SAGE journal articles and teaches students how to read and analyze a journal article;
- A list of **recommend websites** that students can explore for research or their own edification;
- Information on how to create **video and photo essays**;
- And much more!

Visit www/pineforge.com/ballantinestudy to view the site.

We probably share many of the same reasons for choosing sociology as our careers. Our students also share these reasons for finding sociology a fascinating and useful subject: learning about the social world from a new perspective; working with people and groups; developing a range of knowledge, inquiry, and interpersonal skills; and learning the broad and interesting subject matter of sociology, from small groups to societies. In this book, we hope to share that enthusiasm for the subject with students. The following explains what we believe to be unique features of this book and some of our goals and methods for sharing sociology. We hope you share our ideas and find this book helps you meet your teaching and learning goals.

WHAT IS DISTINCTIVE ABOUT THIS BOOK?

What is truly distinctive about this book? This is a text that tries to break the mold of the typical textbook synthesis, the cross between an encyclopedia and a dictionary. *Our Social World* is a unique course text that is a coherent essay on the sociological imagination—understood globally. While we attempt to radically change the feel of the introductory book by emphasizing coherence, current pedagogical knowledge, and an integrating theme, we also present much traditional content. Instructors will not have to throw out the well-honed syllabus and begin from scratch, but they can refocus each unit so it stresses understanding of micro-level personal troubles within the macro-level public issues framework. Indeed, in this book, we make clear that the public issues must be understood as global in nature.

Here is a text that engages students; they say so! From class testing, we know that the structure of chapters and sections, the "Thinking Sociologically" features, the wealth of examples, and other pedagogical aids help students to stay focused, think about the material, and apply it to their lives. It does not bore them or insult their intelligence. It focuses on deep learning rather than memorization. It develops sociological skills of analysis rather than emphasizing memorization of vocabulary. Key concepts and terms are

introduced but only in the service of a larger focus on the sociological imagination. The text is both personal and global; it speaks to sociology as a science as well as applied sociology; it has a theme that provides integration of topics as it introduces the discipline. This text is an analytical essay, not a disconnected encyclopedia.

As one of our reviewers noted,

Unlike most textbooks I have read, the breadth and depth of coverage in this one is very impressive. It challenges the student with college-level reading. Too many textbooks seem to write on a high school level and give only passing treatment to most of the topics; writing in nugget-sized blocks. More than a single definition and a few sentences of support, the text forces the student deep into the topics covered and challenges them to see interconnections.

Normally, the global-perspective angle within textbooks that seemed to grow in popularity in the mid- to late-1990s was implemented by using brief and exotic examples to show that differences between societies existed. They gave, and still give to a large extent, a token nod to diversity. This textbook, however, forces the student to take a broader look at social institutions and functions operating in all cultures and societies.

So our focus in this book is on deep learning: (1) expansion of student's ability to role-take or "perspective-take" and (2) deeper sophistication in their epistemology. Deep learning goes beyond the content of concepts and terms and cultivates the habits of thinking that allow one to think critically. Being able to see things from the perspective of others is essential to doing sociology, but it is also essential to seeing weaknesses in various theories or recognizing blind spots in a point of view. Using the sociological imagination is one dimension of role-taking because it requires a step back from the typical micro-level understanding of life's events and a new comprehension of how meso- and macro-level forces, even global ones, can shape the individual's life. Enhancement of role-taking ability is at the core of this book because it is a prerequisite for deep learning in sociology. Second, how can students become more critical thinkers if they do not know *how we know* when we claim to know something? Developing a more informed understanding of what is (and what is not) considered evidence is at the core of critical thought.

We have made some strategic decisions based on these principles of learning and teaching. We have focused much of the book on higher order thinking skills rather than memorization and regurgitation. We want students to learn to think sociologically: to apply, analyze, synthesize, evaluate, and comprehend the interconnections of the world through a globally informed sociological imagination. However, we think it is also essential to do this with an understanding of how students learn.

Many introductory-level books offer several theories and then provide a critique of the theory. The idea is to teach critical thinking. We have purposefully refrained from extensive critique of theory (although some does occur) for several reasons. First, providing critique to beginning-level students does not really teach critical thinking. It trains them to memorize someone else's critique. Furthermore, it simply confuses many of them, leaving students with the feeling that sociology is really just contradictory ideas and the discipline really does not have anything firm to offer. Teaching critical thinking needs to be done in stages, and it needs to take into account the building steps that occur before effective critique is possible. That is why we focus on the concept of deep learning; we are working toward building the foundations that are necessary for sophisticated critical thought at upper levels in the curriculum.

Therefore, in this beginning-level text, we have attempted to focus on a central higher order or deep learning skill—synthesis. Undergraduate students need to grasp this before they can fully engage in evaluation. While deep learning involves understanding of complexity, some aspects of complexity need to be taught at advanced levels. While students at the introductory level are often capable of synthesis, complex evaluation requires some foundational skills. Thus, we offer contrasting theories in this text, and rather than telling what is wrong with each one, we encourage students through "Thinking Sociologically" features to analyze the use of each and to focus on honing synthesis and comparison skills.

Finally, research tells us that learning becomes embedded in memory and becomes long lasting only if it is related to something that learners already know. If they memorize terms but have no unifying framework to which they can attach those ideas, the memory will not last until the end of the course, let alone until the next higher level course. In this text, each chapter is tied to the social world model that is core to sociological thinking. At the end of a course using this book, we believe that students will be able to explain coherently what sociology is and construct an effective essay about what they have learned from the course as a whole. Learning to develop and defend a thesis, with supporting logic and evidence, is another component of deep learning. A text that is mostly a dictionary does not enhance that kind of cognitive skill.

ORGANIZATION AND COVERAGE

Reminiscent of some packaged international tours, in which the travelers figure that "it is day 7, so this must be Paris," many introductory courses seem to operate on the principle that it is week 4 so this must be deviance week. Students do not sense any integration, and at the end of the course, they have trouble remembering specific topics. This book is different. A major goal of the book is to show the integration between topics in sociology and between parts of the social world. The idea is for students to grasp the concept of the interrelated world; a change in one part of the social world affects all others, sometimes in ways that are mutually supportive and sometimes in ways that create intense conflict.

Although the topics are familiar the text book is organized around levels of analysis, explained through the social world model; this perspective leads naturally to a comparative approach and discussions of diversity and inequality. Each chapter represents a part of the social world structure (society, organizations and groups, and institutions) or a process in the social world (socialization, stratification, and change).

Chapter order and links between chapters clarify this idea. Part I (Chapters 1 and 2) introduces the student to the sociological perspective and tools of the sociologist: theory and methods. Part II examines "Social Structure, Processes, and Control," exploring especially processes such as socialization, interaction, and networks. Part III covers the core issue of inequality in society, with emphasis on class, race or ethnicity, and gender. Part IV turns to the structural dimensions of society, as represented in institutions. Rather than trying to be all-encompassing, we examine family, education, religion, and medicine to help students understand how structures affect their lives. A chapter on "Political Systems: Penetrating Power," with discussion of war, terrorism, and the connections between politics and economics, is available on the book's website. Material on several other topics not included in the text are also available to students; this is because we wanted to limit the number of chapters and keep costs down. If you wish to cover political systems, students can read the chapter on the website for this book. It is organized along the same lines as the rest of the book, examining micro-, meso-, and macro-level dimensions of the political and economic systems. Part V turns to social dynamics: how societies change. Population patterns, urbanization, social movements, technology, and other aspects of change are included.

As instructors and authors, we value books that provide students with a well-rounded overview of approaches to the field. Therefore, this book takes an eclectic theoretical approach, drawing on the best insights of various theories and stressing that multiple perspectives enrich our understanding. We give attention to most major theoretical perspectives in sociology: structural-functional and conflict theories at the meso and macro levels of analysis and symbolic interaction and rational choice theories at the micro to meso levels of analysis. Feminist, postmodern, and ecological theories are discussed where relevant to specific topics. Each of these is integrated into the broad social world model, which stresses development of a sociological imagination.

The book includes 15 chapters plus additional online materials, written to fit into a semester or quarter system. It allows instructors to use the chapters in order, or to alter the order, because each chapter is tied into each other through the social world model. We strongly recommend that Chapter 1 be used early in the course since it introduces the integrating model and explains the theme. Otherwise, the book has been designed for flexible use. Instructors may also want to supplement the core book with other materials such as those suggested in the Instructor's Resource Manual. While covering all of the key topics in introductory sociology, the cost and size of a midsized book allows for this flexibility.

We hope you find this book engaging. If you have questions or comments, please contact us.

Jeanne H. Ballantine   *Keith A. Roberts*
Wright State University   *Hanover College*

Knowledge is improved through careful, systematic, and constructive criticism. The same is true of all writing. This book is of much greater quality because we had such outstanding critics and reviewers. We therefore wish to honor and recognize the outstanding scholars who served in this capacity. These scholars are listed on the next page.

We also had people who served in a variety of other capacities: drafting language for us for boxed inserts, doing library and Internet research to find the most recent facts and figures, and reading or critiquing early manuscripts. Khanh Nguyen deserves special mention as an amazing research assistant. Other contributors include Kate Ballantine, Kelly Joyce, Kent Roberts, Justin Roberts, Susan Schultheis, Vanessa M. Simpson, and an introductory sociology class at Wright State University in the fall of 2005. Authors of short sections within the book include Allen McEvoy, Tony Pickard, Daryl Poole, Elise Roberts, and Rachel Ernst. Scholars who helped with early drafts of some chapters include James W. Burfiend, Timothy Buzzell, Dora Lodwick, and Gregory Weiss. Thanks also to designer Bruce Stiver.

Both of us are experienced authors, and we have worked with some excellent people at other publishing houses. However, the team at Pine Forge/Sage Publications was truly exceptional in support, thoroughness, and commitment to this project. Our planning meetings have been fun, intelligent, and provocative. Ben Penner, Pine Forge acquisitions editor, is a unique and wonderful editor who works hard and plays hard (when he has time), that is, if you call baling hay and harvesting wheat a relaxing vacation. Between helping authors, he catches a few waves on the California coast, but he is always there when the cell phone rings! Deya Saoud, the associate editor on this project, kept us all organized and on schedule with incredible grace and aplomb. She coordinated the work of many people and even managed to keep her sometimes cranky authors in line and in good humor. We had trouble getting Ani Ayvazian, our dedicated copy editor, to leave her computer and take her dog for a walk. She did an outstanding job, and we learned a few of the finer points of punctuation and formatting in the process. Pine Forge's overall project editor, Sanford Robinson, displayed never-flagging patience, exceptional coordination skills, and good humor. He helped us through "too much to do" times. Camille Herrera, the editorial assistant on this project, was often the person who followed through with details and the grit work that such a project entails. Other folks who have meant so much to the quality production of this book include Jennifer Reed, Marketing Manager; Helen Salmon, Director Books Marketing; Steven Martin, Director Books Production; Claudia Hoffman, Managing Editor; Scott Hooper, Manufacturing Manager; Jerry Westby, Executive Editor; Michelle Lee Kenny, Senior Graphic Designer; Ravi Balasuriya, Art Director; Chris Klein, Vice President; Tom Taylor, Vice President; David Horwitz, Vice President; Karen Wiley, Senior Permissions Editor; and Blaise Simqu, President and Chief Executive Officer. We have become friends and colleagues with the staff at Pine Forge/Sage Publications; they are all greatly appreciated.

Thanks to the following reviewers:

Sabrina Alimahomed
University of California, Riverside

Fred Beck
Illinois State University

Obi N. I. Ebbe
The University of Tennessee at Chattanooga

Stephanie Funk
Hanover College

Loyd R. Ganey, Jr.
Western International University

Mary Grigsby
University of Missouri–Columbia

Keith Kerr
Blinn College

Stephen Lilley
Sacred Heart University

Add Akbar Madhi
Ohio Wesleyan University

Meeta Mehrotra
Roanoke College

Melinda S. Miceli
University of Hartford

Leah A. Moore
University of Central Florida

Toni Sims
University of Louisiana–Lafayette

Frank S. Stanford
Blinn College

Tracy Steele
Wright State University

John Stone
Boston University

Stephen Sweet
Ithaca College

Tim Ulrich
Seattle Pacific University

Thomas L. Van Valey
Western Michigan University

Leslie Wang
Saint Mary's College

Chaim I. Waxman
Rutgers University

Jake B. Wilson
University of California, Riverside

John Zipp
University of Akron

UNDERSTANDING OUR SOCIAL WORLD:
The Scientific Study of Society

Why would anyone want to study interactions between friends and family, how groups work, and where a society fits into the global system? What can we learn from scientifically studying our everyday lives? The "scientific study of society" sounds rather official and terribly formal. What exactly does it mean to see the world sociologically? Can sociology make life any better—as the study of biology or chemistry can make life better through new medications? The first chapter of this book helps answer two questions: What is sociology, and Why study it?

The second chapter addresses "how sociologists know what they know." This book and your sociology professor will argue that sociology is valuable. Why is that the case? Because sociology helps give us new perspectives on our personal and professional lives, and sociological insights and skills can help all of us make the world a better place. If sociologists find, for example, that education does not treat all children equally, how would we know that, what can be done about it, and what evidence would be considered reliable, valid, dependable, and persuasive? When sociologists make a statement about the social world, how do they know it is true? What perspective or lens might sociologists employ to make sense of that evidence?

By the time you finish reading the first two chapters, you should have an initial sense of what sociology is, how it can help you understand your social world, why the field is worth taking your time to explore, and how sociologists know what they know. We invite you to take a seat and come for a trip through the fascinating field of sociology, our social world.

CHAPTER 1

SOCIOLOGY: A Unique Way to View the World

What to Expect . . .

What Is Sociology?

Why Study Sociology . . . And What Do Sociologists Do?

The Social World Model

So What?

Sociology involves a transformation in the way one sees the world—learning to recognize the complex connections of our intimate personal lives with large organizations and institutions and with national and global structures and events.

Think About It . . .

1. Why should I study sociology?
2. How might sociology be useful to me?
3. What do sociologists do?
4. What kinds of jobs are available to people who have studied sociology?
4. How might local, national, and global events affect my life?

Macro: Global Community

Macro: National Society

Meso: Institutions and Organizations

Micro: Local Organizations and Community

Micro:
You and
Your Family

Micro: Community civic organizations; local religious congregations; scout troops; athletic teams

Meso: Education or health system for a country

Macro: Canada; Brazil; India; Great Britain; Australia

Macro: United Nations; World Court; World Bank; Google; NATO; The Roman Catholic Church

Several years ago, a man was determined to set a record by sailing across the Atlantic in a tiny, one-person craft powered only by the wind. The sailing vessel was designed and constructed by the man, who would embark alone on this perilous journey. The craft was so small that there was no room for anything other than food and water. He would have no radio or other communication device, and he would be out of contact with other people for the duration of the voyage.

The man departed from the east coast of the United States, and for two months, he sailed in solitude. Although he was feared lost at sea since he was not seen or heard from for many weeks, fortune was with him. His craft was spotted off the Irish coast—his destination. As he sailed into port, the media had been alerted to his arrival and awaited him. When the man disembarked to end this remarkable and sometimes painfully lonely journey, a reporter asked him what he had learned on his solitary voyage. The intrepid sailor thought for a moment and calmly replied, "I learned a lot about people."

Strange as it may seem, the social world is not merely something that exists outside of us. As this story illustrates, the social world is also something we carry inside of us. We are part of it, we reflect upon it, and we are influenced by it, even when we are alone. The patterns of the social world engulf us in both subtle and obvious ways that have profound implications for how we create order and meaning in our lives. By being so totally alone for so long, this sailor learned how very social human beings really are. He learned that even when he was alone, he spent much of his time reflecting on people. He also learned how painful and disorienting it can be to live without human contact. In short, his experiences taught him a basic sociological insight: humans are fundamentally social beings.

Sometimes it takes a dramatic and shocking event for us to realize just how deeply embedded we are in a social world that we take for granted. "It couldn't happen here," read typical newspaper accounts, "This is something you see in Bosnia, Kosovo, the Middle East, Central Africa, and other war-torn areas. . . . It's hard to imagine this happening in the economic center of the United States." Yet on September 11, 2001, shortly after 9:00 a.m., a commercial airliner crashed into a New York City skyscraper, followed a short while later by another pummeling into the matching tower, causing this mighty symbol of financial wealth—the World Trade Center—to collapse. After the dust settled and the rescue crews finished their gruesome work, nearly 3,000 people were dead or unaccounted for. The world as we knew it changed forever that day. This event taught U.S. citizens how integrally connected they are with the international community.

Following the events of September 11, the United States launched its highly publicized "War on Terror," and many terrorist strongholds and training camps were destroyed. Still, troubling questions remained unanswered. Why did this extremist act occur? How can such actions be deterred in the future? How do the survivors recover from such a horrific event? Why was this event so completely disorienting to Americans and to the world community? These terrorist acts shocked and horrified people around the world because they were unpredicted and unexpected in a normally predictable world. They violated the rules that foster our connections to one another. They also brought attention to the discontent and disconnectedness that lies under the surface in many societies—discontent that expressed itself in hateful violence.

These terrorist acts represent, among other things, a rejection of modern civil society. Such acts are carried out

When terrorists attacked New York City's World Trade Center by air, the experience of the people was alarm, fear, grief, and lack of a sense of safety—precisely the emotions causing intimidation and lack of security that the terrorists sought to create. Terrorism disrupts normal social life and daily routines.

Source: © Matt McDermott / Corbis Sygma.

around the world by right- or left-wing political or religious extremists (Smith 1994). The terrorists themselves see their acts as justifiable, but few outside their inner circle can understand the behavior. When terrorist acts occur, we struggle to fit such events into our mental picture of a just, safe, comfortable, and predictable social world. The events of September 11 forced U.S. citizens into the awareness that, as different as they are, they may be grouped together as "all the same" by people in other parts of the world. U.S. citizens may also be despised for what they represent, as perceived by others. In other words, terrorists view U.S. citizens as intimately connected even if citizens do not see themselves that way. For many U.S. citizens, the sense of loyalty to the nation in this adversity was deeply stirred; patriotism abounded. So, in fact, the nation became more connected as a reaction to an act against the United States.

Most of the time, we live with social patterns that seem routine, ordinary, and expected. An airline bombing over Lockerbie, Scotland; suicide bombings in Israel; and the Oklahoma City bombing of a federal building all violated our expectations about what is normal. Without shared expectations between humans about proper patterns of behavior, life would be chaotic, as the terrorist acts demonstrate. Connections require some basic rules of interaction, and these rules create routine and safe normality to everyday interaction. For the people in and around the World Trade Center, the social rules governing everyday life broke down that awful day. How could anyone live in society if there were no rules?

This chapter examines the social ties that make up our social world and the consequences of breakdown in those connections. In this first chapter, you will learn what sociology is, how sociologists view the social world, how studying sociology can help you in your everyday life, and how the social world model is used to present the topics you will study throughout this book.

WHAT IS SOCIOLOGY?

On the tennis court, in a fast food restaurant, in your residence hall, or within your home, you interact with other people. Such interactions are the foundation of social life; they are what interest sociologists. According to the American Sociological Association (2002),

> **Sociology** is the scientific study of social life, social change, and the social causes and consequences of human behavior. Since all human behavior is social, the subject matter of sociology ranges from the intimate family to the hostile mob; from organized crime to religious cults; from the divisions of race, gender, and social class to the shared beliefs of a common culture; and from the sociology of work to the sociology of sports. (p. 1)

As we shall see, sociology is relevant and applicable to our lives in many ways. Sociologists conduct scientific research on social relationships and problems that range from tiny groups of two people to national societies and global social networks.

Unlike the discipline of psychology, which focuses on attributes and behaviors of *individuals*, sociology tends to focus on *group* patterns. While a psychologist might try to explain behavior by examining the personality traits of individuals, a sociologist would examine the position of different people within the group and how positions influence what people do. Sociologists seek to analyze and explain why people interact with others and belong to groups, how groups work, who has power and who does not, and how groups deal with conflict and change. They study factors that influence groups such as wars, trade between countries, and new technology. Sociologists ask questions about the rules that govern group behavior, such as dating or workplace rules; about the causes of social problems, such as child abuse, crime, or poverty; and about why nations declare war and kill each other's citizens.

Two-person interactions—*dyads*—are the smallest units sociologists study. Examples of dyads include roommates discussing their classes, a professor and student going over an assignment, a husband and wife negotiating their budget, and two children playing. Next in size are small groups consisting of three or more interacting people—a family, a neighborhood group, a classroom, a work group, or a street gang. Then come increasingly larger groups—organizations such as sports or scouting clubs, neighborhood associations, and local religious congregations. Among the largest groups within nations are ethnic groups and national organizations or institutions, including economic, educational, religious, health and political systems. *Nations* themselves are still larger and can sometimes involve hundreds of millions of people. In the past several decades, social scientists have also pointed to *globalization*, the process by which the entire world is becoming a single interdependent entity. Of particular interest to sociologists are how these various groups are organized, how they function, why they conflict, and how they influence one another.

THINKING SOCIOLOGICALLY

Identify several dyads, small groups, and large organizations to which you belong. Did you choose to belong, or were you born into membership in the group? How does each group affect decisions you make?

Assumptions Underlying Sociology

As in all disciplines, sociology is based on a few important beliefs, or *assumptions*, that sociologists tend to take for granted about the social world. These ideas about humans

Two-person interaction—a dyad—is the smallest social unit. A student-instructor tutorial is just one example of a dyad.

Source: © Andrei Tchernov.

and social life are supported by considerable evidence, but they are assumptions in that they are no longer matters of debate or controversy because they are taken for granted. Understanding these core ideas will help you see how sociologists approach the study of people in groups.

An athletic team is a social group in which people learn to interact, cooperate, develop awareness of the power of others, and deal with conflict. Here, children experience ordered interaction in the competitive environment of a football game. What values, skills, attitudes, and assumptions about life and social interaction do you think these young boys are learning?

Source: Istockphoto.com.

Sociologists maintain that people are social by nature. This means that humans seek fellowship with other humans, interact with each other, and influence and are influenced by the behaviors of one another. Furthermore, humans need groups to survive. Although a few individuals may become socially isolated as adults, they could not have reached adulthood without sustained interactions with others. The central point here is that we become who we are as humans because we are social beings; other people and groups constantly influence us.

Sociologists assert that people live much of their lives belonging to social groups. It is in social groups that we interact, learn to share goals and to cooperate, develop identities, obtain power, and have conflicts. Your individual beliefs and behaviors, your experiences, your observations, and the problems you face are derived from connections to your social groups.

Sociologists assume that interaction between the individual and the group is a two-way process in which each influences the other. Individuals can influence the shape and direction of groups; groups provide the rules and the expected behaviors for individuals.

Sociologists claim that recurrent social patterns, ordered behavior, shared expectations, and common understandings among people characterize groups. A degree of continuity and recurrent behavior is present in human interactions, whether in small groups, large organizations, or society.

Sociologists hold that the processes of conflict and change are natural and inevitable features of groups and societies. No group can remain stagnant and hope to perpetuate itself. To survive, groups must adapt to changes in the social and physical environment. In the past half century, for example, Asian societies such as Japan, Korea, and Thailand have evolved from agricultural societies to complex, technologically based world economic powers. Yet such rapid change often comes at a price. It can lead to conflict within a society—between traditional and new ideas and between groups that have vested interests in particular ways of doing things.

Rapid change can give rise to protest activities, as in the case of Japanese students protesting the building of a new Tokyo airport that was taking over farmland and polluting the countryside. Moreover, failure to change fast enough or to change in a particular direction can spark conflict, including revolution. Historical examples such as the Russian Revolution come to mind, where the aristocracy seemed unable to understand or respond to the needs of a starving and war-torn nation; the elites were violently overthrown. More recently, the collapse of Soviet domination of Eastern Europe and the violence of citizens against the totalitarian rule of the king of Nepal illustrate the demand for change that sprang from citizens' discontent with authoritarian rule.

As you read this book, keep in mind these basic ideas that form the foundation of sociological ideas: people are social; they live and carry out activities largely in groups; interaction influences both individual and group behavior; people share common behavior patterns and expectations; and processes such as change and conflict are always present. In several important ways, sociological understandings differ from our everyday views of the social world and provide new lenses for analysis.

Sociology versus Common Sense

Consider for a moment some events that have captured media attention, and ask yourself questions about these events: Why do some families remain poor generation after generation? Are kids from certain kinds of neighborhoods more likely to get into trouble with the law than kids from other neighborhoods? Why do political, religious, and ethnic conflicts exist in Bosnia, Kosovo, Northern Ireland, Rwanda, Sudan, East Timor, and the Middle East? Why do some families experience high levels of violence in the home? Why are fewer women than men employed in careers as scientists and mathematicians? Why is the homicide rate in the United States so much higher than that of other developed nations? Why do some people join religious cults? Your answers to such questions reflect your beliefs and assumptions about the social world. These assumptions often are based on your experiences, your judgments about what your friends and family believe, what you have read or viewed on television, and common *stereotypes*, which are rigid beliefs, often untested and unfounded, about a group or a category of people.

Common sense refers to ideas that are so completely taken for granted that they have never been seriously questioned and seem to be sensible to any reasonable person. *Sociologists assume human behavior can be studied empirically; they use scientific methods to test the accuracy of commonsense beliefs and ideas about human behavior and the social world.* Commonsense interpretations based on personal experience are an important means of processing information and deciding on a course of action. While all of us hold such ideas and assumptions, are they necessarily accurate? Would our commonsense notions about the social world be reinforced or rejected if examined with scientifically gathered information?

Sociologists use scientific research methods—planned, systematic, objective, and replicable or repeatable techniques to collect data—to study people's interactions within social groups. Yet how do sociologists' assumptions and research methods differ from what one observes and thinks about every day? For most people, the way in which groups operate seems obvious.

The difference between common sense and sociology is that sociologists test their beliefs by gathering information

An East German border guard shakes hands with a West German woman through a hole in the Berlin Wall. Although their governments were hostile to one another, the people themselves often had very different sentiments toward those on the other side of the divide.

Source: © Peter Turnley / Corbis.

and analyzing the evidence in an objective, systematic, scientific way. Indeed, they set up studies so they can see if what they think is true may in fact be untrue. This is the way science is done. Consider the following commonsense beliefs about the social world and some research findings about these beliefs.

The Geerewol Celebration of Wodaabe men in Niger (Sub-Saharan Africa) illustrates that our notions of masculinity and femininity—something that common sense tells us is innate and universal—are actually socially defined, variable, and learned. Wodaabe men are known for their heavy use of makeup to be attractive to women.

Source: © Carol Beckwith and Angela Fisher / HAGA / The Image Works.

Commonsense Beliefs and Social Science Findings

Belief: Most of the differences in the behaviors of women and men are based on "human nature"; men and women are just plain different from each other. Research shows that biological factors certainly play a part in the behaviors of men and women, but the culture (beliefs, values, rules, and way of life) that people learn as they grow up determines how biological tendencies are played out. For instance, in the Wodaabe tribe in Africa, women do most of the heavy work while men adorn themselves with makeup, sip tea, and gossip (Beckwith 1983). Variations in behavior of men and women around the world are so great that it is impossible to attribute behavior to biology or human nature alone.

Belief: As developing countries modernize, the lives of their female citizens improve. This is generally false. In fact, the status of women in many developed and developing countries is getting worse. Women make up roughly 51 percent of the world's population and account for two-thirds of the world's hours-at-work. However, in no country for which data is available do they earn what men earn, and sometimes the figures show women earning below 50 percent of men's earnings for similar work. Women hold many unpaid jobs in agriculture, and they own only 1 percent of the world's property. Furthermore, a majority of the world's illiterate people—64 percent—are women; only 77 percent of the world's women over age 15 are literate compared to 87 percent of men. Illiteracy rates for women in South and West

Asia are 46 percent and in Sub-Saharan Africa are 54 percent compared to 59 and 61 percent for men. These are only a few examples of the continuing poor status of women in many countries (Population Action International 1993; UNESCO Institute of Statistics 2006).

Belief: Young people in modern industrial societies who join cults are duped through brainwashing or other techniques into changing their beliefs and values; therefore, the key to combating cults is debunking the outrageous beliefs that are passed on to new converts. Extensive research using firsthand observation of new religious movements (and a variety of other methods) have been nearly unanimous in their conclusion: change in a sense of belonging to a group comes before change of ideas. Most recruits to religious movements are recruited through friendship networks or friendship-making strategies (Bromley and Shupe 1981; Lofland and Skonovd 1981; Richardson 1985; Roberts 2004). Once the people in the religious community become a group to which the person wants to belong and wants to conform, the person begins to modify beliefs in line with the group. Change of beliefs and values is a late stage in the conversion process, not the first step. Indeed, the same may be true for members of conventional religious organizations. As sociologist and Roman Catholic Priest Andrew Greeley (1972) puts it, "We might say that instead of Americans belonging to churches because they believe in religion, there may be a strong tendency for them to believe in religion because they belong to churches" (p. 115). So trying to persuade individuals who join cults of the error in their beliefs has little effect if they continue to see the members of the religious group as their primary friendship network.

Literacy is a major issue for societies around the globe. These Chinese children are learning to read. In many developing countries, boys have more access to formal education. The commonsense notion is that most children in the world, boys and girls, have equal access to education, yet many children do not gain literacy.

Source: © Jessica Liu.

Belief: Given high divorce rates and a fear of commitment among American males, marriages (in decline since the 1950s) in the United States and Canada are in serious trouble. Although the divorce rate in North America is high, the rate of marriage is also one of the highest in the world (Coontz 2005). If the fear-of-commitment hypothesis were true, it is unlikely the marriage rate would be so high. Moreover, even those who have been divorced tend to remarry. Despite all the talk about decline and despite genuine concern about high levels of marital failure, Americans now spend more years of their lives in marriage than at any other time in history. Divorce appears to be seen as rejection of a particular partner rather than as a rejection of marriage itself (Coontz 2005; Wallerstein and Blakeslee 1996). The divorce rate reached a peak in the United States in 1982 and has declined modestly since that time (Newman and Grauerholz 2002).

As these examples illustrate, many of our commonsense beliefs are challenged by social scientific evidence. Upon examination, the social world is often more complex than our commonsense understanding of events. Throughout history, there are examples of beliefs that seemed obvious at one time but have been shown to be mistaken through scientific study. For example, people in early Western societies believed that the sun and the planets revolved around the earth, that the earth was flat (if a ship sailed too far, it would fall off), and that ridding the body of "diseased blood" through bloodletting and application of leeches to the skin would cure many illnesses. Each of these beliefs was tested, proven wrong, and modified over time using scientific findings.

Of course, social scientific research may also confirm some common notions about the social world: for example, the unemployment rate among African Americans in the United States is higher than that of most other groups; women with similar education and jobs earn less income than men with the same education and jobs; excessive consumption of alcohol is associated with high levels of domestic violence; people tend to marry others who are of a similar social class. The point is that the discipline of sociology provides a method to assess the accuracy of our commonsense assumptions about the social world.

It used to be taken for granted—a commonsense notion—that the world is flat, yet today the maritime workers on this ship have little fear of falling off the edge of the world. Many things that were once believed to be true have been disproven through empirical investigation in the natural or social sciences, and many more beliefs may be altered in the future.

Source: Photo courtesy of the U.S. Coast Guard.

When beliefs about the social world are inaccurate, they can result in human tragedy. The genocide of the Nazi Holocaust and the existence of slavery both have their roots in false beliefs about racial superiority. If officials and citizens are to improve lives of individuals in societies around the world, there must first be a reliable and accurate understanding of the society. Accurate information gleaned from sociological research can be the basis for more rational and just social policies—policies that better meet the needs of all groups in the social world. The sociological perspective, discussed below, helps gain reliable understanding.

THINKING SOCIOLOGICALLY

What are some commonsense beliefs you hold about your social world? For instance, do you think that criminals are born bad or that rich people work harder to get what they have? How did you develop your beliefs?

The Sociological Perspective and the Sociological Imagination

What happens in the social world affects individual lives. Economic trends, such as inflation or recession, and political decisions, such as allocating national resources to defense or reducing health care spending, affect you and your family. If you are unemployed or lack funds for your college education, your personal problems often have broader social issues at their roots. The sociological perspective holds that you can best understand your personal experiences and problems by examining their broader social context, by looking at the big picture.

As sociologist C. Wright Mills (1959) explains, individual problems or private troubles are rooted in social or *public issues*, what is happening in the social world outside of one's personal control. Mills referred to recognizing the relationship between individual experiences and public issues as the **sociological imagination**. For Mills, many personal experiences can and should be interpreted in the context of large-scale forces in the wider society.

Consider, for example, the personal trauma caused by being laid off—what we might consider a personal trouble. The unemployed person often experiences feelings of inadequacy or lack of worth. This in turn may produce stress in a marriage or even result in divorce. These conditions are not only deeply troubling to the person most directly affected but also related to wider political and economic forces in society. The unemployment may be due to corporate downsizing or to a corporation taking operations to another country where labor costs are cheaper and where there are fewer environmental regulations on companies. Although the causes of stress are social, people blame themselves or each other for personal troubles such as unemployment or a failed marriage, believing that they did not try hard enough. Often, they do not see the connection between their private

lives and larger economic forces beyond their control; they fail to recognize the public issues that incur private troubles.

Families also experience stress as partners assume increasing responsibility for their mate's and their children's emotional and physical needs. Until the second half of the twentieth century, the community and the extended family unit—aunts, uncles, grandparents, and cousins—assumed more of that burden. Extended families continue to exist in countries where children settle near their parents, but in modern urban societies, both the sense of community and the connection to the extended family are greatly diminished. There are fewer intimate ties to call on for help and support, and this puts pressure on family relationships. Divorce is a very personal condition for those affected, but it can be understood far more clearly when considered in conjunction with the broader social context of economics, urbanization, changing gender roles, lack of external support, and legislated family policies.

As you learn about sociology, you will come to understand how social forces shape individual lives, and this will help you to understand aspects of everyday life you take for granted. In this book, you will investigate why much of human behavior is predictable, how group life influences your behaviors and interactions, and why some individuals follow the rules of society and others do not. A major goal of this book, then, is to help you incorporate the sociological perspective into your way of looking at the social world and your place in it. Indeed, the notion of *sociological imagination*—connecting events from the global and national level to the personal and intimate level of your own life—is the core organizing theme of this book.

THINKING SOCIOLOGICALLY

How does poverty, a war, or a recession cause personal troubles for someone you know? Why is trying to explain the causes of these personal troubles by examining only the personal characteristics of those affected not adequate?

Questions Sociologists Ask—and Don't Ask

Sociologists ask questions about human behavior in social groups and organizations—questions that can be studied scientifically. Sociologists, like other scientists, cannot answer certain questions—philosophical questions about the existence of God, the meaning of life, the ethical implications of stem cell research, or the morality of physician-assisted suicide. What sociologists do ask, however, is this: what effect does holding certain ideas or adhering to certain ethical standards have on the behavior and attitudes of people? For example, are people more likely to obey rules if they believe that there are consequences for their actions in an afterlife? What are the consequences—positive and negative—of allowing suicide for terminally ill patients who are in pain? Although sociologists may study philosophical or religious beliefs held by groups, they do not make judgments about what beliefs are right or wrong or about moral issues involving philosophy, religion, values, or opinion; rather, they focus on issues that can be studied objectively and scientifically. Sociology remains descriptive and analytical rather than judgmental or value based. Applied sociologists, those who carry out research to help organizations solve problems, agree that the research itself should be as objective as possible; after the research is completed, then the applied sociologists might use the information to explore policy implications. For background on how applied sociology evolved, see The Applied Sociologist at Work, on page 12.

Consider the following examples of questions sociologists might ask:

- Sociologists might study issues related to abortion, such as who gets an abortion, why they do so, and how society as a whole views abortion. However, they avoid making ethical judgments about whether abortion is right or wrong. Such judgments are questions of values, not ones that can be answered through scientific analysis. The question about the morality of abortion is very important to many people, but it is based on philosophical or theological rationale, not on sociological findings. Still, once the objective analysis has been conducted, applied sociologists on either side of the policy divide might be interested in the relevance of those findings for social policy.
- A sociologist might study the effects of varying cultural standards of beauty on individual popularity and social interaction; however, the sociologist would not judge which individuals are more or less attractive. Such questions are matters of aesthetics, a field of philosophy and art.
- A sociologist might study the processes of becoming drunk and drunken behavior, which is often tied more to social environment than to alcohol itself. Note that a person can be very intoxicated at a wedding reception or at a fraternity party, but the expectations for behavior are very different. While conducting the research, the sociologist does not make judgments about whether use of alcohol is good or bad, right or wrong. At the research stage, the sociologist avoids—as much as is humanly possible—opinions regarding responsibility or irresponsibility. The sociologist does, however, observe the variations in behaviors in the use of alcohol in various situations and the way in which alcohol may result in more unconventional behaviors in certain social settings. An applied sociologist who is researching alcohol use on campus for a college or for a national fraternity may, following the research, offer advice about how research might help to reduce the number of alcohol-related deaths or sexual-assault incidents on college campuses.

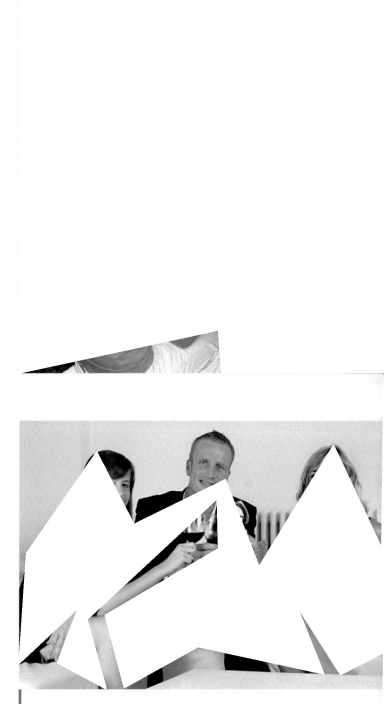

What is acceptable or unacceptable drinking behavior varies according to the social setting. Binge drinking to the point of losing consciousness, vomiting, or engaging in explicitly sexual acts in public may be a source of much good-humored storytelling at a college party. The same act would be offensive at a wedding reception or other events, as illustrated in the photo in which the celebrants may well have consumed more alcohol, but their behavior is restrained.

Source: © Royalty-Free/Corbis; © Kati Neudert.

THE APPLIED SOCIOLOGIST AT WORK

The Study of Society and the Practice of Sociology

by Ruth Pickard and Daryl Poole

The scientific study of social issues and the use of study findings to change society are closely woven together in the history of sociology. August Comte, often considered the father of sociology, and his eighteenth-century contemporaries were intrigued with the idea of applying the new methods of science to social issues; they believed the resulting knowledge could lead to social betterment. Since that early period, the relationship between sociology and its application has remained central to sociology but has taken various forms over time.

During its emergence in the United States in the late nineteenth and early twentieth centuries, sociology had a strong social reform base. Many early sociologists were concerned with the growing disorganization of family and work life that accompanied rapid urbanization and industrialization. They believed that scientific sociology could be used to control such processes and, thus, improve the conditions they considered undesirable. This notion was exemplified by Lester F. Ward, the first president of the American Sociological Society, who in 1906 wrote that the purpose of applied sociology was social improvement.

The early reformist sociology carried the seeds of an internal tension within sociology in the very methods it developed. Surveys and other techniques used by the reformers to gather data soon became the tools of sociologists in universities whose focus turned increasingly toward more academically accepted scientific scholarly work. Establishing credibility in academia meant defining sociology as a quantitatively sophisticated, objective, and value-free science. This concern for pure scientific analysis and reformist sociology goals—using sociological findings to change society—existed side by side and sometimes created conflict between sociologists. At the University of Chicago, which then had the leading sociology program in the nation, an original concern with real-world problems and reform, known as the "Chicago

School," gave way in the 1930s to a research emphasis that dominated both the Chicago program and the discipline of sociology for much of the next four decades. Despite this shift toward abstract, theoretical science, however, there continued to be some sociologists interested in putting sociological findings to use.

In the late 1920s and during the Great Depression of the 1930s, a large number of sociologists were employed by the government to analyze and address the U.S.'s escalating economic and social distress. With the coming of World War II, the research skills of many of these applied sociologists were directed toward finding ways to boost the morale of the country's armed forces, mobilize civilian support, and demoralize the enemy. After the war, issues such as racism, crime, and illiteracy drew the attention of the action-oriented sociologists. This emphasis became a major subdiscipline of sociology with the establishment in 1951 of a new professional organization, the Society for the Study of Social Problems.

The economic good times of the late 1950s, 1960s, and early 1970s supported and even encouraged applied research with social policy implications. During this period, sociology evolved along two lines: those sociologists who emphasized social action and those who pushed for increasingly sophisticated methodological and theoretical purity. Throughout this period, some prominent thinkers advocated the fusion of these scientific and action orientations.

In more recent years, applied sociology has received increased attention due in part to declining opportunities for university employment. Today, sociologists can be found in a wide variety of work situations, and depending on the focus, they may be known as sociological practitioners, applied sociologists, clinical sociologists, policy analysts, program planners, or evaluation researchers, among other titles. This role expansion is generating a vigorous new area of employment but also raising the old debate about the role of sociologists.

Sociologists learn techniques to avoid letting their values influence data gathering and analysis. Still, complete objectivity is difficult at best, and what one chooses to study may be influenced by one's concerns about injustice in society. The fact that sociologists know they will be held accountable by other scientists for the objectivity of their research is a major factor in encouraging them to be objective when they do their research.

THINKING SOCIOLOGICALLY

From the information you have just read, what are some questions sociologists might ask about divorce or cohabitation or gay marriage? What are some questions sociologists would not ask about these topics, at least while in their roles as researchers?

The Social Sciences: A Comparison

Not so long ago, our views of people and social relationships were based on stereotypes, intuition, myths, superstitions, supernatural explanations, and traditions passed on from one generation to the next. Natural sciences first used the scientific method, a model later adopted by social sciences; social scientists use the scientific method to study social relationships, to correct misleading and harmful misconceptions about human behaviors and social relationships, and to guide policy decisions.

An anthropologist works as a cocktail waitress in a bar to study the subculture of that environment and to uncover subtle ways in which gender roles are reinforced. A psychologist wires research subjects to a machine that measures their physiological reaction to a violent film clip, then asks them questions about what they were feeling. A political scientist studies opinion poll results in order to predict outcomes of the next election or how elected officials will vote on proposed legislation. An economist studies the latest stock market trends and tries to predict its movement and its impact on banking practices. A cultural geographer studies housing settlement patterns and migration to help urban planners with more effective land use. A historian reviews documents related to World War II for a book on leading figures who influenced the outcome of the war.

What all of these social sciences—sociology, anthropology, psychology, economics, political science, cultural geography, and history—have in common is that they study aspects of human social life. Social sciences share many common topics, methods, concepts, research findings, and theories, but each has a different focus or perspective on the social world. The following discussion of four social sciences gives an example of how each might study the research topic of family stability and concludes with comments on how sociology might explore this same issue.

Anthropology is closely related to sociology. In fact, the two areas have common historical roots. *Anthropology* is the study of humanity in its broadest context. There are four subfields within anthropology: physical anthropology (which is related to biology), archaeology, linguistics, and cultural anthropology (sometimes called *ethnology*). This last field has the most in common with sociology. Cultural anthropology focuses on the *culture*, or way of life, of the society being studied and uses methods appropriate to understanding culture. (Sociologists are more likely to focus on groups and organizational structures within society and on the patterns that arise out of group relations and culture.) Cultural anthropologists traditionally studied small, preindustrial, preliterate societies, but today, many also study modern communities.

Anthropologists might study the degree of family stability in a society by living in the culture, talking with members, and making observations. How cultures deal with childrearing, sexual behavior, in-law conflicts, and reincorporation of family members into the clan following a divorce are among the many topics an anthropologist might examine to learn about family stability. They are also likely to compare the cultural practices of different societies to gain a broad picture of how family stability emerges in different cultural contexts.

Psychology is the study of individual behavior and mental processes (e.g., sensation, perception, memory, and thought processes). It differs from sociology in that it focuses on individuals, rather than on groups, institutions, and societies, as sociology does. Although there are different branches of psychology, most psychologists are concerned with what motivates individual behavior, personality attributes, attitudes, beliefs, and perceptions. Psychologists also explore stages of human development, abnormal behavior, and the mental disorders of individuals. For example, psychologists would be interested in the effects of family instability and divorce on children. A child's self-esteem, attitudes toward others, and dysfunctional behaviors might be linked to family instability. Early thinking was that parental divorce affected mainly the development of young children. More recent psychological research has shown that adults also can be seriously affected by divorce of their parents (Wallerstein 1996, 2004).

Political science is concerned with government systems and power—how they work, how they are organized, forms of government, relations between governments, who holds power and how they obtain it, how power is used, and who is politically active. Political science overlaps with sociology, particularly in the study of political theory and the nature and the uses of power, but sociology studies a much broader array of social behaviors and institutions. Political scientists who are interested in families might analyze government policies that regulate marriage, divorce, childcare, and other matters. For instance, governments of some countries establish laws for how many children a family may have, and most governments create procedures for obtaining divorce. Of interest to political scientists would be the fact that Italy only recently passed a law permitting divorce; that for a quarter century, China has mandated that urban married couples can have only one child; and that the Netherlands, Britain, Belgium, and Canada approve and recognize same-sex marriages.

Urban Chinese families are allowed to have only one child; having more than one would result in penalties. Thus, families place much attention on their single child.

Source: ©Liu Liqun/Corbis.

Economists analyze economic conditions and explore how people organize, produce, and distribute material goods. They are interested in supply and demand, inflation and taxes, prices and manufacturing output, labor organization, employment levels, and comparisons of industrial and nonindustrial nations. Economists collect and assess data and make predictions about various issues, such as women's roles in the labor force and the costs and benefits to families of having one or two working parents. Sociologists tend to differ from economists in that sociologists ask questions focusing on social relationships, and they do not generally assume that all behavior is motivated solely by a utilitarian calculation of individual costs and benefits.

Finally, *sociologists* assume that human behavior can be studied empirically, and they focus primarily on groups and social structures. Sociologists who are concerned with the effects of economic conditions on families might focus on gender, class, and ethnic implications for social relationships (Healey 2006). For example, what effects do plant layoffs or the lack of jobs have on family stability? Sociologists might explore the effect of social movements on families, like the women's movement or Promise Keepers, an evangelical men's movement with a goal to restore traditional family values to American life. Other sociologists may focus on conditions in the local community and how they affect families or how population trends such as lowered fertility rates or immigration trends influence families. With the rise of two-income couples, sociologists are also interested in negotiation of roles about who does what in the family. Sociologists focus on individuals' connections to groups

(including their roles within families) and the relationships between groups that can be clearly seen when analyzing family instability (Renzetti and Curran 2003).

THINKING SOCIOLOGICALLY

Consider other issues such as the condition of poverty in developing countries or homelessness in North America. What question(s) might each of the social sciences ask about these problems?

WHY STUDY SOCIOLOGY . . . AND WHAT DO SOCIOLOGISTS DO?

Did you ever wonder why some families are close and others are estranged? Why some work groups are very productive while others are not? Why some people are rich and others remain impoverished? Why some people engage in criminal behaviors and others conform rigidly to rules? Although they do not have all the answers to such questions, sociologists do have the perspective and methods to search for a deeper understanding of these and other patterns of human interaction.

There are at least two essential ingredients to the study of the social world: a keen ability to observe what is happening in the social world and a desire to find answers to the question of why it is happening. The value of sociology is that it affords one a unique perspective from which to examine the social world, and it provides the methods to gather data systematically to study important questions about human interaction and group behavior. The practical significance of the sociological perspective is that it

- encourages a more complete understanding of social situations by looking beyond individual explanations to include group analyses of behavior;
- helps people to understand and evaluate problems by enabling them to view the world systematically and objectively rather than in strictly emotional or personal terms;
- cultivates an understanding of the diversity of cultural perspectives and how cultural differences are related to behavioral patterns;
- provides a means to assess the intended and unintended consequences of social policies;
- fosters greater self-awareness, which can lead to opportunities to improve one's life;
- reveals the complexities of social life and provides methods of inquiry designed to sort out the complexities; and
- provides useful skills in interpersonal relations, critical thinking, data collection and analysis, problem solving, and decision making.

Burnouts and Jocks in a Public High School

High schools are big organizations made up of smaller friendship networks and cliques; a careful examination can give us insight into the tensions that exist as the groups struggle for resources and power in the school. Sociologist Penelope Eckert focused on two categories of students that exist in many high schools in North America: "burnouts" and "jocks."

The "burnouts" defied authorities, smoked in the restrooms, refused to use their lockers, made a public display of not eating in the school cafeteria, and wore their jackets all day. Their open and public defiance of authority infuriated the "jocks"—the college prep students who participated in choir, band, student council, and athletics, and held class offices. The burnouts were disgusted with the jocks. By constantly sucking up to the authorities, the jocks received special privileges, and by playing the goody-two-shoes role, they made life much more difficult for the burnouts.

The goal of both groups was to gain more autonomy from the adult authorities who constantly bossed students around. As the burnouts saw things, if the jocks would have even a slight bit of backbone and stand up for the dignity of students as adults, life would be better for everyone. The jocks, for their part, became irritated at the burnouts when they caused trouble and were belligerent with authorities; then the administration would crack down on everyone, and no one had any freedom. Jocks found that if they did

what the adults told them to—at least while the adults were around—they got a lot more freedom. When the burnouts got defiant, however, the principal got mad and removed everyone's privileges.

Eckert's observational field study at Belten High School, located in a community in the Great Lakes region, involved roaming the halls, visiting with students, sitting in the lunchroom, and listening to students talk to each other and to her about life in their high school. Since she was an adult, it took great skill to establish her credibility with the students and convince them that she was not a hall monitor or a spy for the authorities. She took notes on what she saw, overheard, and was told directly; she also went to local fast food restaurants to hang out and talk with students who were "playing hooky" or who stopped by after school. Eckert used this information as the basis for her research into social categories and sense of identity among teenagers in a public high school.

She found that the behavior of both groups was quite logical for their circumstances and ambitions. Expending energy as a class officer or participating in extracurricular activities are rational behavior for

college preparatory students, since those leadership roles help students get into their college of choice. However, those activities do not help one get a better job in a factory in town. In fact, hanging out at the bowling alley makes far more sense, for having friendship networks and acquaintances in the right places are more important to achieving their goals than a class office listed on one's resume. Burnouts maintained their dignity by affirming that they did not recognize bossy adults as authorities. Wearing coats all day was another way to emphasize the idea that "I'm just a visitor in this school."

This method of gathering information was effective in showing how the internal dynamics of schools—conflicts between student groups—were influenced by outside factors such as working- and upper-middle-class status. The study shows that sociological analysis can help us understand some ways that connections between groups—regardless of whether they are in conflict or harmony—shape the perceptions, attitudes, and behaviors of people living in this complex social world.

Source: Eckert (1989). Photos © Istockphoto.com.

This unique perspective has practical value as we carry out our roles as workers, family members, and citizens. For instance, an employee who has studied sociology may better understand how to work with groups and how the structure of the workplace affects individual behavior, how to approach problem solving, and how to collect and analyze data. Likewise, a school teacher trained in sociology may have a better understanding of classroom management, student motivation, causes of poor student learning that have roots outside the school, and other variables that shape the professional life of teachers and scholastic success of students. One example is understanding groups of students: how groups such as jocks and burnouts behave, how the needs of various groups conflict, and why each group's behavior might be quite logical in certain circumstances. Burnouts and Jocks in a Public High School explores one study of a social environment very familiar to many of you, the social cliques in a high school.

What Employers Want

Sociologists have studied what job skills and competencies employers seek in new employees; these are ranked below in order of importance (Ballantine 1991; Brown 1987, 1993). Note that learning the following skills and competencies are part of most sociological training:

1. ability to listen to others, work with peers, and interact effectively in group situations;

2. ability to organize thoughts and information and plan effectively;

3. self-motivation and self-confidence regarding job responsibilities;

4. willingness to adapt to the needs of an organization;

5. ability to handle pressure;

6. ability to conceptualize and solve problems; and

7. effective leadership skills.

Many of these competencies reflect an ability to understand and communicate with others, an obvious concern of the sociological perspective. Keep these skills in mind as you proceed through this book. You might even be interested in a career with a sociology degree.

THINKING SOCIOLOGICALLY

From what you have read so far, how might interaction skills and knowledge of how groups work be useful to you in your anticipated major and career?

What Sociologists Do

Sociologists are employed in a variety of settings. Although students may first encounter them as teachers and researchers in higher education, sociologists also hold nonacademic jobs in social agencies, government, and business. The amount of study completed in sociology, plus the sociologists' areas of specialization, help determine the types of positions they hold. The three typical sociology degrees are bachelor of arts or bachelor of science (BA or BS), master of arts (MA), and doctorate (PhD).

Many sociologists with a bachelor's degree work in the social service sector (such as criminal justice or family services), in government positions, or in business personnel offices. With a master's or a doctorate degree, graduates usually become college teachers, researchers, clinicians, and consultants. For example, the duties of professors vary depending on the type of institution and the level of courses offered. Classroom time fills only a portion of the professor's working days; other activities include preparing for classes, preparing and grading exams and assignments, advising students, serving on committees, keeping abreast of new research in the field, and conducting research studies and having them published; this "publish or perish" task is deemed the most important activity for faculty in some universities.

Most sociologists are employed in colleges and universities, but as Table 1.1 illustrates, and as mentioned above, a significant portion work in business, government, and social service agencies (American Sociological Association 2002; Dotzler and Koppel 1999).

TABLE 1.1 **Where Sociologists Are Employed**	
Places of Employment	**Percentage Employed**
College or university	75.5
Government (all positions)	7.1
Private, for-profit business	6.2
Not-for-profit public service organizations	7.6
Self-employed	3.4

Source: American Sociological Association (2006).

The knowledge and research skills of sociologists are used in business to address organizational needs or problems, in government to provide data such as population projections for education and health care planning, and in social service agencies such as police departments interested in deviant behavior or health agencies concerned with doctor-patient interactions. These latter forms of work are often referred to as *applied sociology*. Applied sociology is an important aspect of the field; each chapter includes boxed inserts discussing the work of an applied sociologist and a section discussing policy examples and implications related to that topic.

Business or Management	Human Services	Education
Market researcher	Social worker	Teacher
Sales manager	Criminologist	Academic research
Customer relations	Gerontologist	Administration
Manufacturing representative	Hospital administrator	School counselor
Banking or loan officer	Charities administrator	Policy analyst
Data processor	Community advocate or organizer	College professor
Attorney		Dean of student life
Research	**Government**	**Public Relations**
Population analyst	Policy advisor or administrator	Publisher
Surveyor	Labor relations	Mass communications
Market researcher	Legislator	Advertising
Economic analyst	Census worker	Writer or commentator
Public opinion pollster	International agency representative	Journalism
Interviewer	City planning officer	
Policy researcher	Prison administrator	
Telecommunications researcher	Law enforcement	
	FBI agent	
	Customs agent	

Figure 1.1   What Can You Do with a Sociology Degree?

Note: Surveys of college alumni with undergraduate majors in sociology indicate that this field of study prepares people for a broad range of occupations. Note that some of these jobs require graduate or professional training. For further information, contact your department chair or the American Sociological Association for a copy of *Careers in Sociology*. 6th edition. Washington, DC: American Sociological Association, 2002.

THINKING SOCIOLOGICALLY

What are some advantages of mayors, legislators, police chiefs, or government officials making decisions based on information gathered and verified by sociological research rather than on using their own intuition or assumptions?

Figure 1.1 provides some ideas of career paths for graduates with a degree in sociology.

You now have a general idea of what sociology is and what sociologists do. It should be apparent that sociology is a very broad field of interest; sociologists study all aspects of human social behavior. The next section of this chapter shows how the parts of the social world that sociologists study relate to each other, and outlines the model you will follow as you continue to learn about sociology.

THE SOCIAL WORLD MODEL

Think about the different groups you depend on and interact with on a daily basis. You wake up to greet members of your family or your roommate. You go to a larger group—a class—that exists within an even larger organization—the college or university. Understanding sociology and comprehending the approach of this text requires a grasp of **levels of analysis**, social groups from the smallest to the largest. It may be relatively easy to picture small groups such as a family, a sports team, or a sorority or fraternity. It is more difficult to visualize large groups such as corporations—The Gap, Abercrombie and Fitch, Eddie Bauer, General Motors Corporation, or Starbucks—or organizations such as local or state governments. The largest groups include nations or international organizations such as the sprawling network of the United Nations. Groups of various sizes shape our lives. Sociological analysis requires that we understand these groups at various levels of analysis.

The **social world model** helps us picture the levels of analysis in our social surroundings as an interconnected series of small groups, organizations, institutions, and societies. Sometimes these groups are connected by mutual support and cooperation; however, sometimes there are conflicts and power struggles over access to resources.

What we are asking you to do here and throughout this book is to develop a sociological imagination—the basic lens used by sociologists. Picture the social world as a linked system made up of increasingly larger units. To understand the units or parts of the social world and their interconnections more clearly, see the social world model at the beginning of this chapter—the concentric rings on page 3.

THINKING SOCIOLOGICALLY

Place yourself at the center of the social world. Now, give examples of each level of analysis in *your* social world.

This social world model will be used throughout this book to illustrate how each topic fits into the big picture, "our social world." No unit of our social world can stand alone; all units affect each other, either because they serve needs of other units in the system or because of intense conflict and tension between different units.

Social Units and Social Structure

Social units are interconnected parts of the social world, ranging from small groups to societies. All these combine to form the **social structure**, the people and groups that bring order to our lives. The social structure holds the social units together and governs the way they work in combination, just as our body's skeleton governs how the limbs are attached to the torso and how they can move. However, sometimes the interconnections between social units are characterized by conflict and divergent self-interests. For example, a religion that teaches that it is wrong to have blood transfusions may conflict with the health care system regarding how to save the life of a child. Business executives want to produce products at the lowest possible cost, but this may mean paying workers low wages and causing damage to the environment. All levels of analysis are linked; some links are supportive, others in conflict.

Social institutions provide the rules, roles, and relationships set up to meet human needs and direct and control human behavior; they are the social units in societies through which organized social activities take place, and they provide the setting for activities essential to human and societal survival. For example, we cannot survive without an economic institution to provide guidelines and a structure for meeting our basic needs of food, shelter, and clothing. Likewise, we would never make it to adulthood as functioning members of society without the family, the most basic of all institutions. Other social institutions that are essential to a national society are educational, religious, political, and health care systems.

Institutions in society are interconnected. Like the system of organs that make up your body—heart, lungs, kidneys, bladder—all social institutions are interrelated; a change in one institution affects the others. When governments pass laws providing money to schools for children's lunches, requiring standardized testing, or limiting extracurricular activities due to lack of funds, it affects both families and schools. Likewise, if many people are unable to afford medical treatment, the society is less healthy and there are consequences for families, schools, and society as a whole.

The **national society**, one of the largest social units in our model, includes a population of people, usually living within a specified geographic area, who are connected by common ideas and are subject to a particular political authority. Although a national society is one of the largest social units, it is still a subsystem of the interdependent global system. France, Kenya, Brazil, and Laos are all national societies on separate continents, but they are all linked as part of the global system of nations. Each national society has its own distinct, relatively permanent geographic and political boundaries, language, and way of life. In most cases, national societies involve countries or large regions where the inhabitants share a common identity as members. In certain other instances, such as contemporary Great Britain, a single national society may include several groups of people who consider themselves distinct nationalities (Welsh, English, Scottish, and Irish within the United Kingdom); such multicultural societies may or may not be harmonious.

THINKING SOCIOLOGICALLY

Think about a significant social conflict or change and how it influences any one of the following social institutions—family, education, religion, politics, economics, science, sports, or health care. How might a significant change in one institution affect stability or change in another institution?

Social Processes

Think of **social processes** as the actions taken by people in social units. Processes keep the social world working, much as the beating heart keeps the body working. The *process of socialization* that takes place through actions of families, educational systems, religious organizations, and other social units, teaches individuals how to become productive members of society. This is essential for the continuation of any society. Similarly, our social positions in society are the result of *stratification*, the process of layering people into social strata based on such factors as income, occupation, and education. *Conflict* occurs between individuals or groups for money, jobs, and other needed resources. The *process of change* is also a continuous pattern in every social unit; change in one unit affects other units of the social world, often in a chain reaction. For instance, change in the quality of health care can impact the workforce, a beleaguered workforce can impact the economy, instability in the economy can affect families as breadwinners lose jobs, and family economic woes can impact religious communities since devastated families cannot afford to give money to the churches, mosques, or temples.

Sociologists generally do not say that these social processes are "good" or "bad." Rather, sociologists try to identify and explain processes that take place within social units. Picture these processes as overlaying and penetrating the whole social world, determining how every unit interacts with every other unit. Social units would be lifeless without the action brought about by social processes, just as body parts would be lifeless without the processes of electrical impulses shooting from the brain to each organ or the oxygen transmitted by blood coursing through our arteries to sustain each organ.

The Environment

Surrounding each social unit is an environment. The **environment** is the setting in which the social unit operates; it includes everything that influences the social unit, such as its physical surroundings and technological innovations. Some parts of the environment are more important to the social unit than others. Your local church, synagogue, or mosque is located in a community. That religious organization may seem like it is autonomous and independent, but it depends on the local police force to protect the building from vandalism, and the health of the local economy influences how much money the organization has available for local benevolent outreach. If the religious education program is going to train children to understand the scriptures, the religious congregation hopes the local schools have already taught the children to read. A religious group may also be affected by other religious bodies, competing with one another for potential members from the community. These religious groups may work cooperatively—organizing a summer program for children or jointly sponsoring a holy-day celebration—or they may define one another as evil, each trying to stigmatize the other. Moreover, if one local religious group is composed primarily of professional and business people and acts as a sponsor for the local Rotary Club, and another group is made up mostly of laboring people and provides space for the local labor union to meet, the religious groups may experience conflict because each one has a different constituency. As you can see, churches, synagogues, and mosques are linked to other local organizations in complex ways.

Think of the environment as part of our social world; each unit has its own environment to which it must adjust, just as each individual has a unique social world, including family, friends, and other social units. Some of those adjustments involve competition and conflict with other units that may want the same resources (time, money, skill, and energy of members); other adjustments involve cooperation as community organizations work together to sponsor a community festival or to raise money for a local teen recreation center.

To understand the human body or a social unit, we must consider the structure and processes within the unit, as well as the interaction with the surrounding environment. No matter what social unit the sociologist studies, the unit cannot be understood without considering the interaction of that unit with its unique environment.

Perfect relationships or complete harmony between the social units is unusual. Social units are often motivated by self-interests and self-preservation, with the result that they compete with others groups and units for resources. Therefore, social units within the society are often in conflict. Whether groups are in conflict or mutually supportive does not change their interrelatedness; units are interdependent. The nature of that interdependence is likely to change over time in each society and can be studied using the scientific method.

Studying the Social World: Levels of Analysis

Picture for a moment your sociology class as a social unit in your social world. Students (individuals) make up the class, the class (small group) is offered by the sociology department, the sociology department (a large group) is part of the university, the university (an organization) is located in a community and follows the practices approved by the social institution (education) of which it is a part, and education is an institution located within a nation. The practices the university follows are determined by the larger unit that provides guidelines for institutions. The national society, represented by the national government, is shaped by global events—technological and economic competition between nations, natural disasters, global warming, wars, and terrorist attacks. Such events influence national goals, including the focus of the educational system. Thus, global tensions and conflicts may shape the curriculum that the individual experiences in the sociology classroom.

Each of these social units—from the smallest (the individual student) to the largest (society and the global system)—is referred to as a level of analysis (Table 1.2). Sociologists employ different theories and methods to explain human behavior, depending on the level of analysis. Therefore, it is important to know the level of analysis in any sociological research.

TABLE 1.2	**The Structure of Society and Levels of Analysis**	
	Level	**Parts of Education**
Micro-level analysis	Interpersonal	Sociology class; individual student
	Local organizations	University; sociology department
Meso-level analysis	Organizations and institution	State boards of education
Macro-level analysis	Nations	Policy and laws governing education
	Global community	World literacy

THINKING SOCIOLOGICALLY

Again, placing yourself at the center of your social world, describe the social units, including small groups, organizations, institutions, and the nation of which you are a part. Now describe your environment.

MICRO-LEVEL ANALYSIS

Sometimes, sociologists ask questions about face-to-face interactions in dyads or among a very small number of people. A focus on individual or small group interaction in specific situations entails **micro-level analysis**. Micro-level analysis is important because face-to-face interaction forms the basic foundation of all social organizations, from families, to corporations, to societies. These personal interactions occur in the organizations and groups to which we belong; therefore, we are members of many groups at the micro level.

To illustrate micro-level analysis, consider the problem of spousal abuse. One might ask why a person remains in an abusive relationship when each year thousands of people are killed by their lovers or mates, and millions more are severely and repeatedly battered. To answer this, several possible micro-level explanations can be considered. One view is that a person has learned from an abusive partner that she is powerless in the relationship or that she "deserves" the abuse; therefore, she gives up in despair of ever being able to alter the situation. The abuse is viewed as part of the interaction—of action and reaction—by which the partners establish expectations of what comprises "normal" interaction.

Another explanation for remaining in the abusive relationship is that the person may have been brought up in a family situation where battering was an everyday part of life. However unpleasant and unnatural this may seem to outsiders, it may be seen by the abuser or by the abused as a "normal" and acceptable part of intimate relationships.

Another possibility is that an abused woman may fear that her children would be harmed or that she would be harshly judged by her family or church if she "abandoned" her mate. She may have few resources to make leaving the abusive situation possible. To study each of these possible explanations involves analysis at the micro level because each focuses on interpersonal interaction factors rather than on society-wide trends or forces. Meso-level concerns, discussed below, lead to quite different explanations for abuse.

MESO-LEVEL ANALYSIS

Analysis of the intermediate-sized social units, called **meso-level analysis**, involves looking at units smaller than the nation but large enough to encompass more than the local community or even the region. This level includes national institutions (such as the economy of a country, the national educational system, or the political system within a country); nationwide organizations (such as a political party, a soccer league, or a national women's rights organization); nationwide corporations (such as Ford Motor Company or IBM); and ethnic groups that have an identity as a group (such as Jews, Mexican Americans, or the Lakota-Sioux in the United States).

Using meso-level analysis to examine changes in women's status within a country, for example, could include study of women's legal, educational, religious, economic, political, scientific, and sports-related opportunities in society. Meso-level changes may create new opportunities for women, but that change in opportunities can also cause conflicts within individual families at the micro level (Newman and Grauerholz 2002).

In discussing micro-level analysis, we used the example of domestic violence. The micro-level explanations of abuse discussed above are sometimes criticized because they "blame the victim"—in this case the abused person—for failing to act in ways that stop the abuse. To avoid blaming victims for their own suffering, many social scientists look for broader explanations of spousal abuse, such as the social conditions at the meso level of society that cause the problem (Straus and Gelles 1990). When a pattern of behavior in society occurs with increasing frequency, it cannot be understood solely from the point of view of individual cases or micro-level causes. For instance, sociological findings show that fluctuations in spousal or child abuse are related to levels of unemployment. Frustration resulting in abuse erupts within families when poor economic conditions make it nearly impossible for people to find stable and reliable means of supporting themselves and their families. Economic issues must be addressed if violence in the home is to be lessened.

MACRO-LEVEL ANALYSIS

Studying the largest social units in the social world, called **macro-level analysis**, involves looking at entire nations, global forces, and international social trends. Macro-level analysis is essential to our understanding of how the larger social forces such as global events shape our everyday lives. A political conflict on the other side of the planet can lead to war, which means that a member of your family may be called up to active duty and sent into harm's way 5,000 miles away from your home. Each member of the family may experience individual stress, have trouble concentrating, and feel ill with worry.

To illustrate the impact of the macro level on our lives, consider the examples of a natural disaster in Indonesia

This photo depicts the damage following the tsunami in Indonesia in 2005. This event not only changed the lives of people living in those countries but had ripple effects on economic exchange, relief efforts around the globe, and international trade that can affect the cost of oil or the foods that are available to put on your table.

Source: U.S. Navy photo by Photographer's Mate 2nd Class Philip A. McDaniel (released).

such as the 2005 tsunami or a military coup in Malaysia; these disasters may change the foods you are able to put on the family dinner table, since much of our cuisine is now imported from other parts of the world.

Indeed, a severe depression in China or a recession in the Middle East may influence whether the bread earners in your own family have a job and can even afford to put food on the table or gas in the car. The entire globe has become an interdependent social unit; if we are to prosper and thrive in the twenty-first century, we need to understand connections that go beyond our communities to other parts of the world. The map on the next page suggests disasters that may have affected you.

Even patterns such as domestic violence, considered as micro- and meso-level issues above, can be examined at the macro level. Worldwide patterns may tell us something about a social problem and offer new lenses for understanding variables that contribute to a problem. A study of 95 societies around the world found that violence against women (especially rape) occurs at very different rates in different societies, with some societies being completely free of rape (Benderly 1982) and others having a "culture of rape." The most consistent predictor of violence against women was a macho conception of masculine roles and personality. Societies that did not define masculinity in terms of dominance and control were virtually free of rape. Some

sociologists believe that the same pattern holds for domestic violence: a society or subgroup within society that teaches males that the finest expression of their masculinity is physical strength and domination is very likely to have battered women (Burn 2005).

The point is that understanding of individual human behavior often requires investigation of larger societal beliefs that support that behavior.

Let us reconsider the following question: Why is it important to understand different levels of analysis? Recognizing the level at which a problem exists helps sociologists to determine appropriate research methods to study sociological questions (keeping in mind that the other levels of analysis will lend depth to the understanding of any topic). All three levels of analysis are discussed throughout this text. Micro-level analysis is most pertinent when discussing face-to-face interaction, small groups, and the process of socialization—learning to become a member of society. Meso-level analysis is necessary for the study of processes such as inequality within the society, and of institutions such as politics and education. Macro-level analysis explores issues for people as members of nations and for nations as they interact in the international arena.

Distinctions between each level are not sharply delineated; the micro level shades into the meso level, and the lines between the meso level and the macro level are blurry.

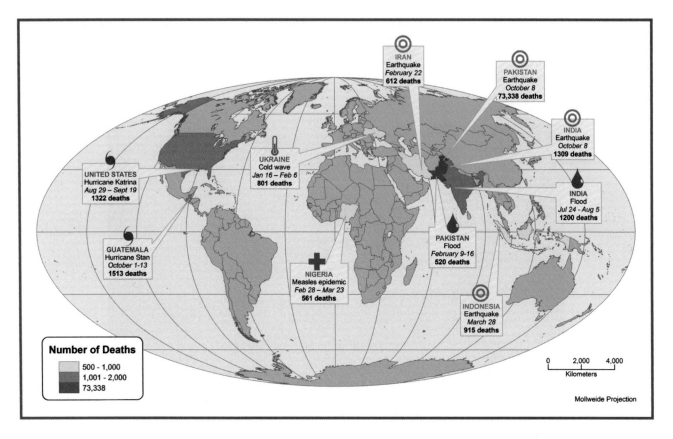

MAP 1.1   The 10 Most Lethal Environmental Disasters of 2005. How might these disasters have touched your own life?

Source: EM-DAT: The OFDA/CRED International Disaster Database (2006). Map by Anna Versluis.

Still, it is clear that in some social units you know everyone or at least every member of the social unit is only two degrees of relatedness away (every person in the social unit knows someone whom you also know). We also all participate in social units that are smaller than the nation but that can be huge; millions of people may belong to the same religious denomination or the same political party. We have connections with those people, and our lives are affected by people we do not even know. Consider political activities that take place on the Internet. In political campaigns, millions of individuals join organizations such as Moveon.com and TrueMajority, participate in dialogue online, and contribute money. The meso level is different from the micro level, but both influence us. The macro level is even more remotely removed, but its impact can change our lives.

The social world model presented in the chapter opening illustrates the interplay of micro-, meso-, and macro-level forces, and Figure 1.2 illustrates that this micro-to-macro model should be seen as a continuum. In Sociology around the World, we examine a village in Tunisia to see how macro-level forces influence a meso-level local community and individual micro-level lives.

Figure 1.2   The Micro-to-Macro Continuum

Building and staffing of this resort in Tunisia—which is patronized by affluent people from other continents—changed the economy, the culture, and the social structure in the local community.

Source: © Sylvie Fourgeot.

THINKING SOCIOLOGICALLY

Place the groups to which you belong in a hierarchy from micro, to meso, to macro levels. Note how each social unit and its subunits exist within a larger unit until you reach the level of the entire global community.

The Social World Model and This Book

Throughout this book, the social world model will be used as the framework for understanding the social units, processes, and surrounding environment. Each social unit and process is taken out, examined, and returned to its place in the interconnected social world model so that you can comprehend the whole social world and its parts. Look for the model at the beginning of every chapter; you can also expect the micro-, meso-, and macro-level dimensions of issues to be explored throughout the text.

The social world engulfs each of us from the moment of our birth until we die. Throughout our lives, each of us is part of a set of social relationships that provide guidelines for how we interact with others and how we see ourselves. This does not mean that human behavior is strictly determined by our links to the social world; humans are more than mere puppets whose behavior is programmed by social structure. It does mean, however, that influence between the individual and the larger social world is

Sociology around the World

Tunisian Village Meets the Modern World

The following case illustrates how the social units of the social world model and the three levels of analysis enter into sociological analysis. It is a story of change as macro-level innovations enter a small traditional village. As you read, try to identify both the units and levels of analysis being discussed and the impact of globalization and modernization on a community that cannot know what these changes will bring.

The workday began at dawn as usual in the small fishing village on the coast of Tunisia, North Africa. Men prepared their nets and boats for the day, while women prepared breakfast and dressed the young children for school. About 10 a.m. it began—the event that would change this picturesque village forever. Bulldozers arrived first, followed by trench diggers and cement mixers, to begin their overhaul of the village.

Villagers suspected something was afoot when important looking officials had arrived two months earlier with foreign businessmen, followed by two teams of surveyors. Their efforts to learn the meaning of these visits had resulted in assurances that nothing would change their way of life. To the villagers, the bulldozers did not look like "nothing." In fact, the foreign businessmen had selected this location for a new multimillion dollar hotel and casino.

Land that the village had held communally for generations was now sold to the outside businessmen by the government, although the contractor from the capital city of Tunis assured concerned citizens that they would still have access to the beach and ocean for fishing. He also promised them many benefits from the hotel project—jobs, help from the government to improve roads and housing, and a higher standard of living.

The contractor set up camp in a trailer on the beach, and word soon got around that he would be hiring some men for higher hourly wages than they could make in a day or even month of fishing. Rivalries soon developed between friends over who should apply for the limited number of jobs, and the economic system of the village was turned upside down.

Residents had mixed opinions about the changes taking place in their village and their lives. Some saw the changes as exciting opportunities for new jobs and recognition of their beautiful village; others viewed the changes as destroying a lifestyle that was all they and generations before them had known.

Today, the village is dwarfed by the huge hotel, and the locals are looked upon as quaint curiosities by the European tourists. Fishing has become a secondary source of employment to hotel and casino work or to selling local crafts and trinkets to souvenir-seeking visitors. Many women are now employed outside the home by the hotel, creating new family structures as grandparents, unemployed men, and other relations take over child-rearing responsibilities.

To understand the changes in this one small village and other communities facing similar change, a sociologist uses the sociological imagination. This involves understanding the global political and economic trends that are affecting this village and its inhabitants (macro-level analysis). It requires comprehension of transformation of social institutions within the nation (meso-level analysis). Finally, sociological investigation explores how change impacts the individual Tunisian villagers (micro-level analysis).

To analyze the process of change, it is important to understand the interconnected parts in this situation. The institutions of politics and economics are represented by the government officials and the international business representatives who negotiated a lucrative deal to benefit both Tunisia and the business corporation. The community and its powerless residents presented few obstacles to the project from the point of view of the government, and in fact government officials reasoned that villagers could benefit from new jobs. However, economic and family roles of the villagers—how they earned a living and how they raised their children—changed dramatically with the disruption to their traditional ways. The process of change began with the demand for vacation spots in the sun. Ultimately, this process reached the village's local environment, profoundly affecting the village and everyone in it. For this Tunisian village, the old ways are gone forever.

reciprocal. We are influenced by and we have influence on our social environment. The social world is a human creation, and we can and do change that which we create. It acts upon us, and we act upon it. In this sense, social units are not static but are constantly emerging and changing in the course of human interaction.

The difficulty for most of us is that we are so caught up in our daily concerns that we fail to see and understand the social forces that are at work in our personal environments. What we need are the conceptual and methodological tools to help us gain a more complete and accurate perspective on the social world. The concepts, theories, methods, and levels of analysis employed by sociologists are the very tools that will give us that perspective. To use an analogy, each different lens of a camera gives the photographer a unique view of the world. Wide-angle lenses, close-up lenses, telephoto lenses, and special filters each serve a purpose in creating a distinctive picture or frame of the world. No one lens will provide the complete picture. Yet the combination of images produced by each lens allows us to examine in detail aspects of the world we might ordinarily overlook. That is what the sociological perspective gives us: a unique set of tools to see the social world with more penetrating clarity. In seeing the social world from a sociological perspective, we are better able to use that knowledge constructively, and we are better able to understand who we are as social beings.

SO WHAT?

Why study sociology and of what use might it be? We live in a complex social world with many layers of interaction. If we really want to understand our own lives, we need to comprehend the various levels of analysis and the dynamic connections between those levels. Moreover, as citizens of democracies, we can influence our city councils, school boards, state legislatures, and congressional or parliamentary policy makers. If we are to do so wisely, we need both perceptive lenses for viewing this complex social system and accurate, valid information (facts) about the society. As the science of society, sociology can provide both tested empirical data and a broad, insightful perspective for analysis.

The next issue, then, is how one gathers this accurate data that informs how we understand the social system. When we say we know something about society, how is it that we know? What is considered evidence in sociology, and what lens (theory) do we use to interpret the data? These are the central issues of the next chapter.

CONTRIBUTING TO YOUR SOCIAL WORLD

At the end of all subsequent chapters, you will find ideas for work and volunteering that relate to the sociological ideas from the chapter you have just read.

Visit www.pineforge.com/ballantinestudy for online activities, sample tests, and other helpful information. Select "Chapter 1: Sociology" for chapter-specific activities.

2 EXAMINING THE SOCIAL WORLD: How Do We Know?

What to Expect . . .

The Development of Sociology as a Science
Empirical Research and Social Theory
How Sociologists Study the Social World
Ethical Issues in Social Research
Sociology's Major Theoretical Perspectives
So What?

Science is about knowing through empirical investigation. Pictured are an astronaut, geologist, archaeologist, biologist, and sociologist. Sociology is a social science because of the way we gather dependable evidence.

Think About It . . .

1. When you say that you know something, how do you know?

2. Why is evidence important when you try to convince someone of something?

3. What does it mean to study society scientifically?

4. How can theories help us make sense of information?

Macro: Global Community

Macro: National Society

Meso: National Institutions and Organizations; Ethnic Subcultures

Micro: Local Organizations and Community

Micro:
You, Close Associates,
and Your Family

Micro level

Meso level

Macro level

Macro level

Micro/Meso Theories

Symbolic Interaction Theory
Rational Choice Theory

Meso/Macro Theories

Structural-Functional Theory
Conflict Theory

Hector is a 16-year-old boy living in a *favela* (slum) in the outskirts of Sao Paulo, Brazil. He is a polite, bright boy, but his chances of getting an education and steady job in his world are limited. Like millions of other children around the world, he comes from a poor family that migrated to the urban area in search of a better life. However, his family ended up in a crowded slum with only a shared spigot for water and one string of electric lights along the dirt road going up the hill on which they live. The sanitary conditions in his community are appalling—open sewers, no garbage collection, disease. Perhaps his family is relatively

Slum dwellers of Sao Paulo, Brazil. Hector lives in a neighborhood like this with shelters made of available materials like boxes and tin.

Source: © Sean Sprague / The Image Works.

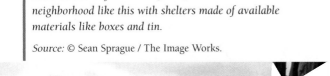

fortunate, for they have cement walls and wood flooring, though no water or electricity. Many adjacent dwellings are little more than cardboard walls with corrugated metal roofs and dirt floors.

Hector wanted to stay in school but was forced to drop out in order to earn money. Since leaving school, he has been picking up odd jobs to help pay the few centavos for the family's dwelling and to buy food to support his parents and six siblings. He works at whatever odd jobs he can find—deliveries, trash pick-up, janitorial work, gardening.

Even when he was in school, Hector's experience was discouraging. He was not a bad student, and some teachers encouraged him to continue, but other students from the city teased the *favela* kids and made them feel unwelcome. Most of his friends had already dropped out. He often missed school because of other obligations—opportunities for part-time work, a sick relative, or a younger sibling who needed care. The immediate need to put food on the table outweighed the long-term value of staying in school.

What is the bottom line for Hector and millions like him? Because of his limited education and work skills, obligations to his family, and limited opportunities, he will continue to live in poverty.

Sociologists are interested in the factors that influence the social world of children like Hector: family, friends, school, community, and the place of one's nation in the global political and economic systems. To understand how sociologists study poverty and many other social issues, consider the ideas and methods they use to do their work. Understanding the *how* helps to see that sociology is more than guesswork or opinion. Rather, it is a scientific study based on a systematic process for expanding knowledge; in the case of sociology, we use scientific methods for studying the social world.

Whatever your area of study or job interests, you are likely to find yourself needing to ask sociological questions. Consider some examples: Why is there binge drinking on college campuses? Do sexually explicit videos and magazines reinforce sexist stereotypes or encourage sexual violence? Do tough laws and longer prison sentences deter people from engaging in criminal conduct? Are workers more productive and more satisfied when they are given a share of company profits? How do we develop our religious and political beliefs? Do classroom teachers treat children from different social classes, races, or ethnic groups the same? Why do people join zealous religious groups that require tremendous self-sacrifice? How are the Internet and other technologies affecting everyday life for people around the world? Is there a *digital divide*, with technology making inequality in the world even worse than it had been previously? How do people in developing countries view national debates in developed countries about limiting immigration? How are people's cultures and their environments affected by the globalization of commerce and production? The list of possible topics is endless.

The point is that this chapter will introduce you to the basic tools used to plan studies and gather dependable information on topics of interest. It will help you to grasp how sociology approaches research questions. To this end, we will consider the development of sociology as a science, the relationship between sociological theories and methods, the process and tools of sociological methods, ethics involved in conducting sociological research, and contemporary sociological theories. To help you understand the link between sociological theory and research and give you a better idea of how sociologists approach the social world, some background on the origins of sociology will be helpful.

THE DEVELOPMENT OF SOCIOLOGY AS A SCIENCE

Throughout recorded history, humans have been curious about how and why people form groups. That should not be surprising since the groups we belong to are so central to human existence and to a sense of satisfaction in life.

Early Sociological Thought

Religion played a major part in influencing the way individuals thought about the world and their social relationships. Christianity dominated European thought systems during the Middle Ages, from the end of the Roman Empire to the 1500s, while Islamic beliefs ruled in much of the Middle East and parts of Africa. North African Islamic scholar Ibn Khaldun (1332–1406) was probably the first to suggest a systematic approach to explain the social world.

Khaldun was particularly interested in understanding the feelings of solidarity that held tribal groups together during his day, which was a time of great conflict and wars. While these issues interested philosophers and theologians,

Plato and Aristotle were early social philosophers in the Western world. Their writings have influenced the social sciences.

Machiavelli, a philosopher, wrote about power and the social control of people.

Ibn Khaldun is so highly regarded as an Islamic scholar and social philosopher and analyst that Tunisia honored him with an artistic depiction on a stamp.

Social contract and individual liberties were primary concerns of John Locke.

they did not develop a scientific approach to study society. They speculated and used pure reason to generalize about human behavior and group solidarity, but they did not use scientific methods to gather data and test their theories, processes that allow us to get closer to the truth.

Sociology has its modern roots in the ideas of nineteenth-century social, political, and religious philosophers who laid the groundwork for the scientific study of society. While it seems likely that humans have always thought about their place in the world, it was not until the nineteenth century that a modern scientific discipline to study society began to emerge.

Until the nineteenth century, social philosophers provided the primary approach to understanding society, one that invariably had a strong moral tone. Their opinions were not derived from scientific evidence but from thinking—abstract reflection—about how the social world works. Often, they advocated forms of government that they believed would be just and good, denouncing those they considered inhumane or evil. For instance, Plato's *Republic*, written around 400 BCE, outlines plans for an ideal state—complete with government, family, economic systems, class structure, and education—designed to achieve social justice. Even today, people still debate the ideal communities proposed by Plato, Aristotle, Machiavelli, Thomas More, and other great philosophers from the past.

Conditions Leading to Modern Sociology

Several conditions in the nineteenth century gave rise to the emergence of sociology (see Map 2.1). First, European nations were imperial powers that were establishing oppressive colonies in other cultures. This exposure to other cultures encouraged at least some Europeans to learn more about the people that had been conquered. Equally important, the social upheaval of revolutions, and sweeping changes brought about by the Industrial Revolution, demanded a deeper understanding of social change. Finally, advances in the natural sciences demonstrated the value of the scientific method as a tool for examining the physical world; applying this scientific method to understand the social world was a logical step.

The social backdrop for the earliest European sociologists was the Industrial Revolution (which began around the middle of the 1700s) and the French Revolution (1789–1799). No one had clear, systematic explanations for why the old social structure that had lasted since the early Middle Ages was collapsing or why cities were exploding with migrants from rural areas. French society was in turmoil. Nobility were being executed, and new rules of justice were taking hold—churches were subordinated to the state, equal rights established for citizens under the law, and democratic rule emerged. These dramatic changes marked the end of the traditional monarchy and the beginning of a new social order. With no methods to collect information on the dramatic changes taking place, leaders in France had to rely on the social philosophies of the time to react to the problems that surrounded them. Some of those philosophies were not informed by facts about social life.

It was in this setting that the scientific study of society emerged. Two social thinkers, Henri Saint-Simon (1760–1825) and Auguste Comte (1798–1857), decried the

The Bastille, a state prison in Paris, France, and symbol of oppression, was seized by the common people in the French Revolution, an upheaval in society that forced social analysts to think differently about society and social stability.

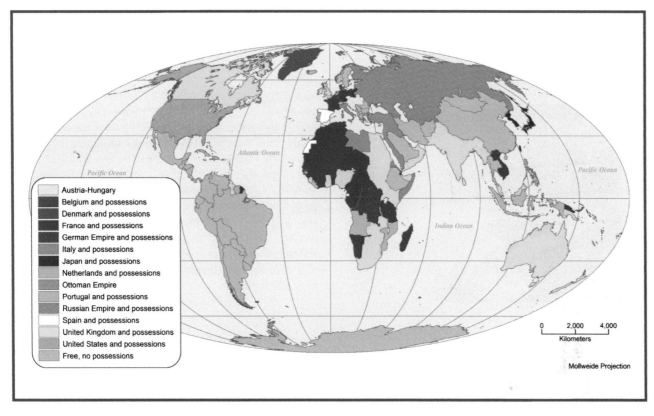

MAP 2.1   Colonial Possessions in 1914

Source: Barraclough (1986:100–1); O'Brien (1999:206); Shepherd (1964:166–67); Stone (1991:243). Map by Anna Versluis.

lack of systematic data collection or objective analysis in social thought. These Frenchmen are considered the first to suggest that a *science of society* could help people understand and perhaps control the rapid changes and unsettling revolutions taking place. Comte officially coined the term *sociology* in 1838. His basic premise was that religious or philosophical speculation about society did not provide an adequate understanding of how to solve society's problems. Just as the natural sciences provided basic facts about the physical world, so too there was a need to gather scientific knowledge about the social world. Only then could we systematically apply this scientific knowledge to improve social conditions.

Comte wanted to use scientific methods to address two basic questions that continue to interest sociologists to this day: What holds society together and gives rise to a stable order rather than anarchy, and why is there change in society? To answer these basic questions, Comte conceptualized society as divided into two parts. *Social statics* referred to aspects of society that give rise to order, stability, and harmony; and *social dynamics* referred to change and evolution in the parts of society and in society itself over time. Simply stated, Comte was concerned with what contemporary sociologists and the social world model in this book refer to as *structure* (social statics) and *process* (social dynamics).

By understanding these aspects of the social world, Comte felt leaders could strengthen the society and could respond appropriately to change. His optimistic belief was that sociology would be the "queen of sciences," guiding leaders to construct a better social order.

Despite helping to found a new discipline, Comte's ideas are not above reproach. While advocating the use of science, Comte still maintained strong philosophical biases toward order and stability, even though the outcomes of that order might reinforce inequality and oppression. Nevertheless, the two main contributions of Comte stand the test of time: the social world can and should be studied scientifically, and the knowledge gained from the scientific study of society can and should be used to improve the human condition.

Sociology continued its evolution as scholars contemplated further changes brought about by the Industrial Revolution. A century ago, scenes of urban squalor were common in Great Britain and other industrializing European nations. Machines replaced both agricultural workers and cottage (home) industries because they produced an abundance of goods faster, better, and cheaper. Peasants pushed off the land by the new technology were flocking to urban areas to find work at the same time that a powerful new social class of industrialists was emerging.

Henri Saint-Simon (above) and Auguste Comte (below) were two contributors to sociology as a science. They insisted that human society could be studied like other sciences, with careful gathering of data using empirical methods.

These massive social and economic changes in the interdependent social world brought about restructuring and sometimes the demise of political monarchies, aristocracies, and feudal lords. Industrialization brought the need for a new skilled class of laborers, increasing demands on what had been an education system serving only the elite. Families were no longer self-sufficient in agriculture or cottage industries but depended on wages from their labor in the industrial sector to stay alive. In short, even from the very beginnings of the discipline, sociologists focused on the relationship between micro-, meso-, and macro-level processes.

These scenes stimulated other social scientists to study society and its problems. Writings of Émile Durkheim, Karl Marx, Harriet Martineau, Max Weber, W.E.B. Du Bois, and many other early sociologists set the stage for development of *sociological theories*—statements of how facts are related to one another. Accompanying the development of sociological theory was the utilization of the *scientific method*—systematic gathering and recording of reliable and accurate data to test ideas. To understand sociology, it is necessary to examine assumptions that underlie the scientific method.

Assumptions of Science

Throughout most of human history, people came to "know" the world by way of traditions being passed down from one generation to the next. Things were so because authoritative persons in the culture said they were so. Often, there was reliance on magical or religious explanations of the forces in nature, and these explanations also became part of tradition. People were interested in the natural world and observed it carefully, but with advances in the natural sciences, observations of cause-and-effect processes became more systematic and controlled. As the way of knowing about the world shifted, tradition and magic as primary means to understand the world were challenged. It was only a little over 200 years ago that people thought lightning storms were a sign of an angry God, not electricity caused by meteorological forces. Some people still believe this.

The scientific approach is based on several core assumptions. The first assumption is that there is a real physical and social world that can be studied scientifically. For example, a hydrogen atom exhibits a particular structure and behaves in a particular way regardless of what we think about it. Second, there is a certain order to the world, and this order results from a series of *causes and effects;* in other words, there are identifiable patterns that can be understood and predicted by examining the sequences that produce them. The world is not merely a collection of unrelated random events but rather events that are causally related and patterned. Third, the way to gain knowledge of the world is to subject it to empirical testing. **Empirical knowledge** means that something can be objectively observed and carefully measured using the five senses (sometimes enhanced by scientific instruments) and that the reality of what is being measured would be the same for all people who observe it.

For knowledge to be scientific, therefore, it must come from phenomena that can be observed and measured. Phenomena that some people presume to exist but that can never be subject to measurement are not within the realm of scientific inquiry; the existence of God, the devil, heaven, hell, and the soul cannot be observed and measured and therefore cannot be examined scientifically. Note that while certain religious notions cannot themselves be subjects of scientific inquiry, religion can be studied in terms of the role it plays in society: its impact on our values and behavior (the sociology of religion), the historical development of specific religious traditions (history of religion), or the emotional comfort and stability it brings to people (psychology of religion).

Finally, science is rooted in **objectivity**, using methods that do not contaminate one's findings while doing research and analysis. Personal opinions or biases should not enter into the collection and analysis of evidence about the world.

Discovery of lightning as a form of electricity has only been understood since 1752, due to an experiment by Benjamin Franklin. There is much we are still learning about the social world, which is why sociological research—using empirical methods—is so exciting.

Harriet Martineau (1802–1876) wrote Society in America, *a critique of America's failure to live up to its democratic principles, especially as they related to women. The book was published in 1837 and was one of many social analyses she published in her lifetime. Her work is a precursor to current feminist work and to conflict theory. It was published 11 years before Karl Marx's most famous work.*

Moreover, scientists are obliged not to distort their research findings so as to promote a particular point of view. The value of scientific research is judged first on whether it passes the test of being conducted without bias.

One way this is done is to see if one's research supports or disproves whatever it is that the researcher thinks is true. The failure to disprove one's ideas offers evidence to support the findings. If I wish to study whether gender is a major factor in whether one is likely to be altruistic, then I must set the research study up in such a way that I could support *or* disprove my hypothesis (educated guess or prediction). In the sciences, **evidence** refers to facts and information that are confirmed through systematic processes of testing—using the five senses.

A failure to meet these standards means that a study is not scientific. Someone's ideas can seem plausible and logical but still not be supported by the facts. This is why evidence is so important. Sociology is concerned with having accurate evidence, and it is important to know what is or is not considered accurate, dependable evidence. You have probably seen one of the *CSI* (Crime Scene Investigation) series on television. You might note how important data and commitment to objective analysis of the data is in that show. Sociologists deal with different issues, but the same sort of concern for accuracy in gathering data guides the work of a sociologist.

Systematic, objective observation proved to be a powerful tool for understanding the natural world and also defined the new approach to understanding the social world. For example, the eighteenth-century English scholar Thomas Malthus was one of the early social scientists who used systematic methods to gather data and present objective scientific methods for analysis of population patterns and growth. Some of his formulae are still used today. However, he was also influenced by philosophical biases; he made judgments about groups of people in social commentaries about "the poor breeding like rabbits," showing the tenuous beginnings of objective social science.

Throughout this book, you will visit the ideas of nineteenth- and twentieth-century sociologists who contributed to the evolution of sociology as a science. Sociologists have come a long way from the early explanations of the social world that were based on the moralizing of the eighteenth- and nineteenth-century social philosophers and the guesswork of social planners. Sociologists and policy makers can now base their policy decisions on solid scientific evidence. Part of the excitement of sociology today comes from the challenge to improve the scientific procedures applied to the study of humans and social behavior.

THINKING SOCIOLOGICALLY

Imagine that you want to understand why people join religious cults and commit their lives to charismatic cult leaders. Why is scientifically gathered data preferable to explanations based on two or three anecdotes told by former members of cults or by speculations on why people join cults?

EMPIRICAL RESEARCH AND SOCIAL THEORY

We all have ideas or beliefs about how our social world works. We tend to take these beliefs, developed throughout our lives, for granted; they serve to define how we see our social world and justify our actions. Social researchers use the scientific method to examine these views of society; they assume that (1) there are predictable social relations in the world, (2) social situations will recur in certain patterns, and (3) social situations have causes that can be understood. If the social world were totally chaotic, little would be gained by scientific study.

It is from these assumptions that sociologists develop preferences for different social theories, just as individuals develop preferences for different religious or political beliefs that guide their lives. The main difference between individual beliefs and social theories is that the latter are subject to ongoing, systematic empirical testing.

Theories are statements regarding how and why facts are related to each other and the connections between these facts. Theories are found at each level of analysis in the social world; which theory a sociologist uses to study the social world depends on the part of the social world to be studied, from the individual in a small group to societies in the global system, as illustrated in the model on page 27.

Each of the major theoretical perspectives discussed in this chapter—symbolic interactionism, rational choice theory, functionalism, and conflict theory—gives a perspective on the way the social world works. For instance, to study Hector's life in Brazil, the questions the researcher asks might focus on the micro-level interactions between Hector and his family members, peers, teachers, and employers that contribute to his situation. One might ask, for example, why Hector finds some activities (working) more realistic or rewarding than others (attending school). A meso-level focus might examine the organizations and institutions—such as the business world, the schools, and the religious communities in Brazil—to see how they shape the forces that affect Hector's life. Alternatively, the focus might be on macro-level analysis—the class structure (rich to poor) of the society and the global forces such as trade relations between Brazil and other countries that influence the opportunities available to poor people.

The poverty Hector experienced can be considered from any of these levels of analysis. Regardless of the level of analysis, however, sociologists look beyond individual explanations to focus on group explanations in understanding issues such as the poverty that haunts Hector's life. Different research methods to collect data are appropriate depending on the level of analysis of the theory being used and the question being researched.

Scientists, including sociologists, use theories to predict why things happen and under what conditions they are likely to happen. Theories explain the relationships between social variables, but these relationships need to be tested. That is why sociologists collect data to test theories. This is where research methods—the procedures one uses to gather data—are relevant. Theory and research are mutually dependent. Theory provides an explanation for the relationship between ideas and facts, and research helps us gather the facts to formulate and test the theory. If a theory—say, an explanation related to Hector's situation—is not supported by the data, it must be reformulated or discarded in favor of a theory that is consistent with the facts that have been uncovered using research methods. The facts (data) collected must be assessed with careful reasoning, as described in the next section.

What factors—personal, institutional, national, and global—cause poverty in a place like Nairobi, Kenya? This grocery store is in a poor section of town.

Source: © Sean Sprague / The Image Works.

Deductive and Inductive Reasoning

Like other scientists, sociologists conduct their investigations using one of two main lines of reasoning. **Deductive reasoning** begins with broad general ideas, or theories, of human social behavior, and from these ideas more specific patterns are identified or "deduced" using logical reasoning. These educated guesses—which still do not have data to support them—are called **hypotheses**. To illustrate, suppose we wish to use deductive analysis to address the problem of why some parents abuse their children. We would begin by determining the level of analysis of the problem—parent-child interactions. Because this is a micro-level problem, a micro-level theory would be our choice for a theory. Previous research has indicated that family abuse is a pattern of violence learned as a child grows up, and violence comes to be seen as "normal." Therefore, our hypothesis (educated guess) to test could be the following: "Abusive parents are more likely than nonabusive parents to have been abused as children and to have learned that violence is an acceptable

method of parenting." We could then gather data on the backgrounds of parents who have been identified as abusive and compare them to a group of nonabusive parents. Then we would compare our data findings with the hypothesis to see if the statement is supported by the evidence.

Inductive reasoning, on the other hand, begins with specific facts (data) or evidence and tries to find or develop a theory—a more generalized set of concepts—to explain the facts. First, the researcher collects facts and then attempts to explain the relationship between these facts. In so doing, the researcher is building up to a generalization, moving from the concrete facts to the abstract theory. The specific facts give rise to a theory, and that theory can then be tested again with new data. A researcher interested in the consequences of child abuse might begin by doing extensive school or playground observations of children who have been abused and review information on these children's academic performance in school. Then a generalization—a theory—would emerge from the data itself. In this case, the research begins

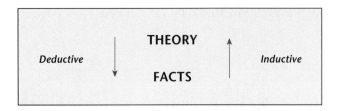

Figure 2.1   Inductive and Deductive Reasoning

with research questions but not a hypothesis. Figure 2.1 illustrates the relationship of inductive and deductive reasoning to theory and facts.

In summary, social scientists use both inductive and deductive reasoning in their work. *Deductive reasoning* tests the theory using scientific research methods to obtain facts (data) relevant to that theory. *Inductive reasoning* connects scientifically collected facts to social theory; it tries to find or create a general theory to explain the facts. Research data may confirm a theory, force its modification, require the scientist to abandon it altogether, or lead to an entirely new theory. Whatever the case, theory and methods work together and cannot be separated in the research process. The following section discusses how sociologists plan research studies to test theories.

THINKING SOCIOLOGICALLY

Imagine that a sociologist collects facts by interviewing Hector and other children from his *favela* to learn about their family lives, educational histories, and work experiences. How would a sociologist approach the problem of poverty in Hector's life using a deductive approach? How would it be different using an inductive approach?

HOW SOCIOLOGISTS STUDY THE SOCIAL WORLD

Since the origins of the discipline, sociologists have designed and refined scientific tools for studying sociological questions. What is presented here is a skeleton of the research process that sociologists and other social scientists spend years studying and perfecting. This section will help to provide a sense of how sociologists study issues and know what they know. If you study more sociology, you will learn more about the research process. It is exciting to collect accurate information and learn answers to important, meaningful questions that can make a difference to people's lives.

To use the scientific method to study the social world, a researcher follows a number of logically related steps.

Step 1: Define a topic or problem that can be investigated scientifically.

Step 2: Review relevant research and theory to refine the topic and define variables.

Step 3: Formulate hypotheses or research questions, and operationalize variables.

Step 4: Design the research method that specifies how the data will be gathered.

Step 5: Select a sample of people or groups from the population.

Step 6: Collect the data using appropriate research methods.

Step 7: Analyze the data, figuring out exactly what the study tells us about the question(s).

Step 8: Draw conclusions and present the final report, including suggestions for future research.

Each of these steps is very important if you become a professional sociologist. However, for our purposes in an introductory course, we will provide a quick summary of the research process: planning a research study, designing the research, doing the analysis, and drawing conclusions.

Planning a Research Study

Planning a research study involves four initial steps: define the problem clearly, find out what is already known about the topic, formulate hypotheses, and operationalize definitions of variables.

The first and most important step is to define a topic or problem that can be investigated scientifically. Without a clear problem, the research will go nowhere. Using poverty as an example of a broad topic area, sociologists could focus on a number of issues—for example, rates of poverty in different countries, poverty and levels of education, race and poverty, gender and poverty, or the relationship between poverty and drug or alcohol abuse. These broad topic areas are a good start, but they must be more specific and defined before they become suitable topics for systematic research. One must clarify specifically what one wants to know about the issue.

Specific research topics, ones that can be measured and tested, are usually posed in the form of questions: Why do some countries have large segments of their populations living in poverty? What causes some students—especially those in poor families—to drop out of school? Why are there disproportionate numbers of women and persons of color living in poverty? Are people who are poor more vulnerable to excessive drug or alcohol use? The research question must be asked in a precise way; otherwise, it cannot be tested empirically. Asking good researchable questions is extremely important in sound scientific research.

THINKING SOCIOLOGICALLY

Pick a topic of interest to you. Now, write a research question based on your topic.

A second step in planning the research is reviewing existing studies to determine what has already been learned about the topic by other researchers. One needs to know how the previous research was done, how terms were defined, and the strengths and limitations of that research. Social scientists can then know what has been done and link their study to existing findings to build the knowledge base. This step usually involves combing through scholarly journals and books on the topic. In the case of Hector, we would need to identify what previous studies tell us about why impoverished young people drop out of school.

In the third step, based on the review of the literature on the topic, social scientists often formulate *hypotheses—* reasonable, educated guesses about the relationship between two or more variables based on the knowledge they have gained on the topic; they then identify the key *concepts,* or ideas, in the hypothesis (e.g., poverty and dropping out of school). These concepts can be measured by collecting facts or data. This process of determining how to measure concepts is called *operationalizing variables.* **Variables** are concepts (ideas) that can vary in frequency of occurrence from one time, place, or person to another. Examples include levels of poverty, percentage of people living in poverty, or number of years of formal education. Variables can then be measured by collecting data; they provide controls for the research, suggesting relationships to test.

A hypothesis predicts the relationship between two or more variables and ways in which variables are related to each other (such as poverty and education). "Poverty *leads* teenagers to drop out of school for opportunities to earn money" is a testable hypothesis that predicts future at-risk young people. Another hypothesis could predict the opposite—that dropping out of school leads to poverty. A hypothesis to study Hector's situation might be as follows: "Poverty is a major cause of teenagers in the *favela* dropping out of school because they need to earn money for the family." That hypothesis provides a statement to be tested.

To o*perationalize* variables, researchers link social concepts such as poverty to specific measurement indicators such as "an annual family income of less than half of the median family income for that country." Using the hypothesis above, concepts such as dropouts and poverty can be measured by determining the number of times they occur.

"Dropouts," for instance, might be defined by the number of days of school missed in a designated period of time according to school records. "Poverty" could be defined by having an annual income that is less than half of the average income for that size of family in Brazil. Our determination of poverty could also include family assets such as ownership of property or other tangible goods such as cattle, automobiles, and indoor plumbing. Poverty may also be examined in terms of access to medical care, education, transportation, and other services available to citizens. It is important to be clear, precise, and consistent about how one measures poverty so that those doing a follow-up study can critique and improve upon one's own study. Background research— including examination of previous studies of poverty—often helps to determine how to operationalize variables.

THINKING SOCIOLOGICALLY

Consider your research question. What are your variables, and how could you operationalize them?

Underlying this discussion of defining the problem is the ability to plan a study that accurately measures what we predict is the relationship between concepts. The following key research terms are important in understanding how two variables (concepts that vary and can be measured) are related:

- **Correlation** refers to relationships between variables, with change in one variable associated with change in another. Poverty and teenagers dropping out of school vary together—happen among the same people.
- **Cause-and-effect relationships** help establish the relationship between two variables. Once we have determined that there is probably a correlation—the fact that the two variables *both* occur in the same situation—we need to take the next step of testing for a causal relationship between variables. The **independent variable** is hypothesized to cause the change; in terms of time sequence, it comes first and affects the **dependent variable**. If we hypothesize that poverty causes Hector and others to drop out of school, "poverty" is the independent variable in this hypothesis, and "dropping out of school" is the dependent variable, *dependent* on the poverty. A *time dimension* is present in determining cause and effect; the independent variable must always precede the dependent variable in time sequence if we are to say one variable causes another.
- **Spurious relationships** occur when there is no causal relationship between the independent and dependent variables, but they vary together, often

due to a third variable working on both of them. For example, if the quantity of ice cream consumed is highest during those weeks of the year when the most swimming pool drownings occur, these two events are correlated. However, eating ice cream did not cause the increase in pool deaths. Indeed, hot weather may have caused more people both to purchase ice cream and go swimming, thus resulting in more chance of drowning incidents—a spurious relationship. **Controls** are used by researchers to eliminate all variables except those related to the hypothesis; using controls helps ensure the relationship is not spurious.

Designing the Research Method

After the researcher has carefully planned the study, the next step is to select appropriate data collection methods; these depend on the research question and the level of analysis (micro, meso, and macro) at which the researcher is working. If the researcher wants to answer a macro-level research question, such as the effect of poverty on school success, they are likely to focus on large-scale social and economic problems in society. To learn about micro-level issues such as the influence of peers on dropping out of school, researchers will focus on small group interactions. Figure 2.2 illustrates different levels of analysis.

Different data collection techniques will be appropriate for studies at different levels of analysis in the social world and will depend on the question the researcher is trying to answer. The method selected is one of the most important decisions in research because the quality of the data collected is directly related to the value of the study findings. Accuracy

in planning can mean the difference between a fruitful scientific study and data that has little meaning.

The primary methods used to collect data for research studies include surveys (both interviews and questionnaires), observation studies, controlled experiments, and use of existing materials. Our discussion cannot go into detail about how researchers use these techniques, but a brief explanation gives an idea of why they use these core approaches.

The **survey method** is used when sociologists want to gather information directly from a number of people regarding how they think or feel, or what they do. Two forms of surveys are common: the interview and the questionnaire. Both involve a series of questions asked of respondents.

Interviews are conducted by talking directly with people, called *respondents,* and asking questions in person or by telephone. *Questionnaires* are written questions to which respondents reply in writing. In both cases, questions may be *open-ended,* allowing the respondent to say or write whatever comes to mind, or *closed-ended,* requiring the respondent to chose from a set of possible answers.

One method to study school dropouts is to survey teenagers about what caused them to leave school. The researcher would have to evaluate whether an interview or questionnaire would provide the best information. Interviews are more time-consuming and labor-intensive than questionnaires but are better for gathering in-depth information. However, if the researcher wants information from a large number of teenagers, questionnaires are often more practical and less costly.

Field studies (also called *observational methods*) are used when systematic, planned observation of interaction is

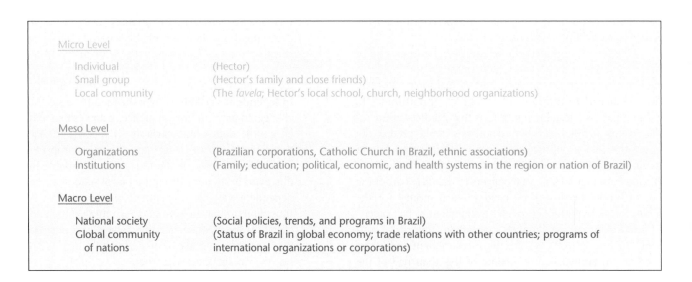

Figure 2.2   The Social World Model and Levels of Analysis

needed to obtain data. *Observation*—the systematic viewing and recording of behavior or interaction in the natural settings where behavior takes place—can take several forms. One form, *detached or nonparticipant observation*, involves the researcher observing as an outsider, without being involved in the activities of the group. For instance, the researcher may observe or videotape a drug-counseling group from behind a one-way mirror in order to study the group dynamics; the individuals or groups may never be aware of the researcher's presence.

Participant observation occurs when the researcher actually participates in the activities of the group being studied. The researcher, for instance, might join Alcoholics Anonymous in order to observe group processes as they occur naturally. Participation is particularly useful when studying illegal or deviant activities where it might be impossible to gain scientifically useful information any other way. The results from such a study are referred to as *qualitative* rather than quantitative research; it provides valuable information that is rich in detail, human context, and social texture, rather than providing hard numerical data that gives percentages or can be illustrated in neat tables.

A problem for participant observers is the possibility of altering group functioning and interaction by their presence—a process called *research effects*—or becoming involved in the group to such a degree that objectivity becomes difficult. This is much less of a problem in large public settings such as religious meetings or watching children on a playground to observe gender segregation. However, in a smaller group, the very presence of the researcher may change things. Furthermore, the researcher's interpretation of the social scene is both especially interesting and especially subject to bias. Despite these potential problems, observation remains a useful way of obtaining information.

Ethnography (also called *ethnographic research*) is a form of field study, but it involves some unique strategies of inquiry and methods of analysis. Ethnographers use self-reflection in research as the research progresses; the researcher pursues any ideas that may shed light on the research problem. Often, the research takes place on site in a natural setting (home, office, playground) and involves using various data collecting techniques, such as interviewing and observing, with writing field notes about observations being primary. Thus, the research process is flexible, often conducted without formal research hypotheses; rather, the researcher poses research questions to guide the observations, and the research evolves in response to what the researcher learns as the research progresses. Unlike research driven by hypotheses to be tested, this method allows the researcher to respond to new ideas that come up during the research (Creswell 2003).

Controlled experiments control all variables except the one being studied. In this way, researchers can study the effects of the variable under study. A controlled experiment usually requires an **experimental group**, in which people are exposed to the variable being studied in order to test its effect, and a **control group**, in which the subjects are not exposed to the variable the experimenter wants to test.

The control group provides a base of data to which the experimental group data can then be compared. By separating the sample into experimental and control groups, the researcher can see if the study's independent variable makes a difference in behavior of people who are exposed to that variable. For example, researchers may want to determine whether viewing violence on television makes children's behavior more aggressive. The control group is exposed to television programming with nonviolent content, and the experimental group is provided with a program involving high levels of violence. The aggression levels of the two groups of children after watching the different shows can then be compared to determine if television violence affects behavior.

Controlled experiments are powerful because they are the most accurate test of cause and effect. Despite the advantages of controlled experiments, there are some drawbacks and they cannot be used to study many sociological research questions. First, many sociological questions cannot be studied in controlled settings because they deal with meso- and macro-level organizations and social forces and cannot be placed in a controlled situation. Hector's situation in the *favela* cannot be studied in a laboratory setting. Second, the mere fact of being in a laboratory setting and knowing one is in an experiment may affect the research results—another form of research effects. Third, because of ethical constraints, social scientists cannot do studies that might harm people. Thus, there are many variables that we cannot introduce in the laboratory.

Existing sources involves use of materials that already exist but are being employed in a new way or to understand a different pattern. There are two approaches involving existing materials: secondary analysis and content analysis.

Secondary analysis uses existing data, that is, information that has already been collected in other studies. Often, large data-collecting organizations such as the United Nations or a country's census bureau, national education department, or a private research organization will make data available for use by researchers. Consider the question of the dropout rate in Brazil. Researchers can learn a great deal about patterns of school dropouts from analysis of information gathered by ministries or departments of education. Likewise, if we want to compare modern dropout rates with those of an earlier age, we may find data from previous decades to be invaluable. Sometimes secondary analysis is the sole method of data collection, and sometimes it is used along with other methods.

Despite its usefulness, secondary analysis cannot be used in some research studies and it has several potential weaknesses. First, not all data sets are representative of the total population being studied; this is especially true in comparing data sets from countries using different definitions of variables (such as levels of poverty) and different data gathering techniques. Second, secondary analysis does not touch the "human side" of research questions in the way interviews or even observation can. Secondary analysis involves no direct observation of the behavior in question. School dropouts, for example, have individual stories and problems that are not told by large, impersonal data sets. Third, the data sets available for secondary analysis are gathered for purposes other than the research questions to which they are now being applied. They may not directly answer the researcher's questions. Finally, any problems or biases that exist in the original data are carried over to the secondary analysis. Despite such limitations, however, secondary analysis can be an excellent way to do meso- or macro-level studies that reveal large-scale patterns in the social world.

Content analysis involves systematic categorizing and recording of information from written or recorded sources. With content analysis, a common method in historical research and study of organizations, sociologists can gather the data they need from printed materials—books, magazines, video recordings, newspapers, laws, letters, memos and sometimes even artworks. A researcher studying variations in levels of concern about child abuse could do a content analysis of popular magazines to see how many pages or stories were devoted to child abuse in 1965, 1975, 1985, 1995, and 2005.

Content analysis has the advantage of being relatively inexpensive and easy to do. It is also *unobtrusive*, meaning that the researcher does not influence the subject being investigated by having direct contact. The written or visual record to be examined is already available. Furthermore, using materials in historical sequence can be effective in recognizing patterns over time—what comes before and what comes after. However, accuracy of the study relies on what content is available.

THINKING SOCIOLOGICALLY

What methods would be appropriate to collect data on your research question?

An example of historical research, using existing materials to examine social patterns, is illustrated in How Do We Know? (page 41). In this case, the researcher, Virginia Kemp Fish, studied records and writings to discover the contributions of early women sociologists in Chicago to sociology and to the betterment of society.

Triangulation, or *multiple methods* of social research, combines two or more methods of data collection to enhance the accuracy of the findings. To study Hector's situation, a research study could use macro-level data on poverty in Brazil and micro-level interviews with Hector and his peers to determine their goals and views. Thus, if all findings point to the same conclusion, the researcher can feel much more confident that the claims are true. Data collection

techniques—survey, field study, controlled experimentation, and analysis of existing sources—represent the dominant methods used to collect data for sociological research.

THINKING SOCIOLOGICALLY

To the question "How do you know?" a sociologist replies that empirical evidence (data) supports certain claims and that is how he or she knows something is true. At this early point in our explorations, how would you describe *empirical evidence*?

Selecting a Sample

It would be impossible to study the reasons for poverty or for dropping out of school of all Brazilian teenagers, so we must select a representative group to study; these findings can help us understand the larger group. A part of the research design is determining how to make sure the study includes people who are typical of the total group. When the research study involves a survey or field observation, sociologists need to decide *who* will be observed or questioned. This involves careful selection of a **sample**, a small and more manageable group of people systematically chosen to represent a much larger group. The objective of sampling is to select a group that accurately represents the characteristics of the entire group (or population) being studied.

Researchers use many types of samples; a common one, the *representative sample*, accurately reflects the group being studied so that the sample results can be generalized or applied to the larger population. In the case of Hector's school, a sample could be drawn from all 13 to 16 year olds eligible for school in his region of Brazil.

The most common form of representative sample is the *random sample;* people from every walk of life and every group within the population have an equal chance of being selected for the study. By observing or talking with this smaller group selected from the total population under study, the researcher can get an accurate picture of the total population and have confidence that the findings do apply to the larger group. Drawing a representative sample is not always simple. In the case of Brazil, people constantly move in and out of the *favela*. Those who have just arrived may not have the same characteristics as those who have been living there a long time. Thus, developing an effective sampling technique is often a complex process.

It is important to have a sample that represents the group being studied. If we wanted to know attitudes toward current foreign policy in Brazil, we would not question people who live in Quebec, Canada, or only people from the city of Sao Paulo, for they do not represent the nation as a whole. If we wanted to understand the views of all Christians in Canada, we cannot ask questions only of those who are affiliated with the conservative Christian Coalition; the majority of Christians hold many other points of view, and their ideas would need to be included in the information gathered. Otherwise, the sample would be *unrepresentative*.

Interpretation of data involves judgment and opinion, often based on the theory guiding the research. As such, it can be challenged by other researchers who might interpret the results differently or challenge the methods used to collect and analyze the data. Discussion and criticism are an important part of science and make possible new ideas, interpretations, and methodological approaches to problems. We sociologists grow through these critiques, as does the field of sociology

itself. Since every research study should be replicable—capable of being repeated—enough information must be given to ensure that another researcher could repeat the study and compare results.

Given that social science research focuses on humans and humans are changeable, findings are seldom seen as absolute or unequivocal. Results do not always have unanimous agreement among scholars, and it is difficult to say that any single study has definitively proven something. Indeed, the word *prove* is not used to describe the interpretation of findings in

How Do We Know?

The Hull House Circle

Historical research can be an important source of data for sociological analysis, for history can demonstrate vividly the causal events. Historical circumstances provide context for understanding why things evolved to the present state of affairs. One fascinating historical study focuses on the contribution of the Hull House women to developing the science of sociology.

Hull House was the base for a group of women social researchers, reformers, and activists, and Jane Addams was one of them. These women had obtained college degrees in some of the few fields then open to women (political science, law, economics), and because they were often excluded from full-time careers in these fields, they used their education and skills to help others and to do research on social conditions.

Some of the earliest social survey research was conducted by the women connected with Hull House, sometimes employing the Hull House residents to help collect data. These women led the first systematic attempt to describe an immigrant community in an American city, a study found in *Hull House Maps and Papers* (Residents of Hull House c.1895/1970).

Virginia Kemp Fish (1986), who originated the designation "Hull House Circle," researched historical literature to learn more about the lives and contributions of these women and their proper place in the sociological literature. She examined records, letters, biographies, and other historical sources to piece together their stories. Fish made an interesting observation about these women's professional styles as compared with those of men.

While men often received their training and support from a mentor (an older, established, and respected man in the field), these women operated within a network of egalitarian relationships and interactions. By studying their written and activist work, Fish shows how they supported each other's work and scholarship and provided emotional encouragement and intellectual stimulation rather than interacting in terms of an unequal power distribution.

Until recently, women sociologists, such as the members of the Hull House Circle, have not received much attention for their contributions to the science of sociology. Fish found that from 1889 to 1935, Jane Addams was head

Jane Addams, social researcher, critic, and reformer.

resident of Hull House, a settlement house in Chicago. Settlement houses were established in urban, immigrant neighborhoods; they created a sense of community and offered a multitude of services.

According to Fish's research, data and documents collected by Addams and other Hull House women provide baseline information that has been used as a starting point or comparison for later studies—for social researchers in the fields of immigration, ethnic relations, poverty, health care, housing, unemployment, work and occupations, delinquency and crime, war, and social movements (Fish 1986). The contributions are extensive, indeed.

Sociology in Your Social World

How to Read a Research Table

A statistical table is a researcher's laborsaving device. Quantitative data presented in tabular form is more clear and concise than the same information presented in several written paragraphs. A good table has clear signposts to help the reader and avoid confusion. For instance, the table below shows many of the main features of a table, and the list that follows explains how to read each feature.*

TABLE 2.1 **Mean Earnings (in dollars)**

Characteristic	Total Persons	Not a High School Graduate	High School Graduate Only	Some College, No Degree	Associate Degree	Bachelor's Degree	Master's Degree	Professional Degree	Doctorate Degree
				Level of Highest Degree					
All persons[a]	37,046	18,734	27,915	29,533	35,958	51,206	62,514	115,212	88,471
Age									
25–34 yrs	33,212	18,920	26,073	28,954	32,276	43,794	51,040	74,120	62,109
35–44 yrs	42,475	22,123	31,479	36,038	38,442	57,438	66,264	126,165	101,382
45–54 yrs	45,908	23,185	32,978	40,291	41,511	59,208	68,344	132,180	92,229
55–64 yrs	45,154	23,602	31,742	38,131	39,147	57,423	66,760	138,845	98,433
65 and over	28,918	17,123	20,618	28,017	23,080	41,323	42,194	77,312	56,724
Sex									
Male	55,455	28,345	40,119	48,812	50,012	71,140	85,700	148,611	105,928
Female	31,024	16,075	23,143	26,720	30,639	40,200	48,535	72,594	73,516
White									
Male	57,075	28,603	41,239	50,262	51,094	73,648	86,718	153,469	111,093
Female	32,344	17,598	23,920	27,329	31,576	39,581	48,746	73,075	71,356
Black									
Male	40,779	24,962	34,334	38,133	43,081	50,793	78,354	—	—
Female	28,171	16,509	21,270	25,919	27,658	42,633	49,330	—	—
Hispanic[b]									
Male	35,160	24,628	31,921	44,397	43,279	52,948	70,747	—	—
Female	23,265	14,414	20,352	24,100	28,060	38,473	48,433	—	—

Source: U.S. Census Bureau, Current Population Survey (2005). Data are extracted from "Table 9: Earnings in 2003 by Educational Attainment of the Population 18 Years and Over, by Age, Sex, Race Alone, and Hispanic Origin: 2004."

Note: The dash means that the base is too small to show the derived measure.
a. Includes other races, not shown separately.
b. Persons of Hispanic origin may be of any race.

TITLE: The title provides information on the major topic and variables in the table.

"Earnings by Highest degree Earned: 1999"

SOURCE: The source note, found under the table, points out the origin of the data. It is usually identified by the label "source."

"Source: U.S. Census Bureau, *Current Population* Survey (2005)

MARGINAL TABS: In examining the numbers in the table try working from the outside in. Begin by looking at the marginals, the figures at the margins of the table. The figures often provide summary information.

In this table note that the column marked "Total persons" provides average income in each category for all levels of education.

CELLS: To make more detailed comparisons, examine specific cells in the body of the table. These are the boxes that hold the numbers or percentages.

In this table the cells contain data on ethnic (white, black, Hispanic), age, and gender difference.

HEADNOTE: Many tables will have a note under the title giving information relevant to understanding the table or units in the table.

For this table, the reader is informed that this includes all persons over the age of 18 who reported an income.

FOOTNOTES: Some tables have footnotes, usually indicating something unusual about the data or where to find more complete data.

In this table several footnotes are provided so the reader does not make mistakes in interpretation.

HEADINGS AND STUBS: Tables generally have one or two levels of headings under the title and headnotes. These instruct the reader about what is in the columns below.

In this table the headnotes indicate the level of education achieved so the reader can identify the average income for persons with that amount of education.

UNITS: Units refer to how the data is reported. It could be in percentages or in number per 100 or 1,000, or in other units.

In this table the data is reported in dollars of income.

FACTS FROM THE TABLE: After reviewing all of the above information, the reader is ready to make some interpretations about what the data mean.

In this table the reader might note that women's income distribution is lower than men's and that women with the same amount of education earn much less than men. Likewise, African Americans and Hispanics earn much less than whites with similar amounts of education.

*Features of the table adapted from Broom and Selznick 1963.

the social and behavioral sciences. Rather, social scientists say that findings tend to support or reject hypotheses.

So, why bother doing social science research if findings can be challenged and nothing is absolute? Systematic, scientific research brings us closer to reality of the social world than guesswork and opinions. When we have supportive findings from numerous studies, not just one, that builds a stronger case for a theory. The search for truth is ongoing—a kind of mission in life for those of us who are scholars. Furthermore, as we get closer to accurate understanding of society, our social policies can be based on the most accurate knowledge available. Most sciences are cautious about claiming that they have the absolute truth.

Now that the appropriate research method for collecting data has been selected, the researher's next step is to collect the data, then analyze that data and see what it says about the research questions and hypotheses.

THINKING SOCIOLOGICALLY

How would you word a questionnaire in a study about the effects of peer influence on dropping out of school? How could you find out whether your questions are good ones?

Analyzing the Data and Drawing Conclusions

Once data is gathered, the next step is to analyze the data to decide what it means. Now that we have, say, 500 questionnaires or a notebook full of field observation notes, what do we do with them? There are multiple techniques used by social researchers to analyze data. The general idea is to evaluate the data to determine the relationship of variables to each other. For instance, if dropout rates are high among Hector's friends, was their school achievement low? What other factors are present? This analysis can become quite complex, but the purpose is the same—to determine the relationship between the variables being examined. After stating the initial hypotheses to test, sociology is not guesswork or speculation. It involves careful, objective analysis of specific data.

A report is developed outlining the research project and analysis of the data collected. The final section of the report presents a discussion of results, draws conclusions as to whether or not the hypotheses were supported, interprets the results, and makes recommendations from the researcher's point of view. As part of the presentation and discussion of results, the report may contain tables or figures presenting summaries of data. Tables presenting information can be extremely useful in understanding the data. The accompanying feature How to Read a Research Table provides useful tips on reading research tables found in journal articles and newspapers.

Applied Sociology

You may have asked yourself, "What can I do with sociology and sociological methods?" Chapter 1 discussed some careers held by sociologists, providing a partial answer to the question.

We add to that the application of sociological theory and research used by applied sociologists to answer questions raised by agencies, organizations, or government. Applied sociology (also known as *sociological practice*) refers to "any use (often client-centered) of the sociological perspective and/or its tools in the understanding of, intervention in, and/or enhancement of human social life" (Steele and Price 2004).

Since the founding of sociology, especially in the United States, some sociologists have had a problem-solving or social-reform orientation to the discipline, always asking about the practical implications of sociological findings (Mauksch 1993; Pickard and Poole 2007). Today, sociologists engaged in applied research use the theories and data collection techniques discussed in this chapter, applying them to address questions and problems of clients in organizations. Table 2.2 outlines key differences between basic (pure) and applied sociology.

TABLE 2.2 **Basic versus Applied Sociology**

	Basic Sociology	**Applied Sociology**
Orientation	Theory building, hypothesis testing	Program effects, focus on consequences of practices
Goal	Knowledge production	Knowledge utilization, problem solving
Source	Self- or discipline-generated	Client-generated

Source: Adapted with permission from the NTL Institute; DeMartini (1982).

In each chapter, you will find a box, The Applied Sociologist at Work, describing a sociologist working in the topic area being discussed. Many of these people have advanced degrees in sociology—a doctorate or a master's degree—but several are applying sociology on the job with a bachelor's degree.

As stated previously, in addition to adhering to the standards and steps of empirical research, researchers studying people must also adhere to standards of ethics so that participants are not harmed, as discussed in the following section.

ETHICAL ISSUES IN SOCIAL RESEARCH

Sociologists and other scientists are bound by ethical codes of conduct governing research. This is to protect any human subjects used in research from being harmed by the research. The American Sociological Association (ASA) code of ethical conduct outlines standards that researchers are expected to observe when doing research, teaching, and publishing; they include points such as being objective, reporting findings and sources fully, making no promises to respondents that cannot be honored, accepting no support that requires violation of these principles, completing contracted work, and delineating responsibilities in works with multiple authors. Related to these standards are the following key ethical issues for sociologists, each a part of the ASA code of ethics:

- How will the findings from the research be used? Will it hurt individuals, communities, or nations if it gets into the hands of "enemies"? Can it be used to aggravate hostilities? In whose interest is the research being carried out? To illustrate the relevance of these questions, in 1964, a number of U.S. social researchers began a study called Project Camelot. The goal was to predict when revolutions would occur in Latin America and to show how governments could stop them. However, the 6 million dollar project was canceled when social scientists complained that it would be unethical for research findings to be used for the United States to intervene in the internal affairs of other countries, especially when such interference might short-circuit movements for human rights.

- How can the researcher protect the privacy and identities of respondents and informants? Is the risk to subjects justified by an anticipated outcome of improved social conditions? For example, in several instances, courts have subpoenaed journalists and social scientists, forcing them to reveal confidential sources and information. Some researchers have spent time in jail to protect the confidentiality of their respondents (Comarow 1993; Scarce 1999).

- Is there informed consent among the people being studied? How much can and should the researcher tell subjects about the purpose of the research without completely biasing the outcome? Does informed consent only mean signing a release form at the beginning of a study? This issue relates to the harm or danger faced by respondents as well as the question of deception by social scientists. Is it acceptable to lie or to mislead participants so they do not change their behavior when they are responding to the situations that the researcher has created? If the public learns that social scientists actively deceive them, what will be the consequences for trusting researchers at a later time when a different study is being conducted?

- Will there be any harm to the participants— including injury to self-esteem or feelings of guilt and self-doubt? Philip Zimbardo (1973) conducted a well-known social psychological experiment in which he designed a mock prison and assigned students to roles of prisoners and guards. The purpose of the study was to gauge the degree to which social roles affect attitudes and behaviors. However, the students took the roles so seriously that they no longer distinguished reality from the artificial situation, and some "guards" became violent and abusive toward the "prisoners." Given these negative reactions, the experiment was discontinued and students were informed about the purpose of the study. Is a research project unethical if it negatively affects a subject's self-esteem? Most social scientists would say yes, such research is beyond the boundaries of ethical conduct.

- How much invasion of privacy is legitimate in the name of research? How much disclosure of confidential information, even in disguised form, is acceptable? For example, a researcher who studies sexual behavior and attitudes may collect data about the most intimate of relationships. How this confidential information is handled to protect respondents is of utmost importance in research ethics.

Codes of ethics cannot answer all ethical dilemmas that arise for researchers, but they do provide general guidelines. In addition, most universities and organizations where research is common have Human Subjects Review Boards whose function is to ensure that human participants are not harmed by the research.

Yet another dilemma is how to get one's findings out into the public so they might influence public policy and the insights of research might be useful to people in their everyday lives. This issue is discussed in The Applied Sociologist at Work (page 45), which presents an essay by a sociologist who was interviewed many times on television and radio, with rather frustrating results.

THINKING SOCIOLOGICALLY

Consider some of the following ethical issues in conducting research. Why is informed consent important? Is it ethical to talk to people when they do not know you are recording their words? Is it ethical to be a researcher in a setting or situation but not inform the group of your research study or that you are studying them? Why?

Research methods work in tandem with sociological theories. The theories suggest how social life is organized and help to shape the questions one asks by suggesting which variables are most important. Knowing this information helps determine appropriate methods to use in a study. The next section summarizes the key ideas in four sociological theories.

SOCIOLOGY'S MAJOR THEORETICAL PERSPECTIVES

Let us return to our opening example of Hector. Sociologists have several perspectives that can help us understand the poverty Hector endures in Sao Paulo, Brazil. Hector's

THE APPLIED SOCIOLOGIST AT WORK

Reporting Research:
A Social Scientist Meets the Press

None of my formal training prepared me for dealing with "media culture" or coping with the media in a manner that would safeguard the integrity of my research findings. Sharing social science findings that have important applications for the public raises ethical concerns and questions. What guidelines should social scientists follow when being interviewed by the media? How can they guard against their research findings being distorted or used to misrepresent an issue? Such questions have no easy answers.

To illustrate, consider the experiences following research and publication of a book (McEvoy and Brookings 2001) directed toward males whose female loved ones are victims of rape; I received scores of invitations to discuss my research with media representatives. Included were many interviews with newspapers having large circulations, radio interviews, regional television appearances, and appearances on over a half-dozen national television programs. These included such shows as *The Oprah Winfrey Show*, ABC's *20/20*, NBC's *The Today Show*, CNN news, and others.

Without exception, I found that interviewers were interested in the story because it was a unique angle on rape. The impact of a rape on males who are close to rape survivors and the role of these males in affecting victim recovery was not something that had been explored previously. Thus, the media sought a fresh approach to an issue that had already become familiar ground. Given market-share considerations, it is usually the kiss of death for the media to revisit an old story when novelty is what sells.

Social scientists, like other scientists, often present their research findings to scholars in journal articles or at professional conferences. It is there that the research is judged to be theoretically and methodologically sound by an audience of scientists who have the expertise to interpret such work. However, highly trained social scientists are not the only audience with interest in this topic. Newspapers, magazines, radio and television talk shows and news programs also take notice of social science research with relevance to a wide audience. The application of social science research to the solution of social problems is of particular interest to the media.

I was expected to package my ideas in the form of sound bites for a mass media motivated by commercial rather than scientific interests. Moreover, I expected that persons conducting interviews would have read the book so that they could ask me relevant questions. A few had; most had not. Some did not even read the one-page press release. As such, questions and comments ranged from intelligent and insightful, to idiotic and insulting. Invariably, I would be asked at least a few questions about topics that were only remotely related to the research. Sometimes, interviewers would fixate on a minor side issue and fail to address the most critical concerns of the book. To compensate for some of these limitations, I soon learned to rephrase the interviewer's questions to allow me to address the issues I thought most relevant or simply to impose my response agenda on the interviewer regardless of what was being asked.

In the dozens of newspaper interviews I experienced, there was never an instance in which the interviewer had gotten all of the quotes right in the published article. Although most of the critically important information was reported accurately, there were always one or more misquotes or comments presented in a way that was misleading. In a few instances, the reporter drew conclusions that did not even remotely resemble comments made during the interview. I was greatly disturbed by this because there was no way to go back to readers and clarify misleading information. Therefore, I was very careful in repeating certain themes and presenting them in very simple terms. In fact, simplicity is what reporters most wanted. Complex and subtle points were usually ignored or dumbed down by the reporter based on the assumption that the readers wouldn't get it.

In television for the local six o'clock news, all that was needed was between 30 and 60 seconds of a talking head. Only the most basic and general message about the research was possible. Moreover, I was always at the mercy of someone in the editing room who was not even present during the interview. That person decided what to present and what to cut. To be honest, I was always worried that either the wrong message would be conveyed or that they would totally misrepresent findings and make me look stupid.

Talk shows such as *The Oprah Winfrey Show* allowed more time to articulate points, but here too, there were difficulties. One thing that bothered me

(Continued)

(Continued)

was a nagging feeling that these shows carried the potential of exploiting human misery, turning it into entertainment and public spectacle. The show formula invariably involved having one or more rape victims or their loved ones describe what happened to them and then cut to the "expert" for insight. The charged emotional content of victim accounts may have made for dramatic and "entertaining" television, but it also made careful analysis very difficult. All of my inclinations were to try to provide comfort to the victims . . . never mind the analysis.

Despite my reservations, however, one overriding consideration compelled me to do these interviews. Quite simply, the information I had to offer could help people deal with trauma in their lives. Where else but

through the mass media could one reach literally millions of people with information that could reduce suffering? Journal articles and presentation of findings at professional conferences would never reach even a tiny fraction of people who could benefit from the message.

I became a social scientist because I wanted to do work that would improve the human condition. However, simply doing the research and reporting it to other social scientists, while important, is not likely to have much impact beyond the profession. If the work of social scientists is to make a difference in the daily lives of citizens, then we must find ways to communicate our knowledge to a broader audience.

Source: By Alan McEvoy, Professor of Sociology, Wittenberg University (McEvoy and Brookings 2001).

interactions with family, peers, school teachers, employers, and religious leaders are studied at the micro level of analysis. Hector's motivation to find work can be understood by studying interpersonal interactions with significant others. By contrast, meso-level analysis focuses on institutions and large organizations; for instance, forces or trends in Brazilian institutions affect the health and vitality of the economy. Macro-level analysis illuminates the larger social context—national and global—within which Hector and his family live. From this perspective, Hector's position in society is part of a total system in which the poor in Brazil and other countries constitute a reserve labor force, available to work in unskilled jobs as

needed. How, for example, might a nationwide human rights organization help the poor by providing legal counsel? International trade, or a change in the Brazilian economy, could have an influence on Hector's job prospects quite independent of his individual motivation to work. Macro-level theories would consider questions related to Brazilian policies as a nation and the position of Brazil in the world system.

Sociologists draw on major theoretical perspectives at each level of analysis to guide their research and to help them understand social behavior and social organizations. A **theoretical perspective** is a basic view of society that guides sociologists' ideas and research. Theoretical perspectives are the broadest theories in sociology, providing overall approaches to understanding the social world and social problems. For example, one theoretical perspective argues that the foundation of a society is the everyday interactions between individuals. Another perspective argues that society is a stable, ongoing structure that provides the framework for our lives. Yet another perspective argues that society is a continual struggle between those with power and privilege and those without. Sociological perspectives help sociologists to develop explanations of organized patterns and to see relationships between patterns.

Micro-level interactions occur in classrooms every day, both among peers and between teacher and students.

Source: © Kurt Gordon.

THINKING SOCIOLOGICALLY

In The Applied Sociologist essay above, do the benefits of using the mass media to get out a message outweigh the risks? Can you think of examples of good and bad presentations of findings by the media?

Recall the social world model presented at the beginning of Chapter 1. It stresses the levels of analysis—smaller social systems existing within larger social systems. We have mentioned that some methods of data collection are more conducive to analysis of micro-level processes of interaction (e.g., participant observation), while other methods work more effectively in understanding macro-level social systems (e.g., secondary data). The same is true of theories and theoretical perspectives; some are especially effective in understanding micro-level contexts, and others illuminate macro-level structures (see the social world model at the beginning of this chapter). Either type of theory—those most useful at the micro or macro levels—can be used at the meso level. Occasionally, functionalism or conflict theory is used to look at micro-level processes instead of the usual macro level, so the distinction is not absolute.

To illustrate how a social problem is approached differently by each of the four major theoretical perspectives, we will further delve into our examination of Hector's circumstances (Ashley and Orenstein 2004; Turner 2003).

Micro- to Meso-Level Theories
Symbolic Interactionism
Symbolic interaction theory (also called social construction or interpretative theory) is concerned with how people give meaning to the events, objects, and individuals in their everyday lives. It focuses on how one defines and responds to events and situations. For example, Hector interacts with his family and friends in the *favela* in ways that he has learned are necessary for survival there. In Hector's world of poverty, the informal interactions of the street and the more formal interactions of the school each carry a set of meanings that guide Hector's behavior.

Symbolic interaction theory assumes that groups form from interacting individuals. Through these interactions, people learn what to expect from others and learn to share common understandings through the use of symbols such as language. In other words, through symbolic communication, people learn to socially construct a meaningful world. This implies that humans are not merely passive agents responding to environmental stimuli but, rather, are actively engaged in creating their own meaningful social world. Based on verbal and nonverbal communication (words and gestures), people interpret interactions with others and then create responses based on these interpretations. In some cases, people may passively accept the social definitions of others. This saves them the effort of making sense of the stimuli around them and of figuring out interpretations (Blumer 1969; Fine 1990). Still, more than any other theory in the social sciences, symbolic interactionism stresses human agency—the active role of individuals—in creating their social environment.

George Herbert Mead (1863–1931) is prominently identified with the symbolic interaction perspective through his influential work, *Mind, Self and Society* (Mead 1934/1962). Mead linked the human mind, the social self, and the structure of society to the process of interaction. He believed that humans have the ability to decide how to act based on their perceptions of the social world, or what sociologists refer to

as their *definition of the situation*. Mead explored the mental processes associated with how humans define situations; he placed special emphasis on human interpretations of gestures and symbols (including language) and the meanings we attach to our actions. He also examined how we learn our social roles in society such as mother, teacher, and friend, and how we learn to carry out these roles. Indeed, as we will see in Chapter 4, he insisted that our notion of who we are—our *self*—emerges from social experience and interaction with others. These ideas of how we construct our individual social worlds and have some control over them come from a perspective known as the Chicago School.

Another symbolic interaction approach—the Iowa School (named after scholars from the University of Iowa)—makes a more explicit link to the meso level of the social system. Manford Kuhn (1964) of the Iowa School sees individual identities as relatively stable because people are connected to roles and positions within organizations. If you hold several positions—honors student, club president, daughter, sister, student, athlete, thespian, middle-class person—those positions form a *core self*, which means that you will interpret new situations in light of those social positions, some of which are very important and anchor how you see things. Once a core self is established, it guides and shapes the way we interact with people in many situations—even new social settings. Thus, if you are president of an organization and have the responsibility for overseeing the organization, part of your self-esteem, your view of responsible citizenship and your attitude toward life will be shaped by that position. Thus, the Iowa School of symbolic interactionism places a bit less emphasis on individual choice, but it does a better job of recognizing the link between the micro, meso, and macro levels of the society (Carrothers and Benson 2003; Stryker 1980).

The following principles summarize the modern symbolic interaction perspective and how individual action results in groups and institutions (Ritzer 2004):

- Humans are endowed with the capacity for thought, shaped by social interaction.
- In social interaction, people learn the meanings and symbols that allow them to exercise thought and participate in human action.
- People modify the meanings and symbols as they struggle to make sense of their situations and the events they experience.
- Interpreting the situation involves seeing things from more than one perspective, examining possible courses of action, assessing the advantages and disadvantages of each, and then choosing one course of action.
- These patterns of action and interaction make up the interactive relations that we call groups and societies.
- Our positions or memberships in those groups and organizations may profoundly influence the way we define our selves and may lead to fairly stable patterns of interpretation of our experiences and of social life.

At the meso level, organizations and governmental agencies provide services that affect individuals with no affiliation to them. A cleaner, more sanitary community affects the health of the community. Here we see workers unloading a sewer tank.

Source: © Jonathan Clark.

To summarize, the modern symbolic interaction perspective emphasizes the process each individual goes through in creating and altering his or her social reality and identity within a social setting. Without a system of shared symbols, humans could not coordinate their actions with one another, and hence society as we understand it would not be possible.

Critique of the Symbolic Interaction Perspective. Although widely used today, symbolic interactionism (especially the Chicago School) is often criticized for neglecting the macro-level structures of society that affect human behavior. By focusing on interpersonal interactions, large-scale social forces such as an economic depression or political revolution that shape human destinies are given less consideration. With the focus on individual agency and the ability of each individual to create meaning, symbolic interaction has often been less attuned to issues of social class position, social power, historical circumstances, or international conflict between societies. Yet these are important issues. (Meltzer, Petras, and Reynolds 1975). In addition, critics point out the difficulty in studying ambiguous ideas such as the development of the self or how the mind works.

Despite these limitations, theorists from the symbolic interaction perspective have made significant contributions to understanding the development of social identities and interactions as the basis for groups and organizations. Many of these studies will be discussed in chapters throughout the book.

Rational Choice Theory

Women decide whether to stay in abusive relationships based on the balance of rewards versus costs. In considering a divorce, do the rewards of escaping a conflicted, abusive marriage outweigh the costs of daily economic and emotional stresses of going it alone? For a lesbian couple, there are potential costs of coming out of the closet to friends, family, and employers. There may also be significant benefits, such as not living in hiding and constant fear of being exposed. These costs and benefits shape the decisions of couples. These are the types of questions addressed by rational choice theorists.

A central premise of micro-level rational choice theory is that human behavior involves choices. On what basis do people make their choices? As the term implies, rational choice approaches assume that people chart a course of action on the basis of rational decisions. From this perspective, rational choices are those that have a *utilitarian* component, wherein people are expected to act in ways that maximize their rewards and minimize their costs. Where the balance lies determines our behavior.

Rational choice, also called *exchange theory*, has its roots in several disciplines—economics, behavioral psychology, anthropology, and philosophy (Cook, O'Brien, and Kollock 1990). It focuses on what people get out of an interaction versus what they contribute to it. Social behavior is seen as an exchange activity—a transaction in which resources are given and received (Blau 1964; Homans 1974). Every interaction involves an exchange of something valued—money, time, material goods, attention, sex, allegiance. People stay in relationships because they get something from the exchange, and they leave relationships that cost them without providing an adequate return. Simply stated, people are more likely to act if they see some reward or success coming from their behavior. The implication is that self-interest for the individual is the guiding element in human interaction.

Applying the rational choice theory to Hector's situation, we could examine how he evaluates his life options. What are the costs and rewards for staying in school versus those associated with dropping out and earning money from temporary jobs? For Hector, the immediate benefit of earning a meager income to put food on his family's table comes at a cost—the loss of a more hopeful and prosperous future. When hungry, the reward of being paid for odd jobs may outweigh the cost of leaving school and losing long-term opportunities.

Critique of the Rational Choice Perspective. Concerns about rational choice approaches are that macro-level analysis and internal mental processes are given little attention. Critics of rational choice challenge the idea that human conduct is always self-centered and that people always seek to maximize rewards and minimize costs. Charitable, unselfish, or altruistic behavior is not easily explained by this view. Why would a soldier sacrifice his or her life to

save a comrade? Why would a starving person in a Nazi concentration camp share a crust of bread with another? The rational choice model seems to imply that such behaviors are irrational. Proponents counter the criticism by arguing that if a person feels good about helping another, that in itself is a benefit that compensates for the cost. Without denying that people often act to maximize their self-interests, people can also be motivated by humanitarian concerns.

Perhaps a more important critique is that humans often do not behave in ways that maximize their own self-interest. In Ohio, some residents have voted against school levies to support the public schools; their rationale is that they do not want to pay the extra hundred dollars or so per year in taxes. Yet the same voters are dismayed when trying to sell their house, only to find that their property value has dropped by as much as $15,000 because it is in a district that does not support education (based on Keith's interviews in 2003 with Ohio residents in communities considering tax levies). In short, acting in our own self-interest requires an accurate definition of the situation, a correct construction of the meaning of various acts.

Some theorists (Denzin 1992; Fiske 1991) have attempted a synthesis between the interaction level of analysis and macro-level theories. For instance, studies of friendships, employee-employer contracts, relations in families, and consumer-salesperson transactions can all be represented as exchange relationships. By combining the millions of exchange relationships, these researchers contend that we can study macro-level patterns in the social world (Fiske 1991).

President George W. Bush delivers his State of the Union address to the nation in the House Chamber at the U.S. Capitol, January 28, 2003. In this address, President Bush said, "In the Middle East, we will continue to seek peace between a secure Israel and a democratic Palestine. . . . Across the earth, America is feeding the hungry; more than 60 percent of international food aid comes as a gift from the people of the United States." Actions taken by a government or by the common people in one country can affect those elsewhere on the planet, as we learn from macro analysis.

Source: White House photo by Susan Sterner.

THINKING SOCIOLOGICALLY

How can symbolic interaction and rational choice perspectives help explain dating behavior? For example, what might a good-night kiss versus sexual intercourse mean to females versus males? How does one learn the cues that indicate attraction to a person of the same or opposite sex? What are some examples of exchange relationships associated with dating? How is the exchange relationship different if one is dating someone of the same sex?

Meso- and Macro-Level Theories

Meso and macro-level theories consider larger units in the social world such as organizations, institutions (such as politics or economics), societies, or global systems. For example, Hector lives in a modernizing country, Brazil, which is struggling to raise the standard of living of its people and compete in the world market. The decisions that are made by his government at a national and international level affect his life in a variety of ways. As Brazil industrializes, the nature of jobs and modes of communication change; local village cultures modify as the entire nation gains more uniformity of values, beliefs, and norms. We can

begin to understand how the process of modernization influences Hector and other poor people by looking at two major macro-level approaches: structural-functional and conflict perspectives. Recall that sociological theories provide possible explanations to help us understand the social world.

Structural-Functional Theory

The structural-functional perspective, also called **functional theory**, assumes that all parts of the *social structure* (such as groups, organizations, and institutions), the *culture* (such as values and beliefs), and *social processes* (such as socialization—learning to be a member of society, stratification—layering of people in society, and change), work together to make the whole society run smoothly and harmoniously. To understand the social world from this perspective, we must look at how the parts of society (structure) fit together and how each part contributes (functions) toward the maintenance of society. For instance, two functions of the family include reproducing children and teaching them to be members of society. These and other functions help perpetuate society, for without reproducing and teaching new members to fit in, societies would collapse.

A Maasai family works together as a unit, and in so doing, they enhance the stability and continuity of their entire society.

Source: © Jeanne Ballantine.

Since the 1950s, functionalism has been dominated by several influential U.S. theorists including Talcott Parsons (1951b) and Robert Merton (1968b). Parsons developed a grand theory of society, so grand that it encompasses all the major parts of society—family, education, religion, politics, economics, and health. Underlying his theory is the assumption that all the parts of the social system are interrelated, and each performs some task or function necessary for a society's survival. The whole is a highly integrated system, cemented together by value consensus, agreement on right and proper actions among individuals who make up the system (Parsons 1951a).

Functions can be manifest or latent. **Manifest functions** are the planned outcomes of social patterns or institutions. The function of the microwave oven, for instance, has been to allow people to prepare meals quickly and easily, facilitating life in overworked and stressed modern families. **Latent**

Structural-functional theory traces its roots to the French Revolution. To Auguste Comte, the question of how to bring about order and harmony out of the chaos of the French Revolution was paramount. He argued that by gaining scientific knowledge about society, leaders could create a better social order. Comte borrowed concepts from the biological sciences, including an analogy between social and biological organisms; this idea held that societies, like biological organisms, develop and become more complex and interdependent. As parts of society grow and change, so do the functions or purposes they serve. To understand why a structure exists, we must understand the needs it meets in society. These ideas are basic to functionalists.

Émile Durkheim (1858–1917) further developed functionalism by theorizing that society is made up of necessary parts that fit together into a working whole. Durkheim (1947) felt that individuals conform to the rules of societies because of a *collective conscience*—the shared beliefs in the values of a group. People grow up sharing the same values, beliefs, and rules of behavior as those around them. Gradually, these shared beliefs and rules are internalized such that a person's behavior is, in a sense, governed from within because it feels right and proper to behave in accord with what is expected. As such, the functionalist perspective of Durkheim and subsequent theorists places emphasis on societal consensus, which gives rise to stable and predictable patterns of order in society. Because people need groups for survival, they adhere to the group's rules so that they fit in. This means that most societies run in an orderly manner with most individuals fitting into their positions in society.

The microwave oven has had many social consequences, some of them expected (manifest), some of them unexpected (latent), and some of them harmful (dysfunctional). What might be some manifest functions, latent functions, and dysfunctional consequences of cell phones or iPods?

Source: © Fred Goldstein.

functions are often unplanned or unintended consequences (Merton 1938). The unplanned consequences of the microwave oven were creation of a host of new jobs and stimulation of the economy as people wrote new cookbooks and as businesses were formed to produce microwavable cookware and prepared foods for the microwave.

Dysfunctions (Merton 1938) are those actions that undermine the stability or equilibrium of society. By allowing people to cook meals without using a convection oven, the microwave oven has contributed to some young people having no idea how to cook, thus making them highly dependent on expensive technology and processed foods. Processed foods as a regular diet are not very good for one's body, and the higher cost for processed food makes it increasingly important for families to have rather substantial incomes in order to survive. The requirement of substantial incomes may limit families from making other kinds of choices (vacations may be limited, cultural opportunities may be curtailed, decisions to allow only one person to work or to job-share may not be an option, and so forth). From a functionalist perspective, it is important to examine the possible functional and dysfunctional aspects of the different parts of society in terms of the maintenance and harmony of society as a whole.

Critique of the Structural-Functional Perspective. Because sociologist Talcott Parsons was a leading scholar and proponent of structural-functional theory, much criticism is directed toward his ideas. His grand theory has been criticized because it is so abstract that it is difficult to test empirically. Moreover, functionalism does not explain social changes in society, such as conflict and revolution. As we try to understand the many societal upheavals in the world, from suicide-bombings in Iraq to the democracy and economic privatization movements in China, it is clear that dramatic social change is possible. The functionalist assumption is that if a system is running smoothly, it must therefore be working well because it is free from conflict. It assumes that conflict is harmful, even though we know that stability sometimes comes from ruthless dictators suppressing the population.

Feminist sociologists criticize functionalism because if the family or economic system of society seems to be functioning smoothly, this does not mean that these systems are fair and equitable or that women and minorities are content with their roles in them. A paradigm that assumes so is making false assumptions, according to feminist theorists. Feminists and others reject the implicit idea of functionalism that orderly society is good, even if not all of its members are treated equally. The point is that a stable system is not the same thing as a healthy system.

Functionalism has had a profound impact on social science analysis. Still, functionalism in the twenty-first century fails to explain many contemporary social situations, according to proponents of a rival macro-level perspective, conflict theory.

THINKING SOCIOLOGICALLY

Are existing social arrangements in a society necessarily desirable, and is dramatic change necessarily dysfunctional as suggested by functional theory?

Conflict Theory

Conflict in any group or society is inevitable. To support this view, conflict theorists advance the following key ideas:

- Conflict and the potential for conflict underlie all social relations.
- Social change is desirable, particularly changes that bring about a greater degree of social equality.
- The existing social order reflects powerful people imposing their values and beliefs upon the weak.

The conflict perspective claims that inequality and injustice are the source of conflicts that permeate society. Since resources and power are distributed unequally in society, some members have more money, goods, and prestige than others. The rich protect their positions by using the power they have accumulated to keep those less fortunate in their places. From the perspective of poor people such as Hector, it seems the rich get all the breaks. Since most of us want more of the resources in society (money, good jobs, nice houses and cars), conflict erupts between the haves and the have-nots. Sometimes, the conflict brings about a change in the society.

Karl Marx was a social analyst who is often identified as the founder of conflict theory.

Modern conflict theory has its origins in the works of Karl Marx (1818–1883), a German social philosopher who lived in England during the height of nineteenth-century industrial expansion; he recognized the plight of exploited underclass workers in the new industrial states of Europe and viewed the ruling elites and the wealthy industrial owners as exploiters of the working class. Marx wrote about the new working class crowded in urban slums, working long hours every day, not earning enough money for decent housing and food, and living and working in conditions that were appalling. Few of the protections enjoyed by workers today—such as retirement benefits, health coverage, sick leave, the 40-hour workweek, and restrictions against child labor—existed in Marx's time.

Capitalism emerged as the dominant economic system in Europe; capitalism is an economic system in which (1) the equipment and property for producing goods is owned privately by wealthy individuals who have the right to use them however they want and (2) the market system (supply and demand) determines the distribution of resources and the levels of income (including wages, rents, and profits). While there are various forms of capitalism, the core principles involve private ownership of industries and nonintervention by government (Heilbroner and Milberg 2002).

Marx believed that two classes, the capitalists (also referred to as *bourgeoisie* or *haves*) who owned the **means of production** (property, machinery, and cash) and the workers (also referred to as *proletariat* or *have-nots*), would continue to live in conflict until the workers shared more equally in the profits of their labor. The more workers came to understand their plight, the more awareness they would have of the unfairness of the situation. Eventually, Marx believed that workers would rise up and overthrow capitalism, forming a new classless society. *Collective ownership*—shared ownership of the means of production—would be the new economic order (Marx and Engels 1848/1969).

The idea of the *bourgeoisie* (the capitalist exploiters who own the factories) and the *proletariat* (the exploited workers who sell their labor) has carried over into analysis of modern-day conflicts between labor and management, between women's and men's interests, and between warring factions within countries such as Rwanda, Darfur, Indonesia, and countries in the Middle East. From a conflict perspective, Hector in Brazil and millions like him in other countries are part of the reserve labor force—a cheap labor pool that can be called on when labor is needed or disregarded when demand is low in order to meet the changing labor needs of industry and capitalism. This pattern results in permanent economic insecurity and poverty for Hector and those like him.

Many branches of the conflict perspective have grown from the original ideas of Marx; here, we mention two contributions to conflict theory, those of American sociologists W.E.B. Du Bois (1899/1967) and Ralf Dahrendorf (1959).

W.E.B. Du Bois was an outstanding contributor to the development of conflict theory and was among the first to apply that theory to American society.

Source: © Bettman/Corbis.

We conclude with two perspectives which cross levels of analysis: feminist theory and the work of Max Weber.

One of the very first American conflict theorists was W.E.B. Du Bois, the first African American to receive a doctorate from Harvard University. Du Bois felt that sociology should be active in bettering society, that while research should be scientifically rigorous and fair-minded, the ultimate goal of sociological work was social improvement—not just human insight. He saw the conflict between haves and have-nots as being based largely on race in the United States, not just social class.

Du Bois (1899/1967) not only wrote on these issues but also acted on them; he was one of the cofounders of the National Association for the Advancement of Colored People (NAACP). He stressed the need for minority ethnic groups to become advocates for their rights, to create conflict where destructive harmony exists, and to change the society toward greater equality and participation. He was—and continues to be—an inspiration to many sociologists who believe that their findings should have real applications and should be used to create a more humane social world (Mills 1956). He was well ahead of his time in recognizing the conflictual nature of American society and the way privilege and self-interest blinded people from seeing the inequities.

A half-century later, Dahrendorf (1959) argued that society is always in the process of change and affected by forces that bring about change. Dahrendorf refined Marx's ideas in several ways: First, he pointed out that Marx's predictions for the overthrow of capitalism had not come about because of changes in conditions for workers (employee organizations, unions); rather, a middle class developed, some workers became part owners, stockholders dispersed the concentration of wealth, and a higher standard of living was achieved for workers. Second, he proposed that class conflict occurs between the haves and the have-nots by adding several new categories of people: quasi-groups, interest groups, and conflict groups.

Quasi-groups include individuals who have similar social positions and interests but do not belong to an organized group. They therefore have little power. For example, residents who live in poverty like Hector, but in different *favelas* surrounding Sao Paulo, are a quasi-group. People in quasi-groups are vulnerable precisely because they lack a social power base.

Interest groups, such as members of Hector's *favela*, emerge from the quasi-groups as a way to seek the power to solve problems. They share interests, like a desire for sanitation, running water, electricity, and a higher standard of living. It is from within these more organized interest groups that conflict groups arise to fight for changes. There is always potential for conflict when those without power realize their common position and form interest groups. How much change or violence is brought about depends on how organized those groups become.

Dahrendorf's major contribution is the recognition that class struggle goes beyond Marx's idea of who controls the means of production; economic interests; and distributions of power, authority, and prestige. A split society—haves and have-nots—become sliced in many directions. Thus, conflict over resources results not just in a conflict between proletariat and bourgeoisie, but in a multitude of divisions including old people versus young people, rich versus poor, one region of the country versus another, Christians versus non-Christians, men versus women, African Americans versus Jews or Hispanics, and so forth. This acknowledges multiple rifts in the society based in interest groups. The notion that men and women can be interest groups, each looking out for its own self-interests, has resulted in one particular version of conflict theory, feminist theory.

While Marx emphasized the divisive nature of conflict, other theorists have modified his theory. His contemporary, Georg Simmel (1858–1918), looked at how conflict could help to hold together groups in society. This idea was also discussed by American theorist Lewis Coser (1956) who took a very different approach to conflict from that of Marx, arguing that it can strengthen societies and organizations within them. According to Coser, problems in a society or group lead to complaints or conflicts—a warning message to the group that all is not well. Resolution of the conflicts shows that the group is adaptable in meeting needs of its members, thereby creating greater loyalty to the group. Thus, conflict provides the message of what is not working to meet people's needs, and the system adapts to the needs for change because of the conflict (Coser 1956; Simmel 1955).

Critique of the Conflict Perspective. First, many conflict theorists focus on the macro level of analysis and lose sight of the individuals involved in conflict situations, such as Hector and his family. Second, empirical research to test conflict propositions is limited. The conflict perspective often paints a picture with rather broad brush strokes, and research to test the picture has often involved interpretations of broad spans of history and is more difficult to claim as scientific. Third, conflict theorists see mostly social stress, power plays, and disharmony; conflict theory is not as effective in explaining social cohesion and cooperation. Fourth, many theorists are not convinced that self-interest is the ultimate motivator of behavior or that altruism and cooperation are uncommon.

THINKING SOCIOLOGICALLY

Imagine that you are a legislator representing your state or province. You have to decide whether to cut funding for a program for senior citizens or slash a scholarship program for college students. You want to be reelected and to avoid offending voters. You know that approximately 90 percent of senior citizens are registered to vote and most do show up on election day, and that only 20 percent of 18 to 22 year olds are registered to vote. What would you do, and how would you justify your decision? How does this example illustrate conflict theory?

Feminist Sociological Theory

Feminists argue that sociology has been dominated by a male perspective and that the male perspective does not give a complete view of the social world. Feminist analysis critiques the hierarchical power structures that feminists argue oppress women and other minorities (Cancian 1992). Much of feminist theory, then, has foundations in the conflict perspective; women are viewed as disadvantaged by the hierarchical way that society is arranged, while men experience privilege because of those arrangements. Men become an interest group intent on preserving their privileges.

Some feminist theories, however, are not based on Marx's writings. Instead, their ideas come from interaction

Gloria Steinem was and is unapologetic about believing that men and women should be treated equally or about being called a feminist. An early leader in the feminist movement, she speaks to hundreds of thousands of demonstrators at the March for Women's Lives in Washington in 2004.

Source: © Krista Kennell / Zuma / Corbis.

perspectives, emphasizing the way gender cues and symbols shape the nature of much human interaction. Thus, feminist theory moves from meso- and macro-level analysis (e.g., looking at national and global situations that give privileges to men) to micro-level analysis (e.g., inequality between husbands and wives in marriage). In particular, feminist theory points to the importance of gender as a variable influencing social patterns.

Feminists contend that there is a disparity between what actually goes on in women's lives and many accounts by social scientists of social relations between males and females; men's explanations of gender relations have not really presented women's lives in a way that is authentic for women themselves. The ideas, work opportunities, and life experiences of women of color are even less understood by traditional sociology (Collins 2000). Men have been doing the studies and writing about experiences that are too far removed from women's own experiences; thus, the reality for women becomes distorted.

In general, feminists point out, women's experiences in social relations involve interdependence with others while males have been taught to be competitive and individualistic

in sports, business competition, and many other social arenas. Males learn early in their lives that vulnerability must be avoided so that one is not exploited by others. This, according to feminist theorists, influences the way men think about society. For example, rational choice theory maintains that each individual is out to protect self-interests and to make choices that benefit only the self. This notion is based on a theory that a male would be more likely to develop than a female. Men are also more likely to view hierarchical social arrangements as normal, and this may contribute to their difficulty, for many decades, in recognizing how patriarchal our society is. Also, some feminists claim that many social commentators have been blinded to the fact that gender roles are socially created, not biologically determined. As a result of these differences in experience and in socialization, women's views on issues of justice, morality, and society lend a different interpretation to society (Brettell and Sargent 2001; Kramer 2001) and can present a more inclusive view of the world (Burn 2004; Lengermann and Niebrugge-Brantley 1990).

It is interesting that many women today will begin a sentence with the disclaimer, "I am not a feminist, but . . ." This seems be because some feminists have had a rather strident style and often focused on men as the cause of problems. Not all feminists are strident or focus on men as oppressors. Indeed, many men call themselves feminists, for a feminist is someone who believes that men and women should be given equal standing and equal opportunities in the society. Feminists have opened the door to understanding how social structures can bind and inhibit the freedom of both men and women; they also recognize that males have generally had more privileges than females in societies around the world. To study sociological questions, feminist methodology puts emphasis on qualitative methods that involve empathetic role-taking with respondents in interviews and trying to understand the world from the female or male respondents' point of view.

Critique of the Feminist Sociological Perspective. Feminists are not the only group with concerns about being fairly and accurately represented in theory and research. Race and ethnic groups and social class groups are also affected. Thus, some theorists argue that theory should represent the intersection between race, class, and gender. When trying to understand minority women in minimum wage jobs or factors affecting homelessness, this intersection can provide a more complete view.

Multi-Level Analysis: Max Weber's Contributions

Max Weber (1864–1920), a German-born social scientist, has had a lasting effect on sociology and other social sciences. He cannot be pigeonholed easily into one of the theoretical categories, for his contributions include both micro- and macro-level analyses. His concept **verstehen** (meaning "understanding") gives him a place in micro-level theory, and his discussions of Karl Marx and of bureaucracies

give him a place in meso- and macro-level theory (Weber 1946).

Verstehen stems from the interpretations or meanings individuals give to parts of their social worlds, to their subjective interpretations or understandings of the social world. Actions that occur outside of individual lives affect these interpretations and our actions. Sociologists try to understand both people's behaviors and the meanings that they attach to their behaviors and their experiences.

From this micro-level base, Weber attempted to understand macro-level processes. For instance, he asked how capitalists understood the world around them, resulting in his famous book, *The Protestant Ethic and the Spirit of Capitalism* (Weber 1904–1905/1958). His work was influenced by Marx's writings and the idea of conflict between groups in society. While Marx focused on economic conditions as the key factor shaping history and power relations, Weber argued that Marx's focus was too narrow, and that politics, economics, religion, psychology, and the military all help explain the social world, power relationships, and conflict. In short, Weber thought that the society was more complex than Karl Marx's core notion that two groups, the haves and the have-nots, are in conflict over economic resources.

The goal-oriented, efficient new organizational form called *bureaucracy* was the focus of much of Weber's writing. This form was based not on tradition but on rationality. In other words, decisions were based on what would best accomplish the organization's goals. Hiring and promotion on the basis of individual merit (getting the most qualified person rather than hiring a friend or relative) is one example of this rational decision making. This is a principle we take

for granted now, but it was not always so. The entire society becomes transformed through a change in how individuals make decisions, especially when that individual is making decisions on behalf of a complex organization.

Opportunities for jobs were changed, the culture became more geared to merit as a basis for decisions, and organizational life became more governed by rules and routines. All of this came from a redefinition of appropriate ways to make decisions. Weber's ideas have laid the groundwork for theoretical understanding of modern organizations.

THINKING SOCIOLOGICALLY

To what extent are human beings free agents who can create their own social world and come up with alternative definitions about life, and to what extent are our lives determined or profoundly shaped by our culture, by the social systems around us, and by our positions of power or powerlessness in the economic and political system?

Using Different Theoretical Perspectives

Each of the theoretical perspectives described in this chapter begins from a set of assumptions about humans. Each makes a contribution to our understanding, but each has limitations or blind spots, such as not taking into account the other levels of analysis (Ritzer 2004). Figure 2.3 provides a summary of cooperative versus competitive perspectives to illustrate how the theories differ.

It is important to understand that there are different and viable perspectives to explain society. None of these is

	Macro analysis	Micro analysis
Humans viewed as cooperative (people interact with others on the basis of shared meanings and common symbols)	*Structural-Functional Theory*	*Symbolic Interactionism Theory*
Humans viewed as competitive (behavior governed by self-interest)	*Conflict Theory* (group interests)	*Rational Choice Theory* (individual interests)

Figure 2.3   Cooperative versus Competitive Perspectives

right or wrong. Rather, a particular theory may be more or less useful when studying some level of analysis or aspect of society. It is also important to learn about the major theoretical perspectives and how each can be used to provide a framework and viewpoint to guide research. The micro-, meso-, and macro-level social world model used in this book does not imply that one of these theories is better than another. The strength of a theory depends on its ability to explain and predict behavior accurately. Each theoretical perspective focuses on a different aspect of society and level of analysis and gives us a different lens on our social world. The social world model helps us picture the whole system

and determine which theory or synthesis of theories best suits our needs in analyzing a specific social process or structure.

THINKING SOCIOLOGICALLY

Consider the issue of homelessness in cities around the world. How could each of the theories discussed in this chapter be used to help understand the problem of homelessness?

SO WHAT?

What makes a discipline scientific is not the subject matter; it is how we conduct our research and what we consider valid evidence. The core features of a science are (1) commitment to empirically validated evidence, facts, and information that are confirmed through systematic processes of testing using the five senses; (2) an effort to disprove whatever it is we think is true, allowing us to be convinced by the evidence rather than by our preconceived ideas; (3) absolute integrity in reporting and in conducting research; and (4) continual openness to how our data are reexamined and new interpretations proposed. It is the fourth feature that causes us to invite and be open to criticism and alternative interpretations. To have credible findings, we always consider the possibility that we have overlooked alternative explanations of the data and alternative ways to view the problem. This is one of the hardest principles to grasp, but it is one of the most important in reaching the truth. Science—including social science—is not facts to

be memorized. Science is a process that is made possible by a social exchange of ideas, a clash of opinions, and a continual search for truth. Knowledge in the sciences is created by vigorous debate. We hope you will not just memorize concepts in this book in order to take a test but will engage in the creation of knowledge by entering into these debates.

Theories serve as lenses to help us make sense of the data that we gather with various research strategies. However, the data themselves can be used to test the theories, so there is an ongoing reciprocal relationship between theory (the lens for making sense of the data) and the research (the evidence used to test the theories). The most important ideas in this chapter are what sociology considers evidence and how sociology operates as a science. In each chapter of this book, we include a study to address the question "How do we know?"

So far, we have focused on what sociology is. The rest of the book examines what the social world is like. The next chapter explores the relationships between culture and society at various levels in our social world.

CONTRIBUTING TO YOUR SOCIAL WORLD

At the Local Level: Conduct a needs-assessment survey in your local community to discover what needs exist that are not currently being addressed. You might want to contact your local *United Way* and other community-based organizations if you would like to help gather data for improvement of community services.

At the National and Global Levels: Help gather census data for your national census bureau. You can learn a great deal about how primary data is gathered and how to do sociological research while providing a service.

Visit www.pineforge.com/ballantinestudy for online activities, sample tests, and other helpful information. Select "Chapter 2: Examining the Social World" for chapter-specific activities.

SOCIAL STRUCTURE, PROCESSES, AND CONTROL

Picture a house. First there is the wood frame, then the walls and roof. This provides the framework or *structure*. Within that structure, activities or *processes* take place—electricity to turn on lights and appliances, water to wash in and drink, and people to carry out these processes. If something goes wrong in the house, we take steps to control the damage and repair it.

Our social world is constructed in a similar way: *social structure* is the framework of society with its organizations, and *social processes* are the dynamic activities of the society. This section begins with a discussion of the *structure of society,* followed by the *processes of culture and social-ization* through which individuals are taught cultural rules—how to function and live effectively within their society. Although *socialization* takes place primarily at the micro-level process, we will explore its implications at the meso and macro levels as well.

If we break the social structure into parts, like the wood frame, walls, and roof, it is the *groups and organizations* (including bureaucracies) that make up the structure. To work smoothly, these organizations depend on people's loyalty to do what society and its groups need to survive; how-ever, smooth functioning does not always happen. Things break down. This means those in con-trol of societies try to control disruptions and deviant individuals in order to maintain control and function smoothly.

As we explore these chapters, we will continue to examine social life at the micro, meso, and macro levels, for each of us as individuals is profoundly shaped by social processes and structures at larger and more abstract levels, all the way to the global level.

SOCIETY AND CULTURE:
Hardware and Software of Our Social World

Computer hardware like the circuit board makes it possible for software to work. Likewise, social structure is the behind-the-scenes "hardware" that makes the culture—in colorful variety—possible.

Think About It . . .

1. Why do people live so differently?

2. Could you be "human" without culture?

3. How do national cultures, subcultures, microcultures, and countercultures influence what you do in your everyday lives?

4. Why are society and culture important in understanding your own life?

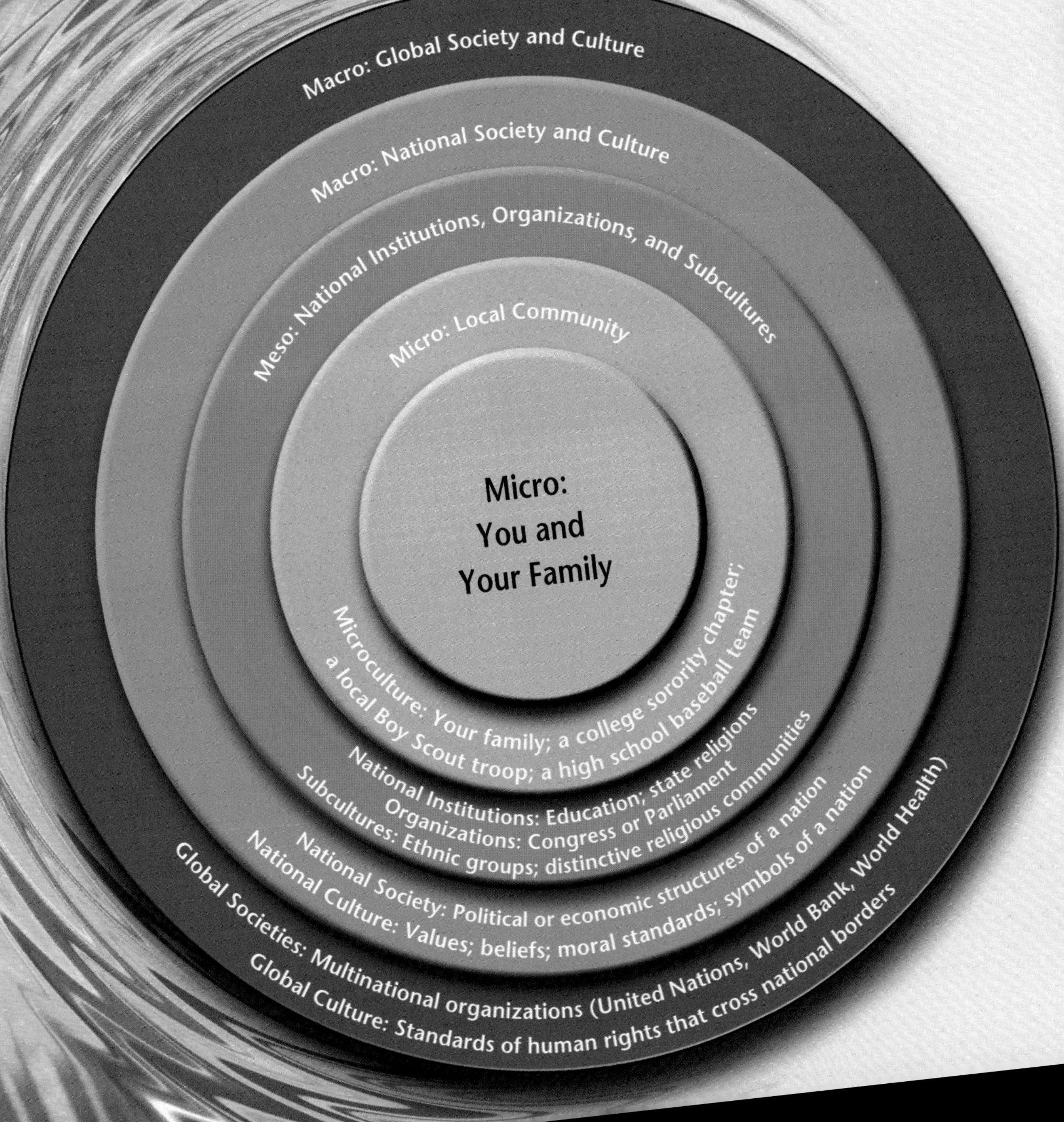

Macro: Global Society and Culture

Macro: National Society and Culture

Meso: National Institutions, Organizations, and Subcultures

Micro: Local Community

**Micro:
You and
Your Family**

Microculture: Your family; a college sorority chapter; a local Boy Scout troop; a high school baseball team

National Institutions: Education; state religions

Organizations: Congress or Parliament

Subcultures: Ethnic groups; distinctive religious communities

National Society: Political or economic structures of a nation

National Culture: Values; beliefs; moral standards; symbols of a nation

Global Societies: Multinational organizations (United Nations, World Bank, World Health)

Global Culture: Standards of human rights that cross national borders

Aisha, an African woman from Sudan, is cooking the evening meal. As she pounds the cassava root into a pulp to make bread dough, she chats with her husband's other wives about the impending marriage of their neighbor to his fourth wife, a young woman who will join his first three wives in the household.

In China, the workday in the fields has ended for the Liu family and the children have returned home from school. The village women are pitching in to prepare the evening meal of rice and vegetables before going to the village square for a farm cooperative meeting.

On an Israeli kibbutz, parents pick up their children after school and play, then join other community members in

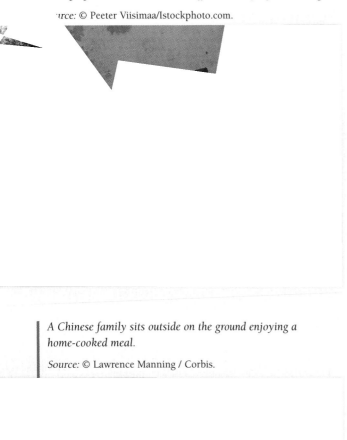

Meal preparation is a communal affair in many African villages.

Source: © Peeter Viisimaa/Istockphoto.com.

A Chinese family sits outside on the ground enjoying a home-cooked meal.

Source: © Lawrence Manning / Corbis.

the central dining hall for an evening meal of dairy products and fresh fruits and vegetables. Families can choose to eat in their own homes, but after a long day, it is convenient to have the meal prepared for them.

In Kansas City, Bethany picks up her children from day care while her husband, Tad, begins to prepare the evening meal. Tonight, they hurriedly heat frozen pizza in the microwave before she goes to the school for a teacher's conference and Tad goes to a ball game where his son—from a previous marriage—is playing third base. On evenings when both Bethany and Tad must work late, the family eats at a neighborhood fast-food restaurant.

Millions of scenarios like these are played out as evening falls around the world. Whether food is prepared over an open fire or in a microwave oven, all humans have the universal need to eat. What foods are available, who prepares them, and how the preparation is done differ from one culture to another. Broad variations may exist even within one society, yet all of these examples have something in common: each represents a society that has a unique culture. A **society** consists of individuals who live together in a specific geographical area, who interact more with each other than they do with outsiders, cooperate for the attainment of common goals, and share a common culture over time. **Culture** is the way of life shared by a group of people—the knowledge, belief, values, rules or laws, language, customs, symbols, and material products within a society that help meet human needs (Tyler 1871/1958).

The way people think and behave in any society is prescribed to a large extent by that society's culture. All activities in the society, whether preparing and eating dinner, selecting leaders for the group, finding a mate, educating young members, or negotiating with other societies, are guided by cultural rules and expectations. In each society, culture provides the social rules for how individuals carry out necessary tasks. Our personal experiences in the world also are determined by the culture provided by our family and society and taught to us beginning at birth.

Whereas culture provides the "software program" or general *guidelines* for the way people live, society provides the "hardware" or the *structure* that provides organization and stability to group life. Each society includes major parts, or *institutions*—family, education, religion, politics, economics, and health—that meet basic human needs. (We will explore specific institutions later in the book.) A society, then, is the group of people who are organized and interdependent. A culture is their way of life. Society cannot exist without culture, and culture does not exist without a society. The two are not the same thing, but they cannot exist without each other, much as computer hardware and software are each useless without the other.

This chapter explores the ideas of society and culture and discusses how they relate to each other. We will look at what society is, how it influences and is influenced by culture, what culture is, how and why it develops, and where we as individuals fit into society and culture in our multileveled social world.

SOCIETY: THE HARDWARE

A society consists of individuals who live together in families and communities. Societies are composed of the *structures*—interdependent positions we hold (parents, workers), groups to which we belong (family, work group, clubs), and institutions as listed above that make up group life. This "hardware" (structure) of our social world provides the framework for "software" (culture) to function.

This section explores ways in which societies are organized, how societies have become more complex over time, and how change influences societies and cultures. Human societies have been in the hunter-gatherer stage for 99 percent of human existence, and a few groups still remain in this stage. In fact, as Table 3.1 illustrates, if all of human history were compressed into the lifetime of a 70-year-old person, humans would have left their cave dwelling only nine months ago. Note the incredible rate of change that has occurred in the past two centuries.

The stage of development that any society has reached depends on a range of factors including availability of resources, contact with other societies, and cultural beliefs. At each developmental stage, changes take place in social structures and relationships between people. It is important to note that not all societies go through all stages. Some are jolted into the future by political events or changes in the global system, and some resist pressures to become modernized.

THINKING SOCIOLOGICALLY

What major changes have taken place in the past 200 years that affect the way people live today? You may want to use your own family's history as a starting point.

Evolution of Societies

The simplest societies have only two or three social positions or statuses. The men can teach their sons everything they need to know, for all of the men do pretty much the same things—hunting, fishing, or farming, and protecting the community from danger. Likewise, girls learn their positions in the society from their mothers—usually child care, fetching water, food preparation, farming, and perhaps building the dwelling in which they live. In more complex societies, such as industrial societies, there are thousands of interdependent statuses and *division of labor*, with each individual holding a specific position with designated tasks. The question here is how societies evolve into new types of societies.

Emile Durkheim (1893/1947), an early French sociologist, pictured a continuum between simple and complex societies. Simple premodern societies are characterized by *mechanical solidarity*, wherein society is held together by common beliefs, values, and emotional ties; division of labor is based largely on male/female distinctions and age groupings.

In a kibbutz in Israel, meals are a community affair, not something individual families do alone.

Source: © Corbis.

Members think the same way on important matters, and everyone fulfills expected social positions providing the glue that holds the society together. The entire society may not have involved more than a few hundred people, so there are no meso-level institutions and subcultures; prior to the emergence of modern countries, there was no macro level either but rather tribal groupings.

As societies transformed, they became more complex. The increasingly complex division of labor and change in the ways people carried out necessary tasks for survival resulted

TABLE 3.1   One Million Years of Human History Compressed into One 70-Year Lifetime

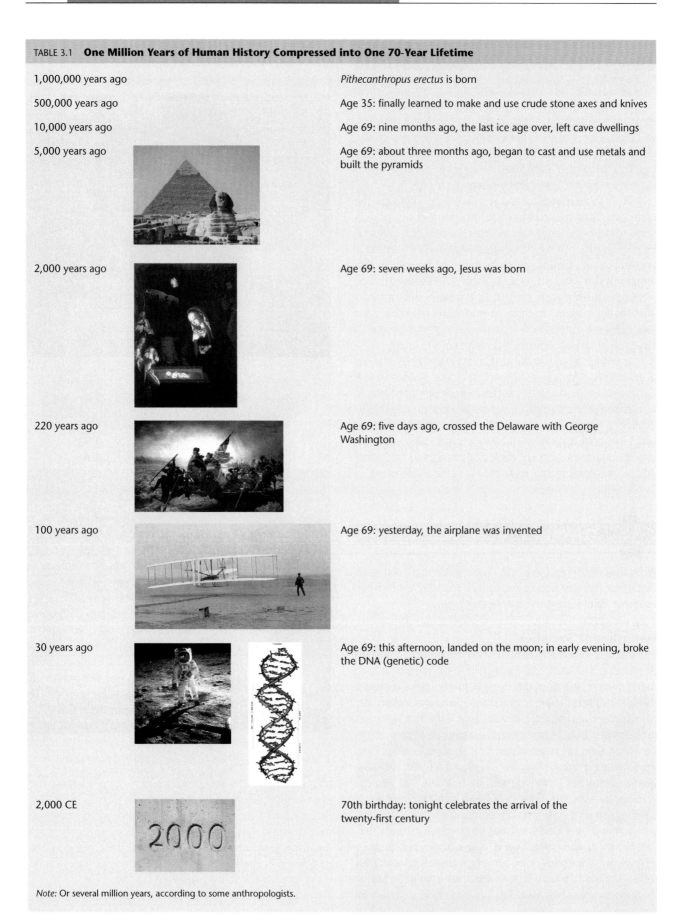

1,000,000 years ago	*Pithecanthropus erectus* is born
500,000 years ago	Age 35: finally learned to make and use crude stone axes and knives
10,000 years ago	Age 69: nine months ago, the last ice age over, left cave dwellings
5,000 years ago	Age 69: about three months ago, began to cast and use metals and built the pyramids
2,000 years ago	Age 69: seven weeks ago, Jesus was born
220 years ago	Age 69: five days ago, crossed the Delaware with George Washington
100 years ago	Age 69: yesterday, the airplane was invented
30 years ago	Age 69: this afternoon, landed on the moon; in early evening, broke the DNA (genetic) code
2,000 CE	70th birthday: tonight celebrates the arrival of the twenty-first century

Note: Or several million years, according to some anthropologists.

A mother in Cote d'Ivoire (West Africa), carrying her load on her head returns to the village with her daughter after gathering wood. Carrying wood and water is typically women's work. In this society, however, the primary social cohesion is mechanical solidarity.

Source: © Olivier Martel / Corbis.

in more complex societies. Each position developed specific tasks and was interdependent with other positions, what Durkheim called *organic solidarity*. To put together a car in a factory takes many individuals carrying out interdependent tasks. One reason the division of labor is critical to new stages of society is that it leads to new forms of social glue based on this interdependence. Changes from mechanical (traditional) to organic (more complex) societies depend on harnessing new forms of energy and finding more efficient ways to use energy; these elements are critical to evolution of societies (Nolan and Lenski 1999).

Also, as societies changed, they become more multi-leveled. The meso level—institutions and large bureaucratic organizations—came to have more influence. Still, as recently as 200 years ago, even large societies had little global inter-dependence, and life for the typical citizen was influenced mostly by local community events at the meso level.

As you read about each of the following types of societies, from most simple to most complex, notice the presence of these variables: division of labor, interdependence of

people's positions, increasingly advanced technologies, and new forms and uses of energy. While none of these variables appears sufficient to trigger evolution to a new type of society, they may all be necessary in order for a transition to occur.

In the simpler, more traditional societies, interpersonal interaction was very important. The economy, religion, educa-tion, political systems, and health care were all largely functions held by the family or individuals serving families, such as shamans for health care. While a specialist—a shaman—might perform healing functions, health care was not a complex institution or even an organization. Developing meso and macro levels of society seems to have been a result of changes in society rather than a cause. As we move through the process of sociocultural evolution, however, the meso- and macro-level institutions of the social world become more organized and have more profound impacts on the lives of individuals.

Types of Societies

Sociologist and anthropologists typically identify five stages in the process of sociocultural evolution (Nolan and Lenski 1999), beginning with foraging societies in which the people hunt and gather in order to survive. Horticultural, agricul-tural, industrial, and then information-age (postindustrial) societies are increasingly complex social systems.

Hunter-Gatherer Societies

From the beginning of human experience until recently, hunting and gathering was the sole means of sustaining life. Other types of societies emerged only recently (Nolan and Lenski 1999), and today, only a handful of societies still rely on hunting and gathering.

Modern industrial societies are often held together through structural interdependence of roles and tasks (organic solidarity). Sharing the same values with others in the same occupation or position is less important than economic interdependence with each other.

Source: © Steve Raymer / Corbis.

A client, consulting for a fertility problem, is sprayed with a medicinal liquid by Abdoulaye, the medicine man in his community in Sereres, Senegal.

Source: © Olivier Martel / Corbis.

In the Kalahari Desert of Southwest Africa live a hunter-gatherer people known as the !Kung San. (The *!* is pronounced with a click of the tongue.) The !Kung live a nomadic life, moving from one place to another as food supplies are used up. They live in temporary huts, settling around water holes for a few months at a time. These settlements are small, rarely more than 20 to 50 people, for food supplies are not great enough to support larger, permanent populations (Lee 1984). A gender division of labor facilitates the effort to obtain food. !Kung women are primarily responsible for gathering nuts and other edible plant matter, while !Kung men are excellent hunters. When a large animal is killed, people gather from a wide area to share in the bounty, and great care is taken to ensure that the meat is distributed fairly. Beyond gender and age, there is little diversity in responsibilities and therefore few choices about what to do.

Because they are a nomadic people, the !Kung San have few personal possessions. All the available resources are shared among the people who live at a water hole and those who come to visit. However, sharing is regulated by a complex system of obligations. A visitor who eats food at another's hearth is expected to repay that hospitality in the future.

The !Kung San are a typical **hunter-gatherer society**, in which people rely on the vegetation and animals occurring naturally in their habitat to sustain life. Several characteristics are common to these societies: group life is organized around kinship ties, and families train the young; fire provides warmth, light, and protection; clothing, shelter, and tools are made of available materials; the people are nomadic, moving periodically to new food sources; and the number of births and deaths are balanced. Weaponry is developed during this stage.

The culture of the !Kung San and the few other hunter-gatherer societies in the world today have changed rapidly in recent years. Much of the wild game on which they subsisted has either disappeared or is now protected on game preserves. In addition, the governments of South Africa and Botswana have attempted to settle the groups on reservations. These nations create a macro-level dimension to the lives of these people that they had not known before. By becoming connected to other ways of life, by choice or force, they will experience change. Thus, the hunter-gatherer lifestyle is becoming extinct.

Herding and Horticultural Societies

The Masai tribespeople inhabit the grasslands of Kenya and Tanzania, depending on their herds for survival. Their animals—cattle and goats—are their primary source of nutrition, providing meat, milk, and blood (which they drink). A semi-nomadic society, the Masai move from settlement to settlement to find grazing land for their animals, setting up semipermanent shelters for the few months they will remain in one area. All of the huts in the village are constructed in a circle; often a fence surrounds the compound to discourage unwelcome animal intruders. The group may return to an old compound after some time has elapsed and the grazing is favorable again. They often grow short-term crops to supplement their diet. The Masai live as they have lived for centuries, in balance with their environment. However, the government of Kenya, a relatively new macro-level influence on their lives, now restricts their territory and practices that overlap with wild animal refuges, and tourism is influencing their economy.

The Masai are a **herding society**: their food-producing strategy is based on their herds of domesticated animals, whose care is the central focus of their activities. Rather than hunt for meat, they tame animals such as sheep, goats, pigs, dogs, and camels, and use them for a food supply. **Horticultural societies** engage in primitive agriculture using digging sticks and wooden hoes to plant and maintain small garden plots. They domesticate beans, corn, squash, and other plants rather than gather wild vegetables. Both herding and horticultural societies are distinguished from hunter-gatherer societies in that their members cultivate food and have some control over its production (Ward 2006).

Without question, the ability to control the source of food was a major turning point in cultural evolution for several reasons. First, because horticultural societies were more settled and surplus food was a possibility, the size of societies increased. A community might now contain as many as 2,000 to 3,000 individuals. Yet because the land became exhausted, many groups still moved periodically, a situation that limited both group size and number of possessions.

Surplus food and possessions brought the advent of private property, status differences, and inequality between individuals and among women and men. Because women were primarily responsible for gardening and raising children, men were free to accumulate wealth and train as warriors. Status for males came to be based on their skill as warriors and on the number of animals, wives, and ornaments they possessed. Historically, the end of the horticultural stage saw advances in irrigation systems, fertilization of land, and rotation of crops. However, the technological breakthrough that moved many societies into the next stage was the plow, introduced about 6,000 years ago. It marked the beginning of the agricultural revolution in Europe and the Middle East and brought massive changes in social structures to many societies.

Agricultural Societies

Pedro and Lydia Ramirez and their four young children live in a small farming village in Nicaragua. They rise early, and while Pedro heads for the fields to do some work before breakfast, Lydia prepares his breakfast and lunch and sees that their eldest son is up and ready to go to school. After school, the boy also helps in the fields. Most of the land in the area is owned by a large company that grows coffee, but the Ramirez family is fortunate to have a small garden plot of their own where they grow some vegetables for themselves. At harvest time, all hands help, including young children. The families receive cash for the crops they have grown, minus rent for the land. The land is plowed with the help of strong animals such as horses and oxen, and fertilizers are used. Little irrigation is attempted, though the garden plots may be watered by hand in the dry season.

The Ramirez's way of life is typical of an agricultural society. Like horticulturalists, agrarian farmers rely primarily on raising crops for food. However, **agriculture societies** are more efficient than horticulture: technological advances such as the plow, irrigation, use of animals, and fertilization allow intensive and continuous cultivation of the same land, thus permitting permanent settlements and greater food surpluses. Through time, as increasingly sophisticated agricultural technology resulted in surplus food, the size of population centers increased to as much as a million or more.

As surpluses accumulated, land in some societies became concentrated in the hands of a few individuals. Wealthy landowners built armies and expanded their empires; during these periods, controlling land took precedence over technological advance. War was prevalent, and societies were divided increasingly into rich and poor classes. Those who held the land and wealth could control the labor source and acquire serfs or slaves. Thus, the feudal system was born. Serfs (the peasant class) were forced to work the land for their survival; food surpluses also allowed some individuals to leave the land and to trade goods or services in exchange for food. For the first time, social inequality became extensive enough that we can refer to social classes. At this point, religion, political power, a standing army, and other meso-level institutions and organizations come to be independent of the family. The meso-level becomes well established.

As technology advanced and goods were manufactured in cities, peasants moved from farming communities to rapidly growing urban areas, where the demand for labor was great. It was not until the late 1700s in England that the next major transformation of society took place, resulting largely from technological advances and harnessing of power.

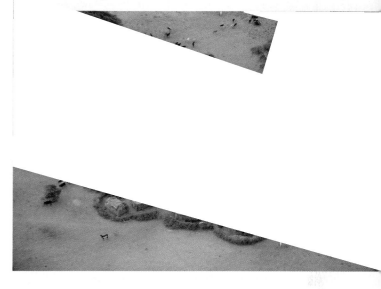

Herds of cattle are led in and out of a Masai village in Kenya. The strategy of domesticating cattle rather than hunting game has been a survival strategy for the Masai, but it also affects the culture in many ways.

Source: © Gavriel Jecan / Corbis.

A child picks coffee in the mountainous region of Northeastern Nicaragua. The campesinos farm cooperatively in the nature preserve Miraflor, but global dips in coffee prices have undermined the economy to the point of brutal poverty, and attempts are being made to develop a tourist economy to replace the traditional livelihood. This will no doubt create a major shift in the culture.

Source: © Jodi Hilton / Corbis.

Industrialization brought major changes in social organization and in culture as production was removed from families to companies with highly organized processes controlled by capitalists. In this photo from the mid-twentieth century, a plant of the American Steel and Wire Company in Cleveland, Ohio, ships goods from Lake Erie and the St. Lawrence River.

Source: Library of Congress.

Industrial Societies

The Industrial Revolution brought the harnessing of steam power and gasoline engines, permitting power-driven machines to replace human and animal power; a tractor can plow far more land in a week than a horse, and an electric pump can irrigate more acres than an ox-driven pump. As a result, raw mineral products such as ores, raw plant products such as rubber, flax or fiber, and raw animal products such as hides could be transformed by chemical or machine power into consumer goods. The Industrial Revolution brought enormous changes in society in both products and structure.

Several characteristics typify **industrial societies**, societies that rely primarily on mechanized production for subsistence. First, the division of labor is more pronounced as industries develop sophisticated machines requiring human expertise. Second, economic resources increase and tend to be distributed more widely among individuals in industrial societies, although inequities are great between the owners and the laborers. Highly skilled workers demand higher wages, whereas unskilled workers receive lower wages. Third, industrialization alters the structure of society as peasants move from rural areas to cities to find work in factories. Most jobs are in the production of machines and products: cars, television sets, washing machines, and so forth. Cities come to be populated by millions of people.

Finally, kinship patterns also change. Whereas agrarian societies favor large, land-based extended family units (recall

that the Ramirez children in Nicaragua all help out at harvest time), family needs are different in industrial societies. Smaller, nuclear families are now preferable because of crowded urban conditions; children become a liability because they contribute less to the finances of the family. The meso- and macro-level dimensions of social life have major impacts on the lives of people.

Perhaps the most notable characteristic of the industrial age is the rapid rate of change compared to other stages of societal development. Whereas the beginning of industrialization in England was gradual, requiring many years of population movement, urbanization, technological development, modernization, and other changes, today societal change is occurring so rapidly that some developing societies virtually bypass the industrial age and move almost directly into the postindustrial era. Much of the rapid change is connected to the increasing complexity of the social world, typical of the postindustrial stage.

Global organizations such as the World Bank, the World Court, the United Nations, and the World Health Organization address problems at a global level and sometimes even make decisions that change national boundaries or national policies. Medical organizations such as Doctors without Borders work cross-nationally; corporations become multinational; and voluntary societies such as Amnesty International lobby for human rights in places around the globe. By the time the next stage is reached, the term *global village* will have become a commonly accepted notion among those who work on social policies.

Postindustrial or Information Societies

In the Japanese metropolis of Osaka, the service industry is booming. The world's most modern **technology**—that is, scientific knowledge used for utilitarian or economic purposes—is produced here. New micro-technology firms open every week, and the entire society feeds on new knowledge in the electronic age. Since World War II, Japan has moved rapidly from agricultural to industrial to postindustrial society, with elements of each stage coexisting. Buddhist monks practice their ancient religion at nearby shrines, and women and men dressed in traditional kimonos perform the ancient ritual tea ceremony next to high-tech companies producing the world's latest electronic gadgets.

The Akamoto family lives in a large apartment building near Osaka. On one side of their building are similar apartments, and on the other side is a rice paddy. From their window, the Akamotos can watch peasant farmers work in the small fields by hand while traffic rushes past on the superhighway. Mr. Akamoto travels to his office in Osaka each day where he works long hours in a banking firm. His college-educated wife is a homemaker. Although an increasing number of Japanese women delay marriage and childbearing in order to work outside the home, few work after they are married and have children.

After World War II, starting in the 1950s, the transition from industrial to postindustrial society began in the United

A nurse from Medecins sans Frontieres (Doctors without Borders) examines an Angolan villager suffering from malnourishment. After Angola gained independence from Portugal in 1975, civil war erupted and a 27-year battle ravaged the country, killing about half a million people and displacing another 4 million before a ceasefire was declared in 2002. People around the world have responded to, and therefore they and their families have been affected by, this civil war in Africa.

Source: © Louise Gubb / Corbis Saba.

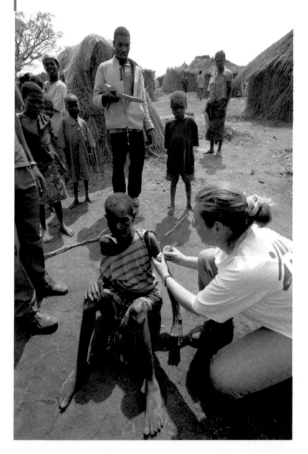

communities and schools with ready access to computers and those without. In 2003, 62 percent of households in the United States had one or more computers, and 88 percent of these had Internet access. However, only 35 percent of householders aged 65 and older, 45 percent of Black or Hispanic householders, and 28 percent of householders with less than a high school education had a computer (U.S. Census Bureau 2005), illustrating the technological gap.

Postindustrial societies rely in part on new sources of power such as atomic, wind, and solar energy; automation; and computer-controlled robots, eliminating all but the most highly skilled technicians. Thus, control of information and ability to develop technologies or provide services rather than control of money or capital become most important.

In the twenty-first century, values of postindustrial societies favor scientific approaches to problem solving, creativity, research, and development. These approaches are becoming dominant in world economies. Although the technological era in which many of us are immersed is in its early stages, its effects are being felt throughout the world through satellites, computers, the Internet, cell phones, and other information systems.

One sociologist has actually chosen to study the relationship of creativity to local cultural climate and to economic prosperity; his research has important applied

This Buddhist monk is quite willing to adopt modern technology, including a cell phone that can connect him with colleagues on the other side of the globe.

Source: © Richard T. Nowitz / Corbis.

States, Western Europe (especially Germany), and Japan. This shift was characterized by movement from human labor to automated production and from manufacturing into service jobs such as computer operators, bankers, scientists, teachers, public relations workers, stockbrokers, and salespeople. More than two-thirds of all jobs in the United States now reside in organizations that produce and transmit information. Daniel Bell (1973) described this transformation of work, information, and communication as "the third technological revolution." As the society transforms, the culture also changes, stimulated by the development of the computer. High levels of technical and professional education are required for those holding key positions; those without technical education are less likely to find rewarding employment (Tapscott 1998). Thus, new class lines are being drawn, based in part on skills and education in new technologies. There is already evidence of a growing divide between

Hybrid buses have been adopted in some cities and in national parks because of the effects of pollution on the globe and its occupants.

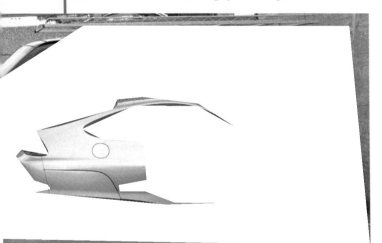

A hybrid Honda Insight parked next to a high gas consumption vehicle. Bicycles, powered by food that is fun to eat rather than gasoline, is even more efficient and cheaper!

Source: Michael Pereckas, Photographer and caption author.

dimensions. The Applied Sociologist at Work (facing page) explores this fascinating research and explains why it is important to policy makers in local communities.

As Richard Florida's research makes clear, the organization of the society and the means of providing the necessities of life have a profound impact on values, beliefs, lifestyle, and other aspects of culture. In much of this book, we focus on this complex, multilayered society, for this is the type of system in which most of us reading this book now live. We turn next to a discussion of the social software that complements the hardware of our society.

THINKING SOCIOLOGICALLY

What are likely to be the growth areas in your society? What competencies (e.g., thinking and analysis) and what skills (e.g., interpersonal abilities and communication skills) will be essential in the future for you to find employment and be successful on the job?

CULTURE: THE SOFTWARE

Each social unit of cooperating and interdependent people, whether at the micro, meso, or macro levels, develops a culture. This culture—including knowledge, beliefs, values, rules or laws, language, customs, and symbols—provides guidelines for the actions and interaction of individuals and groups within the society. For example, consider the cultural guidelines that people follow when they greet another person. In the United States, proper greetings include a handshake, a wave, or saying "hello" or "hi." The greeting ceremony in Japan includes bowing, with the depth of the bow defined by the relative status of each individual. To know the proper bowing behavior, Japanese business people who are strangers exchange business cards upon introduction. Their titles, as printed on their cards, disclose each person's status and thus provide clues as to how deeply each should bow. The proper greeting behavior in many European countries calls for men as well as women to kiss acquaintances on both cheeks.

The definition of culture used in this book differs from the meaning of *culture* in everyday usage. You have probably heard the term *culture* used to refer to the fine arts—classical music, opera, literature, ballet, theater (what some call *high culture*)—or to *pop culture*, including such phenomena as country music, TV sitcoms, professional wrestling, Harlequin romance novels, and other mass entertainment. Although the sociological definition of culture includes both high culture and pop culture, the term has much broader meaning. Everyone shares a culture, and culture is equally important to all people, although there may be different views within and between cultures about what rules and behaviors are most important. No one could survive without culture, for without culture, there would be no guidelines or rules of behavior and societies would be chaotic masses of individuals.

Culture evolves over time. What is normal, proper, and good behavior in hunter-gatherer societies, where cooperation and communal loyalty is critical to the hunt, differs from that in an information age where individualism and competition may be encouraged and enhance one's well-being. Culture provides us with routines, patterns, and expectations for carrying out daily rituals and interactions.

The creation of culture is ongoing and cumulative because individuals and societies build on existing culture. The behaviors, values, and institutions that are natural to us are actually shaped by our culture. In fact, culture is so much a part of our lives that what may strike an outsider as unusual is, for the most part, unseen by members of the culture. We do not think about eating with a fork, but this seems strange to others who eat with chopsticks or with fingers.

Culture is the feature that most separates us from other animals, for only humans have a shared culture. Humans adapt to the environment in a much more flexible manner than animals that use primarily their instincts. *Instincts*, which are a complex series of drives and reflexes that help animals cope with the environment, are programmed into

THE APPLIED SOCIOLOGIST AT WORK

Creativity, Community, and Applied Sociology

Like the transformations of societies from the hunter-gatherer to the horticultural stage or from the agricultural to the industrial stage, our own current transformation seems to have created a good deal of "cultural wobble" in the society. How does one identify the elements or the defining features of a new age—the Post industrial Era or the Information Age or the Age of Creativity—while the transformation is still in process? This was one of the questions that intrigued sociologist Richard Florida.

Dr. Florida (2002) combined several methods. First, he traveled around the country to communities that were especially prosperous and seemed to be on the cutting edge of change in U.S. society. In these communities, he did both individual interviews and focus-group interviews—the latter being a type of group interview with seven or eight people where ideas can be generated from the group, the discussion recorded, and the transcript of the discussion analyzed. These semistructured interviews in which open-ended questions are asked helped Professor Florida identify the factors that caused people to choose the place where they decided to live. His informants discussed quality of life and the way they make decisions. As certain themes and patterns emerged, he tested the ideas by comparing statistical data for regions that were vibrant, had growing economies, and seemed to be integrated into the emerging information economy. He used already existing archival data collected by various U.S. government agencies, especially the U.S. Bureau of Labor Statistics and the U.S. Census Bureau, to compare communities and regions of the country.

In addition to the broad changes occurring in the United States, Florida was interested in the elements of economic prosperity and growth. The economy of the twenty-first century is largely driven by creativity, and creative people often decide where to live based on certain features of the society. He also found that modern businesses flourish when they hire highly creative people. Thus, growing businesses tend to seek out places where creative people locate.

Currently, more than one-third of the jobs in the United States—and almost all of the extremely well-paid professional positions—require creative thinking.

These include not just the creative arts but scientific research, computer and mathematical occupations, educational and library science positions, and many media, legal, and managerial careers. People in this "creative class" are given an enormous amount of autonomy, problems to solve, and freedom to figure out how to solve them. Florida (2002) writes, "Access to talented and creative people is to modern business what access to coal and iron ore was to steel making" (p. 6). The winners in virtually every field—from fashion to architecture, from automobiles to food products, from music to information technology—are those who continually create.

Fairly early in his research, Florida identified regions and urban areas that are especially creative. A young scholar, Gary Gates, was doing research on communities that are open and hospitable to gays and lesbians. Gates and Florida were amazed to find that their lists were nearly identical. Yet the more research Florida did, the more that made sense. Creative people thrive on diversity—ethnic, gender, religious, and otherwise—for when creative people are around others who think differently, it tends to spawn new avenues of thinking and problem solving. Tolerance of difference and even the enjoyment of individual idiosyncrasies is a hallmark of thriving communities. Such communities also have a number of places for creative people to meet and exchange ideas—coffeehouses and wineries that sponsor poetry readings and local musicians, Saturday art markets, and "public squares" or walkways.

Creative and successful businesses have learned that they must be flexible, resulting in businesses that relax the dress codes, allow flexibility in the workday, provide stimulating environments and colleagues, permit a great deal of autonomy to workers to solve problems for themselves, and downplay hierarchical relationships. Just as farmers took great care of the oxen that pulled their plows, creative people and successful businesses seek environments that allow creativity to flourish.

Interestingly, Florida is now very much in demand as a consultant to mayors and urban-planning teams, and his books have become required reading for city council members in places such as Corvalis, Oregon. Some elected officials have decided that fostering an environment conducive to creativity that attracts

(Continued)

(Continued)

creative people will also lead to prosperity, and business will follow. Local music festivals and art chautauquas, the presence of organic food grocery stores, legislation that encourages interesting mom–and-pop stores (and keeps out large "box stores" that crush such small and unique endeavors), encouragement of quaint locally owned bookstores and distinctive coffee shops, provisions for bike and walking paths throughout the town, and ordinances that establish an environment of tolerance for people who are "different" are key elements of creative communities. For policy makers, these become considerations in seeking prosperity for the local community.

Richard Florida teaches regional economic development at Carnegie Mellon University. He earned his bachelor's degree from Rutgers College and his doctorate from Columbia University in Urban Planning.

the brain of the animal from birth. However, humans rely largely on culture. Passing on culture as a means of adapting to the environment is highly useful, for humans are the only mammals that can adapt and manipulate their environment to survive on the equator or in the Arctic.

THINKING SOCIOLOGICALLY

Try playing a game of cards with four people in which each player thinks a different suit is trump. (Trump is a rule that any card from the trump suit wins over any card from a different suit.) In this game, one person believes hearts is trump, another assumes spades is trump, and so forth. What would happen? How would the result be similar to a society with no common culture?

This Japanese schoolgirl might think that eating with a fork or spoon was quite strange. She has been well socialized to know that polite eating involves competent use of chopsticks.

Source: © Karen Kasmauski / Corbis.

The Study of Culture
Real and Ideal Culture

Through the process known as *socialization* (see Chapter 4), we learn from birth the patterns of behavior approved in our society, and for the most part, we hardly question these practices and beliefs that we see around us. Rather like animals who have only lived in a rain forest and cannot imagine a treeless desert, we can fail to notice how much we rely on our culture to make sense of things.

Culture is manifested in two ways. **Ideal culture** refers to those practices and beliefs that are most desirable and are consciously taught to children. Not everyone, however, follows the approved cultural patterns. **Real culture** refers to the way things in society are actually done. For example, the ideal in many societies is to ban extramarital sex (that is, sex outside marriage). This requirement arose for a number of reasons, including the possible consequences of illegitimate children, questions of inheritance, and family jealousies. Historically, it often was found in societies where women were viewed as "sexual property" of men. This traditional ideal that sexual intercourse should occur only within marriage is not always reflected in reality, however. Extramarital sex occurs among a substantial portion of the population in some societies. In the United States, about one-forth of all married men and one-out-of-seven married women have had at least one extramarital affair (Newman and Grauerholz 2002).

Sociologists may learn the ideal rules of a culture by asking questions and reading the laws, but the real behavior patterns are more difficult to discern. Years of living in and observing a group may be needed to sort out the differences between real and ideal culture.

Ethnocentrism and Cultural Relativity

Sociologists must rely on careful use of the scientific method to understand cultures. One issue is particularly important: objectivity in studying other cultures. All humans are raised in a particular culture that they view as normal or natural. Since the study of cultures requires sensitivity to a wide variety of human social patterns, scientists must develop a perspective that reduces bias. This is more difficult than it sounds because human values and behaviors vary so widely and each group thinks its own values are natural and its behaviors are normal and proper. Consider the following example.

The Arapesh of New Guinea, a traditional society, encourage premarital sex; a female who proved her fertility was more attractive as a mate. Anthropologist Margaret Mead (1963) found that the Arapesh not only allowed but encouraged young teens to engage in clandestine premarital sex. The babies resulting from these meetings were absorbed into the matrilineal structure (family ancestry traced through the female line). Their care, support, belonging, and lineage were not major issues for the Arapesh; the babies were simply accepted and welcomed as new members of the mother's family, because the structure was able to absorb them. The society was stable; families were supportive. For the Arapesh, sexual behavior outside of marriage is not a moral issue. Other societies, such as the Bontoc of the Philippines, have similar views.

From studies of 154 societies documented in the *Human Relations Area Files* (Ford 1970) (a valuable source of information on societies around the world), scientists have found that approximately 42 percent of the 154 societies encourage premarital sex, whereas 29 percent forbid such behavior and punish those who disobey this rule. The remainder fall in between. These figures suggest an important point: values, beliefs, and behaviors are created by societies and can vary dramatically from one society to the next. For many people, this variation is highly threatening and even offensive, because most people judge others according to their own perspectives, experiences, and values.

Ethnocentrism describes this tendency to view one's own group and its cultural expectations as right, proper, and superior to others. Many individuals brought up in societies that discourage or forbid premarital sex, for instance, judge groups such as the Arapesh as immoral. In some Muslim societies, for example, offending persons would be severely punished, even killed. In turn, the Arapesh would find rules of abstinence to be strange and even wrong.

This young Bontoc woman from the North Luzon area of the Philippines grew up in a culture with very different norms about sexual morality than are prevalent in the West.

Source: © Charles & Josette Lenars / Corbis.

In 1923, the Hollywood Association started a campaign to expel the Japanese from their community. Signs like these were prominent throughout Hollywood and other California communities. They illustrate ethnocentrism.

Source: © Bettman / Corbis.

It is important for societies to instill a degree of ethnocentrism in their members, for these beliefs make members feel that they belong to the group and help hold the group together. Ethnocentrism promotes loyalty, unity, morale, and conformity to the rules of society. Fighting for one's country, for instance, requires some degree of belief in the rightness of one's own society and its causes. Ethnocentric attitudes also help to protect societies from rapid, disintegrating change. If most people in a society did not believe in the rules and values of their own culture, the result could be dissension, controversy, and widespread crime or deviance.

Unfortunately, however, the same ethnocentric attitudes that strengthen societies may also encourage hostility, racism, slavery, war, and even genocide against others—even others within the society—who are different. Old war movies and propaganda news clips about World War I and World War II labeled enemies as "krauts," "Japs," "barbarians," "savages," and "heathens."

Dehumanizing another group with labels makes it easier to kill them or perform acts of discrimination and destruction. We see this in current conflicts in Iraq in which both sides in the conflict feel hatred for the other combatants. However, as we become a part of a global social world, it becomes increasingly important to accept those who are "different." Bigotry and attitudes of superiority do not enhance cross-national cooperation—which is what the global village and globalization entail.

Ethnocentrism can lead to misunderstandings between members of different cultures. Consider the American businesspeople who go to Japan to negotiate deals and sign contracts. The Japanese way of doing business takes time; it

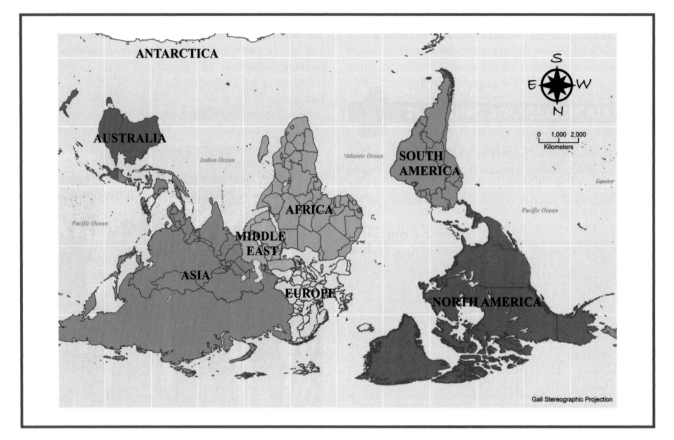

MAP 3.1   "Upside-down" map of the world, where South is up. The fact that this looks "wrong" or disturbing is part of our ethnocentrism.

Source: Map by Anna Versluis.

involves getting to know the other party by socializing over drinks in the evening. It is important not to rush the deal. To the Japanese, the Americans seem pushy, too concerned about contract details rather than trust, and in too much of a hurry. Many an international business arrangement has fallen through because of such cultural misunderstandings.

U.S. foreign relations also illustrate how ethnocentrism can produce hostility. Many U.S. citizens are surprised to learn that the United States—great democracy, world power, and disseminator of food, medicine, and technological assistance to developing nations—is despised in many countries; this is largely because of American dominance and the threat it poses to other people's way of life (Hertsgaard 2003). Americans are regarded by some as thinking ethnocentrically and only about their own welfare as they exploit weaker nations. American tourists are often seen as loudmouthed ignoramuses whose ethnocentric attitudes prevent them from seeing value in other cultures or from learning other languages.

Anti-American demonstrations in South America, the Middle East, and Asia have brought this reality to life through television. Indeed, politicians in several Latin American and European countries have run for office on platforms aimed at reducing U.S. influence. Thus, American ethnocentrism may foster anti-American reactions of ethnocentrism by people from other countries. Note that even referring to citizens of

the United States as Americans—as though people from Canada, Mexico, or South America do not really count as Americans—is seen as ethnocentric by many people from these other countries. *America* and *the United States* are not the same thing, but many people in the United States, including some presidents, fail to make the distinction, much to the dismay of other North and South Americans. Map 3.1 is another illustration of our geographic ethnocentrism; we think the north should always be "on top."

Cultural relativism requires setting aside personal beliefs and prejudices to understand a culture through the eyes of members of that culture and by its own standards. Instead of judging cultural practices as good or bad, acceptable or unacceptable, superior or inferior with reference to ones own cultural practices, the goal is to learn objectively the purpose and the consequences of each practice in the culture under study. Just as we may have preferences for certain software programs to do word processing, we can recognize that other software programs are quite good, may have some features that are better than the one we use, and are ingeniously designed.

Yet being tolerant and understanding is not always easy. For even the most careful observer, the subtleties of other cultures can be elusive. The idea of being "on time," which is so much a part of the cultures of the United States, Canada, and parts of Europe is a rather bizarre concept in many societies.

Sociology around the World

Evolutionary Cuisine

Early Humans' Salad Bar

This menu comes from early hominids who lived in the savannahs of Eastern and Southern Africa from roughly 1.5 to 5 million years ago. Everything was served raw. Cooking with fire had not been invented.

Main Course: Nuts, birds' eggs, roots, tubers, beans, leaves, gum, sap, greens, insects, worms, grubs, termites, and seasonal berries and fruits. (90 percent of the diet.)

Raw Meat Appetizer Tray: Opportunist and gathered delicacies include small mammals, birds, reptiles, fish, shellfish, slow game, dead or dying animals, and infants of species such as antelope, pig, giraffe, or baboons when available. Bone marrow or the contents of animal heads and stomachs are delicious additions to this menu. Season with honey, rock salt, or puree of worms and insects. (10 percent of the diet.)

Ancestral Potluck Dinner

The first members of our own genus, Homo erectus, used these recipes from about 100,000 to 1.5 million years ago in the tropical and temperate zones of Africa and Eurasia. New technologies in fire making, advanced scavenging, and simple hunting as well as social advances in cooperation, sharing, and the gender division of labor provided some very tasty and nourishing meals for our ancestors.

Main Courses: Stew or soup made with vegetables, bird bones, roots, nuts, and foods from the Salad Bar and Raw Meat Appetizer Tray plus other gathered foods as available. Add leftovers and herbal seasonings. (80 percent of the diet.)

Outdoor Barbecue: Sizzling deer haunch, roasted rabbit, shellfish, wild boar, ox, or cattle ribs. (20 percent of the diet.)

Source: Ward (1996, 2006).

Among many Native American people, such as the Dineh (Apache and Navajo), it is ludicrous for people to let a time-piece that one wears on one's arm—a piece of machinery—govern the way one lives life. The Dineh orientation to time, that one should do things according to a natural rhythm of the body and not according to an artificial ticking mechanism, is difficult for many North Americans to grasp. Misunderstandings occur when those of European heritage think "Indians are always late," jumping to an erroneous conclusion that "Indians" are undependable. Native Americans, on the other hand, think whites are neurotic about letting some instrument control them (Basso 1979; Farrer 1996; Hall 1959, 1983).

Another example of ethnocentrism that is hard to overcome is our notions of what is food and what is just not edible. While food is necessary for survival of all humans, there are widespread cultural differences in what people eat, where and how they obtain it, and how they prepare and consume it. The French revere truffles, whereas a New Guinea tribe savors grasshoppers, Europeans and Russians relish raw fish eggs (caviar), Eskimo children find seal eyeballs a treat, Indonesians eat dog, and some Nigerians prize termites. Whether it is from another time period or another society, variations in food can be shocking to us, making it hard to understand other people and other times, as the essay above on Sociology around the World illustrates. Cultural relativism requires that we shrug our shoulders and admit, "Well, they are getting vitamins, proteins, and other nutrients, and it seems to work for them."

Adopting a cultural relativist perspective helps ensure objectivity in studying the widely varying values and social rules that shape people's lives. However, it does not mean that social scientists accept or agree with all the beliefs and practices of the cultures they study. Social scientists may personally oppose acts such as infanticide, head-hunting, slavery, removal of the clitoris from females, gender inequality, forced marriages, cannibalism, terrorism, and genocide. Yet, even though they disagree with such practices, it is important to understand those practices in the context of another society's values and structures. Many social scientists do take strong stands against violations of human rights, environmental destruction, and other policies—basing their positions on what they consider universal human rights and the potential for harm to human beings and to the world community. However, it is important to bear in mind that cultural values in most Western democracies are adaptations to systems that thrive on values of extreme individualism, differentiation, and competition, consistent with very complex society.

THINKING SOCIOLOGICALLY

Small, tightly knit societies with no meso or macro level often stress cooperation, conformity, and personal sacrifice for the sake of the community. Complex societies with established meso- and macro-level linkages are more frequently individualistic, stressing personal uniqueness, individual creativity, and critical thinking. Why might this be so?

In the United States, dogs are family members and are highly cherished and pampered, with dog-care averaging $30 per day becoming a growth industry. In Nanking, China, dogs are valued more as a culinary delicacy, and a good source of protein. If you feel a twinge of disgust, that is part of the ethnocentrism we may experience as our perspectives conflict with those elsewhere in the world.

Sources: Top photo © Istockphoto.com. Bottom photo © Elise Roberts.

SOCIETY, CULTURE, AND OUR SOCIAL WORLD

Whether you are eating termite eggs or chicken eggs, societies always have a culture and culture is always linked to a society. Culture determines the way of life in each level of society, from the global system to the individual family. The social world model at the beginning of the chapter shows that smaller social units such as a college operate within larger social units such as the community, which is also part of a region of the country; what takes place in each of these is determined by the culture. A society's culture provides the guidelines for proper actions—the "software"—for each structural "hardware" unit, from micro-level, two-person relationships to ethnic group subcultures at the meso level to interactions between societies at the macro level.

MICROCULTURES: MICRO-LEVEL ANALYSIS

Micro-level analysis focuses on social interactions in small group or organizational settings. To apply this idea to culture, we look at microcultures. Groups and organizations such as a girl scout troop or a local chapter of the Rotary Club involve a small number of people. These organizations influence only a portion of members' lives; thus, they are not truly subcultures. When the culture affects only a small segment of one's life, affecting a portion of one's week or influencing a limited period of one's life, it is called a **microculture** (Gordon 1970). Additional examples include a street gang, a college sorority, a business office, or a summer camp group.

Hospitals are social units with microcultures. People in different colored uniforms scurry around carrying out their designated tasks as part of the organizational culture. Hospital workers interact among themselves to attain goals of patient care. They have a common in-group vocabulary, a shared set of values, a hierarchy of positions with roles and behaviors for each position, and a guiding system of regulations for the organization—all of which shape the interactions during the 40 hours a week that each member works in the hospital. Yet the hospital culture may have little relevance to the rest of the everyday lives of the employees.

Microcultures may survive over time, with individuals coming in and going out from the group, but no one lives their entire life within a microculture. The values, rules, and specialized language used by the hospital staff continue as one shift ends and other medical personnel enter and sustain that microculture.

Every organization, club, and association has its own set of rules and expectations; these are organizational microcultures. Schools develop their own unique cultures, as do firemen's unions. The microculture of a fraternity impacts current students; as students graduate and move out of that microculture, others move into it. Some microcultures exist for a limited period of time. A summer camp microculture may develop but exists only for that summer; the following summer, a very different culture may evolve because of new counselors and campers. A girl's softball team may develop its own cheers, jokes, insider slang, and values regarding competition or what it means to be a good sport, but next year the girls may be realigned into different teams and the transitory culture of the previous year would not survive. In contrast to microcultures, subcultures continue across a person's life span.

When these people work together in a hospital, they share a common culture: shared terminology, rules of interaction, and values regarding objectifying human body parts so they are not sexualized. However, that only affects a part of each day and each week; it is part of the microculture in which they spend only a segment of their day.

Source: © Tammy Bryngelson / istockphoto.

SUBCULTURE AND COUNTERCULTURES: MESO-LEVEL ANALYSIS

One can be African Canadian, Chinese Canadian, or Hispanic Canadian, living within an ethnic community that provides food, worship, and many other resources, and still be a good Canadian citizen. One can also be a Mormon and live almost all of one's life in Utah, interacting entirely with other Mormons, and still be a good American citizen. Many groups have their own subcommunities within the dominant culture of the larger society.

At the meso level, the social unit plays a more continuous role in the life of members; one can be born, marry, and die in that social unit. The social unit is smaller than the nation but is large enough to sustain people throughout the life span; such a subsociety has its own culture, a **subculture**. A subculture is in some ways unique to that group yet shares the culture of the dominant society (Arnold 1970; Gordon 1970).

Subcultures add their own set of conventions and expectations to the general standards of the dominant culture. Within each subculture, members maintain a feeling of "we" and a belief in the rightness of their customs, rituals, religious practices, dress, food, or whatever else distinguishes them. Note that many categories into which we group people are not subcultures; redheads, left-handed people, tall people, individuals who read *Cosmopolitan Magazine*, and DVD watchers do not make up subcultures because they do not have a common way of life. A motorcycle gang, a college fraternity, and a summer camp are also not subcultures since they affect only a segment of one's life (Gordon 1970; Yablonski 1959). A subculture, on the other hand, influences a person's life in pervasive ways throughout the life span.

In the United States, subcultures include ethnic groups, such as Italian American and Chinese American; religious groups that influence everyday life, such as the Mennonites in Ohio and Orthodox Jews in New York City; and social class groups, including the exclusive culture of the elite upper-class on the East and West coasts of the United States. For example, while Hasidic Jews adhere to the same values and most of the behavioral standards of the predominantly Christian-American culture, they follow additional rules specific to their religion: their clothing and hairstyles follow strict rules, with men wearing beards and temple-locks, and married women wearing wigs; their religious holidays are different from those of the dominant Christian culture; they observe dietary restrictions such as the avoidance of pork and shellfish; and they observe the Sabbath from sunset Friday to sunset Saturday.

This woman is part of a subgroup of the larger society, the Jewish faith community. Her faith influences the way she interacts with people even when she is not in the synagogue and will be a part of her values throughout her life, from infancy to death. Her Jewish community is a subculture rather than a microculture.

Source: © Steven Allan.

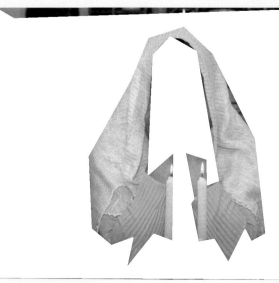

A counterculture such as the Amish, rejects important aspects of the mainstream or dominant culture such as technology and consumerism, replacing it with biblical principles calling for a simple lifestyle.

Source: © Diane Diederich.

In each case, one can live virtually one's entire life under the influence of the values and rules of the subculture.

A give-and-take exists between subcultures and the dominant culture, with each contributing to and influencing the other. Hispanic Americans have brought many foods to American cuisine, including tacos, burritos, paella, salsa, and the custard dessert known as flan.

Subcultural practices can be the source of tensions with the dominant group that has the power to determine cultural expectations in society. In direct conflict with the law, a very small faction of Mormons in the United States believe in and practice polygamy. Having more than one wife violates state laws in Utah, where many live, although polygamists seldom are prosecuted.

When conflict with the larger culture becomes more serious, and laws of the dominant society are violated, we can begin to see a different type of culture. **Countercultures** are groups with expectations and values that contrast sharply with the dominant values of a particular society (Yinger 1960). Driving down back roads of Lancaster County, Pennsylvania, one is likely to encounter horse-drawn buggies of Amish families. The Amish seldom use electricity or modern machines, distinguishing their group from the surrounding society. Conflicts between federal and state laws and Amish religious beliefs have produced shaky compromises on issues of educating children, using farm machinery, and

transportation. The Old Order Amish prefer to educate their children in their own communities, insisting that their children not go beyond an eighth-grade education in the public curriculum. They do not use automobiles or conventional tractors. The Amish are also total pacifists and will not serve as soldiers in the national military. They reject many mainstream notions of success and replace them with their own values and goals. They are one type of counterculture.

In some cases, a counterculture may be interested in bringing about the downfall of the larger culture. Examples of this type of counterculture are numerous: rebellious "survival groups" such as militia and skinheads reject the principles of democratic pluralism; the "old believers" of nineteenth-century Russia committed group suicide rather than submit to the authority of the Czar of Russia on matters of faith and lifestyle (Crummey 1970). The Ranters—a group that arose in sixteenth-century England, when strict puritan attitudes regarding sensuality and sex were common—flaunted the dominant conventional rules and values by running naked through the streets and engaging in sexual acts in open village squares (Ellens 1971; Hill 1991).

Some countercultures continue over time and can sustain members throughout their life cycle—such as the Amish. However, most countercultural groups, like punk rock groups or violent and deviant teenage gangs, are short-lived or are relevant to people only at a certain age. Figure 3.1 graphically illustrates the types of cultures in the social world. Countercultures, as depicted, view themselves and are viewed by others as at least partial outsiders within a nation.

Members of countercultures do not necessarily reject all of the dominant culture, and parts of their culture may eventually come to be widely accepted by the dominant culture. During the Vietnam War, for instance, some antiwar protestors focused their lives on protesting the U.S. involvement in Southeast Asia (and related political and economic issues). By the early 1970s, opposition to the war had become widespread in society, so antiwar protesters were no longer outside of the mainstream; they were less likely to be labeled as unpatriotic or anti-American for their beliefs. Following the war, many counterculture antiwar hippies became active in the mainstream culture and developed conventional careers in the middle class. Thus, ideas, protest songs, emblems, longer hair for men, and the peace symbol from the 1960s civil rights and antiwar movements in the United States, for example, were absorbed into the larger culture

Countercultures are not necessarily bad for society. According to the conflict perspective, introduced in Chapter 2, the existence of counterculture groups is clear evidence that there are contradictions or tensions within a society that need to be addressed. Countercultures often challenge unfair treatment of groups in society that do not hold power. Sometimes, countercultures become social organizations or protest groups. Extremist religious and political groups, whether Christian, Islamic, Hindu, or other, may best

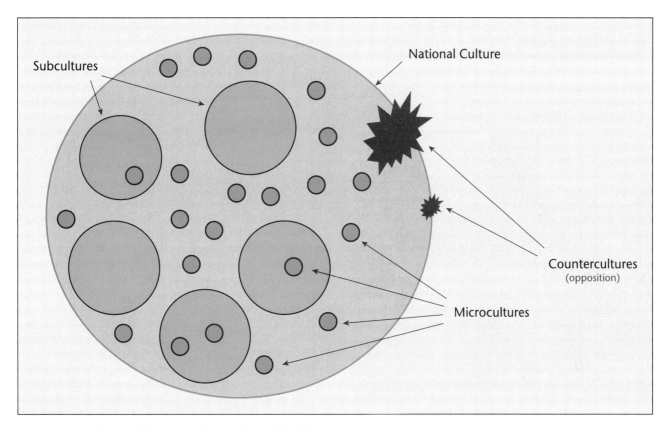

Figure 3.1   Cultures at Various Levels in the Social World

be understood as countercultures against what they perceive as the invasive Western or global culture threatening their ethnic culture. Cultures that operate at each level of our social world may be mutually supportive or they may be in conflict.

THINKING SOCIOLOGICALLY

Describe a counterculture group whose goals are at odds with those of the dominant culture. Do you see evidence that the group is influencing behavioral expectations and values in the larger society? What effect do they have on your life?

MACRO-LEVEL ANALYSIS

Canada is a national society, geographically bounded by the United States on the south, the Pacific Ocean and Alaska on the west, the Atlantic Ocean on the east, and the Arctic on the north. The government in Ottawa passes laws that regulate activities in all provinces, and each province (like states)

passes its own laws. These boundaries and structures make up the national society of Canada.

National Society and Culture

Every culture is intricately related to a society and to social units within that society. The national society is geographically defined by the political boundaries of that nation. The nation itself is made up of a group of people who interact more with each other than with outsiders and who cooperate for the attainment of certain goals. Within the nation, there may be smaller groups, such as ethnic, regional or tribal subcultures made up of people who identify closely with each other. Most nations have a **national culture** of common values and beliefs that tie citizens together, and they may have subcultures within the national culture. The national culture generally affects the everyday lives of the people within the nation, although that impact varies greatly. In some places in Africa and the Middle East, local ethnic or religious loyalties are much stronger than any sense of national culture; consider the loyalties of Shiites, Sunnis, and Kurds in Iraq. Even there, national culture has some influence over citizens through laws, traditions, and sometimes force.

The sense of nation has grown stronger in many industrialized societies over the past century. In colonial

Multinational corporations know no national barriers. With some 50,000 employees, Nike is Vietnam's largest private employer, exporting 22 million pairs of shoes annually. Thousands of products you use every day were likely made or assembled on the other side of the globe.

Source: © Steve Raymer / Corbis.

America, people thought of themselves as Virginians or Rhode Islanders rather than as U.S. citizens. Even during the "war between the states" of the 1860s, the battalions were organized by states and they often carried their state banners into battle. The fact that the southern states still call it *the war between the states* rather than the *civil war* communicates the struggle over recognizing the nation or states as the primary social unit of loyalty and identity. People in the United States today are increasingly likely to think of themselves as Americans (rather than as Ohioans or Floridians), yet the national culture determines only a few of the specific guidelines for everyday life.

Global Society and Culture

Several centuries ago, it would have been impossible to discuss a global culture, but with expanding travel, economic interdependence of different countries, international political linkages, global environmental concerns, and technology allowing for communication throughout the world, people now interact across continents in seconds. Globalization refers to the entire globe becoming "a single socio-cultural place" (Robertson 1997; Robertson and Khondker 1998). The structures such as government and economy that are dominating world patterns make up the global society. These patterns have emerged largely through the process of modernization, the domination of the Western (Europe and U.S.) worldview, and Western control over resources. For example, the very idea of governing a geographic region with a bureaucratic structure known as a nation-state is a fairly

new notion; formerly, many small bands and tribal groupings dominated areas of the globe. However, with globalization, nation-states now exist in every region of the world.

Global culture refers to behavioral standards, symbols, values, and material objects that have become common across the globe. For example, beliefs that monogamy is normal, that marriage should be based on romantic love, and that women should have rights such as voting are spreading across the globe (Leslie and Korman 1989; Newman and Grauerholz 2002). During the twentieth century, the insistence on individual rights and liberties became an increasingly shared notion around the world, although there are backlashes against these and other Western ideas as seen in the acts of small groups from impoverished nations that have embraced terrorism (Misztal and Shupe 1998; Turner 1991a, 1991b). Still, these trends are aspects of the emerging global culture. Clearly, such a global culture did not exist at all as recently as a few hundred years ago.

Even today, global culture probably has fairly minimal impact on the everyday interactions and lives of the average person. As the world community becomes more interdependent and addresses issues that can only be dealt with at the global level (such as global warming or international terrorism), the idea of a common "software" of beliefs, social rules, and common interests takes on importance. Common ideas for making decisions allow for shared solutions to conflicts that previously would have resulted in war and massive killing of people. Global culture at the most macro level will increasingly be a reality in the third millennium.

This section explored how society and culture operate at micro, meso, and macro levels of analysis. Much of this book focuses on social interaction and social structures, including interpersonal networking, the bureaucratic structures, social inequality within the structure, and the core institutions that serve the needs of society. In short, social "hardware"—society—is the focus of many subsequent chapters. The remainder of this chapter will focus on the "software" dimension (culture) and how we study it.

THE COMPONENTS OF CULTURE

Things and thoughts—these make up much of our culture. From our things—**material culture**—to our thoughts (feelings, beliefs, values, attitudes)—**nonmaterial culture**—culture provides the guidelines for our lives.

Material Culture: The Artifacts of Life

Material culture includes all the objects we can see or touch, all the *artifacts* of a group of people—their grindstones for grinding cassava root, microwave ovens for cooking, bricks of mud or clay for building shelters, hides or woven cloth for making clothing, books or computers for conveying information, tools for reshaping their environments, vessels for carrying and sharing food, and weapons used for dominating and subduing others. Material culture includes anything you can touch that is made by humans.

Some material culture is of local, micro-level origins; the kinds of materials with which homes are constructed and the materials used for clothing often reflect the geography and resources of the local area. Likewise, types of jewelry, pottery, musical instruments, or clothing reflect tastes that emerge at the micro and meso levels of family and community. At a more macro level, national and international corporations interested in making profits work hard to establish trends in fashion and style that may cross continents and oceans.

The way we construct our material world, however, has increasingly taken on global proportions. Many of our clothes are now made in Asia or Central American countries; our shoes may well have been produced in the Philippines, the oil used to make plastic devices in our kitchens likely came from the Middle East, and the food itself is imported year-round from around the planet. That romantic diamond engagement ring—a symbol that represents the most intimate tie—may well be imported from South Africa. Our cars are assembled from parts produced on nearly every continent. Moreover, we spend many hours in front of a piece of material culture—our computers—surfing the World Wide Web. Material culture is not just for local homebodies anymore.

THINKING SOCIOLOGICALLY

Think of examples of material culture that you use daily: stove, automobile, telephone, refrigerator, clock, money, and so forth. How do these material objects influence your way of life and the way you interact with others? How would your behavior be different if these material objects, say watches or cars, did not exist?

Nonmaterial Culture:
Beliefs, Values, Rules, and Language

Nonmaterial culture refers to invisible and intangible parts of culture that are of equal or even greater importance than material culture, for they involve the society's rules of behavior, ideas, and beliefs that shape how people interact with others and with their environment. Although you cannot touch the nonmaterial components of your culture, they pervade your life and are instrumental in determining how you think, feel, and behave. Nonmaterial culture is complex, comprising four main elements: beliefs, values, norms or rules, and language.

Beliefs are ideas we hold about life, about the way the society works, and about where we fit into it. Beliefs come from traditions established over time, religious teachings, experiences people have had, and lessons given by parents and teachers or other individuals in authority. Beliefs influence the choices we make. Hindus,

for example, believe that fulfilling behavioral expectations of one's own social caste will be rewarded in the person's next incarnation; in the next life, good people will be born to a higher social status. By contrast, some Christians believe that one's fate in the afterlife depends on whether one believes in certain ideas—for instance, that Jesus Christ is one's personal savior.

Values are nonmaterial shared judgments about what is desirable or undesirable, right or wrong, good or bad. They express the basic ideals of any culture. In industrial societies, for instance, a good education is highly valued. Gunnar Myrdal (1964), a Swedish sociologist and observer of U.S. culture, called the U.S. value system the "American creed," values that are so much a part of the way of life that they are sometimes hard to identify; they are taken for granted. Freedom, equality, individualism, democracy, efficiency, progress, and patriotic loyalty seem to be at the core of the value system of the United States (Macionis 1999; Williams 1970). At the micro level, values related to family loyalty or friendship bonds have high priority and will determine how you spend your days.

At the macro level, conflicts may arise between groups in society because of differing value systems. For example, there are major differences between the values of various Native American groups and the dominant culture—whether that dominant culture is in North, Central, or South America (Lake 1990; Sharp 1991). Consider the story in the Sociology around the World (next page), told by Rigoberta Menchu, about the experiences of Native American populations living in Guatemala. How are different cultural values the source of problems for native peoples?

The conflict in values described in the story of Rigoberta Menchu is not unlike conflicts between Native American meso-level subcultures and other national cultures in North America. Cooperation is a cultural value that has been passed on through generations of Native Americans because group survival depends on group cooperation in the hunt, in war, and in daily life. This value may have led to unwarranted trust in others. As a result, some people believe that Native Americans have received the worst terms in many treaties and other agreements with governments, especially when native populations unintentionally gave up rights to lands that had once been their domain. The value of cooperation can place native children at a disadvantage in North American schools that emphasize competition. Native American and Native Canadian children experience more success in classrooms that stress cooperation and sociability over competition and individuality (Lake 1990; Mehan 1992)

Another Native American value is the appreciation and respect for nature. Conservation of resources and protection of the natural environment—Mother Earth—have always been important because of the dependence on nature for survival. Today, we witness disputes between native tribes and governments of Canada, the United States, Mexico, Guatemala, Brazil and other countries over raw resources

Sociology around the World

Life and Death
in a Guatemalan Village

In her four decades of life, Rigoberta Menchu experienced the closeness of family and cooperation in village life. These values are very important in Chimel, the Guatemalan hamlet where she lives. She also experienced great pain and suffering with the loss of her family and community. A Quiche Indian, Menchu became famous throughout the world in 1992 when she received the Nobel Peace Prize for her work to improve the conditions for Indian peoples.

Guatemalans of Spanish origin hold the power and have used Indians almost as slaves. Some of the natives were cut off from food, water, and other necessities, but people in the hamlet helped to support each other and taught children survival techniques. Most people had no schooling. Her work life in the sugar cane fields began at age 5. At 14, she traveled to the city to work as a domestic servant. While there, she learned Spanish, which helped her to be more effective in defending the rights of the indigenous population in Guatemala. Her political coming of age occurred at age 16 when she witnessed her brother's assassination by a group trying to expel her people from their native lands.

Her father started a group to fight repression of indigenous and poor, and at 20, Menchu joined the movement, Comite de Unidad Campesina (CUC), which the government claimed was communist inspired. Her father was murdered during a military assault, and her mother was tortured and killed. She moved to Mexico with many other exiles to continue the nonviolent fight for rights and democracy.

The values of the native population represented by Menchu focus on respect for and a profound spiritual relationship with the environment, equality of all people, freedom from economic oppression, the dignity of her culture, and the benefits of cooperation over competition. The landowners tended to stress freedom of people to pursue their individual self-interests (even if inequality resulted), the value of competition, and the right to own property and to do whatever one desired in order to exploit that property for economic gain. Individual property rights were thought to be more important than preservation of indigenous cultures; economic growth and profits were held in higher regard than religious connectedness to the earth.

The values of the native population and landowners are in conflict. Only time will tell if the work of Indian activists such as Rigoberta Menchu and her family will make a difference in the lives of this indigenous population.

Source: Burgos-Debray (1984).

found on native reservations. While many other North and South Americans also value cooperation and respect for the environment, these values do not govern decision making in most communities (Brown 2001; Marger 2006). The values honored by governments and corporations are those held by the people with power, prestige, and wealth.

Norms are rules of behavior shared by members of a society and rooted in the value system. Norms range from religious warnings such as "thou shalt not kill" to the expectation that young people will complete their high school education. Sometimes, the origins of particular norms are quite clear. Few people wonder, for instance, why it is a norm to stop and look both ways at a stop sign. Other norms, such as the rule in many societies that women should wear skirts but men should not, have been passed on through the generations and become unconsciously accepted patterns and a part of tradition. Sometimes, we may not know how norms originated or even be aware of norms until they are violated.

Norms are generally classified into three categories—folkways, mores, and laws—based largely on how important the norms are in the society and people's response to the breach of those norms. *Folkways* are customs or desirable behaviors, but they are not strictly enforced: responding appropriately and politely when introduced to someone, speaking quietly in a library, not scratching your genitals in public, using proper table manners, or covering your mouth when you cough. Violation of these norms causes people to think you are weird or even uncouth but not necessarily immoral or criminal.

Mores are norms that most members observe because they have great moral significance in a society. Conforming to mores is a matter of right and wrong, and violations of many mores are treated very seriously. The person who deviates from mores is considered immoral or bordering on criminal. Being honest, not cheating on exams, and being faithful in a marriage are all mores. Table 3.2 provides examples of folkways and mores.

TABLE 3.2	**Types of Norms**
Folkways: Conventional Behaviors	**Mores: Morally Significant Behaviors**
Proper, polite: violators are "weird"	*Right and wrong: violators are "immoral"*
Swearing in house of worship	Lying or being unfaithful to a spouse
Wearing blue jeans to the prom	Buying cigarettes or liquor for young teens
Using poor table manners	Having sex with a professor as a way to increase one's grade
Picking one's nose in public	Parking in handicap spaces when one is in good physical condition

Taboos are the strongest form of mores; they concern actions considered unthinkable or unspeakable in the culture. For example, most societies have taboos that forbid incest (sexual relations with a close relative) and prohibit defacing or eating a human corpse. Taboos are most common and most numerous in societies that do not have centralized governments to establish formal laws and to maintain jails.

Taboos and other moral codes may be of the utmost importance to a group, yet behaviors that are taboo in one situation may be acceptable at another time and place. The *incest taboo* is an example found in all cultures, yet application of the incest taboo varies greatly across cultures (Brown 1991). In Medieval Europe, if a man and woman were within seven degrees of relatedness and wanted to marry, the marriage could be denied by the priest as incestuous. (Your first cousin is a third degree of relatedness from you.) On the other hand, the Balinese permit twins to marry because it is believed they have already been intimately bonded together in the womb (Leslie and Korman 1989). In some African and Native American societies, one cannot marry a sibling but might be expected to marry a first cousin. As Table 3.3 illustrates, the definition of what is and what is not incest varies even from state to state in the United States.

TABLE 3.3	**Incest Taboos in the United States: States that Allow First-Cousin Marriage**	
Alabama	Georgia	Rhode Island
Alaska	Hawaii	South Carolina
California	Maryland	Tennessee
Colorado	Massachusetts	Texas
Connecticut	New Jersey	Vermont
Florida	New York	Virginia

The following states also allow first-cousin marriage but only under certain conditions such as marriage after the age of 60.

Arizona	Illinois	Maine	Wisconsin

All other U.S. states disallow marriages to first cousins within the state. Historically, in the United States, incest laws forbid in-law marriages far more than first-cousin marriages.

Source: Ottenheimer (1996).

Nudity may be considered a violation of law, or mores, or folkways, or simply accepted as normal, as in the case of this nude beach.

Source: © Getty Images.

Laws are norms that have been formally encoded by those holding political power in society, such as laws against stealing property or killing another person. The violator of a law is likely to be perceived not just as a weird or immoral person but as a criminal who deserves formal punishment. Many *mores* are passed into law, and some *folkways* are also made into law. Formal punishments are imposed. Spitting on the sidewalk is not a behavior that has high levels of moral content, yet it is illegal in some cities, with fines to punish violators. Furthermore, behaviors may be folkways in one situation and mores in another. For example, nudity or various stages of near nudity may be only mildly questionable in some social settings (the beach or certain fraternity parties) but would be quite offensive in others (a four-star restaurant or a house of worship).

Sanctions reinforce norms through rewards and penalties. **Formal sanctions** used to enforce the most important norms are those given by official action. Fines for parking in marked spaces, lowered grades in a class for plagiarism, or expulsion for bringing drugs or weapons to school for fighting are *formal negative sanctions* your school might impose. Honors and awards are *formal positive sanctions*. **Informal sanctions** are unofficial rewards or punishments. A private word of praise by your professor after class about how well you did on your exam would be an *informal positive sanction*; gossip or ostracism by other students would be *informal negative sanctions*. Sanctions vary with the importance of the norm and can range from a parent frowning at a child who fails to use proper table manners (a micro-level setting) to a prison term or death sentence. Similarly, when we obey norms, we are rewarded, sometimes with simple acts such as smiles and jokes and pats on the back that indicate solidarity with others. Most often, adherence to norms is

Since 1989, there have been 2,000 reported public executions for drug dealing in Iran. There is little tolerance for deviation from legal and moral boundaries. Formal sanctions are severe. This scene is from the capital, Tehran, in 2001.

Source: © Corbis Sygma.

ingrained so deeply that our reward is simply "fitting in." Your reward for polite social behavior—for asking about someone's interests and activities, for not being overly shy or pushy in conversation—is friendship and fitting into the group. Folkways and many mores are enforced through informal sanctions.

Sometimes, penalties for deviant behavior can be severe. In Iran, any involvement with drugs is punishable by hanging. In other societies such as Saudi Arabia, thieves are punished on the spot by having their fingers or right hand cut off, a sanction that is all the more severe because Saudi society does not approve use of the left hand for common activities such as eating; that hand is used for bathroom hygiene.

Norms concerning sexual behaviors are often very strong and carry powerful sanctions, sometimes even imposed by national governments. A woman who becomes pregnant outside of marriage in societies that condemn premarital and nonmarital sex is likely to be ostracized and her child labeled illegitimate. Such children may be stigmatized for life, living in poverty as outcasts. This was the case in the early 1970s during Bangladesh's war for independence from Pakistan. Many Bangladeshi women were raped by Pakistani army troops and had children as a result. Although they already had suffered the humiliation of rape, some of these women and their children were rejected by their husbands and refused homes with their families. Bangladesh is an Islamic society, and chastity is crucial to the honor of the family and for determining inheritance. Only after these women had endured much suffering and with international pressure did the government declare them national heroines and allow outside agencies to provide for them and their children. The systematic rape of Muslim women by Serbian troops in Bosnia appears to have resulted in another generation of innocent children born to be rejected.

When a society faces change, especially from war, rapid urbanization, industrialization, and modernization, traditional norms that have worked for the society for centuries are challenged. In the past few decades, examples have been seen in many Islamic countries in which modernization has met with a resurgence of religious fundamentalism. A case in point is Iran. The rapid modernization and social changes that took place in the post–World War II era under the Shah of Iran, Mohammed Reza Pahlavi, were met by a backlash from religious fundamentalists. When the Shah was ousted

Mina Talic, 26, lives in this room with 12 other people from the Prijedor region of Bosnia. Mina, her son, and her mother have witnessed many rapes in this refugee camp. An investigative commission concluded that 20,000 women and children were victims of rape by the Serbs during the war in Bosnia.

Source: © Sophie Elbaz / Sygma / Corbis.

in 1979, Ayatollah Ruhollah Khomeini restored traditional Islamic rule. Radio music and drinking of alcoholic beverages were banned, and women were required to again wear the veil, as in previous times. Afghanistan and other Muslim nations are currently struggling with the conflicting values and norms brought about by pressures from the environment, in this case Western nations, for change and modernization, and traditional religious and cultural values.

At the global level, there are fewer norms since this level of interaction is rather new; likewise, there are only newly emerging norms in some areas of technology, such as the Internet and the World Wide Web. In situations in which there are no norms, guidelines are missing for interactions between people. E-mail has existed for civilians since only 1994, so social scientists have been able to watch the emergence of norms in this new social environment. Communication is often mediated and enhanced through nonverbal indicators such as tone of voice, inflection, facial expressions, or other gestures that communicate emotion. In e-mail, the words are just words without context. To establish norms, many listserves now have rules for polite communication to avoid *flaming* someone—insulting them with insensitive words by a faceless person. The development of smileys and emoticons add combinations of characters that represent the emotional context of the message. A few examples of smileys appear in Figure 3.2.

:-)	friendly smile	:-o	shocked or amazed
:-(	sadness or sympathy	:-P	sticking tongue out
;-)	wink	}:(	mad
:'-(	crying	8-)	wide-eyed or glasses

Figure 3.2   Internet Smileys

Norms of Internet communication are still emerging, and you probably have experienced times when messages have been misunderstood because the norms of communication are ambiguous.

THINKING SOCIOLOGICALLY

Think of examples of common folkways and mores in your society. What punishment or sanction would you expect to receive if you violated each of them? What types of behaviors bring the most severe sanctions in your community?

Language is the foundation of every culture. The mini-drama between infant and adult is played out every day around the world as millions of infants learn the language of the adults who care for them. In the process, they acquire an important part of culture. Although many animals can communicate, the ability to speak a language is unique to humans. Human infants have the potential for developing language because the human voice box, tongue, and brain make speech biologically possible. At about one year of age, most infants begin to pronounce recognizable words in the language of their culture. The human infant is capable of making roughly 1,000 sounds, but any given society only considers about 40 or 50 of these to be language sounds. The baby soon learns that some of those sounds elicit enthusiastic responses from the adult caretakers.

Transport a baby from France to the Arapesh tribe in New Guinea and another baby from New Guinea to France, and each will learn to speak the language and adhere to the culture in which it is brought up. The reason is that language, like other components of culture, is learned. Language conveys verbal and nonverbal messages among members of society. Simply put, without language there would be little, if any, culture. Through the use of language, members of culture can pass on essential knowledge to children and can share ideas with other members of their society. Work can be organized; the society can build on its experiences and plan its future. Through language, members express their ideas, values, beliefs, and knowledge, a key ingredient in the ability of humans to sustain social life as we know it.

Language takes three primary forms: spoken, written, and nonverbal. *Spoken language* allows individuals to produce a set of sounds that symbolizes an object or idea. That sound combination is learned by all who share a culture, and it generally holds similar meaning for all members. *Written language* enables humans to store ideas for future generations, accelerating the accumulation of ideas on which to build. It also makes possible communication over distances. Members of a society learn to read these shared symbols, some of which are displayed in Figure 3.3.

福, Поздравляю!, Θεος, בא שר לחם, 십시오, العربية, राम

Figure 3.3   Societies Use Various Symbols to Communicate Their Written Language

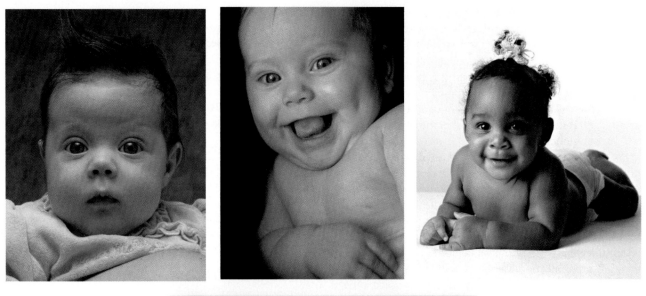

Language development is extremely important to becoming fully human, and it happens very rapidly from about the first year. Still, babies learn to communicate in a variety of other ways. Note how these infants communicate emotions nonverbally. What does each of them seem to be communicating?

Source: © Istockphoto.com.

Nonverbal language consists of gestures, facial expressions, and body postures; this mode of communication may carry as much as 90 percent of the meaning of the message (Samovar and Porter 2003). Every culture uses nonverbal language to communicate, and just like verbal language, those cues may differ widely among cultures. For instance, an A-OK gesture or a hand wave that is positive in one culture may have a negative, even obscene, meaning in another.

The power to communicate nonverbally is illustrated in American Sign Language, designed for the hearing challenged and the mute. Complex ideas can be transmitted without vocalizing a word. Indeed, one can argue that the deaf have a distinctive culture of their own rooted in large part in the unique language that serves them. Technology has aided communication among the hearing-impaired through text messaging.

Misunderstandings can occur between ethnic groups because of cultural differences regarding communication. The Apache Indians in the American Southwest tell "whiteman jokes"—ridiculing white people because they engage in such grossly unacceptable actions as calling one another by name even when they do not know each other intimately, asking about one another's health, complementing one another's clothing, and greeting others who walk into a room. Because so many white U.S. citizens do not understand that these behaviors are viewed as offensive, they may violate expectations and create difficulties for themselves in dealing with Apaches. They may act in ways that are considered ill-mannered and rude (Basso 1979).

Misinterpretation of nonverbal signals can also occur between male and female microcultures in Western societies. When women nod their heads in response to a person who is talking, they often are encouraging the speaker to continue, signaling that they are listening and that they want the speaker to carry on with clarification and explanation. It does not signal agreement. When men nod their heads when another person is speaking, they typically assume the message is "I agree with what you are saying." This can lead to awkward, confusing, and even embarrassing miscues when men and women talk to one another, with a man mistakenly confident that the woman agreed with his ideas (Stringer 2006).

Language also plays a critical role in perception and in thought organization. The *linguistic relativity theory* (Sapir 1929, 1949; Whorf 1956) posits that the people who speak a specific language make interpretations of their reality—they notice certain things and fail to notice certain other things. Many nonindustrial peoples in Asia, Africa, Australia, and South and North America do not keep time in the kinds of simple units used in the industrial world. The smallest units might be sunrise, morning, midday, late afternoon, dusk, and night (Hall 1983). Meeting someone for an appointment requires great patience, for there are no words for what we call "seconds," "minutes," or even "hours." Think about how this would change your life and the pace of everything around you. If you showed up at a predesignated location, your friend might appear three hours later but would be on time since the unit of time would include a four- or five-hour time period. One eats when food is prepared or when one is hungry. One gets up when one is rested. Time-based words cause most of us to organize our days in particular ways and even to become irritated with others who do not adhere to these expectations (Bertman 1998).

To use another example, in the English language, people tend to associate certain colors with certain qualities in a way that may add to the problem of racist attitudes. In Webster's Unabridged English Dictionary, the definition of the word *black* includes "dismal," "boding ill," "hostile," "harmful," "inexcusable," "without goodness," "evil," "wicked," "disgrace," and "without moral light." The word *white*, on the other hand, is defined as "honest," "dependable," "morally pure," "innocent," and "without malice." If the linguistic relativity thesis is correct, it is more than coincidence that bad things are associated with the "black sheep" of the family, the "blacklist," or "Black Tuesday" (when the stock market dropped dramatically).

This association of blackness with negative images and meanings is not true of all languages. The societies that have negative images for black and positive images for white are the same societies that associate negative qualities to people with darker skin. The use of *white* as a synonym for "good" or "innocent"—as in reference to a "white noise machine" or a "white lie"—may contribute to a cultural climate that devalues people of color. In essence, English may influence our perception of color in a manner that contributes to racism.

Children in each different culture will learn about the world within the framework provided by their language. Scientists continue to debate the extent to which language can influence thought, but most agree that while language may contribute to certain ways of thinking, it does not totally determine human thinking (Gumpers and Levinson 1991).

One thing is clear: different language evolves in different settings in the social world. In a prison where inmates are closed off from the larger world, a whole lingo evolves that is incomprehensible to outsiders but essential to survival within the prison: kites, rats, store, punks, wolves, cops, and ballbuster are examples. Even within your own college, there are probably terms used to refer to course sequences, majors, or Greek houses in ways that people at other universities would find bewildering. At Massachusetts Institute of Technology, for example, students often respond to the question "What is your major?" with the number from the catalog: "I'm majoring in 23." That would be a truly bizarre response at some other campuses. Within the medical profession (at the meso level), people may discuss MRIs, brain scans, heart catheterizations, PSA tests, and other processes that are meaningful in that context but may be utterly confusing to a girl scout group or in the World Bank. Discussion of GNP (gross national product) is a phrase generated at the national and global levels to discuss the economic health of a nation or to

Language varies from one social setting to another, and one must learn the language to survive. The prison is a society separated from the larger society, and it develops its own microculture. In prison, one must learn the lingo and the associated values that are applied to "kites, rats, store, punks, wolves, cops, and ballbusters." Inmates, such as these men in the yard of San Quentin State Prison, develop their own insider lingo.

Source: © Kim Kulish / Corbis.

compare the financial vitality of nations. Some terms are relevant to macro-level conversations, and they become necessary for discussing issues that are important at that level.

When grouped together, material and nonmaterial components form cultural patterns. People's lives are organized around these patterns; for example, family life includes patterns of courtship, marriage, child-rearing, and care of the elderly. Table 3.4 illustrates some of the more prominent material and nonmaterial cultural components involved in one pattern of Western society, the ritual of courtship.

TABLE 3.4	**Material and Nonmaterial Cultural Components in Western Courtship**
Material objects	Rings, flowers, candy, and similar tokens of caring are given or displayed.
Nonmaterial cultural components	
Beliefs	Young people date before marriage; marriage is based on romantic love.
Values	Courtship is needed to provide a period for getting to know the partner, for falling in love; couples that are getting close to permanent commitment ought to be exclusive in their romantic and sexual relationships.
Rules	Couple must be officially sanctioned to make the bond permanent.
Language or symbols	Couple expresses their feelings verbally and nonverbally; special names are used: *significant other, boyfriend, fiancée, soul mate.* Couple shows affection through gift giving, exchanging meaningful objects such as a diamond engagement ring, and exclusive dating.

We have seen that material artifacts and nonmaterial beliefs, values, norms, and language are the basic components of culture. Next, we explore theoretical explanations for culture.

THINKING SOCIOLOGICALLY

The words *bachelor* and *spinster* are supposedly synonymous terms, referring to unmarried adult males and females, respectively. Generate a list of adjectives that describe each of these words and that you frequently hear associated with

them (e.g., eligible, swinging, old, unattractive). Are the associated words positive or negative in each case? Does this hold cultural meaning?

CULTURAL THEORY AT THE MICRO LEVEL

When students first read about sociology or other social sciences, the underlying message may seem to be that humans are shaped by the larger society in which they live. External forces do shape us in many ways, but that is not the whole story as we see when we examine the **symbolic interaction** approach to culture.

Symbolic Interaction Theory

How amazing it is that babies learn to share the ideas and meanings of complex cultures with others in those cultures. Symbolic interaction theory considers how we learn to share meanings of symbols, whether material or nonmaterial. Culture is about symbols, such as rings, flags, and words that stand for or represent something else. A ring means love. A flag represents patriotism and love of country. Word symbols conjure up pictures in our heads of what the words symbolize. Symbols summarize shared meanings with others with whom we interact and define what is real and normal. Symbolic interaction theory maintains that our humanness comes from the impact we have on each other through these shared understandings of symbols that humans have created. The meanings of symbols are learned as individuals interact with one another; we learn how to fit into society because of shared perceptions or shared meanings. By interpretation of symbols and their meaning, we *define situations* and determine how we should act.

When people create symbols, such as a new greeting ("give me five") or a symbolic shield for a fraternity or sorority, symbols come to have an existence and importance for a group. This is step one: the symbol is created. Who was it that designed the Star of David and gave it meaning as a symbol of the Jewish people? Who initiated the sign of the cross for Catholics before prayer? Who designed the fraternity's or sorority's shield? Who determined that an eagle should symbolize the United States? Most people do not know the answers to these, but they do know what the symbol stands for. They do share with others the meaning of a particular object. This is step two: the symbol is objectified, assuming a reality independent of the creator. In fact, people may feel intense loyalty to the symbol itself. An entire history of a people may be recalled and a set of values rekindled when the symbol is displayed. This is step three: the group has internalized the symbol. This may be the case regardless of whether the symbol is part of material culture or a nonmaterial gesture. Members of a culture absorb the ideas or symbols of the larger culture—which were originally created by some individual or small group.

Symbolic interaction theory pictures humans as consciously and deliberately creating their personal and collective histories. It emphasizes the part that verbal and nonverbal language and gestures play in the shared symbols of individuals and smooth operation of society. More than any other theory in the social sciences, symbolic interaction stresses the active decision making role of individuals.

This notion that individuals shape culture and that culture influences individuals is at the core of symbolic interaction theory. Other social theories tend to focus at the macro levels.

THINKING SOCIOLOGICALLY

Remember some of the local "insider" symbols that you used as a teenager—friendship bracelets, pet rocks or mood rings? Some individual started each idea, and it spread rapidly from one school to another and one community to another. How are the three steps in the creation of symbols illustrated by this pattern?

CULTURAL THEORIES AT THE MESO AND MACRO LEVELS

How can we explain such diverse world practices as eating grubs and worshipping cows? Why have some societies allowed men to have four wives while others—such as the Shakers—have prohibited sex between men and women entirely? Why do some groups worship their ancestors while others have many gods or believe in a single divine being? How can societies adapt to extremes of climate and geographical terrain—hot, cold, dry, wet, mountainous, flat? Humankind has evolved practices so diverse that we would have trouble imagining a practice that has not been adopted in some society at some time in history.

To explain cultural differences, we will examine two perspectives that have made important contributions to understanding culture at the meso and macro levels: structural-functional and conflict theories.

Structural-Functional Theory

Structural-functional theory seeks to explain why members of a society or an ethnic subculture engage in certain practices. To answer why, structural-functional theorists look for the functions or purposes of these practices. Consider the worship of cows in India: the sacred cow is treated with respect and is not used for food for sensible historical reasons that have become laws over time (Harris 1989). Cows are necessary for agricultural work and therefore must be protected from hungry people for survival of the group.

Functionalists view societies as composed of interdependent parts, each fulfilling certain necessary *functions* or

purposes for the total society (Radcliffe-Brown 1935). Shared norms, values, and beliefs, for instance, serve the function of holding a society—or a subculture—together. Throughout history, societies and subcultures have defended their religious or political beliefs against threats from other societies in their environments. We see this today as fundamentalists from various religions attempt to protect their beliefs from Western ideologies and globalization. At a global macro level, functionalists see the world moving in the direction of having a common culture, potentially reducing "we" versus "they" thinking and promoting unity across boundaries. Synthesis of cultures and even the loss of some cultures are viewed as a natural result of movement into a postindustrial world.

Although most cultural practices serve positive functions for the maintenance and stability of the society, some practices, such as slavery or child abuse, may be dysfunctional for minority groups or individual members of society. The functionalist perspective has been criticized because it fails to consider how much dysfunction or conflict a society can tolerate and how much unity is necessary for a society to survive. Some critics argue that functional theory overemphasizes the need for consensus and integration among different parts of society, thus ignoring conflicts that may point to problems in societies (Dahrendorf 1959).

Conflict Theory

Whereas functionalists assume consensus because all persons in society have learned the same cultural values, rules, and expectations, conflict theorists do not view culture as having this uniting effect. Conflict theorists describe societies as composed of groups—class, ethnic, religious, and political groups at the meso level—vying for power; each group protects its own self-interests and struggles to make its own cultural ways dominant in the society. Instead of consensus, the dominant groups may impose their cultural beliefs on minorities and other subcultural groups, thus laying the groundwork for conflict. Conflict theorists identify tension between meso and macro levels, whereas functionalists tend to focus on harmony and smooth integration.

Actually, conflict may contribute to a smoother-running society in the long run. The French sociologist Georg Simmel (1955) believed that some conflict could serve a positive purpose by alerting societal leaders to problem areas that need attention. This view is illustrated by the political changes that followed the women's movement or by the organic food industry that has arisen in response to corporate agribusiness and massive use of pesticides.

Conflict theorists argue that the people with privilege and power in society manipulate institutions such as religion and education; in this way people learn the values, beliefs, and norms of the privileged group and foster beliefs that justify the dominant group's self-interests, power, and advantage. The needs of the privileged are likely to be met, and their status will be secured. For instance, lower-class schools usually teach obedience to authority, punctuality, and respect for superiors,

Conflict theorists believe that society is composed of groups that each seek their own self-interest, and those groups struggle to make their own cultural values supreme in the society. The recent 2006 conflict over immigration laws is illustrated by the thousands of protesters who expressed their opinions in New York as Democrats and Republicans remained divided over plans to overhaul immigration laws.

Source: © Shannon Stapleton / Reuters / Corbis.

all of which make for good laborers. The children of the affluent, meanwhile, are more likely to attend schools stressing divergent thinking, creativity, and leadership, attributes that prepare them to occupy the most professional, prestigious, and well-rewarded positions in the society. Conflict theorists point to this control of the education process by those with privilege as part of the overall pattern by which the society benefits the rich.

Conflict theory can also help us to understand global dynamics; poor nations feel that the global system protects the self-interests of the richest nations and that those rich nations impose their own culture, including their ideas about economics, politics, and religion, on the less affluent. Many believe there is great richness in local customs that is lost when homogenized by the cultural domination in the macro-level trends of globalization.

Conflict theory is useful for analyzing relationships between societies (macro level) and between subcultures (meso level) within complex societies. It also helps illuminate tensions in a society when local (micro-level) cultural values clash with national (macro-level) trends. Conflict theory is not as successful, however, in explaining simple, well-integrated societies in which change is slow to come about, new ideas are few, and cooperation is an organizing principle. Many societies have little conflict within but

encounter other societies in their environments that challenge their way of life.

POLICY AND CULTURAL CHANGE

Technology is bringing change to societies around the world, often with unanticipated consequences. While technology (an example of material culture) advances rapidly, the non-material culture lags behind, resulting in social disruption. Sociologist William Ogburn (1950) used the term **cultural lag** for this change that occurs unequally between material culture (tangible objects) and nonmaterial culture (ideas, beliefs, and values). Rapid change is opposed by people whose lifestyle is threatened and who wish to preserve the native cultures. Should policy makers respect these differences and reduce the impact of change? That is the policy dilemma.

Imagine living in a remote village on Borneo that, due to its location in the East Indies, has remained largely isolated

Children at a preparatory school play lacrosse and other "exotic" sports that are generally the province of the affluent. Their games are different, as are their academics and their futures, from those of the middle, working, and lower classes. Further, Ivy league colleges provide athletic scholarship for sports like lacrosse and crew, and you can guess who qualifies for those scholarships.

Source: © Kirk Strickland/Istockphoto.com.

from the outside world for hundreds of years. Traditions are well established, and members seldom question how things are done. Then television comes to the village—one set located in a central meeting hut. Initially, it would be used for educational programs, but the village TV receives its share of Western movies and reruns of American situation comedies. The advertisements also expose people to new consumer products. This village in Borneo will never be the same again. Villagers develop a desire for goods hitherto unknown, and young people leave for cities and new opportunities. Refrigerators, dishwashers, and fancy autos become known commodities. They learn that modern medicines can relieve suffering, cure some illnesses, and extend life, making for a higher quality and longer life for many people. Change also challenges the old traditions; without new norms to take their place, disorganization can occur.

Isolation of societies in the global system is rare; most are drawn into the dynamics of the twenty-first century, even if they are not full participants. Societies interact constantly through negotiation, trade, alliances, competition, compromise, conflict, and war. External forces bring about change in political and economic ideologies and make available raw materials, new products, and growing markets.

The social costs of rapid change can be great. During the period of early industrialization, newly arrived peasants lived in an urban squalor hard to imagine today. Karl Marx produced much of his work, which provided the foundation for conflict theory, while living in poverty in London. His wife and two of his daughters died of disease because they could not afford adequate food, housing, or medicines. Even today, these problems exist as people in impoverished regions of the world leave their villages to seek employment in overcrowded urban areas. New technologies have the potential to save lives and to make life less harsh, but introduction of Western technology can also disrupt and even destroy indigenous cultures. This disruption of a culture—called *ethnocide*—can be extremely disorienting to the people. A contributing factor to terrorism is the challenge to traditional culture and values.

Policy makers cannot stop change, but they can determine how to introduce change for the most beneficial and positive results.

THINKING SOCIOLOGICALLY

Is it appropriate to try to change the politics or religion of another culture? Why or why not? Do individual human rights always have supremacy over the rights of a group to determine their own culture? These are tough questions that trouble many people who work in the area of human rights policy.

THE FIT BETWEEN HARDWARE AND SOFTWARE

Computer software may not work with noncompatible machines. Some documents cannot be easily transferred to another piece of hardware, although sometimes a transfer can be accomplished with significant modification in the formatting of the document. The same is true with the hardware of society and the software of culture. For instance, having large extended families, typically valued in agricultural societies, does not work well in industrial and postindustrial societies. Other values such as rewarding people based on individual merit, emphasizing the idea that humans are motivated primarily by their own self-interests, or believing that change in cultures is inevitable and equals progress are not particularly compatible with the hardware of horticultural or herding societies. Values and beliefs ("software") can be transferred to another type of society ("hardware"); however, there are limits to what can be transferred and the change of "formatting" may mean the new beliefs are barely recognizable.

Policies to transport U.S.-style software—individualism, capitalism, and democracy—to other parts of the world illustrate that these ideas are not always successful in other settings. The hardware of other societies may be able to handle more than one type of software or set of beliefs, but there are limits to the adaptability. Thus, we should not be surprised when our ideas are transformed into something quite different when they are imported to another social system. If we are to understand the world in which we live and if we want to improve it, we must first fully understand the societies and cultures, including the links between them and the interconnections between the levels of our social world.

Each society relies on the process of socialization to instill the culture into its members. The next chapter discusses the ways in which we learn to become members of society.

THINKING SOCIOLOGICALLY

Some anthropologists argue that *team sports*, groups organized against each other in competition, was learned by Europeans from Native Americans. How has the diffusion of team sports into U.S. culture influenced the nature of U.S. society and culture? How might our society be different if we had only individual sports?

SO WHAT?

Individuals and small groups cannot live without the supports of a larger society, the hardware of the social world. Without the software—culture—we would be lost. Indeed, without culture, there could be no society for there would be no norms to guide our interactions with others in society. Humans are inherently social and learn their culture from others. Furthermore, as society has evolved to more complex and multitiered social systems, humans have learned to live in and negotiate conflicts between multiple cultures, including those at micro, meso, and macro levels. Life in an information-age society demands adaptability to different sociocultural contexts and tolerance of different cultures and subcultures. This is a challenge to a species that has always had tendencies toward ethnocentrism.

Since there is such variation between societies and cultures in what they see as normal, how do any of us ever adjust to our society's expectations? The answer is addressed in the next chapter. Human life is a lifelong process of socialization to social and cultural expectations.

CONTRIBUTING TO YOUR SOCIAL WORLD

At the Local Level: Italian American, Japanese American or other ethnic group club: Consider exploring your own ethnic background and learning more about it from a local organization relevant to you.

Casa Amiga Communities or other local agencies: Volunteer or serve as an intern in an organization that helps immigrants deal with adjustment to American life.

At the National and Global Levels:
Cultural Survival This is a group interested in helping indigenous cultures around the world to preserve their culture and avoid becoming victims of Westernization or of domination by a more powerful ethnic group in the nation or region. Visit their website at http://www.cs.org.

Visit www.pineforge.com/ballantinestudy for online activities, sample tests, and other helpful information. Select "Chapter 3: Society and Culture" for chapter-specific activities.

CHAPTER

4

SOCIALIZATION:
Becoming Human and Humane

What to Expect . . .

Nature and Nurture
The Importance of Socialization
Socialization and the Social World
Development of the Self: Micro-Level Analysis
Socialization throughout the Life Cycle
Agents of Socialization: The Micro-Meso Connection
Socialization and Macro-Level Issues
Policy and Practice
So What?

Whether at the micro, meso, or macro level, our close associates and various organizations teach us how to be human and humane in that society. Skills are taught as well as values such as loyalty and care-giving.

Think About It . . .

1. What would you be like if you had been raised in isolation or in a different country?

2. What factors influenced the person you are today?

3. What does it mean to have a self? Describe your self.

4. How might globalization or other macro-level events impact you and your sense of self?

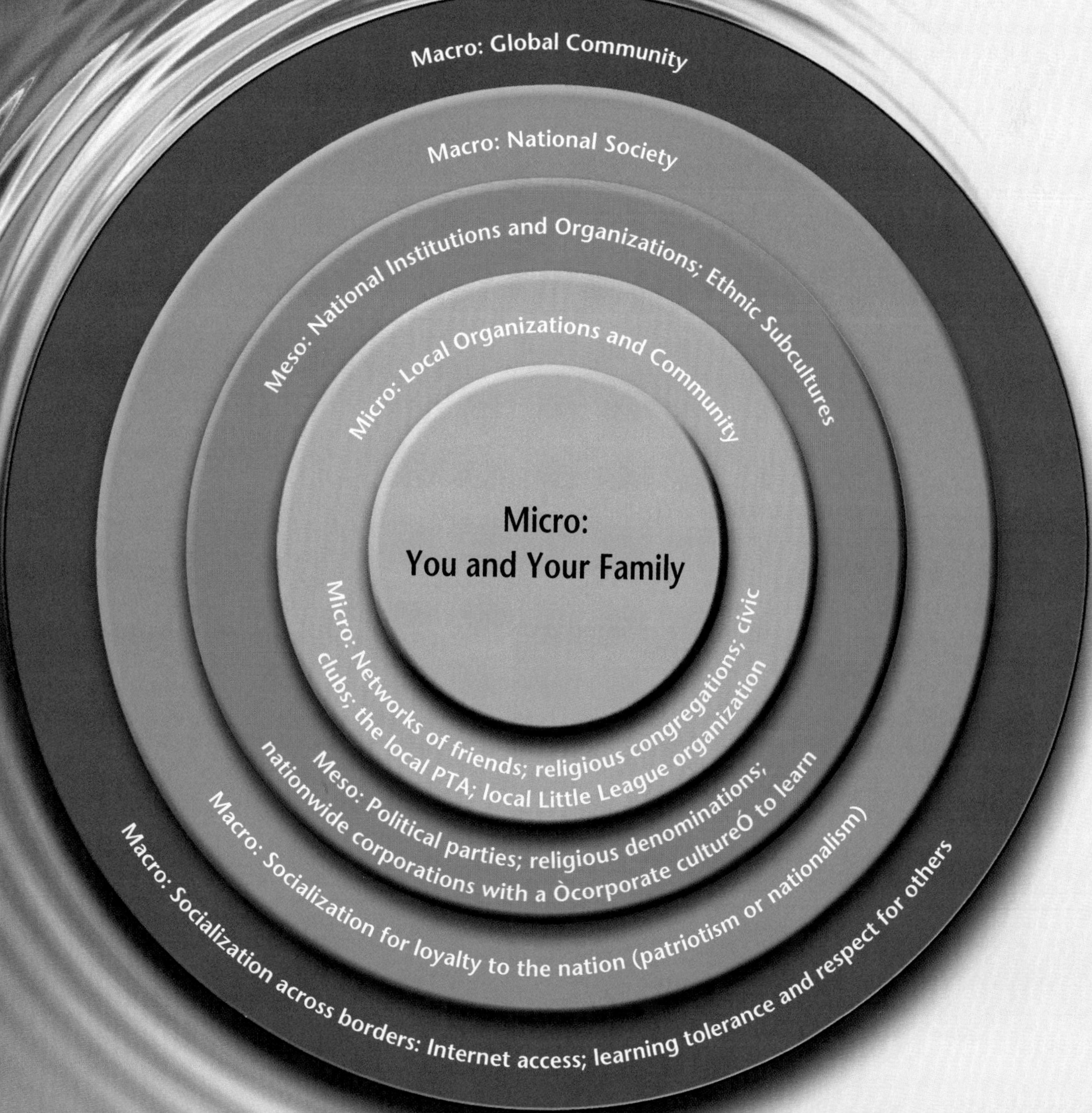

Macro: Global Community

Macro: National Society

Meso: National Institutions and Organizations; Ethnic Subcultures

Micro: Local Organizations and Community

Micro:
You and Your Family

Micro: Networks of friends; religious congregations; civic clubs; the local PTA; local Little League organization

Meso: Political parties; religious denominations; nationwide corporations with a "corporate culture" to learn

Macro: Socialization for loyalty to the nation (patriotism or nationalism)

Macro: Socialization across borders: Internet access; learning tolerance and respect for others

Ram, a first grader from India, had only been in school in Iowa for a couple of weeks. The teacher was giving the first test. Ram did not know much about what that meant, but he rather liked school and the red-haired girl next to him had become a friend. He was catching on to reading a bit faster than she, but she was better at the number exercises. They often helped each other learn while the teacher was busy with a small group in the front of the class.

The teacher gave each child the test, and Ram saw that it had to do with numbers. He began to do what the teacher instructed the children to do with the work-sheet, but after a while became confused. He leaned over to look at the page Elyse was working on. She hid her sheet from him, an unexpected response. The teacher looked up and asked what was going on. Elyse said that Ram was "cheating." Ram was not quite sure what that meant, but it did not sound good. The teacher's scolding of Ram left him baffled, confused, and entirely humiliated. It was his first lesson in the individualism and competitiveness that govern Western-style schools; Ram was being socialized into a new set of values. In his parents' culture, competitiveness was discouraged and individualism was equated with selfishness and rejection of community. Athletic events were designed to end in a tie so that no one would feel rejected; indeed, a well-socialized person would rather lose in a competition than cause someone else to feel bad because they lost.

Socialization is the lifelong process of learning to become a member of the social world, beginning at birth and continuing until death. It is a major part of what the family, education, religion, and other institutions do to prepare individuals to be members of their social world. Like Ram, each of us learns the values and beliefs of our culture. In Ram's case, he literally moved from one cultural group to another and had to adjust to more than one culture within his social world.

Have you ever interacted with a newborn human baby? Infants are interactive, ready to develop into members of the social world; as they cry, coo, or smile, they gradually learn that their behaviors elicit responses from other humans. This exchange of messages—this **interaction**—is the basic building block of socialization. It is out of this process of interaction that a child learns its culture and becomes a member of society, and it is this process of interaction that shapes the infant into a human being with a social *self*—perceptions we have of who we are.

Human biological potential, culture, and individual experiences all provide the framework for socialization. Babies enter this world unsocialized, born totally dependent on others to meet their needs, and completely lacking in social awareness and in an understanding of the rules of their society. Despite this complete vulnerability, they have the potential to learn the language, norms, values, and skills needed in their society. They gradually learn who they are and what is expected of them in their society. Socialization is necessary not only for the survival of the individual but also for the survival of society and its groups. The process continues in various forms throughout our lives as we enter and exit various positions—from school to work to retirement to death.

In this chapter we will explore the nature of socialization and how individuals become socialized. First, however, we briefly examine an ongoing debate: which is more influential in determining who we are—our genes (nature) or our socialization into the social world (nurture)?

Babies interact intensively with their parents, observing and absorbing everything around them and learning what kinds of sounds or actions elicit response from the adults. Socialization starts at the beginning of life.

Source: © Ben German.

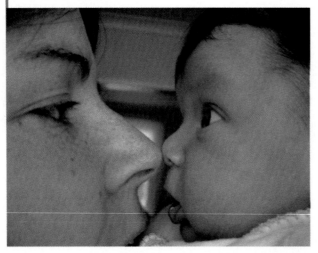

NATURE AND NURTURE

What is it that most makes us who we are? Is it our biological makeup or the environment in which we are raised that guides our behavior and the development of our *self?* One side of the contemporary debate regarding nature versus nurture seeks to explain the development of the self and human social behaviors—violence, crime, academic performance, mate selection, economic success, gender roles, and other behaviors too numerous to mention here—by examining biological or genetic factors (Harris 1998; Winkler 1991). Sociologists call this *sociobiology,* and psychologists refer to it as evolutionary psychology. The theory claims that our human genetic makeup wires us for social behaviors (Wilson Gregory, Silvers and Sutch 1978). For example, according to this theory, altruism—the inclination to share and to cooperate—is at least partially genetically determined.

We perpetuate our own biological family lines and the human species through various social behaviors. Human groups develop power structures, are territorial, and protect their kin. A mother ignoring her own safety to help a child, soldiers dying in battle for their comrades and countries, communities feeling hostility toward outsiders or foreigners, and neighbors defending property lines against intrusion by neighbors are all examples of behaviors that sociobiologists claim are rooted in genetic makeup of the species. Sociobiologists would say these behaviors continue because they result in increased chance of survival of the species as a whole (Lerner 1992; Lumsden and Wilson 1981; Wilson 1980, 1987).

Most sociologists believe that sociobiology and evolutionary psychology explanations have flaws. Sociobiology is a **reductionist** theory; that is, it reduces complex social behaviors to a single factor—in this case to a chromosomal or genetic explanation. There is no evidence for the existence of an altruism gene, an aggression gene, or any other behavioral gene; however, a good deal of evidence does exist to suggest that human behavior is not genetically determined. There are great variations in the way members of different societies and groups behave; persons born in one culture and raised in another adopt social behaviors common to the culture in which they are raised (Gould 1997), as Ram in the opening example is doing. If social behavior is genetically programmed, then it should manifest itself regardless of the culture in which humans are raised. The key is that what makes humans unique is not our biological heritage but our ability to learn the complex social arrangements of our culture. We *learn* what it means to be human in our individual social worlds, and we learn how to behave through our interaction with other people. Still, the nature-versus-nurture controversies continue.

Most sociologists do recognize that individuals are influenced by biology that limits the range of human responses and creates certain needs and drives, but they believe that nurture is far more important as the central force in shaping human behavior through the socialization process. Some sociologists propose theories that consider both nature and nurture. Alice Rossi, former president of the American Sociological Association, argues that we need to build both biological and social theories—or biosocial theories—into explanations of social processes such as parenting. Rather than biology shaping human culture, each society's culture shapes biology to meet its needs (Freese, Powell, and Steelman 1999; Rossi 1984). Socialization is key in this process.

THE IMPORTANCE OF SOCIALIZATION

If you have lived on a farm, watched animals in the wild, or seen television nature shows, you probably have noticed that the young become independent shortly after birth. Horses are on their feet in a matter of hours, and turtles never see their parents when they hatch from eggs. Many species in the animal kingdom do not require contact with adults to survive because their behaviors are inborn and instinctual. Generally speaking, the more intelligent the species, the longer

Intense interaction by infants and their caregivers, usually a parent, occurs in all cultures and is essential to becoming a part of the society and to becoming fully human.

Source: © Peeter Viisimaa.

the period of gestation and of nutritional and social dependence on the mother and family. Humans clearly take the longest time to socialize their young. Even among primates, human infants have the longest gestation and dependency period. Table 4.1 compares human infants and other primate babies. This extended dependency period for humans—what some have referred to as the *long childhood*—allows each human being time to learn the complexities of culture. This suggests that biology and social processes work together.

Normal human development involves learning to sit, crawl, stand, walk, think, talk, and participate in social interactions. Ideally, the long period of dependence allows children the opportunity to learn necessary skills, knowledge, and social roles through affectionate and tolerant interaction with people who care about them. Yet what happens if children are deprived of adequate care or even human contact? The following section illustrates the importance of socialization by showing the effect of deprivation and isolation on normal socialization.

Isolated and Abused Children

Have you ever wondered what children would be like if they grew up without human contact? Among the most striking examples are cases of severely abused and neglected children whose parents kept them isolated in cellars or attics for years without providing even minimal attention and nurturing. When these isolated children are discovered, typically they suffer from profound developmental disorders that endure throughout their lives (Curtiss 1977). Most experience great difficulty in adjusting to a social world

TABLE 4.1	**Dependence on Adults among the Primates**			
Primate Form	Pregnancy Period	Period of Absolute Nutritional Dependency on Mother or Mother-Surrogate	Nursing Period	Social Independence
Human	266 days	1 year or more	1–2 years	6–8 years
Ape: chimpanzee	235 days	3–6 months	2–3 months	12–28 months
Monkey: rhesus	166 days	1–3 weeks	2–4 weeks	2–4 months
Lemur	111–145 days	1–3 days	2–14 days	2–3 weeks

Note: Lemurs and monkeys, among the less complex members of the primate order, depend on adults for food for a much shorter time than do apes and humans. The period of dependence affords human infants time to absorb the extensive knowledge important to the survival of the species.

guided by complex rules of interaction learned from infancy onward.

In case studies comparing two girls, Anna and Isabelle, who experienced extreme isolation in early childhood, Kingsley Davis (1947) found that even minimal human contact made some difference in their socialization. Both "illegitimate" girls were kept locked up by relatives who

Humans and monkeys have very high similarity in DNA structure and are both highly social, but human infants are dependent much longer and humans have far more complex cultural learning needed to function as adults.

Source: © Kirill Zdorov.

wanted to keep their existence a secret. Both were discovered at about age six and moved to institutions where they received intensive training. Yet the cases were different in one significant respect: Anna experienced virtually no human contact; she saw other individuals only when they left food for her. Isabelle had lived in a darkened room but with her deaf-mute mother, so she did have human contact. Anna could not sit, walk, or talk, and learned little in the special school in which she was placed. When she died from jaundice at age 11, she had learned the language and skills of a 2- or 3-year-old. Isabelle, on the other hand, did progress. She learned to talk and played with her peers. After two years, she reached an intellectual level approaching normal for her age but remained about two years behind her classmates in performance levels (Davis 1940, 1947).

Less extreme than the cases of isolation but equally illustrative are the cases of children who come from war-torn countries (Povik 1994), live in orphanages, or are neglected or abused. Although not totally isolated, these children also experience problems and disruptions in the socialization process. These neglected children's situation has been referred to as abusive, violent, and dead-end environments that are socially toxic because of their harmful developmental consequences for children.

What is the message? These cases illustrate the devastating effects of isolation, neglect, and abuse early in life on normal socialization. Humans need more from their environments than food and shelter. They need contact, a sense of belonging, affection, safety, and someone to teach them knowledge and skills. This is children's socialization into the world through which they develop a self. Before we examine the development of the self in depth, however, we consider the complexity of socialization in the multilayered social world.

SOCIALIZATION AND THE SOCIAL WORLD

Sociologists are interested in how individuals become members of the society and learn the culture to which they belong. Through the socialization process, individuals learn what is expected in their society; at the micro level, most parents teach children proper behaviors to be successful in life, and peers influence children to "fit in" and have fun. At the meso level, religious denominations espouse their versions of the Truth, and schools teach the knowledge and skills necessary for functioning in society. At the nationwide macro level, television ads encourage viewers to buy products to be better and happier people, or they entice people to join the military. From interactions with our significant others to dealing with government bureaucracy, most activities are part of the socialization experience that teaches us how to function in our society.

The social world model at the start of the chapter illustrates the levels of analysis in the social world; the process of socialization takes place at each level, linking the parts. Small micro-level groups such as families, peer groups, and voluntary groups like civic clubs; meso-level institutions such as education and political parties; and macro-level units such as the federal government all have a stake in how we are socialized because they all need trained and loyal group members to survive. Organizations need citizens who have been socialized to devote time, energy, and resources that these groups need to survive and meet their goals; for example, charitable organizations cannot thrive unless people are willing to volunteer their energy, time, skills, and money. Lack of adequate socialization increases the likelihood of individuals becoming misfits or social deviants.

Most perspectives on socialization focus on the micro level. However, meso- and macro-level theories add to our understanding of how socialization prepares individuals for their roles in the larger social world. For example, structural-functionalist perspectives of socialization tend to see different levels of the social world operating to support each other. According to this perspective, scouting groups socialize girls and boys by stressing national values and instilling patriotism, thereby enhancing a commitment to the nation and willingness to sacrifice for it. Sports teams often instill values of competition, strategic thinking, and aggression. Education in many Western societies reinforces individualism and an achievement ethic. Families often organize holidays around patriotic themes, such as a national independence day, or around religious celebrations seen to strengthen family members' commitment to the nation and to buttress the moral values emphasized in churches, temples, and mosques. All these values are compatible with preparing individuals to support capitalistic economic systems.

Socialization can also be understood from the conflict perspective, with the linkages between various parts of the social world based on competition with or even direct opposition to another part. Consider the following examples: Socialization into a nation's military forces stresses patriotism and ethnocentrism, sometimes generating conflict and hostility toward other groups and countries. Conflicts between organizations for our resources (time, money, and energy devoted to the Little League, the Rotary Club, and library associations) may leave nothing to give to our religious communities or even our families. Each organization and unit competes to gain our loyalty in order to claim some of our resources.

At the meso level, the purposes and values of organizations or institutions are sometimes in direct contrast with one another or are in conflict with the messages at other levels of the social system. Businesses and educational institutions try to socialize their workers and students to be serious, hardworking, sober, and conscientious, with lifestyles focused on the future. By contrast, many fraternal organizations and barroom microcultures favor lifestyles that celebrate frivolity, playfulness, and living for the moment. This creates conflicting values in the socialization process.

Conflict can occur in the global community as well. For example, religious groups often socialize their members to identify with humanity as a whole ("the family of God") or at least with other members of their religions (e.g., all Christians). However, in some cases, nations do not want their citizens socialized to identify with those beyond their borders. They may need to persuade Christians to kill other Christians or Jews or Muslims who are defined as "the enemy," as in the case of World War II in Europe. If religion teaches that all people are "brothers and sisters" and if religious people object to killing, the nation may have trouble mobilizing its people to arms when the leaders call for war.

In 2006, an Iranian holds a gun in one hand and the holy Muslim book of the Koran in the other during an anti-Israeli gathering in Tehran. Sometimes, distinctions of "we" and "they" are core messages of socialization, and this can lead to hate and violence against "them."

Source: © Abedin Taherkenareh / epa / Corbis.

Conflict theorists believe that those who have power and privilege use socialization to manipulate individuals in the social world to support the power structure and the self-interests of the elite. Individuals compete to meet their own needs; those who have power and privilege are in the best position to get what they need, while having significant influence on the socialization of others through schools and political institutions. Most individuals have little power to control and decide their futures. For example, parents decide how they would like to raise their children and what values they want to instill in their children, but as soon as the school enters into socialization, parents must share the socialization process. Some parents choose to homeschool their children to control external influences on the socialization process.

Each theoretical explanation has merit for explaining some situations. Whether we stress harmony in the socialization process or conflict rooted in power differences, the development of a sense of self through the process of socialization is an ongoing, lifelong process. Individuals make choices that help to construct their reality in a complex social system.

Having considered the multiple levels of analysis and the issues that make socialization complicated, let us focus specifically on the micro level: where does the sense of self originate?

THINKING SOCIOLOGICALLY

Although the socialization process occurs primarily at the micro level, it is influenced by events at each level of analysis shown in the social world model. Give examples of family, community, national, or global events that might influence how you were socialized or how you would socialize your child.

DEVELOPMENT OF THE SELF: MICRO-LEVEL ANALYSIS

The central product of the socialization process is the self. Fundamentally, **self** refers to the perceptions we have of who we are. Throughout the socialization process, our *self-concept* is derived from our perceptions of the way others are responding to us. It is the development of the self that allows individuals to interact with other people and to learn to function at each level of the social world.

Humans are not born with a sense of self; it develops gradually, beginning in infancy and continuing throughout adulthood; it emerges through interaction with others. Individual biology, culture, and social experiences all play a part in shaping the self. The hereditary blueprint each person brings into the world provides broad biological outlines, including particular physical attributes, temperament, and a maturational schedule. However, nature is only part of the picture as shown in our earlier discussion of nature versus

nurture. Each person is also born into a family that lives within a particular culture. This hereditary blueprint, in interaction with family and culture, helps to create each unique person, different from any other person yet sharing the types of interactions, resulting in socialization, by which the self is formed.

Most sociologists, although not all (Irvine 2004), believe that we humans are distinct from other animals in our ability to develop a self and to be aware of ourselves as individuals or objects. Consider how we refer to ourselves in the first person—*I* am hungry, *I* feel foolish, *I* am having fun, *I* am good at basketball; we hold attitudes and feelings toward ourselves. We have a conception of who we are, how we relate to others, and how we differ from and are separate from others in our abilities and limitations. We have an awareness of the characteristics, values, feelings, and attitudes that give us our unique sense of self (James 1890/1934; Mead 1934).

The Looking-Glass Self and Taking the Role of the Other

The theoretical tradition of symbolic interaction, with particular emphasis on the major contributions of Charles H. Cooley (1909/1983: 184) and George Herbert Mead (1934), offers important insights into how individuals develop the self. Cooley believed the self is a social product, shaped by interactions with others from the time of birth. He likened interaction processes to looking in a mirror wherein each person reflects an image of the other.

> "Each to each a looking-glass
> Reflects the other that doth pass."

For Cooley (1909/1983:184), the **looking-glass self** is a reflective process based on our interpretations of the reactions of others. In this process, Cooley believed that there are three principal elements: (1) we imagine how we appear to others, (2) we interpret how others judge that appearance and respond to that interpretation, and (3) we experience feelings such as pride or shame based on this imagined appearance and judgment and respond based on our interpretation. Moreover, throughout this process, we actively try to manipulate other people's view of us to serve our needs and interests. (See Figure 4.1.)

Of course, this does not mean our interpretation of the other person's response is correct, but our interpretation does determine how we respond. Our *self* is influenced by the many "others" with whom we interact, and each of our interpretations of their reactions feeds into our self-concept. Recall that the isolated children failed to develop this sense of self precisely because they lacked interaction with others. The next Sociology in Your Social World (page 100) illustrates the *looking-glass self* process for African American males. This situation experienced by Brent Stables vividly illustrates the impact of the reflection of others on us.

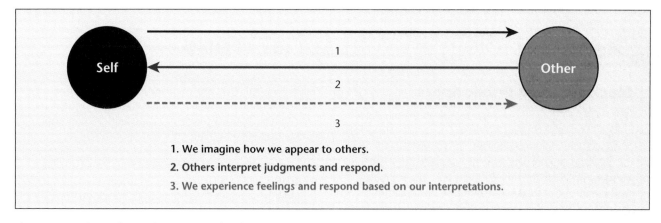

1. We imagine how we appear to others.
2. Others interpret judgments and respond.
3. We experience feelings and respond based on our interpretations.

Figure 4.1   The Looking-Glass Process of Self-Development

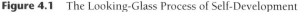

THINKING SOCIOLOGICALLY

Write a character sketch that describes your talents. Who are some of the people who have been most significant in shaping your *self?* How have their actions and responses helped to shape your self conception as musically talented, or athletic, or intelligent, or kind, or assertive, or any of the other hundreds of traits that make up your *self?*

Our sense of self is often shaped by how others see us and what is reflected back to us by the interactions of others. Operating somewhat like a mirror, Cooley (1909/1983) called this process the "looking-glass self."

Source: © Nancy Louie.

Taking the looking-glass self idea a step further, Mead (1934) explained that individuals take others into account by imagining themselves in the position of the other, a process called **role-taking**. When children play mommy and daddy, doctor and patient, or fireperson, they are imagining themselves in another's shoes. Role-taking allows humans to view themselves from the standpoint of others. This requires mentally stepping out of our own experience to imagine how others experience and view the social world. Through role-taking, we begin to see who we are from the standpoint of others; in short, role-taking allows humans to view themselves as objects, as though they were looking at themselves from outside themselves. For Mead, role-taking is a uniquely human behavior and is the foundation for the self and for most interaction in our social world.

Mead also argued that role-taking is possible because humans have a unique ability to use and respond to **symbols**. Symbols, discussed in Chapter 3 on culture, are human creations such as language and gestures that are used to represent objects or actions; they carry specific meaning for members of a culture. Symbols such as language allow us to give names to objects in the environment and to infuse those objects with meanings. Once the person learns to symbolically recognize objects in the environment, the self can be seen as one of those objects. In the most rudimentary sense, this starts with possessing a name that allows us to see our *self* as separate from other objects. Note that the

connection of symbol and object are arbitrary, such as the name John McCain and a specific human being. When we make the sounds that make up that name, most listeners would immediately think of the same person, a U.S. Senator.

Most sociologists do not think other mammals use symbols to communicate, with the exception of a few human-trained chimps and gorillas learning sign language or computer usage. Chimps rely on physical gestures or signs rather than symbolic meaning to communicate. A *sign* indicates some physical object or event that is close at hand—an instinctual cue or stimulus that leads the animal to an automatic, unreflecting, instant response; one that is not pondered before taking action. A dog growling and baring its teeth is a warning or sign that it is prepared to attack.

Sociology in Your Social World

Black Men and Public Space

Many stereotypes—rigid images of members of a particular group—surround the young African American male in the United States. How these images influence the African American male and his social world are the subject of this box. Think about the human cost of stereotypes and their effect on the socialization process as you read the following essay. If one's sense of self is profoundly influenced by the ways others respond, how might the identity of a young African American boy be affected by public images of black males?

* * * *

My first victim was a woman—white, well dressed, probably in her early-twenties. I came upon her late one evening on a deserted street in Hyde Park, a relatively affluent neighborhood in an otherwise mean, impoverished section of Chicago. As I swung onto the avenue behind her, there seemed to be a discreet, uninflammatory distance between us. Not so. She cast back a worried glance. To her, the youngish black man—broad, six-feet-two-inches tall, with a beard and billowing hair, both hands shoved into the pockets of a bulky military jacket—seemed menacingly close. After a few more quick glimpses, she picked up her pace and was running in earnest. Within seconds, she disappeared into a cross street.

That was more than a decade ago. I was 22 years old, a graduate student newly arrived at the University of Chicago. It was in the echo of that terrified woman's footfalls that I first began to know the unwieldy inheritance I'd come into—the ability to alter public space in ugly ways. It was clear that she thought herself the quarry of a mugger, a rapist, or worse. Suffering a bout of insomnia, however, I was stalking sleep, not defenseless wayfarers. As a softy who is scarcely able to take a knife to a raw chicken—let alone hold onto a person's throat—I was surprised, embarrassed, and dismayed all at once. Her flight made me feel like an accomplice in tyranny. It also made it clear that I was indistinguishable from the muggers who occasionally seeped into the area from the surrounding ghetto. That first encounter, and those that followed, signified that a vast, unnerving gulf lay between night-time pedestrians—particularly women—and me. And I soon gathered that being perceived as dangerous is a hazard in itself. I only needed to turn a corner into a dicey situation, or crowd some frightened, armed person in a foyer somewhere, or make an errant move after being pulled over by a policeman. Where fear and weapons meet—and they often do in urban America—there is always the possibility of death.

In that first year, my first away from my hometown, I was to become thoroughly familiar with the language of fear. At dark, shadowy intersections, I could cross in front of a car stopped at a traffic light and elicit the thunk, thunk, thunk, thunk of the driver—black, white, male, or female—hammering down the door locks. On less-traveled streets after dark, I grew accustomed to but never comfortable with people crossing to the other side of the street rather than pass me. Then there was the standard unpleasantness with policemen, doormen, bouncers, cabdrivers, and those whose business it is to screen out troublesome individuals before there is any nastiness.

After dark, on the warren-like streets of Brooklyn where I live, I often see women who fear the worst from me. They seem to have set their faces on neutral, and with their purse straps strung across their chests bandolier-style, they forge ahead as though bracing themselves against being tackled. I understand, of course, that the danger they perceive is not a hallucination. Women are particularly vulnerable to street violence, and young black males are drastically overrepresented among the perpetrators of that violence. Yet these truths are no solace against the kind of alienation that comes of being ever the suspect, a fearsome entity with whom pedestrians avoid making eye contact. . . .

Over the years, I learned to smother the rage I felt at so often being taken for a criminal. Not to do so would surely have led to madness. I now take precautions to make myself less threatening. I move about with care, particularly late in the evening. I give a wide berth to nervous people on the subway platforms during the wee hours, particularly when I have exchanged business clothes for jeans. If I happen to be entering a building behind some people who appear skittish, I may walk by, letting them clear the lobby before I return, so as not to seem to be following them. I have been calm and extremely congenial on those rare occasions when I've been pulled over by the police.

And on late-evening constitutionals, I employ what have proved to be excellent tension-reducing measures: I whistle melodies from Beethoven and Vivaldi and the more popular classical composers. Even steely New Yorkers hunching toward nighttime destinations seem to relax, and occasionally they even join in the tune. Virtually everybody seems to sense that a mugger wouldn't be warbling bright, sunny selections from Vivaldi's Four Seasons. It is my equivalent of the cowbell that hikers wear when they know they are in bear country.

Source: Staples (1992).

What message is reflected back to young black men by those who encounter them on the streets? How does this affect the self-concept of black men?

Source: © Dan Brandenburg.

THINKING SOCIOLOGICALLY

Brent Staples (previous page) goes out of his way to reassure others that he is safe and harmless. What might be some other responses to this experience of being assumed to be dangerous and untrustworthy? How might one's sense of self be influenced by these responses of others? How is the looking-glass self at work in this scenario?

At the micro level, the *symbolic interaction theory* further helps us understand the self. In the process of symbolic interaction, we take the actions of others and ourselves into account. Individuals may blame, encourage, praise, punish, or reward themselves. An example would be a basketball player missing the basket because the shot was poorly executed and thinking, "What did I do to miss that shot? I'm better than that!" Reflexive behavior, being able to look at oneself and one's behaviors as though from the outside, includes the simple act of taking mental notes or mentally talking to one's *self.* Two important ideas are that the self can be both a passive object shaped by the way we think others see us and an active object that can initiate action. The self has *agency*—it is an initiator of action and a maker of meaning. Moreover, to fully comprehend the self, it is necessary to understand that the self develops in stages and is composed of distinct but related parts.

Parts of the Self

According to the symbolic interaction perspective, the self is composed of two distinct but related parts—dynamic parts in interplay with one another (Mead 1934). The most basic element of the self is what George Herbert Mead refers to as the *I,* the spontaneous, unpredictable, impulsive and largely unorganized aspect of the self. These spontaneous,

undirected impulses of the *I* initiate or give propulsion to behavior without considering the possible social consequences. We can see this at work in the "I want it now" behavior of a newborn baby or even a toddler. Cookie Monster on the children's television program *Sesame Street* illustrates the *I* in every child, gobbling cookies at every chance.

The *I* continues as part of the self throughout life, tempered by the social expectations that surround individuals. In stages, humans become increasingly influenced by interactions with others who instill society's rules. Children develop the ability to see the self as others see them and critique the behavior of the *I.* Mead called this reflective capacity of the self the *Me.* The *Me* has learned the rules of society through socialization and interaction, and it controls the *I* and its desires. Just as the *I* initiates the act, the *Me* gives direction to the act. In a sense, the *Me* channels the impulses of the *I* in an acceptable manner according to societal rules and restraints yet meets the needs of the *I* as best it can. When we stop ourselves just before saying something and think to ourselves, "I'd better not say that," it is our *Me* monitoring and controlling

This child is entranced by the messages communicated by Cookie Monster on Sesame Street. *Other than learning letters and numbers, what messages about being human and living in our society are communicated by* Sesame Street *or other children's television programming?*

Source: © Kassie Graves.

the *I*. Notice that the *Me* requires the ability to take the role of the other, to anticipate the other's reaction.

Stages in the Development of the Self

The process of developing a social self occurs gradually and in stages. Mead identified two critical stages, the **play stage** and the **game stage**, each of which requires the unique human ability to engage in role-taking. We can see the emergence of role-taking by observing young children's imitative behaviors in the play stage. Listen to children who are three to five years old play together. You will notice that they spend most of their time telling each other what to do. One of them will say something like, "You be the mommy, and Jose can be the Daddy, and Julie, you be the dog. Now you say 'good morning dear,' and I'll say, 'How did you sleep?' and Julie, you scratch at the door like you want out." They will talk about their little skit for 15 minutes and then enact it, with the actual enactment taking perhaps one minute. Small children can mimic role-taking but only of those events and people familiar to them.

The **play stage** involves a kind of play-acting in which the child is actually "playing at" a role. A child who is playing mommy or daddy with a doll is playing at taking the role of parent. The child is directing activity toward the doll in a manner imitative of how the parents direct activity toward the child. The child is trying to act another role, although the child often does not know what to do when playing the role of a parent "going off to work." Children can only play roles

By imitating roles she has seen, this child is learning both adult roles and empathy with others. This kind of role enactment is an important prerequisite to the more complex interaction of playing a game with others.

Source: © Jaimie Duplass.

they have seen or are familiar with, and they do not know what the absent parent does when not in their presence. The point is that this "play" is actually extremely important "work" for children; they need to observe and imitate the relationships between roles in order to form the adult self.

Society and its rules are initially represented by **particular others**—parents, guardians, relatives, or siblings, whose primary and sustained interactions with the child are especially influential. That is why much of the play stage involves role-taking based on these particular others. The child does not yet understand the complex relations and multiple role players in the social world outside the immediate family. The child may have a sense of how mommy or daddy sees him or her but is not yet able to comprehend how he or she (the child) is seen by the larger social world. They lack the developmental ability to play a role and expect another child to know how to play the reciprocal role. Lack of role-taking ability is apparent when children say inappropriate things such as "Why are you so fat?"

In the **game stage**, the child learns to take the role of multiple others concurrently. Have you ever watched a team of young children play "tee ball" (a pre–Little League baseball game in which the children hit the ball from an upright rubber device that holds the ball), or have you observed a soccer league made up of six year olds? If so, you have seen Mead's point illustrated vividly. In soccer (or football), five- or six-year-old children will not play their positions despite constant urging and cajoling by coaches. They all run after the ball, with little sense of their interdependent positions. Likewise, a child in a game of tee ball may pick up a ball that has been hit, turn to the coach and say, "Now what do I do with it?" Most still do not quite grasp throwing it to first base, and the first base player may actually have left the base to run for the ball. It can be hilarious for everyone except the coach, as a hit that goes seven feet turns into a home run because everyone is scrambling for the ball.

Still, the lesson of incomplete role-taking is clear. Prior to the game stage, the vision of the whole is not possible. When the children enter the game stage at about age seven or eight, they will be able to play the roles of various positions and enjoy a complex game; each child learns what is expected and the interdependence of roles because they are then able to respond to the expectations of several people simultaneously (Hewitt 2007; Meltzer 1978). This allows the individual to coordinate his or her activity with others.

In moving from the play stage to the game stage, children's worlds expand from family and day care to neighborhood playmates, school, and other organizations. This process gradually builds up a composite of societal expectations—what Mead refers to as the **generalized other**. The child learns to internalize the expectations of society—the "generalized other"—over and above the expectations of any "particular others." Initially, behavior is governed by abstract rules ("no running outside of the baseline" or "no touching the soccer ball with your hands unless you are the goalie") rather than guidance from and emotional ties to a "particular other" such as a parent. Children become capable of moving into new social arenas such as school, organized sports, and (eventually) the workplace, and to function with others in both routine and novel interactions. Sociologists see individuals as active in shaping their social contexts, the self, and the choices they make about the future.

An illustration of internalizing the generalized other into one's conception of self is the common human experience of feeling embarrassed. Blushing, a physiological response to feeling embarrassed, may occur when one has violated a social norm and is taking into account how others view that behavior. Spilling a drink at a dinner party, making an inappropriate remark, or even having another call undue attention to one's appearance can cause embarrassment. According to this role-taking view, we see ourselves as objects from the standpoint of others and we judge ourselves accordingly. Very young children, however, do not feel embarrassment when they do such things as soil their pants or make inappropriate comments because they have not incorporated the generalized other; they have not yet learned the perspective of others. The capacity to feel embarrassed is not only an indicator of having internalized the generalized other but also a uniquely human outcome of our role-taking ability (Hewitt 2007).

As we grow, we identify with new in-groups such as a faith community, college sorority, or the military; we learn new ideas and expand our understanding. Some individuals ultimately come to think of themselves as part of the global human community. Thus, for many individuals the social world expands through socialization. However, some individuals never develop this expanded worldview, remaining narrowly confined and drawing lines between themselves and others who are different. Narrow boundaries often result in prejudice against others.

THINKING SOCIOLOGICALLY

Who are you? Write down 15 or 20 roles or attributes that describe who you are. How many of these items are characteristics associated with the *Me*—nouns such as son, mother, student, employee? Which of the items are traits or attributes—adjectives such as shy, sensitive, lonely, selfish, vulnerable? How do you think each of these was learned or incorporated into your conception of your *self*?

The Self and Connections to the Meso Level

Much of the discussion thus far has focused on the Chicago School of symbolic interaction. That perspective emphasizes the role of the *I* and focuses on the active agency of individuals in their own development. The Iowa School of symbolic interaction places more emphasis on the *Me*—on

Very young children who play soccer do not understand the role requirements of games. They all want to chase after the ball, including the goalie. Learning to play positions is a critical step in socialization, for it requires a higher level of role-taking than children can do at the play stage.

Source: © Christopher Knittel.

the role of others and the external social environment in shaping us (Carrothers and Benson 2003).

In the Thinking Sociologically exercise "Who are you?" above, we asked you to think about how you see yourself and what words you might use to portray yourself. If you were describing yourself for a group of people you did not know, we suspect that you would use mostly nouns describing a status—a social position within the society: student, employee, athlete, violinist, daughter, sister, Canadian, Lutheran, and so forth. To a large extent, our sense of who we are is rooted in social positions that are part of organizations and institutions in the society (Kuhn 1964; Stryker 1980). This is a key point made by the Iowa School: selfhood is relatively stable because we develop a *core self*—a stable inner sense of who we are regardless of the immediate setting we are in. This core often centers on the most important social positions we hold in the larger structure of society. You may think of yourself as politically conservative or liberal, and that may influence the way you conduct yourself in a wide range of places and social settings. It may shape your sexual behavior, the honesty with which you conduct business with others, and whether you are willing to cheat on an exam—even though you may not be around other people of your moral or political persuasion at the time (Turner 2003).

The Iowa School stresses that our identities are linked to institutions, organizations, and nations. Because of that, we have a vested interest in the stability of the society and the survival of those organizations that mean a lot to us—whether it is the college where we are a student, the Greek house which we join, the faith community with which we affiliate, or the nation of which we are a citizen. We will voluntarily give up our resources—time, energy, money, or even our lives—in order to preserve an institution or our nation. So the selfhood is not just a function of an individual's identity. Individuals create organizations and institutions, and those social structures take on an independent existence that affects individual actions and thoughts. Selfhood and meso-level structures are linked (Kuhn 1964; Stryker 1980, 2000; Stryker and Stratham 1985; Turner 2003).

SOCIALIZATION THROUGHOUT THE LIFE CYCLE

There are many markers in many developed countries of movement from one stage to the next in the socialization process: starting school at age five or six, obtaining a drivers license at about age 16, becoming eligible for military draft and able to vote at age 18, being legal to consume alcohol at 18 to 21. Most social scientists emphasize the importance of *rites of passage*—celebrations or public recognitions when individuals shift from one status to another. The importance of this shift resides in how others come to perceive the individual differently, the different expectations that others hold for the person, and changes in how the person sees him or her *self*.

Children learn many things in school, but one of the first is to master rules such as standing in lines.

Source: © Matt Matthews.

Infants begin the socialization process at birth. The baby cries, the caregiver responds with a clean diaper, food, a cuddle. The baby coos, and adoring parents ooh and aah. Soon, baby's cries can be distinguished by the parents: baby wants food or has a bubble in the tummy. These are the beginnings of interaction between baby and the social world.

In *childhood*, one rite of passage is a child's first day at school. This turning point marks a child's entry into the larger world. The standards of performance are now defined by the child's teachers, peers, friends, and others outside the home. Increasingly, those others including meso-level organizations, and institutions begin to determine the child's successes and failures in mastering skills. Up until this point, most children are unconditionally accepted and loved by their families, but school begins the sorting process in which the children are judged against others.

Adolescence is an important stage in Western industrial and postindustrial societies, but this stage is far from universal. Indeed, it is largely an invention of complex societies over the past two centuries, characterized by extensive periods of formal education and dependency on parents (Papalia, Olds, and Feldman 2006). In hunter-gatherer and in horticultural societies, there is no period known as adolescence; children generally move into adult roles with the onset of puberty and well-defined rites of passage associated with circumcision or first menstruation (Aries 1965). For example, killing a lion marks a turning point for young Masai males in becoming adults. They are changed in their own eyes and in the eyes of the group. In preindustrial societies, children observe and practice adult roles from an early age and are well prepared to assume these roles when they go through the rite of passage.

Although adolescence as a stage is absent in some cultures, adolescence in the United States, Canada, and much of Europe is a rather stormy period in many households. Tension mounts between the family and peer groups, and struggles arise between parents and their teenagers who seek independence and full standing as adults. Peer groups can become powerful socializing forces that compete with other formal agents of socialization: parents, religious communities, and school officials (Papalia et al. 2006).

Adolescence is, in a sense, a structurally produced mass identity crisis, since Western societies lack clear rites of passage for adolescents. They receive mixed signals about maturity and rites of passage—driving, voting, and joining the military. Thus, teens come to view themselves as a separate and distinct group with their own culture, slang vocabulary, clothing styles, and opinions about appropriate sexual behavior and forms of recreation. Margaret Mead (1973), an anthropologist who studied adolescence, claimed that societies with clear and definitive rites of passage have fewer conflicts between teens and the larger society.

In the United States, at 18 years of age, most people officially enter a world in which macro-level forces are increasingly involved in one's choices and experiences. A war on the other side of the planet may mean that a young person's life is at risk in the military, but even if the individual survives, it will be a different person who returns home. The intense socialization of boot camp is itself a transforming experience. Even if the country is at peace, the graduate may take a job with a transnational corporation; business decisions could cause the company to close a local plant and move production to another part of the globe. Thus, job security can be influenced by national recessions or by cross-national economic factors. With maturity, one becomes increasingly exposed to far-reaching macro-level dimensions of the social world. Keeping one's job may require migration, perhaps even a move to a production plant in another country. This requires retraining and new experiences that one may have been unprepared for in adolescence.

Most of our *adult* years are spent in work- and home-life, including marriage and parenting roles. It is not surprising, then, that graduation from one's final alma mater (whether it be high school, college, or graduate school), marriage, and acceptance of one's first full-time job are rites of passage into adulthood in modern societies. There is considerable variation in how well each society prepares its younger members to assume adult roles. In American society, for example, there is debate regarding how well young people are prepared to become parents or to have a smooth transition from school to work. With some exceptions, such as the bar mitzvah or bat mitzvah transition-to-adulthood in the Jewish tradition, more complex societies have more ambiguous rites of passage into adulthood.

This young Maasai warrior had to prove himself as a man by performing competently as a warrior and hunter. During this ceremony, red ochre is applied to his hair, and it serves as a symbol of his status in the community.

Source: © Louise Gubb / Corbis Saba.

Although smoking is extremely dangerous to one's health and can result in excruciating physical problems later in life, education programs among the young have had little effect. Smoking symbolizes independence from adult control and even adulthood to many teens, so they start the habit largely for social status reasons. This act of rebellion is, ironically, usually started as an act of conformity to peer pressure.

Source: © Istockphoto.com.

If you are an 18- to 22-year-old student, your parents are probably facing the *middle years of adulthood.* Media hype about the aging of the baby boomer generation increases as the number of citizens in the United States over 65 grows (now over 12 percent) (U.S. Census Bureau News 2005). The average life expectancy in 1929 was 57 years; today it is roughly 79 years (Center for Disease Control and Prevention 2006). Television reports, newspaper articles, and popular magazines have focused on the presumed midlife crisis of these baby boomers. Stereotypes about middle-aged men's distress over their sexual virility, or middle-aged women's anguish over menopause, tend to focus on strictly psychological aspects of aging (Sheehy 1995).

Current research asks the following types of questions about socialization: What are the economic and social conflicts associated with caring for one's elderly parents while trying to work and raise one's own family? How do gender role expectations change as one ages, gets divorced, is widowed, or retires? How does one's conception of self evolve as one changes social roles over time? How does one adjust to economic changes brought on by retirement or the death of a spouse? How can one maintain a sense of family continuity and facilitate mutual support when immediate family members live in geographically distant locations? In seeking answers to these questions, we must also consider the sweeping social changes that have accompanied the aging of current generations. Such dramatic social changes are illustrated by the following statement.

If you were born before 1945: We were born before television, before polio shots, frozen foods, Xerox, plastic contact lenses, Frisbees and the Pill. We were born before credit cards, split atoms, laser beams and ballpoint pens; before pantyhose, dishwashers, clothes dryers, electric blankets, air conditioners in our homes, drip-dry clothes and before man walked on the moon. . . . We were before house husbands, gay rights, computer dating, dual careers and commuter marriages. We were before day care centers, group therapy and nursing homes. We never heard of FM radio, tape decks, electric typewriters, artificial hearts, word processors, yogurt, and guys wearing earrings. For us time sharing means togetherness—not computers and condominiums. A chip meant a piece of wood, hardware meant hardware and software wasn't even a word . . . smoking was fashionable, grass was mowed, coke was a cold drink and pot was something you cooked in. And we were the last generation that was so dumb as to think that you needed a husband to have a baby.

Oh my, how the world has changed! (Grandpa Junior 2006)

Socialization varies with age, and one must learn the new expectations of a new age group as one ages. Socialization is a lifelong process of learning through interaction.

Source: © Joseph Jean Rolland Dubé.

THINKING SOCIOLOGICALLY

What are the rites of passage from adolescence into adulthood in your country? Is there ambiguity? Why do adolescents engage in defiant acts against adults? To establish independence? To demonstrate their standing as emerging adults?

Elder status can have rewards (being the source of wisdom and respect) and costs, such as being expected to sacrifice one's life for the good of the society if one could no longer serve a function or keep up with nomadic groups. Historically, Eskimo elders were socialized to be willing to make that sacrifice if the necessity arose.

Source: © Michael T. Sedam / Corbis.

Even the *retired* and *elderly members* of society are constantly undergoing socialization and resocialization, and developing their sense of self. The type of society influences the socialization experience of the elderly and how they carry out their roles. In nomadic subsistence level societies, the elderly may begin to have problems traveling with the group and they may feel they no longer contribute to the group (Cox 1990, 2001). It used to be the case among some Inuit (Eskimo) groups that a time would come when an elderly person would stay behind as the group migrated to a new location to find food for survival. This was a certain death sentence, yet it was the norm, and it aided in survival of the total group that sometimes ran short of resources to support everyone.

The elderly are vitally important to the ongoing group in more settled agricultural societies. They are the founts of wisdom and carry group knowledge, experiences, and traditions that are valued in societies where little change takes place. Councils of elders make the major decisions for the group, and young people listen to and learn from the lessons of

An elder Noctes woman with a grandchild strapped to her back watches traditional dances in her village. The Noctes live in extended family longhouses, so babies and children live under the supervision and care of the elder family members, who are greatly revered.

Source: © Lindsay Hebberd / Corbis.

these elders. Elderly people maintain their active involvement, social identities, and feelings of worth in agricultural societies. They are essentially mentors to the middle-aged and younger members of society, and because of their prestigious position, many children look forward eagerly to the day when they are old and esteemed.

The number of elderly people in industrial and postindustrial countries is growing rapidly as medical science keeps people alive longer, diets improve, and diseases are brought under control. Yet in modern systems, social participation by the elderly often drops after retirement. Retirement is a rite of passage to a new status, like that of marriage or parenthood, for which there is little preparation. As a result, retired persons sometimes feel a sense of uselessness when they abruptly lose their occupational status. One retires *from* something, but *to* what role do they move? The following is a quote from a blue-collar worker: "I've sweated and done a hard day's work in freezing cold and boiling heat, but now all of a sudden one day I'm no good any more. I'm told to take a walk, we don't need you anymore. I hardly missed a day's work, but now I have nowhere

to go and nothing to do but sit and watch soap operas. If that's not a death sentence, I don't know what is."

Retirees in Western societies generally have at least 15 to 20 years of life yet to live. Many retirees develop hobbies, enjoy sports, or have new jobs they can pursue. A recent study followed healthy, active people over time to learn about normal aging. Among the findings were that personality remains stable throughout the years; mental capacity remains consistent, though it may take longer to execute decisions; and cardiac structure does not deteriorate over time unless diseased (Levine 1997). Yet retirement can be the onset of dependency, poverty, loneliness, and ill health; only the ill health is biological. Many problems for the elderly are due to lack of valued roles and formal processes of socialization into elderly roles. However, many elderly become involved in volunteer activities as they adjust to retirement; part-time employment and expert consulting, paid or volunteer work in agencies, and other activities utilize the talents and interests of this large group of individuals (Cox 1990, 2001) This involvement increases respect for the contributions of the older segment of our society and, in turn, influence the self-image and self-esteem of those in this stage of the life cycle.

Death and dying is the final stage of life (Kubler-Ross 1997). Death holds different meanings in different cultures: passing into another life, a time of judgment, a waiting for rebirth, or a void and nothingness. In some religious groups, people work hard or do good deeds because they believe they will be rewarded in an afterlife or with rebirth to a better status in the next life on earth. Thus, beliefs about the meaning of death can affect how people live their lives and how they cope with dying and death.

A body is placed on a pyre at a cremation site next to the Ganges River in India. Cremation is a ritual designed to do much more than dispose of the body; it is intended to release the soul from its earthly existence. Hindus believe that cremation is most spiritually beneficial to the departed soul. The closest relative of the deceased takes charge of the final rite and lights the funeral pyre.

Source: © Harish Tyagi / epa / Corbis.

In the Muslim tradition, the dead are washed and wrapped before burial. In the cemetery in Najaf, Iraq, parlors specializing in the washing of the dead prepare as many as 30 bodies for burial a day. Najaf is regarded as one of the holiest sites to be buried in Iraq. With many bodies, some mutilated from the war, these parlors are hard-pressed to keep up with demand for their services.

Source: © Jehad Nga / Corbis.

U.S. Honor Guards carry a casket bearing the remains of U.S. Air Force personnel at Arlington National Cemetery outside Washington, DC.

Source: © Mike Theiler / epa / Corbis.

In traditional societies, elderly people often die at home with family members present to support the dying person and each other. This provides a socialization experience about

death for those still living. In many modern societies, death has been removed from home and family to the sterile confines of medical facilities (Mitford 2000). Although hospice and other movements allow terminally ill patients to remain at home and make their own decisions about dying and death, people in the West are often reluctant to deal with death. Avoidance of those who are dying is common. Victims of AIDS and cancer speak of the loneliness and isolation they encounter. These experiences of being ignored or shunned cannot help but affect a person's sense of self in the closing months and years of life.

A policy issue currently being debated in many countries is physician-assisted suicide, sometimes called euthanasia, or "good death." (Batavia 2000). Currently, the Netherlands permits the practice, but with many safeguards. Some U.S. states, such as Oregon, have voted on measures to allow euthanasia (Lee and Werth 2000), but these measures are being challenged in the U.S. Supreme Court. So how you die—certainly an intensely personal experience— may be decided by a medical facility, an agency, or decision-making body of the federal government. Even death involves decisions by macro-level social structures.

Each stage of the life cycle involves socialization into new roles in the social world. Many social scientists have studied these developmental stages and contributed insights into what happens at each stage (Clausen 1986; Freud 1923/1960; Gilligan 1982; Kohlberg 1971; Piaget 1989). Although examination of these valuable theories is beyond the scope of this text, information about some theories can be found on this book's website.

Death ends the lifelong process of socialization, a process of learning social rules and roles and adjusting to them. When the individual is gone, society continues. New members are born, are socialized into the social world, pass through roles once held by others, and eventually give up those roles to younger members. Cultures provide guidelines for each new generation to follow, and except for the changes each generation brings to the society, the social world perpetuates itself and outlives the individuals who populate it.

THINKING SOCIOLOGICALLY

How were you socialized to view death and dying? What have you learned in your family about how to cope with death?

The Process of Resocialization

If you have experienced life in the military, a boarding school, a convent, a mental facility, or a prison, or had a major transition in your life such as divorce or the death of a spouse or child, you have experienced **resocialization**. Resocialization is the process of shedding one or more positions and taking on others; it involves changing from established patterns learned earlier in life to new ones suitable to the newly acquired status (Goffman 1961).

THE APPLIED SOCIOLOGIST AT WORK

The Process of Resocialization

Maria Lamb has a bachelor's degree in sociology and is working on a master's degree in applied sociology. She has been working in a resocialization program—a drug rehabilitation and research program. The goal of the program is to work with drug addicts on the streets, to try to get them into treatment, to resocialize them, to study who gets addicted and

This young woman has had several other children placed in foster care as a result of her drug addiction. Her two-year-old falls asleep in her arms while the mother takes a hit of crack. Applied sociologists work at solving problems such as this.

Source: © Brenda Ann Kenneally / Corbis.

how, and to determine what treatments are most successful.

Maria's job is varied. Some days, she is on the streets talking to addicts; she offers them food, shelter, and help in exchange for entering a resocialization program to turn their lives around. She also asks them questions about their past experiences, their initial use of drugs, and their present circumstances to better understand what leads to drug abuse.

To achieve her goals, she uses several techniques to gain access to addicts and collect information: snowballing involves one addict referring her or introducing her to others. To meet addicts, she hangs out in areas frequented by the addicts. Once she works with individuals and gains their trust, she helps them to meet their needs—food, shelter, health care, and possible treatment programs. She also interviews them using a closed and open-ended questionnaire.

Maria has already learned a great deal about street drug culture, what leads individuals to get involved in it, and what might be done to reduce drug dependence. Maria says every day is an exciting challenge. Some days are rewarding, others depressing, but her feeling is that even one improved life is worth the resocialization effort.

We often associate resocialization with major changes in adult life—divorce, retirement, and widowhood. One must adjust to raising children alone, living alone, loneliness, and possible financial problems. One divorcee of three years comments: "There are many things to commend the single life, but I still have not adjusted to eating alone and cooking for myself. But worse than that are Sunday afternoons; that is the loneliest time."

Sometimes, resocialization includes individual's attempts to adjust to new statuses and roles, such as widowhood. In other cases, individuals are forced into resocialization to correct or reform behaviors that are defined as undesirable or deviant. Prison rehabilitation programs provide one example. However, research suggests the difficulty in resocializing prisoners is rooted in the nature of the prison environment itself. Prisons are often coercive and violent environments that may not provide the social supports necessary for bringing about change in a person's attitudes and behaviors.

While resocialization is the goal of self-help groups such as Alcoholics Anonymous, Gamblers Anonymous, Parents Anonymous, drug rehabilitation groups, and weight-loss groups, relapse is a common problem among participants. These groups aim to substitute new behaviors and norms for old undesirable ones, but the process of undoing socialization is difficult. Some applied sociologists work on projects to resocialize clients, as shown above in The Applied Sociologist at Work. Marie Lamb's work illustrates the kind of applied sociology that one can do with a bachelor's degree in sociology.

THINKING SOCIOLOGICALLY

What experiences have you or someone you know had with resocialization? What were the processes, the outcomes, and the difficulties?

There are multiple individuals, groups, and institutions involved in the socialization process. These socialization forces are referred to as *agents of socialization*.

AGENTS OF SOCIALIZATION: THE MICRO-MESO CONNECTION

Agents of socialization are the transmitters of culture—the people, organizations, and institutions that teach us who we are and how to thrive in our social world. Agents are the mechanism by which the self learns the values, beliefs, and behaviors of the culture. Agents of socialization help new members find their place, just as they prepare older members for new responsibilities in society. At the micro level, one's family, the peer group, and local groups and organizations help people to know what is expected of them. At the meso level, education, religion, politics, economics, health, and other sources of learning such as the media and books are all agents that contribute to socialization. They transmit information to children and to adults throughout our lives.

In early childhood, the family acts as the primary agent of socialization, passing on messages about respect for property, authority, and neatness, for example (Elkin and Handel 1991). Peer groups are also important, especially during the teenage years. Some writers even argue that the peer group is most important in the socialization process of children and teens (Aseltine 1995; Harris 1998). Each agent has its own functions or purposes and is important at different stages of

The primary socialization unit for young children is the family, but as the children become teenagers, the reference group becomes increasingly important in shaping the norms, values, and attitudes, especially in highly complex social systems in the West.

Source: © Kevin Russ.

the life cycle, but meso-level institutions play a more active role as one matures. For example, schools and religious bodies become more involved in socialization as children become six years old than was the case when they were preschool age. For us, the authors of this book, other members of the American Sociological Association serve as "significant others" and shape our sense of appropriate behavior for sociologists and professors.

How Do We Know? on the facing page discusses how we know about socialization in schools by exploring an important and widely cited research project. Note what kind of data is viewed as legitimate evidence for understanding gender socialization.

Lessons from one agent generally complement those of other agents; parents work at home to support what school and religion teach. However, at times agents provide conflicting lessons. For example, family and faith community often give teens opposing messages to those of peer groups regarding sexual activity and drug use. This is an instance of mixed messages given by formal and informal agents.

For **formal agents**, socialization is the stated goal. Formal agents usually have some official or legal responsibility for instructing individuals. A primary goal of families is to teach children to speak and to learn proper behavior, school teachers educate by giving formal instruction, and religious training provides moral instruction. (These formal agents of socialization will be discussed in Chapters 10, 11, and 12.)

Informal agents do not have the express purpose of socialization, but they function as unofficial forces that shape values, beliefs, and behaviors. For example, the media, books, the Internet, and advertisements bring us continuous messages even though their primary purpose is not socialization but entertainment or selling products. Children watch countless advertisements on television, many with messages about how to be more attractive, more appealing, smarter, and a better person through the consumption of products. This bombardment is a particularly influential part of socialization at young ages (see Sociology in Your Social World, page 112).

Applying this distinction between formal, intentional socialization and informal, unplanned socialization has important implications for the kinds of messages that are presented and for how such messages are received.

THINKING SOCIOLOGICALLY

What dilemmas do you think might be created for children when the formal and informal agents of socialization provide different messages about values or acceptable behaviors? Is this contradiction something that we should be concerned about? Why or why not?

Gender Socialization in American Public Schools

Pause for a moment as you pass a school yard, and observe the children at play. Children's behavior on the school playground translates into a powerful agent of gender socialization in a world that is very complex. Consider the evidence reported in the ethnographic study of Barrie Thorne, recounted in her award-winning book *Gender Play*.

Many people assume that gender differences are natural and that we are born that way. By contrast, Thorne provides evidence that gender differences are social constructions, influenced by the setting, the players involved in the situation, and the control people have over the situation. As an astute observer and researcher, Thorne suspected that girls and boys have complex relations that play out in the classroom and school yard. Backed by other research findings, Thorne assumed that sex segregation begins in preschool and is well established by middle childhood. It takes place in multiple school settings—in the lunchroom, in classroom activities, in the ways teachers group children (such as lines to go to recess), and in assigning tasks. However, it is on the playground that she chose to do much of her observation on the separate worlds of girls and boys. As her research strategy, she points out that "when adults seek to learn about and from children, the challenge is to take the closely familiar and to render it strange" (Thorne 1993:12).

To test her idea about gender socialization, Thorne used the methodology of participant-observation to write an *ethnography*, a systematic observation of social contexts, in this case of schools in which gender behavior occurs. By doing ethnographic study, Thorne takes us through the process of "gender construction." Kids and adults play an active role in defining and shaping gender expectations through the collective practices of forming lines, choosing seats, teasing, gossiping, and participating in selected activities.

Thorne used two schools for her research. One school was in a small city on the coast of California and the other on the outskirts of a large city in Michigan. Both schools had around 400 students, mostly from working-class backgrounds. Most students were white, with 12 to 14 percent Latino and 5 percent African American. Ethnographer Thorne entered the world of the children, sometimes set apart on the playground taking notes, sometimes participating in their activities such as eating and talking with them in the lunchroom. In each setting, she recorded her observations and experiences in the process of witnessing and "sense-making." For example, she noted what children call themselves and how they think of themselves. She was intrigued by the reference to the *opposite sex*— a term that stresses difference and opposition rather than similarity and sense of "we."

Thorne was struck by the active meaning-construction of children as they gained a notion of "normal" gender behavior. The real focus of her work is in taking seriously how children themselves make sense of sex differences—and how they sometimes ignore any difference as irrelevant to their activities.

Previous studies concluded that boys tend to interact in larger, more age-heterogeneous groups, in more rough and tumble play and physical fighting. Organized sports are both a central activity and a major metaphor in boy's subcultures; they use the language of *teams* even when not engaged in sports, and they often construct interaction in the form of contests. Thorne also found that boys' play involves a much larger portion of the playgrounds, and their play space was generally further from the building, making them less subject to monitoring and sanctioning. Girls played close to the buildings in much smaller areas. Although boys' space was much larger, girls almost never ventured into that region of the playground. By contrast, boys used the entire playground and would often run "sneak invasions" into the girls' space to take things belonging to the girls. Much like those men who harass women by not respecting their private space, many boys felt they had a right to the geographical space that was occupied by females.

Girls' play tended to be characterized by cooperation and turn-taking. They had more intense and exclusive friendships, which took shape around keeping and telling secrets, shifting alliances, and indirect ways of expressing disagreement. Instead of direct commands, girls more often used words like "let's" or "we gotta" (Thorne 1993).

However, Thorne found that these notions of "separate girls' and boys' worlds" used in most previous studies miss the subtleties in the situation—race, class, and other factors. Thorne's major contribution is to alert us to the complexity of the gender socialization process. Especially important is the way her research helps us see the extent to which children are active agents who are creating their own definitions of social relations, not just short automatons who enact adult notions of what gender means. More than most previous researchers, Thorne has shown deep respect for children as social actors.

Source: Thorne (1993).

Sociology in Your Social World

Formal and Informal Agents of Socialization: A Comparison of Schooling and Television

Schooling and television share a basic characteristic: both are purveyors of messages to young people. Despite this similarity, however, there are also many differences. Schools are formal agents of socialization with the express purpose of socializing the young. Television is an informal agent of socialization because the goal is entertaining, selling products, and increasing consumerism; socialization is a secondary result.

Schools	Television
Schooling is formal and bureaucratic; it takes place in specially designed buildings.	TV viewing generally takes place in the informal setting of one's home.
Acquisition of information requires obeying certain rules (e.g., no eating, no talking, no running around).	There are often no rules for watching TV, although parents may put limits on viewing.
School is structured around a sequential, age-appropriate curriculum that intends to inform and to build upon skills.	TV has no structured curriculum but a random content (channel surfing); content is usually designed to entertain; watching TV requires no special skills.
Students are a captive audience, required to attend school for specified periods (8.00–3:00, excluding weekends and certain holidays).	Watching TV is voluntary; programs are available 24 hours per day throughout the year.
There is a power imbalance between teachers and students; students have a role imposed upon them with little control over the requirements of their role; students do not directly control the flow of information from teachers.	There are no role requirements imposed on the viewer from the TV; viewer has power to control flow of information with "on"/"off" switch and choice of channels.
Schools do not provide information to students for commercial purposes (no profit motive).	TV messages are generally provided to viewers for commercial purposes (excepting public TV).
Students are grouped in classes by age or ability; groups of students (15–30) together receive the message.	Viewers watch TV individually or in small groups; millions may receive the same message.
Face-to-face interaction defines the relationship between students and teachers and among students; each takes the other into account throughout the interaction. Face-to-face interaction allows for mutual influence.	Vicarious interaction with an electronic image (rather than a live person) defines the relationship between viewers and media personalities; viewers are not able to interact directly with the millions of other persons receiving the same messages, hence no mutual influence.
Influence of schooling starts when the child begins school (approximately age 5).	Influence of TV begins in infancy when child becomes a new member of the family; impact of TV is significant even before child has entered school.

By Alan McEvoy, Wittenberg University.

Families: Micro-Level Socializing Agents

One way in which families teach children what is right and wrong is through rewards and punishments, called *sanctions*. Children who steal cookies from the cookie jar may receive a verbal reprimand or a slap on the hand, be sent to their rooms, have "time out," or receive a beating, depending on differences in child-rearing patterns; these are examples

of *negative sanctions*. Conversely, children may be rewarded for good behavior with a smile, praise, a cookie, or a special event; these are examples of *positive sanctions*. The amount and types of sanctions dispensed in the family shape the socialization process, including development of the self and the perceptions we have of who we are. Note that family influence varies from one culture to another.

In Japan, the mother is the key agent in the process of turning a newborn into a member of the group, passing on the strong group standards and expectations of family, neighbors, community, and society through the use of language with emotional meaning. The child learns the importance of depending on the group and therefore fears being cast out. The need to belong creates pressure to conform to expectations, and the use of threats and fear of shame helps socialize children into Japanese ways (Hendry 1987; White 1987).

Nonconformity is a source of shame in Japan; the resulting ridicule is a powerful means of social control. In some cases, the outcast is physically punished by peers. Thus, to bring shame on oneself or the family is to be avoided. In the most extreme cases, young people have committed suicide because they did not conform to group expectations and felt profoundly ashamed as a result.

In the United States, most parents value friendliness, cooperation, orientation toward achievement, social competence, responsibility, and independence as qualities their children should learn, in contrast to values of conformity and fitting into the group espoused in Japan. However, subcultural values and socialization practices may differ within the diverse groups in the U.S. population. Conceptions of a "good person" or a "good citizen" and different goals of socialization bring about differences in the socialization of children around the world.

In addition, the number of children in a family and the placement of each child in the family structure can influence the unique socialization experience of the child. In large families, parents typically have less time with each additional child. Where the child falls in the hierarchy of siblings can also influence the development of the self. In fact, birth order is a better predictor of social attitudes than race, class, or gender according to some studies (Benokraitis 2004; Freese et al. 1999), and firstborns are typically the highest achievers (Paulhus, Trapnell, and Chen 1999). Younger children may be socialized by older siblings as much as by parents, and older siblings often serve as models that younger children want to emulate.

Social Class: Meso-Level Socialization

Our educational level, our occupation, the house we live in, what we choose to do in our leisure time, the foods we eat, and what we believe religiously and politically are just a few aspects of our lives that are affected by socialization. Applying what we know from sociological research, the evidence strongly suggests that socialization varies by **social class**, or the wealth, power, and prestige rankings that individuals hold in society (Ellison, Bartkowski, and Segal 1996); meso-level patterns of distribution of resources affect who we become. For example, upper-middle-class and middle-class parents in the United States usually have above-average education and managerial or professional jobs, and they tend to pass on to their children skills and values

Parents and schools are primary agents of socialization in Japan as well as in North America, but the specific values being inculcated and the method for teaching them are different. Below, teachers work with students at a Japanese school.

Source: © Molly E. Rose.

A Japanese mother helps her son at Heian Shinto Shrine during Shichi-go-san Matsuri, also called 7–5–3 Festival, a celebration with prayers of long life for children aged three to seven.

Source: © Tibor Bognar / Corbis.

necessary to succeed in this social class subculture. Autonomy, creativity, and self-direction (the ability to make decisions and take initiative), responsibility, curiosity, and consideration of others are especially important for middle-class success (Kohn 1989). If the child misbehaves, for example, middle-class parents typically analyze the child's reasons for misbehaving, and punishment is related to these reasons; sanctions often involve instilling guilt and denying privileges.

Working-class parents tend to pass on to children their cultural values of respect for authority and conformity to rules, lessons that will be useful if the children also have blue-collar jobs (Kohn 1989). Immediate punishment with no questions asked if a rule is violated functions to prepare children for positions in which obedience to rules is important to success. They are expected to be neat, clean, well-mannered, honest, and obedient students (MacLeod 1995). Socialization experiences for boys and girls are often different, following traditional gender-role expectations. Moreover, these differences in behavior across social classes and parenting styles are apparent cross-culturally as well (Leung, Lau, and Lam 1998).

What conclusions can we draw from these studies? Members of each class are socializing their children to be successful in their social class and to meet expectations for adults of that class. Schools, like families, participate in this process. Although the extent to which schools create or limit opportunities for class mobility is debated, what is clear is that children's social class position upon entering school has an effect on the socialization experiences they have in school (Ballantine 2001). Families and schools socialize children to adapt to the settings in which they grow up and are likely to live.

Electronic Media: Meso-Level Agents within the Home

Television and computers are important informal agents of socialization. In developed countries, there is scarcely a home without a television set, and many homes have computers and Internet access. Fifty-one percent of households in the United States have one or more computers, and nine out of 10 children have computer access (U.S. Census Bureau 2001). Researchers have collected nearly five decades of information on how television has become a way of life in homes.

By the time an average child in the United States reaches 18, he or she will have spent more time watching television than any other single activity besides sleeping. On average, children between ages 8 and 18 spend 3 hours a day watching television, 1 hour and 11 minutes watching videos or DVDs, 1 hour and 44 minutes with audio media, 1 hour using computers, and 49 minutes playing video games, with a total media exposure in a typical day of 8 hours and 33 minutes. Table 4.2 shows total media

exposure of children by several variables (Kaiser Family Foundation 2005).

TABLE 4.2 **Total Media Exposure (average hours per day)**

	Hours per Day
Age	
8- to 10-year-old	8:05
11- to 14-year-old	8:41
15- to 18-year-old	8:44
Gender	
Boy	8:38
Girl	8:27
Race	
White	7:58
Black	10:10
Hispanic	8:52
Parent education	
High school or less	8:30
Some college	8:02
College graduate	8:55
Income	
Under $35,000	8:40
$35,000–$50,000	8:28
Over $50,000	8:34

Source: Kaiser Family Foundation (2005).

THINKING SOCIOLOGICALLY

Considering the table above, how would you describe television-watching patterns among different groups? How might television watching affect other aspects of socialization of children?

Between the ages of 2 and 18, children in the United States spend an average of half an hour a day using computers, including computer use at school. Children ages 8 and older spend more than an hour and a half each day on computers: 22 percent of this time is doing schoolwork; 33 percent is spent on the Internet chatting, surfing the Web, or sending e-mail; and 26 percent is spent playing games (National Parent Information Network 2000). This means that the moguls of mass media—a meso-level social system—are able to influence socialization within the most intimate of environments. "Children (in the U.S.) use computers at very young ages—21 percent of children 2 years and younger, 58 percent of 3- to 4-year-olds, and 77 percent of 5- to 6-year-olds" (National Science Foundation 2005).

A serious concern related to socialization centers around the messages children receive from television and computer games, and the behavioral effects of these messages. There is ample evidence that children are affected in negative ways from excessive television viewing, especially television violence (National Science Foundation 2005), but a direct causal link between television viewing and behavior is difficult to establish. Researchers know, however, that parents who play an active role in helping children understand the content of television shows can have a powerful effect on mitigating television's negative impacts and enhancing the positive aspects of television shows. The television-viewing habits of parents—length of viewing time, types of shows watched, times of day—can also influence how their children respond to television.

Perhaps the most important aspect of television and computers is something that we do not fully understand but that has frightening potential. For the first time in human history, we have powerful agents of socialization in the home from a child's birth onward. Time spent attending to television or computer games is less time spent engaging in interaction with caregivers and peers. Intimate family bonds formed of affection and meaningful interaction are being altered by the dominant presence of electronic media in the home. Television and computer games augment, and potentially compete with, the family as a socializing agent. Those who control the flood of mass media messages received by children may have interests and concerns that are very much at odds with those of parents.

We can conclude that part of the socialization process occurs with the assistance of electronic appliances that share the home with parents and siblings and that command a significant portion of a child's time and attention.

Most formal institutions in modern societies (education, political systems, family, health care, and even religion) socialize people to identify with values and behaviors acceptable in their local and national groups. With globalization, global knowledge and understanding also become important parts of school curricula and media coverage. We move next to a discussion of some of the national and global processes that impact socialization.

THINKING SOCIOLOGICALLY

What other agents of socialization in addition to family, social class, and electronic media are important in teaching you roles, norms, values, and beliefs? What is the impact, for example, of friendship networks or peer groups?

SOCIALIZATION AND MACRO-LEVEL ISSUES

Transnationalism and Sense of Self

Immigration patterns around the world have resulted in a fairly new phenomenon: transnationalism. *Transnationalism* involves an individual or a family that has national loyalty to more than one country (Levitt 2001). Often, it occurs after

migration, when one's roots lie and many of one's close family members continue to live in the country of origin.

Heterogeneous Societies and Effect on Self versus "Other"

For people experiencing transnationalism, there are conflicting messages about culturally appropriate behaviors and the obligations of loyalty to family and nation. However, one need not migrate to another country to experience global pressures. The existence of the Internet and cell phones have increasingly created a sense of connectedness to other parts of the world and an awareness of the global interdependencies (Brier 2004; Roach 2004). Some commentators have even suggested that the Internet is a threat to the nation-state as it allows individuals to maintain traditions and loyalties to relatives and friends in more than one country (Drori 2006). Ideas of social justice or progress in many parts of the world are shaped not just by the government that rules the country but by international human rights organizations and ideas that are obtained from media that cross borders, such as the World Wide Web.

Access to international information and friendships across borders and boundaries are increasingly possible as more people have access to the Internet. Map 4.1, on Internet use around the world, illustrates variability of access but also how widespread this access is becoming. One interesting question is how access or lack of access will influence the strength of "we" versus "they feelings."

In a day and age when people lived in isolated rural communities and did not interact with those unlike themselves, there was little price to pay for being bigoted or chauvinistic toward those who were different. However, we now live in a global village where we or our businesses will likely interact with very different people in a competitive environment. If we hold people in low regard because they are unlike us or because we think they are destined for hell because of their spiritual beliefs, there may be a high cost for this alienation of those who are not like us. Among other problems, terrorism is fermented where people feel alienated. Therefore, diversity training and cultural sensitivity to those "Others" has become an economic and political issue.

The reality is that children in the twenty-first century are being socialized to live in a globalized world. Increasingly, children around the world are learning multiple languages to enhance their ability to communicate with others. Some college campuses are requiring experiences abroad as part of the standard curriculum because faculty members and administrators feel that global perspective is essential in our world today and part of a college education. Socialization to global sensitivity and tolerance of those who were once considered "alien" has become a core element of our day (Robertson 1992; Schaeffer 2003; Snarr and Snarr 2002).

Global Events and Personal Identity

Sometimes, global events can cause a different turn away from tolerance and toward defensive isolation. When 19 young

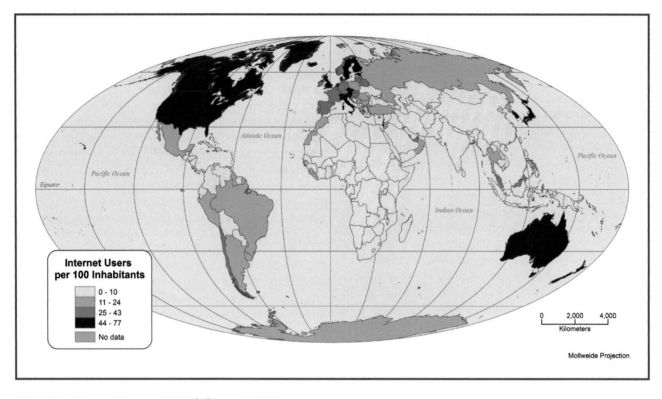

MAP 4.1   Internet Users per 100 Inhabitants in 2004

Source: United Nations International Telecommunication Union (2004).

men from Saudi Arabia and other Middle Eastern countries crashed planes into the World Trade Center in New York City and into the Pentagon in Washington, DC, the United States was shocked and became mobilized to defend itself and its borders. The messages within schools and from the government suddenly took a more patriotic turn. The Secretary of Defense, Donald Rumsfeld, even stated that the problem with America is that citizens do not have a strong enough sense of "we" versus "they."

So this event and other terrorist acts, clearly tragedies rooted in global political conflicts, can intensify boundaries between people and loyalty to the nation-state. Global forces are themselves complex and do not always result in more tolerance. Indeed, the only thing we can predict with considerable certainty is that in this age of sharing a small planet, the socialization of our citizens will be influenced by events at the macro level, whether national or global.

 THINKING SOCIOLOGICALLY

Besides the Internet, what other behaviors or interactions with others are being shaped by macro-level global trends? Which of these are positive, and which are negative? For what reasons?

POLICY AND PRACTICE

What help should be provided to children living in abusive families? Should preschoolers living in poverty be socialized in day care settings? Should adolescents work while going to school? Should new parents be required to take child-rearing classes? How should job-training programs be structured? How can communities use the talents and knowledge of retirees? Can the death process be made easier for the dying person and the family? These are all policy questions— issues of how to establish governing principles that will enhance our common life.

These policy questions rely on an understanding of socialization—how we learn our positions in society. For instance, making decisions about how to provide positive early childhood education experiences at a time when young children are learning the ways of their culture relies on understanding the socialization they receive at home and at school. The quality of child care we provide for young children will affect not only our future workforce but also whether kids turn out to be productive citizens or a drain on society.

Some sociologists do research to try to help policy makers have accurate data and good interpretation of the data so they can make wise decisions. Others are more activist, working in the field as applied sociologists trying to solve the problems through private foundations, consulting firms, or state agencies. An example of someone working in the field, using sociology to solve problems, is Joyce Iutcovich, as revealed in the interesting account of her work in the following The Applied Sociologist at Work.

THE APPLIED SOCIOLOGIST AT WORK

Evaluating Socialization for Young Children

The state of Pennsylvania evaluates early child care facilities (as do most states) to ensure that they are meeting standards set by the state. Part of sociologist Joyce Iutcovich's responsibilities as president of Keystone University Research Corporation is to help plan and oversee the evaluations and training of child care workers. As an applied sociologist, Dr. Iutcovich works with clients such as the state to develop policy, evaluate programs to determine if standards are being met, and recommends interventions to improve child care.

Iutcovich and her colleagues work as a team to design, implement, and evaluate programs in child care training aimed at improving skills of early childhood teachers, and they set up training opportunities for professional development. To evaluate how well child care teachers and facilities are serving children, Keystone collects data on the child care centers, analyzes that data, and makes reports with policy recommendations available to the centers and the state. For instance, Keystone staff members administer an environmental rating scale used in observing child care centers.

Iutcovich's training for her position involved both skill areas of applied research and several content areas of her work: child care, gerontology, juvenile justice, and sex equity. Her PhD degree from Kent State University was in applied sociology, social evaluation research, and social policy. While her content and skill areas are essential to her work, she feels that sociological knowledge of how organizational systems work has proved most important. Another necessary skill for her work is knowledge of computer statistical packages for analysis of data.

As Iutcovich points out, sociologists are ideally suited to do applied research because of their understanding of data and how to work with it, of measuring and analyzing programs, and of turning the findings into recommendations for change or new initiatives. Iutcovich has a useful, satisfying, and fun role; as she says, "there is never a dull day, and no two days are alike." She moves in different contexts and has opportunities to work with a variety of people, from child care teachers to legislators.

 ### SO WHAT?

Human beings are not born as noble savages or as depraved beasts. As a species, we are remarkable in how many aspects of our lives are shaped by learning—by socialization. Human socialization is pervasive, extensive, and lifelong. We cannot understand what it means to be human without comprehending the impact of a specific culture on us, the influence of our close associates, and the complex interplay of pressures from micro, meso, and macro levels. Indeed, without social interaction, there would not even be a self. We humans are, in our most essential natures, social beings. This has been the purpose of this chapter—to open our eyes to the ways in which we become the individuals we are.

Most of the influences that shape us occur in our interactions with others—through networks, groups, organizations, and even bureaucracies. In the next chapter, we turn to an analysis of these aspects of our social world.

CONTRIBUTING TO YOUR SOCIAL WORLD

At the Local Level: *Head Start* centers for poor preschool children provide education and socialization. They often need volunteers.

Boys and Girls Clubs provide socialization experiences for children through their teens. They also need volunteers and frequently provide sites for internships.

Care facilities and hospices for people who are ill or dying help reduce loneliness and provide positive interaction for individuals in these facilities.

They might have volunteer opportunities or part-time work opportunities.

At the National and Global Levels: *Care International, Save the Children,* and other international organizations provide funding for families to send children to school and to provide training. Benevolent fundraising, internships, or eventually jobs with one of these organizations may be a possibility.

Visit www.pineforge.com/ballantinestudy for online activities, sample tests, and other helpful information. Select "Chapter 4: Socialization" for chapter-specific activities.

CHAPTER

5

INTERACTION, GROUPS, AND ORGANIZATIONS: Connections that Work

What to Expect . . .

Networks and Connections in Our Social World

The Process of Interaction: Connections at the Micro Level

Groups in Our Social World: The Micro-Meso Connection

Organizations and Bureaucracies: The Meso-Macro Connection

National and Global Networks: The Macro Level

Policy Issues: Women and Globalization

So What?

Human interaction results in connections—networks—that work to make life more fulfilling and that make our economic efforts more productive. These connections are critical in our social world—from small micro groups to large bureaucratic organizations.

Think About It . . .

1. Are you likely to meet your perfect mate over the Internet?

2. How does interaction with others affect who you are and what you believe?

3. Could you live without groups?

4. How are you connected through networks to people across the globe?

5. Is bureaucratic red tape really necessary?

Macro: Global Community

Macro: National Society

Meso: National Organizations and Institutions; Ethnic Subcultures

Micro: Local Organizations and Community

**Micro:
You and Your Family**

Micro: Networks of school alumni; local religious congregations; scout groups; civic clubs

Meso: Ethnic organizations; political parties; religious denominations

Macro: Citizens of a nation

Macro: Global networks; United Nations; international laws or courts; transnational corporations

Only a few decades ago, we read about cyberspace in science fiction novels written by authors with a little science background and a lot of imagination. Indeed, the word *cyberspace* was coined in 1984 by science fiction writer William Gibson (Brasher 2004). Today, we are well aware that cyberspace is linking the world. In seconds, business people can transact multimillion dollar deals with geographically distant clients who have contracts with multinational corporations. There is no need to wait for the mail or even talk on the phone. The information superhighway is opening new communication routes and networking individuals with common interests.

The implications of the rapidly expanding links in cyberspace are staggering; we cannot even anticipate some of them because change is so rapid. For entertainment, we can talk with friends on listservs or with people we have "met" through cyber social groups. Some of these acquaintances

Each student at Seton Hall University is issued a laptop their first year as part of their tuition. The entire university is wi-fi connected so that the students can access the Internet wireless from any location on campus.

Source: © Najlah Feanny / Corbis.

have never left their own country, which is on the other side of the planet. All of this takes place in the comfort of our homes. Face-to-face communication may or may not ever occur.

Universities now communicate with students and employees by computer. You may be able to register for class by "talking" to the computer. Computers track your registration and grades, and they may even write you letters about your status. They also monitor employee productivity. For doing certain types of research, library books are becoming secondary to the World Wide Web.

Jeanne, one of the coauthors of this book, took a leave of absence in the mid-1980s to do some research in Japan. A benefit of that leave was that she escaped the distractions of ringing phones and could concentrate. Fax was almost unknown, and e-mail did not exist for the civilian population. In 1997, she took a leave of absence in Spain and in 2006 in Italy; she was in instant contact with her office and publisher over the international e-mail superhighway. She could insert a card into a laptop computer and have a mobile phone with voice and data transmission or pick up a mobile phone and call her family or coauthor. Page proofs for this book were sent to her in Italy by the publisher as an e-mail attachment. What a change in only 12 years! Technology is creating a smaller world where time zones are the only thing separating us, but it also may be making the world more impersonal because there is less need to meet face-to-face.

One of our students recently reported that she was ecstatic about having met the perfect man—over the Internet. She expressed reservations about meeting her perfect man in person because it might change this "perfect" relationship. Dating services have sprung up to introduce people via the Internet, and people put pictures and biographies, like home pages, on the Internet. Whether cyberspace is limiting face-to-face contacts is a subject of much debate. Individuals interact with each other whether through cyberspace or face-to-face and form networks linking them to the social world.

This chapter continues the discussion of how individuals fit into the social world, exploring the link between the individual and the social structure. Socialization prepares individuals to be part of the social world, and individuals interact with others to form groups and organizations. Interacting face-to-face and belonging to groups and organizations are the primary focus in the following pages.

NETWORKS AND CONNECTIONS IN OUR SOCIAL WORLD

Try imagining yourself at the center of a web, as in a spider's web. Attach the threads that spread from the center first to family members and close friends, on out in the web to peers, then friends of friends. Some threads to others are close and direct; others are more distant but connect more and more people in an ever-expanding web. Now imagine

Studying Degrees of Separation

I t is not often that a commercial film is made with a theme based on an empirical research project, but *Six Degrees of Separation* is such a film. Perhaps you have heard it said that every American is only six steps (or degrees) from any other person in the country. This assertion is rooted in a study with evidence to support it, although the film conclusion is oversimplified.

Stanley Milgram and his associates (Korte and Milgram 1970; Milgram 1967; Travers and Milgram 1969) studied social networks by selecting several target persons in different cities, just common people that the researcher happened to know. Then they identified "starting persons" in cities more than a thousand miles away. Each starter person was given a booklet with instructions and the target person's name, address, occupation, and a few other facts. The starter person was instructed to pass the booklet to someone he or she knew on a first-name basis who lived closer to or might have more direct networks with the target person than the sender. Although many packages never arrived at their destinations, one-third did. The researchers were interested in how many steps were involved in the delivery of the packages that did arrive. The number of links in the chain to complete delivery ranged from 2 to 10, with most having 5 to 7 intermediaries. This is the source of the reference to "six degrees of separation."

Despite the fact that we interact daily with a fairly small number of people, most Americans actually have a pool of 500 to 2,500 acquaintances. If you were to pick one of those who lived in the general direction of the target person, and that person picked one of her 1,000 or 2,000 acquaintances who lived closer, the numbers multiply very quickly. The numbers of indirect contacts through networks expand geometrically. Clearly, networks are powerful linkages and create a truly small world.

trying to send a letter to someone you do not know. A researcher actually tried this experiment to discover how people are networked and how far removed citizens are from one another within the United States. The How Do We Know? box above will not only explain the empirical evidence behind the film *Six Degrees of Separation* but will also give you a sense of another way to gather empirical evidence to test a hypothesis.

Our **social network** connects us to the larger society, as Milgram's research makes clear. *Networking* refers to using our social network to get jobs or favors, often from people who are not very far removed in the web. Networks begin with micro-level contacts and exchanges between individuals in private interactions, and expand to small groups, and then to large (even global) organizations (Hall 2002:28; Marsden 1987). Together, networks make up the social world. The spider web in Figure 5.1 illustrates that individuals are linked to other people, groups, organizations, and nations in the social world through networks.

Although network links can be casual and personal rather than based on official positions and channels, they place a person within the larger social structure, and it is from these networks that group ties emerge. People in networks talk to each other about common interests. This communication process creates linkages between clusters of people. Today, cyber networks on the Internet bring together people with common interests.

Although they are not designed to catch prey, when networks are drawn out on paper, they look a good deal like a spider's web with connecting parts.

Source: © Caitriona Dwyer.

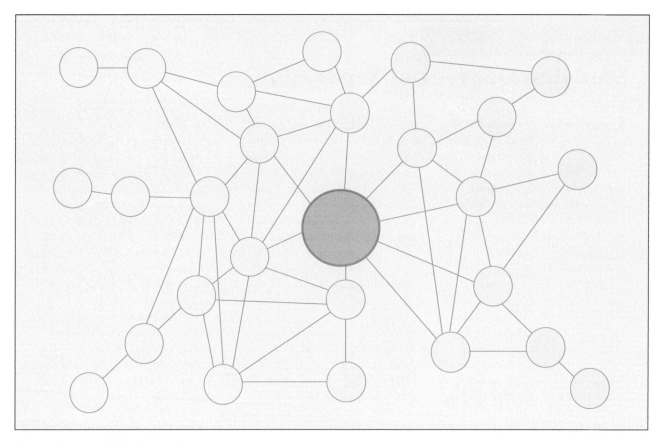

Figure 5.1   Web of Networks

Note: Picture yourself as the circle in the middle. Some of your friends know each other, but some you have known only in high school, others you have met at college, and still others only on the job. Each of these people has connections, creating a web of networks in which you "have a friend who has a friend." Some of these may be important connections for you someday. Note that poor people have fewer friends who are connected to those with resources and influence, reducing their networking capabilities.

Family and Friends: Micro-Level Networks

At the most micro level, you develop close friends in college—bonds that may continue for the rest of your lives. You introduce your friends from theater to your roommate's friends from the soccer team, and the network expands. These acquaintances from the soccer team may have useful information about which professors to avoid, how to make contacts to study abroad, and how to get a job in your field. Membership in food cooperatives, self-help groups such as Alcoholics Anonymous and Weight Watchers, and computer-user groups are examples of networks that connect individuals with common interests (Powell 1990).

All of you—if you are successful at your university— will eventually become part of the university's alumni association, and this may become important to you for social contacts, business connections, or help with settling in a new location. When people refer to the Old Boy network, they are talking about contacts made through general association with people such as alumni. Men have used networks quite successfully in the past, and networks of working women—New Girl networks—are expanding rapidly. One of the reasons for persistent inequality in our

society is that members of certain groups may not have access to these privilege-enhancing networks.

THINKING SOCIOLOGICALLY

Map your social network web. What advantages do you get from your network? What economic benefits might your connections have for you?

Meso- and Macro-Level Networks

Network links create new types of organizational forms, such as those in the opening example of cyberspace and the Internet. These networks cross societal, racial, ethnic, religious, and other lines that divide people. Networks also link groups at different levels of analysis. In fact, you are linked through networks to (1) local civic, sports, and religious organizations; (2) institutions that serve your community and the nation; (3) the nation of which you are a citizen and to which you have formal obligations (such as the requirement that you go to war as a draftee if the government so decides); and (4) global entities such as the United Nations, which use some of your taxes or donated resources to help impoverished people, tsunami victims, and earthquake survivors elsewhere in the world. These networks may open opportunities, or obligations to networks may limit your freedom to make your own choices. As we move from micro-level interactions to larger meso- and macro-level organizations, interactions tend to become more formal. Formal organizations will be explored in the latter half of this chapter. Links with larger organizations have expanded with the Internet.

One of the most interesting developments at the beginning of the twenty-first century is the way Internet technology is influencing networking—including links of individuals to people around the globe. Consider the cases discussed in the opening of the chapter. Internet users have redefined networking through the creation of blogs, chat rooms, message boards, listservs, newsgroups, and dozens of websites devoted to online networking ("Five Rules for Online Networking" 2005). Websites such as LinkedIn.com, WorldWIT.org, and Ryze.com offer business and professional networking, while other sites such as Friendster.com, Myspace.com, Tribe.net, Xanga.com, Classmates.com, Couchsurfing.net, Blogger.com, Facebook.com, and Orkut.com focus on personal and social networking.

LinkedIn.com has over 4 million registered users and allows users to connect with colleagues and clients, list job openings, and reconnect with previous coworkers (www.linkedin.com/static?key=tour_flash). Ryze.com has 250,000 members and allows users to post free networking-oriented home pages and create or join over 1,000 networks based on industry, interests, or location (www.ryze.com/faq.php). WorldWIT, an online networking organization for women in business, has over 30,000 members and, according to its communications director, Kristen Hughes, allows members to find everything "from realtors to dog walkers to employees and new jobs" ("Five Rules for Online Networking" 2005).

Websites dedicated to social networking focus on finding friends, dates, activity partners, or professional contacts. One of the first and largest is Friendster.com (www.friendster.com/info/tour/1_0.htm), which launched in the fall of 2002 and has over 20 million members (Boyd 2004). Like many other social networking sites, it allows users to post a profile and pictures, offer testimonials about others, create and join groups, and link to the profiles of "friends"—often a mixture of friends, colleagues, relatives, and acquaintances of varying levels and from various periods of life. Users can view the profiles of anyone within four degrees of separation—friends of friends of friends of friends—and search the network for people with the same friends, location, hometown, occupation, schools attended, interests, hobbies, or taste in movies, books, or television shows. In many cases, users link to dozens of friends and can access thousands of profiles around the world without reaching beyond the friends-of-friends level of connectivity.

Through online social and business networking, users have been able to expand and access personal networks at unprecedented levels. Users can discover who in their town attended the same college, link college friends to high school friends, search for people with overlapping "friends" and interests in a town where they plan to move or visit, or reconnect with lost friends. Even life partners may be found using the internet, as the illustration on the next page suggests. The networks and their potential uses are virtually unlimited and will continue to reshape networking for the foreseeable future. These networks create connections that can span the globe.

THINKING SOCIOLOGICALLY

How have you or friends used the Internet to expand social or professional networks? How have these networks influenced you or your friends?

THE PROCESS OF INTERACTION: CONNECTIONS AT THE MICRO LEVEL

Each morning as you rouse yourself and prepare for the challenges ahead, you consider what the day might bring, what activities and obligations are on your calendar, and who you will talk to. As you lift your limp, listless body from a horizontal to upright position and blood begins coursing through your veins, thoughts of the day's events begin to penetrate your semiconscious state. A cup of caffeine, cold water on the face, and a mouth-freshening brush bring you to the next stage of awareness. You evaluate what is in store for you, what roles you will play during the day, and with whom you are likely to interact.

Should you wear the ragged but comfortable jeans and tee shirt? No, not today. There is that class trip to the courthouse. Something a bit less casual is in order. Then there is the meeting with the English professor to discuss the last essay. What approach should you take? You could act insulted that she failed to think of you as a future James Joyce. Maybe a meek, mild "please tell me what I did wrong, I tried so hard" approach would work. She seems a nice, sympathetic sort. After class, there is a group of students who chat in the hall. It would be nice to meet them. What strategy should you use? Try to enter the conversation? Tell a joke? Make small talk? Talk to the students individually so you can get to know each before engaging the whole group? Each of these responses is a strategy for interaction, and they each might elicit various interactions.

The Elements of Social Interaction

"Let's have a drink!" Such a simple comment might have many different meanings. We could imagine two children

eHarmony is an online matchmaking agency that uses computers and the Internet to help people find a mate, or at least a good date.

Source: © 2000–2006 eHarmony.com, Inc.

e|Harmony®

fall in love for all the right reasons

HOME   TOUR   **WHY EHARMONY**   PERSONALITY PROFILE   SIGN UP   LOGIN

Scientific Matching | Expert Guidance | Proof it Works | 29 Dimensions of Compatibility

The 29 Dimensions of Compatibility

Most people know that the key to success in a long-term relationship is compatibility. But what does that mean? If you both like foreign movies and Mocha ice-cream, will you still feel the magic in 25 years?

Our proprietary matching model finds people who are compatible with you taking into consideration the following 29 Dimensions that determine long-term success. The power of eHarmony is that we evaluate the key criteria before you begin travelling down the road to commitment.

Dimensions of You
When you take our free personality profile we'll tell you about yourself and where you stand - and help you know who will be compatible with you.

29 Dimensions

Character & Constitution:
Good Character
Dominance vs. Submissiveness
Curiosity
Industry
Vitality & Security
Intellect
Appearance
Sexual Passion
Artistic Passion
Adaptability

Personality:
Obstreperousness
Sense of Humor
Sociability
Energy
Ambition

Emotional Makeup & Skills:
Emotional Health
Anger Management
Quality of Self Conception
Mood Management
Communication
Conflict Resolution
Kindness
Autonomy vs. Closeness

Family & Values:
Feelings About Children
Family Background
Education
Spirituality
Traditionalism
Values Orientation

"eHarmony allowed me to feel secure while meeting and really learning about several men. It took some time, but once I met John, I knew that they had made good on their promise to help me find my Soul Mate."
--Annie in Kansas City, MO

· Read More

Now that you've seen these dimensions, you should realize that it is still next to impossible to correctly evaluate them on your own with each person you think may be right for you. Let eHarmony help you make sure that the next time you fall in love, it's with the right person.

---

playing together, men going to a bar after work, a couple of friends getting together to celebrate an event, fraternity brothers at a party, or a couple on a date. In all these cases, **social interaction** consists of two or more individuals purposefully relating to each other.

"Having a drink," like all interaction, involves *action* on the part of two or more individuals, is directed toward a *goal* that people hope to achieve, and takes place in a *social context* that includes cultural norms and rules governing the situation, the setting, and other factors shaping the way people perceive the circumstances. The action, goal, and

social context help us interpret the meaning of statements such as "Let's have a drink."

The norms governing the particular social context tell what is right and proper behavior. Recall from Chapter 3 that norms are rules that guide human interactions. People assume that others will share their interpretation of a situation. These shared assumptions about proper behavior provide the cues for your own behavior that become a part of your social self. You look for cues to proper behavior and rehearse in your mind your actions and reactions. In the "let's have a drink" scenario, you assume that the purpose for the interaction is understood. What dress, mannerisms, speech, and actions you consider appropriate depend on expectations from your socialization and past experience in similar situations (Parsons 1951), for in modern societies there is a range of possible behaviors and responses in any social situation.

The next Sociology in Your Social World describes norms governing a familiar social interaction: sexual relations. Students at one college developed written norms to reduce the ambiguity that can lead to misunderstanding and even legal problems in gender relationships surrounding sex.

Although most people assume that talking, or verbal communication, is the primary means of communication between individuals, words themselves are actually only a part of the message. In most contexts, they make up less than 35 percent of the emotional content of the message (Birdwhistell 1970). **Nonverbal communication**—interactions using facial expressions, the head, eye contact, body posture, gestures, touch, walk, status symbols, and personal space—make up the rest (Drafke and Kossen 2002). These important elements of communication are learned through socialization as we grow up. Although you may master another written and verbal language, it is much more difficult to learn the nonverbal language.

People who travel to a country other than their own often use gestures in order to be understood. Like spoken language, nonverbal gestures vary from culture to culture as illustrated in Figure 5.2. Communicating with others in one's own language can be difficult enough. Add to this the complication of individuals with different language, cultural expectations, and personalities using different nonverbal messages, and misunderstandings are likely. Nonverbal messages are the hardest part of another language to master because they are specific to a culture and learned through socialization.

The same words, "let's have a drink," may have very different meanings in different social interaction contexts. Humans must learn not only the language but how to read interactional settings.

Source: (Clockwise from left) © Lise Gagne; © Sean Locke; © Tomaz Levstek.

Sociology in Your Social World

Antioch College Sexual Conduct Policy

In the 2005–2006 academic year, Antioch College approved its revised sexual conduct policy—a set of norms to guide behaviors and reduce the incidence of sexual assault. The policy, originally developed by the students themselves in the early 1990s as one of the first of its kind, was referred to as the "ask first" policy; it outlined a protocol for consent to sexual acts to avoid charges of sexual harassment or rape. Whatever you think of this policy, it does attempt to shape interpersonal intimate relations. A summary of key points and other notable content follows:

* * * * * * *

The Sexual Offense Prevention Policy (SOPP) is to ensure the safety and education of the entire Antioch Community, including but not limited to students, faculty, and staff.

Definition of **consent:**

- The act of willingly and verbally agreeing to engage in specific (at each level) sexual behavior.
- Silence must *never* be interpreted as consent.

- A person who is under the influence of drugs and/or alcohol is much less able to—and *may be unable* to—give consent.

Violations fall under the following categories:

Insistent and/or persistent sexual harassment: Unwanted comments, gestures, and other personal attention perceived as sexually intimidating, threatening, and/or denigrating.

Nonconsensual sexual contact II: Sexual contact, including touching or kissing, while knowing the person's judgment is substantially impaired or if the person would be offended by the action if fully aware of the interaction.

Nonconsensual sexual contact I: Sexual contact, including touching or kissing, which is facilitated by intentionally getting another person intoxicated (with drugs and/or alcohol) for the purpose of the sexual contact.

Nonconsensual sexual conduct: Nonconsensual penetration (anal, vaginal, oral) or mouth-to-genital contact.

Unnecessarily endangering the health of another: Knowing or suspecting you have an STD and not telling your partner(s) before engaging in high-risk sexual activity.

THINKING SOCIOLOGICALLY

Would such a policy alter behavior among students on your campus? If so, how?

Consider the following example: You are about to wrap up a major business deal. You are pleased with the results of your negotiations so you give your hosts the thumb-and-finger A-OK sign. In Brazil, you have just grossly insulted your hosts, like giving them "the finger." In Japan, you have asked for a small bribe. In the south of France, you have indicated the deal is worthless. Although your spoken Portuguese, Japanese, or French may have been splendid, your nonverbal language did not cut the deal! Intercultural

understanding is more than being polite and knowing the language.

Consider another example of nonverbal language: *personal space.* Most people have experienced social situations, such as parties, where someone gets too close. One person backs away, the other moves in again, the first backs away again—into a corner or a table with nowhere else to go. Perhaps the approacher was aggressive or rude, but it is also possible that the person held different cultural norms or expectations in relation to personal space.

The amount of personal space an individual needs to be comfortable or proper varies with the cultural setting, gender, status, and social context of the interaction. Individuals from Arab countries are comfortable at very close range. However, people from Scandinavia or the United States need a great deal of personal space. Consider the following four

   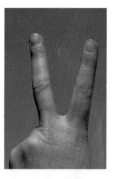

Figure 5.2   Gestures around the World

Gestures are symbolic forms of interaction. However, these gestures can have entirely different meanings in different cultures. A friendly gesture in one culture may be obscene in the next. In some regions in China, the gesture at the second from right means you want four of something. If you held up four fingers in another culture, people might have no idea what you want.

Source: © Mark Coffey; © Anatoly Tiplyashin; © Istockphoto.com.; © Julie Deshaies.

categories of social distance and social space based on a study of U.S. middle-class people. Each category applies to particular types of activity (Hall and Hall 1992):

1. *Intimate distance:* from zero distance (touching, embracing, kissing) to 18 inches. Children may play together in such close proximity and adults and children may maintain this distance, but between adults this intimate contact is reserved for private and affectionate relationships.

2. *Personal distance:* from 18 inches to 4 feet. This is the public distance for most friends and for informal interactions with acquaintances.

3. *Social distance:* from 4 feet to 12 feet. This is the distance for impersonal business relations, such as a job interview or class discussions between students and a professor. This distance implies a more formal interaction or a significant difference in the status of the two people.

4. *Public distance:* 12 feet and beyond. This is the distance most public figures use for addressing others, especially in formal settings and in situations in which the speaker has very high status.

Personal space also communicates one's position in relation to others. The higher the position, the greater the control of space. In social situations, individuals with higher positions spread out, prop their feet up, put their arms out, and use more sweeping gestures (Knapp and Hall 1997). Women and men differ with regard to personal space and other forms of nonverbal language; for instance, women are more sensitive to subtle cues such as status differences and the use of personal space (Henley, Hamilton, and Thorne 2000).

Sociologists study interactions, including verbal and nonverbal communication, to explain this very basic link

You do not need a detailed explanation to know that these two people are romantically interested in one another. Eye contact within close distance tells it all.

Source: © Joseph Justice.

Friends interact at a different distance—one-and-a-half to four feet. In different cultures, distances may seem inappropriately intrusive or cold and removed, and the other person may take offense.

Source: © Istockphoto.com.

A more formal setting calls for a distance of 4 to 10 feet. In a formal context, if one party comes closer than 4 feet, the other party may feel crowded and even offended.

Source: © Sharon Dominick.

between humans and the group. The following theoretical perspectives focus on the micro level of analysis in attempting to explain the social world.

THINKING SOCIOLOGICALLY

What are some complications that you or your friends have had in interactions involving cross-cultural contacts or male-female miscommunication? What might help clarify communication in these cases?

Theoretical Perspectives on the Interaction Process

How many people do you interact with each day, and what happens in each of these interactions? You probably have not given the question much thought or analysis, but that process is exactly what fascinates interaction theorists. Why

do two people interact in the first place? What determines whether the interaction will continue or stop? How do two people know how to behave and what to say around each other? What other processes are taking place as they "talk" to each other? Why do people interact differently with different people? What governs the way they make sense of messages and how they respond to them? These questions interest sociologists because they address the basic interaction processes that result in group formation, ranging in size from dyads (two people) to large organizations.

Rational Choice Theory

Exchange (or rational choice) theory considers why relationships continue, considering the rewards and costs of interaction to the individual. If the benefits of the interaction are high and if the costs are low, the interaction will be valued and sustained. Every interaction involves calculations of

When a respected person speaks in a public setting, listeners would be expected to keep themselves at a greater distance. Los Angeles Mayor Antonio R. Villaraigosa is one public figure who is comfortable at both a public distance and a less formal distance.

Source: Photo by Jim Winstead.

self-interest, expectations of *reciprocity* (a mutual exchange of favors), and decisions to act in ways that have current or eventual payoff for the individual.

Symbolic Interactionism

Symbolic interaction theory focuses instead on how individuals interpret situations, such as "let's have a drink," and how this, in turn, affects their actions. Two theories that are variations on symbolic interaction theory—*ethnomethodology* and *dramaturgy*—explain aspects of symbolic interaction that are part of interpreting situations or manipulating how people perceive interactions.

Ethnomethodology

Suppose an acquaintance greets you with a friendly, "Hi, how ya' doin'?" and you respond with "Rotten, I want to die!" or "Oh, shut up!" rather than the perfunctory "Fine, how's it goin'?" You may have had a really bad day, but you would get a strong reaction because you would be breaching norms related to casual greetings. Similarly, if you violate elevator behavior by singing in the elevator, trying to sell a product to others in the elevator, sniffing the person next to you, or staring at other occupants rather than at the floor numbers, you are breaching elevator norms. These norms are generally understood, even among strangers. Most people take for granted the underlying interaction rules—norms that govern the expected behaviors and the verbal or nonverbal exchanges. However, ethnomethodologists do not take these norms for granted.

Breaking norms is one method used by ethnomethodologists to study the formation of ground rules underlying social interaction and people's responses to violation of norms (Riehl 2001). These researchers use empirical methods to study how people develop shared meanings and consider how common ground rules originated. They question even the most basic aspects of social interactions such as spatial relations, one example of shared assumptions that can be violated especially if you enter a different culture.

THINKING SOCIOLOGICALLY

Try an experiment: Violate rules of elevator behavior or of a game such as checkers or basketball, and observe the reactions. How can you explain the reactions to this situation? Keep in mind that the level of emotion in the response is an indicator of how important the rule is in that setting and to others in the group.

Dramaturgy

Dramaturgy theorists analyze life as a play or drama on a stage, with scripts and props and scenes to be played. The *play* we put on creates an impression for our audience. In everyday life, individuals learn new lines to add to their

Sometimes, social researchers will engage in other atypical behaviors in a setting where that is a violation of norms, observing the reactions to the norm violations to access the nature of the norms. This is called ethnomethodological research.

Source: © Gulliver/zefa/Corbis.

scripts through the socialization process, including influence from family, friends, films, and television. They perform these scripts for social *audiences* in order to maintain certain images, much like the actors in a play.

Every day in high schools, thousands of teenagers go *on stage*—in the classroom or the hallway with friends and peers and with adult authorities who may later be giving grades or writing letters of reference. The *props* these students use include their clothing, a backpack with paper and pen, and a smile or "cool" look. The *set* is the classroom, the cafeteria, and perhaps the athletic field. The *script* is shaped by the actors—authoritarian relationships, competition for grades, or rivalry for social status among peers. The *actors* include hundreds of teens struggling with issues of identity, changing bodies, and attempts to avoid humiliation. Each individual works to assert and maintain an *image* through behavior, clothing, language, and friends.

As individuals perform according to society's script for the situation, they take into consideration how their actions will influence others. By carefully managing the impression they wish the acquaintance to receive—a process called *impression management*—people hope to create an impression that works to their advantage. In other words, the actor is trying to manipulate how others define the situation, especially as it relates to the character of the actor.

Most of the time, we engage in *front stage behavior,* the behavior safest with casual acquaintances because it is scripted and acted for the public and it presents a *definition of self* we hope others will accept as the "real me." A poor or unacceptable performance will be embarrassing both for us and our audience. People develop strategies to cover up their weaknesses or failures such as laughing at a joke even though they do not understand it.

Each part or character an individual plays and each audience requires a different script; interacting with peers at a bar differs from meeting a professor in her office. We learn to avoid those performance activities that are likely to result in humiliation or failure or that contradict the image we have worked to create. At home or with close friends with whom we are more intimate, we engage in *backstage behavior,* letting our feelings show and behaving in ways that might be unacceptable for other audiences (Goffman 1959, 1967). Dramaturgical analysis can be a useful approach to broadening our understanding of interactions.

Social Status: The Link to Groups

Recall the network web you drew. Now add to that web your **social statuses**, positions you hold in the social world. An individual's social status defines how, for example, she interacts with others and how others react to her in a specific situation. We interact differently when in the daughter status with our parents than in a student status with our professor

or peers. Each individual holds many statuses, and this combination held by any individual is called a *status set:* daughter, mother, worker, teammate, student.

Each individual's unique status set is the product of family relationships and groups the individual joins (a university or club) or into which one is born (an ethnic group or gender). Many statuses change with each new stage of life, such as work, student status, or marital status. Statuses at each stage of life and the interactions that result from those statuses form each person's unique social world.

Statuses affect the type of interactions individuals have. In some interactions (as with classmates), people are equals; in other situations, individuals have interchanges with people who hold superior or inferior statuses. If you are promoted to supervisor, your interaction with subordinates will change. Consider the possible interactions shown in Figure 5.3, in which the first relationship is between equals and the others are between those with unequal statuses.

When individuals are in dominant or subordinate positions, power or deference affect interactions. With a friend, these status relationships are constantly being negotiated and bargained: "I'll do what you want tonight, but tomorrow I choose." Studies of interaction between males and females find that in addition to gender, power and hierarchical relationships are important in determining interaction patterns. The more powerful person, such as one who has more wealth or privilege, can interrupt in a conversation with his or her partner and show less deference in the interaction (Kollock, Blumstein, and Schwartz 1985).

People have no control over certain statuses they hold. These **ascribed statuses** are often assigned at birth and do not change during an individual's lifetime; gender or race or ethnicity are examples. Ascribed statuses are assigned to a person without regard for personal desires, talents, or choices. In some societies, one's caste, or the social position into which one is born (e.g., a slave), is an ascribed status since it is usually impossible to change.

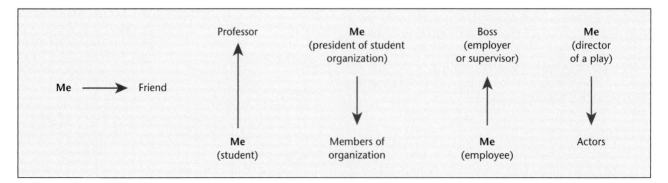

Figure 5.3   Types of Status Relationships Experienced by You

Achieved status, on the other hand, is chosen or earned by decisions one makes and sometimes by personal ability. Attaining a higher education, for example, improves an individual's occupational opportunities and hence his or her achieved status. Being a guitarist in a band is an achieved status but so is being a prisoner in jail, for both are earned positions based on one's own decisions and actions.

At a particular time in life or under certain circumstances, one of an individual's statuses may become most important and take precedence over others. Sociologists call this a **master status**. Whether it is an occupation, parental status, or something else, it dominates and shapes much of an individual's life, activities, self-concept, and position in the community for a period of time. For a person who is very ill, for instance, that illness may occupy a master status needing constant attention from doctors, influencing social relationships, and determining what one can do in family, work, or community activities.

THINKING SOCIOLOGICALLY

What are your statuses? Which ones are ascribed, and which are achieved statuses? Do you have a master status? How do these statuses affect the way you interact with others in your network of relationships?

The Relationship between Status and Role

Every *status* position in your network carries with it certain behaviors and obligations as you carry out the expected behaviors, rights, and obligations of the status—referred to as **roles**. Roles are the dynamic, action part of statuses in a society. They define how each individual in an interaction is expected to act (Linton 1937). The role of a college student includes behaviors and obligations such as attending classes, studying, taking tests, writing papers, and interacting with professors and other students. Individuals enter most statuses with some knowledge of how to carry out the roles dictated by their culture; through the process of socialization, individuals learn roles by observing others, watching television and films, reading, and being taught how to carry out the status. Both statuses (positions) and roles (behavioral obligations of the status) form the link with other people in the social world because they must be carried out in relationships with others. A father has certain obligations (or roles) toward his children and their mother; the position of father does not exist on its own but in relationship to significant others who have reciprocal ties.

Your status of student requires certain behaviors and expectations, depending on whether you are interacting with a dean, a professor, an advisor, a classmate, or a prospective employer. This is because the role expectations of the status of student vary as one interacts with specific people in other statuses. In Figure 5.4, the student is the subject and the others are those with whom the student interacts in the status of student.

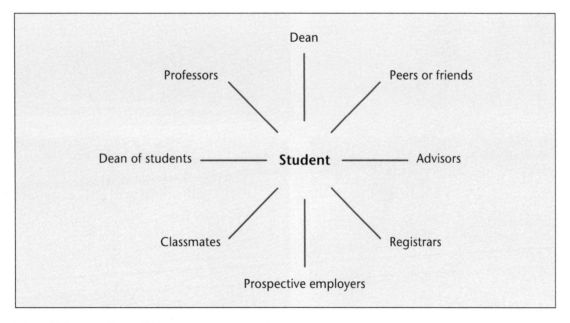

Figure 5.4   Types of Interactions among Students

PHOTO ESSAY

Work Status and Roles around the World

Positions people carry out in different cultures depend on tasks important in that culture. The two women from Ghana carry yams, a staple food, from the fields. Preparing cloth in a traditional method is one man's task. The Asian farmer works long hours in the field planting, sowing, weeding, and harvesting. Men in China use traditional methods to keep the roads open. Formal social control in societies falls to police officers in many societies. The vegetable seller at lower left works on the street in India. At the lower right, fishermen in India put in a catch for their livelihood.

Source: First four photos by Jeanne Ballantine; last three photos © Kate Ballantine.

TABLE 5.1 **Examples of Statuses and Roles**		
Status (position in structure)	**Role (behavior, rights, obligations)**	**Setting and Relationship with Others (environment)**
Student	*Formal* Study, attend class, turn in assignments	Setting: school Others: teachers, students, roommates
	Informal Be a jock, clown, cutup; abuse alcohol on weekends	
Parent	*Formal* Provide financial support, child care	Setting: home and community Others: child, spouse, relatives
	Informal Be a playmate; lead family activities	
Employee	*Formal* Work responsibilities: be punctual, do tasks	Setting: workplace Others: employer, coworkers, clients
	Informal Befriend coworkers; join lunch group; represent company in bowling league	

Within a group, individuals may hold both *formal* and *informal statuses.* One illustration is the formal status of high school students, each of whom plays a number of informal roles in cliques that are not part of the formal school structure. They may be known as jock, nerd, loner, goth, clown, or life-of-the-party. Each of these roles takes place in a status relationship with others: teacher-student, peer-peer, coach-athlete. Examples of complimentary statuses and roles can be seen in Table 5.1.

Social networks, discussed in the beginning of the chapter, link individuals to social groups through their statuses in the social world. In other words, our statuses connect us and make us integral parts of meso- and macro-level organizations. Sometimes, the link is through a status in a family group such as son or daughter, sometimes through an employer, and sometimes through our status as citizen of a nation. Social networks may be based on ascribed characteristics such as age, race, ethnicity, and gender, or on achieved status such as education, occupation, or common interests (House 1994). These links, in turn, form the basis for social interactions and group structures (Hall 2002). However, at times individuals cannot carry out their roles as others expect them to, creating role strain or conflict.

THINKING SOCIOLOGICALLY

In your web, detail your network from close family and friends to distant acquaintances; include your statuses and roles in each part of the network with family members, friends, and school and work acquaintances. What do you notice about your network?

Role Strain and Role Conflict

Every status carries *role expectations*, the way the status is supposed to be carried out according to generally accepted societal or group norms. Most people have faced times in their lives when they simply could not carry out all the obligations of a status such as student—write two papers, study adequately for two exams, complete the portfolio for the studio art class, finish the reading assignments for five classes, and memorize lines for the oral interpretation class, all in the same week. In these cases, individuals face **role strain**, tension between roles *within* one of the statuses. Role strain causes the individual to be pulled in many directions by various obligations of the single status, as in the above case of student.

To resolve role strain, individuals cope in one of several ways: pass the problem off lightly (and thus not do well in classes); consider the dilemma humorous; become highly focused and pull a couple of all-nighters to get everything done; or become stressed, tense, fretful, and immobilized because of the strain. Most often individuals set priorities based on their values and make decisions accordingly: "I'll work hard in the class for my major and let another slide."

Role conflict differs from role strain in that conflict is *between* the roles of two or more statuses. The conflict can come from within an individual or be imposed from outside. College athletes face role conflicts from competing

This couple does not entirely agree on whose job it is to change dirty diapers. Parenting roles often need to be negotiated; in some traditional families in the past, the status had more explicit role expectations and fathers were rarely expected to change diapers.

Source: © Nancy Louie/Istockphoto.com.

demands on their time (Adler and Adler 1991, 2004); they must complete their studies on time, attend practices and be prepared for games, attend meetings of a Greek house to which they belong, and get home for a little brother's birthday. Similarly, a student may be going to school, holding down a part-time job to help make ends meet, and raising a family. If the student's child gets sick, the status of parent comes into conflict with that of student and worker. In the case of role conflict, the person may choose—or be

informed by others—which status is the master status. Figure 5.5 visually illustrates the difference between role conflict and role strain.

THINKING SOCIOLOGICALLY

Using Figure 5.5, fill in the statuses you hold in your social world and roles you perform in these statuses. Then list three examples of role conflicts and three examples of role strains that you experience.

Statuses and the accompanying roles come and go. You will not always be a student, and someday you may be a parent and hold a professional job. You certainly will retire from your job. For instance, as people grow older they disengage from some earlier statuses in groups and engage in new and different statuses and roles.

Our place within the social world is guaranteed, even obligatory, because of statuses we hold at each level of society—within small groups (family and peers), in larger groups and organizations (school and work organizations), in institutions (political or religious groups), and ultimately as citizen of the society and the world. Each of these statuses connects us to a group setting.

GROUPS IN OUR SOCIAL WORLD: THE MICRO-MESO CONNECTION

When Jeanne, one of the coauthors of this book, was a child, the town she lived in had a hermit. He lived in a house on stilts in the bay. He made a big impression on all the kids in the neighborhood. They were fascinated! How does he live? How does he get food? Is he lonely all by himself? Does he get cold without heat? How can he survive without all the conveniences of modern life? One day she was lucky enough to see him rowing to the shore. He was a bearded old man, dressed in a torn plaid shirt and jeans. Although he looked quite harmless and gentle, she remembers feeling a little afraid. Anyone who would choose to live alone, without others, must be very strange indeed.

Few of us could survive as this hermit did—without others. Most of us constantly interact with the people around us. We are born into a family group. Our socialization occurs in groups. We depend on the group for survival. Even hermits depend on others to meet certain needs; no hermit is completely isolated. Groups are necessary for protection, to obtain food, to manufacture goods, to get jobs done. Groups meet our social needs for belonging and acceptance, support us throughout our lives, and place restrictions on us. Groups can be small, intimate environments—micro-level interactions such as a group of friends—or they can become quite large

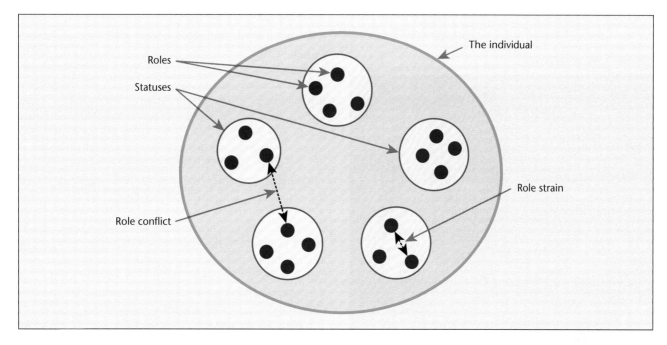

Figure 5.5   Role Strain and Role Conflict

Note: Each individual has many statuses: his or her status set. Each status has many roles: a role set. A conflict between two roles of the same status is a role strain. A conflict between the roles of two different statuses is a role conflict.

as they morph into meso-level organizations. In any case, it is through our group memberships that the micro and meso levels are linked.

Groups are two or more people who interact with each other because of shared common interests, goals, experiences, and needs (Drafke and Kossen 2002). The members feel they belong to the group and are seen by others as thinking, feeling, and behaving with a common goal. Members are in contact, consider each other's behavior, and engage in structured interaction patterns. Groups have defined memberships and ways to take in new members. They also have rules that guide behavior of members. In this section, we look at several questions: What are groups, and how do they vary? How is interaction affected by small groups? What is the importance of groups for individuals?

Not all collections of individuals are groups, however. For instance, your family is a group, but students at your university may or may not be a group depending on their sense of purpose and whether they interact with each other. People shopping at a mall or waiting for a bus are not a group because they do not interact or acknowledge shared common interests.

Groups form through a series of succeeding steps. The first step in group formation is initial interaction. If membership is rewarding and meets individuals' needs, the individuals will attempt to maintain the gratification the group provides (Mills 1984). Consider people in a village: a group of people live near each other and interact to form this village. In the second step, a collective goal emerges; for example, villagers may work together to build an irrigation system or a school. Groups establish their own goals and pursue them, trying to be free from external controls or constraints. In the third and final step, the group attempts to expand its collective goals by building on the former steps and by pursuing new goals. For example, the irrigation system may improve crop production, so the villagers decide to sell the extra produce at the town vegetable market in order to earn money for the school.

The Importance of Groups for the Individual

Groups are essential parts of human life and of organizational structures. They establish our place in the social world, providing us with support and a sense of belonging. Few individuals can survive without groups. This becomes clear when we consider two problems: anomie and suicide.

Anomie and Types of Suicide

With the rapid changes and breakdown of institutional structures in Afghanistan as rival warlords vie for power over territory and in Iraq as religious groups vie for political and economic power, horrific problems abound. Civil disorder, conflicts for power, suicide bombings, murder of police officers, and looting are frequent occurrences. Social controls (police and military forces) are strained and leadership

Men and boys in Bagan, Myanmar, bond with each other as they watch a sporting event and cheer for the home team.

Source: Photo by Elise Roberts

struggles to cope. The result of breakdown is **anomie**, the state of normlessness; the rules for behavior in society break down under extreme stress from rapid social change or conflict (Merton 1968). Consider the example of suicide.

Suicide seems like an individual act, committed because of personal problems or "inherited" weaknesses. However, early sociologist Emile Durkheim took a unique approach. In his volume *Suicide* (1897/1964), he discussed the social factors contributing to suicide. Using existing statistical data to determine suicide rates in European populations, Durkheim looked at such variables as sex, age, religion, nationality, and the season in which suicide was committed. His findings were surprising to many, and they demonstrate that individual problems cannot be understood without also understanding the group context in which they occur—the micro-level social interaction shaped by events and forces at other levels in the social system.

Durkheim found that Protestants committed suicide more often than Catholics, urban folks more often than people living in small communities, people in highly developed and complex societies more frequently than those in simple societies, and people who lived alone more than those situated in families. The key variable linking these findings was *the degree to which an individual was integrated into the group*, that is, the degree of *social bond* with others. During war, for instance, people generally felt a sense of common cause and belonging to their country. Thus, suicide rates were greater during peacetime because it offered less cause for feeling that bond.

Durkheim then went on to describe three distinct types of suicide. *Egoistic suicide* occurs when the individual feels little social bond to the group or society and lacks ties such as family or friends that might prevent suicide. Egoistic suicide is a result of personal despair and involves the kind of motive most people associate with suicide. This is what we often think of when we hear about a suicide.

Anomic suicide occurs when a society or one of its parts is in disorder or turmoil and lacks clear norms and guidelines for social behavior. This situation is likely during major social change or economic problems such as a severe depression. The recent suicides of an Enron executive, Clifford Baxter, and member of a U.S. president's inner circle, Vincent Foster, were related to economic problems and scandal during organizational turmoil.

Altruistic suicide differs from the others in that it involves such a strong bond and group obligation that the individual is willing to die for the group. Self-survival becomes less important than group survival (Durkheim 1897/1964). Examples of altruistic suicide include the young Arab Muslims who hijacked commercial airlines to fly into the World Trade Center and Pentagon, Muslims in Iraq committing suicide missions against American and British military forces and Iraqi police forces, Palestinian suicide bombers in Israel, Buddhist monks who burned themselves to protest the Vietnam War, Japanese Kamikaze pilots who dive-bombed targets during World War II, and Irish Republican Army members who starved themselves to death. These are suicides rooted in extraordinarily high integration into a group—usually occurring in societies or religious groups that have very clear norms and high levels of consensus about values from religious or political commitments.

Durkheim's analysis provides an excellent example of the importance of the group for individuals. Following Durkheim's lead, many sociologists have studied suicide, confirming the importance of group ties for individuals in religious, educational, and social group networks that provide integration of individuals into the society (Hall 2002; Pescosolido and Georgianna 1989).

No individual is an island. Even a hermit cannot think without the language he learned in childhood and cannot organize his life without the cultural categories and skills learned earlier in life. The importance of groups is an underlying theme throughout this text. Groups are essential to human life, but to understand them more fully, we must understand the various kinds of groups in which humans participate.

Types of Groups

Each of us belongs to several types of groups. Some groups provide intimacy and close relationships; others do not. Some are required affiliations; others are voluntary. Some provide personal satisfaction; others are obligatory or necessary for survival. The following discussion points out several types of groups and reasons individuals belong to them.

Primary groups are characterized by close contacts and lasting personal relationships. They operate at the micro level. Your family members and best friends, school classmates and close work associates, and clubs whose members are close friends are all of primary importance in your everyday life. Primary groups provide a sense of belonging and shared identity; group members care about you and you care about them, creating a sense of loyalty. Approval and disapproval from the primary group influence the activities you choose to pursue. Belonging rather than accomplishing a task is the main reason for membership. The group is of *intrinsic value*—enjoyed for its own sake—rather than for some *utilitarian value* such as making money.

For individuals, primary groups provide an anchor point in society. You were born into a primary group—your family. You play a variety of roles in primary relationships—those of spouse, parent, child, sibling, relative, close friend. You meet with other members face-to-face or keep in touch on a regular basis and know a great deal about their lives. What makes them happy or angry? What are sensitive issues? In primary groups you share values, say what you think, let down your hair, dress as you like, and share your concerns and emotions, your successes and failures (Goffman 1959, 1967). Charles H. Cooley, who first discussed the term *primary group*, saw these relationships as the source of close human feelings and emotions—love, cooperation, and concern (Cooley 1909).

Secondary groups are those with formal, impersonal, businesslike relationships. In the modern world, people cannot always live under the protective wing of primary group relationships. Secondary groups are usually large and task oriented because they have a specific purpose to achieve and a focus on accomplishing a goal. As children grow, they move from the security and acceptance of primary groups—the home and neighborhood peer group—to the large school classroom where they become one of the 30 students vying for teacher approval and competing for rewards. Similarly, the job world requires formal relations and procedures: applications; interviews; contracts; employment based on specific skills, training, and job knowledge; and a trial period. In Western cultures, we assume that people should not be hired because of nepotism but rather for their competence to carry out the role expectations in the position.

Fieldworkers in South America work together to gather a mushroom crop.

Source: © Tim Travis, Down the Road Publishing, LLC (www.downtheroad.org).

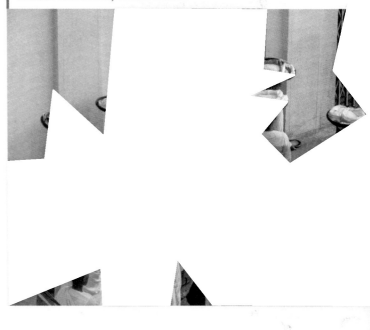

Even Buddhist monks and nuns, who spend much of their lives devoted to private meditation, need the support and solidarity of a group.

Source: Photo courtesy of Elise Roberts.

Relationships in secondary groups are based on accomplishing required tasks and achieving the goals of the group. Because each individual carries out a specialized task, communication between members is often specialized

This Chinese family—a primary group—enjoys one another's company as they play a game of Mahjong. They will not be richer or have more prestige because of the time they spend at this game; the connections are valued for intrinsic reasons.

Source: Photo by Jeanne Ballantine.

The small micro- and large macro-level groups often occur together. Behind most successful secondary groups are primary groups. Consider the small work group that eats together or goes out for a beer Friday afternoons. These relationships help individuals feel a part of larger organizations, just as residents of large urban areas have small groups of neighborhood friends. In mega churches with 30,000 members, the focus of programming is on creating small support groups (primary groups) within the huge congregation (Miller 1997; Sargeant 2000; Wuthnow 1994). In a formal setting such as a university or corporation, primary groups can play a major role in making people feel they belong. For instance, many students live with roommates at the university, study with a small group, go out Friday night with friends, and regularly have meals with close friends. Table 5.2 summarizes some of the dimensions of primary and secondary groups.

Problems in primary groups can affect performance in secondary groups. Consider the problems of a student who has an argument with a significant other or roommate or experiences a failure of their family support system due to divorce or other problems. Self-concepts and social skills diminish during times of family stress and affect group relationships in other parts of one's life (Drafke and Kossen 2002; Parish and Parish 1991).

as well. Contacts with doctors, store clerks, and even professors are generally formal and impersonal parts of organizational life. Sometimes associations with secondary groups are long lasting, sometimes of short duration—as in the courses you are taking this term. Secondary groups operate at the meso and macro levels of our social world, but they affect individuals at the micro level.

As societies modernize, they evolve from small towns and close, primary relationships to predominantly urban areas with more formal, secondary relationships. In the postindustrial world, as family members are scattered across countries and around the world, secondary relationships have come to play ever greater roles in people's lives. Large work organizations may provide day care, health clinics, financial planning, courses to upgrade skills, and sports leagues.

THINKING SOCIOLOGICALLY

In the past, raising children was considered a family task, done by the primary group. Today, many children are in child care settings, often run by secondary groups. Can a secondary group develop love and personal attentiveness formerly provided by families? Can the secondary group provide better care than abusive families? Is this an issue that policy makers should consider?

TABLE 5.2 **Primary and Secondary Group Characteristics**

	Primary Group	Secondary Group
Quality of relationships	Personal orientation	Goal orientation
Duration of relationships	Usually long-term	Variable; often short-term
Breadth of activities	Broad; usually involving many activities	Narrow; usually involving few, largely goal-directed, activities
Subjective perception of relationships	An end in itself (friendship, belonging)	A means to an end (to accomplish a task, earn money)
Typical examples	Families, close friendships	Coworkers, political organizations

Reference groups are composed of members who act as role models and establish standards against which members measure their conduct. Individuals look to reference groups to set guidelines for behavior and decision making. The term is often used to refer to models in one's chosen career field; students in premed, nursing, computer science, business, or sociology programs watch the behavior patterns of those who have become professionals in their chosen career. When people make the transition from student to professional, they adopt clothing, time schedules, salary expectations, and other characteristics of the new role. They emulate those who epitomize success in the field. Professional organizations such as the American Bar Association or American Sociological Association set standards for behavior and achievements. People who already belong to a reference group, such as practicing lawyers, look up to leaders within the field. However, it is possible to be an attorney or an athlete and not aspire to be like others in the group if they are unethical or abuse substances such as steroids; one may instead be shaped by the values of a church group or a political group with which one identifies. Not every group one belongs to is a reference group; it must provide a standard by which you evaluate your behavior for it to be a reference group.

Ethnic groups provide some adolescents with strong reference group standards by which to judge themselves. The stronger the ethnic pride and identification, the more some teens may separate themselves from contact with members of other ethnic groups (Schaefer 2006). This can be functional or dysfunctional for the teens as shown in the next section on in-groups and out-groups. However, a reference group might operate at the meso level of the social system.

One group can serve several purposes, for example as a primary group, a peer group, and a reference group. These different terms refer to different features of a group. For example, a *peer group,* people who share similar age or social status, could also be a reference group. The cross-country team may be Jared's peer group, but his everyday decisions may be based on standards of a religious group or professional society. Note also that someone may have a reference group in which one is not actually a member. The volleyball team or the American Medical Association may be Raluca's reference groups, even though she has not yet attained membership in either one. However, if the standards and judgments of members of those groups influence her own decisions and give her direction, they are reference groups for her.

An **in-group** is one to which an individual feels a sense of loyalty and belonging; it also may serve as a reference group. An **out-group** is one to which an individual does not belong; but more than that, it is a group that is often in competition or in opposition to an in-group.

Membership in an in-group may be based on sex, race, ethnic group, social class, religion, political affiliation, the school one attends, an interest group such as the fraternity

Bloods gang members in Los Angeles use their in-group hand signal to identify one another.

Source: © Steve Starr / Corbis.

or sorority one joins, or the area where one lives. People tend to judge others according to their own in-group identity. Members of the in-group—for example, supporters of a high school team—often feel hostility toward or reject out-group members, boosters of the rival team. The perceived outside threat or hostility is often exaggerated, but it does help create the in-group members' feelings of solidarity. Sometimes, even one's declared major is the source of in-group loyalties, as students from biology ridicule psychology, or history majors bash sociology. Unfortunately, these feelings can result in prejudice and ethnocentrism, overlooking the individual differences of group members. Teen groups or gangs such as the Bloods and the Crips are examples of in-groups and out-groups in action, as are the ethnic and religious conflicts between Sunni and Shiite Muslims in Iraq; Serbs, Bosnian, and Albanian Muslims in the former Yugoslavia; Israeli Jews and Palestinians; Hutus and Tutsis in Rwanda; and Catholics and Protestants in Northern Ireland. In each case, the group loyalty is enhanced by hostility toward the out-group, resulting in gang conflicts and war.

THINKING SOCIOLOGICALLY

What are some examples of your own group affiliations: Primary groups? Secondary groups? Peer groups? Reference groups? In-groups and out-groups?

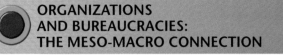

ORGANIZATIONS AND BUREAUCRACIES: THE MESO-MACRO CONNECTION

Our days are filled with activities that involve us with complex organizations: from the doctor's appointment to the college classes; from the political rally for the issue we are supporting to Sabbath worship in our church, temple, or mosque; from paying state sales tax for our toothpaste to buying a sandwich at a fast-food franchise. Figure 5.6 shows institutions of society, each made up of thousands of organizations (your medical organization, educational organization, religious group, economic corporations, political movements, the government itself) and each following the cultural norms of our society. We have statuses and roles in each group, and these link us to networks and the larger social world.

How did these organizational forms develop? Let us consider briefly the transformations of organizations into their modern forms and the characteristics of meso-level organizations today.

The Evolution of Modern Organizations

Empires around the world have risen and fallen since the dawn of civilization. Some economic, political, and religious systems have flourished; others such as monarchies and fascism have withered. We cannot understand our social world at any historical or modern time without comprehending the organizational structures and processes present at that time. Recall the discussion of types of societies, from hunter-gatherer to postindustrial, in Chapter 3. Each type of society entails different organizational structures, from early cities and feudal manors to craft guilds, heavy industries, and web-based companies (Blau 1956).

The development of modern organizations and bureaucracies began with industrialization in the 1700s and was becoming the dominant form of industrial organizations by the 1800s. **Rationality**, the attempt to reach maximum efficiency, became the trend in managing organizations and was thought to be the best way to run organizations—efficiently and with rules that are rationally designed to accomplish goals (Weber 1947). People were expected to behave in purposeful, coordinated ways to reach goals efficiently. No longer were decisions made by tradition, custom, or the whim of a despot but by trained leaders who planned policies to achieve organizational efficiency. Tasks became more specialized, and some manual jobs were taken over by machines. Standardization of products allowed for greater productivity, precision, and speed. These modern rational organizations, called **formal organizations**, are complex secondary groups deliberately formed to pursue and achieve certain goals.

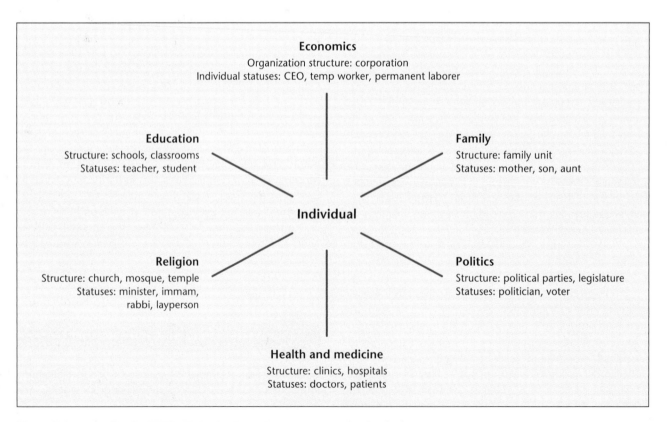

Figure 5.6   Our Social World: Institutions, Organizations, and Individual Status

Cambridge University, General Motors Corporation, and your university are all formal organizations.

Bureaucracies are specific types of very large formal organizations that have the purpose of maximizing efficiency; they are characterized by formal relations between participants, clearly laid out procedures and rules, and pursuit of stated goals. Bureaucracies evolved as the most efficient way of producing products economically for mass markets (Ritzer 2004a).

As societies became dominated by large organizations, fewer people worked the family farm or owned a cottage industry in their homes, and the number of small shopkeepers diminished. Today, some countries are *organizational societies* in which a majority of the members work in organizations. Many other societies around the world are moving in this direction.

Societies making the transition between traditional and modern organizational structures often have a blend of the two, and in many industrializing countries traditional organizational systems mix with newer forms. Bribery, corruption, and favoritism govern some nations as they move toward modern bureaucracies. People in government jobs are promoted based on whom they are connected to in their family tree, not on the basis of their competence as assessed by formal training, examinations, or criteria derived from the needs of the position and organization; breaking down old systems can create disruption, even anomie, in societies undergoing these transitions.

Postindustrial societies feature high dependence on technology and information-sharing. Few people live and work on farms. In the United States today, only 2.5 percent of the civilian labor force, that is 3,479,000 people, are working in agriculture, forestry, and fisheries out of a total civilian labor force of 140,863,000. This is compared to 11.6 percent in farm-related occupations in 1950 and 63.7 percent in 1850 (Europa World Year Book 2005).

THINKING SOCIOLOGICALLY

Make a list of your activities in a typical day. Which of these activities are, and which are not, associated with large formal organizations?

Characteristics of Modern Organizations

Organizations and modern life are almost synonymous. Live in one, and you belong to the other. In this section, we consider types of organizations, some characteristics of bureaucracy, and some processes and problems that occur in organizations.

Think about the many organizations that regularly affect your life: the legal system that passes laws, your college, your workplace, and voluntary organizations to which you belong.

This operations center for the CIA is an example of a modern formal organization, which is not only governed by formal rules and impersonal relations but increasingly involves extensive communication via the impersonal medium of the computer.

Source: © Roger Ressmeyer / Corbis.

Individuals require organizations for human interaction and to meet their needs, and organizations need humans in order to hold positions and carry out tasks or roles. Some organizations, such as the local chapter of the Rotary Club or a chapter of a sorority, function at the micro level. Everyone is in a face-to-face relationship with every other member of the organization. However, those chapters are part of a nationwide organization that is actually a meso-level corporation. At another level in terms of size, the federal government is a very complex organization that influences the lives of every citizen, and some transnational corporations are global in their reach; both operate at the macro level.

All organizations must gain *compliance* from members to follow rules and procedures and obey the orders of persons with authority. Etzioni (1975) compiled information from 60 studies and found that most, but not all, organizations fall into one of the following types based on how they get members to comply with rules:

Utilitarian organizations provide benefits to members in the form of wages or profits; usually they gain compliance by providing income that individuals need to live, in exchange for work to earn a living.

In Philadelphia, people come together for the voluntary civic action of cleaning up the community.

Source: © Nilsen Alan Brian / Corbis Sygma.

Coercive organizations are involuntary. Compliance is by force. Prisons, mental hospitals, some military systems, and schools for young people are examples. Members are generally segregated from the outside world much of the time and forced to behave according to rigid rules.

Normative organizations are most often voluntary associations; people join because they believe in the organization's purposes or goals. Compliance is based on moral or political beliefs, and personal satisfaction is the motive for joining. In other words, people belong to normative organizations because they believe in the message or the value of the organization's purpose. Examples include religious organizations, political parties, and groups representing social causes.

Voluntary organizations have been common in the United States throughout its history. Girl Scouts and Boy Scouts, 4-H clubs, bridge clubs, environmental protection groups, sports leagues, and opera or museum fundraising associations are all examples of voluntary organizations. Membership in voluntary organizations is generally higher in the United States than many other countries (Curtis, Grabb, and Baer 1992; Johnson and Johnson 2006). People join voluntary organizations because they believe in a cause or because they enjoy the social contact or activity. A famous French observer of U.S. culture in the 1830s, Alexis de Tocqueville (1877), noted that citizens join groups, from youth groups and religious groups to veterans and occupational groups, based on common interests, desire for change in their lives, and need to belong.

In recent years, membership in many voluntary organizations has dropped, a factor discussed in the next Sociology in Your Social World; others argue that new types of affiliations and interactions, including the Internet, are replacing some older affiliations.

THINKING SOCIOLOGICALLY

Categorize the organizations to which you belong using Etzioni's typology of organizations (utilitarian, coercive, normative, and voluntary).

Characteristics of Bureaucracy

You need groceries. You probably expect to go into the store, see clearly marked prices on items, even broken down by price-per-unit for comparative purposes. You expect to go to the cashier and pay the set price that is established by the bureaucratic system. Yet if you have been to a Caribbean, African, Asian, or Middle Eastern market, you know that the bartering system is used to settle on a mutually agreeable price. This system is more personal and involves intense interaction between the seller and buyer, but it takes more time, is less efficient, and can be frustrating to the uninitiated visitor accustomed to the relative efficiency and predictability of bureaucracy. As societies transition, they adopt bureaucratic forms of organization.

To get a drivers' license, pay school fees, or buy tickets for a popular concert or game, you may have to stand in a long line. Finally, after waiting in line, you discover that you have forgotten your social security number or they do not take a credit card. The rules and red tape are irksome. Yet what is the alternative? Some institutions have adopted telephone and online registration or ticket purchases, but even with this automated system problems can occur. Frustrations with bureaucracy are part of modern life, but the alternatives (such as bartering) are often even more frustrating or bewildering to those who are used to bureaucratic efficiency.

Most organizations in modern society—hospitals, schools, churches, government agencies, industries, banks, even large clubs—are bureaucracies. Therefore, understanding these complex organizations is critical to understanding the modern social world in which we live.

Max Weber (1864–1920), a famous social scientist who lived and worked in Germany in the early 1900s, looked for reasons behind the massive changes taking place in societies that were transitioning from traditional to bureaucratic, capitalistic society. He wanted to understand why the rate of change was more rapid in some parts of Europe than others and why bureaucracy came to dominate forms of organization in some countries. While traditional society looked to the past for guidance, bureaucratic industrial society required a new form of thinking and behavior, a change in attitude toward rationality; he observed that leadership in

Sociology in Your Social World

Bowling Alone: Individualism versus Sense of Community

The days of bowling leagues are declining with membership down significantly in recent years. Yet more people in the United States bowl than vote today, often enjoying the sport as individuals rather than in organized groups. For sociologists, this points to a broad trend—those who once participated in group activities are turning inward and not joining organized groups (Putnam 1995, 2001).

Does this reflect a breakdown of the U.S. community? Parent-Teacher Associations (PTAs), Red Cross, bowling leagues, and other civic groups were all down in numbers in the mid-1990s. The result is that people get together less often. The enthusiasm for organizational participation that de Tocqueville observed some 200 years ago appears to be dampening. Why are people turning off others and turning inward? Putnam speculates that loss of faith in institutions and the existence of television and computers in many homes keep people from connecting with others. Staying home and watching TV or surfing the net replaces a night out with friends.

In a separate study, a team of University of California, Berkeley, sociologists also analyze the relationship between individualism and sense of community. They conclude that "American individualism, by denying community and history, disables us for citizenship in an interdependent world." As individuals lose contact with others, they face private problems alone. What the United States needs,

This young man spends a wireless evening rather than going out with friends, a pattern that some commentators think is growing as Americans become increasingly insular and satisfied with private "cocoons."

Source: © Oleksandr Gumerov.

according to the authors of this study, is a greater sense of community to give individuals a sense of belonging and to link the micro and macro levels of the social world (Bellah et al. 1991). In other words, individuals should think about bowling together or find other ways to connect and build a sense of community.

Not all agree that individualism has come to dominate U.S. society; different types of groups and affiliations, some based on new technologies, are emerging to replace bowling leagues and similar organizations (Putnam 2001).

business and government was moving from traditional forms with powerful families and charismatic leaders toward more efficient and less personal bureaucracy.

THINKING SOCIOLOGICALLY

If you were on the city council in your city or town, how would you go about creating a stronger sense of connectedness among residents and more investment in the health and vitality of the community? Do local festivals, sports leagues, coffee shops, outdoors music gatherings, or board-walks along rivers help? If not, what can pull people out of

their insulated lives to engage with other citizens and become concerned participants?

Weber's (1947) term, **ideal type bureaucracy**, refers to the dominant and essential characteristics of organizations that are designed for reliability and efficiency. It does not imply a good or perfect organization; it simply describes an organization with a particular set of traits. Any particular bureaucracy is unlikely to have all of the characteristics in the ideal type, but the degree of bureaucratization is measured by how closely an organization resembles the core characteristics of the ideal type. The following characteristics of Weber's ideal type bureaucracy provide an example of how these characteristics relate to schools:

1. *Division of labor based on technical competence:* Administrators lead but do not teach, and instructors teach only in areas of their certification; staff are assigned positions for which credentials make them most qualified; and recruitment and promotion are governed by formal policies.

2. *Administrative hierarchy:* There is a specified chain of command and designated channels of communication, from school board to superintendent to principal to teacher.

3. *Formal rules and regulations:* Written procedures and rules—perhaps published in an administrative manual—spell out system-wide requirements, including discipline practices, testing procedures, curricula, sick days for teachers, penalties for student tardiness, field trip policies, and other matters.

4. *Impersonal relationships:* Formal relationships tend to prevail between teachers and students and between teachers and administrative staff (superintendents, principals, counselors); written records and formal communication provide a paper trail for all decisions.

5. *Emphasis on rationality and efficiency to reach goals:* Use of established processes based on the best interest of the school. Efficiency is defined in terms of lowest overall cost to the organization in reaching a goal, not in terms of personal consequences.

6. *Provision of life-long careers:* Employees may spend their entire careers working for the same organization, working their way up the hierarchy through promotions.

Although the list of characteristics makes bureaucracies sound formal and rigid, informal structures allow organizational members to deviate from rules to both meet goals of the organization more efficiently and to humanize an otherwise uncaring and sterile workplace. The **informal structure** includes the unwritten norms and the interpersonal networks that people utilize within an organization to carry out roles. Likewise, while bylaws, constitutions, or contracts spell out the way things are supposed to be done, people often develop unwritten shortcuts to accomplish goals. The U.S. postal service has rules specifying that letter carriers are not supposed to walk across people's lawns, yet if they did not find shortcuts, it would take many more hours before people would have their mail delivered.

Informal norms are not always compatible with those of the formal organization; consider the following example from a famous classical study. In the Western Electric plant near Chicago, the study found that new workers were quickly socialized to do "a fair day's work," and those who did more or less than the established norm— what the work group thought was fair—were considered "rate busters" or "chiselers" and experienced pressure from the group to conform. These informal mechanisms gave informal groups of workers a degree of power in the organization (Roethlisberger and Dickson 1939).

An example of rational bureaucracy is found in the fast food empires springing up around the world. The next Sociology around the World describes the trend toward the McDonaldization of society.

THINKING SOCIOLOGICALLY

How closely do each of Weber's characteristics of ideal-type bureaucracy describe your college or your work setting? Is your college highly bureaucratized, with many rules and regulations? Are decisions based on efficiency and cost-effectiveness, educational quality, or both? To what extent is your work setting characterized by hierarchy, formal rules governing your work time, and impersonality?

Individuals in Bureaucracies

Lindi England, a young woman from a small town in West Virginia looking for opportunity and adventure, joined the military; she became a victim and a scapegoat of bureaucracy and group pressure. The bureaucracy was the U.S. military; the setting was the Abu Ghraib prison in Iraq; the group pressure was to conform under stressful conditions and "go along with the guards" who were abusing and humiliating prisoners (Zimbardo 2004). When the scandal about the abuse broke in the U.S. news, Lindi England was guilty of atrocities, but she was also the scapegoat, taking the blame for others' atrocities perpetrated against Iraqis, many of whom had not yet been tried or convicted.

Humans can be moral, altruistic, and self-sacrificing for the good of others, but nations and other extremely large organizations (such as corporations or government) are inherently driven by a cost-benefit ratio (Neibuhr 1932). As one moves toward larger and more impersonal bureaucracies, the nature of interaction often changes. A generous person may become anything but forgiving and self-effacing when confronted with group pressures. Caring and humane military officers may order bombing strikes or allow abuse of prisoners, even though they know that some innocent people will be killed or maimed; in the military command in a war, a cold, impersonal cost-benefit analysis takes priority. In bureaucracies, self-preservation is the core value; rational choice or exchange theory is often effective in explaining interactions in these contexts.

Professionals in bureaucracies include doctors, lawyers, engineers, professors, and others who have certain special attributes: advanced education, knowledge and competency in a field, high levels of autonomy to make decisions based on their expertise, strong commitment to their field, a service orientation and a commitment to the needs of the client, standards and regulations set by the profession, and a sense of

Sociology around the World

The McDonaldization of Society

The process of rationalization described by Max Weber—the attempt to reach maximum bureaucratic efficiency—comes in a new modern version, expanded and streamlined, as exemplified by the fast-food restaurant business and chain and "box" stores found around the world. Efficient, rational, predictable sameness is sweeping the world—from diet centers such as Nutri/System to Seven-Elevens and from WalMart to Gap clothing stores with their look-alike layouts. Most major world cities feature McDonalds or Kentucky Fried Chicken in the traditional main plazas or train stations for the flustered foreigners and curious native consumers.

The McDonaldization of society, as George Ritzer (2004b) calls it, refers to several trends: First, *efficiency* is maximized by the sameness—same store plans, same mass-produced items, same procedures. Second is *predictability,* the knowledge that each hamburger or piece of chicken will be the same, leaving nothing to chance. Third, everything

is *calculated* so that the organization can assure that everything fits a standard—every burger is cooked the same number of seconds on each side. Fourth, *increased control* over employees and customers so there are fewer variables to consider—including substitution of technology for human labor as a way to ensure predictability and efficiency.

What is the result of this efficient, predictable, planned, automated new world? According to Ritzer, the world is becoming more dehumanized and the efficiency is taking over individual creativity and human interactions. The mom-and-pop grocery, bed and breakfasts, and local craft or clothing shops are rapidly becoming a thing of the past, giving way to the McClones. This process of the McDonaldization of society, meaning principles of efficiency and rationalization exemplified by fast food chains, are coming to dominate more and more sectors of our social world (Ritzer 1998, 2004a, 2004b). While there are aspects of this predictability that we all like, there is also a loss of uniqueness and local flavor that individual entrepreneurs bring to a community.

---

intrinsic satisfaction from the work (rather than motivation rooted in external rewards, like salary). Professionals also claim authority, power, and control in their work area because of their mastery or expertise in a field (Hall 2002; Pavalko 1988; Ritzer and Walczak 1986). Professionals may face conflicting loyalties to their profession and to the bureaucratic organization in which they are employed. A researcher hired by a tobacco company faced a dilemma when his research findings did not support the company position that nicotine is not addictive. Should he be a whistle-blower and publicly challenge the organization? Several professionals have done so but lost their positions as a result.

Bureaucracy, some argue, is the number one enemy of professionalism, for it reduces autonomy; bureaucrats insist that authority rests in the person who holds an organizational status or title in the hierarchy rather than the person with the most expertise; it tends to reward people with external rewards rather than internal motivations; and it focuses on the needs of the organization as primary rather than on the needs of the client. The potential clash between professionals and bureaucracy raises key concerns as universities, hospitals, and other large organizations are governed increasingly by bureaucratic principles (Roberts and Donahue 2000). Alienation among professionals occurs

when they are highly regulated rather than when they have some decision-making authority and are granted some autonomy (Hall 2002). For example, high-tech companies that depend on engineering designers find that hierarchical structures undermine productivity, whereas factors such as intrinsic satisfaction, flexible hours, and relaxed work environments are central to creative productivity (Florida 2004; Friedman 2005; Molotch 2003).

THINKING SOCIOLOGICALLY

When you shop or eat, is it at McClones or at individually owned stores? Can anything be done to protect the non-McClones, or are they destined to be eliminated by the competition?

Minorities in bureaucracies may come up against a **glass ceiling**, barriers that keep females and other minority group members from reaching high levels of management in organizations. The result is that they are found disproportionately in midlevel positions with little authority and less pay than men and nonminority group members" (Chaffins,

Google Chairman and CEO, Dr. Eric Schmidt (second from right), meets with cofounders Larry Page (on right) and Sergey Brin (on scooter) and two employees at one of the recreation areas around the Google offices in Mountain View, California. Casual environments, comfortable attire, and nonhierarchical relationships characterize many high-tech industries today because creative people demand it.

Source: © Peter DaSilva / Corbis.

Forbes, and Fuqua 1995). When employees have little chance for promotion, they have less ambition and loyalty to the organization (Kanter 1977). Research indicates that women executives bring valuable alternative perspectives, share information readily, give employees greater autonomy, and stress interconnectedness between parts of the organization, resulting in a more democratic type of leadership (Helgesen 1995; Kramer 2001).

Women who reach senior positions share some characteristics that help make them successful. They are familiar with the organizational system and leadership roles, are prepared for competition, capitalize on their strengths, and refuse to yield to pressures. In addition, the number of other women in the organization holding senior positions affects the newcomer's experience. The more senior women there are in the organization, the more likely newcomers are to find support.

The interaction of people who see things differently because of religious beliefs, ethnic backgrounds, and gender experiences increases productivity in many organizations. Having a wide range of perspectives leads to better problem solving (Florida 2004; Molotch 2003).

Problems in Bureaucracies

Bureaucratic inefficiency and red tape are legendary and have been the theme for many classic novels, from Charles Dickens' *Bleak House*, which describes the legal system in England in the 1800s, to George Orwell's (1984), which

depicts a sterile, controlled environment. Yet bureaucracies are likely to stay, for they are the most efficient form of modern organization yet devised. Nonetheless, several individual and organizational problems created by bureaucratic structures are important to understand.

Alienation, feeling uninvolved, uncommitted, unappreciated, and unconnected, occurs when workers experience routine, boring tasks or dead-end jobs with no possibility of advancement. Marx believed that alienation is a structural feature of capitalism with serious consequences: workers lose their sense of purpose and seem to become dehumanized and objectified in the process of creating a product, a product that they often do not see completed and for which they do not get the profits if it is well made (Marx 1964/1844).

Dissatisfaction comes from low pay and poor benefits; routine, repetitive, and fragmented tasks; lack of challenge and autonomy leading to boredom; and poor working conditions. Workers who see possibilities for advancement put more energy into the organization, but those stuck in their positions are less involved and put more energy into activities outside the workplace (Kanter 1977).

Workers' productive behavior is not solely a result of rational factors such as pay and working conditions but is influenced by emotions, beliefs, and norms (Roethlisberger and Dickson 1939). Many organizations have moved toward workplace democracy, employee participation in decision making, and employee ownership plans.

THINKING SOCIOLOGICALLY

How might participation in decision making and increased autonomy for workers enhance commitment and productivity in your place of work or in your college? What might be some risks or downsides to such worker input and freedom?

Oligarchy, the concentration of power in the hands of a small group, is a common occurrence in organizations. In the early 1900s, Robert Michels, a French sociologist, wrote about the **iron law of oligarchy**, the idea that power becomes concentrated in the hands of a small group of leaders in political, business, voluntary, or other organizations. Initially, organizational needs, more than the motivation for power, cause these few stable leaders to emerge. As organizations grow, a division of labor emerges so that only a few leaders have access to information, resources, and the overall picture; this in turn causes leaders who enjoy their elite positions of power to become entrenched (Michels 1911/1967). An example is the Enron Corporation scandal in which Enron executives hid information about financial problems from workers and investors.

Goal Displacement occurs when the original motives or goals of the organization are displaced by new, secondary goals that become primary. Organizations form to meet specific goals. Religious organizations are founded to worship a deity and serve humanity on behalf of that deity, schools are founded to educate children, and social work agencies are organized to serve the needs of citizens who seem to have fallen between the cracks. Yet over time, original goals may be met or become less important as other motivations and interests emerge (Merton 1968; Whyte 1956).

Parkinson's Law, which states that in a bureaucracy work expands to fill the time and space available for its completion, is an example of inefficiency (Parkinson 1957). If we build a new room on our house, we are likely to fill it to capacity. If classes are canceled for a day, our free day gets filled up with other activities. If we have two tests to study for, each takes half a day; but if we have one, it may still take most of the day. Despite the expansion of space or time, we still do not seem to have enough time or room. Organizations work similarly; Parkinson's point is that organizations grow automatically, sometimes beyond efficiency or effectiveness.

Policy makers have explored possibilities of other ways of organizing society. *Alternative organization structures* refer to new approaches that have developed to deal with some of the problems cited above. In 1994, United Airlines turned to Employee Stock Ownership, and the only operating mine in Wales is employee-owned (Blasi and Kruse 1991). In recent years, United Airlines has had problems, some say because management did not cooperate with employees (Schneider 2002). Other companies, *democratic-collective organizations*, rely on cooperation, place authority and decision making in the collective group, and use personal appeals to ensure that everyone participates in problem solving. The rules, hierarchy, and status distinctions are minimized, and hiring is often based on shared values and friendships (Deming 2000). Members believe these organizations are more humane and workers feel connected to the purpose and the product. The hope is that these new forms of organization—nonbureaucratic forms—may actually be more a effective way to organize a postindustrial corporation.

Although we may fantasize about escaping from the rat-race world, about isolating ourselves on an island or living as a hermit in a house on stilts, groups and bureaucracies are a part of modern life that few can escape. These are only a few examples of problems in bureaucracies; some alternatives to bureaucracy are discussed in the next section.

THINKING SOCIOLOGICALLY

In what areas of your college or workplace does Parkinson's Law apply? What policies might lessen the chance that Parkinson's Law will occur?

NATIONAL AND GLOBAL NETWORKS: THE MACRO LEVEL

In one sense, learning to understand people who are unlike us, to network with people who have different cultures, and to make allowances for alternative ideas about society and human behavior have become core competencies in our globalizing social world. Increasingly, colleges have study-abroad programs, jobs open up for teaching English as a second language, and corporations seek employees who are multilingual and culturally competent in diverse settings. One rather recent college graduate with a sociology degree found that she could use her sociology skills in leading groups of college-aged students in international travel experiences. She explains this applied use of sociology in the next The Applied Sociologist at Work.

Of course, macro-level issues go well beyond international travel and networking. With modern communication and transportation systems and the ability to transfer ideas and money with a touch of the keyboard, global networks are superseding national boundaries. Multinational corporations now employ citizens from around the world and can make their own rules. National systems and international organizations, from the United Nations to the World Bank to multinational corporations, are typically governed though rational bureaucratic systems.

One complicating factor at the national and global levels is multilingualism, the reality that many languages are used to communicate. Although Spanish, Chinese, and Arabic are widely used in homes across the globe, English has become the language of commerce; this is because much of the political and economic power and control over the expansion of technology has been located in English-speaking countries.

Technology has some interesting implications for human interaction. E-mail, web pages, chat rooms, and blogs have made it possible for people around the world to talk with each other, exchange ideas, and even develop friendships. When Keith, one of the coauthors, was conducting research in Wales, he was able to set up interviews through the Internet. In other parts of the world, dictators can no longer keep the citizenry from knowing what people outside their country think. In China, as fast as officials censor information on the World Wide Web, computer experts find ways around the restrictions. The process of change is occurring so rapidly that we cannot know what technology will mean for the global world, but it is almost certain that the processes of interaction across national lines will continue to be transformed. The World Wide Web, after all, was not invented until 1989, and e-mail has been available to most citizens—even in affluent countries—only since the early 1990s (Brasher 2004).

Within nations, people with common interests can contact one another, be it organic food interests or peace advocates. Hate groups also set up web pages and mobilize others

THE APPLIED SOCIOLOGIST AT WORK   Elise Roberts

Using Sociology in International Travel and Intercultural Education

After graduating from Macalester College with a bachelor's degree in Sociology, I left the country to backpack through Mexico and Central America. There were times while traveling when I consciously "thought sociologically" as I analyzed Latin American gender roles or observed Mayan-Latino/Latina relations. More than this, my previous studies helped me understand social constructionism. My education helped me become more culturally sensitive and objective in the ways I viewed other societies. Oftentimes, observing a common daily occurrence in Latin America made me question the social construction of my own society, and it made me wonder why I had never thought twice about the way certain things are done and seen in the United States. More than any other experience in my life, international travel helped me examine my own societal assumptions and further understand how society creates so much of one's experience and view of the world.

After almost a year traveling and taking Spanish lessons, I found a job leading groups of teenagers on alternative-education trips abroad. I was excited to get the job, mostly because I was out of money and terrified that I would be forced to return to the States and begin that post-college entry into the real world. What a disheartening thought! Of course, I was soon to learn that leading groups of teenagers in other countries is actually very hard work.

What struck me first upon meeting my first group was that I had very few students who initially understood this sociological perspective that I took for granted, and that was so insightful in dealing with others. At times, my students would point and laugh at local people, convinced that they could not be understood because they were speaking English. They would make fun of the way things were done, calling them "weird" or "stupid." They would mock the local traditions, until we discussed comparable traditions in American culture. These students were not mean or unintelligent; in fact, they loved the places we were seeing and the people we were meeting. They just thought everything was factually, officially *weird*. They had been socialized to understand their own society's ways as "right" and "normal." They were fully absorbed in the U.S. society, and they had never questioned it before.

It was interesting to think about how to teach the concepts of social constructionism in such an applied environment, and it was rewarding to see such a need for concepts that had often seemed just based in textbooks and theory. My coleaders and I learned to have fun while encouraging our students to become more socially conscious and analytical about their travel experience. We sent the groups out on scavenger hunts, where they would inevitably come back and proudly announce what they had paid for a rickshaw ride—and then be shocked to learn that they had paid 10 times the local price. We would use this experience to talk about the role of foreigners, the assumptions that the local population made due to our skin color, and the culture of bartering. The responses to some questions on the hunt were gestures they could not understand, like pointing with the lips and side-to-side nodding. We would use these experiences to discuss nonverbal communication and gestures that we take for granted in U.S. culture. Of course, we would encourage them to interact with the people around them, which naturally helped them understand the struggles facing immigrants and non-English speakers in the United States. We would force them to have conversations while standing toe-to-toe with each other, and they would finish with backaches from leaning away from one another. We would not allow them to explain their behavior with "because it's creepy to stand so close together," even though this was the consensus. "Why?" we would ask, over and over again throughout the semester. "Why do you feel uncomfortable? Why is this weird?" Of course, while traveling internationally, one is surrounded by various other sociological issues, such as different racial or ethnic conflicts, gender roles, or class hierarchies, and learning about these issues was a part of our program as well. Without realizing it, many group conversations and meetings began to remind me of some of my favorite Macalester classes. "Study sociology!" I would say, plugging my major to the most interested students.

I have always thought that travel was an incredibly useful means not only to learn about the society and culture one is visiting but also to learn much about oneself and one's home society. For teenagers who otherwise might never step back to think about the role of being a foreigner or the traditions and social patterns they take for granted, it is even more important. Traveling abroad on my own and leading programs abroad were such extremely rich and rewarding experiences not only due to the cross-cultural exchanges and the intense personal examination that I experienced and saw in my students but also because it was fascinating and rewarding to be able to use my sociology degree every day of my trip.

Elise Roberts graduated from Macalester College with a major in Sociology. Her recent travels took her through Central America, the South Pacific, and many parts of Asia. She is currently working with immigrants in an AmeriCorps program in Chicago and is considering graduate programs in sociology or social work that focus on international social welfare and cross-national ties.

with their view of the world, and terrorists use the Internet to communicate around the world. Clearly, ability to communicate around the globe is transforming the world and our nations in ways that affect local communities and private individuals. Indeed, the Internet has become a major source of consumption—a wide range of products can be obtained through Internet orders from websites that have no geographical home base. There is no actual warehouse or manufacturing plant, and there might not be a home office; business is global and exists in the Ethernet, not in any specific nation (Ritzer 2004b). It makes one rethink national and global loyalties and realities.

In discussing rationalization and the McDonaldization of society in the previous section, we explored the very utilitarian approach to everything that bureaucratization requires. Family loyalties are considered less important than rational choices based on the needs of the corporation. Feelings are subordinated to analytic cognitive processes. Efficiency and calculability are highly prized in the rationalized or McDonaldized social system. However, as these Western notions of how public life should operate are exported to other countries, a severe backlash has occurred. In many Middle Eastern Islamic countries, for example, these values clash with Muslim loyalties and priorities. The result has been high levels of anger at the United States. Many scholars believe that Middle Eastern anger at the United States is not based on opposition to freedom and democracy, as our politicians sometimes say, but to the crass utilitarianism and impersonal organizational structures we tend to import into their micro- and meso-level worlds. They feel that their very culture is threatened. Radical fundamentalist movements—regardless of the specific religion—are mostly antimodernization movements turned militant (Antoun 2001; Davidman 1990; Heilman 2000; Marty 2001; Marty and Appleby 1992, 2004; Shupe and Hadden 1989). So it is that some aspects of global terrorism and international conflict may be based in the way in which the Western world organizes its social life and exports it to other parts of the world.

These conflicts, in turn, have resulted in mobilization of the military in the United States. The result is that members of your own family might be serving abroad even as you read these pages. Our networks, group life, and organizations clearly have implications at all three levels of the social system. We live in a complex web, indeed, and our connections are at work in our lives.

THINKING SOCIOLOGICALLY

How do you think global interaction will be transformed through Internet technology? How will individual connections between people be affected by these transformations at the macro levels of our social world?

POLICY ISSUES: WOMEN AND GLOBALIZATION

Women around the world are viewed as second-class citizens, the most economically, politically, and socially marginalized people on the planet, caught in expectations of religion, patriarchy, and roles needed to sustain life (Schneider and Silverman 2006). Major occupations to help their families survive include street-selling, low-paying factory assembly-line work, piecework (e.g., sewing clothing in their homes), prostitution and sex work, and domestic service. Yet women

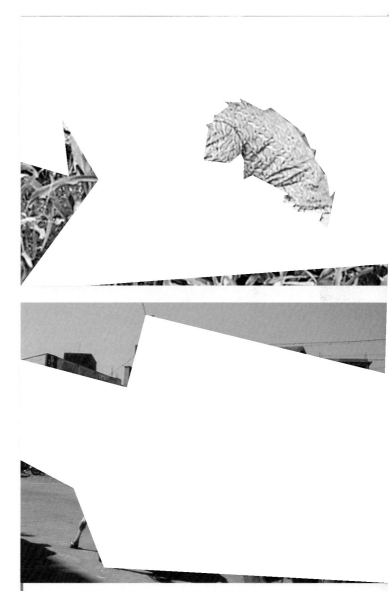

Around the world, two-thirds of the poorest adults are women, even though women produce more than two-thirds of food supplies in the world. A Laotian woman works in the field (top), and an Indian woman transports goods to market (bottom).

Source: Photos courtesy of Clay Ballantine.

produce 75 to 90 percent of the food crops in the world, run households, and are the main determinants of the status of children in poor countries. Due to the "feminization of poverty," two out of three poor adults are women (Enloe 2006; Robbins 2005). Causes of the many problems facing women will be discussed throughout the book.

One organization with policies to help raise the status of women through development is the United Nations; each decade since the 1960s, this global organization has set forth plans to improve conditions in poor countries. Early plans were driven by interests of capitalist countries in the first world; this left women out of the equation and planning. Women suffered more under some of these plans because their positions and responsibilities did not change but conditions got worse as development money went to large corporations with the idea that profits would trickle down to the local level, an idea that did not materialize in most countries (Boulding and Dye 2002). More recently, the United Nations has sponsored conferences on the status of women; the United Nations' Division for the Advancement of Women and other organizations are now developing policies to help educate local women in health, nutrition, basic first aid, and business methods. Many projects have been spawned, including micro-lending organizations (Grameen Bank, Finca), allowing groups of women to borrow money to start cooperatives and other small business ventures. These organizations can have very beneficial effects if they are used wisely by policy makers who care about the people rather than just about their own benefits.

SO WHAT?

Our social lives are lived in small groups and personal networks. The scope of those networks has broadened with increased complexity in the global social world. Indeed, it is easy not to recognize how extensively our networks reach, even to the global level. While bureaucracies existed in eras such as the Roman Empire, the modern world is primarily a phenomenon of the past three centuries. The intimate experiences of our personal lives are far more extensively linked to meso- and macro-level events and to people and places on the other side of the globe than was true for our predecessors. If we hope to understand our lives, we must understand this broad context. Although humans have always depended on groups for survival, it may have been possible to live without global connections and bureaucratic systems several centuries ago. However, these networks are intricately woven into our lifestyles and our economic systems today; the question is whether we control these networks or they control us.

Our networks set norms and curb our behaviors, usually inclining us to conform to the social expectations of our associates; this, of course, contributes to stability of the entire social system, since deviation can threaten the existence of "normal" patterns.

CONTRIBUTING TO YOUR SOCIAL WORLD

At the Local Level: *DARE* or *Alcoholics Anonymous* need supporters to work with persons who are dependent on alcohol, drugs, or tobacco, or who have eating disorders.

At the Organizational or Institutional Level: Participate in an organizational program to reduce conflict or improve intergroup relations.

At the National and Global Levels: *Peace Corps, CARE, Oxfam,* and faith-based organizations work on world issues such as hunger, poverty, and disease such as AIDS.

Visit www.pineforge.com/ballantinestudy for online activities, sample tests, and other helpful information. Select "Chapter 5: Interaction, Groups, and Organizations" for chapter-specific activities.

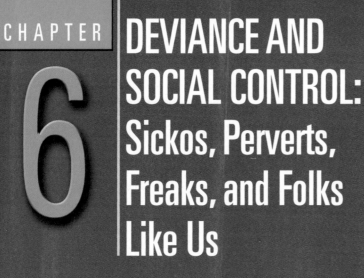

CHAPTER 6

DEVIANCE AND SOCIAL CONTROL:
Sickos, Perverts, Freaks, and Folks Like Us

Deviants are often thought of as perverts and unconscionable rule breakers. We often contrast them to people like us, but the reality is that the line between deviants and conformists is frequently vague, and we may be surprised to learn that "deviants are us."

Think About It . . .

1. Are you a deviant? Who says?

2. Why do people become deviant?

3. What are the costs—and the benefits—of deviance in a society?

4. What should we do about deviance?

Macro: Global Community

Macro: National Society

Meso: National Institutions and Organizations: Ethnic Subcultures

Micro: Local Organizations and Community

**Micro:
You and Your
Family**

Micro: Violations of ordinances; problems with neighbors; theft, burglary, local corruption

Meso: Violations of state laws; white-collar crimes and crimes by corporations; religious clergy malfeasance

Macro: Individual federal crimes (treason, tax fraud, infringement of copyright laws); crimes committed by the state, including domestic terrorism against its own citizens

Macro: Global environmental destruction; international terrorism; human rights violations such as genocide; violations of international treaties about treatment of prisoners

On the corner near the Ballantines' house in Japan was a vending machine. The usual cola, candy, and sundries were displayed, along with cigarettes, beer, whiskey, and pornographic magazines. Out of curiosity, Jeanne and her husband watched to see who purchased what from the machines, and not once did they see teenagers sneaking the beer, cigarettes, or porn. It turns out the Ballantines were not the only ones watching! The neighbors also kept an eye on who did what, the neighborhood watch being an effective form of social control in Japan. Because of the **stigma**, the disapproval attached to disobeying the expected norms, vigilant neighbors help to keep the overall amount of deviance low.

Many communities in various countries have established neighborhood watches as well to help reduce crime and juvenile delinquency. Sometimes, programs include safe houses for children, with people assigned to keep watch and to open their doors to those children in need. Some communities also assign police to particular neighborhoods. As they walk around, they get to know the residents and young people with the idea that they can provide a positive influence. These practices send a signal that deviant behavior is unacceptable; they also provide social control on behaviors of those who might be tempted to commit crimes.

Most people conform to the expected norms of their society most of the time. Occasionally, they may violate a norm, and depending on its importance and on the severity of the violation, the violator may or may not be seen as deviant. Getting drunk on a Saturday night at a party may be tolerated unless it happens often or becomes a nuisance.

Young people in Japan buy soda in vending machines that also carry cigarettes, beer, hard liquor, and pornographic materials, but they do not buy such things. They know someone would be watching.

Source: © B.S.P.I./Corbis.

Wearing strange clothes may be seen as amusing and nonconformist once in a while but is labeled deviant if it becomes a regular occurrence. Adorning oneself with tattoos and rings to be distinctive and individualistic may result in widespread adoption of these behaviors so that they become accepted rather than deviant. Individuals may be seen as deviant if they travel to another culture with different norms and inadvertently violate norms of the host culture.

In this chapter, we discuss **deviance**—the violation of social norms—and the social control mechanisms that keep most people from becoming deviant. We also explore *crime*, the forms of deviance where formal penalties are imposed by the society. The content of this chapter may challenge some of your deeply held assumptions about human behavior and defy some conceptions about deviance. In fact, it may convince you that we are all deviant at some times and in some places. The self-test in the next Sociology in Your Social World illustrates this point. Try taking it to see whether you are deviant.

THINKING SOCIOLOGICALLY

First, read and answer the questions at the top of page 157. Do you think of yourself as being deviant? Why or why not? Are deviants really only those who get caught? For instance, if someone steals your car but avoids being caught, is he or she deviant?

WHAT IS DEVIANCE?

Deviance evokes negative reactions from others because it violates the society's norms. The definition is somewhat imprecise because of constantly changing definitions and ideas about what acts are considered deviant. Some acts are deviant in most societies most of the time: murder, assault, robbery, and rape. Most societies impose severe penalties on these forms of deviance, and if severe formal penalties are imposed by the government, then the deviant actions actually become **crime**. However, under unusual circumstances, these acts may be overlooked or even viewed as understandable, as in the case of looting by citizens following the fall of the Iraqi government in 2003 or the shooting and killing of people—even innocent people—during a war. Other acts of deviance are considered serious offenses in one society but tolerated in another; examples include prostitution, premarital or extramarital sex, gambling, and bribery. Even within a single society, different groups may define deviance and conformity quite differently. The state legislature may officially define alcohol consumption by 19-year-olds as deviant, but on a Saturday night at the fraternity party, the 19-year-old "brother" who does not drink may be viewed as deviant by his peers.

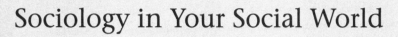

Sociology in Your Social World

Who Is Deviant?

Please jot down your answers to the following self-test questions. No need to share your responses with others.

Have you ever engaged in any of the following acts?

1. stolen anything, even if its value was under $10

2. used an illegal drug

3. misused a prescription drug

4. run away from home prior to age 18

5. used tobacco prior to age 18

6. drunk alcohol prior to age 21

7. engaged in a fist fight

8. carried a knife or gun

9. used a car without the owner's permission

10. driven a car after drinking alcohol

11. (boys) forced a girl to have sexual relations against her will

12. offered sex for money

13. damaged property worth more than $10

14. been truant from school

15. arrived home after your curfew

16. been disrespectful to someone in authority

17. accepted or transported property that you had reason to believe might be stolen

18. taken a towel from a hotel room after renting the room for a night

All of the above are delinquent acts (violations of legal standards), and most young people are guilty of at least one infraction. However, few teenagers are given the label of *delinquent*. If you have answered yes to any of the preceding questions, you have committed a crime in the state of Ohio and in many other states. Your penalty or sanction for the infraction could range from a stiff fine to several years in prison—if you got caught!

Deviance is *socially constructed*. This means that members of groups and societies define what is deviant. Consider the phenomenon of today's young people getting tattoos, tongue studs, and rings anyplace on the body one can place a ring. Is this deviant? It depends on who is judging. Are tattoos and rings symbols of independence and rebellion, a "cool" and unique look if many people begin to adopt the behavior? Do such "deviant" acts then become a symbol of conformity? When the Beatles started the long hair rage in the 1960s, this was deviant behavior to many. Today, we pay no special attention to men with long hair.

THINKING SOCIOLOGICALLY

Are heavy metal rock lyrics, gangster rap's glorification of violence, and hip-hop culture deviant? Who says? Interview your friends or classmates. What are their views?

Some acts are deviant at one time and place and not at others. For instance, in the 1990s the Mexican president of the Democratic Revolutionary Party, Andres Lopez Obrador, proposed to the leading members of his party that in order to strengthen the family, men should be faithful in their roles as husbands and stop keeping mistresses in *casa chica* (or "little homes").

Although this practice is officially considered deviant and condemned in that predominantly Catholic country, men who can afford to keep one or more mistresses often do, a practice that has been overlooked for decades. Obrador's proposal came as a surprise since this form of deviance is seldom mentioned or recognized. His scolding is unlikely to change these patterns of behavior unless legislation is passed, and that is unlikely given the traditions and makeup of the male-dominated government (Dillon 1997). However, as women receive more education, jobs, and power and achieve higher statuses, they are likely to demand change.

Both behaviors and individuals may be defined as deviant. Some individuals have a higher likelihood of being labeled deviant because of the group into which they were born, such as a particular ethnic group, or because of a distinguishing mark or characteristic, such as a deformity. Others may escape being considered deviant because of

Are any of these people deviant? Why or why not?

Sources: Clockwise, © Jennifer Mathews/Istockphoto.com; © Anna Lyubimtseva/Istockphoto.com; © Jordan Chesbrough/Istockphoto.com; © The Image Works; ©Eva Serrabassa/Istockphoto.com.

their dominant status in society. The higher one's status, the less likely one is to be suspected of violating norms and the less likely any violations will be characterized as "criminal." Who would suspect that a respectable white-collar husband and father is embezzling funds or was once in a mental hospital? The Enron scandal of 2001 involved massive fraud and attracted extraordinary attention because many of those involved held highly respectable positions; the "crooks" were very successful, respected businessmen.

Even the looting that happened following Hurricane Katrina was addressed differently when it was done by whites than when African Americans were involved. The media showed photos of black "looters" who stole food, but whites who broke into grocery stories in search of food were described as "resourceful." Likewise, gays and lesbians are often said to be deviant and are accused of flaunting their sexuality; heterosexuals are rarely accused of flaunting their sexuality, regardless of how overtly flirtatious they are. So one's group membership or ascribed traits may make a difference in whether or not one is defined as deviant.

Probably most of us consider deviance problematic for society, representing a breakdown in norms. However, according to structural-functional theory, deviance also serves vital functions by setting examples of what is considered unacceptable behavior, providing guidelines for behavior that is necessary to maintain the social order, and bonding people together through their common rejection of the deviant behavior. Deviance is also "functional" because it provides jobs for those who deal with deviants—police, judges, social workers, and so forth (Gans 2007). Furthermore, deviance can signal problems in society that need to be addressed and can therefore stimulate positive change. Sometimes, deviant individuals break the model of conventional thinking, thereby opening the society to new and creative paths of thinking. Scientists, inventors, and artists have often been rejected in their time but have been honored later for accomplishments that positively affected society. Vincent Van Gogh, for example, lived in poverty and mental turmoil during his life, but he became recognized as a renowned painter after his death, his paintings selling for millions of dollars.

Our tasks in this chapter are to understand what deviance is, how to explain it, where it fits in the social world, how some deviant acts become crimes, and what policies might be effective in controlling or reducing crime.

THINKING SOCIOLOGICALLY

What kind of problems might be created in a society if everyone conformed and no one ever deviated from social standards? In other words, what might be some negative consequences of *total* social conformity?

Misconceptions about Deviance

Many common beliefs about deviance are in fact misperceptions. Using scientifically collected data, the sociological perspective helps dispel false beliefs, as in the examples below.

Popular belief: Some acts are inherently deviant. Fact: Deviance is relative to time, place, and status of the individual. At some place or time, almost any behavior you can mention has been defined as deviant, just as most acts have been legal or even the typical behavior in other times and places. For example, homosexual liaisons were normal for men in ancient Greece and have been acceptable in various societies throughout time. Deviance is not inherent in certain behaviors but is defined by people and their governments (Erikson 1987).

Do these people appear deviant? Why or why not? (They are Ken Lay and Jeffrey Skilling, the executives involved in the massive Enron scandal.)

Sources: © Reuters/Corbis; © Ron Sachs/Corbis.

Those in power have great influence over what is defined as deviant and can often determine punishment for deviant behavior. Some individuals are defined as deviant because they do not fit into the dominant system of values and norms. They may be seen as disruptive, a liability, or a threat to the system. In the Communist regime of mainland China, political indoctrination controls many aspects of the citizens' lives. The rate of deviance is low because of group pressure for conformity; those who commit deviant acts are disgraced and "corrected." However, ongoing protests against Chinese rule and recent violence in Muslim-dominated Western China show that not all agree with the norms of the dominant Han Chinese government. Within dissonant groups, antigovernment protests are heroic rather than deviant.

Some sociologists point out that crime can be "functional" because it creates jobs for people like these above and it unifies the society against the nonconformists.

Sources: © Corbis; © Frances Twitty.

Famous individuals remembered in history books were often considered deviant in their time. In the Middle Ages, for example, anyone who questioned the concept of a flat earth at the center of the universe (with sun and stars circling it) was a deviant and a religious heretic. In the early seventeenth century, Galileo, following Copernicus's lead, wrote a treatise based on empirical observations that upheld the concept of the earth revolving around the sun; he was tried by the Inquisition in Rome and condemned for heresy because of his theory.

Definitions of deviance also vary depending on the social situation or context in which the behavior occurs (Clinard and Meier 2004; McCaghy et al. 2006). If we take the same behavior and place it in a different social context, perceptions on whether the behavior is deviant may well change. In Greece, Spain, and other Mediterranean countries, the clothing norms on beaches are very different from those in most of North America. Topless sunbathing by women is not at all uncommon, even on beaches designated as family beaches. The norms vary, however, even within a few feet of the beach; women will sunbathe topless, lying only 10 feet from the boardwalk where concessionaires sell beverages, snacks, and tourist items. If these women become thirsty, they put on a halter, walk the 15 feet to purchase a cola, and return to their beach blankets where they again remove their swimsuit tops. To walk onto the boardwalk topless would be highly deviant. Yet to be topless on the sand is acceptable. Likewise, drunken behavior at a college party may be acceptable, but conducting oneself in the same manner while sipping champagne at a wedding reception would be cause for disgust. The same behavior can be conventional or deviant depending on where it occurs.

Popular belief: Those who deviate are socially identified and recognized. Fact: Most of us deviate from some norm at some time, as you saw when completing the questionnaire on deviance. (See the preceding Sociology in Your Social World.) However, most behaviors that violate a norm are never socially recognized as deviant. Only about one-third of all crime that is reported to the police in the United States ever leads to an arrest. This means that two-thirds is never officially handled through the formal, legal structure, and the perpetrators escape being labeled deviant.

Popular belief: Deviants purposely and knowingly break the law. Fact: While it is a popular notion that those who engage in deviant behavior make a conscious choice to do so, much deviance is driven by emotion, encouraged by friends, caused by disagreements over norms (as in the case of whether marijuana use should be criminalized), or is a result of conditions in the immediate situation (as in cases of teens spontaneously engaging in a behavior in response to boredom or a struggle for prestige among peers) (McCagh et al. 2006).

Popular belief: Deviance occurs because there is a dishonest, selfish element to human nature. Fact: While surveys show many of us believe this, most people commit deviant acts but do not attribute their own deviance to basic dishonesty or other negative personality factors.

These misperceptions imply that most people believe they have clear understandings of what deviance is and that deviant individuals know when they are being deviant and plan their actions. Yet there is little empirical evidence to support these beliefs, as the research reported in this chapter shows.

THINKING SOCIOLOGICALLY

Think of examples in your life that illustrate the relative nature of deviance. For instance, are there behaviors that are deviant in one setting but not in another or that were deviant when you were younger but are not deviant now?

WHAT CAUSES DEVIANT BEHAVIOR? THEORETICAL PERSPECTIVES

Helena is a delinquent. Her father deserted the family when Helena was 10, and before that he had abused Helena and her mother. Now her mother has all she can cope with; she is just trying to survive financially and keep her three children in line. Helena gets little attention and little support or encouragement in her school activities. Her grades have fallen steadily. As a young teen, she sought attention from boys, but in the process she became pregnant. Now the only kids who have anything to do with her are others who have also been in trouble, and her friends are other young people who have been labeled delinquent. Helena's schoolmates, teachers, and mother see her as a delinquent troublemaker, and it would be hard for Helena to change their views and her status.

How did this happen? Was Helena born with a biological propensity toward deviance? Does she have psychological problems? Is the problem in her social environment? Helena's situation is, of course, only one unique case. Sociologists cannot generalize from Helena to other cases, but they do know from their studies that there are thousands of teens with problems like Helena's.

Throughout history, people have proposed explanations for why some members of society "turn bad"—from biological explanations of imbalances in hormones and claims of innate personality defects to social conditions within individual families or in the larger social structure. Biological and psychological approaches focus on personality disorders or abnormalities in the body or psyche of individuals; they generally do not consider the social context in which deviance occurs.

Social scientists attempt to study questions of deviance scientifically. They examine why certain acts are defined as deviant, why some people engage in deviant behavior, and how other people in the society react to deviance. Sociologists place emphasis on understanding the interactions, social structure, and social processes that lead to deviant behavior, rather than on individual characteristics; they consider the socialization process and interpersonal relationships, group and social class differences, cultural

and subcultural norms, and power structures that influence individuals to conform or deviate from societal expectations (Liska 1999). Theoretical explanations about why people are deviant are important because they influence social policy decisions about what to do with deviants.

This section explores several approaches to understanding deviance and crime. Some theories explain particular categories of crime better than others and some illuminate micro-, meso-, or macro-level processes better than others. Taken together—as complementary perspectives on a complex dimension of human behavior—these theories help us understand a wide range of deviant and criminal behaviors.

THINKING SOCIOLOGICALLY

What common explanations for deviant behavior have you heard? Keep these in mind, and determine whether and how they fit into the following theoretical discussion of deviance.

Micro-Level Explanations of Deviance: Rational Choice and Interaction Theories

No one is born deviant. Individuals learn to be law-abiding citizens or to be deviant through the process of socialization. Thus, behavior is acquired during the processes of interaction and socialization as people develop their social relationships. Why do some people learn to become deviant and others learn to follow the norms of society? A rational choice explanation focuses on cost-benefit analysis of one's choices. Another approach, based in symbolic interaction theory, is that people are exposed to the opportunity to commit delinquent acts through their social relationships with peers and family members, and they come to be labeled deviant. Rational choice and symbolic interaction approaches tend to be micro-level theories.

Social Control Theory and Rational Choice

One of sociology's central concepts is *social control*. In fact, some people argue that social control is the discipline's major area of study (Gibbs 1989; Hagan 2002). Control theory focuses on why most people conform most of the time and do not commit deviant acts. If human beings were truly free to do whatever they wanted, they would likely commit more deviant acts. Yet to live in relationship and proximity to others requires individual control based on social standards and sanctions—in short, social control.

A perpetual question in sociology is the following: How is order possible in the context of rapidly changing society? A very general answer is that social control results from social norms that promote order and predictability in the social world. When people fail to adhere to these norms, or when

Scowls, stares, and gossip—informal sanctions—can deter people from certain kinds of behaviors.

Source: © Amanda Rohde.

The basic idea in rational choice approaches is that when individuals make decisions, they calculate the costs and benefits to themselves. Humans seek to maximize pleasure (benefit) and to minimize pain (costs), and the decision regarding whether to conform or deviate from social norms is determined by the individual's assessment of the pleasure-pain ratio in a given situation. Individuals make rational decisions based on their own mental calculations. From a societal perspective, social control comes from shifting the balance toward more pain and fewer benefits for those who deviate from norms.

The shift in this cost-benefit ratio may mean change in the sanctions provided by society for certain behaviors. *Positive sanctions* reward those behaviors approved by society. This is the reason schools have honor ceremonies, companies reward their top salespeople, and communities recognize civic leadership with "citizen of the year" awards; rewards for conventional behavior are enhanced. *Negative sanctions* (or punishments) increase the cost to those who have deviated from the norm. They range from fines for traffic violations to prison sentences for serious crimes and

the norms are unclear, the stability and continuance of the entire social system may be threatened.

People are bonded to society by four powerful factors:

1. *attachment* to other people who respect the values and rules of the society; individuals do not want to be rejected by those to whom they are close or they admire;

2. *commitment* to conventional activities (such as school and jobs) that they do not want to jeopardize;

3. *involvement* in activities that keep them so busy with conventional roles and expectations that they do not have time for mischief; and

4. *belief* in the social rules of their culture that they accept because of childhood socialization and indoctrination into conventional beliefs.

Should these variables be weakened, there is an increased possibility that the person could commit deviant acts (Hirschi 1969/2002).

Two primary factors shape our tendency to conform. The first is *internal controls*, those voices within us that tell us when a behavior is acceptable or unacceptable, right or wrong; the second is *external controls*, society's formal or informal controls against deviant behavior. Informal external controls include smiles, frowns, hugs, and ridicule from close acquaintances (Gottfredson and Hirschi 1990). Formal external controls come from the legal system through police, judges, juries, and social workers. In both cases, the cost-benefit ratios shift, making either conformity or deviance a rational choice.

Formal sanctions involve the enforcement of rules passed by legitimate officials. This man is being handcuffed for a legal infraction that is fairly serious.

Source: © Frances Twitty.

even death for acts considered most dangerous to society. If one belongs to a subculture or group whose norms conflict with the dominant society's, conformity to the subculture may take precedence over conformity to the larger society.

When rational calculation is at work, deterrence to deviance can be accomplished by increasing the costs (tougher penalties in the courts) by changing awareness of the costs that are already in place, by reducing the benefits (lessening social benefits like admiration), or by changing perception of the cost-benefit balance.

THINKING SOCIOLOGICALLY

Think of a time when you committed a deviant act or avoided one despite tempting opportunity. What factors influence whether you conform to societal norms or to deviant norms?

Differential Association Theory

Keith and Jeanne, coauthors of this, each have children. If someone had offered their children some heroin when they were young, they probably would not have taken it. First, they would not have defined sticking a needle in their arms and injecting heroin as a fun or "cool" thing to do. Second, they would have no idea how to cook the heroin to extract the liquid because they had never seen it done. They would not know the proper technique for how to prepare the drug or how to give the shot. Why? Because they have not associated with drug users and because their family and friends define drug use as deviant.

Differential association refers to the difference in people with whom members of a society interact; some people learn to conform and others learn to deviate, depending on their associations. The theory focuses on the process of learning deviance from family, peers, fellow employees, political organizations, neighborhood groups such as gangs, and other groups in one's surroundings (Akers 1992; Akers et al. 1979; Sutherland, Cressey, and Luckenbil 1992; Warr and Stafford 1991). This theory is a symbolic interaction approach because the emphasis is on how others shape one's definition of what is normal and acceptable. Helena came to be surrounded by people who made dropping out of school and other delinquent acts seem normal; if her close friends and siblings were sexually active as teens, her teen pregnancy might not be remarkable and might even be a source of some prestige with her group of peers.

According to differential association theory, the possibility of becoming deviant depends on four factors: the *duration, intensity, priority,* and *frequency* of time spent with the group (Sutherland et al. 1992). If deviant behavior exists in one's social context and if one is exposed to deviance regularly and frequently (duration and intensity), especially if one is in close association with a group that accepts criminal behavior, the individual is likely to learn deviant ways.

Shooting drugs as a way of spending time and money is a way of life for some young people. Yet some teens would not know the technique for preparing and injecting illegal drugs, nor would they have learned from associates that this is a fun or acceptable way to spend one's time.

Source: © Topham / The Image Works.

Furthermore, individuals learn motives, drives, rationalizations, and attitudes, and develop techniques that influence behavior and cause the individual to commit a deviant act.

Youths of lower socioeconomic status are more likely than their higher status counterparts to engage in violent delinquency because they have learned in their social setting to be more accepting of the use of force, coercion, and violence to solve problems. Elijah Anderson's (2000) book, *Code of the Street*, describes two types of groups that coexist in poor neighborhoods: "decent people" and "street people." The code of the street often involves norms that are opposed to those of mainstream society, yet many children are socialized in areas where this code provides the dominant norms. "Street-oriented people" hang with peers on streets and adopt a certain look with their clothes and jewelry—an image expected by the group. Peers become more important than a society's social control agents. "Decent families" accept mainstream values more fully and often find support systems in church communities or other organizations. Lower status youth are more likely to be suspected, watched, and caught for deviant behavior than higher status youth. Thus, reported delinquency rates may be higher for this group, even if the incidence of violence is not greater (Anderson 2000).

Some theorists contend that lower-class life constitutes a distinctive subculture in which delinquent behavior patterns are transmitted through socialization. The values, beliefs, norms, and practices that have evolved in lower-class communities over time can often lead to violation of laws. These values and norms have been defined by those in power. Just as upper-class youth seem to be expected and destined to succeed, lower-class youth may learn other behaviors that those with privilege have defined as delinquency and crime (Bettie 2003; Chambliss 1973). For instance, in a recent study, Bettie (2003) found that race, class, and gender intersect in important ways to increase the labeling (and decrease the opportunities) for lower-class and minority high school girls.

For some inner-city youth, the local norms are to be tough and disrespectful of authority, to live for today, to seek excitement, and to be "cool"; these are survival techniques. With time, these attitudes and behaviors become valued in and of themselves.

Shoplifting is often done by young people who have yet to be arrested for anything—a form of primary deviance.

Source: © Simon Marcus / Corbis.

Note that differential association theory emerged at a time when social scientists thought most crime was committed by lower-class people; it is now clear that members of all social classes commit different kinds of crimes, but no socioeconomic class has a monopoly on violence, graft, corruption, or dishonesty.

Labeling Theory

Labeling theory is also related to the symbolic interaction perspective, for labels (such as "juvenile delinquent") are symbols that have meanings that affect the self. Labeling theory focuses on how people define reality—what is or is not "normal"—which is a core issue in the symbolic interactionist paradigm. The basic assumption underlying labeling theory is that no behavior or individual is intrinsically deviant. Behavior is deviant because individuals in society label it deviant. The social process is as follows: members of society *create* deviance by *defining* certain behaviors as deviant—smoking pot, wearing long hair, holding hands in public, or whatever is seen as inappropriate at a particular time and place. They then *react* to the deviance by rejection or by imposing penalties. It is this reaction that defines behavior of an individual as deviant more than the act itself; consider the case of the Puritan Witchcraft Trials described in the next How Do We Know?

THINKING SOCIOLOGICALLY

Read about Puritan witchcraft trials on page 165. How does Puritan labeling of deviants parallel labeling today? What purposes does labeling serve?

Labeling theorists define two stages in the process of becoming a deviant. **Primary deviance** is a violation of a norm that may be an isolated act, such as a young teenager shoplifting something on a dare by friends. Most people commit acts of primary deviance. However, few of us are initially labeled deviant as a result of these primary acts. Remember how you marked the deviant behavior test that you took at the beginning of this chapter? If you engaged in deviant acts, you were probably not labeled deviant for the offense.

If an individual continues to violate a norm and begins to take on a deviant identity, this is referred to as **secondary deviance**. Secondary deviance becomes publicly recognized and the individual is identified as deviant, beginning a deviant career. If a teenager such as Helena in the opening example is caught, her act is publicized in the newspaper, she may spend time in a juvenile detention center, and parents of other teens may not want their children associating with her. Employers and store managers may refuse to hire her. Soon there are few options, and in response to society's expectations, the teen may return to the deviant acts and to delinquent acquaintances. Society's reaction, then, is what defines a deviant person (Lemert 1951, 1972).

Witch Hunts in the Puritan Colonies

In a classic study, sociologist Kai Erikson (2005/1966) used historical analysis of records and documents to study deviance that defines boundaries. He looked at cases of conduct that a group considered so dangerous or embarrassing that they brought special sanctions to bear against persons labeled as witches. He hypothesized that boundaries of normality often become more rigid when there is an external threat or internal crisis. Witch hunts in the Puritan colonies of New England came about in exactly this way.

The Massachusetts Bay Colony provided an excellent lab for his historical analysis because the Puritans kept useful and detailed records. Erikson systematically analyzed these historical data and computed crime rates in order to test his hypothesis. Erikson concluded from his analysis that the number of people labeled as deviant offenders in a community at any one time is likely to remain fairly stable. In other words, no community can put such restrictive definitions of acceptable behavior on citizens that large numbers of members fall outside the acceptable boundaries. When the number of people labeled deviant exceeds an acceptable limit, a redefinition of deviance takes place.

Witchcraft was one of the behaviors most feared in the late 1600s. People in the colonies who feared external influences suspected witchcraft when trying to explain social stresses they did not understand. Like many other hysterias, the "enemies" were soon perceived to be everywhere. For a short period in the colonies, around

In early colonial days in New England, some people were accused, tried, and executed for witchcraft. Erikson analyzed legal and political documents from that period to test his hypotheses about deviant behavior in a community.

Source: Crafts (1876).

1692, the witchcraft hysteria labeled and condemned many poor women and a few low-status men to death.

In fact, witchcraft was not the only hysteria that plagued the group. Other hysterias based on beliefs and heresy preceded witchcraft. Erikson points out that waves of hysteria served the purpose of helping the young colony's settlers define the boundaries of their acceptable behavior in their emerging society and served as social control to keep members in-line. The hysteria provided a common enemy— bonding people together in fear— and defined the moral boundaries

beyond which people in this homogeneous setting dare not tread.

Erikson suggests that societies have generally utilized one of three approaches when dealing with deviance:

1. Some societies set aside special days as periods when behavior is permitted that would otherwise be considered deviant. Violation of rules on these occasions are accepted. Mardi Gras, Carnival, and Halloween are examples.

2. Some societies regard deviance as "natural" during one's youth and tolerate it for a specified age group, but not for others in the population.

3. Some societies have special clubs, organizations, or orders whose role is to violate certain norms or rules of the group. Bisexual and homosexual individuals are given special roles in some societies, and some Ivy League colleges have "secret prankster clubs" that engage in disapproved conduct.

Erikson argues that the Puritan attitudes are part of the context of how Americans deal with deviant behavior and that the Puritan heritage is still evident in methods Americans use to handle deviance today, including the practice of capital punishment. Deviation in the United States has often resulted in extraordinarily severe reactions, including termination of life.

Lower-class teens may use alcohol and drugs that are illegal just as middle-class teens do, but since they are on the street in neighborhoods that are frequented by police, they are far more likely to be seen, arrested, prosecuted, and convicted than the college students who actually may consume more alcohol and drugs at their college parties than do their former classmates who are on the street. Only one of the groups gets labeled "deviant."

Source: © Jérome Sessini / In Visu / Corbis.

The *process of labeling* individuals and behaviors takes place at each level of analysis, from individual to society. If community or societal norms define a behavior as deviant, individuals are likely to believe it is deviant. Sanctions for juvenile delinquents can have the effect of reinforcing the deviant behavior by (1) increasing alienation from the social world, (2) forcing increased interaction with deviant peers, and (3) motivating juvenile delinquents to positively value and identify with the deviant status (Kaplan and Johnson 1991).

The *self-fulfilling prophesy* refers to a belief that becomes reality. Individuals may come to see themselves as deviant because of harassment, ridicule, rejection by friends and family, and negative sanctions. James is eight and already sees himself as a failure because his parents, teachers, and peers tell him he is "dumb." In keeping with the idea of self-fulfilling prophesy, James accepts the label and acts accordingly. Unless someone—such as an insightful teacher—steps in to give him another image of himself, the label is unlikely to change. Again, labeling theory focuses on the micro level, the individual and the formation of sense of self.

THINKING SOCIOLOGICALLY

What labels do you carry, and how do they affect your self-concept?

Another explanation of why certain individuals and groups are labeled deviant has to do with their status and power in society. Those who are on the fringes, away from power, and nonparticipants in the mainstream are more likely to be labeled deviants—the poor, minorities, members of new religious movements, or those who in some way do not fit into the dominant system. Since the powerful have the influence to define what is acceptable, they protect themselves from being defined as deviants. People from different subcultures, social classes, or religious groups may be accorded deviant labels.

A study by Chambliss (1973) illustrates the process of labeling in communities and groups. Perhaps during your high school years, you witnessed situations similar to that described in his study. Chambliss looked at the behavior of two small peer groups of boys and at the reactions of community members to their behavior. The Saints, boys from "good" families, were some of the most delinquent boys at Hanibal High School. Although the Saints were constantly occupied with truancy, drinking, wild driving, petty theft, and vandalism, none was officially arrested for any misdeed during the two-year study, partly because they had cars and could go out of town for their pranks. The Roughnecks were constantly in trouble with police and community, even though their rate of delinquency was about equal to that of the Saints. Chambliss found that poor kids, the Roughnecks, may be involved in deviant behavior because the dominant cultural goals seem distant and unattainable. On the other hand, rich kids, the Saints, indulge in delinquent activities to cope with boredom, to rebel, or to seek visibility among peers.

What was the cause of the disparity between these two groups? Community members, police, and teachers alike labeled the boys based on their perceptions of the boys' family backgrounds and social class. The Saints came from stable, white upper-middle-class families, were active in school affairs, and were precollege students whom everyone expected to become professionals. The general community feeling was that the Roughnecks would amount to nothing. They carried around a label that was hard to change, and that label was realized; the Saints almost all became professionals, whereas none of the Roughnecks did. Two Roughnecks ended up in prison, two became coaches, and little is known of the others. For these groups of boys, the prophecy became self-fulfilling (Chambliss 1973). The belief that the Roughnecks would "amount to nothing" came true because that was what was expected by the community, their opportunities were affected by their labels, and the boys came to expect nothing for themselves.

Why do certain behaviors come to be defined as deviant? Again, powerful members of society can label certain behaviors as deviant. While labeling theory is mostly based on micro-level theory, labeling theorists also point toward the role of macro-level social forces—social inequality or lack of access to power as in the case of the Roughnecks—in shaping whether one is labeled or whether one can avoid the label.

Thus, labeling theory is also sometimes used by conflict theorists. When members of the dominant group in society see certain behaviors as potentially threatening or disruptive to the society or to the interests of those who have privileged statuses, the group in power reinforces its position by creating an impossible situation for minority group members. The minority's nonacceptance of the rules becomes deviant; for instance, dissidents opposed to government restrictions or human rights violations in China, Myanmar (Burma), and other countries have been thrown in jail because their protests were labeled deviant by those in power.

Meso- and Macro-Level Explanations of Deviance: Structural-Functional and Conflict Theories

While interpersonal interaction processes can result in deviance, many sociologists believe that meso- and macro-level analysis creates greater understanding of the societal factors leading to deviance. Meso-level analysis focuses on national organizations and institutions and ethnic groups within a nation; macro-level theories focus on societies and global social systems. However, when it comes to deviance and conformity, the same theories tend to operate at meso and macro levels. We look first at structural-functional theories of deviance, those with the longest history in sociology. They include two themes: (1) *anomie*, the breakdown of the norms guiding behavior that leads to social disorganization, and (2) *strain* created by the difference between definitions of success (*goals*) and the *means* available to achieve those goals.

Anomie and Social Disorganization

Villagers from industrializing countries in Africa, Asia, and Latin America were pushed off marginally productive rural lands and were pulled by the lure of the city: new opportunities, excitement, and a chance to change their lives. They flocked to population centers with industrial opportunities, but when they arrived they were often disappointed. Poor, unskilled, and homeless, they moved into crowded apartments or shantytowns of temporary shacks and tried to adjust to the new style of life that often included unemployment. This description could apply to immigrants from 9 months ago or from 90 years ago.

Many industrializing countries face structural changes as their economies move from agriculture to industry. Young men in particular leave behind strong bonds and a common value system that exist in the countryside. In cities, individuals melt into the crowd and live anonymously. Old village norms that provided the guidelines for proper behavior crumble, sometimes without clear expectations emerging to take their places. The lack of clear norms in the rapidly changing urban environment leads to high levels of social disorganization and deviant behavior.

Sociologists use the term *anomie*, or normlessness, to describe the breakdown of norms caused by the lack of

Chinese soldiers tried in vain to stop student protesters in China as the students demanded more freedom to make choices. The students were defined by the government as deviant, many were arrested, and some were shot in Tiananmen Square, the main square in Beijing.

Source: © Peter Turnley / Corbis.

Immigrants are often relegated to the worst housing—such as this shantytown perched along the river in Thailand. These conditions spawn deviance.

Source: © Tim Travis, Down the Road Publishing, LLC (www .downtheroad.org).

shared, achievable goals and lack of socially approved means to achieve goals (Merton 1968). When norms are absent or conflicting, deviance increases as the previous example illustrates. Emile Durkheim (1858–1917) first described this normlessness as a condition of weak, conflicting, or absent norms and values that arise when societies are disorganized. This situation is typical in rapidly urbanizing, industrializing societies, at times of sudden prosperity or depression, during rapid technological change, or when a government is overthrown. Anomie affects urban areas first, but may eventually reach the whole society. Thus, macro-level events, like economic recessions or wars, show how important social solidarity is to an individual's core sense of values.

This general idea of anomie led a group of Chicago sociologists to study the social conditions of that city that are correlated with deviance. The Chicago School, as the research team is known, linked life in transitional slum areas to high incidence of crime. Certain neighborhoods or zones in the Chicago area—generally inner-city transitional zones with recent settlers—have always had high delinquency rates, regardless of the group that occupied the area. Low-economic status, ethnic heterogeneity, residential mobility, family disruption, and competing value systems (because of the constant transitions) led to community disorganization. Although new immigrant groups replaced older groups over time, the delinquency rate remained high because each new generation of newcomers experienced anomie (Shaw and McKay 1929). The high in-migration and out-migration in these communities in itself explains the lack of stability in primary families. Peer group norms became influential, and models of nondeviant behavior were scarce for many teenagers and adults (Anderson 2000).

Strain Theory

Most people in a society share similar values and goals, but those with poor education and few resources have less opportunity to achieve those shared goals than others. When legitimate routes to success are cut off, frustration and anger result and deviant methods may be used to achieve goals. Strain theory focuses on contradictions and tensions between the shared values and goals on the one hand and the opportunity structures of the society on the other.

Strain theory (Merton 1968) suggests that the difference between the societal goals and legitimate means of attaining them can lead to strain in the structure of the society. Individuals may agree with society's definition of success but not be able to achieve it using accepted means; the strain that is created can lead to deviance. Merton uses U.S. society as an example because it places a heavy emphasis on success, measured by wealth and social standing. He outlines five ways individuals adapt to the strain. To illustrate these, we trace potential courses of action for a lower-class student who realizes the value of an education, who knows it is necessary to get ahead, but who has problems competing in the middle-class-dominated school setting.

1. *Conformity* means embracing the society's definition of success and adhering to the established and approved means of achieving success. The student works hard despite the academic and financial obstacles, trying to do well in school to achieve success and a good job placement. She uses legitimate, approved means—education and hard work—to reach goals that the society views as worthy.

2. *Innovation* refers to use of illicit means to reach approved goals. Our student uses illegitimate means to achieve her education goals. She may cheat on exams or get papers from Internet sources. Success in school is all that matters, not how she gets there.

3. *Ritualism* involves strict adherence to the culturally prescribed rules, even though individuals give up on the goals they hoped to achieve. The student may give up the idea of getting good grades and graduating from college but, as a matter of pride and self-image, continues to try hard and to study diligently. She conforms to expectations, for example, but with no sense of purpose; she just does what she is told.

4. *Retreatism* refers to giving up on both the goals and the means. A student either bides her time, not doing well, or drops out, giving up on future job goals. She abandons or retreats from the goals of a professional position in society and on the means to get there. She may even turn to a different lifestyle—for example, a user of drugs and alcohol as part of the retreat.

5. *Rebellion* entails rejecting the socially approved ideas of success and the means of attaining that success but replaces those with alternative definitions of success and alternative strategies for attaining the new goals. Rebelling against the dominant cultural goals and means, a student may join a radical political group or a commune, intent on developing new ideas of how society should be organized and what a "truly educated" person should be.

Figure 6.1 (page 169) shows these five types and their relationship to goals and means.

Deviant behavior results from retreatism, rebellion, and innovation; according to Merton, the reasons individuals resort to these behaviors lie in the social conditions that lead to different levels of access to success, not in their individual biological or psychological makeup.

Structural-functional theories help explain deviance from a social structural point of view, focusing on what happens if deviance disrupts the ongoing social order; it explores how to prevent disruptions, how to keep change slow and nondisruptive, and how deviance can be useful to the ongoing society. However, it fails to account for class conflicts, inequities, and poverty, which conflict theorists argue cause deviance.

Conflict Theory

Protesters gathered near the village of Dannenberg, Germany, to try to prevent the storage of nuclear waste, setting off a confrontation with police. In Serbia, thousands of people

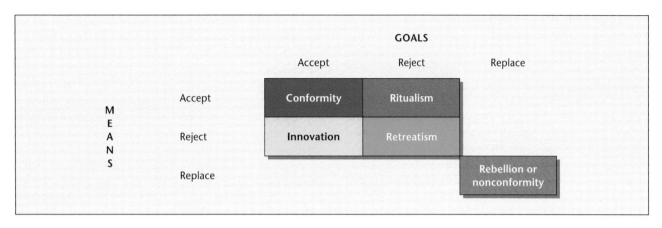

Figure 6.1   Merton's Strain Theory

spent weeks on end in the streets of the capital of Belgrade and other towns to protest the overturning of election results by President Slobodan Milosevic. In Lima, Peru, members of the protest group Tupac Amaru Revolutionary Movement seized the Japanese embassy and took hostages there, demanding amnesty for their comrades being held in prison. Greenpeace, a group fighting to protect the environment, sent their ship to disrupt France's nuclear tests taking place near islands in the South Pacific. Environmentalists in England lived in trees to prevent them from being cut down to make way for a new highway. Protestors in Venezuela blocked oil shipments in attempts to overthrow the government. Some Canadian and American peace advocates went to Baghdad as "human shields" so the Bush administration would not begin the war with Iraq. Are these protesters deviants and criminals, or are they brave heroes? The response depends on who answers the question. Because many societies today are pluralistic, heterogeneous groupings, the differences (goals, resources, norms, and values) between interest groups and groups in power often cause conflict. Conflict theory focuses on macro-level analysis of deviance, looking at deviance as a result of social inequality or of the struggle between groups for power.

Deviance is often related to social class status, interest groups, or cultural conflict between the dominant group and ethnic, religious, political, regional, or gender groups. Wealthy and powerful elites want to maintain their control and their positions (Domhoff 1998); they have the power to pass laws and define what is deviant, sometimes by effectively eliminating opposition groups. Minority groups and subcultures challenge the norms of the dominant groups and threaten the consensus in a society. The greater the cultural difference between the dominant group and other groups in society, the more the possibility of conflict (Huizinga, Esbensen, and Weiher 1991; Huizinga, Loeber, and Thornberry 1994).

Conflict theorists assume that conflict between groups is inevitable; economic and social status differences result

Mannes Ubels gets doused as he clings to the anchor chain of the ship Saga Tide, *while a police patrol boat pulls up to make an arrest. Greenpeace activists, seen as brave heroes by some, prevented the ship from entering the harbor area because it was transporting wood from rare and old forests in western Canada, but in the eyes of the lumber company and the police, they were deviant.*

Source: © Bas Beentjes / epa / Corbis.

in inequality and the motivation to engage in deviance. Therefore, to reduce deviance and crime, we must change the structure of society. For instance, laws in many countries claim to support equal and fair treatment for all, but when one looks at the law in action, another picture emerges. Recall the example of the Saints and Roughnecks; the students from powerful families and higher social classes received favored treatment. Unequal treatment of groups that differ from the dominant group—the laboring class and racial or ethnic minorities in particular—are rooted in the legal, political, and occupational structures of societies.

Some conflict theorists blame the capitalist system for unjust administration of law and argue that the ruling class uses the legal system to further the capitalist enterprise (Quinney 2002). The dominant class defines deviance, applies laws to protect its interests, represses any conflict or protest, and, in effect, forces those in subordinate classes to carry out actions defined as deviant. These actions, in turn, support the ideology that works against subordinate classes. Activities that threaten the interests and well-being of the wealthy capitalist class become defined as deviant. By subordinating certain groups and then defining them as deviant or criminal, the dominant group consolidates its powerful position. Since the dominant class is usually of one ethnic group and those of another race or ethnicity tend to be in the laboring class, the hegemony has racial and ethnic implications as well as social class dimensions.

The fact that subordinate class or race members are apprehended more often than dominant class or race

This young girl is a child prostitute in the frontier border town of Curionopolis, an all-male gold-mining town in Serra Pelada, Brazil.

Source: © Stephanie Maze / Corbis.

members and are prosecuted through the legal system for the same offenses is evidence to support this contention by conflict theorists (Quinney 2002). The result may be that subordinate groups find illegal methods to survive. Moreover, when people feel they are not treated fairly by the society, they have less loyalty to the society and to its rules.

If the structure of society were changed and there were no dominant group exploiting subordinate groups, would crime disappear? To answer this, we can look to patterns of crime in societies that have attempted to develop a communistic classless structure. The rate of crime in China and Cuba, for instance, is lower than that in many Western democracies, in part because of less dramatic inequality and strict social controls. On the other hand, deviance does not disappear in noncapitalist societies. So while capitalistic inequality contributes to deviance, it is only one of many variables at work.

Feminist Theory

The goal of most feminist theorists is to improve women's status, including their treatment by men and those in power. Traditional theories do not give an adequate picture or understanding of women's situations. Consider the case of rape, a threat to every woman. Until recent years in many countries, there have been few serious consequences for the rapists (especially during times of anomie or war), and women often were blamed or blamed themselves for "letting it happen" (Sanday and Reeves 1981). Feminist theorists have attempted to explain this situation in cultural contexts; they argue that we learn our gender roles, part of which is men learning to be aggressive. Women's status in society results in their being treated as sex objects, to be used for men's pleasure. Women around the world fear behaviors from date rape to poor, powerless women becoming sex slaves. Women's race and class identification become relevant in the exploitation of poor ethnically distinct women from developing countries as they become victims of human trafficking.

Although there are several branches of feminist theory, most see the macro-level causes of abuses suffered by women as rooted in the capitalist, patriarchal system. They include the following ideas: (1) women are faced with a division of labor governed by their sex, (2) separation between public (work) and private (home) spheres of social activity create "we" versus "they" thinking between men and women, and (3) socialization of children into gender-specific adult roles has implications for how males and females perceive and relate to each other. One thing is certain: women who have been victimized need help from family and loved ones to feel in control again (McEvoy and Brookings 2001) yet some are blamed for the rape.

Cultural attitudes toward rape differ, often related to the status of women in society. For example, where women are held to high standards of virtue, deviation may be dealt with severely, at least as judged by Western standards. Keep in mind that each cultural practice evolved for a reason in each society;

Sociology around the World

Blaming the Victim: An Extreme Case

Every woman fears being raped—forced into having sex against her will. In most countries, rape is a deviant behavior on the part of the perpetrator, a crime punishable by imprisonment, and the woman is provided medical help and counseling, yet only a small percentage of estimated rapes are reported. In a few countries, the legal system is based on strict interpretations of religious books in order to protect the woman and family from loss of the woman's virtue, shame, and illegitimate children. Although the following example is rare, it does show the extremes to which communities can go to protect the "virtue" of women and the family. In this case, excerpted from *The New York Times*, a woman was blamed for sex outside marriage even though she was raped.

> Chorlaki, Pakistan—The evidence of guilt was there for all to see: a newborn baby in the arms of its mother, a village woman named Zafran Bibi. Her crime: she had been raped. Her sentence: death by stoning. Now Ms. Zafran, who is about 26, is in solitary confinement in a death-row cell in Kohat, a nearby town. The only visitor she is allowed is her baby daughter, now a year old and being cared for by a prison nurse. Ms. Zafran is a tall woman with striking green eyes, a peasant woman of the hot and barren hills of Pakistan's northwest frontier country. Unschooled and illiterate, like most other women there, she may have little understanding of what has happened to her, but her story is not uncommon under Pakistan's strict Islamic laws.

> Thumping a fat red statute book, the white-bearded judge who convicted her, Anwar Ali Khan, said he had simply followed the letter of the Koran-based law, known as *hudood,* that mandates punishments. "The illegitimate child is not disowned by her and therefore is proof of *zina*," he said, referring to laws that forbid any sexual contact outside marriage. Furthermore, in accusing her brother-in-law of raping her, Ms. Zafran had [implicitly] confessed to her crime. "The lady stated before this court that, yes, she had committed sexual intercourse, but with the brother of her husband," Judge Khan said. "This left no option to the court but to impose the highest penalty."

> Although legal fine points do exist, little distinction is made in court between forced and consensual sex. When *hudood* was enacted 23 years ago, the laws were formally described as measures to ban "all forms of adultery, whether the offense is committed with or without the consent of the parties," but it is almost always the women who are punished, regardless of the facts.

Source: Mydans (2002).

the meaning of these standards can only be understood through the eyes of that culture, and Western values make it difficult to understand the reason for certain practices (Mohanty 1988). An extreme example dealing with rape is seen in Sociology around the World (above).

According to feminist theory, women's work in the private sphere—housework, child care, and sexual satisfaction of their husbands—is undervalued, as are the women who carry out these roles. In some societies, women are the property of their husbands, with men's strength and physical force the ultimate means of control over women. Thus, some branches of feminist theory argue that men exploit women's labor power and sexuality in order to continue the current social order; the system is reproduced through new generations that are socialized to maintain the patriarchy and to view inequality between the sexes as "normal" and "natural." Women who deviate from the cultural expectations of "normal" behavior are condemned.

One result of women's status is that they are often victims of crime; what type of victimization varies around the globe, from sex trafficking to date and marital rape (Mohanty 1988). Women are less often in a position to commit crimes. In fact, deviant acts by women have traditionally fallen into the categories of shoplifting, credit card or welfare fraud, writing bad checks (in developed societies), prostitution, and (in some countries) adultery or inappropriate attire. Many Western feminist theorists contend that until women around the world are on an equal footing with men, crimes against women and definitions of various behaviors of women as deviant are likely to continue.

No one theory of why deviance occurs can explain all deviance completely. Some theories consider micro-level processes that shape one's values and self-identity. These approaches examine why certain behaviors and certain individuals are defined as deviant, and they explore the consequences of being labeled deviant. Meso- and macro-level theories attempt to explain structural factors at the community, national, or even the global level that result in deviance being more common among certain groups, in certain areas, or at certain times. Thus, depending on the level of the questions sociologists wish to study (micro, meso, or macro), they select the theory that best meets their needs.

THINKING SOCIOLOGICALLY

Pick a recent example of deviance from your newspaper or television news. Which sociological theories help explain this deviance?

In the United States, up until 1968, this couple would have been violating the law in roughly half of the states. Interracial marriages were illegal until the Supreme Court decided otherwise. Change in definitions of what is illegal has been common in the past 50 years.

Source: © Ana Abejon.

CRIME AND INDIVIDUALS: MICRO-LEVEL ANALYSIS

Crime refers to forms of deviance in which formal penalties are imposed by society. Deviance that violates criminal law is crime. Laws reflect opinions of what is considered right and wrong or good and bad at a particular time and place in a society. Laws change over time, reflecting changing public opinion based on social conditions or specific events.

At the end of the 1920s, 42 of the 48 U.S. states had laws forbidding interracial marriages (Coontz 2005). Interracial marriages violated the state's judicial code. While legislatures in half of these states removed those restrictions by the 1960s, the rest of them became unconstitutional only after a Supreme Court ruling in 1968; today this legal boundary to interracial marriage has been eliminated completely. This pattern is illustrated in Map 6.1. When members of society are in general agreement about the seriousness of deviant acts, these are referred to as **consensus crimes**. Predatory crimes, which are considered wrong in themselves in most nations (premeditated murder, forcible rape, and kidnapping for ransom) are examples of consensus crimes.

By contrast, **conflict crimes** occur when one group passes a law over which there is disagreement or that disadvantages another group (Hagan 1993). Examples include laws concerning public disorder, chemical (drug and alcohol) offenses, prostitution, gambling, property offenses, and political disfranchisement (denying voting rights only to some citizens—females, particular ethnic groups, or those without property). Public opinion about the seriousness of these crimes is often divided, based on people's different social class, status, and interests. The severity of societal response also varies, with high disagreement over the harmfulness of conflict crimes. Consensus or conflict about whether the behavior is harmful has implications for the punishment or support experienced by the person who is accused.

Crimes that affect the individual or primary group seem most threatening to us and receive the most attention in the press and from politicians. Yet these micro-level crimes are only a portion of the total picture and, except for hate crimes, are not the most dysfunctional or dangerous crimes. In the United States, more than 2,800 acts are listed as federal crimes. These acts fall into several types of crime, some of which are discussed below. They may be caused by meso- and macro-level factors but involve individuals (micro level) as the primary actors and victims. In the following section, we will discuss crimes with individual implications.

Predatory or Street Crimes

Crimes committed against individuals or property are called *predatory crimes* by law enforcement agencies and are considered the most serious crimes by the public. In the United States, the *Uniform Crime Report* lists eight serious "index" crimes used to track crime rates. These index crimes are all predatory acts against people (murder, robbery,

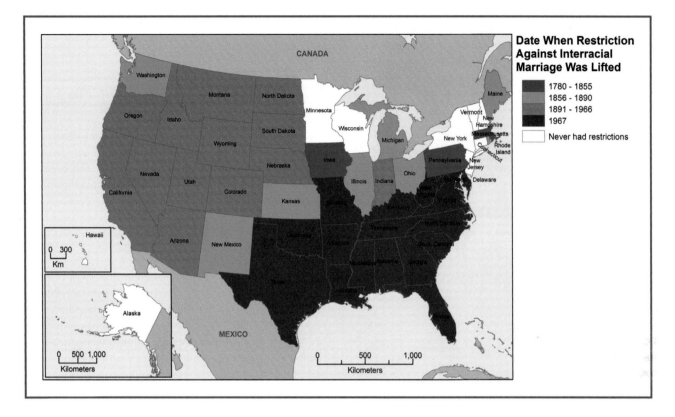

MAP 6.1   Historical Restrictions on Interracial Marriage in the United States

Source: Wallenstein (2002:253–54). Map by Anna Versluis.

assault, and rape) and acts against property (burglary, arson, theft, and auto theft).

Citizens in the United States are increasingly afraid of violent predatory crime, especially by strangers; surveys show that citizens feel they cannot trust others. Some people keep guns. Others, especially women, African Americans, older Americans, and low-income individuals, are afraid to go out near their homes at night (U.S. Bureau of Justice Statistics 2001). Because one's property and bodily safety are at stake, the public fixates on these crimes as the most feared and serious, although the rate of these crimes has been dropping. However, most criminologists do not think they are the most important or the most dangerous crimes. We will discuss the more serious crimes when we discuss meso- and macro-level deviance.

Crimes without Victims

Acts committed by or between consenting adults are known as **victimless** or **public order crimes**; depending on the laws of countries, these can include prostitution, homosexual acts, gambling, smoking marijuana and using drugs, drunkenness, and some forms of white-collar crime. Participants involved do not consider themselves to be victims, but the offense is mostly an affront to someone else's morals. The behaviors labeled deviant by laws fall into the category of conflict crime. These

A woman smokes a marijuana pipe in Amsterdam, Netherlands, where smoking pot is legal. The Dutch do not think there is any victim, and therefore there should be no prohibition of the behavior.

Source: © Jeffrey L. Rotman / Corbis.

Ellen DeGeneres (top) speaks about the tragic murder of Matthew Shepard, a gay student who was beaten and left to die in a hate crime. Counterprotestors (bottom) express their sentiment that Shepard was a deviant who had no moral standing or, seemingly, even the right to live.

Source: © Randa Links / Corbis Sygma; © Adam Mastoon / Corbis.

illegal acts may be tolerated as long as they do not become highly visible. Some prostitution is overlooked in major cities of the world, but if it becomes visible or is seen as a public nuisance, authorities crack down and it is controlled. Even though these acts are called victimless, there is controversy over whether individuals are victims even when consenting to the

act, and whether others such as family members are victims dealing with the consequences of the illegal activities.

THINKING SOCIOLOGICALLY

Can a person be victimized by drugs even if he willingly uses them? Many prostitutes only consent to sex acts because poverty leaves them with few other options and because, like many women without resources, they are vulnerable to domination by men. Are they victims?

Societies respond to victimless crimes such as using and selling drugs with a variety of policies, from execution in Iran and hanging in Malaysia to legalization in Holland. Long prison terms in the United States mean that 3 out of every 10 prison cells are now reserved for the user, the addict, and the drug seller—yet the problem has not diminished (Goode 1997, 2005). Proposals to legalize drugs, gambling, prostitution, and other victimless crimes meet with strong opinions both for and against. Although current U.S. policies and programs toward drugs are not working by almost any measure of success, the various consequences of alternative proposals are also uncertain.

Hate Crimes

Ethnic violence around the world results in reports of hate crimes in communities, at workplaces, and on college campuses. *Hate crimes* are criminal offenses committed against a person, property, or group that are motivated by the offender's bias against a religious, ethnic or national origin, or sexual orientation group. The *Uniform Crime Reports (UCR)* in the United States indicated that hate crimes account for 11.5 percent of total offenses. The majority of hate crimes are directed against property (84.4 percent) and involve destruction, damage, or vandalism; 31.3 percent include direct intimidation, totalling 9,035 hate crimes involving 9,528 victims (U.S. Bureau of Justice Statistics 2005; U.S. Federal Bureau of Investigation 2005b).

Research suggests that most hate crimes are spontaneous incidents, often a case of the victim being in the wrong place at the wrong time. Consider the case of Matthew Shephard, the gay college student who was robbed, tied to a fence post, beaten, and left to die in the cold Wyoming night; 15.7 percent of hate crimes were against those with different sexual orientations. Victims often form supportive in-groups to protect them from others who create a "culture of hate" (Jenness and Broad 1997; Levin and McDevitt 2003).

Hate crimes are often vicious and brutal because the perpetrators feel rage against the victim as a representative of a group they despise. The crimes are committed by individuals or small vigilante groups; the targets are usually

Every 3.1 seconds	1 property crime	Every 36.9 seconds	1 aggravated assault
Every 4.5 seconds	1 larceny, theft	Every 1.3 minutes	1 robbery
Every 14.7 seconds	1 burglary	Every 5.6 minutes	1 forcible rape
Every 25.5 seconds	1 motor vehicle theft	Every 32.6 minutes	1 murder
Every 23.1 seconds	1 violent crime		

Figure 6.2   Crime Clock

Source: U.S. Federal Bureau of Investigation (2005a).

individuals who happen to have certain traits or are part of a particular community.

How Much Crime Is There?

How do sociologists and law enforcement officials know how much crime there is, especially since not all crime is reported to the police? Each country has methods of keeping crime records. For instance, the official record of crime in the United States is found in the FBI's (Federal Bureau of Investigation's) *Uniform Crime Reports (UCR)*. The FBI relies on information submitted voluntarily by law enforcement agencies and divides crimes into two categories: Type I and Type II offenses. Type I offenses, also known as *FBI index crimes,* include murder, forcible rape, robbery, aggravated assault, burglary, larceny theft, motor vehicle theft, and arson. There are hundreds of Type II offenses including fraud, simple assault, vandalism, driving under the influence of alcohol or drugs, and running away from home. The Crime Clock in Figure 6.2 summarizes *UCR* crime records on Type I offenses.

To examine trends in crime, criminologists calculate a rate of crime, usually per 100,000 individuals. Recent data indicate that the rate of violent crime in the United States has been dropping since the mid-1990s. Table 6.1 indicates changes in the rate of Index Crimes from 1985 to 2004 (U.S. Federal Bureau of Investigation 2005a).

Although the *UCR* data provide a picture of how much crime gets reported to the police and leads to arrest, it really does not provide information on how much crime there is in the United States. Sometimes, a crime that *is* reported to the police does not lead to an arrest, or an arrest is made but the case is never prosecuted in court, or a prosecutor will initiate prosecution but the case never comes to trial. Instead, it is *plea-bargained*—a suspect agrees to plead guilty in exchange for being given a lesser charge, perhaps because of guilt or because the person does not have the resources to fight the charges with a good attorney. The reduction of number of cases as the criminal offenses are processed through the criminal justice system is just one of the problems of attempting to determine accurate crime rates.

Another technique to assess crime rates is *self-reporting surveys*—asking individuals what criminal acts they have committed. Such surveys typically focus on adolescents and their involvement in delinquency.

A more respected method among criminologists for finding out how much crime is actually taking place is *victimization surveys*—surveys that ask people how much crime they have experienced. The most extensively gathered victimization survey in the United States is the *National Crime Victimization Survey,* conducted by the Bureau of Justice Statistics. According to these records, the tendency to report crime to the police varies by the type of crime, with violent victimizations having the highest reporting rate. The survey corroborates the data in the Index of Crime, showing that violent crime rates have declined, continuing the downward trend in the Unites States seen since 1994.

How crime is measured affects what and how much crime is reported. While differences in crime reports are often difficult to reconcile, each measurement instrument provides a different portion of the total picture of crime. By using several data-gathering techniques, a more accurate picture of crime begins to emerge. Not only is response to crime more rooted in complex organizations at this level, but crimes themselves are committed within or by organizations.

TABLE 6.1	**Index of Violent Crime, United States**
Year	**Violent Crime Rate (per 100,000 residents)**
1985	558.1
1990	729.6
1995	684.5
2000	506.5
2001	504.5
2002	494.4
2003	475.8
2004	465.5

Source: U.S. Federal Bureau of Investigation (2005a).

Which method discussed above seems like a more accurate way to assess the crime rate and identify theft crime trends? Why is the FBI report usually given attention by the press?

CRIME AND ORGANIZATIONS: MESO-LEVEL ANALYSIS

Understanding criminal behavior is especially important if we wish to understand complex modern societies. First, as societies modernize, there is an almost universal tendency for crime rates to increase dramatically due to *anomie:* normlessness due to breakdown of norms resulting from rapid change in norms, anonymity individuals experience in urban areas, and subcultural differences between urban migrants (Archer and Gartner 1984; Merton 1968). Second, as societies modernize, they become more reliant on formal or bureaucratic mechanisms of control—in other words, a development of the criminal justice system at the meso level of our social world.

Crimes Involving Organizations and Institutions

Organized Crime

Organized crime, on-going criminal enterprises, have the ultimate purpose of personal economic gain through illegitimate means (Siegel 2006). Organized criminals use business enterprises for illegal profit. They engage in violence and corruption in order to gain and maintain power and profit (Adler et al. 2004). Our image of this type of crime is sometimes glamorized, coming from stereotypes in films such as *The Godfather, The Freshman, Goodfellas, The Last Dawn, Casino, Bugsy, Carlito's Way, Prizzi's Honor, Analyze This,* and *Gangs of New York.* Despite this alluring view, organized crime is a serious problem in many countries. It is essentially a *counterculture* with a hierarchical structure, from the boss down to underlings. The operations rely on power, control, fear, violence, and corruption. This type of crime is a particular problem when societies experience anomie and social controls break down.

Marginalized ethnic groups that face discrimination may become involved in a quest to get ahead through organized crime. Early in U.S. history, Italians were especially prominent in organized crime, but today many groups are involved. Organized crime around the world has gained strong footholds in countries in transition. For example, in Russia, anomie resulting from the transition from a socialist economy to a market economy has provided many opportunities for criminal activity.

Organized crime usually takes one of three forms: (1) the *sale of illegal goods and services*, including gambling, loan-sharking, trafficking in drugs and people, selling stolen goods, and prostitution; (2) *infiltrating legitimate businesses and unions* through threat and intimidation, and using bankruptcy and fraud to exploit and devastate a legitimate company; and (3) *racketeering*, the extortion of funds in exchange for protection (i.e., not being hurt). Activities such as running a casino or trash collection service often appear to be legitimate endeavors on the surface but may be cover operations for highly organized illegal crime rings.

Although the cost of organized crime in the United States is impossible to determine exactly, estimates of the annual gross income from organized crime activity is at least 50 billion dollars, more than 1 percent of the gross national product. Some scholars estimate earnings at 90 billion dollars per year (Siegel 2000). Organized crime is responsible for thousands of deaths a year through drug traffic and murders, and it contributes to a climate of violence in many cities (Siegel 2006).

International organized crime has become transnational, using sophisticated electronic communications and transportation technologies. The value of the global illicit drug market is estimated at over 13 billion dollars at the production level, 94 billion dollars at the wholesale level, and 322 billion dollars at the retail level (based on retail prices and taking seizures and other losses into account). The largest market is cannabis, followed by cocaine, the opiates, and other markets (methamphetamine, amphetamine, and ecstasy) (United Nations Development Programme 2005). Many people survive off of the drug trade, from the poppy farmers in Afghanistan, who grow over 75 percent of the world's poppies, to the street drug dealers.

Add other types of crimes (transporting migrants, trafficking in women and children for the sex industry, weapons sales and nuclear material, body parts for transplants) and the estimates of profits for international crime cartels are from 750 billion to over 1.5 trillion dollars a year (United Nations Development Programme 2005).

Occupational Crime

The Arthur Anderson accounting firm employee working with Enron shredded documents, covering a trail of shady dealings. This was illegal. A violation of the law committed by an individual or group in the course of a legitimate, respected occupation or financial activity is called white-collar or *occupational crime* (Coleman 2006; Hagan 2002). Occupational crime can be committed by individuals from virtually any social class, and it can occur at any organizational level. However, most often this refers to white-collar crimes, in the U.S. "estimated to be ten times greater than all the annual losses from all the crimes reported to the police" (Coleman 2006:43). Collapse of the savings and loan industry cost the public billions of dollars. Antitrust violations cost 250 billion dollars. Tax fraud costs 150 billion dollars, and health care industry fraud costs 100 billion dollars. Employee theft adds 2 percent to the retail purchase prices of products we buy (Coleman 2006). Occupational crime receives less attention than violent crimes because it is less visible and because it is frequently committed by people in positions of substantial authority and prestige, as opposed to reports of violent crimes that appear on the television news each night.

Occupational crime is less publicized because it does not always cause *obvious* physical injury to identifiable persons; it occurs in the less visible arena of the meso-level social structure. However, occupational crime can cause death and injuries from lack of safety precautions to malfunctioning machines as seen in cases of mining safety. The cost is tremendous, running into hundreds of billions of dollars a year, far more than violent predatory crimes. Victims of financial scams who have lost their life savings are well aware of this. For instance, in 2001 and 2002, the collapse of major corporations such as Enron left thousands of investors with little stock value; trials have convicted the white-collar executives of wrongdoing in the case.

In addition to occupational crimes such as embezzlement, pilfering, bribery, tax evasion, price fixing, obstruction of justice, and various forms of fraud, computer crime is adding to the losses of businesses and government. Identity theft, embezzlement, international illegal transfers of money, and stock trades cost up to 15 billion dollars worldwide (Rosoff, Pontell, and Tillman 1998). Some banks and trust funds have collapsed due to illegal trading in stocks and bonds.

Sociologists divide occupational crimes into four major categories: crimes against the company, against the employees, against customers, and against the general public (Hagan 2002).

Crimes against the company include pilfering (using company resources such as the photocopy machine for personal business) and employee theft ("borrowing company property," taking from the till, and embezzlement). Most employees are otherwise upstanding citizens, but those who commit occupational crimes say they do so for several reasons. First, they feel little or no loyalty to the organization, especially if it is large and impersonal; it is like stealing from nobody. Second, workers feel exploited and resentful toward the company; stealing is getting back at the company. Third, the theft is seen as a "fringe benefit" or "informal compensation" that they deserve. Making personal long-distance calls on company phones or taking paper and pens are examples. Fourth, workers may steal because of the challenge; it makes the job more interesting if they can get away with it. It is important to note that these people do not see themselves as criminals, especially compared with "street" criminals (Altheide 1978).

The next three types of corporate crime are often done on behalf of the company, and the victims are employees or members of the larger society. *Crimes against employees*

In 2005, this man was rescued after an underground explosion at Dongfeng Coal Mine in northeast China that claimed the lives of 150 miners and left many others severely injured. Similar tragedies have happened in the United States. Often, the cause is a violation of safety regulations by the corporation, a corporate crime against employees that can result in massive deaths.

Source: © Cui Feng / Xinhua / Corbis.

refer to corporate neglect of worker safety. In the United States, the Occupational Safety and Health Act was passed in 1970 to help enforce regulations to protect workers, but there are still many problems. Government agencies estimate that the death rate each year from job-related illness and injuries is fivefold the number from all deaths from street crimes. For example, one out of every five cancer cases have been traced to pollutants in workplaces, and many of these cases were preventable (Simon 2006). Neglect of worker safety is a serious problem in some developing or peripheral countries trying to attract corporations with low taxes, cheap labor, and few regulations.

Why does corporate crime and negligence occur? Several theories of crime are helpful in explaining this pattern. Organizational crimes by executives take place in environments where profits are expected by investors and by one's coworkers (*differential association theory*) and where the benefits of such behavior seem, at the time, to outweigh the costs (*rational choice theory*). The micro-level environment within the larger corporation shapes the decision-making process in a way that fosters crime.

Strain theory points out that corporations are interested in making the greatest short-term profits to achieve their goals; in fact, it is illegal for a U.S. corporation to do anything contrary to the interests of the stockholders. Thus, to install expensive equipment or safety devices cuts those profits, and many employers are concerned with profit, not long-term consequences. Although government agencies in many countries are responsible for reducing environmental hazards and workplace dangers, they do not have sufficient staff to police companies for adherence to laws. Internationally, there is little oversight; when agencies do step in, it is usually after the fact—when complaints are lodged because of serious health and safety problems. Multinational corporations generally look for the cheapest labor costs and lowest environmental regulations to maximize their profits.

One cause of anomie is large numbers of migrants from rural areas coming to urban areas to look for jobs. Without work or hope, they create an unstable population. Governments of these countries try to attract foreign corporations to keep the poor populace employed, regardless of the environmental or workplace consequences.

THINKING SOCIOLOGICALLY

How might conflict theory explain corporate crime?

Crimes against customers involve acts such as selling dangerous foods or unsafe products, consumer fraud, deceptive advertising, and price-fixing (setting prices in collusion with another producer). The purpose of advertising is to convince customers, by whatever means, to buy the product—appealing to vanity, sexual interests, or

Industrial pollution in the Calumet River in Illinois has many causes. However, the U.S. Environmental Protection Agency has documented many cases in which industries violate pollution control laws, and it is the citizenry who suffer—a case of corporate crime against customers.

Source: U.S. Environmental Protection Agency.

competition to keep up with neighbors. Sometimes, these techniques cross the line between honesty and deception. The result can be customers purchasing products that are defective and even highly dangerous—all with the full knowledge of company officials.

Crimes against the public include acts by companies that negatively affect large groups of people. Hospitals or medical offices overbilling Medicare, which costs the taxpayers in the United States an estimated 100 billion dollars a year, is one example. Surreptitiously dumping pollutants into landfills, streams, or the air is another. Proper disposal of contaminants can be costly and time-consuming for a company, but shortcuts can cause long-term effects for the public. One example is Love Canal, New York, the illegal dumping ground for toxic chemicals from the Hooker Chemical Corporation. Years after the dumping, the chemicals injured children and others; Hooker eventually paid 227 million dollars in damages, but cleanup cost taxpayers another 280 million dollars (Coleman 2006). Pollutants from industrial wastes have caused high rates of miscarriages, birth defects, and diseases among residents. These cases demonstrate how lethal crimes against the public can be. The film *Erin Brockovich* illustrated the fight of families against chemical polluters.

After reviewing the evidence, Coleman (2006) draws the conclusion that white-collar crime committed by company executives is by far our most serious crime problem. The economic cost of white-collar crime is vastly greater than the economic cost of street crime. White-collar criminals kill considerably more people than all violent street criminals put together (Coleman 2006).

NATIONAL ISSUES AND GLOBAL COMPARISONS: MACRO-LEVEL ANALYSIS

Crime is a national and global issue as illustrated by *state organized crime*. Overlooked by the public and even by social scientists, this form of crime includes acts defined by law as criminal but committed by state or government officials in the pursuit of their jobs. Examples include a government's complicity in smuggling or assassination, acting as an accessory to crime that is then justified in terms of "national defense," and violating laws that restrict or limit government activities. In some countries including the United States, political prisoners are held without charges, access to lawyers, and trials for long periods, or are tortured, violating both national and international laws. Some countries have also violated their own laws, but it is difficult to cast blame when the guilty party is the government. In places such as Myanmar and Iraq under Saddam Hussein, the government has terrorized the citizenry into conformity and passivity.

Bribery and corruption are the way of life in many governments and businesses. Table 6.2 shows comparative corruption rankings (Transparency International 2003).

TABLE 6.2	**Corruption, 2003**	
	Finland	9.7
	Denmark	9.5
	New Zealand	9.5
	Singapore	9.4
	Sweden	9.3
	Netherlands	8.9
	Norway	8.8
	Switzerland	8.8
	Australia	8.8
	United Kingdom	8.7
	Germany	7.7
	United States	7.5
	Japan	7.0
	France	6.9
	Italy	5.3
	Mexico	3.6
	Thailand	3.3
	Vietnam	2.4
	Indonesia	1.9

Source: Transparency International (2003).

Note: Lower scores indicate more corruption.

THINKING SOCIOLOGICALLY

Sometimes government officials and even heads of state are the perpetrators of crimes. Is there a difference in crime if it is done by an official and justified as necessary for national defense? Why or why not? Is it ever justified for a military or intelligence agency to violate its own country's laws?

Cross-National Comparison of Crimes

Although comparing cross-national data on crime is difficult because there are variations in the measures and definitions of crime, comparisons do give us insight into what types of crimes are committed, under what circumstances, and how often. This information is useful to countries trying to control criminal behaviors in their societies.

Japan and the United States are both modern, urban, industrial countries, but their rates of violent crime are very different. Japan has 21 violent crimes for every 100,000 individuals (including 1 homicide, 2 rapes, 5 robberies), whereas the rate in the United States is 637 for every 100,000 individuals (including 6 homicides, 32 rapes, 149 robberies)— a rate 30 times greater (Interpol Data 2003). How can these differences in crime rates be explained? Researchers look at cultural differences: Japan's low violent crime rate is due in part to Japan's homogeneous society; Japanese people are loyal to a historic tradition of cooperation that provides a sense of moral order, a network of group relations, strong commitment to social norms, and respect for law and order (Westermann and Burfeind 1991). The chapter-opening example about vending machines in Japan illustrates this idea.

Crime rates also reflect a society's methods of dealing with deviance and the level of inequality. Inequality is not as great between people in Japan as it is in some other countries, including the United States; therefore, the economic incentive to commit crime is less. Moreover, the definition of *success* in Japan is not as focused on material possessions and consumption.

Criminologists also consider the causes of economic inequality in different countries. If minority status prevents certain individuals and groups from fitting into the dominant society and getting ahead, this helps explain higher levels of deviance among the disfranchised groups. The overall health of a country's economy—as measured by job opportunities, unemployment, and inflation—also affects the crime rate. When the economy is poor, the crime rates rise. Research shows that the incidence of homicide is higher in countries with greater income inequality.

Detainees sit in a holding area at the Naval Base in Guantanamo Bay, Cuba, during in-processing to the "temporary" detention facility. Four years later, most of the men were still being held without trial. In 2006, the U.S. Supreme Court ruled that the rights of these people have been violated by the U.S. administration. However, little has changed.

Source: © Ron Sachs/CNP/Corbis.

TABLE 6.3   **Crime Rates in Selected Countries for 2001 (incidents per 100,000 individuals)**

Country	Homicide	Rape	Robbery	Burglary	Auto Theft
Albania	16.88	1.65	7.39	8.78	5.44
Argentina	8.24	8.89	135.01	51.22	188.03
Austria	1.96	7.12	85.84	1035.60	48.71
Belgium	5.97	18.82	8.73	736.74	299.78
Brazil	22.98	8.50	88.51		
Bulgaria	6.10	7.00	51.03	454.86	134.94
Canada	4.10	88.20	908.93	547.63	
Colombia (2000)	69.98		6.10	58.10	78.46
Czech Republic	2.27	5.46	42.45	613.27	214.94
Denmark	3.72	9.22	59.67	1776.17	526.06
El Salvador	34.33	17.59	24.14		
Ethiopia	6.33	1.88	5.26	2.04	2.26
Finland	1.71	8.68	40.44		
France	3.91	16.36	229.47	711.39	537.67
Germany	3.21	9.59	69.42	1250.10	91.67
Ghana		2.34	4.77	4.11	2.04
Hong Kong	1.03	1.41	68.00	128.41	16.45
Hungary	4.01	3.20	33.04	681.99	92.41
Ireland	1.60	11.06	48.10	647.17	4.88
Israel	3.43	10.11	30.30	844.20	472.90
Italy	3.75	65.92	408.72		
Jamaica	43.71	35.00	80.93	83.81	3.68
Japan	1.05	1.75	5.02	238.59	49.71
South Korea	2.18	4.29	11.80	6.40	
Mongolia	15.21	26.48	464.72	0.38	
Paraguay	15.56	5.05	3.06	1.85	31.99
Poland	3.50	6.05	129.04	842.88	153.87
Portugal	2.58	3.35	179.84	425.27	253.52
Russia	23.19	5.66	30.94	573.11	26.54
Singapore	0.80	2.81	15.18	23.36	4.55
South Africa	114.84	121.13	468.87	883.83	221.01
Spain	2.90	2.96	250.04	565.07	353.19
Sweden	10.01	23.39	95.83	1323.90	495.21
Switzerland	2.41	6.25	31.08	790.45	885.05
Trinidad/Tobago	14.46	21.62	328.69	385.85	124.85
Turkey	3.89	2.06	4.45	126.76	31.58
United Kingdom					
England and Wales	1.63	16.50	182.69	1605.14	650.47
Northern Ireland	1.60	11.06	48.10	647.17	4.88
Scotland	15.28	11.51	82.59	1652.93	453.35
United States	5.61	31.77	148.50	740.80	430.64
Zimbabwe	10.15	38.38	132.70	485.15	8.68

Source: Interpol Data (2003).

Table 6.3 provides information on crimes in selected countries. Note the differences in crime rates (Interpol Data 2003). As discussed above, these differences are due in part to the much higher disparity in income between rich and poor and the heterogeneity of populations.

THINKING SOCIOLOGICALLY

What can you tell about countries from studying their crime rates? Do the rape rates, especially, tell us anything significant? If so, what?

Global Crimes

Increasingly, crimes are global in nature. Some crimes are committed by transnational conglomerates and may involve organized crime and the smuggling of illegal goods and humans. Other crimes are committed by countries that violate international laws, treaties, and agreements. Consider international agreements regarding protection of the environment that some countries and transnational corporations ignore when these agreements act against their own self-interests; yet these acts may affect the entire global ecological system. The international community has the capacity to try people, organizations, and countries for violation of human rights or international laws, but the process is difficult and politically charged. The 2006 case of Iran's developing nuclear fuel is a case in point.

Some scholars use a *world system perspective*, arguing that the cause of deviance lies in the global economy, inequalities between countries, and competition between countries for resources and wealth. As a result of the capitalist mode of production, an unequal relationship has arisen between core (developed, wealthy nations) and periphery (developing) nations that results in inequality. Core nations often take unfair advantage of peripheral nations; peripheral nations, in turn, must find ways to survive in this global system, and they sometime turn to surreptitious methods to achieve their goals (Chase-Dunn and Anderson 2006). Some nations with lots of resources are semiperiphery nations, benefiting from extensive trade and less vulnerable than the poorest nations. Map 6.2 helps you see where some of these core, peripheral, and semiperipheral nations are located.

As you look at this map, note that the developed or affluent countries are almost all located in the northern hemisphere. While some poor countries are north of the equator, the pattern is obvious; furthermore, the phrase "gone south" is often a colloquialism for an economy that is not strong. To avoid some misleading implications of the words "developed" and "developing," some scholars prefer the term Global South to refer to less affluent nations. If you see or hear the phrase "global south," this Map should help you see why it refers to "developing" poor or countries [see map on next page].

The forms of global corruption are too extensive to catalog here, so we will settle for an illustration of one of the newest manifestations of global crime against people and property: computer crimes involving the Internet.

One team of researchers reports, the Internet "is where crime is rampant and every twisted urge can be satisfied. . . . Fraudsters can tap into an international audience from anyplace in the world" (Sager et al. 2006:261). The illegal "underground web" of businesses such as arms-dealing was estimated at more than 36 billion dollars in 2002; compare that to legitimate business consumers in the United States spending just over 39 billion dollars on the Internet the same year. Of the fraud complaints received by the U.S. government, over 70 percent involved the Internet. Sager and his colleagues write, "The Underground Web, if unchecked, has the potential to undermine the values of society. It enables— even encourages—ordinary citizens to break the law" (Sager et al. 2006:262).

Even legitimate businesses such as Google, Yahoo! or eBay can unwittingly support crime by connecting people to illegal operations. Drug traffic is one of the most common forms of scam; for example, people purchase bodybuilding drugs that are life threatening, find recipes for making illegal methamphetamines, or purchase the date rape drug GHB. Another venue of illegal Internet usage is music and video downloading and sales (Friedman 2005).

Other crimes have also become easier to commit: the FBI reported an increase in online child porn arrests, from 68 in 1996 to 514 in 2001, an increase of 756 percent. Financial fraud costs consumers 22 billion dollars annually according to *Business Week*, and identity theft is running 22 billion dollars annually according to the Identity Theft Resource Center (Sager et al. 2006).

One policy difficulty is that law enforcement gets gridlocked in both national and international jurisdictional confusion. As many as five different federal U.S. agencies can be involved in preventing financial fraud on the Internet, not to mention the state and local agencies that might play a role. If the fraud involves international cybercrime, the customs services and other branches of governments also may enter the investigation. The resulting confusion and lack of clear authority regarding who should prosecute can play into the hands of lawbreakers. Few local authorities feel that identity theft is within their jurisdiction, but government officials may not have the personnel or the interest to pursue these cases (Sager et al. 2006).

THINKING SOCIOLOGICALLY

Why do certain people choose or become forced into a deviant lifestyle? What have you learned so far that helps explain why individuals become deviant?

CONTROLLING CRIME: POLICY CONSIDERATIONS

When people are afraid to walk on the streets because they might be assaulted and when a significant number of individuals are dropping out of society and taking up deviant lifestyles, deviance becomes a topic of great concern. Most governments pass laws and make policies to keep deviance from disrupting the smooth functioning of society. This section discusses mechanisms used by societies to control the amount of deviance.

Dealing with Crime: The Criminal Justice Process

Every society has a process for dealing with criminals. English law sets the ground rules for criminal justice systems in many modern countries. Structural-functionalists see the justice system as important to maintaining order in society. Sometimes, the ground rules and processes of justice respect human rights and represent *blind justice*, meaning that all people are treated equally; often they do not.

Some conflict theorists argue that the criminal justice system presents the threat of crime as a threat from poor people and minorities; it creates fear of victimization in members of society. It is in the interests of those in power to maintain the image that crime is primarily the work of the

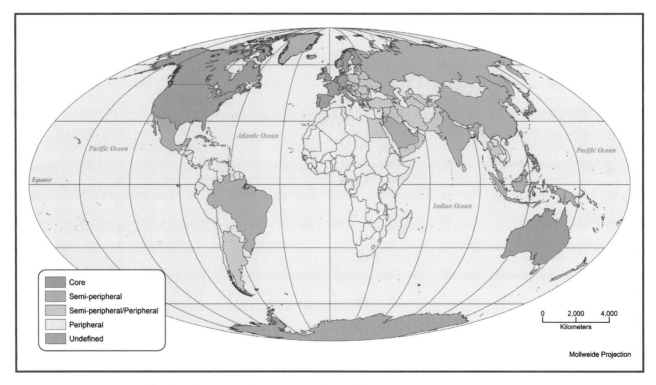

MAP 6.2   Core, Semiperipheral, and Peripheral Countries of the World

Source: Map by Anna Versluis

Note: Some countries are left undefined (in gray). How would you categorize these countries? Do you think the classes of core, semiperipheral, and peripheral work for areas like the Middle East and Eastern Europe?

The public typically hears about "posh conditions," a rare condition. Many prisons are humiliating, degrading, and disorienting for inmates. In most jails, the majority of the people being held have not yet been found guilty of anything, so they are still "presumed innocent."

Source: Photo by Dylan Oliphant from LaMarque, United States.

poor; this deflects discontent and hostility from the powerful and helps them retain their positions (Reiman 1998). Conflict theorists point out that there will always be a certain percentage of crime in society because the powerful will make sure that *something* is labeled deviant. So policy might focus on how to deter deviant acts, or it could focus on the injustices of the system and ways in which the criminal justice system protects and sustains the power structure. In any case, prisons and jails—penal institutions—are currently a primary means of controlling individual criminal behavior.

Prisons and Jails

All modern societies provide some means of protecting individuals from criminals, especially those considered dangerous. Crimes of murder, assault, robbery, and rape usually receive severe penalties. Protection from offenders often means locking people in prisons, a form of *total institution* that completely controls the prisoners' lives and regulates all of their activities. Inmates' lives are drastically changed through the processes of *degradation* that mark the individual as deviant and *mortification* that breaks down the individual's original self as the inmate experiences resocialization (Goffman 1961; Irwin 1985). The inmate is allowed no personal property, there is little communication, verbal abuse of inmates by guards is common, heterosexual activity is prohibited, uniforms and standard buzz cuts are required, and the inmates' schedules are totally controlled.

Social systems that develop within the prison often involve rigid roles, norms, privileges—and informal black markets. In a famous study that simulated a prison situation, Zimbardo illustrated the social organization that develops and the roles that individuals play within the prison system. Students were assigned to roles as prisoners or prison guards. Within a short time, the individuals in the study were acting out their roles. The students playing the role of "guard" became cruel and sadistic, causing Zimbardo to end the experiment prematurely to prevent problems. Participants had taken their roles so seriously that abuse was beginning to have alarming consequences (Zimbardo et al. 1973). The recent abuse of prisoners in Iraq and at Guantanamo prison in Cuba parallel the findings about roles that develop in these social situations from Zimbardo's earlier study (Zimbardo 2007).

Jails in local communities have been called catchall asylums for poor people. Most people in jails are there for their "rabble existence—petty hustlers, derelicts, junkies, crazies, and outlaws" (Irwin 1985). Jails in Europe and the United States house disproportionate numbers of immigrants (especially those with non-European features and skin tones), young men, and members of the poorest class of the citizenry. In the United States, whites make up only 34 percent of the incarcerated population with a sentence of more than one year; their percentage of the U.S. population is around 70 percent. African Americans make up 41 percent of all inmates and around 12 percent of total population, and Hispanics 19 percent of all inmates and approximately 13 percent of the total population (U.S. Federal Bureau of Investigation 2005a).

Numbers of incarcerated individuals have increased rather dramatically in the United States. The reasons for the increase in incarceration rates in the United States have to do with get-tough-on-crime policies, preventative detention policies that lock people up for minor offenses, and the "war on drugs" that increases the number of people put in jails and prisons. The increase in inmates in the United States has meant more jails being built and more people hired to work in the legal system.

THINKING SOCIOLOGICALLY

Why are the people who get sent to jail disproportionately young, poor immigrants, or racial and ethnic minorities?

The Functions and Effectiveness of Prisons

Prisons serve several functions for society. The *desire for revenge or retribution* leads to harsh penalties such as death or life imprisonment. *Removing dangerous people from society* is also seen as a way to protect the public by incapacitating those we think are a threat. *Deterrence* serves the purpose of

preventing an individual from future deviance and deterring others from becoming deviant. Finally, *rehabilitation* efforts are reflected in counseling, education, and work training programs inside prisons (Johnson 2002).

Deterrence is the most common argument underlying the use of the death penalty, more formally known as *capital punishment*. Although most developed countries do not use the death penalty as punishment, the United States still does. In fact, as you can see from Map 6.3, the United States is one of the few countries in North or South America with the death penalty. Capital punishment is most common in Asia, the Middle East, and parts of Africa.

Eighty-one United Nations member nations signed a resolution against the death penalty, declaring it cruel and unusual punishment. Eighty-six countries have laws against the death penalty, 11 more forbid it except for exceptional crimes (such as war crimes), and 27 additional countries have not executed anyone in 10 or more years, although they have no laws forbidding capital punishment. That means 124 countries do not actively employ the death penalty. Seventy-two countries retain the right to use the death penalty, although many of those countries actually do not follow through with the sentence (Amnesty International 2006).

In 2005, there were 2,148 known executions in the world in 22 countries; 94 percent of those occurred in China, Iran, Saudi Arabia, and the United States. Methods of killing included beheading, electrocution, hanging, lethal injection, shooting, and stoning to death. Ironically, research has not shown that the death penalty deters crime, though it serves as retribution (Hood 2002).

U.S. states with the death penalty assume that those contemplating crimes will be deterred by severe penalties, and those who have committed crimes will be justly punished. However, studies on the deterrent effects of capital punishment do not support the first assumption; less than 25 percent of inmates questioned believe the death penalty to be a deterrent to violent crime (Steele and Wilcox 2003). Those who had committed three or more violent crimes indicated that their crimes were not planned, they "just happened," "things went wrong," and they were not thinking or caring about the possible penalty when committing their crimes (Wilcox and Steele 2003). In 2004, the average murder rate per 100,000 people in states with the death penalty was 5.1; the murder rate was much less—2.9—in states that do not have the death penalty (Death Penalty Information Center 2006; Hood 2002). So murder is more likely to happen in states with the death penalty, which is not very good evidence that this penalty has been a deterrent.

THINKING SOCIOLOGICALLY

How can you explain higher murder rates in U.S. states that do have the death penalty?

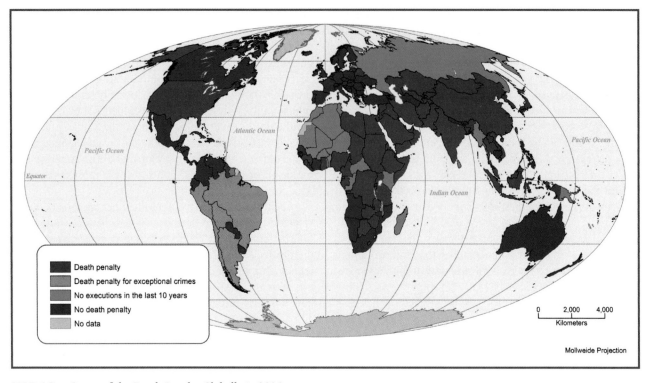

MAP 6.3   Status of the Death Penalty Globally in 2006

Source: Amnesty International (2006). Map by Anna Versluis.

Is the death penalty fairly administered? There is evidence that the death penalty is race and class biased as well; in most U.S. states with capital punishment, a disproportionate number of minority and lower-class individuals are put to death. African Americans make up 42 percent of the death sentence inmates (Bonczar and Snell 2005); in some jurisdictions, African Americans receive the death penalty at a rate 38 percent higher than all others groups. Since 1976, 35 percent of all those executed have been African American, a disproportionate number when considering that they make up less than 13 percent of the population (Amnesty International 2005; Sarat 2001; Siegel 2006).

Furthermore, the death penalty is usually imposed if a white person has been murdered. Homicides in which African Americans, Latinos and Latinas, Native Americans, and Asian Americans are killed are much less likely to result in a death penalty for the murderer, implying that people in society view their loss of life as less serious (Amnesty International 2006). In addition, mistakes are made. Since 1973, 123 prisoners have been released from death row because they were found innocent, and DNA tests are acquitting other death row prisoners and have exonerated people who have already been executed.

Criminals in prison are exposed to more criminal and antisocial behavior, so rehabilitation and deterrence goals are often undermined by the nature of prisons. Consider the case of rape behind bars (Banbury 2004). Nearly 300,000 males are sexually assaulted in U.S. prisons every year, often in gang rapes. Threats of sexual violence and displays of power are a more common motive than actual rape; domination of others to prove manhood prevails in situations in which one cannot otherwise fulfill masculine role expectations (Hanser 2002; Welch 1996). This ongoing problem of assault, rape, and threat of violence in prison so brutalizes inmates that it becomes difficult for them to reenter society as well-adjusted citizens ready to conform to the conventional society they feel has brutalized them (Hensley, Koscheski, and Tewksbury 2005).

Although estimates indicate that only 3 percent of known criminals go to prison, there has been a tremendous increase in incarceration rates in the United States. By the end of 2005, the federal and state prison and local jail population reached well over 2 million prisoners, a total increase of 3.5 percent annually since 1995 (U.S. Bureau of Justice Statistics 2004). Incarceration rates were 724 of every 100,000 U.S. residents in the country (International Centre for Prison Studies 2006). Figure 6.3 illustrates the increase in the prison population since 1925 (Harrison and Karberg 2003).

One in eight African American males between the ages of 25 and 29 are in prison today (12.6 percent); 3.6 percent of the Hispanic population is imprisoned, as opposed to 1.7 percent of whites. In some areas, the rate is much higher; for Blacks in Washington, DC, the rate is 75 percent (The Sentencing Project 2006). Table 6.4 provides a comparison of

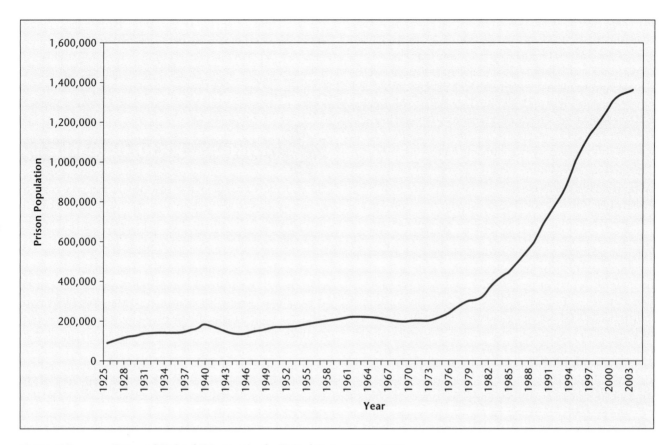

Figure 6.3   State and Federal Prisoners in the United States, 1925–2003

the number of jail and prison inmates in the United States by race.

TABLE 6.4	**Incarceration Rates: Number of Jail Inmates per 100,000 U.S. Residents**		
	Incarceration Rates by Race		
Year	White (non-Hispanic)	Black (non-Hispanic)	Hispanic of Any Race
1990	89	560	245
1995	104	670	263
2000	132	736	280

Source: U.S. Bureau of Justice Statistics (2002).

At 724 per 100,000, the U.S. rate of locking up citizens is the highest in the world, and five to eight times higher than that in other industrial nations (International Centre for Prison Studies 2006; The Sentencing Project 2006). Table 6.5 shows the countries with the highest incarceration rates and compares rates of incarceration in industrial countries.

TABLE 6.5	**World Rates of Incarceration (rates per 100,000 people)**		
Top 10 Countries		**Industrialized Countries**	
United States	724	United Kingdom: England and Wales	144
Russian Federation	594	Spain	143
St. Kitts and Nevis	536	Netherlands	127
Bermuda	532	Australia	126
Virgin Islands (U.S.)	521	Portugal	123
Turkmenistan	489	Austria	108
Cuba	487	Canada	107
Palau	478	Germany	97
Belize	470	Italy	97
Bahamas	462	France	88
		Switzerland	83
		Sweden, Denmark, Finland	78–75
		Japan	62

Source: International Centre for Prison Studies (2006).

The disturbing reality is that, despite the high rates of incarceration in the U.S., **recidivism rates**—the likelihood that someone who is arrested, convicted, and imprisoned will later be a repeat offender—are also very high in the United States. Three out of four men who do time in prison will be confined again for a crime. This means that as a specific deterrent or for rehabilitation, imprisonment does not work very well (National Center for Policy Analysis 2001). This fact has led to a search for alternative means to control crime and has spurred policy analysts to rethink assumptions about what factors are effective in controlling human behavior.

Alternatives to Prison

Social capital refers to social networks, shared norms, values, and understanding that facilitate cooperation within or among groups and access to important resources (Flavin 2004); it encompasses relationships, support systems and services, community resource accessibility, and the interconnections between them, and is embedded in the social structure (Jarrett, Sullivan, and Watkins 2005). Increasing an individual's *social capital* by increasing educational attainment, job skills, and ability to take advantage of available resources can reduce the chances of going to prison in the first place and of recidivism, or repeat offenses and incarceration (Faulkner 2006). Consider the case study in The Applied Sociologist at Work on the facing page.

The tendency to think that the way to control human behavior is through more severe punishments is based on a rational choice theory; if the cost is high enough for deviant acts, people will conform. Yet despite severe punishments, crime rates generally remain higher in the United States than in other countries.

Japan's serious crime rate is roughly one-third that of the United States, yet the lower rate is not attained through harsher penalties. The government actually spends far less of its gross national product on police, courts, and prisons. David Bayley (1991) found in his research that for many crimes in Japan, the offender may simply be asked to write a letter of apology. This is frequently sufficient sanction to deter the person from further violation of the law. The humiliation of writing an apology and the fear of shame and embarrassing one's family are strong enough to restrain the person. This form of social control works in Japan and many other countries. Police in Japan want to be thought of as kind and caring rather than strict in their enforcement of the law (Bayley 1991).

What works in one country cannot necessarily be imported directly into another country. Deterrence is complex; it is influenced by dozens of variables including cultural values and meanings attached to specific behaviors. Not many people think that an apology would work as a deterrent to crimes in the United States. On the other hand, there is a wide range of options available for dealing with crime that countries fail to realize when they think only in terms of harsh (and expensive) punishments. Seeing how crime is controlled in other countries may challenge assumptions in one's own country, causing authorities to come up with creative new solutions that do work. For example,

many criminologists argue that the United States should concentrate on the serious criminals and reduce the number of minor offenders in jails. They also suggest a number of alternatives to sending offenders to jail and prisons such as community service and educational training programs.

THINKING SOCIOLOGICALLY

Do you think changing the cost-benefit ratio so costs of crime are higher will deter crime, or are other policies or methods more effective in enticing people to be responsible, contributing members of society?

Based on the assumption that most criminal behavior is learned through socialization and that criminals can be resocialized—saving tax dollars, increasing productivity of individuals, and making society safer—several sociological theories of crime suggest methods of treatment other than incarceration without rehabilitation. The goal is to reduce both the number of individuals who go to prison and the number who are rearrested after being released—the recidivism rate. Improving social capital is one approach based in theory.

Prison reforms, rehabilitation, training programs, shock probation, and other alternative programs are intended to integrate the less serious offenders into the community in a productive way. If we can reduce discrimination, integrate the potential criminal into the community, and teach at-risk youth acceptable behavior patterns, we may reduce crime and gain productive citizens.

If ex-prisoners have alternative behaviors and educational or job skills, and if they have families to return to, they are less likely to commit further crimes. Therefore, some state penal systems provide education from basic skills to college courses and allow conjugal and family stays to help keep families together. More than one in three prisoners in state correctional facilities around the United States were enrolled in academic programs from adult basic education to college, another third were involved in vocational training, 13 percent were engaged in counseling or therapy programs, and 8 percent received drug and alcohol counseling (U.S. Bureau of Justice Statistics 2003). Other programs included *shock probation* (releasing a first-time offender early in the hope that the shock of prison life would deter them), community service to help develop citizenship and pay restitution for the offense, and day treatment and halfway houses to help inmates readjust to community life and find jobs.

Restitution, for instance, puts the offender in the position of "making it right" with the victim. The offender renders money or service to the victim or community under supervised parole to compensate the victim. This is a positive way of teaching juvenile offenders lessons in responsibility without imprisonment and exposure to more criminal

THE APPLIED SOCIOLOGIST AT WORK

Reducing Recidivism by Increasing Social Capital

James Faulkner is a police department detective. Part of his work is with adults and juveniles, trying to increase their chances of leading productive lives and staying out of prison by increasing their social capital. The following is a case study by Detective Faulkner, at the time a school resource officer, describing his work with one young man.

* * * * * * *

Ray was a 20-year-old male, African American college student who started life with absolutely no social capital and continues to struggle to increase his chances for success. He was the type of offender who continually violated the law. Ray's father left when he was seven years old, and his mother died when he was eight. The father's whereabouts were no longer known. With no information and no parents, this was a prime example of someone with limited resources.

As a school resource officer, I was approached by a school official who was concerned for Ray's long-term future, due to the complexities of his life. As a member of law enforcement and through my personal experiences and observations, I knew Ray was stealing frequently to eat and live. Ray was living with a disabled aunt in deplorable conditions with no food in the house. When I picked him up to help him move in with yet another relative, there was no electricity, water, or phone.

We used my phone as a light as we gathered his items, and I helped him pack what few clothes he had. I began taking Ray food with the assistance of others, a concept not known to Ray.

With his high school graduation approaching, Ray asked me to help him find a job. A simple endeavor proved to be very difficult. It began with a potential employer's request for his social security card. Not only did Ray not have one, but he had no idea how to get one. Initially thinking that this would be relatively simple to solve, I asked him to bring his birth certificate and we would go apply for his social security card; it was then that he asked me how one goes about "getting one of those birth certificate things."

After graduation and the following summer, and with the aid of the assistant school superintendent who took Ray under her wing, we set out to increase Ray's level of social capital. I felt motivated to help Ray because he had been so motivated to try to help himself, yet he had met failure after failure. He continually fell, got back up, and tried something else. This encouraged me to invest in Ray. Small increases in his level of social capital and resources helped Ray establish a network of support for a more successful future. It is my belief that these small increases in Ray's resources will have significant impact on his future lifestyle and reduce his chances for a life of crime. Among other things, we taught him how to apply for loans to get financial help.

With the help of government loans and grants, Ray was admitted and entered college that fall. We helped supply him with housing, toiletries, and clothing. We did our best not to do these things for him but rather show him how to do them himself. There was no family or celebration after his high school graduation, so some school officials and I took Ray to a local steakhouse to celebrate his graduation and entering college, a step he had once perceived as unobtainable. By investing a small amount of social capital in the form of relationships and resources, we were able to steer Ray in the direction of accumulating additional social capital in the form of education.

This could be his ticket out of his previous way of life.

James Faulkner has a master's degree in Applied Social Science/ Criminal Justice.

---

behavior. Restitution is less costly than long incarceration, and victims are often satisfied with this type of program. The likelihood of repeated offense at a later time is also lower in restitution programs than for those who are sent to prison.

Another current trend is toward *privatization of prisons* in an attempt to run them in a more businesslike, cost-effective way. This trend is unlikely to improve the rehabilitation aspects in this age of overcrowded prisons and cost cutting, but several states are experimenting with private facilities, and some federal agencies such as the Immigration and Naturalization Service have contracted with private operators to run facilities. Because sociologists and criminologists study prison programs, make recommendations to improve the correction programs, and help find solutions to deviance, they are highly skeptical of privatization; there are many problems in having any public service administered by people whose primary and perhaps only goal is to make a profit. The current trend seems to be to "warehouse prisoners," with little effort to rehabilitate them or to help them reenter society as productive citizens (Irwin 2005).

At the beginning of the chapter, we said that some of the material presented in this chapter might surprise you, some commonly held assumptions about deviance might be challenged, and a different way of looking at deviance might emerge. Consider what you have read and how this has affected some of your ideas about deviance, crime, and the criminal justice system.

THINKING SOCIOLOGICALLY

What are advantages and drawbacks of various alternatives to prison? Why might rehabilitation and retribution be incompatible and possibly even contradictory goals for a prison organization?

SO WHAT?

Perhaps the answers to some of the chapter's opening questions—what is deviance, why do people become deviant, and what should we do about deviance—have now taken on new dimensions. Deviance as defined by society, communities, and even religion or subcultural groups has many possible explanations, and there are multiple interpretations about how it should be handled. Deviance and crime are issues for any society, for unless most of the people obey the rules most of the time, there can be real threats to stability, safety, and sense of fairness that undermine the social structure. The criminal justice system, then, tends to be a conservative force in society because of its focus on ensuring social conformity.

Regardless of its role, to make the society run more smoothly, we must understand why deviance and crime happen; good policy must be based on accurate information and careful analysis of the information. We must also understand that deviance and conformity operate at various levels in the social world: micro, meso, and macro. In addition, it is important to understand that there may be positive aspects of deviance for any society, from uniting society against deviants to providing creative new ways to solve problems.

One of the dominant characteristics of modern society is social inequality, and as we have seen, that inequality is often an issue in criminal activity. Indeed, many of our social problems are rooted in issues of inequality. Extreme inequality may even be a threat to the deeper values and dreams of the society, especially one that stresses individualism and achievement. In the following three chapters, we look at three types of inequality: socioeconomic, ethnic or racial, and gender-based inequity.

CONTRIBUTING TO YOUR SOCIAL WORLD

At the Local Level: *Boys and Girls Clubs* or halfway houses for teens in trouble provide the opportunity to work one-on-one with juveniles in after-school or weekend programs to provide positive role models and increase their social capital.

Battered women's shelters are one of many community programs that provide safe houses, counseling, and practical help for women and children in abusive situations.

At the Organizational or Institutional Level:
The Date Rape Project provides information and research on date rape on college campuses and in other locations. Consider working to educate college students and others about rape and the spread of disease.

At the National and Global Levels: *The Polaris Project* works to reduce global trafficking in women and children. They work with legislators to crack down on offenders. Volunteers do letter-writing campaigns, support legislation, and do research on the problem.

Visit www.pineforge.com/ballantinestudy for online activities, sample tests, and other helpful information. Select "Chapter 6: Deviance and Social Control" for chapter-specific activities.

INEQUALITY

The underlying question in the next three chapters is why some people rise to the top of society with wealth, power, and prestige at their fingertips, and others languish near the bottom. Why are some individuals and countries rich and others poor? The focus of these chapters is inequality, the process of stratification through which some people "make it" and others do not. At the very bottom of the human hierarchy are those starving and diseased world citizens who have no hope of survival for themselves or their families. This compares with corporate executives and some world politicians or royalty who have billions of dollars at their disposal.

Social inequality is one of the most important processes in modern societies, and the implications extend all the way to the global social network. Sometimes the inequality is based on socioeconomic status, but the basis of differential treatment is often other characteristics: race, ethnicity, gender, sexual orientation, or age. These differences often result in strong "we" versus "they" thinking. One factor runs throughout these patterns of inequality: they have implications for social interaction at the micro, meso, and macro levels of analysis. In this section, we do not try to cover all forms of inequality; rather, we illustrate the patterns by exploring issues of social class, race or ethnicity, and gender.

7

STRATIFICATION:
Rich and Famous—
or Rags and Famine?

What to Expect . . .

In rich countries, like the U.S., Canada, Japan, and Western European nations, we assume there are many economic opportunities, and we like to believe that anyone can become rich and famous, but the reality is that our social world is very brutal for many people, and what they experience is rags and famine.

Think About It . . .

1. Why are some people rich and others poor?

2. Why do you buy what you buy, believe what you believe, and live where you live?

3. Can you improve your social standing? If so, how?

4. How does the fact that we live in a global environment affect you and your social position?

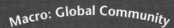

Macro: Global Community

Macro: National Society

Meso: National Institutions and Organizations; Ethnic Subcultures

Micro: Local Organizations and Community

Micro: You and Your Family

Micro: Prestige and power determined by access to resources respect based on leadership and self-confidence

Meso: Institutions support elites and stabilize the stratification system

Macro: The rich, famous, and powerful control resources, tax breaks, health care, religious ideology, and stock markets respond to their needs

Macro: Position in the international system reflects power and access to resources

Not just anyone can belong to a royal family. One must be born as royalty or marry into it. Members of royal families—such as Prince William and Prince Henry of Britain—grow up in a world of the privileged: wealth, prestige, all doors open to them, or so it appears. Their lifestyles include formal receptions, horse races, polo games, royal hunts, state visits, and other social and state functions. The family has several elegant residences at their disposal. However, like most royalty, William and Henry also live within the confines of their elite status, with its strict expectations and limitations. They cannot show up for a beer at the local pub or associate freely with commoners, and their problems or casual antics are subject matter for front pages of tabloids. In today's world, some royalty are figureheads with little political power; others—such as the Ashanti chiefs in West Africa, King Bhumibol Adulyadej of Thailand, King Sihanok of Cambodia, and Emperor Akihito in Japan—have great influence in state affairs.

In Newport, Rhode Island, spacious mansions are nestled along the coast, with tall-masted sailboats at the docks. (see photo on facing page). These are the summer homes of the U.S. aristocracy. They do not hold royal titles, but their positions allow for a life of comfort similar to that of royalty. Members of this class have an elegant social life, engage in elite sports such as fencing and polo, patronize the arts, and are influential behind the scenes in business and politics.

Hidden from the public eye in each country are people with no known names and no swank addresses; some have no address at all. We catch glimpses of their plight through vivid media portrayals, such as those of refugees in Darfur, Sudan, and of impoverished victims of Hurricane Katrina in 2005 along the Gulf of Mexico coast. They are the poor; many of them live in squalor. Economic hard times have pushed some of them from their rural homes to cities in hopes of finding jobs. However, with few jobs for unskilled and semiskilled workers in today's postindustrial service economies, many of the poor are left behind and homeless. They live in abandoned buildings or sleep in unlocked autos, on park benches, under bridges, on beaches, or anywhere they can stretch out and hope not to be attacked or harassed. Beggars stake out spots on sidewalks, hoping citizens and tourists would give them a handout. In the United States, cities such as Houston; Los Angeles; Washington, DC; and New York try to cope with the homeless by setting up sanitary facilities and temporary shelters, especially in bad weather; cities rely on religious and civic organizations such as churches and the Salvation Army to run soup kitchens.

In some areas of the world, such as Sub–Saharan Africa and India, the situation is much more desperate, and families are actually starving. Every morning at daybreak, a cattle cart traverses the city of Calcutta, India, picking up bodies of diseased and starved homeless people who have died on the streets during the night. Mother Teresa, who won the Nobel

Prince Harry and Prince William of the United Kingdom, and King Bhumibol Adulyadej of Thailand (who rarely is photographed in public), live lives of extraordinary privilege, but their status may also limit their understanding of common people and enjoyment of some everyday pleasures of group camaraderie and friendship.

Source: top photo, © Reuters/Corbis.

Peace Prize for her work with those in dire poverty, established a home in India where these people could die with dignity; she also founded an orphanage for children who would otherwise wander the streets begging or die.

Survival, just maintaining life, is a daily struggle for the 37 million people (up 1.1 million from 2003) who live in poverty-stricken parts of the world (U.S. Census Bureau 2005f). These humans are at the bottom of the stratification hierarchy.

This raises the following question: Why do some people live like royalty and others live in desperate poverty? Most of us live between these extremes. We study and work hard for what we have, but we also live comfortably, knowing that starvation is not pounding at our door. This chapter discusses (1) some explanations of stratification systems, (2) the importance and consequences of social rankings for individuals, (3) whether one can change social class positions, (4) characteristics of class systems, (5) social policies to address poverty, and (6) patterns of stability and change.

THE IMPORTANCE OF SOCIAL STRATIFICATION

Social stratification refers to how individuals and groups are layered or ranked in society according to how many valued resources they possess. Stratification is an ongoing process of sorting people into different levels of access to resources, with the sorting legitimated by cultural beliefs about why the inequality is justifiable. This chapter focuses on socioeconomic stratification, and subsequent chapters examine ethnic and gender stratification.

Three main assumptions underlie the concept of stratification: (1) people are divided into ranked categories; (2) there is an unequal distribution of desired resources, meaning that some members of society possess more of what is valued and others possess less; and (3) each society determines what it considers to be valued resources. In an agricultural society, members are ranked according to how much land or how many animals they own. In an industrial society, occupational position and income are two of the criteria for ranking. Most Japanese associate old age with high rank, while Americans admire and offer high status to those with youthful vigor and beauty.

What members of each society value and the criteria they use to rank other members depends on events in the society's history, its geographic location, its level of development in the world, the society's political philosophy, and the decisions of those in power. Powerful individuals are more likely to get the best positions, most desirable mates, and the greatest opportunities. They may have power because of birth status, personality characteristics, age, physical attractiveness, education, intelligence, wealth, race, family background, occupation, religion, or ethnic group—whatever the basis for power is in that particular society. Those with power have advantages that perpetuate their power, and they try to hold onto those advantages through laws, custom, power, or ideology.

Many mansions in places like Newport, Rhode Island, cost several million dollars, and these may be only summer homes for the owners. For people born into wealth, such opulent living seems entirely normal.

Source: © Nicole K. Cioe.

Consider your own social ranking. You were born into a family that holds a position in society—upper, middle, or lower class, for instance. The position of your family influences the neighborhood in which you live and where you shop, go to school, and attend religious services. Most likely, you and your family carry out the tasks of daily living in your community with others of similar positions. Your position in the stratification system affects the opportunities available to you and the choices you make in life. The social world model at the beginning of the chapter provides a visual image of the social world and socioeconomic stratification; the stratification process affects everything from individuals' social rankings at the micro level of analysis to positions of countries in the global system at the macro level.

Micro-Level Prestige and Influence

Remember how some of your peers on the playgrounds were given more respect than others? Their high regard came from belonging to a prestigious family, a dynamic or domineering personality, or symbols that distinguished them—"cool" clothing, a desirable bicycle, expensive toys, or a fancy car. This is stratification at its beginning stage.

Wealth, power, and prestige are accorded to those individuals who have *cultural capital* (knowledge and

A displaced woman and her children sit beneath a temporary shelter at a refugee camp in South Darfur. A disproportionate number of displaced civilians in the camps are women and children. Although such refugees are clean and tidy people, their disrupted lives often result in illness and famine.

Source: USAID.

Even in affluent North America, some people are homeless and spend nights on sidewalks, in parks, or in homeless shelters that are often dangerous, very noisy, and have no privacy. Sleeping on a sidewalk actually offers more safety than being in a isolated area.

Source: © Thania Navarro.

access to important information in the society) and *social capital* (networks with others who have influence). Individual qualities such as leadership, personality, sense of humor, self-confidence, quick-wittedness, physical attractiveness, or ascribed characteristics—such as gender or ethnicity—influence cultural and social capital.

Meso-Level Access to Resources

Often, our individual status in the society is shaped by our access to resources available through organizations and institutions. Our status is learned and reinforced in the family through the socialization process; we learn grammar and manners that affect our success in school. Educational organizations treat children differently according to their social status, and our religious affiliation is likely to reflect our social status. Political systems, including laws, the courts, and police, reinforce the stratification system. Access to health care depends on one's position in the stratification system. Our positions and connections in organizations have a profound impact on how we experience life and how we interact with other individuals and groups.

Macro-Level Factors Influencing Stratification

The economic system, which includes the occupational structure, level of technology, and distribution of wealth in a society, is often the basis for stratification. (See Map 7.1.) Haiti, located on the island of Hispanola, is the poorest country in the western hemisphere and one of the poorest countries in the world; it has little technology, few resources, and an occupational structure based largely on subsistence farming. Even its forest resources are almost gone as desperately poor people cut down the last trees for firewood and shelters, leaving the land to erode (Diamond 2005). The economy is collapsing, leaving many already poor people destitute and in the lowest rungs of the world's stratification system.

The economic position and geographic location of nations such as Haiti affect the opportunities available to individuals in those societies. If the economy is robust and diverse, there is more opportunity for people to raise their status than in poor or stagnant economies. There are simply no opportunities for Haitians to get ahead. Thus, macro-level factors can shape the opportunity structure and distribution of resources.

One problem for Haiti is that it has few of the resources that many other countries in the global system take for granted—a strong educational system, well-paying jobs in a vibrant economy, productive land, an ample supply of water, money to pay workers, and access to the most efficient and powerful technology. Almost all societies stratify members, and societies themselves are stratified in the world system; each individual and nation experiences the world in unique ways. Stratification is one of the most powerful forces that we experience, but we are seldom conscious of how it works or how pervasive it is in our lives. This is the driving question sociologists ask when developing theories of stratification: how does it work?

THINKING SOCIOLOGICALLY

Place yourself in the center of the social world model; working outward from micro-level interactions toward the macro-level institutions, indicate what has influenced where you fall in the stratification system.

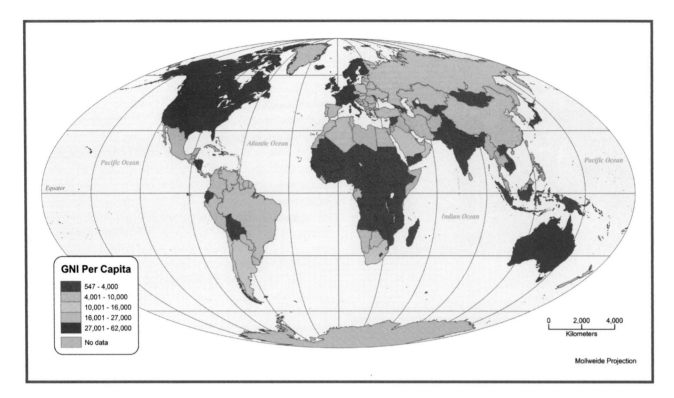

MAP 7.1   Gross National Income (in U.S. dollars) per Capita, 2004

Source: World Development Indicators, World Bank. Map by Anna Versluis.

THEORETICAL EXPLANATIONS OF STRATIFICATION

Why do some people have more money, possessions, power, and prestige than others? We all have opinions about this question. Sociologists also have developed explanations—theories that help explain stratification. Theories provide a framework for asking questions to be studied. Just as your interpretation of a question may differ from your friends' ideas, sociologists have developed different explanations for stratification and tested these with research data. These explanations of social rankings range from individual micro-level to national and global macro-level theories.

Micro-Level Theory
Symbolic Interaction

Most of us have been at a social gathering, perhaps at a swank country club or in a local bar, where we felt out of place. Each social group has norms learned by members through the socialization process; these norms are recognized within that group and can make clueless outsiders feel like space aliens. People learn what is expected in their groups—family, peer group, social class—through interaction with others; for instance, children are rewarded or punished

In India, many people must bathe every day in public in whatever water supply they can find. Homeless people must bathe this way, but here in Calcutta, even some people with homes would not have their own water supply.

Source: Photo by Elise Roberts.

Clothing not only covers our bodies but also acts as a symbol of our social status. Note the difference in the attire of the children on a field trip from a Japanese prep school (top) and the children at play from a low-income school (bottom).

Source: Top photo by Sébastien Bertrand; bottom photo © David Claassen.

for behaviors appropriate or inappropriate to their social position. This process transmits and perpetuates social rankings. Learning our social position means learning values, speech patterns, consumption habits, appropriate group memberships (including religious affiliation), and even our self-concept.

Consider the example of different school socialization experiences of children. Students bring their language patterns, values, experiences, and knowledge they have learned with them from home. These attributes are referred to as their *cultural capital*. Schools place children into courses and academic groups based in part on the labels they receive due

to their cultural capital. Home environments can help children by expanding vocabularies; developing good grammar; experiencing concerts, art, and theater; visiting historical sites; providing reading materials; and modeling adults who like to read. The parents of higher-class families tend to stress thinking skills as opposed to simply learning to obey authority figures. The result of this learning at home is that members of the middle and upper classes or higher castes get the best educations, setting them up to be future leaders with better life chances (Ballantine 2001b). In this way, children's home experiences and education help reproduce the social class systems.

Symbols often represent social positions. Clothing, for example, sets up some people as special and privileged. In the 1960s, wearing blue jeans was a radical act by college students to reject status differences; it represented a solidarity with Laborers and a rejection of the prestige and status games in our society. Today, the situation has changed; young people wear expensive designer jeans that low-income people cannot afford. Drinking wine rather than beer, driving a Jaguar rather than a simpler mode of transportation, and living in a home that has six or eight bedrooms and 5,000 square feet is an expression of *conspicuous consumption*—displaying goods in a way that others will notice and that will presumably earn the owner respect. Thus, purchased products become symbols that are intended to define the person as someone of high status.

Interaction theories help us understand how individuals learn and live their positions in society. Next, we consider theories that examine the larger social structures, processes, and forces that affect stratification and inequality: structural-functional and various forms of conflict theory.

Meso- and Macro-Level Theories
Structural-Functional Theory

Structural-functionalists (sometimes simply called functionalists) view stratification within societies as an inevitable—and probably necessary—part of the social world. The stratification system provides each individual a place or position in the social world and motivates individuals to carry out their roles. Societies survive by having an organized system into which each individual is born and raised and where each contributes some part to the maintenance of the society.

The basic elements of the structural-functional theory of stratification were explained by Kingsley Davis and Wilbert Moore (1945), and their work still provides the main ideas of the theory today. Focusing on stratification by considering different occupations and how they are rewarded, Davis and Moore argue the following:

1. Positions in society are neither equally valued nor equally pleasant to perform; some positions—such as physicians—are more highly valued because

people feel they are very important to society. Therefore, societies must motivate talented individuals to prepare for and occupy the most important and difficult positions, such as being physicians.

2. Preparation requires talent, time, and money. To motivate talented individuals to make the sacrifices necessary to prepare for and assume difficult positions such as becoming a physician, differential rewards of income, prestige, power, or other valued goods must be offered. Thus, a doctor receives high income, prestige, and power as incentives.

3. The differences in rewards in turn lead to the unequal distribution of resources for occupations in society. Therefore, stratification is inevitable. The unequal distribution of status and wealth in society provides societies with individuals to fill necessary positions—such as willingness to undertake the stress of being chief executive officer of a corporation in a highly competitive field.

In the mid-twentieth century, functional theory provided sociologists with a valuable framework for studying stratification (Tumin 1953), but things do change. In the twenty-first century, new criteria such as controlling *information and access to information systems* has become important for determining wealth and status, making scientists and technicians a new class of elites. The society also experiences conflict over distribution of resources that functionalism does not fully explain.

Conflict Theory

Conflict theorists see stratification as the outcome of struggles for dominance and scarce resources, with some individuals in society taking advantage of others. Individuals and groups act in their own self-interest by trying to exploit others, leading inevitably to a struggle between those who have advantages and want to keep them and those who want a larger share of the pie.

Conflict theory developed in a time of massive economic transformation. With the end of the feudal system, economic displacement of peasants, and the rise of urban factories as major employers, a tremendous gap between the rich and the poor evolved. This prompted theorists to ask several basic questions related to stratification: (1) How do societies produce necessities—food, clothing, housing? (2) How are relationships between rich and poor people shaped by this process? and (3) How do many people become alienated in their routine, dull jobs in which they have little involvement and no investment in the end product?

Karl Marx (1818–1883), considered the father of conflict theory, lived during this time of industrial transformation. Marx described four possible ways to distribute wealth: (1) according to each person's need, (2) according to what each person wants, (3) according to what each person earns, or

A McDonald's employee cleans the Thank You sign at the local franchise. Many such workers are paid minimum wage.

Source: Photo by Mark Peterson / Corbis Saba.

(4) according to what each person can take. It was this fourth way, Marx believed, that was dominant in competitive capitalist societies (Cuzzort and King 2002; Marx and Engels 1955).

Marx viewed the stratification structure as composed of two major economically based social classes: The haves and the have-nots. The haves consisted of the capitalist bourgeoisie, while the have-nots were made up of the working class proletariat. Individuals in the same social class had similar lifestyles, shared ideologies, and held common outlooks on social life. The struggle over resources between haves and have-nots was the cause of conflict (Hurst 2004).

The haves control what Marx called the means of production—money, materials, and factories (Marx 1844/1964). The haves dominate because the lower class have-nots cannot earn enough money to change their positions. The norms and values of the haves dominate the society because of their power and make the distribution of resources seem "fair" and justified. Social control mechanisms including laws, religious beliefs, educational systems, political structures and policies, and police or military force ensure continued control by the haves.

The unorganized lower classes can be exploited as long as they do not develop a class consciousness—a shared awareness of their poor status in relation to the means of production (control of the production process). Marx contended that, with the help of intellectuals who believed in the injustice of the exploited poor, the working class would develop a class consciousness, rise up, and overthrow the haves, culminating in a classless society in which wealth would be shared (Marx and Engels 1955). These are some basic ideas underlying Communist philosophy today.

Philadelphia Eagles Terrell Owens is paid millions of dollars each year to carry a football for 16 weeks, while the public school teacher in the bottom photo would take 30 years teaching hundreds of children to read before her total cumulative income for her entire career would add up to one million dollars.

Source: © Tim Shaffer / Reuters / Corbis; © Paul Almasy / Corbis.

Unlike the structural-functionalists, then, conflict theorists maintain that money and other rewards are not necessarily given to those in the most important positions in the society. Can we argue that a rock star or baseball player is more necessary for the survival of society than a teacher or police officer? Yet the pay differential is tremendous. Conflict theorists are not convinced that our social reward system (levels of payment) are rooted in enticing people to make sacrifices to obtain the "most important" tasks in the society. These high prestige positions often go to sons and daughters of elites.

Not all of the predictions of Karl Marx have come true. No truly classless societies have developed: labor unions arose to unite and represent the working class and put them in a more powerful position vis-à-vis the capitalists, manager and technician positions emerged creating a large middle class, some companies moved to employee ownership, and workers gained legal protection from government legislative bodies in most industrial countries (Dahrendorf 1959).

Even societies that claim to be classless such as China have privileged classes and poor peasants. In recent years, the Chinese government has allowed more private ownership of shops, businesses, and other entrepreneurial efforts, motivating many Chinese citizens to work long hours at their private businesses to "get ahead." Only a few small hunter-gatherer societies with no extra resources to allow some to accumulate wealth are classless.

Some theorists criticize Marx for his focus on only the economic system, pointing out that non-economic factors enter into the stratification struggle as well. Max Weber (1864–1920), an influential theorist, amended Marx's theory by considering other elements in addition to economic forces. He agreed with Marx that group conflict is inevitable, that economics is one of the key factors in stratification systems, and that those in power try to perpetuate their positions. However, he added two other influential factors that he argued determine stratification in modern industrial societies: power and prestige, discussed later in this chapter. Sometimes, these are identified as the "three Ps": property, power, and prestige.

Recent theorists suggest that using three Ps we can identify five classes rather than just haves and have-nots: capitalists, managers, the petty bourgeoisie, workers, and the underclass. Capitalists own the means of production and purchase and control the labor of others. Managers sell their labor to capitalists and manage the labor of others for the capitalists. The petty bourgeoisie, such as small shop or business owners, own some means of production but control little labor of others; they have modest prestige, power, and property (Sernau 2001). Workers sell their labor to capitalists and are low in all three Ps. The underclass has virtually no property, power, or prestige.

In the modern world, as businesses become international and managerial occupations continue to grow, conflict theorists argue that workers are still exploited, but in different ways. Owners get more income than is warranted by their responsibilities (note the differential in pay for chief executive officers, CEOs), and better educated and skilled people get more income than is warranted by the differential in education (Wright 2000). Moreover, the labor that produces our clothes, cell phones, digital cameras, televisions, and other products are increasingly provided by impoverished people around the world working for low wages in multinational corporations (Bonacich and Wilson 2005). Service providers in rich countries receive low wages at fast food chains and box stories such as WalMart (Ehrenreich 2001, 2005). One controversial question is whether multinational corporations are bringing opportunity to poor countries or exploiting them as many conflict theorists contend (Wallerstein 2004).

THINKING SOCIOLOGICALLY

Is it possible for a society to be truly "classless" with shared wealth? Why or why not? What empirical evidence might support your position?

The Evolutionary Theory of Stratification: A Synthesis

Evolutionary theory (Lenski 1966; Nolan and Lenski 2005) borrows assumptions from both structural-functional and conflict theories in an attempt to determine how scarce resources are distributed and how that distribution results in stratification. The basic ideas are as follows: (1) to survive, people must cooperate; (2) despite this, conflicts of interest occur over important decisions that benefit one individual or group over another; (3) valued items such as money and status are always in demand and in short supply; (4) there is likely to be a struggle over these scarce goods; and (5) customs or traditions in a society often prevail over rational criteria in determining distribution of scarce resources. After the minimum survival needs of both individuals and the society are met, power determines who gets the surplus: prestige, luxury living, the best health care, and so forth. Lenski believes that privileges (including wealth) flow from having power; and prestige usually results from having access to both power and privilege (Hurst 2004).

Lenski (1966; Nolan and Lenski 2005) tested his theory by studying societies at different levels of technological development, ranging from simple to complex. He found that the degree of inequality increases with technology until it reaches the advanced industrial stage. For instance, in subsistence-level hunting and gathering societies little surplus is available and everyone's needs are met to the extent possible. As surplus accumulates in agrarian societies, those who acquire power also control surpluses, and they use this to benefit their friends and relations. However, even if laws are made by those in power, the powerful must share

some of the wealth or fear being overthrown. Interestingly, when societies finally reach the advanced industrial stage, inequality is moderated; this is because there is greater political participation from people in various social classes and because there are more resources available to be shared in the society.

Lenski's (1966; Nolan and Lenski 2005) theory explains many different types of societies by synthesizing elements of both structural-functional and conflict theory. For instance, evolutionary theory takes into consideration the structural-functional idea that talented individuals need to be motivated to make sacrifices by allowing private ownership to motivate them. Individuals will attempt to control as much wealth, power, and prestige as possible, resulting in potential conflict as some accumulate more wealth than others (Nolan and Lenski 2005). The theory also recognizes exploitation leading to inequality, a factor conflict theorists find in capitalist systems of stratification. The reality is that while some inequality may be useful in highly complex societies, there is far more stratification in the United States than seems necessary. Indeed, extraordinary amounts of differential access to resources may even undermine productivity; it may make upward mobility so impossible that the most talented people are not always those in the most demanding and responsible jobs.

The amount of inequality differs in societies, according to evolutionary theorists, because of different levels of technological development. Because industrialization brings surplus wealth, a division of labor, advanced technology, and interdependence among members of a society, no one individual can control all the important knowledge, skills, or capital resources. Therefore, this eliminates the two extremes of haves and have-nots because resources are more evenly distributed.

The symbolic interaction, structural-functional, conflict, and evolutionary theories provide different explanations for understanding stratification in modern societies. These theories are the basis for micro- and macro-level discussions of stratification. Our next step is to look at some factors that influence an individual's position in a stratification system and the ability to change that position.

THINKING SOCIOLOGICALLY

According to the theories discussed above, what are some reasons for *your* position in the stratification system?

INDIVIDUALS' SOCIAL STATUS: THE MICRO LEVEL

You are among the world's elite. Only about 3 percent of the world's population ever enters the halls of academia, and less than 1 percent has a college degree. Being able to afford the time and money for college is a luxury; it is beyond the financial or personal resources of 99 percent of individuals in the world. Spending time and money now to improve life in the future has little relevance to those struggling to survive each day. Considered in this global perspective, college students learn professional skills and have advantages that billions of other world citizens will never know or even imagine.

In the United States, access to higher education is greater than in many other countries because there are more levels of entry—technical and community colleges, large state universities, and private four-year colleges, to name a few. However, with limited government help, most students must have financial resources to help pay tuition and the cost of living. Many students do not realize that the prestige of the college makes a difference in their future opportunities. Those students born into wealth can afford better preparation for entrance exams and tutors or courses to increase SAT scores, attend private prep schools, and gain acceptance to prestigious colleges that open opportunities not available to those attending the typical state university or non-elite colleges (Persell 2005).

Ascribed characteristics, such as gender, can also affect one's chances for success in life. In Japan and a number of other countries, the imbedded gender stratification system makes it difficult for women to rise in the occupational hierarchy. Many Japanese women earn college degrees but often leave employment after getting married and having children (Japan Institute of Labor 2002). Of 2,396 companies surveyed, the number with women directors was just 72 (less than 3 percent). Furthermore, Japanese women hold only 2 percent of all corporate board seats, and few are on boards of directors (Globe Women's Business Network 2006). Issues of gender stratification will be examined in more depth in Chapter 9, but they intersect with socioeconomic class and must be viewed as part of a larger pattern of inequality in the social world.

Individual Life Chances and Lifestyles

Life chances refer to your opportunities, depending on your achieved and ascribed status in society. That you are in college, probably have health insurance and access to health care, and are likely to live into your late 70s or 80s are factors directly related to your *life chances*. Let us consider several examples of how placement in organizations at the meso level affects individual experiences and has global ramifications.

Education

Although education is valued by most individuals, the cost of books, clothing, shoes, transportation, child care, and time taken from income-producing work may be insurmountable barriers to attendance from grade school through college. Economically disadvantaged students in most countries are more likely to attend less prestigious and less expensive institutions *if* they attend high school or university at all.

One's level of education affects many aspects of life, including political, religious, and marital attitudes and behavior. Generally speaking, the higher the education level, the more active individuals are in political life, the more mainstream or conventional their religious affiliation, the more likely they are to marry into a family with both economic and social capital, the more stable the marriage, and the more likely they are to have good health.

Health, Social Conditions, and Life Expectancy

Pictures on the news of children starving and dying dramatically illustrate global inequalities. The poorest countries in the world are in Sub–Saharan Africa, where most individuals eat poorly, are susceptible to diseases, have great stress in their daily lives just trying to survive, and die at young ages compared to the developed world. (See Table 7.1.)

If you have a sore throat, you can usually get an appointment to see your doctor. Yet many people in the world will never see a doctor. Access to health care requires doctors and

TABLE 7.1 **Life Expectancy**

Poorest Countries	Life Expectancy, 2005 (in years)	Per Capita GNP ($)	Infant Mortality	Richest Countries	Life Expectancy, 2005 (in years)	Per Capita GNP ($)	Infant Mortality
Malawi	36.97	160	103.32	Japan	81.15	37,050	3.26
Mozambique	40.32	270	130.79	San Marino	81.62	N/A	5.73
Namibia	43.93	238	48.98	Singapore	81.62	24,760	2.29
Niger	42.13	210	121.69	Switzerland	80.39	49,600	4.39
Rwanda	46.96	210	98.23	Sweden	80.4	35,840	2.77
Zambia	39.7	400	88.29	United States	77.71	41,440	6.5

Source: World Fact Book (2005).

Note: Infant mortality is per 1,000 live births. (In Canada, the life expectancy is 80.1 years, per capita gross national income is $28,310, and infant mortality rate is 6.5 per 1000 life births.)

medical facilities, money for transportation and treatment, access to child care, and released time from other tasks in order to get to a medical facility. The poor sometimes do not have these luxuries. By contrast, the affluent eat better food, are less exposed to polluted water and unhygienic conditions, and are able to pay for medical care and drugs when they do have ailing health. Even causes of death illustrate the differences between people at different places in the stratification hierarchy. For example, in developing countries shorter life expectancies and deaths, especially among children, are due to controllable infectious diseases such as cholera, typhoid, tuberculosis, and other respiratory ailments. By contrast, in affluent countries, heart disease and cancer are the most common causes of death, and most deaths are of people over the age of 65. So whether considered locally or globally, access to health care resources makes a difference in life chances. To an extent, a chance of a long and healthy life is a privilege of the elite.

The impact of social conditions on life expectancy is especially evident if we compare cross-national data. Countries with the shortest life expectancy at birth illustrate the pattern. These countries lack adequate health care, immunizations, and sanitation; have crises of war and displacement of population resulting in refugees; and experience illnesses, epidemics, and famine. Even a drought has more tragic impact with no other aid resources to help families cope. By studying Table 7.1, you can compare life expectancy with two other measures of life quality for the poorest and richest countries: the GNP per capita income—the average amount of money each person has per year—and the infant mortality rates (death rates for babies).

THINKING SOCIOLOGICALLY

What questions do the data in Table 7.1 raise regarding mortality and life expectancy rates?

Note that average life expectancy in poor countries is as low as 37 years, income as low as $180 a year (many of the people in these populations are subsistence farmers), and infant mortality is as high as 139 deaths in the first year of life for every 1,000 births. Numbers for the richest countries are dramatically different.

The United States has much larger gaps between rich and poor people than most other wealthy countries, resulting in higher poverty rates (more people at the bottom rungs of the stratification ladder). This is, in turn, reflected in health statistics. Sweden has one of the lowest infant mortality rates in the world, a measure of a country's health standards, while the United States trails 40 other developed nations in infant mortality rates (World Fact Book 2005). The life expectancy of men living in Harlem, a predominantly poor African American section of New York City, was shorter in 1992 than the life expectancy of men living in the

The poor around the world often get health care at clinics or emergency rooms, if they have access to care, where they wait for hours to see a health care provider. This is true in the United States as well as in this mother-child health clinic in Kisumu, Kenya.

Source: © Wendy Stone / Corbis.

developing country of Bangladesh. By the age of 65, 55 percent of men in Bangladesh were still alive, but only 40 percent of men in Harlem survived to that age (Himmelstein and Woodhandler 1992). This evidence supports the assertion that health, illness, and death rates are closely tied to socioeconomic stratification. Race and gender interact with social class in ways that often have negative results; these connections are complex, and many white Anglos experience some of the hardships that people of color endure.

THINKING SOCIOLOGICALLY

What are some factors that affect life expectancy in your family, community, and country?

Family Life and Child-Rearing Patterns

In many countries, higher social class correlates with later marriage and lower divorce rates. Members of lower classes tend to marry earlier and have more children; because of tensions from life stresses including money, problems lead to less stable marriages and more instances of divorce and single parenthood.

Child-rearing patterns are also affected by social rankings and serve to reinforce one's social class status. For instance, lower-class families in the United States tend to use more physical punishment to discipline children than middle-class parents, who use guilt, reasoning, time-outs, and other noncorporal sanctions to control children's behavior.

Lifestyles

This includes attitudes, values, beliefs, behavior patterns, and other aspects of your place in the social world; they are shaped through the socialization process. As individuals grow up, the behaviors and attitudes consistent with their culture and family's status in society become internalized through the process of socialization. Lifestyle is not a simple matter of having money. Acquiring money—say by winning a lottery—cannot buy a completely new lifestyle (Bourdieu and Passeron 1977). This is because values and behaviors are ingrained in our self-concept from childhood. You may have material possessions at your disposal, but that does not mean you have the lifestyle of the upper-class rich and famous. Consider some examples of factors related to your individual lifestyle: attitudes toward achievement, political involvement, and religious membership.

Attitudes toward Achievement

These differ by social status and are generally closely correlated with life chances. Motivation to get ahead and beliefs about what you can achieve are in part products of your upbringing and what opportunities you think are available. Even tolerance for those different from yourself is influenced by your social status.

Religious Membership

This also correlates with social status variables of education, occupation, and income. For instance, in the United States upper-class citizens are found disproportionately in Episcopalian, Unitarian, and Jewish religious groups, whereas lower-class citizens are attracted to Nazarene, Southern Baptist, Jehovah's Witnesses, and other holiness and fundamentalist sects. Each religious group attracts members predominantly from one social class, as will be illustrated in Chapter 12 on religion (Kosmin and Lackman 1993; Roberts 2004).

Political Behavior

This is also affected by social status. Around the world, upper-middle classes are most supportive of elite or pro-capitalist agendas because these agendas support their way of life; lower working-class members are least supportive (Wright 2000). Generally, the lower the social class, the more likely people are to vote for liberal parties (Kerbo 2001), and the higher the social status, the more likely people are to vote conservative on economic issues consistent with protecting wealth (Brooks and Manza 1997).

In the United States, members of the lower class tend to vote liberal on economic issues, favoring government intervention to improve economic conditions; however, they vote conservatively on many social issues relating to minorities and civil liberties (e.g., rights for homosexuals) (Gilbert and Kahl 2003; Jennings 1992; Kerbo 2001). The 2004 U.S. presidential election created a conflict for those who vote liberal on economic issues and conservative on moral issues because voters had to make choices about which of these was more important.

The reality is that some people experience high status on one trait, especially a trait that is ascribed, but may experience low status in another area. For example, a professor may have high status but low income. Max Weber called this unevenness in one's status *status inconsistency*. Individuals who experience such status inconsistency, especially if they are treated as if their lowest ascribed status is the most important one, are likely to be very liberal and to experience discontent with the current system (Weber 1946).

People tend to associate with others like themselves, perpetuating and reinforcing lifestyles. In fact, people often avoid contact with others whose lifestyles are outside their familiar and comfortable patterns. Life chances and lifestyles are deeply shaped by the type of stratification system that is prevalent in the nation. Such life experiences as hunger, the unnecessary early death of family members, or the pain of seeing one's child denied opportunities are all experienced at the micro level, but their causes are usually rooted in events and actions at other levels of the social world. This brings us to our next questions: Can an individual change positions in a stratification system?

THINKING SOCIOLOGICALLY

Describe your own lifestyle and life chances. How do these relate to your socialization experience and your family's position in the stratification system? What difference do they make in your life?

SOCIAL MOBILITY: THE MICRO-MESO CONNECTION

The film *Hoop Dreams* followed the story of two talented black teenagers as they pursued their dreams to rise in the basketball world and escape from their bleak neighborhood on the West Side of Chicago (Berkow 1994). Although they faced daily threats from robberies, drug dealers, and peer pressure to commit crimes and to join gangs, the hope of making it big in basketball against astronomical odds drove them on. Such hopes are some of the cruelest hoaxes faced by young African Americans, according to sociologist Harry Edwards (2000), because the chances of success or even of moving up a little in the social stratification system through sports are very small. For example, neither of the young men in *Hoop Dreams* went beyond partial completion of college.

Those few minority athletes who do "make it big" and become models for young people experience "stacking," holding certain limited positions in a sport. When retired from playing, black athletes seldom rise in the administrative hierarchy of the sports of football and baseball, although basketball has a better record of hiring black coaches and managers. Thus, when young people put their hopes and energies into developing their muscles and physical skills, they may lose the possibility of moving up in the social class system, which requires developing their minds and their technical skills; misplaced focus thwarts their dreams of upward social mobility. Of course, systematic discrimination, discussed in the next chapter, also makes upward mobility—even in the world of sports—a difficult prospect.

The whole idea of changing one's social position is called social mobility. **Social mobility** refers to the extent and direction of individual movement in the social stratification system. What is the likelihood that your status will be different from that of your parents over your lifetime? Will you start a successful business? Marry into wealth? Win the lottery? Experience downward mobility due to loss of a job, illness, or inability to complete your education? What factors at the different levels of analysis might influence your chances of mobility? These are some of the questions addressed in this section and the next.

Three issues dominate the analysis of mobility: (1) variations in types of social mobility, (2) factors that affect social mobility, and (3) whether there is a "land of opportunity."

Types of Social Mobility

Most people believe that they can improve their social class ranking with hard work and good education. *Intergenerational mobility* refers to change in status compared to your parents' status, usually resulting from education and occupational attainment. If you are the first to go to college in your family and you become a computer programmer, this would represent intergenerational mobility. The amount of intergenerational mobility in a society measures the degree to which a society has an **open class system**—one that allows movement between classes. In technologically developed countries, there is a severe lack of mobility at the two extremes of the occupational hierarchy—the upper-upper and lower-lower classes—but considerable movement up, down, and sideways in the middle group (Grusky and Hauser 1984; Hauser and Grusky 1988; Slomczynski and Krauze 1987; Treiman 1977). This movement perpetuates the belief that mobility is possible and the system is fair.

Intragenerational mobility (not to be confused with intergenerational mobility) refers to the change in position in a single individual's life. For instance, if you begin your career as a teacher's aide and end it as a school superintendent, that is intragenerational mobility. However, mobility is not always up. *Vertical mobility* refers to movement up or down in the hierarchy and sometimes involves changing social classes. You may start your career as a waitress, go to college part-time, get a degree in engineering, and get a more prestigious and higher paying job, resulting in upward mobility. Alternatively, you could lose a job and take one at a lower status, a reality for many when the economy is doing poorly.

Factors Affecting Mobility

Mobility is driven by many factors, from your family's cultural capital to global economic variables. One's chances to move up depend on micro-level factors such as your

Arthur Agee, one of the two subjects of the documentary film Hoop Dreams, *shows off his ballhandling skills at a neighborhood park in Chicago. Unfortunately, those skills were not the path to upward mobility as he had hoped. He did not make it into the pros.*

Source: Photo by John Zich; Getty Images.

socialization and education and macro-level factors such as the following: the occupational structure and economic status of countries, population changes and the numbers of people vying for similar positions, discrimination based on gender or ethnicity, and the global economic situation.

Socialization

In industrial societies, change of jobs is most likely to occur at the same socioeconomic level because our socialization and training are most applicable to similar jobs (Sernau 2001).

Education, Skills, and Social Ties

Many poor people lack education and skills such as interviewing and getting recommendations needed to get or change jobs in the postindustrial occupational structure (Ehrenreich 2001, 2005). Isolated from social networks in organizations, they lack contacts to help in the job search. The type of education system one attends also affects mobility. In Germany, Britain, France, and some other European countries, children are "streamed" (tracked) into either college preparatory courses or more general curricula, and the rest of their occupational experience reflects this early placement decision in school. In the United States, educational opportunities remain more open to those who can afford them.

Occupational Structure and Economic Vitality

The global structure, a country's position as a rich or poor country in the world system, affects the chances for individual mobility. As agricultural work is decreasing and technology jobs increasing (Hurst 2004), these changes in the

These two men may both be good fathers—caring, supportive, and offering their children the wisdom and skills they know can help their children in the working world. One of these fathers, however, is likely to offer more cultural capital and more opportunities. Capitalistic societies are not completely open systems in which those with the most talent and the strongest work ethic always rise to the top.

Sources: © Lisa F. Young/Istockphoto.com; © Luis Alvarez/ Istockphoto.com.

composition and structure of occupations affect individual opportunity. The health of a country's economy in the global system shapes employment chances of individuals.

Population Trends

The fertility rates, or number of children born at a given time, influence the number of people who will be looking for jobs. The U.S. nationwide baby boom that occurred following World War II resulted in a flood of job applicants and downward intergenerational mobility for the many who could not find work comparable to their social class at birth. By contrast, the smaller group following the baby boomer generation had fewer competitors for entry-level jobs. Baby boomers hold many of the executive and leadership positions today, so promotion has been hard for the next cohort. As baby boomers retire, opportunities will open up and mobility should increase.

Gender and Ethnicity

Many women and ethnic minority groups, locked in a cycle of poverty, dependence, and debt, have little chance of changing their status. Women in the U.S. workforce, for instance, are more likely than men to be in dead-end clerical and service positions with no opportunity for advancement. In the past three decades, the wage gap between women and men has narrowed and women now earn 81 percent of what men earn (U.S. Census Bureau 2005f; U.S. Department of Labor 2005) compared to 60 percent in 1980. The competition for jobs among baby boomers is more intense because more women are looking for jobs; in most cases, the economy has adjusted to the larger workforce. Special circumstances such as war have often allowed women and others who were denied access to good jobs to get a "foot in the door" and actually enhance the upward mobility prospects of women and ethnic groups.

Some people experience privilege (e.g., white, European-born, native-speaking males who are in the middle class or higher); some experience *disprivilege* due to socioeconomic status, ethnicity, gender, or a combination of these. Be aware that various forms of inequality intersect in our society in highly complex ways.

The Interdependent Global Market and International Events

If the Asian stock market hiccups, it sends ripples through world markets. If high-tech industries in Japan or Europe falter, North American companies in Silicon Valley, California, may go out of business, costing many professionals their lucrative positions. In ways such as these, the interdependent global economies affect national and local economies, and that affects individual families.

Whether individuals move from "rags to riches" is not determined solely by their personal ambition and work ethic. Mobility for the individual, a micro-level event, is linked to a variety of events at other levels of the social world.

THINKING SOCIOLOGICALLY

Do you know individuals who have lost jobs because of economic slowdowns or gotten jobs because of economic booms and opening opportunities? What changes have occurred in their mobility and social class?

Is There a "Land of Opportunity"?
Cross-Cultural Mobility

Would you have a better chance to improve your status in England, Japan, the United States, or some other country? If there is a land of opportunity where individuals can be assured of improving their economic and social position, it is not simple to identify. Countless immigrants have sought better opportunities in new locations. Perhaps your parents or ancestors did just this. The reality of the land of opportunity depends on the historical period and economic conditions, social events, and political attitudes toward foreigners when the immigrants came, their personal skills, and their ability to blend into the new society.

During economic growth periods, many immigrants have found great opportunities for mobility in the United States and Europe. Early industrial tycoons in railroads, automobiles, steel, and other industries are examples of success stories. Today, the number of millionaires in the United States has skyrocketed to 5 million, four times the number a decade ago. Yet such wealth eludes most people who immigrate and must work multiple low-paying jobs just to feed their families and stay out of poverty.

Opportunities for upward mobility have changed significantly with globalization. Many manufacturing jobs in the global economy have moved from developed to developing countries with cheap labor, reducing the number of unskilled and low-skilled jobs available in developed countries (Krymkowski and Krause 1992). Multinational corporations look for the cheapest sources of labor, mostly in developing countries with low taxes, no labor unions, few regulations, and workers needing jobs. Today, only 14 percent of U.S. workers are in manufacturing jobs, while the percentage of workers grows in low-level service jobs and in high-skilled, high-tech jobs careers. The high-tech positions are good news for those with college degrees and technical skills, but the loss of laboring positions and replacement in fast-food and box store chains (e.g., WalMart, K-Mart, Home Depot, Lowe's) means a severe loss of genuine opportunity for living wages.

Although the new multinational industries springing up in developing countries such as Malaysia, Thailand, and the Philippines provide opportunities for mobility to those of modest origins, much of the upward mobility in the world is taking place among those who come from small, highly educated families with "get-ahead" values and who see education as a route to upward mobility (Blau and Duncan 1967; Featherman and Hauser 1978; Jencks 1979; Rothman 2005). They are positioned to take advantage of the changing

Despite significant progress in gender inequality in the United States and Canada, women and men professionals, such as these architects, often get quite different financial compensation for their work.

Source: © Paul Barton / Corbis.

These immigrants arrived at Ellis Island more than a century ago, hoping that in North America they could get a new start in life with more economic opportunity than they had in the old country.

Source: Library of Congress.

occupational structure and high-tech jobs. As the gap between rich and poor individuals and countries widens, more individuals are moving down than up in the stratification system.

What Are Your Chances for Mobility?

College education is the most important factor in moving to high-income status in developed countries. In fact, the

Poverty on the Hopi reservation in Arizona is such that much of this town looks like it is part of a developing country.

Source: Photo by Keith Roberts.

However hard he and his wife and children work, they will always be in debt; they cannot pay the total amount due for their hut or food from the owner's store. Basically, they are slaves—they do not have control over their own labor. They were born into this status, and there they will stay!

Imagine being born into a society in which you have no choices or options in life. You could not select an occupation that interested you, could not choose your mate, could not live in the part of town you favor. You would see wealthy aristocrats parading their advantages and realize that this would never be possible for you. You could never own land or receive the education of your choice.

The situation described above is reality for millions of people in the world; the situation into which they are born is where they spend their lives. All individuals are born with certain characteristics over which they have no control

These Aboriginal boys in Australia seem to be having fun as children, but their futures are determined by their place and family of birth. It is highly unlikely they will ever experience much affluence. Still, they may have rewarding lives surrounded by family if they are not absorbed into the larger world system that makes them dependent on a cash income. That is often what makes families vulnerable and forced to trade their children into slavery.

Source: Photo by Elise Roberts.

economic rewards of a college degree have increased; those with degrees become richer, and those without become poorer. This is because of *changes in occupational structures*, creating new types of jobs and a new social class with skills for the computer information age. These "social-cultural specialists" who work with ideas, knowledge, and technology contrast with the old middle class of technocrats, manufacturers, business owners, and executives (Brint 1984; Florida 2002; Hurst 2004).

With the rapid growth of postindustrial economies and computer technologies, fewer unskilled workers are needed, resulting in underemployment or unemployment for this group, who will continue to live at the margins in information societies, forming the lower class. Do you know individuals who are being nickel-and-dimed in today's economic environment? The next Sociology in Your Social World discusses this situation (page 207).

THINKING SOCIOLOGICALLY

What social factors in your society limit or enhance the likelihood of upward social mobility for you and your generation? Explain.

MAJOR STRATIFICATION SYSTEMS: MACRO-LEVEL ANALYSIS

Barak's family works on a plantation in Mozambique. He tries in vain to pay off the debts left by his father's family.

Sociology in Your Social World

Nickel-and-Dimed

Have you or has someone you know held a minimum wage job? Did you have to support yourself and maybe other family members on that wage, or was it just pocket money? Millions in the United States live in this world of unskilled laborers, getting from $5.15 to $7 an hour for their work. Author Barbara Ehrenreich asked how individuals and families, especially those coming off welfare and onto workfare programs, survive on these wages. To find out, she tried it herself. Living in several cities—Key West, Florida; Portland, Maine; and Minneapolis, Minnesota— she held jobs as a waitress, retail clerk at WalMart, hotel housekeeper, and nursing home aide. Each job demanded special skills, and each was physically and mentally demanding.

After describing the details of each job and the lives of her coworkers, Ehrenreich concludes that people are earning far less than they need to live on. Her coworkers struggled to meet minimum housing costs (sometimes living in cars), bought cheap food, shopped at thrift stores, and often had to piece together their lives. Transportation, child care, and health care were problems, and these individuals and families were constantly in debt.

"The Economic Policy Institute recently reviewed dozens of studies of what constitutes a living wage and came up with an average figure of $30,000 a year for a family of one adult and two children, which amounts to a wage of $14 an hour" (Ehrenreich 2001:214). This budget includes health insurance, a telephone, and child care, but no extras, and more than most minimum wage workers have. Upward mobility for this large group in the population is difficult if not impossible. Ehrenreich's research makes it clear: to be a society of at least minimal opportunity for all, we must reconsider economic policies to better address underpaid workers as well as the unemployed.

Source: Ehrenreich (2001).

(e.g., family background, age, sex, and race); in **ascribed stratification systems**, these characteristics determine one's position in society. In contrast, **achieved stratification systems** allow individuals to earn positions through their ability and effort. For instance, in a class system, it is sometimes possible to achieve a higher ranking by working hard, obtaining education, gaining power, or doing other things that are highly valued in that culture.

Ascribed Status: Caste and Estate Systems

Caste systems, the most rigid ascribed systems, are maintained by cultural norms and social control mechanisms that are deeply imbedded in religious, political, and economic institutions. Individuals born into caste systems have predetermined occupational positions, marriage partners, residences, social associations, and prestige levels. A person's caste is easily recognized through clothing, speech patterns, family name and identity, skin color, or other distinguishing characteristics. Individuals learn their place in society through the process of socialization that begins in their earliest years. To behave counter to caste prescriptions would be to go against religion and social custom, and religious ideas dictate that one's status after death (in Christian

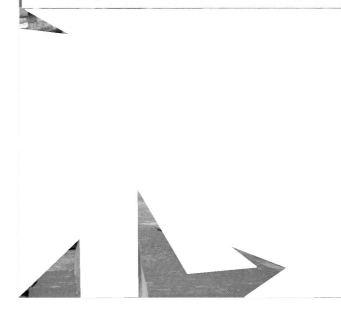

The caste system, which prevailed in India for many years, has weakened in urban areas with influence from the global social system.

Source: Photo by Elise Roberts.

Sociology around the World

The Outcastes of India

The village south of Madras in the state of Tamil Nadu was on an isolated dirt road, one kilometer from the nearest town. It consisted of a group of mud and stick huts with banana leaf thatched roofs. As our group of students arrived, the Dalit villagers lined the streets to greet us—and stare. Many had never seen Westerners. They played drums and danced for us and threw flower petals at our feet in traditional welcome.

Through our translator, we learned something of their way of life. The adults work in the fields long hours each day, plowing and planting with primitive implements, earning about eight cents from the landowner, often not enough to pay for their daily bowl of rice. Occasionally, they catch a frog or bird to supplement their meal. In the morning, they drink rice gruel, and in the evening eat a bowl of rice with some spices. Women and children walk more than a kilometer to the water well—but the water is polluted during the dry season. There are no privies but the fields. As a result of poor sanitation, inadequate diet, and lack of health care, many people become ill and die from easily curable health problems. For instance, lack of vitamin A, found in many fruits and vegetables to which they have little access, causes blindness in many village residents. Although the children have the right to go to the school in the closest village, many cannot do so because they have no transportation, shoes, or money for

paper, pencils, and books. Also, the families need them to work in the fields alongside their parents or help care for younger siblings. Many taboos rooted in tradition separate the Dalit from other Indians. For instance, they are forbidden to draw water from the village well, enter the village temple, or eat from dishes that might be used later by people of higher castes. The latter prohibition eliminates most dining at public establishments. Ninety-five percent are landless and earn a living below subsistence level.

Dalits who question these practices have been attacked and their houses burned. In one instance, 20 houses were burned on the birthday of Dr. Ambedkar, a leader in the Dalit rights movement. Official records distributed by the Human Rights Education Movement of India state that every hour, two Dalits are assaulted, three Dalit women are raped, two Dalits are murdered, and two Dalit houses are burned (*Dalit Liberation Education Trust* 1995; Thiagaraj 1994; Wilson 1993). This group in the bottom rung of the stratification system has a long fight ahead to gain the rights that many of us take for granted.

A few Dalit have migrated to cities where they blend in, and some of these have become educated and are now leading the fight for the rights and respect guaranteed by law. Recently, unions and interest groups have been representing the Dalit, and some members turn to religious and political groups that are more sympathetic to their plight, such as Buddhists, Christians, or Communists.

denominations) or one's next *reincarnation* or rebirth (in the Hindu tradition) might be in jeopardy. Stability is maintained by the belief that one can be reborn into a higher status in the next life if one fulfills expectations in their ascribed—socially assigned—position in this life. Thus, believers in both religions work hard in hopes of attaining a better life next time around. The institution of religion works together with the family, education, economic and political institutions to shape (and sometimes reduce) both expectations and aspirations and to keep people in their prescribed places in caste systems.

The clearest example of a caste system is found in India. The Hindu religion holds that individuals are born into one of four *varna*, broad caste positions, or into a fifth group below the caste system, the *outcaste* group. The first and highest varna, called Brahmans, originally was made up of

priests and scholars; it now includes many leaders in society. The second varna, Kshatriyas or Rajputs, includes the original prince and warrior varna, and now makes up much of the army and civil service. The Vaishyas, or merchants, are the third varna. The fourth varna, the Sudras, include peasants, artisans, and laborers.

The final layer, below the caste system, encompasses profoundly oppressed and broken people—"a people put aside"—referred to as untouchables, outcastes, Chandalas (a Hindu term), and Dalits (the name preferred by many "untouchables" themselves). Although the Indian Constitution of 1950 granted full social status to these citizens, and a law passed in 1955 made discrimination against them punishable, deeply rooted traditions are difficult to change. Caste distinctions are still very prevalent, especially in rural areas, as seen in the discussion in Sociology around the World (above).

Just as the position of individuals in caste systems is ascribed, estate systems are similarly rigid in stratifying individuals. **Estate systems** are characterized by the concentration of economic and political power in the hands of a small minority of political-military elite, with the peasantry tied to the land (Rothman 2005). During the Middle Ages, knights defended the realms and the religion of the nobles. Behind every knight in shining armor were peasants, sweating in the fields and paying for the knights' food, armor, and campaigns. For farming the land owned by the nobility, peasants received protection against invading armies and enough of the produce to survive. Their life was often miserable; if the crops were poor, they ate little. In a good year, they might save enough to buy a small parcel of land. A very few were able to become independent in this fashion.

Estate systems are based on ownership of land, the position one is born into, or military strength; an individual's rank and legal rights are clearly spelled out, and arranged marriages and religion bolster the system. Estate systems existed in ancient Egypt, the Incan and Mayan civilizations, Europe, China, and Japan. Today, similar systems exist in some Central and South American, Asian, and African countries with large banana, coffee, and sugar plantations, as exemplified in the earlier example of Barak in Mozambique. Over time, development of a mercantile economy resulted in modifications in the estate system. Now, peasants often work the land in exchange for the right to live there and receive a portion of the produce.

Achieved Status: Social Class Systems

Social class systems of stratification are based on achieved status. Members of the same social class have similar income, wealth, and economic position. They also share comparable styles of living, levels of education, cultural similarities, and patterns of social interaction. Most of us are members of class-based stratification systems, and we take advantage of opportunities available to our social class. Our families, rich or poor, educated or unskilled, provide us with an initial social ranking and socialization experience. We tend to feel a kinship and sense of belonging with those in the same social class—our neighborhood and work group, our peers and friends. We think alike, share interests, and probably look up to the same people as a reference group. Our social class position is based on the three main factors determining positions in the stratification system: property, power, and prestige.

Compared with systems based on ascribed status, achieved status systems maintain that everyone is born with common legal status; everyone is equal before the law. In principle, all individuals can own property and choose their own occupations. However, in practice, wealth affords better legal representation; similarly, most class systems pass privilege or poverty from one generation to the next, and individual upward or downward mobility is never guaranteed.

The Dalits—sometimes called "untouchables"—are the most impoverished people in India. While they live in incredible hardship, they are beginning to mobilize and demand rights as citizens of India and the world.

Source: Photo by Kate Ballantine.

Property, Power, and Prestige

This is the trio that, according to Max Weber, determines where individuals rank in relation to each other (Weber 1946, 1947). Positions in social stratification systems, according to Weber, are determined by these three elements and the opportunities the individual has to gain these. By *property* (wealth), Weber refers to owning or controlling the means of production. *Power*, the ability to control others, includes not only the means of production but also the position one holds. *Prestige* involves the esteem and recognition one receives, based on wealth, position, or accomplishments. Table 7.2 gives examples of households in the upper and lower social classes; it illustrates the variables that determine a person's standing in the three areas listed above.

Although these three dimensions of stratification are often found together, this is not always so. Recall the idea of status inconsistency: an individual can have a great deal of prestige yet not command much wealth (Weber 1946). Consider winners of the prestigious Nobel Peace Prize such as Wangari Maathai of Kenya, Rigoberta Menchu of Guatemala, or Betty Williams and Mairead Corrigan of Northern Ireland; none of them is rich, but each has made contributions to the world that have gained them prestige around the world. Likewise, some people gain enormous wealth through crime or gambling, but this wealth may not be accompanied by respect or prestige.

TABLE 7.2   **Basic Dimensions of Social Stratification**

	Class Variables (Economic)	Prestige Variables	Power Variables (Political-Legal)

	Income
	Wealth
	Occupation
	Education
	Family Stability
	Education of Children
		Occupational Prestige
		Respect in Community
		Consumption
		Participation in Group Life
		Evaluations of Race, Religion,
		  Ethnicity
			Political Participation
			Political Attitudes
			Legislation and Governmental
			  Benefits
			Distribution of Justice

Households in the upper social class	Affluence: economic security and power, control over material and human investment Income from work but mostly from property	More integrated personalities, more consistent attitudes, and greater psychic fulfillment due to deference, valued associations, and consumption	Power to determine public policy and its implementation by the state, thus giving control over the nature and distribution of social values
Households in the lower social class	Destitution: worthlessness on economic markets	Unintegrated personalities, inconsistent attitudes, sense of isolation and despair; sleazy social interaction	Political powerlessness, lack of legal recourse or rights, socially induced apathy

Source: Rossides (1997:15).

Note: Contains examples of values in the top and bottom classes within each dimension and examples of subdimensions. For expository purposes, religious and ethnic or racial rankings are omitted.

The Economic Factor

One's income, property, and total assets comprise one's **wealth**. These lie at the heart of class differences. The contrast between the royal splendor described in the opening of this chapter and the daily struggle for survival of those in poverty is an example of the differences extreme wealth creates. Another example is shown in the income distribution in the United States by quintiles (see Table 7.3). Note that there has been minimal movement between the groups over the years.

TABLE 7.3   **Share of Household Income in Quintiles**

	1995	2000	2003	2004
Lowest quintile	3.7	3.6	3.4	3.4
Second quintile	9.0	8.9	8.7	8.7
Third quintile	15.0	14.9	14.7	14.8
Fourth quintile	23.3	23.0	23.2	23.4
Highest quintile	49.0	49.7	50.1	49.8
Ratio of highest fifth to lowest fifth	13.2	13.8	14.7	14.6

Source: U.S. Census Bureau (2000, 2005f).

Although income distribution in the United States has not changed dramatically over time, there has been an increase in overall inequality as the middle class has decreased by over 8 percent since 1969. A majority of the 8 percent have experienced a downward movement, although a few have moved up in the stratification system (Duncan, Rodgers, and Smeeding 1993; Rose 2000).

The Power Factor

Power refers to the ability to control or influence others, to get them to do what you want them to do. Positions of power are gained through family inheritance, family connections, political appointments, education, hard work, or friendship networks. Two theories dominate the explanations of power—power elite and pluralist theories.

We discussed previously the conflict theorists' view that those who hold power are those who control the economic capital and the means of production in society (Ashley and Orenstein 2005). Consistent with Marx, many recent conflict theorists have focused on a *power elite*—individuals with powerful positions in political, business, and military arenas (Domhoff 2001; Mills 1956). These people interact with each other and have a kind of conspiracy to ensure that their power is not threatened; they each tend to protect the power of the other. The idea is that those who are not in this interlocking elite group do not hold real power (Dye 2002).

Pluralist theorists argue that power is not held exclusively by an elite group but is shared among many power centers, each of which has its own self-interests to protect (Ritzer and Goodman 2004). Pluralists contend that well-financed special interest groups (e.g., dairy farmers or truckers' trade unions) and professional associations (e.g., the American Medical Association) have considerable power through collective action. Officials who hold political power are vulnerable to pressure from influential interest groups,

TABLE 7.4 **Prestige Rankings of 17 Professions and Occupations**

OCCUPATIONS (Base: All Adults)	Very Great Prestige %	Considerable Prestige %	Some Prestige %	Hardly Any Prestige at All %	Not Sure/ Refused %
Scientist	51	25	20	2	3
Doctor	50	30	17	1	2
Military officer	47	27	21	3	2
Teacher	47	23	20	7	2
Police officer	40	32	20	7	1
Priest/minister/clergyman	36	25	24	11	3
Engineer	34	32	28	4	2
Architect	27	34	31	4	4
Member of Congress	27	30	29	11	3
Athlete	21	24	37	15	3
Entertainer	19	29	34	15	3
Journalist	19	25	41	12	4
Business executive	18	29	36	13	4
Lawyer	15	25	38	20	2
Banker	15	29	44	10	2
Union leader	14	22	37	23	5
Accountant	13	23	42	17	4

Source: Taylor (2002).

and each interest group competes for power with others. Creating and maintaining this power through networks and pressure on legislators is the job of lobbyists. For example, in the ongoing U.S. debate over health care legislation, interest groups from the medical community, insurance lobbies, and citizens' groups wield their power to influence the outcome, but since these major interests conflict and no one group has the most power, no resolution has been reached.

The Prestige Factor

Prestige refers to an individual's social recognition, esteem, and respect commanded from others. An individual's prestige ranking is closely correlated with the value system of society; chances of being granted high prestige improve if one's patterns of behavior, occupation, and lifestyle match those that are valued in the society. Among high-ranked occupations across nations are scientists, physicians, military officers, lawyers, and college professors. Table 7.4 shows selected occupational prestige rankings in the United States. Obtaining material possessions or increasing one's educational level can boost prestige but in themselves cannot change class standing.

THINKING SOCIOLOGICALLY

Describe your own wealth, power, and prestige in society. Does your family have one factor but not others? What difference does each of the factors make in your life?

Social Classes in the United States

When asked about their social class, most people in the United States identify themselves as middle class, and in the current economic structure, most people are middle class. However, there is slight movement to the upper class and somewhat more movement to the lower class, resulting in a shrinking middle class. As noted previously, the U.S. system allows for mobility within the middle class, but there is little movement at the very top and very bottom of the social ladder. People in the top rung often use the power and wealth to insulate themselves and protect their elite status, and the bottom group is insulated because of vicious cycles of poverty that are hard to break (Gilbert and Kahl 2003).

The middle class, as defined by sociologists, makes up about 40 percent of the population in the United States, depending on what economic criteria are used (Rose 2000). Since most people identify themselves as "middle class," this section focuses on characteristics of that group, although much research has been done on each social class. Wages and salaries in the middle classes have declined since the 1980s, but those of the upper classes have risen. Reasons for middle-class decline include downsizing and layoffs of workers, technological shifts, competition, free trade, and trade deficits between countries, immigration, and deregulation— all macro-level economic trends that mean lower incomes for middle-class workers. The top 20 percent of income earners increased their percentage of the total income available in the United States by almost 6 percent between 1977 and 2005, with the top 5 percent receiving 22 percent of all income. Changes in class groups are due largely to structural changes in society; the upward movement among the few who have received huge gains in earning power is causing wages and earnings to become more unequal.

Upper middle-class families typically have high income, high education, high occupational level (in terms of prestige and other satisfactions), and high participation in political life and voluntary associations. Families enjoy a stable life, stressing companionship, privacy, pleasant surroundings in safe neighborhoods, property ownership, and stimulating associations. They stress internalization of moral standards of right and wrong, taking responsibility for one's own actions, learning to make one's own decisions, and training for future leadership positions.

The *lower middle class* includes small businesspeople and farmers; semiprofessionals (teachers, local elected officials, social workers, nurses, police officers, firefighters);

This little boy sits at the feet of an aid worker. How much power do you imagine this little African boy's parents have to make sure their child's needs are met? This boy and his family have personal troubles because the meso and macro systems of his society have failed to work effectively.

Source: © Istockphoto.com.

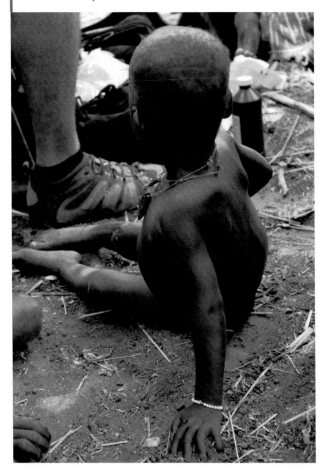

middle-management personnel, both private and public; and sales and clerical workers in comfortable office settings. Families are relatively stable; they participate in community life, and while they are less active in political life than the upper classes, they are more political than those in classes below. Children are raised to work hard and obey authority. Therefore, childrearing patterns more often involve swift physical punishment for misbehavior than talk and reasoning that is typical of the upper middle class.

THINKING SOCIOLOGICALLY

How does today's popular culture on TV, films, magazines, and popular music groups depict different social classes? How are poor people depicted, and who is responsible for their poverty? Do any of these depictions question the U.S. class system? What kinds of music are class based?

POVERTY: MULTI-LEVEL DETERMINANTS AND POLICY

Stories about hunger and famine in Third World countries fill the newspapers, but one hardly expects to see hunger in rich countries. Eighty-eight percent of U.S. households had enough food for the family in 2004. However, 13.5 million U.S. households (11.9 percent of all households) did not have enough food at some time during the year due to lack of money or other resources. In 4.4 million households (3.9 percent), people were hungry (U.S. Department of Agriculture 2005b). The poor come from disenfranchised groups such as the homeless, unemployed, single parents, disabled, elderly, and migrant workers. On average, about 23.9 million people living in 10.3 million households receive food stamps in the United States each month (U.S. Department of Agriculture 2005a). With downturns in employment, low wages, and reduced aid to poor families, hunger and poor health are likely to continue. Consider the case of adolescents growing up poor, discussed in the next How Do We Know?

The poor—the underclass—have no permanent or stable work or property-based income, only casual or intermittent earnings in the labor market. They are often dependent on help from government agencies or private organizations to survive. In short, they have personal troubles in large part because they have been unable to establish linkages and networks in the meso- and macro-level organizations of our social world. They have no collective power and, thus, little representation of their interests and needs in the political system.

Sociologists recognize two basic types of poverty: absolute poverty and relative poverty. **Absolute poverty**, not having resources to meet basic needs, means no prestige, no access to power, no accumulated wealth, and insufficient means to survive. While absolute poverty in the United

Growing Up Poor

Adolescents have quests; they want love, work, thrills, mentors, and mastery over the social world. Yet for poor adolescents with few advantages, there is little chance of making it in today's competitive world with shrinking economic opportunities. An award-winning study by Terry Williams and William Kornblum (1985) documents the lives and experiences of young people in the United States. The study, *Growing Up Poor*, sought to understand how racial and ethnic segregation influence the ability of youths to seek jobs outside their own residential areas, and how local community institutions—especially schools, voluntary civic associations, churches, political associations, federally sponsored programs, and small-scale institutions of the neighborhoods—facilitate or impede the entry of disadvantaged youth into the labor market.

Using ethnographic community research, the researchers wanted to present a balanced picture of community life for teens. The study,

conducted in four U.S. cities (New York City; Louisville, Kentucky; Cleveland, Ohio; and Meridian, Mississippi) included field observations on street corners, pool halls, classrooms, smoke shops, project apartments, parks, and other hangouts in seven communities within the four cities.

First, the researchers found quantitative data on youth unemployment and other indicators of the status of youth. They then focused on the lives behind the statistics—the young people actually living in these community contexts. The researchers focused on school dropouts, young mothers' work and family patterns, street life and crime, ghetto life, Manpower program experience, and alternative routes out of poverty.

One of the research techniques was to hire 86 disadvantaged youth from these communities as research assistants; these teens were trained in skills needed for the project. They wrote down observations, wrote about their experiences and

those of others, and drew maps of the immediate neighborhoods with places teens congregate.

A key finding was that for those who do poorly in school, success is illusory. In the past, they could make up for school failure with early earnings at manual labor. Now, many of those industrial options are closed, and they become prime candidates for chronic unemployment, crime, homicide, depression, and exploitation. Yet some, a very few, do succeed—despite all odds.

The study has implications for the teens, the communities, and the nation at large. Based on their research, Williams and Kornblum recommend strategies and programs to policy makers for dealing with the teens in impoverished families. Unless research like this on the causes of teen poverty is conducted and the process of impoverishment understood, it is unlikely that solutions will ever be found.

States is quite limited, the Dalit of India, described earlier in The Outcastes of India, provide an example; they often die of easily curable diseases because their bodies are weakened by chronic and persistent hunger and almost total lack of medical attention.

Relative poverty refers to those whose income falls below the poverty line, resulting in an inadequate standard of living relative to others in a given country. In most industrial countries, relative poverty means shortened life expectancy, higher infant mortality, and poorer health, but not many people die of starvation or easily curable diseases, such as influenza.

The feminization of poverty refers to the trend in which single females, increasingly younger and with children, make up a growing proportion of those in poverty. Vicki's situation

provides an example. Her life has been hard! After her parents divorced, she quit high school to take odd jobs to help her mother pay the bills. Eighteen, pregnant, and the baby's father out of the picture, she lived on welfare, then workfare because without a high school degree she could not get a job that paid enough to support herself and her baby. She became homeless, living out of her defunct car that would not run because she lacked the money to repair it. Her life spiraled out of control, and she is now in a mental facility, her daughter placed in foster care.

While we do not like to admit that this can happen in the United States or Canada, and we try to blame the victim (why did she not just finish high school, not get pregnant, have an abortion), people do what they must to survive. The fact is that social policies such as workfare affect poor people's chances of success. This problem is heightened as many middle-class women are pushed into poverty through divorce; they sacrificed their own careers for husbands and family so their earning powers are often inadequate and many are unable to collect on child support. The numbers in poverty are highest in and around large central cities such as Paris, France; Mexico City, Mexico; Sao Paulo, Brazil; and Caracas, Venezuela. In the United States, numbers are highest in cities such as New York, Chicago, Detroit, Cleveland, and Los Angeles, where the percentage of poor African American families headed by females reaches close to 50 percent in some cities. Girls who grow up in female-headed households or foster homes, without a stable family model, are more likely to become single teen mothers and to live in poverty, causing disruption in their schooling, employment possibilities, and marital opportunities (Duncan et al. 1998; Gans 1995). Conflict theorists argue that poor women, especially women of color, in capitalistic economic systems are used as a reserve labor force that can be called on when labor is needed and dismissed when not needed (Ehrenreich 2001). They are an easily exploited group (Newman 1999).

Why does poverty persist? The elite groups in each culture define what it means to be a success; one major way this is perpetuated is via popular entertainment, which is run and financed by wealthy companies and individuals (Aquirre and Baker 2000). Those who cannot live up to the expectations are labeled "failures" and blamed for their misfortune; they live under constant stress that can cause mental or physical breakdowns and humiliating alienation from the social system. Some turn to alcohol or drugs to escape the pressure and failure or to crime to get money to pay the bills. Poor physical and mental health, inadequate nutrition, higher mortality rates, obesity, low self-esteem, feelings of hopelessness, daily struggle to survive, and dependence on others are a few of the individual consequences of poverty within our social world. Costs to the larger society include the following:

- It loses the talents and abilities that these people could contribute.
- It must expend tax dollars to address their needs or to regulate them with social workers and police.
- People live with a contradiction of cultural values which claim that all citizens are "created equal" and are worthy of respect, yet not all can "make it" in society.

Welfare programs in developed countries are often thought of as programs for the poor. However, there are massive programs of government support for people in all levels of the social system: university students pay nothing in some countries to roughly one-third of the cost of their education at other state-supported universities (taxpayers picking up the rest of the cost); grants and subsidies to farmers; and tax breaks for businesses. Interestingly, only the programs for the poor are stigmatized as unearned giveaway programs.

THINKING SOCIOLOGICALLY

Why is it that only the programs to help the poor are stigmatized as unearned giveaway programs?

The elimination of poverty takes money and requires choices by policy makers to *do* something about poverty. Some argue poverty will never be eliminated because poor people are needed in society. Consider the position put forth in the accompanying Sociology in Your Social World.

Eliminating Poverty: Some Policy Considerations

Some policy makers suggest attacking the problem of poverty institution by institution, offering incentives for family stability, for students to finish high school, and for job training. The Joint Center for Poverty Research, among other think tanks, has set forth policies to reduce poverty based on research (Poverty Research News 2002). Yet all these programs, public and private, require either massive commitment of funds or remodeling of our social institutions. For instance, government programs in the United States and other countries are designed to help individuals through difficult times during economic downturns. The goal of most welfare programs is to eliminate poverty by changing the factors that perpetuate poverty, but without money and jobs, this is impossible. Can welfare reform plans such as workfare in the United States "end welfare as we know it" as policy makers claim?

Workfare and Other Aid Programs

For most societies, poverty means loss of labor, a drain on other members in society to support the poor, and extensive health care and crime prevention systems. Some of the U.S. Great Society programs of the 1960s and 1970s were successful in reducing poverty by attacking the root causes. The Women, Infants, and Children Program provides nutritional help, and Head Start provides early childhood education; both programs have received good grade cards for helping poor women and children, but funding to some of these programs has been cut back due to other funding priorities and their effectiveness reduced (which will surely lead to criticism of its ineffectiveness). Other programs—Aid to Families with Dependent Children, Medicaid, Medicare, food stamps—helped many who had short-term problems but were criticized as creating dependence of families on aid (Corbett 1994/1995).

Work incentive programs such as *workfare* offer job training and food stamps. Able-bodied unemployed or underemployed adults must work, be receiving on-the-job training, or be getting education in basic skills to qualify. Work incentive programs have gained adherents who argue that many welfare recipients would work if provided support and motivation. This idea works in theory, but

Sociology in Your Social World

The Functions of Poverty

Surely wealthy countries such as the United States have the means to eliminate poverty if they chose to. Its persistence is subject for debate. Some sociologists argue that poverty serves certain purposes or *functions* for society (Gans 1971, 1995), and these make it difficult to address the problem directly and systematically. Some people actually benefit from having poor people kept poor. Consider the following points:

1. The fact that some people are in poverty provides us with a convenient scapegoat for societal problems; we have individuals to blame for poverty—the poor individuals themselves—and can ignore meso- and macro-level causes of poverty that would be expensive to resolve.

2. Having poor people creates many jobs for those who are not poor, including "helping" professions such as social workers and law enforcement such as police, judges, and prison workers.

3. The poor provide an easily available group of laborers to do work; they serve as surplus workers to hire for undesirable jobs.

4. The poor serve to reinforce and legitimate our own lives and institutions. It also allows the rest of us to feel superior to someone, enhancing our self-esteem.

5. Their violation of mainstream values helps to remind us of those values, thereby constantly reaffirming the values among the affluent.

From this perspective, the poor serve a role in the structure of society, so some group of people will always be at the bottom of the stratification ladder.

Source: Gans (1995).

---

success in helping people out of poverty depends on the macro-level economic conditions: Are there jobs available at living wages? When the public is attracted to politicians who cut taxes, there is no money for social programs and little hope of helping the "invisible" poor out of poverty. In fact, institutions such as prisons absorb public funds that could go to poverty reduction, yet crime is often a result of people feeling that they have no other options for survival.

Social research centers provide a major service to policy makers; data collected on social problems such as poverty, drug problems, and welfare affect governmental decisions about how to deal most effectively with problems. The next The Applied Sociologist at Work provides an example of one research center and its work.

THINKING SOCIOLOGICALLY

Recalling what you have learned about poverty, how would you develop a plan to attack the problem of poverty within your community or country? Is it a matter of job training, family values, breaking the cycle, welfare support, or something else?

NATIONAL AND GLOBAL DIGITAL DIVIDE: MACRO-LEVEL STRATIFICATION

Two of Jeanne's African student friends, Mamadou from Niger and Eric from Ghana, answer their cell phones to the sound of chimes from London's Big Ben clock tower and a Bob Marley song. One speaks in Kanuri and French and the other in Twi to friends thousands of miles away. They are the future generation of elites from developing countries, fluent in the languages of several countries, of computers, and of the digital age. Many of their fellow country citizens are not so fortunate; they live subsistence lives and have little contact with the digital world swirling overhead through satellite connections.

The global social world is increasingly based on producing and transmitting information through digital technology. Few tools are more important in this process than the computer, Internet, and cell phones. In nearly every salaried and professional position, computer knowledge and ability to navigate the Internet are critical employment skills; therefore, individuals with insufficient access to computers and lack of technical skills face barriers to many professions and opportunities. Since computer skills are important for personal success, this is an important micro-level issue; the

THE APPLIED SOCIOLOGIST AT WORK   Kenneth Nyberg

The Applied Research Center

At some universities, students receive hands-on experience doing applied community research. Applied Research Center (ARC) is a multimillion-dollar research organization in a university setting. The main office is on the campus of California State University, Bakersfield, with branch offices in Fresno and Hanford. Its principle interests are public policy research and public health issues (welfare reform, child health, drug abuse, education, and crime), all issues related to social class status. ARC employs more than 65 people including research scientists, research assistants, students, and staff. Most of the revenues to run ARC come from grants and contracts, from agencies such as NASA, California Department of Social Services, California Department of Alcohol and Drug Programs, and Children and Families Commissions in six California counties. As executive director and chief scientist of ARC, Dr. Kenneth Nyberg is responsible for the applied science, ethics, performance and quality of the work, and professional relationships with funding agencies.

Recent projects in the center include analyses of the impacts of welfare reform on welfare client populations, the relative merits (both efficiency and benefit-cost) of drug treatment programs versus incarceration, and organizational performance work for NASA, which focused on improving the efficiency of flight testing.

To be successful in carrying out this diverse agenda, Nyberg stresses the need to keep "a vivid sociological imagination" in the forefront of his work as well as exploring what each social science can bring to the understanding of problems. Necessary components in the research process include understanding methodologies that can answer questions, having secure computer facilities for confidential information and a secure server large enough to handle multiple projects at one time, and being familiar with methods of data analysis.

The most exciting part of this work, according to Nyberg, is discovering important information and knowing it first. ARC often knows answers to important policy questions and can inform policy makers a year or more before agencies and others work on solutions. ARC, therefore, has an impact on policy matters and on the lives and prospects of people. He points out the tremendous responsibility involved in learning and dealing with information that affects people's lives directly. The downside is the myriad of pressures, from timelines to political intrusions on the work and findings.

Dr. Kenneth Nyberg received his doctorate from the University of Utah. His areas of research include families and children, welfare reform, public health and disease, and social change. He has taught many methods courses, and students participate actively in the center's research.

---

digital divide is breaking down for some young and elite members of developing society such as Mamadou and Eric, but few individuals and countries have sufficient technology and educated population to participate in this new economy (Drori 2006; Nakamura 2004).

The recent growth in both the development and use of technology has taken place mostly in developed countries and among well-educated elite from developing countries. The number of Internet users around the globe increased from 16 million in 1995 to over 500 million in 2001—in just six years (Drori 2006). As William Gibson (1999) put it, "The future is already here. It's just not evenly distributed." In the United States, the most wired country in the world, many poor people do not have access to computers or mentors to teach them how to use computers. This digital divide is beginning to close, but it still creates barriers for many (McChesney, Wood, and Foster 1998; Nakamura 2004; Shade 2004).

Comparing countries cross-nationally, only 5 percent of the world's population is online, but 50 percent of those who *are* live in either North America or Scandinavia (Sweden, Norway, Finland, Denmark, and Iceland). Seventy-nine percent

of the online population lives in nations that belong to the Organization for Economic and Cooperative Development—countries that comprise 14 percent of the people on the planet. By contrast, in Sub–Saharan Africa and in India, only 4 out of every 1,000 citizens uses the Internet (Drori 2006). Ninety-seven percent of Internet hosts are in the developed countries (which have only 16 percent of the world's population), and 66 percent of income from royalties and licensing fees go to two countries: the United States receives 54 percent and Japan 12 percent. In some countries, the monthly access fee for hooking up to the Internet is stunningly high compared to average monthly income: in Bangladesh, 191 percent; in Nepal, 278 percent; and in Madagascar, 614 percent. This may be why 35 of the poorest countries in the world have less than 1 percent of the Internet users (Drori 2006).

An additional difficulty is that most websites and e-mail services use English, the computer keyboards are designed with a Western alphabet, and some of the digital systems in computers are established on the basis of English symbols and logic. It is difficult to even use the Internet in other languages—a fact that many of us may not think about as we use the system (Drori 2006). For people who are struggling for the very survival of their culture, the dominance of English may feel like a threat, one more example of Western dominance. So resistance to the use of computers and the Internet is more than a matter of finances or technology; there may be cultural reasons as well.

Policy decisions at the international level affect the status of developing countries. The United Nations, the International Monetary Fund, and other international organizations have pressured countries to develop their Internet capacities; indeed, this is sometimes used as a criterion for ranking countries in terms of their "level of modernization" (Drori 2006). Countries that have not been able to get "in the game" of Internet technology cannot keep pace with a rapidly evolving global economy.

Internet technology has created a digital divide, but it also has had some beneficial economic impact, stimulating jobs in poor countries. In 1999, computer component parts were a substantial percentage of production in some developing countries: 52 percent of Malaysia's exports, 44 percent of Costa Rica's and 28 percent of Mexico's. The high-tech revenue for India increased from 150 million U.S. dollars in 1990 to 4 billion dollars in 1999. On the less positive side, e-waste from electronic equipment is extremely toxic, and it is almost always shipped to poor countries, where extremely poor people must deal with the consequences of toxic pollution (Drori 2006).

Digital technology is an example of one important force changing the micro- and macro-level global stratification system—a spectrum of people and countries from the rich and elite to those that are poor and desperate.

![THINKING SOCIOLOGICALLY]

THINKING SOCIOLOGICALLY

What evidence of the digital divide do you see in your family, community, nation, and world? For instance, can your grandparents program their VCR? Do they know how to work a cell phone or navigate the Internet?

The Global "Digital Divide" and Policy

As poor countries become part of the electronic age, some are making policies that facilitate rapid modernization. They are passing over developmental stages that rich countries went through. As an illustration, consider the telephone. In 2002, 90 percent of all telephones were cell phones, many using satellites. Some countries never did get completely wired for landlines, thus eliminating one phase of phone technology. With satellite technology in place, some computer and Internet options will be available without expensive intermediate steps (Drori 2006). Engineers in India, working through an organization called Simputer Trust, have been designing a simple computer (a "simputer") that will be less expensive and will have more multilingual capacities than the PC. Such efforts will enhance access of poor

In rural villages in Laos where people live in grass houses such as this one, there is no reliable electricity or other support systems for Internet technology. Few people in such communities have ever been online or even know about the resources made available through the World Wide Web.

Source: Photo by Elise Roberts.

countries to the computer and Internet and will provide the means for poor countries to become part of the competitive global stratification system; technology is leveling the world playing field (Drori 2006; Friedman 2005).

The changing global economic landscape is affecting nations' internal economic competition as well. Bangalore is home to India's booming digital industries that are successfully competing in the global high-tech market. Yet many villages and cities in India provide examples of the contrasts between the caste system and the emerging class system. In rural agricultural areas, change is extremely slow despite laws forbidding differential treatment of outcastes and mandating change. In urban industrial areas, new opportunities are changing the traditional caste structures; intercaste and intracaste competition for wealth and power is increasing with the changes in economic, political, and other institutional structures. The higher castes were the first to receive the education and lifestyle that create industrial leaders; now shopkeepers, wealthy peasants, teachers, and others are vying for power. Within the world system, India is generally economically poor but developing certain economic sectors rapidly. Thus, India is in transition both internally and in the global world system.

A small percentage of societies control most world resources. Because of this, the gap between the rich and poor countries is large and in most cases growing. Competition over unequal distribution of power, wealth, and resources creates tensions between countries. These tensions can stimulate development or cause bitter conflicts and hostilities that include terrorism, civil wars, revolution, and other forms of hostility and protest. For instance, Middle Eastern countries have a key world resource at their core—oil. This creates the possibility of conflicts both between Middle Eastern countries and in the world, as exemplified by the 1989 Gulf War between Iraq and Kuwait and the current Middle Eastern conflicts involving Iraq, the United States, and the United Nations.

SO WHAT?

Perhaps your understanding of why you are rich or poor—and what effect your socioeconomic status has on what you buy, what you believe, and where you live—has taken on new dimensions. Perhaps you have gained some insight into what factors affect your ability to move up in the social class system. The issue of social stratification calls into question the widely held belief in the fairness of our economic system. By studying this issue, we better understand why some individuals are able to experience *prestige* (respect) and to control power and wealth at the micro, meso, and macro levels of the social system, while others have little access to those resources. Few social forces affect your personal life at the micro level as much as stratification. That includes the decision you make about what you wish to do with your life, who you might marry, and the fact that you are reading this book.

We leave this discussion of stratification systems, including class systems, with a partial answer to the question posed in the beginning of this chapter: Why are some people rich and others poor? In the next two chapters, we expand the discussion to include other variables in stratification systems—race and ethnicity, and gender. By the end of these chapters, the answer to the opening questions should be even clearer.

CONTRIBUTING TO YOUR SOCIAL WORLD

At the Local Level: Remember to tip generously when you are being served by people in minimum-wage jobs—housekeeping maids that have cleaned your room, breakfast servers at the continental breakfast, employees at fast food restaurants, and so forth.

Local homeless shelters or soup kitchens for the poor often need volunteer help or interns.

At the Organizational or Institutional Level: After graduation, consider doing a one-year service with *AmeriCorp*. The pay is not good, but the experience and contribution to those in need provides other rewards.

At the National and Global Levels: Consider doing a paid internship sponsored by *Sociologists without Borders* (or *Sociólogos sin Fronteras*; http://www.sociologistswithoutborders.org). This experience, or joining Peace Corps or another international agency, will give you a wonderful experience in an impoverished country helping people in need of resources.

Grameen Bank (www.grameen-info.org/bank or www.grameenfoundation.org) was started in Bangladesh by Professor Muhammad Yunus, winner of the 2006 Nobel Prize for Peace. It makes small business loans to people who live in impoverished regions of the world and who have no collateral for a loan. The default rate on these loans is one of the lowest of any bank anywhere. Rather than collateral, the promise to repay is based on social ties to others in one's community who will not receive loans unless the first party pays regularly on their loan. Consider doing a local fundraiser with friends for the Grameen Bank or other micro-credit organization.

Purchase only coffee and chocolate that are Fair Trade products. Among other things, this will ensure that you are not supporting slavery someplace around the globe with your purchases.

Visit www.pineforge.com/ballantinestudy for online activities, sample tests, and other helpful information. Select "Chapter 7: Stratification" for chapter-specific activities.

CHAPTER

8 RACE AND ETHNIC GROUP STRATIFICATION: Beyond "We" and "They"

As we travel around our social
world, the people we encounter
gradually change appearance.
As human beings, we are all
part of "we," but there is a
tendency to define those who
look different as "they."

Think About It . . .

1. Why do you look different from those around you? What importance do these differences make?

2. Is everyone prejudiced? If so, why? Why do people categorize others?

3. Why are minority group members in most countries poorer than dominant group members?

4. What can you do to make the world a better place for all people?

Macro: Global Community

Macro: National Society

Meso: National Institutions and Organizations; Ethnic Subcultures

Micro: Local Organizations and Community

Micro: You and Your Family

Micro: Local reference groups; deliberate exclusion of ethnic group members

Meso: Laws that intentionally or unintentionally discriminate; educational-testing biases

Macro: Laws or court rulings that set policy for state and local levels

Macro: Racial and ethnic hostilities at the national and global levels result in wars, genocide, or ethnic cleansing

When Siri wakes it is about noon. In the instant of waking she knows exactly who and what she has become . . . the soreness in her genitals reminds her of the fifteen men she had sex with the night before. Siri is fifteen years old. Sold by her impoverished parents a year ago, she finds that her resistance and her desire to escape the brothel are breaking down and acceptance and resignation are taking their place. . . . Siri is very frightened that she will get AIDS . . . as many girls from her village return home to die from AIDS after being sold into the brothels. (Bales 2002:207–09)

Siri is a sex slave, just like millions of other young women around the world. Slavery is not limited to Third World countries: Dora was enslaved in a home in Washington, DC, and domestic slaves have been discovered in London, Chicago, New York, and Los Angeles. The CIA reports thousands of women and children are smuggled into the United States each year as sex and domestic slaves or locked away in sweat shops (Bales 2004). International agencies estimate that over one million children in Southeast Asia have been sold into bondage, mostly into the booming sex trade.

It may be surprising to know that slavery is alive and flourishing around the world (*Modern Slavery* 2005). An estimated twenty-seven million people, mostly women and children from poor families in poor countries, are auctioned off or lured into slavery each year by kidnap gangs, pimps, and cross-border syndicates (Bales 2004; Kyle and Koslowski 2001). "As a global phenomenon, human trafficking in slaves from such places as Ukraine, Myanmar (Burma), Laos, Nepal, and the Philippines, mostly for commercial sex industry, is so profitable that criminal business people invest in involuntary brothels much as they would in a mining operation" (Kyle and Koslowski 2001:1). In Africa, the primary use of slaves is in the chocolate industry. In Asia, young girls from Bombay (India) or Myanmar become unwilling "wives"; if the man grows tired of the girl, she has little option but to turn to prostitution to survive (Bales 2004).

International events such as the Olympics and major soccer matches bring new markets for the sex trade. Young foreign girls are chosen for sex slaves because they are exotic, free of AIDS, and cannot escape due to insufficient money and knowledge of the language or the country to which they are exported (Moritz 2001). Sometimes, poor families sell their daughters for the promise of high wages and perhaps money sent home. As a result, girls as young as six are held captive as prostitutes or as domestic workers. Child labor, a

In Calcutta's red light district, over 7,000 women and girls work as prostitutes. Only one group has a lower standing: their children. Zana Briski became involved in the lives of these children in 1998 when she first began photographing prostitutes in Calcutta. Living in the brothels for months at a time, she quickly developed a relationship with many of the kids who, often terrorized and abused, were drawn to the rare human companionship she offered. Since the children were fascinated by her camera, Zana thought it would be great to see the world through their eyes. It was at that moment that she had the idea of teaching photography to the children of prostitutes. She produced a film based on her work that became a crusade to keep these children of prostitutes, pictured here, out of a life of prostitution. Her film won the Oscar for Best Documentary in 2006. Learn more about her organization, Kids with Cameras, at www.kids-with-cameras.org.

In India, many slaves are used to make bricks. Young children who have no family are often sucked into slavery, such as these children. One of the most common uses for slaves in the world is to make chocolate; very little chocolate is produced without slave labor.

Source: © Valli/Summers/Corbis Sygma.

The Fair Trade Certified symbol signifies that products such as coffee, tea, and chocolate (made from cacao) meet sustainable development goals, help support family farmers at fair prices, and are not produced by slave labor. Much of the work on cacao plantations is done by child slaves smuggled from poor countries.

problem in many parts of the world, requires poor young children to do heavy labor for long hours in agriculture, brick-making, match-making, and carpet factories, earning little but helping families pay debts. Many argue that this is slavery, although others say it is necessary for the families' survival. The children dare not complain, for the sanctions may involve severe injury or death (Bobin 1995). Much of the chocolate and coffee bought (unless they are Fair Trade Certified products) also supports slavery; chocolate, especially, is grown and harvested at slave camps where young boys are given a choice between unpaid hard labor (with beatings for any disobedience) and death by starvation or shooting (Bales 2000, 2004).

Debt bondage is another form of modern-day slavery. Extremely poor families—often people with differences in appearance or culture than those with power—work in exchange for housing and meager food; they often find themselves in severe debt that passes from generation to generation or that is incurred when farmers face drought, need cash to keep their families from starving, and borrow money. The only collateral they have on the loan is themselves, put up for bondage until they can pay off the loan. No one but the wealthy landowner keeps accounting records, which results in there being no accountability; therefore, the poor families may find themselves enslaved. The lack of credit available to marginal people contributes to fraud and its consequence: slavery. Because those in slavery have little voice and no rights, the world community hears little about this tragedy (Bales 2004). A recent successful international movement in impoverished areas provides small loans—micro credit—mostly to women, to help them start small businesses and move out of desperate poverty and slavery.

In the slavery of the nineteenth century, slaves were expensive and there was at least some economic incentive to care about their health and survival. In the new slavery, humans are cheap and replaceable; there is little concern about working them to death, especially if they are located in remote cacao (used to make chocolate) or coffee plantations (Bales 2000). By current dollars, a slave in the southern United States would have cost as much as $40,000, but contemporary slaves can be procured from poor countries for as little as $90 (Bales 2004). Employers can legally exploit and abuse them with long hours and without legal interference because the slaves owe money.

What all of these human bondage situations have in common is that poor minority groups are victimized. Because many slaves are members of ethnic, racial, religious, tribal, gender, age, caste, or other minority groups and have obvious physical or cultural distinctions from the people who exploit them, they are at a distinct disadvantage in the stratification system. Although all humans have the same basic characteristics, few people have a choice about being born into a minority group, and it is difficult to change that minority status because of visible barriers—physical appearance, names, dress, language, or other distinguishing characteristics. Historical conditions and conflicts rooted in religious, social, political, and historical events set the stage for dominant or minority status, and people are socialized into their dominant or subservient group.

Minority or dominant group status affects most aspects of people's experiences in the social world. These include the family's status in the community, socialization experience, where one can live, opportunities for success and achievement in education and occupation, the religious group to which one belongs, and the health care one receives. In fact, it is impossible to separate minority status from one's position in the stratification system (Aguirre and Turner 2004; Farley 2005; Rothenberg 2004).

In this chapter, we explore race and ethnic group membership that leads to differential placement in stratification systems. The next chapter considers ascribed status based on gender. The topics in this chapter and the next continue the discussion of stratification: who is singled out for differential treatment, why they are singled out, results for both the individuals and the society, and some actions or policies that deal with differential treatment.

THINKING SOCIOLOGICALLY

AIDS is a major problem in South Africa, especially for poor populations. What role might the new puppet character, Kami, who has HIV on the South African version of *Sesame Street*, play in children's attitudes toward the disease?

WHAT CHARACTERIZES RACE AND ETHNIC GROUPS?

Migration, war and conquest, trade, and intermarriage have left virtually every geographical area of the world populated by groups of people with varying ethnicities. In this section, we consider characteristics that set groups apart, especially groups that fall at the lower end of the stratification system.

Minority Groups

Several factors characterize **minority groups** and their relations with dominant groups in society (Dworkin and Dworkin 1999):

1. Minority groups are distinguishable from dominant groups due to factors that make them different from the group that holds power.

2. Minority groups are excluded or denied full participation in economic, political, educational, religious, health, and recreational institutions of society.

3. Minority groups are defined and valued usually less favorably by the dominant group based on their characteristics as minority group members.

4. Minority groups are stereotyped, ridiculed, condemned, or otherwise defamed, allowing dominant group members to justify and not feel guilty about unequal and poor treatment based on political or religious ideologies and ethnocentric beliefs.

5. Minority groups develop collective identities among members to insulate themselves from the unaccepting world; this in turn perpetuates their group identity by creating ethnic or racial enclaves, intra-group marriages, and segregated group institutions such as churches.

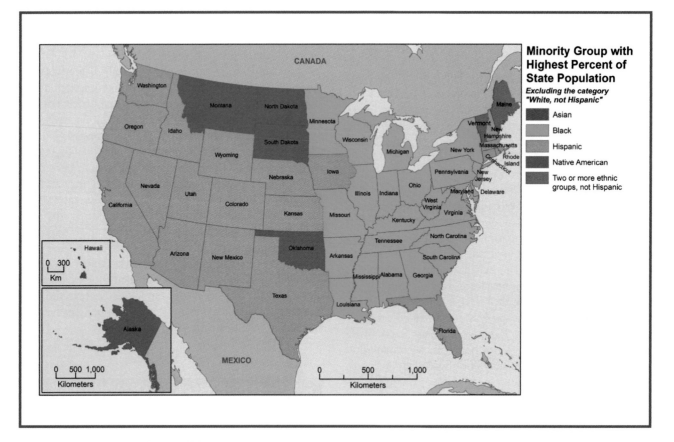

MAP 8.1   Minority prevalence, 2000.

Source: U.S. Census Bureau, Census 2000 Redistricting Data (PL 94-171) Summary File. Cartography: Population Division, U.S. Census Bureau. American FactFinder at factfinder.census.gov provides census data and mapping tools. Map by Anna Versluis.

Native Americans often are stereotyped and treated with disrespect. Not all "Indians" wore these elaborate war bonnets. Indeed, these were characteristic of only about a dozen tribes (all in the American plains) out of more than 500 distinctive native peoples in North America. Each feather in a war bonnet was earned through an act of incredible bravery, and it is a sacrilege to wear a bonnet unless one has earned each feather. This is why Native Americans from the plains find the wearing of these bonnets for sporting events to be such a profound insult. Yet they have too little power to demand respect for their cultures and their sacred traditions.

Source: © Peter Turnley/Corbis.

THINKING SOCIOLOGICALLY

Where do you and your family fall in the dominant-minority stratification system in your community? What minority group characteristics listed above helped you determine this?

Because minority status is determined by history and ideology, the minority group could be the dominant group in a different time or society. Throughout England's history, wars and assassinations changed the ruling group from Catholic to Protestant and back several times. In Iraq, Shiite Muslims are dominant in numbers and now also in power but were a minority under Saddam Hussein's Sunni rule.

Dominant groups are not always a numerical majority. In the case of South Africa, advanced European weapons placed the native Bantu population under the rule of a small percentage of white British and Dutch descendants in what became a complex system of planned discrimination called Apartheid.

The Concept of Race

Racial minority is one of the two types of minority groups most common in the social world. A **race** is a group within the human species that is identified by a society as presumably having certain biologically inherited physical characteristics. However, in practice, it is impossible to accurately identify racial types. Most attempts at racial classifications have been based on combinations of appearance, such as skin color and shade, stature, facial features, hair color and texture, head form, nose shape, eye color and shape, height, and blood or gene type. Our discussion of race focuses on three issues: (1) origins of the concept of race, (2) the social construction of race, and (3) the significance of race versus class.

Origins of the Concept of Race

In the eighteenth and nineteenth centuries, scientists attempted to divide humans into four major groupings—Mongoloid, Caucasoid, Negroid, and Australoid—and then divided them into more than thirty racial subcategories. In reality, few individuals fit clearly into any of these types. The next Sociology in Your Social World provides insight into the origins of racial categories that have had a major impact on history and form the basis for many conflicts today.

From the earliest origins in Africa, humans slowly spread around the globe. Map 8.2 shows the likely human migration patterns. Physical adaptations of isolated groups to their environments originally resulted in some differences in physical appearance—skin color, stature, hair type—but mixing of peoples over the centuries has left few if any isolated "pure" races, only gradations as one moves around the world. Thus, the way societies choose to define race has come about largely through what is culturally convenient for the dominant group.

In the 1970s, the United Nations, concerned about racial conflicts and discrimination, issued a "Statement on Race" prepared by a group of eminent scientists from around the world. This and similar statements by scientific groups point out the harmful effects of racist arguments, doctrines, and policies. The conclusion of their document upheld that (1) all people are born free and equal both in dignity and in rights, (2) racism stultifies personal development, (3) conflicts (based on race) cost nations money and resources, and (4) racism foments international conflict. Racist doctrines lack any scientific basis as all people belong to the same species and have descended from the same origin. In summary, problems arising from race relations are social, not biological, in origin; differential treatments of groups based on "race" falsely claim a scientific basis for classifying humans. One anthropologist sums it up: "Human populations . . . are all mongrels" (Wheeler 1995). So what is the problem?

Sociology in Your Social World

Historical Attempts to Define Race

T hroughout history, political and religious leaders, philosophers, and even scientists have struggled with the meaning and significance of race. The first systematic classification of all living phenomena was published in 1735 by Carl von Linne (Linnaeus). His hierarchy of species was actually quite complex, including monkeys, elephants, and angels! His work was based on the study of fossil remains of various species, implying evolution of the species over time. Then in 1758, he published *Systema Naturae*, in which he suggested four human types: Americanus (Native Americans), Asiaticus, Africanus, and Europeanus (Cashmore and Troyna 1990); other scientists proposed other divisions. Johann Blumenbach was the first to use the word *race* in his 1775 classification system: Caucasian, Mongolian, Ethiopian, American, and Malay.

By the nineteenth century, race began to take on a biological meaning and to signify inherent physical qualities in humans (Goldberg 1990). From there, it was a short step to theorizing about inherent inequalities between races. For instance, Joseph Arthur, known as Count de Gobineau (1816–1882), questioned why once great societies had declined and fallen. He argued that each race has specific characteristics, and he attributed the demise of societies to the inequality of races. His book published in 1865 earned him the title "father of modern racism."

A major event in theories of race was the publication of Charles Darwin's *The Origin of Species* (originally published in 1858). Among his many ideas was that human races *might* represent stages or branches of a tree of evolution (Darwin 1858/1909). This idea implied that those groups of humans who were biologically best suited to the environment would survive. He argued that "natural selection," or "survival of the fittest," was true of all races in the human species, not of individuals within a species. However, from Darwin's ideas emerged the concepts of *survival of the fittest* and *ever-improving races*.

These two late-nineteenth-century concepts were taken out of context and became the foundation for a number of theories of superior races. For instance, in 1899, the Brit-turned-German Houston Stewart Chamberlain published an aristocratic, anti-Semitic work in which he argued that northern and western European populations, Teutonic in particular, were superior. He argued for racial purity, a theme the Nazis of the 1930s and 1940s adopted. Gustaf Kossina introduced the idea of "Volk" in his writings, claiming a commonality of traits among Germans that, he felt, qualified the German people to become the "ruling elite" (Cashmore and Troyna 1990).

Mein Kampf (1939) was Adolf Hitler's contribution to the concept of a superior race. In it, he conceptualized two races, the Aryans and Others. He focused attention on several groups, in particular the Jews. German economic and social problems were blamed on the Jews. What followed in the name of German purity was the extermination of millions of Jews, Poles, Catholics, Gypsies, homosexuals, and other groups and individuals who were deemed "less human" or who opposed the Nazis. The extent to which Hitler succeeded exemplifies what can happen when one group needs to feel superior to others, blames other groups for its shortcomings, and has the power to act against those minorities. More recent attempts to classify groups have been based not on external characteristics but on blood or gene type, even though blood types or genome usually do not correlate with other traits.

As applied to mammals, the term *race* has biological significance only when it refers to closely inbred groups in which all family lines are alike—as in pure breeds of domesticated animals. These conditions are never realized in humans and are impossible in large populations of any species (Witzig 1996). Many groups have been mislabeled "races" when differences are actually cultural. Jews, Poles, Irish, and Italians have all erroneously been called "races." In short, when it comes to humans, scientists do not agree about how many races there are in the biological sense of that word or whether race is a biological reality at all.

Source: www.aaanet.org/press/an/cfp_race05.htm (retrieved July 5, 2006).

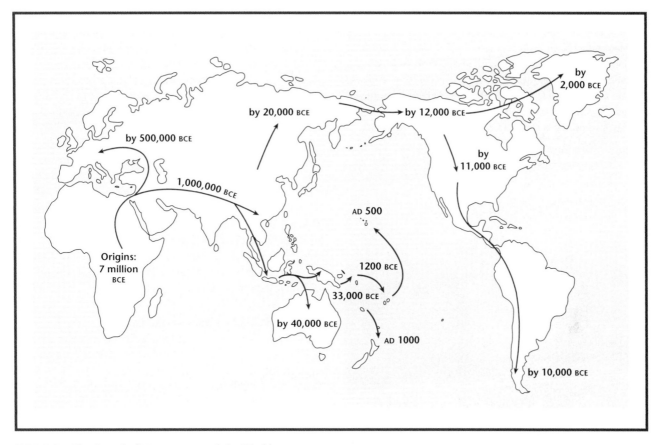

MAP 8.2 The Spread of Humans around the World

Source: Diamond (1999:37).

Social Construction of Race:
Symbolic Interaction Analysis

Why are sociologists concerned about a concept that has little scientific accuracy and is ill defined? The answer is its social significance. The social reality is that people are defined or define themselves as belonging to a group based in part on physical appearance. As individuals try to make meaning of the social world, they may learn from others that some traits—eye or nose shape, hair texture, or skin color—are distinguishing traits that make people different. Jean Piaget, famous cognitive psychologist, described the human tendency to classify objects as one of our most basic cognitive tools (Piaget and Inhelder 1955/1999); this inclination has often been linked to classifying "racial" groups. Motives for classifying individuals into racial groups have ranged from the scientific study of humans to the desire to subjugate and exploit minority groups. Once in place, racial categories provide individuals with an identity based on ancestry—"*my* kind of people have these traits."

Symbolic interaction theory contends that if people believe something is real, it may be real in its consequences. It does not matter whether scientists say that attempts to classify people into races are inaccurate and that the word is biologically meaningless; people on the streets of your hometown think *they* know what the word *race* means. Moreover,

people do look different as we traverse the globe. That people *think* there are differences has consequences. As a social concept, race has not only referred to physical features and inherited genes but has carried over to presumed psychological and moral characteristics, thus justifying discriminatory treatment. The following examples illustrate the complex problems in trying to classify people into "races."

With the enactment of Apartheid Laws in 1948, the white government in South Africa institutionalized differential laws based on their definitions of racial groups and specified the privileges and restrictions allotted to each group (Stanford University Webpage 2006). Bantu populations—the native Africans—lived in restricted areas; Coloreds—those of mixed blood—were restricted to other living areas and types of work; Asians—descendants of immigrants from India and other Asian countries—received higher salaries than the Bantu groups but less than whites; and whites of European descent, primarily Dutch and English, had the highest living standard and best residential locations. Under the Apartheid system, race was determined by tracing ancestry back for fourteen generations; a single ancestor who was not Dutch or English caused an individual to be considered "colored" rather than white. Physical features mattered little; individuals carried a card indicating their race based on genealogy. Although this

South African Riots: Blacks charge toward the photographer during a riot in which police opened fire to disperse 10,000 demonstrating black students in Soweto township, 15 miles south of Johannesburg, after tear gas failed to curb them. At least six persons, including four whites, were killed and at least 40 injured in the day-long rioting. The students were continuing a two-week protest against the compulsory teaching of Dutch-based Afrikaans in black schools. (Johannesburg, South Africa; June 16, 1976)

Source: © Bettmann/Corbis.

system began to break down in the 1990s due to international pressure and under the leadership of the first black president (Nelson Mandela, elected in 1994), vestiges of these notions of "reality" will take generations to change.

By contrast, in Brazil, an individual's race is based on physical features—skin tone, hair texture, facial features, eye color, and so forth—rather than on the "one drop of blood" rule in South Africa. Brothers and sisters who have the same parents and ancestors may be classified as belonging to different races. The idea of what determines one's race is based on nearly opposite criteria in Brazil and South Africa, illustrating the arbitrary nature of racial classification attempts. That lighter skinned blacks often have higher education, occupational standing, and income than their darker fellow citizens illustrates this fact (Keith and Herring 1991; Walker and Karas 1993).

Before civil rights laws were passed in the United States in the 1960s, there were a number of states with laws that spelled out differential treatment for racial groups. These were commonly referred to as Jim Crow laws. States in the South passed laws defining who was African American or Native American. In many cases, it was difficult to determine in what category to place an individual. For instance, African Americans in Georgia were defined as people with any ascertainable trace of "Negro" blood in their veins; in Missouri, one-eighth or more Negro blood was sufficient; whereas, in Louisiana, one-thirty-second Negro blood defined one as black. Differential treatment was spelled out in other states as well. In Texas, for example, the father's race determined the race of the child. In Vermont,

newborn babies of racially mixed parentage were listed as "mixed" on the birth certificate. In West Virginia, a newborn was classified as "black" if either parent was considered black. Until recently, several U.S. states still attempted to classify the race of newborns by the percentage of black blood or parentage (Lopez 1996). Federal law now prohibits discrimination on the basis of "racial" classifications, and most of these state laws have been challenged and dropped.

Arbitrary classifications such as those in the examples above are frequently used as justification for treating individuals differently despite the lack of scientific basis for such distinctions (Williams 1996). The legacy of "race" remains even in countries where discrimination based on race is illegal. Poverty and discrimination justify and reinforce differential treatment in poor schools, employment, and other areas of life, thus resulting in a vicious cycle of more poverty and discrimination. The question remains: why is a baby with any African or Native American heritage classified by minority status?

The Significance of Race versus Class

From the time of slavery until the late twentieth century, race has been the determining factor in social stratification and opportunity for people of African descent in the United States, the Caribbean, and Brazil. Whether this is changing in the twenty-first century is a question that has occupied sociologists, politicians, educators, and other scientists in recent years. Some scholars argue that race is a primary cause of different placement in the stratification system; others insist that race and social class are both at work, with socioeconomic factors (social class) more important than race.

An influential participant in the debate, sociologist William Julius Wilson, states that the racial oppression that characterized the African American experience throughout the nineteenth century was caused first by slavery and then by a lingering caste structure that severely restricted upward mobility for African Americans. However, the breakdown of the plantation economy and the rise of industrialism created more opportunities for African Americans to participate in the economy (Wilson 1978, 1993a, 1993b).

Wilson (1978) argues that after World War II, an African American class structure developed with characteristics similar to those of the white class structure. Occupation and income took on ever greater significance in social position, especially for the African American middle class. However, as black middle-class professionals moved up in the stratification structure, lower-class African American ghetto residents became more isolated and less mobile. Limited unskilled job opportunities for the lower class have resulted in poverty and stagnation so severe that some families are almost outside of the functioning economic system. Wilson (1978, 1984, 1993a) calls this group the *underclass*.

The United States cannot escape poverty because well-paid, unskilled jobs are disappearing from the economy and because the poor are concentrated in segregated urban areas (Massey, Gross, and Shibuya 1994). Poorly educated African American teenagers and young adults from the inner-city see their job prospects limited to the low-wage sector (e.g., fast food work), and they experience record levels of unemployment (Wilson 1987). Movement out of poverty becomes almost impossible.

Wilson's point is illustrated by the following: more than two in five African Americans are now middle-class, compared to one in twenty in 1940. Thus, there is an ever-widening gap between poor African Americans and their middle-class counterparts. On the other hand, most adults in many inner-city ghetto neighborhoods are not employed in a typical week. Thus, children in these neighborhoods may grow up without ever seeing someone go to work (Wilson 1996). The new global economic system is a contributing factor as unskilled jobs go abroad to cheaper labor (Massey and Denton 1993; McFate, Lawson, and Wilson 1995; Smith and Feagin 1995). Without addressing these structural causes of poverty, we cannot expect to reduce the number of people in the underclass—whether they are white or black (Massey 1990).

Has race declined in significance and class become more important in determining placement in the stratification system? Tests of Wilson's thesis present us with mixed results (Jencks 1992). For instance, African Americans' average educational levels (12.4 years in school) are almost the same as whites' (12.7 years), showing comparable qualifications for employment. However this equity stops at the high school level; 27.6 percent of whites are college graduates compared to 17.3 percent of blacks (U.S. Census Bureau 2005i, Table 212). More important, African Americans earn less than whites in the same occupational categories. As Table 8.1 makes clear, income levels for African Americans and whites are not even close to being equal. Unemployment and poverty affect a higher percentage of black families than white ones, so economics alone does not seem a complete answer to what people are in the underclass.

Although racial bias has decreased at the micro (interpersonal) level, it is still a significant determinant in the lives of African Americans, especially those in the lower class. The data are complex, but we can conclude that for upwardly mobile African Americans, class may be more important than race. Still, physical traits such as skin color cannot be dismissed; they can be crippling for the underclass.

THINKING SOCIOLOGICALLY

Look around you. On what basis do you classify people into social groups? Do you use "racial" criteria? What other distinctions do you use, and why?

Ethnic Groups

The second major type of minority group—the **ethnic group**—is based on cultural factors: language, religion, dress, foods, customs, beliefs, values, norms, a shared group identity or feeling, and sometimes loyalty to a homeland, monarch, or religious leader. Members are grouped together because they share a common cultural heritage, often connected with a national or geographical identity. Some social scientists prefer to call racial groups ethnic groups because the term *ethnic* encompasses most minorities and avoids problems with the term *race* (Aguirre and Turner 2004).

Visits to ethnic enclaves in large cities around the world give a picture of ethnicity. A Little Italy, Chinatown, Greek Town, and Polish neighborhood may have non-English street signs and newspapers, ethnic restaurants, culture-specific houses of worship, and clothing styles that reflect the ethnic subculture. Occasionally, an ethnic group shares power in the pluralistic societies, but most often they hold a minority status with little power.

TABLE 8.1 **Race and Family Income**

Median Family Annual Income*		
	White	$55,768
	Black	$34,369 (62% of white-family income)
	Hispanic	$34,272 (61% of white-family income)

Source: U.S. Census Bureau (2006e, Table 679).

Income (in dollars) by Educational Level and Race/Ethnicity*

Education	White	Black	Hispanic
Not a High School Graduate	19,110	16,201	18,349
High School Graduate	28,708	23,777	23,472
Some College, No Degree	30,316	25,616	27,586
College Graduate	52,259	42,968	43,676
Master's Degree	62,981	57,449	56,486
Professional Degree	119,712	87,713	78,190

Source: U.S. Census Bureau (2006e, Table 217).
* 2003 figures.

Ethnic enclaves have a strong sense of local community and often hold festivals such as this Italian American celebration of Saint Joseph, held in Little Italy in the North End of Boston. In many nations, it is a day of sharing with the poor and needy. In many Italian villages, people of any means contribute to a table spread in the public square as an offering for favors received from prayers to this kindly saint. This statue replaces the table found in public squares but fulfills the same goal.

Source: © Todd Gipskin/Corbis.

How is ethnicity constructed or defined? Many very different ethnic groups have been combined in government categories, such as the census, yet they speak different languages and often have very different religions. For example, in North America, group members did not view themselves as "Indian" or "Native American." Instead, they used 600 independent tribal nation names to define themselves, including the Ojibwa (Chippewa), Dine (whom we call the Navajo), Lakota (whom we tend to call the Sioux), and many others (see Map 8.3). Likewise, Koreans, Filipinos, Chinese, Japanese, and Malaysians come from very different cultures but were identified as "Asian Americans" in the census. People from Brazil, Mexico, and Cuba were grouped together in a category called "Hispanics" or "Latinos."

When federal funds for social services were made available to "Asian Americans" or "American Indians," these diverse people began to think of themselves as part of a larger grouping for political purposes (Esperitu 1992). The federal government essentially created an ethnic group by naming and providing funding to that group. If people wanted services (health care, legal rights, and so forth), they had to become a part of a particular group. This process of merging many ethnic groups into one broader group further emphasizes that ethnic identity is itself socially shaped and created.

THINKING SOCIOLOGICALLY

Identify one dominant and one minority group in your community or on campus. Where do they fall in the stratification system? Does this placement reflect a similar racial, ethnic, or other minority group status in the nation as a whole? How are the life chances of individuals in these groups influenced by factors beyond their control?

● PREJUDICE AND RACISM: MICRO-LEVEL ANALYSIS

Have you ever found yourself in a situation in which you were viewed as different, strange, undesirable, or "less than human"? Perhaps you have felt the sting of rejection, based not on judgment of you as a person but solely because of the ethnic group into which you were born. Then again, you may have been insulated from this type of rejection if you grew up in a homogeneous community or in a privileged group; you may have even learned some negative attitudes about those different from yourself. It is sobering to think that where and when in history you were born determine how you are treated, your life chances, and many of your experiences.

Racial and ethnic minorities experience disproportionate prejudice and racism. Several processes act to keep minority groups among the have-nots of society. Consider the following factors:

Process	Result
Stratification	Minority status
Prejudice	Poor self-concept, negative relations with others
Racism	Negative attitudes, stereotypes, self-fulfilling prophecy
Discrimination	Poor jobs, income, education, housing
Negative contact	Hostilities, war, conflict between groups

Prejudice

When minority groups are present within a society, prejudice influences dominant-minority group relations. **Prejudice** refers to attitudes that prejudge a group, usually negatively and not based on facts. Prejudiced individuals lump together people with certain characteristics as an undifferentiated group without considering individual differences. Although prejudice can refer to positive attitudes and exaggerations (as when a mother is prejudiced in thinking her own child is gifted), in this chapter we refer to the negative aspects of prejudice; we also focus on the adverse effects brought on minority group members by prejudice. While prejudice can be stimulated by events such as conflicts at the institutional level and war at the societal level, attitudes are held

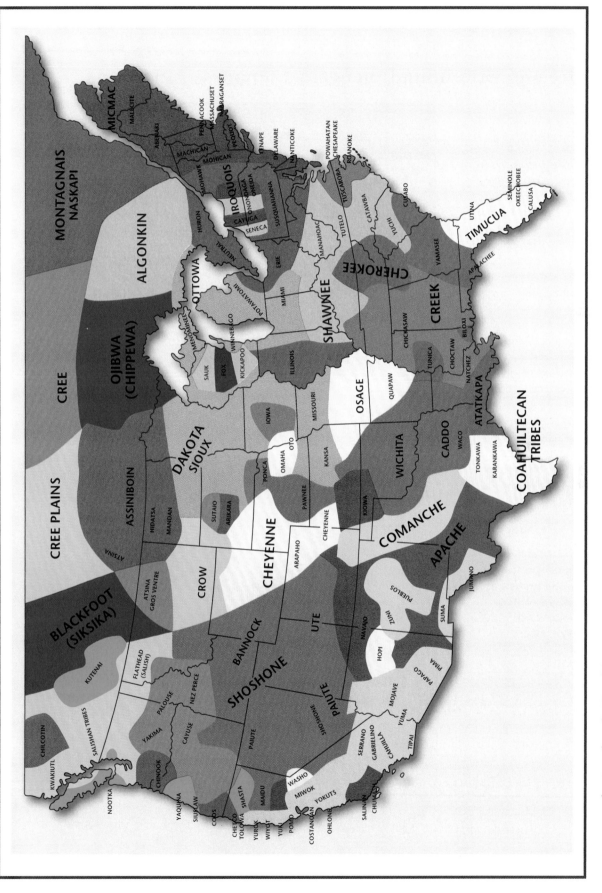

MAP 8.3 "Indian" Lands in the United States.

Source: Adapted from Smith (1989). Courtesy of Cherokee Publications, Cherokee, NC.

Note: Long before "white people" set foot in the Americas, many thriving societies of Native Americans lived in groups on the North and South American continents. Each group developed a lifestyle compatible with the geographical area and material goods available to it. Many different cultures, languages, religions, value systems, economies, and political systems emerged. Thus the term Native American refers to many different societies, each with its own identity.

PHOTO ESSAY

Prejudice and Discrimination against Japanese Americans

On December 7, 1941, Japan bombed Pearl Harbor. Fear of a Japanese invasion and of subversive acts by Japanese Americans prompted President Franklin D. Roosevelt to sign Executive Order 9066 on February 19, 1942. The order designated the West Coast as a military zone from which "any or all persons may be excluded." Although not specified in the order, Japanese Americans were singled out for evacuation. More than 110,000 people of Japanese ancestry were removed from California, southern Arizona, and western Washington and Oregon and sent to ten relocation camps. Those forcibly removed from their homes, businesses, and possessions included Japanese immigrants who were legally forbidden to become U.S. citizens (Issei), the American born (Nisei), and children of the American born (Sansei).

▲ After the internment of Japanese Americans from the Seattle region, barber G. S. Hante points proudly to his bigoted sign that reads, *We Don't Want Any Japs Back Here . . . EVER!*

Source: © Bettmann/Corbis.

▼ Persons of Japanese ancestry arrive at the Santa Anita Assembly Center from San Pedro. Evacuees lived at this center at the former Santa Anita race track before being moved inland to relocation centers. (Arcadia, CA; April 5, 1942)

Source: © Corbis/Clem Albers.

▼ Dust storm blows at this War Relocation Authority center (Manzanar) where evacuees of Japanese ancestry spent the duration of World War II. (California; July 3, 1942)

Source: © Corbis/Dorothea Lange.

by individuals and can be best understood as a micro-level phenomenon.

When prejudiced attitudes are manifested in actions, they are referred to as **discrimination**, differential treatment and harmful actions against minorities. These actions at the micro level might include refusal to sell someone a house because of the religion, race, or ethnicity of the buyer, or employment practices that treat groups differently based on minority status (Feagin and Feagin 2003). Both prejudice and discrimination affect the lives of both discriminators and those discriminated against. Discrimination, such as laws that deny opportunities or resources to members of a particular group, operates largely at the meso or macro level, discussed later in the chapter.

The Nature of Prejudice

Prejudice is an understandable response of humans to their social environment. To survive, every social group or unit—a sorority, a sports team, a civic club, or a nation—needs to mobilize the loyalty of its members. Each organization needs to convince people to voluntarily commit energy, skills, time, and resources so the organization can meet its needs. Furthermore, as persons commit themselves to a group, they invest a portion of themselves and feel loyalty to the group.

Individual commitment to a group influences one's perception and loyalties, creating preference or even bias for the group; this commitment is often based on stressing distinctions from other groups and deep preference for one's own group. However, these loyalties may be dysfunctional for out-group members and the victims of prejudice.

One reason people hold prejudices is that it is easier to pigeonhole the vast amount of information and stimuli coming at us in today's complex societies, and to sort information into neat unquestioned categories, than to evaluate each piece of information separately for its accuracy. Prejudiced individuals often categorize large numbers of people and attribute to them personal qualities based on their dress, language, skin color, or other identifying racial or ethnic features. This process is called **stereotyping**.

Stereotypes, or the pictures in our heads, are often distorted, oversimplified, or exaggerated ideas passed down over generations through cultures. They are applied to all members of a group, regardless of individual differences, and used to justify prejudice, discrimination, and unequal distribution of power, wealth, and opportunities. Often, the result is unfair and inaccurate judgments about individuals who are members of the stereotyped groups.

Prejudice is difficult to change because it is rooted in traditions and cultural beliefs and is based on culturally imbedded stereotypes of groups. Individuals grow up learning these ingrained beliefs that often go unchallenged. Yet when studied scientifically, stereotypes seldom correspond to facts.

Social scientists know, for instance, that prejudice is related to the history and to the political and economic climate in a region or country, part of the macro-level cultural and social environment. For instance, in some southern U.S. states where African Americans constitute a majority of the population, there is evidence that white racial attitudes are more antagonistic due to perceived or real economic and political competition for jobs and power (Farley 2005; Glaser 1994).

In wartime, the adversary may be the victim of racial slurs or be depicted in films or other media as villains. During World War II, American films often showed negative stereotypes of Japanese and German people, stereotypes that likely reinforced the decision to intern more than 110,000 Japanese Americans, the majority of whom were U.S. citizens, in detention camps following the bombing of Pearl Harbor. Similar issues and stereotypes have arisen for American citizens with Middle Eastern ancestry since the attacks on the New York World Trade Center on September 11, 2001.

Sometimes, minority group members incorporate prejudiced views about themselves into their behavior. This process, an example of a *self-fulfilling prophesy*, involves the adoption of stereotypical behaviors. (See Chapter 4.) No group is born dumb, lazy, dirty, or money hungry, but they can be conditioned to believe such depictions of themselves or be forced into acting out certain behaviors based on expectations of the dominant group.

Source: www.politicalcartoons.com, No. 257. Courtesy of Brian Farrington.

 THINKING SOCIOLOGICALLY

Watch the Oscar-winning movie *Crash*. In what ways does this video raise issues of majority-minority stereotypes? How does it highlight labeling done by each group?

Explanations of Prejudice

We have all met them, the people who express hostility toward others. They tell jokes about minorities, curse them, and even threaten action against them. Why do these individuals do this? The following theories have attempted to explain the prejudiced individual.

Frustration-Aggression Theory. In Greensboro, North Carolina, in 1978, a group of civil rights activists and African American adults and children listened as a guitarist sang

The Ku Klux Klan march against Martin Luther King Day.
(January 1990)

Source: © Mark Peterson/Corbis.

freedom songs. A nine car cavalcade of white Ku Klux Klan (KKK) and American Nazi Party members arrived. The intruders unloaded weapons from the back of their cars, approached the rally, and opened fire for 88 seconds; they left as calmly as they arrived. Four white men and a black woman were dead (Cashmore and Troyna 1990). According to frustration-aggression theory, many of the perpetrators of this and other heinous acts feel angry and frustrated because they cannot achieve their work or other goals. They blame any vulnerable minority group—religious, ethnic, sexual orientation—and members of that group become targets of their anger. Frustration-aggression theory focuses largely on poorly adjusted people who displace their frustration with aggressive attacks on others.

Scapegoating. When it is impossible to vent frustration toward the real target—one's boss, teachers, the economic system—frustration can take the form of aggressive action against minority group members who are vulnerable because of their low status. They become the scapegoats. The word *scapegoat* comes from the Bible, Leviticus 16:5–22. Once a year, a goat (which was obviously innocent) was laden with parchments that people had used to write their sins on. The goat was then sent out to the desert to die. This was part of a ritual of purification, and the creature took the blame for others.

Scapegoating occurs when a minority group is blamed for others' failures or shortcomings. It is difficult to look at oneself to seek reasons for failure but easy to transfer the cause for one's failure to others. Individuals who feel they are failures in their jobs or other aspects of their lives may blame minority groups. From within such a prejudiced mindset, even violence toward the out-group becomes acceptable. One example is the hostility represented in a notice distributed to a college campus's mailboxes: "Earth's Most Endangered Species: The White Male. Help Preserve It." The notice expressed frustration with the "plight" of white males and blamed policies favoring minorities for their perceived problems.

Today, jobs and promotions are harder for young adults to obtain than they were for the baby boom generation, but the reason is mostly demographic. The baby boom of the 1940s and 1950s resulted in a bulge in the population; there are so many people in the workforce at each successive step on the ladder that it will be another few years before those baby boomers start retiring in large numbers. Until that happens, there will be a good deal of frustration about apparent occupational stagnation. It is easier—and safer—to blame minorities or affirmative action programs than to vent frustration at the next oldest segment of the population or at one's grandparents for having a large family. Blacks, Hispanics, other minorities, and affirmative action policies become easy scapegoats.

Although this theory helps explain some situations, it does not predict when frustration will lead to aggression, why only some people who experience frustration vent their feelings on the vulnerable, and why some groups become targets (Marger 2006).

Racism

Racism is any attitude, belief, or institutional arrangement that favors one racial group over another, and this favoritism may result in intentional or unintentional consequences for minority groups (Farley 2005). Racism is often embedded in institutions of society and supported by people who are not aware of the social consequence of their actions. Many people without social science training see racism as a micro-level issue—one involving individual initiative and individual bigotry—while most social scientists see the problem as at the meso and macro levels. Still, issues at the micro level continue to be real.

Ideological racism involves the belief that humans are divided into innately different groups, some of which are biologically inferior. Those who hold these views see biological differences as the cause of most cultural and social differences (Marger 2006), as Hitler's actions against the Jews and other groups illustrate. (Discussed in Sociology in Your Social World, p. 226)

Symbolic racism is the insistence that one is not prejudiced or racist, that one is color-blind and committed to equality; however, this insistence is often accompanied by opposition to any social policies that would eliminate racism and make true equality of opportunity possible.

Institutional racism involves discrimination that is hidden within the system, and symbolic racism allows it to remain in place. Symbolic racists reject ideological racism as blatant, crude, and ignorant but fail to recognize that their actions may perpetuate institutional inequalities.

Racism has psychological and social costs both to those on the receiving end and to the perpetrators. There is a waste of talent and energy of both minorities and of those who justify and carry out discriminatory actions. In the 1990s, individual membership in white supremacy groups in Europe and North America grew, as did attacks on blacks, Jews, immigrants, and those whose religious and cultural practices were different from the majority. For instance, in 1996 in the United States, racism resulted in a rash of African American church

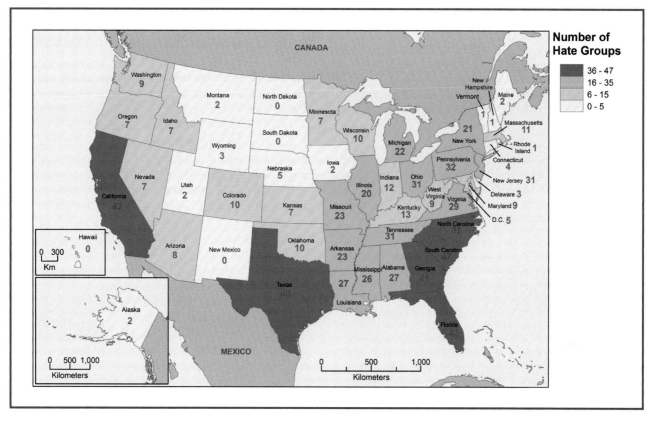

MAP 8.4   Number of Active U.S. Hate Groups in 2004

Source: Map courtesy of The Southern Poverty Law Center.

Note: Please visit www.pineforge.com/ballantinestudy and choose "Chapter 8: Race and Ethnic Group Stratification" to access this map interactively.

bombings (Feagin, Vera, and Batur 2001; Sack 1996), and in 2005 alone, there were 1,757 anti-Semitic incidents involving vandalism, assaults, or threats directed at Jewish citizens or Jewish establishments (Anti-Defamation League 2006). Unfortunately, until there are better economic opportunities for more people, individual racism is likely to be one result of economic competition for jobs (Feagin et al. 2001).

Although social-psychological theories shed light on the most extreme cases of individual or small group prejudice and racism, there is much these theories do not explain. They say little about the everyday hostility and reinforcement of prejudice that most of us experience or engage in, and they fail to deal with institutional discrimination.

DISCRIMINATION: MESO-LEVEL ANALYSIS

Dear Teacher,

I would like to introduce you to my son, Wind-Wolf. He is probably what you would consider a typical Indian kid. He was born and raised on the reservation. He has black hair, dark brown eyes, and an olive complexion. And, like so many Indian children his age, he is shy and quiet in the classroom. He is 5 years old, in kindergarten,

In 1966, the Rough Rock Demonstration school was begun on the Navajo Reservation. It became the model for many other tribally run schools. It taught reverence for Navajo ways, along with a typical grade school curriculum of English and mathematics skills.

Source: © Monty Roessel.

and I can't understand why you have already labeled him a "slow learner."

He has already been through quite an education compared with his peers in Western society. He was bonded to his mother and to the Mother Earth in a traditional native childbirth ceremony. And he has been continuously cared for by his mother, father, sisters, cousins, aunts, uncles, grandparents, and extended tribal family since this ceremony. . . .

Wind-Wolf was strapped (in his baby basket like a turtle shell) snugly with a deliberate restriction on his arms and legs. Although Western society may argue this hinders motor-skill development and abstract reasoning, we believe it forces the child to first develop his intuitive faculties, rational intellect, symbolic thinking, and five senses. Wind-Wolf was with his mother constantly, closely bonded physically, as she carried him on her back or held him while breast-feeding. She carried him everywhere she went, and every night he slept with both parents. Because of this, Wind-Wolf's educational setting was not only a "secure" environment, but it was also very colorful, complicated, sensitive, and diverse.

As he grew older, Wind-Wolf began to crawl out of the baby basket, develop his motor skills, and explore the world around him. When frightened or sleepy, he could always return to the basket, as a turtle withdraws into its shell. Such an inward journey allows one to reflect in privacy on what he has learned and to carry the new knowledge deeply into the unconscious and the soul. Shapes, sizes, colors, texture, sound, smell, feeling, taste, and the learning process are therefore functionally integrated—the physical and spiritual, matter and energy, and conscious and unconscious, individual and social.

It takes a long time to absorb and reflect on these kinds of experiences, so maybe that is why you think my Indian child is a slow learner. His aunts and grandmothers taught him to count and to know his numbers while they sorted materials for making abstract designs in native baskets. And he was taught to learn mathematics by counting the sticks we use in our traditional native hand game. So he may be slow in grasping the methods and tools you use in your classroom, ones quite familiar to his white peers, but I hope you will be patient with him. It takes time to adjust to a new cultural system and learn new things. He is not culturally "disadvantaged," but he is culturally different. (Lake 1990:48–53)

This letter expresses the frustration of a father who sees his son being labeled, discriminated against by the school system before even being given a chance. *Discrimination* refers to actions taken against members of a minority group; it can occur at individual and small group levels but is particularly problematic at the organizational and institutional levels, the meso level of analysis.

THINKING SOCIOLOGICALLY

How does the discrimination experienced by the boy described in this letter relate to labeling and the self-fulfilling prophesy?

Discrimination is based on race, ethnicity, age, sex, sexual orientation, nationality, social class, religion, or whatever other category members of a society choose to make significant (Feagin and Feagin 2003; McLemore, Romo, and Baker 2001). **Individual discrimination**, actions taken against minority group members by individuals, can take many forms, from avoiding contact by excluding individuals from one's club, neighborhood, or even country, to physical violence against minorities as seen in hate crime attacks on Asian Americans perceived to be taking jobs from white Americans.

Institutional discrimination, or meso-level discrimination, is often a normal or routine part of the way an organization operates; it includes both intentional actions, such as laws restricting minorities, and unintentional actions, which have consequences that restrict minorities. Institutional discrimination is built into organizations and cultural expectations in the social world. Even nonprejudiced people can participate in institutional racism quite unintentionally. For example, many schools track students into classes based on standardized test results. Yet minority children end up disproportionately in lower tracks for a number of reasons (see Chapter 11). Thus, a

Jim Crow laws playing out in a Florida movie house: This was the rear entrance for African Americans. (Pensacola, FL; 1930s)

Source: © Bettmann/Corbis.

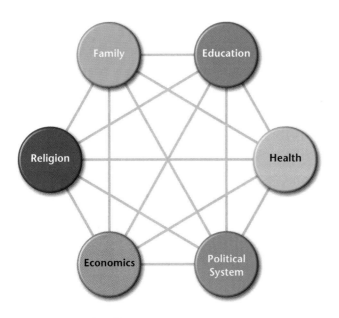

Figure 8.1   Side-Effect Discrimination

Source: Feagin and Feagin (1986).

Notes: Because institutions are interdependent, discrimination in one results in unintentional discrimination in others.

policy that is meant to give all children an equal chance ends up legitimizing the channeling of some minorities into the lower-achieving classroom groupings.

Purposeful discrimination that is built into the law or is part of the explicit policies of an organization is called *de jure discrimination*. Jim Crow laws, passed in the late 1800s in the United States, and laws that forbad Jewish people in Germany from living, working, or investing in certain places are examples. By contrast, *unintentional discrimination* results from broad policies that favor one group and disadvantage another. This is sometimes called *de facto discrimination*, for there is discrimination "in fact" even if not in intent; it can be more damaging than discrimination by individuals because it is often done by people who are not the least bit prejudiced and may not recognize the effects of their actions (Merton 1949a).

Unintentional discrimination usually occurs through one of two processes: side-effect discrimination or past-in-present discrimination (Feagin and Feagin 1986). **Side-effect discrimination** refers to practices in one institutional area that have a negative impact because they are linked to practices in another institutional area. Figure 8.1 illustrates this idea. Each institution uses information from the other institutions to make decisions. Thus, discrimination in the criminal justice system, which has in fact been well documented, may influence decisions in other parts of society.

Consider the following examples of side-effect discrimination in the criminal justice and employment systems and of the Internet and job opportunities. In a 1999 interview conducted by one of your authors, a probation officer in a

moderately sized city in Ohio said that he had never seen an African American in his county get a not-guilty verdict and that he was not sure it was possible. He had known of cases in which minorities had pled guilty to a lesser charge because they did not think they could receive a fair verdict in that city. When the person applies for a job, however, she or he is required to report the conviction on the application form. By using information about one's criminal record, employers who may or may not intend to discriminate end up doing so whether or not the individual was guilty. The side-effect discrimination is unintentional discrimination; the criminal justice system has reached an unjust verdict, and the potential employer is swayed unfairly.

The Internet also plays a role in institutional discrimination and privilege. For example, in Alaska, 15 percent of the population is Native, but Natives hold only 5 percent of state jobs (U.S. Census Bureau 2003a). Consider that the State of Alaska uses the Internet as its primary means of advertising and accepting applications for state jobs (State of Alaska, Workplace Alaska 2006). One-hundred-sixty-four predominantly Native villages in Alaska lack affordable Internet access (Denali Commission 2001). Other options for application include requesting applications by mail, if one knows about the opening; however, this process is limited by the reliability and speed of mail service to remote villages and the often short application periods for state jobs. State officials may not intentionally use the mechanism to prevent Aleuts, Inupiats, Athabaskans, or other Alaska Natives from gaining access to state jobs, but the effect can be institutionalized discrimination. Here, Internet access plays a role in participation of minorities in the social world (Nakamura 2004).

The point is that whites, especially affluent whites, benefit from privileges not available to low-income minorities.

Children play on the porch of their rustic home with no plumbing in the rural Alaska village of Akhiok, among the Aleutian Islands.

Source: © Phil Schermeister/Corbis.

The privileged members may not purposely disadvantage others and may not be prejudiced, but the playing field is not level even though discrimination may be completely unintentional. Peggy McIntosh (2002) identifies several dozen privileges of being white in North America. Put yourself in the position of a person who does not have these privileges:

> I can avoid spending time with people who mistrust people of my color. I can protect my children most of the time from people who might not like them. I can criticize our government and talk about how I fear its policies and behavior without being seen as a cultural "outsider." I can easily buy posters, postcards, picture books, greeting cards, dolls, toys, and children's magazines featuring people of my race. I can arrange my activities so that I will never have to experience feelings of rejection owing to my race. (p. 97–101)

Past-in-present discrimination refers to practices from the past that may no longer be allowed but that continue to affect people today. In Mississippi in 1951–1952, the average state expenditure to educate a white child was $147 per pupil; the average was $34 per black pupil in segregated schools (Luhman and Gilman 1980). Such blatant segregation and inequality in use of tax dollars is no longer legal. This may seem like ancient history, yet some of those African Americans who were in school in the 1950s and 1960s are now in their 50s, trying to support a family and pay for their children's college expenses. To those who received a substandard education and did not have an opportunity for college, it is not ancient history because it affects their opportunities today.

Stanley Lieberson (1980) asked a difficult question: Why do some minority groups do better than others? He used multiple methods of gathering data to test various explanations. His study and conclusion are explained in How Do We Know? on the opposite page. As you read it, think about the special structural circumstances that made things different for African Americans than for many other minority groups. How are side-effect discrimination and past-in-present discrimination at work?

Some countries have attempted to make amends for past institutional discrimination by passing laws that prohibit differential treatment on the basis of race, age, sex, or sexual preference. India has legal protection and education quotas for outcaste members, forbids discrimination on the basis of caste, and encourages the hiring of lower and outcaste members. However, tradition and unintentional discrimination make change a slow process.

Remember that prejudice is an attitude, discrimination an action. If neighbors do not wish to have minority group members move onto their block, that is prejudice. If they try to organize other neighbors against the newcomers or make the situation unpleasant once the minority family has moved in, that is discrimination. If minorities cannot afford to live in the neighborhood because of discrimination in the marketplace, that is institutional discrimination.

Burakumin ("people of the hamlet"), also known by the more negative term Eta (outcastes or "full of filth"), are a minority in the homogeneous country of Japan. They live in approximately 5,000 settlements and comprise 2 percent of the population, between two and three million people. Historically, they did the dirty work: butchers, executioners, leather workers, and "entertainers" or minstrels. Today, although discrimination is outlawed, they have low education and poor jobs.

Source: © The Cover Story/Corbis. Photographer: James Nelson.

Discrimination can cause prejudice and vice versa, but they are most often found working together, reinforcing one another (Merton 1949a; Myers 2003).

THINKING SOCIOLOGICALLY

Think of some events in history that might have an effect on attitudes toward particular groups. Why might the events cause inter-group hostility? How does discrimination discussed above help us to understand world conflicts such as the intense hostility between Palestinians and Jews in Israel?

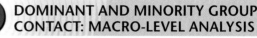

DOMINANT AND MINORITY GROUP CONTACT: MACRO-LEVEL ANALYSIS

Economic hard times hit Germany in the 1930s; to distract citizens from the nation's problems, a scapegoat was found—the Jewish population. The German states began restricting Jewish activities and investments; gradually hate rhetoric intensified, but even then most Jews had little idea about the fate that awaited them. Millions of these citizens perished in gas chambers because they were defined as an undesirable race (although being Jewish is actually a religious or ethnic identification, not biology) by the ruling Nazi party.

Japanese policies have resulted in a relatively homogeneous population over time, but one group, the Burakumin, have been treated as outcasts because their ancestors were relegated to performing work considered ritually

A Piece of the Pie

Why did new immigrant groups from South, Central, and Eastern Europe fare so much better than did African Americans in the United States? Frequently heard explanations point out that the handicaps faced by blacks were more severe than those faced by whites, that blacks could not shed their skin color, making them more recognizable as "different" and more subject to discrimination. Yet Japanese and Chinese people have fared well. They, too, have faced discrimination and can be singled out because of their physical features. To address these difficult questions, Stanley Lieberson (1980) consulted vast numbers of historical writings about immigrants, slavery, and the economic and educational systems of the 1800s. He studied secondary data, mostly collected from census data, and analyzed explanations by other social scientists, thus developing an overview of the economic and social circumstances that have affected different groups in the United States.

Lieberson (1980) concludes that the new immigrants and blacks who were arriving in the North did not differ greatly in their aspirations to get an education and good jobs. Just after slavery, the prospects for blacks looked promising. In fact, while many immigrants favored jobs over pursuit of education, blacks were initially fairly successful in narrowing the gap in education. So what caused African Americans to fall behind? Just before World War II, discrimination against blacks was intense. In the hierarchy of respect, blacks were lower than Asian or European immigrants, probably as a result of unfavorable attitudes during the slave period—another case of the past-in-present influence. Immigrants were preferred over blacks for jobs, especially in those positions that required minimal skills. Immigrants received more of the jobs in manufacturing that had future possibilities for mobility, while blacks could only get service jobs such as sweeping floors where promotion possibilities were nonexistent. Asian groups also experienced periods of severe discrimination, but their groups were limited in numbers due to immigration laws, and they posed little economic threat. Meanwhile, labor unions discriminated against African Americans, and realtors enforced segregation in housing.

Another factor identified by Lieberson (1980) was the context of inter-group contact. Slaves and Native Americans were forced into contact with whites, whereas immigrants came voluntarily, usually for economic betterment. Voluntary immigrants perceived the economic conditions to be better because they chose to come. They started out with better economic prospects and more "cultural capital"—education, useful language skills, knowledge of how the social system works, and established kinship or friendship networks.

Ethnic groups often develop certain occupational niches. Greek immigrant men ran eating and drinking establishments; Swedish immigrants were carpenters; Russian immigrants were furriers. However, any niche can absorb only so many workers, and most of these groups could not continue beyond the niche capacity. However, black migration to the northern industrial states did not stop, flooding the job market in certain fields.

Comparing African Americans with other nonwhites brings up several other points: Chinese and Japanese were treated with hostility and severity just as blacks were, but their immigration was less intense and sustained, the economic threat eventually lessened, and after some decades, these groups began to advance. As a smaller percentage of the population than blacks, these other nonwhite groups could occupy special niches that did not threaten other groups.

unclean—butchering animals, tanning skins, digging graves, and handling corpses. Today, discrimination is officially against the law, but customs persist. Ostracized and kept within certain occupations and neighborhoods (Kristof 1995), there is little intermarriage or even socializing between Burakumin and others. They remain a minority.

Mexico, Guatemala, and other Central American governments face protests by their Indian populations, descendants of Aztecs, Maya, and Inca, who have distinguishing features and are generally relegated to servant positions. These native groups have been protesting against government policies and their poor conditions—absentee land ownership, usurping of their land, poor pay, inability to own land, and discrimination by the government (DePalma 1995).

These examples illustrate contact between governments and minority groups. The Jews in Germany faced genocide;

Genocide	Subjugation	Population Transfer	Assimilation	Pluralism
Extermination of minorities	Oppression; slavery	Removal to new location	Cultural blending of groups	Groups share power

Figure 8.2   Types of Dominant–Minority Group Relations

Burakumin in Japan, segregation; and Native Americans, population transfer. The form these relations take depends on the following:

1. who has more power;

2. the needs of the dominant group for labor or other commodities that could be provided by the minority group;

3. the cultural norms of each group, including level of tolerance of outgroups;

4. the social histories of the groups, including their religious, political, racial, and ethnic differences;

5. physical and cultural identifiers that distinguish the groups; and

6. the times and circumstances (wars, economic strains, recessions).

Where power between groups in society is unequal, the potential for differential treatment is always present. Yet some groups live in harmony whether their power is equal or unequal (Kitano 1997). The Pygmies of the Ituri rainforest have traded regularly with nearby local African settlements by leaving goods in an agreed place in exchange for other needed goods; there is often only minimal direct contact between these groups.

Whether totally accepting or prone to conflict, dominant-minority relations depend on time, place, and circumstances. Figure 8.2 indicates the range of dominant-minority relationships and policies.

Genocide is the systematic effort of a dominant group to destroy a minority group. Christians were thrown to the lions in ancient Rome. Hitler threw Jews and other non-Aryan groups into concentration camps to be gassed. Turks slaughtered Armenians in 1915. To varying degrees, genocide has existed throughout history, and it still exists today. Iraqis used deadly chemical weapons against the Kurdish people within their own country. Members of the Serbian army massacred Bosnian civilians to rid towns of Bosnian Muslims, an action referred to as *ethnic cleansing* (Cushman and Mestrovic 1996). In Rwanda, Tutsi and Hutu tribespeople carried out mass killings against each other in the late 1990s. In Darfur, a section of western Sudan in Africa, massive genocide is occurring while powerful nations of the world do little to stop it. The United Nations estimates that two million Sudanese people have died, disappeared, or become refugees in other countries (Smith 2005).

Subjugation refers to the subordination of one group to another that holds power and authority. Haiti and the Dominican Republic are two countries sharing the island of Hispanola in the Caribbean. Because many Haitians are poor, they are lured by promises of jobs in the sugar cane fields of the Dominican Republic. However, they are forced to work long hours for little pay and are not allowed to leave until they have paid for housing and food, sometimes impossible on their low wages.

Slavery is one form of subjugation that has existed throughout history. When the Roman Empire captured other lands, captives became slaves. This included many Greeks

The Rwandan genocide began in April 1994 when the Rwandan president's plane was shot down. In the next 100 days, over 800,000 Rwandans were slaughtered in the ethnic fighting between the Hutu and Tutsi tribespeople, and the genocide continued for the next several years. Tens of thousands of refugees fled into neighboring Tanzania, Burundi, and Zaire. The United Nations and the world stood by, not able to agree on a strategy or funding to support troops. Many argue the same thing is happening in the Darfur region of Sudan, where the international community has not been effective in stopping the slaughter.

Source: © David Turnley/Corbis.

who as a nation also kept slaves at various times in their history. African tribes enslaved members of neighboring tribes, sometimes selling them to slave traders, and slavery has existed in Middle Eastern countries such as Saudi Arabia. As mentioned in the opening story for this chapter, slavery is flourishing today (Bales 2000, 2004).

Segregation, another form of subjugation, keeps minorities powerless by formally separating them from the dominant group and depriving them of access to the dominant institutions. Jim Crow laws, instituted in the southern United States after the Civil War, legislated separation between groups—separate facilities, schools, neighborhoods (Bobo and Smith 1998; Feagin and Feagin 1986; Massey and Denton 1993). Around the world, barrios, reservations, squatters quarters, and *favela* are sometimes maintained by the dominant group, usually unofficially but sometimes officially, and serve to isolate minorities in poor or overcrowded areas.

Domestic colonialism refers to exploitation of minority groups within a country (Blauner 1972; Kitano 1997). African Brazilians and Native Americans in the United States and Canada have been "domestically colonized groups"—managed and manipulated by dominant group members.

Population transfer refers to the removal, often forced, of a minority group from a region or country. Generally the dominant group wants land, resources, or economic power held by the minority. In 1972, Uganda's leader, General Idi Amin, gave the 45,000 Asians in that country, mostly of Indian origin, thirty-six hours to pack their bags and leave under threat that they would be arrested or killed. Many found homes in England; others went to India. Yet for the thousands who were born and raised in Uganda, this expulsion was a cruel act, barring them from their homeland. Since the Asian population had great economic power, the primary motivation for their expulsion was to regain economic power for Africans; however, their departure left the country in economic chaos with a void in the business class.

Examples of other population transfers are numerous: Native Americans in the United States were removed to reservations. The Cherokee people were forced to walk from Georgia and North Carolina to new lands west of the Mississippi—a "Trail of Tears" in which approximately 40 percent of the people perished. During World War II, Japanese Americans were forcibly moved to "relocation centers" and had their land and property confiscated. Many Chinese were forced to flee from Vietnam on small boats in the 1970s; homeless and even nation-less people, they were dubbed "the boat people" by the press. In 2001, many Afghani people fled to Pakistan to escape U.S. bombing; many others departed earlier to escape oppression by the ruling Taliban.

Movements of people across borders can result in **transnationalism**, people who fully participate in and have loyalty to two nations and cultures and often hold dual citizenship. An increasing number of naturalized U.S. citizens are

Trail of Tears.

also tax-paying members of their countries-of-origin, and they return often to help families and neighbors with financial needs or immigration plans (Levitt 2001). Yet dual citizenship can create dilemmas of identity and sense of belonging.

Assimilation refers to the structural and cultural merging of minority and majority groups, a process by which minority members may lose their original identity. It occurs when ethnic groups in a region disregard distinctions between groups. Interaction among racial and ethnic groups occurs in housing, schooling, employment, political circles, family groups, friendship, and social relationships (Kitano 1997). *Forced assimilation* occurs when a minority group is forced to suppress its identity. This happened in Spain around World War II when the Basque people were forbidden by the central government from speaking or studying the Basque language. For several centuries—ending only a few decades ago—the British government tried to stamp out the Welsh language from Wales. However, assimilation is often a voluntary process in which a minority group such as immigrants chooses to adopt the values, norms, and institutions of the dominant group.

Assimilation is more likely to occur when the minority group is culturally similar to the dominant group. For instance, in the United States, the closer a group is to being white, English speaking, and Protestant, or what is referred to as WASP (white Anglo Saxon Protestant), the faster its members will be assimilated into the society, adopting the culture and blending in biologically through intermarriage.

Pluralism occurs when each ethnic or racial group in a country maintains its own culture and separate set of institutions. In Malaysia, for example, three groups share power—Malays, Chinese, and Indians. Although the balance is not completely stable because Chinese and Indians hold more political and economic power than the native Malays, there is a desire to maintain a pluralistic society. Switzerland also has three dominant cultural language groups: French, German, and Italian. Three official languages are spoken in the government and taught in the schools. Laws are written in three languages. Each group respects the rights of the other groups to maintain a distinctive way of life. While tensions do exist, both Malaysia and Switzerland represent examples of pluralist societies.

Legal protection is often necessary in order to have pluralism. This occurs when governments act to protect a distinct, sometimes endangered, group. The government of the Philippines has restricted contact of Filipinos and archaeologists with tribes living on remote islands of the Philippines in order to protect their way of life from westerners and developers.

Many individuals in the world face disruptions during their lifetimes that change their position in the social structure. The dominant-minority continuum illustrates the range of relations that can affect people's lives as transitions take place.

THINKING SOCIOLOGICALLY

Think of examples from current news stories of positive and harmful intercultural contact. Where do your examples fit on the continuum from genocide to pluralism? What policies might address issues raised in your examples?

Theoretical Explanations of Dominant-Minority Group Relations

Are human beings innately cruel, inhumane, greedy, aggressive, territorial, or warlike? Some people think so, but the evidence is not very substantial. To understand prejudice in individuals or small groups, psychological and social-psychological theories are most relevant. To understand institutional discrimination, studying organizations is helpful; to understand the pervasive nature of prejudice and stereotypes over time in various societies, cultural explanations are useful. Although aspects of macro-level theories relate to micro- and meso-level analysis, their major emphasis is on understanding the national and global systems of group relations.

Conflict Theory

In the 1840s, when the United States had a railroad to build, large numbers of laborers immigrated from China to do hard manual work at low wages. When the railroad was completed and competition for jobs became tight, the once-welcomed Chinese became targets of bitter prejudice, discrimination, and sometimes violence. Between 1850 and 1890, whites in California protested against Chinese, Japanese, and Chicano workers. Members of these minority groups banded together in towns or cities for protection, founding the Chinatowns we know today (Kitano 1997,

Chinese men were invited and encouraged to come to North America to help build railroads. However, prejudice was extremely prevalent, especially once the railroads were completed and the immigrants began to settle into various jobs in the U.S. economy.

Source: © Underwood & Underwood/Corbis.

2001). Non-Chinese Asian groups suffered discrimination as well because the prejudiced generalizations were applied to all Asians (Son 1992; Winders 2004).

Why does discrimination occur? Conflict theorists argue that creating a "lesser" group protects the dominant group's advantages. Since privileges and resources are usually limited, those who have them want to keep them. One strategy used by privileged people, according to conflict theory, is to perpetrate prejudice and discrimination against minority group members. A case in point is the *gastarbeiter* (guest workers) in Germany and other Western European countries, who immigrate from Eastern Europe, the Middle East, and Africa to fill positions in European economies. They are easily recognized because of cultural and physical differences and are therefore ready targets for prejudice and discrimination, especially in times of economic competition and slowing economies; this helps perpetuate them in low-level positions.

Karl Marx argued that exploitation of the lower classes is built into capitalism because it benefits the ruling class. Unemployment creates a ready pool of labor to fill the marginal jobs; the pool is often made up of identifiable minority groups. This pool protects those in higher-level positions from others moving up in the stratification system.

One conflict theorist identifies three critical factors that contribute to hostility over resources (Noel 1968): first, if two groups of people are identifiably different in appearance, clothing, or language, then we-versus-they thinking may develop. However, this by itself does not establish long-term hostility between the groups. Second, if the two groups come into conflict over scarce resources that both groups want for themselves, hostilities are very likely to arise; the resources might be the best land, the highest paying jobs, access to the best schools for one's children, or positions of prestige and power. Conflict over resources is likely to create stereotypes and animosity. If the third element is added to the mix—one group having much more power than the other—then intense dislike between the two groups and misrepresentation of each group by the other is virtually inescapable. What happens is that the group with more power uses that power to ensure that they (and their offspring) get the most valued resources. However, since they do not want to feel badly about themselves as unfair and brutish people, they develop stereotypes and derogatory characterizations of "those other people" so the lack of access provided to "them" seems reasonable and justified. Discrimination comes first, and prejudiced ideology comes later to excuse the discrimination (Noel 1968). Thus, macro- and meso-level conflicts can lead to micro-level attitudes.

Split labor market theory, a branch of conflict theory, characterizes the labor market as having two levels: the *primary market* involves clean jobs, largely in supervisory roles, and provides high salaried wages and advancement possibilities; the *secondary market* involves undesirable hard dirty work, compensated with low hourly wages and few benefits or career opportunities. Minorities, especially those from the urban underclass, are most likely to find dead-end jobs in the secondary market. For instance, when Mexicans work for little income picking crops as migrant laborers, they encounter negative stereotypes because they are poor and take jobs for low wages. Prejudice and discrimination build against the new, cheaper workers who threaten the next level of workers as the migrant workers seek to move up in the economic hierarchy. Thus, competition for low jobs pits minorities against each other and low-income whites against minorities. By encouraging division and focusing antagonism between worker groups, employers reduce threats to their dominance and get cheaper labor in the process. Workers do not organize against employers who use this dual system because they are distracted by the antagonisms that build up between workers—hence the split labor market (Bonacich 1972, 1976). This theory maintains that competition, prejudice, and ethnic animosity serves the interests of capitalists because it keeps laboring classes from uniting.

Conflict theory has taught us a great deal about racial and ethnic stratification. However, conflict theorists often focus on people with power intentionally oppressing others in order to protect their own self-interests. They depict the dominant group as made up of nasty, power-hungry people. As we have seen in the meso-level discussion of side-effect discrimination and past-in-present discrimination, discrimination and privilege are often subtle and

Mexicans in Canada: Manuel Sanchez from Michuacan, Mexico, at the head of a line of workers at the sorting table at Louis Keursten's tobacco farm in Ontario. Each leaf is individually sorted by color and grade, pressed into 50 lb bales, and prepared for sale.

Source: © Paul A. Souders/Corbis.

unconscious, which means they can continue even without prejudice or ill-will by those who are in the dominant group; the privilege is institutionalized. Conflict theorists sometimes miss this important point.

Structural-Functional Theory

From the structural-functional perspective, maintaining a cheap pool of laborers who are in and out of work serves several purposes for society. Low-paying and undesirable jobs for which no special training is needed—busboys, janitors, nurse's aides, street sweepers, and fast food service workers—are often filled by minority group members of societies, including immigrant populations seeking to improve their opportunities.

Not only does this cheap pool of labor function to provide a ready labor force for dirty work, the menial unskilled jobs, but these individuals also serve other functions for society: they make possible occupations that service the poor, such as social work, public health, criminology, and the justice and legal systems; they buy goods others do not want—day-old bread, old fruits and vegetables, secondhand clothes; they set examples for others of what not to be; and they allow others to feel good about giving to charity (Gans 1971, 1994).

Sociologist Thomas Sowell (1994) contends that history and the situation into which one is born create the major differences in the social status of minority groups; minority individuals must work hard to make up for their disadvantages. Sowell's contentions are controversial in part because of the implication that institutional discrimination can be overcome by hard work. Conflict theorists counter his argument by saying that discrimination that reduces opportunities is built into institutional and organizational structures and must be dealt with through structural change. They argue that hard work is necessary, but not sufficient, for minorities to get ahead.

Prejudice, racism, and discrimination are dysfunctional for society, resulting in loss of human resources, costs to societies due to poverty and crime, hostilities between groups, and disrespect for those in power (Bowser and Hunt 1996; Schaefer 2006).

THINKING SOCIOLOGICALLY

What are some micro-, meso-, and macro-level factors that enhance the chances that minority persons can move up the social ladder to better jobs?

Cultural explanations point out that prejudice and discrimination are passed on from generation to generation through cultural transmission. Stereotypes about groups limit our perceptions of what these groups can do and thereby limit the opportunities available to minority group members. Cultural beliefs are passed on through micro-level socialization processes and macro-level institutional structure, aided by media stereotypes. Even when we see cases of minorities who do not conform to the prevalent images, selective vision reinforces stereotypes, prejudices, and labels we have learned.

Sudanese children: Young victims of famine wait in line to receive food in the Sudanese camp of Narus. A worldwide study released May 2, 2006, by UNICEF reveals that some 5.6 million children die every year in part because they do not consume enough of the right nutrients, and 146 million children are at risk of dying early because they are underweight.

Source: © William Campbell/Sygma Corbis.

Cultural beliefs help to explain why racism remains in place and why inequality is sustained over a long period of time. From this perspective, cultural beliefs serve to stabilize inequality once it is created in a society; beliefs alone do not cause inequality to form in the first place. The phenomenon of *symbolic racism* in contemporary North America is a good example: the assertion that the society is already fair prevents an honest look at institutional discrimination that operates so subtly and so pervasively at the meso and macro levels of a society.

THE EFFECTS OF PREJUDICE, RACISM, AND DISCRIMINATION

Pictures of starving orphans from Sudan and Ethiopia and broken families from war-torn Bosnia remind us of the human toll resulting from prejudice and discrimination. This section discusses the results of prejudice, racism, and discrimination for minority groups and societies.

The Costs of Racism

Individual victims of racism suffer from the destruction of their lives, health, and property, especially in societies where racism leads to poverty, enslavement, conflict, or war. Poor self-concept and low self-esteem result from constant reminders of a devalued status in society.

Prejudice and discrimination result in costs to organizations and communities as well as to individuals. First, they lose the talents of individuals who could be productive and contributing members because of poor education, substandard housing, and inferior medical care. Table 8.2 shows the differences in health care for ethnic groups in the United States.

THINKING SOCIOLOGICALLY

How might lack of health care affect other aspects of one's life (work, family life)?

TABLE 8.2 **Health Care in the U.S.**			
	White	Black	Hispanic
U.S. Citizens Not Covered by Health Care	14.2%	20.2%	32.4%
Average Expenditure per Customer for Health Care in the United States	$2,490	$1,339	$1,366

Source: U.S. Census Bureau (2005i, Table 125).

Second, government subsidies in the form of welfare, food stamps, and imprisonment cost millions but are made necessary in part by the lack of opportunities for minority individuals. Representation of ethnic groups in the U.S. political system can provide a voice for concerns of groups. Table 8.3 shows the representation of ethnic groups in Congress.

TABLE 8.3	**Representation in Congress, 2006**			
	Native American	Asian	Black	Hispanic
Senate	0	2 (2%)	1 (1%)	2 (2%)
House	1 (0.2%)	5 (1%)	42 (9.6%)	22 (5%)
Percentage of Population	1.5%	3.8%	12.7%	12.8%

Source: U.S. Census Bureau (2006e).

THINKING SOCIOLOGICALLY

How might one's self-interests be underrepresented in policy decisions if there is low representation of one's ethnicity?

Continued attempts to justify racism by stereotyping and labeling groups have *cultural costs*, too. There are many talented African American athletes who are stars on college sports teams, but very few of them have been able to break into the ranks of coaches and managers, though there has been more opportunity in basketball than in other sports (Edwards 1994; Eitzen and Sage 2003; Sage 2005). The number of African American and Mexican American actors and artists has increased, but the numbers of black playwrights and screenwriters who can get their works produced or who have become directors remains limited. African American musicians have found it much more difficult to earn royalties and therefore cannot compose full-time (Alexander 2003). Since these artists must create and perform their art "as a sideline," they are less able to contribute their talents to society. The rest of us in the society are the poorer for it.

THINKING SOCIOLOGICALLY

Think of a specific example of cultural costs of racism in your community. What might be done to address these costs?

Minority Reactions to Prejudice, Discrimination, and Racism

How have minority groups dealt with their status? Five different reactions are common: assimilation, acceptance, avoidance, aggression, and change-oriented actions directed at the social structure. The first four do not address the meso- and macro-level issues; they are micro-level responses.

An accommodation to prejudice and discrimination is *assimilation.* Some minority group members attempt to pass or assimilate as members of the dominant group so as to avoid bigotry and discrimination. Although this option is not open to many because of their distinguishing physical characteristics, this strategy usually involves abandoning one's own culture and turning one's back on family roots and ties, a costly strategy in terms of self-esteem and sense of identity. People who select this coping strategy are forced to deny who they are and to live their lives in constant anxiety, feeling as though they must hide something about themselves.

In the 1960s, popular items advertised in African American magazines were "whitening creams" or "skin bleaches." Light-colored persons with African ancestry would bleach their skins to pass as white. Skin-whitening creams can be found today on pharmacy shelves in many countries. Dissatisfaction with one's body has an impact on one's self-concept.

Passing also has been a common response of gays and lesbians who are afraid to come out. Homosexuals experience the costly impact on self-esteem and the constant fear that they may be discovered. Likewise, assimilated Jews have changed their religion and their names in order to be accepted. Despite the wrenching from one's personal history, passing has allowed some individuals to become absorbed into the mainstream and to lose the stigma of being defined as a minority; to these people, it is worth the high cost.

Acceptance is another common reaction to minority status. Some minority groups have learned to live with their minority status with little overt challenge to the system. They may or may not hold deep seated hostility, but they ultimately conclude that change in the society is not very likely; acceptance may be the rational means to survive within the existing system.

There are many possible explanations for this seeming indifference. For example, religious beliefs allow poor Hindus in India to believe that if they accept their lot in life, they will be reincarnated in a higher life-form. If they rebel, they can expect to be reincarnated into a lower life-form. Their religion is a form of social control.

Unfortunately, many children are socialized to believe that they are inferior or superior because minority group members are *expected* by the dominant group to behave in certain ways and often live up to that expectation because of the self-fulfilling prophesy (Farley 2005). Evidence to support stereotypes is easily found in individual cases—"inferior" kids live in shabby houses, dress less well, speak a different dialect. At school and on the job, minority position is reaffirmed by these characteristics.

Avoidance means shunning all contact with the dominant group. This can involve an active and organized attempt to leave the culture or live separately as some political exiles have done. In the United States, Marcus Garvey organized a Back-to-Africa movement in the 1920s, encouraging blacks to give up on any hope of justice in American society and to return to Africa. Native Americans continually moved west in the nineteenth century—trying to or being forced to get away from white Anglo settlers who brought alcohol and deadly diseases. In some cases, withdrawal may mean dropping out of the society as an individual—escaping by obliterating consciousness in drugs or alcohol. The escape from oppression and low self-concept is one reason why drug use is higher in minority ghettos and alcohol abuse is rampant on Native American reservations.

Aggression resulting from anger and resentment over minority status and subjugation may lead to retaliation or violence. Because the dominant group holds significant power, a direct route such as voting against the dominant group or defeating them in war is not always possible. Indeed, direct confrontation could be very costly to those lacking political or economic power.

Aggression usually takes one of two forms, indirect aggression and displaced aggression. *Indirect aggression* takes the form of biting assertiveness in the arts—literature, art, racial and ethnic humor, and music—and in job related actions such as inefficiency and slowdowns by workers. *Displaced aggression*, on the other hand, involves hostilities directed toward individuals or groups other than the dominant group, as happens when youth gangs attack other ethnic gangs in nearby neighborhoods. They substitute aggression against the other minority group for their frustrating circumstances.

The four responses discussed thus far address the angst and humiliation that individual minorities feel. They each allow an individual person to try to cope, but they do not address the structural causes of discrimination. The final strategy is change-oriented action: minority groups pursue social change in the meso- and macro-level structures of society. In the United States, Martin Luther King, Jr., followed in the nonviolent resistance tradition of India's Mohandas K. ("Mahatma") Gandhi, who sought to change India's laws so minorities could have equal opportunities within the society. King's strategy involved nonviolent popular protests, economic boycotts, and challenges to the current norms of the society. The NAACP (National Association for the Advanced of Colored People) sought to bring about similar kinds of change at the legislative level through legal suits that create new legal precedents on behalf of racial equality. Often, these lawsuits address side-effect discrimination—a meso-level problem. Many other associations for minorities—including the Anti-Defamation League (founded by Jews) and La Raza Unida (a Chicano organization) also seek to address problems both within organizations and institutions (meso level) and in the nation as a whole (macro level).

Minority groups in some countries embrace violent tactics as a means to bring about change—riots, insurrections, hijackings, and terrorist bombings aimed at the dominant group. Their hope is either to destroy the dominant power structure or to threaten the stability of the current macro-level system such that the group in power is willing to make some changes.

Sometimes minority reactions result in assimilation, but often the goal is to create a pluralistic society in which cultures can be different yet have economic opportunities open to all. Often minority groups want to preserve their traditions, in all their colorful variety, colorful variety, as in the HIndu ceremony depicted in the photo below.

THINKING SOCIOLOGICALLY

Do you think hip-hop or rap brings people together or tears them apart? Does it contribute to stereotyping or alleviate it? Explain.

POLICIES GOVERNING MINORITY AND DOMINANT GROUP RELATIONS

Between 1860 and 1920, the United States received 30 million immigrants from central and southeastern European countries. In the 1980s, refugees from war-torn countries such as Afghanistan, Lebanon, Cambodia, and El Salvador sought political asylum in the United States, Canada, Australia, France, Norway, and several Latin American countries (Omi and Winant 1989). In the 1990s, residents fled from Albania, Bosnia, Cuba, Haiti, Rwanda, Zaire, and other nations, mostly into neighboring countries such as Chad. In the early twenty-first century, Sudanese are

Thaipusam is an annual Hindu festival which draws the largest gathering in multi-racial Malaysia—nearly a million people in 2000. Several hundred devotees spear their cheeks with long, shiny steel rods—often a metre long—and pierce their chests and backs with small, hook-like needles in penance. Bleeding and pain appear minimal; the devotee remains in a trance after preparatory spiritual cleansing. Such festivals preserve long-standing and even sacred cultural traditions of indigenous/minority peoples.

Source: © Photo courtesy Sonia Nicholl.

fleeing to refugee camps in neighboring countries. These movements, brought about by war, famine, and economic dislocation, force families to seek new locations where they can survive and perhaps improve their circumstances. The degree of acceptance children and their families find in their newly adopted countries varies depending on the government's policies, the group's background, and economic conditions in the host country (Rumbaut and Portes 2001). Some formerly refugee-friendly countries are closing their doors to immigration because of the strain on their economy and threats of terrorism. In this section, we consider the policies that emerge as dominant and minority groups come into contact and interact.

Policies to Reduce Prejudice, Racism, and Discrimination

In the preceding pages, we considered some of the costs to individuals, groups, societies, and the global community inflicted by discriminatory behavior and policies. Discrimination's influence is widespread, from slavery and subjugation to unequal educational and work opportunities, to legal and political arenas, and to every other part of the social world. If one accepts the premise that discrimination is destructive to both individuals and societies, then ways must be found to address the root problems effectively. However, solutions to ethnic tensions around the world have many experts baffled. Consider ethnic strife in Bosnia and Croatia; conflicts between Palestinians and Israelis; conflicts between Shiites and Sunni Muslims in Iraq; tribal genocide in Rwanda and conflicts between religious groups in Northern Ireland. In places such as these, each new generation is socialized into the prejudice and antagonisms that perpetuate the animosity and violence. Social scientists and policy makers have made little progress in resolving conflicts that rest on century-old hostilities.

From our social world perspective, we know that no problem can be solved by working at only one level of analysis. A successful strategy must bring about change at every level of the social world—individual attitudes, organizational discrimination, cultural stereotypes, societal stratification systems, and national and international structures. However, most current strategies focus on only one level of analysis. Figure 8.3 shows some of the programs enacted to combat prejudice, racism, and discrimination at the individual, group, societal, and global levels.

Individual or Small Group Therapy

Programs to address prejudice, racism, and stereotypes through human relations workshops, group encounters, and therapy can achieve goals with small numbers of people. For instance, African American and white children who are placed in interracial classrooms in schools are more likely to develop close interracial friendships (Ellison

Thousands of refugees fled Vietnam in the 1970s to escape violence and possible death. Most left in whatever vessels they could crowd on. These Vietnamese boat people, rejected by the Malaysian authorities, take refuge on the Indonesian archipelago of Anambas.

Source: © Jacques Pavlovsky/SIGMA CORBIS.

and Powers 1994). Also, the higher the people's education levels, the more likely they are to respect and like others and to tolerate—even appreciate and enjoy—differences. Education gives a broader, more universal outlook, reduces misconceptions and prejudices, shows that many issues do not have clear answers, and encourages multicultural understanding.

However, these strategies do not address the social conditions underlying the problems because they reach only a few people: those who are exposed through school or other programs, who voluntarily seek help, or who are required to participate in prejudice reduction programs. Thus, this approach alone achieves only limited results. It also does not begin to address dilemmas that are rooted in meso- and macro-level discrimination. Micro-level solutions are often blind to the structural causes of problems.

Group Contact

Many social scientists advocate organized group contact between dominant and minority group members to improve relations. Consider the following example from a classroom in an all-white farming district in Iowa. The teacher, Jane Elliot, divided her third-grade class into two groups: brown-eyed and blue-eyed children. Then she told the class that brown-eyed children were "superior," were more intelligent, and would be given more privileges. The blue-eyed children wore collars for identification, sat in the back of the room, and were treated as "inferiors." The next day, the tables turned and the blue-eyed children were superior and brown-eyed children became inferior. The blue-eyed children, superior for the day,

Types of Problems at Each Level	Types of Solutions or Programs
Individual level: stereotypes and prejudice	Therapy; tolerance-education programs
Group level: negative group interaction	Positive contact; awareness by majority of their many privileges
Societal level: institutional discrimination	Education, media, legal-system revisions
Global level: deprivation of human rights	Human rights movements; international political pressures

Figure 8.3   Problems and Solutions

took their new roles even more to heart than the brown-eyed superior children had. Children who had formerly been friends were hostile toward each other. In each case, the inferior group for the day, whether blue- or brown-eyed, could not concentrate, did poorly on their work and tests, and seemed sullen and disinterested. The teacher had the children evaluate what it was like and how it felt to be in the minority (Peters 1972/1987).

In another classic example of group contact, social psychologists Muzafer Sherif and Caroline Sherif (1953) and their colleagues ran summer camps for boys aged 11 and 12 and studied how groups were established and reestablished. Upon arrival, the boys were divided into two groups that competed periodically. The more fierce the competition, the more hostile the two cabins of boys became toward each other. The experimenters tried several methods to resolve the conflicts and tensions:

1. Appealing to higher values (be nice to your neighbors). This proved of limited value.

2. Talking with natural leaders of the groups (compromises between group leaders). Group leaders agreed, but their followers did not go along.

3. Bringing groups together in a pleasant situation (a mutually rewarding situation). This did not reduce competition; if anything, it increased it.

4. Introducing a superordinate goal that could be achieved only if everyone cooperated. This technique worked. The boys were presented with a dilemma: the water system had broken or a fire needed to be put out, and all were needed to solve the problem. The group not only worked together, but their established stereotypes eventually began to fade away. Such a situation in the larger society might arise from efforts to get a candidate elected, a bill passed, or a neighborhood improved.

Programs involving group contact to improve conditions for minorities have been tried in many areas of social life, including integrated housing projects, job programs to promote minority hiring, and busing children to schools to achieve a higher level of racial and socioeconomic integration. For instance, the Chicago Housing Authority opened a refurbished mixed-income housing experiment with resident participation in decision making; although many predicted failure, the project thrived with long waiting lists of families wanting to participate (McCormick 1992). Positive contact experiences do tend to improve relations on a micro level by breaking down stereotypes, but in order to solidify gains, we must also address institutionalized inequalities.

Institutional and Societal Strategies to Improve Group Relations

Sociologists contend that institutional and societal approaches to reduce discrimination get closer to the core of the problems and affect larger numbers of people than do micro-level strategies. For instance, voluntary advocacy organizations pursue political change through lobbying, watchdog monitoring, educational information dissemination, canvassing, protest marches, rallies, and boycotts (Minkoff 1995). Two such groups are the Anti-Defamation League and the Southern Poverty Law Center's Teaching Tolerance Program. Both groups provide schools and community organizations with their literature, videos, and other materials aimed at combating intolerance and discrimination toward others. Some local efforts have been made through AmeriCorps and other agencies to do problem solving, provide institutional support for schools, and create linkages across ethnic and racial boundaries, as illustrated in The Applied Sociologist at Work on page 250. With a bachelors' degree in sociology, Rachel Ernst was able to make a difference in her hometown.

The Civil Rights Commission, Fair Employment Practices Commission, and Equal Employment Opportunity Commission are government organizations that protect rights and work toward equality for all citizens. These agencies oversee practices and hear complaints relating to racial, sexual, age, and other forms of discrimination. Legislation, too, can modify behaviors; laws requiring equal treatment of minorities have resulted in increased tolerance of those who are "different" and have opened doors that previously were closed to minorities.

In the United States, executive action to end discrimination has been taken by a number of presidents. In 1948, Harry Truman moved to successfully end military segregation, and subsequent presidents have urged passage of civil rights legislation and equal employment opportunity legislation. Affirmative action laws were first implemented during Lyndon

Piles of garbage have accumulated behind new housing projects in the Iztapalapa area of Mexico City, Mexico.

Source: © Sergio Dorantes/Corbis.

Johnson's administration; they have been used to fight pervasive institutional racism (Crosby 2004; Farley 2005).

Affirmative action. One of the most contentious policies in the United States has been affirmative action. The following discussion addresses the intentions and forms of the policy (Gallagher 2004). A societal policy for change, affirmative action actually involves three different policies. Its simplest and original form, which we call *strict affirmative action*, involves affirmative or positive steps to make sure that unintentional discrimination does not occur. It requires, for example, that an employer who receives federal monies must advertise a position widely and not just through internal or friendship networks; if one needs an employee with a college education, then by federal law one must recruit through minority and women's colleges as well as state and private colleges in the region. If hiring in the suburbs, one is obliged to contact the unemployment agencies in the poor and minority communities as well as those in the affluent neighborhoods. After taking these required extra steps, one is expected to hire the most qualified candidate that applies, irrespective of race, ethnicity, sex, religion, or other external characteristics. The focus is on

providing opportunities for the best qualified people. For many people, this is the meaning of *affirmative action*, and it is inconceivable that this could be characterized as reverse discrimination, for members of the dominant group will be hired if they are in fact the most qualified. These policies do not overcome the problem that qualified people who have been marginalized may be competent but do not have the traditional paper credentials that document their qualifications.

The second policy is a *quota system*, a requirement that employers *must* hire a certain percentage of minorities. For the most part, quotas are now unconstitutional. They apply only in cases in which a court has found a company to have a substantial and sustained history of discrimination against minorities and in which the employment position does not really have many requirements (if the job entails sweeping floors and cleaning toilets, there would not be an expectation of a specific academic degree or a particular grade point average).

The third policy and the one that has created the most controversy among opponents of affirmative action is *preference policies*, sometimes called *set-aside policies*. Preference policies are based on the concept of equity, the belief that sometimes people must be treated differently in order to treat them fairly and to create equality. This policy was enacted because of institutional racism in order to level the playing field.

The objectives of preference policies are to (1) eliminate qualifications that are not substantially related to the job but that unwittingly favor members of the dominant group and (2) foster achievement of objectives of the organization that are only possible through enhanced diversity. To overcome these inequalities and achieve certain objectives, employers and educational institutions take account of race or sex by making special efforts to hire and retain workers or accept students from groups that have been underrepresented because of race. In many cases, these individuals bring qualifications others do not possess. Consider the following examples.

A goal of the medical community is to provide access to medical care for underserved populations. There is an extreme shortage of physicians on the Navajo reservation. Thus, a Navajo applicant for medical school might be accepted even if her scores are slightly lower than another candidate because she speaks Navajo and understands the culture. One could argue that she is more qualified to be a physician on the reservation than someone who knows nothing about Navajo society but has a slightly higher grade point average or test score. Some argue that tests should not be the only measure to determine successful applicants.

Likewise, an African American police officer may have more credibility in a minority neighborhood and may be able to diffuse a delicate conflict more effectively than a white officer who scored slightly higher on a paper-and-pencil placement test. Sometimes being a member of a particular ethnic group can actually make one more qualified for a position.

A 1996 proposition in California to eliminate affirmative action programs in the state passed in a popular referendum. The result was that colleges in California are allowed to offer preference based on state residency, athletic competency,

Reducing Racism in a Racial Tinderbox

In April 2001, Cincinnati, Ohio, received national and international attention as the shooting death of an unarmed black teenager by a white city police officer sparked three days of civil unrest, during which predominantly African American crowds broke windows, looted stores, and challenged police practices. Rachel explains her role:

My community work in Cincinnati began several months after the unrest, when as a fresh college graduate I joined an AmeriCorps program called Public Allies in order to apply my undergraduate sociology degree to community development. Although almost six months had passed, the issue of race relations within the Cincinnati community still touched upon fresh wounds and unanswered questions. My work with the National Conference for Community and Justice (NCCJ) connected me with students and adults seeking racial healing in their communities, and I spent much of my time facilitating interracial dialogues and coordinating high school programs on topics such as stereotyping, social justice, and local and international human relations.

My sociological background provided me with a conceptual foundation as I engaged participants in exploring the complex dynamics of inequality and power. I utilized the sociological imagination in challenging misconceptions of white students with limited experience outside of suburbia, who stated, "Racism doesn't really exist anymore." My understanding of micro, meso, and macro facets of power and privilege enabled me to address the hidden dimensions of contemporary racism and to illustrate the powerful role that poverty played in fueling April's "race riots."

As I worked with community members, I soon realized that my greatest contribution toward racial healing was in acting as an ally and activist within the white community. There is a certain power in white individuals acknowledging their own privilege within social systems and yet fighting for change and equity. The biggest challenges to contemporary race relations are not overt acts of discrimination and prejudice. Rather, the most pervasive obstacles to justice and equity reflect patterns of denial within the white community—denial that racism and inequalities persist, denial of white privilege, and denial that the Civil Rights laws only partially addressed the legacies of slavery. Sociology teaches me to explore the roots of this denial and to view the world through a theoretical lens. As a white individual I have incredible influence within my own community when I move beyond my own privilege and share with others the tools for understanding social dynamics. As a student of sociology I explored the systems—at various levels—behind poverty and racism. Racism is much larger than prejudice and discrimination—it is manifest in systems of segregation, poverty, and institutionalized inequality and disadvantage compounded over generations.

In Cincinnati, the April 2001 unrest prompted dozens of community efforts, including dialogue series, ballot initiatives on police profiling, prejudice-reduction programs, and changes in city governance. However, in a town where whites consider themselves free from blame if they do not wear KKK robes, efforts that do not address power dynamics and historical discriminatory practices fail to truly tackle the underlying issues. Combining this sociological knowledge with my passion for justice within my hometown allowed me to dive deeper into the complexities of racism, white privilege, and civil unrest to fight for change at several levels of the social system.

Rachel Ernst graduated in 2001 from Hanover College in Indiana with a Bachelor of Arts degree in Sociology. She has now enrolled in a doctoral program in Sociology at Indiana University.

musical skill, having had a parent graduate from the school, and many other factors—but not race. Many colleges and universities admit students because they need an outstanding point guard on the basketball team, an extraordinary soprano for the college choir, or a student from a distant state for geographic diversity; these students were shown preference by being admitted with lower test scores than some other applicants.

A lawsuit filed in a Detroit district court in 1997 alleged that the University of Michigan gave unlawful preference to minorities in undergraduate admissions and in the law school admissions. In this controversial case, the court ruled that undergraduate admissions were discriminatory because they used numbers rather than individualize judgment to make the determination (University of Michigan Documents Center 2003). Consider Sociology in Your Social World, page 251, and decide whether you think the policy was unfair, and whether only race and ethnicity should have been deleted from the preferences allowed.

The question remains, should preferences be given to accomplish diversity? Some people feel that programs involving any sort of preference are reverse discrimination. Others believe such programs have encouraged employers, educational institutions, and government to look carefully at hiring policies and minority candidates and that many more competent minority group members are working in the public sector as a result of these policies.

Sociology in Your Social World

Preference Policies at the University of Michigan

To enhance diversity on the campus—a practice that many argue makes a university a better learning environment and enhances the academic reputation of the school—many colleges have preference policies in admissions. However, the University of Michigan was sued by applicants who felt they were not admitted because others replaced them on the roster due to their racial or ethnic background.

The University of Michigan is a huge university where a numbering system is needed to handle the volume (tens of thousands) of applicants; they cannot make a decision based on personal knowledge of each candidate. Thus, they give points for each quality they deem desirable in the student body. A maximum of 150 points is possible, and a score of a 100 would pretty much ensure admission. The university felt that any combination of points accumulated according to the following formula would result in a highly qualified and diverse student body.

For academics, up to 110 points possible:

80 points for grades (a particular grade point average in high school resulted in a set number of points; a 4.0 resulted in 80 points; a 2.8 resulted in 56 points.)

12 points for standardized test scores (ACT or SAT)

10 points for the academic rigor of high school (so all students who went to tougher high schools earned points)

8 points for the difficulty of the curriculum (e.g., points for honors curriculum vs. keyboarding courses)

For especially desired qualities, including diversity, up to 40 points possible of any combination

of the following (but no more than 40 in this category):

Geographical distribution (10 for Michigan resident; 6 for underrepresented Michigan county)

Legacy (a relative had attended Michigan (4 pts for a parent; 1 pt for grandparent or sibling)

Quality of submitted essay (3 points)

Personal achievement—a special accomplishment that was noteworthy (up to 5 points)

Leadership and service (5 points each)

Miscellaneous (only one of these could be used):

- Socioeconomic disadvantage (20 points)
- Racial or ethnic minority (20 points; disallowed by the court ruling)
- Men in nursing (5 points)
- Scholarship athlete (20 points)
- Provost's discretion (20 points; usually the son or daughter of a large financial donor or of a politician)

In addition to ethnicity being given preference, athleticism, musical talent, having a relative who is an alum, or being the child of someone who is noteworthy to the university were also considered. Some schools also give points for being a military veteran or for coming from a distant state. The legal challenge to this admissions system was based only on the racial and ethnic preference given to some candidates, not to the other items that are preferenced.

Does this process seem reasonable as a way to get a diverse and highly talented incoming class of students?

Source: Kantrowitz and Wingert (2003).

THINKING SOCIOLOGICALLY

Should colleges consider an applicant's state of origin, urban or rural background, ethnicity, musical or athletic ability, alumni parent, or other factors in admitting students if it helps the college achieve its goals? Should men with lower scores be admitted because the college wants to have balanced gender enrollment? Is ethnic diversity so central to the learning environment that it must be an admissions criterion? Why?

Leaders of India's resistance in parley before being jailed. Mohandas K. Gandhi hears the whispered suggestion of Mahadev Desai, his secretary, while Pandit Jawaharlal Nehru sits serenely in the foreground. The meeting resulted in a campaign of civil disobedience against British rule. All the men in this picture were jailed as a result of the decisions of the Congress. (Bombay, India; July 8, 1942)

Source: © Bettmann/Corbis.

Cesar Chavez leads a supermarket protest. (August 1990)

Source: © Najlah Feanny/Corbis.

Nonviolent resistance: Institutional and societal policy for change. Another technique for bringing about change at the institutional and societal level is nonviolent resistance by minority groups. The model for this technique comes from India where, in the 1950s, Mahatma Gandhi led the struggle for independence from Britain. Although Britain clearly had superior weapons and armies, boycotts, sit-ins, and other forms of resistance eventually led to British withdrawal as the ruling colonial power. Jesse Jackson, a U.S. presidential candidate in 1984 and 1988, led his Chicago-based organization, PUSH, in economic boycotts against companies such as Coca-Cola to force them to hire and promote blacks, and Cesar Chavez led boycotts against grape growers to improve the working conditions of migrant workers. This strategy has been used successfully by workers and students to bring about change in many parts of the world.

Global Movements for Human Rights

A unique coalition of world nations has emerged from a recent international event—the terrorist attack of September 11, 2001, on the World Trade Center in New York City, a center housing national and international businesses and workers. Citizens from ninety countries were killed when two hijacked commercial jetliners flew into the towers. In addition to the world condemnation, many countries' governments have pledged to fight against terrorism. Yet why did such a heinous act occur? Many social scientists attempting to identify a cause point to the disparities between rich and poor peoples of the world; the perpetrators likely felt Muslims were treated as inconsequential players in the global world and they struck out to make a dramatic impact on the world community and the United States. The point is that global issues and ethnic conflicts in the social world are interrelated.

The rights granted to citizens of any nation used to be considered the business of each sovereign nation, but after the Nazi holocaust, German officers were tried at the Nuremberg Trials and the United Nations passed the Universal of Declaration Human Rights. Probably more than any other U.S. president, Jimmy Carter made human rights the centerpiece of his foreign policy. In addition, the United Nations, several national governments (Britain, France, and Canada), and privately funded advocacy groups speak up for international human rights as a principle that transcends national boundaries. The most widely recognized private group is Amnesty International, a watchdog group that does lobbying on behalf of human rights and supports political prisoners and ethnic group spokespersons. When Amnesty International was awarded the Nobel Peace Prize in 1997, the group's visibility was dramatically increased. Even some activist sociologists have formed Sociologists without Borders, or SSF (Sociólogos sin Fronteras; http://www.sociologistswithoutborders.org).

Everyone can make a positive difference in the world, and one place to start is in our community (see Contributing to Your Social World); we can counter prejudice, racism, and discrimination in our own groups by teaching children to see beyond "we" and "they" and by speaking out for fairness and against stereotypes and discrimination.

SO WHAT?

Why are minority group members in most countries poorer than dominant group members? This and other chapter opening questions can be answered in part by considering individual causes of prejudice and racism; physical and cultural differences that distinguish groups of people; and the fact that human beings have a tendency to create "we" and "they" categories and to treat those who are different as somehow less human. The categories can be based on physical appearance, cultural differences, religious differences, or anything the community or society defines as important. Once people notice differences, they are more inclined to hurt "them" or to harbor advantages for "us" if there is competition over resources that both groups want. Even within a nation, where people are supposedly all "us," there can be sharp differences and intense hostilities.

Indeed, "we" and "they" thinking can invade some of the most intimate settings. Inequality is not limited to social classes, race or ethnic groups, or religious communities; it can infect relations between human males and females in everything from the home to the boardroom and from the governance of nations to the decisions of global agencies. More on this in the next chapter: "Gender Stratification."

CONTRIBUTING TO YOUR SOCIAL WORLD

At the Local Level: *Big Brothers Big Sisters* helps a child with few resources and little cultural capital get a broader picture of society. By becoming a mentor, you could provide advice, support, and know-how to help develop skills that could make for success.

Commission on human relations: Most communities have organization(s) working for positive ethnic relations. Contact them to ask how you can become involved.

At the Organizational or Institutional Level: *Teaching Tolerance* (www.splcenter.org/center/tt/teach.jsp) is a program of the Southern Poverty Law Center that has curriculum materials for teaching about diversity and a program for enhancing cross-ethnic cooperation and dialogue in schools. Consider using their ideas and materials to enhance ethnic relations on a campus.

AmeriCorps (www.americorps.org) is a network of national service programs involving over 70,000 people in education, public safety, health, the environment. . . . Members are selected by and serve with local and national organizations such as Habitat for Humanity, the American Red Cross, and Big Brothers Big Sisters.

At the National and Global Levels: *Free the Slaves* (http://www.freetheslaves.net) fights slavery worldwide by helping people to freedom and helps to abolish slavery around the world.

Sociologists without Borders (http://www.sociologistswithoutborders.org) promotes human rights globally. Advocates that sociologists participate, democratically, with others to set standards for human well-being and devote energies to understanding how to achieve these standards.

Amnesty International (www.amnestyusa.org or www.amnesty.org) is a worldwide movement of people who campaign for internationally recognized human rights.

Kids with Cameras (www.kids-with-cameras.org) can be successful in fulfilling its mission of empowering children through the art of photography only when people are involved and excited about the work! Assist Kids with Cameras gain momentum and strength; donate, volunteer, buy a print, e-mail the kids, and join the e-mail list.

Visit www.pineforge.com/ballantinestudy for online activities, sample tests, and other helpful information. Select "Chapter 8: Race and Ethnic Group Stratification" for chapter-specific activities.

GENDER STRATIFICATION: *She/He*—Who Goes First?

What to Expect . . .

Social inequality is especially evident in gender relations, and while women in some societies are treated with deference, they are rarely given first access to positions of significant power or financial reward. While they may play many work roles, they often *carry the load* of child care by themselves. Because they have more role strains, this photo essay focuses on women.

NATIONAL LEAGUE FOR DEMOCRACY

Think About It . . .

1. How does being female or male affect your thoughts and behaviors?

2. Why do women have second-class status in your society? Other societies?

3. Why do some people face violence because of their sexuality?

4. Can anything be done to make men and women more equal?

Macro: Global Community

Macro: National Society

Meso: National Institutions and Organizations; Ethnic Subcultures

Micro: Local Organizations and Community

**Micro:
You and Your Family**

Micro: Peers, neighbors, teachers, coaches, and religious education instructors socialize children into gender roles

Meso: Leadership positions limited for women; segregation of boys and girls or men and women limits access to resources

Macro: National policies provide sex-based privileges

Macro: Women often have lower status, hold fewer positions of power and influence, and rarely hold leadership positions

Y ou name it, and some society has probably done it! Gender relations are no exception. Since the social roles we play and identities we create for ourselves are influenced by our societies, variations around the world show that most roles and identities are not biological but rather socially constructed. We have now discussed factors that stratify individuals into social groups (castes and classes) and the role race and ethnicity play in stratification. Add the concepts of sex and gender, and we have a more complete picture of how class, race and ethnicity, and gender together influence who we are and our positions in society. Consider the following examples from societies that illustrate some unusual human social constructions based on sex and gender; these examples illustrate that gender roles are created by humans to meet needs of their societies. We will then move to more familiar societies.

Men of the Wodaabe society in Niger, Africa, would be defined as effeminate by most Western standards because of

Wodaabe men in Niger (Africa) go to great pains with makeup, hair, and jewelry to ensure that they are highly attractive, a pattern that is thought by many people in North America to be associated with females.

Source: © Frans Lemmens / zefa / Corbis.

their behavior patterns. The men are like birds, showing their colorful feathers to attract women. They take great care in doing their hair, applying makeup, and dressing to attract women. They also gossip with each other while sipping their tea. What are the women doing? They are cooking meals, caring for the children, cleaning, tending to the animals, planting small gardens, and preparing for the next move of this nomadic group (Millenium Television Series No. 5 1992).

People in industrial societies might seem unacceptably aggressive and competitive to people of the Arapesh tribe in New Guinea where gentleness and nonaggression are the rule for both women and men. Yet nearby, women of the Tchambuli people are assertive, businesslike, and the primary economic providers; men of the Tchambuli exhibit expressive, nurturing, and gossipy behavior.

The Mbuti and !Kung peoples of Africa value gender equality in their division of labor and treatment of women and men, and among the Agta of the Philippines, women do the hunting. In West African societies such as the Ashanti and Yoruba kingdoms, women control much of the market system (Dahlberg 1981; Mead 1935/1963; Turnbull 1962).

Women under the Taliban in Afghanistan could not be seen in public without total covering that met strict requirements. Anyone not obeying could be stoned to death. Women could not hold public positions or even work. If they became ill, women could not be examined by a physician because all doctors are male but instead would have to describe their symptoms to a doctor through a screen (*Kandahar* 2003).

In China, adults work in the factories and fields. Children are cared for in state-run child care settings. Equality between the sexes is the goal, although many women claim they serve in the public work arena and do a disproportionate amount in the private home setting.

Certain tasks must be carried out by individuals and organizations in each society for members to survive. Someone in the society must be responsible for raising children, someone must provide people with the basic necessities (food, clothing, shelter), someone needs to lead, someone must help resolve conflicts. One's presumed sex is often used to determine who holds what positions and who carries out what tasks; one's life chances in the stratification system are profoundly affected by the combination of sex and age. For instance, obligations of the youngest daughter in some Mexican households mean she may be required to forego marriage, to stay at home, and to care for her mother as she ages (Esquivel 2001).

In this chapter, we will explore the implications of one's sex combined with race and class in the stratification system, one's sexuality, and the concept of gender.

SEX, GENDER, AND THE STRATIFICATION SYSTEM

Women in some parts of the world are treated in ways that might be unthinkable to you. Some women are considered unclean during menstruation and are segregated in special huts. Other women are thought to have extra powers during menstruation. Some women who work outside the home in strict Muslim societies are stigmatized as "bad wives" or "immoral Muslims." Some societies believe women should shave their armpits and legs; if they do not, they are thought to be unattractive. In others, hair is natural and considered desirable, even beautiful. Some men trade sisters or cousins to obtain wives. Some women must be completely covered when in public; women elsewhere are expected to wear next to nothing at the beach. Historically, some women bound their feet to keep them small and attractive to men (Daly 1978). Other women's clitorises are removed so they would not have sexual urges or be temptresses to men. Some wives burned themselves on the funeral pyres of their dead husbands (*sati*, "virtuous" women being burned alive with their dead husbands). Some girls are killed at birth so they will not be a burden to their families. A few women are elected to premier leadership roles, such as prime minister or president of the nation; others are kept isolated from the world outside of their homes.

All of the above are cultural creations, and these beliefs and practices in societies around the world affect the lives of individual females. Although gender identities and roles change slowly, they do change over time, reflecting the economic, political, and social realities of the society and the influence of other societies. For instance, today women in India seldom commit suicide on their husband's funeral pyre, but before the practice of *sati* was outlawed, the practice was common as a way to deal with widows who no longer had a role in society or a means of support. A woman who refused to comply might be stigmatized and dishonored as a bad or unfaithful wife (Weitz 1995).

Muslim girls in the town of Kargil (in Ladakh, a district in India near Pakistan) cover their faces when in public. The display of bodies, even in a college classroom, would be immoral to many Muslims.

Source: Photo by Steve Evans.

Sex, Gender, and Sexuality

At birth when a doctor says, "It's a . . . ," they are referring to the distinguishing primary characteristics that determine **sex**, the penis or vagina. Sex is a biological term referring to ascribed genetic, anatomical, and hormonal differences between males and females. Right? Partly! Sex is also "a determination made through the application of socially agreed upon biological criteria for classifying persons as females or males" (West and Zimmerman 1987:127). This means that sometimes this binary male-female categorization by biological criteria is not clear; occasionally people are born with ambiguous genitalia (the *intersexed*), up to 1 in 1,000 births (Fausto-Sterling 1993, 2000). Whether male, female, or intersexed, anatomical differences at birth or chromosomal typing before birth result in attempts to clearly categorize sex; in some societies great lengths are taken to assign a sex.

In adolescence, secondary characteristics further distinguish the sexes, with females developing breasts and hips, and males developing body hair, muscle mass, and

The bound foot of an elderly Chinese woman in Yunnan Province illustrates the bodily mutilation that women experienced in the interest of being considered desirable and high status.

Source: © Kazuyoshi Nomachi / Corbis.

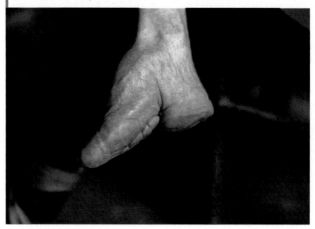

Many women today are in major leadership positions. On the left is Michelle Bachelet, the president of Chile, who won almost 54% of the popular vote in 2006. In the center photo, German Chancellor Angela Merkel addresses the press in a news briefing. On the right is Ellen Johnson-Sirleaf, president of Liberia, who was honored and awarded the 2006 Africa Prize for Leadership for the Sustainable End of Hunger.

Source: © Presidencia de Chile / Nancy Coste; © Senate.de; © CDU Deutschlands

deep voices. Individuals are then expected to adopt the behaviors appropriate to their anatomical features. In addition to the physical sex differences between males and females, a few other physical conditions are commonly believed to be sex-linked, such as a prevalence of color-blindness, baldness, learning disabilities, autism, and hemophilia in males. Yet some traits that members of society commonly link to sex are actually learned through socialization. There is little evidence, for instance, that emotions, personality traits, or ability to fulfill most social statuses are determined by inborn physical sex differences. Although the terms *sex, gender,* or even *sexuality* are often used interchangeably, it is useful to understand the technical difference.

A person's sex—male, female, or other—is a basis for stratification around the globe, used in every society to assign positions and roles to individuals; however, what is defined as normal behavior for a male, female, or intersexed person in one society could get one killed in another.

Gender identity is learned and created. It refers to a society's notions of masculinity and femininity—socially constructed meanings associated with male or female—and how individuals construct their gender identity within these constraints. These meanings determine proper behaviors and placement in the stratification system (Rothenberg 2004), and individuals are expected to act appropriately for their sex category. **Gender roles** are those commonly assigned tasks or expected behaviors of individuals because of their sex category; they vary greatly as illustrated in the opening examples (Lips 2005). Members of society learn the psychological, social, and cultural guidelines for each gender. In many societies, these distinctions are the way they are

because "men are men and women are women—a division perceived to be natural and rooted in biology." (West and Zimmerman 1987:128). Yet constructed gender identities vary depending on an individual's circumstances. You may expect to open the door or have it be opened, but your friend may be offended by the gesture. As is apparent from the opening examples, gender may vary by one's position in society and ethnic or racial group. Our cultural beliefs define what is right and wrong, and our identities are constructed within this framework; there is not some absolute truth governing gender roles and identities.

Sexuality refers to how we experience our own bodies and our bodies in relation to others. In the nineteenth century, medical science began to study sexuality and sexual behavior; most often, sexuality was defined in binary terms (Colligan 2004), and behaviors falling outside heterosexual boundaries were often defined as perverse. In the twentieth century, researchers such as Kinsey (Kinsey, Pomeroy, and Martin 1948; Kinsey et al. 1953) and Masters and Johnson (1966, 1970) conducted studies that uncovered actual sexual behaviors, not just those that had been defined as normal. These studies considered a range of sexual practices, from premarital sex and homosexuality to orgasm and masturbation (Lindsey 2005). In summary, while the terms *sex, gender,* and *sexuality* are often used interchangeably, they do have distinct meanings. One can be a masculine heterosexual female, a masculine homosexual male, or any of a number of possible combinations.

The distinctions between these terms are not always as clear-cut as the definitions would imply. Individuals and organizations are continually negotiating the meanings attached to gender and sexuality; that is, they are "doing gender," a concept discussed later in this chapter (West and Zimmerman 1987).

Sex, Gender, and Sexuality at the Micro Level

"It's a boy!" brings varying cultural responses. In many Western countries, that exclamation results in blue blankets; toys associated with males such as footballs, soccer balls, and trucks; roughhousing; and gender socialization messages. In some Asian societies, boys are sources for great rejoicing whereas girls may be seen as a burden; they occasionally even face *female infanticide* (killing of newborn girl babies). Beginning at birth, each individual passes through many stages; at each, there are messages that reinforce appropriate gender behavior in that society. Although gender socialization differs in each society, proper roles are established by the culture and learned from birth. These gender expectations are inculcated into children by parents, siblings, grandparents, neighbors, peers, and even day care providers. If we fail to respond to the expectations of these significant people in our lives, we may experience teasing, isolation and exclusion, harsh words, and stigma. To avoid these informal sanctions, which can be extremely uncomfortable, we usually learn to conform, at least in our public behavior.

Once we reach school-age and become more involved in activities separate from our parents, other people in the community—teachers, religious leaders, coaches—also begin to influence us. We are grouped by sex in many of these social settings, and we come to think of ourselves as like *this* group and unlike *that* group: boys versus girls, we versus they. Even if our parents are not highly traditional in their gender expectations, we still experience many influences at the micro level to conform to traditional gender notions.

Differential treatment and stratification of the sexes continues as we reach adulthood. Men traditionally have more networks, statuses, and access to resources outside of the home; this has resulted in women having less power because they are more dependent on husbands or fathers for resources. Even spousal abuse is related to imbalance of power in relationships. Lack of connections to the larger social system makes it difficult to remove oneself from an abusive relationship.

The subtitle of this chapter asks, Who goes first? When it comes to the question of who walks through a door first, the answer is that in many Western societies *she* does—or at least formal etiquette would suggest this is proper. The strong man steps back and defers to the weaker female, graciously holding the door for her (Walum 1974). Yet when it comes to who walks through the metaphorical doors to the professions, it is the man who goes first. Women are served first at restaurants and at other micro-level settings, but this seems little compensation for the fact that doors are often closed to them at the meso and macro levels of social intercourse.

Some scholars even think that language is powerful in shaping the behavior and perceptions of people, as discussed in the chapter on culture. Women often end sentences with tag questions, a pattern that involves ending a declarative statement with a short tag that turns it into a question: "That was a good idea, don't you think?" This pattern may cause male business colleagues to think women are insecure or uncertain about themselves. The women themselves may view it as an invitation to collaboration and dialogue. Yet a perception of insecurity may prevent a woman from getting the job or the promotion. On the flip side, when women stop using these "softening" devices, they are perceived by men to be strident, harsh, or "bitchy" (Wood and Reich 2006).

Other aspects of language may also be important. The same adverb or adjective, when preceded by a male or female pronoun, can take on very different meanings. When one says, "He's easy" or "He's loose," it does not generally mean the same thing as when someone says, "She's easy" or "She's loose." Likewise, there are words such as *slut* for women for which there is no equivalent for men. There is no female equivalent for the term for a man whose wife is making a fool of him by having an affair, a *cuckold*. Why is that? To use another example, the word *spinster* is supposed to be the female synonym for *bachelor*, yet it has very different connotations. Even the more newly coined *bachelorette* is not usually used to describe a highly appealing, perhaps lifelong, role. What might be the implications of these differences?

Those who invoke the biological argument that women are limited by pregnancy, childbirth, or breast-feeding from participating in public affairs and politics ignore the fact that in most societies women play a variety of roles in addition to keeping the home and hearth. They also ignore those societies in which males are deeply involved in nonaggressive and nurturing activities such as child rearing.

THINKING SOCIOLOGICALLY

Some people always write "he" first when writing "he and she." Does this influence gender roles, or is this just fussiness about insignificant matters? Explain.

Sex, Gender, and Sexuality at the Meso Level

By whatever age is defined as "adulthood" in our society, we are expected to assume leadership roles and responsibilities in the institutions of society—carrying out family roles, educating the young, providing health care, teaching principles of one's faith, providing for support through the economic institution, and participating in government. The roles we play in these institutions often differ depending on our sex or gender, which determine our placements and many of our experiences in the social world (Brettell and Sargent 2005).

In most societies, sex and age stipulate when and how we experience *rites of passage* (rituals and formal processes that acknowledge a change of status); these include anything that admits one to adult duties and privileges. Rites of passage are institutionalized in various ways: religious rituals such as bar mitzvah or bat mitzvah ceremonies, which are a bit different for males and females; educational celebrations such as graduation ceremonies, which often involve caps and gowns of gender-specific colors or place females on one side of the room and males on the other; and different ages at which men and women are permitted to marry.

Other institutions segregate us by sex as well: traditional Greek Orthodox Christian churches and Orthodox Jewish synagogues, for example, do not have families seated together. Men sit on one side of the sanctuary and women on the other. Many institutions, including religious, political, and economic organizations, have historically allowed only males to have leadership roles. Only men are to teach the scriptures to the young among traditional Jews, but few men fill that role in contemporary Christian congregations.

Often, women's reduced access to power in micro-level settings has to do with a lack of power and status in meso-level organizations and institutions. This is one reason why policy makers concerned about gender equality have focused so much on inclusion of women in social institutions. For example, micro-credit organizations around the world make small financial loans, primarily to women, to start small businesses in order to support their families. One of these organizations is described in the next Sociology around the World.

Sex, Gender, and Sexuality at the Macro Level

Going to school, driving a car, voting, working—people around the world engage in these necessary activities; yet in some parts of the world, these activities are forbidden for women. When we turn to the national and global level, we again witness inequality between the sexes that is quite separate from any form of personal prejudice or animosity toward women. Patterns of social action that are imbedded in the entire social system may influence women and men, providing unrecognized privileges or disadvantages (McIntosh 1992). This is called *institutionalized discrimination*.

In hunter-gatherer and agricultural societies, women increase their power relative to men as they age and as people gain respect for their wisdom. Especially within a clan or a household, women become masters over their domains (Taylor 1990). Men move from active roles outside the home to passive roles after retirement, while women do the opposite.

The winds of change are influencing the roles of women in many parts of the world as is seen in governing structures. Although women are still denied the right to vote in a few countries, voting is a right in most. In the United States, women have voted for a little over 80 years. Yet in the entire history of the United States, only 32 women have served in the Senate. As of 2005, the number is at an all-time high, with 14 out of 100 senators being women (U.S. Senate 2005 [http://www.senate.gov/index.htm]). Still, the United States is far behind many other countries in this area. The nation with the highest percentage of women in the national parliament or congress is Rwanda (sub–Saharan Africa) at 48.8 percent. The other countries in the top ten, with women constituting at least 35 percent of members in the national legislature, are Sweden (45 percent), Costa Rica and Norway (38 percent), Finland (37.5 percent), Denmark (37 percent), Netherlands (37 percent), Cuba and Spain (36 percent each), and Argentina and Mozambique (35 percent each). Canada is 50th among nations at 21 percent, and the United States ranks 83rd at 15 percent, right between the Cape Verde and Angola and well below Suriname, Bosnia, and Zimbabwe (Inter-Parliamentary Union 2006).

Several factors have been especially effective in increasing women's positions in national parliaments in Africa: the existence of a matriarchal culture (where women may have increased authority and power in decision making), political systems that stress proportional representation, and the adoption of gender quotas for government positions (Yoon 2004). One researcher found that democratization is often linked to a *decrease* in representation by women, a sad reality for those committed to democratization around the world (Yoon 2001). Globally, women's access to power and prestige is highly variable, and northern European countries have a position of leadership when it comes to gender equity in government. (See Table 9.1, Map 9.1.)

(Text continues on page 264)

Sociology around the World

Micro Credits and Empowerment of Women

The 30 village women gather regularly to discuss issues of health, crops, their herds, the predicted rains, goals for their children, and how to make ends meet. They are from a subsistence farming village in southern Niger on the edge of the Sahara desert. Recently, a micro-credit organization was established with a small grant of $1,500 from abroad; with training from Care International, an international nongovernmental organization (NGO), the women selected a board of directors to oversee the loans. Groups of five or six women have joined together to explain their projects to the board and request small loans. Each woman is responsible for paying back a small amount on the loan each week after the project is established and bringing in money.

The women are enthusiastic; in the past they had no funds, and banks charged enormous interest rates on loans. A loan of between $20 and $50 from the micro-credit organization is a tremendous sum considering that for many of these women that is equivalent to six months' earnings. With the new possibilities for their lives, they have big plans: for instance, one group plans to buy a press to make peanut oil, a staple cooking oil in the region. Currently, they must pay a great deal for oil imported from Nigeria. Another group will buy baby lambs, fatten them, and sell them for future festivals at a great profit. Yet another group plans to set up a small bakery. They are also discussing the possibility of making local craft products to sell to foreign fair-trade organizations such as *10,000 Villages* (an organization that markets products made by villagers and returns the profits to the villagers).

Some economists and social policy makers claim that grassroots organizations like micro credits may be the way out of poverty for millions of poor families and that women are motivated to be small entrepreneurs to help support their families and buy education and health care for their children ("Small Fortunes" 2005). Indeed, in 2006, Muhammad Yunus, who founded Grameen Bank—a microcredit lender for the very poor—received the Nobel Prize for Peace.

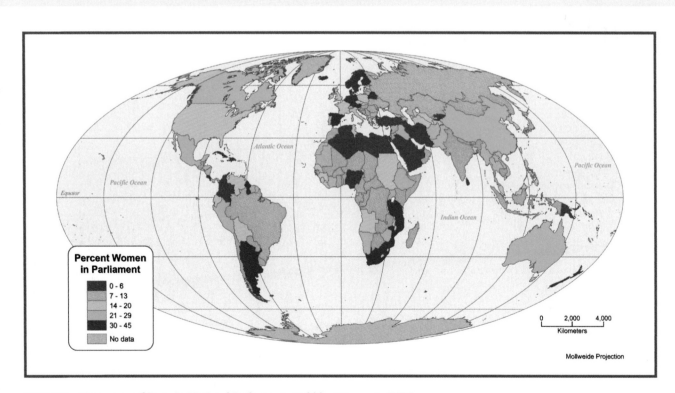

MAP 9.1 Percentage of Seats in National Parliaments Held by Women in 2006

Source: Inter-Parliamentary Union (2006). Map by Anna Versluis.

TABLE 9.1   **Women in National Governments**

Rank	Country	Lower House or Single Chamber			Upper House or Senate		
		Seats	Women	% Women	Seats	Women	% Women
1	Rwanda	80	39	48.8	26	9	34.6
2	Sweden	349	158	45.3	—	—	—
3	Costa Rica	57	22	38.6	—	—	—
4	Norway	169	64	37.9	—	—	—
5	Finland	200	75	37.5	—	—	—
6	Denmark	179	66	36.9	—	—	—
7	Netherlands	150	55	36.7	75	22	29.3
8	Cuba	609	219	36.0	—	—	—
8	Spain	350	126	36.0	259	60	23.2
10	Argentina	257	90	35.0	72	30	41.7
11	Mozambique	250	87	34.8	—	—	—
12	Belgium	150	52	34.7	71	27	38.0
13	Austria	183	62	33.9	62	17	27.4
14	Iceland	63	21	33.3	—	—	—
15	South Africa	400	131	32.8	54	18	33.3
16	New Zealand	121	39	32.2	—	—	—
17	Germany	614	195	31.8	69	13	18.8
18	Guyana	65	20	30.8	—	—	—
19	Burundi	118	36	30.5	49	17	34.7
20	United Republic of Tanzania	319	97	30.4	—	—	—
21	Seychelles	34	10	29.4	—	—	—
22	Peru	120	35	29.2	—	—	—
23	Belarus	110	32	29.1	58	18	31.0
24	Andorra	28	8	28.6	—	—	—
25	Uganda	321	89	27.7	—	—	—
26	Afghanistan	249	68	27.3	102	23	22.5
26	Vietnam	498	136	27.3	—	—	—
28	Namibia	78	21	26.9	26	7	26.9
29	Grenada	15	4	26.7	13	4	30.8
30	Mexico	500	129	25.8	128	28	21.9
31	Iraq	275	70	25.5	—	—	—
32	Suriname	51	13	25.5	—	—	—
33	Timor-Leste	87	22	25.3	—	—	—
34	Switzerland	200	50	25.0	46	11	23.9
35	Australia	150	37	24.7	76	27	35.5
36	Liechtenstein	25	6	24.0	—	—	—
37	Honduras	128	30	23.4	—	—	—
38	Luxembourg	60	14	23.3	—	—	—
39	Laos Democratic Republic	109	25	22.9	—	—	—
40	Tunisia	189	43	22.8	112	15	13.4
41	Bulgaria	240	53	22.1	—	—	—
42	Eritrea	150	33	22.0	—	—	—
42	Lithuania	141	31	22.0	—	—	—
44	Ethiopia	529	116	21.9	112	21	18.8
45	Republic of Moldova	101	22	21.8	—	—	—
46	Croatia	152	33	21.7	—	—	—
47	Pakistan	342	73	21.3	100	17	17.0
48	Portugal	230	49	21.3	—	—	—
49	Latvia	100	21	21.0	—	—	—
50	Canada	308	64	20.8	100	35	35.0
51	Monaco	24	5	20.8	—	—	—
52	Nicaragua	92	19	20.7	—	—	—
53	Poland	460	94	20.4	100	13	13.0
54	China	2980	604	20.3	—	—	—
55	Democratic People's Republic of Korea	687	138	20.1	—	—	—

TABLE 9.1 (Continued)

Rank	Country	Lower House or Single Chamber			Upper House or Senate		
		Seats	Women	% Women	Seats	Women	% Women
56	Bahamas	40	8	20.0	16	7	43.8
57	United Kingdom	646	127	19.7	721	126	17.5
58	Trinidad and Tobago	36	7	19.4	31	10	32.3
59	Guinea	114	22	19.3	—	—	—
60	Senegal	120	23	19.2	—	—	—
60	Macedonia	120	23	19.2	—	—	—
62	Singapore	95	18	18.9	—	—	—
63	Estonia	101	19	18.8	—	—	—
64	Saint Vincent and the Grenadines	22	4	18.2	—	—	—
65	Equatorial Guinea	100	18	18.0	—	—	—
66	Venezuela	167	30	18.0	—	—	—
67	Tajikistan	63	11	17.5	34	8	23.5
68	Uzbekistan	120	21	17.5	100	15	15.0
69	Italy	630	109	17.3	322	44	13.7
70	Mauritius	70	12	17.1	—	—	—
71	Czech Republic	200	34	17.0	81	10	12.3
72	Bolivia	130	22	16.9	27	1	3.7
73	Bosnia and Herzegovina	42	7	16.7	15	0	0.0
73	El Salvador	84	14	16.7	—	—	—
73	Panama	78	13	16.7	—	—	—
73	San Marino	60	10	16.7	—	—	—
73	Slovakia	150	25	16.7	—	—	—
78	Ecuador	100	16	16.0	—	—	—
79	Turkmenistan	50	8	16.0	—	—	—
80	Zimbabwe	150	24	16.0	66	21	31.8
81	Philippines	236	37	15.7	24	4	16.7
82	Cape Verde	72	11	15.3	—	—	—
83	United States	435	66	15.2	100	14	14.0
84	Angola	220	33	15.0	—	—	—
85	Chile	120	18	15.0	38	2	5.3
86	Bangladesh	345	51	14.8	—	—	—
87	Sudan	450	66	14.7	50	2	4.0
88	Sierra Leone	124	18	14.5	—	—	—
89	Cyprus	56	8	14.3	—	—	—
90	Israel	120	17	14.2	—	—	—
Lowest rankings							
	Oman	83	2	2.4	58	9	15.5
	Egypt	442	9	2.0	264	18	6.8
	Haiti	99	2	2.0	29	4	13.8
	Kuwait	65	1	1.5	—	—	—
	Papua New Guinea	109	1	0.9	—	—	—
	Yemen	301	1	0.3	111	2	1.8
	Bahrain	40	0	0.0	40	6	15.0
	Kyrgyzstan	72	0	0.0	—	—	—
	Micronesia	14	0	0.0	—	—	—
	Nauru	18	0	0.0	—	—	—
	Palau	16	0	0.0	9	0	0.0
	Qatar	35	0	0.0	—	—	—
	Saint Kitts and Nevis	15	0	0.0	—	—	—
	Saudi Arabia	150	0	0.0	—	—	—
	Solomon Islands	50	0	0.0	—	—	—
	Tuvalu	15	0	0.0	—	—	—
	United Arab Emirates	40	0	0.0	—	—	—

Source: Inter-Parliamentary Union (2006).

Cross-cultural analyses do confirm that gender roles either evolve over centuries or transform by sweeping reform laws such as voting rights. The fact that women in China generally work outside the home while women in some Muslim societies hardly venture from their homes, is due to differences in cultural norms dictating gender roles that are learned through the socialization process.

GENDER SOCIALIZATION: MICRO- AND MESO-LEVEL ANALYSES

The old adage says, "Sugar and spice and everything nice–that's what little girls are made of. Snips and snails and puppy dog tails–that's what little boys are made of." As the verse implies, different views of little girls and little boys start at birth, based on gender and stereotypes about what is biologically natural. Behavioral expectations stem from cultural beliefs about the nature of men and women, and these expectations guide socialization from the earliest ages and in intimate primary group settings.

Socialization into gender is the process by which people learn the cultural norms, attitudes, and behaviors appropriate to their gender; that is, they learn how to think and act as boys or girls, women or men. Socialization reinforces the "proper" gender behaviors, and punishes the improper behaviors. This process, in turn, reinforces gender stereotypes. In many societies, traits of gentleness, passivity, and dependence are associated with femininity, while boldness, aggression, strength, and independence are identified with masculinity. For instance, in most Western societies, aggression in women is considered unfeminine, if not inappropriate or disturbed; likewise, the gentle, unassertive male is often looked upon with scorn or pity, stigmatized as a "wimp." Expectations related to these stereotypes are rigid in many societies (Pollack 1999).

Stages in Gender Socialization
Gender socialization takes place through a series of life stages, discussed in Chapter 4 on socialization. Examples from infancy and childhood show how socialization into gender roles takes place.

Infancy
Learning about our gender roles begins at birth. Parents in the United States describe their newborn daughters as soft, delicate, fine-featured, little, beautiful, pretty, cute, awkward, and resembling their mothers. They depict their sons as strong, firm, alert, and well-coordinated (Lindsey 2005; Rubin 1974). Clothing, room decor, and toys also reflect notions of gender; for instance, in Spain, parents and grandparents dress babies and their carriages in pink or blue, proudly showing off the little ones to friends as they promenade in the evenings.

Although these stereotypes have declined in recent years, they continue to affect the way we handle and treat male and female infants (Karraker 1995). When people know they are holding baby girls, they are gentle; when they are holding boys, they are more likely to bounce them or to roughhouse with the child.

Childhood
Once out of infancy, research shows that many boys are encouraged to be more independent and exploratory, while girls are protected from situations that might prove harmful. More pressure is put on boys to behave in "gender appropriate" ways. Boys are socialized into "the boy code" that provides rigid guidelines (see How Do We Know?). Cross-cultural studies show boys often get more attention than girls because of their behavior, with an emphasis on achievement and autonomy for boys (Kimmel and Messner 2004).

THINKING SOCIOLOGICALLY

First, read The Boy Code essay on the facing page. What evidence to you see of the boy code when you observe your friends and relatives? What is the impact of the boy code?

In a majority of societies, the stereotype of soft, nonaggressive, noncompetitive, diminutive women is reinforced in many subtle ways, including the names parents select. Boys are more often given strong, hard names that end in consonants, such as Bill, Tom, Peter, and John. Girls are more likely to be given soft pretty names with vowel endings such as Linda, Wendy, Patricia, Christina, Debbie, Kathy, or Susie. Alternatively, they may be given feminized versions of boys' names—Roberta, Jessica, Josephine, Nicole, Michelle, or Donna. Sometimes, boys' names are given to girls without first feminizing them. Names such as Lynn, Stacey, Tracey, Faye, Dana, Jody, Lindsay, Robin, and Carmen used to be names exclusively for men, but once they were applied to girls, the use for boys dropped off within a decade or two. So a name that is a male's name may for a time be given to either sex, but then is relegated primarily to girls. The pattern rarely goes the other direction because once feminized the names seem to be less acceptable for males (Berry and Harper 1993; Lieberson, Dumais, and Bauman 2000).

In the early childhood years, children become aware of their own gender identity; as they reach school-age, they learn that their sex is permanent and they begin to categorize behaviors that are appropriate for their sex. As children are rewarded for performing proper gender roles, these roles are reinforced. That reinforcement solidifies gender roles, setting the stage for later life gender-related interactions, behaviors, and choices.

The Boy Code

In Chapter 5, we mentioned the Old Boy network in American society—a system that favors adult men through networks. This system actually starts with "the boy code," the rules about boys' proper behavior. Young boys learn "the code" from parents, siblings, peers, teachers, and society in general. They are praised for adhering to the code and punished for violating its dictates. The boy code is ingrained in society; by five or six years of age, boys are less likely than girls to express hurt or distress. They have learned to be ashamed of showing feelings and of being weak. William Pollack (1999) writes that boys learn several stereotyped behavior models exemplifying the boy code.

1. "The sturdy oak": men should be stoic, stable and independent; a man never shows weakness.

2. "Give 'em hell": from athletic coaches and movie heroes, the consistent theme is extreme daring, bravado, and attraction to violence.

3. "The 'big wheel'": men and boys should achieve status, dominance, and power; they should avoid shame, wear the mask of coolness, and act as though everything is under control.

4. "No sissy stuff": Boys are prohibited from expressing feelings or urges perceived as feminine—dependence, warmth, empathy.

This gender straitjacket, according to Pollack, causes boys to conceal feelings in order to fit in and be accepted and loved. As a result, some boys, especially in adolescence, become silent, covering any vulnerability and masking their true feelings. This affects boys' relationships, performance in school, and ability to connect with others. Since not all cultures define masculinity in this way, social scientists do not believe these traits are rooted in biological programming.

Pollack (1999) suggests that we can help troubled boys reconnect by

1. giving some undivided attention each day just listening to boys;

2. encouraging a range of emotions;

3. avoiding language that taunts, teases, or shames;

4. looking behind the veneer of "coolness" for signs of problems;

5. expressing love and empathy;

6. dispelling the "sturdy oak" image; and

7. advocating a broad, inclusive model of masculinity.

To obtain his information for his study, reported in *Real Boys*, Pollack (1999) relied on several data collection methods. He used his notes from over 20 years of working with men and boys as codirector of the Center for Men at McLean Hospital and Harvard Medical School. This provided data and professional notes on the lives of hundreds of young and adolescent boys. In addition, he observed boys in various situations from homes to sports fields, and he interviewed parents of boys.

His questions to boys evoked candid responses on questions about home life, school, friends, and emotional lives. Pollack's involvement in the project, Listening to Boys' Voices, provided information that spurred him to find more information about boy's lives. For instance, boys are two times as likely as girls to be labeled "learning disabled" and as having ADD (attention deficit disorder); in addition, 67 percent of students in special education classes are boys. The complexity of the issues related to studying boys led Pollack to use multiple methods to study and write about boys' lives.

With the women's movement and shifts in gender expectations have come new patterns of male behavior. Some men are forming more supportive and less competitive relationships with other men, and there are likely to be continued changes in and broadening of "appropriate" behavior for men (Kimmel and Messner 2004; Nardi 1992; Stoltenberg 1993).

Babies are often treated quite differently by parents, even if they are not consciously aware they are doing so. The child picks up the messages about what is appropriate or inappropriate for someone of her or his sex.

Source: © Darama / Corbis.

THINKING SOCIOLOGICALLY

Identify a particular gender-specific ritual or activity you have seen or have participated in. What peer, family, or societal expectations surrounded it?

Meso-Level Agents of Gender Socialization
Clues to proper gender roles surround children in materials produced by corporations (books, toys, games), in mass media images, in educational settings, and in religious organizations and beliefs. In Chapter 4 on socialization, we learned about agents of socialization. Those agents play a major role in teaching children proper gender roles. The following examples demonstarate how organizations and institutions in our society teach and reinforce gender assumptions and roles.

Corporations
Corporations have produced materials that help socialize children into proper conduct. Publishers, for example, produce books that present images of expected gender behavior; language and pictures in preschool picture books, elementary children's books, and school textbooks are steeped in gender role messages reflecting society's expectations and stereotypes. In a classic study of award winning children's books from the United States that have sold more than 3,000,000 copies, Weitzman (Weitzman et al. 1972) made several observations: (1) males appear more often in stories, sometimes as male animal characters; (2) activities of male and female characters in books differ, with boys playing active roles and girls being passive or simply helping brothers, fathers, or husbands; (3) adult women are pictured as more passive and dependent, and few women are depicted as working outside the home; and (4) males are depicted carrying out a range of activities and jobs (Weitzman et al. 1972).

A young man gives a young woman an old fashioned noogie, rubbing his knuckle against the top of her head, much to her dismay. Such physically dominating behavior is common for boys and is laughed off in many cases; a girl who did the same thing is likely to be scolded for the behavior.

Source: © Rasmus Rasmussen.

Boys and girls begin to conform to gender expectations even more once they are old enough to understand that their sex is rather permanent, that boys are not capable of becoming "mommies." They become even more conscious of adhering to norms of others in their gender category.

Source: © Lucas Hrubizna; © Jostein Hauge.

Although more recent books show some expansion in the roles book characters play, studies confirm a continuing pattern of gender role segregation in children's books (Anderson and Hamilton 2005; Diekman and Murmen 2004; Williams et al.1987). Whether Peter Rabbit, Curious

George the Monkey, or Babar the Elephant (popular childhood book characters), the male animal characters in books outnumber females. Males of any species most often are portrayed as adventurous, brave, competent, clever, and fun, while female counterparts are depicted as incompetent, fearful, and dependent on others (Davis 1984; Purcell and Stewart 1990). Moreover, even though authors and publishers have begun producing books presenting unbiased gender roles, the tens of thousands of older, classic, books in public and school libraries mean that a parent or child picking a book off of the shelf is still likely to select a book that has stereotypical views of boys and girls.

Producers of toys and games also contributed to traditional messages about gender. Store-bought toys fill rooms in homes of children in the Western world, and it is usually quite clear which are boys' rooms and which are girls.' Boys' rooms are filled with sports equipment, army toys, building and technical toys, and cars and trucks. Girls' rooms have fewer toys, and most are related to dolls and domestic roles. Boys have more experience manipulating blocks, Tinker Toys, Legos, and Erector sets—toys paralleling masculinized activities outside the home in the public domain, from constructing and building trades to military roles and sports. Girls prepare for domestic roles with toys relating to domestic activities. Barbie dolls stress physical appearance, consumerism, and glamour. Only a few Barbies are in occupational roles; the Ken dolls that Mattel designed to match Barbie (and recently discontinued) were often doctors or other professionals. An analysis of Barbie Computers for girls and Hot Wheels Computers for boys reveals differences in what they teach children, as illustrated in Table 9.2:

A young girl picks out the Barbie dolls she wants. Mattel's Barbie dolls have been heavily criticized for extremely traditional and highly sexualized images of young women.

Source: © Lynn Goldsmith / Corbis.

TABLE 9.2 **Toys That Teach**

In 2000, a major toy company, the Mattel Corporation, produced two computers. The Barbie model was designed with girls as the target market, and a Hot Wheels model was developed for boys. These models differed in more than simple appearance. The two computers had different software installed in them, including different educational programs. Researchers found the following:

Only Barbie Has	Only Hot Wheels Has	Both Models Have
Fashion designer	Cluefinders math 9–12	A 3D world atlas
Detective Barbie	Compton's complete reference collection	Math workshop
Miscellaneous Barbie accessories	Kid pix studio	Typing tutorial
	Logical journey	National geographic: The 90s
	Zoombinis (thinking game)	Writing and creativity center
	A human anatomy and 3D visualization program	

The Mattel Corporation claimed that the popular Barbie software, involving "accessories" for Barbie, consumed too much space on the Barbie model computer to include the educational software that was on the Hot Wheels computer.

Source: Headlam (2000); Kramer (2001).

Each toy or game helps enact *anticipatory socialization* for future gender roles. Toys that require building, manipulating, and technical skills provide experiences for later life. Choices ranging from college major and occupational choice to activities that depend on visual-spatial and mathematical interests and abilities appear to be affected by these early choices and childhood learning experiences (Tavris and Wade 1984). Consider the example of Dungeons and Dragons, a popular game primarily among adolescent boys in Europe, Japan, and North America. The participants role-play their way through scenarios full of demons and dragons, using a vast array of weapons and magical spells. The boys develop characters that they impersonate throughout the game as they negotiate, bargain, create, imitate, and develop a variety of other social or cognitive skills. They must calculate complex mathematical formulae and use logic and imagination—all skills that will aid them in coping with the adult public world. The packaging of this product makes it clear it is a boys' activity; only a few girls become players.

Mass Media

Mass media in their many forms—magazines, ads, films, music videos, Internet sites—are major agents of socialization into gender roles (Walters 1999). Young men and women, desiring to fit in, are influenced by messages from the media. For instance, the epidemic of steroid use among boys and dieting among girls is a health concern in the United States (Taub and McLorg 2007); yet manufacturers advertise such products with promises to remake teens into more attractive people.

Video games that dehumanize women teach and perpetuate stereotypes about women. A scandal arose in 2003 over a video game, "Hunting for Bambi," and subsequent claims that the game was being played "in reality."

This video game featured men hunting in a forest for naked women and shooting them with paintballs; critics condemned it as violent, degrading, and voyeuristic—a dehumanizing of women. Women in such videos become objects to be exploited. They raise the question of whether society would allow videos called "Hunting Italian Americans," "Hunting African Americans," or "Hunting Jewish Americans" (Glass 2003).

Some action films produced within the past decade include adventurous and competent girls and women, helping to counter images as the ones the video described above. Hermoine in *Harry Potter* is intelligent and creative; Queen of Naboo and Senator Amidala in *Star Wars: Episode II* is strong, brave, intelligent (and beautiful); and Lara Croft in *Tomb Raiders* holds her own against evil. However, videos depicting highly competent females are few, and most of those few women are highly attractive and unrealistically thin.

Television is another powerful socializing agent. By the time they start school, average English, Canadian, and U.S. children will have spent more time in front of a television than in classrooms in the coming 12 years. Television presents a simple, stereotyped view of life, from advertisements to situation comedies to soap operas. Male characters outnumber women two-to-one on prime-time television (Davis 1990; Gerbner 1998). Women in soap operas and ads, especially those working outside the home, are often depicted as having problems in carrying out their role responsibilities (Benokraitis and Feagin 1995). Even the extraordinary powers of superheroes on Saturday morning television depict the female characters as having gender-stereotyped skills such as super-intuition. Notice the next time you are in a video game room that the fighting characters are typically male and often in armor. When fighting women do appear, they are usually clad in skin-revealing bikini-style attire—odd clothing in which to do battle!

Films and television series in the United States seldom feature average-sized or older women (although one does see more variety of ages and body types in the British Broadcasting Company productions). Movie stars are attractive and thin, presenting an often unattainable model for young women, making many feel inadequate and feeding the diet frenzy (Kramer 2005; Taub and McLorg 2007). Women who are quite large are almost entirely comic figures in U.S. television.

How do social scientists know that television affects gender role socialization? Studies have shown that the more television children watch, the more gender stereotypes they hold. From cartoons to advertisements, television in many countries provides enticing images of a world in which youth is glorified, age is scorned, and female and male roles are stereotyped and/or unattainable (Kilbourne 2000; Tuchman 1993, 1996).

THINKING SOCIOLOGICALLY

Think of recent mass media examples that you have seen. How do they depict women and men? How might the depictions affect young men and women, if at all?

Educational Systems

Even centers of learning bolster sex-specific expectations and limitations. Educational systems are socialization agents of children through textbooks, classroom activities, playground games, and teachers' attitudes. For example, boys are encouraged to join competitive team sports and girls to support them (Gilligan 1982; Kramer 2001); these simulate hierarchical adult roles of boss/secretary and physician/nurse. Furthermore, the team sports that the boys learn teach them *strategic thinking*—a critical skill that involves anticipating the moves of the opponent and countering with one's own strategy. This is a very useful skill in the business world and is not explicitly taught in other places in the school curriculum. Girls' games rarely teach this skill.

Children's experiences in grade and middle school reinforce boundaries of "us" and "them" in classroom seating and activities, in the lunchroom, and in playground activities, as girls and boys are seated, lined up, and given assignments by sex (Sadker and Sadker 1994). Those who go outside the boundaries, especially boys, are ridiculed by peers and sometimes teachers, reinforcing stereotypes and separate gender role socialization (Sadker and Sadker 2005; Thorne 1993).

Boys act out and receive more attention in school classrooms than girls do, even though it may be negative attention. In classrooms, boys are called on more often to do physical chores such as erasing the boards and emptying the trash. Teachers reward girls for being passive and obedient (Sadker and Sadker 1985, 1993, 2005).

Actress Lindsay Lohan, star of the film Mean Girls, *poses (top) as she arrives at the film's premiere in Hollywood. Lohan portrays a 15-year-old girl, and like most actresses, she must conform to the image of very thin, shapely femininity. Roseanne Barr (bottom) is also a successful actress, but as a much fuller figured woman, her roles are limited to comedic figures.*

Source: © Fred Prouser / Reuters / Corbis; © Lynn Goldsmith / Corbis.

High school and college women's athletics are much less reliable paths to being known and visible on campus since so few people come to the games. Even at the professional level, Shannon Johnson of the Connecticut Sun drives to the hoop against Annie Burgess of the Washington Mystics before a rather small crowd.

Source: © Greg Fiume / NewSport / Corbis.

Boys begin at young ages to work and play together as teams. Girls also join team sports, but their play more frequently involves one-on-one activities. Boys learn the skills of competition, negotiating, bargaining, aggressiveness, good sportsmanship, and strategic thinking. Girls learn good nurturing skills in their play and are often on the sidelines as cheerleaders and supporters for boys activities.

Part of the issue of male-female inequality in schools is tied to the issue of popularity, which it seems has less to do with being liked than with being known. For a girl, if everyone knows her name, she is popular (Eder, Evans, and Parker 1995). At the middle-school level, there are more ways that boys can become known. Even when there are both boys' and girls' basketball teams, many spectators come to the boys' contests and very few to the girls' games. Thus, few people know

the female athletes' names. In fact, a far more visible position is cheerleader—standing on the sidelines cheering for the boys—because those girls are at least visible (Eder et al. 1995). The other major way in which girls are visible or known is physical appearance, a major standard of popularity and esteem (Eder et al. 1995). There are simply far more visible positions for the boys than for girls in middle school.

Title IX of the U.S. Educational Amendments Act of 1972 was a major legislative attempt to level the educational playing field. Passed to bar gender discrimination in schools receiving federal funds, this legislation mandates equal opportunity for participation in school-sponsored programs (Lindsey 2005). The law has reduced or eliminated blatant discrimination in admissions, health care, counseling, housing, sex-segregated programs, financial aid, dress codes, and other areas that were of concern. However, the biggest impact of Title IX legislation has been in athletics. Women's athletic programs and scholarships benefited from the law with a resulting increase in women's opportunities and participation. Forty percent of college women participate in sports programs (Fox 1995); one-third of high school women participate in sports compared to 45 percent of males. In performing arts, academic clubs, yearbook, and student government, about one-third of women and 20 percent of men in high school participate (National Center for Education Statistics 2004). However, some men's programs such as wrestling have been cut back to save money in order to provide more equitable funding for all sports programs.

Religious Beliefs

Religious beliefs serve as agents of socialization by reinforcing and perpetuating gender role stereotypes and cultural beliefs. Religious teachings provide explanations of birth, death, and the reason for living, so it is only natural to find notions of proper male/female roles. Although the specific teachings vary, the three major monotheistic religions that affirm that there is only one God—Christianity, Islam, and Judaism—are traditionally patriarchal, stressing separate female and male spheres (Ahmed 1993; Kramer 2005). The following are examples of some of these traditional role expectations and the status of women in various religions.

Some interpretations of the Adam and Eve creation story in the Hebrew Bible (which is the Old Testament of the Christian Bible) state that because man was created first, men are therefore superior; because Eve, created from the rib of man, was a sinner, her sins keep women forever in an inferior, second-class position. For these reasons, in some branches of these religions, women are restricted in their roles within family and religious organizations; they cannot be priests in Catholic churches and cannot vote on business matters in some religious organizations. However, recent work by feminist scholars is challenging the notion of patriarchy in Judaic and Christian history, pointing out that women may have played a much broader role in religious development than currently recognized (Hunter College

Women's Studies Collective 2005; Murphy 1993). Even the name Yahweh—the name for God in the Hebrew Bible—had both male and female connotations, and when God is referred to as a source of wisdom, feminine pronouns and references were used (Borg 1994). Increasingly, denominations are allowing women greater roles in the religious hierarchies, ministries, and priesthood.

Women in Judaism lived for 4,000 years in a patriarchal system where men read, taught, and legislated while women followed (Lindsey 2005). Today, three of the four main branches of Judaism allow women equal participation, illustrating that religious practices do change over time. However, Hasidic and Orthodox Jews have a division of labor between men and women following old laws, with designated roles for the home and religious life.

Some Christian teachings have treated women as second-class citizens, even in the eyes of God. For this reason, some Christian denominations have excluded women from a variety of leadership roles and told them they must be subservient to their husbands. Other Christians point to the admonition by Saint Paul that theologically speaking, "There is no such thing as . . . male and female, for you are all one in Christ Jesus." This suggests that women and men are not to be stratified as spiritually different (Galatians 3:28).

Traditional Hindu religion painted women as seductresses, strongly erotic, and a threat to male spirituality and asceticism. To protect men from this threat, women were kept totally covered in thick garments and veils and seen only by men in their immediate families. Today, Hinduism comes in many forms, most of which honor the domestic sphere of life—mothers, wives, and homemakers—while accepting women in public roles, depending on the woman's caste position (Lindsey 2005).

Traditional Islamic beliefs also portrayed female sexuality as dangerous to men. The Quran (also spelled Qur'an or Koran), the Muslim sacred scriptures, includes a statement that men are superior to women because of the qualities God has given men. Hammurabi's Code, written in the Middle East between 2067 and 2025 BCE, is the earliest recorded legal system; the laws about women's status were written to distinguish between decent women, belonging to one man, and indecent or public women. Aspects of this tradition have carried over to present times.

Women in fundamentalist Muslim societies such as Algeria, Iran, Syria, and Saudi Arabia are separated from men (except for fathers and brothers) in work and worship. They generally remain covered. *Purdah,* which means curtain, refers to practices of seclusion and separate worlds for women and men in Islamic cultures. Screens in households and veils in public enforce female modesty and prevent men from seeing women (Ward and Edelstein 2006). Today, some women argue that the veil they wear is for modesty, cosmetic purposes, or to protect them from stares of men; others claim that the veil is a symbol of oppression and subservience, showing that women must keep themselves in submissive positions.

By contrast to women athletes who are the stars of the action in front of minuscule crowds, women in very sexy outfits are highly visible when they perform as cheerleaders in front of 80,000 fans at the Dallas Cowboys games.

Source: © S. Carmona / Corbis.

Most major religious groups have branches, both traditional fundamentalism adhering to literal interpretations of religious texts and modern branches that have changed to accommodate to the modern world. Even governments and legal systems interpret and enforce religious laws differently, as seen in news stories replete with conflicts between modern and fundamentalist Christian, Muslim, Jewish, and Hindu groups.

A major reason most societies have laws, taboos, and other cultural expectations to control the sexual behavior of their members is so that family lines are secure. Some religions condone a man divorcing a woman who does not produce a male heir or the severe punishment or death of a woman who has sex before or outside of marriage. Recent reports tell of a woman in Nigeria who had a child out of wedlock and another woman in Pakistan who was a rape victim; both were condemned to death by stoning; this is an example of strict Islamic law, called Sharia. In both cases, the women suffered social humiliation and degradation and potentially the ultimate sacrifice of death. Protests from within and outside the societies have postponed these death penalties (Mydans 2002).

Religious laws often provide the justifications to keep women servile, and public shaming and threat of severe punishments reinforce the laws. Meso-level religious systems influence how different societies interpret proper gender roles and how sometimes these belief systems change with new interpretations of scriptures.

All of these agents of socialization—corporations, mass media, schools, and religious groups—reinforce "appropriate" gender roles in each society.

THINKING SOCIOLOGICALLY

What are some books, toys, childhood games, television shows, school experiences, religious teachings, and peer interactions that influenced your gender role socialization? In what ways did they do so?

GENDER STRATIFICATION: MESO- AND MACRO-LEVEL PROCESSES

The invisible glass ceiling and the "sticky floor" restrain women from reaching high levels in corporate structures and keep women around the world in low-paying jobs since they are not part of the network (Hunter College Women's Studies Collective 2005; Kimmel 2003). "The *glass ceiling* keeps women from reaching the highest levels of corporate and public responsibility, and the 'sticky floor' keeps the vast majority of the world's women stuck in low-paid jobs" (Hunter College Women's Studies Collective 2005:393). Men on the other hand face the "glass escalator," especially in traditionally female occupations; even if they do not seek to climb in the organizational hierarchy, occupational social forces push them up the job ladder into higher echelons (Williams 1992). Women make up more than 40 percent of the world's paid workforce but hold only around 20 percent of managerial

jobs, and for those they are often compensated at lower pay than their male counterparts. Only 5 percent of the top corporate jobs are held by women. However, companies with women in leadership positions do realize high profits (Adler 2001; Hunter College Women's Studies Collective 2005).

Gendered Organizations

"People have a gender, which rubs off on the jobs they do. The jobs in turn have a gender character that rubs off on the people that do them" (Cockburn 1988:38). At each level of analysis in organizational settings, gender is a major factor in our personal and work lives; it pervades all aspects of organizations, from day-to-day practices of organizations to gender ideologies to distributions of power (Acker 1990, 1992). For instance, what do women who are breastfeeding their babies do when the organization does not provide space or place for this? Must they quit their jobs or alter their family schedules? Many women have multiple responsibilities: work to support their families, be good mothers, and be good workers. Men do not face the same issues because most corporations assume the average worker is male.

Research in organizations has considered a number of issues related to the experiences of individuals; for example, in occupations that are predominantly one sex or the other, is there gender bias? One finding is that workers are more satisfied when the sex composition of their work group and distribution of men and women in power is balanced (Britton 2000:430). Whether or not our gendered behaviors in organizations reproduce inequality in organizations influences the experiences and opportunities we have in organizations. Feminists propose ideas to minimize gender differences in organizations, that is, to "degender" organizations, so that all members have equal opportunities (Britton 2000).

THINKING SOCIOLOGICALLY

If corporate structures were reversed so that women structured and organized the workplace, how might the workplace environment change?

Institutionalized Gender Discrimination

Gender stratification at the meso level—like race and ethnic stratification—can occur quite independently of any overt prejudice or ill-will by others. It becomes part of the social system, and we are not even conscious of it, especially if we are one of the privileged members of society. Most of what has been discussed so far is *de jure* discrimination, done deliberately because of cultural images of women as inferior or fundamentally different from men. The more subtle process of *de facto* discrimination (which is not intended) also needs our attention. When inequality is woven into the web of the macro-level social structure and becomes taken for

Little girls learn to use their voices and to hold their bodies and gesture in ways that communicate deference. Note the earlier photo of Roseanne Barr; she is a comedian, but she tilts her head to the side—a sign of deference—in promotional shots. This makes her more acceptable to the public.

Source: © Pathathai Chungyam.

TABLE 9.3	**U.S. Income by Educational Level and Sex (in dollars)**	
Education	**Men**	**Women**
Not a high school graduate	28,345	16,075
High school graduate	40,119	23,143
Some college; no degree	48,812	26,720
College graduate (bachelor's)	71,140	40,200
Master's degree	85,700	48,535
Doctorate	105,928	73,516
Professional degree	148,611	72,594

Source: U.S. Census Bureau, Current Population Survey (2005).

granted, it is called *institutional discrimination*. It can include intentional actions such as bank policies requiring single women, compared with single men, to have three times as much money up-front for a house down payment in order to receive a homeowners loan; but it also includes unintentional actions that have consequences that disadvantage women. Unintentional (de facto) inequity usually happens through side-effect discrimination or through past-in-present discrimination (Feagin and Feagin 1986, 2003). *Side-effect discrimination* involves practices in one institution that are linked to practices in another institution; they have an effect that is not anticipated or even recognized by most people in the society. For instance, if family life is highly regulated by gender expectations, as research shows it to be, then women find it more difficult to devote themselves to gaining job promotions. Furthermore, as long as little girls learn to use their voices and to hold their bodies and gesture in ways that communicate deference, employers assume a lack of the self-confidence necessary for major leadership roles. If women are paid less despite the same levels of education (see Table 9.3), they are likely to have less access to expensive health care or to be able to afford a $20,000 down payment for a house unless they are married. This makes women dependent on men in a way that most men are not dependent on women.

A factor affecting differences in incomes is the type of degree that men and women receive (engineering rather than education) as well as a difference in the typical number of years women have spent in their professional fields; that is, there are fewer women senior law partners in part because women who are now in their 50s or older were often not

admitted to professional graduate programs in the 1960s and 70s. However, even when these human capital differences are factored in, men still make considerably more on average than women with identical levels of experience and training.

Men often get defensive and angry when people talk about sexism in society because they feel they are being attacked or asked to correct injustices of the past. However, the empirical reality is that the playing field is not level for men and women. Most men do not do anything to intentionally harm women, and they may not feel prejudiced toward women. Sexism can operate so that men are given privileges they never asked for and may not recognize.

Past-in-present discrimination refers to practices from the past that may no longer be allowed but that continue to affect people today. At an appliance industry in the Midwest investigated by one of the authors, there is a sequence of jobs one must hold to be promoted up the line to foreman. This requirement ensures that the foreman understands the many aspects of the production at the plant. One of the jobs involves working in a room with heavy equipment that cuts through and bends metal sheets. The machine is extremely powerful and could easily cut off a leg or hand if the operator is not careful. Because of the danger, the engineers designed the equipment so it would not operate unless three levers were activated at the same time. One lever was triggered by stepping on a pedal on the floor. The other two required reaching out with one's hands so that one's body was extended. When one was spread-eagled to activate all three levers, there was no way one could possibly have a part of one's body near the blades. It was brilliant engineering. There was one unanticipated problem: the hand-activated levers were 5 feet 10 inches off the ground and 5 feet apart. Few women had the height and arm span to run this machine, and therefore no women had yet made it through the sequence of positions to the higher paying position of foreman. The equipment cost millions of dollars, so it was not likely to be replaced. Neither the engineers who designed the machine nor the upper-level managers who established the sequence of jobs to become foreman

In some countries, there is a huge gender digital divide; in others, nearly as many women as men use computers. However, research shows that they tend to use computers in different ways. These women in India are learning computer skills.

Source: © Owen Franken / Corbis.

had deliberately tried to exclude women. Indeed, they were perplexed when they looked at their employee figures and saw so few women moving up through the ranks. The cause of women's disadvantage was not mean-spirited men but features of the system that had unintended consequences. The barriers women face, then, are not just matters of socialization or other micro-level social processes. The nature of sexism is often subtle and pervasive in the society, operating at the meso and macro levels as institutional discrimination.

Gender Differences in Internet Use

One specific form of institutionalized difference in access to resources at the global level has to do with the Internet. Knowledge of events in the world, job skills, awareness of job openings, networks that extend beyond national borders, and other resources are available through the Internet. Yet globally,

there is a larger digital divide in gender than any other category (Drori 2006). The difference in Internet use by women as a percentage of all users varies significantly by country: Swedish and Danish women are roughly 45 percent of Internet users in their countries, Israelis a bit over 40 percent, Chinese around 30 percent, Senegalese 17 percent, and Ethiopians 14 percent. In the Arab world, women account for only 4 percent of the online population; in Kenya, a 1999 survey in two provinces found that 99 percent of the women had never heard of the Internet. Several other countries are close to equal in usage by women: Mexico at 46 percent, South Africa and Thailand each at 49 percent, and the United States at 51 percent (Drori 2006). Even in these countries, it has only been in the past few years that women's usage has climbed to that level; in 1996, U.S. women's usage was only 38 percent (Drori 2006:53).

Chapter 7, on stratification, explored global differences in Internet usage and found that the largest variance was based on wealth of the country and access to technology. The same principle holds for women's usage. While many African countries may have only half of 1 percent of the population online, in none of the African countries cited by Drori (2006) do women have more than 15 percent of that tiny share. So of the women in most African countries, fewer than 7 out of 10,000 have used the Internet. Clearly, the majority of women are "out of the digital loop."

Internet-related gender stratification exhibits itself not just in terms of whether a person uses the Internet but also in terms of how a person uses the Internet. Even within industrialized countries such as the United States, women tend to use mostly e-mail services, with the intent of keeping up with family and friends (Shade 2004). For men, the Internet is used to gather information and to exchange ideas and facts relevant to professional activities. Thus, "women are using the internet to reinforce their private lives and men are using the internet for engaging in the public sphere" (Shade 2004:63). The difference has to do with choices men and women make but also reflects differences in the professional positions men and women hold. For men, the Internet is enhancing their careers; this is far less true for women. However, things do change very rapidly in the world of the Internet.

THINKING SOCIOLOGICALLY

Ask several people from different generations how they use computer technology and the Internet and how they learned these skills. What do you conclude?

GENDER STRATIFICATION: MICRO-TO MACRO-LEVEL THEORIES

In recent years, some biologists and psychologists have considered whether there are innate differences in the make-up of

A newborn infant rests in his father's embrace. Some biologists have argued that this is a role that is more natural and comfortable for females, but this father seems very at ease in the caretaker role.

Source: © Tari Faris.

interaction perspective has been forceful in insisting that notions of gender are not intrinsically related to a person's sex. The bottom line is that gender is a socially created or constructed idea, not one that emanates from one's biological traits (Mason-Schrock 1996).

Who should open the door? Traditional notions of gender are hard to change because confusion over proper masculine and feminine roles creates anxiety and even anomie. People want guidelines; thus, it is easier to adhere to traditional definitions. Traditional notions of gender are often reinforced by religious dogmas and beliefs, making those ideas appear sacred, absolute, and beyond human change. Absolute answers are comforting to those who find change disconcerting. Others believe the male prerogatives and privileges of the past were established by men to protect their rights. Any change in concepts of gender or of roles assigned to males and females will be hard to bring about precisely because they are part of the meaning system in the social world.

Not only do some cultures suggest that women are helpless and need the door held for them, but women's stylish attire—such as many forms of shoes and many dresses—actually does make them more vulnerable and helpless.

Source: © Royalty-Free / Corbis.

women and men. For instance, males produce more testosterone, a hormone found to be correlated with aggression. Research does show that in many situations, males tend to be more aggressive and concerned with dominance, whether the behavior is biologically programmed or learned or both; but other traits, such as nurturance, empathy, or altruism, show no clear gender difference (Fausto-Sterling 1992; Pinker 2002). Although biological and psychological factors are part of the difference between females and males, our focus here is on the major contribution that social factors make in social statuses of males and females in human society. This section explores social theories that explain gender differences.

Symbolic Interactionism: Micro-Level Analysis

Symbolic interactionists look at gender as socially constructed. While sex is the biological reality of different "plumbing" in our bodies, interactionists are interested in how those physical difference come to be symbols, resulting in different social rights and rewards. This chapter's discussions of micro-level social processes have pointed out that the meaning connected to one's sex produces notions of masculinity and femininity. The symbolic

By contrast to the clothing and gestures that create vulnerability in women, men are encouraged to use gestures that communicate strength and self-assurance, and their clothing and shoes would allow them to defend themselves or flee danger.

Source: © Lisa Kyle Young.

Symbolic interaction—more than any other theory—stresses the idea of human agency, with the notion that humans not only are influenced by the society in which they live but actively help to create it (Charon 2007; Hewitt 2007). In a study of elementary children in classrooms and especially on playgrounds, Barrie Thorne (1993) found that while teachers influenced the children a great deal, the children themselves were active participants in creating the student culture that encompassed their play. As children played with one another, Thorne noticed the ways in which they created words, nicknames, distinctions between one another, and new forms of interaction. This is a very important point: humans do not just passively adopt cultural notions about gender, they "do gender." They create it as they behave and interact with others in ways that define "normal" male or female conduct (West and Zimmerman 1987). "Doing gender" is an everyday, recurring, and routine occurance. It is a constant ongoing process that defines each situation, takes place in organizations and between individuals, and becomes part of institutional arrangements. Social movements such as civil rights and the women's movement challenge these arrangements and can bring about change. Understanding the process of doing gender helps us understand why we think and act as we do.

When children are in an ambiguous situation, they may spontaneously define one's sex as the most relevant trait about themselves or others. Indeed, even when children are enacting something they have heard elsewhere, they are helping to make it a reality for those around them. The very fact that they act as if gender matters helps to make the notion of gender more concrete and real to the other children. As the next child adopts the "definition of reality" from the first, acting as if sex is more important than hair color or eye color

or ear lobe attachment to the cheek, this makes gender the most prominent characteristic in the mind of the next child. Yet each child, in a sense, could choose to ignore gender and decide that something else is more important—nationality, dress, or ability to speak the same language. The same principle applies to adults. Human life is largely about where we draw lines between things and between "us" and "them." When a person "chooses" to recognize gender as a critical distinction between two individuals or two groups, that person is doing gender (Hewitt 2007; O'Brien 2006)

It is through interaction that people do gender, and while this process begins at a micro level, it has implications all the way to the global level. The Iowa School of symbolic interactionism places more stress on meso-level reinforcement of social constructions of gender (Carrothers and Benson 2003; Stryker 1980), emphasizing individuals conforming to or rebelling against the messages that pervade our institutions. The next section explores meso- and macro-level forces that shape gender and stratification based on sex.

THINKING SOCIOLOGICALLY

How do you "do gender"? How did you learn these patterns of behavior? Are they automatic responses, or do you think about "who opens the door"?

Structural-Functional and Conflict Theories: Meso- and Macro-Level Analyses
Structural-Functional Theory

From the structural-functional perspective, each sex has a role to play in the interdependent groups and institutions of society. Some early theorists argued that men and women carry out different roles and are, of necessity, unequal because of needs of societies and practices that have developed since early human history. Social relationships and practices that have proven successful in the survival of a group are likely to continue and be reinforced by society's norms and laws. Thus, relationships between women and men that are believed to support survival are maintained. In traditional hunter-gatherer, horticultural, and pastoral societies, for instance, the division of labor is based on sex and age. Social roles are clearly laid out, indicating who performs which everyday survival tasks. The females often take on the primary tasks of child care, gardening, food preparation, and other duties near the home. Men do tasks that require movements farther from home, such as hunting or fishing.

As societies industrialize, roles and relationships change due to structural changes in society. Durkheim (1947/1893) described a gradual move from traditional societies held together by *mechanical solidarity* (common values and emotional ties between members) to modern societies that cohere due to *organic solidarity*. The glue that holds modern society together is based less on common values and more on division of labor and the interdependence of statuses within the social world. According to early functionalists, gender division of labor exists in modern societies because it is efficient and useful to have different-but-complementary male and female roles. They believed this accomplishes essential tasks and maintains societal stability (Lindsey 2005; Moen, Downey, and Bolger 1990).

More recent structural-functional theorists describe society as an integrated system of roles that work together to carry out the necessary tasks in society; they argue that two complementary types of roles are needed in the modern industrial and postindustrial family. The female plays the *expressive role* through childbearing, nursing, and caring for family members in the home. The male carries out the *instrumental role* by working outside the home to support the family (Anderson 1994; Parsons and Bales 1953).

Although this pattern was relevant during the industrial revolution and again after World War II when men returned to take jobs women had held during the war, it currently characterizes only a small percentage of families in Western industrial and postindustrial societies (Ramazanoglu 1992) and less than 10 percent of families in the United States (Aulette 2002). In reality, gender segregation has seldom been total because in most cultures women's work has combined their labor in the *public* sphere—that is, outside the home—with their work in the *private sphere*—inside the home (Lopez-Garza 2002). Poor minority women in countries around the world must often work in low-paying service roles in the public sphere and carry the major burden for roles in the private sphere. Gender analysis through a structural-functional perspective stresses efficiencies that are believed to be gained by specialization of tasks (Waite and Gallagher 2000).

Conflict Theory

Conflict theorists view males as the haves—controlling the majority of power positions and most wealth—and females as the have-nots. Women have less access to power and have historically depended on males for survival. This is the case even though they raise the next generation of workers and consumers, provide unpaid domestic labor, and assure a pool of available, cheap labor during times of crisis, such as war. By keeping women in subordinate roles, males control the means of production and protect their privileged status.

A classical conflict explanation of gender stratification is found in the writings of Karl Marx's colleague Friedrich Engels (1884/1942). In traditional societies where size and strength were essential for survival, men were often dominant, but women's roles were respected as important and necessary to the survival of the group. Men hunted, engaged in warfare, and protected women. Over time, male physical control was transformed into control by ideology, by the dominant belief system itself. Capitalism strengthened male dominance by making more wealth available to men and their sons. Women became dependent on men, and their roles were transformed into "taking care of the home" (Engels 1884/1942).

Functionalists have argued that traditional divisions of labor are constructive in that they encourage the efficiencies of specialization and they ensure that all tasks, including child care, are fulfilled.

Source: © Bruce Burkhardt / Corbis.

Ideologies based on traditional beliefs and values have continued to be used to justify the social structure of male domination and subjugation of women. It is in the interest of the dominant group, in this case men, to maintain their position of privilege: political and economic power and greater access to resources. Conflict theorists believe it unlikely that those in power by virtue of sex, race, class, or political or religious ideology will voluntarily give up their positions as long as they are benefiting from them. By keeping women in traditional gender roles, men maintain control over institutions and resources (Collins 1971; Ramazanoglu 1992).

While Marx and especially Engels wrote about oppression of women under capitalistic systems, modern conflict theorists put less emphasis on class conflict and much more on the "we"/"they" thinking that occurs between the sexes and the way power is used by men to perpetuate their privileges.

Feminist Theory

Feminist theorists agree with Marx and Engels that gender stratification is based on power struggles, not biology. Yet some feminist theorists argue that Marx and Engels failed to include a key variable in women's oppression: patriarchy. *Patriarchy* involves a few men dominating and holding authority over all others, including women, children, and less powerful men (Arrighi 2000). According to feminist theory, women will continue to be oppressed by men until patriarchy is eliminated.

A distinguishing characteristic of most feminist theory is that it actively advocates change in the social order, whereas many other theories we have discussed try only to explain

Men who play golf together or join men's-only clubs develop networks that enhance their power and their ability to "close deals." When women are not part of the same networks, they are denied the same insider privileges. Many conflict theorists would argue this is purposeful; others point to it as a reality even if it is not intentional.

Source: © George Shelley / Corbis.

When women have less power at the meso level, they may also be more vulnerable at home. This girl attends to her injured mother at a hospital in Hyderabad, Pakistan, after the woman's husband chopped off her nose with an axe and broke all her teeth. According to the Pakistan Institute of Medical Sciences, over 90% of married women report being severely abused when husbands were dissatisfied by their cooking or cleaning or when the women had given birth to a girl instead of a boy or had been unable to bear a child at all.

Source: © Nadeem Khawer / epa / Corbis.

the social world (Anderson 2006; Lorber 1998). Some variations of feminist theory complement each other, and others have contradictory ideas (Kramer 2005). However, all feminist theories argue for bringing about a new and equal ordering of gender relationships to eliminate the patriarchy and sexism of current gender-stratification systems.

Feminist theorists try to understand the causes of women's lower status and seek ways to change systems to provide opportunities for women in education and work, to improve the standard of living, and to give women control over their bodies and reproduction. Feminist theorists also feel that little change will occur until group consciousness is raised so that women understand the system that limits their status and do not blame themselves for their situations (Sapiro 2003).

As societies become technologically advanced and need an educated workforce, women of all social classes and ethnic groups around the world are likely to gain more equal roles. Women are entering institutions of higher education in record numbers, and evidence indicates they are needed in the world economic system and the changing labor force of most countries. Feminist theorists look at these global and national patterns, but they also note the role of patriarchy in interpersonal situations—such as domestic violence, another key topic in feminist theory. For example, women in the United States who are struggling to make ends meet for their families often face limited-time welfare benefits yet may not be able to gain stable employment; thus, they may feel no option but to return to an abusive relationships out of desperation. They often have few economic or social resources to do otherwise (Scott, London, and Myers 2002).

THINKING SOCIOLOGICALLY

Why do women and men in relationships behave the way they do? If these behaviors are hurtful or destructive, what might be done to change the situation?

Violence against women perpetuates gender stratification, as is evident in the intimate environment of many homes. Because men have more power in the larger society, they have more resources within the household as well (side-effect discrimination). Women are often dependent on the man of the house for his resources, meaning they are willing to yield on many decisions. Power differences in the meso- and macro-level social systems also contribute to power differentials and vulnerability of women in micro-level settings. In addition, poor women have fewer options when considering whether to leave an abusive relationship. Although there are risks of staying in an abusive relationship, many factors enter into a woman's decision to stay or leave. The following Sociology in Your Social World discusses one form of violence around the world that is perpetuated predominantly against women: rape.

Sociology in Your Social World

Rape and the Victims of Rape

For many women around the world, rape is the most feared act of violence and the ultimate humiliation. Rape is a sexual act, but closely tied to macho behavior, and often a power play to intimidate, hurt, and dominate women. Rape has been used by "owners" as a method to subdue women slaves (Brown 2001), by Serbian army troops to humiliate Bosnian Muslim men who are expected to protect their women, and by prison inmates against other inmates to establish power hierarchies. Consider the case of South Africa's AIDS epidemic. Some men believe—beyond all logic or science—that having sex with a virgin will help cure AIDS; hence, the rate of rape of young girls is high. Some societies are largely free from rape, while others are prone toward rape. What is the difference?

Rape provides an example of the impact of cultural practices, beliefs, and stereotypes. When a society is relatively tolerant of interpersonal violence, holds beliefs in male dominance, and strongly incorporates ways to separate women and men, rape is more common (Sanday 1981; Sanday and Goodenough 1990; Shaw and Lee 2005). Rape is also more common when gender roles and identities are changing and norms about interaction between women and men are unclear. What does this say, then, about the United States, where women have a 1 in 5 chance of being raped in their lifetimes (Burn 2005), where someone is sexually assaulted or raped every two-and-a-half minutes, averaging over 2,000 rapes daily and 204,370 rapes or sexual assaults annually. Most rape victims are under 30 years of age (Shaw and Lee 2005; U.S. Department of Justice 2004). These figures are probably much lower than reality; even though the rape and sexual assault rates have been dropping in the past 10 years, the estimates are that only 1 in 10 rapes in the United States are reported (U.S. Department of Justice 2004).

An alarming problem is rape on college campuses in the United States. Researchers report that "Nearly one of every four women on college campuses has experienced sexual violence" (Shaw and Lee 2005:424). Women report being sexually assaulted while few males define their behavior as assault; this discrepancy points to the stereotypes and misunderstandings that can occur because of different beliefs and attitudes. Rape causes deep and lasting problems for women victims as well as for men accused of rape because of "misreading" women's signals. Groups of college men report thinking of gang rape as a form of male bonding; to them, it was no big deal. The woman was just the object and instrument; her identity was immaterial (Martin and Hummer 1989; Sanday and Goodenough 1990). Sometimes, alcohol and roofie (date-rape drugs) are involved. This mentality kept the Duke University Lacrosse team on the front pages of newspapers across the country in spring 2006 because of definitions of what is *rape* differ between groups.

Men who hold more traditional gender roles view rape very differently than women and less traditional men. They tend to attribute more responsibility to the female victim of the rape, believe sex rather than power was the motivation for rape, and look less favorably on women who have been raped. In a strange twist of logic, one study showed that some men actually believe that women want to be forced into having involuntary sex (Szymanski et al. 1993).

Many citizens and politicians see rape as an individualized, personal act, while social scientists tend to see it as a structural problem that stems from negative stereotypes of women, subservient positions of women in society, and patriarchal systems of power. Until there is better understanding on the part of both men and women about gender and rape, the culture of rape is likely to continue (McEvoy and Brookings 2001). A number of sociologists and anthropologists believe that rape will not be substantially reduced unless our macho definitions of masculinity are changed (Sanday and Goodenough 1990).

THINKING SOCIOLOGICALLY

Using a sociological perspective, how would you recommend policy makers deal with domestic violence and rape?

In summary, feminist analysis finds gender patterns imbedded in social institutions of family, education, religion, politics, economics, and health care. If the societal system is patriarchal, ruled by men, the interdependent institutions are likely to reflect and support this system. Feminist theory helps us to understand how patriarchy at the meso and macro level can influence patriarchy at the micro level and vice versa.

Class, Race, and Gender

While the different branches of feminist theory agree on their goals, the means they propose to bring about that change differ (Walby 1990). One current trend is to view the social world as an intersection of class, race, and gender (Glenn 1999; Smith 1999). In this way, one can look at the variety of ways that many common citizens are controlled by those who have monopoly on power and privilege. The reality is that some women are quite privileged. Not all women live in poverty. Some are extremely wealthy. However, these women still often have less power than their husbands or other men in their lives. It is also true that some women—in any given country—are privileged because of their race or ethnicity (Rothenberg 2006). In many respects, they have more in common with men of their own ethnicity or race than they do with women of less esteemed groups, and they may choose to identify with those statuses that enhance their privilege.

Race, class, and gender have cross-cutting lines that may modify one's subjugation in the society or may intensify it. Sexual orientation, age, nationality, and other factors may have similar effects of diminishing or increasing minority status of specific women, and theorists are paying increasing attention to these intersections (Rothenberg 2004, 2006). Chapter 8 discussed the fact that racial and class lines may be cross-cutting or parallel. In the case of gender, there are always cross-cutting lines with race and social class. However, gender will still affect one's prestige and privilege within that class or ethnic group. Thus, these three variables should be considered simultaneously (Hossfeld 2006; Kirk and Okazawa-Rey 2007).

Because daughters are a financial liability in India and China, there is a longstanding preference for sons. This results in extended families in which there are far more boys than girls.

Source: Photo courtesy of Kate Ballantine.

GENDER AND MINORITY GROUP STATUS

Women as a Minority

Couples in the United States, India, China, and many other countries would like their first child to be a boy, and most couples want more boys than girls; in some societies, families are more likely to continue to have children until they have boys. In countries around the world, people have found ways to cull girl babies if the family already has girls, if there is not enough food to feed the family, or if the father is absent (Ward and Edelstein 2006). For instance, in India and China, daughters have traditionally been considered a liability because they are additional mouths to feed as children, they require a dowry to marry, and they move away before they can contribute to the family as parents age. Hence, many female fetuses are aborted each year. Furthermore, even if few girls are actively killed at birth today, adequate nourishment or medical attention may be withheld when girls are ill, resulting in a higher death rate (Bumiller 1990; Burn 2005; Ward and Edelstein 2006).

Women make up over 50 percent of the world's population, yet their experience often parallels that of other smaller minority groups. Recall that a minority group has less power and influence in the society, not necessarily fewer people. Consider the characteristics of minority groups and the similarities between the position in the United States and Great Britain of poor minority women (e.g., people of African and West Indian descent) of either sex:

1. *Physical, cultural, or social characteristics* distinguish minority group members from the dominant group. Women are distinguished by physical (sex) characteristics, just as people of color are distinguished by physical characteristics.

2. Women's share of *desired goods and positions* (power) in society is limited because dominant groups control these. Around the world, United Nations statistics tell the story of women and other minorities: poor education, higher mortality, and less access to health care and other valued resources. Income for men and women varies significantly depending on ethnicity within the United States, but even when ethnicity is considered, women get paid less than men (see Table 9.4). Voting rights for women and African Americans did not occur until the twentieth century in most countries and only after persistent struggles. Both blacks and women are underrepresented in politics, with African American women facing double jeopardy. Both groups are also disproportionately found in low-paying jobs that have little opportunity for advancement.

3. *Ideological or other justifications* are used by the dominant group to deny equal treatment. Both

blacks and women have been stereotyped in books and the media—blacks as "lazy" or "inferior," women as "emotional and unstable due to imbalances in hormones." Religious, political, and pseudoscientific ideologies have been used to keep women and blacks in inferior positions, with women of color experiencing additional burdens.

4. *Collective identity* among minority group members develops to help insulate them from the discriminatory acts of the dominant group. Both women and blacks have organizations and social movements with goals to better their position in society. Both have engaged in consciousness-raising efforts, ranging from coffee klatches and women's auxiliaries to protest movements. However, many women experience more isolation from each other than do blacks because of the nuclear family's residential patterns—isolated in apartments or suburban housing that serve to separate women in their individual homes. This reduces the possibility for consciousness raising and cohesiveness among women from different social classes or groups, a pattern that is parallel to the differences that separate people of color into lower-, middle-, and upper-class.

5. *Minority group status* is generally determined by rules of descent, with members born into a status they cannot change. Race and sex are ascribed statuses of minority groups into which individuals are born and which are with them for life. In developing countries, differences in the status of men and women are more extreme; women rank lower than men on indicators of well-being, from education and health to employment status (United Nations 2002).

Putting these characteristics together suggests that women are indeed a "minority group," subject to stereotypes, prejudice, and discrimination, and women of color can face the triple status determinants of being poor women of color. Consider the global example in Sociology around the World on page 182.

TABLE 9.4 **Income by Educational Level and Ethnicity or Race, 2003 (in dollars)**

Education	Male	Female
Asian American	32,291	17,679
White	30,732	17,259
African American	21,986	16,581
Hispanic	21,053	13,642

Source: U.S. Census Bureau (2006e, Table 684).

Gender, Homosexuality, and Minority Status

One group of people who faces particular discrimination in many countries is homosexuals. Homosexuality has always existed and has been accepted and even required at some times and places. In some cases, homosexuals have been placed in a separate sexual category with special roles; some societies ignore its existence; a few consider it a psychological illness or form of depraved immorality; and a very few even consider this form of sexuality a crime (as in some Muslim societies today and in most states in the United States during much of the twentieth century). In each case, the government or dominant religious group determines the status of this group. The reality is that deviation from a society's gender norms, such as attraction to a member of the same sex, may cause one to experience minority status.

Lesbians (female homosexuals) are women attracted to other women. Because these women do not follow traditional gendered expectations of femininity of many societies, they often experience prejudice and discrimination. Women's status is typically based on their relationship with men, and in most societies they are economically dependent on men. Therefore, lesbians may go against norms of societies and are in some instances perceived as dangerous, unnatural, or a threat to men's power (Burn 2005; Ward and Edelstein 2006).

Sexism affects the lives of gay men as well. *Homophobia* (intense fear and hatred of homosexuality and homosexuals) is highly correlated with and perhaps a cause of traditional notions of gender and gender roles (Lehne 1995; Morin and Garfinkle 1978; Pharr 1997; Price and Dalecki 1998; Shaw and Lee 2005). Some homosexuals deviate from traditional notions of masculinity and femininity and therefore from significant norms of many societies. This results in hostile reactions and stigma. Indeed, homosexual epitaphs are often used to reinforce gender conformity and to intimidate anyone who would dare to be different from the norm (Lehne 1995; Price and Dalecki 1998). Still, the whole issue of homophobia focuses on prejudice held and transmitted by individuals.

It is important to recognize that sex and sexuality are not binary (male-female) concepts but are broader concepts including various combinations of masculine, feminine, heterosexuals, homosexuals, and a range of other variations. This is normal in human sexuality. It is societal expectations developed over time that impose categories on human sexuality.

Heterosexism is the notion that the society reinforces heterosexuality and marginalizes anyone who does not conform to this norm. Heterosexism focuses on social processes that define homosexuality as deviant and legitimize heterosexuality as the only normal lifestyle (Oswald 2000, 2001). In short, heterosexism operates very often at the meso and macro levels of society, through privileges granted to persons who are heterosexual and denied to those who are not.

Homosexuality has been an issue in recent political elections in the United States and has spawned debates about family life and whether homosexuals should be allowed to

Sociology around the World

North African Women in France: The Intersection of Class, Race, and Gender

Zouina is Algerian, but she was born in France to her immigrant parents. She lived with them in a poor immigrant suburb of Paris in the Saint-Denis region until she was forced to return to Algeria for an arranged marriage to a man who already had one wife. That marriage ended, and she returned to her "home" in France. In 2003, there were an estimated 70,000 forced and polygamous marriages in immigrant communities of France, considered illegal under French law. Since she returned to France, Zouina has been working wherever she can find work. The high unemployment and social and ethnic discrimination, especially against foreign women, makes life difficult (*The Perfumed Garden* 2000).

The situation is complex. Muslim women from Tunisia, Morocco, and Algeria living in crowded slum communities outside Paris face discrimination in French society, in the workplace, and within their own communities (*Le Monde Diplomatique* 2004). Expected to be both good Muslim women and good family coproviders—which necessitates working in French society—they face ridicule when they wear their *hijabs* (coverings) to school or work and encounter ridicule in their community if they do not wear them. They are caught between two cultures, not able to express their own religious and cultural identity in either.

Because of high unemployment in the immigrant communities, many youth roam the streets. Gang rapes by young North Africans against young women has been a topic in the news in France and abroad; negative press against the North African youths should not hide the economic impact causing problems for French youths, who also face problems from high unemployment in France.

North African women are faced with rejection and disdain in both communities. With the conflicting messages due to their ethnic differences (race), their poor status (class), and their sex, these women attempt to construct and manage their identities under difficult circumstances (Killian 2006).

---

marry, to adopt or have children, or to have the same rights as heterosexuals. In short, many institutions in the social world have been influenced by this debate over sexuality and gender. The notion of allowing gays and lesbians the right to a legal marriage has been extremely controversial in the United States, and more than 30 states have passed legislation defining marriage as between a man and a woman, some even approving amendments to their constitutions to ensure that same-sex marriages will not happen in those states (Newman and Grauerholz 2002). The point is not to argue for or against same-sex marriage but to note that homosexuals do not have many of the rights that heterosexuals enjoy; the discrepancy is based on sexuality characteristics.

Heterosexuals in the United States have a variety of rights—ranging from insurance coverage and inheritance rights for life-long partners, to jointly acquired property, hospital visitation rights as family, rights to claim the body of a deceased partner, and rights to have the deceased prepared for burial or cremation. The U.S. federal government confers 1,138 rights to heterosexuals that they normally take for granted, but often these rights do not extend to same-sex partners in a life-long relationship. Most states also bestow more than 200 specific rights to persons who "marry," but since most states do not allow same-sex marriages, homosexuals do not have these same rights (U.S. General Accounting Office 2003). In Canada and many European countries, citizens do have a right to same-sex marriage, and this has reduced the number of discrepancies in the rights of gays and heterosexuals.

THINKING SOCIOLOGICALLY

Why do gays and lesbians have different rights in countries around the world? Why do some societies provide equal protection under the laws while others do not?

COSTS AND CONSEQUENCES OF GENDER STRATIFICATION

In rapidly changing modern societies, role confusion abounds. Men hesitate to open doors for women, wondering if gallantry will be appreciated or scorned. Women are torn between traditional family roles on the one hand and working to support the family and fulfill career goals on the other. As illustrated in the examples below, sex-based stratification limits individual development and causes both psychological and social problems in behaviors, education, health, work, and other parts of the social world.

Psychological and Social Consequences of Gender Stratification: Micro-Level Implications

For both women and men, rigid gender stereotypes can be very constraining. Individuals who hold highly sex-typed attitudes feel compelled to behave in stereotypic ways, ways that are consistent with the pictures they have of proper gender behavior (Basow 1992, 2000). However, individuals who do not identify strongly with masculine or feminine gender types are more flexible in thoughts and behavior, tend to score higher on intelligence tests, have greater spatial ability, and have higher levels of creativity. Because they allow themselves a wider range of behaviors, they have more varied abilities and experiences and become more tolerant of others' behaviors. High masculinity in males sets up rigid standards for male behavior and has been correlated with anxiety, guilt, and neuroses, whereas less rigid masculine expectations are associated with emotional stability, sensitivity, warmth, and enthusiasm (Bellisari 1990). Rigid stereotypes and resulting sexism affect everyone and curtail our activities, behaviors, and perspectives.

Superwoman Image

Women in many societies are expected to be beautiful, youthful, and sexually interesting and interested, and at the same time to prepare the food, care for the children, keep a clean and orderly home, and sometimes bring in money to help support the family. Some are also expected to be competent and successful in their careers. Multiple, sometimes contradictory, expectations for women cause stress and even serious psychological problems.

Women who work outside the home are often expected to keep up with the domestic tasks as well. Evidence indicates that when women enter the labor force, there are not parallel changes or redistribution of responsibilities in family life. On the contrary, working generally leads to an increase in what is expected of women. The "superwoman syndrome," a pattern by which women assume multiple roles and try to do all well, takes its toll (Faludi 1993). The resulting strain contributes to depression and certain health problems such as headaches, nervousness, and insomnia (Wood 2003).

Beauty Image

Disorders including anorexia and bulimia nervosa relate to societal expectations of the ideal woman's appearance. About 1 out of every 100 American women suffers from these severe eating disorders, and the numbers have been growing since the 1970s. It occurs most frequently in females between 12 and 18 years of age. This serious problem is caused by distortions in body image, brought on by what the women,

Women are often expected to be superwomen: competent professional women who also are nurturing and attentive moms. Men do not face the same dual message.

Source: © Poppy Berry / zefa / Corbis.

especially white middle- and upper-middle-class women, see as societal images of beauty, often images created in magazines that are unattainable in real life (Doyle and Paludi 1998; Kilbourne 1999; Taub and McLorg 2007).

THINKING SOCIOLOGICALLY

Why are eating disorders found primarily in the United States and some Western societies?

Men also suffer psychological costs of stereotyping. Fitness magazines picture the "perfect" male body and advertise exercise equipment and steroids. In addition, men die earlier than women, in part due to environmental, psychological, and social factors. Problems in developed countries such as heart disease, stroke, cirrhosis, cancers, accidents, and suicides are linked in part to the male role that dictates that males should appear tough, objective, ambitious, unsentimental, and unemotional—traits that require men to assume great responsibility and suppress their feelings.

The concept of *androgyny,* "the integration of feminine and masculine characteristics," suggests a social world in which individuals are free to express all qualities, not only rigid sex-typed attitudes and behaviors (Bem 1974, 1983; Lindsey 2005). The more healthy attitude for both men and women is flexibility rather than rigidity that limits expression and opportunity.

The idea of androgyny is that men and women should just be people, with nurturant abilities and vulnerability as well as strength and desire for achievement.

Source: © Alberto Perez Veiga; © Teresa Hurst.

THINKING SOCIOLOGICALLY

Why do some men and women resist androgyny, power sharing, and equality of roles? What have they to gain or lose from resistance?

Societal Costs and Consequences of Gender Stratification: Meso- and Macro-Level Implications

Gender stratification creates costs for societies around the world in a number of ways: poor educational achievement of female children; loss of human talents and resources of half of the population; lack of health care coverage for women, which affects both the women and their children; and social divisiveness leading to alienation, if not hostility. Discrimination and violence against women, whether physical or emotional, has consequences for all institutions in a society (Pan American Health Organizaton 2003).

Consider how the ratio of women to men in an occupational field affects the prestige of the occupation. As more men enter predominantly female fields such as nursing and library science, the fields gain higher occupational prestige and salaries tend to increase. It seems that men take their gender privilege with them when they enter female professions (Kramer 2001; Williams 1992). However, the evidence indicates that as women enter male professions such as law, the status tends to become lower, making women's chances of improving their position in the stratification system limited (Kemp 1994).

Women in the economic sphere may also face a glass ceiling, limiting their contributions to the professions and management. Resistance to expanding women's professional roles in traditional societies is often strong. For example, 40 percent of Japanese women work, but only 9 percent hold managerial positions. Although their education levels are generally high, Japanese women's wages are about 65 percent of their male counterparts' wages. Breaking through the glass ceiling continues to be a barrier for individual women but also a challenge for entire societies that could benefit from talents and abilities never fully maximized (French 2003).

CHANGING GENDER STRATIFICATION AND POLICY CONSIDERATIONS

Women in factories around the globe face dangerous conditions and low pay. Sweatshops exist because poor women have no other options to support their families and because we in rich countries want to buy the cheap products that perpetuate the multinational corporate system. Just a few years ago, maquiladoras (foreign-owned assembly plants) in Mexican border towns worked for 2,000 multinational companies that paid $3.75 to $4.50 an hour (Burn 2000). Two-thirds of the workers were poor women. Consider the following figures in Table 9.5 on wages in the textile industry from world countries:

TABLE 9.5	Labor Cost Comparisons in the Textile Industry, 2004–2005	
Region/ Country	Average Hourly Wages and Benefits U.S. $ (2004)	Ratio to U.S. Cost (%)
North America (NAFTA)		
Canada	18.61	118
Mexico	2.19	14
United States	15.78	100
South America		
Argentina	2.86	18
Brazil	2.83	18
Colombia	1.97	13
Venezuela	2.85	18
Western Europe		
France	21.03	133
Germany	27.69	175
Greece	11.67	74
Portugal	6.87	89
Switzerland	35.33	224
United Kingdom	20.17	128
Central and Eastern Europe		
Bulgaria	1.50	10
Czech Republic	3.94	25
Poland	3.80	24
Turkey	2.88	18
Northeast Asia		
China (coastal)	0.76	5
China (inland)	0.48	3
Hong Kong	6.21	39
South Korea	7.10	45
Taiwan	7.58	48
Southeast Asia		
Indonesia	0.55	4
Malaysia	1.18	7
Thailand	1.29	8
Vietnam	0.28	2
South Asia		
Bangladesh	0.28	2
India	0.67	4
Pakistan	0.37	2
Sri Lanka	0.46	3
Middle East and Africa		
Egypt	0.82	5
Israel	9.35	59
Kenya	0.67	4
Mauritius	1.57	10
Morocco	2.56	16
South Africa	3.80	24

Source: Werner International Management Consultants (2005).

Women in Thailand produce shoes at extremely low rates. These jobs are better than no employment at all, but before pressures from Western societies changed their cultures, most people were able to feed their families quite adequately in small villages. Changes in the entire world system have made that form of life no longer feasible, but working for multinational corporations also keeps them impoverished.

Source: © UNESCO, photo by Dominique Rogers.

In El Salvador, women employees of the Taiwanese maquiladora Manderin are forced to work shifts of 12 to 21 hours during which they are seldom allowed bathroom breaks; they are paid about 18 cents per shirt, which is later sold for $20 each. Manderin makes clothes for The Gap, J. Crew, and Eddie Bauer. In Haiti, women sewing clothing at Disney's contract plants are paid 6 cents for every $19.99 101 Dalmatians outfit they sew; they make 33 cents an hour. Meanwhile, Disney makes record profits and could easily pay workers a living wage for less than one half of 1 percent of the sales price of one outfit. In Vietnam, 90 percent of Nike's workers are females between the ages of 15 and 28. Nike's labor costs for a pair of basketball shoes (which retail for $149.50) are $1.50, 1 percent of the retail price (Burn 2000:120).

These women often earn less than half of what is needed to survive in their areas. Yet corporations can pay low wages and in many cases continue poor and even dangerous working environments because these areas have high unemployment and families have no other options.

What can be done about the abusive treatment of women around the world? This is a tough issue: governments have passed legislation to protect workers, but governments also want the jobs that multinational corporations bring and therefore do little to enforce regulations. International labor standards are also difficult to enforce. Multinationals are so large that it is difficult to influence their practices. Trade unions have had little success entering companies to attract workers to join because they are squashed immediately.

THE APPLIED SOCIOLOGIST AT WORK | Eleanor Lyon

Women and Violence

What influences a woman to stay with a violent partner or to leave that partner? How should the courts treat cases of domestic violence? Dr. Eleanor Lyon, an applied sociologist, conducted a study for the National Institute of Justice in which she interviewed women whose partners were accused of domestic violence. The results of the study may help courts respond more effectively to cases of domestic violence. For instance, some question why an abused woman does not leave her abusing partner. Research finds a number of reasons: loss of financial resources and even a home for her children, disruption of her children's schooling, anxiety about being seen as a family breaker, fear of deportation if the woman is an illegal immigrant, dread that child protective services might become involved, concern about rejection by her family and church group, or alarm she would be committing a sin (Glass 2003).

One conclusion from Lyon's study was that officials need to use a holistic approach to understand when a woman will leave her husband and the implications of leaving for her and her family. These issues are complex, but they need to be understood fully if sociologists are to make useful recommendations to help agencies serving abused women and policy makers seeking solutions.

Lyons uses qualitative and quantitative methods in her current work. She notes that effective work in human services agencies requires a strong background in research methodology as well as writing and listening skills. In fact, if she were to go back to school, she would focus on building skills not only in sociological methodology but also in other social science methodologies to enhance her interdisciplinary investigations.

The most rewarding aspects of her research include working on an agenda for change in issues she cares about, the excitement of new learning that takes place when doing research, and the strong collaborative relations she builds with others who care about the same issues. Despite the rewards, however, there are uncertainties about being self-employed, especially since there is an uneven flow of work. Still, the rewards of making a contribution through action-research outweigh the stresses and strains of the work.

Dr. Eleanor Lyon spends half of her working time as director of Lyon and Associates, her consulting firm. She specializes in issues concerning violence against women and criminal justice policy and hires research assistants as needed to do interviews, help design instruments, and enter data for analysis. She also teaches courses at the University of Connecticut, School of Social Work.

One place to start is to adopt practices that have worked for other groups facing discrimination in the past; consider the following possibilities for bringing about change: holding nonviolent protests, sit-down strikes, and walkouts to protest unequal and unfair treatment; women working together in support groups to help their children and neighborhoods; using the Internet to carry the message to others; carrying out boycotts against companies that mistreat employees; following traditions that have succeeded in the past such as using the arts, preachers, storytellers, and teachers to express frustration and resistance, educate others, and provide ideas and strategies for resistance; and building on traditions of community and religious activism (Collins 2000). Most of these strategies require organized groups.

At women's conferences around the world, policy makers debate the means to create solutions to women's problems. Most United Nations member countries have at least fledgling women's movements fighting for improved status of women and their families; the movements attempt to change laws that result in discrimination, poverty, abuse, and low levels of education and occupational status. Although the goals of eliminating differential treatment of women, especially minority women, are jointly affirmed by most women's groups, the means to improve conditions for women are debated between women's groups. For instance, some advocate working within existing institutions in societies to bring about equal rights. Others push for complete overhauling of existing systems to bring about a new order that would ignore sex as a variable in assigning power. Whether any of these efforts will change women's individual lives and the lives of their children is debatable.

We grow up being socialized into patterns of behavior, even if those patterns include discrimination. In Western countries with relatively high wages, many young women are afraid of change and of the protests implied in being an active feminist. Familiar patterns are comfortable, even if they limit opportunities. Being an activist is risky, especially if one is living a comfortable life. Restrictions caused by gender stratification become clearer as young women enter the public sphere (Hogeland 2004).

We would be too optimistic to predict that grassroots efforts or boycotts by those who are enjoying the fruits of poor women's labor will change the system. The best hope may lie in increased opportunities for women as countries modernize and in efforts of countries like Cambodia (Kampuchia) that strive to enforce labor laws and improve conditions and wages for workers. These efforts will only work if other countries join in, if Cambodia remains a competitive labor market, and if

buyers support products made in countries with fair labor practices (betterfactories.com 2006).

Policy is informed by social science research. Some applied feminist sociologists have worked in shelters for battered women, rape response centers, and other agencies that deal with concerns of women. The Applied Sociologist at Work on page 286 explores the work of one such sociologist dealing with feminist issues in an applied setting.

SO WHAT?

In the beginning of this chapter, we asked how being born female or male affects our lives. Because sex is a primary variable on which societies are structured and stratification takes place, being born male or female affects our public and private sphere activities, our health, our ability to practice religion or participate in political life, our educational opportunities, and just about everything we do. As sociologists with a focus on empirical ways of knowing and scientific methods, we can only focus on description and analysis of what is. Other disciplines, such as philosophy and theology, may be more useful in articulating what it "ought" to be. Applied sociologists may move from an analysis of empirical

data to questions of how to improve the quality of people's lives by suggesting solutions. Likewise, policy recommendations are those that take what is known about gender relations and offer plans for changing and improving the society. Gender inequality clearly exists; what should be done is a matter of debate.

Inequality based on class, race, ethnicity, and gender is a process taking place at all levels of analysis. It takes place in a social context within our social world: institutions. Institutions are the stable patterns of roles, statuses, and groups which meet the basic needs of individuals and society in an orderly way; they include family, education, religion, political structures, and economics, and processes such as inequality. In complex societies, there are other necessary institutions including health care and science and technology.

CONTRIBUTING TO YOUR SOCIAL WORLD

At the Local Level: *Battered women shelters:* most communities have shelters that need volunteers.

At the Organizational or Institutional Level: Research those companies that exploit women in their production of products sold in this country. Boycott those companies, send a letter to the company president informing her or him of your objections to the company's policies, and encourage friends to do the same.

At the National and Global Levels: Contribute to *FINCA International, the Grameen Bank,* or another nonprofit organization that provides small micro-credit loans to women in impoverished countries who are starting their own small businesses. Information is available at www.villagebanking.org. Buy products made or supported by *10,000 Villages* or other fair trade nonprofit organizations.

Visit www.pineforge.com/ballantinestudy for online activities, sample tests, and other helpful information. Select "Chapter 9: Gender Stratification" for chapter-specific activities.

INSTITUTIONS

Picture a house, a structure in which you live. Within that house there are processes—the action and activities that bring the house alive. Flip a switch and the lights go on because the house is well-wired. Adjust the thermostat, and the room becomes more comfortable as the structural features of furnace or air-conditioning systems operate. If the structural components of the plumbing and water heating systems work, you can take a hot shower when you turn the knob. These actions taken within the structure make the house livable. If something breaks down, you need to get it fixed so that everything works smoothly.

Institutions, too, provide a framework or structure of society; processes are the action part of both institutions and society, where activities take place. These include the interactions between people in groups that make society work. Institutions of family, religion, education, health, politics, and economics are interdependent and mutually supportive, just as the processes in a house work together. However, breakdown in one institution or conflict between institutions of society for limited resources affect the whole society. The structures in any society—including institutions—are fairly stable, while the processes within society and institutions are dynamic and often lead to significant change.

Rather than trying to be all-encompassing in this book, we attempt to illustrate how various aspects of society work. The following four chapters examine four of the institutions that make up society. As you read these chapters, notice the interdependencies; change in one institution affects others. Information about the connection of these institutions, including observations on the political and economic systems, will be discussed in detail. A complementary chapter on "Political Systems: Penetrating Power" is available on the website for this book, if you would like to explore that institution in more depth. Sociologists studying economics, sport, or science as institutions would raise questions similar to the ones raised as we discuss family, education, religion, medicine, and politics at the micro, meso, and macro levels of analysis. We begin with the institution of family.

CHAPTER

10

FAMILY:
Partner Taking,
People Making,
and Contract
Breaking

What to Expect . . .

What Is a Family?

Theoretical Perspectives on Family

Family Dynamics: Micro-Level Processes

The Family as an Institution: Meso-Level Analysis

National and Global Family Issues: Macro-Level Analysis

Marriage, Divorce, and Social Policies

So What?

Appearing in rich variety, the family is often referred to as the "most basic" institution. In this social relationship we take partners and "make people"—both biologically and socially speaking. In the modern world, these intimate "basic" unions often experience conflict, violence, and contract breaking as well.

Think About It . . .

1. Why is family important to you?
2. Why are families around the world so different?
3. How do people find mates?
4. What, if anything, should be done to strengthen families?

Macro: Global Community

Macro: National Society

Meso: National Institutions and Organizations; Ethnic Subcultures

Micro: Local Organizations and Community

**Micro:
You and Your Family**

Micro: Family is the unit of action in local community; supports churches; spends money on entertainment and commodities

Meso: States regulate marriage and divorce; economy influences family prosperity; families are responsible for education, religious training, family values

Macro: Governments develop family policies; family instability is threat to national stability

Macro: International organizations establish guidelines to support women, children, and families; global events (e.g., wars) take lives of family members

In a village in India, the family is preparing for the day's chores. Chetana and Daya work with other women in the end of the long house that is used for cooking for the entire group. Other rooms along the house are designated for sleeping, greeting guests, and caring for children. Many people of all ages come and go—children, middle-aged adults, and elderly members. In this system, family units live together in an *extended family*; several generations of blood relatives share a single household.

It is morning in Sweden; Anders and Karin Karlsson are rushing to get to their offices on time. The children, a boy of 12 and a girl of 8, are being scurried out the door to school. All will return in the evening after a full day of activities and join together for the evening meal. In this dual-career family, common in many postindustrial societies, both parents are working professionals.

The gossip at the African village water well this day is about the rich local merchant, Azi, who has just taken his fourth and last wife. She is a young, beautiful girl of 15 from a neighboring village. She is expected to help with household chores and bear children for his already extensive family unit. Several of the women at the well live in affluent households where the husband has more than one wife.

Tom and Henry recently adopted Ty into their family. The couple share custody of the five-year-old boy, attend his school events, and teach him what parents are expected to teach their children.

WHAT IS A FAMILY?

What do these very different scenes have in common? Each describes a family, yet there is controversy about what

In recent decades, the definition of family has broadened; no longer is it necessarily limited to heterosexual couples. These gay men are parents to this baby.

Source: © Tomas Van Houtryve / Corbis.

constitutes a family. Those groupings that are officially recognized as families tend to receive a number of privileges and rights, such as health insurance and inheritance rights (Degenova and Rice 2002). The U.S. Census Bureau (2005e) defines the family as "a group of two or more people (one of whom is the householder) related by birth, marriage, or adoption and residing together; all such people (including related subfamily members) are considered as members of the family." Thus, a family might be composed of siblings, cousins, a grandparent and grandchild, or other groupings. Some sociologists define family as those sharing economic property, sexual access among the adults, and a sense of commitment among members (Collins and Coltrane 2001). This definition would include same-sex couples as families.

How do you define family? Answering the questions in the Sociology in Your Social World on page 293 will indicate the complexity of this question.

THINKING SOCIOLOGICALLY

First, use the survey on page 293. Were your answers different from your friend's or relative's? Why do you hold these particular views of "the ideal family"? Why might others in the world have answered differently?

The family is often referred to as the most basic institution of any society. First, an *institution* is a system of norms; the place where we learn many of the norms for functioning in the larger society is the family. Second, most of us spend our lives in the security of a family; we are born, raised, and will die in family settings. Through good and bad, sickness and health, most families provide for our needs, both physical and psychological. Therefore, families meet our primary, our most basic, needs. Third, major life events—marriages, births, graduations, promotions, anniversaries, religious ceremonies, holidays, funerals—take place within the family context and are celebrated with family members. In short, family is where we invest the most emotional energy and spend much of our leisure time. Fourth, the family is capable of fulfilling a number of other functions—economic support, education or training, religious socialization and rituals, our major social statuses and roles, resolution of conflicts, and so forth. One cannot conceive of the economic system providing emotional support for each individual or the political system providing socialization and personalized care for each child. Family can perform the functions of many other systems. Finally, in many nonindustrialized societies and in some ethnic groups within modern cultures, the family is the key to social organization of the entire society. The institution of family is important to the survival of individuals and the society. It is the place where we confirm our partnerships as adults, and it is where we make people—not just biologically, but socially. In the family, we take an organism that has the potential to be fully human, and we model this tiny bit of humanity into a caring, compassionate, productive person.

Sociology in Your Social World

The Ideal Family

What is "the ideal family"? Does it have one adult woman and one adult man? One child or many? Grandparents living with the family? Ask a friend or relative to answer the questions below, and compare the answers with your own. Note that all of these options are found in some societies.

1. How many adults should the ideal family contain? _____

2. How many children should the ideal family contain? _____

3. What should be the sex composition of the adults in the ideal family?
   a. 1 female and 1 male
   b. Male-male or female-female
   c. Several males and several females
   d. Other ___ (Write in): _____

4. What should be the sexes of the child(ren) in the ideal family? _____

5. Who should select the marriage partner?
   a. The partners should select each other.
   b. The parents or close relatives should select the partner.
   c. A matchmaker should arrange the marriage.
   d. Other _____

6. What is the ideal number of generations living in the same household?
   a. One generation: partners and no children
   b. Two generations: partners and children
   c. Three or more generations: partners, children, grandparents, and great-grandparents
   d. Other _____

7. Where should the couple live?
   a. By themselves
   b. With parents
   c. With brothers or sisters
   d. With as many relatives as possible

8. What should the sexual arrangements be? (Check all that apply.)
   a. Partners have sex only with each other.
   b. Partners can have sex outside of marriage if it is not "disruptive" to the relationship.
   c. Partners are allowed to have sex with all other consenting adults.
   d. Male partners can have sex outside marriage.
   e. Female partners can have sex outside marriage.
   f. Other _____

9. Which person(s) in the ideal family should work to help support the family?
   a. Both partners
   b. Male only
   c. Female only
   d. Both, but the mother only after children are in school
   e. Both, but the mother only after children graduate from high school
   f. All family members including children
   g. Other _____

10. Should the couple have sex before marriage if they wish? Yes ___ No ___ Other_____

11. Should physically disabled aging parents
    a. be cared for in a child's home?
    b. be placed in a nursing care facility?
    c. Other _____

Note: Adapted from a classroom questionnaire created by Charles Green, University of Wisconsin, Whitewater.

We are born and raised in our **family of orientation**, which consists of our parent(s) and possibly sibling(s). In this family, we receive our early socialization and learn the language, norms, core values, attitudes, and behaviors of our community and society. When we find a life mate and/or have our own children, we establish our **family of procreation**. The transmission of values, beliefs, and attitudes from our family of orientation to our family of procreation preserves and stabilizes the family system. Because family involves emotional investment, we have strong feelings about what form it should take.

PHOTO ESSAY

Family Interactions

Families vary a great deal from one culture to another, but if they work well together, they provide support for members, a sense of identity, and feelings of belonging and caring.

Sources: (Clockwise from top) © Jelani Memory/Istockphoto.com; © Andrei Tchernov/Istockphoto.com; © Philip Langley/Istockphoto.com; © Jupiter Images; © Kate Ballantine; © Kate Ballantine.

Whether we consider families at micro, meso, or macro levels, sociological theories can help us understand the role of families in the social world.

THEORETICAL PERSPECTIVES ON FAMILY

Consider the case of Felice, a young mother locked into a marriage that provides her with little satisfaction. For the first year of marriage, Felice tried to please her husband, Tad, but gradually he seemed to drift further away. He began to spend evenings out; sometimes he came home drunk and yelled or hit her. Felice became pregnant shortly after their marriage and had to quit her job. This increased the financial pressure on Tad, and they fell behind in paying the bills.

Then came the baby. They were both ecstatic at first, but Tad soon reverted to his old patterns. Felice felt trapped. She was afraid and embarrassed to go to her parents; they had warned her against marrying so young without finishing school, but she was in love and had gone against their wishes. She and Tad moved away from their hometown, so she was out of touch with her old support network and had few friends in her new neighborhood. Her religious beliefs told her she should try to stick it out and that it was partly her fault for not being a "good enough wife." She could not live on her own with a baby with no job or skills. She thought of marriage counseling, but Tad refused to consider this and did not seem interested in trying to work out the problems. He had his reasons for behaving the way he did, including feeling overburdened with the pressures of caring for two dependents. The web of this relationship seems difficult to untangle. Sociological theories provide us with tools to analyze such family dynamics.

Micro-Level Theories of Family and the Meso-Level Connection
Rational Choice or Exchange Theory

Rational choice or **exchange theory** can help us understand situations like Felice's: why people seek close relationships, why they stay in abusive relationships, and why they seek quasi-family relations in foster parenting, alternative family groups, or communal living arrangements. As discussed in Chapter 2, rational choice or exchange theory evaluates the costs and rewards of engaging in interaction. We look for satisfaction of our needs—emotional, sexual, and economic—through interaction. Patterns in the family are reinforced to the extent that exchanges are beneficial to members. When the costs outweigh the rewards, the relationship is unlikely to continue. Women in abusive relationships weigh the costs of suffering abuse against the rewards of having social legitimacy, income, social acceptance, not going against religious beliefs, a home, and companionship. Many factors enter into the complex balance of the exchange. Indeed, costs and benefits of various choices are often established by meso-level organizations

We invest much of our emotional energy and spend most of our leisure time with our families.

This Romanian family does not have much money, but the children learn many survival skills and the most basic needs of the children, physical and psychological, are met.

Source: © Kate Ballantine.

and institutions: insurance programs, health care options, and legal regulations that make partnering decisions easy or difficult.

According to rational choice theorists, even the mate-selection process is shaped by a calculation of exchange. People estimate their own assets—physical, intellectual, social, and economic—and try to find the "best deal" they can make, with attention to finding someone with at least the

No other institution can fulfill the functions of the family, but the family can fulfill many functions of other institutions. At left, family members in Ecuador work together as an economic team to produce food for the market. At the right, a family reinforces religious conviction through mealtime prayer.

Source: Photo by Downtheroad.org; © Glenda Powers/Istockphoto.com.

Some of our most rewarding and memorable times are spent in families. It is no wonder it is called the most basic institution.

Source: © Viktor Kitaykin.

Symbolic Interaction Theory

Symbolic interaction theory also helps to understand Felice's situation because it explains how individuals learn their particular behavior patterns and ways of thinking. Culture dictates the language we learn and how we interpret various situations; we are taught proper behavior patterns through socialization. Our role relationships are developed through interaction with others. Felice, for example, developed certain expectations and patterns of behavior by modeling her experiences on her family of orientation, observing others, and developing expectations from her initial interactions with Tad. He developed a different set of expectations; his father had hopped bars after work, had affairs with other women, and expected "his woman" at home to accept this without question. Tad modeled his role of husbands after his father's behavior.

Two related concepts in symbolic interaction theory are the *social construction of reality* and the *definition of a situation*. What we define as real or as normal is shaped by what others around us accept as ordinary or acceptable. Our ideas about family, like anything else, are socially shaped by our experiences and our significant others. Children who grow up in homes where adults hit one another or shout at one another with sarcastic put-downs may come to think of this behavior as typical or normal family life. They simply have known no other type of interaction. Thus, without seeing other options, they may create a similar pattern of family interaction in their own homes. Interaction with others, according to this theoretical model, is based on people's shared meanings. Concepts such as "family" or "wife" or "parenting" carry meaning to you and your siblings

level of resources they possess, even if those assets are in different areas. If someone marries another person with far more assets, the one with fewer assets is likely to have little power and to feel dependent on that relationship, often putting up with things that equal partners would not tolerate. *Cost/benefit*, according to this view, affects the forming of the relationship and the power and influence later in the relationship.

but may mean something very different to the person sitting beside you in class or to a potential mate.

One of the great challenges of newlyweds is meshing their ideas of division of labor, family holidays, discipline of children, spousal relations, economic necessities, and their assumptions about being in a committed relationship. A new couple socially constructs a new relationship, blending the models of life partnership from their own childhood homes. Of course, the couple can also create an entirely new model as they jointly define their relationship. This brings us back to a central premise of symbolic interactionism: humans are active agents who create their social structure through interaction. We not only learn family patterns, we *do* family in the sense that we create roles and relationships and pass them on to others as "normal." It is the sum total of all our actions that makes family into meso- and macro-level social patterns.

Our identities are shaped by institutional arrangements at the meso level. Family life is harder for couples when meso-level corporations, religious bodies, legal systems, and other government entities define the roles of "wife" and "husband." For example, each U.S. state actually spells out in its legal codes the duties of husbands and wives; those who do not fulfill these duties may be in "neglect of duty." In some societies, the official state religion dictates proper roles. So our conceptions of these family roles are embedded in the larger structure in ways that many people do not realize.

This grandmother is building bonds in the extended family by taking several of her grandchildren on an outing.

Source: © Marzanna Syncerz.

![thinking icon] **THINKING SOCIOLOGICALLY**

What did you learn about spouse and parenting roles from your family of procreation? How will what you learned affect your current or future family roles?

Meso- and Macro-Level Theories of the Family
Structural-Functional Theory

Structural-functional theory points out the common purposes of families in every society. Although the families described at the beginning of this chapter vary greatly, their members have a number of common needs and problems. For instance, they all must secure food and shelter, raise children, and care for dependents. Despite great variations, most human family systems serve similar purposes, or *functions*, for their members and for society.

Why do all societies have families? One answer is that families fulfill certain functions or purposes for societies and enhance their survival. Traditionally, there have been at least six ways the family has helped stabilize the society, according to structural-functional theory:

Sexual regulation. Physically speaking, any adult human could engage in sex with any other human; however, in

Introduction of a baby to a household changes the interpersonal dynamics, the topics of conversation, the amount of sleep people are able to get, the sense of responsibility for the future, the larger community and the quality of local schools, and many other aspects of social life.

Source: © Joshua Blake.

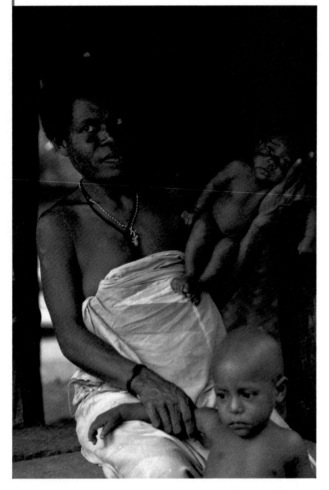

This mother in New Guinea was actually more attractive as a mate in that culture once she had proven her fertility.

Source: © Brian A. Vikander / Corbis.

practice, no society allows total sexual freedom and most of us are particular about our mates! Every society attempts to regulate the sexual behavior of its members in accordance with its own particular values, often through marriage. The **incest taboo** (prohibition against sex with a close relative) is a virtually universal restriction on sexual behavior, for instance.

Premarital sexual practices vary greatly from culture to culture. In New Guinea, premarital sex is not only tolerated but encouraged. A girl who has had a child as a teenager is a more desirable mate because she has proven her fertility. This practice is acceptable because the child is absorbed into the extended family that cares for any children. In other societies, women are protected, even cloistered, before marriage to protect their virtue and the reputation of the families.

In a few cultures, the bride must spend the first night after her marriage with the chief or leader of the group, and only thereafter does she live with her husband. This custom reinforces the authority and power of the patriarch. The Dani of Indonesia require women and their newborns to live away from their husbands for up to five years after the birth of the child. This regulation, most often in societies where men have more than one wife, serves to control population and to space children. In each example above, the sex regulation practice appears to serve some function in society (Ward and Edelstein 2006).

Reproduction and replacement. Societies need children to replace members who die. Reproduction is controlled to keep family lineage and inheritance clear. Parent and caretaker roles are clearly defined and reinforced in many societies by ceremonies: baby showers, birth nnouncements, christenings, and naming ceremonies that welcome the child as a member of the family.

Socialization. The family is the main training ground for children. It is in our families that we begin to learn values and norms, proper behavior, roles, and language. Later socialization in most societies is carried out by schools, religious organizations, and other institutions, but the family remains the most important initial socializing agent to prepare us for roles in society.

Emotional support and protection. Families are our main source of love and belonging, giving us a sense of identity, security, protection, and safety from harm. Unfortunately, not all of us receive these supports from our families. Problems of children in homeless shelters and incidents of family violence and neglect are reminders that societal functions typically met by the family are not always successfully provided in families.

Status assignment. Our family of birth is the most important determinant of our social status, life chances, and lifestyles. It strongly affects our educational opportunities, access to health care, and religious and political affiliations. In fact, in societies with caste systems, the ascribed position at birth is generally the position at death. Although in class societies, individuals may achieve new social statuses, our birth positions and the early years of socialization have a strong impact on who and what we are.

THINKING SOCIOLOGICALLY

In what ways does your family's reputation in the community and financial situation affect other aspects of your life?

Economic support. Historically, the family was a unit of production—running a farm or a bakery or a cobbler shop. Although this function is still predominant in many societies, the economic function carried out in individual families has pretty much disappeared in most Western families. However, the family remains an economic unit of *consumption.* Who paid for your clothing, food, and other needs as you were growing up? Who helps many of you pay your college tuition and expenses? Families usually provide these necessities by buying them. Taxing agencies, advertising and commercial enterprises, workplaces, and other social institutions also treat the family as the primary economic unit.

Functional theorists ask about the consequences of what takes place in the family for other parts of the society; they are likely to recognize ways that the micro-level processes of the family (e.g., socialization of Japanese children to be cooperative and members of groups and U.S. children to be competitive and individualistic) are compatible with structural needs of society at the meso and macro levels (e.g., need for motivated workers who thrive on competition). At the macro level, competition is valuable to the economic processes of the nation, for it stimulates the capitalistic system of production. Each part of the system, according to functionalists, works with other parts to create a functioning society.

Changing family functions. In some societies, the family is the primary unit for educating children, practicing religion, structuring leisure time activities, caring for the sick and aged, and even conducting politics. However, as societies modernize, many of these functions are transferred to other institutions.

As societies change, so do family systems. The sociohistorical perspective of family tells us that changes in intimate relationships—sexuality, marriage, and family patterns—have occurred over the centuries. Major transitions from agricultural to industrial to postindustrial societal systems change all of the institutions within those societies. Families in agricultural societies are often large and self-sufficient, producing their own food and providing their own shelter, but this is not the case in contemporary urban societies.

Industrialization and urbanization typical in eighteenth- and nineteenth-century Europe and the United States created a distinct change in roles; the wife and child became dependent on the husband who "brought home the bread." The family members became consumers rather than independent and self-supporting coworkers on a farm. This male breadwinner notion of family has not lasted long in the Western world (Coontz 2005). In addition to role shifts, other changes in society have brought shifts to the family: advances in technology brought medical advances, new knowledge to be passed on in schools, recreation organized according to age groups, and improved transportation are examples.

As many families moved to urban areas, tasks once carried on within the family unit moved to other institutions. The economic function has gone to the factory, store, and office. Social prestige is increasingly centered around a family member rather than the family surname. Socialization is increasingly done in schools, as teachers have become substitute parents; they do a great deal of the preparation of the child for the larger world. The traditional protection and care

A member of the Brotherhood of the Cross and Star kneels beside the altar holding a bowl of holy water while a clergyman tends to an infant during its naming ceremony in London. Bringing a new member into the community through birth is a cause for celebration in almost all societies.

Source: © Homer Sykes / Corbis.

function has been partially replaced by police, reform schools, unemployment compensation, social security, health care systems (e.g., Medicare and Medicaid), and other types of services provided by the state. Little League baseball, industrial bowling teams, aerobic exercise groups, television, and computer games have replaced the family as the source of leisure activities and recreation. Although many would argue that the family still remains the center of the affectional life and is the only recognized place for producing children, one does not have to look far to discover that these two functions are also increasingly found outside the boundaries of the traditional family unit.

These changes have shifted the family's role in modernizing societies and made the family's functions more specialized. Still, it remains a critical institution in society. Most families still function to provide stable structures to carry out early childhood socialization and to sustain love, trust, affection, acceptance, and an escape from the impersonal world.

THINKING SOCIOLOGICALLY

Does reduction of traditional family functions mean a decline in the importance of family or merely an adaptation of the family to changes in society? Is the modern family, based largely on emotional bonds rather than structural interdepency, a healthier system, or is it more fragile?

Sociology around the World

Body Mutilation for Marriage

To marry into a wealthy, high-status family, women's families around the world have done whatever it takes to make their daughters more desirable mates. We learn through socialization which parts of the body have sexual connotations. In some societies, fat is sexy; in others, legs or breasts are focal points. In other societies, tattoos and piercings are marks of beauty. Consider the following two examples of body alterations to enhance the marriage prospects of women.

For centuries in China, women with tiny feet were considered sexually attractive, a prize catch for men. Besides the sexual appeal, the status for the man lay in the fact that women with tiny bound feet could not work in the fields or do hard labor, thus demonstrating to all that the man was wealthy. Women bound their little girls' feet starting at about age two so that the feet would not grow; sometimes the feet of adult women were no more than three inches long (Levy 1990; Levy, Waley, and Eberhard 1992; Yung 1995). This practice was outlawed when Communists came to power in the 1950s, and only a few elderly women remain as evidence of the practice.

To those in Western societies, one of the most abhorrent examples of altering the body for sexual purposes is the practice of clitorectomy, carried out in some African, Middle Eastern, and Asian societies. Those practicing female circumcision or excision (removal of the clitoris) believe it eliminates base sexual desire and keeps the woman from "straying," leaving only the vagina, or "source of life" (Burn 2005; "A Painful Tradition" 1999). They also believe tightening the vagina increases pleasure for the male, although it can be deadly for women who hemorrhage as a result.

In some traditional societies, circumcision is a significant rite of passage in a young woman's life, accompanied by singing, dancing, and new clothes, and above all signifying her eligibility for marriage. In Guinea, for instance, women are married by age 14, sometimes given to their husbands as gifts. Some women in this society believe the female circumcision rite shows beauty and courage and is a means of achieving recognition and power. Any woman who does not go through the procedure would be an outcast and not marriageable—and marriage is a ticket to survival.

However, many women around the world protest the practice as a dangerous mutilation of the body causing health and reproductive problems and violating human rights. Several cases of women trying to escape the procedure by seeking refugee status have come before foreign courts; a young Ghanaian woman who sought asylum in the United States to avoid the ritual of circumcision made front-page news in several countries; after over two years in U.S. detention, she was granted asylum, setting a precedent for other women in similar situations (Hu 1999).

Many women, including feminist theorists, who oppose female genital mutilation see it as a power struggle favoring males, resulting in females' bodies becoming objects to control for the sexual attraction and pleasure of men.

Conflict Theory

Conflict theorists study both individual family situations and broad societal family patterns. They argue that conflict in families is natural and inevitable; it results from the struggle for power and control in the family unit and in the society at large. As long as there is an unequal allocation of resources, conflict will arise.

Family conflicts take many forms. For instance, conflicts occur over allocation of resources, a struggle that may be rooted in conflict between men and women in the society: Who makes decisions, who gets money for clothes or a car, who does the dishes? On the macro level, family systems are a source of inequality in the general society,

sustaining class inequalities by passing on wealth, income, and educational opportunities to their own members, or perpetuating disadvantages such as poverty and lack of cultural capital (Benokraitis 2004).

Yet some conflict theorists argue that conflict within the family can be important because it forces constant negotiation among individual family members and may bring about change that can strengthen the unit as a whole. Believing that conflict is both natural and inevitable, these theorists focus on root causes of conflict and how to deal with the discord. For conflict theorists, there is no assumption of a harmonious complementary family; the social world is characterized more by tension and power plays than by social

This is an X-ray of the feet of a woman whose feet were bound when she was a child to make her attractive to a wealthy suitor. Her disability was a status symbol for her husband, who had clear proof that he could provide for wife and family without help, but she paid the price of limited mobility for his prestige.

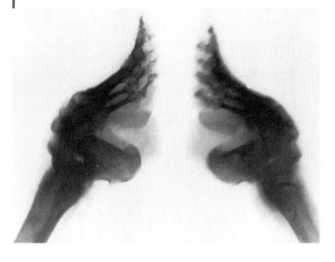

accord. Sociology around the World on page 300 provides an example of women being used in family power relations.

 THINKING SOCIOLOGICALLY

How do men or women mutilate their bodies in your society in order to be sexually appealing to others? For example, are breast implants (by which women lose feeling and perhaps the euphoria of orgasm) a similar phenomenon? Why or why not? What about the painful ritual of placing metal braces on ones teeth to pull them into different locations in order have a better smile? Are there any painful self-mutilating rituals that men (but not women) do for greater attractiveness? If so, what are those activities? If not, why not?

Feminist Theory

The feminist approach is based on sociological studies done on, by, and for women. Because women often occupy very different places in society from men, feminist theorists argue the need for a feminist perspective in order to understand family dynamics. Feminist scholars begin by placing women at the center, not to suggest their superiority but to spotlight them as subjects of inquiry and as active agents in the working of society. The biases rooted in male assumptions are uncovered and examined (Eshleman and Bulcroft 2006; Olin 1996).

One micro-level branch of feminist theory, the interpretive approach, considers women within their social contexts—the interpersonal relations and everyday reality facing women as they interact with other family members. It does not ignore economic, political, social, and historical factors but focuses on the ways women construct their reality, their opportunities, and their place in the community. According to feminist theorists, this results in a more realistic view of family and women's lives than many other theories provide. Applying this feminist approach to understand Felice's situation, the theorists would consider the way she views her social context and the way she assesses her support systems.

With roots in conflict theory, many feminist theorists argue that patterns of patriarchy and dominance lead to inequalities for women. One of the earliest conflict theorists, Friedrich Engels (Karl Marx's close associate), argued that the family was the chief source of female oppression and that until basic resources were reallocated within the family, women would continue to be oppressed. However, he said that as women become aware of their collective interests and oppression, they will insist on a redistribution of power, money, and jobs (Engels 1902).

One vivid example of how women and men can be viewed as groups with competing interests is through a feminist analysis of domestic violence. In the United States, a woman is assaulted or beaten every nine seconds (Tjaden and Thoennes 2000); someone is sexually assaulted every two-and-a-half minutes (U.S. Department of Justice 2002); 60 percent of all married women will experience battering at some time in their lives (CALCASA 2006); and four women are murdered each day by boyfriends or husbands (Tjaden and Thoennes 2000). In Western societies, men are under pressure to be successful; when they are not, home may be the place where they vent their frustrations. When socialization results in a hypermasculine sense of identity, and this is combined with an emotional dependency on a female, it is a lethal combination. Cultural messages tell men that they are to be in charge, but knowing they are emotionally and sometimes economically dependent on their wives may result in violence to regain control.

Women are most severely exploited in societies that treat them as property and in which the family is a key political unit for power and status. Where men are the heads of families and women are dependent, women might be treated as less than equal both within the family and in the labor market. Consider the practice of *sati;* although outlawed now, it lingers in some areas of India. The widow is expected to (or was forced to) throw herself on her husband's funeral pyre because there was no structural place for her in the family after her husband's death. In some societies, the practice of wife beating is expected if the husband is dissatisfied with her cooking, housekeeping, or child care. This can happen in groups such as the Masai or in countries such as Brazil. In some cultural situations, the woman's life is only valuable as it relates to the economic situation and the needs of men. Changes in the patriarchal family structure, education and employment opportunities for women, and child care availability can lead to greater freedom of choice, equality, and autonomy for women, according to feminist theorists (Shaw and Lee 2005).

FAMILY DYNAMICS: MICRO-LEVEL PROCESSES

The Abubakar family belongs to the Hausa tribe of West Africa. They share a family compound composed of huts or houses for each family unit of one wife and her young children, plus one building for greeting guests, one for cooking, one for the older children, and one for washing. The compound is surrounded by an enclosure. Each member of the family carries out certain tasks: food preparation, washing, child care, farming, herding—whatever is needed for the group. Wives live with their husbands' families. Should there be a divorce, the children generally belong to the husband's household because the family lineage is through the father's side.

The eldest male is the leader. He makes decisions for the group. When a child is born, the eldest male within the family presides over a ceremony to name the child and welcome him or her into the group. When the child reaches marrying age, he plays a major role in choosing a suitable mate. Upon his death, the power he has held passes to his eldest son, and his property is inherited by his sons.

However, Abubakar's eldest son has moved away from the extended family to the city where he works in a factory to support himself. He lives in a small room with several other migrants. He has met a girl from another tribe and may marry her, although his family does not approve of his marrying outside their group and without their blessing. He will probably have a small family because of money and space pressures in the city; his lifestyle and even values have already altered considerably. In the social world, the global trend toward the Western model of industrialization and urbanization is altering cultures around the world and changing family life.

The story indicates the extensive interdependencies of family as a micro-level social unit, a meso-level institution, and a macro-level social system. Many individual family issues that seem very intimate and personal are actually affected by norms and forces at another level (such as migration and urbanization), and decisions of individuals affect meso- and macro-level social structures (such as size of families).

THINKING SOCIOLOGICALLY

What kinds of changes in families would you anticipate as societies change from agricultural to industrial economies and as individuals move from rural to urban areas? What changes has your family undergone over several generations?

Mate Selection: How Do New Families Start?

At the most micro level, two people get together to begin a new family unit. There are more than 6 billion people in the world, but it is highly unlikely that your mate was or will be randomly selected from the entire global population. Even in Western societies where we think we are responsible for choosing our marriage partners, mate selection is seldom an entirely free choice. Indeed, our mate selection is highly limited by geographical proximity, ethnicity, age, social class, and a host of other variables. So like all of the other micro-level processes we will examine here, macro-level factors also play a part. What are some factors in the mate-selection process?

Norms Governing Choice of Marriage Partners: Societal Rules and Intimate Choices

A number of norms and social constraints—meso- and macro-level expectations—govern the choice of a mate in any society. Most are unwritten, and they vary somewhat from culture to culture, but we all learn them from an early age. One of the cultural rules is **exogamy**—a norm that requires individuals to marry outside of their own immediate group. The most universal form of exogamy is the *incest taboo,* including restrictions against father-daughter, mother-son and brother-sister marriages. Some countries, including about half the U.S. states, forbid first cousins to marry, while others, such as some African groups, encourage first cousin marriages to solidify family ties and property holdings (Ottenheimer 1996). As we saw in Chapter 3, there is considerable cultural variation in whether first cousins are forbidden or preferred mates On the other hand, some societies require *village exogamy* (marriage outside the village) because it bonds together villages and reduces the likelihood of armed conflict between them.

Anthropologists have suggested several hypotheses to explain why all societies develop norms governing, and usually prohibiting, incestuous relations. These range from intuitive recognition of the negative biological results of inbreeding to necessity for families to make ties with outside groups for survival. One clear issue is that rights to sexual access can cause jealousy that rips a social unit apart. If father and son became jealous about who was sleeping with the wife/mother, relationships would be destroyed and parental authority sabotaged. Likewise, if the father was always going to the daughter for sexual satisfaction, the mother and daughter bond would be severely threatened (Davis 1960; Williams, Sawyer, and Wahlstrom 2006). No society can allow this to happen to its family system; any society that has failed to have an incest taboo self-destructed long ago.

On the other hand, norms of **endogamy** require individuals to marry inside certain boundaries, whatever the societal members see as protecting the homogeneity of the group. Endogamous norms may require individuals to select mates of the same race, religion, social class, ethnic background, or clan (Williams et al. 2006). Whether marriages are arranged or entered into freely, both endogamy and exogamy limit the number of possible mates. In addition to marrying within a group, most people choose a mate with similar social characteristics—age, place of residence, educational background, political philosophy, moral values, and psychological traits—a practice called *homogamy*.

Going outside the limits in mate selection can make things tough for newlyweds who need family and community support. Few take this risk. For instance, in the United States, close to 90 percent marry people with similar religious values (Williams et al. 2006); 80 to 90 percent of Protestants marry other Protestants, and 64 to 85 percent of Catholics marry within their religious faith. For Jews, the figure is as high as 90 percent (Eshleman and Bulcroft 2006), but the figure has dropped in recent decades to as low as 50 percent for Jews, depending on the type of Judaism (Newman and Grauerholz 2002). In Canada, only one person in five enters into religious intermarriages (Heaton 1990). However, with increased tolerance for differences, cross-denominational marriage is more likely today than a century ago. It is also higher among individuals who grew up as Catholics but are not now practicing (Sander 1993). Intermarriage between Catholics and Protestants in the United States was rare in the 1920s, but as prejudice against Catholics has declined and differences in educational levels between the groups have decreased, educational homogamy has become more important than religious endogamy (Kalmijn 1991).

Each group may have different definitions of where the exogamy boundary is. For Orthodox Hasidic Jews, marriage to a Reform Jew is exogamy—strictly forbidden. For the Amish, the marriage of a Hostetler Amish woman to a Beachy Amish man is beyond consideration. Marriage of a Hopi to a Navajo has also been frowned upon as marriage to an Other—even though many Anglos would think of this as an endogamous marriage of two Native Americans.

So cultural norms of societies limit individual decisions about micro-level matters such as choice of a spouse, and they do so in a way that most individuals do not even recognize. Exogamy and endogamy norms and expectations generally restrict the range of potential marriage partners, even though some of these norms are weakening. Still, the question remains: How do we settle on a life partner?

Finding a Mate

In most societies, mate selection is achieved through either arranged marriages, free-choice unions, or some combination of the two. In either case, selection is shaped by cultural rules of the society.

Arranged Marriages

In this pattern of mate selection, someone other than the couple—elder males, parents, a matchmaker—selects the marital partners. This method of mate selection is most common in traditional, often patriarchal, societies. Some examples follow.

Many traditional girls in Muslim societies don a veil at puberty and wear it throughout their adult years. Custom dictates that she should not look into the eyes of men outside of her immediate family. Marriage for her is a matter of necessity, for her support comes from the family system. Economic arrangements and political alliances between family groups are solidified through marriage; daughters are valuable commodities in negotiations to secure these ties between families (Burn 2005). Beauty, youth, talent, and pleasant disposition bring a high price and a good match. Should the young people like each other, it is icing on the cake. Daughters must trust that the male elders in their families will make the best possible matches for them. Clearly, the men hold the power in this vital decision.

In the Tiwi tribe of Australia, no female child is born without a husband. The father of the child-to-be betroths the unborn to an older man. Should "she" be a "he," the arrangement is cancelled. All females are married in utero because it is believed that the female can become pregnant at any time after birth. For a woman to have a child if she is unmarried is a serious offense. At puberty, the girl goes to live with her husband. Should the husband die, the girl is immediately transferred to another man. Although age spans between husbands and their several wives may be great, this arrangement assures everyone a home and security. It has been the tradition for the Tiwi tribe for thousands of years (Nanda and Warms 2007).

Seated front and center with the bride and groom at many Japanese weddings is the matchmaker, the person responsible for bringing the relationship into being. After both families agree to the arrangement, the couple meets over tea several times to decide whether the match is agreeable. Roughly 30 percent of marriages in Japan are still arranged this way, the rest being called "love marriages" ("Getting Married in Japan" 2002).

Where arranged marriages are the norm, love has a special meaning. The couple may never have set eyes on each other before the wedding day, but respect and affection generally grow over time as the husband and wife live together. People from these societies are assured a mate and have difficulty comprehending marriage systems based on love, romance, and courtship, factors that they believe to be insufficient grounds for a lifelong relationship. They wonder why anyone would want to place themselves in a marriage market, with all of the uncertainty and rejection? Such whimsical and unsystematic methods would not work in many societies where the structure of life is built around family systems.

Free Choice and Romantic Love

When the partners in a marriage select each other based primarily on romance and love, they are participating in free-choice marriage. Sonnets, symphonies, rock songs, poems, and plays have been written to honor love and the psychological and physiological pain and pleasure that the mating game brings. However impractical romance may

During this Shinto-style wedding in Japan, a shrine maiden (left) pours Japanese rice wine into a nuptial cup held by the bride. During the ceremony, the bride and groom each take three sips while exchanging the cup three times; this symbolizes the bond between the couple. In roughly a third of these weddings, the marriage was arranged by a matchmaker.

Source: © Yuriko Nakao / Reuters / Corbis.

seem, marriage choice based on **romantic love** is becoming more prevalent as societies around the world become more Westernized and families exert less control over their children's choice of mates (Eshleman and Bulcroft 2006). Industrialized societies tend to value love and individualism and tend to have high marriage rates, low fertility rates, and high divorce rates (Levine et al. 1995).

Free-choice mate selection is found in most Western societies; couples in the United States tend to put more emphasis on romantic love and the process of attracting a mate than most other societies. Romantic love is most common in wealthy countries where individuals are emphasized over community interests (Eshleman and Bulcroft 2006). For example, 86 percent of U.S. college students say they would not marry without love.

The old adages about women "hooking a man" and men being "snagged or caught" are challenged by data that suggest that men are more likely than women to prefer marriage over the single status for life; 66 percent of men agreed that "it is better to get married" compared to 51 percent of women in a recent U.S. survey. In response to the statement, "it is more important for a man to spend a lot of time with his family than be successful at his career," 76 percent of men agreed, compared to 72 percent of women (Centers for Disease Control and Prevention 2006). These sentiments are comparable in many European countries where fewer women are marrying than in the past.

E-romance is helping to facilitate mate selection in free-choice systems. By allowing people of all ages to enter into relationships on the Internet, some find compatible mates. This facilitates what those in arranged marriage systems find bewildering about free-choice systems—How do you meet possible mates? The burgeoning business in e-romance introduces people with common interests, backgrounds, ages, and other variables. For example, eHarmony has participants fill out an extensive 436-question personality profile that it claims is a "scientifically proven" compatibility-matching system. Over 9 million users hope for one or more matches from the system. The matches can then communicate electronically and may eventually decide to meet in person.

Many of the e-dating services claim that their profiles and processes are based on social science research; Pepper Schwartz, a well-known sociologist on relationships, helped design PerfectMatch's system. Many services have sprung up, including Match.com, PerfectMatch.com, Chemistry.com, and a number of more specialized services such as Goodgenes.com and conservativematch.com.

Are these services successful in matching up potential mates? A recent study found that one in three respondents was unattached, and 7 percent of the population were actively looking for partners. Thirty-seven percent of those had tried online dating sites, and about half had been out on a date as a result of online services. About one-third of those had formed long-term relationships. Because online dating is relatively new, it is unclear whether it will become a dominant form of mate selection (Gottlieb 2006).

THINKING SOCIOLOGICALLY

Is e-dating a modern-day form of the matchmaker? Is it replacing other forms of finding a mate? Why or why not?

In this interdependent global society, the dominant Western model tends to infiltrate and to be adopted in other parts of the world. Once again, the social world model helps us to understand that even mate-selection processes are shaped by macro-level influences that filter to the national, institutional, community, and individual family levels. A very private and personal process is becoming transformed by global forces and trends.

Starting with the assumption that eligible people are most likely to meet and be attracted to others who have similar values and backgrounds, sociologists have developed various mate-selection theories that view dating as a three-stage process.

1. Stimulus: We meet someone to whom we are attracted by appearance, voice, dress, similar ethnic background, sense of humor, or other factors. Something serves as a stimulus that makes us take notice. Of course, sometimes the stimulus is simply knowing the other person is interested in us.

2. Value comparison: As we learn about the other's values, we are more likely to find that person

compatible if she or he affirms our own beliefs and values toward life, politics, religion, and roles of men and women in society and marriage. If values are not compatible, the person does not pass through our filter; we look elsewhere.

3. Roles and needs stage: Another filter comes at this stage in which the couple explores roles of companion, parent, housekeeper, and lover. This might involve looking for common needs, interests, and favored activities. If roles and needs are not complementary to one's own, desire for a permanent relationship wanes.

The mate-selection process varies somewhat from person to person, but social scientists believe that a sequential series of decisions, in a pattern such as that described above, is often part of the process (Eshleman and Bulcroft 2006; Murstein 1987).

THINKING SOCIOLOGICALLY

Conduct a small survey of dating and married couples you know. Ask them about how they became involved in their relationship and the process of deciding to get together or marry. How do their comments mesh with the three-stage process described above?

The mate-selection process complete, the couple moves on to the challenges of marriage. Certain adjustments must be made as the couple maneuvers through various stages of life. What affects marital adjustment? The next How Do We Know? describes findings from research that studied marriages that have lasted 20 or more years; the researchers asked just that question.

Who Holds the Power?
Authority Relations in Marriage

Power relations, another micro-level issue shaped by cultural norms, affect the personal interactions and decision making in individual families. Two areas that have received particular sociological attention are decision making in marriage and work roles.

Decision Making in Marriage

Cultural traditions establish the power base in society and family: patriarchy, matriarchy, or egalitarianism. The most typical authority pattern in the world is *patriarchy,* or male authority. *Matriarchy,* female authority, is rare; even where the lineage is traced through the mother's line, males generally dominate decision making. Some analysts have suggested reasons for male dominance: males are physically larger, they are free from childbearing, and they are not tied to one place by homemaking and agricultural responsibilities. However, social scientists find no evidence that there are any inherent

intellectual foundations for male authority as opposed to female authority (Kramer 2001; Ward and Edelstein 2006).

Egalitarian family patterns, in which power, authority, and decision making are shared between the spouses and perhaps with the children, are emerging, but they are not yet a reality in most households. For example, research indicates that in many U.S. families, decisions concerning vacation plans, car purchases, and housing decisions are reached democratically. Still, most U.S. families are not fully egalitarian; males generally have a disproportionate say in major decisions (Lindsey 2005).

Resource theory attempts to explain power relations by arguing that the spouse with the greater resources—education, occupational prestige, income—has the greater power. In many societies, income is the most important factor because it represents identity and power. If only one spouse brings home a paycheck, the other is usually less powerful (Blumstein and Schwartz 1985; Tichenor 1999). In families in which the wife is a professional, other factors in addition to income such as persuasion and egalitarian values may enter into the power dynamic (Lindsey 2005; Lips 1991). Regardless of who has greater resources, men in two-earner couples tend to have more say in financial matters and less responsibility for children and household tasks. U.S. women spend on average 11 hours a week on child care, while men spend 3.3 hours; women also spend a weekly average of 19.4 hours on housework other than child care, while men devote 10.4 hours (Bianci et al. 2000; Newman and Grauerholz 2002).

Who Does the Housework?

Is there a typical division of labor in households? In many societies, couples exhibit highly sex-segregated family work patterns, even when the male contributes many hours to housework. Women take responsibility for most of the household and childcare (Coltrane 2000). When men do participate, they tend to do dishes, grocery shopping, repairs, work outside the house, and care for the car (Bianci et al. 2000; Ferree 1991). Table 10.1 shows a typical division of household tasks for married couples.

TABLE 10.1	Housework and Gender: Hours per Week	
Task	Husband	Wife
Cleaning	2.1	8.0
Cooking	1.4	5.3
Laundry	0.3	2.4
Bill paying	1.6	1.1
Outdoor work	2.1	0.8
Repairs	2.2	0.8
Pet or plant care	0.8	1.0
Total hours per week	10.4	19.4

Source: Bianci et al. (2000).

Marital Adjustment and Marriages that Last

What makes a marriage last? How do people reach 25 and 50 years together? Richard Mackey and Bernard O'Brien (1995) sought to answer this question using in-depth analysis of long-lasting marriages. Issues that especially interested them were how couples adjust to one another, the relationship over time, and patterns that make for lasting relationships. The researchers gathered marital histories from 120 husbands and wives in 60 marriages. They interviewed people in their own homes but talked with each person separately. Interviews averaged about two hours. Each couple was recruited through community organizations (civic clubs, churches, synagogues, professional and trade union organizations, and so forth), and each couple was selected using the following criteria: (1) the couple had been married at least 20 years, (2) the youngest child was at least 18 and out of high school, (3) there was no current or historical pattern of extensive marriage trouble or counseling, and (4) the sample represented racial, ethnic, educational, and religious diversity. Interviews allowed for flexibility and openness in the responses, and each one was then transcribed for analysis. Each respondent was asked a variety of questions about the early phases of marriage, the child-rearing years, and the later empty-nest stage. Key concepts were coded to see how often certain themes or patterns occurred; the coded data were then entered into

a computer statistical program for quantitative analysis. The findings from the study were then published in the book, *Lasting Marriages: Men and Women Growing Together.*

The authors found many interesting patterns, but the analysis of marital adjustment was especially intriguing. The study examined satisfaction in the areas of communication, sex, trust, empathy, emotional intimacy, marital conflict, and mutual decision making. Marriages go through stages related to age of children. For instance, the authors found some long-term decline in the intensity of satisfaction with sex, although it did improve a bit right after all the children left the home. Conflict was more intense when children entered the picture and improved after the parents had the home to themselves. Communication declined while the children were around and then improved as the couple entered the later stage. Emotional intimacy generally improved over the course of the marriage, although it did suffer while the children were in the adolescent stage. Mutual decision making, empathy, and trust all improved somewhat over the years.

This was not a study based on a random sample of all couples, so its findings are limited to healthy—or at least lasting—marriages. However, adjustment was not an all-or-nothing matter; it fluctuated over time but did not decline overall over many years. Some aspects of marital adjustment improved with age,

others deteriorated slightly, and others suffered until the empty-nest stage and then improved. By using both qualitative and quantitative methods of data analysis, Mackey and O'Brien (1995) improved our knowledge of how lasting marriages adjust and adapt over time.

The authors found that stable marriages survive for a number of reasons, including ethnic group beliefs about divorce, religious commonality, and comfortable family income. However, one predictor of lasting marriage is overall satisfaction with the marriage. Decision making in lasting marriages was mutual and collaborative, with emphasis on equity; communication was open and direct and became more comfortable in times of crisis as time passed; mutual respect was maintained throughout the relationship, while trust and understanding of the other seemed to grow over the years; frequency of sexual intimacy declined over the years, but psychological intimacy improved as successful couples learned to depend on each other for support. In the long run, the latter form of intimacy seemed most important. Conflicts were not a problem as long as the partners tried to solve them in ways that led to win-win resolutions (rather than rancorous win-lose contests). This conflict-resolution skill was highly related to overall satisfaction. These seemed to be the key elements of stable and fulfilling marriages.

THINKING SOCIOLOGICALLY

Analyze the division of labor in your family. How did it evolve? Is it considered fair by the participants? How does it compare to the Table 10.1?

The Second Shift, a term coined by Hochschild (1989), refers to the housework and child care that employed women do after their first-shift jobs; studies over the years indicate that women take on more household responsibilities. Employment schedules also affect the amount of time each spouse contributes to household tasks; husbands who are at home during hours when their wives are working tend to take on more tasks. Employment, education, and earnings give women more respect and independence and a power base for a more equitable division of labor across tasks (Cherlin 2002; Kramer 2001). Egalitarian shared work is most common in dual-wage families where there is agreement over an equitable division of labor.

Interestingly, husbands who do an equitable share of the household chores actually report higher levels of satisfaction with the marriage (Stevens, Kiger, and Riley 2001). The success or failure of a marriage depends in large part on patterns that develop early in the marriage for dealing with the everyday situations including power relationships and division of labor.

While women generally are economically dependent on men, giving men the power, men are often dependent on women emotionally, for they are less likely to have same-sex friends with whom they share feelings and vulnerabilities. Men bond with one another, but they seldom develop truly intimate ties that provide support in hard times. So women are not entirely without power; it is just that their power frequently takes a different form (and results in fewer privileges) (Newman and Grauerholz 2002)

THINKING SOCIOLOGICALLY

Interview couples you know about what keeps them together and what causes tensions. Find a couple(s) that have been together for 20 or more years, and ask what they feel has kept them together.

THE FAMILY AS AN INSTITUTION: MESO-LEVEL ANALYSIS

We experience family life at a very personal level, but consider all families together and we have the family as an institution—a stable pattern of social relationships at the meso level of society.

According to the U.S. census, the total number of households involves residential units, irrespective of family or kinship ties. This number was 113.1 million households in 2005; 32 percent of those households were nonfamily units, compared to only 10 percent nonfamilies in 1950 (U.S. Census Bureau 2005a). The average number of members living in a household decreased from 3.14 persons in 1970, to 2.76 in 1980, then rose to 3.24 in 2000 and fell to 2.57 in 2005. In the year 2005, 18.2 percent of the households were single-parent female householders with no spouse present. The number of children living with a single parent was up to 28 percent in 2005 (U.S. Census Bureau 2005a). These figures give us some idea about capacity for change in *the family* as an institution—as a collective entity that meets needs of individuals and society as a whole. Some of the changes in this institution have resulted from—or caused—changes in other institutions.

Marriage and Family Structure: The Components of Family as an Institution

Although the family is an element in the larger social system, it does vary in interesting ways from one society to another. How many mates does a society think a man or woman should have, for instance? Some societies believe that several wives provide more hands to do the work and establish useful political and economic alliances between family groups. They bring more children into the family unit and provide multiple family members for emotional and physical support and satisfaction. On the other hand, having one spouse per adult probably meets most individuals' social and emotional needs very effectively, is less costly, and eliminates the possibility of conflict or jealousy among spouses. It is also easier to relocate a one-spouse family to urban areas, a necessity for many families in industrialized societies. Let us examine the issue of adult partners in a family.

Types of Marriages

Monogamy and polygamy are the main forms of marriage found around the world. **Monogamy**, the most familiar form to those of us in industrial and postindustrial societies, refers to marriage of two individuals. *Polygamy*, in which a man or woman has more than one spouse, is most often found in agricultural societies where multiple spouses and children mean more help with the farmwork. There are two main forms of polygamy—*polygyny* and *polyandry*. Anthropologist George Murdock found that **polygyny**, a husband having more than one wife, was allowed (although not always practiced) in 709 of the 849 societies he cataloged in his classic *Ethnographic Atlas*. Only 16 percent (136 societies) were *exclusively* monogamous (Barash 2002).

Although many societies allow polygyny, only a small percentage of families in the world actually practice it because of the expense of maintaining a large family, high prices that men's families must pay to the bride's family in some societies, and religious and political pressures from other powerful

An extended family works their farm together in Chelsea, Michigan.

Source: © Andrew Sacks / Corbis.

THINKING SOCIOLOGICALLY

Some popular films and television series have depicted forms of polygamy. Consider hit series such as *Big Love.* What is the appeal of such entertainment for those in monogamous societies? What are examples of shows that depict serial monogamy?

Extended families include two or more adult generations that share tasks and living quarters; this may include brothers, sisters, aunts, uncles, cousins, and grandparents. In most extended family systems, the eldest male is the authority figure. This is a common patten around the world, especially in agricultural and developing societies. Some ethnic groups in the United States, such as Mexican Americans and some Asian Americans, live in extended monogamous families with several generations under one roof. This is financially practical and helps group members maintain their traditions and identity by remaining somewhat isolated from Anglo society.

As societies become more industrialized and fewer individuals and families engage in agriculture, the **nuclear family**, consisting of two parents and their children—or any two of the three—becomes more common. This worldwide trend toward nuclear family occurs because more individuals live in urban areas where smaller families are more practical, mate selection is based on love, and couples establish independent households after marriage; marriage is less of an economic arrangement between families; fewer marriages take place between relatives such as cousins; and equality between the sexes increases (Burn 2005; Goode 1970).

The family can be found in many forms. No matter how it manifests itself structurally, a society's family institution is interdependent on each of the other major institutions. For example, if the health care system is unaffordable or not functioning well, families may not get the care they need to prevent serious illness. If the economy goes into a recession and jobs are not available, families experience stress, abuse rates increase, and marriages are more likely to become unstable. If the government fails to support families, as occurred when Hurricane Katrina hit New Orleans and Southern Mississippi in the summer of 2005, families may suffer, be torn apart, and experience wrenching disorientation and dislocation. Interdependence with the economy, the next topic, illustrates this point.

countries for monogamy. Indeed, only a limited number of men in polygynous societies can afford to support several wives. Since the number of men and women is usually fairly balanced in a society, there are seldom enough extra women to go around. Polygyny does increase at times of war when the number of men is reduced due to war causalities.

Polyandry, a wife having more than one husband, is practiced in less than 1 percent of the world's societies. Among the Todas of Southern India, brothers can share a wife, and the Marquesan Islanders allow wives to have more than one husband. A Tibetan practice originating in the country's system of land ownership and inheritance allows a woman to marry several men, usually brothers (O'Connel 1993). This often happens when the men are poor and must share a single plot of land to eke out a meager livelihood, so they decide to remain a single household with one wife. Murdock found only four societies in the world that practice polyandrous marriage.

Members of Western societies often find the practice of polygamy hard to understand, just as those from polygamous societies find monogamy strange. Some societies insist on *strict monogamy:* marriage to one other person is lifelong, and deviation from that standard is prohibited. Yet most Western societies practice what could be called a variation of polygamy—*serial monogamy.* With high divorce and remarriage rates, Western societies have developed a system of marrying several spouses, but one at a time. One has spouses in a series rather than simultaneously.

Extended and Nuclear Families

The typical ma-pa-and-kids monogamous model that is familiar in many industrialized parts of the world is not as typical as it appears. From a worldwide perspective, it is only one of several structural models of family.

THINKING SOCIOLOGICALLY

Under what social circumstances would an extended family be helpful? Under what circumstances would it be a burden?

The Economic Institution and the Family

The family is the primary economic unit of consumption, so what happens in the economy has a major impact on the structure and quality of family life. When economic times are rough, employment instability and uncertainty, economic strain, and deprivation can cause strained family relations. Low-income families, especially single-parent families headed by women, are particularly hard-hit and often have to struggle for survival (Staples 1999; Willie 2003).

Poverty and Families in the United States

The poverty threshold in 2005 for a family of four was $19,806 (U.S. Census Bureau 2006d). In 2004, there were 26.5 million families (11 percent) that lived below the poverty level (U.S. Census Bureau 2005f). Table 10.2 shows the percentage of individuals and families in poverty. Table 10.3 shows the increase in single-parent families between 1970 and 2002 (Hamilton et al. 2006).

The "feminization of poverty," discussed in earlier chapters, is a global problem. It occurs where single motherhood is widespread, as shown in Table 10.3, and where there are few policies to reduce poverty (Goldberg and Kremen 1990; Williams et al. 2006). Single mothers, whether in capitalist or socialist countries, have some

When couples have divorced and are no longer units of economic cooperation, there is much more stress on the primary caretaker to perform multiple roles.

Source: © Jason Lugo.

common experiences, including dual roles as workers and mothers, lower earnings than men, irregular paternal support payments, and underrepresentation in policymaking bodies. What differs around the world are governmental policies to help mothers with child support, child care, health care, maternity leave, and family allowances. Single mothers are as prevalent in Sweden as in the United States, but U.S. single mothers are six times more likely to be poor because of fewer support systems (Casper, McLanahan, and Garfinkel 1994; Goldberg and Kremen 1990). For single teens, early motherhood, lack of education, and insufficient income lead to a multiproblem family pattern. One reason for the increase in single-parent households among African American women is that there are 1.75 million more African American women than men (U.S. Census Bureau 2005g), due in large part to high mortality rates of African American males. Although African Americans value family, many poor men cannot fulfill the economic role of husband and father because the number of jobs available to less-educated men is decreasing (McLeod 2004; Wilson 1987). The percentage of births to unmarried mothers varies considerably by ethnicity as shown in Table 10.4. Although the percentage of births has increased over time, it has leveled off for African Americans in recent years.

Some argue that a *culture of poverty*, a set of attitudes and values including a sense of hopelessness and passivity, low aspirations, feelings of powerlessness and inferiority, and *present-time orientation* (concern only for the present), is

TABLE 10.2 **Poverty Status of U.S. Families by Family Type**

Poverty Status and Family Type	Total Percentage Below Poverty Level
Total families[a]	10.2
Married-couple families	5.5 (3.2 million)
Female householder, no spouse present	28.4 (4 million)

Source: U.S. Census Bureau (2005f).
a. Data includes families in group quarters.

TABLE 10.3 **Percentage of Births to Unmarried and Married Women: United States (in percentages)**

Year	Births to Unmarried Women (%)	Births to Married Women (%)
2004	35.8	64.2
2000	33.2	66.8
1995	32.2	67.8
1990	28.0	72.0
1985	22.0	78.0
1980	18.4	81.6

Source: Hamilton et al. (2006, Table 4).

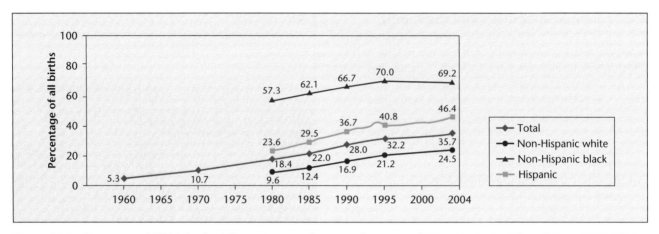

Figure 10.1   Percentage of All Births that Were to Unmarried Women, by Race and Hispanic Origin, Selected Years, 1960–2004

Source: Child Trends DataBank (http://www.childtrendsdatabank.org, retrieved August 22, 2006).

TABLE 10.4	**Percentage of Births to Unmarried Mothers**
African American	68.5
Native American	58.4
Hispanic	42.5
White (non-Hispanic)	27.1
Asian	14.8

Source: Child Trends Data Bank (2005).

When both parents have full-time jobs, one solution to the stress is to hire other people to do some of the familial jobs, including care of children. Many people who use child care feel it has been very good for the children, and studies confirm this—depending on the quality of the care agency.

Source: © Jacques M. Chenet / Corbis.

passed from one generation to the next (Lewis 1961, 1986). However, many sociological researchers support the argument that poverty itself causes the values and attitudes that develop in poor communities as survival mechanisms (McLeod 2004). In a field study of an African American ghetto community, Carol Stack (1998) found some creative adaptations to unhealthy environmental conditions. Relatives and intimate friends shared money, child care, food, and housing to meet each other's needs in times of crisis. In this example, the notion of family is expanded to include a network of people who provide mutual care. On the flip side, when someone does succeed in escaping the slum, close friends and relatives lean on the person for support and contacts, and the person can get drawn back into the impoverished networks. So the same networks can be both supportive and entrapping.

Dual-Worker Families

A different kind of economic influence can be seen in dual-career marriages. Two incomes may relieve economic strain on a household, but family life may be quite complicated. Browse through the checkout-line magazine racks next time you are in a grocery store. Note the number of articles offering advice on how to cope with stress and overload or how to budget time, cook meals in minutes, rise to the top, and "make it" together. Stress, role conflict, and work overload are common, but most couples are aware of these strains and have chosen to combine marriage, sometimes children, and the intense involvement required by a career.

In many industrialized societies, government and industry support dual-career families with various family-friendly policies: readily available child care facilities, parenting leaves for childbirth and illness, and flexible work hours or telecommuting (working from one's home). However, many corporations in the United States have been slow to respond to dual-career family needs. Company-sponsored day-care and paternity leave are still rare. A few businesses are experimenting with family-friendly policies such as *flextime*, allowing individuals to schedule their own work hours within certain time frames, and *job sharing*, allowing individuals to split a job with one family member working in the morning and the other in the afternoon.

Family is a diverse and complex social institution. It interacts with other institutions and in some ways reinforces them. Families prepare the next generation. Adult family members socialize children and teach national loyalty; mentor the children on the use of money; and tutor children in reading, math, and social studies. Families pray together and talk as families about what happens after death; they provide care of disabled, infirm, or sick members of the family. As a basic institution, the family plays a role in the vitality of the entire nation. So it should not be surprising that at the macro level, many national and global policy decisions concern how to strengthen the family.

 ## NATIONAL AND GLOBAL FAMILY ISSUES: MACRO-LEVEL ANALYSIS

The most effective way to explore macro-level issues pertaining to families is to explore policy matters that affect the family or that are intended to strengthen families. After exploring issues of national concern—teen pregnancies, cohabitation, homosexual relationships, and divorce—we look at some global trends in marriage and family life.

Teen Pregnancies and Their Consequences

High rates of premarital sex, teenage pregnancy, and teen marriage are ongoing concerns are in the United States, Canada, and many other countries. In the United States, approximately one-third of all births in recent years have been to unmarried women. Of teenagers who become pregnant, 26 percent have abortions; 22 percent marry before childbirth; and 52 percent have out-of-wedlock births, resulting in single-parent families (Eshleman and Bulcroft 2006). The rate of births to teenagers in the United States is among the highest in the world at 45.9 births per 1,000 females in the 15-to-19 age group (Health in Schools 2002), but overall rates have been dropping slowly since 1991, with a 45 percent drop for African American teens.

Why are U.S. premarital-sex and teen-pregnancy rates so high? One variable stands out: the United States is less open than most countries (excluding Muslim societies) about sexual matters, reducing the amount of information teens receive about sex. In addition, compared to other developed countries, teens in the United States have less access to contraception and more restrictions on obtaining contraception, higher costs for contraception, and no national health care to help cover costs. High religiosity of some segments of American society results in less open

The rate of teen births in the United States is one of the highest in the world, despite more conservative attitudes toward premarital sex. One contributing factor is the restrictions on access to birth control.

Sources: © Anatoly Tiplyashin/Istockphoto.com; © Jorge Sá.

discussion about sex and less contraceptive education provided in schools.

Combine these factors with explicit portrayals of sex in the media, peer pressures, sexual desire, and lack of contraception, and we have a perfect recipe for high rates of teen pregnancy. In sum, restrictive attitudes toward sex education and an economically deprived underclass make teenage pregnancy more likely. However, education programs in some schools have helped reduce rates dramatically.

The biggest concern around the world is not sex outside of marriage but births out of marriage and care of the mother and child. Thus, teen pregnancy is not just a North American problem. In a study of 37 countries, those with low teen-birth rates had

1. high levels of socioeconomic modernization,

2. openness about discussing sex,

3. relatively low levels of inequality in the society as measured by family income,

4. an older minimum legal age for marriage,

5. awareness of the dangers of sexually transmitted diseases, and

6. a growing economy, which makes young women more optimistic about their futures (Sommerfeld 2002).

The number of teens who are sexually active is highest among Swedish and Danish adolescents; England, France, Netherlands and the United States have similar and somewhat lower rates. Despite this, the failure to use contraceptives is much higher with U.S. teenage girls: 20 percent in the United States, 4 percent in Britain, 6.5 percent in Sweden, and 13 percent in Canada (Sommerfeld 2002).

Teenage parents in industrial societies face extreme difficulties, for both themselves and their children. Often, neither parent has finished high school or developed the skills to earn a living wage. They cannot provide for health care, adequate nutrition, household and family stability, or other needs of their child. Births outside marriage result in less education for mother and child; less prestigious and more dead-end jobs; and children with poor test scores, grade retention, early sexual activity, and problem behaviors such as truancy and delinquency. Thus, we see that within our social world, factors at the macro level, such as contraceptive availability or cultural attitudes about discussing sex, influence pregnancy rates among teens. In turn, decisions about sexual behavior by individual teens have consequences for the macro-level systems, such as the welfare system and social services at the national, institutional, and local levels.

Teenage pregnancy is a national, macro-level issue because the stability of families is critical to a nation. Teen parents often have low levels of education, have few job skills, and cannot provide adequate health care, nutrition, and stability for a family. This puts pressure on governments to provide support for economically unstable units. When only one teenager must fulfill the parenting roles, an even more tenuous family is formed.

Because teenage families are so fragile, the result can be poorly socialized children, unhappy adults whose needs are not being met, and demands on taxpayers to provide support to these weak units and these vulnerable children. It is not surprising that policies to deter teen pregnancies are a public issue for many nations. The debate is usually whether to provide inexpensive birth control, allow abortion, or deter teenage pregnancy by making the costs for sexual activity very high. In the United States, there is little consensus about what policies at the macro level would best strengthen families.

THINKING SOCIOLOGICALLY

Some people think that making birth control, especially condoms, readily available will bring down teen pregnancy rates. Others argue that making birth control available would provide an enticement or an invitation to sexual experimentation at a young age and would undermine strong families. What is your view, and why?

Cohabitation

Another family issue is cohabitation, a significant macro-level trend in many European and North American countries. In the United States, unmarried couples living together nearly doubled in the 1990s, from 2.9 million in 1990 to nearly 4.85 million in 2005 (U.S. Census Bureau 2005a). As Table 10.5 shows, the increases in cohabiting households (same-sex and different-sex couples) in the United States over 20 years are dramatic.

TABLE 10.5	Cohabiting Households in the United States, 1980–2005
1980	1,589,000
1985	1,983,000
1990	2,856,000
1995	3,668,000
2000	5,475,768
2005	4,855,000

Source: U.S. Census Bureau (2005a).

Why do heterosexual couples decide to *cohabit*—live together in a sexual relationship without marriage? Cohabitors cite a number of reasons:

- rejection of the superficial dating game,
- a desire to enter more meaningful relationships with increased intimacy but with freedom to leave the union,
- emotional satisfaction and reduced loneliness,
- a chance to clarify what individuals want in a relationship and try out a relationship before permanent commitment,

- financial benefits of sharing living quarters, and
- sexual gratification (the latter cited more often by men than women) and some protection against disease by having one partner. (Bumpass and Lu 2000; Bumpass, Sweet, and Cherlin 1991; Lamanna and Riedmann 2003; Schoen and Weinick 1993).

For some, cohabitation is part of the mate-selection process. In 1987, 33 percent of the adult population between the ages of 19 and 44 had cohabited at some point, and by 2000 that percentage had increased to 41 percent. By the 2005, 4,855,000 households were made up of unmarried couples (Newman and Grauerholz 2002; U.S. Census Bureau 2005a). However, at any given point in time, only about 7 percent of the population in the United States is cohabiting (Benokraitis 2004). Countries with the highest percentage of women between 20 and 24 years in cohabiting relationships include Sweden (77 percent), New Zealand (67 percent), Austria (64 percent), France (63 percent), Netherlands and Norway (each 57 percent), and Canada (46 percent) (United Nations 2003). Latin American and Caribbean surveys have indicated that more than one in four women between the ages of 15 and 49 are in relationships they call *consensual unions*, living together without official sanction. However, such women typically have far less legal protection than European women during or after such unions. The rates of cohabitation seem to be declining in many African countries, where the rates are often below 15 percent of women (United Nations 2003).

Marriage versus cohabitation rates and reasons vary significantly by ethnicity. For whites in the United States, cohabitation is often a precursor to marriage; for African Americans, it may be an alternative to marriage. Financial problems encourage cohabitation in African American families, since many African American men avoid marriage if they do not think they can support a family and fulfill the breadwinner role. Sixty-eight percent of Hispanic families were married-couple households, while 83 percent of white households and only 48 percent of African American households were officially married families in 2000 (Fields and Casper 2001). Although childbearing increases the chance of marriage, it is a much stronger impetus to white than to black cohabitors (Manning and Smock 1995).

We might assume that cohabiting would allow couples to make more realistic decisions about entering permanent relationships. However, studies show little relationship between cohabitation and ensuing marital satisfaction, emotional closeness, sharing of roles, or amount of conflict. Some studies from Canada, Sweden, and the United States have even found evidence of lower quality marriages, lower commitment, and greater likelihood of divorce among those who cohabited before marriage (Bennett, Blanc, and Bloom 1988; Waite and Gallagher 2000). Indeed, one study found that the longer a couple cohabited before marriage, the greater the

likelihood that their marriage would eventually end in divorce (DeMaris and Rao 1992). The next Sociology in Your Social World discusses some reasons why cohabiting couples may have higher divorce rates than those who have not lived together prior to marriage.

Social analysts such as Waite and Gallagher (2000) and various scholars belonging to the conservative Council on Families in America believe that cohabitation is a threat to the stability of society. The council believes that the government should create more enticements to marry (e.g., tax breaks) and that the society should make cohabitation less acceptable and more stigmatized. This, they believe, would make for a stronger family system.

THINKING SOCIOLOGICALLY

First, read Sociology in Your Social World on page 314. How do you evaluate the argument that cohabitation is a threat to the stability of all marriages? Is reducing cohabitation an effective step to strengthening marriage?

Homosexual Relationships and Civil Unions

A hotly-debated macro-level policy matter concerning the family is homosexuality. As homosexual relationships become more widely acknowledged in the Western world, many gay and lesbian couples are living together openly as families. The 2000 U.S. Census reports 601,209 declared gay or lesbian households, but most scholars acknowledge that this is probably a substantial underreporting because of the stigma in many communities of reporting that one is homosexual (Smith and Gates 2001). Estimates are that 99.3 percent of all counties in the United States have same-sex couples, and approximately 3.1 million people live in same-sex relationships. One in three lesbian couples and one in five gay male couples are raising children (Human Rights Campaign 2003). In some places, these unions are officially recognized by state or religious organizations, but recognition is controversial at the national level. The Hawaiian Supreme Court ruled in 1993 that prohibitions against same-sex marriages are discriminatory; Alaska followed with a similar ruling a few years later; Vermont, spurred by a unanimous state supreme court ruling, passed a law in 2000 allowing civil unions for gays and lesbians; and Connecticut followed with civil union legislation in 2005.

However, many religious groups believe homosexuality is unacceptable, condemn it in a variety of ways, and deny the right to legal marriage (Laythe, Finkel, and Kirkpatrick 2001; McNeil 1993; Rodriguez and Lupfer 2000). More recently, the citizens in Hawaii and Alaska have voted to amend the state constitution so that marriage is limited to legal unions between a man and a woman. Furthermore, as of 2005, 44 states passed laws to not recognize same-sex

Sociology in Your Social World

Cohabiting: Facts and Fiction

I t seems reasonable—and many people believe—that if a couple lives together before marriage, they are more likely to have a marriage that lasts. Yet research shows that those who cohabit prior to marriage have higher divorce rates than those who do not. Several attempts have been made to explain this pattern, but Linda Waite and Maggie Gallagher (2000) have offered an interesting set of data and an intriguing interpretation to explain this puzzle. They point out that marriage has many benefits. Married people have better physical and mental health, have more frequent and more satisfying sex, and are substantially better off financially by the time of retirement than single people (they have more than double the money invested per person). Interestingly, the same benefits do not accrue to people who cohabit.

Much of this is because marriage links two people together in a way that makes them responsible to each other. If one smokes or drinks excessively, their partner has the right to complain about it—to essentially nag them into better health patterns—because their health has a direct impact on their partner, and vice versa. Likewise, if one likes to spend money very freely on vacations, the more frugal person is likely to restrain the spending habits of the spendthrift. This is acceptable because their financial futures are closely intertwined. As each person restrains the habits of the other, the couple is likely to end

up with more savings. As a result, at the end of their careers, the couple is likely to have more money put away for retirement. Also, people tend to be more adjusted when they have unqualified and unambiguous emotional support from another person whose life is inextricably tied to their own.

Couples who cohabit typically keep their finances separate and their options open. Moreover, they do not feel as if they have the right to nag the other person about health habits or finances. Their bond is emotional, but they are not committed in a way that they know their futures are intertwined. Thus, many of the advantages that come with marriage are lost. Moreover, according to Waite and Gallagher (2000), when such a couple does marry, they are shocked to find the other person beginning to nag them or to restrain their spending habits. The relationship is quite different, and they are irritated by the changed behavior of the other. So cohabitation is not really a trial marriage after all; the nature of the relationship changes with marriage.

Waite and Gallagher also feel that all marriages are threatened by cohabitation and by the higher divorce rate in the society. As people come to enter relationships with less certainty that it will be lifelong, they lose some of the benefit of behaviors that are based on an assumption of permanently intertwined futures. Thus, cohabitation is not really a prelude to more lasting marriage; it actually may imperil the benefits of marriage in surprising ways.

---

marriages or civil unions contracted in other states as legally binding (Religious Tolerance 2005).

Marriage was approved for gays and lesbians in Massachusetts in 2003, although opponents have been trying to pass legislation reversing this pattern as this text is being written. The California legislature has been seriously considering legalization of same-sex marriage, with one house of the legislature approving it in 2005.

Despite the mixed messages on civil unions and same-sex marriages, polls in the United States show increased public acceptance of homosexuality as well as a rise in support of marriage benefits to gay and lesbian couples; 60 percent believe gay and lesbian couples should have the same rights as heterosexual married couples. The United States is evenly split on allowing gay and lesbian couples to legally form civil unions. Fifty-two percent of the public accept homosexuality

as a legitimate lifestyle (Human Rights Campaign 2003), while 90 percent support equal opportunity for homosexuals on the job (Johnson 2005). Yet in 2003, it was still legal to fire someone based on their sexuality in 36 states (Human Rights Campaign 2003). In the mass media, inclusion of gay characters and even themes in films such as *In and Out* (1997) and *Brokeback Mountain* (2005) plus television features such as *Ellen* and *Will and Grace* show popular culture's evolution in acceptance of portraying homosexuality.

In many other countries, same-sex couples are gaining rights that are similar to those of a heterosexual married couple. The Netherlands was the first to approve such marriages in 2001, followed shortly thereafter by Belgium. When Canada approved gay and lesbian marriages in 2005, 8 out of the 10 Canadian provinces had already approved such policies. Denmark, France, Germany, Iceland, Norway, and

Sweden offer a legal status similar to Vermont's civil unions, entailing most of the privileges of marriage, such as inheritance rights, health benefits, and family-only visitation rights in hospitals or prisons. In most of these countries, the new laws are controversial and have been challenged in court, but attitudes in Europe seem to be gradually shifting toward more acceptance of same-sex unions (Religious Tolerance 2005).

Those who favor allowing gay and lesbian marriages claim that supportive lifelong dyadic relationships are good for individuals and good for society. They see the fact that homosexuals want stable socially sanctioned relationships as an encouraging sign about how important the family is to society and how homosexuals want to fit in. Moreover, since many societies offer all kinds of tax benefits, insurance coverage, and other privileges, the denial of marriage on the basis of gender attraction is seen as discriminatory and may be costly to partners who are denied rights.

Those opposed insist that marriage has been a function of the church, temple, and mosque for centuries. None of the religious traditions have historically recognized gay relationships as legitimate, although a few are doing so now. Sometimes, biology is appealed to, with the assertion that marriage is a legitimate way to propagate the species; since homosexual unions do not serve this purpose, they do not serve the society, according to this view.

The question of same-sex marriage has been enormously controversial in the United States. It is legal as of this writing only in Massachusetts, although two other states provide civil unions as an alternative. Same-sex marriage is legal now throughout Canada.

Source: © Cameron Pashak.

THINKING SOCIOLOGICALLY

Should gays and lesbians in permanent committed relationships, where they care for each other and perhaps even raise children, be considered a family? Why or why not?

Divorce—Contract Breaking

Is the family breaking down? Is it relevant in today's world? Although most cultures extol the virtues of family life, the reality is that not all partnerships work. Support is not forthcoming for the partner, trust is violated, and relationships deteriorate. So we cannot discuss family life without also recognizing the often painful side of family life that results in contract breaking.

Some commentators view divorce rates as evidence that the family is deteriorating; they see enormous problems created by divorce. There are costs to adults who suffer guilt and failure, to children from divided homes, and to the society that does not have the stabilizing force of intact lifelong partnerships. Many children around the world are raised without both natural parents present. For example, nearly half of all U.S. children today live at least part of their lives in single-parent families.

Others argue that marriage is not so much breaking down as adapting to a different kind of social system. They claim that the family of the 1950s, depicted in television shows such as *Leave it to Beaver, Ozzie and Harriet,* and *Father Knows Best*

As much as we sentimentalize and romanticize marriage in North America, a very high percentage of marriages do not last "til death do us part." Contract breaking has become virtually an American tradition.

Source: © Peter Dazeley / zefa / Corbis.

TABLE 10.6 **Why People Divorce**	
Societal and Demographic Factors	**Personal Factors**
Family, religion, law, social disintegration, individual cultural values, education, income, age at marriage, cohabiting pregnancy before marriage, existence of children, ethnic differences, history of family divorce, and multiple marriages and divorces	Communication problems, infidelity, constant conflict, emotional abuse, falling out of love, unsatisfactory sex, insufficient income, physical abuse, someone else, bored
Source: Williams, Sawyer, and Wahlstrom (2006).	

as white, middle-class, and suburban, would be ill suited to the societies we have today. Indeed, more people today express satisfaction with marriage than at any previous time period, and there are more silver (50 year) wedding anniversaries now than ever before (Gelles 1995; Kain 1990). Even late in the nineteenth century, the average length of a marriage was only 13 years—mostly because life expectancy was so short. "Til death do us part" was not such a long time then as it is today when average life expectancy is in the late 70s (Coontz 2005; Gelles 1995; Newman and Grauerholz 2002).

 THINKING SOCIOLOGICALLY

In what ways do television shows such as *The Simpsons* or *The Family Guy* depict family? How do these shows compare to shows about the Black American family of the 1980s such as *The Crosby Show,* or those mentioned above from the 1950s?

Why do people divorce? Some contributing factors are social, and some are very personal, as is indicated in Table 10.6 above.

If we grant that not everyone is temperamentally suited to sustain a nurturing marriage for 50 years, and if we acknowledge that people do change over time, what would be an acceptable divorce rate for our society? Five percent of all marriages? Twenty percent? Forty percent? This is difficult for governments to decide, but many people feel that the current rate, someplace between 40 and 50 percent, is too high (Ahrons 2004; Newman and Grauerholz 2002). When people say that more than half of all today's marriages will end in divorce, they are pointing out that with upward divorce trends, by the time people now in their 20s reach their 70s, the rates could be 50 to 55 percent. However, it is also possible that such predictions will not come true; we do know that social predictions can become self-negating as people and societies change their behaviors and their policies. Still, the trend is long and strong in an upward direction (Coontz 2005).

One reason for the increases in the U.S. divorce rate in the past 35 years is a policy change: no-fault divorce laws. For centuries in North America, one had to prove that

the other party was in breach of contract. Marriage was a lifelong contract that could only be severed by one party having violated the terms of the contract (Riley 1997). Each state spelled out those acts that were so odious that they justified ending such a sacred vow. Even then, if both parties had done something wrong (he was an adulterer, but she did not clean the house and was therefore in "neglect of duty"), the judge was obligated to rule that, since they both violated the contract, the divorce would be denied. This resulted in ugly and contested divorces and in people being forced to live together in unloving, nonnurturing relationships.

In 1970, the state of California was the first to initiate no-fault divorce, wherein a couple could end a marriage without proving that the other person was in breach of contract. A bilateral no-fault divorce (often called *dissolution*) requires both parties to agree that they want out of the marriage. If they agree to the terms of settlement (child custody, child visitation rights, split in property, and so forth), the marriage would be dissolved (Gilchrist 2003). A second form, unilateral no-fault divorce, allows one person to insist that the marriage has *irreconcilable differences;* the two do not have to agree. Many women feel this arrangement protects vulnerable women from staying in an unloving relationship; they do not have to give up everything to get him to sign the agreement. Still, this does make divorce much easier to obtain. Some critics believe this has led to a *divorce culture*—a society in which people assume that marriages are fragile rather than assuming that marriages are for life (a *marriage culture*). This raises the following questions: To what extent are divorces being sought for the slightest offense? Is this a chronic problem or a highly atypical pattern? Also, is divorce really a problem; does it have lasting consequences?

Divorce and Its Social Consequences

The highest rates of divorce in the world are among young couples. Marriages that occur at later ages have lower divorce rates. In the United States, the highest rates are for women in their teens and men between 20 and 24. The rate of divorce has leveled off and even dropped since the high mark in 1981, as shown in Table 10.7.

The emotional aspects of divorce are for many the most difficult. Divorce is often seen as failure, rejection, even punishment. Moreover, a divorce often involves a splitting with family and many close friends, with one's church or synagogue, and from other social contexts in which one is known as part of a couple (Amato 2000; Ebaugh 1988). No wonder divorce is so wrenching. Unlike simple societies, most modern societies have no ready mechanism for absorbing people back into stable social units such as clans.

Adjustment to divorced status varies by gender: men typically have a harder time emotionally adjusting to singlehood or divorce than women. Divorced men must often leave not only their wives but their children, and while many women have support networks, fewer men have developed or sustained friendships outside of marriage. Finances, on the other hand, are a bigger problem for divorced women than for men, especially if women have children to support. One major study shows that women's standard of living declined 27 percent one year after divorce, while men's increased by 10 percent (Peterson 1996). Almost 40 percent of divorced and widowed women fall into poverty during the first 5 years of being single (McManus and DiPrete 2001).

There are also costs for children, 1 million of whom experience their parents' divorce each year in the United States. These children's lives are often turned upside down: many children move to new houses and locations, leave one parent and friends, and make adjustments to new schools. Reduced resources can have negative consequences for children; only about 41 percent of custodial parents receive the full child support payments due them. One-fourth receives less than the specified amount, and one-third receives none at all (U.S. Census Bureau 2006d).

Adjustment depends on the age of the children and the manner in which the parents handle the divorce. Children in families with high levels of marital conflict may be better off long-term if parents divorce (Booth and Amato 2001). If the children are torn between two feuding

parents or if they are the focus of a bitter custody battle, they may suffer substantial scars.

Many studies indicate divorce lowers the well-being of children in the short-term, affecting school achievement, peer relationships, and behavior. However, more important may be the long-term or lasting effects on their achievement and quality of life as these children become adults (Amato and Keith 1991; Amato and Sobolewski 2001). The studies offer quite variable findings on this. One study that followed children of divorce for 15 years showed that through adolescence and into adulthood, many children continue to feel anxious and have fears, anger, and guilt (Sun 2001; Wallerstein and Blakeslee 2004). Adults may experience depression; lower levels of life satisfaction; lower marital quality and stability; more frequent divorce; poorer relationships with parents; poorer physical health; and lower educational attainment, income, and occupational prestige (Eshleman and Bulcroft 2006). Other studies suggest that later in life, individuals whose parents divorced during their childhood have a higher probability of teen marriage, divorce, peer problems, delinquency, truancy, and depression (Chase-Lansdale, Cherlin, and Kierman 1995; Newman and Grauerholz 2002).

On the other hand, some studies find that children who are well-adjusted to begin with have an easier time with divorce, especially if they can remain in their home and in their familiar school, with both parents part of their lives, and if they maintain their friendship networks. Grandparents, too, can provide stability during these traumatic times. For instance, Ahrons (2004) found that adults whose parents were divorced are actually very well-adjusted and happy. She found no general long-term negative consequences of parental divorce in her extensive longitudinal study that traced people into their middle years. Seventy-nine percent of her respondents said their parents' decision to divorce was a good one, and 78 percent indicated that they were not affected by the divorce. The key, she found, is the nature of the postdivorce relationships. Large numbers of divorcees have very civil relationships and continue to cooperate and collaborate on behalf of the children. In these cases, there are few, if any, long-term wounds.

TABLE 10.7	**How the U.S. Divorce Rate in 2000 Compared with Previous Decades**
Year	**Divorces per 1,000 Population**
1950	2.6
1960	2.2
1970	3.5
1980	5.2
1981	5.3 (highest rate)
1990	4.7
2000	4.2
2001	4.0
2002	3.9
2003	3.8
2004	3.7

Sources: U.S. Census Bureau (2003c, Table 83); Centers for Disease Control (2005); National Vital Health Statistics Report (2005).

THINKING SOCIOLOGICALLY

Would making it harder to get a divorce create stronger and healthier families? Would it create more stable but less healthy and nurturing families? If you were making divorce policies, what would you do? What are the positive and negative aspects of your policy?

Global Family Patterns and Policies

Family systems around the world are changing in similar ways, pushed by industrialization and urbanization, by changing kinship and occupational structures, and by influences from outside the family. The most striking changes include

1. free choice of spouse,
2. more equal status for women,
3. equal rights in divorce,
4. neolocal residency (living separate from either sets of parents),
5. bilateral kinship systems (tracing lineage through both parents), and
6. pressures for individual equality (Sado and Bayer 2001).

However, countermovements in some parts of the world call for strengthening of marriage through modesty of women, separation of the sexes (in both public and private spheres), and rejection of high divorce rates and other Western practices.

National policies limiting availability of birth control and lack of knowledge about family planning affect the economic circumstances of families that are forced to raise many children; this has resulted in an increase in out-of-wedlock birth rates and thereby creates more single-parent families. Likewise, as individuals and couples at the micro level make decisions such as choosing a spouse based on love, rejecting multiple wives, or establishing a more egalitarian family, the collective impact may rock the foundations of the larger society. Because legislatures make policies to support families or to influence family decisions such as fertility rates, the interaction between policy makers and social scientists can lead to laws based on better information and more comprehensive

Global forces, such as ethnic holocausts that create refugees, can strain and destroy families. This is a scene of refugees at Korem Camp in Ethiopia.

Source: USAID.

analysis of possible consequences. This is part of the public contribution of applied sociology—providing accurate information and analysis for wise public policy.

Family life, which seems so personal and intimate, may actually be linked to global patterns. Global aid is activated when draught, famine, or other disasters affects communities and a country is not able to provide for families. In such cases, international organizations such as the United Nations, Doctors without Borders, Oxfam, and the Red Cross mobilize to support families in crises. Support varies from feeding starving children to opposing the slavery that occurs when parents are reduced to selling their children in order to survive. International crises can lead to war, perhaps removing the main breadwinner from the family or taking the life of a son or daughter who was drafted to fight. Homes and cultivated fields may be destroyed and the families forced into refugee status.

Do marriage and divorce rates indicate the family is in crisis? To answer these questions, we need information on current patterns, historical trend lines, and patterns in other parts of the world. The next Sociology around the World provides cross-cultural data on marriage and divorce ratios.

THINKING SOCIOLOGICALLY

Considering the chart on page 319, should we be alarmed about rates of marriage and marriage dissolution? Why or why not?

MARRIAGE, DIVORCE, AND SOCIAL POLICIES

In an effort to strengthen marriages and reduce divorce rates, should countries make divorce more difficult to obtain? All the 50 U.S. states now have no-fault provisions based on "irreconcilable differences" or "irreconcilable breakdown of the marriage" (Aulette 2002; Gelles 1995). The conservative U.S. organization, Council on Families in America, has said that we should go back to fault divorce in order to make it less easy to end a marriage in this divorce culture. They argue that many couples enter marriages assuming that the marriage will probably not last. An assumption of impermanence is no way to begin a marriage. They insist that profamily policies that promote stability are a precursor to healthy relationships (Coontz 1997; Hunter College Women's Studies Collective 2005; Popenoe, Elshtain, and Blankenhorn 1996). Other scholars think that limiting the divorce process would leave many women in highly vulnerable positions in relationship to abusive men, and while it may create more marriages that stay together, it would not necessarily create healthy ones. Healthy marriages are what help the society, not unhappy ones, say the defenders of no-fault divorce.

Sociology around the World

Cross-Cultural Differences in Family Dissolution

Is the family breaking down around the world? Perhaps this is the wrong question. We may, instead, need to consider how the family copes with changing demands. Family conflict and disorganization occur when members of the family unit do not carry out roles expected of them by spouses, other family members, the community, or the society. This may be due to voluntary departure (divorce, separation, desertion); involuntary problems (illness or other catastrophe); a crisis caused by external events (death, war, depression); or failure to communicate role expectations and needs. Many of these role failures are a direct consequence of societal changes due to globalization. Once again, the social world model helps us understand macro-level trends and patterns that affect us in micro-level contexts.

Divorce is still very limited in some parts of the world and is only an option for one gender. In some Arab countries, only the husband has the right to pronounce "I divorce thee" in front of a witness on three separate occasions, after which the divorce is complete. The wife returns, sometimes in disgrace, to her family of procreation, while the husband generally keeps the children in the patriarchal family and is free to take another wife. Despite this seemingly easy process, the divorce rate is comparatively low in most countries because family ties and allegiances are severely strained when divorces take place. Thus, informal pressures and cultural attitudes restrain tendencies to divorce.

Still, when family turmoil and conflict are too great to resolve or when the will to save the family disappears, the legal, civil, and religious ties of marriage may be broken. The methods for dissolving marriage ties vary, but most countries have some form of divorce. Table 10.8 compares marriage and divorce rates in selected industrial countries. Notice that while the divorce rate in the United States is highest by a good margin, the marriage rate is also high.

TABLE 10.8   **Marriage and Divorce Ratios in Selected Countries, 1960–2002**

Country	1960	1970	1980	1990	2002	Country	1960	1970	1980	1990	2002
	Marriages per 1,000 persons in population						Divorces per 1,000 persons in population				
United States	8.5	10.6	10.6	9.8	7.5	United States	2.2	3.5	5.2	4.7	3.9
Belgium	7.2	7.6	6.7	6.5	4.0	Belgium	0.5	0.7	1.5	2.0	4.0
Denmark	7.8	7.4	5.2	6.1	6.5	Canada	0.4	1.4	2.6	2.9	NA
France	7.0	7.8	6.2	5.1	4.6	Denmark	1.5	1.9	2.7	2.7	6.5
Germany	9.4	7.3	5.9	6.5	4.6	France	0.7	0.8	1.5	1.9	4.6
Greece	7.0	7.7	6.5	5.9	5.5	Germany, Former West	0.8	1.2	1.6	1.9	4.6
Ireland	5.5	7.0	6.4	5.1	5.1	Italy	NA	NA	0.2	0.5	4.5
Italy	7.7	7.3	5.7	5.6	4.5	Japan	0.7	0.9	1.2	1.3	5.8
Luxembourg	7.1	6.3	5.9	6.1	4.4	Luxembourg	0.5	0.6	1.6	2.0	4.4
Netherlands	7.8	9.5	6.4	6.4	5.0	Netherlands	0.5	0.8	1.8	1.9	5.0
Portugal	7.8	NA	7.4	7.3	5.1	Portugal	0.1	0.1	NA	0.9	5.1
Spain	7.7	7.3	5.9	5.7	5.0	Sweden	1.2	1.6	2.4	2.3	4.4
United Kingdom	7.5	8.5	7.4	6.5	5.1	United Kingdom	0.5	1.2	3.0	2.9	5.1

Source: United Nations (2003, Tables 23 and 25).

Note: NA = not available.

THE APPLIED SOCIOLOGIST AT WORK | Steven L. Nock

Covenant Marriage

Dr. Steven Nock, professor of sociology at the University of Virginia, had initially been interested in the impact of social stratification on American families. His interest in families grew from a concern that family issues be incorporated into our thinking about the American class system. From this base of research, he became intrigued when several states instituted the new legislation—covenant marriages—to try to strengthen and stabilize marriages.

Nock realized that this legal innovation was the first time in history that individuals would be offered a choice regarding which system of laws would govern their marriages. He wanted to know who desires a more restrictive form of marriage—men or women, rich or poor, black or white, young or old? Furthermore, he wanted to determine whether government can predictably alter something like divorce rates through the actions of law.

Nock and his coresearchers are conducting *focus groups* (a type of open-ended group interview) and interviews with a large number of state power brokers (legislators, governors, and other officials) about why the law was passed. They also have interviewed those charged with implementing the law (court clerks, judges, clergy) and those charged with providing the mandatory counseling (marriage counselors, ministers). In addition, the researchers set up several rounds of interviews with a scientifically selected sample of covenant marriage and standard marriage couples. Approximately 350 couples of each type were selected, and both partners in each marriage completed lengthy questionnaires at three points in the first few years of the marriage. This policy is so new that there is virtually no data on its successes or failures, and as this book goes to press, the research team is still analyzing the data.

Writing his findings for policy makers, Nock has to understand the law and the state policies involved. Applied researchers must also be sensitive to the political and economic implications of the findings.

(Will implementation require additional taxes? Will policies be acceptable to voters? Will they be possible given the existing system of laws in a state? Will they achieve the desired outcome?)

Applied research must be able to convince others that a policy or law will have a predicable consequence. The research must be understandable to the nonsociologist, and it must be done objectively, without any appearance of bias or preformed conclusions. Note that Nock has a policy agenda in his work.

Because of his research, Nock is consulted by legislators and others involved in family policy decisions and passage of laws, especially if they are thinking about implementing covenant marriage in their state. While data about the policy are not yet definitive, Nock knows more about the debates and variations in covenant marriage law than perhaps anyone else in the country or world. Regarding the challenges and the rewards of this work, Nock wrote to us:

> I began my career in sociology with a desire to influence public policy and change social conditions. I saw the field of sociology as offering guidance to those seeking to change our society. My work on covenant marriage, and on marriage more generally, is slowly being incorporated into policy and thinking about policy. There is no doubt that people face many challenges in forming stable relationships in which to raise children. Anything that might help couples should be investigated. The work on covenant marriage takes a small step in this direction. This is one of the most rewarding aspects of my work. The other reward is the chance to collaborate with colleagues who share similar goals and objectives. Working with such valued colleagues is the most rewarding aspect of any research effort.

Dr. Steven L. Nock, University of Virginia, did his undergraduate work at the University of Richmond, followed by a doctorate in sociology at the University of Massachusetts, Amherst.

 THINKING SOCIOLOGICALLY

Would it strengthen marriages to remove all no-fault divorce laws and return to a fault divorce where one member of the couple must prove that the other person was in breach of contract? Why or why not?

Yet another social policy proposal is to change the marriage contract itself. With the new Covenant Marriage Law implemented in Louisiana (1997), Arizona (1998), and Arkansas (2002), people can choose whether they want a standard marriage or an "upgraded" covenant marriage. If they opt for covenant marriage, premarital counseling is required before the wedding, a year of counseling is necessary before a fault divorce is permitted, and the availability of no-fault divorce is restricted by longer requirements of counseling (Laconte 1998; Nock 1999; Nock, Wright, and Sanchez 1999). Contracts mean marriages are less easily dissolved. The Applied Sociologist at Work on page 320 discusses policies on covenant marriage.

We have been talking about a national trend (divorce rates) regarding an institution (the family) and the impact it has on individuals. Processes at the macro and meso levels affect the micro level of society, and decisions at the micro level (i.e., to dissolve a marriage) affect the community and the nation. The various levels of the social world are indeed interrelated in complex ways.

SO WHAT?

Our happiest and saddest experiences are integrally intertwined with family. Family provides the foundation, the group through which individuals' needs are met. Societies depend on families as the unit through which to funnel services. It is the political, economic, health, educational, religious, and sexual base for most people. These are some of the reasons family is important to us. Despite those who lament the weakening of the family, the institution of family is here to stay. Its form may alter as it responds and adapts to societal changes, and other institutions will continue to take on functions formerly reserved for the family. Still, the family is an institution crucial to societal survival, and whatever the future holds, the family will adapt in response to changes in other parts of the social world. It is an institution that is sometimes vulnerable and needs support, but it is also a resilient institution—the way we partner and make people in any society.

The next three chapters continue to examine institutions and their interconnections. When a child grows up and leaves the embrace of the family, the social environment they experience is the local school. It is to education and schools that we turn next.

CONTRIBUTING TO YOUR SOCIAL WORLD

At the Local Level: Vulnerable families often need support. You might consider working or volunteering with a battered women's shelter, *Big Brother Big Sister* program, homeless shelters with families, or an after-school recreational program for children in your local community.

At the Organizational or Institutional Level: *United Way* has contacts with other family-oriented organizations that may need help.

Religious congregations and human services agencies sometimes offer courses in premarital counseling, parenting skills, or marriage enrichment retreats. They often seek paid or volunteer assistance.

At the National and Global Levels: Write a letter to your government officials concerning an issue about which you feel strongly. For example, if you think covenant marriage or some other idea is good, or if you have strong feelings about restricting or expanding no-fault divorce options or same-sex marriage policies, consider writing a letter to your representatives. In the United States, for example, almost all marriage and divorce laws are under the control of state government.

Check the *United Nations–UNESCO* website. There are many international organizations that work with refugees, orphans of wars, and immigrant families.

Visit www.pineforge.com/ballantinestudy for online activities, sample tests, and other helpful information. Select "Chapter 10: Family" for chapter-specific activities.

eFfGgh
RrSsT
7890

E=
☺

What to Expect . . .

In schools, there is much being
learned by students besides the
classic three Rs, and there is
much that sociologists have
learned about the place of
education within our social
system. Even the buildings
themselves tell us something
about who is served by the
schools in that society.

Think About It . . .

1. What do we learn—both formally and informally—in schools?

2. Is education the road to opportunity in societies, or does it protect the interests of the privileged?

3. Do families help or hurt children's school achievement?

4. How is education changing in your own local community, in your society, and globally?

5. Why is education a major concern around the world?

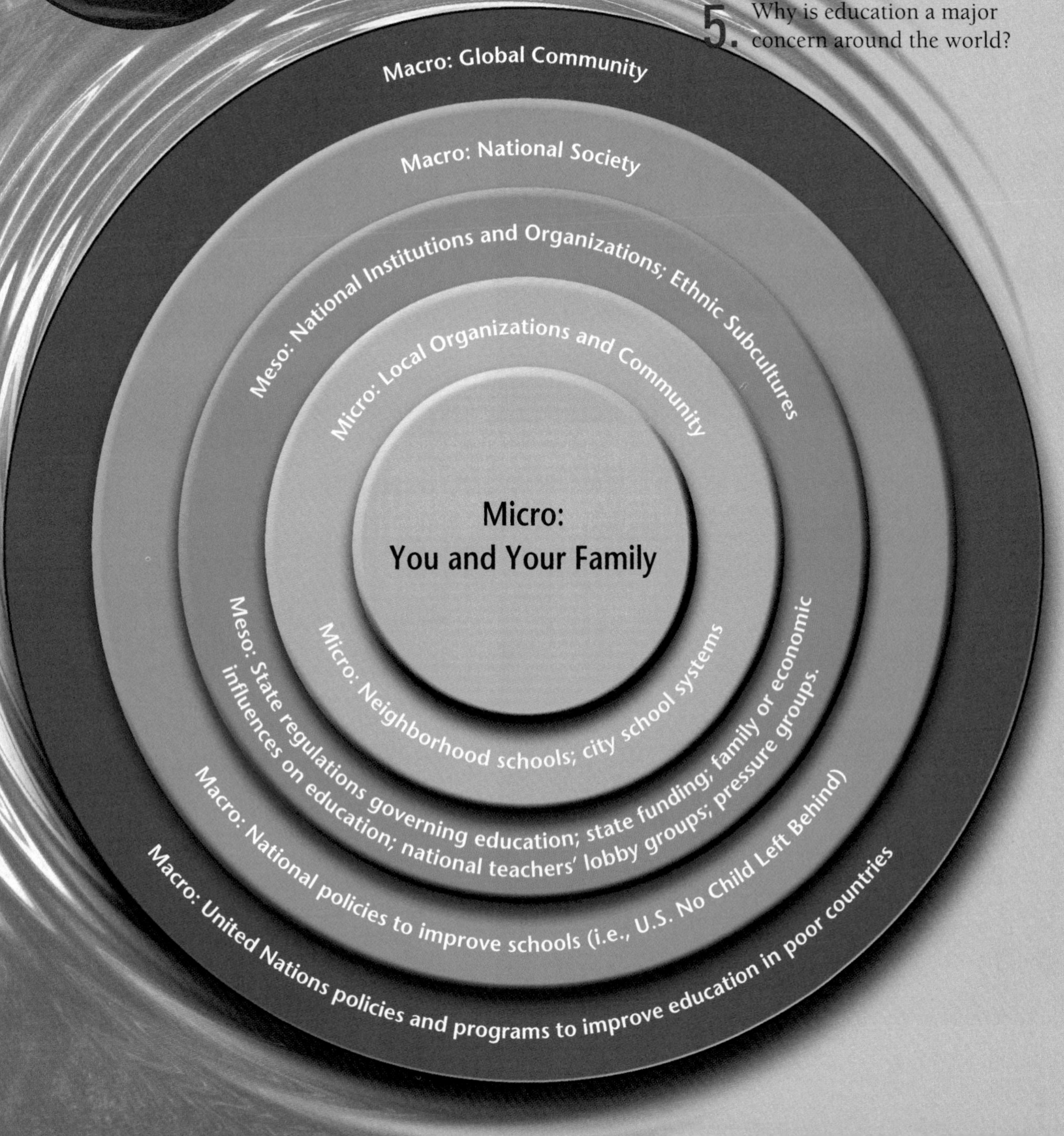

Macro: Global Community

Macro: National Society

Meso: National Institutions and Organizations; Ethnic Subcultures

Micro: Local Organizations and Community

**Micro:
You and Your Family**

Micro: Neighborhood schools; city school systems

Micro: family or economic influences on education; national teachers' lobby groups; pressure groups.

Meso: State regulations governing education; state funding;

Macro: National policies to improve schools (i.e., U.S. No Child Left Behind)

Macro: United Nations policies and programs to improve education in poor countries

Tomás is a failure. At nine years old, he cannot read, write, or get along with his peers, and out of frustration he sometimes misbehaves. He has been a failure since he was three, but his failure started earlier than that; his parents say so. They have told Tomás over and over that he will not amount to anything if he does not shape up. His teachers have noticed that he is slow to learn and does not seem to have many friends. They, too, define him as a failure. Tomás believes his parents and teachers, for he has little evidence to contradict their judgment.

For some children, school is an exercise in daily frustration and humiliation.

Source: © Royalty-Free / Corbis.

Children volunteer to participate during an arithmetic lesson in the village school in Lalibela, Ethiopia. This kind of overcrowding is not uncommon in poor countries.

Source: © Earl and Nazima Kowall / Corbis.

Two strikes against him are the judgments of his parents and his school teachers. The third strike is Tomás's own acceptance of the label "failure." Tomás is an *at-risk* child, identified as having characteristics inclining him toward failure in school and society. Probably, he will not amount to anything and may even get in trouble with the law unless a caring, sensitive teacher or friend encourages him and makes him realize that he has abilities and is not the worthless person he believes himself to be. These are micro-level issues.

Tomás goes to school in Toronto (Ontario), Canada, but he could live in any country. In every community, there are Tomáses. Although successful children receive encouragement and praise from parents and teachers and develop a positive self-concept to counter disappointments and failures, the Tomáses know little of encouragement from their environments and regard themselves as failures. Most young children succeed in negotiating the rules and regulations of school, and school provides them with skills necessary for future occupations. Yet the label Tomás carries with him through school will affect or even determine his success in life because, next to home, schools play the biggest role in socializing children into their self-images, attitudes toward success, and place in the social world.

For most people across the globe, survival comes first, and education is an informal process of training children so they know how to survive and help their families survive. *Schooling*—learning skills such as reading and math in a building via systematic instruction by a trained professional—is a luxury some children will never know. On the other hand, in most urban areas around the world and in affluent countries, formal education is necessary for success—and survival. Education of the masses in a school setting is a modern concept; it became necessary when literacy became essential to many jobs (even if just to read instructions for operating machinery) and to democratic governments where informed citizenry elect officials and vote on public policies.

STATE OF THE WORLD'S EDUCATION: AN OVERVIEW

Every society educates its children; in most societies, there are national education systems created for this task. Global organizations concerned with education also contribute. For the past 50 years, UNESCO (United Nations Educational, Scientific, and Cultural Organization) has become the "global center for discussion and implementation of educational ideas and organization models" (Boli 2002:307). It provides teacher training, curricular guidance, and textbook sources, and gathers international statistics on educational achievement. Many countries have adopted UNESCO (2003) standards, including the organizational model of six years of primary school, and three years of intermediate and secondary school; vocational education has decreased at the secondary level in favor of comprehensive training, but it is an option for specialized training later on.

Formal education—schooling that takes place in a formal setting with the goal of teaching a predetermined curriculum—has expanded dramatically in the past several decades as higher percentages of the population in many countries attend school. Although major educational gaps still exist between elite and poor individuals and between females and males, these gaps are narrowing. Girls' enrollments worldwide are now close to half of students at the primary levels in most countries, and girls' secondary school enrollment rose from 32 percent in 1950 to 45 percent in the 1990s (Boli 2002:311). Women are also entering more male-dominated fields of higher education and attending university at levels equal to or exceeding men in some countries.

Education has become a global issue. What is considered essential knowledge to be taught in schools is based largely on a country's level of development, political ideology, and guidelines from international standards. Leaders believe that a literate population is necessary for economic development and expansion, a thriving political system, and the well-being of the citizenry. Global trends in schooling influence education systems in Africa, Asia, Latin America, Europe, and the Middle East, regardless of political system or level of affluence. As Boli (2002) writes, "Education has become a global social process that both reflects and helps create the global society that is under formation" (p. 312).

Student-teacher ratios, one measure of educational quality, vary from a low of 13 to 1 in several Western European countries and 15.8 to 1 in the United States, to a high of 72 to 1 in Ethiopia and over 60 to 1 in Chad, Congo, Malawi, Mozambique, and Rwanda. The highest numbers of students per teacher at all levels of education were in sub-Saharan Africa, with an average at all levels of education of 41 to 1 pupils per teacher, and in South and West Asia, with a ratio of 44 to 1 (National Center for Education Statistics 2002; UNESCO 2003, 2006).

Literacy is another measure of quality of education. In developing countries, 76 percent of the population is literate, including 64 percent of women (UNESCO 2006); but there is variation among these countries: in the least economically developed countries, only 38 percent of the women are literate. Developed countries have rates of 99 percent literacy for men and women. (See Table 11.1.) In some math and science courses, males achieve at higher levels than females, especially in countries where women's status is lower, but females often have higher achievement in language and reading.

Mass education is spreading around the world. As communication, transportation, and globalization continue to make countries more interdependent and more accessible to each other, developed countries influence levels and types of education worldwide. The national education curricula of many poor countries is similar to models of mass education used in colonial powers and developed countries (Benavot 1992; Benavot, Meyer, and Kamens 1991; Chabbott and Ramirez 2000; McEneaney and Meyer 2000; Meyer et al. 1992). International organizations, from the United Nations to other nongovernmental bodies concerned with education,

TABLE 11.1 **Adult Literacy (age 15 and over) by Gender and Region, 2000–2004**					
	Adult Literacy Rates %			**Adult Illiterates**	
	Total	**Male**	**Female**	**Total (thousands)**	**Percentage Who Are Female**
World	82	87	77	799,147	64
Developing countries	76	83	69	788,999	64
Developed countries	99	99	99	9,151	62
Countries in transition	100	100	99	998	70
Sub-Saharan Africa	62	70	54	137,000	61
Arab States	62	73	51	69,298	64
Central Asia	99	100	99	339	70
East Asia and the Pacific	91	95	88	134,978	71
South and West Asia	58	71	45	402,744	64
Latin America and the Caribbean	89	90	88	39,383	55
North America and Western Europe	99	99	99	6,946	61
Central and Eastern Europe	97	99	96	8,464	77

Source: UNESCO (2006:129).

Note: Figures may not add to totals because of rounding. 2000–2004 data are derived from the March 2004 literacy assessment by the UNESCO Institute for Statistics, which uses directly reported national figures together with UIS estimates. For countries that did not report literacy data for the 2000–2004 reference period, UIS estimates for 2002 were used.

While Nicaragua shares the commitment to mass education of all young people, its resources are very meager, as we can see from this photo of an impoverished school building in a Nicaraguan village.

Source: Photo by Daniel O. Conkle.

have provided central points for development of educational models. Social sciences add knowledge about the role of education in economic growth, stratification, and political behaviors (Boli 2002). Mathematics, for instance, is taught universally, and science has been taught in most schools since World War II (Kamens and Benavot 1991), although more science is taught in countries with a higher standard of living (Baker 2002). Whether this trend toward similar curricula meets the needs of individuals in all countries is a matter of debate.

Education can be studied through several different lenses or perspectives. The next section provides a summary of how symbolic interaction, rational choice, functional theory, conflict theories, and approaches specific to education each offers an angle for understanding education in society. Sociologists use theory to provide a framework for explaining what they find in their research; the theory used is based on the level of analysis of the problem being examined and on what the researcher judges to be most applicable to the problem.

THEORETICAL PERSPECTIVES ON EDUCATION

As shown in each chapter so far, theory provides a lens for stating problems, interpreting data, making sense of information that we gather, and explaining causal relationships. This section examines several theories used in analyzing educational systems, looking first at micro-level theories and then at meso- and macro-level theories.

Education and Individuals: Micro-Level Theories

Who were the popular kids in your school? Those who studied hard and excelled academically? Those who excelled on the sports field? Those who showed talent in the arts or a specific subject? Those who eschewed education in favor of partying?

Who hung out together at lunch? How did different individuals and groups distinguish themselves—clothing or hair styles, social positions that offered social visibility and therefore popularity, or different language or slang used by students—often leading to labeling one another? Sociologists of education focus on many questions concerning interaction in classrooms and schools between student peers, students and staff members, and students and teachers. Consider micro-level theories that can help to understand individuals in classrooms and schools.

Social Interaction within the Classroom: Symbolic Interaction Perspective

The focus in the symbolic interaction perspective is often on how symbols affect sense of self or shape social hierarchies (Eder, Evans and Parker 1995). Children are active in creating distinctions between one another and are therefore agents in creating the social reality in which they live. Popularity, a major issue for many children, especially in middle-school years, is mostly a function of being visible and having everyone know who you are by representing the school in an athletic contest, by being attractive, or by being

The struggle for a sense of self worth is much more pronounced for middle-school girls than for boys, probably because boys have more ways of being visible and known than girls, who are often highly visible only for their physical appearance.

Source: © Kevin Dodge / Corbis.

seen in a leadership position. The difficulty is that there are few such positions; competition is created, and some individuals are going to be "losers." Indeed, in the United States, children from families who cannot afford to purchase the required clothing or other status symbols or send their children to sports training or camp are more likely to be the "losers." Those who "win" and have access to symbolic resources that are highly visible are given special privileges in the classroom or the school and are more likely to develop leadership skills and generally feel very good about themselves (Eder et al. 1995).

Research findings indicate that girls have more struggles with self-esteem, especially in middle school, than do boys (American Association of University Women Educational Foundation 2001). Sense of self—an intensely personal experience—is shaped by the micro interactions of the school.

For young people from 6 to 18 years old, spending much of their time in school or school-related activities, *student* is a status that has enormous impact on how individuals see themselves. Interaction with others in each school status affects the student's sense of self. The image that is reflected back to someone—as student or as teacher, for example—can begin to mold one's sense of competence, intelligence, and likeability.

The larger school organization creates a structure that influences how individuals make sense of their reality and interact with others. The Iowa School of symbolic interaction emphasizes the link between the self and meso-level positions or statuses (Stryker 1980, 2000). Official school positions—such as president of the student council or senior-class president—come to be important elements of one's self.

Making Choices in Educational Settings: Rational Choice Theory

The rational choice theory focuses on individuals undertaking a cost-benefit analysis of virtually everything they do. What are the costs—in terms of finances, physical well-being, emotional health, relationships, self-esteem, or other factors—and what are the benefits? If benefits outweigh costs, the individual is likely to make the decision to act in the specified way to continue receiving benefits; if costs outweigh benefits, the individual will seek other courses of action. In education, the question is how weighing of costs and benefits influences decisions about education.

Individuals who are considering dropping out of school go through some analysis of costs to themselves, for instance, their battered self-esteem in schools. Whether we would agree that they have assessed the costs and the benefits correctly is not the point; the issue is how the individual evaluates the benefits and costs at a given moment in making a decision.

The issue of teacher retention is a similar case; currently, roughly half of all new teachers in the United States leave the profession within five years, an extremely high rate (Lambert 2006). Rational choice theorists explain this in terms of the perceived costs—poor salary for a college graduate; lack of

Males have many ways of becoming known and respected. Male athletics draw bigger crowds than female athletics, and one can become a local celebrity based on one's skill on the field or court.

Source: © Crystal Chatham.

A teacher or school administrator interacting with a student can shape the sense of self of the student, positively or negatively. However, student receptiveness, or rejection and hostility, can also shape the self-image of the school official—building a self-image as a compassionate and caring person, a failure with students, or a mean ogre. Interaction influences the self-image of both parties.

Source: © Lisa F. Young.

respect from parents, students, and administrators; 12- to 14-hour days for nine months of the year; and lack of professionalism in treatment of teachers in the No Child Left Behind (NCLB) federal program. Teachers compare these to the benefits of teaching—the feeling of making a contribution to society and helping children, time off in the summer, and enjoying many aspects of teaching, coaching, or directing. The costs today are seen by many teachers as higher than they used to be for professionals in teaching, so they leave the profession.

THINKING SOCIOLOGICALLY

What other kinds of processes within a school are influenced by costs and benefits? Do you think most behavior in schools is shaped by this kind of rational choice calculation?

Why Societies Have Education Systems: Macro-Level Theories

Wherever it takes place and whatever the content, education prepares individuals to live and work in their particular societies. In a rural Indian village in Uttar Pradesh, children gather in a lean-to shelter for their morning lessons before going to the fields to help with the animals. The average years of schooling in India is eight (UNESCO 2005). In some rural areas, little more than basic literacy is considered necessary or possible, especially for girls. Village children go to the community school, tablets in hand, but when the family needs help in the fields or with child care, older children often stay at home. Even though several years of school are required, not all people become literate. Learning to survive—how to grow crops, care for the home, treat diseases, and make clothing—are essential survival skills that come before formal education; they take most of an individual's available time and

These children take the only viable mode of transportation, a gondola school bus.

Source: Photo by Elise Roberts.

A mother in Madagascar pounds tapioca in her house yard as one young child watches and learns, an example of informal education. Someday, this may be the daughter's task, unless the society changes so dramatically that the traditional survival strategies and roles become irrelevant.

Source: © Wolfgang Kaehler / Corbis.

energy. Basic literacy is a goal, but it is sometimes limited to urban areas of developing countries where basic academic skills (literacy, mathematics, science) are essential in order to find employment. Mass education was not even a goal until the 1900s (Benavot et al. 1991), when it became clear that skilled labor and a literate citizenry are necessary for economic development and informed political participation.

The Purposes of Education: Functionalist Perspective

Functional theorists argue that formal and informal education serve certain crucial purposes in society, especially as societies modernize (Boli 2002).

Socialization: Teaching children to be productive members of society.
Societies use education to pass on essential information of a culture—values, skills, and knowledge necessary for survival. Sometimes this process occurs in formal

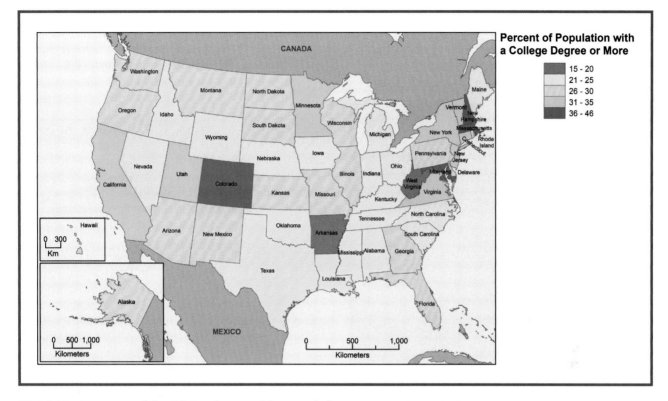

MAP 11.1 Percentage of the U.S. Population Holding a Bachelor's Degree or More in 2004

Source: U.S. Census Bureau (2006f, Table 18). Map by Anna Versluis.

classrooms, sometimes in informal places. In West African villages, children may have several years of formal education in a village school, but they learn rights, wrongs, values, and future roles informally by observing their elders and by "playing" at the tasks they will soon undertake for survival. The girls help pound cassava root for the evening meal, while the boys build model boats and practice negotiating the waves. Mainly the elite—the sons and daughters of the rulers and the wealthy—receive formal education beyond basic literacy in less prosperous countries.

By contrast, elders and family members in developed societies cannot teach all the skills necessary for survival. Formal schooling emerged to meet the needs of industrial and postindustrial societies, furnishing the specialized training required by rapidly growing and changing technology. Schools also provide the cultural socialization important in heterogeneous societies, where diverse groups must learn rules that maintain the social order. Children receive socialization messages from teachers, formal curricula, and the routine practices and rules of everyday classroom life (Brint, Contreras, and Matthews 2001; Gracey 1977).

Selecting and training individuals for positions in society. Most of us have taken standardized tests, have received grades at the end of the term or the year, and have asked teachers to write us

recommendation letters. These activities are part of the selection process prevalent in competitive societies with formal educational systems. We accumulate credentials—grades, test scores, and degrees—that determine the college or job opportunities available to us, the fields of study we pursue, and ultimately our positions in society. Map 11.1 above indicates the distribution of college degrees within the United States.

Promoting change and innovation. Citizens expect schools to respond to the constant changes in societies. In multicultural societies such as Israel, France, and England, schools help to integrate immigrants by teaching them the language and customs and by working to reduce intergroup tensions. The challenge is to provide educational opportunity to all groups. In Israel, for instance, many recent Jewish immigrants from Africa and the former Soviet Union work hard to master Hebrew and to move successfully through the educational system.

Institutions of higher education are expected to generate new knowledge, technology, and ideas, and to produce students with up-to-date skills and knowledge to lead industry and other key institutions in society. In our age of computers and other electronic technology, critical thinking and analytical skills are essential as workers face issues that require problem solving rather than rote memorization. Thus, the curriculum must change to meet the needs of

Schools provide an education, but from the standpoint of job enhancement, getting the credential—the degree—is equally important. Sometimes, the pursuit of the credential becomes primary and learning becomes secondary.

Source: © Nancy Louie.

the social circumstances. Familiarity with technological equipment—computers, Internet resources, electronic library searches, and so forth—become critical survival skills. Lack of training in these areas fosters further division of social classes and reduced chances for social mobility.

India has top-ranked technical institutes, and the highly skilled graduates are employed by multinational companies around the world. Companies in Europe and the United States also send information to India for processing and receive it back the next morning because of the time difference. Well-trained, efficient engineers and computer experts working in India for lower wages than many developed countries have become an essential part of the global economy (Friedman 2005).

Enhancing personal and social development. Most of us remember our first day of elementary school. It marked a transition between the warm, loving, accepting world of the family and a more impersonal school world that emphasized discipline, knowledge, skills, responsibility, and obedience. In school, children learn that they are no longer accepted regardless of their behaviors as they were in their families. They must meet certain expectations and compete for attention and rewards. They also must prepare to participate in their society's political and economic systems, in which a literate populace is necessary to make informed decisions on issues.

Latent functions of education. In addition to these planned, formal functions, education has several *latent*

functions—unintended, unorganized, informal results of the educational process. For example, schools keep children off the streets until they can be absorbed into productive roles in society. They provide young people with a place to congregate, which in turn fosters a "youth culture" of music, fashion, slang, dances, dating, and sometimes gangs. At the ages when social relationships are being established, especially with the opposite sex, schools are the central meeting place for the young—a kind of mate selection market. Education also weakens parental control over youths, helps them begin the move toward independence, and provides experience in large, impersonal secondary groups.

Functional theorists believe that when these social functions are not adequately addressed, the educational system is ripe for change. Government proposals for educational reforms are stimulated by new knowledge and technologies and indications of falling behind in international comparisons or high unemployment and poorly trained labor force. The structure and the processes within the educational institution remain stable only if the basic functions are met.

Going off to school is a huge step in the life of a child. Children learn how to cooperate with others, how to get along without their families there all the time for support, and who one is in the pecking order of the peer group.

Source: © Jan Tyler.

Critics of functionalism challenged the idea of elite social control of education and competition between class and ethnic groups.

Stratification and Education: Conflict Perspective

Schools participate in the stratification process in societies; some students receive elite educations and others do not in part because of class, race, and gender differences (Kerckhoff 2004). One mechanism for attaining high status in a society is attending an elite school. Graduates of British "public schools," American preparatory (prep) high schools, and private high schools and international schools in countries around the world attend the best universities and become leaders of government, business, and the military. Because these schools are very expensive and highly selective, elite members of society have the most access to them. Persell and Cookson (1985) write, "The internal processes (what goes on within the schools) and external networks (connections outside the school) operate to construct class privileges as well as to transmit class advantages, thereby helping to produce structured stratification within society" (p. 126). Many leaders of former colonized countries have the opportunity to study abroad, continuing Western influence in these countries. Those not born into positions of advantage have very limited chances to participate in elite education.

Conflict theorists see institutions, including education, as tools of powerful and affluent groups to ensure that their own self-interests are met. The schools, they believe, are manipulated in ways that keep the sons and daughters of the haves in positions of privilege, while lower-class children are prepared for less prestigious and rewarding positions in society. If schools do not provide equal educational opportunities for all children in a society—and conflict theorists contend that schools do not—then students cannot compete equally in the job market. Because the elites of society protect their educational advantages, the **reproduction of class** occurs; the socioeconomic positions of one generation pass on to the next generation. This process takes place in part through socialization of young people into adult work roles and compliance to the modern corporation and its needs; schools teach students from lower socioeconomic positions to obey authority and accept the dominant ideology that justifies social inequality. If citizens believe that those with the best educations and jobs in their society actually earned or deserve them, then they are unlikely to attempt to change the system. In these ways, schools serve the interests of the privileged (Bowles 1977; Bowles and Gintis 2002; Collins 2004; Passeron and Bourdieu 1990).

The cultural values and social norms of the dominant group (ideas of etiquette, proper ways of speaking and writing, notions of deference to superiors, and so forth) are transmitted to all social classes and legitimated through formal schooling; other definitions of reality from other ethnic or socioeconomic groups are marginalized. According to the conflict theorists, this process enhances power and

Schools provide additional latent functions, such as a place to meet other young people with a shared nonacademic interest!

Source: © Eileen Hart.

confirms the privileges of the dominant group. The educational system is not equally beneficial to all or even to the majority of citizens in society.

Having explored some lenses through which sociologists analyze educational systems, we now turn to a focus on the classrooms, corridors, local schools, and key players where the everyday drama of teaching and learning is played out.

THINKING SOCIOLOGICALLY

Do you think education enhances upward social mobility and serves both individuals and society, or does it mostly serve the affluent, reproducing social class and training people to fulfill positions at the same level as their parents?

WHO DOES WHAT? MICRO-LEVEL INTERACTIONS IN EDUCATIONAL ORGANIZATIONS

Most of us have had some especially important learning experience in which one person helped us master a skill, whether it was a scout leader, a grandmother, a choir director, a coach, a neighbor, or an elementary school teacher. We know how important one-on-one mentoring can be to the learning process. Education is often an intimate exchange between two people. Education can change the way we think about the world around us, influence our sense of competency, and affect our self-esteem and our most personal outlooks on self and society.

We learn in different social contexts skills that are important beyond the classroom, sometimes with one-on-one mentoring and sometimes in groups. Often, such learning environments and interactions are more important than formal schooling for our sense of competency.

Source: © Rohit Seth.

Education is also an important organization in local communities. It is often the source of pride and unifying symbol of identity as local communities rally around the success of their school. Moreover, in small towns, the school system is often a large employer in the community, so it has real economic importance to the financial vitality of the area. At the micro level, much sociological analysis has focused on the statuses we occupy and the roles we play, so our discussion here focuses on our positions or statuses within educational settings and on the informal rules of behavior and interaction that evolve in those micro settings.

Who Does What? Statuses and Roles in the Educational System

Students, teachers, staff, and administrators are major statuses in educational systems; the roles associated with each status bring both obligations and inherent problems. When the independent status holders agree on expected behaviors, schools function smoothly. When they do not agree, conflicts can arise as to how to meet the differing expectations and goals of the system. Let us look at several statuses and accompanying roles in schools.

Students and the Peer Culture of Schools

In some countries, going to school is a privilege; in others, it is a necessary part of life that many students resist. In either case, children understand the school system well. They know how they must behave to be considered "good kids" and how one comes to be labeled a "bad kid," although they do not know how to change that label once it is in place.

In a Rwandan secondary school, Ecole des Sciences (School of Sciences) in Byimana, 45 students are crowded onto benches; they are quiet, respectful, and very hard-working. They know the norms and rules, and peer culture supports this behavior. They are in a privileged position, and many students are lined up to take their place on the bench should they not work hard and succeed. Although they have no written texts, they write down the lectures in their notebooks and memorize the material (Schlueter 2006).

This section considers lessons children learn in the micro culture of the classroom. Classrooms are small societies of peers; they reflect the patterns and the problems of the larger world (Durkheim 1956). For instance, studies indicate that female peer friends are closely knit and egalitarian, sharing confidences and problems, whereas male friends are loosely knit, with clear status hierarchies based on shared activities such as sports (Corsaro and Eder 1990; Wood 2005). Society's racial and gender patterns also reflect friendship patterns in many schools; for example, studies in the United States have found that students are only one-sixth as likely to choose a cross-race peer as a same-race peer for a friend (Grant 2004; Hallinan and Williams 1990).

Children worldwide begin learning what is expected of them in preschool and kindergarten, providing the basis for schooling in the society (Neuman 2005). For example, Gracey (1977) describes early school socialization as "academic boot camp." Kindergarten teachers teach children to follow rules, to cooperate with each other, and to accept the teacher as the boss who gives orders and controls how time is spent. All of this is part of what young children learn, lessons instilled in students even though it is not yet the formal curriculum of reading, writing, and arithmetic. These less formal messages form the hidden curriculum, examined in more detail below.

In schools around the world, students play a variety of roles; *jocks, geeks (brainy ones), burnouts,* and *gang members* are some labels applied to U.S. students. These roles make up the *student peer culture,* "a stable set of activities or routines, artifacts, values, and concerns that children produce and share in interaction with peers" (Corsaro and Eder 1990:197). Peer cultures have a major effect on the future roles of their members (Waller 1932/1965). For instance, *jocks* in the United States or *ear 'oles* in Britain—college-bound middle-class students—have an investment in the school system, whereas *burnouts* or *lads*—working-class students who often feel hostile or alienated toward the school environment—may engage in behaviors that prevent them from succeeding in high school and can lead to dropping out (Eckert 1989; Jackson 1968; MacLeod 1995; McNeal 1995; Willis 1979).

Class, race, and gender are all interactive factors that can affect a child's experience. While many experts acknowledge that girls and boys have different experiences in school, a recent debate in Britain and the United States focuses on whether boys or girls have a harder time in school. The masculinizing of schools refers to hiring male

PHOTO ESSAY

Student Roles

S tudents in schools play a variety of roles and often are identified by labels. What labels might apply to the students in these photos, and what were some of the labels applied to students in your high school?

Source: © John Carleton.

Source: © Kevin Russ.

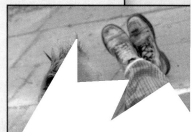

Source: © Istockphoto.com.

Source: © Tomaz Levstek.

Source: © Istockphoto.com.

Source: © Bonnie Jacobs.

Source: © Istockphoto.com.

Source: © Joel Natkin.

Zimbabwe once had one of the best education systems in Africa, but after severe economic crisis in the country, educational conditions have declined rapidly. Still, some children are privileged over other children who do not get any education.

Source: © Gideon Mendel / Corbis.

The micro culture of a classroom will shape children's learning and their image of society and relationships, but that micro culture is also shaped by the prejudices and attitudes in the larger society. In the United States, fewer than 20 percent of children will have a friend of another race.

Source: © Bonnie Jacobs.

teachers at higher pay levels than female teachers; more male-dominated extracurricular activities, especially sports; and increased practical, vocational curricula. These trends help to keep boys from dropping out by making schools more "boy-friendly" (Lesko 2001). The next Sociology in Your Social World discusses concerns that have been raised about boys in U.S. schools.

Sexual harassment is also a gender issue in schools. According to studies by the American Association of University Women Educational Foundation (1993, 2001), four out of five students report some type of sexual harassment in school; girls experience "hostile hallways" in more physically and psychologically harmful ways than boys. The following summarizes findings from a recent AAUW study of 2,064 U.S. public school students in 8th through 11th grades and from the Gay, Lesbian, and Straight Network:

- 83 percent of girls and 79 percent of boys report having experienced harassment. More than 1 in 4 students experienced it *often.*

- 76% of students have experienced nonphysical harassment, while 58% have experienced physical harassment. Nonphysical harassment includes taunting, rumors, graffiti, jokes, or gestures.

- There has been a sea change in awareness of school policies about harassment since the first American Association of University Women Educational Foundation study in 1993. Seven in 10 students (69%) say that their school has a policy on sexual harassment, compared to only 26% of students in 1993. Nearly all students (96%) say they know what harassment is, and boys' and girls' definitions do not differ substantially.

- Substantial numbers of students fear being sexually harassed or hurt in school. Eighteen percent are afraid some or most of the time; fewer than half (46%) report *never* being afraid in school. One-third of students fear being sexually harassed in school.

- In 2005, slightly more than 75 percent (3 out of 4) of high school students heard derogatory remarks such as "faggot" or "dyke" frequently or often at school, 89 percent reported *frequently* hearing "that's so gay" or "you're so gay"—with the implication of stupidity or worthlessness. Nearly 4 out of 10 gay, lesbian, bisexual, or transgendered students experienced physical bullying at school, and half of those students had actually been assaulted because of their sexual orientation (Gay, Lesbian, and Straight Education Network 2006).

- In summary, "sexual harassment is a part of everyday life for boys and girls at school. . . . Parents, teachers, and administrators need to do a better job educating our children on what is and what isn't appropriate" (American Association of University Women Educational Foundation 2001).

Students from different social class, religion, ethnic or racial backgrounds, or sexual orientations need safe places where they can be themselves and not face constant ridicule. Perhaps, the greatest insult in many schools is to be called a "fag"—a shortening of "faggot" or "flaming faggot." A *faggot* is actually a bundle of sticks, used to feed the fire that burned witches and homosexuals. While many youngsters

Sociology in Your Social World

Where the Boys Are

The Myth of the Fragile Girl; The War against Boys; Failing at Fairness: How America's Schools Cheat Girls; and At Colleges, Women are Leaving Men in the Dust—these are just a few subjects in a debate about whether boys or girls, rich or poor, minorities or whites, have the biggest advantage or disadvantage in schools in Western societies. For many years, concern focused on factors that inhibited girls' educational attainment in school. Recently, some authors are turning the tables and focusing their concern on adolescent boys, but this is controversial as we shall see.

The picture looks grim for some groups of young men, as shown in analyses that focus on differences in the experiences of girls and boys from elementary grades through higher education. Statistics indicate that the state of educational achievement varies greatly by sex, age, race or ethnicity, and socioeconomic status. Why is this so? Among the many reasons for the differences, researchers point to the incredible gains made by women and the fact that women tend to study more. In the United States, African American, Hispanic, and low-income males lag behind all other groups, including females from their own ethnic group (King 2000).

African Americans and Hispanics had lower high school graduation rates (56 and 52 percent, respectively) than white students (78 percent) in 2002. In 2003, Asian or Pacific Islanders had a higher high school completion rate (94.9 percent) than whites (91.9 percent), blacks (85 percent), or Hispanics (69.2 percent); the gap has been narrowing in recent years (Laird, DeBell, and Chapman 2006; National Center for Education Statistics 2005). College attendance rates are shown in Table 11.2.

A study by the National Urban League (2006) indicates that one-third of the poorly educated young

black men end up in prison, further reducing their chances for education, good jobs, and stable family life. They feel disconnected from a society that helps women with children but ignores the vulnerabilities of men (Mincy 2006). The following figures provide a partial picture:

- An estimated 2 to 3 million youth ages 16 through 24 are without postsecondary education and are disconnected—neither in school nor employed.
- Among those between ages 16 and 24 who are not enrolled in school, only about half are working and one-third are involved with the criminal justice system. Roughly three in ten will spend some time in prison or jail during their lives.
- As few as 20 percent of black teens are employed at any time, and education has not been a path to better jobs for neighbors and family members (Mincy 2006).

Women have surpassed men in college attendance, and men, regardless of race or class, get lower grades, take more time to graduate, and are less likely to get a bachelor's degree (Lewin 2006). Between 1969 and 2000, men undergraduates increased by 39 percent; female undergraduates increased by 159 percent. Females became the majority of undergraduates in 1978, and the percentage of male undergraduates in 2006 had continued to drop to 42 percent of the college total (Lewin 2006). However, men from the highest income groups attend college at a slightly higher rate than women in that group, and men from low-income families—disproportionately African American and Hispanic—are the most underrepresented. The gender gap in favor of females has been most pronounced among low-income whites and Hispanics. The imbalance is of such concern to college admissions officers that some colleges are turning away more qualified females in favor of males (Britz 2006). Some colleges are even adding activities such as football to attract more male students (Pennington 2006).

Research shows a growing disparity between the number of women and men receiving bachelor's degrees and the resulting decline in achievement of men (Lewin 2006). Data indicate that while women do not score as high on achievement tests as men in math and science, they hold higher educational aspirations, are more likely to enroll in college, and more likely to attain a college degree

TABLE 11.2 **College Attendance Rates**

Race	College Attendance Rate % (2004)
White, non-Hispanic	68.8
Black	62.5
Hispanic	61.8

Source: National Center for Education Statistics (2005, Table 181).

(Continued)

(Continued)

(National Center for Education Statistics 2000). The figures for gender and education are even more severe when race is considered; black women earned twice as many bachelor's degrees as black men (National Center for Education Statistics 2002); yet females who are racial or ethnic minorities lag behind white women (King 2000).

Despite the sex differences, some researchers argue that the gender gap is not nearly as significant as the differences for race or ethnicity and social class. Furthermore, men still dominate math and science fields that pay more money and result in more power. Perhaps concern over boys' performance simply reflects nervousness about women's achievements (Lewin 2006).

What do we do? Girls and women face serious educational problems in many developing countries, and women in developed countries are still at a disadvantage in hiring for high-paid jobs and equal wages. Concern about boys is a relatively new twist in the equity issue. Books and articles suggest the problems start early; they bemoan the fate of young men—especially those from racial or ethnic minorities—pointing out the greater difficulty males have paying attention in class, sitting still, seeking help when they need it, and sustaining a positive attitude toward school. Suggestions for improving the situation include more games and competition that boys like, more outdoor exercise, and more male role models as teachers.

who use the word are not familiar with the origins of the word, it does create terror for people who are gay. It is a death threat—a form of terrorism.

Finally, educators are deeply concerned about disruptive or deviant students, not only because they disrupt learning but because many are at risk of dropping out of school. Some educators suggest no-fail, cooperative learning classrooms for at-risk students, allowing them to establish more positive peer networks and minimizing individual failure. Still, the environment outside the school also powerfully affects students' achievements and behaviors within the school. Disorganization in the community and family is related to lack of school commitment and is reflected in delinquent behavior (Jenkins 1995; Ogbu 1998). The students at highest risk for dropping out of school in Western countries are also at high risk for joining gangs and engaging in violent behavior (Noguera 1996; Willis 1979); they feel the system is stacked against them. Gangs are also an issue in a number of Western countries—especially in Europe (McEvoy 1990). The peer cultures of gangs often interfere with learning inside the school.

There are many factors that affect students, but the degree of success they experience is often dependent on their role-partners: teachers.

Teachers: The Front Line

We all remember certain teachers with fondness and think of others with fear or anger. In *Life in Classrooms*, Philip Jackson (1968) estimated that teachers have more than a thousand interchanges a day in their roles as managers of the classroom. Teachers serve as gatekeepers, controlling the

classroom flow of students, activities, resources, and privileges; act as timekeepers and traffic managers; and spend a great deal of time in "neutral" gear—not accomplishing much. Many teachers complain that they are so bogged down with paperwork and forms—attendance, tardiness, student behavior, and other required reports for the state—that they have little time to address the primary objectives of the school: student learning.

Teachers are in the middle of the educational hierarchy between the micro and meso levels. They occupy the front line

Middle-school students crowd around a teacher's desk in Nagano, Japan. The teacher may experience intense role strain, dealing with the roles of disciplinarian, supporter, confidant, and judge of academic quality.

Source: © TWPhoto/Corbis.

PHOTO ESSAY

Teacher Roles

Teachers hold the core roles in schools, but it is a challenging role that must delicately balance the curriculum, the needs of students, the policies of the school, the ideas of the larger community, and the concerns of parents or other constituencies.

Source: © Dean Conger / Corbis.

Source: © Keith Dannemiller / D70s / Corbis.

Source: © Olivier Martel / Corbis.

Source: © Bonnie Jacobs.

Source: © Jamie Wilson.

in implementing the goals of the school and the state. As the primary socializers and role models for students, teachers are expected to set good examples, yet they are often in the awkward situation of being the students' supporters and encouragers at the same time they are their judges—giving grades and recommendations as part of the selection and allocation functions. This creates an important role strain that can interfere with the task of teaching and can contribute to teacher burnout, discussed below (Dworkin 2001, 2007; Dworkin, Saha and Hill 2003).

Teacher status varies from society to society, depending on the value placed on their role and pay they receive relative to other occupations. In Japan, where education is considered extremely important for training future generations, teachers are treated with great respect and honor; they receive salaries competitive with those in industry and professions like law and medicine (Ballantine 2001b). In Europe, many high schools are organizationally more like universities. Teachers think of themselves as akin to professors, and in African secondary schools, teachers hold high status in their profession.

In the United States, high schools are under local control with the same school board as the elementary and middle schools; teachers are part of the professional organizations with teachers of lower grades. Therefore, secondary teachers think of themselves as more like middle-school teachers than like university professors. The reference groups of high school teachers in the United States and European schools differ (Clark 1985; Legters 2001).

U.S. teachers complain of feeling unappreciated, frustrated, and dissatisfied; the morale issues are rooted in low salaries, low status of teaching as a profession, unmotivated students, problems of discipline in the classroom, lack of support from students' families and the community, criticism of schools, and interruptions of classroom work for time-consuming special programs. However, the public gives teachers high marks and disapproves of their being forced to "teach to the tests" and limit curricular offerings by No Child Left Behind (NCLB) policies (Phi Delta Kappa/Gallup Poll 2001, 2005).

A major issue facing U.S. teachers is accountability for students' progress. The accountability movement gave rise to two types of tests: standardized tests to measure students' achievements and competency tests to determine teachers' own knowledge and skills (Grant and Murray 1999). Achievement or proficiency tests are controversial because they put pressure on teachers to teach primarily what will help students pass the tests so that they can move up in the school system and graduate from high school. Competency tests seem insulting for teachers who have already been licensed and are performing well.

Teachers are criticized for everything from their lack of skills to poor preparation to problems with motivation, yet the organizational context of teachers' work is a key source of problems. Studies in Australia and the United States show teachers feel they are unappreciated (Saha and Dworkin 2006); poor

social standing and respect for the teaching occupation require more than better recruiting and training but also upgrading the status of teachers (Ingersoll 2005). Several sociologists suggest that teachers' dissatisfactions can be addressed through organizational and structural changes, allowing teachers more autonomy and control over their environments (Dworkin 2007; Dworkin et al. 2003; Ingersoll 2005).

Still, the majority of the public and many politicians want teachers held to high standards of competence and conduct (Phi Delta Kappa/Gallup Poll 2001). The question is who should enforce high standards: the profession itself or legislators and the public?

THINKING SOCIOLOGICALLY

How do you think students affect the sense of self, the confidence, the effectiveness, and the quality of teachers' lives?

One reason teachers' organizations oppose government standards imposed on educators is that they deprofessionalize teachers (Ingersoll 2004). Two key features of being a professional are autonomy on the job and self-regulation by the profession. Lawyers can be disbarred by the American Bar Association for incompetence, and doctors can have their medical licenses revoked by the medical establishment, but control of teachers often comes from outside teacher organizations. In most professions, there is a sense of calling and commitment that motivates, not just by money but by self-respect, a sense of contribution, and pride in being a member and serving others. The accountability movement assumes that teachers are not professionals, should not have much autonomy, should be closely supervised, and should not be allowed to regulate competence among themselves. When government regulates standards for teachers, the result is deprofessionalization (Roberts and Donahue 2000). Thus, quality might actually decrease as teachers face lack of status as professionals and lack of control over their work and opt for other occupations.

THINKING SOCIOLOGICALLY

Who should enforce high teacher standards? Who should decide what these standards are?

Administrators: The Managers of the School System

Key administrators—superintendents, deans, principals, or headmasters and headmistresses—hold the top positions in the educational hierarchy of local schools. They are responsible for a long list of tasks: issuing budget reports; engaging in staff negotiations; hiring, firing, and training staff members; meeting with parents; carrying out routine approval of projects; managing public relations; preparing reports for boards of directors, local education councils, legislative bodies, and national agencies; keeping up with new regulations; making recommendations regarding the staff; and many other tasks. Depending on the size of the system, they also may oversee discipline and act as buffers between parents and teachers when conflicts arise. In some countries, a lay board of education oversees decisions including hiring of administrators and expenditures.

Administrators operate one step removed from the actual educational functions of the classroom, and they mediate between the local community school and the larger bureaucracy at the state and national levels. A key finding is that school organization and administrative structures around the world are becoming more similar.

The Informal System: What Really Happens inside Schools?

It is the first day of class, and the teacher asks a question. Should we respond or let someone else answer? If we respond, the teacher might be impressed, but the other students might think we are brown-nosing or too bold. What if we answer incorrectly and sound foolish?

The **informal system** of schooling includes the unspoken, unwritten, implicit demands that we must learn, whether in kindergarten or college, in order to master the system. These unwritten norms of the classroom may be imposed by teachers or by the student culture. The informal system does not appear in written goal statements or syllabi but, nonetheless, is an important part of our experiences in school. It exists along with the formal bureaucratic structure and influences what happens in that structure. Consider several dimensions of the informal system: the hidden curriculum, the educational climate, the value climate, and power dynamics and coping strategies within the classroom.

The **hidden curriculum** refers to the implicit demands found in every learning institution; students have to learn and respond to these in order to succeed within the education system (Snyder 1971). For instance, when we enter a college classroom for the first time and receive a syllabus, several questions probably go through our minds, as shown below.

According to functional theorists, it is through the hidden curriculum that students learn the expectations, behaviors, and values necessary to succeed in school and society. For conflict theorists, the hidden curriculum is a social and economic agenda that is responsible for differentiating social classes: more is expected of members of elite classes, and they are given greater responsibility and opportunities for problem solving that result in higher achievement (Brookover and Erickson 1975), whereas schools teach nonelite students to obey rules and to accept their lot as responsible, punctual workers. Many working-class schools do indeed stress order and discipline over achievement (Willis 1979). Studies comparing working-class schools with upper-middle-class schools reveal differences in structures that reinforce social class behaviors (Anyon 1980; Hargreaves 1978; Kalmijn and Kraaykamp 1996; Kozol 2005; Lubeck 1985).

Educational Climate of Schools

Sometimes, we feel comfortable and even stimulated when we walk into a school. Other schools seem cold and unfriendly. Some schools have an atmosphere of excitement about learning, with artwork and posters on the walls and excited noises coming from classrooms. In some schools, uniformed students walk in columns and sit up straight in neat rows. Other schools concentrate on enforcing rigid rules and have posted warnings on the walls and guards in the halls barking orders. All of these factors are aspects of *school climate*, "a general social condition that characterizes a group, organization, or community" such as a school (Brookover, Erickson, and McEvoy 1996; Brookover et al. 1979).

The school's architecture, teachers' expectations, open-versus-closed classroom structure, ability grouping, age grading, and team teaching all affect the climate of the school.

Syllabus for Course	
Actual or Visible Curriculum	**Hidden Curriculum**
Instructor: Name	What should I call the instructor? (This may be formally established.)
Texts: Names	Do we really have to buy them and read them?
Course topics: Listed	What is the instructor really going to teach? What is he or she really interested in?
Requirements:	
Readings	What do I really have to do to get by?
Projects	Will it help if I speak up in class?
Exams	Will it help if I go see the instructor?
Bibliography	Am I really supposed to use this?

Kenyan schoolgirls wait for classes to begin. Children like this, whose parents can afford to send them to school, will likely grow up with enough education to postpone marriage and childbirth and have better economic prospects. Note the mural. What messages are communicated in this photo about the influence of this African school?

source: © Karen Kasmauski / Corbis.

Many schools also have ceremonies and rituals that contribute to the school climate—logos, symbols, athletic events, pep rallies, award ceremonies—but in some countries like Japan, extracurricular activities are often held outside school hours, often Saturday afternoons, sponsored by private clubs.

Classrooms, too, have climates. The teachers' use of discipline and encouragement, the way teachers organize tasks and plan student interactions, and the seating arrangement and wall décor play a large role in creating an atmosphere that influences student achievement (Cohen 1997). Consider British infant schools for beginning students, often structured so that the youngest five-year-old students are socialized and taught by the older students of six or seven. Everyone learns and takes responsibility for others' learning. Jeanne's son Andy attended this type of school when he had just turned five; he was soon learning the routines from older children and reading about Roger Red Hat and Billy Blue Hat, followed by fairy tales with dragons.

Class, ethnicity or race, and gender also have subtle but pervasive impacts on students' experiences in different educational climates. For instance, studies indicate that boys get more attention, are called on more often, and are given instructions about how to accomplish tasks, while teachers sometimes do the tasks *for* the girls in the class (Sadker and Sadker 1995; Spade 2004).

Equitable treatment of students from diverse class and race backgrounds is another concern of educational climate studies. In multicultural societies, teachers teach children from many subcultural backgrounds and learning styles. Do students have equal access to materials and technology? Are all students active and influential participants in the learning process, shown by similarities in student achievement? These goals for equitable teaching and learning face challenges in the increasingly diverse classrooms around the world as more heterogeneous groups of immigrant students with linguistically and culturally diverse backgrounds come into schools. "Different" students tend to end up in lower ability groups, guaranteeing their poorer achievement (Cohen 1997; Lucas and Berends 2002).

Native American children have often been raised in ways incompatible with U.S. teacher expectations and the requirements of U.S. policies laid out in NCLB; these differences that the government does not take into account can be a recipe for failure. Table 11.3 illustrates the problems students from different backgrounds may have in schools that provide unfamiliar experiences; even the brightest children can be failures in such circumstances.

Another study of the informal system is revealing of the effects of students' race and gender on teacher expectations:

> White girls are being groomed for academic attainment in a context of dependence and loyalty, while African American girls receive encouragement to emphasize social relationships over academic work. White boys are being groomed for high attainment and high status social roles, without the concomitant training for social conformity. African American boys are carefully monitored and controlled in classrooms, as teachers' expectations for their academic futures diminish. (Grant 2004:296)

This does not imply conscious or intended bias on the part of teachers; the expectations are subtle and can be recognized only by careful empirical study and analysis.

The friendships made by students and the overall climate of support depend in part on how schools and classrooms are organized and on teachers' policies (Vandell and Hembree 1994). For instance, some schools track students on the basis of their tested ability in certain subjects, thus creating friendship groups within these tracks (Hallinan and Williams 1989). Tracking systems tend to create and maintain racial, ethnic, and social class segregation in schools and classrooms (Lucas and Berends 2002).

Value Climate of Schools

The *value climate* refers to students' motivations, aspirations, and achievements. Why is achievement significantly higher in some schools than in others? How much influence do the values and outlooks of peers, parents, and teachers have on students? Sociologists know that a student's home is influential in determining educational motivation; recall the opening case of Tomás who received only negative comments and little encouragement. Neighborhood racial,

TABLE 11.3 **The Mismatch between No Child Left Behind Programs and the Research Base on Native American Learning**

Native American Learning Styles	*No Child Left Behind (NCLB) Requirements?*
Best Practices	**No Child Left Behind Programs**
Hands-on, experience-based	Abstract, "drill and kill"
Use of culturally appropriate materials	Culturally bland/generic
Informal, flexible learning environment	Highly structured, extreme inflexibility
Collaborative, teamwork	Highly individualistic, isolating
Teacher as facilitator or coach	Teacher-centered, top-down
High levels of dialogue	Scripted, unnatural interactions
Learning Styles (Preferences)	**No Child Left Behind Programs**
Holistic approach, whole-to-part	Fragmented learning, part-to-whole
Reflective meaning-making	Rote learning, memorizing
Visual learning mode, including pictures and illustrations	Heavy print emphasis
Culturally Appropriate Programs	**No Child Left Behind Programs**
Based in culture's values and beliefs	Dominant culture's values and beliefs
Both/and approach (local and global)	Dominant culture only
Begins but does not end with community	Content irrelevant to community
Environmental Conditions That Support Resiliency	**No Child Left Behind Programs**
Promotes close bonds	Not addressed in NCLB
Uses high-warmth, low-criticism style of interaction	Failure-focused
Sets and enforces clear boundaries using democratic principles	Uses top-down imposed rules
Encourages sharing of responsibilities, service to others, expectation of helpfulness	Not addressed in NCLB
Supports development of autonomy/independence	Teacher-controlled
Expresses high and realistic expectations	Expectations are low
Encourages personal goal setting and future focus	Not addressed in NCLB
Encourages development of values and life skills	Not addressed in NCLB
Encourages development of leadership, allows for decision making and other opportunities for meaningful participation	Scripted participation and decision making
Appreciates unique talents of each individual	Group-focused
Emphasizes creativity	Emphasizes conformity
Encourages development of sense of humor	Absent

Source: Starnes (2006).

ethnic, and class composition also can affect value climate within the school. Segregation of schools along social class lines, for example, can lower expectations of teachers and achievement for students from some lower-class neighborhoods. Classes integrated along ethnic or class lines can raise the level of motivation and achievement for members of minorities (Garner and Raudenbush 1991; Lucas and Berends 2002; Mickelson 1990).

Students' and teachers' perceptions of the learning environment also influence school value climate and achievement. In the United States, studies show that when students perceive themselves to be members of and involved in their schools, they perform better than those who are not attached to school (Smerdon 2002). If students feel a sense of futility and hopelessness and if they are convinced that their teachers do not believe in their ability, are indifferent to their academic achievement, or are obsessed with discipline, high levels of achievement are less likely. If teachers have negative expectations, students are likely to have lower aspirations

and achievement levels (Rosenthal and Jacobson 1968). Expectations and rankings by others can become a *self-fulfilling prophecy*, affecting how children feel about their own abilities; this, in turn, influences their motivation to achieve and ultimately their life chances. Students who are expected to do very well generally rise to meet these expectations (Cohen 1997; Weber and Omotani 1994).

Many factors related to class, race, and gender affect teacher expectations (Morris 2005). The next Sociology in Your Social World outlines some of the expectations that affect teachers' judgments of students in the United States; most of these apply to any country.

Taking into consideration the finding that teachers' expectations account for 5 to 10 percent of students' achievements (Brophy 1983), a group of researchers undertook to raise the value climate and expectations of teachers and students in a group of Chicago public schools. They based their plan on three goals for creating an effective academic learning climate: schools need to be safe and orderly with no

Sociology in Your Social World

Sources of Teacher Expectations

We need to guard against the following factors that create lower expectations for certain groups of students:

- *Sex:* Boys and girls are sometimes the recipients of low academic expectations because of mistaken beliefs about boys' maturation and sex-role discrimination against girls.
- *Socioeconomic status level:* Low expectations are typically held for children from families with low-level income and education, low-status jobs, and undesirable neighborhood residence.
- *Race and ethnic identifiers:* Teachers may have lower expectations for African American, Hispanic, and Native American students than other students. Asian American students receive high expectations.
- *The status of the school:* Rural and inner-city schools often have lower expectations than suburban schools. The racial, ethnic, and income level of the school is often a factor in such prejudice, with a negative "can't do anything" climate.
- *Appearance and neatness:* Lower expectations are associated with clothes and grooming that are out of style, made of cheaper material, not brand name, or purchased at thrift or discount stores, and with poor handwriting and other sloppiness in presentation.

- *Oral language patterns:* Nonstandard English often is the basis for holding lower expectations for students.
- *Halo effect:* There is a tendency to label a student's current achievement based on past performance evaluations of a child. Therefore, blind grading—evaluation of student work without knowledge of who wrote the material until after it is graded—is important.
- *Readiness:* There are negative effects when teachers assume that maturation rates or prior lack of knowledge or experience are unchanging phenomena, thus precluding improvement.
- *Seating position:* Lower expectations are typically transmitted to students who sit on the sides and in the back of a classroom.
- *Student behavior:* Students with nonacademic behaviors that are inappropriate by middle-class standards also tend to receive lower academic expectations from teachers.
- *Teacher education textbooks and training institutions:* Some textbooks and professors perpetuate notions among teachers-in-training that certain kinds of students have limitations, which reinforce low expectations for those students.
- *Tracking or grouping:* Students in lower academic tracks are presumed to have been placed there for a good reason (i.e., they have limited capacities and can never be expected to learn critical knowledge and skills), yet in some cases placements may have been arbitrary or incorrect.

Source: Brookover, Erickson, and McEvoy (1996:75–76).

---

violence or disruptions; schools need to be organized so that they become true academic learning communities with no ability groupings that result in large numbers of failures; and schools need to be clear on what students will learn at each level in math, science, social studies, language, and technical skills such as computer literacy.

Although eliminating ability grouping (tracking) is controversial in some school districts, in Chicago the school achievement levels rose significantly with this plan (Brookover and Erickson 1975; Brookover et al. 1996). Another reform plan in Chicago is Renaissance 2010, a movement to create 100 new small schools in neighborhoods across the city to relieve crowding, increase students'

feelings of belonging, and bring in new leadership (Ayers and Klonsky 2006; Duncan 2006). These are only two of many plans to improve school achievement levels; plans need to take into consideration the educational and value climates of schools in order to be successful. Whether throughout the school or in a particular classroom, the atmosphere that pervades the learning environment and expectations has an impact on students' educational achievement.

Power Dynamics and Coping Strategies in the Classroom

Obedience, cooperation, responsibility, and punctuality are characteristics important to schools and to society. How rules are enforced and who has control are part of the power dynamics in classrooms. The students who are most successful in meeting achievement and behavioral expectations do best in school. Most often, they come from families that understand how the system works. The rules and standards are typically based on norms and values of groups in power, so students from these backgrounds have already been socialized into proper modes of conduct and are certified by the school as "most qualified" for leadership roles in the society (Bowles and Gintis 1976).

Both students and teachers develop strategies to cope with pressures and difficult situations. Coping strategies, part of the hidden curriculum, range from complete compliance to outright rebellion. For instance, college students set priorities for studying various subjects, deciding which test is most important, and figuring out where to cut corners. Do the following four strategies sound familiar? They are taken in part from Merton's (1968a) strain theory of deviance (see Chapter 6) and represent strategies used by students to cope with school pressures:

- *Conformity:* Acceptance of goals and means—doing the school work expected.
- *Innovation:* Finding alternative or unapproved methods to achieve conventional goals—cheating or plagiarizing to pass a course or to win an academic contest.
- *Retreatism:* Rejection of goals and means—rebelling against school establishment by not conforming or cooperating.
- *Ritualism:* Indifference toward goals—getting by following rules but not excelling in school.
- *Rejection with replacement:* Rejection of goals and means in favor of another strategy—being a discipline problem or dropping out of school to pursue other activities (Hammersley and Turner 1980; Merton 1968b).

Teachers use incentives to obtain student compliance. In some settings, grades and the threat of dismissal are enough, especially if others are waiting in the wings to take one's place as was the case in the Rwandan School of Sciences. In other settings, positive feedback, pizza parties for good behavior, and even no-attendance days for students who have never had a detention are necessary incentives to co-opt students into learning. Teachers' methods of discipline are based largely on creating costs (punishments) and benefits (rewards, teacher appreciation, privileges that others do not enjoy). The teacher tries to elicit cooperation and participation from students by creating a ratio that favors compliance.

Because teachers in some countries cannot force students to comply with incentives, they develop coping strategies, techniques they use to maintain control over the classroom and to accomplish their goals and influence the climate of the classroom. When students challenge a teacher's authority, the teacher can decide to appear tough and savvy, kind and caring, or friendly and joking, depending on what they think is likely to be effective for the particular situation. Manipulating the structure of the classroom is one effective means of control: putting students at tables or in a circle, breaking up groups of chattering friends, or leading a discussion by standing right beside the most disruptive child. Teachers study educational discipline techniques, but they rely most strongly on classroom experience for effective classroom management.

THINKING SOCIOLOGICALLY

What examples of the informal system can you see in the courses you are currently taking? How do these affect your learning experience?

AFTER THE SCHOOL BELL RINGS: MESO-LEVEL ANALYSIS

Schools can be like mazes, with passages to negotiate, hallways lined with pictures and lockers, and classrooms that set the scene for the educational process. However, they are mazes in a much larger sense; they involve complex

> *The school bell is a symbol of meso-level control over participants in schools. It interrupts lessons, tells people when to change rooms or switch topics of study, indicates when one is late (reinforcing punctuality, especially in industrialized societies), and imposes order on the day. It rings based on a clock that ignores what else is happening when time has come for a change. How does this represent meso-level control?*
>
> *Source:* © Thomas Peter.

interwoven social systems at the meso level. It is at this level that we encounter the formal structure of the school system.

Formal Education Systems

Formal education came into being in the Western world in sixteenth-century Europe; schools were seen as a way for Catholics and Lutherans to win souls to religious beliefs. The first compulsory education was in Lutheran Weimar in 1619. By the nineteenth century, schooling was seen as necessary to teach the European lower classes better agricultural methods, skills for the rapidly growing number of factory jobs, patriotism, and obedience to authorities.

By 1900, national state school systems were common in Europe and most former colonies of collapsed colonial empires—Ottoman, Austro-Hungarian, British, and French. These systems shared many organizational structures, curricula, and methods because leaders shared their ideas about what works. The Prussian model with strict discipline and ties to the military became popular. However, the two-track system—one for rich and one for poor—was debated worldwide—and still is.

Thus, formal education systems came into being when other social institutions required new skills and knowledge. When knowledge needed by the young became too complex to be taught informally in families through examples, moral lessons, and stories, a change was needed. Industrializing societies required workers with basic literacy and math skills. Schooling that formerly served only the elite gradually became available to the masses, and some societies began to require schooling for basic literacy (usually third-grade level). Schools emerged as major formal organizations and eventually developed extensive bureaucracies. The postwar period from 1950 to 1992 brought about a rapid rise in education worldwide, as shown in Table 11.4 (Boli, 2002:309).

Sometimes, differing goals for educational systems lead to conflict. Former colonial countries struggle with the legacies of European educational systems that served the needs of only a small, elite segment of the population. What need, for example, does a subsistence farmer in Nigeria or Kenya have for Latin? Yet Latin was often imposed on curricula of colonial nations as part of the colonial standard curriculum. Some countries are now revising curricula based on goals and needs of agriculturally based economies.

The Bureaucratic School Structure

The formal bureaucratic atmosphere that permeates many schools arose because it was cost-effective, efficient, and impersonal; it provided a way to process masses of students coming from different backgrounds. Recall Weber's bureaucratic model on groups and organizations, discussed in Chapter 5:

1. Schools are characterized by a division of labor among administrators, teachers, students, and support personnel. The roles associated with the statuses are part of the school structure. Individual teachers or students hold these roles for a limited time and are replaced by others coming into the system.

2. The administrative hierarchy incorporates a chain of command and channels of communication.

3. Specific rules and procedures in a school cover everything from course content to discipline in the classroom.

4. Personal relationships are downplayed in favor of formalized relations among members of the system, such as placement on the basis of tests and grading.

5. Rationality governs the operations of the organization; people are hired and fired on the basis of their qualifications and how well they do their jobs.

A result of bureaucracy is that some children are not helped with personal problems or learning difficulties (Kozol 2006; Sizer 1984). Impersonal rules can lock people into rigid behavior patterns, leading to apathy and alienation. In schools, these feelings cause passivity among students, which in turn frustrates teachers. Children like Tomás in the opening example do not fit into neat cubbyholes that bureaucratic structures invariably create. These children view school not as a privilege but as a requirement imposed by an adult world. Teachers, caught between the demands of an impersonal bureaucracy and goals for their students, cannot always give these children the personal help they need. Thus, we see that organizational requirements of educational systems at a meso level can influence the personal student-teacher relationship at the micro level. This is another example of how the social world model helps us to understand human behavior in organizations.

A bureaucratic model for schools encourages—and even demands—rigid organizational structure. In her humorous book, *Up the Down Staircase*, Bel Kaufman (1964) gives a striking example of dysfunctional bureaucracy. The following memo instructs teachers about their responsibilities.

TABLE 11.4 **World Educational Enrollment Rates 1950–1992 (in percentages)**

Year	Primary Schooling	Secondary Schooling	Tertiary Schooling (University)
1950	58	13	1.4
1960	77	27	6.0
1970	84	36	11
1980	96	45	11
1992	98	53	14

Source: Boli (2002:309).

Program for Today's Homeroom Period (Check off each item before leaving the building today.)

- Make out attendance cards and seating plan.
- Take attendance.
- Fill out attendance sheets.
- Send out absentee cards.
- Make out three sets of students' program cards (yellow) from master program card (blue); alphabetize and send to office.
- Make out five copies of teacher's program card.
- Sign transportation cards.
- Request supplies.
- Assign lockers, and send names and numbers to office.
- Fill out age-level reports.
- Announce and post assembly schedule, and assign rows in auditorium.
- Announce and post fire, shelter, and dispersal drills regulations.
- Check last term's book and blacklists.
- Check library blacklist.
- Fill out condition of room report.
- Elect class officers.
- Urge joining student council, and begin collecting money.
- Appoint room decorations monitor, and begin decorating room.
- Salute flag (only for nonassembly or Y2 sections).
- Point out the nature and function of homeroom: literally, a room that is a home, where students will find a friendly atmosphere and guidance.
- Teachers with extra time are to report to the office to assist with activities that demand attention.

(adapted from Kaufman 1964)

The bottom line is that formal bureaucratic structures can thwart the goals of an education system. Even colleges and universities face controversies over control of decision making and direction of programs. For instance, funding from business and government organizations allows many university employees to concentrate on research, but it also determines the research agenda they must follow and takes staff away from other functions of the university, such as teaching (Gamson 1998).

Education and the Social Institution of Family

Interconnections between meso-level institutions are a common refrain in this book. Consider interconnections between the institution of family and education. When children enter kindergarten or primary school, they bring many prior experiences, including socialization experiences from parents, brothers, sisters, and other relatives. Family background, according to many sociologists, is the most important single influence on children's school achievement (Jencks 1972). Studies show that parents' encouragement and concern about schoolwork are key factors in achievement. Children

These chairs represent the bureaucracy or hierarchy of the school, with every student facing the teacher as though she or he is the only one who is expected to speak and is worthy of undivided attention. Look through other photos in this chapter, especially ones in nonindustrialized countries. What do you notice that is different about the arrangement of students that suggests differences in relationships in the school?

Source: © Joe Sacher.

succeed in large part because of what their parents do to support them in education (Lee 1991; MacLeod 1995; Schneider and Coleman 1993).

Although most families stress the importance of education, they do so in very different ways. Many middle-class parents in developed societies tend to "manage" their children's education, visiting schools and teachers, having educational materials in the home, and holding high expectations for their children's achievement. In these families, children learn the values of hard work, good grades, and deferred gratification for reaching future goals. Jeanne, one of the coauthors, lived with a family in Germany where she helped the three children with their lessons, improving her German in the process. The parents, both highly educated, visited their children's teachers and provided their children with extra tutoring to help them pass exams into college preparatory tracks.

In Korea, parents select an academic or vocational track for their children after middle school. Some send their youngsters to private, competitive, specialized high schools that focus on foreign language, natural sciences, or the arts. At the end of high school, any student who wishes to go on to the university may take the very difficult and competitive entrance exam once. Concern in Korea centers around the number of suicides among young people who do not pass this exam for university entrance, hence the phrase, "life or death competition." The situation in Japan is similar, but

Marisol attends a middle-school computer class and is mentored by one of her favorite teachers. Marisol currently aspires to become an artist or a lawyer. This dream is fragile since her parents want Marisol to drop out of school and work to help the family survive. Nonetheless, her goal is to finish school and take a different path from her sisters who dropped out of school and started families at a young age.

Source: © Janet Jarman / Corbis.

Recent controversy in France concerned Islamic girls and women wearing the head covering to schools and creating some "we" versus "they" polarization between Muslims and non-Muslims. At this school fair organized by the French League of Muslim Women, women join in on the fun of hula-hoop challenge.

Source: © Alain Nogues / Corbis.

students who do not pass the first time often study for an additional year and take the exam again. In Israel, students receive either a plain or university-qualifying diploma, also based on an exam (Ayalon and Shavit 2004).

Involvement of parents from lower socioeconomic status and first-generation new immigrant families can have significant impact on their children's educational outcomes (Bankston 2004; Domina 2005), yet these parents tend to look to schools as the authority and less involved in their children's schooling, leaving decisions to the school. If they are recent immigrants they may have language difficulties communicating, and they may be intimidated and uncomfortable in dealing with principals and teachers. Much of the disadvantage experienced by children from immigrant families, however, is rooted in the core problem—poverty. Children whose parents are uninvolved with their education and who therefore must make educational decisions on their own are more likely to do poorly or to drop out of school (Kalmijn and Kraaykamp 1996).

Changes in family and work structures put parents under more stress; for example, busy single parents often have little time to help their children with schoolwork. Children who live in homes with single parents or stepparents tend to receive "less encouragement and attention with respect to educational activities than children who live with both biological parents" (Astone and McLanahan 1991:318–19; Mulkey, Crain, and Harrington 1992).

THINKING SOCIOLOGICALLY

How do religion, health, politics, economics, and other institutions in your community influence education, and vice versa? What are examples of links between schools and other social institutions?

Goals: What and Whose?

Various social groups, from religious to ethnic groups, have goals for the schools. At each level of analysis, we see these goals played out. For example, individuals want to enhance their status in society through education. *Community leaders* expect schools to produce youths who will conform and contribute to the well-being of the community. *Ethnic and religious groups* want their values and their worldview represented in the curriculum and instilled into their children. *Societal leaders'* goals for education are to strengthen knowledge, skills, and patriotic or religious values in young people; to train them to be contributing members of society; to prepare them to defend their country; and to teach them their place in the stratification system. Recent controversy in France over Muslim girls' wearing the *hijab* (head covering) to school is an example of the clash of cultures that can occur in goals when race, class, and gender conflict.

Goals in *decentralized school systems* (sometimes called site or school-based management systems) are set by each school or school district; even individual teachers set goals and make their own decisions within broad parameters set by the state. Many interest groups prefer this model because their members can influence educational goals at the community level, which is more responsive to local needs. In the United States, however, where up to one family in five changes residence every year and many families are recent immigrants (Noguera 2004), lack of standardized curricula results in inconsistencies across districts in curriculum, texts, financing, and other educational matters that cause disruptions in children's educations. Some educational professionals select packaged texts to provide continuity in the curriculum for the mobile society (Ballantine 2001b; Wong 1991).

Decision Making at the Meso Level

Who should have the power to make decisions about what children learn? In relatively homogeneous countries such as Japan and Sweden, where centralized goal setting and school decisions are possible, educational decision making typically causes little controversy. Centralized ministries of education are also common in Latin American, Asian, and African countries, where educational standards and funding are controlled by the national government. However, heterogeneous societies, such as Canada, Israel, and the United States, include many different racial, ethnic, and religious subcultures, each with its own needs and interests. Teachers, administrators, school boards, parents, and interest groups all claim the right to influence the curriculum. Consider influences from micro and macro levels on the meso-level organization.

Local-Level Influences

At the U.S. local community level, curriculum conflicts over selection of reading material and sex education courses represent two of the most controversial areas of decision making. Obscenity, sex, nudity, political or economic bias, profanity, slang or nonstandard English, racism or racial hatred, and antireligious or presumed anti-American ideas have all been reasons for censoring texts and library books in schools (Delfattore 2004). *Harry Potter* is a current target. The group Family Friendly Libraries argues that the Potter books should be banned from school libraries because they believe the series promotes the religion of witchcraft (DeMitchell and Carney 2005).

In Yucaipa, California, a set of schoolbooks called *Impressions* was called "satanic, immoral, and violent" by a group of conservative religious parents. The books contained excerpts from children's stories such as Walter Farley's *The Black Stallion* and C. S. Lewis's *The Lion, the Witch and the Wardrobe* (Warren 1990). Similar dramas are played out elsewhere in school board meetings and superintendents' offices around the United States.

Fights over textbooks and library books represent a local issue over which families and community groups hope to exert power. Groups who feel their lifestyles are being threatened want to have a say in how knowledge reaching

TABLE 11.5 **The 10 Most Challenged Books of 2005**

The following are the 10 books that were most often challenged in public schools in 2005 and the reasons they were being contested.

1. *It's Perfectly Normal,* by Robie Harris, for homosexuality, nudity, sex education, religious viewpoint, abortion, and being unsuited to age group.
2. *Forever,* by Judy Blume, for sexual content and offensive language.
3. *The Catcher in the Rye,* by J. D. Salinger, for sexual content, offensive language, and being unsuited to age group.
4. *The Chocolate War,* by Robert Cormier, for sexual content and offensive language.
5. *Whale Talk,* by Chris Crutcher, for racism and offensive language.
6. *Detour for Emmy,* by Marilyn Reynolds, for sexual content.
7. *What My Mother Doesn't Know,* by Sonya Sones, for sexual content and being unsuited to age group.
8. *Captain Underpants* series, by Dav Pilkey, for antifamily content, being unsuited to age group and violence.
9. *Crazy Lady!,* by Jane Leslie Conly, for offensive language.
10. *It's So Amazing! A Book about Eggs, Sperm, Birth, Babies and Families,* by Robie H. Harris, for sex education and sexual content.

Source: American Library Association 2006.

their children is constructed (Delfattore 1992; Page and Clelland 1978). Books including *The Wizard of Oz, Rumpelstiltskin, The Diary of Anne Frank, Madame Bovary, Soul on Ice, Grapes of Wrath, Huckleberry Finn,* Shakespeare's *Hamlet,* Chaucer's *The Miller's Tale,* and Aristophanes's *Lysistrata* are on the hit lists of groups attempting to ban books (Ballantine 2001b). Table 11.5 shows the most frequently challenged books in 2005.

Sex education is another hot topic because of conflicts over the roles and goals of education. The number of sexually active teens in the United States has risen substantially since 1980, increasing the number of citizens advocating sex education. Most teens who have had sex have used at least one method of birth control—98 percent claiming such usage in one survey (Abma et al. 2004). A growing number of large city school districts, concerned with teen pregnancy and sexually transmitted disease, including AIDS, now provide teens with sex education, information about contraception, counseling, and sometimes condoms. Those opposed to sex education in schools cite many reasons; for example, they fear that a nonjudgmental discussion about sexual behavior and information about how to engage in responsible sex will simply increase the amount of premarital teen sex. Critics also believe that sex education should be left to families and religious institutions.

National-Level Influences

Because the constitution of the United States leaves education in the hands of each state, the involvement of the federal government (macro level) has been more limited than in most countries. Yet when the federal government makes funds available for special programs such as mathematics and science, reading, or special education, these funds have a major impact on school programs. Consider the cases of formerly all-male military academies Virginia Military Institute and the Citadel and the power of the federal government, courts, and public monies to change institutions, in this case forcing them to become coeducational. The Americans for Disability Act is another example of federal government mandates affecting local schools.

Policy decisions by federal lawmakers influence what and how children learn. Since 1965 and the establishment of the U.S. Department of Education, presidents have put their mark on the U.S. education system. The policy of President George W. Bush's administration is the NCLB initiative that sets the stage for nationwide standards for learning. Commenting on the "soft bigotry of low expectations," President Bush established an initiative to tie school performance to federal funds and require annual testing for accountability of student competence. So even in the decentralized United States where only $1 in $14 is from the federal government, the national government has an impact on what happens in the intimate environment of classrooms.

There are both positive and negative aspects of the controversial NCLB initiative, with research on the outcomes showing mixed results. On the one hand, it is healthy to set high standards, constructive to expect every child to succeed, and helpful to have some consistency between school systems in a society where students are often geographically mobile. On the other hand, the initiative ignores much of what educators and social scientists know from research; also, the critics argue that it overemphasizes testing, presents unrealistic timetables for schools to meet, and does not provide the funding necessary to carry out the mandates. One critic says, "Bush replaced it [soft bigotry] with the hard bigotries of inadequate funding, a poor understanding of the nature of educational and social inequality, and an even worse implementation plan . . . his plans for reforming education have ignored sociological research on the role of schools and communities in challenging and reinforcing discrimination and inequality" (Karen 2005:165).

THINKING SOCIOLOGICALLY

What other positive or negative consequences might occur from having increased levels of national control over education and schools?

IS EDUCATION THE ROAD TO OPPORTUNITY? STRATIFICATION AT THE MACRO LEVEL

Carlos Muñoz was born in San Diego, the only child of Rafael and Yolanda Muñoz. Both of Carlos's parents were born in Mexico, but they met and were married in the United States. They divorced several years ago, and Carlos alternates living with his mother and father. His mother has long worked as a teacher's aide in the local school district; she lives in a tidy house in a working-class, mostly Mexican area near downtown San Diego. She periodically takes Carlos on trips to Mexico.

Mrs. Muñoz graduated from a high school in the same district where she is now employed, and she is knowledgeable about the educational system here. She is happy with Carlos's high school, which is not overcrowded and understaffed as his junior high school had been, but she is worried about his school performance, saying that he lacks *ganas* (desire) and is not spending enough time or effort on his studies. "He tries to do everything fast. . . . He's getting an F in biology and Cs in most other classes." Of her career hopes for Carlos, she says, "It would be perfect for him to be a lawyer, but he needs to work harder. I don't think that he can do it." His father has now taken a more active role in Carlos's education, hoping to get him on the right track again (Portes and Rumbaut 2001:14–15).

Mrs. Muñoz and millions of other immigrant parents in countries around the world have high hopes for their children, hopes that can be realized through education. Immigrant families from around the globe view education as essential to success in their new cultures. Many groups push their children to achieve in order to improve their opportunities in the new country (Kao 2004). This section focuses on the role of education in the stratification system. While it has implications regarding individual families' chances to succeed, the reality is that education is deeply interwoven into the macro-level inequalities of the society.

Can Schools Bring about Equality in Societies?

Equal opportunity exists when all people have an equal chance of achieving high socioeconomic status in society regardless of their class, ethnicity or race, or gender. James Coleman (1968, 1990) describes the goals of equal educational opportunity:

- to provide a common curriculum for all children regardless of background;
- to provide that children from diverse backgrounds attend the same school; and
- to provide equality within a given locality.

In the United States, equal opportunity means that children are provided with equal facilities, financing, and access to school programs (Kozol 1991). Schools in poor neighborhoods or in rural villages in the United States and around the world, however, often lack the basics—safe buildings, school supplies and books, and funds to operate. Lower-class minority students who live in these areas fall disproportionately at the bottom of the educational hierarchy. Many children face what seem to be insurmountable barriers to educational success: increasing numbers of children living in poverty; lack of health care and immunizations; missing school due to illness or homelessness; or dropping out to help the family (Kozol 2005; Stallings 1995).

Two widely cited classical studies on equal educational opportunity—the Coleman Report and Jencks's study of inequality (Coleman et al. 1966; Jencks 1972)—have had a major impact on policy in education and stand out because of their comprehensive data collection, analysis, and contribution to the understanding of inequality.

The Coleman Report

The Coleman Report was the first of these important studies. The purpose of Coleman and colleagues' study was to compare the opportunities and performance of minority students with those of white students. Covering about five percent of U.S. schools and surveying 645,000 students at five grade levels, researchers collected results from several tests, and gathered information on the children's backgrounds and attitudes toward schooling. School administrators also filled out questionnaires about their schools. Some key findings follow:

1. Minority students (except for Asian American) scored lower on tests at each level of schooling than did white students, and this disparity increased from the 1st to the 12th grades. Coleman attributed the disadvantage of minority students to a combination of out-of-school factors, including parents' educational levels and other environmental factors.

2. The majority of children studied attended segregated schools with same-race teachers.

3. The socioeconomic makeup of the school, the home background, and the background of other students in the school made the biggest difference in students' school achievement levels. This led to the recommendation that schools should be integrated in order to have a mix of students from various class and ethnic groups.

4. Curriculum and facilities made little difference in student achievement levels.

5. White children had somewhat greater access to physics, chemistry, language labs, textbooks, college curricula, and better qualified and higher paid teachers, but the differences were not very great (Coleman et al. 1966).

On the basis of these findings, Coleman recommended that one way to improve the academic achievement of poor and minority children would be to integrate schools, thereby producing a climate for achievement. Based on his findings and recommendations, busing plans were implemented in many large school districts, resulting in controversy and court challenges (Orfield et al. 1997). Today, busing and other methods to desegregate schools such as magnet schools and choice plans are in place. How Do We Know? on page 350 describes a study of magnet schools.

THINKING SOCIOLOGICALLY

In Metz's study reported on page 350, what are the advantages or disadvantages of using several different ways of gathering data?

The Jencks Study

In the second major study of equal educational opportunity cited above, Jencks (1972) concluded that schools alone cannot create equal opportunity. Even if schools reduce the educational attainment gap, economic inequality among adults continues to exist.

> The evidence suggests that equalizing educational opportunity would do very little to make adults more equal. If all elementary schools were equally effective, cognitive inequality among sixth-graders would decline less than three percent. . . . Cognitive inequality among twelfth-graders would hardly decline at all and disparities in their eventual attainment would decline less than one percent. Eliminating all economic and academic obstacles to college attendance might somewhat reduce disparities in educational attainment, but the change would not be large. (Aronson 1978:409)

No one likes to hear that schools make little difference, and Jencks's (1972) findings caused controversy. Most people agree, however, that schools alone cannot solve societal problems.

Tests of Coleman's and Jencks's data confirm one basic finding: a student's family background and peers are vitally important in educational achievement. The schools do not operate in a vacuum, and the success of schools is influenced by local neighborhoods, reference groups of each student, sense of hope, perceived likelihood of success of each child, and the values and expectations of the child's family. These are not variables that are under the control of schools. Thus, a combination of factors influences the chances for equality of opportunity.

Who Gets Ahead and Why?
The Role of Education in Stratification

Remember Tomás, the boy in our opening example who was labeled a failure? What is the role of schools in giving him a

How Do We Know?

Life and Learning in Magnet Schools

Mary Haywood Metz studied three magnet schools in a city school district that she identifies as Heartland, U.S.A.; the overall goal for establishing the magnet schools was to accomplish court-ordered desegregation and to stimulate innovative education. By closing some black neighborhood schools and locating magnet schools in black areas of town, the city achieved desegregation without mandatory reassignment of students.

Each of the three magnet schools offered a different type of program to attract students. The first offered Individually Guided Education, with special organization of the curriculum, instructional techniques, and roles of staff members. The second offered "open education" developed by the staff—with a highly flexible curriculum that required and encouraged very self-directed students. The third school—for gifted and talented students—had a policy of selective admissions and promised an enriched traditional curriculum.

Ethnographic studies are useful when one wishes to learn how organizations work within their settings or environments. Metz's goal was to understand the character, atmosphere (climate), and influences shaping the lives of these three magnet schools—what really

happened in these schools—and to learn about the experiences of the schools' participants. She used multiple research strategies— interviewing, participant observation, and documents—both in the schools and the school district.

Metz spent a semester in each school and three years in the district doing observation, open-ended formal and informal interviews, and analysis of documents as described below:

To describe and explain the character of the life of each school in a holistic way, the researcher needed to participate in that life, to observe and in some measure experience the life the adults and students led. She used open-ended interviews which allowed students, teachers, administrators, and parents to respond to questions in their own words and at length made it possible to explore their perspectives. . . . Observation was conducted in classrooms, halls, cafeterias, playgrounds, girls' bathrooms, and in teachers' lounges and dining-rooms . . . formal interviews were conducted with a small sample of students, most teachers and administrators, and a few

parents. . . . Documents used for analysis included student and faculty handbooks from each school, bulletins for students and faculty, announcements of meetings, and a variety of other written statements. (Metz 1986:13–14)

In addition, Metz considered the historical context of desegregation in which the schools developed, as well as the community climate.

In her book, Metz describes aspects of the daily lives within the schools, the faculty culture, principal-teacher relations, the development of school loyalty, and other characteristics of the three magnet schools. In Heartland, the magnet school concept was only partially successful in desegregating schools; most children bused were black, and many parents sent their children to the closest school regardless of the program offered. Magnet schools made desegregation palatable, and each of these three schools enjoyed some success in dealing with diverse student populations.

Metz provides researchers, school personnel, policy makers, and practitioners an understanding of daily life in these schools as experienced by the participants.

---

chance for success in life? Looking to macro-level theories for explanations, functionalists see the educational system determining where Tomás falls in the stratification system and training him for that position. Education is a **meritocracy**, a social group or organization in which people are allocated to positions according to their abilities and credentials. As long as schools provide everyone with an equal chance to

achieve to their ability, schools are doing their job. The fact that minority students currently are completing more years of schooling indicates a decline in inequality, according to functionalists.

Yet in societies around the world, we see evidence that middle-class and elite children, especially boys in developing countries, receive more and better education than equally intelligent poor and minority children. Children do not attend school on an equal footing, and in many cases meritocracy does not exist. Conflict theorists look at the system for the roots of inequalities. Why is Tomás "unlucky," while others succeed? Explanations go beyond a focus on the children's abilities to analyses of background factors, ethnic groups, and the placements of their families in the stratification system. Conflict theorists feel education creates and perpetuates inequality. The haves hold the power to make sure that institutions, including schools, serve their own needs and protect their access to privileges (Bowles 1977; MacLeod 1995; Sadovnik 2004). The parents in this group have social and cultural capital—language skills, knowledge of how the social system works, and networks—to ensure that their children succeed (Kao 2004; Lareau and Horvat 1999).

Policy makers in some countries, recognizing inequalities, have set up special programs to help girls and ethnic minorities attend schools, providing incentives to them and their families and eliminating school fees. In the United States, *compensatory education* helps to narrow the opportunity gap.

Early Childhood Education and Opportunity

Early childhood education research in China, India, Brazil, Canada, and Europe demonstrate similar findings:

1. Children from birth to age five develop rapidly in linguistic and cognitive gains, emotional development, social regulatory development, and other capacities.

2. In the child's early years, the growth trajectory in learning, health, and emotional development should not be interrupted.

3. Needs of young children are not always adequately addressed.

4. In developing countries, child survival programs that concentrate on reducing infant mortality rates, increasing immunization rates, improving nutrition, and providing clean water and sanitation services have produced long-term economic benefits (Levine 2005; UNICEF 2004).

Evaluations of the Head Start program in the United States, designed for three to five year olds from disadvantaged backgrounds, show that it increases the likelihood that enrolled children will stay in school, will receive preventive health care, will avoid later remedial classes, and will not become juvenile delinquents. Parental education is also part of the program. Yet fewer than half of the eligible children take part in the program due to fluctuations in support as political administrations change (Schweinhart 1997; Zigler, Styfco, and Gilman 1993). Although support increased during the 1990s, funding under the current administration is less vigorous.

Sources of Inequality

Three sources of inequality in schools—testing, tracking, and funding—illustrate how schools reproduce and perpetuate social stratification; they also give clues as to what might be done to minimize the repetitious pattern of poverty.

Testing. Testing is one means of placing students in schools according to their achievement and merit and of determining progress being made. Is this an accurate way to assess student competency? Critics of testing argue that the test questions, language differences, and the testing situation itself are biased against lower-class, minority, and immigrant students, resulting in lower scores and relegating these students to lower tracks in the educational system.

Two types of tests have been at the root of the controversy: intelligence (IQ) tests and achievement tests. IQ tests, which were originally developed to diagnose mental retardation, have been used to place armed service recruits in jobs and students in academic programs. Yet scientists know that intelligence is complex and that the paper-and-pencil tests only measure selected types of intelligence (Gardner 1987, 1999). Many scholars also question whether the tests are unbiased for boys and for girls from different class and ethnic backgrounds.

Achievement tests are supposed to measure how much a student has learned. In many countries, scores on achievement tests for college entrance determine a student's future life chances. Critics of tests point out that higher-class students with better schooling and enriched backgrounds do better on the tests, even if they have not gained as much knowledge. Table 11.6 shows differences in ACT (American College Test) and SAT (Scholastic Assessment Test) scores based on sex, race, and ethnic group.

THINKING SOCIOLOGICALLY

Evaluate your testing experience on variables mentioned above. Were your scores an accurate measure of your ability or achievement? Why or why not? What other factors entered in? Have your scores affected your life chances?

Tracking or Streaming. Placing students in groups based on their ability levels is another way in which schools contribute to the stratification process. Many educators believe that tracking allows students to be taught in ways appropriate to their needs, but others point out problems. Tracking begins in primary school; intelligence and achievement tests and teacher judgments are typically used to track students into groups (Kilgore 1991; Wells and Oakes 1996). Research finds that tracking correlates directly with the child's background and ethnic group, language skills, appearance, and other socioeconomic variables (Oakes 1985, 1990; Rosenbaum 1999). In other words, it is not always a measure of a student's ability.

TABLE 11.6   **ACT and SAT SCORES**

ACT Scores: 2004	Average	SAT Scores: 2004–2005	Average
Composite, total scores	20.9	SAT verbal, all students	508
Male	21.0	Male	513
Female	20.9	Female	505
Race/ethnicity		White	532
White, non-Hispanic	21.8	Black	433
Black, non-Hispanic	17.1	Hispanic/Latino	463
Mexican American/		Mexican American	453
Chicano	18.4	Puerto Rican	460
Puerto Rican	18.8	Asian American	511
Asian American/		American Indian	489
Pacific Islander	21.9	Other	495
American Indian/			
Alaska Native	18.8	SAT math, all students	520
		Male	538
		Female	504
		White	536
		Black	431
		Hispanic/Latino	469
		Mexican American	463
		Puerto Rican	457
		Asian American	493
		American Indian	493
		Other	513

Source: National Center for Education Statistics (2005, Table 126).

Track placement, some believe, is arbitrary and based on teachers' impressions or questionable test results. Even language differences between teachers and students can affect placement (Mehan 1992). Over time, differences in children's achievement become reinforced through the selection process and differences in track programs (Spade, Columba, and Vanfossen 1997). The result is that students from lower social classes and minority groups are clustered in the lower tracks and complete fewer years and lower levels of school (Gamoran 1987; Hallinan 1994; Lucas and Berends 2002; Oakes et al. 1997). School failure in early adolescence leads to other problems in later adolescence and adulthood such as poor mental health and high rates of deviant behavior, all of which affect employment and socioeconomic status (Chen and Kaplan 2003).

The negative effects of tracking can be reduced if the system of placement is flexible, allowing students to be placed in different tracks by subject matter and ensuring reevaluation of students frequently so that they are not locked into placements (Ballantine 2001a; Lucas 1999).

School Funding. The amount and sources of money available to fund schools affect the types of programs offered, an important issue for nations that must compete in the global social and economic system. Money for education comes from central governments in some societies, and from a combination of federal, state, and local government and private sources like religious denominations in others. In countries such as Uganda in Africa, the government runs the schools, but most funding comes from tuition paid by each student or by the student's parents. Whatever the source, schools sometimes face budget crises and must trim programs.

In the United States, unequal school spending results from reliance on local property taxes as well as state and federal funds; about 50 percent of the money for schools comes from state funds; most of the rest is derived from property taxes. Inequality in spending corresponds to racial and class composition of schools and achievement levels, with poor students particularly disadvantaged by smaller tax bases and fewer local school resources (Condron and Roscigno 2003). Questions of how to fund schools in the United States have created an ongoing controversy that has reached the courtroom in a number of states. Overall, the United States spends less money per student on education than most other industrialized nations. Wealthier districts in the United States have more money to finance schools and can afford better education for their children because more money is collected from property taxes; higher-class students have advantages not available in poor districts (Kozol 2005, 1991; Wenglinsky 1997).

THINKING SOCIOLOGICALLY

Were you tracked in any subjects? What effect, if any, did this have? What effect do you think it had on friends of yours who were placed in higher or lower tracks?

Public and Private Schools

Elite preparatory (prep) schools in England, Japan, the United States, and many other countries traditionally have been the training ground for the sons and daughters of the elite to maintain their high positions. Chile's privatization of schools takes the form of parental choice and vouchers, in line with the transition of the country to a market-oriented economy; however, inequality persists in educational opportunity and outcomes, especially in the transition to secondary schools. Advantages come to those in private-voucher and private-paid schools as opposed to public schools (Torche 2005).

In the United States, private Catholic parochial schools are the most prevalent private schools; other religiously affiliated schools are the next most common; and private preparatory schools are third. About 10 percent of U.S. students attend private schools.

Studies have found that achievements of low-income and minority students attending Catholic schools, especially in inner-cities, are closer to white middle-class students' achievements than are the achievements of similar students attending public schools (Hoffer, Greeley, and Coleman 1987; MacFarlane 1994; Morgan 2001; Walsh 1991). In general, private schools are more academically demanding, more stringent, more disciplined, and more orderly; they assign more homework; and they demand more parental involvement than do public schools (Cookson and Persell 1985); and they can expel children who do not perform or are disruptive.

However, much of the reason private schools have generally had higher levels of achievement is the select population they admit. A massive study released in the summer of 2006 by the U.S. Department of Education compared 7,000 public schools and 530 private schools. The study controlled for student socioeconomic backgrounds in a way that is often not done, and it found that children performed roughly on par in the two types of schools, either private or public schools excelling slightly in either math or reading depending on grade level. The only group that lagged significantly was children attending conservative Protestant Christian schools (Schemo 2006).

Proposed choice and voucher plans allowing students and parents to choose their schools have been controversial in part because public schools might well be left with the least capable students and teachers, further stratifying an already troubled system (Chubb and Moe 1990; Witte and Thorn 1996). Private schools could also become sanctuaries

This elementary school in New York City is strapped for funds, lacking in supplies and services for the students. The teacher has tried to compensate by at least making the room colorful.

Source: © Mark Peterson / Corbis.

This computer class is held at a formerly failing inner-city British school, transformed by new management and increased governmental funding. Many students come from situations that present educational challenges: refugee status, children in temporary shelters, or non-English speaking homes. However, the school is highly successful and has become a government beacon school.

Source: © Gideon Mendel / Corbis.

for those who do not want integrated schools and could perpetuate religious and racial segregation.

A teacher assists a student at the Pennington Preparatory School in New Jersey. This school, as you might guess by the children's clothing, serves the elite and is a pathway to elite colleges and further privilege.

Source: © David H. Wells / Corbis.

EDUCATIONAL TRENDS AND SOCIAL POLICY ISSUES

In the early twenty-first century, school systems around the world face dramatic changes: pressures for equal educational opportunity for all groups—classes and castes, race and ethnic groups, females and males. The need for technological training of citizenry, increased demand for more access to higher education, changes in the student composition of the classroom, and accountability and testing of students and teachers are but a few of the many issues. Because education reflects societal politics and problems, policies swing from conservative to more liberal and back again, depending on who is in power and what their agenda is for change. Consider the current concerns about world

tensions that are resulting in internationalizaton of the classroom (King 2006). Within our lifetimes, we are likely to experience several of these swings; for example, currently in the United States, the issues of accountability, standardized testing, and teaching basic skills are at the forefront, but movements toward individualization of education and developing the whole child are reappearing (Gamoran 2001). Although the past century brought some improvement in equality in education, much remains to be done to level the playing field. The greatest barrier to equal education in the twenty-first century within and between countries may prove to be class, with many minorities represented in lower classes. Sociologists of education contribute to the policy discussions in their roles as researchers, consultants, policy analysts, and applied sociologists, as illustrated in the next The Applied Sociologist at Work.

Education of Girls

Gene Sperling (2005) writes, "One of the silent killers attacking the developing world is the lack of quality basic education for large numbers of the poorest children in the world's poorest countries—particularly girls" (p. 213). In 2005, over 110 million children—60 percent of them girls from ages 6 to 11—received no schooling at all; another 150 million dropped out of primary school. Fifty percent of girls in sub-Saharan Africa do not complete primary school, and only 17 percent are in secondary school. In Niger, for instance, only 12 percent of girls in rural areas are in primary school compared to 83 percent in the capital city, Niamey. In refugee camps in Africa, only 6 percent of children receive any secondary education due to hardships from lack of teachers to AIDS to orphaned status. Even when children do receive some primary education, the quality is such that many children leave school without basic skills (UNESCO 2005).

What is clear is that when girls are educated, the consequences are great: "What is striking is the breadth of benefits derived from educating girls—not only economic benefits in terms of higher wages, greater agricultural productivity, and faster economic growth, but also health benefits, HIV prevention, and women's empowerment" (Sperling 2005:214; Sperling and Herz 2004). We know that girls in Uganda "with some secondary education were three times less likely to be HIV-positive, and those with some primary school were about half as likely to be HIV-positive" (Sperling 2005:214). Sexual activity is dramatically reduced when girls are in school and learn about AIDS. When school fees were abolished in Uganda, Kenya, and Tanzania in East Africa, enrollments increased dramatically. Additional incentives to parents to compensate for the loss of labor of their children also increases enrollment as shown in the cases of Bangladesh, Mexico, and Brazil. In China, better educated citizens hold more egalitarian gender attitudes (Shu 2004), and in Turkey, gender inequalities in education are lessened in metropolitan areas and in less patriarchal families (Rankin and Aytac 2006). In Taiwan, researchers find that the social

THE APPLIED SOCIOLOGIST AT WORK

Government Comprehension and Planning in Education

How do local, regional, and national educational officials know about children's achievements in school? How do children in different countries compare academically? What number of schools and teachers will be needed in future years? What is the effect of race, class, and gender on school experiences? Dr. Carl Schmitt has worked for the U.S. Department of Education's National Center for Education Statistics (NCES) for more than 20 years. During this time, he has used *longitudinal* data to research many of these questions that help officials from the national government to local schools plan for school children and their needs.

From 1972 to 1996, the NCES sponsored five national longitudinal studies that obtained data from students and educators through repeated surveys over time. These studies looked at the educational experiences of elementary, secondary, and postsecondary students. The first, done in 1972, focused on a cohort of high school seniors; the second in 1980 included both high school sophomores and seniors. A third study completed in 1988 focused on eighth graders. Then in 1990 and 1993, the agency conducted research on students' lives and successes after graduation. A sixth study in 1995 focused on early childhood kindergarten cohorts.

These studies were motivated by a number of issues in education: declining test scores, the dropout rate, increased vocational education opportunities, and access to postsecondary and vocational education. Together, they provide rich data on students' experiences and help answer why some fail. Data were collected from students and on student academic and testing records, data on school policies, teacher practices, family involvement, persistence in school, participation in postsecondary education, and information on current educational issues.

One of Schmitt's tasks is to produce data files that can be used by others for policy formation and publications. To prepare the data, he must understand complex statistical data analyses and be able to communicate the key findings to a professional audience. One of his research projects drew insights and information from two studies to examine the institution of education as a system that has an impact on the larger society. When dealing with information about public schools, districts, and state education agencies, he looks at the data in ways that make the findings useful to others. Managing and analyzing large amounts of data are key tools for his work.

To carry out his work, Schmitt uses computers to write, calculate with spreadsheets using statistical packages such as SPSS and SAS, do graphics work, and manipulate database tools. Rewards of his work come from providing valuable information that could make a difference in the lives of children and school officials and from making complex data accessible for large audiences. However, there are some frustrations in a government agency where he does not always have control over what is produced from his work.

Dr. Carl Schmitt received his graduate degrees from New York University. He specialized in methodology and quantitative analysis, social stratification and inequality, and complex organizations. He learned both substantive information and methodological skills that are essential for his work.

---

class and education level of the parents plays a major role in the educational attainment of their children, especially daughters. The education of girls is raising the standards of living for them and their families (Jao and McKeever 2006).

Educational Policies in the United States

"If an unfriendly foreign power had attempted to impose on America the mediocre educational performance that exists today, we might well have viewed it as an act of war. As it stands, we have allowed this to happen to ourselves" (p. 1). These words come from an influential U.S. report from the 1980s titled *A Nation at Risk: The Imperative for Educational Reform*. It outlines a number of serious problems in the U.S. education system. The report received a great deal of attention from the press and from educators, some arguing that it overstated the problems (Bracey 2003), others using the report as a call for reform.

A flood of reports and government plans have followed *A Nation at Risk*, each lamenting the sorry state of education and suggesting methods to redress the problems in schools: strengthen high school graduation requirements, raise college entrance requirements, emphasize basic skills, require a longer school day and year-round schooling, improve the training and status of teachers, hold educators responsible for students' performance, provide the funds necessary to improve the educational system, and hold families accountable.

"The Little Red School Bus," sponsored by the nonprofit Christian Appalachian Project, helps residents in rural Kentucky prepare for high school equivalency certificates and a better chance of finding a job. This may be the only chance for an education these people will experience.

Source: © Karen Kasmauski / Corbis.

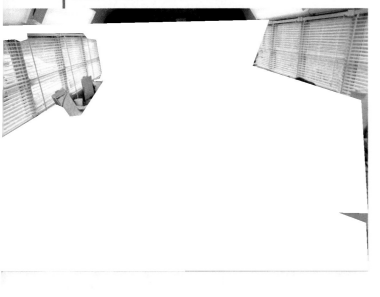

Today, despite numerous U.S. government policies and reports, the data on school success shows a worsening picture. There are 27 million functionally illiterate Americans, with many 17 year olds unable to write well or solve mathematical problems and lacking the basic skills needed to enter business and the military.

Each new presidential administration proposes educational reforms to address the same problems; under the Bush administration plan, NCLB (U.S. Department of Education 2006), schools are required to administer achievement tests for accountability—tests that focus on math and reading. Schools failing to meet guidelines are penalized. The result is that 70 percent of schools are reducing instructional time in other subjects to teach more reading and math. The greatest reduction is in social studies, followed by science, art, music, and physical education (Center for Education Policy 2006).

Critics argue that these are extremely important fields for the twenty-first century and should not be shortchanged for a test. Numerical gains based on math and reading achievement tests do not measure learning in many other areas, and they certainly to not measure ability to think critically. In addition, many critics find the expectations of NCLB impossible for schools to reach, and therefore the program is demoralizing. The policy makes no provision for differences in family backgrounds, socioeconomic status, preschool education, or the community context (Bracey 2005); critics argue it can actually perpetuate and

intensify disparities between groups and communities. Rural and small schools often are disadvantaged by NCLB; while schools were promised funds to help implement NCLB, these funds have not been forthcoming, disadvantaging poorer school districts. Yet the schools are penalized if they do not meet standards. Some affluent school districts have decided to ignore the federal policy, with the risk of losing federal funds, but they think local autonomy is worth that loss. Whether NCLB is really improving achievement levels is also in dispute (Bracey 2005; Karen 2005). So education remains a hot topic in political circles.

THINKING SOCIOLOGICALLY

If you had a position of influence to improve public education, what policies would you recommend? What might be some unintended negative consequences of the policy you propose?

Global Issues in Education

Most societies view the education and training of young people as an economic investment in the future. Countries with capitalist economic systems are more likely to have an educational system that stresses individualism and competition, pitting students against one another for the best grades and the best opportunities. The elites often ensure that their own children get a very different education than the children of the laboring class. Socialist and traditional economic systems often encourage cooperation and collaboration among students, with the collective needs of society viewed as more important than those of individuals. The social economic values of the society are reflected in approaches to learning and in motivation of students.

Just as countries are divided by economic systems and wealth into center or core areas and poorer peripheral areas, so too do educational systems reflect the economic and political institutions of a given society and its place in the world system. Distinctions between countries lie at the base of many global studies and sometimes reflect the former colonial status of countries. Education of women also differs, with girls getting higher education if they live in urban areas and come from less patriarchal families (Rankin and Aytac 2006).

Other studies compare the curricula of nations and changes in those curricula to determine how similar and different they are. Findings generally support a convergence of curricular themes across nations, reflecting the interdependence of nations. However, many researchers question whether that convergence is good for all people in all societies, especially students from peripheral developing countries.

Governments compare their academic test scores on the International Assessment of Educational Progress and the International Association for the Evaluation of Educational Achievement (IEA); these are tests of children around the world in literacy, mathematics, science, civic education, and foreign language. Recently, IEA published results from the Third International Mathematics and Science Study, in which 40 countries tested children at the 4th-, 8th-, and 12th-grade levels (Baker 2002). These rankings provide information on the similarities, differences, and effects of development on education (Ballantine and Spade 2004). Country groupings fall into several categories, with some doing very well in math and science but not always the same ones doing well in reading (Baker 2002). East Asian countries score highest on math and science achievement; however, for other countries to try to copy their educational systems is not the answer, for education occurs in cultural contexts (Zhao 2005). Gleaning ideas from studying other successful systems and adapting those aspects that are culturally compatible may help raise scores of all, but cultural contexts determine what will be successful (Houlihan 2005; Kagan and Stewart 2005; Stewart 2005; Suarez-Orozco 2005).

Political and economic trends outside of a country can also have an impact on the educational system within the country. Examples of external influences include world educational and technological trends, new inventions, and new knowledge. Even an event like the terrorist attacks on the World Trade Center and the Pentagon on September 11, 2001, shape the school curricula as schools give greater weight to patriotism.

A country's level of education is a key indicator of quality of life and placement in the global social world. Industrialized countries want to trade with poor countries and therefore are interested in creating trained workers, markets for their products, and people with resources to purchase their products. Education is one route to creating productive employees and consumers. Education around the globe has become a concern in international organizations such as the United Nations and within the business communities of developed countries to develop trained workers competent in technology.

THINKING SOCIOLOGICALLY

How might education be important to countries competing in the world system? How might education be affected by global events, such as a war or a worldwide economic recession?

The Future of Education in the Global System

Educational issues are in the news daily. The search for the perfect model of education is never ending. School systems around the world are under pressure to meet the diverse needs of the societies as a whole and their individual citizens—such as Tomás.

A major concern in developed countries that are moving from the Information Age into "learning societies"

In Namibia, as elsewhere around the world, an education is increasingly necessary as the economy is globalized and skills in literacy and numeracy become critical to survival and hopes of prosperity.

Source: © Anthony Bannister/Corbis

is this: what will become of those students who do not complete enough education to fit into the technological and economic needs in the twenty-first century (Von Holzen 2005)? In developed countries, high school used to prepare most young people for a job and marriage. By the 1990s, high school was preparation for college, which was itself necessary to find a decent job in the globalizing world (Attewell 2001; Schneider and Stevenson 1999). In the United States, educators, corporations, wealthy individuals, and philanthropies concerned that minority groups are falling behind support special programs to reduce cyber-segregation of haves and have-nots (Attewell 2001), the latter composed of poor and minority families. Some companies are donating funds and computers to schools in poor countries to reduce the digital divide (Williams 2000).

The cyber-gap may be slowly closing, and although access is improving, there are differences in the implementation of new innovations and ways computers are used—some for education and others for entertainment. Electronic textbooks and materials give the developed and developing world alike access to new knowledge and ideas that can continually be updated through e-textbooks (Rossman 2005). Even video games are used by corporations, the government, and the military to educate. Advocates argue, "They let people participate in the world. They let players think, talk, and act in new ways . . . to *inhabit* roles that are otherwise inaccessible to them" (Shaffer et al. 2005:105). Much learning will take place without walls, clocks, or age segregation as students learn through digital lessons on their own time (Lundt 2004).

Computer and Internet skills are essential to success in college and most jobs in this globalized social world. Many courses, even degrees, can now be done online.

Source: © Luis Alvarez; © Paulus Rusyanto.

Classrooms of the future will incorporate technological innovations and use of information networks; teachers learn new technologies with social pressure and access to expertise and help (Frank, Zhao, and Borman 2004). Those who do not master technology will be left behind in the workforce of the twenty-first century. However, we can put money into technology, but this alone is not the answer to reducing inequalities.

One form of technology that is bound to impact the future is the Internet. The next Sociology in Your Social World discusses the "virtual university"—an application of Internet technology to higher education.

THINKING SOCIOLOGICALLY

First, read about the Virtual University on the next page. How might this new form of higher education affect segments of the population—the poor, the working class, the middle class—differently? What implications does it have for equal access to education for ethnic groups? People of color? Men and women? In what ways would it be beneficial, and in what ways might it cause new problems?

The link between school completion and work, or what is referred to as the *school-to-work transition,* is clearly defined and planned by public policy in most European countries and Russia, with postsecondary options such as vocational school and associate degrees to prepare young people for skilled positions (Kerckhoff 2001; Kerckhoff and Bell 1998) and numbers of needed engineers or dentists determining the educational slots available in these fields. However, these options are poorly defined in other countries, especially the United States (Altbach and Davis 1999).

How students make the transition from their education to the workforce is an important issue that affects equal opportunity, counseling, tracking, preparation for the future, high school dropout rates, vocational (versus academic) curricula, and the need for two-year community college programs. Although the numbers of minority students entering high schools and colleges around the world are increasing, the issue of how to provide equal educational opportunity will continue well into the third millennium.

In the process of governments developing their educational policies, we again see the interconnections of our social world. Curricula respond to global events and international markets. However, they are also shaped by the relative effectiveness or ineffectiveness of teachers and students in individual classrooms around the world. The macro-level concerns and the micro-level processes come together in education, with the ultimate objective to prepare individuals in each classroom to meet the needs of the community, the state, the nation, and the world.

Sociology in Your Social World

Internet Technology and the Virtual University

Imagine a university that comes to all citizens who have a desire to learn and wish to take courses, from high school age to senior citizens. The setting can be the home, a library, or any place with Internet access.

No need to imagine! In Kentucky and several other states, this scenario is reality. Faced with the changing state, national, and global economy that made former occupations in coal mining and growing tobacco obsolete, Kentucky's virtual university is being used as one solution to the problem of unemployment and poverty.

How does the process work? The virtual university has a staff of 20, sitting in an office with cubicles and computers, and arranges for services to be delivered online to students around the state and beyond. Public and private universities in Kentucky offer up to three-quarters of required degree credits online. Other services include contracts with professional course designers, online library resources, student counseling services, and bookstore services. The role of faculty changes from lecturing to mentoring—from discussing issues and problems with students to using services such as online writing assistance and of course grading student work.

In the virtual university, students as consumers have control over the process of learning, are able to register and carry out all tasks online, move at an individually comfortable pace, watch and interact with professional online courses that include projects and assignments, read the text from online bookstores, and interact with the professors online. According to Susman, president of Kentucky Commonwealth Virtual University, virtual universities involve an "orbital shift." No longer do students need to be on site, running around between offices to register or to obtain professor permissions and parking passes. No longer are they concerned with getting to class on time—the Internet has 24-hour access. On the down side, these students do not have the personal interaction with a professor or the rich interaction of a classroom where knowledge itself is often created.

Looking for recreation as a part of the college experience? Join the virtual football team. Michigan Virtual University has challenged Kentucky's team to a match. Other opportunities for games such as chess, book clubs, and chat rooms in courses are being created as you read this; the possibilities are endless.

Critics express concern about the lost interaction and lack of "control" over student learning. The roles of teacher and student change rather dramatically when face-to-face interaction with the professor and class members takes place on a computer screen.

Whether or not we approve, the university experience for some students is likely to be a very different one in the future, with technology leading the way.

Source: Taken in part from a lecture by Mary Beth Susman, President, Kentucky Commonwealth Virtual University, Bethesda, MD, at the meeting of the Society for Applied Sociology, August 11, 2000.

SO WHAT?

It is common for people to think that institutions are major sources of social reform and improvement. Educational systems are typically viewed as the channel for reduction of inequality, the source of upward mobility, the way to improve the economy, and the path for reduction of prejudice in societies. However, institutions such as education have a vested interest in lack of change, or stability. Schools foster patriotism and loyalty toward the political system, families support schools and education, and education is expected to support the economic vitality of the nation. Institutions and organizations are also driven by interest in their own survival, and risk-taking behaviors on behalf of change are not necessarily ones that foster survival; taking risks may threaten those who have power, privilege, and influence. It should not be surprising, therefore, that education does more to enhance stability than to create change. Still, those who seek to improve the society see tremendous potential in education as an agent of change if its influence can be harnessed; it works largely with young minds in the socialization process—carrying out what powerful policy makers feel is important.

Another institution that socializes individuals has a meaning system that believers feel is the ultimate reality and is at the core of goodness and transformation of the world. We turn in the next chapter to a sociological perspective on religion.

CONTRIBUTING TO YOUR SOCIAL WORLD

At the Local Level: Volunteer to read at a local school or a community tutoring center. Many children need individual support to make it through school, and some parents are unable to help them.

At the Organization or Institutional Level: Consider teaching English abroad through one of many organizations that sponsor teachers. Visit

www.globaltesol.com, www.soyou wanna.com, www.teachabroad.com, and related websites.

At the National and Global Levels: Support educational organizations, from *UNICEF* to *Care International*.

Teach in *Peace Corps*.

Visit **www.pineforge.com/ballantinestudy** for online activities, sample tests, and other helpful information. Select "Chapter 11: Education" for chapter-specific activities.

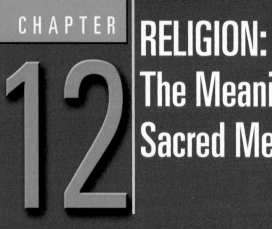

What to Expect . . .

Religion takes many forms and is expressed in various ways but it is always about a sense of meaning—and that meaning both generates and bestows sacredness.

Think About It . . .

1. How did you become committed to a faith and a church—or not become so?

2. How did you develop your views toward religion?

3. How does religion affect your family, education, political system, social position, and other aspects of your life?

4. How does religion help solve world problems (war, poverty, hunger, disease, bigotry) or contribute to them?

Macro: Global Community

Macro: National Society

Meso: National Institutions and Organization; Ethnic Subcultures

Micro: Local Organizations and Community

Micro: You and Your Family

Micro: Your local church, temple, or mosque; outreach programs that impact the local community

Meso: Churches impact the economy, family life, education, government; regional denominational divisions make church policy

Macro: Denominational positions on national policies; religiously-based social movements; religious television programming influencing national culture

Macro: Cross-national religious organizations; global outreach programs to address hunger or human rights at the international level

Every night before going to bed Nandi Nwankwo from Nigeria sets out a bowl of milk and some food for the ancestors who, he believes, are present outside the family's dwelling at night. Respected ancestors protect family members, but they are also a powerful and even frightening force in guiding social behavior. Children are told that they must behave or the ancestors will punish them.

Kisra, an Iranian Muslim woman, gains status when she produces sons; her community values sons highly and often identifies them as among the best of God's blessings. From the time they are young children, Muslim boys and girls know their place in the family, community, and society. Many social expectations, including sex roles, are clear in the Quran (sometimes spelled *Koran*), and values are gleaned from its teachings.

Tuneq, knowledgeable Netsilik Eskimo hunter that he is, apologizes to the soul of the seal he has just killed. He shares the meat and blubber with his fellow hunters, and he makes sure that every part of the seal is used or consumed—skin, bones, eyes, tendons, brain, and muscles. If he fails to honor the seal by not using every morsel or if he violates a rule of hunting etiquette, an invisible vapor will come from his body and sink through the ice, snow, and water. This vapor will collect in the hair of Nuliajuk, goddess of the sea. In revenge, she will call the sea mammals to her so the people living on the ice above will starve. Inuit religion provides rules that help to enforce an essential ecological ethic among these arctic hunters to preserve the delicate natural balance.

These are but three examples from the world's many and varied religious systems. What they have in common is that each system provides directions for appropriate and expected behaviors and serves as a form of social control for individuals within that society. Whether ancestors, gods, one God, prophets, or elders are watching over us, the sanctions that encourage conformity are strong; indeed, they are made *sacred*, a realm of existence different from mundane everyday life. Religion, according to Andrew M. Greeley, the well-known priest and sociologist, pervades the lives of persons of faith. It cannot be separated from the rest of the social world (Greeley 1989). Members of societies believe so strongly in their religions that conquests and wars throughout history have been based on dissemination or defense of religious beliefs.

Sociologists are interested in these relationships, in the consequences of religion for society and for members of society, and in the way social relationships and structures affect religions. In this chapter, we explore religion as a complex social phenomenon, one that is interrelated with other processes and institutions of society. We investigate a variety of types of religious groups, see how religion can influence social values and attitudes, and explore religious trends. We also discuss the role of religion in the larger world context.

WHAT DOES RELIGION DO FOR US?

We began this chapter by looking at examples of daily experiences in which religion and society have enormous power over an individual. Why do people engage in religious practices, beliefs, and organizations? In short, they do so because religion meets certain very basic needs.

Human questions about the meaning of life, the finality of death, or whether injustice and cruelty will ever be ended cannot normally be answered by science or by everyday experience. Religion helps explain the meaning of life, death, suffering, injustice, and events beyond our control. As sociologist Emile Durkheim pointed out, humans generally view such questions as belonging to a realm of existence different from the mundane or profane world of experience. He called this separated dimension the *sacred realm*. This sacred realm elicits feelings of awe, reverence, and even fear. It is viewed as being above normal inquiry and doubt. Religious guidelines, beliefs, and values dictate "rights and wrongs," provide answers to the big questions of life, and instill moral codes and ideas about the world in members of each society or subculture. For that reason, religions are extremely important in controlling everyday behavior (Durkheim 1915/2002).

Thus, religion is more than a set of beliefs about the supernatural. It often *sacralizes* (makes sacred and unquestionable) the culture in which we live, the class or caste position to which we belong, the attitudes we hold toward other people, and the morals to which we adhere. Religion is a part of our lifestyle, our gender roles, and our place in society. We are often willing to defend it with our lives. It is sobering to know that around the world, many different people believe quite as strongly as we do that they have found the Truth—the ultimate answers—in their religions. They, too, are willing to die for their religion, which they are convinced is "the only way."

Note various wars between Hindus and Muslims in India, or between two Muslim sects of Sunni and Shi'ite in the Muslim country of Pakistan. Although the root causes of these wars are political and economic, religious differences help to polarize we-versus-they sentiments. Such conflicts are never exclusively about religion, but religion can convince each antagonist that God is on its side. Thus, religion is an integral part of most societies and is important in helping individuals define reality and determine what is worth living or dying for.

THINKING SOCIOLOGICALLY

Consider your own beliefs. Which of the purposes or functions of religion mentioned above does your religious faith address?

Components of Religion

Religion normally involves at least three components: a faith or worldview that provides a sense of meaning and purpose in life (which we will call the *meaning system*), a set of interpersonal relationships and friendship networks (which we will call the *belonging system*), and a stable pattern of roles, statuses, and organizational practices (which we will call the *structural system*) (Roberts 2004).

Meaning System

The meaning system of a religion includes the ideas and symbols it uses to provide a sense of purpose in life and to help explain why suffering, injustice, and evil exist. It provides a big picture to explain events that would otherwise seem chaotic and irrational. For example, although the loss of a family member through death may be painful, many people find comfort and hope and a larger perspective on life in the idea of life after death. Most religious people find that deep love of God gives purpose and deep satisfaction to life (discussed later in this chapter).

Because each culture has different problems to solve, the precise needs reflected in the meaning system vary. Hence, different societies have developed different ways of answering questions and meeting needs. In agricultural societies, the problems revolve around growing crops and the elements necessary for crops—water control, sunlight, and good soil. Meaning systems often reflect these concerns. Among the Zuni of New Mexico and the Hopi of Arizona, water for crops is a

Buddhist monks pray at Bayon Temple in Angkor Thom.

Source: © Chris Lisle/Corbis.

critical concern. These Native American people typically grow corn in a climate that averages roughly ten inches of rain per year, so it is not surprising that the central focus of the dances and the supernatural beings—kachinas—is to bring rain. In many societies, the death rate is so high that high fertility has been necessary to perpetuate the group. Thus, fertility goddesses take on great significance. In other societies, strong armies and brave soldiers have been essential to preserve the group from invading forces; hence, gods or rituals of war have been popular. Over time, meaning systems of religion have reflected needs of the societies in which the religion is practiced.

Belonging System

Belonging systems are profoundly important in most religious groups. Many people remain members of religious groups not so much because they accept the meaning system of the group but because that is where their belonging system—their friendship and kinship network—is found; their religious group is a type of extended family. In fact, church membership increases as people get older and move through the family life cycle of marriage, childbearing, and childrearing (Sherkat and Ellison 1999; Stolzenberg, Blair-Loy, and Waite 1995). A prayer group may be the one

Clan totems are part of the cultural and religious tradition of native peoples in northwest North America, from Oregon to Alaska. This photo from a church in Alaska is interesting because it blends a local cultural and religious symbol with a Christian symbol (the Cross) in a Christian sanctuary.

Source: Photo by Keith Roberts.

area in their lives in which they can be truly open about their personal pain and feel safe to expose their vulnerabilities (Wuthnow 1994). Irrespective of the meaning system, a person's sense of identity may be very much tied up with being a Muslim, a Buddhist, or a Christian.

In the United States, the religious groups that have grown the fastest in recent years are those that have devised ways to strengthen the sense of belonging and have fostered friendship networks within the group, including emphasis on endogamy—marrying within one's group. If a person is a member of a small group in which interpersonal ties grow strong—a church bridge club, a Quran study group, or even a working committee—he or she is likely to feel a stronger commitment to the entire organization. In short, the belonging system refers to the interpersonal networks and the emotional ties that develop between adherents to a particular faith community.

Structural System

A religion involves a group of people who share a common meaning system. However, if each person interprets the beliefs in his or her own way and if each attaches his or her own meanings to the symbols, the meaning system becomes so individualized that *sacralization* of common values can no longer occur. Therefore, some system of control and screening of new revelations must be developed. Religious leaders in designated statuses must have the authority to interpret

Kwanzaa, which means "first fruits of the harvest" in Kiswahili, was initiated in 1966 by Dr. Maulana Karenga. It is an African American celebration of the traditional African values of family, community responsibility, and self-improvement. This family celebrates Kwanzaa, which runs from December 26th to January 1st. Such rituals create in children a sense of sacredness about certain values and outlooks on life.

Source © Corbis.

the theology and define the essentials of the faith. The group also needs methods of designating leaders, of raising funds to support their programs, and of ensuring continuation of the group. To teach the next generation the meaning system, they need to produce educational resources and to develop a formal structure to determine the content and form of those materials. In short, if the religion is to survive past the death of a charismatic leader, it must undergo institutionalization.

Thus, religions are institutions in the social world, comprising several interrelated components: the meaning subsystem, mostly operating at the micro level; the belonging subsystem, critical at the micro level but also part of various meso-level institutions; and the structural subsystem that tends to have its major impact at the macro level of societies and global systems. These may reinforce one another and work in harmony toward common goals, or there may be conflict between them. When change occurs, it usually occurs because of disruption at one of these subsystem levels.

Since religion itself is one institution in the larger society, it is interdependent and interrelated with the political, economic, family, education, health, and technology systems. Changes in any one of these areas can bring change to religion, and changes in religion can bring changes to other institutions of society. Consider examples of the furor that is occurring in parts of the United States over teaching of intelligent design as part of the science curriculum in public schools; the conflict is reverberating in congregations, schools, legislative chambers, courts, and scientific communities.

While some people dislike the idea of organized religion, the fact remains that a group cannot survive in the modern world unless it undergoes *routinization of charisma;* that is, the religious organization must develop established roles, statuses, groups, and routine procedures for making decisions and obtaining resources (Weber 1947).

Like any other formal organization in society, religious structures consist of various smaller groups and individuals, each of which has its own specialized task. Contemporary Christian denominations in the United States, for example, may have national commissions on global outreach, religious education, evangelism, theological training, worship, world peace, social justice, and so forth. In addition, bishops, presbyters, or other leaders oversee the work of several hundred pastors who lead their own congregations. The formal organization may be caught in some of the dysfunctions of any organization: goal displacement, the iron law of oligarchy, alienation, and other problems discussed in Chapter 5.

At the local level, too, a formal religious structure develops, with committees doing specific tasks, such as overseeing worship, maintaining the building, recruiting religious educators, and raising funds. These committees report to an administrative board that works closely with the clergy (the ordained ministers) and has much of the final responsibility for the life and continued existence of the congregation. The roles, statuses, and committees make up the structural system. Just as any organization needs data on its effectiveness,

THE APPLIED SOCIOLOGIST AT WORK

Research for Religious Organizations

My interest in research on and for religious institutions began when I worked with my graduate school mentor on a grant studying the growth and decline of denominations. I explored demographic change and church growth, denominational switching, and the impact of new church development on the growth of established denominations.

I am a church research officer, a position which entails everything from mundane gathering of statistics to serious social research. Our office of six persons collects membership, attendance, and giving data from all United Church of Christ (UCC) churches, and analyses that data. We do surveys among our churches, pastors, staff and lay leaders on a wide variety of topics (issues related to congregational health, leadership, use of denominational resources, beliefs and attitudes, and so forth). I also conduct research on the state of religion/churches in modern society and on social trends that might impact our churches. This research is written up in reports and published in books that give advice to our churches and pastors. I speak to clergy groups regularly on related topics. My clients get an

interpretation of data based on broader, sociologically based understanding of the religious trends.

I have studied church trends (patterns of growth and decline) using data from local congregations and studies of religious participation and religious marginality. Also, I have conducted large-scale surveys with pastors from several denominations as key informants. It is particularly gratifying to see theories confirmed with real data on real churches.

The most rewarding aspect of my work is the ability to help church leaders see their situation from a different perspective and use that perspective and information to make a positive difference in their work. The least rewarding facets are grunt work (providing routine information) and other aspects of life in a bureaucracy (forms to fill out, committee meetings, staff retreats, performance evaluations, and having one's work ignored due to other agendas).

Dr. C. Kirk Hadaway received his Ph.D. in Sociology from the University of Massachusetts, Amherst. He has worked for various boards and agencies of the Southern Baptist Convention, has been director of research at the United Church of Christ, and currently is director of research for the Episcopal Church.

religious organizations collect information to help inform policy. The Applied Sociologist at Work above describes the work of a sociologist who does research within such a denominational structure.

THINKING SOCIOLOGICALLY

Outline the meaning, belonging, and structural systems of a religion with which you are familiar. Illustrate how these subsystems influence and are influenced by the larger social world, from individual to national and global systems.

HOW DO INDIVIDUALS BECOME RELIGIOUS? MICRO-LEVEL ANALYSIS

We are not born religious, although we may be born into a religious group. We learn our religious beliefs through socialization, just as we learn our language, customs, norms and values. Our family usually determines the religious environment in which we grow up, whether it is an all pervasive or one-day-a-week aspect of socialization. We start imitating religious

practices such as prayer before we understand these practices intellectually. Then, as we encounter the unexplainable events of life, religion is there to provide meaning. Gradually, religion becomes an ingrained part of many people's lives.

It is unlikely that we will adopt a religious belief that falls outside the religions of our society. For instance, if we are born in India, we will be raised in and around the Hindu, Muslim, or Sikh faiths; in most Arab countries, we will become Muslim; in South American countries, Catholic; and in many Southeast Asian countries, Buddhist. Even if we had been born into the family next door or the next village, our religion and politics might be different. Indeed, although our religious affiliation may seem normal and typical to us, none of us is part of a religion that is held by a majority of the world's people, and we may in fact be part of a rather small minority religious group when we think in terms of the global population. Map 12.1 and Table 12.1 show this vividly.

Learning the meaning system of a religious group is both a formal and an informal process. In some cultures, religious faith pervades everyday life; for the Amish, farming without machines or use of electricity is part of religious teachings that affect the total lifestyle. Formal teaching in most religions takes place primarily in the temple, church, or mosque, and is limited to certain holy days or special times. The formal teaching

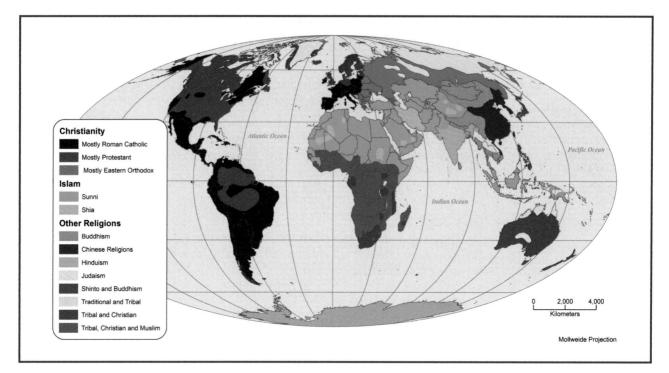

MAP 12.1   Dominant Religious Groups around the World

Source: World Religions, 5th ed., W. Matthews, copyright © 2007. Reprinted with permission of Wadsworth, a division of Thomson. Map by Anna Versluis.

TABLE 12.1   **Religious Membership around the Globe**

Religion	Membership (in millions)	Percentage of World Population
Christian Total	2,107.0	24.4
Roman Catholic	*1,105.8*	*12.8*
Protestant	*369.8*	*4.3*
Orthodox	*218.4*	*2.5*
Anglican	*78.7*	*0.9*
Muslim	1,283.4	14.9
Hindu	851.3	9.9
Nonreligious	767.2	8.9
Buddhist	375.4	4.3
Chinese Folk Religion (Universist)	402.0	4.7
Ethnic Religion	252.8	2.9
Atheist	150.7	1.7
New Religious Movement	107.3	1.2
Tribal Religion (2001 figures)	96.6	1.8
Sikh	25.0	0.3
Jewish	15.0	0.2
Spiritist	12.9	0.1
Baha'i	7.5	0.9
Confucianist	6.4	0.1
Jain	4.5	0.1
Shintoist	2.8	0.0
Zoroastrian	2.6	a
Other Religion	1.2	a
Independent	416.5	4.8

Source: Park (2006).

Note: Numbers add up to more than the 6 billion people in the world because many people identify themselves with more than one religious tradition. Thus, the percentages will also add up to more than 100%; percentages are rounded.

[a]Less than 0.05 percent.

may take the form of Bar or Bat Mitzvah classes, Sunday school, or Parochial school. Informal religious teaching occurs when we observe others "practicing what they preach."

One church member may be committed to the meaning system; another to the belonging system, strong friendship networks; and a third to the structural system, making large financial donations to a church even though he or she has no close personal ties to the group or the theology of that church. In most cases, however, commitment to one of these systems will reinforce commitment to the others. They usually go together.

Most people do not belong to a religious group because they believe; rather they come to believe because they want to belong and are socialized into belonging, to feel a part of the group (Greeley 1972). People generally accept the explanation provided by the religious group about whether there is life after death or why one has suffered from illness or a serious accident; they feel comfortable sharing similar feelings and beliefs.

Switching religious affiliations or joining new religious movements (NRMs) indicates that loyalty to a friendship network usually comes first, followed by commitment to the meaning and structural systems. In many cases, accepting a new meaning system is the final stage rather than the initial stage of change (Roberts 2004).

Since changing religious groups occurs most often through change of friendship networks, religious groups frequently try to control the boundaries and protect their members from outside influences. The Amish in the United States have done this by living in their own communities and attempting to limit schooling of their children by outside authorities. To help perpetuate religious beliefs and practices, most religious groups encourage endogamy, marrying within the group. For example, Orthodox Jews have food taboos and food preparation requirements that limit the likelihood that they will share a meal with "outsiders."

Religious groups also try to socialize members to make sacrifices of time, energy, and financial resources on behalf of their faith. If one has sacrificed and has devoted one's resources and energy for a cause, one is likely to feel a commitment to the organization—the structural system (Kanter 2005; Sherkat and Ellison 1999). Many young men in the Church of Jesus Christ of the Latter-Day Saints (Mormons) devote two years of their lives to being missionaries, and young women devote one to one-and-a-half years. They must save money in advance to support themselves. This sacrifice of other opportunities and investment of time, energy, and resources in the church creates an intense commitment to the organization. Few of them later feel that they have wasted those years or that the investment was unwise.

The survival of a religious group depends in part on how committed its members are and whether they share freely of their financial and time resources. Most religious groups try, therefore, to socialize their members into commitment to the meaning system, the belonging system, and the structural system of their religion.

The Bat Mitzvah, shown here, is the initiation ceremony into the faith for Jewish girls.

Source: © Corbis.

Amish family at the beach; their faith influences their beach attire.

Source: © Kevin Fleming/Corbis.

THINKING SOCIOLOGICALLY

How did you or individuals you know become religious? Did you think about the process as it occurred?

Symbols and the Creation of Meaning: A Symbolic Interactionist Perspective

Dina is appalled as she looks around the Laundromat. The *gaje* (the term Gypsies use to refer to non-Gypsies) just do not seem to understand cleanliness. These middle-class North

A Romanian Gypsy woman uses different tubs to wash upper- and lower-body clothing and men's and women's apparel separately so they will not become spiritually defiled.

Source: © Peter Turnley/Corbis.

never again be considered *wuzho*—ritually clean. Food that touches the floor becomes filthy and inedible.

Ideally, a Gypsy woman would have separate wash tubs for men's upper-body clothing, men's lower-body clothing, women's upper-body clothing, women's lower-body clothing, and children's clothing. Gypsies know too well that the spirit of Mamioro brings illness to homes that are *marime*. The lack of spiritual cleanliness of non-Gypsies causes Gypsies to minimize their contact with *gaje*, to avoid sitting on a chair used by a *gaje*, and generally to recoil at the thought of assimilation into the larger culture (Southerland 1986; Sway 1988). How we make sense of the world takes place through meaning systems, as illustrated in the above example. For the Gypsies, things have meaning in ways that differ from the ideas that are prominent in the larger society, and the different meanings result in different behaviors and sometimes separation.

Symbolic interaction theory focuses on micro-level interaction, the primary concern being how people make sense of the meaning of things and how we construct our worlds. In an ambiguous situation, we seek help from others: is the situation funny, scary, bizarre, normal, or mysterious? Think about how you feel attracted to, or perhaps put off by, someone who wears

American neighbors of hers are very concerned about whether their clothes are *melalo*—dirty with dirt. By contrast, they pay no attention to whether they are *marime*—defiled or polluted in a spiritual sense. She watches in horror as a woman not only places the clothing of men, women, and children in a single washing machine but also includes clothing from the upper and lower halves of bodies together! No respectable Gypsy would allow such mixing; if it did occur, the cloth could be used only as rags. The laws of spiritual purity make clear that the lower half of the body is defiled. Anything that comes in contact with the body below the waist or that touches the floor becomes *marime* and can

The yarmulke (skullcap or kippah) has been worn by Jewish men since roughly the second century C.E. It symbolizes respect for and fear of God and serves to remind the wearer that there is always some distance between himself and God—and the need for humility. These caps are also a sign of belonging and commitment to the Jewish community.

Source: © Corbis.

Prayer beads are symbols of faith in Catholicism and other religions and serve as a reminder of one's reference group.

Source: © Roy Morsch/Corbis.

a cross as a necklace or who has other religious symbolism such as a yarmulke worn by Orthodox Jewish men to cover the crown of the head or a Muslim woman with head scarf. Symbols affect the way we feel about people and whether we are inclined to form a relationship.

It is the *meaning system* that most interests symbolic interactionists—the worldview or conceptual framework by which people make sense of life and cope with suffering and injustice. Religious meaning systems are made up of three elements: myths, rituals, and symbols.

Myths are stories embodying ideas about the world. When sociologists of religion use the word *myth*, they are not implying that the story is untrue. A myth may relate historical incidents that actually occurred, it may involve fictional events, or it may communicate abstract ideas such as reincarnation. Regardless of the literal truth or fiction of these stories, myths transmit values and a particular outlook on life. If a story such as the exodus from Egypt by ancient Hebrew people elicits some sense of sacredness, communicates certain attitudes and values, and helps life make sense, then it is a myth. The Netsilik Eskimo myth of the sea goddess Nuliajuk reinforces and makes sacred the value of conservation in an environment of scarce resources. It provides messages for appropriate behavior in that group. Thus, whether a myth is factual or not is irrelevant; myths are always "true" in some deeper metaphorical sense.

Rituals are group activities in which myths are reinforced with music, dancing, kneeling, praying, chanting, storytelling, and other symbolic acts. A number of religions, such as Islam, emphasize rituals of *orthopraxy* (conformity of behavior) more than *orthodoxy* (conformity to beliefs or doctrine) (Preston 1988; Tipton 1990). Praying five times a day while facing Mecca, mandated for the Islamic faithful, is an example of orthopraxy.

Often, rituals involve an enactment of myths. In some Christian churches, the symbolic cleansing of the soul is enacted by actually immersing people in water during baptism. Likewise, Christians frequently reenact the last supper of Jesus (Communion or Eucharist) as they accept their role as modern disciples. Among the Navaho, rituals enacted by a medicine man may last as long as five days; an appropriate myth is told and sand paintings, music, and dramatics lend power and unique reality to the myths.

The group environment of the ritual is important. Ethereal music, communal chants, and group actions such as kneeling or taking off one's shoes when entering the shrine or mosque create an aura of separation from the everyday world and a mood of awe so that the beliefs seem eternal and beyond question; they become *sacralized*. Rituals also make ample use of symbols, discussed in Chapter 4.

A *symbol* is anything that can stand for something else. Since religion deals with a transcendent realm, a realm that cannot be experienced or proven with the five senses, sacred symbols are a central part of religion. They have a powerful emotional impact on the faithful and reinforce the sacredness of myths.

Muslims pray to God (whom they call Allah) five times a day, removing their shoes and prostrating themselves as they face Mecca. This is an important ritual, and it illustrates that orthopraxy is central for Muslims. Personal devotion, which is expressed in actions, is emphasized in Islam.

Source: © Robert van der Hilst/Corbis.

Sacred symbols have been compared to computer chips that can store an enormous amount of information and deliver it with force and immediacy (Leach 1979). Seeing a cross can flood a Christian's consciousness with a whole series of images, events, and powerful emotions concerning Jesus and his disciples. Tasting the bitter herb during a Jewish Seder service may likewise elicit memories of the story of slavery in Egypt, recall the escape under the leadership of Moses, and send a moral message to the celebrant

Removal of shoes and kneeling before entering Leh Mosque in India is an expression of sacred respect for the Holy.

Source: © Nevada Wier/Corbis.

to work for freedom and justice in the world today. The Mezuzah, a plaque consecrating a house on the doorpost of a Jewish home, is a symbol reminding the occupants of their commitment to obey God's commandments and reaffirming God's commitment to them as a people. Since symbols are often heavily laden with emotion and can elicit strong feelings, they are used extensively in rituals to represent myths.

Myths, rituals, and symbols are usually interrelated and interdependent. Together, they form a set of ideas about life or about the cosmos that seem uniquely realistic and compelling; they reinforce rules of appropriate behavior and even political and economic systems by making them sacred. They can also control social relationships between different groups. The Gypsy revulsion at the filthy *marime* practices of middle-class Americans, like the Kosher rules for food preparation among the Jews, create boundaries between "us" and "them" that nearly eliminate prospects of intermarriage or even of close friendships outside of the religious community. Some scholars think these rituals and symbolic meanings are the key reason why Gypsies and Jews have survived for millennia without being assimilated or absorbed into dominant cultures. The symbols and meanings created barriers that prevented the obliteration of their cultures.

When symbolic interactionists study religion, they tend to focus on how symbols influence people's perception of reality and on the role rituals and myths play in defining what is "really real" for people. Symbolic interactionists stress that humans are always trying to create, determine, and interpret the meaning of events. Clearly, no other institution focuses as explicitly on determining the meaning of life and its events as religion.

THINKING SOCIOLOGICALLY

In a tradition with which you are familiar, how do symbols and sacred stories reinforce a particular view of the world or a particular set of values and social norms?

A Rational Choice Perspective

People with religious freedom make rational choices to belong to a religious group or change to another religion after weighing the costs (financial contributions, time involved) and benefits of belonging (eternal salvation, a belonging system, and a meaning system) (Finke and Stark 1993; Miller 1997; Sargeant 2000; Warner 1993). *Rational choice theory* is based on an economic model of human behavior. The basic idea is that the process people use to make decisions is at work in religious choices: What are the benefits and what are the costs? Do the benefits outweigh the costs? The benefits, of course, are

This advertisement ran in The Sundial, *the daily paper at the California State University, Northridge (CSUN). The church is located only a few miles from the university and hoped to catch, with their student-friendly service (and their targeted marketing), the interest of CSUN students.*

Source: Used with permission from the First Presbyterian Church of Granada Hills.

Wanna meet cool CSUN students just like YOU?

It's the 11th Hour, and you're invited!

Starting Sunday, September 9th, we're hosting a life-changing, roof-raising, Lord-praising, new worship service, and we want you to be a part of this exciting beginning.

1th HOUR

First Presbyterian Church of Granada Hills
10400 Zelzah Ave. (just North of Devonshire)
Northridge, CA 91326
(818) 360-1831   URL: www.fpogh.org

Come get involved in dynamic community that many CSUN students are already enjoying.
It's about getting real. It's about going deeper. It's the 11th Hour. **Are you ready?**

The 11th Hour kicks off at **11 a.m. Sundays.**

nonmaterial when it comes to religious choices—feeling that life has meaning, confidence in an afterlife, sense of communion with God, and so forth. This approach views churchgoers as consumers who are out to meet their needs or obtain a "product." It depicts churches as entrepreneurial establishments, or "franchises," in a competitive market, with "entrepreneurs" (ministers) as leaders. Competition for members leads churches to "market" their religion to consumers. Converts, and religious people generally, are thus regarded as active and rational agents pursuing self-interests, and growing churches are those that meet "consumer demand" (Finke 1997; Finke and Stark 2005; Iannaccone 1994). Religious groups produce religious "commodities" (rituals, meaning systems, sense of belonging, symbols, and so forth) to meet the "demands" of consumers (Sherkat and Ellison 1999).

Rational choice theorists believe that aggressive religious entrepreneurs who seek to produce religious "products" that appeal to a "target audience" will reap the benefits of a large congregation. Churches, temples, and mosques are competitive enterprises, and each must make investments of effort, time, and resources to attract and keep potential "buyers." There are many religious entrepreneurs out there seeking to meet individual needs; the challenge is for the various groups to beat the competition by meeting the demand of the current marketplace (Finke and Stark 2005).

For instance, when the United States separated church from state so that most individuals were not automatically members of a state religion, organized religions had to offer a "product" that would "sell" to consumers (Moore 1995).

Indeed, some scholars argue that where religion is an ascribed identity (adopted based on one's family of birth or the country's official religion), it is likely to be much less vigorous than in places where there is a competitive religious marketplace and religion is an achieved identity (chosen freely from many options) (Finke 1997; Finke and Stark 2005; Iannaccone 1994, 1995; Sargeant 2000).

When there are more religious groups competing for the hearts and minds of members, concern about spiritual matters is invigorated and commitment is heightened. Religious pluralism and spiritual diversity increase rates of religious activity as each group seeks its "market share" and as more individual needs are met in the society (Finke and Stark 2005; Iannaccone 1994, 1995; Warner 1993).

Not everyone agrees that religion is a competitive enterprise (Stark 2000). This strictly utilitarian economic analysis of religion seems counter to the way most religious people understand their own behavior. As one religious scholar puts it, "It is one thing to describe a person's decision to join a church *as if* the person were trying to maximize his or her benefits; it is something different to claim that the person's *actual* thought in joining measured his or her potential gains against potential losses" (McGuire 2002:298–99).

THINKING SOCIOLOGICALLY

Does the rational choice approach seem to you to make sense of religious behavior? Is religious behavior similar to self-interested economic behavior?

RELIGION AND MODERN LIFE: MESO-LEVEL ANALYSIS

In this section, we explore how religion as an institution interacts with other institutions and what kinds of organizational forms religion takes as it interacts with the larger social environment.

The Yaqui youth was very ill. He had been bitten by a rattler in the hot Arizona desert just outside his village. Although there was a medical clinic staffed by nurses and a visiting doctor, the family decided to use traditional Yaqui medicine, a blend of Native American rituals and what is referred to as *pagan Catholicism*. The medicine man broke eggs, mixed curative potions, and chanted incantations over the sick boy. These familiar rituals gave comfort to the family waiting anxiously for signs of the boy's recovery. After the boy had received the medicine man's treatment, he went to the clinic as well. He did recover, and the people believe that what led to the recovery was adherence to their traditional method of healing (Ballantine observation). The interaction of traditional religious practices and modern health care institutions illustrate these interconnections at the meso level.

Yaqui dancers, who blend Christian and indigenous beliefs, appeal to the supernatural for healing.

Source: Ken Matesich, photographer. Courtesy of the Arizona State Museum and the University of Arizona.

Religion and Other Social Institutions

In traditional societies, religion is not separated from other social institutions, as in the case above, but is an integral part of people's social world. In complex societies, on the other hand, religion is a distinctive group or organization. The dominant religion(s) in any complex society generally supports the political system and ideology of the dominant group. It is closely related to the economic system, linked to the education system, and legitimates the family system through sacred rites of passage for marriage, birth, and death. Even the health system, as shown in the Yaqui example, is closely linked to religious beliefs about the healing process, disease, and death.

Religion not only supports other institutions but may also experience support or pressure from these other institutions. The Catholic church has faced increasing criticism from international organizations, political movements, governments, religious groups, and educational institutions for its ban on birth control. Due to rapid population growth, especially in poor Catholic nations, many interested parties are putting pressure on the Catholic church to ease its strict ban in these countries. The church cannot ignore these pressures, for they undermine the legitimacy of the church if they are not addressed or countered. Even if the church does not change, it must expend considerable effort to defend its position to keep from losing credibility in the eyes of

Promise Keepers worship together as they reaffirm their faith and their masculine social roles.

Source: © Les Stone/Sygma Corbis.

members and nonmembers alike. Some Catholic clergy and a number of lay-members have defected over positions of the church. Let us consider the relationship between religion and other social institutions: family, politics, and economics.

Religion and Family

Everyone was dressed in their colorful finery to welcome the baby into the religious community. The naming ceremony in this Nigerian village takes place when the baby reaches six weeks and is considered a viable human being. After the ceremony, the bonds of religious community are solidified with food, music, and dancing.

Iran's supreme leader, Ayatollah Ali Khamenei, speaks to ethnic Arabs during a visit to Dehlavieh in the southern oil province of Khuzestan. (Dehlavieh, Iran; March 25, 2006)

Source: AFP/Getty.

Our parents provide our first contacts with religion. They may say prayers, attend worship services, and talk about proper behavior as defined by their religious group. Religious congregations make marriages sacred through ceremonies. Mother's Day, Father's Day, and Grandparents' Day are now recognized by many religions and societies, thereby honoring and legitimating parenting. Many of the sacred ceremonies in religion are family affairs: births, christenings or naming of new members, and funerals. Jews, Muslims, and Latter-Day Saints (Mormons) are especially known for their many ceremonies and gatherings designed specifically for family units.

Religiosity, a person's degree of religious involvement, is positively associated with moral beliefs and behavior in youth and influences interaction with children and support of spouses in marriages (Brody et al. 1994). For instance, young women in the United States who are religious are less likely than other adolescents to become sexually active prior to marriage (Sherkat and Ellison 1999). Some religious groups such as conservative Protestants are also involved in childrearing, producing parenting manuals to guide families. Some of these manuals have created controversy because of their emphasis on hierarchical and authority-centered parenting models (Bartkowski and Ellison 1995).

Tensions can arise between family and religion over social control. Among the Amish, if the bishop orders a member of the church to be shunned, the family must comply and must refuse to speak to or associate with that person. If they do not cooperate with the shunning, the members of their community will also shun them. This sometimes leads to intense tension as the church tries to determine communication patterns and interactions within a family.

The New Right and other conservative organizations sometimes argue that if society could reinstitute the family and religious values of the past, today's societal problems would be reduced; if parents would spend more time with their children, instilling proper values, things would be better. However, working parents today often spend more time with their children than parents did in past times. Stereotypes of the families and the religious values of the "good old days" come from a small segment of the total population: those upper-middle class families in which only one parent had to work (Coontz 1997, 2005; Woodberry and Smith 1998). Today, many problems and pressures facing families occur at different levels of analysis and are out of the control of the family or local religious group. However, religiously affiliated social movements may also attempt to transform or strengthen other institutions; the conservative Christian men's movement Promise Keepers (see photo on top left) is one example of an effort to restore a traditional model of family life.

Although religion cannot solve all family problems, most religions encourage stable family life and checks and balances for "moral" behavior in other institutions.

Religion and Politics: Theocracies and Civil Religion

Jan, a Swede, belongs to a state religion: Lutheranism. He was raised a Lutheran and does not really think about the

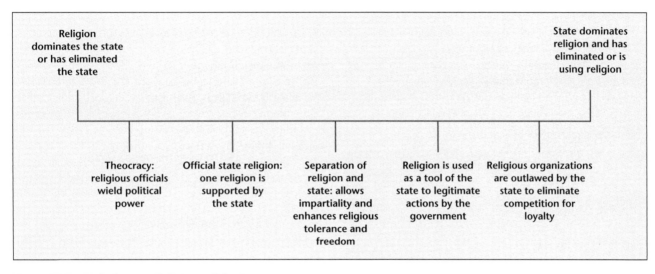

Figure 12.1 Links between Religion and the State

possibility of other religious beliefs, although there is a large Pentacostal movement in Sweden. The Nwankwo family, mentioned in the chapter opening, practices an ancient tribal religion, also with no thought that another religious belief might have something better to offer. Most of us are raised in a particular belief system from childhood and adhere to that religion because it is part of the custom and tradition most familiar to us and because those close to us expect us to adhere to those beliefs. We seldom question our "choice."

In a pure **theocracy**, or rule by God, religious leaders rule society in accordance with God's presumed wishes. Iran is one example where religion clearly has a privileged position. In some situations, religion is used as a tool of the state to manipulate the citizenry and to maintain social control. A *state religion*, on the other hand, has some autonomy but receives support from tax money; Sweden, Britain, and Italy are examples. Some countries, such as the former Soviet Union, have outlawed religion altogether so that no loyalty competes with loyalty to the nation. The continuum in Figure 12.1 shows possible relationships between church and state.

Countries with diverse religious groups experience multiple pressures on their political systems: religious voting blocs, conflicts over definitions of public morality, and lobbying efforts for policies that have moral implications—abortion, euthanasia, rights for homosexuals, care of the poor, war and peace, and so forth. Sometimes religious groups form the basis for political parties and pressure groups lobbying for policies that support their beliefs (Hayes 1995). Even in the United States, which professes separation between church and state matters, religious groups influence policies such as prayer in school, selection of textbooks and reading matter, and abortion. In some countries, religious groups strongly oppose the government and seek to undermine the authority and power of political leaders. In Nazi Germany, some church leaders formulated the Barmen Declaration in opposition to Hitler; many Christian groups in South Africa opposed Apartheid; and in some parts of Latin America, church leaders

work for human rights and more equitable distribution of land and resources. While religion often reinforces the power of the state, it may also be a source of conflict and tension on issues regarding morality, justice, and legitimate authority.

In simple homogeneous societies, religion serves as a kind of glue, sacralizing the current social system by offering it supernatural legitimacy. In complex and heterogeneous societies, on the other hand, no one religion can provide the core values of the culture. In such circumstances, an alternative mode called **civil religion** frequently evolves. Civil religion is based on a set of beliefs, symbols, and rituals that pervade many aspects of secular life and institutions. It involves a shared public faith in the nation and what that nation stands for. While civil religion lacks the structural system of organized religion in industrial societies, it is often supported by various types of patriotic groups. Not only do these small voluntary associations develop intense belonging systems, civil religion also tends to strengthen the sense of belonging of all citizens as members of that society (Bellah 1992; Gehrig 1981; Roberts 2004).

Rituals of civil religion include the pledge of allegiance, saluting the flag, and singing the national anthem. For example, American civil religion is not explicitly Christian, for it must appeal to those who are non-Christian as well (Bellah 1970), but it involves reference to God in many areas of civilian life and a legitimation of the political system. It attempts to give the nation and the government supernatural blessing and authority. It also calls the nation to a higher standard of justice and may be used by change agents such as Martin Luther King, Jr., to make social change more acceptable and compelling.

In Ireland, part of the intense conflict between Protestants and Catholics is over civil religion. Protestants and Catholics not only come from different economic strata and different ethnic backgrounds but also have different visions for the future of the country and different ideas about what gives the country its special place in history. Although civil religion is supposed to unite a country, in Ireland and other divided

Civil religion blends reverence for the nation with more traditional symbols of faith. Pictured is the chapel at Punchbowl, the Pacific cemetery for U.S. military personnel, located in Hawaii. Note that two U.S. flags are inside the altar area and are more prominent than two of the three religious symbols that also adorn the chancel: the Christian cross, the Jewish Star of David, and the Buddhist wheel of Dharma.

Source: Photo by Keith Roberts.

countries, civil religion can itself be a point of intense conflict (Bellah and Greenspahn 1987; McGuire 2002).

THINKING SOCIOLOGICALLY

How does civil religion manifest itself in your country? Give specific examples.

Religion and the Economy:
The Protestant Ethic and Capitalism

Why do most of us study hard, work hard, and strive to get ahead? Why are we sacrificing time and money now—taking this and other college courses—when we might spend that money on an impressive new car? Our answers probably have something to do with our moral attitudes about work, about those who lack ambition, and about convictions regarding the proper way to live. Max Weber (1904-05/1958) saw a relationship between the economic system, particularly capitalism, and ideas about work and sacrifice. He gathered information by studying many documents, including diaries of Calvinists (a branch of Protestantism), sermons and religious teachings, and other historical papers. The following is his argument in a nutshell.

Noting that the areas of Europe where the Calvinists had strong followings were the same areas where capitalism grew fastest, Weber (1904-05/1958) argued that four elements in the Calvinist Protestant faith created the moral and value system necessary for the growth of capitalism: belief in predestination, a calling, self-denial, and individualism.

1. *Predestination* meant that one's destiny was predetermined. Nothing anyone could do would change what was to happen. Since God was presumed to be perfect, he was not influenced by human deeds or prayer. People's chances for salvation, or going to Heaven, were decided by God even before they were born. Those people who were chosen by God were referred to as *the elect* and were assumed to be a small group. Therefore, people looked for signs of their status—salvation or damnation. High social status was sometimes viewed as a sign of being among the elect, so motivation was high to succeed in *this* life.

2. *The calling* referred to the concept of doing God's work. Each person was put on earth to serve God, and each had a task to do in God's service. One could be called by God to any occupation, so the key was to work very hard and with the right attitude. Since work was a way to serve God, laziness or lack of ambition came to be viewed as a sin. These ideas helped to create a society in which people's self-worth and their evaluation of others were tied to a work ethic. Protestants became workaholics!

3. *Self-denial* involved living a simple, unshowy life. If one had a good deal of money, one did not spend it on a lavish home, or expensive clothing, or various forms of entertainment. Such consumption would be offensive to God. Therefore, if people worked hard and began to accumulate resources, they simply saved them or invested them in a business. This self-denial was tied to an idea that we now call *delayed gratification*, postponing the satisfaction of one's present wants and desires in exchange for a future reward. The reward they sought was in the afterlife. Because Calvinists believed in predestination, they did not expect to earn salvation, but they believed that they could demonstrate to themselves and others that they were among the elect.

4. *Individualism* meant that each individual faced his or her destiny alone before God. Much previous Christian theology had emphasized group salvation, the idea that an entire community would be saved or damned together. The stark individualism of Calvinistic theology stressed that each individual was on his or her own before God. Likewise, in the economic system that was emerging, individuals were on their own. The person who thrived was an individualist who planned wisely and charted his or her own course. Religious individualism and economic individualism reinforced one another.

The Protestant ethic that resulted from these elements stressed hard work, simple living, and rational decision making by daring individualists. Although business people and laborers spent long hours working at their calling, the earnings and profits were not spent on worldly indulgences but reinvested for new equipment. Individualism allowed people to pursue their own course of action and not to feel guilty for doing so. This combination was ideal for the growth of capitalism. Religion resulted in major changes in cultural values that, in turn, transformed the economic system. Weber (1904-05/1958) saw both systems as dynamic, interrelated, and ever-changing.

Gradually, the capitalistic system, stimulated by the Protestant ethic, spread to other countries and to other religious groups. Many of the attitudes about work and delayed gratification no longer have supernatural focus, but they are part of our larger culture nonetheless. They influence our feelings about people who are not industrious and our ideas about why some people are poor. In fact, some religious sects see individuals as responsible for their own fates, believing the poor and jobless got into their circumstances and should solve their own problems rather than depend on government aid (Davis and Robinson 1999).

Weber recognized that other factors also had to be present for capitalism to arise, but he believed that the particular set of moral values and attitudes that Calvinism instilled in the people was critical. While Marx argued that religion kept workers in their places and allowed the capitalists to exploit the system and maintain their elite positions, Weber focused on the change brought about in the economic system as a result of religious beliefs and values.

Religion interacts with the economy in other ways as well. For one thing, religion is big business. In the United States, at the turn of the twenty-first century, members donated an average of $440 per year to religious organizations, with contributions to the top 15 denominations topping $18 billion (Sherkat and Ellison 1999). In most countries, religions (1) employ clergy and other people who serve the church, (2) own land and property, and (3) generate millions through collections and fundraising. Some of this money goes to upkeep of the building, some to charitable activities, and some to investments. Religious ventures continue to expand into many areas, from shopping centers to homes and apartment buildings for the elderly. In the United States, televangelism is a multimillion dollar industry involving the sale of books and tapes; donations of hundreds of millions of dollars; establishment of colleges, hospitals, and amusement parks; and provision of jobs in a wide variety of technical electronic areas.

There are other ways in which religion and the economic institutions are linked. When large religious organizations take moral stands on poverty, they may influence the economy. Moreover, when the economy is especially bad, certain kinds of religious movements are more likely to be spawned: millenarian movements that expect the end of the world soon almost always occur when economic prospects are bleak (Roberts 2004).

Although religion today may not have the power to transform the economy or other social institutions, each institution does affect others. Society also shapes the kind of organization and the relationship to other institutions that the religious group adopts, as discussed in the next section.

THINKING SOCIOLOGICALLY

Religion is influenced not only by other institutions in society but also by the media. What messages can we learn from the media (movies, TV, music) that reflect the state of religion in society?

Types of Religious Associations

From denominations to sects to new religious movements (NRMs), religious organizations take many forms. The following discussion explores *ideal types*, that is, models that summarize the main characteristics of types of religious organizations. Any specific religious group may not fit all of the characteristics exactly.

The Ecclesia

Official state religions are called **ecclesia**, referring to religious groups that claim as members everybody within the boundaries of a particular society (Chalfant, Beckley, and Palmer 1994). Ecclesia includes all members of a society. They try to monopolize religious life in that society, have a close relationship with the power structure, have a formal structure with officially designated full-time clergy, and have membership based on birth into the society.

Many countries have official state religions. Norway and Sweden are Lutheran. Spain, France, Italy, and many Latin American countries are Roman Catholic. Greece is Greek Orthodox. Iran, Egypt, and other Middle Eastern countries are Islamic. England is Anglican. India is predominantly Hindu, although Muslims share power. Because ecclesias represent the interests of the state and those in power, disfranchised groups often seek other religious outlets; in Great Britain, 80 percent of the people of Wales in

The west facade of St. Paul's Cathedral, in London. St. Paul's is part of the Anglican Church—the official "state church" in Britain.

Source: © Angelo Hornak/Corbis.

the early twentieth century affiliated with Nonconformist Christianity, not with the Church of England where the Queen is officially the head of the church.

In societies that do not have official religions such as the United States, religion takes several forms: denominations, sects, and NRMs (or cults).

Denominations

In the United States, Congregationalist, Episcopalian, Presbyterian, Lutheran, Baptist, Methodist, and other mainline Christian religious groups are denominations. They all have certain characteristics in common. The denomination is seen as a legitimate form of religious expression but does not have religious dominance or monopoly in the society. Each religious group appeals to a particular segment of the population, often related to class, race, ethnicity, and sometimes regional area; they coexist with and usually are accepting of other denominations (Christiano, Swatos, and Kivisto 2002; Roberts 2004). The largest denominations in the United States are indicated on Map 12.2.

Most denominations have formal bureaucracies with hierarchical positions, specialization of tasks, and official creeds. This hierarchy extends even to the international level in some denominations such as the Anglicans. The leadership is trained, and there is often a professional church staff. Worship typically involves formal, ritualized, and prescribed ceremonies. Note that the Roman Catholic Church is an ecclesia in Spain because it is the official state religion, but it is a denomination in the United States and Canada where it is one of many religious groups and is not affiliated with or supported by the state.

While denominations vary somewhat in the values and beliefs they advocate, they usually support the basic values and social arrangements of the larger society. They may work for moderate changes, but they seldom call for radical or revolutionary restructuring of the society. Thus, the membership tends to be made up of those people who have benefited from the existing social arrangements and who hold positions of power and influence. Most of these denominations are large and financially secure, in part because they attract a middle- and upper-class clientele. This comfortable accommodation between denominations and the existing social order is precisely what made Marx feel that religion was used to keep the social structure from changing.

While the key characteristic of a denomination is its accommodation to the state, disfranchised members of society are more likely to be attracted to sects or cults.

Sects

John Wesley (1703–1791), founder of a movement now known as the Methodist Church, began a renewal movement in the Church of England. He wanted to call people back to the basics of the faith; his evangelical revival called followers to lead Christian lives through a method of strict discipline—prayer, worship, study, and mutual support groups. Hence, the name *Methodists* arose—a term that was originally derogatory. It referred to people whose worship was much too "enthusiastic" to be decent and orderly, the standard of worship among Anglicans and Presbyterians of the day. Because church authorities disapproved of Wesley's new *methods*, he was marginalized and refused an Anglican church to lead; he took his movement to the streets. As a person of deep commitment and a skilled organizer, Wesley formed associations in Great Britain and North America; today, Methodists have become one of the largest Christian bodies in the new world and a mainstream denomination in the United States.

Sects, such as the early Methodists, form in protest against their parent religion. Sometimes, they are begun by dissatisfied members who form splinter groups and break away from denominations. Those splitting off do so because of theological concerns or because they feel the church has surrendered to secular authority (Roberts 2004; Stark and Bainbridge 1985). They believe that the true religious

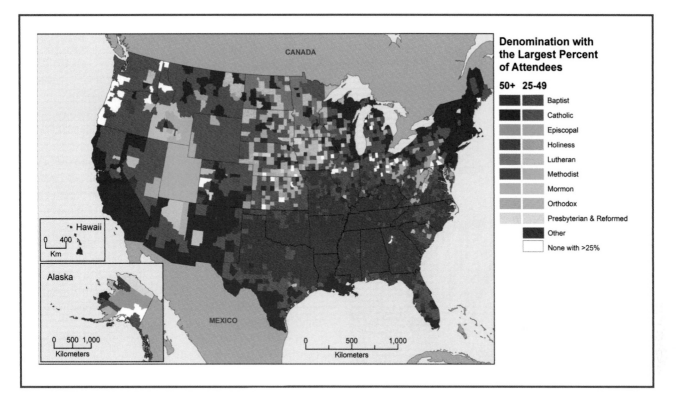

MAP 12.2   Denominational Distribution in the United States

Source: Religious Congregations and Membership Study, 2000. Map by Anna Versluis.

Note: This map shows the largest religious denomination by attendance for each county. In some cases the largest denomination receives less than a majority of the county's religious adherents. The map thus underrepresents the diversity in any area, but it does demonstrate regional variation. Only one county—in Virginia—has a majority of adherents that are Muslim; in all other counties with a majority, a Christian denomination is the largest religion.

doctrines are being abandoned, people are becoming contaminated by worldly ways, and the group must save itself by returning to the true religion. Often, the break has other underlying social dimensions. Sect members may feel the denomination has come to embrace the existing power structure too closely; part of the membership feels the unjust social arrangements are condemned by God and should be condemned by the faithful. In other instances, the splinter group is simply alienated by the bureaucracy and hierarchical structure of the religious group itself (Niebuhr 1929).

There are more than 400 sects in the United States. Tennessee has the highest sect membership per population; the lowest region in sectarianism is New England. However, Africa has six times as many sects as the United States (Stark and Bainbridge 1985).

Sects are characterized by their separation from other religious and even social groups. (See Table 12.2.) There is exclusive commitment to one body of teaching and a claim of monopoly over religious Truth. Sects typically demand total allegiance to the organization (Wilson 1982).

TABLE 12.2   **Distinguishing Sects from Denominations or Ecclesia**

The following are characteristics that distinguish a sect from a denomination or an ecclesia:

1. Exclusive membership policy: Only the saved or those who meet high standards of membership are admitted.

2. Conflict with the host society: The outside secular society is usually viewed as depraved or evil, values of the larger society are rejected, and there is often deep suspicion of the state.

3. Lack of a complex organizational structure: Little or no national organization exists, clergy are often not educated in seminaries and have no formal ordination beyond the local congregation, and there may not be a larger affiliated institution that produces religious education materials.

Source: Yinger (1970).

Tofuni members of the sect of Heavenly Christians kneel in worship during a ceremony. The sect was founded in 1947, in Benin, by Samuel Oshofa and has more than 10 million followers throughout the countries bordering the Gulf of Guinea, Africa.

Source: © Juan Echeverria/Corbis.

Members of Christian sects in North America are often socially separated from those of higher social classes. As Liston Pope (1942/1965) stated, sectarians "substitute religious status for social status." For those who are less well off, a sect gives the feeling that members are among God's chosen, even if they do not have much social prestige in this world. Because most people who join sects feel deprived, there is a high degree of tension between the values of members and those of the larger society (Stark 1985).

As sects grow in membership, coordination becomes necessary, leadership succession occurs, a hierarchy develops, and members become less alienated as social class positions change. Any of these factors can be the catalyst to move the sect toward becoming a denomination. The process of institutionalization occurs and helps survival, but it is fraught with difficulties as the intimacy of a small group is overwhelmed by the impersonality of the emerging large organization.

Sects are often formed because groups split from denominations or individuals feel deprived, but over time, most sects become another denomination. Few contemporary groups are pure sect or pure denomination; they are on a continuum between the two and may be moving toward sectarianism or toward denominationalization.

New Religious Movements (NRMs) or Cults

NRMs, like sects, are protest or splinter groups; but unlike sects, if NRMs survive for several generations, become established, and gain some legitimacy, they become new religions in the society rather than new denominations of the existing

faith. *Cult* was once the common term for this kind of movement, but the media and the public have so completely misused the word that its meaning has become unclear and often negative. The term *cult*, as sociologists have historically used it, is not a negative term; it is simply descriptive. Most sociologists of religion now prefer NRMs to describe these religious forms (Barker 1989; Robbins 1988).

NRMs are founded on a new revelation (or insight) or on a radical reinterpretation of an old teaching. They are usually out of the mainstream religious system, at least in their early days. Christianity, Buddhism, and Islam all began as NRMs or cults. Either Jesus started a new cult, or else we must conclude that Christianity is a denomination of Judaism—an idea which few Christians or Jews would accept!

The estimated number of NRMs in North America is between 1,500 and 2,000. The Institute for the Study of American Religion lists 1,667 different religious groups that are nonconventional religions (Melton 1992). There could be 10,000 more NRMs in Africa and an undetermined but large number in Asia.

An NRM is often started by a charismatic leader, someone who claims to have received a new insight, often directly from God. For example, Reverend Sun Myung Moon founded an NRM called the Unification Church, the members of which are often referred to as *Moonies*. Some sensational NRMs have ended in tragedy: Reverend Jim Jones led his devoted followers to a retreat in Guyana and ultimately to their suicides in the belief that heaven was awaiting them (Lacayo 1993; Wright 1995), and a group suicide occurred in California by a band of believers who thought that supernatural beings were coming to take them away in a flying saucer (see the next Sociology in Your Social World).

Dead members of Heaven's Gate were uniformly and neatly laid out on the beds when found.

Source: © Koester-Soqui/Corbis.

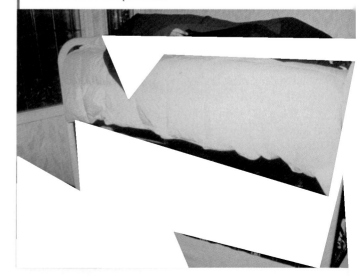

Sociology in Your Social World

Heaven's Gate

In late March of 1997, thirty-nine bodies of members from a religious movement known as Heaven's Gate were found. Founded in 1973 by Marshall Applewhite and Bonnie Nettles, this NRM was a millenarian movement (meaning that the members expected the end of the world to be approaching very soon) that blended literal interpretation of the Christian Bible, theosophical doctrines, Hindu ideas from the Bhagavad Gita, and belief in UFOs and supernatural space aliens. Applewhite and Nettles believed that Jesus had been picked up by a flying saucer and that his human body was transformed into a divine body. They taught their followers that they must have little interest in their human bodies and must overcome physical desires in order to be worthy of entering "the level above human." Their bodies, they believed, were nothing more than a suit of clothes that needed to be shed. Evil space aliens that misled humans were called *Luciferians*, and the temptations of Luciferians had to be avoided. Beginning in 1993, to avoid physical desire, eight of the men voluntarily had themselves castrated.

Applewhite, called *Do* by members of the group, waited on a pier in Santa Monica in 1994 with other members of this flying saucer religion, expecting a saucer to pick them up. When it failed to happen, they decided that they might have to kill their earthly bodies to be transported to the "next level." Ridiculed for their beliefs, they became increasingly insulated from nonbelievers. Since members of this group believed that the earth was to be destroyed soon anyway and only a small window for escape existed, drastic action seemed justified. They believed that the otherworldly spaceships would be coming behind the cover of the spectacular comet, Hale-Bopp. When Do, a charismatic figure, son of a Christian minister, and a one-time professor of music, gave the word, the faithful were to shed the external shell (their bodies) in order to attain heaven. This seemed logical to those passionate believers (Wessinger 2000). Interestingly, this group had been studied by sociologists since the mid-1970s (Balch 1982, 1995).

Heaven's Gate, like other spectacular groups in which people commit suicide or violate social norms, draws attention because the media love to explore their unusual beliefs and behaviors.

Sect	→	Established Sect	→	Denomination
Cult or NRM	→	Established Cult	→	New Religious Tradition

Figure 12.2   The Evolution of Sects and Cults (New Religious Movements: NRMs)

Source: Roberts (2004).

Most new religious groups are not dangerous to members; furthermore, most religious groups that are now accepted and established were stigmatized as weird or evil when they started. Early Christians were characterized by Romans as dangerous cannibals, and in the early decades of the twentieth century in the United States, Roman Catholics were depicted in the media as dangerous, immoral, and anti-American (Bromley and Shupe 1981). When we encounter media reports about NRMs, we should listen to and read these with a good dose of skepticism and recognize that not all cults are like the sensational ones.

Many NRMs are short lived, lasting only as long as the charismatic leader does. The Jim Jones movement died with his death and the cyanide poisoning of its members. Only those groups that institutionalize and prepare for their futures, as did the early Christians, are likely to survive. So both sects and NRMs find that developing a complex organization enhances survival, but in the process, they are usually transformed as religious groups. Figure 12.2 illustrates the parallel evolution of these two types of religious groups.

The social conditions in the late twentieth century were ripe for NRMs; many young people, often from middle-class families in industrialized nations, have been attracted to NRMs in their search for who and what they are. These religious communities provide meaning and belonging systems with friendship bonds and clear-cut answers for people seeking meaning and direction in life. This choice has been especially evident in urban areas and on the West Coast of the United States and Canada.

Nonconventional religious movements, however, are hard to study since the members know they might be persecuted for their faith perspective. Witchcraft is one example of a religion that has been forced to remain secretive, and the next How Do We Know? explores the strategies of one sociologist to examine this interesting religious community.

THINKING SOCIOLOGICALLY

What factors might cause the birth and success of new religious movements (NRMs)?

RELIGION IN SOCIETY: MACRO-LEVEL ANALYSIS

As an integral part of society, religion meets the needs of individuals and of the social structure. In this section, we explore functionalist and conflict theories as we consider some functions of religion in society and the role of religion in stratification systems of the society.

The Contribution of Religion to Society: A Functionalist Perspective

Religions have survived many attempts at destruction, ridicule, ostracism, or torture of believers. Some religions seem to become stronger as a result of adversity. Consider the Jewish people under Hitler, the Christians during Roman times and the tortures they endured, and the Puritans, Mormons, and Huguenots who gave up homelands to seek religious freedom. To endure through adversity, religion must be a powerful force for the believers.

Regardless of their personal belief or disbelief in the supernatural, sociologists of religion acknowledge that religion has important social consequences. Functionalists contend that religion has positive consequences—helping people answer questions about the meaning of life and providing part of the glue that helps to hold a society together. Let us look at some of the social functions of religion, keeping in mind that the role of religion in societies varies.

Social Cohesion

Religion helps individuals feel a sense of belonging and unity with others, a common sense of purpose with those who share the same beliefs. It serves to hold any social unit together and gives the members a sense of camaraderie. Durkheim's widely cited study of suicide stresses the importance of belonging to a group; contemporary research shows that a high rate of congregational membership and religious homogeneity in a community are associated with lower rates of suicide (Ellison, Burr, and McCall 1997; Stark, Doyle, and Rushing 1983). Thus, religion serves society well as long as religious views are consistent with other values of society (Bainbridge and Stark 1981). If there are competing religions, cohesion may be reduced and even be a source of conflict and hatred. Societies with competing religions often develop a civil religion—a theology of the nation—that serves to bless the nation and to enhance conformity and loyalty.

Legitimating Social Values and Norms

The values and norms in a culture need to be seen not just as random or arbitrary if they are to be compelling to members of the society. Religion often sacralizes social norms—grounds them in a supernatural reality or a divine command that makes them larger than life. Whether those norms have to do with care for the vulnerable, the immorality of extramarital sex, the sacredness of a monogamous heterosexual marriage, the proper roles of men and women, or "false witness" regarding a neighbor, foundations of morality from scripture create feelings of absoluteness. This lends stability to the society: agreement on social control of deviant behavior is easier, and the society can rely less on coercion and force to get citizens to behave themselves. Of course, the absoluteness of the norms also makes it more difficult to change them as the society evolves. This inflexibility is precisely what pleases conservatives and distresses liberals, the latter often seeking new ways to interpret the old norms.

Social Change

Depending on the time and place, religion can work for or against social change. Some religions fight to maintain the status quo or return to simpler times. This is true of many fundamentalist religions—be they branches of Christian, Jewish, Hindu, or Islamic faiths—that seek to simplify life in the increasingly complex industrial world. Other religious traditions support or encourage change. Japan was able to make tremendous strides in industrialization in a short time following World War II, in part because the Shinto, Confucian, and Buddhist religions provided no obstacles and, in fact, supported the changes. In the United States, the central figures in the civil rights movement were nearly all African American religious leaders. As the first nationwide organizations controlled by black people, African American religious organizations established networks and communication channels that were utilized by those interested in change (Lincoln and Mamiya 1990; McAdam 1999; Wilmore 1973).

Witchcraft in the United States

In *A Community of Witches: Contemporary Neo-Paganism and Witchcraft in the United States* (1999), Helen Berger applies sociological analysis to conduct a fascinating study of contemporary Wicca. To study this movement, Berger used several methods of gathering information. First, for two years she did participant-observation in a newly formed coven in New England. A *coven* is a small congregation of witches, usually comprising no more than ten or twelve members. It took considerable effort to establish trust with the members, but this method of gathering data allowed her to experience firsthand the close-knit support group and the actual behaviors and interactions within the group. A national organization provided her with a wealth of printed material produced by Neo-Pagans and allowed her entry to several national Neo-Pagan festivals where she observed the rituals. She also did in-depth, open-ended interviews with forty members from a variety of covens. By using a variety of methods, Berger was able to gain in-depth information, but she was also able to get an idea of whether her experiences were generalizable to all parts of the country.

While Berger found Wicca to be a rather healthy and vibrant movement, she also found that it experiences some of the same dilemmas of any other church or temple. Wicca is feminist, believing in a goddess and involving an emphasis on gender equality. It also celebrates spiritual unity of humans with nature and therefore has a strong ecology ethic. Wicca encourages an intuitive approach to decision making (using intuition rather than focusing on logic) and celebrates the senses; this sensuousness embraces sexuality, fertility, and being at one with the universe. Most rituals are conducted outside, and the cycles of the moon, the solstice (cycles of the sun), and other natural seasons are central to this religion.

Berger finds that Wicca is a product of the globalized world, for the religion involves bits and pieces selected from religions around the world. It has spread with modern technology including Internet communication, desktop publishing, and fax machines. Furthermore, it is a religion about self-fulfillment, in keeping with a contemporary obsession with self-awareness and self-transformation.

Wicca attracts rather well-educated people, a high proportion of them having college degrees. Most members were originally attracted to this movement while in their twenties, although a substantial number are now older and have children. Eighty-five percent of the members are from urban or suburban communities; covens are rare in rural areas and small towns.

Berger finds that the strong sense of community and mutual support that members feel are a major draw and a significant factor in keeping people in the movement. The sense of family is remarkably like what Christians describe as the tone and feel of their churches or their prayer groups. Indeed, the support has helped many people get through hard times in their lives, and they see Wicca as a very loving and caring community.

Rites of the Wiccan religion in Texas: saluting the four cardinal points.

Source: © Rebecca McEntee/Corbis Sygma.

Wicca has several branches: one strand of the movement is exclusively feminist (with no men admitted); those members who have heterosexual marriages and families find they cannot celebrate their faith easily as a family. Thus, socialization of the next generation becomes a problem, since the religious community does not embrace one's entire family. Other strands of Wicca actively involve men, women, and children. Berger believes that this organizational dilemma is so severe that the continuance of these Wiccan movements that exclude men is questionable. Inclusive Wiccan movements are much more likely to survive, for these create structures that will sustain the group and pass along the faith to each new generation. Even this routinization is not without its problems, however, since one of the central emphases in Wicca is spontaneity. Establishing stable organizations and routines is a bit of a contradiction. Like all other religious groups in a complex society, organization and adaptation to the surrounding society are critical to the group's survival.

Which religious groups in your community have a stabilizing influence, sacralizing the existing system? Which groups advocate change in the society, pushing for more social equality and less ethnocentrism toward others? Are there mosques, temples, or churches that oppose the government's policies, or do they foster absolute loyalty?

The Link between Religion and Stratification: A Conflict Perspective

Our religious ideas and values and the way we worship are shaped not only by the society into which we are born but also by our family's position in the stratification system. Religion serves different primary purposes for individuals, depending on their positions in the society. People of various social statuses differ in the type and degree of their involvement in religious groups.

At times, religions reinforce socially defined differences between people, giving sacred legitimacy to racial prejudice, gender bias, and inequality. Conflict theory considers ways in which religion relates to stratification and the status of minority groups.

The Class Base of Religion

Conflict theorist Karl Marx (1844/1963) states clearly his view of the relationship between religion and class—that religion helps perpetuate the power structure. For the proletariat or working class, religion is a sedative, a narcotic that dulls people's sensitivity to and understanding of the plight in their life situation. He calls religion the "opiate of the people." It keeps people in line and provides an escape from reality, the tedium, if not suffering, of daily life. At the same time, it helps those in power keep other people in line because it promises that if laborers serve well in this life, then the hereafter or the next incarnation will be better. Some religions justify the positions of those who are better off by saying they have earned it.

Because the needs and interests of classes differ, religion is class-based in most societies. In the United States, different denominations and sects show corresponding differences in social class measures such as education, occupation, and income (Pyle 2006; Smith and Faris 2005). For instance, people with higher social status attend worship more regularly than do people with less education and income, but people with lower socioeconomic status pray and read the Bible more frequently (Albrecht and Heaton 1984; Roberts 2004). States with larger Jewish populations have higher per capita income levels, whereas states with larger fundamentalist Protestant populations are associated with lower income levels (Waters, Heath, and Watson 1995). The specific links

between denominational affiliation and socioeconomic measures in the United States at the beginning of the twenty-first century are indicated in Table 12.3. The sectarian religions (sects) tend to attract lower- and working-class worshippers because they focus on the problems and life situations faced by people in lower social classes.

Max Weber (1946) referred to this pattern of people belonging to religious groups that espouse values and characteristics compatible with their social status as *elective affinity*. For example, people in laboring jobs usually find that obeying rules of the workplace and adhering to the instructions of the employer or supervisor are essential for success on the job (Bowles and Gintis 1976; McLeod 2004). The faith communities of the poor and the working class tend to stress obedience, submission to "superiors," and the absoluteness of religious standards. The values of the workplace are reenacted and legitimated in the churches and help to socialize children to continue in noncreative laboring jobs.

Many people in affluent congregations are paid to be divergent thinkers, to be problem solvers, and to break the mold of conventional thinking. They will not do well professionally if they merely obey rules; instead, they are expected to be rule-makers while trying to solve organizational or management problems (Bowles and Gintis 1976). It is not surprising, then, that the denominations of the affluent are more likely to value tolerance of other perspectives, religions, or values, and view factors that limit individual opportunity (e.g., institutional racism and sexism) as evil. They embrace tolerance of differences and condemn rigidity, absolutism, and conventionalism. Critical thinking, creativity, and even a streak of independence are valuable characteristics; their religious communities are likely to encourage each member to work out his or her own theology, within limits (Roberts 2004; Roof 1999).

Stratification is found in various world religions, not just Christianity. For example, Hinduism in the upper classes of India conforms much more to the official beliefs of the religion; it is monotheistic and stresses concepts of transmigration of souls, reincarnation. The lower castes believe in a sort of Hindu folk religion that is polytheistic, belief in multiple gods. Lower-class Hindus tend to identify Hindu statues as gods in themselves (rather than as symbols), and they believe in heaven and hell rather than in reincarnation. In fact, in some areas, the folk Hinduism of the lower castes can hardly be recognized as Hinduism at all (Noss and Noss 1990). Supernatural realms in classical Hindu societies are stratified as well. Individuals are born into a caste based on their behavior in a previous incarnation. Their task in their current life is to do the work assigned to their particular caste well and prove themselves worthy of higher caste status in the next life.

Whatever the particular belief, the relationship between one's religion and one's social status affects everything from life expectancy, likelihood of divorce, and mental health to attitudes regarding sexual behavior, abortion, and stem cell research.

TABLE 12.3   **Socioeconomic Profiles of American Religious Groups**

Religious Group	Mean Years of Education	Percentage of College Graduates	Median Annual Household Income (in $)
Unitarian	16.39	61.1	46,158
Jewish	15.69	60.2	51,871
Episcopalian	14.84	45.5	42,953
Presbyterian USA	14.59	39.7	40,300
Congregationalist (United Church of Christ)	13.82	35.3	32,269
United Methodist	13.65	27.0	33,893
Evangelical Lutheran	13.59	23.6	29,044
No Religion	13.58	27.1	29,086
Latter-Day Saint (Mormon)	13.50	28.1	43,515
Catholic	13.15	21.7	35,788
Adventist	13.44	12.0	30,094
American Baptist	13.24	22.0	23,321
Black Baptist	12.59	19.9	23,793
Southern Baptist	12.58	16.4	28,528
Nondenominational Protestant	12.52	12.9	38,901
Jehovah's Witness	12.19	7.0	27,081
Assemblies of God	12.17	10.3	30,346
Other Pentecostal	11.81	7.0	23,174

Source: Smith and Faris (2005).

THINKING SOCIOLOGICALLY

How do the social class and religious affiliation of people you know relate to the discussion here? How do denominations with higher average levels of education (Unitarians, Jews, Episcopalians, Presbyterians, and Congregationalists) in your community differ from those with less education?

Racial Bias, Gender Prejudice, and Religion

Most religious groups profess to welcome all comers, yet most have practiced discrimination against some group at some time, often related to political and economic factors in the society. In fact, some studies show positive relationships between religion, prejudice, and discrimination (Hunsberger 1995). It is important to recognize that religion has multiple and even contradictory effects on societies. For example, most Christian denominations have formal statements that reject racial prejudice as un-Christian. The meaning system teaches tolerance. However, informal group norms in a local congregation—the belonging system—may be tolerant of ethnic jokes and may foster distrust of certain races (Woodberry and Smith 1998). Among United States whites, for instance, active church members display more prejudice than inactive church members or the unchurched (Chalfant and Peck 1983; Roberts 2004).

Prejudice may be perpetuated because promotions to larger churches are usually awarded to those ministers who are well-liked, who have growing and harmonious churches, and whose churches are financially sound.

Ministers are sometimes reluctant to speak out forcefully on controversial issues or for racial equality for fear of offending their parishioners. Bishops may not promote a minister to a larger church if his or her current congregation is racked with dissention and donations have declined. Even though the

A Methodist minister blesses the cup before offering the sacrament of communion to her congregation.

Source: Photo courtesy of Reverend Vickie Perkins. Photographer: Keith Roberts.

denomination's meaning system may oppose prejudice, the structural system may reward clergy who do not defend that meaning system (Campbell and Pettigrew 1959; Quinley 1974; Roberts 2004; Thomas 1985).

Women have often been the main volunteers and the most faithful attendees in congregations, and in some denominations they hold leadership positions (Woodberry and Smith 1998); yet they have often been denied entrance into the halls of power or equality within religious organizations. In many Islamic religious groups, the religion gives men the dominant position, though women must be treated with respect. They must be covered, including their faces, and cannot enter certain areas of the mosque when men are present. In some Christian denominations, religious rules regarding attire and hair length also help to reinforce differentiation. Men may enter a Christian cathedral in Europe with very few restrictions, but women must cover their heads so God will not be offended; this symbolizes and communicates the presumed differences between women and men before God (Douglas 1966). Literal teachings of many religions legitimate treating women differently, often in ways that disallow leadership opportunities and imply inferiority.

Within Christian groups, women have traditionally played one of two roles: silence and obedience to men in religious authority or specialized subordinate roles within the religious group. Many deeply religious women have been concerned over the lack of really significant roles for women and have fought for reformation within their religions. Ordination of women is a newly won right in several denominations (Dudley 1996); for instance, a study of Seventh-Day Adventists found very positive attitudes toward female pastors, and female Anglican clergy in the United Kingdom felt they brought important skills and strengths to their ministries (Robbins 1998).

Seventy-one percent of the public in the United States who express a religious preference favor having women as pastors, ministers, priests, or rabbis, compared to 42 percent in 1977 (Gallup Poll 2000). Still, some religious groups do not ordain women into the ministry or the priesthood. Because such leadership statuses are important symbolic positions, many women feel that this refusal helps sacralize the social stereotype of women as less capable.

While most mainline Christian denominations now have official statements on the equality of women and formal policies against discrimination in ordaining or hiring women pastors, the official meaning system does not tell the whole story. Local congregational search committees who screen and hire new ministers care deeply about the survival and health of the local church. While studies show that such persons are themselves not opposed to women in the pulpit, they believe that others in their church would be offended and would stop coming and giving money to the church. Thus, local belonging and structural systems of the religion may perpetuate unequal treatment of clergywomen even if the meaning system says they are equal (Chaves 1999; Lehman 1980, 1981, 1985; Robbins 1998).

Given these frustrations, some women have been uncomfortable working for reform from within and have left traditional religions to form new structures in which they can worship as equals, including NRMs. Indeed, women in the Western world have, throughout history, been more likely than men to opt for unconventional forms of religion (McGuire 2002).

In some instances, religion may reinforce and legitimate social prejudices toward racial groups or toward women; in others, religion may be a powerful force for change and for greater equality in a society. Seldom does religion take a passive or entirely disinterested position on these matters. Consider conflicts around the world, many of which are based on religious and class differences; people are fighting and dying for their religious beliefs. In Rwanda, Tutsi and Hutu tribespeople slaughtered each other. In Belfast, Ireland, bombs sent civilians to their graves or to hospitals, maimed for life. In India, Muslims and Hindus continue to massacre each other. Protestant against Catholic, Shiite Muslim against Sunni Muslim, Jew against Muslim, Christian against Jew—religion elicits strong emotions and influences people's definition of reality. Ethnocentric beliefs can be reinforced by religious beliefs. Religion has been the apparent cause of wars and social strife, but it has also been the motivation for altruism and a major contributor to social solidarity.

THINKING SOCIOLOGICALLY

From what you know about the status of minority groups and women, how are problems they face in religion and other institutions (education, politics, economics) similar?

RELIGION IN NORTH AMERICA

Name almost any religion and a group representing that belief system can probably be found in the United Kingdom, United States, Canada, Kenya, and several other countries where religious tolerance is the norm. Consider the United States; religious pluralism was a founding principle since Roger Williams settled in Rhode Island.

Is Religion Dying or Revitalizing?

"Is God Dead?" was the question on the cover of *Time Magazine* on April 8, 1966. The headline put into focus a question many were asking and continue to ask about religious life: is it declining? Although it has appeared at various times that society was becoming secular and religion was fading in influence, religion is a fundamental, integral part of the American culture (Christiano et al. 2002; Stark 2000). While the demise of religion may appear at times to be imminent, religion readjusts to changes in society and takes on new forms. The latter half of the twentieth century saw a wide range of religious groups forming and growing in

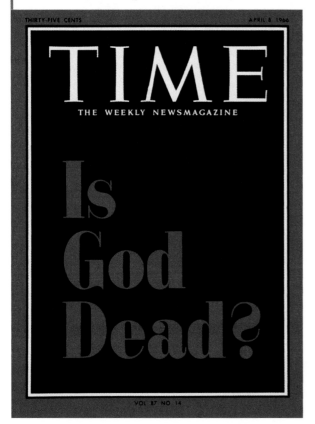

people's lives. Map 12.3 also shows that Americans report high levels of attendance at religious worship services, but as you can see, there are significant geographical variations.

TABLE 12.4	**Leading Religious Indicators**
Belief in God	81%[a]
Member of a church	64%[a]
Attended church in past 7 days	35%[a]
Religion *very important* in life	61%[b]
Religion answers problems	65%[c]
High confidence in organized religion	56%[c]

[a]Gallup Poll (2006).
[b]Gallup Poll (2004).
[c]Gallup Poll (2001).

How important is religion in your life? (in %)			
	Very	**Fairly**	**Not Very**
2005	59	25	16
2000	59	29	12
1995	58	29	12

Source: Newport (2006).

Not only do 56 percent of Americans sampled indicate a high confidence in organized religion, more confidence than in politics and other institutions, but religious membership has shown an increase over the past three centuries (Gallup Poll 2001). In the "good old days" of American colonialism, only about 17 percent of the population belonged to a church. Religious membership rose fairly steadily from the 1770s until the 1960s. While there has been a modest decline in the past 30 years, membership has fluctuated between 64 and 70 percent since 1992 (Newport 2006; Roberts 2004); 2005 membership in mosques synagogues, or churches, was reported at 64 percent of the adult population (Newport 2006). Another measure of religious strength is belief in God. Gallup Poll results have for three decades indicated that 93 percent of the population in the United States believes in God or a universal spirit or higher power (Newport 2004). Attendance at weekly worship is shown in Figure 12.3.

The relative vibrancy of religion in North America is also seen in the work of Canadian sociologist Reginald Bibby (1987a, 1987b, 2002); he confirms that religion remains strong as an influence in Canadian life. Religious adherence in that country has remained at nearly 90 percent for the past four decades; half the population reports having had a personal religious experience, three out of four claim to pray at least occasionally, and overall religious membership in Canada has continued to increase every decade (Bibby 2002). These rates are higher than that for other religiously pluralistic nations and higher than most nations with state religions. In relation to other countries the United States and Canada are religious; current trends show mainline denominations

North America, from the occult and astrology to Moonies and from New Age spirituality to Zen Buddhism. Furthermore, middle-class Catholics and Episcopalians were "speaking in tongues" and "the fervent evangelical culture could not be classified as 'marginal' when successive presidents"—Ford, Carter, Reagan, and Bush—openly claimed membership in it and to being born-again (Marty 1983). The religiosity of President George W. Bush was a political factor in his reelection in the 2004 election (Green and Silk 2005).

Many sociologists of religion document the vitality of American religion with an array of empirical data (Finke and Stark 1993; Hadden 1987; Stark 2000). Polling data indicate that 41 percent of U.S. Christians identify themselves as born-again or Evangelical Christians (Gallup Poll 2006). This means that roughly 60 million Americans attest to some sort of personal religious experience or personal commitment, and that does not include those who are Jewish, Muslim, or New Age who have had profound religious experiences (Roberts 2004).

A look at the data gives a picture of trends in religion over time. Those trends show more stability than the "God is dead" fear warrants. Table 12.4 shows results from a Gallup Poll regarding indicators of the importance of religion in

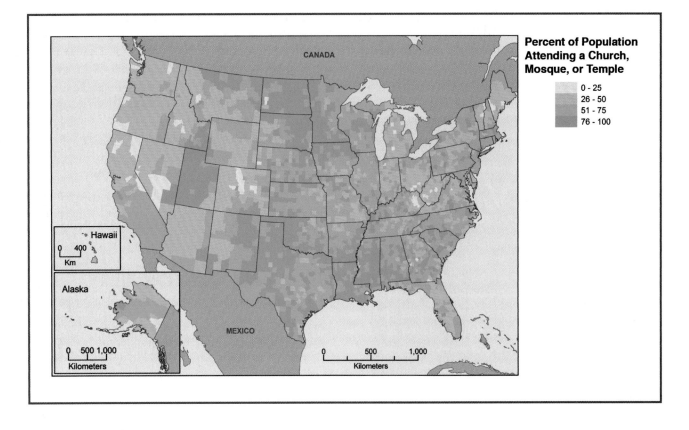

MAP 12.3   Percent of U.S. Population Affiliated with a Church, Mosque, or Temple

Source: Religious Congregations and Membership Study, 2000. Map by Anna Versluis.

Note: This map is based on data reported by local congregations and includes both members and other regular attendees; it does not represent weekly attendance. The numbers indicate an over-reporting, but that does not change the overall geographical pattern of religious affiliation.

losing members while fundamentalist and Pentecostal groups are growing, as are Evangelical megachurches (congregations with 10,000 to 35,000 members).

Antimodern religious groups, those favoring old, traditional values, have prospered in recent years in North America. Attempts to counter the bureaucratic denominational structures and to meet the longing for a simple, ordered, homogeneous world without complications, complexity, or pluralism have increased. Such groups appeal to those who want clear meaning, interpretations, and answers, and who want an authority to dictate right and wrong and a community of like-minded individuals who share beliefs (Ammerman 1988, 1990).

Among Protestants and Catholics, the largest groups in the United States, there are fluctuations but not dramatic declines in members. Almost two-thirds of Protestants and over 80 percent of Catholics say they are members of a particular church. Although there has been some decline in church attendance (mostly among Catholics) and in church membership (mostly among Protestants), religion is still important to most Americans (Bibby 2002; Gallup and Lindsay 1999).

The Process of Secularization

Secularization refers to the diminishing influence and role of religion in everyday life; instead of religion being the dominant institution, it is but one. Secularization involves a movement away from supernatural and sacred interpretations of the world and toward decisions based on empirical evidence and logic. Before modern scientific explanations and technology, religion helped explain the unexplainable. However, the scientific method, emphasis on logical reasoning, and the belief that there are many different religious interpretations rather than one have challenged religious and spiritual approaches to the world. Although religion is still strong in the lives of individuals, it does not have the extensive control of education, health, politics, or family that it once did; it is an institution among others rather than being the dominant one.

Some scholars have argued that secularization is an inevitable and unstoppable force in the modern and post-industrial world (Berger 1961, 1990; Beyer 2000; Dobbelaere 1981, 2000). Others argue that secularization is far from inevitable and has almost reached its limit (Hadden 1987; Stark 2000; Swatos and Gissurarson 1997; Warner 1993).

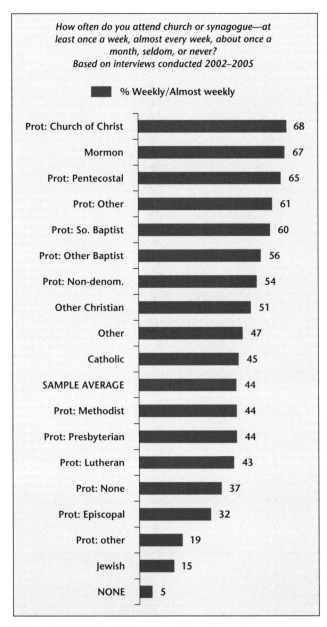

Figure 12.3 Church/Synagogue Attendance

Source: Newport (2006)

Our social world model helps us understand that, like religion, secularization is a complex phenomenon that occurs at several levels and affects each society differently (Beyer 2000; Chaves and Gorski 2001; Yamane 1997).

Secularization may be occurring at the societal level but not at the individual level in the United States (Bellah et al. 1996; Chaves 1993; Chaves and Gorski 2001). Thus, when faith does not guide people's everyday lives—their conduct on the job, in political choices, in regard to sexual behavior, in the science classroom, or in attitudes toward racial relations—then secularization at the micro level would have occurred. Three out of four U.S. citizens believe that "a

person should come to their moral views independent of any church or synagogue" (Yamane 1997:116), and many people insist they are "spiritual but not religious" (Roof 1999).

Within church-related organizations (Baptist hospitals, Presbyterian colleges, Jewish social service foundations), if the decisions about how to deliver services or who will be hired or fired are based on systematic policies designed for organizational efficiency, then meso-level secularization is present within a religious organization (Chaves 1993). If policies in the society at large are made with little discussion of theological implications—decisions being based on human rights arguments rather than on what is sinful—then society has become secular at the societal level (Chaves 1993; Dobbelaere 1981, 2000; Yamane 1997). (See Table 12.5.) Debates about prayer in schools, court decisions about "one nation under God" in the pledge of allegiance to the flag, and involvement of religious leaders in political issues suggest that societal-level secularization is a point of controversy in the United States. Still, few will deny that the bureaucratic structures of the United States and virtually every other postindustrial nation are thoroughly secularized. Macro, meso, and micro secularization do not seem to be in harmony.

Most sociologists of religion believe that religion continues to be a powerful force at the individual level and that it has some influence in the larger culture (the macro level). They maintain there is a trend toward secularization in most Western societies but that the trend is neither inevitable nor uniform across societies (Dobbelaere 2000; Lambert 2000; Sommerville 2002; Wilson 1982; Yamane 1997).

At a global level, no particular theological authority has power to define reality or to determine policies, religious authority structures are minimal, and secularization is well established. Perhaps, this is one reason why conservatives of nearly every religious faith are leery of global processes and global organizations, such as the United Nations; our global organizations are governed by rational-legal authority, not religious doctrines.

THINKING SOCIOLOGICALLY

Do you think it creates problems in a society if that society is secularized at the meso and macro levels but not at the micro level? Why?

SOCIAL POLICY: THE HOMOSEXUALITY DEBATES

Gays in the church, gay marriage, ordination of gay ministers—these issues make for heated debate over church policy and even threaten to split some denominations. Most established religious groups assume the normality of heterosexuality. Marriage is sanctified by religious ceremony in all major

PHOTO ESSAY

Prayer in Schools?

Secularization involves the diminishing influence of religion in everyday life. In many places and in the United States in the past, prayer in schools was commonly accepted; public institutions and religious life were merged. Today in the United States, pluralism and separation of church and state have led to secularization at the macro and meso levels, even though religion still has profound influence at the micro level. This has led to great controversies about religious expression within schools, where children are socialized into the values of the society.

▲ Mongolian children praying at school.

Source: © Setboun/Corbis.

▼ A group of young students pray in a classroom in Hossein Abad, Iran.

Source: © Jean Guichard/Sygma Corbis.

▼ First graders share a moment of silent prayer at the start of their school day in a South Carolina school in 1966.

Source: © Betttmann/Corbis.

TABLE 12.5	**The Complexity of Secularization in the Social World**	
	Institutional Differentiation	**Rational/Utilitarian Decision Making**
Macro Level	Institutions in the society, including government and education, and the economy, are functionally independent and autonomous of religious organizations.	Decision making about social policies are based on cost-benefit analyses, using logic and empirical data rather than scripture or proclamations of religious authorities.
Meso Level	Organizations look to other social associations and units that have similar functions and goals for accepted practices of how to operate the organization, and not to religious organizations and authorities.	Decision making about an organization's policies and goals are based on utilitarian analyses and consequences, rather than on scripture, theological arguments, or proclamations of religious authorities.
Micro Level	Individuals emphasize being "spiritual rather than religious," formulate their own meaning system or theology, and may believe that spirituality has little to do with other aspects of their lives.	Decision making about life decisions is based on individual self-interest without concern for the teachings of the religious group or the clergy; calculations of cost and benefit to the individual are foremost in individual decisions.

Source: Roberts (2004).

religious groups, but recently some denominations have openly debated the possibility of recognizing church weddings for gays and lesbians. In the Christian tradition, there are six passages in scripture that condemn homosexual relationships, only one of which condemns lesbian relationships (Genesis 19:1–28; Leviticus 18:22, 20:13; Romans 1:26–27; I Corinthians 6:9; I Timothy 1:10). Opposition to homosexuality is especially high among religious fundamentalists. In recent years, there have been strident conflicts in the Presbyterian (U.S.) and United Methodist denominations, but in the most conservative denominations few questions are even raised by homosexuality (such as ordination of clergy; same-sex marraige by an ordained minister; and formal statements condemning homosexuality as a sin). The rightness of absolute heterosexuality is taken for granted.

THINKING SOCIOLOGICALLY

The film *Brokeback Mountain* depicting two gay men struggling with their sexuality and with societal expectations shows the power of norms, including religious beliefs, to influence the lives of gay and bisexual men and women. How is this conflict depicted in the film, and what role does religion play in the conflict?

Liberals in the churches tend to see this issue as one of prejudice against persons for a characteristic that is immutable; they assume that homosexuality is an inborn trait. Conservatives argue that homosexuality is a choice that has moral implications. They tend to see homosexuality as a behavior that is acquired through socialization; therefore acceptance of homosexuality will likely increase the numbers of people who engage in this lifestyle. Conservatives see liberal notions about

homosexuality and gender roles as a threat to society and family, a threat to the moral social order, whereas liberals often feel that sexuality within a committed relationship is not a moral issue but shows lack of tolerance of other lifestyles.

Some mainstream denominations have developed policies supportive of lesbian, gay, and bisexual persons in local churches: More Light (Presbyterian), Open and Affirming (United Church of Christ and Christian Church), Reconciled in Christ (Lutheran), and Reconciling Congregations (Methodist). These designations apply to approximately 300 congregations that wish to be known as "gay and lesbian friendly" (www.mlp.org/resources/history). A new denomination, Universal Fellowship of Metropolitan Community Churches (UFMCC), affirms homosexuality as a legitimate lifestyle for Christians (Rodriguez and Ouellette 2000). It has more than 300 local churches in the United States. One study conducted on a UFMCC congregation in New York found that homosexuals affiliated with this church have exceptionally positive personal adjustment; they are more likely to have an integrated self-concept as both a gay person and as a religious person (Rodriguez and Ouellette 2000). Religious persons who are homosexual and members of traditional congregations struggle with a lesser sense of self-integration.

One of the most controversial issues in several mainline denominations is over ordination of homosexuals as ministers. A Gallup Poll shows a shift toward acceptance of homosexual clergy by the majority of Americans: 53 percent approved in 1996 as opposed to 36 percent in 1977 (Gallup and Lindsay 1999: 87). In 2005, 49 percent of a sample felt homosexuals should be ordained as clergy (Gallup Poll 2004). Still, most denominations do not knowingly ordain homosexuals as ministers and do not allow their ministers to perform marriages or "holy unions" of two gay men or two lesbian women. If ministers do so, they may be defrocked as ministers.

The right of same-sex couples to marry continues to be controversial in the United States, but it has been settled as law in Canada, where this couple ties the knot.

Source: © Reuters/Corbis.

Some ministers continue to perform marriage ceremonies as a protest against a policy they think is immoral. They may take a "don't ask, don't tell" position with their bishops. One retired minister estimated that even in his very conservative Midwestern state, there are roughly 50 homosexual holy unions performed by Methodist pastors each year. He stated,

> Back in the 1950s, ministers could lose their ordination and ministerial privileges if they married someone in a church wedding who had been divorced. Performing a marriage of someone who had been divorced was a serious offense in the Methodist church—and in most other Protestant churches, too. If a divorced person wanted to marry a second time, a civil wedding was supposedly the only option. Many of us in the pastorate thought that the policy was inhumane. These were people whom we pastored; they had made a mistake in a previous selection of a spouse and wanted to start again. Many clergy secretly went against formal policy of the church, but we did not tell our bishops. By the 1960s, if the church purged all of us who had done this, the Methodist church would have lost more than half of its ministers. In another 20 years, the same thing will be true with holy unions. If you have two people in your congregation who really care for each

other and want to ritually affirm their lifelong commitment, how can we not honor that commitment and caring? I think it is a matter of time before this will become widely accepted. (Roberts 2004:299)

One study has documented a softening of opposition to homosexual rights among religiously committed people (Petersen and Donnenwerth 1998). Even where there are strong reservations about marriage of gays or lesbians, there is support for nondiscrimination in other areas such as jobs.

In our social world, religious organizations influence society and the larger society influences religious groups. Moreover, attitudes in a local community or a region of the country influence attitudes within a congregation, irrespective of the positions of the official denomination (Koch and Curry 2000). Two catalysts are creating tension for change in religious organizations: (1) the emphasis on the equality of all people before God in Christian theology and (2) an impetus in the larger society that legitimates people in leadership roles based on competence and commitment rather than on traits beyond their control (skin color, gender, or sexual orientation).

Thus, the policy issues for all religious communities are (1) whether a homosexual person can ever have the spiritual qualities to lead a congregation as its minister; (2) whether that faith community should or should not endorse and permit same-sex marriages in their churches, mosques, or temples; and (3) whether faith groups should be involved in government policy regarding the right of the state to grant marriage licenses to homosexuals or other civil unions—a secular equivalent to the marriage contract that would allow over 1,000 rights and privileges that heterosexuals enjoy. One proposed solution is that, since marriage has historically been "owned" by religious communities, the state could grant licenses for civil unions (not marriages) for both homosexuals and heterosexuals. Faith communities alone would decide whether they acknowledge a couple as married. The notion that the state should have any say in the matter of marriage only began with Martin Luther, who insisted that marriage was not a sacrament. These highly contested areas of public policy continue to be contentious.

THINKING SOCIOLOGICALLY

How is hostility toward homosexuals similar and different from sexism and racism? Does religion play a role in heterosexism and homophobia? Why?

RELIGION IN THE MODERN WORLD

Religion and Peace

Can religion bring peace to the world? Most religious systems advocate living in harmony with other humans and with nature, yet often peace is not the reality. Some religions that believe they have the only Truth defend themselves or try to spread "the true word" by force. Other religious groups lie at the roots of cultural differences, which cause ethnocentrism and sometimes hatred, and individuals fight and die to defend their belief systems and way of life. Fundamentalist religious groups use strategies to attempt to preserve their distinctive identity as a people or group (Marty and Appleby 1991, 2004); they seldom believe in pluralism or tolerance of other beliefs but rather believe they are the only true religion. Consequently, they resist and defend themselves against modernism that threatens their beliefs and way of life or try to spread the "true word," sometimes by force (Billings and Scott 1994; Lamy 1996; Stern 2003; Wessinger 2000). Members of fundamentalist groups—be they Orthodox Jews, traditional Muslims, or born-again Christians—generally believe in a literal interpretation of their holy books and a personal experience with Allah or God. Some fundamentalist groups remove themselves from the secular world, including politics, but other fundamentalist groups are active in politics.

Conflict between religious groups is especially intense if ethnic, economic, and religious differences enter in. Consider Ireland where the main landowners are Protestants of Scottish descent. The laborers are predominantly native Irish in ethnicity and are Roman Catholic. Hatred between Protestants and Catholics is exacerbated by the lack of cross-cutting loyalties or friendships (McGuire 2002). Frustrations of groups not in power lead to ethnocentrism and sometimes hatred against others. Those in power similarly develop stereotypes about those unlike themselves whose ideology and values are different. Cross-cutting social cleavages reduce social hostilities, as Figure 12.4 illustrates.

British soldiers watch as Orange men gather in front of a security wall that was constructed by soldiers at Drumcree Church in Portadown, Northern Ireland. (July 5, 2000)

Source: © Reuters/Corbis.

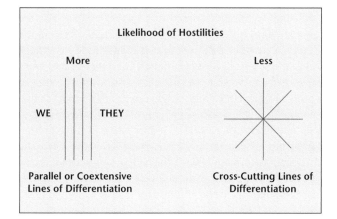

Figure 12.4 Lines of Differentiation between "We" and "They"

Note: Imagine that each line represents a division in the society between groups based on religion, ethnicity, political party, economic status, language spoken, skin color, or other factors. Parallel lines of differentiation divide people in each conflict along the same lines. *Cross-cutting lines* cut the differences so that people who were part of "they" in a previous antagonism become part of "we" in the present discord. This lessens the likelihood of deep and permanent hostilities within a social unit.

Religion has the greatest potential for reducing hatred between groups when those groups share some type of common identification. If the conflict is over ethnicity and economics, a common religious heritage can lessen the likelihood of violent confrontation. Some religious groups have joined together in peaceful enterprises such as attempts to ban nuclear weapons or to bring about peace in the Middle East. This common purpose provides for cooperation and collaboration, thus lessening animosity and we-versus-they thinking.

Perhaps the core reason that some countries are secular is because of history; the conflicts in Europe between religions were very brutal, beginning with the bloodletting in the Hundred Years' War. From that time, "religion was the sixteenth century word for nationalism" (Wallerstein 2005:125), the intense religious in-group loyalties led to a willingness to kill those who were Other. The horrific religious conflicts in European societies did not reach closure until the Enlightenment; at this time, tolerance of other religions became dominant and a primary foundation for determining national policy (Dobbelaere 1981, 2000; Lambert 2000).

As we have seen, the disconnect between micro and macro levels—religious passion at the micro level and secular domination at the macro level—has resulted in severe tensions around the world (Wallerstein 2005). For instance, in the United States, the movement is toward increasing religiosity at the micro level and increasing secularism at the macro level.

Christian, Islamic, Jewish, and other world faiths sponsor a variety of programs aimed at health care, hunger relief, and easing of suffering caused by natural disasters. Prior to

This is a large Buddha image in the famous Wat Xieng Thong temple complex in Luang Prabang, Laos. Wat Xieng Thong was built by King Saisetthathirat in 1560 and is located on a peninsula between the Mekong and Khan rivers in northern Laos.

Source: Photo courtesy of Elise Roberts.

the 1700s, remarkably few efforts had been made to reach out to persons in other cultures. Moreover, from 1700 until well into the twentieth century, outreach programs were aimed almost exclusively at trying to convert the "heathen," those with belief systems that differed (Hunter 1983; Lee 1992).

Liberal theologies suggest that God may speak to people through a variety of channels, including scientific findings and revelations proclaimed by other religious traditions. While leaders may feel their beliefs provide the fullest and most complete expression of God's Truth, leaders recognize that other beliefs also provide paths to Truth. Many global religious programs today are ecumenical and aimed at humanitarian relief rather than proselytizing.

The rise of religious fundamentalism in the twentieth century, whether Islamic, Buddhist, Hasidic Jewish, Evangelical Christian, or Malaysian Dukway, appears to be a reaction against global modernization (Davidman 1990; Robertson

1989; Robertson and Garrett 1991; Shupe and Hadden 1989; Turner 1991a). Rapid global change has resulted in anomie as people confront change—fear obliteration of their own culture, encroaching secularization of the society as the supernatural realm shrinks, threat to the material self-interests of religious organizations, and fear of interdependence with powerful nations of the Western world. All of these threats have strengthened fundamentalism.

THINKING SOCIOLOGICALLY

What specific religious beliefs or behaviors might influence the way in which religions and countries relate to one another? How might religious organizations influence international relations?

Religion, Technology, and the World Wide Web

Religion not only impacts nations but is also impacted by social trends and global networks. Consider technology and the Internet. From television broadcasts of megachurch services to Muslim chat rooms using technology to communicate, religious messages travel in new ways.

The printing press is an interesting example. Prior to the wide distribution of religious texts to people who are not ordained ministers, the hierarchies of Christendom controlled what was disseminated as Truth. The common (and typically illiterate) member of the local church did not have any basis for challenging the Pope or other church leaders. Those leaders were the authority. However, Martin Luther used the printed word in many powerful ways. He and other reformers claimed that the Bible alone was the ultimate source of Truth and religious authority. The church leaders were to be believed only insofar as they were faithful to the scriptures. Luther himself used the printed word to spread his version of Christian Truth, and he did so with a vengeance. He not only wrote more than other dissenters, he out-published the entire legion of defenders of the Vatican (Brasher 2004). He published in the common languages of the people rather than in Latin, and the Protestant Reformation was launched. It is doubtful that this could have happened without the printing press. The printing press had similar revolutionary effects within Judaism (Brasher 2004).

Today, television and multimedia worship have enhanced the marketing of religion, including the modification of the product to meet "consumer" demand (Frankl 1987; Hadden and Shupe 1988; Roberts 2004; Sargeant 2000). The Internet is the most recent technology with potential for enormous impacts. Brasher (2004) reports that there are more than a million religion websites and they cover an extraordinarily wide range of religious beliefs and practices. Even conservative Christians such as Jerry Falwell—who dubbed the internet an evil Tower of Babel—have used it to spread their message. Indeed, the panic over whether the turn of the millennium (Y2K) would result in massive crashes in computers around the world was related to the end of the world by some conservative Christians (Brasher 2004; Lamy 1996). The computer, in short, would be the medium to bring an end to life in this world.

Inherent contradictions exist between the notions of time and authority, and between technology and tradition (Brasher 2004). The medium of the Internet is fast-paced and oriented to the now. Technology is often outdated in a few years if not in a few months. The past hardly seems a source of authority or of Truth. Yet traditional religious communities often excel in maintaining and propagating memories of past events that give meaning to life or that defined notions of sacredness and Truth. It is too early to tell for sure what impacts these most recent technologies might have on religions around the world. One thing is clear: the Internet allows instant access to information about religions that otherwise might be obscure or nonexistent for many people.

SO WHAT?

Religion is a powerful force in the lives of people around the world. It typically elicits passions and deep loyalties, and in so doing it can stimulate people to great acts of self-sacrificing charity or it can elicit horrible atrocities and intergroup bigotries. People's religious affiliation is strongly related to their nationality, ethnic and racial group, and lifestyle. Religion is the one institution in most societies that consistently professes a desire for peace and good will, yet there may be inconsistencies between what people say and what they do. At its very best, religion provides us with hope that the world's problems can be dealt with in humanitarian ways.

Religion provides a sense of meaning in life regarding the big questions, and that is why things religious come to have sacred meaning. They address our spiritual life and our sense of purpose. Humans, however, are not just spiritual; they are also deeply concerned about their physical health—their bodies. The final institution we will examine in this text is medicine, and as in this chapter on religion, we will find that social dynamics and social patterns are extremely important in understanding health and illness in our complex social world.

CONTRIBUTING TO YOUR SOCIAL WORLD

At the Local Level: Most religious groups sponsor social service outreach in their local communities, their nations, or around the world. They jointly sponsor soup kitchens, food pantries, or thrift stores for the poor, and they welcome help. Individual religious groups have service and peace projects. Check groups' websites for volunteer or work opportunities.

At the Organizational or Institutional Level: Consider getting involved with the housing problem in the United States through a service organization founded by a religious group. One of these is *Habitat for Humanity* (www.habitat.com), "a nonprofit (international) ecumenical Christian housing organization building simple, decent, affordable housing in partnership with people in need." It is a global macro-level organization working at the community micro level.

At the National and Global Levels: Some religious groups are committed to working for justice and peace at the national and global levels. The following are just two examples of peace and justice organizations.

Tikkun Community (www.tikkun.org) is an ecumenical organization, started in the Jewish community to "mend, repair, and transform the world. . . . International community of people of many faiths calling for social justice and political freedom in the context of new structures of work, caring, communities and democratic social and economic arrangements."

American Friends Service Committee (www.afsc.org) is "a Quaker organization which includes people of various faiths who are committed to social justice, peace, and humanitarian service." Sponsors many relief and peace projects around the world.

Visit **www.pineforge.com/ballantinestudy** for online activities, sample tests, and other helpful information. Select "Chapter 12: Religion" for chapter-specific activities.

CHAPTER

13

MEDICINE:
An Anatomy
of Health
and Illness

What to Expect . . .

**Health and illness are fundamentally social matters,
influenced by social interactions, affected by complex
organizations intended to provide health care, and
shaped by social policies at national and global
levels. A true anatomy of health and illness involves
comprehension of the social implications of medicine.**

Think About It . . .

1. What does it mean to be sick? Healthy?

2. How are you diagnosed and cared for?

3. Which health care systems keep people healthiest?

4. Is health care a right for all or a privilege for those who can afford it?

5. What are variations in health care around the world?

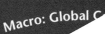

Macro: Global C

Macro: National Society

Meso: State and National Institutions; Ethnic Subcultures

Micro: Local Organizations and Community

**Micro:
You and Your Family**

Micro: Local health care providers; health influences churches, community schools, and the local business world

Meso: State governments regulate health care; economy influences health care availability; political elections hinge on government responses to problems such as epidemics

Macro: National governments develop policies to support those with serious illnesses; federal governments fund research to cure diseases

Debbie, a 20-year-old woman in Portland, Oregon, lay in pain, dying from ovarian cancer. She had not eaten or slept in two days and was struggling for air. Her words to the physician were, "Let's get this over with." In this case of *medical futility*, in which treatment "fails to end total dependence on intensive medical care," the physician relieved her suffering with a syringe of morphine sulfate; she began breathing normally and shortly thereafter died as a result of the physician-assisted suicide (American Medical Association 1988). This case and others like it raise great controversy in medical, legal, and religious communities.

Allowing individuals to choose death to relieve the irreversible suffering of an incurable disease and allowing physicians to hasten the death of terminally ill patients is accepted by proponents of *active euthanasia* ("good death"). This involves aiding the dying individual by prescribing or administering a lethal dose of drugs to patients who request it, usually under legally controlled conditions. A majority of deaths of terminally ill individuals are planned and sometimes hastened by medical interventions (Working Group on Assisted Suicide and End-of-Life Decisions 2000). In addition, anyone can sign a living will or right-to-die form requesting that no extraordinary efforts be made to help one stay alive (passive euthanasia). However, opponents see aiding death as a sin or even murder.

Those who favor euthanasia argue that (1) physicians should be able to create comfortable environments for death to occur; (2) terminally ill individuals have a right—without interference by the state—to determine how they die and to make the decision to die; (3) legal safeguards are available to prevent abuse of physician-assisted suicide; (4) high rates of self-induced suicide already exist among terminally ill patients; (5) a majority of the public favors legalization of physician-assisted suicides; and (6) extending life with no hope of recovery is costly to the medical care system and to families.

Those opposed to euthanasia argue that (1) physicians are responsible to sustain life and relieve suffering; (2) medical measures are available to relieve pain so few have to suffer; (3) religious beliefs often point to the sanctity of life and allowing life to take its natural course; (4) some terminally ill individuals may request to die because they are depressed or they feel pressured into suicide; and (5) allowing terminally ill patients to commit suicide may make suicide a more acceptable option for those people who are depressed, disabled, elderly, or retarded (Weiss and Lonnquist 2006).

Some countries and states have passed laws legalizing and controlling euthanasia. In the Netherlands, doctors can assist patients in dying but only under very strict regulations. In Oregon, a law that has been challenged in the courts requires that two or more doctors must agree that the patient has six or fewer months to live, and the patient must also ask to die at three different times, the last time in writing, in order for doctors to be able to act on the request. Doctors have to wait 15 days before complying with the patient's wishes (Werth et al. 2002).

Dying is not something that just happens. How we die, where we die, who is with us when we die, and whether we have choice about when to die are decisions bound in cultural values, beliefs, and laws. Death and its various issues are but one aspect of the interrelationship between our physical condition and our social system. This chapter illustrates that events surrounding health, illness, and death are social events governed by rules of the social world.

Dr. Kevorkian (right) is accompanied to court in Michigan. He was tried and found guilty of helping people who were in severe pain and who no longer wanted to live to commit suicide.

Source: © Mears D / Corbis Sygma.

WHY IS HEALTH A SOCIAL ISSUE?

In the West African country of Nigeria, fundamentalist religious leaders in the northern part of the country refused to allow international medical teams to immunize children against polio, resulting in an outbreak of this crippling disease that had almost been eradicated in the world. The religious leaders had little trust in the motives of Western medical teams. However, when the epidemic broke out and children began dying, the leadership relented and allowed the immunization programs to take place. This illustration of health at the global level points out how individual decisions have an effect on health of a community and shows the importance of medical organizations and their efforts to control world pandemics such as polio, AIDS, SARS, bird flu, and other epidemics.

Health is a state of physical, mental, and social well-being, or the absence of disease. Illness, or lack of health, affects the way we perform our individual responsibilities in the social world. Like any key social issue, effective health care affects individuals and groups at the micro, meso, and macro levels.

The Micro Level

Sociologists are concerned with how our state of health affects our individual ability to carry out social responsibilities. Everyday lives are shaped by our own state of health or illness and that of our loved ones and close associates. If a roommate, significant other, or child is ill, it affects our lives in a number of ways: it alters our schedules, takes time as we deal with the illness, causes us to worry, and costs us in terms of medical care and lost work time. If a parent is dying of cancer or a child has epilepsy, our lives are influenced in profound and disruptive ways.

Communities are responsible for providing adequate health care, sanitation, and clean drinking water to citizens, services that affect the health of citizens. Community activities are also affected by the health of citizens; a serious case of influenza in the public schools may force schools to close for several days, causing repercussions in workplaces throughout the community as parents struggle to deal with child care issues. Thus, health status affects other institutions in the community, from family to schools to the workplace.

The Meso Level

The institution of health care provides for the physical, mental, and social well-being of citizens; this includes prevention, diagnosis, and treatment of illness and regulation of the dispensing of medicine. The health care institution works together with families, education, religion, politics, and economics; what happens in the system of health care affects every part of the social world, as shown in the example of assisted suicide. The economic well-being of individuals in a society relates to health care access and who can pay. This often determines who lives, who dies, who is healthy, and who is not. Education about health care influences health and life expectancy; well-educated citizens are more likely to develop health-enhancing lifestyles. Families attempt to prevent illness and care for sick individuals and often have responsibility to care for the ill and ailing. Political systems determine standards for health care and regulate medicinal drugs. Religious organizations establish support systems and health services, sometimes offer faith healing alternatives to supplement the established medical system, and offer solace in times of illness and death.

The Macro Level

Each *society* has a vested interest in the health of its citizenry because the general state of health affects the quality of life of the people and the state of the economy. Imagine the society in which citizens had "permission" to be sick frequently. How would that society continue to function? Societies have social policies that influence the way medicine is organized and health services are delivered. Beliefs about who is ill with what kinds of illness and for how long vary by society.

Consider the case of the now dissolved Soviet Union. After the Soviet victory over Czarist Russia in 1917, the new revolutionary government was faced with an

After walking many miles, homecare volunteer Thulile Dlamini arrives at her HIV-positive client's home in Swaziland. "I wash her clothes in the river, sometimes even the blankets, because she can't even walk to the toilet" says Dlamini, who works with the Global Fund in Swaziland.

Source: © Gideon Mendel for the Global Fund / Corbis.

Other institutions, like schools, can also affect health in a variety of ways. In the case here, one must wonder about sanitation and health, since this is the toilet facility in a Chinese school.

Source: © Kate Ballantine.

underdeveloped nation that essentially still produced its food with human-pushed plows and simple hoes. The task of leading the country out of the sixteenth century and into the twentieth was formidable. It called for a total effort from the nation's workforce. Confronted with a severe

One way to combat diarrhea diseases in India is through provision of safe drinking water by the government. This is a primary concern of the World Health Organization. However, the World Bank and International Monetary Fund have been pushing for privatization of water, meaning that water is not affordable for many.

Source: © World Health Organization (2006).

shortage of labor, the new government determined that absenteeism at work, regardless of excuse, had to be kept very low. Accordingly, they instituted rules that required workers to obtain a certificate allowing them to be absent from work because of illness (Field 1953, 1957; Weiss and Lonnquist 2006). These certificates could only be obtained from government clinics, and each clinic was limited in the number of permits it could issue. In some cases, physicians were actively encouraged to compete with one another to see how few certificates they could issue. Thus, absence due to illness was controlled and the human resources needed for rebuilding the nation were augmented.

Global health focuses on several issues: possible pandemics such as highly contagious diseases that have become worldwide threats as global travel increases, distribution of immunizations and drugs, and concerns about bioterrorism threats. One example is the HIV/AIDS epidemic that has become a *pandemic,* a disease that is prevalent throughout an entire country and may infect a continent or reach around the world. The global nature of this pandemic is illustrated

in Map 13.1. Such diseases require cooperation across national boundaries by organizations such as the United Nations if they are to be controlled. For instance, smallpox remained a serious global threat from the Middle Ages until the mid-twentieth century; the World Health Organization of the United Nations eliminated the disease completely in the 1960s. River Blindness afflicted thousands of West Africans but has been eradicated due to international cooperation. Funding by organizations such as the Bill and Melinda Gates Foundation provide for research, treatment, and eradication of killer diseases such as malaria, AIDS, and even tuberculosis. However, the threat of bioterrorism has raised the specter of other diseases such as smallpox and polio reappearing.

Illness may seem like an individual problem, but as shown in the above examples, it is far more than that. It is a national and global issue. This chapter examines health care at each level of analysis, from individual behaviors and decisions; to religious, political, and economic aspects; to the effect of stratification and ethnic status on the quality of health care one receives. Keep the social world model in mind as you read about health, illness, and medical care.

THINKING SOCIOLOGICALLY

Why do pandemic diseases require international solutions?

THEORETICAL PERSPECTIVES ON HEALTH AND ILLNESS

As in the analysis of each institution, it is important to understand how each of the major paradigms or perspectives in sociology approaches the analysis of medicine and health care. Each offers a lens for seeing or noticing different aspects of health and illness in a given society and within the global system.

Micro-Level Theoretical Perspectives

Unruly school children were once considered *ill-mannered* or *ill-behaved;* now they are often labeled as *hyperkinetic* or having *attention deficit disorder* (ADD), suffering from conditions that can be controlled by appropriate medication. Heavy gamblers, alcoholics, and drug abusers are now defined as *addicts* rather than as people lacking self-discipline. How conditions are labeled can result in social stigma of varying degrees (Freund and McGuire 1999) and to different policies to treat problems.

The Symbolic Interaction Perspective and Labeling Theory

To symbolic interactionists, illness is whatever powerful individuals in society, such as doctors, define or label it to be. In recent years, the definition of illness has expanded to

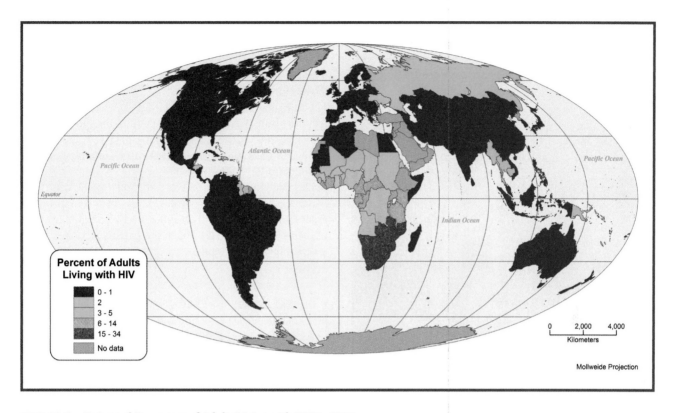

MAP 13.1 Estimated Percentage of Adults Living with HIV in 2005

Source: World Health Organization/UNAIDS (2006). Map by Anna Versluis.

encompass substance abuse and some forms of deviant behavior, giving physicians even more power and authority over broad areas of social life. Illness used to be viewed as a *physical* condition—germs, viruses, bacteria—causing the body to malfunction. Through the labeling process, behaviors that were once seen as criminal or "bad" are now defined as illness—unruly behavior, mental illness, and various addictions such as gambling and alcoholism. Some see the change in authority as a positive step toward treating these conditions, but others see it as an increase in the control and power of the medical profession.

Medicalization and Labeling
Medicalization refers to the shift in handling of some forms of deviance as well as some normal human functions (such as pregnancy and childbirth) from the familial, legal, or religious arenas to the health care system. In some cases, the shift is away from the issue of individual self-control and toward medical diagnosis and treatment. Consider addictive behaviors such as alcoholism and drug abuse. There is considerable debate about how we define *alcoholism* because this influences the interpretation of the problem, the physician's role in treatment, whether we hold the patient to blame for the problem, and how it will be treated (Cockerham 2004; Fingarette 1988; Keller 1991).

HIV-positive orphan, eight-year-old Zamokuhle Mdingwe (wearing maroon jacket), poses with his friends in the doorway of his grandmother's house in South Africa. Zamo's mother died more than a year earlier from AIDS-related infections. Since the death of his grandfather six months earlier, his grandmother has been struggling to support the family. His drugs are being provided by a nonprofit organization.

Source: © Gideon Mendel / Corbis.

There is some controversy among scholars as to the advisability of listing gambling as a medical problem, a form of addiction that needs medical diagnosis and treatment. What might be some pros, and some cons, of considering gambling a medical issue?

Source: © Diane White Rosier.

or health at the micro level is shaped by forces at other levels in our social world.

Meso- and Macro-Level Theoretical Perspectives

The institution of health care in Western culture differs dramatically from that of many other cultures around the world. Consider the conflicting ideas of illness between the Hmong culture in the United States, made up of immigrants from Vietnamese hill tribes, and the medical community. In the book, *The Spirit Catches You and You Fall Down,* Anne Fadiman (1997) describes the contacts between an immigrant Hmong family with an epileptic child and the hospital in their U.S. community. When the parents take their child for treatment of her epileptic seizures, everything from the

The label alcoholic *has a number of implications, including the fact that the stigma associated with the term may prevent some people from seeking help. This is one reason many alcohol treatment centers have recast alcoholism as a disease, hoping that the redefinition would remove stigma. Other problems arise when the issue is medicalized.*

Source: © Royalty-Free / Corbis.

Symbolic interactionists emphasize the social definitions or labels such as *alcoholic* or *drug addict* and examine the effect such labels have on the life of the individual. Medical conditions can be treated, and less stigma may be attached to these "illnesses" if they are not labeled as "moral degeneracy" (White 2002). On the other hand, labeling the alcoholic as *sick* creates another type of stigma that may never be erased, and seeing alcoholism as a medical condition takes away individual responsibility, putting control in the hands of the health care system. The next Sociology in Your Social World explores the issue of policy toward alcoholism.

Some "problems" may not be problems at all; movements to "demedicalize" various social behaviors has resulted in homosexuality being removed from the American Psychiatric Association's list of mental disorders. Furthermore, social critics argue that once conditions are medicalized, they come to be controlled and exploited by powerful experts. On the other hand, some scholars conceptualize medicalization of health issues as part of a healthy, working social system because the individual's responsibility is reduced and illness is not their fault. They argue that with stigma and blame lessened, the issues can be more effectively addressed.

Having some sense of the issues raised by the symbolic interactionists, we turn now to how the experience of illness

Sociology in Your Social World

Alcoholism and Policy

Perhaps you know someone who struggles with an alcohol problem. A hotly contested debate in the medical and psychological fields is how to define *alcoholism*, for that definition affects everything from treatment procedures to who has responsibility for rehabilitation. Is the alcoholic to be held responsible, or is this a condition beyond the individual's control? The classic disease conception of alcoholism, for instance, was first proposed in the 1930s by two reformed drinkers and given scientific support in the work of E. M. Jellinek (Jellinek 1960). In the aftermath of social and political debates (Acker 1993), key professional groups officially labeled alcoholism a disease.

The medical definition of alcoholism now includes three dimensions: biophysical, psychological, and social: "Alcoholism is a primary, chronic disease with genetic, psycho-social, and environmental factors influencing its development and manifestations. The disease is often progressive and fatal. It is characterized by impaired control over drinking, preoccupation with the drug alcohol, use of alcohol despite adverse consequences, and distortions in thinking, mostly denial. Each of these symptoms may be continuous or periodic" (Meyer 1996:163). The medical view of alcoholism has several implications: unless there is intervention, alcoholics suffer physical and emotional breakdown and an early death. Schoeman (1991) writes about those who are vulnerable:

1. There is physiological predisposition in the way their bodies process alcohol.

2. Once a person takes up drinking, he or she will become ill.

3. Drinking leads to consumption in ever greater amounts with increasingly severe consequences.

4. The disease produces a distinctive disability: loss of ability to choose when it comes to alcohol consumption.

5. Alcoholism progresses through a predictable sequence of stages, independent of individual characteristics.

Many health care professionals, however, are reluctant to treat alcoholism as a problem drug (Meyer 1996). Some argue that the disease concept is the wrong approach, that what is really at stake is "heavy drinking" as a way of life. Rather than treating a "disease," they feel that professionals should be concerned with approaches that will change the way in which individuals organize their behaviors. These researchers and practitioners argue that heavy drinkers can become nondrinkers or moderate drinkers and can control their drinking.

Changing the alcoholic by altering perceptions, routines, attitudes, and habits of behavior gives the individual responsibility in a context of supportive family or friends, economic opportunities, and alternative role models. A third possibility exists—that there is truth in both models based on individual differences. Treatment programs can be found based on both of these models, and the debate is still going strong.

---

concepts of what causes the problem, to the cures, to communication about the disease are problematic. The medical staff treats the epileptic seizures with Western medical techniques, whereas the Hmong family attribute the seizures to spirits (Fadiman 1997). Concepts of health and disease vary greatly in different ethnic groups. Theories and cross-cultural knowledge help to understand this and other cultural differences in approaches to health care.

The Functionalist Perspective

Functional theorists focus primarily on the macro level of the health care system. Studies of suicide, carried out by the early French sociologist, Emile Durkheim, illustrate that social conditions and events in the larger society and people's group affiliations affected inclinations to commit suicide. Other studies have linked illnesses such as heart disease, kidney failure, stroke, mental illness, and infant mortality to macro-level processes and trends in societies, especially economic conditions that are correlated with physical and mental health. For example, economic recessions cause social stress and disruption in lifestyles that can activate mental problems; these in turn can result in health problems.

According to functionalists, social norms define what counts as illness and how to treat it. The purpose of the health care system in society is to maintain the social structure and a harmonious balance between individuals and institutions in society; illness is potentially disruptive to the balanced social world. The sick role is sometimes considered a deviant one because it "robs" the society of normal role functioning. As we saw in the Soviet example, if too many people claim the sick role at the same time, the tasks necessary to maintain the society cannot be performed. The primary task, or function, of the medical profession is to control illness and prevent individuals from being unable to perform their social roles.

Despite the harmonious view of functionalists, ambivalence does exist in the doctor-patient relationship. Paul Starr (1982) in an award-winning book about American medicine (see How Do We Know? on page 417) notes that physicians hold power over patients in the doctor-patient relationship, and patients may have contradictory expectations for their treatment (Hughes and Griffiths 1999). We turn to conflict theory for a different perspective on the health care system.

THINKING SOCIOLOGICALLY

What duties and responsibilities do you relinquish when you occupy a sick role? Which ones do you continue during your illness?

The Conflict Perspective

Poverty, unemployment, low wages, malnutrition, and a host of other economic conditions affect people's access and ability to compete for health care and medicines in many countries; differential access is a key theme in conflict theorists' approach to health issues. Consider the case of Nkosi, a four-year-old boy in a rural, Ghanaian village. He came down with an infection from the polluted water, causing diarrhea and vomiting. Already weakened by malnutrition and parasites, by the time help came, dehydration was so extensive that it was too late and he died, one of millions of similar casualties. Why was health care not available?

Nkosi had less access to medical treatment, immunizations, antibiotics, vitamins, and a balanced diet than children in major urban areas of developing countries and in developed countries. Children in poor countries around the world suffer from malnutrition and chronic disease before succumbing to pneumonia, normally a curable disease. The explosion in new "emerging infectious diseases" such as AIDS, Brazilian Purpuric fever, new strains of Ebola, and various insect- and bird-transported diseases such as SARS and bird flu add to the problems faced by health care workers treating the sick in developing countries (Farmer 1999). In fact, life expectancy (average length of life) is as low as 35 years in some drought-ridden and war-torn countries

such as regions of Sudan where disease has ideal conditions to spread.

In the world system of rich and poor countries, individuals suffer different illnesses depending on the level of development of their society and their position in it; poor people in poor countries die from ailments that are curable infectious diseases in rich countries. Consider the case of Swaziland in sub–Saharan Africa. Weakened from poor nutrition and hungry because their land has been ravaged by drought, many people die of treatable diseases. However, the real killer is AIDS. Forty percent of parents are infected by AIDS. Life expectancy in Swaziland is 38 years (meaning the average age of the population is 38 years) and dropping rapidly; it is expected to be 30 years by 2010. What little governmental health care system exists cannot cope with the crisis. The numbers of orphans, now at 40 million, is growing rapidly. Forget education; children are concerned with trying to survive on the little food available and to raise their younger siblings. International aid organizations provide most of the meager food they do consume (Senate Democratic Policy Committee Hearing 2004).

At the national level, many governments officially proclaim that health care is a basic right of all citizens, although many do not have the means to meet the health needs of citizens. However, some poor countries are trying. Every child in China, for instance, receives medical attention and is immunized against a number of childhood diseases. Cuba has also developed a system to reach all of its citizens, as explained in the Sociology around the World on page 405.

At the global level, multinational companies that build plants in the poor Global South provide examples of the profit motive's influence on health conditions. As they look for large profit margins and cost-cutting opportunities, health and safety standards are sometimes lower than those in developed countries that have strict health regulations. Although many multinational companies provide health clinics for workers, lower safety standards can lead to long-term illnesses, eye problems, lung disease, and other debilitating health problems. Moreover, multinational pharmaceutical companies have resisted generic drugs or inexpensive vaccines that are crucial to combating disease in developing countries. Poor countries are places to save money in manufacturing labor costs and raw materials but are not places to provide services since they contribute little to company profits—the bottom line for most huge capitalistic corporations. A few countries such as India are developing their own cheaper versions of drugs for AIDS and other diseases, bypassing pharmaceutical companies.

A consistent theme in Parsons's (1975). functional model of the sick status is the physician's need for total authority in the relationship in order to meet the health needs of clients. Some conflict theorists argue that this power is really so that physicians can decide whom they might treat. Some physicians prefer not to locate in poor or rural areas or countries, treat elderly patients, or spend time on those with AIDS. The

Sociology around the World

Health Care, Cuba's Pride

One thing all Cubans were promised under the Communist regime of Fidel Castro was access to good health care, seen as a basic right of all people. When Cuba had many European Eastern Block trading partners and support from the former Soviet Union, its system was considered a model, especially for a Global South country. Now, the country has lost external support due to the collapse of the Soviet system; Cuba has fallen on hard economic times primarily because of the U.S.-imposed embargo on goods going to Cuba, with the health care system being one victim. Shortages of drugs, diagnostic equipment, and medical supplies have forced Cuba's well-trained doctors to be creative; they use herbal remedies, hypnosis, and acupuncture in place of needed supplies and equipment.

The health care system still has an ample supply of doctors (58.2 for every 10,000 inhabitants); hospitals and clinics are spread throughout the country; and infant mortality and life expectancy rates are comparable to those of developed countries (Pan American Health Organization

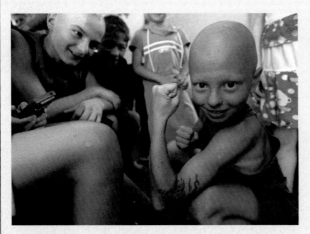

A Ukrainian boy jokes while surrounded by friends at a pediatric hospital near Havana, Cuba. This child is one of thousands Cuba has treated since 1990 free of charge for loss of hair, skin disorders, cancer, leukemia, and other illnesses attributed to the radioactivity unleashed by the Chernobyl nuclear power plant reactor meltdown in Ukraine in 1986, years before they were born.
Source: © Claudia Daut/Reuters/Corbis.

2000). However, under the economic hardships and due to lack of medicine and equipment that could easily control some illnesses and diseases, these figures are beginning to slip. Typhoid fever and tuberculosis, once almost nonexistent, are more common now, and water contamination is increasing. These problems illustrate the interrelationship between health, economic resources, and global links between countries (Golden 1994).

Health statistics have a human face; diary entries of a recent visitor to Cuba tell of the impact economic sanctions have on the health of ordinary citizens:

> I visited Dr. Barbara, a young family doctor, in her neighborhood *consultorio* in Havana, Cuba. Her waiting room was full of young mothers holding plump and healthy babies, sitting against a wall covered with a hand-painted wall mural. A portrait of Fidel Castro (Cuba's head of government) hung next to a painted caricature of Mickey Mouse on the wall behind her desk. Her eyes bright, her long hair bouncing against her shoulders, she said she was very proud to be a Cuban physician and to care for a patient community of 200 families. But, she added with a pause, sometimes she felt helpless to provide the care that her patients needed. She explained that diagnostic tests were often missed or delayed because of shortages of X-ray film or replacement parts for equipment. Blood work was limited by lack of reagents needed in the labs. Her prescription choices were restricted to the medicines available at the time, a situation that she found very frustrating when her patient had multiple medical problems that dictated the use of one medicine rather than another. Prozac and other state-of-the-art antidepressants were unheard of, and only a few drugs for treating depressive and anxiety disorders were available. Many anticancer medicines were difficult or impossible to get. She said that people were dying sooner than necessary because of these scarcities. (Lemkau 2006).

Despite the problems caused by the embargo, highly trained Cuban health care workers can be found in needy areas around the world, and Cuban medical training facilities have international student bodies.

most lucrative positions with the most prestige are generally located in major global urban areas and at well-known clinics, treating people who can pay for private care. This leads some conflict theorists to discuss the doctor-patient relationship as an association in which the doctor exercises social control, and loyalty of the doctor to the patient depends in part on the social status of the patient (White 2002).

Feminist Theory

For *feminist theorists*, gender is a key variable that affects health and illness. Feminist theorists argue that the patriarchal control of women carries over to health care systems and reinforces dependence, submission, and definitions of what is *illness* for women. Western women are profitable for the health care system because they are seen more often and have more expensive procedures such as hysterectomies (White 2002). Controlling women's reproductive health and defining women's normal biological experiences as medical problems is rooted in Western society's class interests and in maintaining patriarchal authority. However, in some countries, women are important and respected healers and doctors. Consider one example, Gujarat, India, where women medical practitioners hold significant and autonomous places in the medical establishment, giving women power and a voice in their health care.

Women have been kept in inferior social positions through much of history because powerful members of society said that their bodies limited them (Shorter 1991); this is especially true in Western societies. For instance, drugs to control depression keep women in situations that cause depression. Menopause is treated as an illness or is brushed aside. Women, then, are defined in the medical profession by their reproductive life cycle (White 2002). One result is that more women than men are patients because of medicalization of women's normal life cycles.

To regain control of women's health, some feminists have formed health organizations concerned with reproductive health: midwifery, natural childbirth, home deliveries, and menopause (Clarke and Olesen 1999). With increasing numbers of women physicians, attitudes toward women's health and communication practices between women and physicians are changing.

Conflict theorists argue that the institution of health care creates the conditions that contribute to sickness through low employment opportunities, stress, health hazards at work, poor living conditions, and lack of access to medical care. We now consider the institutionalization of medicine.

THINKING SOCIOLOGICALLY

How might each of the theoretical perspectives deal with attention deficit disorder (ADD) or addictions such as gambling, sex, or drugs?

THE STATUS AND ROLES OF THE SICK PERSON: MICRO-LEVEL ANALYSIS

What constitutes *illness behavior* rests on the signs, symptoms, and circumstances defined by our social group rather than on a set of universally recognized bodily malfunctions. Cultural definitions combined with physical symptoms help us understand illness (Furnham 1994; Krieger 1994; Weiss and Lonnquist 2006). The words of a poor Central American woman who was asked if she has been sick illustrate this point:

> I wish I really knew what you meant about being sick. Sometimes I felt so bad I could curl up and die but had to go on because the kids had to be taken care of and besides, we didn't have any money to spend for a doctor. How could I be sick? How do you know when someone is sick, anyway? Some people can go to bed most any time with anything, but most of us can't be sick, even when we need to be. (Koos 1954).

To this woman, being sick was not just a physical condition or how she felt or any physical symptoms she displayed. From a cultural perspective, she had responsibilities that could not be ignored, little access to health care, and no money to buy medicine or care. So who defines the poor woman above as sick? She herself? Her friends and family? Her employer? A health care professional? What is necessary before we can say, from the sociological point of view, that someone is sick?

Illness, or being sick, is a complex matter resulting from changes in the body. Try comparing illness to an iceberg: the whole iceberg is not what we see. Similarly, most illness lies under the surface and may never come to public attention unless it forces the person to alter routines or fail in carrying out responsibilities. Generally, physical disorders can be identified and a health professional can relieve pain or discomfort and return individuals to a healthy state (Kurtz and Chalfant 1991).

However, for the sociologist, the view of illness as only a physical disorder is too limited; as a social condition, definitions in the society influence who is considered sick and under what conditions. Illness, then, is in part socially constructed. The health establishment, schools, and workplaces acknowledge illness only if certain societally defined conditions are present.

Surveys of health in populations around the world indicate that few people are totally free from some degree of physical disorder. Yet the presence of such disorders does not mean that individuals will seek treatment or that the illness will be recognized and treated. Both individual (micro) and structural (meso or macro) factors are important in health care decisions and treatment. The political and economic environment, access to the health care system that provides services, and the predisposition by an individual to seek medical care all enter into health care decisions (Andersen 1995).

Being sick is more than a physical problem of fever, aches and pains, loss of energy, and other symptoms. Being sick changes relationships, how other people spend their time and how other people respond to you, including lowered expectations of what you can do. In short, being sick involves a change to a new role.

Source: © Jamie Wilson.

THINKING SOCIOLOGICALLY

The Central American woman felt like she could "curl up and die," but she survived. Was she sick? Would you be sick if you felt the way she did? Why might your definition of your situation be different from hers?

The Sick Role

Think of all the social relationships, engagements and responsibilities that are affected when you are sick. You miss class, have to cancel other engagements, avoid your friends so that you do not infect them with your germs, and cannot carry out your usual responsibilities. Most people are sympathetic for a couple of days, but then expect you to get back to your usual routines and responsibilities. Let us consider this "role" of being sick.

Those who are ill occupy a special position or status in society—the sick role (Parsons 1975). They are *deviant* in that they are not carrying out their role expectations; other members must pick up those responsibilities. Unlike other deviance, however, the sick role is not punished but is tolerated as long as the sick individual cooperates and acts to overcome illness, returning as soon as possible to fulfill their usual social roles.

In an early contribution to the sociology of health, Parsons's (1951a) presented a functional theoretical model of the "sick role," outlining four interrelated behavioral expectations—two rights and two obligations:

Right 1: The sick person has the right to be *excused from normal social responsibility* as needed to be restored to normal functioning in the society. For example, sick students expect to receive permission to miss class or to make up a missed exam.

Right 2: The *sickness is not the individual's fault.* The sick person did not mean to deviate from normal social expectations and cannot become well by self-decision or by willing it so.

Obligation 1: The *sick person should define being sick as undesirable.* To avoid the accusation of laziness or malingering, the sick person must not prolong illness unnecessarily to avoid social obligations.

Obligation 2: Those in the sick status are *expected to seek technically competent help and cooperate in getting well.* In Western countries, the help is most often a medical doctor.

Parsons (1951a) describes the physicians' roles as complementing the "sick role"—to restore routine behavior and "orderliness" in patients. The models presented by Parsons are clearly related to functionalist thought. They focus on integrating all aspects of medical care into a working social system.

One problem is that some individuals might like being excused from tasks and allowed to deviate from social responsibility (such as taking tests or doing a really arduous task). Certainly, being sick can be a less demanding lifestyle than going to work or school or taking care of a family. The sick role can also *legitimize failure* by providing a ready excuse for poor performance at some task (Cole and Lejeune 1972); people who believe they are permanently unable to fulfill their normal social roles may be motivated to define themselves as sick. Yet an excess of sick people could be disruptive to the social fabric, so it is necessary to develop means to control who enters the sick status, as did the Soviet regime, and to guard against misuse of illness as an excuse for avoiding social responsibility.

Individuals make choices about their own health and lifestyles—decisions about leisure time activities; exercise; the amount and type of food they consume; use of alcohol, drugs, and tobacco; and sexual behavior. All of these choices affect health. Any of these taken to extremes can result in illness. Health and lifestyle choices are influenced by socialization patterns, family backgrounds, peers, jobs, and cultural expectations.

Eating patterns are a concern for U.S. public health officials. Both children and adults fall into the couch potato syndrome of a sedentary life as flab accumulates into excess weight, a recipe for certain illnesses. Fast food has become a convenient time-saver and a recipe for gaining weight. Health care workers have developed education campaigns to change eating patterns, and schools are removing pop machines from cafeterias.

Many people in industrialized societies, especially in the United States, are extremely overweight, a serious health hazard that brings with it many risks. This is a concern to the society as a whole since it means lowered productivity and increased health care costs.

Source: Photo by Malingering.

THINKING SOCIOLOGICALLY

Do you feel the problem depicted in the film *Super Size Me* is a serious one related to health of a nation? Do changes need to be made, and if so, what would you recommend to policy makers?

Another concern are the millions of people with negative body images that result in health problems as some men and women abuse their bodies with excessive and unhealthy eating and behavior patterns, such as steroid use. Individual behaviors that influence risk factors for illness include high stress, substance abuse problems, poor diets, and lack of exercise.

Determining who is sick goes beyond physical symptoms and feelings of discomfort. Symptoms such as distress, anxiety, or perceived seriousness of the symptoms often result in seeking health care. Individuals may postpone health action or not seek health care because of lack of availability and affordability or because they deny the existence of the ailment.

Social Factors in Illness and Health

An American Peace Corps volunteer in a South American village could not understand the resigned attitude of a mother, Mónica, as she held her dying baby. He offered to help Mónica get the baby to the clinic 15 miles away, but she seemed resigned to its death. The expectations that shaped Mónica's

behavior were learned in her cultural setting; three of her seven children had died. In this rural Global South setting, up to half of the babies born will die in infancy because of illness, poor sanitation, lack of clean water, and lack of health care and medicine; people come to accept infant deaths, often easily preventable, as normal. Many children are not even named until their parents determine that they are likely to live.

Thus, individual beliefs, experiences, and decisions about health and illness may be deeply rooted in meso- and macro-level structural factors that shape availability of health services as well as factors that shape one's lifestyle and attitudes toward health care. Consider some of the social dimensions that are relevant to individual health.

Cultural Belief Systems and Health

Western scientific medicine centers on physicians who use medical technology to heal those who are sick and return them to society as contributing members. In non-Western parts of the world, quite different healing approaches are used. In North Africa, for example, members of the Azande tribe believe in a spiritual system of healing centered on the activities of the local shaman. Illness occurs, they believe, when an offended individual arranges for a "sickness pellet" to be placed in the body of the offender. Through spiritual ceremonies, the sorcerer sees that the pellet is withdrawn from the body and restores the person to health.

Some Hispanic cultures practice a unique ancient complex of healing known as *curanderismo*. The origins are found in indigenous herbal medicine, indigenous religious belief systems, witchcraft, and Spanish Catholicism. Good health and a strong body are viewed as God's blessing for the faithful. Illness comes either when one has sinned or as a message from God to help the person learn to be good. The relationship between the *curandero*, or healer, and the patient is close, relying on psychological and spiritual as well as physical treatment. Many Hispanics combine Western medicine and curanderismo; for "non-Hispanic illnesses," the physician is the healer of choice. However, for culture-specific conditions such as *susto* (characterized by extreme fright), the curandero may be consulted since many believe that such conditions are impervious to even the highest technology of the scientific physician (Weiss and Lonnquist 2006). The role of the curandero combines elements of psychologist and healer.

Even definitions of who is considered mentally ill and who is put away for their own and society's protection vary greatly across societies (Basaglia 1992). Manuel is a schizophrenic who "goes crazy" when the moon is full (the concept of *lunacy*) and is put in a Nicaraguan mental hospital during that time. Otherwise, he lives a relatively normal life with his parents. In another culture, he might be put in long-term hospital care, or a different definition might be given to his mental instability (Fernando 2002).

Pain is a universal experience, yet how it is perceived, experienced, and reacted to varies by cultural background, ethnic group membership, and socialization experience

(Showalter 2002). In a U.S. hospital-based study of reactions to pain, researchers observed that patients' responses fell into two main categories: stoic and emotive. Patients with Jewish and Italian cultural backgrounds responded to pain emotionally, while patients of Yankee background were stoical and tried to bravely endure pain; those of Irish descent denied pain altogether. Although the Jewish American and Italian American patients exhibited similar reactions to pain, their reasons for these reactions were different. The Jewish American patients took a long-term view toward pain; they were concerned about its meaning for their future, and their reactions did not subside when pain-relieving drugs were administered. The Italian American patients, on the other hand, were mainly concerned with the pain itself, and drugs both relieved the pain and their complaints (Thomas and Rose 1991; Zborowski 1952).

Other studies have found that expressive, emotive responses came from Hispanic, Middle Eastern, and Mediterranean patients, while stoic patients were more often from Northern European and Asian backgrounds (Davidhizar, Shearer, and Giger 1997; Thomas and Rose 1991). Decisions we make and experiences we have are directly related to our socialization, culture, and how we define reality.

Group Factors in Health Care

Age, gender, ethnicity, economic factors, social status, and urban or rural residence are important in determining patterns of health and illness as well. A discussion of these group factors follows.

Age, not surprisingly, affects health in several ways. People age 65 and older need medical intervention and hospitalization more often that any other age group; they also receive more preventative care than other age groups. As the size of the world's senior population has grown, this age cohort has increased as the population most utilizing the health care system; in the United States, those 65 and older averaged 11.7 visits to physicians per year (National Center for Health Statistics 2002b). Figure 13.1 on the next page shows the number of visits by females and males to physicians between 1996 and 2003.

Gender patterns are clear too: in Western cultures, women report more health problems than do men. They use more physician services on a regular basis and receive more preventive and reproductive care, take more medications, and are more likely to be hospitalized (Anson 1998; Weiss and Lonnquist 2006). By contrast, men use emergency services more.

Ethnic groups, as illustrated by the cases of Hispanic *curanderismo*, Hmong concepts of illness, and experiences of pain discussed above, provide socialization to possible health care options ranging from modern medical practitioners to alternative medical practitioners (from traditional folk healers to modern chiropractors who are not part of the medical establishment), nonmedical professions (e.g., social workers and clergy), lay advisors, and self-care (Pescosolido 1992).

Gerardo Queupukura, a renowned shaman of the Mapuche tribe in Chile, attends to the line of patients and looks at the urine sample to determine a patient's health status. The medicine man holds consultations twice a week.

Source: © Erwin Patzelt / dpa / Corbis.

Although pain is universal, the way we respond to it is influenced by ethnicity, socialization experiences, and other cultural messages about pain.

Source: © Tom and Dee Ann McCarthy / Corbis.

As we saw in Chapter 8, disadvantage experienced by Blacks is often rooted in indirect institutional discrimination—discrimination that is part of the social system and not a result of individual prejudice. This certainly operates in the case of differential health care. In the United States, African Americans are still less likely to have regular health care

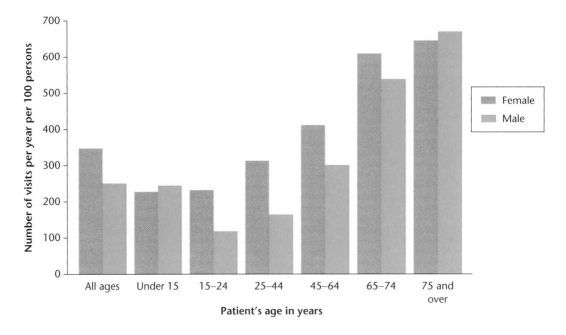

Figure 13.1   Number of Visits Per Year by U.S. Females and Males to Physicians, 1996–2003

Source: National Center for Health Statistics (2005).

The affluent have much better health care, especially in countries such as the United States where individuals often pay for their own health service or at least pay through their employers. This is the Eisenhower Medical Center in Rancho Mirage, California.

Source: Derek Baird.

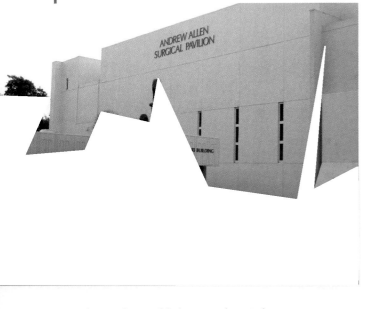

African Americans, and other minorities in the United States (i.e., the number of live-born infants who die in their first year) is increasing as Table 13.1 shows (National Vital Statistics Report 2001). The high infant-mortality rate of the United States compared with other developed countries is due largely to social class differentials between minorities and whites in the United States, as shown in Table 13.1.

African Americans also have higher rates of cancers and shorter survival times than whites at all stages of cancer diagnosis (American Cancer Society 2006; Ries et al. 2000).

Social status affects health because wealthier individuals are more likely to seek professional help early for physical or psychological distress, partly because they can afford treatment. However, contact with physicians is highest among the lowest income categories (7.6 doctor visits per year compared to an average of 6 for the entire population) (Weiss and Lonnquist 2006; Williams and Collins 1995). Lower income citizens' perceptions of necessary health consultation often involve response to crises. The "working poor" who do not qualify for Medicaid but cannot afford private insurance or medical care delay care (Weiss and Lonnquist 2006). Without universal access to health care, income affects health status.

providers and more likely to use hospital emergency rooms and health clinics than the majority of the population. Health care is less available in inner cities and rural areas where there are concentrations of minority residents. Minority women are less likely to receive prenatal care than other women, and the infant mortality gap between whites,

THINKING SOCIOLOGICALLY

Why do some people in the world have more access to health care than others? What does this mean for health and productivity of individuals and societies?

TABLE 13.1	Infant Deaths per 1,000 Live Births by Race of Mother, 2001

Race or Ethnic Origin	Percentage
All races	6.6
White	5.7
American Indian	9.7
Asian or Pacific Islander	4.7
Black	13.3

Source: U.S. Department of Health and Human Services (2005).

Differences in access to health care relate to meso and macro levels of the social system, discussed in the next sections.

 ## MODERN HEALTH CARE SYSTEMS: MESO-LEVEL ANALYSIS

At one time, health care was largely an issue addressed in homes by families. Today in wealthy countries, health care has become institutionalized. The bustling hospital, the efficient nurses and nurse's aides, and the technically proficient physicians have replaced home care, visiting doctors, folk remedies, and homes as the setting for births, deaths, and many health issues in between. Much of the treatment of diseases depends on research that is funded by governments or foundations, and health delivery is performed by organizations that are bureaucratized corporations. This section explores the institution of medicine: organization of health care systems, hospitals as complex organizations, and changes of professional status for physicians.

The Organization of Health Care Systems

Citizens' access to health care depends on several factors: the cultural values concerning the government's role in providing health care, whether health care is seen as a human right for all citizens or a privilege for those who can pay, the amount and source of funding to provide health care, and the type of health care available. Societies around the world struggle with issues of cost, quality and access to care, and medical technology (Gallagher, Stewart, and Stratton 2000; Gallagher and Subedi 1995; Schieber and Maeda 1999). In developed countries, these struggles result from aging populations with more health needs and smaller numbers of citizens in the taxable working population to support health care programs. Developing countries struggle with problems that result in high death rates from curable diseases and from epidemics. Nations develop health care philosophies and systems based on population needs and their ability to address them.

Types of Health Care Systems

The two most common national models for providing health care—socialized medicine and decentralized national health care programs—are based on the philosophy of health care as a human right. Add to that the U.S. fee-for-service plan. Table 13.2 summarizes key aspects of these three types of systems.

Socialized medicine programs provide a government-supported consumer service with equal access to health care for all citizens of a country (Cockerham 2004). The political system controls the organization and financing of health services and owns most facilities, pays providers directly, and allows private care for an extra fee. Although there are variations in systems, developed countries that have socialized medicine systems include Canada, Great Britain, Israel, Norway, Sweden, and several other European countries.

Countries with *decentralized national health programs* have many of the same characteristics but differ in the government's role; the government has less direct control over health care systems and acts to regulate the system, not operate it (Cockerham 2004). Countries with decentralized systems include France, Germany, Japan, and the Netherlands. The United States, unique among developed countries, has a fee-for-service system, financed by a mix of private and public purchasers.

TABLE 13.2	Types of Health Care Delivery Systems around the World

Role of Government	Fee-for-Service	Socialized Medicine	Decentralized National Health
Regulation	Limited	Direct	Indirect
Payment to providers	Limited	Direct	Indirect
Ownership of facilities	Private and public	Private and public	Private and public
Public access	Not guaranteed	Guaranteed	Guaranteed
Private care	Dominant	Limited	Limited

Source: Cockerham (2004).

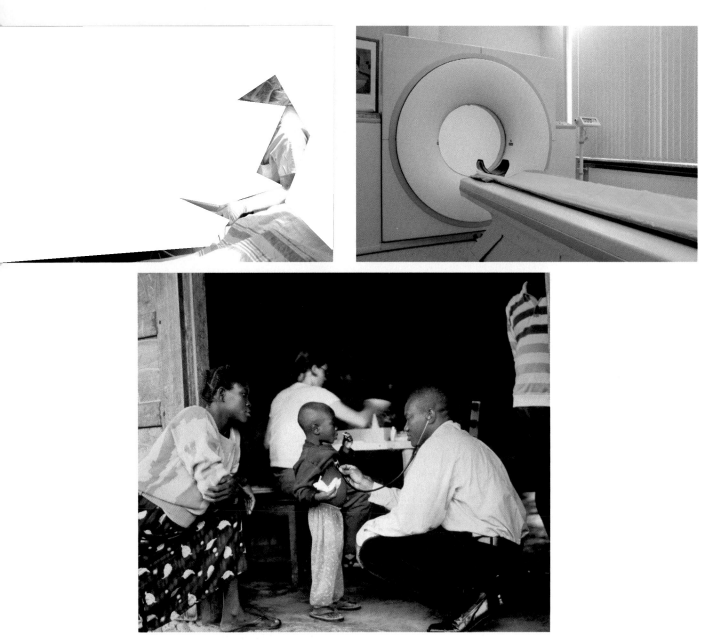

High-tech equipment is expensive (top two photos), but in places like Ghana (lower photo), physicians must use what little technology they have available.

Source: © David Elfstrom; © Sławomir Jastrzębski; © Mika/zefa/Corbis.

Most governments in Europe decided to support health care as a human right for all citizens and put these systems into place in the late 1800s and early 1900s; their motivations were to develop healthier populations, to strengthen their military forces and their economic systems, and to reduce the possibility of revolution by the poor and working classes by providing for basic health care needs. By providing health insurance and protection for the injured or unemployed, financial security in case of illness was increased.

Health care systems in developing countries are often patterned after former colonial systems. However, most countries struggle to provide for basic health care needs, to ensure access to health care for citizens living in rural areas, and to deal with costly diseases such as AIDS. Because of the lack of physicians, especially in rural areas, most developing countries rely on a combination of Western and indigenous medical practices using herbs and other local remedies. Trained midwives deliver babies, and health education workers travel to villages to teach about the spread of diseases such as AIDS, sometimes making condoms available. In Ugandan villages where a high percentage of the adult working population has been infected or died from AIDS, social workers visit regularly to be sure orphaned children are eating and sowing crops.

The World Health Organization and other international organizations help provide immunizations and treatment for epidemics but not for ongoing health needs. For example, Kenya, in East Africa, has a rapidly growing population, 85 percent of which lives in rural areas. Kenya has a socialized health care system based on the British model, with a national health service that employs doctors and owns hospitals. However, these services are available primarily in the largest cities of Nairobi and Mombasa. In fact, 80 to 85 percent of the health care budget goes to these urban areas. Rural areas are served by only 10 percent of the doctors in the national health system, and citizens in remote areas rely on folk healers and herbalists for care (Cockerham 2004).

Hospitals as Complex Organizations

Hospitals are places for the care and treatment of the sick and injured, providing centralized medical knowledge and technology for treatment of illnesses and accidents. The industrial revolution in Western Europe and the United States caused population shifts to urban areas. These shifts, in turn, precipitated new and threatening environmental and health conditions from crowding and lack of sanitation. Rational, systematic approaches to health care as opposed to individual folk remedies became imperative. In the late 1800s, there was an explosive growth in the number of hospitals, many of which were sponsored by religious organizations; the focus of these early hospitals was on segregating the destitute and terminally ill who might be contagious and were likely to die. At this time, most hospitals were still small, but improvements in medical knowledge and competency were changing the old system.

The status of the hospital shifted dramatically in the early 1900s due to advances in medical science. Trained staff, sterile conditions, and more advanced techniques and technology changed hospitals from being the last resort of the urban poor and the dying to places of healing for all classes. Small community hospitals were an essential element of town life. As hospital care has become more available, the structure of hospitals also changed.

The post–World War II period produced huge growth in health care facilities and numbers of employees in the health care system. Medicines and vaccines controlled many infectious diseases that had formerly killed and disabled individuals. This period also saw the growth and funding of medical schools and large medical facilities that provided not only patient care but also education and research. Thus began the dominance of the hospital in providing medical care. Today, many hospitals are centers of medical knowledge and technology, housing not only patients and surgical units but laboratories and diagnostic centers, specialty clinics, and rehabilitation centers.

Although medical health systems differ across societies, hospitals exhibit many characteristics similar to other large, bureaucratic organizations: hierarchical structures, rules and regulations, positions (doctors, nurses) based on competency and training, hiring and promotion based on merit,

and contracts for work performed. Primary care physicians and other gatekeepers control client access to hospitals.

Historically, hospitals were designed for the convenience of physicians. However, today two rather independent bureaucracies function within modern large-scale hospital organizations. Physicians dominate the medical operations, while lay administrators operate the everyday functioning.

Health care systems are major employers in most developed nations. In the United States, for instance, more than 4 million people are employed in a variety of hospital jobs as nurses, hospital administrators, pharmacists, physical therapists, physician's assistants, and imaging specialists (those who do X-rays). Nurses are the largest group of health care workers with licensed registered nurses (at 2,449,000) and licensed practical nurses (at 531,000), followed by physicians (at 819,000) (U.S. Census Bureau 2005i). Seventy-five percent work in hospitals and nursing homes (U.S. Census Bureau 2001a). In the hospital, the nurse manages the patient care team under the authority of the physician, who is the prime decision maker. Under the nurse's authority in this hierarchical structure come increasing numbers of ancillary personnel.

As hospitals and other medical facilities in the United States are increasingly owned and operated by for-profit corporations, the overwhelming power of the professional or medical line is giving way to powerful corporate management—the lay or administrative line. Physicians have become the "customers" of the hospital, buying space and time to carry out their functions. Sometimes, the physician's orders contradict those of the administrative line, especially with regard to medical decisions versus cost-saving decisions.

Early in the morning, a lot of patients are already lining up to see a medical professional at this Phelophepa health train. It crosses the Western Cape countryside in South Africa periodically, providing what little medical consultation is available to the black community in that area.

Source: © Joao Luis Bulcao / Corbis.

Some hospitals, such as Guy's Hospital in London—seen here from across the Thames River—are huge bureaucracies with complex role structures and have many of the problems and dilemmas of any other bureaucracy.

Source: © WildCountry/Corbis.

THINKING SOCIOLOGICALLY

What type of medical facilities are available in your community? Who controls them? Do you see evidence of hospitals' corporate structures being geared to efficiency and profit? What effect, if any, has this had on service and commitment to clients?

Changing Professional Status of Employees in the Health Care System

Special features distinguish the hospital from other large-scale organizations. The division of labor in the hospital is extensive and even more highly specialized than other formal organizations. The hospital has a well-established hierarchical system of stratification affecting power and prestige. Hospitals depend on the cooperation of highly skilled people whose work must be coordinated. Not only are patterns of authority rigidly followed, but the clothing and symbols peculiar to particular positions are recognizable and, as in the army, serve as status badges. The physicians, at the top of the stratification ladder, exercise the most power and receive the highest financial and prestige rewards. Signs of their superior status include wearing long, white coats or not wearing special uniforms at all. Since the physician's position has not always been so exalted and appears to be changing in modern societies, let us consider the status of *physician*. Physicians rank among the most respected professionals in

most societies. Although trust and prestige seem to decline each year for all professions, physicians continue to command great respect, based on an assumption that they have special esoteric knowledge and humanitarian intent (Goode 1990; Starr 1982; Weiss and Lonnquist 2006).

The widespread acceptance of physician authority is relatively recent. Before the nineteenth century, too little medical knowledge was established and too few means of practice were successful to command such recognition. Physicians gained status from the discovery that some diseases were caused by bacteria and could be treated with antiseptics, from the introduction of anesthesia, and from the idea that specially trained persons could treat illnesses. Coupled with scientific advances and more sophisticated diagnostic tools, these beliefs began to elevate the status of physicians and scientific medicine (Pescosolido and Boyer 2001).

The transformation of physicians to a position of professional recognition in the United States came when some 250 physicians meeting in Philadelphia in May 1847 established the American Medical Association (AMA). This umbrella organization became the means to gain legitimacy and power over health care practice (Cockerham 2004). The predominantly female health care areas such as midwifery and other holistic approaches such as osteopathy, chiropractic medicine, and homeopathy were delegitimized by the powerful new AMA. Only one approach was granted credibility: **allopathy,** the approach used by the dominant groups of physicians in Western societies.

Physicians entering practice in the United States today are faced with several major changes. First, it is now a system shaped by the purchasers of care and the competition for profits, where it was once run by doctors who knew their patients and were committed to the Hippocratic oath of healing. Second, there has simultaneously been a decline in the public's trust of physicians, with willingness to question them and even outright distrust by some people. Third, an emphasis on specialization and subspecialization has arisen where previously there had been prestige and rewards in primary care (family doctors). Fourth, outpatient care in homes and doctors' offices is once again becoming more common, where the middle part of the twentieth century saw an emphasis on hospitalization. Finally, there is a demand by payers (especially insurance companies) for detailed accounts of medical decision making, fixed prepayment rates established by insurers, and less willingness to pay doctors based solely on their decisions about patients' needs (Cockerham 2004).

Deprofessionalization means that the work of physicians is increasingly controlled by nonprofessional outside forces—financial concerns, government regulation, technological changes, new medical administrators, and a more knowledgeable public. Many physicians now work for managed care systems (Hafferty 2000; Waitzkin 2000), so their own autonomy is limited by bureaucrats for whom they work. Moreover, bureaucratization of hospitals and controls

PHOTO ESSAY

Clothing and Status in the Hospital

Note the difference in how each of these people dresses. The outfits they wear are not insignificant, for they distinguish status, authority, and rights to certain prerogatives within the hospital or clinic.

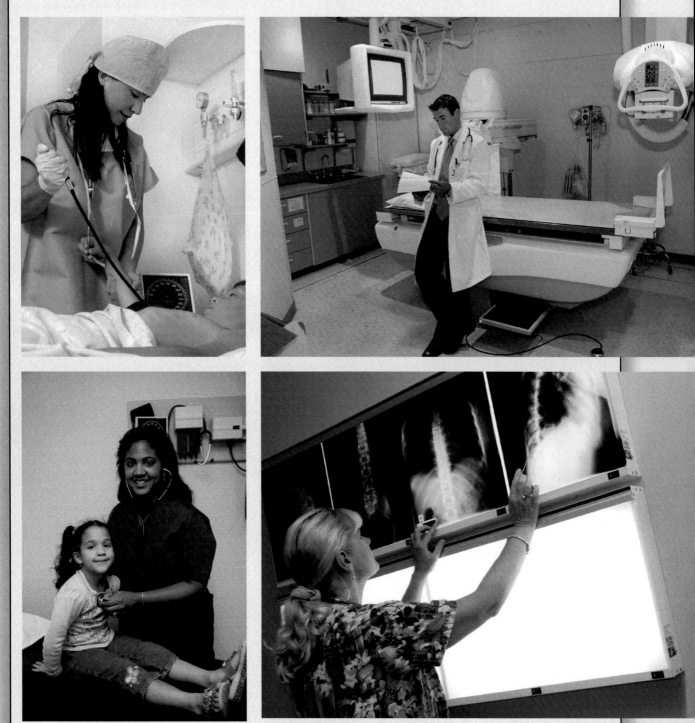

Source: © Sean Locke; © Leah-Anne Thompson; © Joseph Abbott; © Istockphoto.com.

Television shows about doctors, such as Grey's Anatomy, *depict doctors as highly autonomous and respected professionals. While there is some truth to this, physicians are increasingly working in bureaucratic settings in which the bureaucracy governs many of their decisions, causing deprofessionalization.*

Source: © 2006 CNET Networks, Inc.

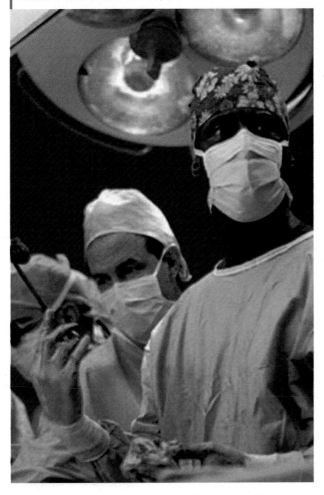

by insurance companies on doctors' decisions have reduced the autonomy of physicians to make decisions they think are best for the patient, another element of deprofessionalization.

THINKING SOCIOLOGICALLY

Doctors have been depicted in many television shows over the past five decades. How accurate are TV depictions about the U.S. medical system? How might they affect people's expectations of doctors and hospitals? In what ways are TV doctors and nurses different from real-life doctors and nurses?

We have explored issues of health care at the micro level (the role of sick people) and at the meso level (organization

of health care and hospitals as complex organizations). We now move to macro-level policy issues at national and global levels.

HEALTH CARE AND POLICY ISSUES AT NATIONAL AND GLOBAL LEVELS: MACRO-LEVEL ANALYSIS

Eloise knew something was seriously wrong when she lost her appetite, vomited when she ate more than a few bites, and lost her usually abundant energy. Without health insurance and fearing to lose her job if she missed work to sit in the out-patient waiting room of the hospital to see a doctor, she tried home remedies, and hoped the symptoms would go away. When she finally did go to the hospital she was in serious condition. Eloise spent a few days in intensive care and is now on treatments, but without income from her job she cannot pay the bills for herself and her child. Similar medical emergencies occur across the United States for over 46 million people in who lack medical insurance (Quinn 2006).

The Health Care System in the United States

The United States has the best system and the worst! It is one of the best in the world in terms of quality medical care, trained practitioners, facilities, and advanced medical technology. People from around the world seek training and care in the United States. It is also the worst system: it requires the highest cost per capita in the world to provide care (discussed in more detail later), does not provide equal access to citizens, is inefficient, has competing interests, and is fragmented. Some critics claim that the U.S. health care system is a social problem. It developed without specific direction and responded to demands piecemeal, allowing practitioners, medical facilities, and insurance and drug companies to establish themselves and then protect their self-interests, sometimes at the expense of citizens. In a discussion of the development of the U.S. health care system (see How Do We Know?), Starr uses historical analysis to determine key elements in its transformation.

Health Care Achievements

Medical research into gene therapy, understanding of the human genome, and research into new drug and technological therapies makes research one of the most rapidly advancing medical fields. New therapies will help people live longer, more comfortable, and productive lives—if they can afford the care. As science moves rapidly, ethical questions about use of fetal tissue in experiments and treatments, cloning, and other issues challenge ethicists and lawmakers (Mike 2003).

In addition to advances in medical science, there have been *achievements in public health* that prolong lives:

Historical Content Analysis in Sociology:
The Social Transformation of American Medicine

In this Pulitzer Prize–winning book, Paul Starr (1982) documents and analyzes the development of medicine in America from the 1700s to the 1980s. The research was a massive undertaking; Starr consulted books, journals, historical documents and accounts of medical practice, government reports, public health documents and records of specific diseases, hospital records, medical cost reports, medical school histories and catalogs, information on medical organizations, biographies and autobiographies, and other documents that shed light on the history and development of medicine in the United States. By doing *content analysis* on each historical period—that is, systematically studying the written materials available about medicine— he pieced together a picture of the themes and trends at different time periods. Starr used many sociological concepts and theories throughout his research to give his analysis depth.

His book represents two long movements: (1) the rise of medical profession sovereignty and (2) the transformation of medicine into an industry with the expansion of corporate influence and the state

control. Starr examines a number of issues about the institution of medicine. Why, for example, did Americans change from being wary of medicine to being devoted to it? Doctors who were previously deeply divided became united—and prosperous; why was that? Hospitals, medical schools, clinics, and other medical organizations assumed forms in the United States that were unlike those institutions in other countries, an intriguing difference. In the process, hospitals became the central institutions in medical care while public health became marginalized, unlike other places in the world. Similarly, there is no national health insurance in the United States, and commercial indemnity insurance now dominates the private health insurance market. In an interesting twist, some physicians are now taking part in the creation of corporate health care systems, a new development that is interesting to understand. Why did they evolve the way they did? Medicine is now a business as well as a cultural phenomenon in the United States, and Starr's investigation helps us understand that reality.

During the early years of U.S. history, the medical profession was

not yet established. Many "doctors" were educated persons who had no coursework in the sciences, and hospitals were places where people went to die, not to be healed. With the advent of modern medicine— sanitation and sterilization, understanding of disease, medicines, and vaccines—medicine grew in stature and people turned to doctors and hospitals for their medical needs. Starr documents the changing trends in medicine and ends with a discussion of recent problems with insurance systems and the debates between private insurance, medical systems, and public programs. Concerns today center around privatization of health care, hospital and physician services, insurance, and containment of costs.

By using historical analysis, Starr was able to give both an overview of trends and a detailed account of medicine throughout U.S. history. Only such a long-term perspective could help us so deeply understand many of the issues regarding medical care, the status of physicians, and the institutionalization of medicine.

Source: Starr (1982).

motor-vehicle safety, safer workplaces, control of infectious diseases, decline in heart problems, healthier foods, healthier mothers and babies, family planning, clean drinking water, and education of citizens about the dangers of tobacco and other substances as health hazards (Morbidity and Mortality Weekly Report 1999).

Problems in the U.S. Health Care System
The fragmented way in which the U.S. health care system has developed has led to two major problems: lack of universal access to health care and constantly escalating health care costs along with a sizeable uninsured population, resulting in lack of health care security (LeBow 2004; Oberlander 2002).

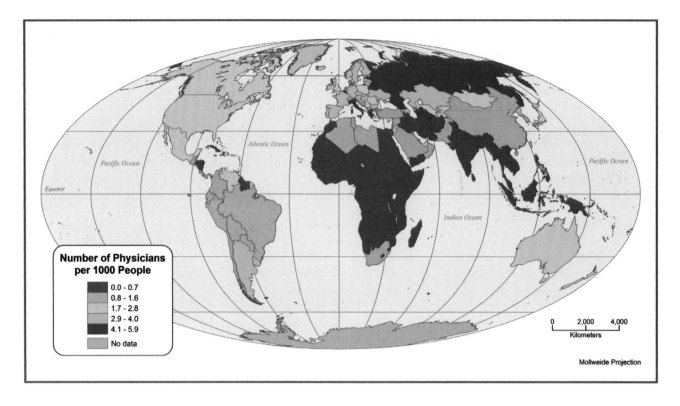

MAP 13.2   Number of Physicians per 1,000 People

Source: World Health Organization (2006). Map by Anna Versluis.

Access to health care. No matter how advanced technical-medical skills may be, they are of little use to society if they are not available to those who need them. In the United States, services are not necessarily distributed according to the needs of the people (Andersen, Rice, and Kominski 2001).

First, there is a *maldistribution of services.* The shortage of physicians in rural areas in the United States and many other countries is particularly serious (White 2002), and there is no indication that this will change soon. See Map 13.2 for an illustration of the maldistribution of physicians globally. Some free enterprise advocates contend that an oversupply of physicians will lead to a trickle-down to rural areas, but data analysis shows that this is not occurring. The expectation that family or primary care physicians would gravitate to rural areas is not occurring either. The U.S. has followed the lead of some other countries that cover physician education costs in exchange for a commitment to work in poor or rural areas for a set time period. Called the National Health Service Corps (NHSC), it encourages better distribution of health services but also brings less experienced and nonpermanent physicians to poor and rural locations (Gallagher and Johnson 2001; Ginsberg 1999).

Within cities, physicians are concentrated in certain neighborhoods—and outside certain neighborhoods. As a hospital's service area becomes increasingly populated by poorer residents, the facility faces a higher demand for free care. Closure and relocation to more profitable areas are particularly common among for-profit hospitals, and poor minority populations suffer.

Another aspect of maldistribution is the lack of family practice physicians; many physicians choose to enter one of

A woman receives a physical at the DayBreak Community Health Center in Houston, Texas. DayBreak is run by the Bread of Life outreach program, which offers meals, shelter, medical care, and counseling for homeless and poor people.

Source: © Greg Smith / Corbis.

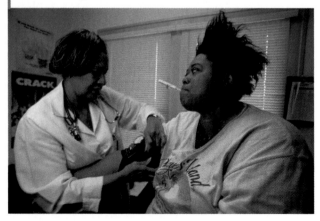

over 30 specialty areas in medicine. The reward system of medicine in terms of prestige, income, and lifestyle makes specialty practice more appealing than general medicine; moreover, most specialists are found in urban areas. The result of lack of access to medical care in rural areas and urban poor areas, especially for the poor and uninsured, is less frequent care, fewer regular physician visits and procedures, and a higher chance of serious illness and of dying in hospital once they do get admitted.

Health care cost and funding. Perhaps the most serious problem for health care systems and consumers in the United States, however, is the escalating cost of health care. Since 1947, expenditures for health care (now at 14.9 percent of the Gross National Product) have increased more rapidly than expenditures for other areas of the economy, and the U.S. spends twice as much per year on health care as other countries. Approximately 30 percent of health care costs in the United States go to administration; this cost is much lower in other countries, for example 16 percent in Canada (Woolhandler, Campbell, and Himmelstein 2004). Table 13.3 shows the increases in costs over time in the United States.

THINKING SOCIOLOGICALLY

Develop several hypotheses to explain why health care costs are rising rapidly. How would you test these hypotheses?

The United States is now the only developed country in the world that does not have a national health insurance program providing health care coverage for all citizens. Proposals for universal coverage plans have failed primarily because of opposition from private insurance companies, physicians, and drug companies and philosophical differences between politicians

The medical profession fought against the first proposed government medical insurance programs—Medicare and Medicaid (Marmor 1999); the programs passed mainly because they allowed physicians to retain their autonomy and to control their financial rewards (McKinlay and Marceau 1998). More recent attempts to nationalize health care have failed due in part to lobbying from physician advocates such as the AMA, insurance companies, and drug companies.

Managed health care plans developed quickly to fill the gap after the 1994 national health plan failed to pass in Congress ("Why Comprehensive Health" 1994). Health Maintenance Organizations (HMOs) and Preferred Provider Organizations (PPOs) arose to manage the care of a majority of patients who receive insurance through an employer (Gold 1999; Gold et al. 1998; Pescosolido and Boyer 2001).

TABLE 13.3	**National Health Expenditures: United States**		
Year	In Billion Dollars	Percentage of Domestic Product	Yearly Amount per Capita (in $)
1960	26.9	5.1	141
1970	73.2	7.1	341
1980	247.2	8.9	1,051
1990	699.5	12.2	2,689
2000	1,309.4	13.3	4,670
2002	1,553.0	14.9	5,440

Source: Centers for Medical and Medicaid Services (2004).

Escalating costs, the newer burden of chronic and degenerative diseases, the increasing number of Americans not covered by any form of health insurance, and only a modest relationship between health care spending and important markers of "success" (e.g., the infant mortality rate) compared to other countries led to a major federal government effort of restructuring the American health care system (during the Clinton presidency). Its failure led to the private health insurance market launching initiatives that greatly transformed the structure and financing of health services. (Pescosolido and Boyer 2001:180)

For-profit HMOs now enroll 29 percent of insured, and PPOs enroll 41 percent (Oberlander 2002). The PPOs differ in that clients typically have fewer restrictions in getting treatment. These managed care companies control costs by limiting visits to specific physicians on their network, requiring referrals for specialists and demanding preauthorization for hospital stays. Each insured individual is guaranteed care in exchange for a monthly sum paid by the employer and employee. Approximately 61 percent of insured patients are in managed health care plans. These recent developments in administration and cost containment have controlled but not reduced costs because of increased demand for care, rising numbers of senior citizens who need more health care, and expensive new technologies.

Managed care tries to integrate two goals—efficiency and high-quality care—with two means—financing and care delivery (Gold et al. 1998). Evidence indicates that these corporations are making profits and that 43 percent of consumers are satisfied with their health care (Burda 2001; Health Confidence Survey 2001; Vandenburgh 2001). Today, there are a variety of plans, and some states are now attempting to control costs by managing health services for their citizens through managed care systems.

In the current health care system, 80 percent of physicians work under fee-for-service plans (private insurance and direct payment by clients), retaining physicians' autonomy. The other 20 percent are employed primarily as hospital staff. Hospitals receive payment by fee-for-service and third-party insurance (government Medicare and Medicaid) plans. For clients who cannot pay, the shrinking numbers of public hospitals, county and state facilities, and free clinics are their options. Table 13.4 shows sources of funding for health care.

TABLE 13.4	**Sources of Payment for Health Services, 2003 (in billions of dollars)**
National health expenditures	$1,678.9
Annual percentage change	7.7 higher
Percentage of gross domestic product	15.3
Private expenditures	$913.2 (about 54.1%)
Private insurance	$600.6 (35.4%)
Out-of-pocket	$230.5 (13.7%)
Other	$61.5 (5.0%)
Paid by the government	$765.7 (about 45.9%)
Medicare	$283.1

Source: U.S. Census Bureau (2006e, Table 119).

Managed care has its critics who argue that for-profit corporations do not belong in the business of health care because health is a human right. Some in the medical field object to corporations making decisions about their clients' care. The provision of U.S. health care by profit-oriented organizations, sometimes referred to as *corporatization,* means that a network of private corporations now supplies health care to clients for a profit. In addition, costs of for-profit care are high and rising, leading to demands for a national health plan that would provide universal coverage at less expense. Meanwhile, the federal government is passing piecemeal legislation to deal with problems.

Controversies such as extending health benefits to *domestic partners*—unmarried cohabiting heterosexual and homosexual couples—has further clouded the issues of insurance coverage. However, some city and state government employees receive partner benefits; New York City granted benefits to its employees' domestic partners, but in 1999 Pennsylvania voted to deny such benefits to homosexual partners.

Lack of health care security. The biggest criticism of the U.S. system is that 46 million Americans, including 11.2 percent of U.S. children and 18.9 percent of children in poverty, remain uninsured (Quinn 2006; U.S. Census Bureau 2005h). This figure was up from 45 million people in 2003. 15.7 percent of citizens had no insurance coverage in 2004 compared to 13.6 percent in 2001, and the numbers of uninsured keep rising (U.S. Census Bureau 2005h). Even those who rely on Medicaid (45 million) and Medicare are likely to see reductions in benefits in insurance coverage. Of the poor people with no insurance, a disproportionate number are unmarried women, often with children, or members of ethnic groups (Meyer and Pavalko 1996; Mills

2001). Numbers of uninsured grow with unemployment, the drop in the number covered by employment-based health insurance and a drop in median income in the United States. Approximately 6 percent of people applying for coverage were refused, usually due to preexisting conditions, and another 7 percent were charged higher rates due to prior medical conditions. Insurance companies can deny medical claims in order to reduce their costs if they deem a procedure unnecessary (Levinson 1993).

At this time, there is no plan before the U.S. Congress that attempts to cover all uninsured, as did the last major attempt under the Clinton administration in 1994 (Oberlander 2002). Barriers to health care and lack of health insurance keep many from using services, even with the payments of Medicare and Medicaid. Table 13.5 shows the differences and disparities in health insurance coverage between groups in the United States. Note the numbers of uninsured, lowest for white citizens at 12.5 percent, and the number of privately insured, highest for whites at 79.3 percent.

TABLE 13.5	**Health Insurance Coverage for Persons under Age 65, Hispanic Origin and Race, U.S. 2000.**				
Insurance Type	Total U.S.	White Non-Hisp.	Black Non-Hisp.	Mexican American	Puerto Rican	Cuban American
Private	71.7%	79.3%	57.0%	46.6%	52.6%	63.6%
Medicaid	9.4	6.3	19.3	12.5	27.6	9.7
Other Public	2.1	1.9	3.7	1.0	3.4	1.5
Uninsured	16.8	12.5	20.0	39.9	16.4	25.2

Source: National Center for Health Statistics (2002a).

Medicare and Medicaid—services for the growing percentage of citizens 65 and over (estimated to be one in five by 2050) and for the poor—were legislated without cost limits on these services (National Center for Health Statistics 2002a). Whatever the medical profession charged was what the government paid. Since the original legislation, Congress has had some success in regulating and limiting charges and the length of hospital stays, but "creative billing" has thwarted government attempts to control the costs of the services. Thus, efforts to reform the system and control costs continue.

Lack of universal access and escalating costs are adversely affecting the quality of care offered to some citizens. For example, many uninsured clients such as Eloise, the woman discussed at the beginning of this section, defer care due to unaffordable fees. This compounds their health risks, increasing the likelihood of more expensive emergencies later. Financial considerations may also affect the type of services offered to clients. Socioeconomic status influences the decision to perform some surgical procedures like Caesarian deliveries.

When government money is supporting health care programs, evaluation is required to be sure that dollars are being spent effectively. The Applied Sociologist at Work describes the role sociologists can play in this process.

Policy Issues and Social Reforms in the United States' System

We return to this question: Is medical care a right or a privilege? Some argue it is a human right that cannot be bought and sold to the highest bidder or richest segments of society. Others argue that it is a privilege, a commodity to be purchased in a free market and that competition will both improve quality and reduce costs (Navarro 1996). The human rights argument provides the model for most developed countries, whereas the market-driven system is the main model in the United States for all but the elderly and poor who qualify for some government insurance (Harrington and Estes 2004).

THE APPLIED SOCIOLOGIST AT WORK

Evaluating and Improving Health Services

When organizations or communities receive money from government or foundations for health care projects, some form of accountability is required. Grant recipients must show that they have used the money effectively and for the intended purpose. Thus, grant applications have built-in checks for evaluating the project. This is where Dr. Harry Perlstadt comes in. As a faculty member affiliated with the Michigan State University Institute for Public Policy and Social Research, he has conducted many evaluation studies, mostly in the area of medical sociology. Below are three examples.

The Kellogg Foundation gives grants to local health projects, and Professor Perlstadt has helped to keep these projects on track. For instance, in the Comprehensive Community Health Models of the Michigan project, three communities were given funds to increase access to health insurance. Perlstadt met biweekly to advise those involved in carrying out the project. He looked at each of the three sites independently and at the overall project. At each site, there was a local director with whom he worked. In many cases, coordinating between grantors (Kellogg Foundation), project directors at each site, and evaluators required careful balancing as each participant in the project had different goals.

The federal Centers for Disease Control and the Michigan Department of Community Health asked Perlstadt and fellow sociologists Stan Kaplowitz and Lori Post to solve a problem. They needed to develop a better method to tell health care providers whether or not to screen young children for elevated blood lead levels. At the time, five standard (but not very predictive) questions were used in diagnosis. The researchers first developed an extensive survey that was given to parents at the time that blood was drawn from their child. It turned out that having the street address enabled the researchers to draw on census data on housing conditions and neighborhood poverty levels that was more accurate than what the parents were reporting. The researchers then developed a website where health providers could type in the street address; answer a few questions about ethnicity, income, and insurance; and then receive back the probability of the child having elevated blood lead levels.

The World Health Organization has organized ministerial (cabinet level) conferences to develop programs to improve environmental health in European countries. The World Health Organization hired Perlstadt as an advisor to assess the work of the conference planning committee. A small group developed a pilot study and then conducted a survey of people who had served or worked with the conference planning committee. The instruments contained both quantitative items and many opportunities for respondents to write in their opinions and suggestions. Perlstadt analyzed the data using a computer statistical program and in his reports illustrated the numerical findings with quotes from the written comments. The *quantitative data* made his findings applicable to a broad range of situations, but the *qualitative reports* from respondents gave a human dimension and made the report more convincing.

To carry out these evaluations, Perlstadt utilizes multiple research tools and draws on extensive knowledge and experience about medical sociology. He travels frequently to meet with all parties involved in a perplexing issue. Each project has its challenges; Perlstadt points out that that is part of the fun—learning new information on each new project and looking at the evaluation as a puzzle to be solved. His job is rather like being a detective discovering information to solve problems.

Dr. Harry Perlstadt received his doctorate in Sociology from the University of Chicago and his master's in Public Health from the University of Michigan. He directs the Program in Bioethics, Humanities, and Society at Michigan State University.

Current proposals for reform of the U.S. health care system take several forms:

1. Revise the partly public, partly private system with a mix of governmental and private insurers. This model would be the simplest reform since it is most compatible with the current system.

2. Vote in reforms one at a time; this is currently happening. For instance, in 1983 Medicare set fixed-fee amounts for services at hospitals, and in 1989 it fixed rates for physicians. In 1996, Congress passed legislation that individuals cannot be denied health insurance when changing jobs. In 2005, a new prescription drug benefits program was launched. These legislative efforts have moved the system piecemeal toward guaranteed insurance for some in the population.

3. Pass a comprehensive reform package that would provide national health insurance and government oversight and administration. Some states have passed programs to provide access and contain costs for their residents. In 1974, Hawaii was the first to have a comprehensive plan covering about 90 percent of the population; Tennessee followed, and now Vermont provides insurance to poor residents for a low fee that covers free medical and dental care for those under 18. In 2006, Massachusetts also adopted a program for health coverage that may be the most comprehensive of all. It requires every citizen to have health insurance, but provides subsidies to cover costs for the lowest income people and requires insurance companies to provide reduced rates for them. The fact that everyone must buy insurance made the proposal acceptable to the insurance companies. Several other states including Florida, Minnesota, Oregon, and Washington are following with plans to help the uninsured.

THINKING SOCIOLOGICALLY

What are the advantages and disadvantages of each proposal above? What effect would each proposal have on different groups of people in a society?

A significant problem for state and federal governments and for individuals is the high cost of drug prescriptions. The pharmaceutical industry does not cap costs in the United States as it does in many other countries as required by governments, partly due to what they argue are research costs connected with developing new drugs; for this reason also, only brand label drugs can be sold for a certain period before generic drugs can be sold to allow companies to recoup their development costs. Many individuals and even states have turned to Canada and other countries for cheaper drugs in order to control costs. However, the U.S. administration opposes purchases outside of the United States, pointing out possible problems with quality control.

Social scientists say that three factors must be present for a major social initiative such as universal health insurance to pass: common understanding of the problem, general agreement on the approach to solving the problem, and positive political ramifications for legislators taking a position on the problem. The last major attempt to pass a comprehensive reform plan in the United States during the Clinton presidency failed in 1994 (Oberlander 2002). Although there was agreement on the problem, the policy issues—how to approach and solve the problem—never coalesced.

Thus, the crisis in U.S. health care continues, and there are likely to be continuing efforts to reform the system. Many reformers look to Canada's system as a possible model. (See Sociology around the World on the facing page).

Experts in health care predict that several trends will affect the future direction of U.S. health care (Coile 2002; Morrison 2000; Weber 2003):

1. Response to the threat of bioterrorism means hospitals must be prepared to be first responders in emergency, and public health officials and the Centers for Disease Control have taken on new importance with the national threats from terrorism.

2. PPOs have gained enrollment (about 92 million enrollees), while HMOs have lost enrollees (less than 80 million).

3. Hospitals are growing to meet increased demand for services, advertising their services, and changing their images to please clients.

4. Use of computer technology for record keeping and medical tests is growing.

5. Medical advances are changing the way physicians and hospitals treat clients. For example, gene testing and therapy, stem-cell therapy, and individualized drugs are imminent.

6. Employers are fighting the rapid increases in health care insurance costs; many are dropping HMOs and shifting more cost for health care to employees.

7. Growing numbers of citizens without health insurance and reformers are reviving debates about national health insurance. Several organizations have plans ready to present to Congress (Physicians' Working Group for Single-Payer National Health Insurance 2003).

Although it is difficult to predict whether change will mean dramatic restructuring or tinkering with the current

Sociology around the World

Comparing Health Care Systems: The Canadian Model

Two principles underlie Canada's system: all Canadians should have the right to health care and financial barriers to care should be eliminated. After World War II, the Canadian government established universal health insurance to improve the health of all Canadians, with costs shared 50–50 by federal and provincial governments. Physicians are paid by the national health insurance in a fee-for-service or per-patient-fee plan, not a government salary. The plan has led to improved productivity and prosperity (Bolaria and Dickinson 2001).

As a publicly funded insurance plan in a privately controlled system, physicians are not government employees. They maintain autonomy, are well-paid, and have high prestige. The government, in consultation with the medical professionals, sets prices for services. This plan contains costs by determining the level of reimbursement for services, controlling the number of physicians entering medical schools, and limiting private insurance to supplemental plans for vision, dental, and drug coverage.

Comparing major health indicators in Canada and the United States, Canada has lower infant mortality (4.7 deaths per 1,000 live births in Canada versus 6.6 in the United States), and higher life expectancy (80.2 years in Canada versus 77.9 years in the United States) (U.S. Census Bureau 2006b). Canada pays for the system with taxes that are 15 to 20 percent higher than the United States, but at one-third percent less cost per capita for health care than the United States. Canada spent 10.4 percent of its GDP in 2005 on health expenditures, while the United States commits 15.3 percent of its GDP

(Canadian Institute for Health Information 2005). Comparing Canada and the United States with 16 developed countries, the United States spent the most per capita ($5,635 in 2003). Norway, Switzerland, and Canada follow with $3,807 to $3,001 per capita (Canadian Institute for Health Information 2005).

The Canadian system is the one most often mentioned as a model for a future U.S. system (Cockerham 2004). Problems of care denied because of lack of insurance, discrimination, and geographic maldistribution—major issues in the U.S. system—have been largely solved.

In a comparison of access in the U.S. and Canadian systems, 13 percent of Americans are unable to get needed care, many for financial reasons. In Canada, 3.7 percent cannot get care, almost none for financial reasons. In addition, controls by corporations result in hospital stays in the United States that are 20 to 40 percent shorter than in most other countries for similar procedures. Some attribute this to the profit motive that undermines attention to services and to client needs as foremost. Yet in Canada, waiting periods for nonessential procedures are longer and tests such as MRIs are given less often.

Fewer people in the United States report being satisfied with their health system than in Canada. A comparison of public opinion regarding the health care systems resulted in the following:

	Canada (%)		United States (%)	
	1988	2001	1988	2001
Only minor changes needed	56	21	10	18
Fundamental changes needed	38	59	60	51
Completely rebuild system	5	18	29	28

Source: Blendon et al. (2002).

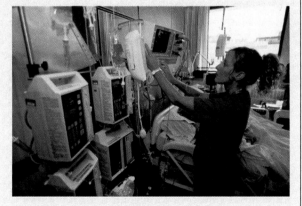

An intensive care nurse checks the monitors for a patient at Lion's Gate Hospital in Vancouver, Canada. In Canada, medical care is guaranteed by citizenship.

Source: © Christopher J. Morris / Corbis.

Since the Canadian system has many positive qualities, why have Americans not adopted it? A proposal for a similar system has been put before Congress, but controversy continues. Concern among conservatives in the United States about government control—combined with lobbying by physicians, insurance companies, and drug companies—have helped to keep the U.S. system in private hands. Other concerns raised about the Canadian system have to do with access to some types of care, waiting periods for nonessential surgeries, and rationing of care for some procedures (Cockerham 2004; Schiff, Bindman, and Brennan 1994). No system is perfect, including the Canadian one. The question is which one provides better care of the citizenry in the long run.

Depicted above is the process of creating traditional medicines, from start to finish, in Ethiopia. First the plants are cultivated or picked from wild herbs. Then the medicine is extracted from the plants. This is sold in the equivalent of pharmacies or prescribed by traditional healers.

system, these and other trends make change inevitable— leaving the health care system of the United States with three main challenges: (1) what to do about the rising uninsured population; (2) how to control costs, especially in a managed care system; and (3) what the physician-client relationship will be under new structures of health care (Pescosolido and Boyer 2001). The next section looks at change in health care at the global level of the social world.

THINKING SOCIOLOGICALLY

Do profit motive and competition create higher quality in a service field such as health care, as they seem to in production of products? Why or why not? What are some positive and some negative consequences of a competitive system with the "winners" rewarded by higher profits?

Health Care around the Globe

The doctor lived in a modest house in rural Kenya. His herbal garden produced many of the medicinal plants that were drying in front of the house and that he used in treatment in lieu of modern medicines that were in short supply. This Western-trained physician combined modern and traditional medicine to meet his clients' needs, and villagers came from miles around, bringing food and livestock in payment for services. This is but one example of medical care around the world.

Each society organizes its health care system in ways congruous with its culture. Although societies have developed different ways of dealing with illness, Western scientific medicine is spreading throughout the world. The demographic makeup, value systems, and financial status of each country will have an effect on how health care is delivered.

Developed societies with a high proportion of elderly and a low proportion of young people have very different needs from developing societies with many children. In "older" societies, special care for chronic illness is more necessary, whereas "younger" societies must deal with childhood illnesses.

Great Britain: Socialized Medicine

During a year-long sabbatical in England, the Ballantine family was signed up with a local "surgeon," as the British call family physicians. Their sore throats, upset tummies, and bruised feet visited the doctor at no direct cost. The school referred their daughter to the hospital eye clinic for glasses, again at no cost. Their son was diagnosed and treated for "glandular fever" (mononucleosis), once again at no cost.

In Great Britain, all citizens have access to treatment by family physicians and dentists, to the dispensing of prescribed drugs, to eye care, and to community nursing and health visitor services. Although citizens can pay extra for private care, the system is geared toward providing mass care through local "surgeries." The general practitioner is the initial contact for almost everyone entering the medical care system. Each general practitioner provides primary care for approximately 2,500 registered patients and receives a substantial salary directly from the government based on the number of patients registered. Doctors also enjoy high prestige. People can register with the general practitioner of their choice, as long as the physician is willing to accept them. Family doctors refer patients to secondary (hospital) care when needed. Once registered, individuals use this one primary care option within the system of free care.

The health care system of Great Britain removes economic factors from the health marketplace. The government has created the National Health Service (NHS), which controls almost all general and specialized health services. The establishment of the NHS in 1948 represented the decision that health care is a human right. The shift in values was from a market system (pay as you can) to social equity system (equal health care for all). It reflected the modified socialistic economic philosophy of the government (Cockerham 2004; Lassey, Lassey, and Jinks 1997).

Since physician participation in the NHS is not mandatory, some private practices still exist, and doctors can accept private paying patients. However, as employees of the state, most health personnel receive a government salary; government medical boards have almost total responsibility for planning and control of medical care. Although the maintenance of standards in such a system is a government responsibility, monitoring these standards has been delegated to the health professionals. Some individuals complain about waits for visits and surgery and about aging facilities, but recent changes are improving public opinion of the health care system (Cockerham 2004; Weiss and Lonnquist 2006).

The results of the British system have been high life expectancy, low infant mortality, and the percentage of the GNP spent on health care held to 8 percent. Recent proposals for reforms have resulted in some decentralization of decision making, more competition between care providers, and more efficiency in the system.

The People's Republic of China: Medicine in a Communist State

Jeanne, one of the coauthors, met Xi (pronounced "She") on a train in China. He was returning to his village after completing a medical training course that covered first aid treatment, giving immunizations, and recognizing serious symptoms. He is one of over 1.8 million *barefoot doctors* or *countryside doctors*, paramedics trained in basic medicine who provide health care for rural residents in China's villages.

Barefoot doctors are generally peasants selected by fellow members of their agricultural communes. They continue to work on the farm, but after some training take responsibility for preventive medicine and some aspects of primary care in the local neighborhood. Their income is determined in the same manner as other agricultural workers. The barefoot doctor is the only medical practitioner that many of the 800 million people living in rural areas ever see. From a sociological perspective, a strength of these practitioners is their within-the-culture socialization; given the homogeneity of peasant neighborhoods, the barefoot doctor should have little difficulty understanding the local culture.

Little was known outside China about its health care system until the 1970s when Western visitors, including health observers, were welcomed by the government. When the "bamboo curtain" was raised in 1971, the outside world learned that, against a background of poverty, a primary network of health services had been established. However, health care delivery faced major problems due to the country being so large in area and the population so spread out and rural. In addition, the political leaders were determined to bring industrialization and a modern lifestyle to the country in a very short time. This put severe pressures on all of China's institutions, including the health care system.

Western-style medicine expanded rapidly in China. From 1978 to 1980, the number of traditional Chinese medical personnel increased slightly, but the number of higher level medical personnel increased significantly.

Today, clinics for preventive care, birth control, and first aid are scattered throughout rural areas; the very sick go to regional hospitals. Although the numbers of barefoot doctors has declined, there seems to be no government plan to eliminate these practitioners. On the contrary, the government is attempting to upgrade their training with formal educational programs such as the one Xi had attended. Participants are tested and licensed under close supervision by local departments of public health. Today, these practitioners take formal training for a minimum of six months. Many have taken courses in specific areas of Western medicine such as minor surgery as well as Chinese practices. So although Western medicine is not supplanting the old system, it is being integrated into traditional medicine; doctors are trained in both. Consider the example of acupuncture, an ancient practice that has spread around the world.

Acupuncture is an ancient Chinese method for treating certain physical problems and relieving pain. It is part of a healing system that understands health and the human body in relation to nature; the body seeks a balance between itself and the world around it; when imbalance occurs, disease results. Thus, the goal of Chinese medicine is to restore internal balance to the body.

Acupuncture along with related treatments is based on the idea that the body has certain points that ease and control pain and stimulate body functions. The process of inserting fine sharp needles into selected points (there are 700 possible points) related to affected organs in the body is essentially painless, and doctors have even done operations without chemical anesthesia using acupuncture to block pain. The procedures are widely practiced in Asia and are gaining popularity in many Western countries.

Although acupuncture has been practiced for over 5,000 years in China, only in the 1970s when relations with China improved did this treatment become known and practiced in the West. Many Western doctors reject the

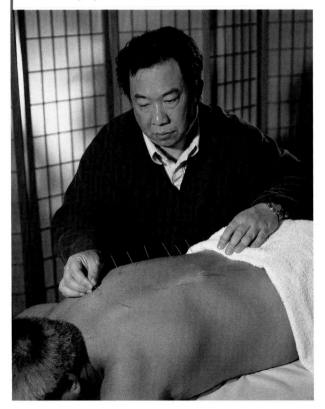

This acupuncturist is inserting needles on the back of his patient. This is an ancient and highly respected medical system in China, and it has gained significant headway in the United States.

Source: © Royalty-Free / Corbis.

practice as unscientific and ineffective, and some regulating agencies have put limits on its practice. However, many patients feel otherwise. An increasing number of acupuncture pain clinics are opening around the world; about 8.2 million U.S. adults have used acupuncture (Barnes et al. 2004). Some insurance companies also cover the costs of acupuncture, and the World Health Organization recognizes over 40 conditions that can be effectively treated by acupuncture (Weiss and Lonnquist 2006). In Australia, 15 percent of the general practitioners offer acupuncture (Lupton 2001). Diffusion of medical knowledge throughout the world brings new practices to all countries.

The Chinese health care system does face problems. In rural areas, many people practice traditional folk medicine. Disease, poor sanitation, pollution, ignorance, and smoking result in lowered life expectancy. Chinese account for about 30 percent of the world's tobacco consumption, or 300 million smokers; about 70 percent of China's male population smokes. Smoking-related deaths are increasing, with lung cancer deaths increasing 4.5 percent a year (Lin et al. 1998). Government efforts to control smoking have been ambivalent because the government receives money from foreign tobacco sales.

A brief look at China's urban areas shows Red Cross health workers, formerly known as *street doctors*, practicing under the supervision of doctors in local hospitals. The Red Cross health workers also focus on health promotion and disease prevention. Doctors functioning in similar capacities in factories are known as *worker doctors*.

Today, China's health care system is financed by the government, patient fees, and health insurance. Although only 155 million of 1.2 billion people are covered by health insurance, with the increasingly comprehensive health care network, China has brought down the death rate. Average life expectancy is now 70.9 years, compared to Japan at over 80 years (U.S. Census Bureau 2006b) and compared to the period after the Chinese Cultural Revolution in 1955 with an average life expectancy of 40.8 years.

Nicaragua: Revolutionary Changes

An elderly Nicaraguan woman, Lucia, came to a rural clinic with the complaint of "sadness in my body and fear in my chest." Was this a heart problem? Arthritis? Some other sickness? Knowing the cultural context of the woman's description, the doctors determined her problem. After checking her physical condition and charging her a modest fee based on her income, they found that her complaint was not symptomatic of a heart attack, but rather of missing her children, who had all left to work in foreign countries. The patient, with limited access to psychological care, had found what help she could.

Nicaragua provides a case study of how political and economic changes transform a health care system. The story begins with the Sandinista revolution. After a massive popular uprising ousted Somoza, the dictator whose family had controlled the country (with U.S. backing) since 1936, the Government of National Reconstruction was formed. Before that time, health care for the poor had been limited or nonexistent. However, the new leaders of the Sandinista People's Revolution declared that the entire population would receive free medical assistance, with clinics and hospitals throughout the nation (Garfield and Williams 1992). Help came from West Germany in the form of immunizations for children; medical brigades arrived first from Cuba, then from Mexico, Panama, Costa Rica, Argentina, and Honduras; money from regional and international organizations helped pay for medicine. Medical care became widespread.

The United States boycotted the Nicaraguan government because of its socialist-leftist leanings and was instrumental in funding the so-called "contra war." Eventually, in 1990, the demoralized country voted to end the war by supporting a new government, the UNO coalition. This coalition of center- and right-wing parties won a majority of seats in the parliament, and the reins of government were turned over to the rightist parties. Under the leadership of Violetta Chamora, the health care system returned to privatization. The wealthy could afford to go to Miami or Houston for care, but for others privatization meant finding money to pay for care in their own country, money many did not have. Once again, quality of care in Nicaragua became income-contingent.

One stark example of this differential access is seen in the nation's only psychiatric hospital, located in the capital city of Managua. No drugs or technological equipment are available, and the facility serves as a holding pen for the 200 chronically mentally ill and unmanageable patients. In the middle of the compound, surrounded by barbed wire and a locked gate, is a modern facility with drugs and treatment programs for the few who can pay.

The nationwide infant mortality rate decreased under the health care system that was available to all but grew again under the privatized system; the current rate is about 35 per 1,000 live births (PHNIP 2002). Among the indigenous cultures of eastern Nicaragua, diseases eliminated in the 1980s have come back. With no medicines to treat them, measles, whooping cough, malaria, and tuberculosis are again becoming widespread and reducing life expectancy. Medical personnel have the skills to treat the problems, but there are no tools or medicines. As a hospital administrator put it, "We are like a car with no gas."

The primary care and lay community health workers under the government-funded health care system extended care into rural communities; the current government ministry is stressing specialized medical training. In the face of prohibitive cost and lack of availability of medical care, people in rural areas are today returning to traditional folk practices and home remedies such as teas and herbal plants. Some of these remedies, like the use of herbal teas for diarrhea, work well. However, other folk beliefs are harmful. One belief is that women should not eat milk products, eggs, or beans for 40 days after giving birth. This harmful misinformation could be corrected with proper

In Esteli, Nicaragua, political murals and graffiti celebrate the Sandinista movement, which many Nicaraguans felt was a movement on behalf of the people. Access to health care expanded for common people under this revolutionary and pro-Marxist government. Health treatment has become less accessible under privatization, with medical care more dependent on ability to pay.

Source: www.downtheroad.org.

health care and education. However, this requires a vibrant educational system that reaches into the countryside.

The cases of Cuba, the United States, Kenya, Great Britain, China, Nicaragua, and other countries illustrate the impact of national and global political and economic factors on the health care available to citizens. The political system of countries and their economic status influence the philosophy toward health care and the money they have to put into health care. International policies such as embargoes between countries influence availability of health care *within* countries; and international organizations, such as the World Health Organization, focus on epidemics and pandemics throughout the world.

Globalization of Medical Problems

A dramatic worldwide health problem illustrating the interconnectedness between countries is the international sale of body parts. In some countries, people at the bottom of the stratification system are so desperately poor that they sell their body parts to help their families survive. Witness the example of mothers and fathers in poor slums of Mumbai and other cities in India who sell their kidneys for money to pay for housing, food, education for their children, and dowries to marry off daughters. In the process, their health often deteriorates, and when the money is gone, life is even more difficult. Although laws were passed in India in 1994 banning the sale of human organs (Kumar 2001), few violators are caught and punished.

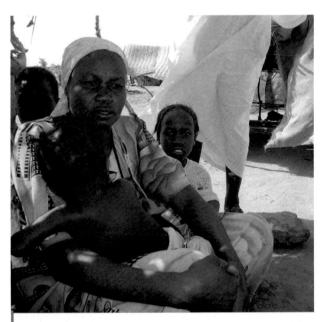

These two women are of similar age, both in their 30s. Health facilities make an enormous difference in one's life chances, health, and how one ages. The woman at the top lives in North America; the woman in the bottom photo raises a family in Senegal, West Africa.

Source: © Jordan Chesbrough; © USAID Dakar, Senegal.

Wealthy individuals in need of kidneys buy these body parts to improve their chances of survival and a normal life; for example, the transplant trade attracts medical tourists from Europe who visit developing countries in Latin America and Asia for transplants and other "cheap" treatments. This is a dramatic illustration of the differences in health attitudes and behavior between rich and poor.

The black market in body parts is spreading to many countries. An international "transplant Mafia" based in Moldova (once part of the Soviet Union) smuggles live donors to the United States to sell their lungs and kidneys because the market for body parts exceeds the supply (Kates 2002). Even officials in coroners' offices have been apprehended harvesting body parts without consent of family members, often making a profit from the sales (Mashberg 2002). Reports from Nigeria indicate that mortuary and cemetery workers are selling body parts at markets (Ananova 2001), and a survey of students in the United Kingdom found that one in four would sell a kidney to help pay for their educations (Ananova 2002). This issue emphasizes the global differences between rich and poor people and countries; where there is a need and a market for goods, those in need will step in to fill the gap, and many sick individuals will pay handsomely for body parts.

The status of a nation's health and medical care are often measured by key international markers—decrease in infant mortality and increase in life expectancy. *Infant mortality* indicates the availability of and access to prenatal care and care for infants, and *life expectancy* shows the overall health conditions in a country. These basic data tell us a great deal about the health and health care of a nation. Consider the health statistics in Table 13.6 and 13.7.

THINKING SOCIOLOGICALLY

First examine Tables 13.6 and 13.7. Select several countries with the highest and lowest infant mortality and life expectancy. What do the figures tell you; that is, what might one conclude about health care or quality of life from these figures?

Globalization and the Mobility of Disease

Thus far, we have looked at comparisons of health care around the world; we now focus on issues of global change and interconnectedness as health issues. The density and mobility of the world's population (discussed in Chapter 14) affects human health; for instance, use of land and space determines the number of rodents and insects, the water supplies, and the direct contact people have with one another. Currently, about half of the world's population lives in urban areas, many in slums surrounding major cities. Problems such as open sewers, inadequate sanitation, lack of electricity, and polluted water pervade these slums. Most infections spread more readily where there is a population of at least 150,000, although more than 1 million is even more favorable for infectious germs

| TABLE 13.6 | **Infant Mortality Rates in 2006 in Countries with 5+ Million Persons** |

Number of Deaths Under 1 Year per 1,000 Live Births

Lowest		Highest	
Sweden	2.8	Angola	185.4
Japan	3.2	Sierra Leone	160.4
Finland	3.6	Afghanistan	160.2
Czech Republic	3.9	Mozambique	129.2
Germany	4.1	Niger	118.3
France	4.2	Somalia	114.9
Switzerland	4.3	Mali	107.6
Spain	4.4	Tajikistan	106.5
Denmark	4.5	Tanzania	96.5
Austria	4.6	Malawi	94.4
Belgium	4.6		
Canada	4.7		
Netherlands	5.0		
United Kingdom	5.1		
Ireland	5.3		
Greece	5.4		
Italy	5.8		
Cuba	6.2		
Taiwan	6.3		
United States	6.6 (21st)		

Source: United States Bureau of the Census, Population Division, International Programs Center, "International Data Base." www.census.gov/ipc/www/idbnew.html, 2006.

| TABLE 13.7 | **Life Expectancy in the Year 2006 in Countries with 5+ Million Persons** |

Highest		Lowest	
Japan	81.3	Angola	37.5
Australia	80.5	Mozambique	39.8
Switzerland	80.5	Zambia	40.0
Sweden	80.5	Zimbabwe	40.4
Canada	80.2	Malawi	41.7
Italy	79.8	Niger	43.8
France	79.7	Rwanda	47.3
Spain	79.7	Cote d'Ivoirie	48.8
Israel	79.5	Ethiopia	49.0
Greece	79.2	Uganda	52.7
Netherlands	79.0		
Belgium	78.8		
United Kingdom	78.5		
Finland	78.5		
Jordan	78.4		
United States	77.9		
Germany	77.4		
Austria	76.2		

Source: United States Bureau of the Census, Population Division, International Programs Center. "International Data Base." www.census.gov/ipc/www/idbnew.html.2006.

(Wilson 2006) by increasing the chances that the germs will find hosts that are not already immune. Our globe has increasing numbers of cities that exceed 1 million.

Other factors that help the spread of disease are the increasing numbers of settings with shared circulated air (airplanes, doomed stadiums, air-conditioned buildings). In addition, most diseases travel by direct contact with other infected people. A World Health Organization study indicates that of the infections leading to death, 65 percent are due to person-to-person contact. Another 22 percent come from food, water, or soil contamination; 13 percent are transmitted by insects; and just 0.3 percent are acquired directly from animals (bird flu, rabies, etc.) (Wilson 2006). Because people are moving around the globe much more today than in the past, they are exposed to more people in more environments. For example, business trips take people all over the globe. More than 5,000 airports now host international travelers, and more than 1 million people cross international borders each day, counting only commercial airline travel (Wilson 2006).

When the West Nile virus—a deadly mosquito-borne disease—was first discovered in New York City in 1999, it killed seven people before any action could be taken. Within a year, it had spread to 12 states, and within two years was found in mosquitoes, 60 species of birds, and a dozen mammals (Wilson 2006). Although health officials acted quickly to stem the spread of the disease, other pandemics are a constant threat. The world is highly connected, and diseases anywhere in the world can quickly spread to other continents, overpowering the medical communities' ability to diagnose, isolate, and treat diseases. Other examples of contagious diseases have been SARs, bird flu, and AIDS. The AIDS pandemic took the lives of 2 million people in sub–Saharan Africa alone in 2005, and an additional 2.7 million people in the region became infected with HIV (UNAIDS-Joint United Nations Programme on HIV/AIDS 2006).

AIDS is spread in part by local traditions. For example, in sub–Saharan Africa where AIDS is rampant and some villages have only children and elderly people remaining, cultural practices enhance the spread of AIDS. One reason is that men often travel from their rural villages to urban areas for work, are infected with AIDS by prostitutes, and return to infect their wives. In 2006, the Bill and Melinda Gates Foundation funded a new initiative to help combat AIDS and malaria in poor countries.

This leads to the issue of lack of resources for medications. When the South African government passed a law that would make lifesaving HIV/AID medicines available to the 4 million persons suffering from the disease in that country, the pharmaceutical giants from the developed countries united and used their clout to crush the law. Only intense negative publicity caused them to finally relent. Seven countries (the United States, Britain, Japan, Germany, Canada, France, and Italy) control 70 percent of the world's monetary resources. Those resources are used to benefit their own populations—12 percent of the world's people; as a result, there will be places in the world where diseases are not being controlled (Booker and Minter 2006). Yet given our global mobility and the mobility of infection, the problem is worldwide. To rephrase Martin Luther King, Jr.'s, statement about injustice, we might say: disease anywhere is disease everywhere.

The issue of global health is not limited to diseases and their treatment. Use of tobacco is a major issue, with perhaps a trillion "sticks"—mostly American made—being sold to and smuggled into countries around the world. Mark Schapiro (2006) documents the active involvement of a number of American Tobacco companies in illegal smuggling activity, and the top U.S. tobacco companies now earn more from cigarette sales abroad than at home. So these companies have a vested interest in the globalization of their product, which is made difficult by countries that bar or severely limit the importation of tobacco products. The World Health Organization considers smuggling tobacco products a major world health issue, and the nations involved also see it as a major health issue. Governments have mixed reactions: they gain tremendous revenue from taxes and tariffs on tobacco products, but health care costs also increase due to diseases. Criminal justice systems have little leverage over companies that operate abroad. It is rare that action to curb sales of tobacco products is ever taken (Schapiro 2006).

Indigenous Medicine: Traditional and Modern Medical Practices

In India, an ancient Hindu approach to medical care focuses on the link between mind and body. It suggests that health can be achieved if there is an adequate balance between the two and that balance can be brought about through meditation and medication, a combination of Western medicines and appropriate relaxation and exercise. Such beliefs are consistent with the overall pattern of Indian culture and religion.

In a rural Mexican–Native American village in Arizona, a gravely ill young boy named Yas is being treated by the shaman of the village for a rattlesnake bite. Prayers are chanted by all present as the shaman pours a mixture of herbs and other ingredients over Yas's head. After this procedure, Yas is taken to a local health care clinic for Western treatment.

In an African village in Ghana, the local shaman, Kofa, mixes herbs for each patient from recipes passed down through the generations. There are herbal mixtures for infection, impotence, infertility, asthma, stomach ailments, and numerous other problems. Using combinations of traditional and Western treatments, he gains legitimacy. He points out that the herbal medicines he uses are very effective and, in fact, form the basic substances of many Western medicines.

Down the road from the shaman, patients can visit Amma, the priestess, for a small gift or sum of money. The closest role in Western medicine to Amma's services would be a psychologist or psychiatrist. Her visitors include the lovesick, the lonely, the hypochondriacs, and the bereaved. She sings chants, prescribes potions (mixtures of herbs, often sedatives), and gives advice.

People around the world rely on a variety of medical models and practitioners to meet their needs. As migrations occur, practices spread. Western medicine has learned from folk medicine traditions; tested many of the traditional herbal remedies; incorporated acupuncture, pressure point, and massage therapies; and used other procedures adopted from traditional medicine. *Allopathy* (medicine practiced by MDs in Western societies) retains dominance over alternative medical practices—homeopathy, chiropractic, acupuncture, and other types of medical practices that those in authority often label *quackery*. Yet folk medicines in many societies combined with Western medicine effectively treat people's illnesses in their social contexts. Medicine itself has become globally informed, delivered with awareness of local social setting.

Unfortunately, around the world, many preventable and curable diseases go untreated because of the lack of access to medicines and health care. Dehydration from diarrhea caused by water-borne diseases such as cholera, blindness caused by vitamin A deficiency, and other preventable diseases are unnecessary afflictions in today's world. Some developing countries have few physicians per capita. For instance, in Malawi, there is 1 doctor for every 100,000 people, in Ethiopia and Niger 3 doctors for every 100,000 citizens, and in Mali 4 doctors per 100,000 citizens. The few doctors in these countries are located mostly in urban areas (United Nations Development Programme

2005a). Folk remedies are the only health care most of these citizens have.

As long as there is inequality in our social world, adequate health care is unlikely to reach all people and all countries (Garrett 2000). In spite of increasingly sophisticated medical technology and medicines available, cost, distribution, and policies of governments are the determinants of who receives health care around the world.

THINKING SOCIOLOGICALLY

We live in a global world, yet our most immediate experiences are local. What are benefits you and your family might receive if international agencies resolve health problems in Africa, Asia, and South America?

SO WHAT?

When you are sick and when you are diagnosed and cared for, the norms that allow you to be sick and the expectations of you in the sick role vary from the expectations placed on others around the world. Although health is a private, personal concern, it is also a public concern, delivered through organizations dispensing health care and government practices determining access and funding of health care. Distant from your daily life but important to your well-being are the global health organizations that concern themselves with global epidemics. In addition,

whether you have insurance or money to pay doctors depends in part on the economic conditions in society and the global marketplace of health care delivery.

Our social institutions—from family, education, and religion to politics, economics, and health—maintain stability in societies; however, the world in which we live is a dynamic one. In the final two chapters, we turn to an examination of how change occurs. First, we examine two forces that have changed exponentially in the past two centuries—population patterns and urbanization. We close with an examination of social change in its many manifestations.

CONTRIBUTING TO YOUR SOCIAL WORLD

At the Local Level: *Local health clinics* sometime need volunteers or interns.

At the Organizational or Institutional Level: *Relay for Life* and other health-related support agencies involve fundraising for cancer treatment, research, and other causes. There are fundraisers for AIDS, for example, that can enhance both medical research centers and delivery of medication nationally and globally.

At the National and Global Levels: The *World Health Organization* sometimes takes interns, especially if you are willing to work outside your own country.

Sister villages with third world countries help improve the lives of residents and provide exchange opportunities. Ask your community representatives about opportunities to help raise funds, build wells, or work on other facilities in developing countries.

Visit www.pineforge.com/ballantinestudy for online activities, sample tests, and other helpful information. Select "Chapter 13: Medicine" for chapter-specific activities.

SOCIAL DYNAMICS

S ocial structures such as institutions—family, education, religion, health, politics, and economics—incline toward stability; they tend to resist change. Yet this entire book shows that societies are dynamic and changing. They are characterized by processes, and those processes are fluid and vibrant. Globalization itself, a major theme in this book, is not only a force for transformation but also evidence of the changing nature of our social world. We do not live in the same sort of world our grandparents inhabited. The macro- and meso-level dimensions of the world have become increasingly powerful, which is exactly why we need a sociological imagination to understand how the events in our own micro worlds are influenced by the larger society.

This section looks at some of those processes that are dynamic, fluid, and vibrant—population changes, urbanization, expansion of technology, social movements, and more. We live in exciting and challenging times, and we will thrive best if we understand the micro-, meso-, and macro-level dimensions of our lives and the linkages between parts of our social world. We turn next to population dynamics and urbanization.

POPULATION AND URBANIZATION:
Living on Spaceship Earth

What to Expect . . .

The human population is limited to this one moderately sized sphere, on which it depends for survival. The question is whether human groups can cooperate with each other and use the resources of the planet responsibly. In the meantime, humans are concentrated in dense urban areas, illustrated by the night shot in the background of these pages, in which bright lights beam from urban areas in Europe but from fewer places in Africa.

Think About It . . .

1. Why is your family the size it is?

2. Why might you or your family decide to move to another location?

3. What characterizes your home town or city? What makes you feel comfortable or uncomfortable there?

4. Why do people move from rural areas to urban areas? What problems does this urbanization trend create?

5. How do global issues relating to urbanization, the environment, and technology affect your family and your local community?

Macro: Global Community

Macro: National Society

Meso: National Institutions and Organizations: Ethnic Subcultures

Micro: Local Organizations and Community

Micro: You and Your Family

Micro: Population trends affect schools, churches, businesses, and communities

Meso: Family, education, religion, health, politics, and economics all affect and are affected by population growth and movement

Macro: National policies on population: birth incentives, birth control, abortion

Macro: Global migrations, epidemics, wars; United Nations policies that affect population

I magine that we are looking down from our satellite at a spherical object drifting through space. It appears to be a beautiful mix of greens and blues, and at night, parts of the sphere glows with lights while other parts are dark. That is home—our little (relatively speaking) planet. The controlling inhabitants of the planet are humans, all 6.5 billion of them. The topic of this chapter is the spread and distribution of those humans living on spaceship earth (Diamond 1999/2005).

Since the emergence of Homo sapiens in East Africa, human populations have grown in uneven surges and declines. The World Population Clock (see Table 14.1) illustrates the process.

Despite some sporadic growth for millennia, the explosion of human beings on the planet in the past two centuries is stunning. If we collapsed all of human history into one 24-hour day, the time period since 1750 would consume one minute. Yet 25 percent of all humans have lived during this "one-minute" time period. In the 200 years between 1750 and 1950, the world's population mushroomed from 800 million to 2.5 billion. On October 12, 1999, the global population reached 6 billion. It has now expanded to over 6.5 billion, growing at the rate of 74.2 million in 2006; estimates put the world population at 7.6 billion by 2020. This means the world is growing each year by the number of people in the country of Germany, Philippines, or Vietnam. Every minute, 249 children are born and 108 people die around the world, resulting in a net increase of 141 people per minute (U.S. Census Bureau 2006b). Between 2000 and 2030, nearly 100 percent of the world growth will occur in developing countries in Africa, Asia, and Latin America (Population Reference Bureau 2006), where 81 percent of the world's population lives and 90 percent of the births occur each year.

TABLE 14.1 **World Population Timetable, 2002**

	World	More Developed Countries	Less Developed Countries	Less Developed Countries (less China)
Population	6,214,891,000	1,197,329,000	5,017,562,000	3,736,850,000
Births per				
Year	133,144,457	13,280,363	119,864,094	102,728,168
Month	11,095,371	1,106,697	9,988,675	8,560,681
Week	2,560,470	255,392	2,305,079	1,975,542
Day	364,779	36,385	328,395	281,447
Hour	15,199	1,516	13,683	11,727
Minute	253	25	228	195
Second	4.2	0.4	3.8	3.3
Deaths per				
Year	53,930,540	12,168,652	41,761,888	33,526,910
Month	4,494,212	1,014,054	3,480,157	2,793,909
Week	1,037,126	234,013	803,113	644,748
Day	147,755	33,339	114,416	91,855
Hour	6,156	1,389	4,767	3,827
Minute	103	23	79	64
Second	1.7	0.4	1.3	1.1
Natural increase per				
Year	79,213,917	1,111,711	78,102,206	69,201,258
Month	6,601,160	92,643	6,508,517	5,766,772
Week	1,523,345	21,379	1,501,966	1,330,793
Day	217,024	3,046	213,979	189,592
Hour	9,043	127	8,916	7,900
Minute	151	2	149	132
Second	2.5	0.04	2.5	2.2
Infant deaths per				
Year	7,254,371	94,505	7,159,866	6,621,798
Month	604,531	7,875	596,656	551,817
Week	139,507	1,817	137,690	127,342
Day	19,875	259	19,616	18,142
Hour	828	11	817	756
Minute	14	0.2	14	13
Second	0.2	0.003	0.2	0.2

Source: Haupt and Kane (2003).

Let us start by focusing on one area of our world, a place called Kenya in East Africa. We focus here partly because East Africa, where Kenya and Tanzania are located, was—according to many scientists—home to spaceship earth's earliest human inhabitants. Scientists believe bones found in the dry Olduvai Gorge area are the oldest remains of Homo sapiens ever found. We also focus here because today Kenya is making human history for another reason. With a population of about 34.7 million people and a natural increase of 2.57 percent annually (*World Fact Book* 2006), Kenya is among the most rapidly growing populations on earth. Let us transport ourselves to this country and attempt to understand the situation of the Kenyan to see if that holds some explanation for Kenya's ballooning population. Although Kenya is made up of many groups of people with different religions and value systems, there are several themes that pervade most subcultures.

Wengari, like Kenyan girls of most tribal affiliations, married in her teens. She has been socialized to believe that her main purpose in life is to bear children, to help with the farming, and to care for parents in their old age. Children are seen as an asset in Kenya; religious beliefs and cultural value systems encourage large families. However, the population of Kenya is 45 percent dependent (people under 15 or over 65) (*World Fact Book* 2006); they rely on working-age citizens to support them. Arable farmland is becoming scarce and cannot continue to feed the growing population. Added to that are severe droughts in parts of the country—droughts that are killing animal herds and preventing growth of crops. These facts, however, have little meaning to young women like Wengari who have been socialized into their role within their subcultures.

By contrast, to the north in many of the industrialized, urbanized countries of Europe, birthrates are below population replacement levels, meaning population size eventually may begin to drop. Germany, Hungary, and Latvia, for instance, are losing population. "While Asia's share of world population may continue to hover around 55 percent through the next century, Europe's portion has declined sharply and could drop even more during the twenty-first century. Africa and Latin America each will gain part of Europe's portion. By 2100, Africa is expected to capture the greatest share. Countries growing by less than 1 percent annually include Japan, Australia, New Zealand, Russia, and much of Europe" (Population Reference Bureau 2006).

In industrialized societies, children in the middle class and above are dependent until they leave home; the typical European boy or girl often waits until the late 20s or even 30s to start a family after education is complete and a job is in hand. Many limit their family size because societal values support small families; it is difficult to house large families in small urban apartments where the majority of the population live. Workers must support and feed their families on earned wages rather than through farming. Both mother and father often work, and contrary to many children in developing countries, most children born will survive to old age. Life expectancy, the average age at death, is 47 years in Kenya; in some European countries, it is over 80 years.

Anthropologists sift for fossils in the Olduvai Gorge in Tanzania, site of the famous Leakey discoveries that reveal so much about human origins.

Source: Enright / Corbis.

Changes in the environment and in the global economy make it difficult for this Kenyan family to provide for itself. Some of these children and their cousins may find it necessary to move to urban centers, a worldwide migration trend. Much of the socialization they received in villages will not be relevant to their adult urban lives.

Source: © USAID.

India is the second largest country in the world, but it has one of the fastest growth rates. This is a typical street in Calcutta, a crowded urban center of 15,656,000 people.

Source: © Thierry Prat / Sygma / Corbis.

On yet another continent, China, the country with the largest population in the world at 1.306 billion people, had the greatest drop in population growth in the late twentieth century due to strict governmental family planning practices (U.S. Census Bureau 2006b). India, the second largest country, has a population growth rate (increase in a country's population during a specified period of time) of 1.38 percent a year, just over replacement level (*World Fact Book* 2006).

While some countries have birth rates below population replacement levels, the world's population continues to grow because of the skyrocketing growth rate in other countries and because of *population momentum* caused by the large number of individuals of childbearing age having children; even though birth rates per couple drop, the number of women of childbearing age is still very high, resulting in continued growth in population size. Unfortunately, most of the countries with the highest growth rates are developing countries with the fewest resources to support the additional population.

What we have been discussing is the study of human populations, called **demography**. All permanent societies, states, communities, adherents of a common religious faith, racial or ethnic groups, kinship or clan groups, professions, and other identifiable categories of people are **populations**. The size, geographical location, and spatial movement of the population; its concentration in certain geographical areas; and changing characteristics of the population are important elements in the study of demography and constitute a core subfield within sociology.

With growing populations and limited farmland to support the population, hungry people move to cities in hopes of finding jobs. This pattern of movement is called **urbanization**. The second half of this chapter will consider the evolution, growth, and development of populated areas, including movements from rural areas to cities, the organization of urban life, the relationship between individuals and the city, and some problems facing cities.

The previous chapters have been organized by moving from micro- to macro-level analysis. Because demographic work has focused on societies and global trends, we will reverse the order in this section and discuss macro-level patterns first, followed by meso-level causes for change, and micro-level implications.

THINKING SOCIOLOGICALLY

Do you have choice in how many children you have? What factors go into your decision? How might your decision differ if you were in a different country? What might work against your having the number of children you want?

MACRO-LEVEL PATTERNS IN WORLD POPULATION GROWTH

For thousands of years, early Homo sapiens roamed the plains of Africa, their survival and growth depending on the environment in which they lived. Over thousands of years, they mastered fire and tools, and agriculture and animals, and with these skills slowly increased control over the environment, allowing their numbers to expand. This evolution in the growth patterns of human populations is worth closer examination.

Patterns of Population Growth over Time

Members of the small band of early Homo sapiens who inhabited the Olduvai Gorge moved gradually, haltingly, from this habitat into what are now other parts of Africa, Asia, and Europe. The process took thousands of years. At times, births outnumbered deaths and populations grew, but at other times, plagues, famines, droughts, and wars decimated populations. From the beginning of human existence, estimated from perhaps one million years ago until modern times, the number of births and deaths balanced each other over the centuries (Diamond 2005). The large population we see now results from population evolution that consisted of three phases:

1. Humans, because of their thinking ability, competed satisfactorily in the animal kingdom to obtain the basic necessities for survival of the species.

2. With the agricultural revolution that occurred about 10,000 years ago and the resulting food surplus, mortality rates declined and the population grew as more infants survived and people lived longer.

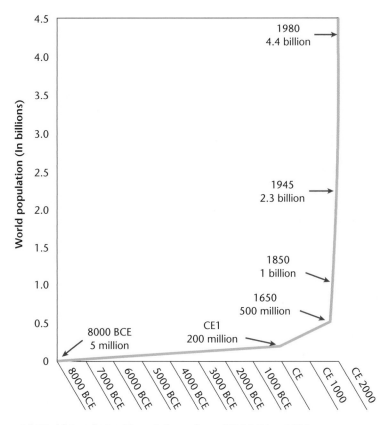

Figure 14.1   The Exponential World Population Growth from about 8000 BCE to 1980

Source: Abu-Lughod (2001:50).

3. The biggest increase came with the industrial revolution, beginning about 300 years ago. Improved medical knowledge and sanitation helped bring the death rate down.

When industrialization made its debut, it brought the social and economic changes discussed in Chapter 3 (e.g., machines replacing human labor and mass production using resources in new ways), but it also augmented urbanization of societies. The population explosion began with industrialization in Europe and spread to widely scattered areas of the globe. With trade and migrations came the diffusion of ideas and better medical care, influencing population growth rates in all parts of the world by keeping people alive longer. Figure 14.1 shows population growth throughout history.

The worldwide rate of population growth reached its peak in the 1960s and has decreased to a current rate of approximately 1.14 percent per year, resulting in a leveling off of increases in world population (*World Fact Book* 2006). (See Figure 14.2.)

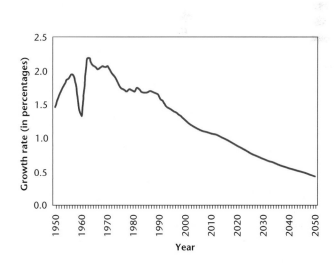

Figure 14.2   World Population Growth Rate, 1950–2050

Source: World Fact Book (2006).

Predictors of Population Growth

Children in some Sub–Saharan and East African countries with the highest rates of HIV/AIDS in the world are forced to fend for themselves. With large percentages of the working aged population dead (or dying) from AIDS, orphaned children take care of their younger siblings. In some villages

Children in Uganda and elsewhere in Africa often have to raise their siblings because their parents have died of AIDS. These six children are siblings and AIDS orphans.

Source: © Gideon Mendel / ActionAid / Corbis.

(*World Fact Book* 2006). Working adults in developing countries have a tremendous burden to support the dependent population, especially if a high percentage of the population is urban and not able to be self-supporting through farming.

Similarly, high percentages of older dependent people over 64 are found in most developed countries. In the European countries of Norway, Sweden, Denmark, the United Kingdom, and Germany, between 15 and 19 percent of the population is in the age group over 64. These countries have low death rates, resulting in the average life expectancy at birth being as high as 80 (*World Fact Book* 2006).

The percentage of dependent elderly people is growing, especially in developed countries. Consider the case of Japan, which faces a grave "graying," or aging of its population, problem. In 2007, 20 percent of its population is over 65, and the average life expectancy is 81.3 years (Population Reference Bureau 2006). The Japanese population is graying nearly

Palestinian children attempt to fly the flag of a Palestinian group. With half of the Palestinian population under age 15, younger Palestinians are taking active roles in politics, and many are responsible for helping to support their families.

Source: © Micah Walter / Corbis.

in Uganda, for instance, social workers visit periodically to bring limited food for survival and see that children are planting crops. These children must learn survival skills—and gender roles—at a very young age. They have little chance to experience the childhood age-role.

Think for a moment about the impact that your age and sex have on your position in society and your activities. Are you of childbearing age? Are you dependent on others for most of your needs? If so, is this largely due to your age and what that age means in your society? Are you supporting others? These matters greatly influence your behavior and that of others like you, and collectively they shape the population patterns of an entire society. In the analysis of age and sex on human behavior, three sets of concepts can be very useful: dependency ratios, sex ratios, and age-sex population pyramids.

The *youth dependency ratio* is the number of children under age 15 to the number between 15 and 64; the number of those over 64 to those between 15 and 64 is called the *aged dependency ratio*. While many of the world's young people under 15 help support themselves and their families, and many over 64 are likewise economically independent, these figures have been taken as the general ages when individuals are not contributing to the labor force. They represent the economic burden (especially in developed countries), the people in the population who must be supported by the working-age population. The **dependency ratio**, then, is the ratio of those in both the young and aged groups compared to the number of people in the productive age groups between 15 and 64 years old.

In several developing countries such as the Gaza Strip (formerly Israeli occupied territory), Benin, and Rwanda, close to 50 percent of the population is under 15 years of age

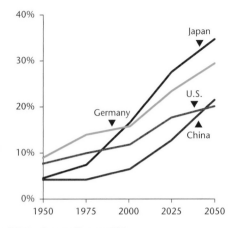

Figure 14.3   Japan Grows Old

Source: Moffett (2003).

Note: Japan's percentage of population over 65 is growing faster than any other nation.

twice as fast as many other nations, in large part because the birth rate is very low, only 1.3 children per woman. There simply are not enough replacement workers to support the aging population. Japan provides a glimpse into the future for other rapidly aging societies including Germany, the United States, and China (Moffett 2003). (See Figure 14.3.)

The sex ratio refers to the ratio of males to females in the population. For instance, the more females, especially females in or soon to be in the fertile years, the more potential there is for population growth. The sex ratio also affects population growth patterns by determining the supply of eligible spouses. Marriage patterns are affected by economic swings, wars in which the proportion of males to females may decrease, and migrations that generally take males from one area and add them to another. **Population pyramids** illustrate sex ratios and dependency ratios (see Figure 14.4 on page 442).

The graphic presentation of the age and sex distribution of a population tells us a great deal about that population. The structures are called pyramids because that is the shape they took until several decades ago. By looking up and down the pyramid, we can see the proportion of population at each age level. Looking to the right and left of the center-line tells us the balance of males to females at each age. The bottom line shows us the total population at each age.

The first pyramid shows populations that have fairly low birth and death rates, typical of developed countries. The second pyramid illustrates populations with high birth rates and large dependent youth populations, typical of developing countries. The third pyramid, "other less developed countries," shows countries in the middle. The world population has been getting both younger (developing countries) *and* older (developed countries), resulting in large numbers of dependent people.

In a number of European countries, 20 percent of the population is over age 64, and life expectancy is nearly 80. This creates a different set of social dilemmas and problems than in countries with large young populations under age 15. This elderly couple strolls along the waterfront in Seaton, England.

Source: © Peter Elvidge.

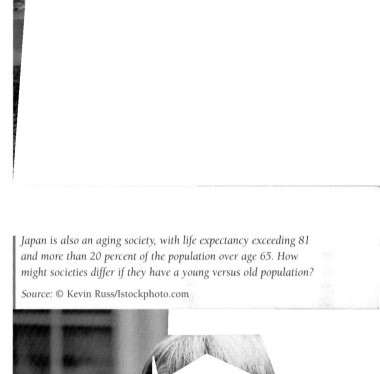

Japan is also an aging society, with life expectancy exceeding 81 and more than 20 percent of the population over age 65. How might societies differ if they have a young versus old population?

Source: © Kevin Russ/Istockphoto.com

As developing nations have more and more children, they are creating more potential parents in later years, adding momentum to the world's population growth. Because today young children live, whereas in the past they might have died of disease and malnutrition, they are likely to reproduce,

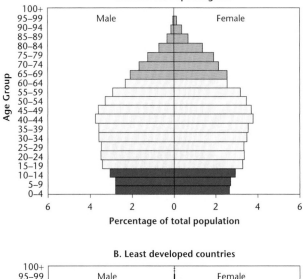

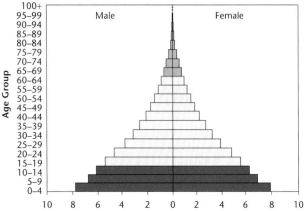

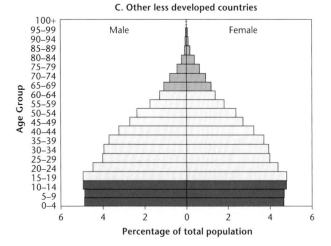

Figure 14.4   Population Pyramids, by Development Group, 2005

Source: United Nations Department of Economic and Social Affairs, Population Division (2005:23).

adding to the population size. Fewer deaths of infants and children due to immunizations and disease control lower mortality rates, resulting in younger populations and higher potential numbers of births in the future.

THINKING SOCIOLOGICALLY

What can you tell about different countries' levels of development by studying the population pyramid?

Explaining Population Patterns: Theoretical Explanations

From the earliest historical writings, we find evidence of interest in population size and growth. Scriptures such as the Quran and the Bible have supported population growth to increase the ranks of the faithful. Of course, population expansion made sense at the time these holy tracts were written. Government leaders throughout the ages have adopted various philosophies about the best size of populations. The ancient Greek philosopher Plato (350 BCE/1960) argued that the city-state should have 5,040 citizens and that measures should be taken to increase or decrease the population to bring it in line with this figure. However, the first significant scholarly analysis that addressed global population issues came from Thomas Malthus (1766–1834), an English clergyman and social philosopher.

Malthus's Theory of Population

In his "Essay on the Principle of Population" (1798/1926), Malthus argued that humans are driven to reproduce and will multiply without limits if no checks are imposed. An unchecked population increases geometrically: 2 parents could have 4 children, 16 grandchildren, 64 great-grandchildren, and so forth—and that is simply with a continuous average family size of 4. Since the means of subsistence (food) increase at best only arithmetically or lineally (5, 10, 15, 20, 25), the end result is a food shortage and possible famine.

Malthus recognized several *positive checks* on populations, factors that would keep populations from excessive growth, including wars, diseases and epidemics, and food shortages leading to famine (a drastic, wide-reaching shortage of food). Looking at historical factors and at the world today, we see examples of these population checks. War decimated the populations of several countries during the world wars and has taken its toll on other countries in Eastern Europe, Africa, and the Middle East since then through constant conflicts. The AIDS virus, SARS, Ebola, and bird flu have raised fear of new plagues (epidemics of often fatal diseases). Waterborne diseases such as cholera and typhus strike after floods, and the floods themselves are often caused by the environmental destruction resulting from too many humans in a geographic area. Consider the effects of typhoons, tsunamis, mud slides from heavy rains, and hurricanes, some of which result in massive loss of life. Famine in Ethiopia and countries in the horn of Africa during the latter part of the twentieth century

Sacred scriptures, including the Quran and the Bible, have embraced population expansion. This made a great deal of sense at the time these scriptures were written, but sacred support for large families is more problematic in today's resource-taxed world.

Source: © The British Library Board.

resulted in massive relief efforts but too little and too late to save thousands who died of starvation. Over 20 million people in Eritrea, Ethiopia, northern Kenya, Somalia, and Tanzania in East Africa (Popline 2006b), and part of Sudan and Niger in West Africa are experiencing famines. Famines are caused in part by erosion and stripping the earth of natural protections such as forests and grasslands by people in need of more land to grow food and graze animals and of firewood to cook. Today, there are also economic factors in checks on population. For example, imported cheap food is driving local farmers out of business in some areas.

Malthus held strong political views based in part on his population theory. He suggested preventive checks on rapid population growth, primarily in the form of delayed marriage and practice of sexual abstinence until one could afford a family. Contraception technology was crude and unrealistic in his day, and therefore, he did not present it as an option for population control.

Although we see evidence of Malthus's population checks today, his ideas stemmed from ethnocentric capitalistic class-based "blaming the poor" for their plight and their contributions to population growth; this ignored the role capitalism plays in the process, exploiting raw materials and laborers. In fact, having large families made sense to many families; having more children provided more workers as a source of economic security (Robbins 2005).

Four other main criticisms have been raised about Malthus's theory. First, his idea that food production would grow arithmetically and could not keep up with population growth must be modified in light of current agricultural techniques, at least in some parts of the world. Second,

Health workers collect the bodies of some 64,000 chickens destroyed at a farm in Hong Kong after an outbreak of avian flu in 2002 in an effort to stop the spread of the flu. Chicken is a protein mainstay of the Chinese diet, so the disease affected their health in more than one way.

Source: © REUTERS / Bobby Yip / Corbis.

Malthus saw abstinence from sex, even among the married, as the main method of preventing births and did not recognize the potential for contraception. Third, poverty has not always proven to be an inevitable result of population growth. Fourth, Malthus ignored the consumption patterns

Near Alem Kitmama in Ethiopia, scarcity of fresh water and other resources threaten survival. In the nineteenth century, Thomas Malthus predicted such shortages due to population increases.

Source: © 2006 World Health Organization.

of industrialized nations, ultimately blaming the scarcity of resources on the rapid population growth of the poor developing nations. There seemed to have been a good deal of ethnocentrism in blaming those in poverty, when much of the problem has to do with excessive consumption patterns in the developed nations.

Two neo-Malthusians, scientists who accept much of his theory but make modifications based on current realities, are Garrett Hardin and Paul Ehrlich. Hardin (1968), a biologist, argues that individuals' personal goals are not always consistent with societal goals for population growth; an individual may decide to have many children, but this could be detrimental to the whole society. If many people act solely on their own individual interests, social tragedy may well ensue. The dilemma between individual reproductive decisions and limited resources is one Malthus predicted.

Ehrlich and Ehrlich (1990) adds to the formula of "too many people and too little food" the problem of a "dying planet" from environmental damage. To hold on to economic gains, population must be checked, and to check population, family planning is necessary. Ehrlichs' ideas can be summed up as follows:

> America and other rich nations have a clear choice today. They can continue to ignore the population problem and their own massive contributions to it. Then they will be trapped in a downward spiral that may well lead to the end of civilization in a few decades.

More frequent droughts, more damaged crops and famines, more dying forests, more smog, more international conflicts, more epidemics, more gridlock, more drugs, more crime, more sewage swimming, and other extreme unpleasantness will mark our course. It is a route already traveled by too many of our less fortunate fellow human beings. (p. 23)

The neo-Malthusians favor contraception rather than simple reliance on the moral restraint that Malthus proposed (Weeks 2005). They also acknowledge that much of the environmental damage is caused by corporate pollution and excessive consumption habits in developed countries such as the United States, Canada, and Europe.

THINKING SOCIOLOGICALLY

What are contemporary examples of Malthus's checks on population growth—war, disease, famine? Are family planning and contraception sufficient to solve the problem of global overpopulation by humans? Can you think of any other alternatives?

Demographic Transition: Explaining Population Growth and Expansion

Why should a change in the economic structure such as industrialization and movement from rural agricultural areas to urban cities have an impact on population size? One explanation is found in the **demographic transition theory**.

The idea of demographic transition, first developed in the early 1900s, involves comparing countries' stages of economic development with trends in birth and death rates. Three stages of development are identified in this theory:

- *Stage 1:* These populations have high birth and death rates that tend to balance each other over time. Births may outpace deaths until some disaster diminishes the increase. This has been the pattern for most of human history. These include preindustrial, non-urban societies such as the Wodaabe tribe described in Chapter 3 of this text.
- *Stage 2:* Populations still have high birth rates, but death rates decline (i.e., more people live longer) because of improvements in health care and sanitation, establishment of public health programs, disease control and immunizations, and food availability and distribution. These factors are especially important in declining death rates of less developed countries today. This imbalance between continuing high births and declining deaths means that the population growth rate is very high. Our opening example of Kenya represents a society at this stage of development.
- *Stage 3:* Populations level off at the bottom of the chart (below) with low birth rates and low death rates. Most industrial and postindustrial societies are in this stage. Population growth rates in these countries are very low because nuclear families are small.

These stages are illustrated in Figure 14.5.

Overpopulation not only is a challenge to resources for food and water but large populations damage the environment and provide little ecological recovery time. This photo shows pollution of a stream in Yunnan, China.

Source: © Kate Ballantine.

Demographic transition theory helps explain the developmental stage and population trends in countries around the world, but it does not consider some important factors that affect the size of populations: (1) people's age at marriage determines how many childbearing years they have (late marriage means fewer years until menopause); (2) contraceptive availability determines whether families can control their number of children; (3) a country's

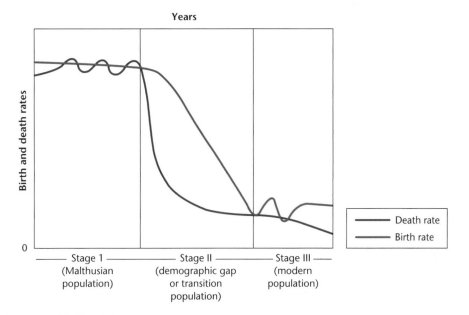

Figure 14.5 The Demographic Transition

resources and land may determine how much population a country can support; (4) the economic structure of a country, religious beliefs, and political philosophies affect attitudes toward birth control and family size; and (5) economic expansion rates influence a country's need for labor.

Not all societies go through the same time frame in transition from one stage to another. For example, demographic transition occurred rapidly in Europe, where notions of modernization, urbanization, and progress evolved naturally from the cultural values; people generally married later, and the value of having children varied with resources available; in addition, many deadly diseases that at one time kept population growth in check were under control.

Critics argue that there is a built-in assumption that modernization in the second and third stages will result in rational choices about family size. Yet unless women gain status by having smaller families, they are likely to continue to have large families (Robbins 2005).

Economic development generally results in a decline in the birth rate. The process of modernization that parallels economic development puts pressure on extended families to break apart into smaller nuclear family units, especially as families move to crowded urban areas; urban families tend to have fewer children because children are a liability and cannot help support the family. Also, the family support systems found in rural areas are less available in urban areas because of the distance between family members, contributing to the desire for smaller families. Economic development, modernization, and urbanization did not occur together in all parts of the world, so the outcome of the three-stage transition has not always occurred as predicted in the theory.

This billboard in Shanghai is advertising the Chinese government's "One Child Only" policy. The government decided three decades ago that their rate of population growth was a threat to the viability of the country.

Source: © Wolfgang Kaehler / Corbis.

The *wealth flow theory* suggests that two strategies are operating in families in decisions about family size: When wealth flows from children to parents, that is, when children are an asset working on the family farm or laboring, parents have larger families. When wealth flows from parents to children, families are likely to have fewer children (Caldwell 1982). To raise a child to 17 years in the United States, for instance, costs over $200,000 (Robbins 2005).

Conflict Theorists' Explanations of Population Growth

Karl Marx and Fredrick Engels did not agree with Malthus's idea that population growth outstrips food and resources because of people's fertility rates, resulting in poverty. They felt that social and structural factors built into the economic system were the cause of poverty. *Capitalist structures* resulted in wealth for the capitalists and created overpopulation and poverty for those not absorbed into the system. Workers were expendable, kept in competition for low wages, used when needed, and let go when unprofitable to capitalists.

However, *socialist societies*, Marx argued, could absorb the growth in population, so the problem of overpopulation would not exist. In a classless society, all would be able to find jobs and the system would expand to include them. Engels asserted that population growth in socialist societies could be controlled by the central government. This regulation is, in fact, what is happening in most present-day socialist countries through such methods as strict family planning and liberal abortion policies. In China, for instance, a couple should not marry until their combined age is 50, and they may have only one child without penalty; exceptions are made for rural citizens and some ethnic minorities. Those who exceed the state birth limits in planned societies may receive fewer state benefits and be ostracized.

Modern conflict theorists point to many factors that influence population growth, both capitalist policies and large families: unfair distribution of resources; dumping goods to put local farmers out of business; exploiting natural resources by nonlocal companies, multinationals, and other countries; and systems of patriarchy that prevent women from controlling their reproductive choices.

Policy Implications: Population Patterns and Economic Development

Does rapid population growth retard the economic development of a country? This question has been a subject of debate among demographers and policy makers in recent years. It is important because the beliefs of decision makers affect the policy decisions and solutions that are advocated. For instance, if policy makers feel population growth does not retard economic development, then there is less inclination by policy makers to curb population growth. On the other hand, if they feel population growth does retard economic development, family planning efforts are more likely since economic prosperity is of more immediate concern to political office holders (Solow 2000).

This issue has caused heated debate at several World Population Conferences. Some socialist and Catholic countries argue that capitalistic economic exploitation and political control, not population growth, cause poverty in Global South countries. Multinational companies and foreign countries exploit poor countries' resources, sometimes with payoffs to government officials, leaving the citizens with no gains. Most nations, policy makers and demographers agree that high population growth contributes to poverty. Rapid population growth is bad for economic growth because countries cannot adjust quickly enough to provide the infrastructure (housing, health care, sanitation, education) for so many additional people (United Nations Population Division 2005). Better sex education, access to contraceptives, and birth control advice help reduce population growth and spread of disease. As important to limiting population growth is providing opportunities for citizens, especially women, to obtain education and jobs.

INSTITUTIONAL INFLUENCES IN POPULATION CHANGE: MESO-LEVEL ANALYSIS

Populations change in *size* (overall number of people); *composition* (the makeup of the population, including sex ratio, age distribution, and religious or ethnic representation in the population); and *distribution* (density or concentration in various portions of the land). The key variables that cause changes in the size, composition, or distribution are major population processes. Populations change when births and deaths are not evenly balanced or when significant numbers of people move from one area to another. So the most important demographic processes are **fertility** (the birth rate), **mortality** (the death rate), and **migration** (movement of people from one place to another). While migration does not change the size or composition of the world as a whole, it can affect size or makeup in a local or national population. The most unpredictable yet controllable population factor in the world or in a nation is fertility.

Factors Affecting Fertility Rates

Jeanne, one of the coauthors, was riding in the back of a "mammy wagon," a common means of transport in Africa. Crowded in with the chickens and pigs and people, she did not expect the conversation that ensued. The man in his late 20s asked if she was married and for how long. Jeanne responded, "Yes, for three years." The man continued, "How many children do you have?" Jeanne answered, "None." The man commented, "Oh, I'm sorry!" Jeanne replied, "No, don't be sorry. We planned it that way!" This man had been married for 10 years to a woman three years younger than he and had eight

In an urban area in Cambodia (Kampuchia) residents crowd onto this truck, a common form of transportation. With a high fertility rate and migration from rural to urban areas, crowded transportation is common.

Source: www.downtheroad.org.

These Roma in Romania move from place to place, settling in open areas and selling their wares. Migration is one of the key demographic processes, sometimes due to displaced populations squatting on land as refugees.

Source: © Kate Ballantine.

children. The ninth was on the way. In answer to his pointed questions, Jeanne explained that she was not being cruel to her husband and that birth control was what prevented children, and no, it did not make sex less enjoyable. He expressed surprise that limiting the number of children was possible and rather liked the idea; he jumped at the suggestion of visiting the family planning clinic in the city. With his meager income, he and his wife were finding it hard to feed all the little mouths.

Demographers consider micro-, meso-, and macro-level factors in attempting to understand fertility rates around the world. We know that individuals' personal decisions are key. People deciding to marry, couples' decisions to use contraception, their ideas about the acceptability of abortion, and whether they choose to remain childless can have an impact on national and global rates of population change. So choices at the meso level do make a difference.

Fertility also fluctuates with what is happening in meso-level institutions such as economic, political, and family systems. During depressions, for example, the rate of fertility tends to drop. However, macro-level structural factors also affect fertility: population policies and level of economic development of the nation; the government's commitment to providing (or restricting) contraception; changes in norms and values about sexuality within a society; and environmental factors such as the availability of food, water, and health care.

Economic Factors

As discussed earlier, several factors contribute to overpopulation; poverty, status of women, and exploitation of resources and labor are some of these. Note the cyclical nature of the problem—overpopulation leads to poverty, which leads to overpopulation, which makes agreeing on a solution tricky. The relationship between poverty and population reduction is very complex.

The worldwide fertility rate is 2.65 children per woman. We know that one of the most significant distinguishing characteristics between developed and developing countries is their fertility rates—an average of 2.1 children per woman in developed countries and 5 or more children per woman in the least developed category. Figure 14.6, below, compares more developed regions of the world with the least developed and less developed regions.

THINKING SOCIOLOGICALLY

What does Figure 14.6 (age-specific fertility rates by development levels) tell you about the lives of individuals in these different regions of the world?

Although women's fertile years are roughly 15 to 44 (United Nations 2006), women in developed countries have 80 percent of their children between the ages of 20 and 35. In developing countries, fertility rates are as high for those age 15 to 19 as they are for 45- to 49-year-old women. This has changed in recent years in some developing regions where rates for women 30 and older are as low as in developed regions. Still, 21 percent of births in developing regions occur at age 35 or older, ages when there is greater risk in pregnancy, labor, and delivery, compared to 11.8 percent in developed regions. An important point in this section, however, is how various organizations and institutions affect fertility rates.

Government Influence

Some governments provide incentives for having children; others discourage high fertility. Thus, meso-level social policies shape decisions of families at the micro level. A state's

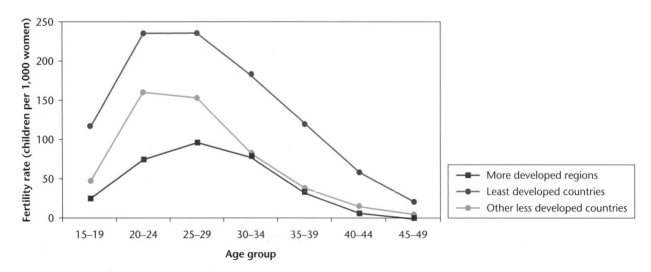

Figure 14.6 Age-Specific Fertility Rate, by Development Group, 2000–2005

Source: United Nations Department of Economic and Social Affairs, Population Division (2005:33–34).

pronatalist policies (those that encourage fertility) or *antinatalist* policies (those that discourage fertility) may be expressed in several ways: by manipulating contraceptive availability; by promoting change in factors that affect fertility such as the status of women, education, and degree of economic development; through propaganda for or against having children; by creating incentives (maternity leaves, benefits, and tax breaks) or penalties (such as fines); and by passing laws governing age of marriage, size of family, contraception, and abortion.

Antinatalist policies arise out of concern over available resources and differences in birth rates among population subgroups. Singapore, a country in Asia located off the Malay peninsula, consists of one main island and many smaller islands. It is one of the most crowded places on earth, with 17,496 persons per square mile (Population Reference Bureau 2005). This is compared to 80 in the United States, 8 in Canada, and 876 in Japan. One hundred percent of the population of Singapore is urban, and 90 percent live in the capital city. The country has little unemployment and one of the highest per capita incomes in Asia; however, it is dependent on imports from other countries for most of its raw materials and food. Singapore is but one example of a country that needs to control population growth.

Some years ago, the central government started an aggressive antinatalist plan. Birth control was made available, and residents of Singapore who had more than one or two children were penalized with less health care, smaller housing, and higher costs for services such as education. Singapore now claims the second lowest *natural increase rate* (the birth rate minus the death rate) in Southeast Asia, at 0.8 percent a year, just behind China. Governmental policies really can affect the natural increase rate.

China's antinatalist policy has been in effect since 1962. The government discourages traditional preferences for early marriage, large families, and many sons by using group pressure, privileges for small families, and easy availability of birth control and abortion. The government has reduced the natural increase rate in China, the most populous nation on earth, to only 0.6 percent annually (Population Reference Bureau 2005). Unfortunately, there are side effects to such a stringent policy among a people who value male children; there has been an increase in selective abortions to have sons, and there are instances of *female infanticide*—killing of female infants when they are born—so that families can try for a male child.

An example of pronatalist government policies can be seen in Romania. Many Romanian men were killed in World War II, creating a sex imbalance. Marriage and birth rates plummeted. Concerned about the low birth rate, in 1966 the government banned abortions and the importation of most contraceptives. Within eight months, the birth rate doubled, and within 11 months it tripled.

Individuals and governments vary in their opinions concerning the rights of government to determine the number of children families should or may have. Sometimes, citizens are unhappy with population programs. In 1991, the Japanese government, concerned about the dropping Japanese birth rate and the increasing dependent age of the population, one of the lowest rates of natural increase in the world (now 0.1 annual percent), provided incentives to encourage women to have more children. Bonuses for education and other benefits for these children were proposed. However, this raised angry voices both from feminists who argued the plan was to keep women in the home and from those who were concerned about the large population (127.7 million) on the small amount of habitable land space (Population Reference Bureau 2005).

In the United States, citizens like to think that decisions about fertility are entirely a private matter left to the couple. Indeed, it is sometimes hard to pin a simple label of antinatalist or pronatalist on the current administration. President George W. Bush reinstated the "gag rule" that Presidents Ronald Reagan and George H. W. Bush, had implemented, limiting the availability of birth control for teens in the United States unless parents are informed that the teen has applied for contraception, a policy that contributed to the increased teen pregnancy rates in the United States. The administration also blocked U.S. funding to international family planning groups that offer abortion and abortion counseling (Blackman 2001) and proposed a 19 percent cut in international family planning contributions for 2006 (Popline 2006c). Both limits to contraceptive availability and prohibitions on abortion are pronatalist since they encourage fertility. Many conservatives who oppose birth control measures and abortion may not intentionally be pronatalist, since this is not the rationale for their policy, but the policy still has the latent consequence of encouraging population increases. On the other hand, pronatalist governmental policies that might encourage larger families, such as tax breaks or access to day care centers, are not available. Thus, U.S. government policies do affect fertility rates in the United States.

Policies of governments are sometimes variable depending on ethnic group as well, and we do not need to go to Iraq or Darfur to find such policies. In the United States, there have been programs—even well into the twentieth century—that encouraged sterilization of black women. While white women were being encouraged to have large families in the 1950s, poor women of color were being discouraged from reproducing. Legal scholar Dorothy Roberts has found a continuing legacy of dual treatment of black and white fertility and motherhood in the United States. This has lead to a continuing distrust of governmental family policies in some parts of the African American community (Roberts 1997, 2002).

THINKING SOCIOLOGICALLY

Is it appropriate for governments to use enticements or penalties to encourage or discourage fertility? Why or why not? What are positive factors and problems with different policies?

In Indonesia, Nur Azizah binti Hanafiah, 22, receives a caning, having been found by a citizen having illegal sex with her boyfriend at her house. This Aceh region of Indonesia has practiced Islamic Sharia law since 2001. In some societies, she would have been stoned to death for having premarital sex.

Source: © Nani Afrida / epa / Corbis.

Religious and Cultural Norms

Norms and customs of a society or subculture also influence fertility. In some cultures, pronatalist norms support a woman having a child before she is married so she can prove her fertility. In other societies, a woman can be stoned to death for having a child or even sex out of wedlock.

A primary shaper of morality and values in most societies is religion. Some religious groups oppose any intervention such as birth control or abortion in the natural processes of conception and birth. Roman Catholics, for instance, are taught that large families are a blessing from God and that birth control is undesirable. The Roman Catholic Church officially advocates the rhythm method to reduce conception, a less reliable method in lessening birth rates than contraception technology. It might be noted, however, that a great many Catholics in the Western world are not following these teachings and are little different from their neighbors in use of contraception. Islam also encourages births; many children increase the likelihood that families will continue to produce the faithful to carry the religion into future generations. Such policies were created when populations were kept in check by high death rates.

Nonreligious cultural customs affect fertility as well. Couples may be pressured to delay marriage until they are in their late 20s or even 30s when they are economically secure. In Ireland, the mean age at first marriage for men was 32.9

and for women 30.3 years in 2000 (Council of Europe 2001, 2004). Although Ireland is a predominantly Catholic country, delayed marriage helps to keep the birth rate down. Another antinatalist custom in some groups is sexual abstinence after birth of a child, usually during the lactating (breast-feeding) period, which lasts anywhere from one to five years. In polygamous societies, the wife and newborn may live with the wife's family while the husband continues to live with his other wives.

Education

It is a straightforward relationship; the higher the women's status in society as measured by education level and job opportunities, the lower their fertility. If a country wants to control population growth, raising the status of women is key. Figure 14.7 shows the relationship between education and family size in eight developing countries (Population Reference Bureau 2001). Note that the higher the educational level, the lower the fertility rate and population growth. So, again, education and reduction of poverty are major variables contributing to moderation in population size.

Studies repeatedly show that investing in education of girls and women raises every index of a country's progress toward economic growth and development; yet 300 million children are without access to education, two-thirds of them girls. Of 771 million illiterate adults in the world, two-thirds are women. Although this gender gap has narrowed, it persists in sub–Saharan Africa, Arab states, and South and West Asia where only 6 in 10 adults are literate (UNESCO Institute for Statistics 2005). Two-thirds of the world's illiterate adults live in 9 countries, and 45 percent live in India and China.

Family planning programs resulted in a significant decline of up to one-third in global fertility between 1972 and 1994, over and above such factors as education (Rao and Mohanam 2003). Availability of contraception may determine a woman's ability to control the number of children she has during the fertile years. For instance, in the 1990s, the prevalence of contraceptive use globally increased from 57 to 67 percent; usage doubled in the least developed countries, resulting in a decline of fertility in all regions of the world and a total world decline from 3.2 to 2.7 percent. However, availability of contraception is spotty; in Africa, only 27 percent of married women are using any method of contraception, and only 20 percent are relying on modern methods. In some parts of Africa, under 5 percent use modern methods, yet the region has the highest levels of fertility (and AIDS) in the world. Globally, 201 million women lack access to effective contraceptives, but many would practice family planning if given the option (United Nations Population Fund 2005).

As seen above, many factors affect fertility rates, but they also have important consequences. Increases in numbers of humans and consumption patterns of citizens in wealthy developed countries deplete the environmental resources and cause more pollution. Lower population growth means

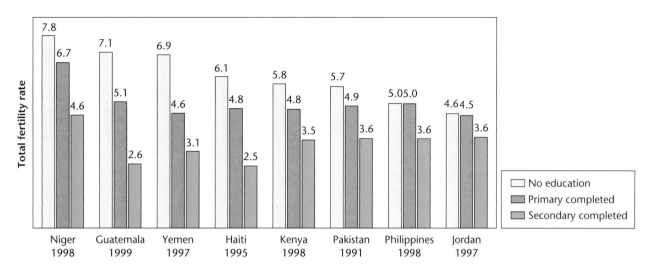

Figure 14.7 Women's Education and Family Size in Selected Countries, 1990s

Source: Demographic and Health Surveys, 1991–1999. © 2001 Population Reference Bureau.

less pressure on governments to provide emergency services for booming populations and means more attention given to services such as schools, health care, and jobs. Most population experts are concerned about these consequences, and they encourage governments and other meso-level institutions in fast-growing countries to act aggressively to control population size. Critics argue that wealthy countries need to curb excesses as well.

There are consequences of population fluctuations in affluent parts of the world as well as for poor parts. The impact of the baby boom in the United States illustrates this, as discussed in the next Sociology in Your Social World.

THINKING SOCIOLOGICALLY

First, read about the baby boom on page 452. What impact have the baby boom and baby boomlet had on your opportunities for education and a career?

Mortality Rates and National Health Care Organizations

Imagine living in Sierra Leone, West Africa, where the life expectancy at birth is 40 years and women have an average of 6.5 children. Those who survive to adulthood may well live longer, but of every 1,000 babies born alive, 165 will die within the first year. Seventy-five percent of the population lives on less than $2 a day. At 20, life would be half over (Population Reference Bureau 2005). Although the country's natural resources include a flourishing diamond industry, a British company controls part of it and private contractors the rest. Little wealth flows to the average person or to the government to improve the lot of its people. Most men and

women are subsistence farmers, working small plots that may not provide enough food to keep their families from starving. When one plot is overfarmed, the family moves to another and clears the land, depleting more arable land. A low 28 percent of the population lives in urban areas, primarily in the capital of Freetown; thus, Sierre Leone is an agricultural country as most of the population are farmers or fishers.

Some other African countries face similar situations. Life expectancy in Botswana, Lesotho, and Swaziland is 35 years; Zambia 37; and Angola 40 (Population Reference Bureau 2005). Average life expectancy for Africa as a whole is 54 years; the low life expectancy is due to epidemics such as AIDS, wars, and malnutrition. Table 14.2 shows the infant mortality rate around the world, meaning the number of infant deaths (children under one year) per 1,000 births; this is a key indicator of a country's status in the world.

TABLE 14.2 **Infant Mortality Rates around the World**	
Region	**Infant Mortality Rate**
World	54
More developed countries	6
Less developed countries	59
Less developed (excluding China)	64
Africa	88
Northern America	7
Latin America	27
Asia	51
Europe	7
Oceania	29

Source: Population Reference Bureau (2005).

Sociology in Your Social World

The Significance of the Baby Boom

At the end of World War II, the birth rate shot up temporarily in most countries involved in the war as many young people who had been forced to delay marriage made up for lost time. The postwar economy was growing, people were employed in relatively well-paying positions, and the norms supported large families. While this baby boom lasted about only 3 years after World War II in Britain, it lasted 17 years in the United States, from 1946 to 1963.

The baby boom phenomenon has had many impacts. During the late 1960s, school boards and contractors were busy building schools to educate the growing number of children; by the 1980s, student numbers declined and towns were consolidating schools and closing buildings. When the baby boomers entered the job market starting in the mid-1960s, there were great numbers of applicants for jobs and employers could pay less; the supply was so great they were assured that someone would take the job. Two decades later, it was much easier for young people to find jobs since there were fewer of them in that age range looking for starting-level positions. However, that generation is finding it hard to get promotions because the baby boomers have dominated so many of the high-level positions. In addition, trends in marketing and advertising have, for years, been dictated by the baby boom generation because they are such a large segment of the consumer public.

By the 1960s, changes in people's views of the ideal family size and the proper age for marriage changed; zero population growth movements and environmental concerns slowed the rate of growth. The period from the late 1960s to early 1970s has been referred to as a "baby bust" or the "birth dearth." (This fluctuation resulted in a population structure that did not look very much like a pyramid, as shown in Figure 14.8a, on page 457.)

In the mid-1970s and into the 1980s, when the baby boom generation started having babies, there was another baby boom—or "baby boomlet"—but it was much smaller since the baby boomers had smaller families. The result is

A temporary classroom (top) was added on behind an elementary school to accommodate the overcrowding in the 1960s. This was common when baby boomers were of school age. More recently, schools have been abandoned (bottom) due to fertility declines in the latter part of the twentieth century.

Source: © Kevin Russ.

that population growth in many developed countries has remained below the replacement level. Growth in the overall size of populations in Global North at this point is due largely to immigration; otherwise, many populations would be declining more significantly. The point is that extreme fluctuations in fertility rates can affect societies in a number of ways.

An infant suffering from AIDS receives care at a Salvation Army hospital in Chikankata, Zambia. By the start of the twenty-first century, over 34.3 million people in the world were infected with HIV/AIDS, with almost 25 million of them in Africa.

Source: © Joel Stettenheim / Corbis.

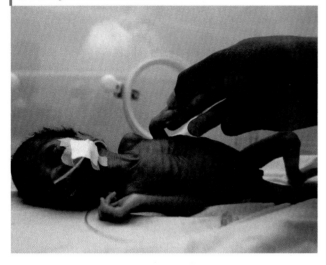

What causes the stark contrast in life expectancy and infant mortality rates between developed and developing countries? This is a complex issue involving the world economic system, exploitation of natural resources by foreign companies, corruption, lack of access to basic resources, poverty, malnutrition, and lack of opportunity. Access to health care, discussed in Chapter 13, is one key factor accounting for the difference. For instance, in many poor countries, rural families have no access to doctors or Western medicine and drugs such as antibiotics; they rely on local healers and herbal remedies that are effective for some illnesses but cannot cure other medical problems. People frequently die from problems that are easily cured in more developed countries. Note the different causes of death in developed versus developing countries in Table 14.3 (World Health Organization 2002).

Even in developed countries such as the United States, some groups have less access to health care and are less likely than others to receive prenatal care. These are also the groups at highest risk for problem births and infant deaths: those under 18, the unmarried, African Americans, Hispanics, the poor, and women with little education. Infants born to minority teenage mothers living in poverty are of particular concern in the United States; these infants come into the world with many strikes against them, and their mortality rate is especially high. They often have low birth weight, the most common direct or indirect cause of infant mortality. The U.S. infant mortality rate improved from 12.5 deaths per 1,000 births in 1980 to 10.0 in 1990 to 6.6 in 2005 (Population Reference Bureau 2005), but it is still higher than many other developed countries.

Migration: Why and Where People Move

Most of us have moved one or more times in our lives. Perhaps, we have moved to a larger house down the block, maybe to another area of our country for a job opportunity or school, or even to another country altogether. If we have changed our residence, we have been part of the process called **geographic mobility**.

Over the history of the human race, people have migrated to the far reaches of the globe. Because of adaptability to climatic and geographic barriers, humans have dispersed to more areas of the globe than any other species. Even inhospitable locations such as the North and South poles have been explored and have human settlements.

The *push-pull theory* points out that some people are pushed from their original locations by wars, plagues, famine, political or religious conflicts, economic crises, or other factors, and pulled to new locations by economic opportunities or political and religious tolerance. Most people do not leave a location unless they have been either forced out, or they have a viable alternative in the new location and the benefits of moving outweigh the costs (Weeks 2005). In some cases, the push factors are especially strong; in others, the pull factors dominate.

TABLE 14.3 **Leading Causes of Death in 2001**

Developing Countries	Number of Deaths	Developed Countries	Number of Deaths
HIV/AIDS	2,678,000	Ischemic heart disease	3,512,000
Lower respiratory infections	2,643,000	Cerebrovascular disease	3,346,000
Ischemic heart disease	2,484,000	Chronic obstructive pulmonary disease	1,829,000
Diarrhoeal diseases	1,793,000	Lower respiratory infections	1,180,000
Cerebrovascular disease	1,381,000	Trachea/bronchus/lung cancers	938,000
Childhood diseases	1,217,000	Road traffic accidents	669,000
Malaria	1,103,000	Stomach cancer	657,000
Tuberculosis	1,021,000	Hypertensive heart disease	635,000
Chronic obstructive pulmonary disease	784,000	Tuberculosis	571,000
Measles	674,000	Self-inflicted	499,000

Source: World Health Organization (2002).

This vessel containing over 300 immigrants from Eritrea, East Africa, was spotted by an Italian customs police helicopter. Every year, thousands of illegal immigrants departing from the Mediterranean coasts of Africa try to reach Europe through Sicily. The commute is dangerous, and many immigrants are found dead on the Sicilian shoreline, but the desire for a better future keeps the masses coming.

Source: © Mimi Mollica / Corbis.

When we are young, we go where our parents go. If a parent receives a lucrative job offer in another location, the family moves. If the family grows and the dwelling becomes too small, it moves. If a relative needs help or a family member's health requires a different climate, the family moves. What sets the stage for migration is an individual's personal traits, such as the willingness to take risks, and the perceived advantages of living in a different place. If an opportunity is present, the individual may move. However, if the risks are high, if the information about migration is scarce, or if negative factors such as leaving family behind are present, individuals may decide not to move.

While the decision to move is often a personal or family one, it is also influenced by the sociocultural environment. History is replete with examples of large groups of people who left an area because of aspirations to improve their life chances, hopes of retaining a way of life, or expulsion of groups by political, economic, or religious forces. Chinese workers came to the United States for economic reasons, to help build the railroad. Amish and Mennonite settlers from Europe sought religious freedom and preservation of their way of life; the Amish, a group originating in Germany, left Germany en masse, and the members of this group now live entirely in North America. Italian immigration to the United States took place in groups; when a family left Italy, they would usually move to a U.S. city where a relative or a previous acquaintance lived. Thus, residents of entire apartment buildings in the North End of Boston were from the same extended family, or entire city blocks of people came from the same town or

region of Southern Italy (Gans 1962). Also, former colonial powers have numerous immigrants from colonized countries; this has helped make many European cities like London and Paris the multicultural environments they are today.

Migrations can be *internal*, within a country, or *international*, from one country to another. Moves from rural farm communities to urban areas are a common internal migration pattern found around the world. International moves are often influenced by political unrest or discrimination against a group of people such as the Nazi persecutions of the Jewish population. For people who depend on the land, drought and other adverse environmental conditions force movement.

In the contemporary world situation, international migration is especially common where wars and famines ravage a country. In the 1970s and 1980s, refugees from Kampuchea (Cambodia) fled military offensives and moved to refugee camps on the Thailand border. In the past several decades, Kurds flocked to Turkey and Iran to escape the former Iraqi military. Israelis worked secretly to transport Ethiopian Jews to Israel. Tamils from northern Sri Lanka fled to India. Nigerians expelled Ghanaian migrant workers. Continuing today, indigenous Central American refugees fleeing guerilla warfare have entered Mexico and the United States. Hindu and Muslim hostilities in India have led to mass migrations among the countries of India, Pakistan, and Bangladesh as residents look for safe havens, and refugees from war-torn Sudan have sought refuge in camps in neighboring countries such as Chad. The list of international population movements due to internal crises is extensive and constant.

International migrations in modern times are also motivated by economic opportunities abroad or by fluctuations in the local and world economy. Since the 1960s, most movement has been from less developed to more developed countries. Demand for cheap labor has brought many "guest workers" from developing countries to European nations and immigrants to other industrialized countries. Illegal human trafficking, especially of women and children, also brings immigrants. However, two factors curb migrations: restrictive immigration laws of receiving countries and economic depressions. During recessions, many countries restrict immigration by passing strict immigration quotas, even for political refugees from war-torn countries, and open-door immigration policies tend to diminish or disappear.

Prior to 1914, when World War I began, it was not standard practice for nations to require a passport in order to enter a country (Friedman 2005). Since most people could not afford intercontinental travel, controlling the flow of people was not an issue. There has been a more restrictive stance in the United States than in Canada or most European countries regarding immigration during the past century (Farley 2005). Strict policies have not entirely stemmed the tide, however. Eleven million illegal migrants from Mexico and other south and central American countries now live in the United States, and half a million illegal immigrants enter the country each year. Some people are so desperate to cross over to the United States that they risk everything; 400 Mexicans died in 2005 trying to cross the desert to the U.S. border (*The Economist* 2006). Many people fear job competition by illegal immigrants who will work for very little and flood the job market.

THINKING SOCIOLOGICALLY

Think about your own grandparents or great grandparents and where they came from. How long have your ancestors occupied the same land? Do they go back more than one generation on that land? If they have been mobile, what factors were critical to their mobility? How has their mobility or stability influenced your family's experiences?

Since the terrorist attacks of September 11, 2001, the idea that the U.S. borders are porous has been highly divisive as the U.S. Congress struggles to find an appropriate policy—Republicans against Democrats, the House against the Senate, and a Republican President against his Republican congressional allies. One proposal even suggested building a wall the entire length of the Mexican-U.S. border, an expensive proposition that most analysts think would be futile.

A bill that passed in the House of Representatives would make all illegal aliens felons and would make it a crime (akin to smuggling) for U.S. citizens (including church and social workers who help immigrants) to help anyone who is in the United States illegally. This led to protest marches in many cities, including a 500,000 person demonstration in Los Angeles. In contrast to the House bill, some leading senators favor giving some long-term illegal residents a path to citizenship. President Bush has endorsed a "guest worker" program for people who

Two women refugees from Eritrea walk past their refugee camp in east Sudan. Ethnic cleansing and political turmoil have left many people around the world not only homeless but country-less.

Source: © Peter Turnley / Corbis.

work at jobs that other Americans are not willing to do, at least for the wages currently being paid. The debate is intense, and the solutions will not be easy (*The Economist* 2006).

The rate of internal migration in the United States is high compared with most places in the world; patterns have primarily involved individual "pull" migration to economic opportunities and better housing. People's reasons for moving fall into several categories, as seen in Table 14.4.

During different historical periods, movement directions have varied. For many years, rural residents in the

TABLE 14.4 **Reasons for Moving by Type of Move, 2002–2003 (in percentages)**				
Reason	All Movers	Intracounty	Intercounty	From Abroad
Family-related reasons: changed marital status, to establish own household, and so on	26.3	24.7	28.5	29.4
Work-related reasons: new job or transfer, to look for work, closer to work, retired, and so on	15.6	6.0	28.3	38.1
Housing-related reasons: want own home, better house or neighborhood, cheaper housing, and so on	51.3	65.3	33.5	8.8
Other reasons: attend or leave college, change of climate, health, and so on	6.8	3.9	9.9	23.7

Source: U.S. Census Bureau (2004).

At the conclusion of their careers, many American retirees have moved to the Sunbelt—to California, the Southwest, and here to in Palm Springs, California. Indeed, an entire industry has developed around senior citizen migration. This has left some states with especially high or especially low ratios of older citizens.

extremely important for comprehending social processes very close to your everyday life. While most developed countries do not have massive famines or population explosions, population fluctuations influence us in many ways.

In 1969, Keith, one of the coauthors, lived in Boston and his wife taught in a suburban school system there. The elementary school where she taught had four first-grade classrooms, with 28 children per room—112 first graders in the school. By the next year, the decline in the fertility rate six years earlier was being felt, and the number of first graders declined. Within four years, the number of first graders in her school was reduced to 40, with two classrooms and only 20 students per class. Some school systems lost half of their student population in a short time. One year, first-grade teachers were losing their jobs or having to move to another grade, and the next year it was second-grade teachers who were scrambling. The third year, third-grade teachers were in oversupply, and so forth. With low demand, these were not times for college students to be pursuing teaching careers.

We have already mentioned the impact of the baby boom (the high fertility rates from 1946 to about 1963) and

In a few years, as the baby boomers become the "bingo boomers," the field of gerontology will be the booming industry. You might consider this growth field for your own career.

Source: © Robert Kyllo.

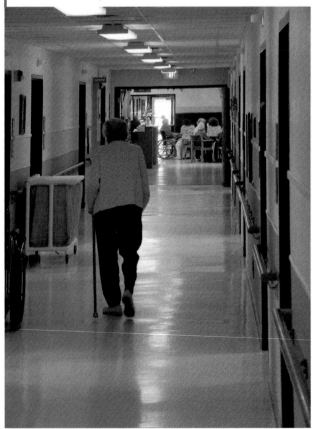

United States moved to higher-income urban areas. Until the 1950s, people moved out of the southern states and into the northern—especially north central—states. Then the pattern reversed, and the flow started south and west. Movement since the 1960s has been toward the Sunbelt, especially to California, Arizona, Texas, and Florida. Movement to the Pacific Coast and even Alaska has also increased due to economic opportunities there.

Although decisions about family size and migration are individual ones, they are influenced by what happens at the meso and macro levels.

THINKING SOCIOLOGICALLY

What are the benefits and cost for individuals and governments of extensive internal migration? What are the advantages and disadvantages of having large numbers of immigrants?

MICRO-LEVEL POPULATION PATTERNS

You might get the impression that population studies are mostly about other places and problems (hunger and population explosion in developing countries) that do not affect your country. However, understanding demography can be

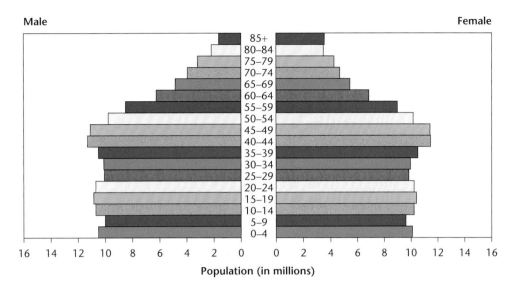

Figure 14.8a   United States, 2005

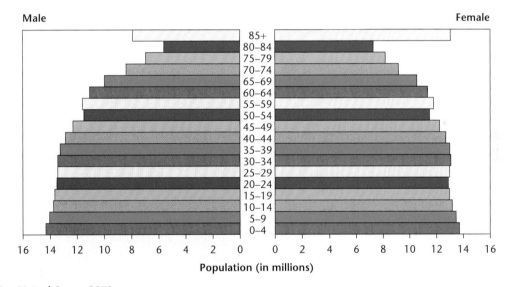

Figure 14.8b   United States, 2050

Source: U.S. Census Bureau, International Database.

the following baby bust (the drop in fertility for more than a decade following the baby boom). The impact on the population is graphically represented in the population pyramid of the United States (see Figure 14.8a). As you can see, the U.S. population no longer looks anything like a pyramid, and this odd population pattern affects job prospects, retirement security, career decisions, and deviance rates, to name only a few of the outcomes. Note the projected implications for 2050 in Figure 14.8b.

The decision about your career is a deeply personal decision, but population trends also shape that decision. For example, if a business that produces children's products expands its production shortly after a birth dearth dip in fertility rates, the timing of the business expansion may cause severe financial hardships or even bankruptcy for the company. Smart business people pay a great deal of attention to characteristics of the population. That same information might be relevant to an individual deciding on a career. For example, this is an incredibly good time for students who enjoy working with older people (gerontology) or in the medical field to think about a career in gerontology or health care.

Retirement is another topic for which population patterns are critical. Most developed countries are struggling with how young working people are going to support the nonworking aging populations. The number of working people contributing to pensions compared to retirees who depend on support is changing dramatically systems in many countries are in trouble because of low birth rates and increasing numbers of nonworking elderly people.

Consider the U.S. example; when social security was established in the United States in the 1930s, life expectancy was 59. The number of people in the age-dependent categories of under 15 or over 65 was low. For each person who received social security, 20 paid into the federal coffers. Twenty people each paying $500 a year could easily support a retired person who might receive $10,000 per year. However, the average life expectancy has shifted and the age-dependent population increased. Currently in the United States, roughly 12.5 percent of the population is over the age of 65 (Central Intelligence Agency 2006), as opposed to 4 percent in the 1930s. Moreover, predictions are that by 2035, 20 percent of the population will be over 65. When the baby boomers are collecting social security, the people born during the birth dearth will be the ones in their prime earning years, but there are far fewer of them paying into the system. When commentators and politicians say social security is in trouble, therefore, they are not generally saying it has been mismanaged. They are pointing to problems created by changes in the composition of the U.S. population.

In the 1980s, the U.S. administration and Congress saw the problem coming and for the first time began to save funds in a social security account for the baby boomers. They also passed laws requiring baby boomers to work longer before they qualify for social security. That there are so many baby boomers—and that an extremely high percentage of citizens over the age of 65 vote—makes it unlikely that Congress or the president would cut back on benefits to this group once they have retired. Still, with the federal budget squeezed by war and natural disasters (such as Hurricane Katrina) causing the deficit to grow, some members of Congress have voiced interest in "borrowing" from the social security reserves. Members of the younger generations will be the ones to pay if insufficient funds are available for the baby boomers, and their future pensions may be in jeopardy.

 THINKING SOCIOLOGICALLY

You have probably not thought much about economic security after retirement. What plans can you make now for this long period of life after work? Why is this planning important?

Rates of deviance and juvenile delinquency are also influenced by population patterns. In the 1960s and 1970s, these rates climbed precipitously. When the amount of juvenile delinquency began to decline in the 1980s and 1990s, members of both major U.S. political parties claimed it was their policies that made the difference. However, most deviant acts are committed by young people in their mid-teens to early twenties. Thus, when the baby boom generation was in

their teens and early twenties, the overall rates of deviance were higher. Many of those same delinquents became upright citizens—even law-and-order conservatives—once they had families and careers. When the birth dearth group was in their teens, overall rates of crime dropped, because there were fewer teenagers.

Understanding how *immigration* and internal migration patterns affect individuals can help you make location decisions. Enhanced or weakened economic prospects of certain countries or regions change the demand for workers. For example, representation in the U.S. Congress is based on the census done every 10 years; if a state loses population, it may have fewer representatives to Congress the following year. Shifts in the distribution of the population, therefore, can mean shifts in the amount of power a state holds in national policymaking.

This former gang member is like many teenage delinquents. He eventually developed role responsibilities of adulthood and began to work within the system. He now helps young men change their lives. When a large percentage of the population is between 16 and 24, the deviance rates in the society increase.

Source: © Rob DeLorenzo / ZUMA / Corbis.

Sociology in Your Social World

Population Pyramids and Predicting Community Needs and Services

tudy the Population Pyramid graphs below. Based on what you see, answer the following questions:

1. Which community would be likely to have the lowest crime rate?

2. Which would be likely to have the most cultural amenities (theaters, art galleries, concert halls, and so forth)?

3. Imagine you were an entrepreneur planning on starting a business in one of these communities.
   a) Name three businesses that you think would be likely to succeed in each community.
   b) Name one business that you think would be unlikely to succeed in each community.

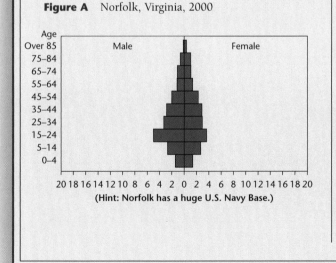

Figure A Norfolk, Virginia, 2000

(Hint: Norfolk has a huge U.S. Navy Base.)

Figure B Bloomington, Indiana, 2000

(Hint: Bloomington is a town of about 65,000 and is the home of Indiana University, a large Big Ten university.)

Figure C Naples, Florida, 2000

(Hint: Naples is a major retirement location.)

Source: U.S. Census Bureau (2006a).

Demography is relevant to job prospects and career planning, to policy decisions about pension plans such as social security, to market research for businesses, and to understanding political power and influence within a country. Because population trends will shape your life, understanding those trends can help you use that knowledge to your advantage.

To illustrate the power of demographic trends on individual decisions, Sociology in Your Social World provides an exercise in problem solving using information from population pyramids of U.S. cities. Our next topic continues the discussion of population by focusing on growth of urban areas.

PHOTO ESSAY

World Cities

C ities are vibrant places: rich in cultural diversity, artistic creativity, fine cuisine, high-paying jobs, and exciting nightlife for young people. The world cities pictured here illustrate variations *and* similarities.

Sources: (Clockwise from top left) © Timothy Babasade; www.downtheroad.org; © Carsten Madsen; © Leon Bonaventura; © Jeannette Meier Kamer; © Ralph Paprzycki.

URBANIZATION: MOVEMENT FROM RURAL TO URBAN AREAS

Mumbai (Bombay), India; Caracas, Venezuela; Lagos, Nigeria; Shanghai, China; and New York City, United States, are all bustling *megacities* (cities with over 10 million people) with traffic congestion and people rushing to their destinations on foot or in various types of motorized and nonmotorized vehicles. Carts, bicycles, and taxis weave in and out of traffic jams; the local spices and other aromas scent the air; sidewalk merchants display vegetables and fruits unique to the country; beggars and the homeless, often migrants from rural areas, dot the sidewalks; merchants sell colorful wares; and prostitutes solicit business. Cities are vibrant places with diversity and contributions of a variety of ethnic traditions coming together. The amazing sights, sounds, smells, tastes, cultural activities such as arts, theater, clubs, music, and events mean there is always excitement. There is also the draw of exciting and high-paying jobs. These few impressions convey the excitement of city life—factors that lure people to cities.

These megacities around the world are part of a global trend that has gained momentum over several centuries—*urbanization.* This process involves "1. the movement of people from rural to urban places, where they engage in primarily non-rural occupations, and 2. the change in lifestyle that results from living in cities" (Brunn, Williams, and Zeigler 2003:5). Urbanization accompanies (1) *modernization*—transformation from traditional, mostly agrarian societies, to contemporary bureaucratized states; and (2) *industrialization*—transformation from an agricultural base and handmade goods to manufacturing industries. We explore urbanization in this chapter as a very specific demographic trend that has major social implications for how people live and interact.

Most people live their lives in *communities:* locations that provide residents with a place to live; a sense of identity and belonging; neighbors and friends; activities and social involvements; and access to basic necessities such as food, jobs, schools, and health care. Our most intimate micro-level interactions take place in these communities, and we are connected to larger meso- and macro-level social structures such as political and religious organizations, world health organizations, and international relief agencies (e.g., UNICEF)—through our communities. In this section, we consider the development of communities, from rural areas and small towns to urban areas such as megacities. The next Sociology around the World (page 462) outlines major urbanization trends in the world (Brunn et al. 2003; United Nations Population Division 2003).

THINKING SOCIOLOGICALLY

First, read about World Urbanization Trends on page 262. How does global urbanization affect you?

The second half of this chapter is a continuation of the discussion of demographic patterns; however, we will return here to the pattern used in previous chapters of discussing micro-level analysis first, followed by meso- and macro-level analyses. First, how do urban environments affect us as individuals? We turn to that topic next.

CITIES AS MICRO-LEVEL LIVING ENVIRONMENTS

In the seventeenth and eighteenth centuries, when Europe was undergoing dramatic changes, small, bucolic villages contrasted sharply with the rapidly growing urban centers. Tonnies (1855–1936) described these two extreme types on a continuum from **Gemeinschaft**, meaning small traditional community in German, to **Gesellschaft**, meaning large, impersonal urban areas. He saw social life as an evolution from family units to rural villages, towns, cities, nations, and finally cosmopolitan urban life (Tonnies 1887/1963). Family, friendship, relations to the land, common values, traditions, and experiences are key elements of Gemeinschaft. Gesellschaft, a product of urban industrial society, is characterized by formal relations, contracts, laws, and economies built on money. People in urban areas do not necessarily know one another or share common values; they tend to be employees of bureaucratic organizations; and they tend to be more isolated as individuals rather than members of a collectivity.

A number of other theorists living in the Europe of the nineteenth century suggested similar contrasts. Durkheim (1858–1917) described the social bonds that held society together and the changes that arose from industrialization and urbanization. **Mechanical solidarity** was his term for the glue that held a society together through shared beliefs, values, and traditions typical of rural areas and simple societies. In mechanical solidarity, social bonds were formed by homogeneity of thought.

Think of any large business in which each employee has a specific task to perform in the division of labor. The social glue that holds these people together is **organic solidarity**, a division of labor with each member playing a highly specialized role in the society; each person is dependent on others with interrelated, interdependent tasks. This interdependence of specialized tasks is the key to unity in more complex societies with organic solidarity.

The ways in which order is maintained in society illustrate the differences between the two types of societies; in mechanical solidarity, legal systems are concerned with moral order, upheld by shared beliefs and values and a desire to be well regarded in the community. Organic solidarity stresses *restitutive law,* that is, making amends for a wrongdoing by paying fines or spending time in jail (Durkheim 1893/1947). So even the notion of how to maintain conformity varies as this transformation in the society occurs.

Sociology around the World

World Urbanization Trends

World Urbanization Prospects: The 2003 Revision and The 2001 Revision, are reports published by the United Nations Population Division. They provide a valuable data set on past, present, and future urbanization trends in regions and subregions of the world. They also provide data on individual cities and urban areas. The major findings of these most recent editions are as follows:

1. The world's population reached 6.5 billion in February 2006 and is expected to increase to between 9 and 12 billion by 2050. Whereas 40 percent (3 billion people) of the world population lived in urban areas in 1950, that percentage increased to 48 percent (5 billion people) by 2003 and will increase further, to an estimated 60 percent by 2030.

2. The rural population is anticipated to decline slightly from 3.3 billion in 2003 to 3.2 billion in 2030. Based on current projections, the number of rural and urban dwellers was expected to be about equal by 2007. The proportion of the population that is urban is expected to rise to 61 percent by 2030. The majority of all urban dwellers is living in smaller urban settlements, while less than 5 percent of the world population is living in megacities.

3. During the 2000–2030 period, the world's urban population is projected to grow at an average annual rate of 1.8 percent, which is nearly double the projected growth rate for the world (1.0 percent per year). The urban population reached 1 billion in 1960, 2 billion in 1985, and 3 billion in 2002. It is projected to attain 4 billion in 2017 and 5 billion in 2030. Based on these rates, the urban population of the world will double in 38 years.

4. Marked regional differences exist in the level and pace of urbanization; Latin America and the Caribbean had a level approximating 75 percent in 2000, which was higher than the level in Europe and almost twice that in Asia and Africa. By 2030, over half the populations of Asia and Africa will be living in urban areas, while the figure for Latin American and the Caribbean will reach 84 percent, a level similar to North America, the most urbanized region by 2030.

5. In both Europe and the United States and Canada, the percentage of those living in urban areas is expected to increase, respectively, from 71 percent and 77 percent in 2000 to 81 percent and 85 percent in 2030. Oceania's increase will be somewhat smaller, from 74 percent to 77 percent.

6. Despite high levels of urbanization in Europe, North America, Latin America and the Caribbean, and Oceania, the combined urban population of those areas in 2000 (1.2 billion) were less than that of Asia (1.4 billion). By 2030, Asia will have more urban residents than all other regions of the world combined (rising to 54 percent from 48 percent in 2000); Africa will be the second most urbanized continent in the world.

7. Asia will retain its position as having the world's largest rural population (2.3 billion) in the 2000–2030 period. Africa, with nearly 500 million rural residents in 2000, will see an increase by 2030 to 702 million, the second largest share. Only Africa and Oceania among the world regions will experience increases in rural residents. Overall, the world's rural population will remain relatively stable from 2000 to 2030, at around 3.2 billion.

8. The numbers of people living in smaller cities is greater than the numbers living in very large urban areas. In 2000, about 25 percent of the world's population lived in areas with fewer than 0.5 million, and by 2015, that number is expected to be about 27 percent.

9   High urban population growth is not necessarily associated with population size. In fact, some of the highest growth rates are in cities with small populations, for as population size increases, the growth rate tends to decline. Megacities will experience low growth, with some growing less than 1 percent per year.

Source: United Nations Population Division (2002, 2003).

Major population shifts from rural to urban areas came with industrialization in Europe and North America, followed by the same process in other areas of the world. As urbanization continues to sweep the world, many rural areas are disappearing and those that remain are taking on aspects of metropolitan life as they move away from mechanical and toward organic solidarity. Even the remotest villages are influenced by urban and global concerns (Bowler, Bryant, and Nellis 1992). For instance, decisions about what crops to grow are often tied to nonlocal demand; poor farmers in South America and Afghanistan can make more money growing poppies for drug suppliers in big cities than they can from food crops to feed the local population.

The early interpretations of urbanization, especially by European sociologists, were through a rather pessimistic lens. The trend was seen largely as a decline of civil society. However, there are pluses as well as minuses in quality of life as people inhabit more densely populated areas.

Life in the City

On warm evenings, the residents come out of their oppressive apartments to sit on the front steps. Children play ball in the street or splash in front of open fire hydrants. Neighbors chat about work and politics and other things neighbors share. Across the interstate highway, the professional couple is having cocktails with friends from work in their renovated, air-conditioned Victorian home. In the nearby suburb, families are returning from sports practices, mowing their lawns, and preparing dinner. Political, economic, and cultural factors all help to shape these different scenarios in the inner city and its surrounding area. Three major urban organizational trends emerged in the latter part of the twentieth century: urban residential patterns, gentrification, and suburbanization.

Urban Residential Patterns

Neighborhoods are identifiable areas within the larger metropolitan area. Four characteristics help define neighborhoods:

1. A neighborhood can meet most of the needs of residents: food, schools, religions.

2. Neighborhoods are "natural areas"; that is, to a great degree, residents are homogeneous with respect to income, interests, ethnicity or race, and other shared characteristics.

3. There is a high degree of social interaction among the residents of a neighborhood.

4. There is substantial *symbolic commitment*, the feeling of belonging to a meaningful sociogeographic area.

Some neighborhoods in cities, especially in ethnic immigrant concentrations, are closely knit. This is especially true when members of extended families live in the same area and provide support for one another (Guest and

rban life in New York (top) is more individualistic and ureaucratic. Life in small towns, such as the Tibetan village (bottom), is more communal and personal, but one has much less privacy.

Source: © Perry Kroll, Manhattan; © Kate Ballantine.

Stamm 1993; Logan and Spitze 1994). In major cities around the world, ethnic enclaves offer security, familiarity, and protection. For new migrants to cities, neighborhoods provide gradual adaptation to the strange new society and the dominant group; immigrant groups often attempt to recreate their former more intimate village-type settings within their urban neighborhood (Gans 1962). Ethnic communities can provide job opportunities and gradual acculturation into language and customs.

Despite the sometimes impersonal environment of cities, local neighborhoods in urban areas often have a sense of community, where children play in the street in the spray of open fire hydrants on the hottest days of summer.

Source: © Craig Veltri.

Supportive *ethnic enclaves* are also found in African American inner city neighborhoods of predominantly single mothers and children; Stack (1974) found that women created support networks—sustaining each other through sharing of child care and resources. However, in some low-income tenement areas, little interaction has been found because of high turnover of residents and fear of violence (Renzetti 2003).

Homogeneous middle-class city and suburban dwellers often have an active neighborhood life as well. A *suburb* is an area immediately adjacent to a city, extending outward beyond the city limits or the core of the city (Flanagan 2001). The variables that create a sense of community are complex, and generalizations that apply to all types of communities are difficult to make.

City dwellers become accustomed to the fast pace of life, the danger of stepping off the curb to cross the street, the crowds jostling and pushing them along as they rush to work, the impersonal attitudes of clerks, the impatience with inconveniences. The thrill of city life outweighs the problems for many residents who are sentimentally attached to the unique nature of life in cities. Let us look at some of the variables that affect how people experience city life.

Human Relationships in Cities

Sociologist Georg Simmel (1902–17/1950) was concerned with the experience of urban life, with what it does to people's thoughts and behavior. He argued that two factors—the intensity and stimulation of city life and the market effects on urban relations—cause people to have different attitudes, beliefs, and values from those in rural areas. City dwellers have no choice but to be somewhat insensitive, avoid intense relationships, and keep social relationships superficial to protect their privacy. However, he did not feel this was necessarily negative. Cities free people from the social constraints of close relationships in small towns.

Sociologist Louis Wirth (1964) also argued that because urban residents live in heterogeneous, high-density areas, they develop coping mechanisms for dealing with the situation. They become sophisticated, removed from others in order to insulate themselves from too many personal claims and expectations of others. The depersonalization that results from lower commitment to a common community "goal" also leads to a higher tolerance for nonconformity in cities, resulting in more individual freedom—and as a result more deviance.

Urban sociologist Claude Fischer (1984) argues that urbanism shapes social life rather than leaving residents as alienated individuals in a sea of traffic, noise, and pollution. City life strengthens social groups, promotes diverse subcultures, and encourages intimate social circles. These urban groups share similar activities or traits. The larger numbers of people make it possible for individuals with similar interests—from ethnic subcultures to gay communities to artist groups—to draw together as clubs, organizations, or neighborhoods. These little social worlds "touch but do not interpenetrate" (Fischer 1984:37); as long as there are enough members of a group, they can maintain their own identity. When different groups come in contact with each other, the result may be positive sharing of cultures or it may be conflict, causing members to associate all the more closely with their own group. Gangs fall into this latter category. So rather than creating isolated individuals who interact defensively with others, urban life may create choices about lifestyle and enhance a different kind of community base, intensifying the interactions.

Despite these benefits of urban life in countries where cities have substantial resources to provide services, urbanization can have very different consequences, especially in poor regions of the world. Rapidly growing cities in developing countries often face challenges to provide services—shelter, water, electricity, sanitation, schools, health care—for the increasing numbers of residents.

THINKING SOCIOLOGICALLY

What do you see as the most important consequences—for individuals or groups—of urban residence?

HOW DID CITIES EVOLVE? MESO-LEVEL ORGANIZATIONAL STRUCTURES

Human settlements have gone through massive transitions over the past 10,000 years, from small agricultural settlements

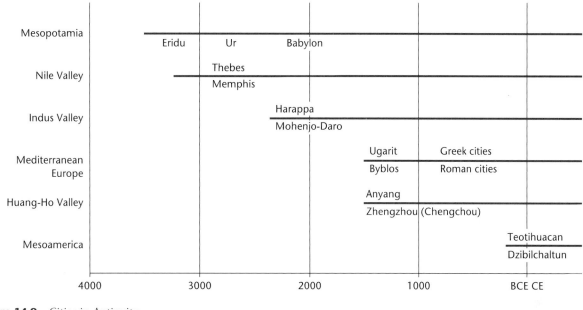

Figure 14.9 Cities in Antiquity

Source: Sjoberg (1965:56–57).

to bustling crowded metropolises with millions of people. The first step in the development of urban life came when those living nomadic lives became more settled. Archeological evidence indicates that there may have been early settlements in southern Russia as early as 15,000 years ago (Zimolzak and Stansfield 1983). Starting about 10,000 years ago with the advent of agriculture, domestication of animals, and the shift from food gathering to food production, small groups developed permanent settlements. Among the first was Eridu in Iraq, a settlement of some 25 permanent compounds with a population of up to 200 in each compound and a grain storage facility in the center (see Figure 14.9). The people grew wheat and barley and domesticated dogs, goats, and sheep.

These settlements were not cities as we think of them today, however, because they had different cultural and economic structures and there was little division of labor. Everyone shared roles, worked the land to support the population, and banded together for protection. Cities, by contrast, are large permanent settlements with nonagricultural specialists, a literate elite, and surplus food to support the social classes that are not involved in food production (Sjoberg 1960). They have been the source of intense fascination for many social science theorists.

Theories of Urban Development

Among the first sociologists in the United States were a group of scholars who studied problems in the city of Chicago. The Chicago School, founded by Robert Ezra Park and Ernest W. Burgess in 1916, with major contributions by Roderick McKenzie, Amos Hawley, Jane Addams, and others, dominated urban sociology until the final decades of the twentieth century. Their studies of urban ecology focused on the patterns of land use and residential distribution of people in urban areas. These theorists pictured the city's growth pattern as a series of circles. Moving out from the center, each circle was dominated by a particular type of activity and residential pattern, from central city ghettoes and rooming houses to working-class apartments and bungalows, to middle-class housing, to upper-class suburbs (Park, Burgess, and McKenzie 1925/1967). See Figure 14.10 for an illustration of this pattern.

Urban ecologists further refined the Chicago School's original ideas by exploring social, economic, political, and technological systems of cities' spatial patterns (Abu-Lughod 1991). Several processes constantly take place in urban areas: residential segregation; invasion by a new ethnic, religious, or socioeconomic group; and succession by that group. These processes are part of dynamic city life (Berry and Kasarda 1977).

In the past three decades, very new and different theories of urban development have emerged, spurred in part by the decay, riots, and disturbances in cities around the world that dramatized inequalities and forced sociologists to find new explanations for urban problems. Two controversial books, *The Urban Question* (Castells 1979) and *Social Justice and the City* (Harvey 1973), challenged the urban ecology approach and outlined a new direction. These authors contend that urban space is both socially defined and in scarce supply; therefore, political-economic conflict

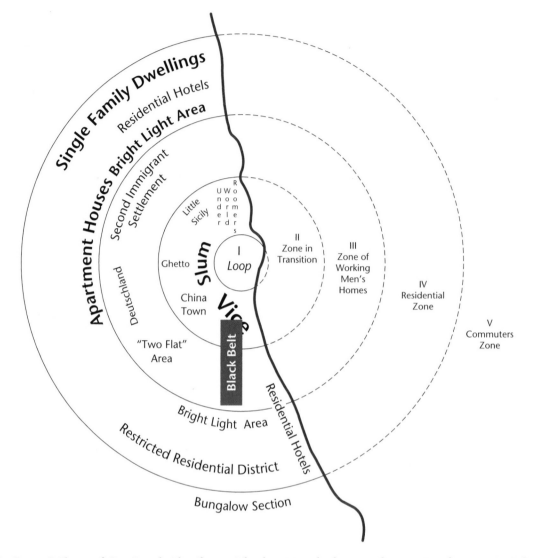

Figure 14.10   Burgess's Theory of City Growth: The Chicago School envisioned urban growth as a series of concentric circles, with ethnicity, class, residential patterns, and types of activity evolving with each ring removed from the central city.

Source: Park, Burgess, and McKenzie (1925/1967:55).

will arise over how space gets allocated and by whom; any effective solution to urban problems must address inequalities between groups and allocations of resources in urban areas (Abu-Lughod 1991; Harvey 1973).

Some conflict theorists see growing city problems as a result of domination by elites, creating poverty and exploitation of the poor (Flanagan 1993, 2001; Gottdiener and Hutchison 2006). Cities produce profits for those who buy and sell property and for investors and politicians who redevelop urban areas. Sometimes, poor urban residents are displaced in the process (Gottdiener 1987; Hannigan 1998; Logan and Molotch 1987). In short, conflict theorists see urbanization and modernization as a cause of poverty among city residents around the world.

Types of Cities

Although organizational structures of cities have changed and evolved over time, in the following section, we will focus on industrial and several variants of postindustrial cities.

Industrial Cities

The onset of industrialization in seventeenth- and eighteenth-century Europe started the trend toward *urbanized nations,* countries in which more than half of the population live in urban areas. Rural peasants migrated to the cities in search of opportunities and to escape the tedium and poverty of agricultural existence and shortage of available farmland. Often, the urbanization process was rapid and unplanned. Today, developed countries are over 75 percent urban, and developing countries are on average 40 percent urban; by 2030, this imbalance will be even greater.

Industrial cities became primarily commercial centers motivated by competition, a characteristic that differentiated them from preindustrial cities. The advent of power-driven machinery and the new capitalist factory system transformed and replaced the former craft and cottage industries and guild structures (Abu-Lughod 1991). Roads, waterways, and railroads made travel and communication between towns and cities easier and faster; cities became fast-paced as power-run vehicles took to the streets.

Cities served the rapidly advancing industrial sector, but crowded conditions, poor sanitation, polluted water supplies, and poor working conditions all contributed to the misery of poor urban residents and short life expectancy compared to those living in the countryside. Urban systems became overwhelmed by the large numbers of migrants, and conditions became as desperate as those the people had tried to escape in the rural areas.

By 1850, profound changes began taking place in many European countries and in the United States. A shift from predominantly rural to urban living was underway. In about 1870, Great Britain became the first truly urban nation with over 50 percent of the population in urban areas. Economically changing conditions on the British Isles were conducive to urbanization and industrialization; Parliament had passed "reorganization of land acts" that pushed many rural citizens from the countryside to cities. In addition, raw materials were available from colonies; new technology was rapidly advancing manufacturing techniques; and the banking facilities, credit, stock and other financing for industry were falling into place (Benevolo 1995; Mumford 1961).

Consider residential population patterns in the United States. Ninety percent of the U.S. population lived on farms in the 1790s; today, only 1.84 percent of the population work in farming (3 million workers), and only 6.5 percent of rural households are working farms (U.S. Department of Agriculture 2002). Agribusiness conglomerates have bought out family farmers who could not compete with these large businesses. Young people have left farms, resulting in an older population in rural areas than in urban areas.

Between 1940 and 2000, the number of urban areas in the United States increased from 33 to 453 (The Federal Register 2002), and many cities have become global economic centers (Abbott 1993; Abu-Lughod 2001). Urban growth was aided by an increase in agricultural productivity that made food available to support urban dwellers and by the development of an adequate distribution system to get the produce to markets to feed those in urban areas.

With the advent of public transportation in the late 1800s, people in many countries began to escape crowded city conditions by moving out into emerging suburbs. As private automobiles and means of communication such as the telephone became available in the early 1900s, movement to the suburbs increased rapidly. Road systems were developed

Despite the many jobs created, one of the downsides of industrialized cities is phenomenal pollution, as this photograph of Pittsburgh in the mid-twentieth century illustrates.

Source: © Bettmann/Corbis.

to accommodate the growing numbers of autos, and more businesses and services relocated to suburban areas.

Since the 1990s, the U.S. census shows that some rural areas are once again gaining population. This is especially the case in recreation areas where urban residents relocate to *exurbs* (rural areas within commuting distance of city jobs), and retired persons look for new locations with clean air, space, interpersonal civility, and a slower pace than the city (Johnson and Fuguitt 2000).

Postindustrial Cities

Postindustrial cities (Bell 1976/1999) have a high percentage of employees in the service sector—business headquarters, government and intergovernmental organizations, research and development, tourism, finance, health, education, and telecommunications. They are found in the most technologically advanced, wealthy nations. Washington, DC, fits most of these characteristics, as does La Defense, an urban center on the outskirts of Paris, built as a commercial, service, and information-exchange center to serve France.

Postindustrial cities are closely tied to the economic structures of capitalism, with global production systems and instant exchanges of information (Abu-Lughod 2001;

Apartment buildings surround this back alley that serves as a bathroom in the major Indian city of Mysore. Some poor residents have no other facilities to use.

Source: © Kate Ballantine.

Vito Bruno, an elderly resident of Boston, can be found every day reading the paper outside Cafe Vittoria. Boston's North End is the oldest neighborhood in the city and one of the oldest in America. First settled by colonists, the streets have seen waves of Irish and Jewish immigrants, and in the recent past, it has been a tight-knit Italian American community. As in many ethnic areas in the heart of major cities, property values are going up as the neighborhood is gentrified.

Source: ©Andrew Lichtenstein / Corbis.

Castells 1989; Friedman 2005). In the transformation from industrial to postindustrial economies, from manufacturing to service economies, some people get left behind; there are often severe income disparities between those trained for the new economies and those with less training and in lower level positions (Fainstein, Gordon, and Harloe 1992). Cities such as Bangalore, India, illustrate the disparities between high-tech industries and poor agricultural peasants in the surrounding areas.

Some urban areas are carefully planned. *New towns,* for example, are cities built from scratch as economically self-sufficient entities with all the needed urban amenities. Urban planners believed that these cities could relieve the congestion of urban areas, provide new economic bases and residences near jobs, and solve many problems faced by older cities. Some "new towns" have been success stories: Columbia, Maryland; Brazilia, Brazil (the relatively new capital); Canberra, Australia. Others have not lived up to expectations. Americans thought this was a new and innovative idea, but Sociology around the World on page 269 discusses archeological research indicating that large planned cities existed in North America before white Europeans even knew the continent existed.

As people move to the suburbs, and manufacturing firms, services, commerce, and retail trade follow (Meltzer 1999), these movements lock cities and suburbs into competition over jobs and tax revenues (Stanback 1991). When this happens, farmland and open lands disappear; quality of construction is often shoddy since builders want to make big profits; energy and water demands increase, often straining public utilities; and sprawl leads to vast, crowded freeway systems. Such a "suburbanization of industry" took place between 1970 and 1990, as many industries relocated out of central city areas, looking for favorable tax rates.

In some urban areas, neatly manicured lawns and freshly painted exteriors reflect new directions away from either suburbanization or deterioration of inner-city neighborhoods. The process of **gentrification** refers to members of the middle and upper class, mostly young white professionals, buying and renovating rundown properties in central-city neighborhoods. The process begins when affluent urban residents leave their stylish homes and move to suburbs. Poorer residents are left behind to rent once-fashionable homes from absentee owners. Later, affluent professionals buy the rundown homes at bargain rates, renovate them, and live in these newly gentrified areas (Feagin 1983).

In recent years, these neighborhoods that are often adjacent to the central business districts have become the new "fashionable" residential areas; Georgetown in Washington, DC, and German Village in Columbus, Ohio, are examples. Beautiful old classic homes have become affordable to mostly young upper-middle-class professionals who decide they want ready access to the cultural opportunities of the city. Relocating downtown makes this possible. They bring consumers, leadership, and a tax base to the city, but they also

Sociology around the World

City Planning in Prehistoric Central America: Teotihuacan

Teotihuacan was a Mesoamerican city (between the American continents) created by a society that had no metal tools, had not invented the wheel, and had no pack animals. At its height, Teotihuacan covered 8 square miles (20 square kilometers), which made it larger than imperial Rome. Its central religious monument, the Temple of the Sun, was as broad at its base as the great pyramid of Cheops in Egypt. Its population may have reached 100,000.

Strategically located astride a valley that was the gateway to the lowlands of Mexico, Teotihuacan flourished for 500 years as a great urban commercial center. Yet it was more than that. It was the Mecca of the New World, a religious and cultural capital that probably housed pilgrims from as far away as Guatemala. Perhaps most startling, Teoihuacan was a totally planned city. Its two great pyramids, its citadel, its hundred lesser religious structures, and its 4,000 other dwellings were laid out according to an exact design. Streets (and many of its buildings) were organized on a perfect grid aligned with the city center. Even the shape of the river that divided the city was changed to fit the grid pattern.

Planning for the construction of Teotihuacan's major temples must have been an incredible undertaking. The Temple of the Sun, for instance, rises to a height of 215 feet and has a base of 725 square feet. These dimensions mean that it took about 1 million tons of sun-baked mud bricks to build the temple. When the Spaniards conquered Mexico in the sixteenth century, they were amazed to find Teotihuacan's ruined temples. Local inhabitants claimed that the temples had been built by giants. They showed the Spaniards the bones of giant elephants (which had lived there in prehistoric times) to prove their point.

Small buildings as well as large ones were cleverly conceived in Teotihuacan. Houses were apparently

Teotihuacan was a pre-European city in the heart of North America, a city of 100,000 people.

planned for maximum space and privacy. Apartments were constructed around central patios, with each patio designed to give dwellers light and air, as well as an efficient drainage system. In a Teotihuacan housing complex, a person could indeed have lived in relative comfort (Jordan-Bychkov and Domoch 1998).

---

force poor residents to leave the area as rents soar and landlords can make more profit by selling the properties.

If professional people are taking over the low-rent districts and fixing them up, where are the low-income people to turn for housing? The poor are pushed into less attractive parts of town with fewer services and recreational areas and often pay higher rents for less adequate housing. Alternative housing for displaced residents may be difficult to find, contributing to problems of homelessness. Conflict theorists view gentrification and other urban developments that favor the wealthy and displace or exclude the poor as control by real estate capitalists, who sometimes engineer the takeover of poor areas where fine old homes still stand. By contrast, others argue that wealthy residents who choose the lifestyle of the city over suburbia are helping to support viable, livable cities (Caulfield 1994).

THINKING SOCIOLOGICALLY

What are some positive and negative aspects of gentrification for individuals and cities? Explain.

Megacities

As we look at earth from space, some areas glow. These urban areas of 10 million or more residents, called megacities, dot the globe as rural residents leave agriculture to seek opportunities in urban areas. In the 1950s, only New York City had 10 million people; there were 75 cities in the world with 1 to 5 million residents, mostly in developed countries. Table 14.5 shows the rapid change in this pattern with the 10 largest population centers in 2000 and for 2005 (United Nations Population Division 2002, 2003).

As the world becomes more congested and cities continue to attract residents, cities start to merge or to become continuous urban areas without rural areas between them. Those who have driven from Boston to Washington, DC, an area sometimes called Boswash, know the meaning of *megalopolis*, a spatial merging of two or more cities along major transportation corridors (Brunn et al. 2003; Knox and Taylor 1995).

Global Urban Variations

Many people around the globe live in cities with long, often glorious histories. Some live in relatively new suburbs surrounding central cities, and others live in new urban areas, recently planned and constructed. Cities' spatial arrangements vary by their histories, as the following examples illustrate.

Kabul, Afghanistan, is an example of a traditional, *indigenous city* in the developing world. Indigenous cities usually predate European cities. Kabul dates back to 500-300 BCE, and it became the capital of Afghanistan in 1776. In the old section, bazaars and flat-roofed houses crowd the narrow winding streets made for foot and cart traffic. The newer sections have wide, tree-lined streets. Land use is mixed, with small businesses and residences sharing the same dwellings. In many indigenous cities, certain occupational types occupy distinctive areas. The centers of indigenous cities usually include a market or bazaar, monuments, government buildings, and a religious mosque, church, or temple. While some of the elite live in the heart of these cities, the poor live on the periphery of the city or the city streets, a pattern vastly different from North American affluent urban and suburban areas.

Developing countries often have *dual cities* such as Delhi–New Delhi, India, in which a modern Westernized colonial central city is located next to a traditional, indigenous city. Abijan, Ivory Coast, which served as the hub for French colonial administrators and economic activities, is such a city. On one side is located an exclusive French quarter, fancy hotels, the commercial and service centers, and the beachfront. Across the bridge is a bustling traditional African city with markets and social networks structured to meet the needs of the indigenous inhabitants, and hidden in back alleys behind the bustling shops are many slum dwellings.

From cities built on ancient foundations to new urban centers, cities are a main organizational structure in modern life. How do these urban areas develop? This leads us to a discussion of macro-level issues.

TABLE 14.5	**Ten Largest Population Centers (population in millions)**					
2000				**2005**		
Rank	**Center and Country**	**Population**		**Rank**	**Center and Country**	**Population**
1	Tokyo, Japan	34,450		1	Tokyo, Japan	35,327
2	Mexico City, Mexico	18,066		2	Mexico City, Mexico	19,013
3	New York/Newark, USA	17,846		3	New York/Newark, USA	18,498
4	Sao Paulo, Brazil	17,099		4	Mumbai (Bombay), India	18,336
5	Mumbai (Bombay), India	16,086		5	Sao Paulo, Brazil	18,333
6	Calcutta, India	13,058		6	Delhi, India	15,334
7	Shanghai, China	12,887		7	Calcutta, India	14,299
8	Buenos Aires, Argentina	12,583		8	Buenos Aires, Argentina	13,349
9	Delhi, India	12,441		9	Jakarta, Indonesia	13,194
10	Los Angeles area, USA	11,814		10	Shanghai, China	12,665

Source: United Nations Population Division (2003).

URBAN PROBLEMS, THE ENVIRONMENT, AND SOCIAL POLICY: MACRO-LEVEL PERSPECTIVES

The mountains rise from the sea, dotted with pastel-colored shanties. On the drive from the port city of La Guiara up into the mountains to the capital city of Caracas, Venezuela, one sees settlements nestled into the hillsides. The poor, who have come from throughout the country to find opportunities in the capital, make shelters in the hills surrounding Caracas, often living with no running water, electricity, or sewage disposal. The laundry list of urban problems is overwhelming: excessive size, overcrowding, shortages of services, education, and health care, slums and squatters, traffic congestion, unemployment, and effects of global restructuring, including loss of agricultural land, environmental degradation, and resettlement of immigrants and refugees (Brunn et al. 2003; Jacobs 1961, 1969). This section considers several of the many problems facing urban areas such as Caracas.

Rural Migrants and Overcrowding

Barriadas surround the outskirts of Caracas, a situation found in many cities where migrants find any available space within or around the city to squat. For example, in Cairo, Egypt, a huge, sprawling graveyard full of large mausoleums, The City of the Dead, has become home to thousands of families transplanted from rural areas, and in cities in India such as Chennai (Madras), Mumbai (Bombay), and Calcutta, thousands of homeless migrants live on the sidewalks, on highway medians, and in river channels that can flood.

Overcrowding exists in cities throughout the world but causes special problems in developing countries where rural residents seek opportunities in urban areas. Squatters with hopes for a better future set up shacks of any material available—tin, cardboard, leaves, mud, and sticks—in settlements known as *barriadas* in Spanish, *shantytowns* in English, *bidonvilles* in French, *favelas* in Portuguese-speaking Brazil, and *bustees* in India. The majority of migrants to the city are young. They are pulled to the city in hopes of finding jobs and often have been pushed from the rural areas because of limited land on which to farm.

The hills surrounding Caracas, the capital of Venezuela, are densely packed with migrants from rural areas looking for opportunities in the urban area.

Source: © Loic Bernard.

These and other children sleep in streets in Bombay each night.

Source: © Louie Psihoyos / Corbis.

In the past three decades, the urban populations in Africa, Asia, and Latin America have mushroomed, and as Map 14.1 shows, nine of the largest cities in the world are now in the Global South. Rural-to-urban migration and development of megacities dominates the economic and political considerations in many countries. The newcomers spill out into the countryside, engulfing towns along the way. Figure 14.11 shows the population numbers living in urban areas by region of the world, indicating trends from 1950 to 2000 and making projections through 2030 (United Nations Population Division 2002).

Countries have little time or money to prepare infrastructures and provide services for the rapidly increasing numbers of urban residents. Technological development, job opportunities, and basic services have not kept up with the large migrations of would-be laborers; providing services such as water, electricity, sanitation, schools, transportation, and health services to these people has become a major

problem—even impossible for some poor governments. Health and disease, especially contagious diseases, cause deadly epidemics due to the lack of services and poor sanitary conditions. Sociology around the World on page 474 describes one plague that ravaged much of Europe.

Lack of adequate housing is a worldwide problem, not helped by high birth rates and lower death rates in developing countries, causing population increase that is greater than the rate of economic growth or the capacity of society to absorb the migrants into urban areas. Since residents of the squatter settlements hold traditional rural values, adaptation to urban bureaucracy and overcrowding become even more difficult, resulting in *anomie* (normlessness) and exacerbating urban problems. Planning and social policy have failed poor migrants in rapidly growing slums of many world cities.

Environment, Infrastructure, and Urban Ecosystems

"Life on Earth in 2050 will be marked by struggles for food, water, and energy security," according to a recent study of the link between human well-being and health of the planet (Popline 2006a). The study, involving 1,360 scientists from 95 nations, asserts, "Sixty percent of the ecological systems that sustain life on Earth are being degraded or used unsustainably" (Popline 2006a:1). Extinction of species, lack of water and water pollution, resource exploitation, collapse of some global fisheries, and new diseases result from this breakdown. Urbanization by 2050 will stretch resources to their limits. Cities will have no way to dispose of wastes, resulting in epidemics. We cannot address environmental problems in detail here; suffice it to say that humans are causing most of the problems that are killing people now and will kill many in the future. The problems are exacerbated by an increase in natural disasters (e.g., hurricanes), which scientists believe to be a result of global warming. We can ignore the problems or call them nonexistent because life has improved for many people, but this is a short-sighted response. This increase in quality of life is actually magnifying the problems and hastening the demise of cities and the environments that support cities.

Additional infrastructure problems threaten to immobilize cities in developing countries. Traffic congestion is so intense in some cities that the slow movement of people and goods reduces productivity, jobs, health, and vital services. Pollution of the streets and air are chronic problems, especially with expansion of automobile use around the world. Older cities face deteriorating infrastructures, with water, gas, and sewage lines in need of replacement. In developed countries, concern for these problems has brought action and some relief, but in developing countries where survival issues are pressing, environmental contamination is a low priority. Thus, the worst air pollution is

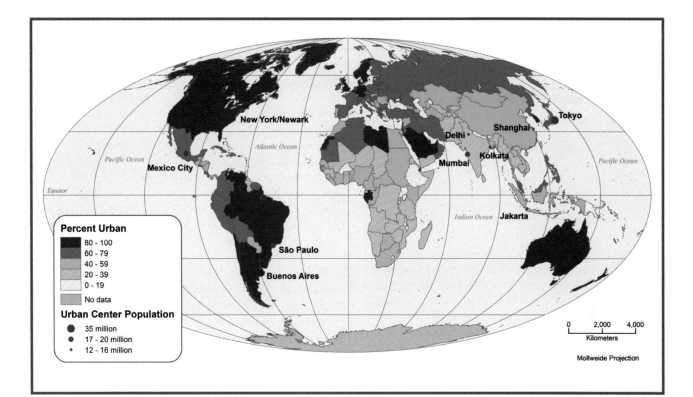

MAP 14.1 World Urban Populations

Source: World Development Indicators (2006). Map by Anna Versluis.

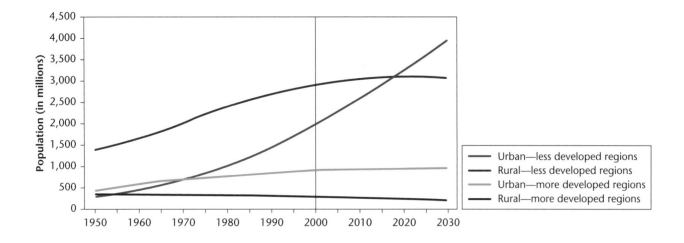

Figure 14.11 Urban and Rural Populations, 1950–2030

Source: United Nations (2002).

Sociology around the World

"Ring around the Rosey" and the Plague

Ring around the Rosey,

Pockets full of posies,

Ashes, Ashes,

We all fall down!

Remember this nursery school rhyme? You probably did not understand the meaning of the rhyme as a child; it refers to the bubonic plague that was ravaging England and Europe in the early to mid-1600s, leaving dead and dying people in its wake. One account says that people infected with the plague got red circular sores that smelled very bad. People would put flowers (posies) in their pockets or on their bodies somewhere to cover up the smell. Because people were dying so rapidly, it was difficult to keep up with burials and the dead were burned to reduce the spread of the disease (ashes, ashes). So many people were sick and dying that "we all fall down." Although there are variations on this story, it is probably true that the rhyme related to the plague.

From 1603 to 1849, the clergy had the task of recording the deaths, burials, and the cause of deaths that occurred; these were circulated weekly with a summary put out before Christmas. This process is one of the earliest records of vital statistics. In 1662, John Graunt from London analyzed the records for the first known statistical analysis of demographic data; among his findings was that "for every 100 people born in London, only 16 were still alive at age 36 and only 3 at age 66" (Weeks 1999:61). The plague had an impact on social relationships; many citizens avoided anyone who was a stranger, and some who contracted the disease died miserable lonely deaths because of others' fears of the disease. As the industrial revolution advanced, so did income, housing, sanitation, and nutrition; all these improvements in people's lives reduced the incidence of plague and increased life expectancy. Today, cases of the plague can be found in several places, including India and the rural southwest United States. Antibiotics are effective treatment for people who have access to them, but many poor people cannot afford expensive medications from affluent countries.

Source: Barefoot (2003).

---

now found in major cities in developing countries such as Seoul, Korea; Mexico City; Sao Paulo, Brazil; and several Chinese cities.

Water, an essential resource for survival, illustrates the complex urban ecosystem. Cities pipe in millions of gallons of water each day to residents from lakes or reservoirs, sometimes located at a distance from the city. Through a complex network of pipes, the water is connected to each establishment. After use—cooking, cleaning, showering, disposing of wastes—the water is discarded and becomes an output. Some of the water is used in products or for industrial uses and some is stored, but most waste water—about 95 percent—is piped out to sewer plants, rivers, or other disposal sites. Among other plans, environmental scientists are working on methods to purify and recycle greywater (waste water) for reuse.

When water into the system comes from contaminated sources, individuals complain and demand that more money and effort be expended to protect the water supply. Yet external strains from floods, droughts, or various contaminants can cause water supplies to be less than safe (Jordan-Bychkov and Domoch 1998). Water is but one example of the complex urban ecosystem with its interdependent parts. (See Figure 14.12.)

To understand the urban ecosystem, its growth and its decay, we must understand that there are pressures on the city both from both external sources and internal dynamics.

Poverty in the World's Cities

Poor people are often invisible. Around the world, they are tucked away in enclaves most people do not see. Until something brings attention to the poor, leaders and most of the citizenry can ignore them. Invisibility of urban poverty results because these residents have little power to make their problems public and little energy beyond that needed for survival. Earlier chapters addressed reasons for poverty and the groups who fall disproportionately into poverty (Gans 1991; Wilson 1978, 1987). Urban

Figure 14.12   Detail of an Urban Water System

Source: © Istockphoto.com.

residential patterns generally reflect the same reasons for poverty.

The *permanent underclass* refers to the poor worldwide who do not have education or skills to become part of the local or world economy (Jones 1992). Children leave school at young ages to help support their families, reducing their opportunities to get out of poverty; however, modernizing economies have little need for unskilled labor.

The *feminization of poverty*, the increase of women and their children in the ranks of the impoverished, is a growing problem in developed and developing countries. The increasing numbers of teen mothers who have low education, are unemployed, and have few prospects to get out of poverty result in their disproportionate representation among the homeless. (See How Do We Know? on page 476 for a discussion of the circumstances and coping strategies of homeless people.) One cause of feminization of poverty is divorces that leave women with small children and poor job prospects. Single-parent homes with a woman as the bread-earner are far more likely than other types of households to be in economic trouble, with poor housing, lack of education, and scant job opportunities.

In some cities, residents are working collectively for survival and improvement in their conditions. In Harlem, New York, some residents live in cooperatives and rental buildings that they manage, taken over after landlords abandoned the buildings. The "community household model" in which residents control their own housing may provide a new method of organization and leadership by tenants and community activists (Leavitt and Saegert 1990).

THINKING SOCIOLOGICALLY

First, read the essay about urban homeless people on page 476. Are there homeless people in your community? Why are they homeless? What, if anything, can or should be done about the problem?

Crime and Delinquency in the City

Social disruption and crime are not intrinsic to cities; one can walk through many areas of Toronto, London, or Paris at night with little likelihood of problems. Traditional African cities had very low crime rates but today are much less safe because of high levels of new migrants. When people are transient, when they move frequently, they are more likely to experience *anomie*, to have less commitment to community norms, and to lack of a sense of commitment to the norms and the well-being of the local community. Add to that the desperate situation of poor, and you have a recipe for crime.

As young people move from rural to urban life, juvenile delinquency becomes a problem. In rural communities and tribal cultures, strict norms govern behavior; but in urban areas, cohesiveness of families and ties with tribal groups are lessened. When education, economic security, and social services increase, conformity again becomes a norm for these newcomers, replacing the anomie of the transition.

A key message from the study of urbanization is that people's lives are influenced by the environment in which they live. Applied sociologists can play a role in improving the conditions of urban areas, as described in The Applied Sociologist at Work on page 477.

THINKING SOCIOLOGICALLY

Some scholars argue that crime and delinquency are not intrinsic to cities but that crime is shaped by anomie, transience, and lack of connectedness. How might we begin to build a sense of community, belonging, and attachment in urban areas?

Urban Planners and Social Policy in the Global Social World

Try planning an ideal city. First, list everything you need to consider. Now think of organization: who will handle what? Consider services, maintenance, financing, and leadership. This would be quite a task. The problem is that most urban planners do not have the luxury of starting from scratch. They must work with decaying areas, being cognizant of the meaningful landmarks and treasured sites. Planners may also have to undo hasty or inadequate planning from previous actions. Among other things, they attempt to maximize technical efficiency such as getting water from point A to point B.

How Do We Know?

Understanding Urban Homeless People

Immigration to urban areas can result in homeless people sleeping under bridges, in parks, in vacant lots, in unused subway tunnels, or even on the sidewalks of main thoroughfares. Although homelessness was frequently observed in Third World countries, this was uncommon in North American and European cities until the early 1980s. Two sociologists, David Snow and Leon Anderson, undertook a study at the macro, meso, and micro levels of analysis to understand the processes of homelessness in America.

Since any one source of data might not provide the whole picture, and understanding contributing factors at each level of analysis would help, Snow and Anderson (1993) used *triangulation* by collecting several forms of data. First, they did an ethnographic study, making friends and becoming "buddy-researchers" with the homeless people they came to know in Austin, Texas. They did interviews, made extensive observations, listened in on conversations, and asked homeless people to help them understand the implications and the processes of homeless living in a modern American city. Second, they used "tracking data" by contacting homeless people through a variety of organizations and institutions in the city and state. This provided them with access to official files and data, allowed them to confirm stories, enabled them to identify how homeless people drew on resources, and provided information on how street people related to social service and religious agencies.

In trying to make sense of homelessness, the researchers identified key variables that distinguished different types of homelessness; they uncovered a wide range of causes, circumstances, and coping methods. Clarifying eight key variables helped them to identify several types of homeless people and to prevent overgeneralization about any one kind of homelessness.

Snow and Anderson's (1993) work was a form of detective work—sorting through information and trying to understand the many dimensions of homelessness. Using macro-level perspectives, they looked at employment trends and wage labor issues in the larger society, social policies of the government designed to address poverty and homelessness. Meso-level issues involved study of family life and care-giving organizations. They also considered the micro culture of street people, how they lend each other support and help each other make sense of their circumstances. They point to many forces at work on the homeless, from global economic trends to the way their families relate to them.

Perhaps the most intriguing findings of this study involved how people affirmed a sense of self in this humiliating situation. After all, to be a person of worth in American society is to (1) own some property, (2) have someone who cares about you enough to take you in if you are really desperate, and (3) occupy a significant status in society by earning some money and have a career or position deserving of respect. The homeless not only lack all of these, their master status—"homeless person"—is one that elicits disrespect. "Dignity and worth are not primarily individual characteristics, but instead flow from the roles we play," write the authors (Snow and Anderson 1993:9). To be homeless, then, is far more than to be without a residence or shelter. It is to be without a place to restore one's dignity. So how did they cope?

This research showed a number of coping strategies, only a few of which can be reported here. Sometimes, the homeless people explained away their circumstances as *temporary "bad luck"* or part of a normal cycle in which they just happened to be on the down end of the cycle for a while. Sometimes, they would distance themselves from the *role of homelessness*, pointing out that they were "different" than other homeless people, "didn't really belong," and did not really deserve to be seen as homeless at all. Some people coped by *fictive story-telling*, pointing to pronounced achievements in the past (often fictionalized or embellished), or creating stories of their phenomenal accomplishments when they finally do get on their feet. By affirming another identity in the past or the future, their self-esteem was salvaged. However, perhaps the most surprising strategy to preserve self worth was to *embrace the role* of being homeless with pride—to boast about how one was the best at being a survivor, the best at being a friend to the homeless, or the best at rejecting shallow values of materialism in our commercial society. They could thus affirm themselves for coping skills, for caring qualities, or for deep spirituality. They had defined reality in a way that allowed them to see themselves in a positive light. They had changed the social construction of reality, at least among themselves.

This research not only used multiple methods to check accuracy of findings and insights but also explored social interaction and processes at more than one level of analysis in the social world.

THE APPLIED SOCIOLOGIST AT WORK

Improving Quality of Life by Transforming Community Structure

As is true of many urban centers, Detroit, Michigan, has its share of distressed neighborhoods. Dr. Jay Weinstein has been director of an interdisciplinary team attempting to bring about economic, social, and physical restructuring of some of these areas. By developing long-term relationships in several urban neighborhoods, the team has had success working with residents and others to improve conditions. Weinstein calls this approach *relationship brokering*—bringing people together to share perspectives and to clear up misperceptions between residents, local officials, service providers, and police. These efforts have helped to empower residents to take action and improve their neighborhoods.

A major project along these lines, which began in 1990 and continues to the present, is in the Detroit suburb of Taylor, Michigan. For decades, residents of Taylor and the surrounding Down River area were painfully aware of the problems of their neighborhood, known by uncomplimentary names such as "Crack Ridge," "Hooker Heaven," and "Sin City." With about 7,500 people packed into an area of one-half square mile, most residents were living in rental units controlled by the U.S. Department of Housing and Urban Development Section 8 program (subsidized private housing).

In 1989, an influential local newspaper published a series of articles showing that the neighborhood had earned the labels applied to it. The series exposed the high incidences of drug trafficking and use, prostitution, alcoholism, and violent crimes in the neighborhood. The people living in Down River were only too familiar with the situation. Nevertheless, the articles inspired local and federal political leaders to demand action.

In the spring of 1990, Weinstein and his colleagues were awarded an applied research grant by the City of Taylor Department of Community Development. The purposes of the work were to assess the problems by providing reliable data and to make recommendations to improve the community. The fact-finding stage revealed that the problems of "Crack Ridge" were every bit as serious as portrayed by the media. However, it was also shown that the residents of the neighborhood were not the main perpetrators. Instead, for as long as anyone could remember, the area had been under siege by nonresidents who came

and went, drifted from apartment to apartment, or illegally occupied residences under threat of harm to the rightful owners.

Based on these and other findings, the research team recommended a plan for a thorough physical, economic, social, and political reconstruction of the neighborhood. Fortunately, city and federal officials understood the value of such sociological expertise. With few reservations, they accepted the recommendations of the sociological team and set out on a 10-year program of implementation. Working with residents of the neighborhood and other citizens of the city, Taylor's mayor, city council, Department of Human Resources, police department, and many others tackled the problem. Weinstein and his colleagues helped to guide the rebirth of this community.

Today, the neighborhood has a new name (The Villages of Taylor), a new human services center, a new residential owner (a private nonprofit corporation established by the city), and many new or redesigned buildings. The population density has been reduced by more than 20 percent and all this without one person being displaced against his or her will, other than drug dealers. In fall 2001, in one of the most treasured moments of his life, Weinstein attended the official dedication of The Villages of Taylor.

For Weinstein, sociological theory is at the root of his neighborhood work. He tries to identify the "definitions of reality" held by the residents and then helps residents examine those definitions, a symbolic interaction approach. Only by understanding their definitions can residents begin to act to change the situation.

In his work, Weinstein uses a multiple-methods approach: surveys, participant observation, census data, and other large data sets. Each technique has strengths and limitations. Using a variety of approaches in combination brings him closer to the elusive truths of social life.

Dr. Jay Weinstein, a professor at Eastern Michigan University, specializes in urban sociology, demography, and social change. He received his doctorate from University of Illinois, Champaign-Urbana He has been doing private consulting for over 20 years, with contracts from international and local governments and nonprofit organizations. His studies have included analysis of demographic trends and changes in India, Albania, Bulgaria, and Jamaica.

Planners must meet needs for housing, sanitation, education, food distribution, jobs, family life, and recreation. Planning efforts need to take into consideration what will happen to various groups, including the poor, elderly, women, and homeless populations.

In the early twenty-first century, a number of global trends affect urban planning (Brunn et al. 2003):

1. The process of urbanization—people migrating to cities—will continue, exacerbating the already difficult situation for many of the world's crowded urban areas.

2. Information and transportation technologies allow people in any part of the globe to be in contact; however this may also reduce the feelings of belonging to a specific place, reducing commitment to work on city problems.

3. International boundaries will diminish in importance as flow of information, goods, services, labor, and capital increasingly ignore national boundaries. For example, migration of Asians to cities around the world will continue and will have an impact on these cities.

4. Economies will increasingly rely on brainwork, including invention of new technologies, rather than on brawnwork of older manufacturing; thus, the gap between haves and have-nots is likely to continue.

5. Conflicts between cultural and political groups, including religious and political extremists, will continue to affect urban life.

6. *McDonaldization*—creation of a consumer world dominated by major Western food, music, fashion, and entertainment—will continue even as we see an increasing diversity of people within Western nations and communities.

Awareness of these trends can help urban planners in their efforts to design cities to meet the needs of the future (Friedman 2006; Garreau 1991).

In the past, men were designers of cities, but women also experience them; some analysts believe that women's experiences in the city are quite different from men's. Spaces that have been designed with women in mind emphasize opportunities for participation, involvement in community development, and leisure activities such as informal places for meeting (Andrew and Milroy 1991; Renzetti 2003; Wilson 1993a). Unfortunately, profit is often the motivation in planning, and few planning efforts consider cities in a holistic fashion. Urban planners in socialist countries with centralized national plans for urban areas may find it easier to consider the needs of all residents (Flanagan 2001).

Millions of people live satisfying lives in cities, but for others, life is misery. Whether the economic base and urban planners can keep up with the demands for even basic services in developing countries remains to be seen. This is especially true in areas of the world where population is outstripping the land and people are flocking to cities for survival. This basic population pattern—urbanization—has consequences at the most global levels and at the most micro levels of human life. Our social world model—which looks at the connections of micro, meso, and macro levels of the social system—makes us cognizant of the consequences of decisions made by millions of individuals and families. It makes us mindful of the human consequences of global trends and forces.

 ## SO WHAT?

Population trends, including migration resulting in urbanization, provide a dynamic force for change in societies. Whether one is interested in understanding social problems, social policy, or factors that may affect one's own career, demographic processes are critical forces. We ignore them at our peril—both to us individually and as a society. Family businesses can be destroyed, retirement plans obliterated, and the health of communities sabotaged by population factors if they are overlooked. If they are considered, however, they can enhance planning that leads to prosperity and enjoyment of our communities. Urban living creates problems, but it can have enormous benefits as well, and this is but a single example of a population trend.

Many other factors create change in a society, and the factors contributing to social dynamics are interactive, some of them contributing to change in a particular direction and others retarding change. The next chapter examines the larger picture of social transformation in our complex and multileveled social world.

CONTRIBUTING TO YOUR SOCIAL WORLD

At the Local Level: Your community, whether a large city or a small town, may have neighborhood recreation departments, crime watch, or community-organizing agencies that need volunteers to provide services or to help neighbors solve problems and apply pressure to city hall to get things done. Such volunteers are especially needed in working-class and poor neighborhoods.

At the Organizational or Institutional Level: Some cities have urban-planning offices that welcome internships, a place you could make a contribution and explore interest in this field.

Homeless shelters and soup kitchens welcome volunteers.

At the National and Global Levels: International organizations dealing with refugees need contributions of money and school supplies. Other organizations need volunteers to help tutor children or teach language skills to adults from war-torn countries.

Population census projects take place in most countries and require workers to collect data.

Visit www.pineforge.com/ballantinestudy for online activities, sample tests, and other helpful information. Select "Chapter 14: Population and Urbanization" for chapter-specific activities.

15 THE PROCESS OF CHANGE: Can We Make a Difference?

Humans are profoundly influenced by the macro structures around them, but people are also capable of creating change, especially if they band together with others and approach change in an organized way. Social movements such as those depicted in the pictures are one powerful way to bring about change.

Think About It . . .

1. Can you as an individual change the world?

2. How does change at one level of the social world model affect other levels?

3. What conditions enhance or retard social change?

4. How does technology affect the process of change?

Macro: Global Community

Macro: National Society

Meso: National Institutions and Organizations; Ethnic Subcultures

Micro: Local Organizations and Community

Micro: You and Your Family

Micro: Plant closings, hate crimes, business scandals

Meso: Family instability from economic recessions; church scandals; failures of schools to provide quality education

Macro: Government decisions about homosexual marriages, going to war, trade agreements, or tariffs

Macro: Actions by United Nations, the World Court, or the International Monetary Fund; agreements by international alliances; business decisions of multinational corporations

Illegal drug deals involve a worldwide network and have spawned a big business—from the societies whose peasants survive by growing and supplying the raw materials for making drugs to street vendors and middle-level dealers, from individuals who see their loved ones devastated by the effects of drugs to large organizations that oversee the drug production and distribution process. To create change in the drug trade—production, trafficking, and consumption—each level of the social world, from the most micro-level interactions to the global, must be included in the effort.

Most production of opium and heroin takes place in just a few countries: Afghanistan produces about 89 percent of the world's opium production. This is followed by Myanmar (Burma) and Lao People's Democratic Republic, but the production is dropping in these countries. Opium poppy production decreased for the first time in 2005, but cultivation increased in some areas in 2006 (United Nations Office on Drugs and Crime 2006a, 2006b). Poppy production had fallen off dramatically under the Taliban regime in Afghanistan because it banned production and cut opium production by 94 percent (United Nations Office on Drugs and Crime 2003). (See Figure 15.1.)

Global trafficking as measured by confiscated drugs has increased slightly in the past few years; the most commonly seized drug was cannabis, followed by opiates and stimulants (see Figure 15.2). The most commonly consumed (and confiscated) drug was cannabis (160 million people), followed by amphetamine-type stimulants (34 million people), opiates such as heroin (close to 15 million people), and cocaine (over 14 million people). This means 200 million people, close to 5 percent (4.7 percent) of the world's population over fourteen years of age, use some form of drugs that most experts and many countries define as dangerous and illegal.

Governments and communities around the world are concerned with illicit drug trafficking and consumption because drug trade results in loss of labor, increased crime, ruined lives, and costs for rehabilitation. Understanding the process of social change from a multilevel approach is essential for those interested in dealing with the drug trade. We have begun with a discussion of drugs because this social issue illustrates many other problems such as poverty and crime, where social change is occurring and where micro, meso, and macro dimensions are interactive.

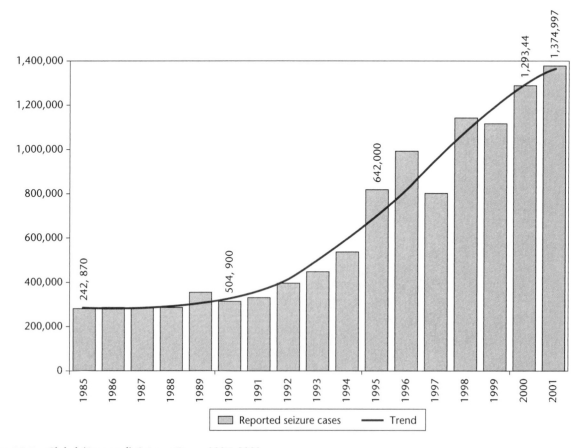

Figure 15.1   Global (Reported) Seizure Cases, 1985–2001

Source: United Nations Office on Drugs and Crime (2003:47, 2006a, 2006b).

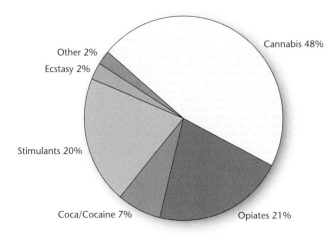

Figure 15.2 Breakdown of Reported Global Seizure Cases in 2001

Source: United Nations Office on Drugs and Crime (2003:47, 2006a, 2006b).

Turn on the morning or evening news, and we have a lesson in our changing social world. We see headlines of medical advances and cures for disease; biological breakthroughs in cloning and the DNA code; terrorist bombings in Israel, Iraq, Chechnya, and other parts of the world; famine in drought-afflicted Sub–Saharan Africa; disasters such as earthquakes, hurricanes, tsunamis, and floods; and social activists calling for a boycott of Wal-Mart (see photo on next page) or of oil companies or other corporations. The society's problems bombard us, depress us; they also point out that social, political, environmental, and biological events bring change into the lives of people. Some events seem far away and hard to imagine: thousands killed by a tidal wave in India or hundreds swept away by mud from an erupting volcano in Colombia. Some of these are natural events; others are due to human actions: a rise in terrorism reflecting divisions in world economic, political, and religious ideologies; or biological advances that revolutionize the meaning of life—cloning, stem cell therapies, and DNA testing. Regardless of source, these events bring about change.

Social change is defined as variations or alterations over time in the behavior patterns, culture (including norms and values), and structure of society. Some change is controllable, and some is out of our hands, but change is inevitable and ubiquitous. Change can be rapid, caused by some disruption to the existing system, or it can be gradual and evolutionary, such as the breeding of new types of dogs, cattle, or crops over several centuries. Very often, change at one level in the social world occurs because of change at another level; micro, meso, and macro levels of society may work together in the change process or be out of sync.

Whatever change we choose to examine—the global demand for exotic tourist locations, the nation into which tourist trade is being introduced, the institutions that regulate and routinize everyday life for people, the village and villagers for whom life is changed by an influx of strangers on vacation—the social world model helps us conceptualize the process of change. This chapter explores causes of change and some strategies for bringing about desired change.

THE COMPLEXITY OF CHANGE IN OUR SOCIAL WORLD

The Yir Yorant, a group of Australian aborigines, have long believed that if their own ancestors did not do something, then they must not do it. It would be wrong and might cause evil to befall the group (Sharp 1990). Obviously, this is not a people who favor change or innovation. By contrast, *progress* is a positive word in much of Australia and in other countries where change is seen as normal. The traditions, cultural beliefs of a society, and internal and external pressures all affect the degree and rate of change in society.

Our social world model is based on the assumption that change, whether evolutionary or revolutionary, is inevitable

U.S. coast guard officers guard 13 tons of cocaine found stashed in secret compartments on a fishing boat off San Diego in 2001. Illegal drugs are not only a personal issue but involve several institutions (including government and family) at the meso level, and control of drugs is a national and international policy issue. Treating it only as a micro issue ("Just say No") leads to misunderstanding of the nature of the problem.

Source: © Reuters / Corbis / Mike Blake.

Bill Gates holds a child who is receiving a trial Malaria vaccine at a medical research centre in Mozambique. Gates announced a grant of $168 million to fight malaria, a disease that kills more than 1 million people a year, 90% of them children in Africa. Sometimes, social change occurs because of individual initiatives.

Source: © Jon Hrusa / epa / Corbis.

and ever present in the social world. The impetus for change may begin at the micro, meso, or macro level of analysis. (See the thematic model on the opening pages of this chapter.) Studies of the change process are not complete, however, until the level under study is understood in relation to other levels in the model. Consider examples of change at various levels.

Change and Micro-Level Analysis
Change at the Individual Level
One of the nation's top entrepreneurs, Microsoft's Bill Gates combines intelligence, business acumen, and philanthropy, qualities that appeal to American individualism. Gates has power to influence others because of his fame, wealth, and charisma. He is able to bring about change in organizations through his ability to motivate people and set wheels in motion. Many people have persuasive power to influence decision making, but it is not always based on charisma; for some, it is due to expertise; for others, influence comes

from holding wealth, privileged positions, or needed information, or even from power by force.

Most organizations—schools, businesses, volunteer organizations—use one or more of the following strategies to persuade individuals to accept change: they appeal to individuals' values, they use persuasion by presenting hard data and logic, they convince individuals that the existing benefits of change outweigh the costs, they remove uncooperative individuals from the organization, they provide rewards or sanctions for acceptance of change in order to change the cost-benefit ratio, or they compel individuals to change by an order from authority figures. In any case, individuals are active agents that initiate and bring about change.

Change at the Community Level
Picture for a moment a beautiful quiet fishing village on the Mediterranean coast of Africa. In this traditional village, most of the inhabitants go about their daily routines much as they have for generations. However, things change the day the strangers arrive. This quiet village is just the spot for development of a large Mediterranean resort hotel complex, one that will attract wealthy visitors from around the world.

The strangers who came brought with them government officials interested in national economic growth. Soon, other strangers with surveying equipment set up camp, and the digging begins. A few residents are displaced—paid a small amount to move from their huts along the beachfront. Some villagers see change as exciting, bringing new adventures and opportunities. Others see it as a disruption to the peaceful life that they value; they protest the change, but there is no one to listen and they have no legal recourse. An enormous resort hotel is built, and this beachfront

Protesters at Oakland's new Wal-Mart want the public to be aware of the toll they feel Wal-Mart's unfair and allegedly illegal treatment of employees, as well as their business practices, will have on the community. Social movements are one way for citizens to influence their communities and social policy.

Source: © Rachel Epstein.

area becomes the playground of the superrich from around the globe.

Life in this village and society will never be the same due to the influence of the world economy; the village changes because of forces outside its boundaries. Individuals, families, and community groupings will find their lives undergoing dramatic change with the influx of tourists from different countries, new ideas, changing job structures, an economy based on world currencies, threats to traditional belief systems and morality, and a new way of life.

THINKING SOCIOLOGICALLY

Imagine yourself as a villager engaged in subsistence farming or fishing. How would your life change with global tourism coming to your village?

Change and Meso-Level Analysis
Change at the Institutional Level

We have learned in other chapters, especially the chapters on institutions, that institutions are interrelated with each other. Except for state terrorism, which is instituted by a government to control the citizens of its own or another nation, contemporary terrorism is a meso-level phenomenon, even though it has both personal and global implications. Most modern terrorist organizations are not nations; they are ethnic or religious subgroups that have elicited passionate loyalty from followers—even to the point of suicide on behalf of the group and its ideology.

The terrorist attacks of September 11, 2001—which killed 3,025 innocent people from 68 nations—resulted in immediate instability in both the United States and international markets. Governments responded in a variety of ways as they sought to deter any further attacks and to seek out and punish the guilty parties. Religious services had high attendance in the weeks that followed the attacks, and religious leaders tried to make sense of the suffering and the feelings of injustice. Many families were devastated; other families were soon separated as people in the military or the National Guard were called into action. Health care facilities and professionals began to make plans for biological and chemical terrorist attacks, changing the way monies were allocated in the health care industry.

Terrorism refers to "the use of indiscriminate violence to cause mass fear and panic to intimidate a population and advance one's political goals, whatever they may be" (Nolan 2002:1648). This usually refers to acts of violence by private nonstate groups to advance revolutionary political goals. In 2000, there were 423 terrorist acts around the world that killed 405 people and injured 791. According to the U.S. Department of State (2001), almost half of these acts were against the United States.

A member of the Marine Corp gets a final embrace from his girlfriend at Camp Pendleton, California, before he leaves with his unit on a seven-month deployment to Iraq. Change at the meso level can have global consequences as well as disrupting intimate relationships at the micro level.

Source: Photo by Lance Cpl. Ray Lewis.

Revolutionary groups with terrorist tactics operate at the meso level, trying to change the society by intimidating the citizens and government so they will change policies. In this photo, Israeli rescue workers search the wreckage of a destroyed bus in Jerusalem in 2003. A suicide bomb blew apart the bus packed with Orthodox Jews returning from a holy shrine in Jerusalem.

Source: REUTERS / Nir Elias, © Reuters/Corbis.

Obviously, terrorism has consequences for economies. Not only do terrorist acts destabilize economies, but they change the kinds of jobs that are available, with new jobs created in airport and seaport security. Investors also become hesitant to invest if they think the economy will be negatively affected, and this lack of investment can spawn a recession. However, it is not only the economics of the rich nations that are important when we discuss terrorism; the ripple effects affect all countries. Economic realities are core motivating factors for terrorists who commit horrific acts.

To understand why terrorism occurs, we must look at some of the underlying factors. The unequal distribution of world resources has created a source of deep anger toward the United States and other affluent countries. U.S. citizens make up only 5 percent of the total world population, yet the United States consumed 26 percent of world energy resources in 2000 (Ad Hoc Committee on Environmental Stewardship 2000), 30 percent more than it produced (World Almanac Education Group 2001). The average U.S. citizen consumes six times more energy than the world average (U.S. Department of Energy 2006). This seems grossly unfair to people who can barely feed their families or provide even minimal shelter for their children. Furthermore, wealthy countries have considerable economic influence over developing nations because poor countries are dependent on the income, employment, and loans from the core affluent countries. Citizens of poor countries may work for multinational corporations, often for very low wages; however, the profits are returned to wealthy countries, helping to perpetuate the gross inequity in distribution of resources. Whether or not we think it is justified, this inequity leads to hostilities—and sometimes terrorism—against more powerful countries.

Terrorism both affects political institutions and is a political statement in itself. The events of September 11 changed the Bush presidency, establishing the core issues and direction of its programs. His administration proposed, and Congress approved, a Patriot Act that channeled resources into heightened security and military preparedness. The provisions of the bill also greatly restricted civil liberties and allowed the government to snoop into the private lives of citizens in ways that had never before been tolerated, from monitoring home telephone connections of Americans to scrutinizing the books they checked out of the library. Following September 11, many state governments mandated more intense patriotism training and rituals in the schools, with additions to the curriculum and daily loyalty ceremonies. In Wisconsin, for example, every classroom was required to either recite the pledge of allegiance or listen to the national anthem (Ladson-Billings 2006). The No Child Left Behind education bill that was passed by Congress in 2002 also mandated that school personnel turn over personal information about students to military recruiters, including private information that had previously not been available to anyone but the student and school personnel (Ayers 2006; Westheimer 2006).

Other institutions are affected by terrorism as well. Health care organizations have had to anticipate possible implications of further attacks and have had difficulty deciding how to focus their resources in preparation. According to an analysis by O'Toole and Henderson (2006), the United States has done very little to protect against the threats of bioterrorism; most resources have gone to airport security and to fighting terrorists in other parts of the world (Flynn 2006). In many ways, North America would be an easy target for swamping the medical capacity to deal with biological or chemical attacks on water supplies, subways, or other high-density population areas (Flynn 2006; O'Toole and Henderson 2006). Thus, terrorism is a concern of the medical institution as well. The ground rules of institutional life in the United States had clearly changed because of the attacks.

However, to understand the events of September 11, we also need to comprehend that this was a politically motivated act performed by Saudi Arabians and other Middle Easterners who were intensely pro-Palestinian and anti-Israeli. From the terrorist perspective, the attack on the New York City World Trade Center was an effort to punish the United States. September 11 was a symbolic date for Palestinians, the date when Britain declared control of Palestine. This set off a chain of events leading to the United Nations' granting the land to Jews to establish Israel; many Middle Easterners felt this was unjust because the Palestinians lost the country in which they had been living. Moreover, the Camp David Accords that established Israel's right to exist in the Middle East was signed on September 11, 1979. So on two counts, this date had powerful symbolic meaning to the people who were displaced from Palestine, just as the date has new and powerful meaning today for Americans. Political acts, mostly those supported and implemented by the United States, undergirded the rage of terrorists who saw the United States and its supporters as evil.

Meso-level movement (terrorism) has created change that ripples through our institutions and affects both our individual lives and the national and global macro-level systems in which we all live.

THINKING SOCIOLOGICALLY

How has terrorism affected institutions with which you are familiar? How is your life being changed by threats of terrorism?

Change and Macro-Level Analysis
Change at the Societal Level

Our social world becomes increasingly more complex and more biologically interdependent. Pollution of the environment by any one country now threatens other countries. Carcinogens, acid rain, and other airborne chemicals carry across national boundaries (Brecher, Costello, and Smith 2006). They also can pollute the air that surrounds the entire planet, destroying the ozone that protects us from intense sun rays and warming the planet in ways that could threaten all of us. In the past century, scientists claim, the earth's surface has warmed by one degree. That does not sound like much, until one considers that during the last ice age, the earth's surface was only seven degrees lower than today. Small variations can make a huge difference, and we do not know what all of those consequences might be if the earth's surface increases by another two or three degrees. Currently, sea ice is melting each year at a rate that equals the size of Maryland and Delaware combined (Lindsay 2006). It is alarming to visit the glaciers on the South Island of New Zealand (closest to Antarctica) and realize that glaciers there are melting so fast that they have receded by as much as 10 or 12 miles in just a couple of decades. While some of the environmental change may be rooted in natural causes, the preponderance of the evidence suggests that human activity—the way we consume and the way we live our lives—is the primary cause.

Obviously, this is a global issue, but it has implications for nations, which must work together for change. Only 5 percent of the world's population emits 25 percent of the heat-trapping gases (Lindsay 2006). Many nations do not want to change. U.S. President Bush rejected the Kyoto Treaty on global warming because it "does not make economic sense," and his trusted advisor Condoleezza Rice bluntly asserted, "Kyoto is dead" (Lindsay 2006).

Fixing the environmental issues will be expensive, it may hinder the economy and slow the rate of growth, and it may even stimulate a recession. Since recessions are terrifying for any elected politician who must keep the public happy. Change is not easy. Still, most of the rest of the world's nations have signed the Kyoto Treaty, and there is continuing pressure on the United States to concede. Since nations are still the most powerful units for allocating resources and for setting policy—especially the wealthy developed nations that produce most of the products and most of the pollution—change in our society that will address the issues of a shared environment is of critical importance. The two big quandaries are (1) the costs and benefits to various nations of participating in a solution and (2) the matter of time—will nations respond before it is too late to make a difference? Currently, most of the cost of pollution is accruing to impoverished countries, while rich nations benefit from the status quo.

Change in Global Systems
As the world becomes increasingly interconnected and interdependent, impetus for change comes from global organizations, national and international organizations and governments, and multinational corporations. New and shifting alliances between countries link together nations, form international liaisons, and create changing economic and political systems. The following international alliances between countries, for example, are based primarily on economic ties:

SADC: Southern African Development Community
NAFTA: North American Free Trade Agreement
CEFTA: Central European Free Trade Agreement
CAFTA: Central American Free Trade Agreement
ASEAN: Association of Southeast Asian Nations
WIPO: World Intellectual Property Organization
G8: Group of Eight
OPEC: Organization of Petroleum Exporting Countries
ADP: Asian Development Bank
EFTA: European Free Trade Association
EEA: European Economic Area
APEC: Asia-Pacific Economic Cooperation
EU: European Union
SEATO: Southeast Asian Treaty Organization

The goal of NAFTA—the North American Free Trade Agreement, which was begun in 1993—was to establish a free trade area between Canada, the United States, and Mexico in order to facilitate trade in the region. Promoters, including many global corporations, promised the agreement would create hundreds of thousands of new high-wage jobs, raise living standards in each of the countries, improve environmental conditions, and transform Mexico from a poor developing country into a booming new market. Opponents (including labor unions, environmental organizations, consumer groups, and religious groups) argued the opposite—that NATFA would reduce wages; destroy jobs; undermine democratic policy making in North America by giving corporations free reign; and threaten health, environment, and food safety (American Cultural Center Resource Service 2004; Public Citizen's Global Trade Watch 2003; U.S. Trade Representative 2003). Ross Perot, former candidate for presidency, indicated there would be a great whooshing sound as jobs were sucked away from the United States. How can one trade agreement have such differing potential outcomes? The issue of immigration from poorer to wealthier countries is also causing bitter debate within and between countries involved.

Analyses of the agreement show mixed results. There is some indication that tariffs are down and there are increased U.S. exports, some Mexican markets are doing well and have weathered global economic crises, there is growth in manufacturing in Mexico, and there is improvement in some areas of environmental protection and labor rights. On the other hand, it does appear that regulations on quality of products and environmental pollution have been reduced, U.S. trade deficits have increased, income inequality has increased, and perhaps as many as 3 million—one in six—manufacturing jobs in the United States have been lost. It is clear that NAFTA has resulted in change at all levels in the social world, from restructuring of economies at the national and global levels to affecting individual job security and availability. The overall verdict on NAFTA's effect is still out.

The principle is that change at one level of the social world leads to change in other levels as it did in the global example of

NAFTA, the societal example of environmental problems, and the community example of development in a Mediterranean African village. Changes at the macro level affect individuals, and initiation of or resistance to change at the micro level has repercussions at the meso and macro levels.

THINKING SOCIOLOGICALLY

Give an example of how individual resistance to changes initiated by the national government or by an international agency may influence the course of change.

SOCIAL CHANGE: PROCESS AND THEORIES

The Process of Social Change

Something always triggers a social change. That something may come from outside the organization, which sociologists call **stress**, or the impetus may come from within the organization, the source called **strain**.

Two examples of strain are conflicting goals and different belief systems within the organization. *Conflicting goals* are seen in the case of the steel industry and its workers; most individuals' goals are to meet their basic needs for food and shelter for their families by holding jobs. In Pittsburgh and Cleveland, many steel companies have closed down or moved to less costly sites due to lack of profits from changing economic demands and competition. Their profit goals led to decisions to downsize or move to other less costly production sites, creating massive unemployment in Cleveland and Pittsburgh. People who had created hopeful futures for themselves and their families were left without jobs.

Belief systems (political, religious, economic, and social beliefs) within a society can also have a major effect on the type and rate of change that takes place. For example, some religious groups expect their members to obey moral dictates of their belief system, yet the values of the surrounding society stress individual freedoms, often in ways disapproved of by the religion. These conflicting goals create strain. Some religious groups oppose stem cell research that uses cells of fetuses, most of which were created in test tubes. Others within the same congregation believe this research will lead to alleviation of suffering and save lives. While both sides believe they are pro-life, the internal strain in the religious group emanates from events and forces in other institutions—science and medicine.

Stresses, those pressures for change that come from the organization's external environment, can be traced to several sources: the natural environment, population dynamics, leaders, technologies, other institutions, and major historical events.

The natural environment can bring about slow or dramatic change in a society. Floods, hurricanes, tsunamis, heavy snows, earthquakes, volcanic eruptions, mud slides,

tornados, and other sudden events are not planned occurrences, but they can have dramatic consequences. Disease epidemics, such as the SARS (Severe Acute Respiratory Syndrome) outbreak in 2002 or the potential bird flu epidemic, are also often unpredictable.

SARS is the first severe transmissible disease to emerge in the twenty-first century. The first case occurred in Guangdong Province, China, in November 2002, and the outbreak, affecting 305 persons, caused 5 deaths. Many of the cases involved medical staff treating patients with SARS. It was reported to the World Health Organization in February of 2003. The disease began spreading around the world along international air travel routes, several of which became hot spots. In May 2003, half a year after the first case was discovered, 7,761 probable cases in 30 countries on 6 continents had been reported, with 623 deaths from the disease (Wilson 2006; World Health Organization 2003, 2006).

The SARS threat brought about change in the World Health Organization, global medical reporting systems, and response networks. For instance, the Global Public Health Intelligence Network scans Internet communications for rumors and reports of suspicious diseases. This way, health organizations from the local to global levels can act quickly to contain the spread of deadly epidemics.

Less rapid natural changes also can have incremental but dramatic effects. For example, some scientists predict that the climatic changes resulting from the *greenhouse effect* are warming our atmosphere, transforming agricultural land areas into deserts, raising sea levels about one meter in this century, causing ice sheets to melt, increasing rainfall in the currently dry areas, and intensifying the strength of hurricanes. This warming of the earth's atmosphere results from a buildup of carbon dioxide or other gases (Environmental Protection Agency 2004). The majority of scientists are convinced that global warming is real, is a human-generated problem, and is a genuine threat to our survival, but it is the responsibility of political powers to bring about change in policies (Lindsay 2006).

Without human intervention to address the causes, change in the climate will affect habitable land areas, very possibly create disasters that cost great amounts of money, and increase the cost of fuel, thus changing people's lifestyles. In the film *An Inconvenient Truth* (2006), former U.S. vice president and presidential candidate Al Gore addresses the threat and what the world needs to do to save the environment. Natural disasters are so important that the sociology of disasters has become a specialty field within the discipline, as indicated by one of the classic sociological studies of disasters, reported in the next How Do We Know?

Population dynamics—birth and death rates, size of populations, age distribution, and migration patterns—can be important contributors to external stress on organizations. Where populations are growing at extremely rapid rates, strains on government systems result in inability to meet basic needs of the people. Values and beliefs regarding childbearing, knowledge of birth control, and the position of women in society are some of the crucial social variables in

Research on Disasters and Their Aftermath

A series of small villages were settled along a mountain creek of West Virginia known as Buffalo Creek. This was mining country, and at the top of the creek, there was a substantial bank of land that held in a reservoir of wastewater; a coal company poured more than 1 million tons of wastewater and coal waste into this company-created basin. The restraining embankment of shale, clay, slag, and low-quality coal that created the reservoir was referred to by the coal company as an "impoundment," but the people themselves referred to it as a "dam." Whatever one calls it, this restraining wall was weakened by heavy rains in the winter of 1972, and on February 26, it broke, setting forth a massive flood of black sludge and oily, slag-filled wastewater down the valley toward the homes of five thousand residents in the mountain villages. The first village hit was not just crushed, it disappeared entirely. This meant that the villages farther down the creek-bed had not just filthy water coming at them but the remains of homes, churches, stores, vehicles, and bodies descending on them. By the time the water subsided, the flood had taken with it almost everything in its path.

Newspapers reported on the economic loss and the staggering death toll, but lawyers, psychologists, and sociologists were interested in the human cost to survivors—costs to their sense of self, their mental and emotional well-being, and their family and friendship ties. Yale sociologist Kai Erikson's (1976) research is one of

the classic pieces of investigation regarding the human and social toll of disasters. Here was a community that had an extraordinarily close-knit social network, where crime was virtually nonexistent, divorces were extraordinary, chemical abuse and mental problems were far below national norms, and neighborhoods were like extended families. Yet the community had been ripped apart by the flood. Time had not healed the social and emotional wounds, even years after the flood: few marriages remained intact, problems of deviance and delinquency were rife, and more than 90 percent of the people interviewed were judged to be in need of psychological counseling.

Erikson used several methods to gather data. He read depositions and other existing materials gathered by a law firm that was engaged in litigation against the coal company, he conducted extensive interviews with many of the survivors, and he did observations in the devastated communities.

Many findings are similar to those following other disasters and give us insight into the aftermath of hurricanes such as Katrina, earthquakes, or terrorist attacks such as those on September 11, 2001.

The federal government's response to the flood in Buffalo Creek was mostly to immediate needs for survival. Thus, mobile homes were brought in and emergency food was provided, but people were placed in these shelters with no attentiveness to

neighborhoods or preexisting kinship ties. Thus, people found themselves surrounded by strangers at a time when they desperately needed support but when they also had few interpersonal resources needed to forge new relationships.

The mental health symptoms tied to individual trauma include psychic numbness (feeling mentally blank and emotionally limp), constant death anxiety, feeling of guilt for having survived when so many members of one's family have not, experiencing guilt for not having saved people who were seen being swept down the river, losing the "furniture of self" (the symbols of one's life that might include one's home, family heirlooms, photographs of loved ones, and other artifacts that connect one to others and to a personal history), and loss of trust in the order of the universe or a loving God that people believed was in control of life's events. Everything from personal identity to religious faith was severely affected by this flood. The personal devastation was far more disturbing and long lasting than the economic loss, even though only the latter got press coverage.

Erikson (1976) argued that the "collective trauma" was more important to understand than the individual trauma: "People find it difficult to recover from the effects of individual trauma so long as the community around them remains in shreds. It is a general theory in psychiatry that time heals . . . wounds, but . . . time can work its special therapy only if it acts in

(Continued)

(Continued)

concert with a nurturing communal setting" (p. 155). The collective trauma included five dimensions:

- *Disorientation:* Erikson (1976) found that many persons were so socially displaced that they could hardly orient themselves in time and space, even two or three years after the flood. He writes, "It was a common occurrence for survivors to give vital statistics about themselves as of the day of the flood, as if that were the last day on which they measured their existence . . . (and) knew themselves to be living" (p. 212).

- *Loss of morale and morality:* Following the flood, people were more likely to commit deviant acts and to think they were surrounded by immoral people. The most important principle learned is that evacuations and relocations should be done by neighborhoods, because people who know one another are far less likely to commit crimes and are more capable of helping one another with recovery. When this basic finding is ignored, the recovery will almost certainly be more difficult.

- *Loss of connection:* Marriages began to disintegrate, and people

lost their sense of connection to others. "Members of a family find that intimacy and gentleness are hard to sustain in an emotional atmosphere as dry as this one. The general community validated . . . bonds and gave them shape," reports Erikson (1976:221). Yet when the community is gone, the interpersonal bonds seem to wither up as well. A people known for generosity of spirit seemed incapable of reaching out to others when their community was utterly destroyed.

- *Illness and identity:* The people seemed to feel that the land was polluted and untrustworthy, with some people being afraid to till the soil lest they find a body part of a family member or a neighbor buried there. Because the land was polluted, many people felt their own bodies were polluted too.

- *Lost sense of safety:* People slept in their clothes and boots; whenever it rained, many residents would run to the creek every hour to check on the water levels. Again, Erikson (1976) summarizes, "One of the crucial jobs of a culture is to edit reality in such a way that it seems

manageable, and that can mean to edit it in such a way that its perils are at least partially masked. . . . [The flood] stripped people of their communal supports, and, in doing so, it stripped them of the illusion that they could be safe" (pp. 240–41).

This disaster at Buffalo Creek indicates how much of our personal mental health rests in the health of the larger community. It helps us understand how anomie (normlessness) can create anxiety and disorientation. Most of all, it helps us understand that natural disasters and human catastrophes, such as the September 11 terrorist attacks and devastating storms such as Hurricane Katrina and the daily killings in Iraq can have pervasive consequences on individuals and communities. It forces us to be aware of the extent to which we depend on a larger community to regain our footing when a disaster disrupts our lives. We humans are, indeed, profoundly social beings. Changes that disrupt our social ties can have severe and wide-ranging consequences.

Source: Erikson (1976).

addressing this issue. Immigration due to political upheavals or for economic opportunities creates stress on societies receiving the newcomers as resources go to adjustment; for example, Haitians attempting to flee from the 2004 rebellion in Haiti sought refuge in neighboring countries including the United States, creating stresses, and many refugees from the Darfur region in Sudan are fleeing to camps in the nearby country of Chad. Maps 15.1 and 15.2 show visually the hot spots globally for refugees and other persons who have been uprooted or displaced from their homelands.

THINKING SOCIOLOGICALLY

What lessons can we take from Erikson's (1976) findings to shed light on the Katrina hurricane disaster in New Orleans in 2005?

Leaders or dominant individuals influence change through their policy decisions or social movements they help generate. Mohandas K. (Mahatma) Gandhi in India taught the modern world ways of bringing about change in political systems through nonviolent methods. Mikhail Gorbachev created new relations between the United States and the U.S.S.R. through glasnost—open communication and thawing tense relations. Policies of Charles Taylor, former military dictator of Liberia, created long-term war and resulted in thousands of deaths. These leaders' actions created internal strains and external stressors leading to change in the international community, in foreign policies of countries, and in meso-level institutions such as the political and economic systems.

Technology provides the tools for change, and societal changes have been strongly influenced by technological innovations. For example, the invention of the plow allowed more land to be used for agriculture, creating greater food surpluses and allowing for new classes of people to move into towns and then urban areas. The steam engine drove looms and spinning jennys that helped develop factories and cities around those factories. The computer makes possible the management of worldwide production, investments, and banking systems.

William F. Ogburn compiled a list of 150 social changes in the United States that resulted from the invention of the radio, such as instant access to information (Ogburn 1933). Other lists could be compiled for the telephone, automobile, television, and computers. Some of these changes give rise to secondary changes; for example, automobile use led to the development of paved highways, complex systems of traffic patterns and rules, and need for gasoline stations. The next *Sociology in Your Social World* explores several issues involving the automobile and change.

THINKING SOCIOLOGICALLY

What might be some long-term social consequences for our individual lives and societies of the expanded use of the computer, the microwave oven, or the cell phone?

The diffusion or spread of the technology is likely to be uneven, especially in the early stages of the new technology. For example, computer technology is advancing rapidly, but those advances began in corporate boardrooms, military bases, and university laboratories. Policies of governments and leaders such as funding for school computers, determine the rate of public access. Thus, only gradually are computers reaching the world's citizenry.

The social environment includes the institutionalized patterns of relationships that develop in organizations and nations. For example, historically, Timbucktou in northwest Africa developed a strong interdependent relationship with England. They exchanged gold and slaves for woven cotton cloth. As can be imagined, these interdependencies were also sources of stress. In Timbucktou, bolts of cloth became symbols of prestige; greater conflicts were created as more people from Timbucktou sought to enslave others and to exchange humans for cloth. In England, greater separation developed between those with access to gold and slaves and those without such resources. Both situations resulted in changes in the social structure of society.

Major historical events—wars, economic crises, assassinations, political scandals, and catastrophes—can change the course of world events. For instance, the triggering event that actually started World War I was the assassination of Archduke Franz Ferdinand of the Austro-Hungarian empire; this assassination resulted in the German invasion of several other countries and the beginning of the war. So a micro-level act, the murder of an individual, had global ramifications. Clearly, internal strains and external stressors give impetus to the processes of change. The question is, how do these processes take place?

Theories of Social Change

Social scientists seek to explain the causes and consequences of various types of social change; many do so with the hope that change can be controlled or guided. Theories of change often reflect the events and belief systems of particular historical time periods. Conflict theory, developed during periods of change in Europe, began to gain adherents in the United States during the 1960s when intense conflict over issues of race and ethnic relations, the morality of the Vietnam war, and changes in social values peaked. Theories that focused on social harmony were of little help.

Major social change theories fall into seven approaches: symbolic interaction, rational choice, evolutionary, cyclical, functional, conflict, and world systems theories. As we review these theories, some will be familiar from previous chapters.

Micro-Level Theories of Change
Symbolic interactionism. According to symbolic interaction theory, human beings are always trying to make sense of the things they experience; they are continually trying to figure out what an event or interaction means and what action is required of them. Humans are active agents capable of constructing meaning that agrees with or diverges from what others around them think. This capacity to redefine one's situation—such as concluding that one is oppressed, even though others have accepted the circumstances as normal—can be a powerful impetus to change. It can be the starting point of social movements, cultural changes, and revolutions.

Some sociologists believe that all social behavior is essentially micro-level social action. Individuals are always, they believe, at the core of any social trends or movements, even if those movements are national or global (Blumer 1986; Giddens 1986; Simmel 1902-17/1950). After all, it is individuals who act, make decisions, and take action. Neither

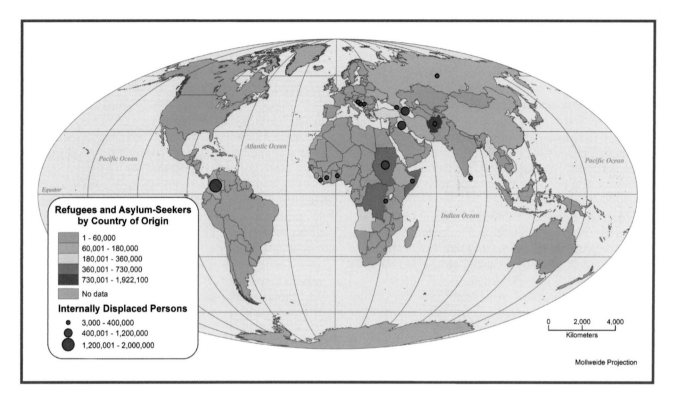

MAP 15.1   Number of Refugees, Asylum Seekers, and Internally Displaced Persons by Their Country of Origin, December 2005

Source: UNHCR (2006). Map by Anna Versluis.

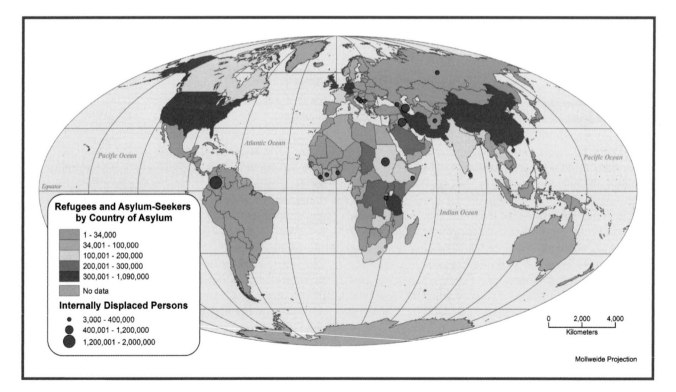

MAP 15.2   Number of Refugees, Asylum Seekers, and Internally Displaced Persons by Their Country of Asylum, December 2005

Source: UNHCR (2006). Map by Anna Versluis.

Sociology in Your Social World

Technology and Change: The Automobile

When we think of technology and its impact on society, the innovation of the past two decades that is especially prominent is the computer and accompanying Internet. However, it was only a century ago that a newfangled novelty was spreading quickly from urban areas to the countryside: the automobile. At the turn of the twentieth century, this strange horseless carriage was often referred to as the "devil wagon" in rural areas. The introduction of this self-propelled vehicle was controversial, and it sent ripples though the society in a number of ways. In the 1890s and early 1900s, some cities and counties had rules forbidding motorized vehicles. In Vermont, a walking escort had to precede the car by an eighth of a mile with a red warning flag, and in Iowa, motorists were required to telephone ahead to a town they planned to drive through to warn the community. This was so people could take action lest their horses be alarmed (Berger 1979; Clymer 1953; Glasscock 1937; Morris 1949). In most rural areas, motorists were expected to pull their cars to a stop or even to shut down the motor when a horse-drawn buggy came near. Legislation known as "pig and chicken clauses" meant that in most states, the automobilist was liable for any accident that occurred when passing an animal on or near the road, even if the injury was due to the animal having run away in fright (Scott-Montagu 1904). Such norms were considered the decent way to conduct oneself only a hundred years ago.

Automobiles were restricted to cities for nearly a decade after their invention because roads were inadequate outside of the urban areas. "Keith's (one of your coauthors) grandfather, . . . ", Owen G. Roberts, invented a seatbelt in about 1915 because on an all-day drive westward from Columbus, Ohio (the family covered about 80 miles in eight hours that day), his wife Mary was knocked unconscious when the rough roads caused her head to hit the roof of the car with great force. Cars in the first decade of the twentieth century often slid off muddy roads into ditches or got caught in deep tracks; these conditions had not deterred horses. Paving of roads became a necessity for automobile travel, and, of course, made automobile travel much faster and more common. The expansion was stunning. An estimated 85,000 motored vehicles were in use in rural American in 1911. By 1930, the number was nearly 10 million (Berger 1979).

Forms of entertainment began to change when people were able to go longer distances in shorter periods of time. As the Model T made cars affordable, families no longer had only each other for socializing. Thus, the complete dependence on siblings and parents was lessened over the course of the twentieth century, possibly weakening the intense bonds in some families (Berger 1979). Furthermore, entertainment gradually became available virtually any night of the week, whereas previously socializing had been done on Saturdays in town or at special events such as the county fair or a corn husking (Berger 1979; McKelvie 1926). Even courting was substantially changed, as individuals could go farther afield to find a possible life partner, as couples could go more places on dates, and as two people could find more privacy.

Transportation that made transversing distances more possible changed how people related to a number of other institutions as well. Since people could drive farther to churches, they often chose to go to city churches where the preachers were more skilled as public speakers and where the music was of higher quality. Small country churches began to consolidate or to close. However, many people found that a country drive was a more interesting way to spend Sunday mornings, and preachers often condemned cars for leading people away from church (Berger 1979). Still, once pastors could afford cars, many people received services such as pastoral calls that had previously been unknown in more remote rural areas (Wilson 1924). Likewise, motorized vehicles made transportation to schools possible. Once the busing of students to school was instituted, the attendance rates of rural children increased substantially (U.S. Department of Interior 1930). In addition, small rural hospitals with fewer special services began to close, so even the delivery of medical services was changed. Moreover, one of the banes of life for farm women was loneliness and isolation, sometimes becoming so severe in the western states as to lead to "madness" (Berger 1979; McNall and McNall 1983). The automobile was a boon to mental health by helping to solve this problem of isolation.

As people could live in less congested areas but still get to work in a reasonable amount of time via an automobile, the suburbs began to develop around major cities. No longer did people, of necessity, locate homes with close access to shopping, schools, churches, or places

(Continued)

(Continued)

to socialize. Yet this very dispersion of the population has made it mandatory that far more gasoline be consumed, thereby creating pollution. As the wealthy moved to expensive suburbs and paid higher taxes to support outstanding schools, socioeconomic and ethnic stratification between communities increased.

When Owen G. Roberts built one of the first automobiles in Ohio and then a couple of decades later

established a very large automobile dealership in Columbus, it was not his intent to heighten segregation, to create funding problems for inner cities where mostly the poor now live, or to pollute the environment. Yet these are some of the unintended consequences of the spread of the automobile. It sometimes takes decades before we can identify the consequences of the technologies we develop and adopt.

---

corporations, nor nations, nor bureaucracies make decisions. Individual actors may hold positions within organizations, but they are still persons. The way in which an individual defines the reality he or she is experiencing makes a huge difference in how that person will respond.

From this perspective, social institutions and structures are considered rather fragile, for they are always subject to maverick individuals "thinking outside the box" and changing how others see things. Individuals can cause cultural change, riots, social movements, planned change by organizations, and a host of other actions that transform the society. That people may construct reality in new ways can be a serious threat to the status quo, and conservatives are therefore often committed to ensuring that the next generation will see the world the same way by being socialized into existing ideas.

Individual members of a group or organization can also be a source of resistance to change. If change feels threatening to some members who have a vested interest in the current arrangements, the leaders who advocate change may face resistance. For that reason, providing opportunities for group members to participate in suggesting, planning, and implementing change helps create acceptance and positive attitudes toward change. This collaborative process is often used when a firm or a public agency is planning a major project, such as the development of a shopping mall or a waste-disposal site, and cooperation and support by other parts of the community become essential. Symbolic interactionists would see this as an effort to build a consensus about what the social changes mean and to implement change in a way that is not perceived as threatening to the members. This notion that people are active agents who can advocate for change has been taken very seriously by applied sociologists who do community action research—involving residents in research that can improve the community. The Applied Sociologist at Work on page 495 provides a vivid illustration.

THINKING SOCIOLOGICALLY

First, read the Applied Sociologist at Work. Then think of a change that is needed in your community. How could you use participatory action research to address this issue?

Rational choice. Rational choice theorists insist that behaviors are largely driven by individuals seeking rewards and limiting costs. Because of this, most individuals respond to positive or negative sanctions; they engage in those activities that bring positive rewards and try to avoid the negative. A group seeking change can attempt to set up a situation in which desired behavior is rewarded. The following typology (see Figure 15.3) shows the relationship between behaviors and sanctions.

		Sanction	
		Formal	**Informal**
Behavior	**Positive**	Bonuses, advances, fringe benefits, recognition	Praise, smile, pat on the back
	Negative	Demotion, loss of salary	Ridicule, exclusion, talk behind back

Figure 15.3   Relationship between Behaviors and Sanctions

Bringing about change may not require a change in costs or rewards; it may be sufficient simply to change the people's perception of the advantages and disadvantages of certain actions. Sometimes people do not know all the rewards, or they have failed to accurately assess the expenditures.

THE APPLIED SOCIOLOGIST AT WORK

Participatory Action Research

We started this chapter with a question: Can you as an individual change the world? Here, we focus on a research method, not an individual case study. It involves community members in action research. When bringing about change requires action that disrupts the lives and routines of some citizens, the disruption will make the change controversial. However, if change is planned with individuals in mind, it can be a smooth process. "Participatory action research . . . is not simply about change, but about change of a particular kind. . . . This form of research aspires to communitarian and egalitarian politics: people working together toward rationality, justice, coherence, and satisfactoriness in workplaces and in other areas of people's lives" (McTaggart 1997:6).

Also referred to as empowerment evaluation, collaborative research, and action research, this activist research is different from many of the other research projects we have described. The researchers involve people in the organization or community being studied throughout the research process (Kemmis and McTaggart 2000). In the process, the participants help to meet the research and action goals. Some of the earliest sociology in the United States, carried out by Jane Addams and the

Hull House settlement in Chicago (described in Chapter 2), asked for advice from women in the community; it provided these women with data to help local residents "understand community patterns in order to make better decisions" (Adler and Clark 2003; Feagin and Vera 2001:66). The goal is that the research be relevant to those being studied and result in social change and social justice for all people, especially those deprived of food, clothing, shelter, health, and human freedom or dignity (Adler and Clark 2003).

Contrary to much research in which the organization or community members are *subjects* of the research, in participatory action research, all members have something to contribute. Success of the process is in the ability to communicate with and be responsive to community members (Esposito and Murphy 2000:181).

Any of the research methods used in traditional research can be used in participatory action research, but the most frequently used are participant observation and interviewing. In addition, group discussions, community meetings and seminars, and video productions may be used to conduct research that fosters change.

For example, few citizens in the United States realize all the benefits of marriage. To change marriage rates, we may not need more benefits; we may do just as well to change the population's appraisal of the benefits already available.

Change, according to this perspective, is enhanced through doing a *force-field analysis.* What are the forces or payoffs in favor of change, and what are the forces rewarding the status quo? How do we change the balance in each direction? These are the issues that influence an individual's support for, or opposition to, change.

Meso- and Macro-Level Theories of Change

Cyclical theories. Cyclical theories present societies as going through cycles similar to the rise and fall of civilizations or humans moving from birth to death; the powerful civilizations of Egypt, Greece, and Rome are classic examples of societies that were born, grew, matured, declined, and died. Arnold Toynbee (Toynbee 1934–61/1988), for example, suggests that societies move from a passive to an active state in response to external challenges (stresses). A challenge from an outside threat may mobilize a society, but the activism

eventually slows down as patterns become institutionalized. Events within a country (strains) can also begin a cycle; when one ethnic or ideological group becomes a ruling elite following a time of social turmoil, the society often stabilizes and calms down. However, it is not uncommon for the regime to become increasingly oppressive until a part of the general population decides to rebel. A new leader surfaces as a result, perhaps someone from a different ethnic group or political faction, and the process begins again. According to Toynbee, all civilizations follow this process of passivity or stability followed by activism and turbulence (Ashley and Orenstein 2004).

Social evolutionary theories. Social evolutionary theories assume that societies move slowly from simple to more complex forms. Early *unilinear theories* maintained that all societies moved through the same steps and that advancement or progress was desirable and would lead to a better society. These theories came to prominence during the industrial revolution when European social scientists sought to interpret the differences between their own societies and the "primitive societies" of other continents.

Europe was being stimulated by travel, exposure to new cultures, and a spawning of new philosophies, a period called the Enlightenment. Europeans witnessed the developments of mines, railroads, cities, educational systems, and rising industries, which they defined as "progress" or "civilization." World travelers reported that other peoples and societies did not seem to have these developments. These reports provided the empirical evidence that early sociologist Auguste Comte used in proposing his theory of unilinear development from simple to complex societies. Unilinear theories came to legitimate colonial expansion and exploitation of other people and lands that were seen as "inferior."

Gerhard Lenski and colleagues (Lenski, Nolan, and Lenski 1998) offer a more recent version of evolutionary theory. They discuss four stages through which societies progress: hunter-gatherer, horticultural, agrarian, and industrial (see Chapter 3). Lenski claims this does not suggest that some stages are "higher" or "better" than others but that this is the typical pattern of development due to expansion of technology and more efficient harnessing of energy sources. Despite his claim that this theory is not judging some as "better," Lenski does use the term *progress*. This phrase refers to greater technological sophistication rather than to moral superiority; still, in terms of technology, he does think the later stages are more advanced.

Evaluations of evolutionary theories suggest that there are many modern cases that do not fit this singular pattern. A number of societies are skipping steps or being selective about what aspects of technology they wish to adopt. Developing countries such as India and China are largely agricultural but are importing and developing the latest technology. Furthermore, some religious, social, and political ideologies question the assumption that "material progress" (which is what technology fosters) is desirable.

Even the phrase "developing countries" has been controversial with some scholars, since it might imply that all societies are moving toward the type of social system characterized by the affluent or developed societies. Some prefer the term *global south* as a metaphorical term, since poor countries are disproportionately in the southern hemisphere. Note that the term is a metaphor for all poor countries, for some prosperous countries are in the south and some poor ones in the north, but the term is meant to avoid an assumption of inevitable evolution toward Western cultures.

Contemporary evolutionary theories are *multilinear*. These theories also maintain that simple societies go through a process of change to become large, complex, technologically advanced societies. These models of change acknowledge variations in the way change takes place. The rapid spread of ideas and technologies means that societies today may move quickly from simple to complex, creating modern states with pockets of contrasting cultures. Consider the mass of contradictions of the Middle East today. Due to the world demand for their oil, several countries in this region have among the highest per capita incomes in the world. In 2002, average per capita income for the entire world was $6,328. Saudi Arabia had a per capita income of $10,140, Kuwait $22,470, and the United Arab Emirates $23,770 (World Bank 2006). Especially the urban elite have access to modern conveniences such as computers, jets, and cell phones. Yet other Middle Eastern people still live traditional lives as nomads or herders in small villages or earn their living from the desert. Not all segments of society change at the same rate. This makes it nearly impossible to categorize some societies as being in one stage.

Functionalist theories. Functional theorists assume that societies are basically stable systems held together by the shared norms and values of their members. The interdependent parts work together to make the society function smoothly. A change in one part of the society affects all the other parts, each changing in turn until the system resumes a state of equilibrium. Change can come from external or internal sources, from contact with other societies or from strains within. Slow, nondisruptive change occurs as societies become more complex, but any change may be seen as a threat to the equilibrium of a system. Rapid change is seen as especially dysfunctional or disruptive for the system. For example, the downfall of the former Soviet Union resulted in economic chaos that is still unresolved. Since sudden, disruptive change is difficult to explain using functional theory and since any change is viewed with some suspicion, some sociologists have turned to conflict theories to help explain change, especially rapid or violent changes.

Conflict theories. Conflict theorists assume that societies are dynamic and that change and conflict are inevitable. According to Karl Marx, socioeconomic class conflict is the major source of tension leading to change in any society. Karl Marx and Friedrich Engels (1848/1969) argued that the antagonistic relationship they saw developing between the workers (proletariat) and the owners of the production systems (bourgeoisie) in nineteenth-century England would lead to social revolution. From this, a new world order would emerge in which the workers themselves would own the means of production. Thus, conflict between the owners and the workers would be the central factor driving social change.

Other conflict theorists study variables such as gender, religion, politics, and ethnic and interest group problems in their analyses, feeling that these factors can also be the grounds for oppression and "we" versus "they" differences (Dahrendorf 1959). Some see conflict as useful for society because it forces societies to adapt to new conditions and leads to healthy change (Coser 1956); conflict over slavery or over gender inequality are examples of problems that caused stresses and strains, eventually resulting in improved society. The current conflict over health care in the United States may also eventually lead to a better system.

World systems theory of change. World systems theorists focus on the historical development of the whole world and how that development has influenced individual countries today. Capitalist economies first appeared around 1500; since then, except for a few isolated tribal groupings, almost all societies have been at least indirectly influenced by dominant capitalist world economic and political systems (Wallerstein 1974).

This theory divided the world system into three main parts (see Figure 15.4); the core, semiperipheral, and peripheral areas (Wallerstein 1974). The *core* areas are economically and politically powerful. Core countries include European states, Australia and New Zealand, Japan, Canada, the United States, and a few others. Historically, they have controlled global decision making, received the largest share of the profits from the world economic system, and dominated *peripheral* areas both economically and culturally by controlling the flow of technology and capital into those countries. Peripheral countries, many of which are in Africa and Asia, provide cheap labor and raw materials for the core countries' needs. The *semiperipheral* countries are in an intermediate position, trading with both the core and the peripheral countries. Former republics of the Soviet Union generally are considered semiperipheral. Since most semiperipheral countries are industrializing, they serve as areas to which core-country businesses and multinational corporations can move for continued growth, often in partnerships, as semiperipheral states aspire to join the core countries. The core and semiperipheral countries process raw materials, often from peripheral countries, and may sell the final products back to the peripheral countries. The semiperipheral countries and the peripheral countries need the trade and the resources of the core countries, but they are also at a severe disadvantage in competition and are exploited by those at the core, resulting in an uneasy relationship. (See Figure 15.4.)

These basic relationships between the core, semiperipheral, and peripheral countries have endured since the 1700s. However, several "Asian Tigers" (Korea, Thailand,

In this typical situation, these South African miners are all black, while the supervisors and managers are white. These gold mines are part of a multinational corporation and the larger world economic system, with stockholders from around the globe.

Source: © Gideon Mendel / Corbis.

Taiwan) and China may challenge the existing relationships with their expanding economies.

Since the 1960s, however, these relationships have been dramatically modified. Changes in technology and in international global institutions have allowed corporations to break their production processes into smaller segments; these segments are then scattered over the world to take advantage of the lower manufacturing costs in the periphery. This process creates *commodity chains*—worldwide networks of labor resources and production processes that create a product. Each piece of the chain can be located in a core,

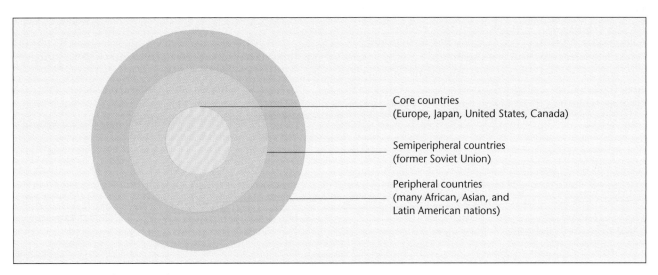

Core countries
(Europe, Japan, United States, Canada)

Semiperipheral countries
(former Soviet Union)

Peripheral countries
(many African, Asian, and
Latin American nations)

Figure 15.4 World Systems Theory

semiperipheral, or peripheral country. Because manufacturing processes are often performed in semiperipheral countries, their share of the world's manufacturing and trade production has risen sharply. By contrast, the distribution of profits from multinational corporations still benefits the core countries.

The core countries have been a major force in the development of global institutions, such as the International Monetary Fund (IMF), that facilitate and attempt to control international capital flow. By increasing frameworks for debt restructuring for peripheral countries, the IMF attempts to restore sustainability and growth to countries that default on their loans. At least 30 countries have restructured their debt under IMF guidelines (International Monetary Fund 2003).

However, the IMF leaves countries little economic autonomy; the restructuring plans even control what countries do within their own national boundaries, creating debt dependencies on core countries that the poorer countries can never overcome. For example, the IMF has demanded and instituted freezes on salaries and minimum wages in places such as Brazil and Argentina, has mandated opening of borders to imports, and has unintentionally undermined the economies of some very poor countries. The problem has been one of insisting on application of economic theories that work in affluent counties but not always in poor ones (The Dollars and Sense Collective 2006; Friedman 2006; Weidenbaum 2006; Weller and Hersh 2006).

In one sense, world systems theory is a conflict theory that is global in nature, with core countries exploiting the poor countries. As we might expect from conflict theory, some groups of noncore countries have increased their collective power by forming alliances such as OPEC (Organization of Petroleum Exporting Countries), OAS (Organization of African States), and SEATO (Southeast Asia Treaty Organization). These alliances present challenges to the historically core countries of the world system because of their combined economic and political power.

The price we pay for petrol at the gas pump reflects the power of OPEC to set prices. Other types of alliances such as the NAFTA (North American Free Trade Agreement) are being forged between core countries and their neighbors. These alliances can lead to sharing of resources and reduction of hostility toward core nations in "we" versus "they" polarities. For instance, under former President Bill Clinton's leadership, the United States gave Mexico a loan to strengthen its peso. To protect U.S. investors, Mexico was to place all of its money from the sale of oil in U.S. banks. Mexico recently paid off its restructured loans (Stevenson 2003). However, when we understand these international treaties and alliances as part of a larger issue of conflict over resources and economic self-interests, the animosity by noncore countries toward core countries such as the United States begins to make sense. Likewise, the mistrust of the United States toward countries that seem to be getting U.S. jobs is not entirely unfounded. The problem is an extraordinarily complex system that always leaves the most vulnerable more at risk and the wealthiest even richer.

THINKING SOCIOLOGICALLY

Where is your clothing made? Did a multinational corporation have it assembled in the "global south"? Who benefits from companies buying cheap labor in developing countries: You? The workers? Governments? The companies that manufacture the products? Who, if anyone, is hurt?

COLLECTIVE BEHAVIOR: MICRO-LEVEL BEHAVIOR AND CHANGE

The following incident occurred in Chicago during riots in the 1960s and provides an example of *collective behavior*, a form of unplanned action that can be understood at a micro level.

On Saturday, July 15, [Director of Police Dominick] Spina received a report of snipers in a housing project. When he arrived he saw approximately 100 National Guardsmen and police officers crouching behind vehicles, hiding in corners and lying on the ground around the edge of the courtyard.

Since everything appeared quiet and it was broad daylight, Spina walked directly down the middle of the street. Nothing happened. As he came to the last building of the complex, he heard a shot. All around him the troopers jumped, believing themselves to be under sniper fire. A moment later a young Guardsman ran from behind a building.

The Director of Police went over and asked him if he had fired the shot. The soldier said yes, he had fired to scare a man away from a window; that his orders were to keep everyone away from windows.

Spina said he told the soldier: "Do you know what you just did? You have now created a state of hysteria. Every Guardsman up and down this street and every state policeman and every city policeman that is present thinks that somebody just fired a shot and that it is probably a sniper."

A short time later more "gunshots" were heard. Investigating, Spina came upon a Puerto Rican sitting on a wall. In reply to a question as to whether he knew "where the firing is coming from?" the man said:

"That's no firing. That's fireworks. If you look up to the fourth floor, you will see the people who are throwing down these cherry bombs."

By this time four truckloads of National Guardsmen had arrived and troopers and policemen were again crouched everywhere looking for a sniper. The Director of Police remained at the scene for three hours, and the only shot fired was the one by the Guardsman.

Nevertheless, at six o'clock that evening two columns of National Guardsmen and state troopers were directing mass fire at the Hayes Housing Project in response to what they believed were snipers. (Report of the National Advisory Commission on Civil Disorders 1968:3–4)

Collective behavior refers to actions that are spontaneous, unstructured, disorganized, and often violate norms; they arise when people are trying to cope with stressful situations and unclear or uncertain conditions (Goode 1992; Smelser 1963, 1988). Collective behavior falls into two main types: crowd behavior and mass behavior. It often starts as a response to an event or stimulus—a perceived threat as in the above example, a shooting or beating, a speech, a sports event, or a rumor. The key is that as individuals try to make sense of the situations they are in and respond based on their perceptions, collective social actions emerge.

Crowd behaviors—mobs, panics, riots, and demonstrations—are all forms of collective behavior in which a crowd acts, at least temporarily, as a unified group (LeBon 1895/ 1960). Crowds are often made up of individuals who see themselves as supporting a just cause; because the protesters are in such a large group, they may not feel bound by the normal social controls—either internal (normal moral standards) or external (fear of police sanctions).

Mass behavior occurs when individual people communicate or respond in a similar manner to ambiguous or uncertain situations, often based on common information from the news or on the Internet. Examples include public opinion, rumors, fads, and fashions. Unlike social movements, these forms of collective behavior generally lack a hierarchy of authority and clear leadership, a division of labor, and a sense of group action.

Theories of Collective Behavior

Social scientists trying to explain disruptions in the social world have studied group and crowd dynamics. Researchers find that most members of crowds are respectable, law-abiding citizens, but faced with specific situations, they act out (Berk 1974; Turner and Killian 1993). Several explanations of individual involvement dominate the modern collective behavior literature.

The *minimax strategy* (Berk 1974) is based on principles of rational choice theory; it suggests that individuals try to minimize their losses or costs and maximize their benefits; people are more likely to engage in behavior if they feel the rewards outweigh the costs. Individuals may become involved in a riot if they feel the outcome—drawing attention to their plight, the possibility of improving conditions, solidarity with neighbors and friends, looting goods—will be more rewarding than the status quo or the possible negative sanctions.

Emergent norm theory (Turner and Killian 1993) addresses the unusual situations and breakdown of norms in which most collective behavior takes place. Unusual situations may call for the development of new norms and even new definitions of what is acceptable behavior. Individuals in crowds do have different emotions and attitudes that guide their decisions and behaviors than if they act alone. The implication of this theory is that in ambiguous situations, people look to others for clues about what is happening or what is acceptable, and norms emerge in ambiguous contexts that may be considered inappropriate in other contexts.

Crowds can stimulate change in a society, but they can also become unruly and unpredictable. Government officials spend a good deal of money and time equipping and training officers in how to control angry and radicalized members of crowds.

Source: © Dušan Jankovic.

The value-added theory describes conditions for crowd behavior and social movements. Key elements are necessary, with each new variable adding to the total situation until conditions are sufficient for individuals to begin to act in common and collective behavior emerges (Smelser 1963). These are the six factors Smelser (1963) identified:

1. *Structural conduciveness:* Existing problems create a climate that is ripe for change (tensions between religious and ethnic groups in Iraq).

2. *Structural strain:* the social structure is not meeting the needs and expectations of the citizens, which creates widespread dissatisfaction with the status quo—the current arrangements (the government is unable to control violence and provide basic services).

3. *Spread of a generalized belief:* common beliefs about the cause, effect, and solution of the problem evolves, develops, and spreads (U.S. troops may leave; militias are killing members of other groups).

4. *Precipitating factor:* A dramatic event or incident occurs to incite people to action (groups of men from different religious groups are kidnapped, bound, and shot).

5. *Mobilization for action:* Leaders emerge and set out a path of action, or an emergent norm develops that stimulates common action (citizens gather to protest the killings and lack of security and services).

6. *Social controls are weak:* If police, military, or strong political or religious leaders are unable to counter the mobilization, a social movement or other crowd behavior (e.g., a riot or mob) is likely to develop (Iraq could erupt into civil war, depending on social controls).

On the southern outskirts of Basra in Iraq, British soldiers monitor a checkpoint leading into the city, checking people for weapons. A young Iraqi girl experiences the tense and hostile realities of war as her relative is checked by British soldiers. This kind of military presence is often scary for residents and is very dangerous work for soldiers.

Source: © Peter Turnley / The Denver Post / Corbis.

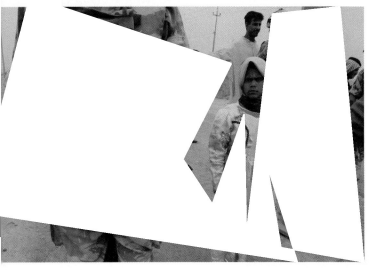

Charlie Hunnan and Ray Winstone star in the drama Cold Mountain, *which depicts vigilantes and lawlessness that existed during the U.S. Civil War.*

Source: © Miramax Films / ZUMA / Corbis.

When all six factors are present, some sort of collective behavior will emerge. Those interested in controlling crowds that are volatile must intervene in one or more of these conditions (Kendall 2004; Smelser 1963).

Types of Collective Behavior

Collective behavior ranges from spontaneous violent mobs to temporary fads and fashions. Figure 15.5 shows the range of actions.

Mobs are emotional crowds that engage in violence against a specific target. Examples include lynchings, killings, and hate crimes. Near the end of the U.S. civil war, self-appointed vigilante groups roamed the countryside in the South looking for army deserters, torturing and killing both those who harbored deserters and the deserters themselves. There were no courts and no laws, just "justice" in the eyes of the vigilantes. Members of these groups constituted mobs. The film *Cold Mountain* (Frazier 1997) depicts these scenes vividly.

Riots—an outbreak of illegal violence against shifting targets, committed by individuals expressing frustration or anger, against people, property, or both—begin when certain conditions occur. Often a sense of deprivation sets the stage for a riot—hunger, poverty, poor housing, lack of jobs, discrimination, poor education, or an unresponsive or unfair judicial system. If the conditions for collective behavior are present, there are many types of incidents that can be the precipitating factor setting off a riot. Participants can come not only from poor neighborhoods but also from middle-class areas in which residents feel frustrated with an emotionally charged issue that is not being solved by the leaders of the city or nation. For example, residents of many towns in Iraq have been rioting over lack of jobs, poor pay, and the limited resources available to sustain a decent life.

In 1969, when the police raided a New York gay bar, Stonewall Inn, they were seeking arrests on immorality charges. The frustration of being under attack for their sexuality finally led homosexuals at the bar to erupt; a three-day riot ensued. Eventually, this angry energy was transformed into a social movement for change, the international Stonewall Movement for gay, lesbian, and bisexual rights. The distinction between riots and mobs is illustrated in Figure 15.6.

Panic occurs when a large number of individuals become fearful or try to flee threatening situations that are beyond their control, sometimes putting their lives in danger. Panic can occur in a crowd situation such as a restaurant or theater in which someone yells "fire," or it can occur following rumors or information spread by the media. Panic started by rumors set off the run on the stock market in October 1929, causing the stock market crash in the United States and repercussions around the world. It all involved a large number of actions by individuals.

Rumors are a form of mass behavior in which unsupported or unproven reports about a problem, issue, or concern circulate widely throughout the public. Rumors may spread only in a local area, but with electronic means

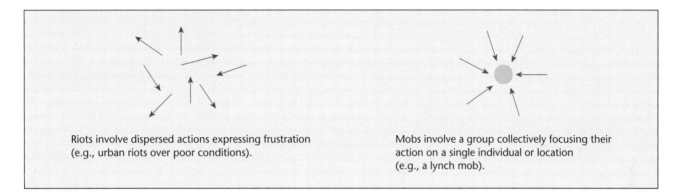

Spontaneous and often violent			Less spontaneous and seldom violent		
Crowd behavior			Mass behavior		
Mob	Riot	Panic	Rumor	Fad	Fashion

Figure 15.5   Types of Collective Behavior

Riots involve dispersed actions expressing frustration (e.g., urban riots over poor conditions).

Mobs involve a group collectively focusing their action on a single individual or location (e.g., a lynch mob).

Figure 15.6   The Difference between Riots and Mobs

available, rumors are spreading more widely and rapidly. *Urban legends*, one example of widely spread but unverified messages, are unsubstantiated stories that sound plausible and become widely circulated. People telling them usually believe them (Henslin 2005). The next Sociology in Your Social World provides an example.

THINKING SOCIOLOGICALLY

What role is the Internet playing in spread of information and rumors? How is e-mail changing the way we communicate and our interpersonal relationships?

Fads are temporary items or activities that spread rapidly and are copied enthusiastically by large numbers of people. American Girl dolls and accessories were all the rage in 2003. Holiday sales were brisk, and the company struggled to keep up with orders. Like its predecessors, Barbie and Cabbage Patch dolls, American Girl was the current fad. Sometimes, fads become institutionalized; that is, they gain a permanent place in the culture. Other fads die out, replaced by the next hot item.

Fashions refer to a social pattern favored by a large number of people for a limited period of time; examples would include clothing styles, music genres, color schemes in home decor, types of automobiles, and architectural designs. They typically last longer than fads but sometimes survive only a season as can be seen in the clothing industry. Music styles such as "post hard core," "conscious hip hop," "screamo," and "UK 2-step garage" were popular among

A young woman in New York, wearing a dildo atop her forehead, celebrates the anniversary of the Stonewall uprising. On June 26, 1969, gay men and women barricaded themselves in Manhattan's Stonewall Inn and united against sexual discrimination and police brutality in the first act of unity for gay rights. Since then, gays, lesbians, bisexuals, and transgendered people have been more assertive in claiming rights as citizens and more willing to express themselves in public.

Source: © Viviane Moos / Corbis.

Sociology in Your Social World

Exam Stories Put Truth to the Test

College exams are quickly approaching, so it is a good time to take a look at the latest chapter in the tome of teacher-student legend and rumors.

The first one was reported from Calgary, Alberta, by a civil-engineering student at the University of Manitoba. It describes a professor who announces an open-book final examination in which the students "may use anything they could carry into the exam room." The story that was passed around was that one crafty undergraduate took the professor at his word and carried in a graduate student to write his exam for him.

Another legend was reported from North Carolina. Supposedly, on the day before the final exam, the professor stepped out of his office for a few minutes, leaving the door open and the pile of next day's examinations on the desk. A student came by to ask a question and found the room empty, so he stole one of the exams. However, the professor had counted the exams, and the next morning, he checked them again

before going to the classroom. Discovering that one was missing, he cut one-half inch from the bottom of the remaining exams. When the exam papers were turned in, the student whose paper was one-half inch longer than the others received a failing grade.

Another classic exam story was about a philosophy professor at Harvard who allegedly was teaching a class in metaphysics. When the students were settled for the final exam, the teacher placed a chair on the desk in front of the room. "Prove that this chair exists," he says. "You have two hours." One student is said to have written, "What chair?" and left the room while others frantically composed their essays. As the story goes, the student who wrote the two-word challenge got an A.

Campus legends such as these help reduce the strains of college life and spread the reputations of legendary professors. Furthermore, they keep alive hopes of someday outfoxing the professors—or the students, depending on which side you are on.

Abridged and edited from an article by Jan Harold Brunvand, United Feature Syndicate. These and other urban legends about exams and college experience can be reviewed at http://www.snopes.com.

---

some groups as this book was being written but may be passé by the time you read this, replaced by new styles resulting from change in mass behavior.

THINKING SOCIOLOGICALLY

Why have body adornments and piercings become so popular with today's younger generation? Does this influence or is it influenced by change in the larger society?

Each of these forms of collective behavior involves micro-level individual actions that cumulatively become collective responses to certain circumstances. However, ripples are felt in other levels of the social world. Insofar as these various types of collective activity upset the standard routines of the society and the accepted norms, they can unsettle the entire social system and cause lasting change.

The separation of each of the forms of change into levels is somewhat artificial, of course, for individuals are also acting in organizations and in national social movements.

However, when we move to meso- and macro-level analyses, the established structures and processes of the society become increasingly important; much of the change at these levels is planned change.

PLANNED CHANGE IN ORGANIZATIONS: MESO-LEVEL CHANGE

The following five real examples represent problems in organizations and illustrate why organizations attempt to plan for change.

The board of trustees of a small liberal arts college has witnessed recent drops in student enrollments that could cause the college to go out of business, but the college has a long tradition of fine education and devoted alumni. How does the college continue to serve future students and current alumni? The problem is how to plan change to keep the college solvent.

A company manufactures silicon chips for computers, but recently the market has been flooded with inexpensive

Fashions are established largely at fashion shows like this one. Such events cannot occur unless there is a very high level of affluence where people can afford to throw away perfectly good clothing for something more stylish. In developing countries where it is a gift just to have clean, warm clothing, the very existence of such displays of wealth is evidence of decadence in wealthy societies.

Source: © Istockphoto.com.

chips, primarily from Asia where they are made more cheaply than this North American firm can possibly make them. Does the company succumb to the competition, figure out ways to meet it, or diversify its products? What steps should be taken to facilitate the change? Many companies in Silicon Valley, California, face exactly this challenge.

A nonprofit organization concerned with research into a rare disease has held fundraising drives for many years to support research regarding the causes of and cures for this disease. However, the breakthrough has come and vaccines are now being produced to prevent the disease. Does the nonprofit agency close shop or find another cause to support? Such was the problem faced by the March of Dimes, which collected money for poliomyelitis research and helped support the discovery of a cure. Except for a few hot spots where ethnic groups refuse vaccinations, the disease has been eradicated. The nonprofit organization had become

an effective fundraiser for a charitable cause; should it just fold up the charity and lay off its employees?

A Native American nation within the United States is facing unemployment among its people due in large measure to discrimination by Anglos in the local community. Should the elders focus their energies and resources on electing sympathetic politicians, boycotting racist businesses, filing lawsuits, becoming entrepreneurs as a nation so they can hire their own people, or begin a local radio station so they will have a communication network for a social movement? What is the best strategy to help this proud nation recover from centuries of disadvantage?

All these are real problems faced by real organizations. Anywhere we turn, organizations face questions involving change, questions that arise because of internal strains and external stresses. How organizational leaders and applied sociologists deal with change will determine the survival and well-being of the organizations.

Planned Change in Organizations

Some organizations are well prepared to meet the challenge of change; they spend time and money writing long-range strategic plans and doing self-studies to determine areas for ongoing change. Other organizations may be unable to cope, and they decline in influence. Sometimes, change is desired, and sometimes it is forced on the organization by stresses from society, more powerful organizations, or individuals

Genea Rednose works as the cage cashier at a native-owned casino on New Mexico's Pueblo San Felipe. Casinos bring needed cash to reservations, but some native people have serious moral concerns about an enterprise that makes money on the basis of taking what others have without producing a socially useful product. Moreover, many impoverished native people frequent the casino and lose money they cannot afford to give up.

Source: © Miguel Gandert / Corbis.

THE APPLIED SOCIOLOGIST AT WORK   Stephen Steele

Local Community Research Center

Dr. Stephen Steele started using sociology to help a business he was working for solve a problem and bring about needed change; he has been in the business of helping organizations solve problems with sociological knowledge ever since.

"If someone has knowledge and fails to use it, that is a terrible waste," comments Steele. The idea of being involved in social betterment and making a difference were guiding principles that led Steele to a life of sociological research. In 1978, he used his research skills to help set up a Community Research Center at the local community college. The goals were for the nonprofit center to help community organizations solve their problems, train students to use research skills, help bring about needed change, and provide a service to all. In 1982, he became director, a position he still holds.

Many students have developed sophisticated analytical and research skills by working on projects in the community, and the center has supported itself by contracting its high-quality, low-cost research services to community organizations. Although the range of the center's research is broad, the main foci have been on community change, economic development, and

county government issues. For instance, Steele's company, Applied Data Associates, received one federal grant to evaluate an antidrug project and another to evaluate ways to increase the active involvement of Hispanic Americans in community civic organizations.

The interaction between theory and research is crucial in his work. Consider the four basic sociological theories: he looks for systems of interaction (functionalism), for power centers (conflict), for interaction patterns and definitions of reality within corporate cultures (symbolic interactionism), and for costs and benefits of various choices (rational choice).

Steele likens applied sociology to being a "social plumber"—there is a specific problem, so he uses his tools to fix it. He finds being a social plumber rewarding and exciting, using sociological knowledge and tools to change groups, organizations, and environments, and in the process improving the quality of life for people.

Dr. Stephen Steele received his bachelor's and master's degrees from Eastern Michigan University and his doctorate from Catholic University of America. He teaches sociology at Ann Arundel Community College in Maryland and runs his own research center. His students gain practical experience working in the center.

(Kanter 1983, 2001a, 2001b; Olsen 1968) Rosabeth Kanter (1983) points out that planned change in organizations or whole societies is filled with contradictions, tensions, and dilemmas, because the pieces of a system are connected and not easily "decoupled." Change in one aspect of the system, even of a minor nature, can send ripples through the rest of the organization. A problem solved in one area creates unanticipated problems someplace else. The structures that work with the original organizational scheme may begin to deteriorate, even when only minor modifications were intended. The speed of change due to our modern communication and transportation technologies makes the unexpected outcomes of minor changes even more complex.

Planned change such as strategic planning is the dream of every organizational leader. It involves deliberate, structured attempts, guided by stated goals, to alter the status quo of the social unit (Bennis, Benne, and Chin 1985). Some applied sociologists devote their careers to combining research and advocacy of change, as illustrated in the Applied Sociologist at Work at the top of this page.

There are several important considerations as we think about planned change: How can we identify the need for change? How can we plan or manage the change process successfully? What kind of systems adapt well to change? Here, we briefly touch on the topic and outline three approaches advocated by experts to plan change.

Models for Planning Organizational Change

Change models fall into two main categories: closed system models that deal with the internal dynamics of the organization and open system models (such as our social world model) that consider the organization and its environment.

The *closed system models,* often called classical or mechanistic models, focus on the internal dynamics of the organization. The goal of change using closed models is to move the organization closer to the ideal of bureaucratic efficiency and effectiveness. An example is "time and motion studies" that analyze how much time it takes a worker to do a certain task and how it can be accomplished more efficiently. Each step in McDonald's process of getting a hamburger to you, the customer, for instance, has been planned and timed for greatest efficiency. In some closed system models, change is legislated from the top executives and filters down to workers.

The *human resources organic model* also focuses on internal dynamics, taking into account the individuals working in the organization. The famous Hawthorne studies at the Western Electric plant gave rise to a new model of organizations that emphasized human needs and the importance of the informal work group in satisfaction and performance of workers (Roethlisberger and Dickson 1939).

The *human relations approach* or "Theory Y," as it came to be known, and the *organizational development (OD) movement* stem from this early work. The idea is that participants in the organization should be involved in decision making leading to change; the leadership is more democratic and supportive of workers, and the atmosphere is *transparent*—open and honest. This model emphasizes that change comes about through adjusting workers' values, beliefs, and attitudes regarding new demands on the organization.

Current efforts include team building and change of the organizational culture to improve worker morale. Closed-system models tend to focus on group change that occurs from within the organization; an alternative approach is to look more broadly at the interaction between internal processes and external forces.

Open system models combine both internal processes and the external environment. The latter provides the organization with inputs (workers and raw materials) and feedback (acceptability of the product or result). In turn, the organization has outputs (products) that affect the larger society. There are several implications of this model: (1) change is an ever-present and ongoing process, (2) all parts of the organization and its immediate environment are linked, and (3) change in one part has an effect on other parts. The model in Figure 15.7 illustrates the open system.

THINKING SOCIOLOGICALLY

Using the model in Figure 15.7, fill in the parts as they relate to your educational institution. For example, inputs might include faculty members and students.

The Process of Planned Change

The process of planned change is like a puzzle with a number of pieces that differ for each organization but must fit together for the smooth operation of the organization. The goal of most organizations is to stay balanced and avoid threats or conflict. Change is generally perceived as desirable if it is evolutionary or planned; otherwise, it can be disruptive to the balance of the system.

When planned change occurs in organizations, the leaders direct most of the action. At the societal and global macro levels, change is often stimulated by those outside the chambers of power, and there is much less control over how the change evolves. We turn next to an exploration of change at the macro level.

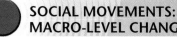

SOCIAL MOVEMENTS: MACRO-LEVEL CHANGE

The antinuclear power movement emerged as a significant force in 1975 after the potentially catastrophic accident at Three Mile Island in Pennsylvania. A worker accidentally caused a fire in wiring, risking loss of protection against meltdown. Meltdown occurs when the power plant's nuclear reactor core overheats and uranium fuel escapes, endangering the lives of nearby workers and local residents. Afraid of possible consequences of meltdown, citizens joined together in protest against nuclear power.

Nuclear power looked like a promising way to meet future energy needs, but as problems started to mount, lawsuits cost millions, and public safety was at risk.

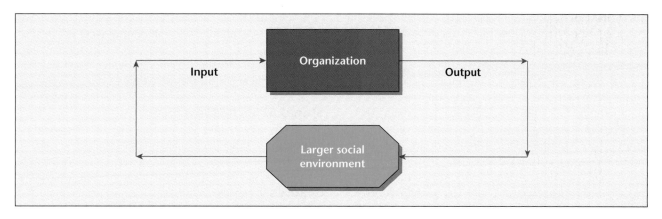

Figure 15.7 Open Systems Model

Questions arose, and the protests grew. Prominent scientists and Hollywood stars joined with environmental groups such as The Sierra Club, Citizens Against Nuclear Power, and Friends of the Earth to attract attention to the growing movement. Public attitudes regarding the dangers of nuclear contamination, accidents, and meltdown were influenced further by media and films such as *The China Syndrome*.

In the years to follow, other events served to reinforce the movement. The Clamshell Alliance in New Hampshire delayed opening of a nuclear power plant in Seabrook, and the Three Mile Island nuclear accident that occurred near Harrisburg, Pennsylvania, in March 1979, required evacuation of 150,000 people from the region. This led to antinuclear demonstrations in Washington, DC, and around the country (Walsh and Warland 1983).

The movement has also had global dimensions, including environmental protests following the Chernobyl nuclear disaster in the then–Soviet Union near Kiev. This accident caused contamination of agricultural lands across Europe and resulted in disabilities and deaths of some residents near the plant. The ultimate toll can be seen only after years of suffering by those who were exposed to the contamination. Japan is heavily dependent on nuclear power because of its lack of fuel resources. On September 30, 1999, a privately owned nuclear power plant at Tokaimura, Japan, had a uranium accident; 300,000 residents in the areas were told to stay indoors, and many workers were exposed to potentially lethal doses of radiation (Amodeo 1999; Larimer 1999). Such events helped to keep the antinuclear social movement alive, although advocates of nuclear power argue that new protections at plants make this form of energy safe.

What Is a Social Movement?

From environmental protection and women's rights to animal rights and prayer in schools, individuals seek ways to express their concerns. **Social movements** are consciously organized attempts outside of established institutional mechanisms to enhance or resist change through group action; social movements focus on a common interest, such as nuclear power. They have an organization, a leader, and one or more goals. These goals aim to correct some perceived wrongs existing in the society or even around the globe. Social movements are most often found in industrial or postindustrial societies with diverse groups that advocate for their own goals and interests.

Movements are begun by individuals, usually persons outside the power structure who might not otherwise have an opportunity to express their opinions (Greenberg 1999). The problems leading to social movements often result from the way resources—jobs, income, housing, education, and power—are distributed. In turn, they often stimulate the formation of *countermovements*—a social movement against the goals of the original movement (McCarthy and Zald 1977).

Many individuals join social movements to change the world or their part of the world and the direction of history. In fact, social movements have been successful in doing just that. Consider movements around the world that have protected lands, forests, and rivers for the people whose survival depends on those natural resources. For example, the Chipko Movement (meaning "embrace") in a number of areas of India has been fighting the logging of forests by commercial industries. Villagers, mostly women, use Gandhian nonviolent methods to oppose the deforestation. A movement by local peasants in Bihar, India, fought efforts to control their fishing rights in the Ganges River. Labor movements around the globe also fight for workers rights. In Cambodia, garment workers who sew many of the clothes sold in developed countries are receiving better working conditions through a joint effort of the International Labor Organization and the U.S. government. The project started in 2001 to alleviate problems in sweatshops; periodic unannounced visits by inspectors, interviews with workers, and new training opportunities for workers are all part of the agreement that guarantees Cambodia access to U.S. markets (Better Factories Movement in Cambodia 2006).

In the United States, ACORN (Association of Community Organizations for Reform Now) is a grassroots neighborhood-based antipoverty group, started in each community by concerned residents, that now has offices in over 100 U.S. cities with over 200,000 members—and growing. Community members knock on doors to inform neighbors about issues, get petitions signed, and get people on the streets to protest against the severe inequality in society. They are funded by foundations, private donations, and organizations working jointly to bring about change. In Gary, Indiana, this group paid its utility bills in pennies to protest the quick shut off of power to financially strapped customers. In Chicago, members gathered signatures for a law requiring Wal-Mart to pay employees $10 per hour plus benefits. Each community's issues involve populist organizing that can affect policies and bring about change in society. As social scientist Peter Dreier says, ACORN combines local projects with national action on larger issues. This type of grassroots organizing has the potential to be a major force for change in many communities (Eckholm 2006).

Consider the suffragettes without whom women would still be sitting at home on election days or other branches of the women's movement that have made great strides and continue the struggle for equal pay, promotions, and job opportunities. Recent movements in Europe and the United States focus on immigration. Some protesters are against illegal aliens and high immigrant rates, but the countermovement supports allowing recent immigrants to stay and work, regardless of how they arrived.

Stages of Social Movements

Social movements take the time and energy of individual volunteers, but these personal resources must be focused as the movement evolves. In the *preliminary stage*, the context for a movement is set. Historical or recent events may have created dissatisfaction and discontent in the general public or a part of the public. This discontent can galvanize people through a single event.

In the *popularization stage*, individuals coalesce their efforts, define their goals and strategies, develop recruitment tactics, and identify leaders; the social movement enters the public arena. The leaders present the social problems and solutions as seen by the members of the social movement.

During its third stage, the social movement is *institutionalized* into a formal organization. This organized effort generates the resources and members for the social change efforts.

In some movements, the final stage is *fragmentation and demise.* The group may or may not have achieved its goals, but fragmentation breaks apart the organization because the resources may be exhausted, the leadership may be inept or may have lost legitimacy, or the leaders may be co-opted by powerful mainline organizations. In this latter case, radical renewal movements may arise among those still strongly committed to the original cause (Mauss 1975).

THINKING SOCIOLOGICALLY

What evidence can you see in your local area, your country, or the world of stages in the women's movement?

Conditions for Social Movements

Sociologists have identified several conditions that give rise to a social movement. First, social movements need to have a "preexisting communication network" that allows alienated or dissatisfied people to share their discontent (Farley 2000; Freeman 1975; Snow, Zurcher, and Ekland-Olson 1980). This network may then become co-opted for use by disaffected citizens, even if that was not the original purpose of the network. Several recent political movements such as MoveOn.com and TrueMajority.com were carried out primarily on the Internet.

Second, the people in this network must share some basic values and ideals; often, they occupy similar social statuses or positions (Freeman 1975). Third, a strain and a precipitating event galvanizes the people around the issue (Freeman 1975). Fourth, effective leadership emerges— someone who can mobilize people, organize the movement, and garner resources to fund the movement (Farley 2000). Finally, the people in the movement develop a sense of efficacy, a sense that they actually can be successful and change the system. Sometimes, as in the case of the civil rights movement, a sense of confidence in success comes from a religious conviction that God will not let the movement fail (Farley 2000).

In the case of the women's movement, interested women were linked into "preexisting communication networks" by serving on state Commissions on the Status of Women (Ferree and Merrill 2000). The refusal of the Equal Employment Opportunities Commission to consider women's rights as equal to those of racial minorities became the strain and precipitating event that led women to form the National Organization for Women (NOW), a group that continues to fight for women's rights today (Freeman 1975). The Equal Rights Amendment (ERA) provided a major issue around which women's groups rallied. Many women spent tremendous

Social movements have protested against immigrants and on behalf of more open immigration laws. Young people in this photo demonstrate in Paris against Pasqua's laws that seek to restrain immigration and French citizenship. The lower banner reads "Prison + expulsion = double pain."

Source: © Antoine Gyori / Corbis Sygma.

Former NOW President Eleanor Smeal and former First Ladies Betty Ford and Lady Bird Johnson urged ratification of the Equal Rights Amendment at a rally on the Lincoln Memorial Grounds in Washington, DC, in 1981. The Women's Movement has changed American society dramatically, but the Equal Rights Amendment to the Constitution that would enshrine gender equality in law did not pass.

Source: © Bettmann/Corbis.

time and effort in attempts to have the ERA ratified by the necessary number of states. Spokespersons emerged, and fundraiser events provided resources. For a long time, advocates were convinced that the campaign would be successful. However, when the realization of failure came, an era

Two members of the environmental group Earth First hold a sign in front of the Lincoln Memorial in Washington, DC, to protest the destruction of the earth's rainforests and to advocate for the rights of various species that are endangered. Such movements use nonviolent protest, legislative means, and appeals to the public or to the courts to accomplish their goals.

Source: © Bettmann/Corbis.

in the women's movement ended. Some women's organizations fragmented and faded from the scene, while others revised their goals and strategies and moved forward.

Social movements begin because of cultural conflicts in society and because people come together who have social change as their goal.

Proactive social movements promote change; for example, Stonewall is a gay, lesbian, and bisexual rights movement—discussed earlier in the chapter—that began when patrons fought back against a police raid of a gay bar in New York in 1969. From that incident, the concern about gay rights erupted from a small number of activists into a widespread movement for rights and acceptance. Stonewall now has gone global, with chapters in other countries and continents. *Reactive social movements* resist change. While homosexuality has not been its only concern, Focus on the Family, headed by evangelist James Dobson, has organized lobbying efforts and rallies to ensure that homosexuality is not normalized and is not given equal status to heterosexual married relationships.

Social movements sometimes focus on regional or even organizational modification, but typically their focus is on national or global issues. Amnesty International's primary interest is on human rights violations by nations; they publish information on violations around the world. Another way to classify social movements is by their purpose or goals. Four types are usually singled out.

Types of Social Movements

Expressive movements are group phenomena, but they focus on changing individuals and saving people from corrupt lifestyles. Many expressive movements are religious, such as the born-again Christian movements and new religious movements such as Transcendental Meditation. Expressive movements also include secular psychotherapy movements and self-help or self-actualization groups.

Social reform movements seek to change some aspect of society, but members generally support the society as a whole. These movements focus on a major issue such as environmental protection, women's rights, same-sex marriage, non-corporate and just globalization, gay rights, or civil rights. Typically, these movements use nonviolent, legislative means or appeals to the courts to accomplish their goals, although splinter groups may resort to more aggressive methods.

Revolutionary movements attempt to transform society, to bring about total change in a society by overthrowing existing power structures and replacing them with new ones. These movements often resort to violent means to achieve their goals as has been the case with many revolutions throughout history. When we read in the paper that there has been a coup, we may be looking at a revolutionary movement that has ousted the government in power. Although it was not violent, Nelson Mandela's African National Congress succeeded in taking power in South Africa in 1994, rewriting the constitution, and purging a racially segregated apartheid social system that had oppressed four-fifths of the South African population.

Resistance or regressive movements try to protect an existing system or part of a system. They see societal change as a threat to values or practices and wish to maintain the status quo or return to a former status by reversing the change process (Inglehart and Baker 2001). The Council on Families in America seeks to preserve functions and structure of the family from the middle of the twentieth century; the movement to pass a constitutional amendment on the definition of marriage is a current effort. The Islamic movement under the Ayatollah Khomeini in Iran sought to restore fundamentalist Islam and eliminate Western influences; the current regime in Iran is challenging condemnation from many developed nations and antinuclear movements over its uranium enrichment efforts.

Global transnational movements focus on large-scale, often global issues. They take place across societies as international organizations seek change in the status of women, child labor, rights of indigenous peoples, global warming, and animal rights around the world. An example is any movement to improve the working conditions and environmental effects resulting from actions of multinational corporations (The Durban Accord 2003; Flavin 2001; World Resources Institute 2003). Another example is Free the Slaves, a global antislavery organization started by sociologist Kevin Bales (1999, 2000). This kind of movement is explored in more detail in the next section.

Figure 15.8 summarizes the types of movements and focus of each, from the micro to the macro level.

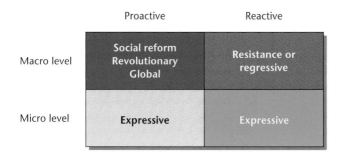

Figure 15.8 Types of Movements

THINKING SOCIOLOGICALLY

Consider a social movement with which you are familiar. What type of movement is it, and what was or is it trying to accomplish?

Globalization and Social Movements

Social movements are about people trying to improve their societies. They are intriguing in part because they are such compelling evidence that however strong macro- and meso-level social forces are in shaping our lives, humans still make choices and are capable of countering those forces. As Eitzen and Zinn (2006) put it,

> Social structures constrain what we do, but they do not determine what we do. While these structures are powerful, human beings are not totally controlled. . . . Individuals acting alone, or with others, can shape, resist, challenge, and sometimes change the social structures that impinge on them. These actions constitute *human agency.* (p. 322)

Since World War II, power in the global system has come to be dominated by a group of industrial giants called the Global 8 (G-8); they control world markets and regulate economic and trading policies (Henslin 2005). Included in this elite group are the dominant three (Japan representing the East, Germany representing central Europe, and the United States representing the Western Hemisphere) and five other important but less dominating powers (Canada, France, Great Britain, and Italy, and more recently Russia). The G-8 (previously called the G-7) are the core countries that have the most power in the World Trade Organization, the World Bank, the IMF, and other regulatory agencies that preside over the global economy. These agencies have often demanded that poor countries must adhere to their

demands or lose the right to loans and other support, referred to as "globalization from above." Yet the imposed policies from above have often been disastrous for poor countries, creating situations in which a debt burden is created that can never be paid off. If these were individuals rather than countries, we would call them indentured servants or slaves (Brecher et al. 2006; Cockburn 2006; Eitzen and Zinn 2006; Stein 2006; Weidenbaum 2006; Weller and Hersh 2006). They are trapped by their indebtedness, and newly created policies of global agencies like the World Bank and the IMF make it impossible to ever pay those debts. This creates nations where hopelessness would seem to reign supreme. Yet social movements are arising in precisely these places and are often joining forces across national boundaries; even some with groups within the G-8 nations—labor unions, college student groups, and

Nelson Mandela voted for the first time in his life in South Africa on April 27, 1994. This was the first democratic election open to all races in South Africa after segregation was abolished. A political prisoner for 26 years, Nelson Mandela was held by the apartheid-based government as a dangerous revolutionary for his beliefs in racial equality. He was elected president of the country in this election and was co-recipient of the Nobel Peace Prize for his work for democracy and equality. His nonviolent movement brought revolutionary change.

Source: © Louise Gubb / Corbis Saba.

Some social movements are regressive; they seek to reverse social trends and return to a previous set of social arrangements. Here, veiled women and children in Lebanon march in support of the Iranian leader Ayatollah Khomeini to restore traditional values and modest roles and image for women and against Westernization.

Source: © Francoise de Mulder / Corbis.

religious bodies concerned about social justice—are joining the movements.

Some of the most interesting social movements in the twenty-first century are globalization movements by those who are weakest and most vulnerable. Some of these movements are small, but many of them have created networks with other groups around the world, using the Internet to communicate and to find common ground. Moreover, a group of the poorest nations have now formed their own organization to counter what was then called the G-7. Calling themselves the G-77, the alliance has existed since the 1970s, but the first meeting of the heads of state of these poor nations occurred in 2000. The countries are now uniting, rather like a labor union seeking collective unity by workers, and hope they have some power to determine their own destinies by challenging what they experience as the "tyranny" of the G-8 (Brecher et al. 2006; Hayden 2006). Map 15.3 displays the location of G-8 and G-77 countries.

Globalization as it now exists—with corporate profits as the ruling principle of most decision making—has lowered environmental standards, lessened consumer protection, decreased national sovereignty and local control of decisions, and reduced safety and other protections for workers. However, in the competition to find cheaper labor for higher profits, there is a "race to the bottom" as communities must lower standards or else lose jobs to some other part of the world that is even more impoverished. When jobs move elsewhere, the people who had come to depend on

those jobs are devastated and often thrust into poverty and homelessness. This leads to migration, either as illegal aliens in another country or as squatters in slums of cities in their own countries.

Nations no longer have the same power to regulate the multinational industries when they produce much of their product elsewhere on the planet. Industries can simply exercise their option of exiting the country, leaving that country without the jobs or the tax revenue. The result has been a rise in countermovements. *Globalization from below* refers to the efforts by common people—in small groups and protest movements—to fight back. Rather than globalization being controlled solely by the pursuit of profits, these countermovements seek to protect workers, to defend the environment, and to combat the bone-crunching poverty that plagues so much of the global south where poverty has actually increased in the past 30 years and continues to rise.

The argument goes like this:

> It is the activity of people—going to work, paying taxes, buying products, obeying government officials, staying off private property—that continually re-creates the power of the powerful. . . . [The system, for all its power and resources, is dependent on common people to do the basic jobs that keep the society running.] This dependency gives people a potential power over the society—but one that can be realized only if they are prepared to reverse their acquiescence. . . . Social movements can be understood as the collective withdrawal of consent to established institutions. The movement against globalization from above can be understood as the withdrawal of consent from such globalization (Brecher et al. 2006:337).

Some social movements deal with global issues and organizations. Demonstrators here protest the policies of the World Trade Organization because of what they think policies do to American jobs and to increase poverty in the poorest countries of the world.

Source: © Christopher J. Morris / Corbis.

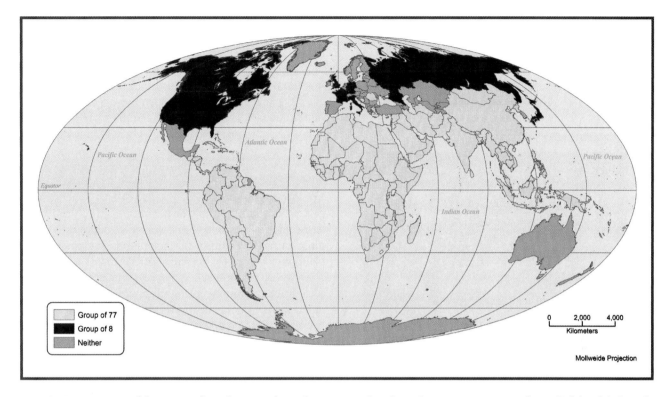

MAP 15.3   Countries of the Group of 8 and Group of 77. The pattern makes clear why poor countries are often called the global south.

Source: http://www.g77.org; retrieved August 19, 2006. Map by Anna Versluis.

The authors go on to describe the Lilliputian strategy named after the tiny Lilliputians who—in *Gulliver's Travels*—captured Gulliver by tying him up with hundreds of tiny threads. The tiny threads in this case are thousands of small resistance actions to the oppressive policies of the G-8 and transnational corporations. The following are just four examples:

> Under heavy pressure from the World Bank, the Bolivian government sold off the public water system of its third largest city, Cochabamba, to a subsidiary of the San Francisco-based Bechtel Corporation, which promptly doubled the price of water for people's homes. Early in 2000, the people of Cochabamba rebelled, shutting down the city with general strikes and blockades. The government declared a state of siege and a young protester was shot and killed. Word spread all over the world from the remote Bolivian highlands via the Internet. Hundreds of e-mail messages poured into Bechtel from all over the world demanding that it leave Cochabamba. In the midst of local and global protests, the Bolivian government, which had said that Bechtel must not leave, suddenly reversed itself and signed an accord accepting every demand of the protestors (Brecher et al. 2006:341–42).

In April 2000, AIDS activists, unions, and religious groups were poised to begin a lawsuit and picketing campaign denouncing the Pfizer Corporation as an AIDS profiteer for the high price it charges for AIDS drugs in Africa. Pfizer suddenly announced that it would supply the drug fluconazole, used to control AIDS side effects, for free to any South African with AIDS who could not afford it (Brecher et al. 2006:342).

Groups in Europe, Japan, and the U.S. that had been involved in support for development and popular movements in third world countries found that those developing countries were increasingly being used as production platforms by global corporations. They began calling attention to the growth of sweatshops and pressuring companies like the Gap and Nike to establish acceptable labor and human rights conditions in their factories around the world. Their efforts gradually grew into an anti-sweatshop movement with strong labor and religious support and tens of thousands of active participants. In the U.S., college students took up the anti-sweatshop cause on hundreds of campuses, ultimately holding sit-ins on many campuses to force their colleges to ban the use of college logos on products not produced under acceptable labor conditions (Brecher et al. 2006:333).

Many concerned citizens in the developed world now buy Fair Trade goods such as coffee, cocao, and fruits.

Global protests often focus on actions of American and multinational corporations. Women demonstrators including Bhopal Gas victims in India hold a "Wanted" poster of former Union Carbide Chairman Warren Anderson, arguing that he be tried for crimes. More than 3,000 people were killed and tens of thousands injured when a tank at the Union Carbide pesticide plant leaked five tons of poisonous gas.

Source: © REUTERS / Corbis / Raj Patidar.

Many individuals in G-8 countries have been extremely generous in donating to international organizations helping victims of disasters and in joining in solidarity with those in dire straights in the developing global south. However, governments have often been unsympathetic. The United States spends 0.13 of 1 percent of its gross national product on United Nations programs that address poverty, famine, illiteracy, and disease. That represents a decrease of 90 percent from the Kennedy administration era, more than 40 years ago. Still, those who believe in the Lilliputian strategy think that actions by individuals and small groups can have a real impact.

THINKING SOCIOLOGICALLY

What are cases in which the Lilliputian strategy has made a difference in local, national, or international events with which you are familiar?

In summary, some social change is planned by organizations, some is initiated by groups that are outside the organizational structure (social movements), and some is unplanned and spontaneous (collective behavior). The most important point, however, is that actions by individuals affect the larger social world, sometimes even having global ramifications. Likewise, national and international changes and social movements influence the lives of individuals.

TECHNOLOGY, ENVIRONMENT, AND CHANGE

At the edge of the town of Bhopal, India, looms a subsidiary plant of the American-based Union Carbide Company; the plant provides work for many of the town's inhabitants. However, on December 3, 1984, things did not go as normal. A storage tank from the plant, filled with the toxic chemical liquid methyl isocyanate, overheated and turned to gas that began to escape through a pressure-relief valve. The gas formed a cloud and drifted away from the plant. By the time the sirens were sounded, it was too late for many people; the deadly gas had done its devastating work: more than 2,500 dead and thousands ill, many with permanent injuries from the effects of the gas. Put in perspective, the number of casualties was about equal to the number in the terrorist attack on the Twin Towers of New York City on September 11, 2001.

The legal systems became tangled in battles that prevented many of the victims from receiving any needed compensation for their injuries or the deaths of wage earners. The company settled with the government of India for a fraction of the claims put forth by individuals, and many people were never compensated for their medical expenses or their losses. (Not all multinational companies have been such poor citizens.)

This example illustrates change at multiple levels of analysis. We see a *global* multinational company (Union Carbide) in a *society* (India) that welcomed the jobs for its citizens. A *community* within that larger society benefited from the jobs until many residents were killed or disabled, leaving shattered *families* and devastated *individual* lives. The accident also spawned a number of forms of collective behavior. The immediate aftermath of the accident at Bhopal included panic, as people tried to flee the deadly gas. Like many environmental and nuclear crises, this one later resulted in several social movements as activists demanded accountability and safety measures. The disaster also brought about planned change in the way Union Carbide does business and protects workers and citizens.

Technology refers to the practical application of tools, skills, and knowledge to meet human needs and extend human abilities. However, nuclear disasters that have occurred also make clear that technology and environment cannot be separated. The raw products that fuel technology come from the environment, the wastes resulting from technology return to the environment, and technological mistakes affect the environment. This section discusses briefly the development and process of technology, the relationship between technology and environment, and the implications for change at each level of analysis.

Human abilities enable scientists to invent new and better ways to make life more comfortable and safe. Throughout human history, there have been major transition periods or *waves* when changes in the material culture brought about revolutions in human social structures and cultures (Toffler and Toffler 1980). The *agricultural revolution* used technology in the form of a plow to till the soil, establishing new social arrangements, and eventually resulting in food surpluses that allowed cities to flourish. The *industrial revolution* brought machines powered by steam and petrol, resulting in mass society, divisions of labor in manufacturing, and socialist and capitalist political-economic systems. Today, *postindustrial technology*, based on the microchip, is fueling the spread of information, communication, and transportation on a global level. This *postindustrial revolution* is producing new technologies that can move information and people rapidly around the globe; explore space; and analyze, store, and retrieve masses of information in seconds. Even exploration of Mars is underway as this chapter is being written. However, each wave affects only a portion of the world, leaving other people and countries behind and creating divisions between developed and developing, and rich and poor nations, regions, communities, and individuals.

According to sociologist William Ogburn (1922/1938, 1961, 1964), change is brought about through three processes: discovery, invention, and diffusion. *Discovery* is a new way of seeing reality; the material objects or ideas have been present, but they are seen in a new light when the need arises or conditions are conducive to the discovery. It is usually accomplished by an individual or small group, a micro-level activity.

Invention refers to combining existing parts, materials, or ideas to form new ones. There was no light bulb or combustion engine lying in the forest waiting to be discovered; they required human ingenuity to put together something that had not previously existed. Social inventions of the past 300 years include democracy, capitalism, bureaucracy, and the right to privacy. Technological innovations often result from research institutes and the expansion of science, increasingly generated at the meso level of the social system.

Diffusion is the spread of an invention or discovery from one place to another; the spread of ideas such as capitalism, democracy, and religious beliefs has brought changes in human relationships around the world. Likewise, the spread of various types of music, film technology, telephone systems, and computer hardware and software across the globe have had important ramifications for global interconnectedness. Diffusion often involves expansion of ideas across the globe, but it also requires individuals to adopt ideas at the micro level.

Technology and Science

Science is the systematic process of producing human knowledge; it uses empirical research methods to discover

We would never have made it to the moon or had two Exploration Rovers (robotic geologists) exploring the surface of Mars if science had not become an institution. It used to be that science was something a few affluent people did in their spare time and with spare resources. Only in the past century has science become fully institutionalized, and this has dramatically accelerated the rate of social change.

Source: Photo courtesy of NASA.

facts and test theories. *Technology* applies scientific knowledge in order to solve problems. Early human technology was largely a result of trial and error, not scientific knowledge or principles; humans did not understand why boats floated or fires burned. Since the industrial revolution, many inventors and capitalists have seen science and technology as routes to human betterment and happiness. With the emphasis on science, the scientific process is a major social institution in twenty-first century industrial and postindustrial societies, providing the bases of information and knowledge for sophisticated technology.

Indeed, one of the major transformations in modern society is due to science becoming an institution. Prior to the eighteenth century, science was an avocation. People like Benjamin Franklin experimented in their backyards with whatever spare cash they had in order to satisfy their own curiosity. Franklin discovered that lightening was actually electricity by flying a kite in a thunderstorm. It was impossible then to imagine that we would now have a vehicle exploring Mars or that a human would walk on the moon.

Institutionalization means creating a stable pattern of roles, statuses, and groups that address some basic societal need—in this case science and the need for new resources and new ways of understanding the natural world. *Science* in the contemporary world is a social process. It involves mobilizing financial resources and employing the most highly trained people (which in turn required the development of educational institutions).

Social conditions can be conducive or deleterious to scientific or technological innovation (Robertson 1992). Innovation resulting in change will be very slow until a society has institutionalized science and accepted change. This involves providing extensive training, paying some people simply to do research, and funding the investigations. Specialization in science speeds up the rates of discovery; people focus in one area and get much more in-depth understandings. Effective methods of communication across the globe mean that we do not need to wait six years for a research manuscript to cross the ocean and to be translated into another language. Competition in science means that researchers move quickly on their findings. Delaying findings may mean that the slowpoke does not get tenure at his or her university, promotion in the research laboratory, or awards for innovation.

We would not have automobiles, planes, missiles, space stations, computers, the Internet, and many of our modern conveniences without the institutionalization of science and without scientific application (technology). Science is big business, funded by industry and political leaders. University researchers and some government-funded science institutes engage in *basic research* designed to discover new knowledge, often on topics that receive funding. Industry and some governmental agencies such as the military and the Department of Agriculture employ scientists to do *applied research* to discover practical uses for existing knowledge.

Scientific knowledge is usually cumulative with each study adding to the existing body of research. However, radical new ideas can result in scientific revolutions (Kuhn 1970); Galileo's finding that the earth revolves around the sun and Darwin's theory of evolution are two examples of radical new ideas that changed history.

THINKING SOCIOLOGICALLY

Imagine what your life would have been like before computers, e-mail, and the Internet. What would be different? (Note that you are imagining the world from only 10 to 20 years ago!)

Technology and Change

The G-8, discussed earlier, holds yearly meetings to determine the world's markets and regulate global economic policy: interest and currency rates and tariffs. The group's power enables those countries to control technology by obtaining cheap raw products, especially oil; in the process, they profoundly influence which countries will be rich or poor. While politicians like to tell us they believe in a free market economy, uninhibited by governmental interference, they actually intervene regularly in the global market.

New technological developments can be a force for world integration but also for economic and political disintegration (Schaeffer 2003). The technological revolution in communications has brought fiber optic cable and wireless microwave cell phones and satellite technologies that make it easier to communicate with people around the world. We now live in a global village, a great boon for those fortunate enough to have the education and means to take advantage of it (Drori 2006; Howard and Jones 2004; McLuhan and Powers 1992; Salzman and Matathia 2000).

However, the changes in technology do not always have a positive effect on developing countries. For example, by substituting fiber-optic cable for old technologies, the demand for copper, used for more than 100 years to carry electrical impulses for telephones and telegraphs, has bottomed out. Countries such as Zambia and Chile that depended on the copper trade have seen major negative impacts on their economies. New developments resulting in artificial sweeteners reduced demand for sugar, the major source of income for 50 million people who work in the beet and cane sugar industries around the globe. As new technologies bring substantial benefits to many in the world, those benefits actually harm people in other parts of the world.

Some societies are attempting to replace the old economies with new service industries such as tourism; however, with violence and terrorist threats, many potential tourists prefer not to travel to peripheral countries. Money spent on travel often goes to airlines, first-class hotels, and cruise ship lines based in core countries rather than to local businesses in the peripheral countries (Schaeffer 2003). Changes in technology and the economy have forced many individuals to leave their native villages in search of paid labor positions in the urban factories and the tourism industry, disrupting family lives.

With the changes brought about by technology come changes in the nonmaterial culture—the values, political ideologies, and human relationships. Note that the social world is interdependent as functionalists have claimed; but relations are not necessarily harmonious, and people are often exploited based on competition over resources, as conflict theories point out.

In the opening questions, we asked whether you as an individual can make a difference. In closing, we present the final Sociology in Your Social World, a plan you can follow to make a difference.

THINKING SOCIOLOGICALLY

First, read "Making a Difference" on page 515. Then use the steps to plan how you would bring about a change that would make a difference in your community, region, nation, or world.

Sociology in Your Social World

Making a Difference

To develop sociological interventions that will bring about change, applied sociologists and individuals like you can take certain steps (Glass 2004). Because bringing about change requires cooperation, working in a group context is often essential. Flexibility, openness to new ideas, and willingness to entertain alternative suggestions are also key factors in successful change. The following steps provide a useful strategy for planning change:

1. *Identify the issue:* Be specific and focus on what is to be changed. Without clear focus, your target for change can get muddied or lost in the attempt.

2. *Research the issue and use those findings:* Learn as much as you can about the situation or problem to be changed. Use informants, interviews, written materials, observation, existing data (such as Census Bureau statistics), or anything that helps you understand the issues. That will enable you to find the most effective strategies to bring about change.

3. *Find out what has already been done and by whom:* Other individuals or groups may be working on the same issue. Be sure you know what intervention has already taken place. This can also help determine whether attempts at change have been tried, what has been successful, and whether further change is needed.

4. *Change must take into account each level of analysis:* When planning a strategy, you may focus on one level of analysis, but be sure to consider what interventions are needed at other levels to make the change effective or to anticipate the effects of change on other levels.

5. *Determine the intervention strategy:* Map out the intervention and the steps to carry it out. Identify resources needed, and plan each step in detail.

6. *Evaluate the plan:* Get feedback on the plan from those involved in the issue and from unbiased colleagues. If possible, involve those who will be affected by the intervention in the planning and evaluation of the change. When feasible, test the intervention plan before implementing it.

7. *Implement the intervention:* Put the plan into effect, watching for any unintended consequences. Ask for regular feedback from those affected by the change.

8. *Evaluate the results:* Assess what is working, what is not, and how the constituents that experience the change are reacting. Sociological knowledge and skills should help guide this process.

SO WHAT?

Can you change the world? The underlying message of this chapter and the text is that choices we as individuals make facilitate change at each level in our social world. Understanding sociology provides knowledge and tools to make informed decisions and allows us to work with groups to make a difference.

As you face individual challenges to bring about change in your social world, keep in mind this message: change at one level affects all others. Sociology as a discipline is focused on gathering accurate information about the society in which we live. Still, sociologists as citizens often use their knowledge to advocate for changes that they think will make a better society, and applied sociologists help organizations bring about change. While you are not yet a sociologist, we hope you have gained important insights that will help you to contribute to the dialogue about how to make our social world a better, more humane, place!

CONTRIBUTING TO YOUR SOCIAL WORLD

At the Local Level: Work with the *Student Life* staff to start a new social movement or club to address issues that concern you.

Be aware of your buying power—the products you buy, the box stores you patronize, the kinds of foods you consume. Some of these may involve exploitation of people or destruction of the environment. You can decide that you are going to be a part of the Lilliputian strategy in which you refuse to support those businesses and policies that offend your own moral scruples. The net effect of many people making such choices can make a difference.

At the Organizational or Institutional Level: *ACORN* works on community issues. See if your community has an office, and if not, explore the possibility of setting one up.

Your community probably has a number of social movement organizations devoted to an issue you care about and committed to influencing an institution within the larger society. Consider getting involved with one of these groups so you can be proactive in shaping the society in which you live.

Volunteermatch.org has suggestions for getting involved in your local area.

At the National and Global Levels: The Lilliputian strategy at the micro level can be part of an overall effort at the macro level to influence global policies and decisions. Decide what issues concern you, search the web or join a group that knows about networks and policies, and become part of the solution rather than part of the problem of acquiescence. This can be a better world, but each of us must act on our principles.

Consider working with an international organization helping with disaster relief or in an orphanage run by an organization such as *Mary Knoll*.

Visit www.pineforge.com/ballantinestudy for online activities, sample tests, and other helpful information. Select "Chapter 15: The Process of Change" for chapter-specific activities.

Abbott, Carl. 1993. *The Metropolitan Frontier: Cities in the Modern American West*. Tucson: University of Arizona Press.

Abma, J. C., G. M. Martinez, W. D. Mosher, and B. S. Dawson. 2004. "Teenagers in the United States: Sexual Activity, Contraceptive Use, and Childbearing, 2002." *Vital Health Statistics* 23 (24). National Center for Health Statistics.

Abu-Lughod, Janet L. 1991. *Changing Cities: Urban Sociology*. New York: Harper Collins.

Abu-Lughod, Janet L. 2001. *New York, Chicago, Los Angeles: America's Global Cities*. Minneapolis: University of Minnesota Press.

Acker, C. 1993. "Stigma or Legitimation? A Historical Examination of the Social Potentials of Addition Disease Models." *Journal of Psychoactive Drugs* 25: 13–23.

Acker, Joan. 1990. "Hierarchies, Jobs, Bodies: A Theory of Gendered Organizations." *Gender and Society* 4: 139–58.

Acker, Joan. 1992. "Gendered Institutions: From Sex Roles to Gendered Institutions. *Contemporary Sociology* 21: 565–69.

Ad Hoc Committee on Environmental Stewardship. 2000. "Green Facts for the U.S. and the World at Large." Atlanta, GA: Emory University.

Adler, Emily Stier, and Roger Clark. 2003. *How It's Done: An Invitation to Social Research*. 2nd ed. Belmont, CA: Wadsworth.

Adler, Freda, Gerhard O. W. Mueller, William S. Laufer, and E. Mavis Hetherington. 2004. *Criminology*. 5th ed. New York: McGraw-Hill.

Adler, Patricia A., and Peter Adler. 1991. *Backboards and Blackboards: College Athletes and Role Engulfment*. New York: Columbia University Press.

Adler, Patricia A., and Peter Adler. 2004. "The Gloried Self." Pp. 117–126 in *Inside Social Life*, 4th ed., edited by Spencer E. Cahill. Los Angeles: Roxbury.

Adler, Roy D. 2001. "Women in the Executive Suite Correlate to High Profits." *Harvard Business Review*, 79:3 (November 16).

Aguirre, Adalberto, Jr., and Jonathan H. Turner. 2004. *American Ethnicity: The Dynamics and Consequences of Discrimination*. 4th ed. Boston: McGraw-Hill.

Ahmed, Leila. 1993. *Women and Gender in Islam: Historical Roots of a Modern Debate*. New Haven, CT: Yale University Press.

Ahrons, Constance. 2004. *We're Still Family*. New York: Harper Collins.

Akers, Ronald. 1992. *Deviant Behavior: A Social Learning Approach*. 3rd ed. Belmont, CA: Wadsworth.

Akers, Ronald L., Marvin D. Krohn, Lonn Lanza-Kaduce, and Marcia Radosevich. 1979. "Social Learning and Deviant Behavior." *American Sociological Review* 44 (August): 635–54.

Albrecht, Gary. 2002. *The Disability Business: Rehabilitation in America*. Thousand Oaks, CA: Sage.

Albrecht, Stan L., and Tim B. Heaton. 1984. "Secularization, High Education, and Religiosity." *Review of Religious Research* 26 (September): 43–58.

Alexander, Victoria D. 2003. *Sociology of the Arts: Exploring Fine and Popular Forms*. Malden, MA: Blackwell.

Altbach, Philip G., and Davis, Todd M. 1999. "Global Challenge and National Response: Note for an International Dialogue on International Higher Education." *International Higher Education* 14: 2–5.

Altheide, David, Patricia A. Adler, Peter Adler, and Duane Altheide. 1978. "The Social Meanings of Employee Theft." Pp. 90 in *Crime at the Top*, edited by John M. Johnson and Jack D. Douglas. Philadelphia: Lippincott.

Amato, Paul R. 2000. "The Consequences of Divorce for Adults and Children." *Journal of Marriage and the Family* 62 (November): 1269–287.

Amato, Paul R., and Bruce Keith. 1991. "Parental Divorce and the Well-Being of Children: A Meta-Analysis." *Psychological Bulletin* 110 (1) 26–46.

Amato, Paul R., and Juliana M. Sobolewski. 2001. "The Effects of Divorce and Marital Discord on Adult Children's Psychological Well-Being." *American Sociological Review* 63 (December): 697–713.

American Association of University Women Educational Foundation. 2001. "Hostile Hallways: Bullying, Teasing, and Sexual Harassment in School." Retrieved August 26, 2006 (www.aauw.org).

American Cancer Society. 2006. "Cancer Facts and Figures for African Americans 2005–2006." Atlanta, GA: American Cancer Society.

American Cultural Center Resource Service. 2004. "North American Free Trade Agreement." Retrieved September 29, 2006 (http://usinfo.org/law/nafta/chap-01.stm.html).

American Library Association. 2006. "Ten Most Frequently Challenged Books of 2005." Office of Intellectual Freedom. Retrieved August 26, 2006 (http://www.ala.org/ala/of/bannedbooks/challengedbanned/challenged banned.htm).

American Medical Association. 1988. "It's Over, Debbie." *Journal of the American Medical Association* 259 (14): 2094–98.

American Sociological Association. 2002. *Careers in Sociology*. 6th ed. Washington, DC: American Sociological Association.

American Sociological Association. 2006. "Trend Data on the Profession." Retrieved July 28, 2006 (www.asanet.org/page.ww?section=Profession+Trend+Data&name=Trend+Data+on+the+Profession).

Ammerman, Nancy Tatom. 1988. *Bible Believers: Fundamentalists in the Modern World*. New Brunswick, NJ: Rutgers University Press.

Ammerman, Nancy Tatom. 1990. *Baptist Battles: Social Change and Religious Conflict in the Southern Baptist Convention*. New Brunswick, NJ: Rutgers University Press.

Amnesty International. 2005. "Abolish the Death Penalty: The Death Penalty Is Racially Biased." Retrieved August 4, 2006 (http://www.amnestyusa.org/abolish/factsheets/racialprejudices.html).

Amnesty International. 2006. "Facts and Figures on the Death Penalty." June. Retrieved August 8, 2006 (http://web.amnesty.org/pages/deathpenalty-facts-eng); (http://web.amnesty.org/pages/deathpenalty-countries-eng).

Amodeo, Karrin. 1999. "Japan Nuke Update." Federation of American Scientists. Retrieved September 29, 2006 (www.fas.org/news/japan/990930-jpn.htm).

517

Ananova. 2001. "Death Workers Sell Body Parts for Extra Christmas Cash." Retrieved December 4, 2005 (www.ananova.com/news/sm_465113 .html).

Ananova. 2002. "Students Willing to Sell Body Parts to Fund Education." April 8. Retrieved August 26, 2006 (www.ananova.com).

Andersen, Ronald M. 1995. "Revisiting the Behavioral Model and Access to Medical Care: Does it Matter?" *Journal of Health and Social Behavior* 36 (1): 1–10.

Andersen, Ronald M., Thomas H. Rice, and Gerald F. Kominski. 2001. *Changing the U.S. Health Care System: Issues in Health Services, Policy and Management.* 2nd ed. San Francisco: Jossey-Bass.

Anderson, David A., and Mykol Hamilton. 2005. "Gender Role Stereotyping of Parents in Children's Picture Books: The Invisible Father." *Sex Roles: A Journal of Research* 52 (3/4): 145.

Anderson, Elijah. 2000. *Code of the Street: Decency, Violence, and the Moral Life of the Inner City.* New York: W. W. Norton.

Anderson, Margaret L. 2006. *Thinking about Women: Sociological Perspectives on Sex and Gender.* 7th ed. Boston: Allyn & Bacon.

Anderson, Michael. 1994. "What Is New about the Modern Family?" Pp. 67–90 in *Time, Family and Community: Perspectives on Family and Community History,* edited by Michael Drake. Oxford, UK: The Open University.

Andrew, Caroline, and Beth Moore Milroy, eds. 1991. *Life Spaces: Gender, Household, Employment.* Vancouver: University of British Columbia Press.

Anson, Ofra. 1998. "Gender difference(s) in health perceptions and their predictors." *Social Science and Medicine* 36 (4): 419–27.

Anti-Defamation League. 2006. *2005 Audit of Anti-Semitic Incidents.* Retrieved June 29, 2006 (www.adl.org/PresRele/ASUS_12/audit-2005 .htm).

Antoun, Richard T. 2001. *Understanding Fundamentalism: Christian, Islamic, and Jewish Movements.* Walnut Creek, CA: AltaMira.

Anyon, Jean. 1980. "Social Class and the Hidden Curriculum of Work." *Journal of Education* 162 (1): 67–92.

Aquirre, Adalberto, and David V. Baker. 2000. *Structured Inequality in the United States.* Englewood Cliffs, NJ: Prentice Hall.

Archer, Dane, and Rosemary Gartner. 1984. *Violence and Crime in Cross-national Perspective.* New Haven, CT: Yale.

Aries, Philippe. 1965. *Centuries of Childhood: A Social History of Family Life.* New York: Knopf.

Arnold, David O., ed. 1970. *The Sociology of Subcultures.* Berkeley, CA: Glendessary.

Aronson, Ronald. 1978. "Is Busing the Real Issue?" *Dissent* 25 (Fall): 409.

Arrighi, Barbara A. 2000. *Understanding Inequality: The Intersection of Race, Ethnicity, Class, and Gender.* Lanham, MD: Rowman & Littlefield.

Aseltine, Robert H., Jr. 1995. "A Reconsideration of Parental and Peer Influences on Adolescent Deviance." *Journal of Health and Social Behavior* 36 (2): 103–21.

Ashley, David, and David Michael Orenstein. 2004. *Sociological Theory.* 6th ed. Boston: Allyn & Bacon.

Astone, Nan Marie, and Sara S. McLanahan. 1991. "Family Structure, Parental Practices and High School Completion." *American Sociological Review* 56 (3): 318–19.

Attewell, Paul. 2001. "The First and Second Digital Divides." *Sociology of Education* 74 (3): 252–S59.

Aulette, Judy Root. 2002. *Changing American Families.* Boston: Allyn & Bacon.

Ayalon, Hanna, and Yossi Shavit. 2004. "Educational Reforms and Inequalities in Israel: The MMI Hypothesis Revisited." *Sociology of Education* 77 (2): 103–20.

Ayers, William. 2006. "Hearts and Minds: Military Recruitment and the High School Battlefield." *Phi Delta Kappan* 87 (8): 594–99.

Ayers, William, and Michael Klonsky. 2006. "Chicago's Renaissance 2010: The Small Schools Movement Meets the Ownership Society." *Phi Delta Kappan* February: 453–56.

Bainbridge, William S., and Rodney Stark. 1981. "Suicide, Homicide, and Religion: Durkheim Reassessed." *Annual Review of the Social Sciences of Religion* 5: 33–56.

Baker, David P. 2002. "International Competition and Education Crises: Cross-National Studies of School Outcomes." Pp. 393–98 in *Education and Sociology: An Encyclopedia,* edited by David L. Levinson Peter W. Cookson, Jr., and Alan R. Sadovnik. New York: RoutledgeFalmer.

Balch, Robert W. 1982. "Bo and Peep: A Case Study of the Origins of Messianic Leadership." Pp. 13–72 in *Millennialism and Charisma,* edited by Roy Wallis. Belfast, Northern Ireland: The Queen's University.

Balch, Robert W. 1995. "Waiting for the Ships: Disillusionment and the Revitalization of Faith in Bo and Peep's UFO Cult." Pp. 137–66 in *The Gods Have Landed: New Religions from Other Worlds,* edited by James R. Lewis. Albany: State University of New York Press.

Bales, Kevin. 1999. *Disposable People: New Slavery in the Global Economy.* Berkeley: University of California Press.

Bales, Kevin. 2000. *New Slavery: A Reference Handbook.* 2nd ed. Santa Barbara, CA: ABC-CLIO.

Bales, Kevin. 2002. "Because She Looks Like a Child." Pp. 207–29 in *Global Woman: Nannies, Maids, and Sex Workers in the New Economy,* edited by Barbara Ehrenreich and Arlie Russell Hochschild. New York: Henry Holt.

Bales, Kevin. 2004. *Disposable People: New Slavery in the Global Economy.* Rev. ed. Berkeley: University of California Press.

Ballantine, Jeanne H. 1991. "Market Needs and Program Products: The Articulation between Undergraduate Applied Programs and the Market Place." *Journal of Applied Sociology* 8 (3/4): 1–19.

Ballantine, Jeanne H. 2001a. "Education." Pp. 277–93 In *Social Problems: A Case Study Approach,* edited by Norman A. Dolch and Linda Deutschmann. Dix Hills, NY: General Hall.

Ballantine, Jeanne H. 2001b. *The Sociology of Education: A Systematic Approach.* 5th ed. Englewood Cliffs, NJ: Prentice Hall.

Ballantine, Jeanne H., and Joan Z. Spade. 2004. *Schools and Society.* 2nd ed. Belmont, CA: Wadsworth.

Banbury, Samantha 2004. "Coercive Sexual Behavior in British Prisons as Reported by Adult Ex-Prisoners. *The Howard Journal* 43 (2): 113–30.

Bankston, Carl L., III. 2004. "Social Capital, Cultural Values, Immigration, and Academic Achievement: The Host Country Context and Contradictory Consequences." *Sociology of Education* 77 (2): 176–80.

Barash, David. 2002. "Evolution, Males, and Violence" *The Chronicle Review,* May 24, B7.

Barefoot, Coy. 2003. "Our Childhood Memories." *Attaché.* U.S. Airways, November.

Barker, Eileen. 1989. *New Religious Movements: A Practical Introduction.* London: HMSO.

Barnes, Patricia M., Eve Powell-Griner, Kim McFann, and Richard L. Nahin. 2004. "Complementary and Alternative Medicine Use among Adults: United States, 2002." *CDC Advance Data Report,* No. 343.

Barraclough, Geoffrey, ed. 1986. *The Times Concise Atlas of World History.* Rev. ed. London: Times Books Limited.

Bartkowski, John P., and Christopher G. Ellison. 1995. "Divergent Models of Childrearing in Popular Manuals: Conservative Protestants vs. the Mainstream Experts." *Sociology of Religion* 56 (1): 21–34.

Basaglia, Franca Ongaro. 1992. "Politics and Mental Health." *International Journal of Social Psychiatry* 38 (1): 36–39.

Basow, Susan A. 1992. *Gender: Stereotypes and Roles.* 3rd ed. Belmont, CA: Wadsworth.

Basow, Susan A. 2000. "Gender Stereotypes and Roles." Pp. 101–15 in *The Meaning of Difference: American Constructions of Race, Sex and Gender, Social Class, and Sexual Orientation,* 2nd ed., edited by Karen E. Rosenblum and Toni-Michelle C. Travis. New York: McGraw-Hill.

Basso, Keith H. 1979. *Portraits of the Whiteman: Linguistic Play and Cultural Symbols Among the Western Apache.* Cambridge: Cambridge University Press.

Batavia, A. I. 2000. *So Far So Good: Observations on the First Year of Oregon's Death with Dignity Act.* Washington, DC: American Psychological Association.

Bayley, David. 1991. *Forces of Order: Policing Modern Japan*. Berkeley: University of California Press.

Beckwith, Carol. 1983. "Niger's Wodaabe: People of the Taboo." *National Geographic* 164 (4): 483–509.

Bell, Daniel. 1973. *The Coming of Post-Industrial Society: A Venture in Social Forecasting*. New York: Basic Books.

Bell, Daniel. [1976] 1999. *The Coming of Post-Industrial Society: A Venture in Social Forecasting*. Special anniversary ed. New York: Basic Books.

Bellah, Robert N., ed. 1970. "Civil Religion in America." Pp. 168–215 in *Beyond Belief: Essays on Religion in a Post-Traditionalist World*. New York: Harper & Row.

Bellah, Robert N. 1992. *The Broken Covenant: American Civil Religion in Time of Trial*. Chicago: University of Chicago Press.

Bellah, Robert N., and Frederick E. Greenspahn, eds. 1987. *Uncivil Religion: Interreligious Hostility in America*. New York: Crossroad.

Bellah, Robert N., Richard Madsen, William M. Sullivan, Ann Swindler, and Steven M. Tipton. 1996. *Habits of the Heart: Individualism and Commitment in American Life*. Updated edition. Berkeley: University of California Press.

Bellisari, Anna. 1990. "Biological Bases of Sex Differences in Cognitive Ability and Brain Function." Unpublished paper.

Bem, Sandra L. 1974. "The Measurement of Psychological Androgyny." *Journal of Consulting and Clinical Psychology* 42 (2): 155–62.

Bem, Sandra L. 1983. "Gender Schema Theory and Its Implications for Child Development: Raising Gender-Aschematic Children in a Gender-Schematic Society." *Signs: Journal of Women in Culture and Society* 8 (Summer): 598–616.

Benavot, Aaron. 1992. "Curricular Content, Educational Expansion, and Economic Growth." *Comparative Education Review* 36 (2): 150–74.

Benavot, Aaron, John Meyer, and David Kamens. 1991. "Knowledge for the Masses: World Models and National Curricula: 1920–1986." *American Sociological Review* 56 (1): 85–100.

Benderly, Beryl Lieff. 1982. "Rape Free or Rape Prone." *Science* 82 (3): 40–3.

Benevolo, Leonardo. 1995. *The European City*. Cambridge, MA: Blackwell.

Bennett, Neil, Ann Blanc, and David Bloom. 1988. "Commitment and the Modern Union: Assessing the Link between Premarital Cohabitation and Subsequent Marital Stability." *American Sociological Review* 53 (1): 127–38.

Bennis, Warren G., Kenneth D. Benne, and Robert Chin. 1985. *The Planning of Change*. 4th ed. New York: Holt, Rinehart and Winston.

Benokraitis, Nijole V. 2004. *Marriages and Families: Changes, Choices, and Constraints*. 5th ed. Englewood Cliffs, NJ: Prentice Hall.

Benokraitis, Nijole V., and Joe R. Feagin. 1995. *Modern Sexism: Blatant, Subtle, and Covert Discrimination*. 2nd ed. Englewood Cliffs, NJ: Prentice Hall.

Berger, Helen A. 1999. *A Community of Witches: Contemporary Neo-Paganism and Witchcraft in the United States*. Columbia: University of South Carolina Press.

Berger, Michael L. 1979. *The Devil Wagon in God's Country: The Automobile and Social Change in Rural America, 1893–1929*. Hamden, CT: Archon.

Berger, Peter L. 1961. *The Noise of Solemn Assemblies*. Garden City, NY: Doubleday.

Berger, Peter L. 1990. *The Sacred Canopy*. Garden City, NY: Anchor Books.

Berk, Richard A. 1974. *Collective Behavior*. Dubuque, IA: Brown.

Berkow, Ira. 1994. "Dreaming Hoop Dreams." *The New York Times*, October 9, sec. 2, p. 1.

Berry, Brian J. L., and John Kasarda. 1977. *Contemporary Urban Ecology*. New York: Macmillan.

Berry, Herbert, III, and Aylene S. Harper. 1993. "Feminization of Unisex Names from 1960 to 1990." *American Name Society* 41 (4): 228–38.

Bertman, Stephen. 1998. *Hyperculture: The Human Cost of Speed*. Westport, CT: Praeger.

Better Factories Movement in Cambodia. 2006. Retrieved September 29, 2006 (www.betterfactories.com).

Bettie, Julie. 2003. *Women without Class: Girls, Race, and Identity*. Berkeley: University of California Press.

Beyer, Peter. 2000. "Secularization from the Perspective of Globalization." Pp. 81–93 in *The Secularization Debate*, edited by William H. Swatos, Jr., and Daniel V. A. Olson. Lanham, MD: Rowman and Littlefield.

Bianci, Suzanne M., Melissa A. Milkie, Liana C. Sayer, and John P. Robinson. 2000. "Is Anyone Doing the Housework? Trends in the Gender Division of Household Labor." *Social Forces* 79 (1): 191–228.

Bibby, Reginald W. 1987a. *Fragmented Gods: The Poverty and Potential of Religion in Canada*. Toronto, Canada: Irwin.

Bibby, Reginald W. 1987b. "Religion in Canada: A Late Twentieth Century Reading." Pp. 263–67 in *Yearbook of American and Canadian Churches*, edited by Constant H. Jacquet, Jr. Nashville, TN: Abington.

Bibby, Reginald W. 2002. *Restless Gods: The Renaissance of Religion in Canada*. Toronto, Canada: Stoddard.

Billings, Dwight B., and Shaunna L. Scott 1994. "Religion and Political Legitimation." *Annual Review of Sociology* 20: 173–202.

Birdwhistell, Raymond L. 1970. *Kinesics and Context: Essays on Body Motion Communication*. Philadelphia: University of Pennsylvania Press.

Blackman, Ann. 2001. "Bush Acts on Abortion 'Gag Rule.'" *Time*, January 22. Retrieved September 20, 2006 (http://www.time.com/time/nation/article/0,8599,96275,00.html).

Blasi, Joseph Raphael, and Douglas Lynn Kruse. 1991. *The New Owners: The Mass Emergence of Employee Ownership in Public Companies and What it Means to American Business*. New York: Harper Collins.

Blau, Peter M. 1956. *Bureaucracy in Modern Society*. New York: Random House.

Blau, Peter M.1964. *Exchange and Power in Social Life*. New York: John Wiley.

Blau, Peter, and Otis Dudley Duncan. 1967. *The American Occupational Structure*. New York: John Wiley & Son.

Blauner, Robert. 1972. *Racial Oppression in America*. New York: Harper & Row.

Blendon, Robert J., Cathy Schoen, Catherine M. DesRoches, Robin Osborn, Kimberly L. Scoles, and Kinga Zapert. 2002. "Inequities in Health Care: A Five-Country Survey." *Health Affairs* 21 (3): 182–91.

Blumer, Herbert. 1969. *Symbolic Interactionism: Perspective and Method*. Englewood Cliffs, NJ: Prentice Hall.

Blumer, Herbert. 1986. *Symbolic Interactionism: Perspective and Method*. Berkeley: University of California Press.

Blumstein, Philip, and Pepper Schwartz. 1985. *American Couples: Money, Work, Sex*. New York: Pocket Books.

Bobin, Frederic. 1995. "Pakistan Divided by Child Labor Row." *Guardian Weekly*, September 3, 11.

Bobo, Lawrence, and Ryan A. Smith. 1998. "From Jim Crow Racism to Laissez-Faire Racism: An Essay on the Transformation of Racial Attitudes in America." Pp. 182–220 in *Beyond Pluralism: Essays on the Conceptions of Groups and Identities in America*, edited by Wendy Freedman Katkin, Ned C. Landsman, and Andrea Tyree. Urbana: University of Illinois Press.

Bolaria, Singh, and Harley D. Dickinson. 2001. "The Evolution of Health Care in Canada: Toward Community or Corporate Control?" Pp. 199–213 in *The Blackwell Companion to Medical Sociology*, edited by William C. Cockerham. Malden, MA: Blackwell.

Boli, John. 2002. "Globalization." Pp. 307–13 in *Education and Sociology: An Encyclopedia*, edited by David L. Levinson, Peter W. Cookson, Jr., and Alan R. Sadovnik. New York: RoutledgeFalmer.

Bonacich, Edna. 1972. "A Theory of Ethnic Antagonism: The Split Labor Market." *American Sociological Review* 37 (October): 547–59.

Bonacich, Edna. 1976. "Advanced Capitalism and Black-White Race Relations in the United States: A Split Labor Market Interpretation." *American Sociological Review* 41 (February): 34–51.

Bonacich, Edna, and Jake B. Wilson. 2005. "Hoisted by Its Own Petard: Organizing Wal-Mart's Logistics Workers." *New Labor Forum* 14: 67–75.

Bonczar, Thomas P., and Tracy L. Snell. 2005. "Capital Punishment, 2004." *Bureau of Justice Statistics Bulletin*. Washington, DC: U.S. Department of Justice: NCJ 211349.

Booker, Salih, and William Minter. 2006. "Global Apartheid: AIDS and Murder by Patient." Pp. 517–22 in *Beyond Borders: Thinking Critically about Global Issues,* edited by Paula S. Rothenberg. New York: Worth.

Booth, Alan, and Paul R. Amato. 2001. "Parental Predivorce Relations and Offspring Postdivorce Well-Being." *Journal of Marriage and the Family* 63 (February): 197–212.

Borg, Marcus J. 1994. *Meeting Jesus Again for the First Time.* San Francisco: Harper San Francisco.

Boulding, Elise, with Jennifer Dye. 2002. "Women and Development" in *Introducing Global Issues,* edited by Michael T. Snarr and D. Neil Snarr 2nd ed. Boulder, CO: Lynne Rienner Publ.

Bourdieu, P., and J. C. Passeron. 1977. *Reproduction in Education, Society and Culture.* London: Sage.

Bowler, I. R., C. R. Bryant, and M. D. Nellis, eds. 1992. *Contemporary Rural Systems in Transition, Volume 1: Agriculture and Environment, Volume 2: Economy and Society.* Wallingford, Oxforshire, UK: C.A.B. International.

Bowles, Samuel. 1977. "Unequal Education and the Reproduction of the Social Division of Labor. P. 137 in *Power and Ideology in Education,* edited by Jerome Karabel and A. H. Halsey. New York: Oxford University Press.

Bowles, Samuel, and Herbert Gintis. 1976. *Schooling in Capitalist America.* New York: Basic Books.

Bowles, Samuel, and Herbert Gintis. 2002. "Schooling in Capitalist America Revisited." *Sociology of Education* 75 (1): 1–18.

Bowser, Benjamin, and Raymond Hunt, eds. 1996. *Impacts of Racism on White Americans.* Thousand Oaks, CA: Sage.

Boyd, Danah. 2004. "Friendster and Publicly Articulated Social Networks." Conference on Human Factors and Computing Systems, Vienna, April 24–29. Retrieved September 29, 2006 (www.danah.org/papers/CHI2004 Friendster.pdf).

Bracey, Gerald W. 2003. "April Foolishness: The 20th Anniversary of *A Nation at Risk.*" *Phi Delta Kappan* April: 616–21.

Bracey, Gerald W. 2005. "The 15th Bracey Report on the Condition of Public Education." *Phi Delta Kappan* October: 138–53.

Brasher, Brenda E. 2004. *Give me that On-Line Religion.* New Brunswick, NJ: Rutgers University Press.

Brecher, Jeremy, Tim Costello, and Brendan Smith. 2006. "Globalization and Social Movements." Pp. 330–47 in *Globalization: The Transformation of Social Worlds,* edited by D. Stanley Eitzen and Maxine Baca Zinn. Belmont, CA: Wadsworth.

Brettell, Caroline B., and Carolyn F. Sargent. 2001. *Gender in Cross-Cultural Perspective.* 3rd ed. Englewood Cliffs, NJ: Prentice Hall.

Brettell, Caroline B., and Carolyn F. Sargent. 2005. *Gender in Cross-cultural Perspective.* 4th ed. Englewood Cliffs, NJ: Prentice Hall.

Brier, Noah Rubin. 2004. "Coming of Age." *American Demographics* 26 (9): 16.

Brint, Steven. 1984. "'New Class and Cumulative Trend Explanations of the Liberal Political Attitudes of Professionals." *American Journal of Sociology* 60 (July): 30–71.

Brint, Steven, Mary F. Contreras, and Michael T. Matthews. 2001. "Socialization Messages in Primary Schools: An Organizational Analysis." *Sociology of Education* 74 (July) 157–80.

Britton, Dana M. 2000. "The Epistemology of the Gendered Organization." *Gender and Society* 14 (3): 418–34.

Britz, Jennifer Delahunty. 2006. "Are Today's Girls Too Successful?" *Dayton Daily News,* March 31, A7.

Brody, Gene H., Zolinda Stoneman, Douglas Flor, and Chris McCrary. 1994. "Religion's Role in Organizing Family Relationships: Family Process in Rural, Two-Parent African American Families." *Journal of Marriage and the Family* 56 (November): 878–88.

Bromley, David G., and Anson D. Shupe, Jr. 1981. *Strange Gods: The Great American Cult Scare.* Boston: Beacon.

Brookover, Wilbur B., and Edsel L. Erickson. 1975. *Sociology of Education.* Homewood, IL.: Dorsey.

Brookover, Wilbur B., Edsel L. Erickson, and Alan McEvoy. 1996. *Creating Effective Schools: An In-Service Program.* Holmes Beach, FL: Learning Publications.

Brookover, Wilbur B., C. Beady, P. Flood, J. Schweitzer, and J. Wisenbaker. 1979. *School Social Systems and Student Achievement: Schools Can Make a Difference.* New York: Praeger. Retrieved August 26, 2006 (http://www.nwrel.org/scpd/re-engineering/ryco/ReferenceDetails.asp?RefID=68).

Brooks, Clem, and Jeff Manza. 1997. "Social Cleavages and Political Alignments: U.S. Presidential Elections, 1960–1992." *American Sociological Review* 62 (December): 937–46.

Broom, Leonard, and Philip Selznick. 1963. *Sociology: A Text with Adapted Readings.* 3rd ed. New York: Harper & Row.

Brophy, Jere E. 1983. "Research on the Self-Fulfilling Prophesy and Teacher Expectations." *Journal of Educational Psychology* 75: 631–61.

Brown, Dee. 2001. *Bury My Heart at Wounded Knee: An Indian History of the American West.* 30th-anniversary ed. New York: Holt.

Brown, Donald E. 1991. *Human Universals.* Philadelphia: Temple University Press.

Brown, Louise. 2001. *Sex Slaves: The Trafficking of Women in Asia.* London: Virago/Little, Brown.

Brown, William. 1987. Identification and Application of Competencies for Applied Sociologists. Paper presented at the Southern Sociological Meetings, Atlanta, GA.

Brown, William. 1993. "A Proposed Multi-Level Plan to Market Sociological Competencies." *The American Sociologist* 24 (3/4): 87–105.

Brunn, Stanley D., Jack F. Williams, and Donald J. Zeigler. 2003. *Cities of the World: World Regional Urban Development.* 3rd ed. Lanham, MD: Rowman and Littlefield.

Bryant, A. L. 1993. "Hostile Hallways: The AAUW Survey on Sexual Harassment in America's Schools." Washington, D.C. AAUW Foundation.

Bumiller, Elisabeth. 1990. *May You be the Mother of a Hundred Sons: A Journey among the Women of India.* New York: Fawcett Columbine.

Bumpass, Larry L., and Hsien-Hen Lu. 2000. "Trends in Cohabitation and Implications for Children's Family Contexts in the United States." *Population Studies* 51 (1): 29–41.

Bumpass, Larry L., James A. Sweet, and Andrew Cherlin. 1991. "The Role of Cohabitation in Declining Rates of Marriage." *Journal of Marriage and the Family* 53 (November): 913–27.

Burda, D. 2001. "Hospital Operating Margins Hit 5.2%." *Modern Healthcare* 31 (45): 10.

Burgos-Debray, Elisabeth, ed. 1984. *I, Rigoberta Menchu: An Indian Woman in Guatemala.* Translated by Ann Wright. London: Verso.

Burn, Shawn Meghan. 2000. *Women across Cultures: A Global Perspective.* Mountain View, CA: Mayfield.

Burn, Shawn Meghan. 2005. *Women across Cultures: A Global Perspective.* 2nd ed. New York: McGraw-Hill.

CALCASA (California Coalition against Sexual Assault). 2006. "Statistics about Rape and Sexual Assault, 2006." Retrieved September 15, 2006 (www.denimdayinla.org/documents/RapeSexualStats2006.doc).

Caldwell, John C. 1982. *Theory of Fertility Decline.* New York: Academic Press.

Campbell, Ernest Q., and Thomas F. Pettigrew. 1959. *Christians in Racial Crisis.* Washington, DC: Public Affairs Press.

Canadian Institute for Health Information. 2005. "National Health Expenditure Trends, 1975–2005." Retrieved August 30, 2006 (www.cihi.ca).

Cancian, Francesca M. 1992. "Feminist Science: Methodologies that Challenge Inequality." *Gender and Society* 6 (4): 623–42.

Carrothers, Robert M., and Denzel E. Benson. 2003. "Symbolic Interactionism in Introductory Textbooks: Coverage and Pedagogical Implications." *Teaching Sociology* 31 (2): 162–81.

Cashmore, Ellis, and Barry Troyna. 1990. *Introduction to Race Relations.* London: Routledge.

Casper, Lynne M., Sara S. McLanahan, and Irwin Garfinkel. 1994. "The Gender-Poverty Gap: What We Can Learn from Other Countries." *American Sociological Review* 59 (August): 594–605.

Castells, Manuel. 1977. *The Urban Question: A Marxist Approach.* Cambridge, MA: MIT Press.

Castells, Manuel. 1989. *The Informational City: Information Technology, Economic Restructuring and the Urban-Regional Process.* Cambridge, MA: Basil Blackwell.

Caulfield, Jon. 1994. *City Form and Everyday Life: Toronto's Gentrification and Critical Social Practice.* Toronto: University of Toronto Press.

Center for Education Policy. 2006. "Survey on Hours Spent on Subjects." Menlo Park, CA: SRI International. Retrieved August 26, 2006 (www.sri.com/policy/cep/edreform).

Centers for Disease Control and Prevention. 2006a. *Average Life Expectancy 2006.* Retrieved July 20, 2006 (www.voanews.com/english/2006–04–27-voa32.cfm).

Centers for Disease Control and Prevention. 2006b. "Survey of Childless People Ages 15 to 44." *Dayton Daily News,* June 1, 1A.

Centers for Medical and Medicaid Services. 2004. "Health Care Indicators." Baltimore, MD: Office of the Actuary, Office of National Health Statistics.

Chabbott, Colette, and Francisco O. Ramirez. 2000. "Development and Education." Pp. 163–87 in *Handbook of Sociology of Education,* edited by Maureen T. Hallinan. New York: Kluwer Academic Publishers/Plenum.

Chaffins, Stephanie, Mary Forbes, Harold E. Fuqua, Jr. 1995. "The Glass Ceiling: Are Women where they should be?" *Education* 115 (3) Spring: 380–87.

Chalfant, H. Paul, and Charles W. Peck. 1983. "Religious Affiliation, Religiosity, and Racial Prejudice: A New Look at Old Relationships." *Review of Religious Research* 25 (December): 155–61.

Chalfant, H. Paul, Robert E. Beckley, and C. Eddie Palmer. 1994. *Religion in Contemporary Society.* 3rd ed. Palo Alto, CA: Mayfield.

Chambliss, William J. 1973. "The Saints and the Roughnecks." *Society* 11 (December): 24–31.

Charon, Joel M. 2007. *Symbolic Interactionism: An Introduction, an Interpretation.* 9th ed. Upper Saddle River, NJ: Prentice Hall.

Chase-Dunn, Christopher, and E. N. Anderson. 2006. *The Historical Evolution of World-Systems.* New York: Palgrave Macmillan.

Chase-Lansdale, P. Lindsay, Andrew J. Cherlin, and Kathleen E. Kierman. 1995. "The Long-Term Effects of Parental Divorce on the Mental Health of Young Adults: A Developmental Perspective." *Child Development* 66 (6) 1614–634.

Chaves, Mark. 1993. "Denominations as Dual Structures: An Organizational Analysis." *Sociology of Religion* 54 (20): 147–69.

Chaves, Mark. 1999. *Ordaining Women: Culture and Conflict in Religious Organizations.* Cambridge, MA: Harvard University Press.

Chaves, Mark, and Philip S. Gorski. 2001. "Religious Pluralism and Religious Participation." *Annual Review of Sociology* 27: 261–81.

Chen, Zeng-Yin, and Howard B. Kaplan. 2003. "School Failure in Early Adolescence and Status Attainment in Middle Adulthood: A Longitudinal Study." *Sociology of Education* 76 (2): 110–27.

Cherlin, Andrew J. 2002. *Public and Private Families.* Boston: McGraw-Hill.

Child Trends Data Bank. 2005. "Percentage of Births to Unmarried Women." Retrieved August 22, 2006 (http://www.childtrendsdatabank.org/pdf/75_PDF.pdf).

Christiano, Kevin J., William H. Swatos, Jr., and Peter Kivisto. 2002. *Sociology of Religion: Contemporary Developments.* Walnut Creek, CA: AltaMira.

Chubb, John E., and Terry M. Moe. 1990. *Politics, Markets and America's Schools.* Washington, DC: Brookings Institution.

Clark, Burton R. 1985. "The High School and the University: What Went Wrong in America?" *Phi Delta Kappan* February: 391–97.

Clarke, Adele E., and Virginia L. Olesen. 1999. *Revisioning Women, Health, and Healing.* London: Routledge.

Clausen, John A. 1986. *The Life Course: A Sociological Perspective.* Englewood Cliffs, NJ: Prentice Hall.

Clinard, Marshall B., and Robert F. Meier. 2004. *Sociology of Deviant Behavior.* 12th ed. Belmont, CA: Wadsworth/Thomson Learning.

Clymer, Floyd. 1953. *Those Wonderful Old Automobiles.* New York: Bonanza.

Cockburn, Andrew. 2006. "21st Century Slaves." Pp. 299–307 in *Globalization: The Transformation of Social Worlds,* edited by D. Stanley Eitzen and Maxine Baca Zinn. Belmont, CA: Wadsworth.

Cockburn, Cynthia. 1988. "The Gendering of Jobs: Workplace Relations and the Reproduction of Sex Segregation." Pp. 59–76 in *Gender Segregation at Work,* edited by Sylvia Walby. Philadelphia: Open University Press.

Cockerham, William C. 2004. *Medical Sociology.* 9th ed. Englewood Cliffs, NJ: Prentice Hall.

Cohen, Elizabeth G. 1997. "Equitable Classrooms in a Changing Society." Chapter 1 in *Working for Equity in Heterogeneous Classroom: Sociological Theory in Practice,* edited by E. Cohen, and R. Lotan. New York: Teachers College, Columbia University Press.

Coile, Russell C., Jr. 2002. "Top 10 Trends in Health Care for 2002." *Health Trends* 14 (3): 2–12.

Cole, Stephen, and Robert Lejeune. 1972. "Illness and the Legitimation of Failure." *American Sociological Review* 37 (3): 347–56.

Coleman, James S. 1968. "The Concept of Equality of Educational Opportunity." *Harvard Educational Review* 38 (Winter): 7–22.

Coleman, James S. 1990. *Equality and Achievement in Education.* Boulder, CO: Westview.

Coleman, James S., Ernest Q. Campbell, Carol J. Hobson, James McPartland, Alexander M. Mood, Frederic D. Weinfeld, and Robert L. York. 1966. *Equality of Educational Opportunity.* Washington, DC: U.S. Government Printing Office, Department of Education.

Coleman, James William. 2006. *The Criminal Elite: Understanding White Collar Crime.* 6th ed. New York: Worth.

Colligan, S. 2004. "Why the Intersexed Shouldn't Be Fixed: Insights from Queer Theory and Disability Studies." Pp. 45–60 in *Gendering Disability,* edited by B. G. Smith and B Hutchinson. New Brunswick, NJ: Rutgers University Press.

Collins, Patricia Hill. 2000. *Black Feminist Thought: Knowledge, Consciousness, and the Politics of Empowerment.* 2nd ed. New York: Routledge.

Collins, Randall. 1971. "A Conflict Theory of Sexual Stratification." *Social Problems* 19 (Summer): 2–21.

Collins, Randall. 2004. "Conflict Theory of Educational Stratification." *American Sociological Review* 36: 47–54.

Collins, Randall, and Scott L. Coltrane. 2001. *Sociology of Marriage and the Family: Gender, Love, and Property.* 5th ed. Belmont, CA: Wadsworth.

Coltrane, Scott. 2000. "Research on Household Labor: Modeling and Measuring the Social Embeddedness of Routine Family Work." *Journal of Marriage and the Family* 62 (November): 1208–233.

Comarow, Murray. 1993. "Point of View: Are Sociologists above the Law?" *The Chronicle of Higher Education,* December 15, A44.

Condron, Dennis J., and Vincent J. Roscigno. 2003. "Disparities within: Unequal Spending and Achievement in an Urban School District." *Sociology of Education* 76 (January): 18–36.

Cook, Karen S., Jodi O'Brien, and Peter Kollock. 1990. "Exchange Theory: A Blueprint for Structure and Process." Pp. 158–81 in *Frontiers of Social Theory: The New Syntheses,* edited by George Ritzer. New York: Columbia University Press.

Cookson, Peter W., Jr., and Caroline Hodges Persell. 1985. *Preparing for Power: America's Elite Boarding Schools.* New York: Basic Books.

Cooley, Charles Horton. 1902. *Human Nature and the Social Order.* New York: Scribner.

Cooley, Charles Horton. [1909] 1983. *Social Organization: A Study of the Larger Mind.* New York: Schocken Books.

Coontz, Stephanie. 1997. *The Way We Really Are: Coming to Terms with America's Changing Families.* New York: Basic Books.

Coontz, Stephanie. 2005. *Marriage, A History: From Obedience to Intimacy, or How Love Conquered Marriage.* New York: Viking.

Corbett, Thomas. 1994–95. "Changing the Culture of Welfare." *Focus* 16 (2): 12–22.

Corsaro, William A., and Donna Eder. 1990. "Children's Peer Cultures." *Annual Review of Sociology* 16: 197–220.

Coser, Lewis A. 1956. *The Functions of Social Conflict.* New York: The Free Press.

Council of Europe. 2001, 2004. *Recent Demographic Developments in Europe 2001, 2004.* Strasbourg, France: Council of Europe Publishing.

Cox, Harold G. 1990. "Roles for Aged Individuals in Post-industrial Societies." *International Journal of Aging and Human Development* 30 (1): 55–62.

Cox, Harold G. 2001. *Later Life: The Realities of Aging.* 5th ed. Englewood Cliffs, NJ: Prentice Hall.

Crafts, William A. 1876. *Pioneers in the Settlement of America.* Vol. 1. Boston: Samuel Walker.

Creswell, John W. 2003. *Research Design: Qualitative, Quantitative, and Mixed Methods Approaches.* 2nd ed. Thousand Oaks, CA: Sage.

Crosby, Faye J. 2004. *Affirmative Action is Dead; Long Live Affirmative Action.* New Haven, CT: Yale University Press.

Crummey, Robert O. 1970. *The Old Believers and the World of Antichrist: The Vyg Community and the Russian State, 1694–1855.* Madison: University of Wisconsin Press.

Curtis, James E., Edward G. Grabb, and Douglas Baer. 1992. "Voluntary Association Membership in Fifteen Countries: A Comparative Analysis." *American Sociological Review* 57 (2): 139–52.

Curtiss, S. 1977. *Genie: A Psycholinguistic Study of a Modern-Day "Wild Child."* New York: Academic Press.

Cushman, Thomas, and Stjepan G. Mestrovic. 1996. *This Time We Knew: Western Responses to Genocide in Bosnia.* New York: New York University Press.

Cuzzort, R. P., and Edith W. King. 2002. *Social Thought into the Twenty-First Century.* 6th ed. Belmont, CA: Wadsworth.

Dahlberg, Frances. 1981. *Woman the Gatherer.* New Haven, CT: Yale University Press.

Dahrendorf, Ralf. 1959. *Class and Class Conflict in Industrial Societies.* Palo Alto, CA: Stanford University Press.

Dalit Liberation Education Trust: 10th Anniversary Newsletter. 1995 No. 2. May. Madras: Human Rights Education Movement of India.

Daly, Mary. 1978. *Gynecology: The Metaethics of Radical Feminism.* Boston: Beacon.

Darwin, Charles. [1858] 1909. *The Origin of Species.* New York: P. F. Collier.

Davidhizar, R., R. Shearer, and J. N. Giger. 1997. "Pain and the Culturally Diverse Patient." *Today's Surgical Nurse* 19 (6): 36–39.

Davidman, Lynn. 1990. "Accommodation and Resistance to Modernity: A Comparison of Two Contemporary Orthodox Jewish Groups." *Sociological Analysis* (Spring): 35–51.

Davis, A. J. 1984. "Sex-Differentiated Behaviors in Nonsexist Picture Books." *Sex Roles* 11: 1–16.

Davis, D. M. 1990. "Portrayals of Women in Prime-Time Network Television: Some Demographic Characteristics." *Sex Roles* 23: 325–32.

Davis, Kingsley. 1940. "Extreme Social Isolation of a Child." *American Journal of Sociology* 45: 554–65.

Davis, Kingsley. 1947. "A Final Note on a Case of Extreme Isolation." *American Journal of Sociology* 52: 432–37.

Davis, Kingsley. 1960. "Legitimacy and the Incest Taboo." Pp. 398–402 in *A Modern Introduction to the Family,* edited by Norman W. Bell and Ezra F. Vogel. Glencoe, IL: The Free Press.

Davis, Kingsley, and Wilbert Moore. 1945. "Some Principles of Stratification." *American Sociological Review* 10 (April): 242–45.

Davis, Nancy J., and Robert V. Robinson 1999. "Their Brothers' Keepers? Orthodox Religionists, Modernists, and Economic Justice in Europe." *American Journal of Sociology* 104 (6): 1631–65.

De Tocqueville, Alexis. 1877. *Democracy in America.* New York: Barnes.

Death Penalty Information Center. 2006. "Nationwide Murder Rates." Retrieved August 4, 2006 (www.deathpenaltyinfo.org).

Degenova, Mary Kay, and Philip F. Rice. 2002. *Intimate Relationships, Marriages, and Families.* 5th ed. New York: McGraw-Hill.

Delfattore, Joan. 1992. *What Johnny Shouldn't Read: Textbook Censorship in America.* New Haven, CT: Yale University Press.

Delfattore, Joan. 2004. "Romeo and Juliet Were Just Good Friends." Pp. 177–83 in *Schools and Society,* 2nd ed., edited by Jeanne H. Ballantine and Joan Z. Spade. Belmont, CA: Wadsworth.

DeMaris, Alfred, and K. Vaninadha Rao. 1992. "Premarital Cohabitation and Subsequent Marital Stability in the United States: A Reassessment." *Journal of Marriage and the Family* 54 (February): 178–90.

DeMartini, Joseph R. 1982. "Basic and Applied Sociological Work: Divergence, Convergence, or Peaceful Coexistence?" *The Journal of Applied Behavioral Science* 18 (2): 205–6.

Deming, W.E. 2000. *Out of the Crisis.* Cambridge, MA: MIT Press.

DeMitchell, Todd A., and John J. Carney. 2005. "Harry Potter and the Public School Library." *Phi Delta Kappan* October: 159–65.

Denali Commission. 2001. *Telecommunications Inventory Survey.* Retrieved June 29, 2006 (www.commonwealth.north.org/transcripts/denalicom .html).

Denzin, Norman K. 1992. *Symbolic Interactionism and Cultural Studies: The Politics of Interpretation.* Cambridge, MA: Blackwell.

DePalma, Anthony. 1995. "Racism? Mexico's in Denial." *The New York Times,* June 11, E4.

Diamond, Jared. 1999. *Guns, Germs and Steel: The Fates of Human Societies.* New York: W. W. Norton.

Diamond, Jared. 2005. *Collapse: How Societies Choose to Fail or Succeed.* New York: Viking.

Dickens, Charles. 1948. *Bleak House.* London: Oxford University Press.

Diekman, Amanda B., and Sarah K. Murmen. 2004. "Learning to Be Little Women and Little Men: The Inequitable Gender Equality of Nonsexist Children's Literature." *Sex Roles: A Journal of Research* 50 (5/6): 373.

Dillon, Sam. 1997. "How to Shock a Mexican Politician: Assail Adultery." *International Herald Tribune,* January 27, 1, 6.

Dobbelaere, Karel. 1981. *Secularization: A Multidimensional Concept.* Beverly Hills, CA: Sage.

Dobbelaere, Karel. 2000. "Toward an Integrated Perspective of the Processes Related to the Descriptive Concept of Secularization." Pp. 21–39 in *The Secularization Debate,* edited by William H. Swatos, Jr., and Daniel V. A. Olson. Lanham, MD: Rowman and Littlefield.

The Dollars and Sense Collective. 2006. "The ABCs of the Global Economy." Pp. 82–92 in *Globalization: The Transformation of Social Worlds,* edited by D. Stanley Eitzen and Maxine Baca Zinn. Belmont, CA: Wadsworth.

Domhoff, G. William. 1998. *Who Rules America? Power and Politics in the Year 2000.* Mountain View, CA: Mayfield Publishing.

Domhoff, G.William. 2001. *Who Rules America? Power, Politics, and Social Change.* 4th ed. New York: McGraw-Hill.

Domhoff, G.William. 2005. *Who Rules America? Power, Politics, and Social Change.* 5th ed. New York: McGraw-Hill.

Domina, Thurston. 2005. "Leveling the Home Advantage: Assessing the Effectiveness of Parental Involvement in Elementary School." *Sociology of Education* 78 (3): 233–49.

Dotzler, Robert J., and Ross Koppel. 1999. "What Sociologists Do and Where They Do It—The NSF Survey on Sociologists' Work Activities and Work Places." *Sociological Practice: A Journal of Clinical and Applied Sociology* 1 (1): 71–83.

Douglas, Mary. 1966. *Purity and Danger.* London: Routledge and Kegan Paul.

Doyle, James A., and Michele A. Paludi. 1998. *Sex and Gender: The Human Experience.* 4th ed. New York: McGraw-Hill.

Drafke, Michael and Stan Kossen. 2002. *The Human Side of Organizations.* 8th ed. Englewood Cliffs, NJ: Prentice Hall.

Drori, Gili S. 2006. *Global E-Litism: Digital Technology, Social Inequality, and Transnationality.* New York: Worth.

DuBois, W. E. B. [1899] 1967. *The Philadelphia Negro: A Social Study.* New York: Schocken.

Dudley, R. L. 1996. "How Seventh-Day Adventist Lay Members View Women Pastors." *Review of Religious Research* 38 (2): 133–41.

Duncan, Arne. 2006. "Chicago's Renaissance 2010: Building on School Reform in the Age of Accountability." *Phi Delta Kappan* February: 457–58.

Duncan, Greg J., Willard Rodgers, and Timothy M. Smeeding. 1993. "W(h)ither the Middle Class? A Dynamic View." Pp. 240–71 in *Poverty and Prosperity in the USA in the Late Twentieth Century*, edited by Dimitri B. Papadimitriou and Edward N. Wolff. New York: St. Martin's.

Duncan, Greg J., W. Jean Yeung, Jeanne Brooks-Gunn, and Judith R. Smith. 1998. "How Much Does Childhood Poverty Affect the Life Chances of Children?" *American Sociological Review* 63 (3): 406–23.

The Durban Accord. 2003. "Our Global Commitment for People and Earth's Protected Areas." World Commission on Protected Areas. Retrieved September 16, 2006 (www.iun.org/themes/wcpa/wpc2003/pdfs/outputs/wpc/dur banaccord.doc).

Durkheim, Emile. [1893] 1947. *The Division of Labor in Society*. Translated by George Simpson. New York: The Free Press.

Durkheim, Emile. 1947. *Elementary Forms of Religious Life*. Glencoe, IL: The Free Press.

Durkheim, Emile. 1956. *Education and Society*. Translated by Sherwood D. Fox. Glencoe, IL: The Free Press.

Durkheim, Emile. [1897] 1964. *Suicide*. Glencoe, IL: The Free Press.

Durkheim, Emile. [1915] 2002. *Classical Sociological Theory*. Edited by Craig Calhoun. Malden, MA: Blackwell.

Dworkin, Anthony Gary. 2001. "Perspectives on Teacher Burnout and School Reform." *International Education Journal* 2 (2): 69–78.

Dworkin, Anthony Gary. 2007. "School Reform and Teacher Burnout: Issues of Gender and Gender Tokenism." Pp. 69–78 in *Gender and Education: An Encyclopedia*, edited by Barbara Banks, Sara Delamont, and Catherine Marshall. New York: Greenwood.

Dworkin, Anthony Gary, and Rosalind J. Dworkin. 1999. *The Minority Report: An Introduction to Racial, Ethnic, and Gender Relations*. 3rd ed. Fort Worth, TX: Harcourt Brace.

Dworkin, Anthony Gary, Lawrence J. Saha, and Antwanette N. Hill. 2003. "Teacher Burnout and Perceptions of a Democratic School Environment." *International Education Journal* 4 (2): 108–20.

Dye, Thomas R. 2002. *Who's Running America? The Bush Restoration*. 7th ed. Englewood Cliffs, NJ: Prentice Hall.

Ebaugh, Helen Rose Fuchs. 1988. *Becoming an Ex: The Process of Role Exit*. Chicago: University of Chicago Press.

Eckert, Penelope. 1989. *Jocks and Burnouts: Social Categories and Identity in High School*. New York: Teacher's College Press.

Eckholm, Erik. 2006. "City by City, an Antipoverty Group Plants Seeds of Change." *The New York Times*, June 26, A.12.

The Economist. 2006. "The United States and Mexico: Sense, Not Sensenbrenner" and "Immigration: Don't Fence Us Out". April 1–7, pp. 10 and 41.

Eder, Donna, Catherine Colleen Evans, and Stephen Parker. 1995. *School Talk: Gender and Adolescent Culture*. New Brunswick, NJ: Rutgers University Press.

Edwards, Harry. 1994. "Black Youth's Commitment to Sports Achievement: A Virtue-Turned-Tragic-Turned-Virtue." *Sport* 85 (7): 86.

Edwards, Harry. 2000. "Crisis of the Black Athlete on the Eve of the 21st Century." *Society* 37 (3): 9–13.

Ehrenreich, Barbara. 2001. *Nickel and Dimed: On (Not) Getting By in America*. New York: Henry Holt.

Ehrenreich, Barbara. 2005. *Bait and Switch: The (Futile) Pursuit of the American Dream*. New York: Henry Holt.

Ehrlich, Paul, and Ann Ehrlich. 1990. *The Population Explosion*. New York: Simon and Schuster.

Eitzen, D. Stanley, and George H. Sage. 2003. *Sociology of North American Sport*. Boston: McGraw-Hill.

Eitzen, D. Stanley, and Maxine Baca Zinn. 2006. *Globalization: The Transformation of Social Worlds*. Belmont, CA: Wadsworth.

Elkin, Frederick, and Gerald Handel. 1991. *The Child and Society: The Process of Socialization*. 5th ed. New York: McGraw-Hill.

Ellens, G. F. S. 1971. "The Ranting Ranters: Reflections on a Ranting Counter-Culture." *Church History* 40 (March): 91–107.

Ellison, Christopher G., and Daniel A. Powers. 1994. "The Contact Hypothesis and Racial Attitudes among Black Americans." *Social Science Quarterly* 75 (2): 385–400.

Ellison, Christopher G., John P. Bartkowski, and Michelle L. Segal. 1996. "Do Conservative Protestant Parents Spank More Often?" *Social Science Quarterly* 77 (3): 663–73.

Ellison, Christopher G., J. A. Burr, and P. L. McCall 1997. "Religious Homogeneity and Metropolitan Suicide Rates." *Social Forces* 76 (1): 273–99.

EM-DAT: The OFDA/CRED International Disaster Database. 2006. Brussels, Belgium: Université Catholique de Louvain. Retrieved August 12, 2006 (http://www.em-dat.net).

Engels, Friedrich. 1902. *The Origin of the Family, Private Property, and the State*. Chicago: Charles H. Kerr.

Engels, Friedrich. [1884] 1942. *The Origin of the Family, Private Property, and the State*. New York: International Publishing.

Enloe, Cynthia. 2006. "Daughters and Generals in the Politics of the Gobalized Sneaker." Pp. x-x in *Beyond Borders: Thinking Critically about Global Issues*, edited by Paula S. Rothenberg New York: Worth.

Environmental Protection Agency. 2004. "Terms of Environment." Retrieved (www.epa.gov/OCEPAterms/gterms.html).

Erikson, Kai T. 1976. *Everything in Its Path: Destruction of Community in the Buffalo Creek Flood*. New York: Simon & Schuster.

Erikson, Kai. 1987. "Notes on the Sociology of Deviance." Pp. 9–21 in *Deviance: The Interactionist Perspective*, 5th ed., edited by Earl Rubington and Martin S. Weinberg. New York: Macmillian.

Erikson, Kai T. [1966] 2005. *Wayward Puritans: A Study in the Sociology of Deviance*. Boston: Pearson Education.

Eshleman, J. Ross, and Richard A. Bulcroft. 2006. *The Family*. 11th ed. Boston: Allyn & Bacon.

Esperitu, Yen Le. 1992. *Asian American Panethnicity: Bridging Institutions and Identities*. Philadelphia: Temple University Press.

Esposito, L., and J. W. Murphy. 2000. "Another Step in the Study of Race Relations." *The Sociological Quarterly* 41 (2): 171–87.

Esquivel, Laura. 2001. *Like Water for Chocolate*. New York: Anchor.

Etzioni, Amitai. 1975. *A Comparative Analysis of Complex Organizations*. New York: The Free Press.

The Europa World Year Book. 2005. London: Europa Publications Limited. p. 4231.

Fadiman, Anne. 1997. *The Spirit Catches You and You Fall Down*. New York: Noonday.

Fainstein, Susan S., Ian Gordon, and Michael Harloe, eds. 1992. *Divided Cities: New York and London in the Contemporary World*. Oxford, UK: Blackwell.

Faludi, Susan. 1993. *Backlash: The Undeclared War against American Women*. New York: Anchor.

Farley, John E. 2005. *Majority-Minority Relations*. 5th ed. Englewood Cliffs, NJ: Prentice Hall.

Farley, Reynolds. 2000. *Strangers to these Shores*. 6th ed. Boston: Allyn & Bacon.

Farmer, Paul. 1999. *Infections and Inequalities: The Modern Plagues*. Berkeley: University of California Press.

Farrer, Claire R. 1996. *Thunder Rides a Black Horse: Mescalero Apaches and the Mythic Present*. 2nd ed. Prospect Heights, IL: Waveland.

Faulkner, James B. 2006. "Social Capital, Social Services and Recidivism." Thesis for Applied Behavioral Science Program, Wright State University.

Fausto-Sterling, Anne. 1992. *Myths of Gender: Biological Theories about Women and Men*. 2nd ed. New York: Basic Books.

Fausto-Sterling, Anne. 1993. "The Five Sexes: Why Male and Female Are Not Enough." *The Sciences* (March/April): 20–24.

Fausto-Sterling, Anne. 2000. *Sexing the Body: Gender Politics and the Construction of Sexuality*. New York: Basic Books.

Feagin, Joe R. 1983. *The Urban Real Estate Game: Playing Monopoly with Real Money*. Englewood Cliffs, NJ: Prentice Hall.

Feagin, Joe R., and Clairece Booher Feagin. 1986. *Discrimination American Style: Institutional Racism and Sexism*. Malabar, FL: Krieger.

Feagin, Joe R., and Clairece Booher Feagin. 2003. *Racial and Ethnic Relations*. 7th ed. Englewood Cliffs, NJ: Prentice Hall.

Feagin, Joe R., and H. Vera. 2001. *Liberation Sociology*. Boulder, CO: Westview.

Feagin, Joe R., Hernan Vera, and Pinar Batur. 2001. *White Racism: The Basics*. New York: Routledge.

Featherman, David L., and Robert Hauser. 1978. *Opportunity and Change*. New York: Academic Press.

The Federal Register. 2002. Office of the Federal Register, National Archives and Records Vol. 67.

Fernando, Suman. 2002. *Mental Health, Race and Culture*. 2nd ed. New York: Palgrave.

Ferree, Myra Marx. 1991. "The Gender Division of Labor in Two-Earner Marriages: Dimensions of Variability and Change." *Journal of Family Issues* 12 (2): 158–80.

Ferree, Myra Marx, and David A. Merrill. 2000. "Hot Movements, Cold Cognition: Thinking about Social Movements in Gendered Frames." *Contemporary Sociology: A Journal of Reviews* 12: 626–48.

Field, Mark. 1953. "Structured Strain in the Role of the Soviet Physician." *American Journal of Sociology* 58 (5): 493-502.

Field, Mark. 1957. *Doctor and Patient in Soviet Russia*. Cambridge, MA: Harvard University Press.

Fields, Jason, and Lynne Casper. 2001. "America's Family and Living Arrangements: March 2000." Pp. 20–537 in *Current Population Reports*. Washington, DC: U.S. Census Bureau.

Fine, Gary Alan. 1990. "Symbolic Interactionism in the Post-Blumerian Age." Pp. 117–57 in *Frontiers of Social Theory: The New Synthesis*, edited by George Ritzer. New York: Columbia University Press.

Finfacts. 2005. "From World Bank Development Indicators 2005." Retrieved August 21, 2006 (http://www.finfacts.com/biz10/global worldincomepercapita.htm).

Fingarette, Herbert. 1988. *Heavy Drinking: The Myth of Alcoholism as a Disease*. Berkeley: University of California Press.

Finke, Roger. 1997. "The Consequences of Religious Competition: Supply-Side Explanations for Religious Change." Pp. 45–64 in *Rational Choice Theory and Religion: Summary and Assessment*, edited by L. A. Young. New York: Routledge.

Finke, Roger, and Rodney Stark. 1993. *The Churching of America, 1776–1990: Winners and Losers in Our Religious Economy*. New Brunswick, NJ: Rutgers University Press.

Finke, Roger, and Rodney Stark. 2005. *The Churching of America, 1776–2005: Winners and Losers in Our Religious Economy*. New Brunswick, NJ: Rutgers University Press.

Fischer, Claude S. 1984. *The Urban Experience*. 2nd ed. San Diego: Harcourt Brace Jovanovich.

Fish, Virginia Kemp. 1986. "The Hull House Circle: Women's Friendships and Achievements." Pp. 185–227 in *Gender, Ideology, and Action: Historical Perspectives on Women's Public Lives*, edited by Janet Sharistanian. Westport, CT: Greenwood.

Fiske, Alan Page. 1991. *Structures of Social Life: The Four Elementary Forms of Human Relations*. New York: The Free Press.

"Five Rules for Online Networking." 2005. *CNN*, April 1. Retrieved July 25, 2006 (www.cnn.com/2005/US/Careers/03/31/online.networking).

Flanagan, William G. 1993. *Contemporary Urban Sociology*. New York: Cambridge University Press.

Flanagan, William G. 2001. *Urban Sociology: Images and Structure*. 4th ed. Boston: Allyn & Bacon.

Flavin, Christopher. 2001. "Rich Planet, Poor Planet." Pp. 1–410 in *State of the World 2001*, edited by Lester R. Brown, Christopher Flavin, and Hilary French. New York: W. W. Norton.

Flavin, Jeanne. 2004. "Employment, Counseling, Housing Assistance . . . and Aunt Yolanda? How Strengthening Families' Social Capital Can Reduce Recidivism." *Fordham Urban Law Journal* 3 (2): 209–16.

Florida, Richard. 2002. *The Rise of the Creative Class*. New York: Basic Books.

Flynn, Stephen. 2006. "Why America Is Still an Easy Target." Pp. 246–52 in *Globalization: The Transformation of Social Worlds*, edited by D. Stanley Eitzen and Maxine Baca Zinn. Belmont, CA: Wadsworth.

Ford, Clennan S. 1970. *Human Relations Area Files: 1949–1969—A Twenty Year Report*. New Haven, CT: Human Relations Area Files.

Fox, Mary F. 1995. "Women and Higher Education: Gender Differences in the Status of Students and Scholars." Pp. 220–37 in *Women: A Feminist Perspective*, 5th ed., edited by Jo Freeman. Mountain View, CA: Mayfield.

Frank, Kenneth A., Yong Zhao, and Kathryn Borman. 2004. "Social Capital and the Diffusion of Innovation within Organizations: The Case of Computer Technology in School." *Sociology of Education* 77 (2): 148–71.

Frankl, Razelle. 1987. *Televangelism: The Marketing of Popular Religion*. Carbondale: Southern Illinois University Press.

Frazier, Charles. 1997. *Cold Mountain*. New York: Atlantic Monthly Press.

Freeman, Jo. 1975. *The Politics of Women's Liberation: A Case Study of an Emerging Social Movement and its Relation to the Policy Process*. New York: McKay.

Freese, J., B. Powell, and L. C. Steelman. 1999. *Rebel without a Cause or Effect: Birth Order and Social Attitudes*. Washington, DC: American Sociological Association.

French, Howard W. 2003. "Challenges for Japan: The Glass Ceiling Starts at the Floor." *International Herald Tribune,* June 25, 1, 4.

Freud, Sigmund. [1923] 1960. *The Ego and the Id*. New York: W. W. Norton.

Freund, Peter E. S., and Meredith B. McGuire. 1999. *Health, Illness, and the Social Body*. 3rd ed. Englewood Cliffs, NJ: Prentice Hall.

Friedman, Thomas L. 2005. *The World Is Flat: A Brief History of the Twenty-First Century*. New York: Farrar, Straus, and Giroux.

Friedman, Thomas L. 2006. "Opening Scene: The World Is Ten Years Old." Pp. 21–29 in *Globalization: The Transformation of Social Worlds*, edited by D. Stanley Eitzen and Maxine Baca Zinn. Belmont, CA: Wadsworth.

Furnham, Adrian. 1994. "Explaining Health and Illness: Lay Perceptions on Current and Future Health, The Causes of Illness, and the Nature of Recovery." *Social Science and Medicine* 39 (5): 715–25.

Gallagher, Charles. 2004. "Transforming Racial Identity through Affirmative Action." Pp. 153–70 in *Race and Ethnicity: Across Time, Space and Discipline*, edited by Rodney D. Coates. Leiden, Holland: Brill.

Gallagher, Eugene B., and Janardan Subedi, eds. 1995. *Global Perspectives on Health Care*. Englewood Cliffs, NJ: Prentice Hall.

Gallagher, Eugene B., Thomas J. Stewart, and Terry D. Stratton. 2000. "The Sociology of Health in Developing Counties." Pp. 389–97 in *Handbook of Medical Sociology*, 5th ed., edited by C. Bird, P. Conrad, and A. Fremont. Englewood Cliffs, NJ: Prentice Hall.

Gallagher, Timothy J., and Robert J. Johnson. 2001. "A Model for Unmet Medical Care Needs." Paper presented at the American Sociological Association meetings, August, Anaheim, CA.

Gallup Poll. 2000. Retrieved February 15, 2003 (http://www.gallup.com/poll/indicators/indreligion.asp).

Gallup Poll. 2001. *Gallup Poll Topics: Religion*. Retrieved July 10, 2006 (http://www.gallup.com/poll/indicators/indreligion4.asp).

Gallup Poll. 2004. *Gallup Poll Social Series: Values and Beliefs*. Retrieved July 10, 2006 (http://brain.gallup.com/documents/question.aspx?question=152992&Advanced=0&SearchConType=1&SearchTypeAll=homo sexual%20clergy).

Gallup Poll. 2006. *Gallup Poll Topics: A-Z*. Retrieved July 10, 2006 (http://poll.gallup.com/content/default/aspx?ci=1690&pg=2).

Gallup, George, Jr., and D. Michael Lindsay. 1999. *Surveying the Religious Landscape: Trends in U.S. Beliefs*. Harrisburg, PA: Morehouse.

Gamoran, Adam. 1987. "The Stratification of High School Learning Opportunities." *Sociology of Education* 37: 19–35.

Gamoran, Adam. 2001. "American Schooling and Educational Inequality: A Forecast for the 21st Century." *Sociology of Education* (Extra Issue: Currents of Thought: Sociology of Education at the Dawn of the 21st Century) 60 (3): 135–55.

Gamson, Zelda F. 1998. "The Stratification of the Academy." Pp. 67–73 in *Chalk Lines: The Politics of Work in the Managed University*, edited by Randy Martin. Raleigh, NC: Duke University Press.

Gans, Herbert J. 1962. *The Urban Villagers: Group and Class in the Life of Italian-Americans*. New York: The Free Press.

Gans, Herbert J. 1971. "The Uses of Poverty: The Poor Pay All." *Social Policy* 2 (2): 20–24.

Gans, Herbert J. 1991. *People, Plans, and Policies: Essays on Poverty, Racism, and Other National Urban Problems*. New York: Columbia University Press.

Gans, Herbert J. 1994. "Positive Functions of the Undeserving Poor: Uses of the Underclass in America." *Politics and Society* 22 (3): 269–83.

Gans, Herbert J. 1995. *The War against the Poor*. New York: Basic Books.

Gans, Herbert J. 2007. "No, Poverty Has Not Disappeared." Reprinted in *Sociological Footprints*, edited by Leonard Cargan and Jeanne Ballantine. Belmont, CA: Wadsworth.

Gardner, Howard. 1987. "The Theory of Multiple Intelligences." *Annual Dyslexia* 37: 19–35.

Gardner, Howard. 1999. *Intelligence Reframed: Multiple Intelligences for the 21st Century*. New York: Basic Books.

Garfield, Richard, and Glen Williams. 1992. *Health Care in Nicaragua: Primary Care Under Changing Regimes*. New York: Oxford University Press.

Garner, Catherine L., and Stephen W. Raudenbush. 1991. "Neighborhood Effects on Educational Attainment: A Multilevel Analysis." *Sociology of Education* 64 (4): 251–60.

Garreau, Joel. 1991. *Edge City: Life on the New Frontier*. New York: Doubleday.

Garrett, Laurie. 2000. *Betrayal of Trust: The Collapse of Global Public Health*. New York: Hyperion.

Gaustad, E. S., and Phillip L. Barlow. 2001. *New Historical Atlas of Religion in America*. Oxford, UK: Oxford University Press.

Gay, Lesbian, and Straight Education Network (GLSEN). 2006. "GLSEN's 2005 National School Climate Survey Sheds New Light on Experiences of Lesbian, Gay, Bisexual and Transgendered (LGBT) Students." Retrieved June 27, 2006 (www.glsen.org).

Gehrig, Gail. 1981. "The American Civil Religion Debate: A Source of Theory Construction." *Journal for the Scientific Study of Religion* 20 (1): 51–63.

Gelles, Richard J. 1995. *Contemporary Families: A Sociological View*. Thousand Oaks, CA: Sage.

Gerbner, George. 1998. "Casting the American Scene." Screen Actors Guild.

"Getting Married in Japan." 2002. *Japanese Language*. Retrieved September 15, 2006 (http://japanese.about.com/library/weekly/aa080999.htm).

Gibbs, Jack P. 1989. *Control: Sociology's Central Notion*. Urbana: University of Illinois Press.

Gibson, William. 1999. "Science and Science Fiction." *Talk of the Nation*. National Public Radio, November 30.

Giddens, Anthony. 1986. *The Constitution of Society*. Rep. ed. Berkeley: University of California Press.

Gilbert, Dennis, and Joseph A. Kahl. 2003. *The American Class Structure in an Age of Inequality: A New Synthesis*. 6th ed. Belmont, CA: Wadsworth.

Gilchrist, John. 2003. *Anderson's Ohio Family Law*. Cincinnati, OH: Anderson.

Gilligan, Carol. 1982. *In a Different Voice: Psychological Theory and Women's Development*. Cambridge, MA: Harvard University Press.

Ginsberg, E. 1999. "U.S. Health Care: A look ahead to 2025." *Annual Review of Public Health* 20 (1): 55–67.

Glaser, James M. 1994. "Back to the Black Belt: Racial Environment and White Racial Attitudes in the South." *The Journal of Politics* 56 (1): 21–41.

Glass, John. 2003. "Hunting for Bambi. Hoax? Reality? Does It Matter?" *Common Dreams* (online journal) July 31.

Glass, John. 2004. "Developing Sociological Interventions." Retrieved September 29, 2006 (www.geocities.com/solviolence/frame.htm).

Glasscock, C. B. 1937. *The Gasoline Age: The Story of the Men Who Made It*. Indianapolis, IN: Bobbs-Merrill.

Glenn, Evelyn Nakano. 1999. "The Social Construction and Institutionalization of Gender and Race: An Integrative Framework." Pp. 3–43 in *Revisioning Gender*, edited by Myra Marx Ferree, Judith Lorber, and Beth B. Hess. Thousand Oaks, CA: Sage.

Globalis Interactive World Map. 2006. Retrieved August 30, 2006 (http://globalis.gvu.unu.edu/indicator_detail.cfm?Country=CN@IndicatorID=18).

Globe Women's Business Network. 2006. "Corporate Women Directors International." Retrieved August 21, 2006 (http://www.globe women.com).

Goffman, Erving. 1959. *Presentation of Self in Everyday Life*. Garden City, NY: Anchor.

Goffman, Erving. 1961. *Asylums: Essays on the Social Situation of Mental Patients and other Inmates*. New York: Anchor.

Goffman, Erving. 1967. *Interaction Ritual*. New York: Anchor.

Gold, Marsha R. 1999. "The Changing U.S. Health Care System: Challenges for Responsible Public Policy." *Milbank Quarterly* 77 (1): 3–37.

Gold, Marsha R., L. Nelson, T. Lake, R. Hurley, and R. Berenson. 1998. "Behind the Curve: A Critical Assessment of How Little Is Known about Arrangements between Managed Care Plans and Physicians." Pp. 67–100 in *Contemporary Managed Care: Readings in Structure, Operations, and Public Policy*, edited by M. R. Gold. Chicago: Health Administration Press.

Goldberg, David Theo, ed. 1990. *Anatomy of Racism*. Minneapolis: University of Minnesota Press.

Goldberg, Gertrude Schaffner, and Eleanor Kremen. 1990. *The Feminization of Poverty*. New York: Praeger.

Golden, Tim. 1994. "Health Care, Cuba's Pride, Falls on Hard Times." *The New York Times*, October 30, p. 1.1.

Goode, Erich. 1992. *Collective Behavior*. New York: Harcourt Brace Jovanovich.

Goode, Erich. 1997. *Between Politics and Reason: The Drug Legalization Debate*. New York: St. Martin's.

Goode, Erich. 2005. *Drugs in American Society*. 6th ed. Boston: McGraw-Hill.

Goode, William J. 1970. *World Revolution and Family Patterns*. New York: The Free Press.

Goode, William J. 1990. "Encroachment, Charlatanism, and the Emerging Profession: Psychiatry, Sociology, and Medicine." *American Sociological Review* 25 (6): 902–14.

Gordon, Milton. 1970. "The Subsociety and the Subculture." Pp. 150–63 in *The Sociology of Subcultures*, edited by David O. Arnold. Berkeley, CA: Glendessary.

Gottdiener, Mark. 1987. *The Decline of Urban Politics: Political Theory and the Crisis of the Local State*. Newbury Park, CA: Sage.

Gottdiener, Mark, and Ray Hutchison. 2006. *The New Urban Sociology*. 3rd ed. Boston: McGraw-Hill.

Gottfredson, Michael R., and Travis Hirschi. 1990. *A General Theory of Crime*. Palo Alto, CA: Stanford University Press.

Gottlieb, Lori. 2006. "How Do I Love Thee?" *The Atlantic* 297 (2): 58–70.

Gould, Stephen J. 1997. *The Mismeasure of Man*. New York: W. W. Norton.

Gracey, Harry L. 1967. "Learning the Student Role: Kindergarten as Academic Boot Camp." Pp. 215–226 in *Readings in Introductory Sociology*, 3rd ed. Edited by Dennis Wrong and Harry L. Gracey. New York: Macmillan.

Grandpa Junior. 2006. *If You Were Born before 1945*. Retrieved July 20, 2006 (www.grandpajunior.com/1945.shtml).

Grant, Gerald, and Christine E. Murray. 1999. *Teaching in America: The Slow Revolution*. Cambridge, MA: Harvard University Press.

Grant, Linda. 2004. "Everyday Schooling and the Elaboration of Race-Gender Stratification." Pp. 296–308 in *Schools and Society: A Sociological Approach to Education*, 2nd ed., edited by Jeanne H. Ballantine and Joan Z. Spade. Belmont, CA: Wadsworth.

Greeley, Andrew M. 1972. *The Denominational Society*. Glenview, IL: Scott, Foresman.

Greeley, Andrew M. 1989. *Religious Change in America*. Cambridge, MA: Harvard University Press.

Green, John C., and Mark Silk. 2005. "Why Moral Values Did Count." *Religion in the News* 8 (1): 5–8.

Greenberg, Edward S. 1999. *The Struggle for Democracy*. 3rd ed. New York: Addison-Wesley.

Grusky, David B., and Robert M. Hauser. 1984. "Comparative Social Mobility Revisited: Models of Convergence and Divergence in 16 Countries." *American Sociological Review* 49 (February): 19–38.

Guest, Avery M., and Keith R. Stamm. 1993. "Paths of Community Integration." *Sociological Quarterly* 34 (4): 581–95.

Gumpers, John J., and Levinson, Stephen C. 1991. "Rethinking Linguistic Relativity." *Current Anthropology* 32 (5): 613–23.

Hadden, Jeffrey K. 1987. "Toward Desacralizing Secularization Theory." *Social Forces* 65: 587–611.

Hadden, Jeffrey K., and Anson Shupe. 1988. *Televangelism: Power and Politics on God's Frontier.* New York: Henry Holt.

Hafferty, Frederic. 2000. "Reconfiguring the Sociology of Medical Education: Emerging Topics and Pressing Issues." Pp. 238–57 in *Handbook of Medical Sociology,* 5th ed., edited by C. Bird, P. Conrad, and A. Fremond. Englewood Cliffs, NJ: Prentice Hall.

Hagan, Frank E. 2002. *Introduction to Criminology.* 5th ed. Belmont, CA: Wadsworth.

Hagan, John L. 1993. "The Social Embeddedness of Crime and Unemployment." *Criminology* 31: 465–91.

Hall, Edward T. 1959. *The Silent Language.* New York: Doubleday.

Hall, Edward T. 1983. *The Dance of Life.* Garden City, NY: Anchor Books/Doubleday.

Hall, Edward T., and Mildred Reed Hall. 1992. *An Anthropology of Everyday Life.* New York: Doubleday.

Hall, Richard H. 2002. *Organizations: Structures, Processes, and Outcomes.* 7th ed. Englewood Cliffs, NJ: Prentice Hall.

Hallinan, Maureen T. 1994. "Tracking: From Theory to Practice." *Sociology of Education* 67 (2): 79–91.

Hallinan, Maureen T., and Richard A. Williams. 1989. "Interracial Friendship Choices in Secondary Schools." *American Sociological Review* 54 (February): 67–78.

Hallinan, Maureen T., and Richard A. Williams. 1990. "Students' Characteristics and the Peer-Influence Process." *Sociology of Education* 63 (2): 122–32.

Hamilton, Brady E., Stephanie J. Ventura, Joyce A. Martin, and Paul D. Sutton. 2006. "Final Births for 2004." *National Center for Health Statistics.* Retrieved September 15, 2006 (www.cdc.gov/nchs/products/pubs/pubd/hestats/finalbirths04/finalbirths04.htm).

Hammersley, Martyn, and Glenn Turner. 1980. "Conformist Pupils." In *Pupil Strategies: Explorations in the Sociology of the School,* edited by Peter Woods. London: Croom Helm.

Hannigan, John. 1998. *Fantasy City: Pleasure and Profit in the Postmodern Metropolis.* London: Routledge.

Hanser, Robert D. 2002. "Labeling Theory as a Paradigm for the Etiology of Prison Rape: Implications for Understanding and Intervention." *Professional Issues in Counseling On-line Journal* (April). Retrieved August 4, 2006 (http://www.shsu.edu/~piic/summer2002Hanser.htm).

Hardin, Garrett. 1968. "The Tragedy of the Commons." *Science* 162: 3859 (December): 1243–48.

Hargreaves, D. H. 1978. "The Two Curricula and the Community." *Westminster Studies in Education* 1: 31–41.

Harrington, Charlene, and Carroll L. Estes. 2004. *Health Policy: Crisis and Reform in the U.S. Health Care Delivery System.* 2nd ed. Sudbury, MA: Jones and Bartlett.

Harris, Judith Rich. 1998. *The Nurture Assumption: Why Children Turn Out the Way They Do.* New York: The Free Press.

Harris, Marvin. 1989. *Cows, Pigs, War, and Witches: The Riddles of Culture.* New York: Random House.

Harrison, P. M., and J. C. Karberg. 2003. *Prison and Jail Inmates at Midyear 2002.* Washington, DC: Bureau of Justice Statistics.

Harvey, David. 1973. *Social Justice and the City.* London: Edward Arnold.

Haupt, Arthur, and Thomas T. Kane. 2003. *Population Reference Bureau Report, 2003.* Washington, DC: U.S. Population Bureau.

Hauser, Robert, and David Grusky. 1988. "Cross-National Variation in Occupational Distributions, Relative Mobility Chances, and Intergenerational Shifts in Occupational Distributions." *American Sociological Review* 53 (November): 723–41.

Hayden, Tom. 2006. "Seeking a New Capitalism in Chiapas." Pp. 348–54 in *Globalization: The Transformation of Social Worlds,* edited by D. Stanley Eitzen and Maxine Baca Zinn. Belmont, CA: Wadsworth.

Hayes, Bernadette C. 1995. "The Impact of Religious Identification on Political Attitudes: An International Comparison." *Sociology of Religion* 56 (2): 177–94.

Headlam, Bruce. 2000. "Barbie PC: Fashion over Logic." *The New York Times,* January 20, G4.

Healey, Joseph F. 2006. *Race, Ethnicity, Gender and Class: The Sociology of Group Conflict and Change.* 4th ed. Thousand Oaks, CA: Pine Forge.

Health Confidence Survey. 2001. "2001 Health Confidence Survey: Summary of Findings." Pp. 1–9. Washington, DC: Health Confidence Survey/Employee Benefit Research.

Health in Schools. 2002. "Annual Summary of Vital Statistics Shows Continued Decline in Teen Pregnancies." *Health and Healthcare in Schools* 3 (10). Retrieved August 22, 2006 (www.healthinschools.org/ejournal/2002/dec02_2.htm).

Heaton, Tim B. 1990. "Religious Group Characteristics, Endogamy, and Interfaith Marriages." *Sociological Analysis* 51 (4): 363–76.

Heilbroner, Robert L., and William Milberg. 2002. *The Making of Economic Society.* 11th ed. Englewood Cliffs, NJ: Prentice Hall.

Heilman, Samuel. 2000. *Defenders of the Faith: Inside Ultra-Orthodox Jewry.* Berkeley: University of California Press.

Helgesen, Sally. 1995. *The Female Advantage: Women's Ways of Leadership.* New York: Doubleday.

Hendry, Joy. 1987. *Becoming Japanese: The World of the Preschool Child.* Honolulu: University of Hawaii Press.

Henley, Nancy, Mykol Hamilton, and Barrie Thorne. 2000. "Womanspeak and Manspeak: Sex Differences in Communication, Verbal and Nonverbal." Pp. 111–15 in *Sociological Footprints,* edited by Leonard Cargan and Jeanne Ballantine. Belmont, CA: Wadsworth.

Hensley, Christopher, M. Koscheski, and Richard Tewksbury. 2005. "Examining the Characteristics of Male Sexual Assault Targets in a Southern Maximum-Security Prison." *Journal of Interpersonal Violence* 20 (6): 667–79.

Henslin, James M. 2005. *Sociology: A Down-to-Earth Approach.* 8th ed. Boston: Allyn & Bacon.

Hertsgaard, Mark. 2003. *The Eagle's Shadow: Why America Fascinates and Infuriates the World.* New York: Picador.

Hewitt, John P. 2007. *Self and Society: A Symbolic Interactionism Social Psychology.* 10th ed. Boston: Allyn & Bacon.

Hill, Christopher. 1991. *The World Turned Upside Down: Radical Ideas during the English Revolution.* New York: Penguin.

Himmelstein, David U., and Steffie Woodhandler. 1992. *National Health Program Chartbook.* Cambridge, MA: Center for National Health Program Studies.

Hirschi, Travis. [1969] 2002. *Causes of Delinquency.* New Brunswick, NJ: Transaction Publishers.

Hitler, Adolf. 1939. *Mein Kampf.* New York: Reynal and Hitchcock.

Hochschild, Arlie. 1989. *The Second Shift: Working Parents and the Revolution at Home.* New York: Viking.

Hoffer, Thomas, Andrew M. Greeley, and James S. Coleman. 1987. "Catholic High School Effects on Achievement Growth." Pp. 67–88 in *Comparing Public and Private Schools,* Vol. 2, Student Achievement, edited by Edward H. Haertel, Thomas James, and Henry M. Levin. New York: Falmer.

Hogeland, Lisa Maria. 2004. "Fear of Feminism: Why Young Women Get the Willies." Pp. 565–68 in *Women's Voices, Feminist Visions,* 2nd ed., edited by Susan M. Shaw and Janet Lee. Boston: McGraw-Hill.

Homans, George C. 1974. *Social Behavior: Its Elementary Forms.* New York: Harcourt, Brace Javanovich.

Hood, Roger. 2002. *The Death Penalty: A World-wide Perspective.* 3rd ed. Oxford: Claredon Press.

Hossfeld, Karen J. 2006. "Gender, Race, and Class in Silicon Valley." Pp. 264–70 in *Beyond Borders: Thinking Critically about Global Issues,* edited by Paula S. Rothenberg. New York: Worth.

Houlihan, G. Thomas. 2005. "The Importance of International Benchmarking for U.S. Educational Leaders." *Phi Delta Kappan* November: 217–18.

House, James S. 1994. "Social Structure and Personality: Past, Present and Future." Pp. x-x in *Sociological Perspectives on Social Psychology*, edited by Karen Cook, Gary Fine, and James S. House Boston: Allyn & Bacon.

Howard, Philip N., and Steve Jones, eds. 2004. *Society On-Line: The Internet in Context*. Thousand Oaks, CA: Sage.

Hu, Winnie. 1999. "Women Fearing Mutilation Savors Freedom." *The New York Times*, August 20, A21.

Hughes, David, and Lesley Griffiths. 1999. "On Penalties and the Patient's Charter: Centralism V. De-centralised Governance in the NHS." *Sociology of Health and Illness* 21 (1): 71–94.

Huizinga, David, Finn-Aage Esbensen, and Anne Wylie Weiher. 1991. "Are there Multiple Paths to Delinquency?" *The Journal of Criminal Law and Criminology* 82: 83–118.

Huizinga, David, Rolf Loeber, and Terence P. Thornberry. 1994. "Urban Delinquency and Substance Abuse: Initial Findings." *OJJDP Research Summary*. Washington, DC: USGPO.

Human Rights Campaign. 2003. *Answers to Questions about Marriage Equality*. Washington, DC: Human Rights Campaign, Family Net Project.

Hunsberger, B. 1995. "The Role of Religious Fundamentalism, Quest, and Right-Wing Authoritarianism." *Journal of Social Issues* 51 (2): 113–29.

Hunter College Women's Studies Collective. 2005. *Women's Realities, Women's Choices: An Introduction to Women's Studies*. 3rd ed. New York: Oxford University Press.

Hunter, James Davidson. 1983. *American Evangelicalism*. New Brunswick, NJ: Rutgers University Press.

Hurst, Charles E. 2004. *Social Inequality: Forms, Causes and Consequences*. 5th ed. Boston: Allyn & Bacon.

Iannaccone, Laurence R. 1994. "Why Strict Churches Are Strong." *American Journal of Sociology* 59 (5): 1180–211.

Iannaccone, Laurence R. 1995. "Voodoo Economics? Reviewing the Rational Choice Approach to Religion." *Journal for the Scientific Study of Religion* 34 (1): 76–88.

Ingersoll, Richard M. 2004. "The Status of Teaching as a Profession." Pp. 102–18 in *Schools and Society: A sociological approach to education*, 2nd ed., edited by Jeanne H. Ballantine and Joan Z. Spade. Belmont, CA: Wadsworth.

Ingersoll, Richard M. 2005. "The Problem of Underqualified Teachers: A Sociological Perspective." *Sociology of Education* 78 (2): 175–79.

Inglehart, Ronald, and Wayne E. Baker. 2001. "Modernization's Challenge to Traditional Values: Who's Afraid of Ronald McDonald?" *The Futurist* 35 (2): 16–22.

International Centre for Prison Studies. 2006. "Entire World: Prison Population Rates per 100,000 of the National Population." London: King's College. Retrieved August 4, 2006 (www.kcl.ac.uk.depsta/rel/icps/worldbrief/highest_to_lowest_rates.php).

International Monetary Fund. 2003. "Proposal for a Sovereign Debt Restructuring Mechanism: A Factsheet." Retrieved September 29, 2006 (www.imf.org/external/np/exr/facts/sdrm.htm).

Inter-Parliamentary Union. 2006. "Women in Parliament." Retrieved July 10, 2006 (http://www.ipu.org/wmn-e/classif.htm).

Interpol Data. 2003. Retrieved August 4, 2006 (www.interpol.int/public/drugs).

Irvine, Leslie. 2004. *If You Tame Me: Understanding our Connection with Animals*. Philadelphia: Temple University Press.

Irwin, John. 1985. *The Jail: Managing the Underclass in American Society*. Berkeley, CA.: University of California Press.

Irwin, John. 2005. *The Warehouse Prison: Disposal of the New Dangerous Class*. Los Angeles: Roxbury.

Jackson, Philip W. 1968. *Life in Classrooms*. New York: Holt, Rinehart & Winston.

Jacobs, Jane. 1961. *Life and Death of Great American Cities*. New York: Random House.

Jacobs, Jane. 1969. *Economy of Cities*. New York: Random House.

James, William. [1890] 1934. *The Principles of Psychology*. Mineola, NY: Dover.

Jao, Jui-Chang, and Matthew McKeever. 2006. "Ethnic Inequalities and Educational Attainment in Taiwan." *Sociology of Education* 79 (2): 131–52.

Japan Institute of Labor. 2002. "Women's work patterns and the M-shaped curve." Retrieved August 22, 2006 (http://www.jil.go.jp/index-e.htm).

Jarrett, R. L., P. J. Sullivan, and N. D. Watkins. 2005. "Developing Social Capital through Participation in Organized Youth Programs: Qualitative Insights from Three Programs." *Journal of Community Psychology* 33 (1): 41–55.

Jellinek, E. M. 1960. *The Disease Concept of Alcoholism*. New Haven, CT: Hillhouse.

Jencks, Christopher. 1972. *Inequality: A Reassessment of the Effects of Family and Schooling in America*. New York: Basic Books.

Jencks, Christopher, ed. 1979. *Who Gets Ahead? The Determinants of Economic Success in America*. New York: Harper & Row.

Jencks, Christopher. 1992. *Rethinking Social Policy: Race, Poverty and the Underclass*. Cambridge, MA: Harvard University Press.

Jenkins, Patricia H. 1995. "School Delinquency and School Commitment." *Sociology of Education* 68 (July): 221–39.

Jenness, Valerie, and Kendal Broad. 1997. *Hate Crimes*. New York: Aldine de Gruyter.

Jennings, Jerry T. 1992. "Voting and Registration in the Election of November 1992." *Current Population Reports*, P-20–466. Washington, DC: U.S. Department of Commerce, Economics and Statistics Administration, U.S. Bureau of the Census.

Johnson, David W. and Frank P. Johnson. 2006. *Joining Together: Group Theory and Group Skills*. 9th ed. Boston: Allyn & Bacon.

Johnson, Kenneth M., and Glenn V. Fuguitt. 2000. "Continuity and Change in Rural Migration Patterns, 1950–1995." *Rural Sociology* 65 (1): 27–49.

Johnson, Paul. 2005. "Majority of Americans Believe Homosexuality Should Not Be Illegal, Support Partner Rights: Gallup Poll." Retrieved August 22, 2006 (www.sodomylaws.org/usa/usnews141.htm).

Johnson, Robert. 2002. *Hard Time: Understanding and Reforming the Prison*. Belmont, CA: Wadsworth/Thompson Learning.

Jones, Jacqueline. 1992. *The Dispossessed: America's Underclasses from the Civil War to the Present*. New York: Basic.

Jordan-Bychkov, Terry G., and Mono Domoch. 1998. *The Human Mosaic*. 8th ed. New York: W. H. Freeman.

Kagan, Sharon Lynn, and Vivien Stewart. 2005. "A New World View: Education in a Global Era." *Phi Delta Kappan* November: 185–87.

Kain, Edward L. 1990. *The Myth of Family Decline: Understanding Families in a World of Rapid Social Change*. Lanham, MD: Lexington.

Kaiser Family Foundation. 2005. *Generation M: Media in the Lives of 8 to 18 Year-Olds—Report*. Retrieved July 20, 2006 (www.kff.org/entmedia/7251.cfm).

Kalmijn, Matthijs. 1991. "Shifting Boundaries: Trends in Religious and Educational Homogamy." *American Sociological Review* 56 (December): 786–800.

Kalmijn, Matthijs, and Gerbert Kraaykamp. 1996. "Race, Cultural Capital, and Schooling: An Analysis of Trends in the United States." *Sociology of Education* 69 (1): 22–34.

Kamens, David H., and Aaron Benavot. 1991. "Elite Knowledge for the Masses: The Origins and Spread of Mathematics and Science Education in National Curricula." *American Journal of Education*. 99:2 (February) 137–180.

Kandahar: The Sun behind the Moon. 2003. Film. Mohsen Makhmalbaf. Retrieved September 29, 2006 (http://en.200/wikipedia.org/wiki/kandahar) (www.cduniverse.com/productinfo.asp?pid=5603736).

Kanter, Rosabeth Moss. 1977. *Men and Women of the Corporation*. New York: Basic Books.

Kanter, Rosabeth Moss. 1983. *The Change Masters: Innovation for Productivity in the American Corporation*. New York: Simon and Schuster.

Kanter, Rosabeth Moss. 2001a. "Creating the Culture for Innovation." Pp. x-x in *Leading for Innovation: Managing for Results*, edited by Frances

Hesselbein, Marshall Goldsmith, and Iain Somerville. San Francisco: Jossey-Bass Publishers.

Kanter, Rosabeth Moss. 2001b. "From Spare Change to Real Change: The Social Sector as Beta Site for Business Innovation." *Harvard Business Review on Innovation*. 153–178.

Kanter, Rosabeth Moss. 2005. *Commitment and Community*. Cambridge. MA: Harvard University Press.

Kantrowitz, Barbara, and Pat Wingert. 2003. "What's at Stake?" *Newsweek*, January 27, 30–37.

Kao, Grace. 2004. "Social Capital and its Relevance to Minority and Immigrant Populations." *Sociology of Education* 77 ( ): 172–76.

Kaplan, Howard B., and Robert J. Johnson. 1991. "Negative Social Sanctions and Juvenile Delinquency: Effects of Labeling in a Model of Deviant Behavior." *Social Science Quarterly* 72 (1): 117.

Karen, David. 2005. "No Child Left Behind? Sociology Ignored!" Dworkin, A. Gary. "The No Child Left Behind Act: Accountability, High-Stakes Testing and Roles for Sociologists." Ingersoll, Richard M. "The Problem of Underqualified Teachers: A Sociological Perspective." Epstein, Joyce L. "Attainable Goals? The Spirit and Letter of the No Child Left Behind Act on Parental Involvement." *Sociology of Education*. (April) 78:2. 165–182.

Karraker, Katherine Hildebrant. 1995. "Parent's Gender-Stereotyped Perceptions of Newborns: The Eye of the Beholder Revisited." *Sex Roles* 33 (9/10): 687–701.

Kates, Brian. 2002. "Black Market in Transplant Organs." *New York Daily News*, August 25.

Kaufman, Bel. 1964. *Up the Down Staircase*. Englewood Cliffs, NJ: Prentice Hall.

Keith, Verna M., and Cedric Herring. 1991. "Skin Tone and Stratification in the Black Community." *American Journal of Sociology* 97 (3): 760–78.

Keller, Mark. 1991. "On Defining Alcoholism." *Alcohol Health and Research World* 15 (4): 253–59.

Kemmis, S. and R. McTaggart. 2000. "Participatory Action Research." Pp. x-x in *Handbook of Qualitative Research*, 2nd ed., edited by Norman K. Denzin and Yvonna S. Lincoln. Thousand Oaks, CA: Sage: 567–606.

Kemp, Alice Abel. 1994. *Women's Work: Degraded and Devalued*. Englewood Cliffs, NJ: Prentice Hall.

Kendall, Diane. 2004. *Sociology in Our Times: The Essentials*. 4th ed. Belmont, CA: Wadsworth.

Kerbo, Harold R. 2001. *Social Stratification and Inequality*. 4th ed. Boston: McGraw Hill.

Kerckhoff, Alan C. 2001. "Education and Social Stratification Processes in Comparative Perspective." *Sociology of Education* (Extra Issue: Currents of Thought: Sociology of Education at the Dawn of the 21st Century): 3–18.

Kerckhoff, Alan C., and Lorraine Bell. 1998. "Hidden Capital: Vocational Credentials and Attainment in the United States." *Sociology of Education* 71(2): 152–74.

Kilbourne, Jean. 1999. *Deadly Persuasion: Why Women and Girls Must Fight the Additive Power of Advertising*. New York: The Free Press.

Kilbourne, Jean. 2000. *Killing Us Softly, III*. Video. Northampton, MA: Media Education Foundation.

Kilgore, Sally B. 1991. "The Organizational Context of Tracking in Schools." *American Sociological Review* 56 (2): 201–2.

Killian, Caitlin. 2006. *North African Women in France: Gender, Culture, and Identity*. Palo Alto, CA: Stanford University Press.

Kimmel, Michael S. 2003. *The Gendered Society*. 2nd ed. New York: Oxford University Press.

Kimmel, Michael S., and Michael A. Messner. 2004. *Men's Lives*. 6th ed. Boston: Allyn & Bacon.

King, Edith W. 2006. *Meeting the Challenges of Teaching in an Era of Terrorism*. Belmont, CA: Thomson.

King, Jacqueline E. 2000. "Gender Equity in Higher Education." Washington, DC: American Council on Education, Center for Policy Analysis.

Kinsey, Alfred E., Wardell B. Pomeroy, and Clyde E. Martin. 1948. *Sexual Behavior in the Human Male*. Philadelphia: Saunders.

Kinsey, Alfred E., Wardell B. Pomeroy, Clyde E. Martin, and H. Gephard. 1953. *Sexual Behavior in the Human Female*. Philadelphia: Saunders.

Kirk, Gwyn, and Margo Okazawa-Rey. 2007. *Women's Lives: Multicultural Perspectives*. 4th ed. Boston: McGraw-Hill.

Kitano, Harry H. L. 1997. *Race Relations*. 5th ed. Englewood Cliffs, NJ: Prentice Hall.

Kitano, Harry H. L. 2001. *Asian Americans: Emerging Minorities*. 3rd ed. Englewood Cliffs, NJ: Prentice Hall.

Knapp, Mark L., and Judith A. Hall. 1997. *Non-verbal Communication in Human Interaction*. 4th ed. Fort Worth: Harcourt Brace College Publishers.

Knox, Paul L., and Peter J. Taylor, eds. 1995. *World Cities in a World-System*. Cambridge, England: Cambridge University Press.

Koch, Jerome R., and Evans W. Curry. 2000. "Social Context and the Presbyterian Gay/Lesbian Debate: Testing Open Systems Theory." *Review of Religious Research* 42 (2): 206–14.

Kohlberg, Lawrence. 1971. "From Is to Ought." Pp. 151–284 in *Cognitive Development and Epistemology*, edited by T. Mischel. New York: Academic Press.

Kohn, Melvin. 1989. *Class and Conformity: A Study of Values*. 2nd ed. Chicago: University of Chicago Press.

Kollock, Peter, Philip Blumstein, and Pepper Schwartz. 1985. "Sex and Power in Interaction: Conversational Privilege and Duties," *American Sociological Review*, 50 (February): 34–66.

Koos, Earl. 1954. *The Health of Regionville*. New York: Columbia University Press.

Korte, Charles and Stanley Milgram. 1970. "Acquaintance Networks between Racial Groups." *Journal of Personality and Social Psychology* 15: 101–08.

Kosmin, Barry A., and Seymour P. Lackman. 1993. *One Nation under God: Religion in Contemporary American Society*. New York: Harmony Books.

Kozol, Jonathan. 1991. *Savage Inequalities: Children in America's Schools*. New York: Crown.

Kozol, Jonathan. 2005. "Confections of Apartheid: A Stick-and-Carrot Pedagogy for the Children of Our Inner-City Poor." *Phi Delta Kappan* December: 265–75.

Kozol, Jonathan. 2006. *The Shame of the Nation: The Restoration of Apartheid Schooling in America*. New York: Crown.

Kramer, Laura. 2001. *The Sociology of Gender: A Brief Introduction*. Los Angeles: Roxbury.

Kramer, Laura. 2005. *The Sociology of Gender: A Brief Introduction*. 2nd ed. Los Angeles: Roxbury.

Krieger, Nancy. 1994. "Epidemiology and the Web of Causation: Has Anyone Seen the Spider?" *Social Science and Medicine* 39 (7): 887–903.

Kristof, Nicholas D. 1995. "Japan's Invisible Minority: Better Off than in Past, but Still Outcasts." *The New York Times International*, November 30, A18.

Krymkowski, Daniel H., and Tadeusz K Krause. 1992."Occupational Mobility in the Year 2000: Projections for American Men and Women." *Social Forces* 71 (1): 145–57.

Kubler-Ross, Elizabeth. 1997. *Death, the Final Stage of Growth*. Rep. Ed. New York: Scribner.

Kuhn, Manford. 1964. "Major Trends in Symbolic Interaction Theory in the Past Twenty-Five Years." *Sociological Quarterly* 5: 61–84.

Kuhn, Thomas. 1970. *The Structure of Scientific Revolutions*. 2nd ed. Chicago: University of Chicago Press.

Kumar, Sanjay. 2001. "Despite Ban, Organs Still Sold in India." *Reuters Health*, March 9. Retrieved September 20, 2006 (http://www.geocities.com/somewherereal/bodyparts.html).

Kurtz, Richard A., and H. Paul Chalfant. 1991. *The Sociology of Medicine and Illness*. Boston: Allyn & Bacon.

Kyle, David, and Rey Koslowski, eds. 2001. *Global Human Smuggling: Comparative Perspectives*. Baltimore, MD: Johns Hopkins University Press.

Lacayo, Richard. 1993. "Cult of Death." *Time*, March 15, 36.

Laconte, Joe. 1998. "I'll Stand Bayou: Louisiana Couples Choose a More Muscular Marriage Contract." *Policy Review* 89: 30–35.

Ladson-Billings, Gloria. 2006. "Once Upon a Time When Patriotism Was What You Did" *Phi Delta Kappan* (87:8) April: 585–588.

Laird, J, S. Lew, M. DeBell, and C. Chapman. 2006. "Dropout Rates in the United States: 2002 and 2003" (NCES 2006–062). Washington, DC: U.S. Department of Education, National Center for Education Statistics.

Lake, Robert. 1990. "An Indian Father's Plea." *Teacher Magazine* 2 (September): 48–53.

Lamanna, Mary Ann, and Agnes Riedmann. 2003. *Marriages and Families: Making Choices throughout the Life Cycle.* 8th ed. Belmont, CA: Wadsworth.

Lambert, Lisa. 2006. "Half of Teachers Quit in Five Years: Working Conditions, Low Salaries Cited." *Washington Post,* May 9, A7.

Lambert, Yves. 2000. "Religion in Modernity as a New Axial Age: Seculariazation or New Religious Forms?" Pp. 95–125 in *The Secularization Debate,* edited by William H. Swatos, Jr., and Daniel V. A. Olson. Lanham, MD: Rowman and Littlefield.

Lamy, Philip. 1996. *Millennium Rage.* New York: Plenum.

Lareau, Annette, and Erin McNamara Horvat. 1999. "Moments of Social Inclusion and Exclusion: Race, Class, and Cultural Capital in Family-School Relationships." *Sociology of Education* 72 (1): 37–53.

Larimer, Tim. 1999. "The Japan Syndrome." *Time.* Oct. 11: 50–51.

Lassey, Marie L., William R. Lassey, and Martin J. Jinks. 1997. *Health Care Systems around the World.* Englewood Cliffs, NJ: Prentice Hall.

Laythe, Brian, Deborah Finkel, and Lee A. Kirkpatrick. 2001. "Predicting Prejudice from the Religious Fundamentalism and Right–Wing Authoritarianism" *Journal for the Scientific Study of Religion* 41 (1): 1–10.

Le Monde Diplomatique. 2004. "France: Outsider Women." Retrieved July 4, 2006 (http://mondediplo.com/2004/10/12women).

Leach, Edmund R. 1979. "Ritualization in Man in Relation to Conceptual and Social Development." Pp. 333–37 in *Reader in Comparative Religion,* 3rd ed., edited by William A Lessa and Evon Z. Vogt. New York: Harper & Row.

Leavitt, Jacqueline, and Susan Saegert. 1990. *From Abandonment to Hope: Community-Households in Harlem (Columbia History of Urban Life).* New York: Columbia University Press.

LeBon, Gustave. [1895] 1960. *The Crowd: A Study of the Popular Mind.* New York: Viking.

LeBow, Bob. 2004. *Health Care Meltdown: Confronting the Myths and Fixing our Failing System.* Chambersburg, PA: Alan C. Hood.

Lee, B. C., and J. L. Werth. 2000. *Observations on the first year of Oregon's Death with Dignity Act.* Washington, DC: American Psychological Association.

Lee, Richard B. 1984. *The Dobe !Kung.* New York: Holt, Rinehart & Winston.

Lee, Richard Wayne. 1992. "Christianity and the Other Religions: Interreligious Relations in a Shrinking World." *Sociological Analysis* (Summer): 125–39.

Lee, Seh-Ahn. 1991. "Family Structure Effects on Student Outcomes." *Resources and Actions: Parents, Their Children and Schools.* Report to National Science Foundation and National Center for Educational Statistics, August.

Legters, Nettie E. 2001. "Teachers as Workers in the World System." Pp. 417–26 in *Schools and Society: A Sociological Approach to Education,* edited by Jeanne H. Ballantine and Joan Z. Spade. Belmont, CA: Wadsworth.

Lehman, Edward C., Jr. 1980. "Patterns of Lay Resistance to Women in Ministry." *Sociological Analysis* 41 (4): 317–38.

Lehman, Edward C., Jr. 1981. "Organizational Resistance to Women in Ministry." *Sociological Analysis* 42 (2): 101–18.

Lehman, Edward C., Jr. 1985. *Women Clergy: Breaking through Gender Barriers.* New Brunswick, NJ: Transaction.

Lehne, Gregory K. 1995. "Homophobia among Men: Supporting and Defining the Male Role." Pp. 325–36 in *Men's Lives,* 3rd ed., edited by Michael Kimmel and Michel Messner. Boston: Allyn & Bacon.

Lemert, Edwin M. 1951. *Social Pathology.* New York: McGraw-Hill.

Lemert, Edwin M. 1972. *Human Deviance, Social Problems, and Social Control.* 2nd ed. Englewood Cliffs, NJ: Prentice Hall.

Lemkau, Jeanne Parr. 2006. "Fences, Volcanoes and Embargoes." Unpublished Manuscript.

Lengermann, Patricia, M., and Jill Niebrugge-Brantley. 1990. "Feminist Sociological Theory: The Near-Future Prospects." Pp. 316–44 in *Frontiers of Social Theory: The New Synthesis,* edited by George Ritzer. New York: Columbia University Press.

Lenski, Gerhard E. 1966. *Human Societies.* New York: McGraw-Hill.

Lenski, Gerhard, Patrick Nolan, and Jean Lenski. 1998. *Human Societies: An Introduction to Macrosociology.* 8th ed. New York: McGraw Hill.

Lerner, Richard M. 1992. "Sociobiology and Human Development: Arguments and Evidence." *Human Development* 35 (1): 12–51.

Lesko, Nancy. 2001. *Act Your Age.* London: Routledge/Taylor and Francis.

Leslie, Gerald R., and Sheila K. Korman. 1989. *The Family in Social Context.* 7th ed. New York: Oxford University Press.

Leung, K., S. Lau, and W. L. Lam. 1998. *Parenting Styles and Academic Achievement: A Cross-Cultural Study.* Detroit, MI: Wayne State University Press.

Levin, Jack, and Jack McDevitt. 2003. *Hate Crimes Revisited: America's War on Those Who Are Different.* Boulder, CO: Westview.

Levine, Leslie. 2004. *If You Tame Me: Understanding Our Connection with Animals.* Philadelphia: Temple University Press.

Levine, Michael H. 2005. "Take a Giant Step: Investing in Preschool Education in Emerging Nations." *Phi Delta Kappan* November: 196–200.

Levine, Robert, Suguru Sato, Tsukasa Hashimoto, and Jyoti Verma. 1995. "Love and Marriage in Eleven Cultures." *Journal of Cross-Cultural Psychology* 26 (5): 554–71.

Levine, Susan. 1997. "Down the Ages, a Look at Aging." *International Herald Tribune,* February 11, 1.

Levinson, Arnold R. 1993. "Outcomes Assessment." *National Law Journal* 16 (6): S8.

Levitt, Peggy. 2001. *The Transnational Villagers.* Berkeley: University of California Press.

Levy, Howard S. 1990. *Chinese Footbinding: The History of a Curious Erotic Custom.* Taipei, Taiwan: SMC Pub. Inc.

Levy, Howard S., Arthur Waley, and Wolfram Eberhard. 1992. *The Lotus Lovers: The Complete History of the Curious Erotic Custom of Footbinding in China.* New York: Prometheus.

Lewin, Tamar. 2006. "At Colleges, Women Are Leaving Men in the Dust." *The New York Times,* July 9, A1, 18.

Lewis, Oscar. 1961. *The Children of Sánchez: Autobiography of a Mexican Family.* New York: Random House.

Lewis, Oscar. 1986. *La Vida: A Puerto Rican Family in the Culture of Poverty.* New York: Irvington.

Lieberson, Stanley. 1980. *A Piece of the Pie: Blacks and White Immigrants since 1880.* Berkeley: University of California Press.

Lieberson, Stanley, Susan Dumais, and Shyon Bauman. 2000. "The Instability of Androgynous Names: The Symbolic Maintenance of Gender Boundaries." *American Journal of Sociology* 105 (5): 1249–87.

Lin, BoQi, Richard Peto, Zheng-Ming Chen, Jillian Boreham, Ya-Ping Wu, Jun-Yao Li, T. Colin Campbell, and Jun-Shi Chen. 1998. "Emerging Tobacco Hazards in China: Retrospective Proportional Mortality Study of One Million Deaths." *British Medical Journal* 317 (7170): 1411–22.

Lincoln, Erik, and Laurence Mamiya. 1990. *The Black Church in the African American Experience.* Durham, NC: Duke University Press.

Lindsay, James M. 2006. "Global Warming Heats Up." Pp. 307–313 in *Globalization: The Transformation of Social Worlds,* edited by D. Stanley Eitzen and Maxine Baca Zinn. Belmont, CA: Wadsworth.

Lindsey, Linda L. 2005. *Gender Roles: A Sociological Perspective.* 4th ed. Englewood Cliffs, NJ: Prentice Hall.

Linton, Ralph. 1937. *The Study of Man.* New York: D. Appleton-Century.

Lips, Hilary M. 1991. *Women, Men and Power.* Mt. View, CA: Mayfield.

Lips, Hilary M. 2005. *Sex and Gender: An Introduction.* 5th ed. Boston: McGraw-Hill.

Liska, Allen E. 1999. *Perspectives in Deviance.* 3rd ed. Englewood Cliffs, NJ: Prentice Hall.

Lofland, John, and Norman Skonovd. 1981. "Conversion Motifs." *Journal for the Scientific Study of Religion* 20 (4): 373–85.

Logan, John, and Harvey Molotch. 1987. *Urban Fortunes: The Political Economy of Place.* Berkeley: University of California Press.

Logan, John R., and Glenna D. Spitze. 1994. "Family Neighbors." *American Journal of Sociology* 100 (2): 453–76.

Lopez, Ian F. Haney. 1996. *White by Law.* New York: New York University Press.

Lopez-Garza, Marta. 2002. "Convergence of the Public and Private Spheres: Women in the Informal Economy." *Race, Gender and Class* 9 (3): 175–92.

Lorber, Judith. 1998. "Reinventing the Sexes: The Biomedical Construction of Femininity and Masculinity." *Contemporary Society* 27 (5): 498–99.

Lubeck, Sally. 1985. *Sandbox Society: Early Education in Black and White America.* London: Falmer.

Lucas, Samuel R. 1999. *Tracking Inequality: Stratification and Mobility in American High Schools.* New York: Teachers College Press.

Lucas, Samuel R., and Mark Berends. 2002. "Sociodemographic Diversity, Correlated Achievement, and De Facto Tracking." *Sociology of Education* 75 (4): 328–48.

Luhman, Reid, and Stuart Gilman. 1980. *Race and Ethnic Relations: The Social and Political Experience of Minority Groups.* Belmont, CA: Wadsworth.

Lumsden, Charles J., and Edward O. Wilson. 1981. *Genes, Mind, and Culture: The Coevolutionary Process.* Cambridge, MA: Harvard University Press.

Lundt, John C. 2004. "Learning for Ourselves: A New Paradigm for Education." *The Futurist* November-December: 22.

Lupton, Deborah. 2001. "Medicine and Health Care in Australia." Pp. 429–40 in *The Blackwell Companion to Medical Sociology,* edited by William C. Cockerham. Malden, MA: Blackwell.

Macaulay, David. 1978. *Underground.* Boston: Houghton Mifflin.

MacFarlane, Ann G. 1994. "Racial Education Values." *America* 17 (9): 10–12.

Macionis, John J. 1999. *Sociology.* 7th ed. Englewood Cliffs, NJ: Prentice Hall.

Mackey, Richard A., and Bernard A. O'Brien. 1995. *Lasting Marriages: Men and Women Growing Together.* Westport, CN: Praeger.

MacLeod, Jay. 1995. *Ain't No Makin' It: Aspirations and Attainment in a Low-Income Neighborhood.* Boulder, CO: Westview.

Malthus, Thomas R. [1798] 1926. *First Essay on Population 1798.* London: Macmillan.

Manning, Wendy D., and Pamela J. Smock. 1995. "Why Marry? Race and the Transition to Marriage among Cohabitors." *Demography* 32 (4): 509–20.

Marger, Martin N. 2006. *Race and Ethnic Relations: American and Global Perspectives.* 7th ed. Belmont, CA: Wadsworth.

Marmor, Theodore R. 1999. *The Politics of Medicare.* 2nd ed. Hawthorne, NY: Aldine de Gruyter.

Marsden, Peter V. 1987. "Core Discussion Networks of Americans." *American Sociological Review* February: 122-131.

Martin, Patricia Yancey, and Robert A. Hummer. 1989. "Fraternities and Rape on Campus." *Gender and Society* 3 (4): 457–73.

Marty, Martin E. 1983. "Religion in America since Mid-Century." Pp. x-x in *Religion and America,* edited by Mary Douglas and Stephen Tipton. Boston: Beacon.

Marty, Martin E. 2001. "The Logic of Fundamentalism." *Boston College Magazine* (Fall): 44–46.

Marty, Martin E., and R. Scott Appleby, eds. 1991. *Fundamentalism Observed.* Chicago: University of Chicago Press.

Marty, Martin E., and R. Scott Appleby, eds. 1992. *The Glory and the Power: The Fundamentalist Challenge to the Modern Age.* Boston: Beacon.

Marty, Martin E., and R. Scott Appleby. 2004. *Accounting for Fundamentalism: The Dynamic Character of Movements.* Chicago: University of Chicago Press.

Marx, Karl. [1844] 1963. "Contribution to the Critique of Hegel's Philosophy of Right." Pp. 43–59 in *Karl Marx: Early Writings,* translated and edited by T. B. Bottomore. New York: McGraw-Hill.

Marx, Karl. [1844] 1964. *The Economic and Philosophical Manuscripts of 1844.* New York: International Publishers.

Marx, Karl, and Friedrich Engels. 1955. *Selected Work in Two Volumes.* Moscow: Foreign Language Publishing House.

Marx, Karl, and Friedrich Engels. [1848] 1969. *The Communist Manifesto.* Baltimore: Penguin.

Mashberg, Tom. 2002. "Med Examiner's Office Has Secret Body-Parts Deal." *Boston Herald,* May 20, 1.

Mason-Schrock, Douglas. 1996. "Transsexual's Narrative Construction of the 'True Self.'" *Social Psychology Quarterly* 59 (3): 176–92.

Massey, Douglas S. 1990. "American Apartheid: Segregation and the Making of the Underclass." *American Journal of Sociology* 96 (2): 329–57.

Massey, Douglas S., and Nancy A. Denton. 1993. *American Apartheid: Segregation and the Making of the Underclass.* Cambridge, MA: Harvard University Press.

Massey, Douglas S., Andrew B. Gross, and Kumiko Shibuya. 1994. "Migration, Segregation, and the Geographic Concentration of Poverty." *American Sociological Review* 59 (June): 425–45.

Masters, William H., and Virginia Johnson. 1966. *Human Sexual Response.* Boston: Little, Brown.

Masters, William H., and Virginia Johnson. 1970. *Human Sexual Inadequacy.* Boston: Little, Brown.

Mauksch, Hans. 1993. "Teaching of Applied Sociology: Opportunities and Obstacles." Pp. 1–7 in *Teaching Applied Sociology: A Resource Book,* edited by C. Howery. Washington, DC: American Sociological Association Teaching Resources Center.

Mauss, Armand. 1975. *Social Problems as Social Movements.* Philadelphia: Lippincott.

McAdam, Doug. 1999. *Political Process and the Development of Black Insurgency, 1930–1970.* 2nd ed. Chicago: University of Chicago Press.

McCaghy, Charles H., Timothy A. Capron, California J. D. Jamieson, and Sandra Harley Carey. 2006. *Deviant Behavior: Crime, Conflict, and Interest Groups.* 7th ed. Boston: Allyn & Bacon.

McCarthy, John D., and Mayer N. Zald. 1977. "Resource Mobilization and Social Movements: A Partial Theory." *American Journal of Sociology* 82 (6): 1212–41.

McChesney, Robert W., with Ellen Meiksins Wood, and John Bellamy Foster. 1998. *Capitalism and the Information Age: The Political Economy of the Global Communication Revolution.* New York: Monthly Review Press.

McCormick, John. 1992. "A Housing Program that Actually Works." *Newsweek,* June 22, 61.

McEneaney, Elizabeth H., and John W. Meyer. 2000. "The Content of the Curriculum: An Institutionalist Perspective." Pp. 189–211 in *Handbook of the Sociology of Education,* edited by Maureen T. Hallinan. New York: Kluwer Academic/Plenum.

McEvoy, Alan W. 1990. "Confronting Gangs." *School Intervention Report* (Learning Publications) 3/4 (February/March): 1–20.

McEvoy, Alan W., and Jeff B. Brookings. 2001. *If She Is Raped: A Book for Husbands, Fathers, and Male Friends.* 3rd ed. Holmes Beach, FL: Learning Publication.

McFate, Katherine, Roger Lawson, and William Julius Wilson, eds. 1995. *Poverty, Inequality, and the Future of Social Policy.* New York: Russell Sage.

McGuire, Meredith. 2002. *Religion: The Social Context.* 5th ed. Belmont, CA: Wadsworth.

McIntosh, Peggy. 1992. "White Privilege and Male Privilege: A Personal Account of Coming to See Correspondences through Work in Women's Studies." Pp. 70–81 in *Race, Class, and Gender: An Anthology,* edited by Margaret L. Anderson and Patricia Hill Collins. Belmont, CA: Wadsworth.

McIntosh, Peggy. 2002. "White Privilege: Unpacking the Invisible Knapsack." Pp. 97–101 in *White Privilege: Essential Readings on the Other Side of Racism,* edited by Paula S. Rothenberg. New York: Worth.

McKelvie, Samuel R. 1926. "What the Movies Meant to the Farmer." *Annals of the American Academy of Poetical and Social Science* 128 (November): 131.

McKinlay, John B., and L. D. Marceau. 1998. "The End of the Golden Age of Doctoring." Presented at the American Public Health Association, November, Washington, DC.

McLemore, S. Dale, Harriett Romo, and Susan Gonzalez Baker. 2001. *Racial and Ethnic Relations in America.* 6th ed. Boston: Allyn & Bacon.

McLeod, Jay. 2004. *Ain't No Makin' It: Aspirations and Attainment in a Low-Income Neighborhood.* 2nd ed. Boulder, CO: Westview.

McLuhan, Marshall, and Bruce R. Powers. 1992. *The Global Village: Transformations in World Life and Media in the 21st Century.* New York: Oxford University Press.

McManus, Patricia A., and Thomas A DiPrete. 2001. "Losers and Winners: The Financial Consequences of Separation and Divorce for Men." *American Sociological Review* 66 (April): 246–68.

McNall, Scott G., and Sally Allen McNall. 1983. *Plains Families: Exploring Sociology Through Social History.* New York: St. Martin's.

McNeal, Ralph B. 1995. "Extracurricular Activities and High School Dropouts." *Sociology of Education* 68 (January): 62–81.

McNeil, John J. 1993. *The Church and the Homosexual.* 4th ed. Boston: Beacon.

McTaggart, R. 1997. *Participatory Action Research: International Contexts and Consequences.* Albany: SUNY Press.

Mead, George Herbert. [1934] 1962. *Mind, Self and Society.* Chicago: University of Chicago Press.

Mead, Margaret. [1935] 1963. *Sex and Temperament in Three Primitive Societies.* New York: William Morrow.

Mead, Margaret. 1973. *Coming of Age in Samoa.* New York: Morrow Quill.

Mehan, Hugh. 1992. "Understanding Inequality in Schools: The Contribution of Interpretive Studies." *Sociology of Education* 65 (1): 1–20.

Melton, J. Gordon. 1992. *Encyclopedic Handbook of Cults in America.* Revised and Updated Edition. London: Routledge.

Meltzer, B. 1978. "Mead's Social Psychology." Pp. 15–27 in *Symbolic Interactionism: A Reader in Social Psychology,* 3rd ed., edited by J. Manis and B. Meltzer. Boston: Allyn & Bacon.

Meltzer, B., Meltzer, B., J. Petras, and L. Reynolds. 1975. *Symbolic Interactionism: Genesis, Varieties and Criticism.* London: Routledge and Kegan Paul.

Meltzer, Jack. 1999. *Metropolis to Metroplex: The Social and Spatial Planning of Cities.* Baltimore: Johns Hopkins University Press.

Merton, Robert K. 1938. "Social Structure and Anomie." *American Sociological Review* 3 (October): 672–82.

Merton, Robert K. 1949a. "Discrimination and the American Creed." Pp. 99–126 in *Discrimination and National Welfare,* edited by Robert M. MacIver. New York: Harper.

Merton, Robert K. 1968a. "Social Structure and Anomie." *American Sociological Review* 3 (October): 672–82.

Merton, Robert K. 1968b. *Social Theory and Social Structure.* 2nd ed. New York: The Free Press.

Metz, Mary Haywood. 1986. *Different by Design: The Context and Character of Three Magnet Schools.* New York: Routledge & Kegan Paul.

Meyer, John W., David Kamens, Aaron Benavot, Yun-Kyung Cha, and Suk-Ying Wong. 1992. *School Knowledge for the Masses: World Models and National Primary Curriculum Categories in the Twentieth Century.* London: Falmer.

Meyer, Madonna H., and Eliza K. Pavalko. 1996. "Family, Work, and Access to Health Insurance among Mature Women." *Journal of Health and Social Behavior* 37 (4): 311–25.

Meyer, R. 1996. "The Disease Called Addiction: Emerging Evidence in a Two Hundred Year Debate." *The Lancet* 347 (8995): 162–66.

Michels, Robert. [1911] 1967. *Political Parties.* New York: The Free Press.

Mickelson, Roslyn Arlin. 1990. "The Attitude-Achievement Paradox among Black Adolescents." *Sociology of Education* 63 (January): 44–61.

Mike, Valerie. 2003. "Evidence and the Future of Medicine." *Evaluation and the Health Professions* 26 (2): 127–52.

Milgram, Stanley. 1967. "The Small World Problem." *Psychology Today* 1: 61–67.

Millenium Television Series No. 5. 1992. "Tribal Wisdom and the Modern World." *The Art of Living.*

Miller, Donald E. 1997. *Reinventing American Protestantism.* Berkeley: University of California Press.

Mills, C. Wright. 1956. *The Power Elite.* New York: Oxford University Press.

Mills, C. Wright. 1959. *The Sociological Imagination.* New York: Oxford University Press.

Mills, Robert J. 2001. "Health Insurance Coverage 2000." *Current Populations Reports.* Washington, DC: U.S. Census Bureau.

Mills, Theodore M. 1984. *The Sociology of Small Groups.* 2nd ed. Englewood Cliffs: Prentice Hall.

Mincy, Ronald B. 2006. *Black Males Left Behind.* Washington, DC: The Urban Institute Press.

Minkoff, Debra C. 1995. *Organizing for Equality.* New Brunswick, NJ: Rutgers University Press.

Misztal, Bronislaw, and Anson D. Shupe. 1998. *Fundamentalism and Globalization: Fundamentalist Movements at the Twilight of the Twentieth Century.* Westport, CT: Praeger.

Mitford, Jessica. 2000. *The American Way of Death Revisited.* New York: Alfred A. Knopf.

Modern Slavery. 2005. A Production of "Free the Slaves." Retrieved June 29, 2006 (www.freetheslaves.net).

Moen, Phyllis, Geraldine Downey, and Niall Bolger. 1990. "Labor Force Reentry among U.S. Homemakers in Midlife: A Life-Course Analysis." *Gender and Society* 4 (2): 230–43.

Moffett, Sebastian. 2003. "Going Gray: For Ailing Japan, Longevity Begins to Take its Toll." *The Wall Street Journal,* February 11, A1, 12.

Mohanty, Chandra Talpade. 1988. "Under Western Eyes: Feminist Scholarship and Colonial Discourses." *Feminist Review* 30 (Autumn): 61–88.

Molotch, Harvey. 2003. *Where Stuff Comes From: How Toasters, Toilets, Cars, Computers, and Many Other Things Come to Be as They Are.* London: Routledge.

Moore, Laurence. 1995. *Selling God: American Religion in the Marketplace of Culture.* New York: Oxford University Press.

Morbidity and Mortality Weekly Report. 1999. "Ten Great Public Health Achievements—United States, 1900–1999." *JAMA* 281 (16): 1481–84.

Morgan, Stephen L. 2001. "Counterfactuals, Causal Effect Heterogeneity, and the Catholic School Effect on Learning." *Sociology of Education* 74 (4): 341–73.

Morin, Stephen F., and Ellen M. Garfinkle. 1978. "Male Homophobia." *Journal of Social Issues* 34 (1): 29–47.

Moritz, Owen. 2001. "Trafficking in Humans Is Thriving Business in Africa." *Daily News,* April 17, 4.

Morris, Edward W. 2005. "From "Middle Class" to "Trailer Trash": Teachers' Perceptions of White Students in a Predominately Minority School." *Sociology of Education* 78 (2): 99–121.

Morris, Lloyd R. 1949. *Not So Long Ago.* New York: Random House.

Morrison, J. Ian. 2000. *Health Care in the New Millennium.* San Francisco: Jossey-Bass.

Mulkey, Lynn M, Robert L. Crain, and Alexander J. C. Harrington. 1992. "One-Parent Households and Achievement: Economic and Behavioral Explanations of a Small Effect." *Sociology of Education* 65 (January): 48–65.

Mumford, Lewis. 1961. *The City in History: Its Origins, Transformations, and Prospects.* New York: Harcourt, Brace, and World.

Murphy, Cullen. 1993. "Women and the Bible." *Atlantic Monthly* 272 (2): 39–64.

Murstein, Bernard I. 1987. "A Clarification and Extension of the SVR Theory of Dyadic Pairing." *Journal of Marriage and the Family* 49 (November): 929–33.

Mydans, Seth. 2002. "In Pakistan, Rape Victims Are the 'Criminals.'" *The New York Times,* May 17, A3.

Myers, John P. 2003. *Dominant-Minority Relations in America: Linking Personal History with the Convergence in the New World.* Boston: Allyn & Bacon.

Myrdal, Gunnar. 1964. *An American Dilemma.* New York: McGraw-Hill.

Nakamura, Lisa. 2004. "Interrogating the Digital Divide: The Political Economy of Race and Commerce in the New Media." Pp. 71–83 in

Society On-Line: The Internet in Context, edited by Philip N. Howard and Steve Jones. Thousand Oaks, CA: Sage.

Nanda, Serena, and Richard L. Warms. 2007. *Cultural Anthropology.* 9th ed. Belmont, CA: Wadsworth.

Nardi, Peter M., ed. 1992. *Men's Friendships.* Newbury Park, CA: Sage.

National Center for Education Statistics. 2000. "Distribution of Undergraduate Enrollment among Students Aged 24 or Younger, by Race/Ethnicity, Gender, and Income." Washington, DC: U.S. Department of Education. Retrieved August 26, 2006 (nces.ed .gov/fastfacts/dailyarchive.asp?StatCat).

National Center for Education Statistics. 2002. *Digest of Education Statistics 2002.* Table 207. Washington, DC: U.S. Department of Education.

National Center for Education Statistics. 2004. "Trends in Educational Equity of Girls and Women: 2004." November. Retrieved August 25, 2006 (http://nces.ed.gov/pubsearch/pubsinfo.asp?pubid=2005016).

National Center for Education Statistics. 2005a. *The Condition of Education.* Washington, DC: U.S. Department of Education.

National Center for Education Statistics. 2005b. *Digest of Education Statistics Tables and Figures 2005.* Washington, DC: U.S. Department of Education.

National Center for Health Statistics. 2002a. *Health: United States 2002.* Washington, DC: U.S. Government Printing Office.

National Center for Health Statistics. 2002b. "Physician Visits Increase for Older Patients." News Release. Retrieved August 26, 2006. (www.cdc .gov/nchs/releases/01news/olderpat.htm).

National Center for Health Statistics 2005. *Health: United States, 2005.* Washington, DC: U.S. Government Printing Office.

National Center for Policy Analysis. 2001. "Crime and Gun Control." Retrieved August 4, 2006 (http://www.ncpa.org/pi/crime/pd042501e.html), (http://www.ncpa.org/iss/cri/2002/pd060302c.html).

National Parent Information Network. 2000. "Kids and Media at the New Millennium." *Parents News.* May-June.

National Science Foundation. 2005. *Children, TV, Computers and More Media: New Research Shows Pluses, Minuses.* Retrieved July 20, 2006 (http://www.eurekalert.org/pub_releases/2005-02/nsf-ctc021005.php).

National Urban League. 2006. "The State of Black America." New York. Retrieved August 26, 2006 (www.nul.org/thestateof blackamerica.html).

National Vital Statistics Report. 2001. "Infant Mortality Rates by Race: United States, 1940–1999." 69 (8).

Navarro, Vicente.1996. "Why Congress Did Not Enact Health Reform." *Journal of Health Politics, Policy and Law* 20: 455–62.

Neuman, Michelle J. 2005. "Global Early Care and Education: Challenges, Responses, and Lessons." *Phi Delta Kappan* November: 188–92.

Newman, David M., and Liz Grauerholz. 2002. *Sociology of Families.* 2nd ed. Thousand Oaks, CA: Pine Forge.

Newman, Katherine S. 1999. *No Shame in my Game: The Working Poor in the Inner City.* New York: Knopf and the Russell Sage Foundation.

Newport, Frank. 2004. "A Look at Americans and Religion Today." *Speaking of Faith: American Public Media webpage.* Retrieved July 7, 2006 (http://speaking offaith.publicradio.org/programs/godsofbusiness/gallup poll.shtml).

Newport, Frank. 2006. "Mormons, Evangelical Protestants, Baptists Top Church Attendance List." *Gallup Poll.* Retrieved April 14, 2006 (http://brain.gallup.com/content/?ci=22414).

Niebuhr, H. Richard. 1929. *The Social Sources of Denominationalism.* New York: Henry Holt.

Niebuhr, Reinhold. 1932. *Moral Man and Immoral Society.* New York: Scribner.

Nock, Steven L. 1999. "The Problem with Marriage." *Society* 36 (5): 20–27.

Nock, Steven L., James D. Wright, and Laura Sanchez. 1999. "America's Divorce Problem." *Society* 36 (4): 43–52.

Noel, Donald. 1968. "A Theory of the Origin of Ethnic Stratification." *Social Problems* 16 (Fall): 157–72.

Noguera, Pedro A. 1996. "Preventing and Producing Violence: A Critical Analysis of Responses to School Violence." *Sociology of Education* 56 (3): 189–212.

Noguera, Pedro A. 2004. "Social Capital and the Education of Immigrant Students: Categories and Generalizations." *Sociology of Education* 77 (2): 180–84.

Nolan, Cathal J. 2002. "Terrorism." Pp. 1648–49 in *The Greenwood Encyclopedia of International Relations.* London: Greenwood.

Nolan, Patrick, and Gerhard Lenski. 1999. *Human Societies: An Introduction to Macrosociology.* 8th ed. New York: McGraw-Hill.

Nolan, Patrick, and Gerhard Lenski. 2005. *Human Societies: An Introduction to Macrosociology.* 10th ed. Boulder, CO: Paradigm.

Noss, David S., and John B. Noss. 1990. *A History of the World's Religions.* New York: Macmillan.

Oakes, Jeannie. 1985. *Keeping Track: How High Schools Structure Inequality.* New Haven, CT: Yale University Press.

Oakes, Jeannie. 1990. *Multiplying Inequalities: The Effects of Race, Social Class, and Tracking on Opportunities to Learn Mathematics and Science.* Santa Monica, CA: The Rand Corporation.

Oakes, Jeannie, Amy Stuart Wells, Makeba Jones, and Amanda Datnow. 1997. "Detracking: The Social Construction of Ability, Cultural Politics, and Resistance to Reform." *Teacher's College Record* 98 (3): 482–510.

Oberlander, Jonathan. 2002. "The U.S. Health Care System: On a Road to Nowhere?" *Canadian Medical Association Journal* 167 (2): 163–69.

O'Brien, Jody. 2006. *The Production of Reality.* 4th ed. Thousand Oaks, CA: Pine Forge.

O'Brien, Patrick K., ed. 1999. *Atlas of World History.* New York: Oxford University Press.

O'Connel, Sanjida. 1993 "Meet My Two Husbands." *Guardian,* March 4, Sec. 2:12.

Ogbu, John U. 1998. "Understanding Cultural Diversity and Learning." *Educational Researcher* 21 (8): 5–14.

Ogburn, William F. 1933. *Recent Social Trends.* New York: McGraw-Hill.

Ogburn, William F. [1922] 1938. *Social Change, with Respect to Culture and Original Nature.* New York: Viking.

Ogburn, William F. 1950. *Social Change.* New York: Viking.

Ogburn, William F. 1961. "The Hypothesis of Cultural Lag." Pp. 1270–73 in *Theories of Society: Foundations of Modern Sociological Theory,* Vol 2, edited by Talcott Parsons, Edward Shils, Kaspar D. Naegele, and Jesse R. Pitts. New York: The Free Press.

Ogburn, William F. 1964. *On Culture and Social Change: Selected Papers.* Edited by Otis Dudley Duncan. Chicago: University of Chicago Press.

Olin, Susan Moller. 1996. "Families and Feminist Theory: Some Past and Present Issues." Pp. 13–26 in *Feminism and Families,* edited by Hilde Lindemann Nelson. New York: Routledge.

Olsen, Marvin E. 1968. *The Process of Social Organization.* New York: Hold, Rinehart, and Winston.

Omi, Michael, and Howard Winant. 1989. *Racial Formation in the United States: From the 1960s to the 1980s.* New York: Routledge.

Orfield, Gary, Mark D. Brachmeier, David R. James, and Tamela Eitle. 1997. "Deepening Segregation in American Public Schools." *Equity and Excellence in Education* 30 (2): 5–24.

Oswald, Ramona Faith. 2000. "A Member of the Wedding? Heterosexism and Family Ritual." *Journal of Social and Personal Relationships* 17 (June): 349–68.

Oswald, Ramona Faith. 2001. "Religion, Family, and Ritual: The Production of Gay, Lesbian, and Transgendered Outsiders-Within." *Review of Religious Research* 43 (December): 39–50.

Ottenheimer, Martin. 1996. *Forbidden Relatives: The American Myth of Cousin Marriages.* Urbana: University of Illinois Press.

O'Toole, Tara, and Donald A. Henderson. 2006. "A Clear and Present Danger: Confronting the Threat of Bioterrorism." Pp. 239–45 in *Globalization: The Transformation of Social Worlds,* edited by D. Stanley Eitzen and Maxine Baca Zinn. Belmont, CA: Wadsworth.

Page, Ann L., and Donald A. Clelland. 1978. "The Kanawha County Textbook Controversy: A Study of the Politics of Life Style Concern." *Social Forces* 57 (September): 265–81.

"A Painful Tradition." 1999. *Newsweek,* July 5, 32–33.

Pan American Health Organization. 2000. "Physicians per 10,000 Inhabitants Ratio for Year 1999." Washington, DC: Division of Health Systems and Services Development, Human Resources Development Program.

Pan American Health Organization. 2003. *Violence against Women: The Health Sector Responds.* Washington, DC: PAHO Publications Program.

Papalia, Diane E., Sally Wendkos Olds, and Ruth Duskin Feldman. 2006. *A Child's World: Infancy through Adolescence*. 10th ed. Boston: McGraw-Hill.

Parish, Thomas S., and Joycelyn G. Parish. 1991. "The Effect of Family Configuration and Support System Failures during Childhood and Adolescence on College Students' Self-concepts and Social Skills," *Adolescence* (26:102) Summer: 441.

Park, Ken. 2006. *World Almanac and Book of Facts*. Mahway, NJ: World Almanac.

Park, Robert Ezra, Ernest W. Burgess, and Roderick D. McKenzie. [1925] 1967. *The City*. Chicago: University of Chicago Press.

Parkinson, C. Northcote. 1957. *Parkinson's Law*. Boston: Houghton Mifflin.

Parsons, Talcott. 1951a. *The Social System*. New York: The Free Press.

Parsons, Talcott. 1951b. *Toward a General Theory of Action*. New York: Harper & Row.

Parsons, Talcott. 1975. "The Sick Role and Role of the Physician Reconsidered." *Milbank Memorial Fund Quarterly* 53 (3): 257–78.

Parsons, Talcott, and Robert F. Bales. 1953. *Family, Socialization and Interaction Process*. Glencoe, IL: The Free Press.

Passeron, Jean Claude, and Pierre Bourdieu. 1990. *Reproduction in Education, Society, and Culture*. 2nd ed. Newbury Park, CA: Sage.

Paulhus, D. L., P. D. Trapnell, and D. Chen. 1999. *Birth Order Effects on Personality and Achievement within Families*. Malden, MA: Blackwell.

Pavalko, Ronald M. 1988. *Sociology of Occupations and Professions*. 2nd ed. Itasca, IL: F. E. Peacock.

Pennington, Bill. 2006. "Small Colleges, Short of Men, Embrace Football." *The New York Times*, July 12, A1.

The Perfumed Garden. 2000. Brooklyn, NY: First Run Icarus Films. (info@frif.com).

Persell, Caroline Hodges. 2005. "Race, Education, and Inequality." Pp. 286–24 in *Blackwell Companion to Social Inequalities*, edited by M. Romero and E. Margolis. Oxford, UK: Blackwell.

Persell, Caroline Hodges, and Peter W. Cookson, Jr. 1985. "Chartering and Bartering: Elite Education and Social Reproduction." *Social Problems* 33 (2): 114–129.

Pescosolido, Bernice A. 1992. "Beyond Rational Choice: The Social Dynamics of How People Seek Help." *American Journal of Sociology* 97 (4): 1113.

Pescosolido, Bernice A., and Carol A. Boyer. 2001. "The American Health Care System: Entering the Twenty-first Century with High Risk, Major Challenges, and Great Opportunities." Pp. 180–98 in *The Blackwell Companion to Medical Sociology*, edited by William C. Cockerham. Malden, MA: Blackwell.

Pescosolido, Bernice A., and Sharon Georgianna. 1989. "Durkheim, Suicide, and Religion: Toward a Network Theory of Suicide," *American Sociological Review* 54 (February): 33–48.

Peters, William. [1972] 1987. *A Class Divided*. New York: Doubleday.

Petersen, Larry R., and Gregory V. Donnenwerth. 1998. "Religion and Declining Support for Religious Beliefs about Gender Roles and Homosexual Rights." *Sociology of Religion* 59 (4): 353–71.

Peterson, Richard R. 1996. "A Re-evaluation of the Economic Consequences of Divorce." *American Sociological Review* 61 (June): 528–36.

Pharr, Suzanne. 1997. *Homophobia: A Weapon of Sexism*. Expanded ed. Berkeley: Chardon.

Phi Delta Kappa/Gallup Poll. 2001. "The 33rd Annual Phi Delta Kappa/Gallup Poll of the Public's Attitudes toward the Public Schools." Retrieved August 26, 2006 (www.pdkintl.org/kappan).

Phi Delta Kappa/Gallup Poll. 2005. "The 37th Annual Phi Delta Kappa/Gallup Poll of the Public's Attitudes Toward the Public Schools." *Phi Delta Kappan* September: 41–57.

PHNIP Country Health Statistical Report: Nicaragua. 2002. Retrieved October 4, 2006 (www.constellafutures.com/abstract.cfm/2830).

The Physicians' Working Group for Single-Payer National Health Insurance. 2003. "Proposal of the Physicians' Working Group for Single-Payer National Health Insurance." *Journal of the American Medical Association* 290 (13): 798–805.

Piaget, Jean. 1989. *The Child's Conception of the World*. Savage, MD: Littlefield, Adams Quality Paperbacks.

Piaget, Jean, and Barbel Inhelder. [1955] 1999. *Growth of Logical Thinking*. London: Routledge and Kegan Paul.

Pickard, Ruth, and Daryl Poole. 2007. "The Study of Society and the Practice of Sociology." Previously unpublished essay.

Pinker, Steven. 2002. *The Blank Slate: The Denial of Human Nature*. New York: Viking.

Plato. [circa 350 B.C.] 1960. *The Laws*. New York: Dutton.

Pollack, William. 1999. *Real Boys: Rescuing Our Sons from the Myths of Boyhood*. New York: Owl Books.

Pope, Liston. [1942] 1965. *Millhands and Preachers*. New Haven, CT: Yale University Press.

Popenoe, David, Jean Bethke Elshtain, and David Blankenhorn. 1996. *Promises to Keep: Decline and Renewal of Marriage in America*. Lanham, MD: Rowman and Littlefield.

Popline. 2006a. "Ecosystems Report Links Human Well-Being with Health of Planet." Washington, DC: Population Institute. 28 (January/February): 1.

Popline. 2006b. "Millions Vulnerable to Famine in Africa." Washington, DC: Population Institute. 29 (March/April): 1.

Popline. 2006c. "Overseas Population Spending Threatened." Washington, DC: Population Institute. 29 (March/April): 1.

Population Action International. 1993. *Closing the Gender Gap: Educating Girls*. Report on Progress toward World Population Stabilization. Washington, DC: Population Action International.

Population Reference Bureau. 2001, 2005. *World Population Data Sheet*. Washington, DC: Population Reference Bureau. Retrieved September 29, 2006 (www.prb.org/pdf05/05WorldDataSheet_Eng.pdf).

Population Reference Bureau. 2006. "Human Population: Fundamentals of Growth: Population Growth and Distribution." Retrieved September 29, 2006 (www.prb.org/Content/NavigationMenu/PRB/Educators/Human_Population/Population_Growth).

Portes, Alejandro, and Ruben G. Rumbaut. 2001. *Legacies: The Story of the Immigrant Second Generation*. Berkeley: University of California Press.

Poverty Research News. 2002. Retrieved August 22, 2006 (www.jcpr.org/newsletters/index.html).

Povik, Fili. 1994. *Zlata's Diary: A Child's Life in Sarajevo*. New York: Viking.

Powell, Walter W. 1990. "Neither Market Nor Hierarchy: Network Forms of Organization." *Research in Organizational Behavior* 12: 295–336.

Preston, David L. 1988. *The Social Organization of Zen Practice: Constructing Transcultural Reality*. Cambridge, UK: Cambridge University Press.

Price, Jammie, and Michael G. Dalecki. 1998. "The Social Basis of Homophobia: An Empirical Illustration." *Sociological Spectrum* 18 (2): 143–59.

Prime Time. 1991. "Dignity for Sale: Selling Kidneys in India." August 1.

Public Citizen's Global Trade Watch. 2003. "The Ten Year Track Record of the North American Free Trade Agreement: U.S. Workers' Jobs, Wages and Economic Security." Retrieved September 29, 2006 (http://www.citizen.org/documents/NAFTA_10_jobs.pdf).

Purcell, Piper, and Lara Stewart. 1990. "Dick and Jane in 1989." *Sex Roles* 22 (3/4): 177–85.

Putnam, Robert D. 1995. "Bowling Alone, Revisited." *The Responsive Community* (Spring): 18–33.

Putnam, Robert D. 2001. *Bowling Alone: The Collapse and Revival of American Community*. New York: Simon and Schuster.

Pyle, Ralph E. 2006. "Trends in Religious Stratification: Have Religious Group Socioeconomic Distinctions Declined in Recent Decades?" *Sociology of Religion* 67 (Spring): 61–79.

Quinley, Harold. 1974. *The Prophetic Clergy*. New York: John Wiley.

Quinn, Jane Bryant. 2006. "Health Care's New Lottery." *Newsweek*, February 27, 47.

Quinney, Richard. 2002. *Critique of Legal Order: Crime Control in Capitalist Society*. New Brunswick, NJ: Transaction Publishers.

Radcliffe-Brown, A. R. 1935. "On the Concept of Functional in Social Science." *American Anthropologist* 37 (3): 394–402.

Rama Rao, Saumya and Raji Mohanam. 2003. "The Quality of Family Planning Programs: Concepts, Measurements, Interventions, and Effects." *Studies in Family Planning* (34:4) December: 227–248.

Ramazanoglu, Caroline. 1992. "What Can You Do with a Man? Feminism or the Critical Appraisal of Masculinity" *Women's Studies International Forum* 15 (3): 339–50.

Rankin, Bruce H., and Işik A. Aytaç. 2006. "Gender Inequality in Schooling: The Case of Turkey." *Sociology of Education* 79 (1): 25–43.

Reiman, Jeffrey. 1998. *The Rich Get Richer and the Poor Get Prison.* 5th ed. Boston: Allyn & Bacon.

Religious Congregations and Membership Study, 2000. Association of Religion Data Archives (ARDA). Collected by the Association of Statisticians of American Religious Bodies. (http://www.thearda.com/Archive/Files/Descriptions/RCMSCY.asp). Accessed August 26, 2006.

Religious Tolerance. 2005. Ontario Consultants on Religious Tolerance website. Retrieved August 22, 2006 (www.religioustolerance.org).

Renzetti, Claire. 2003. "Urban Violence against Women." Speech September 30. Dayton, Ohio: Wright State University.

Renzetti, Claire M., and Daniel J. Curran. 2003. *Women, Men and Society.* 5th ed. Boston: Allyn & Bacon.

Report of the National Advisory Commission on Civil Disorders. 1968. New York: Bantam.

Residents of Hull House. [c. 1895] 1970. *Hull House Maps and Papers.* New York: Arno.

Richardson, James. T. 1985 "Active Versus Passive Converts: Paradigm Conflict in Conversion/Recruitment Research." *Journal for the Scientific Study of Religion* 24 (2): 163–79.

Riehl, Carolyn. 2001. "Bridges to the Future: Contributions of Qualitative Research to the Sociology of Education." *Sociology of Education.* Extra Issue: 115–34.

Ries, L. A. G., M. P. Eisner, C. L. Kossary, B. F. Hankey, B. A. Miller, and B. K. Edwards, ed., 2000. *SEER Cancer Statistics Review, 1973–1997.* Bethesda, MD: National Cancer Institute.

Riley, Glenda. 1997. *Divorce: An American Tradition.* Lincoln: University of Nebraska Press.

Ritzer, George. 1998. *The McDonaldization Thesis: Explorations and Extensions.* Thousand Oaks, CA: Pine Forge.

Ritzer, George. 2004a. *The Globalization of Nothing.* Thousand Oaks, CA: Pine Forge.

Ritzer, George. 2004b. *The McDonaldization of Society.* New Century edition. Thousand Oaks, CA: Pine Forge.

Ritzer, George, and Douglas J. Goodman. 2004. *Sociological Theory.* 6th ed. New York: McGraw-Hill.

Ritzer, George, and David Walczak. 1986. *Working: Conflict and Change.* 3rd ed. Englewood Cliffs NJ: Prentice Hall.

Roach, Ronald. 2004. "Survey Reveals 10 Biggest Trends in Internet Use." *Black Issues in Higher Education,* October 21.

Robbins, Mandy. 1998. "A Different Voice: A Different View." *Review of Religious Research* 40 (1): 75–80.

Robbins, Richard H. 2005. *Global Problems and the Culture of Capitalism.* 3rd ed. Boston: Allyn & Bacon.

Robbins, Thomas. 1988. *Cults, Converts and Charisma: The Sociology of New Religious Movements.* London and Newbury Park, CA: Sage.

Roberts, Dorothy. 1997. *Killing the Black Body: Race, Reproduction, and the Meaning of Liberty.* New York: Pantheon.

Roberts, Dorothy. 2002. *Shattered Bonds: The Color of Child Welfare.* New York: Basic Books.

Roberts, Keith A. 2004. *Religion in Sociological Perspective.* 4th ed. Belmont, CA: Wadsworth.

Roberts, Keith A. and Karen A. Donahue. 2000. "Professing Professionalism: Bureaucratization and Deprofessionalization in the Academy" *Sociological Focus.* (33:4) Fall: 365–83.

Robertson, Roland. 1989. "Globalization, Politics, and Religion." Pp. 1–9 in *The Changing Face of Religion,* edited by James A. Beckford and Thomas Luchmann. London: Sage.

Robertson, Roland. 1992. *Globalization: Social Theory and Global Culture.* London: Sage.

Robertson, Roland. 1997. "Social Theory, Cultural Relativity and the Problem of Globality." Pp. 69–90 in *Culture, Globalization and the World System,* edited by Anthony King. Minneapolis: University of Minnesota Press.

Robertson, Roland, and William R. Garrett, eds. 1991 *Religion and Global Order.* New York: Paragon.

Robertson, Roland, and H. H. Khondker 1998. "Comparative Sociology, Global Sociology and Social Theory" *Sociology* 13 (1): 25–40.

Rodriguez, Eric M., and Michael B. Lupfer. 2000. "Gay and Lesbian Christians: Homosexual and Religious Identity Integration in the Members of a Gay-Positive Church." *Journal for the Scientific Study of Religion* 39 (3): 333–47.

Roethlisberger, Fritz J., and William J. Dickson. 1939. *Management and the Worker.* Cambridge: Harvard University Press.

Roof, Wade Clark. 1999. *Spiritual Marketplace: Baby Boomers and the Remaking of American Religion.* Princeton, NJ: Princeton University Press.

Rose, Stephen. 2000. *Social Stratification in the United States.* New York: The New Press.

Rosenbaum, James E. 1999. "If Tracking Is Bad, Is Detracking Better? A Study of a Detracked High School." *American Schools* Winter: 24–47.

Rosenthal, Robert, and Lenore Jacobson. 1968. *Pygmalion in the Classroom.* New York: Holt, Rinehart & Winston.

Rosoff, Stephen M., Henry N. Pontell, and Robert Tillman. 1998. *Profit without Honor: White Collar Crime and the Looting of America.* Englewood Cliffs, NJ: Prentice Hall.

Rossi, Alice S. 1984. "Gender and Parenthood." *American Sociological Review* 49 (February): 1–19.

Rossides, Daniel W. 1997. *Social Stratification: The Interplay of Class, Race, and Gender.* Englewood Cliffs, NJ: Prentice Hall.

Rossman, Parker. 2005. "Beyond the Book: Electronic Textbooks Will Bring Worldwide Learning." *The Futurist* 39 (January/February): 18–23.

Rothenberg, Paula S. 2004. *Race, Class and Gender in the United States: An Integrated Study.* 6th ed. New York: Worth.

Rothenberg, Paula S. 2006. *Beyond Borders: Thinking Critically about Global Issues.* New York: Worth.

Rothman, Robert A. 2005. *Inequality and Stratification: Race, Class and Gender.* 5th ed. Englewood Cliffs, NJ: Prentice Hall.

Rubin, Jeffrey Z. 1974. "The Eye of the Beholder: Parents' Views on Sex of Newborns." *American Journal of Orthopsychiatry* 44 (4) 512–19.

Rumbaut, Ruben G., and Alejandro Portes. 2001. *Ethnicities: Children of Immigrants in America.* Los Angeles: University of California Press.

Sack, Kevin. 1996. "Burnings of Dozens of Black Churches across the South Are Investigated." *The New York Times,* May 21, A6.

Sadker, Myra, and David Sadker. 1985. "Sexism in the Schoolroom of the 1980s." *Psychology Today* 19 (March): 54–57.

Sadker, Myra, and David Sadker. 1993. "Fair and Square?" *Instructor* 102 (7): 44–46.

Sadker, Myra, and David Sadker. 1994. "Surprising Ways to Help Your Daughter Succeed." *McCall's* 121 (12): 62–66.

Sadker, Myra, and David Sadker. 1995. *Failing at Fairness: How Our Schools Cheat Girls.* New York: Touchstone.

Sadker, Myra, and David Sadker. 2005. *Teachers, Schools, and Society.* 7th ed. New York: McGraw-Hill.

Sado, Stephanie, and Angela Bayer. 2001. "Executive Summary: The Changing American Family." Population Resource Center. Retrieved August 22, 2002 (www.prcdc.org/summaries/family/family/html).

Sadovnik, Alan R. 2004. "Theories in the Sociology of Education." Pp. 7–26 in *Schools and Society: A Sociological Approach to Education,* 2nd ed., edited by Jeanne H. Ballantine and Joan Z. Spade. Belmont, CA: Wadsworth.

Sage, George H. 2005. "Racial Inequality and Sport." Pp. 266–75 in *Sport in Contemporary Society,* 7th ed., edited by Stanley D. Eitzen. Boulder, CO: Paradigm.

Sager, Ira, Ben Elgin, Peter Elstrom, Faith Keenan, and Pallavi Gogoi. 2006. "The Underground Web." Pp. 261–70 in *Globalization: The*

Transformation of Social Worlds, edited by D. Stanley Eitzen and Maxine Baca Zinn. Belmont, CA: Wadsworth.

Saha, Lawrence, and A. Gary Dworkin. 2006. "Educational Attainment and Job Status: The Role of Status Inconsistency on Occupational Burnout." Presented at the International Sociological Association, July 23–29, Durban, South Africa.

Salzman, Marian, and Ira Matathia. 2000. "Lifestyles of the Next Millennium: 65 Forecasts." Pp. 466–71 in Sociological Footprints, edited by Leonard Cargan and Jeanne Ballantine. Belmont, CA: Wadsworth.

Samovar, Larry A., and Richard E. Porter. 2003. Intercultural Communication. Belmont, CA: Wadsworth.

Sanday, Peggy Reeves. 1981. "The Socio-Cultural Context of Rape: A Cross-Cultural Study." Journal of Social Issues 37 (4): 5–27.

Sanday, Peggy, and Ruth Gallagher Goodenough, eds. 1990. Beyond the Second Sex. Philadelphia: University of Pennsylvania Press.

Sander, William. 1993. "Catholicism and Intermarriage in the United States." Journal of Marriage and the Family 55 (November): 1037–41.

Sapir, Edward. 1929. "The Status of Linguistics as a Science." Language 5: 207–14.

Sapir, Edward. 1949. Selected Writings of Edward Sapir in Language, Culture, and Personality. Edited by David G. Manddelbaum. Berkeley: University of California Press.

Sapiro, Virginia. 2003. Women in American Society: An Introduction to Women's Studies. 5th ed. Mountain View, CA: Mayfield.

Sarat, Austin. 2001. When the State Kills: Capital Punishment and the American Condition. Princeton, NJ: Princeton University Press.

Sargeant, Kimon Howland. 2000. Seeker Churches: Promoting Traditional Religion in a Nontraditional Way. New Brunswick, NJ: Rutgers University Press.

Scarce, Rik. 1999. "Good Faith, Bad Ethics: When Scholars Go the Distance and Scholarly Associations Do Not." Law and Social Inquiry 24 (4) 977–86.

Schaefer, Richard T. 2006. Racial and Ethnic Groups. 10th ed. Englewood Cliffs, NJ: Prentice Hall.

Schaeffer, Robert K. 2003. Understanding Globalization: The Social Consequences of Political, Economic, and Environmental Change. 2nd ed. Lanham, MD: Rowman and Littlefield.

Schapiro, Mark. 2006. "Big Tobacco." Pp. 271–84 in Globalization: The Transformation of Social Worlds, edited by D. Stanley Eitzen and Maxine Baca Zinn. Belmont, CA: Wadsworth.

Schemo, Diana Jean. 2006. "Public Schools Close to Private in U.S. Study." The New York Times, July 15, A10, 1.

Schieber, George, and Akiko Maeda. 1999. "Health Care Financing and Delivery in Developing Countries." Health Affairs 18 (3): 193–206.

Schiff, Gordon D., Andrew B. Bindman, and Troyen A. Brennan. 1994." A Better-Quality Alternative: Single-payer National Health System Reform." Journal of the American Medical Association 272 (10): 803–7.

Schleuter, Albert. 2006. Personal interview, July.

Schneider, Barbara, and James S. Coleman. 1993. Parents, Their Children and Schools. Boulder, CO: Westview.

Schneider, Barbara, and David Stevenson. 1999. The Ambitious Generation: Imagining the Future. New Haven, CT: Yale University Press.

Schneider, Greg. 2002. "Owner Role Always Tense for United Employees." Washington Post. December 10: E01.

Schneider, Linda, and Arnold Silverman. 2006. Global Sociology. 4th ed. Boston: McGraw-Hill.

Schoeman, Ferdinand. 1991. "Book Review: Heavy Drinking: The Myth of Alcoholism as a Disease." The Philosophical Review 100 (3): 493–98.

Schoen, Robert, and Robin M. Weinick. 1993. "Partner Choice in Marriages and Cohabitations." Journal of Marriage and the Family 55 (May): 408–14.

Schweinhart, Lawrence J. 1997. "Child-Initiated Learning Activities for Young Children Living in Poverty." ERIC Digest. Washington, DC: Office of Educational Research and Improvement, October.

Scott, Ellen K., Andrew S. London, and Nancy A. Myers. 2002. "Dangerous Dependencies: The Intersection of Welfare Reform and Domestic Violence." Gender and Society 16 (6): 878–97.

Scott-Montagu, John. 1904. "Automobile Legislation: A Criticism and Review." North American Review 179 (573): 168–77.

Senate Democratic Policy Committee Hearing. 2004. "America's Uninsured: Myths, Realities and Solutions." Retrieved September 29, 2006 (democrats.senate.gov/dpc/hearings/hearing9/Pollack.pdf).

The Sentencing Project. 2006. "International Rates of Incarceration 2003." Retrieved August 4, 2006 (http://www.sentencingproject.org/pdfs/pub9036.pdf).

Sernau, Scott. 2001. Worlds Apart: Social Inequalities in a New Century. Thousand Oaks, CA: Pine Forge.

Shade, Leslie Regan. 2004. "Bending Gender into the Net: Feminizing Content, Corporate Interests, and Research Strategy." Pp. 57–70 in Society On-Line: The Internet in Context, edited by Philip N. Howard and Steve Jones. Thousand Oaks, CA: Sage.

Shaffer, David Williamson, Kurt R. Squire, Richard Haverson, and James P. Gee. 2005. "Video Games and the Future of Learning." Phi Delta Kappan October: 95–112.

Sharp, Henry S. 1991. "Memory, Meaning, and Imaginary Time: The Construction of Knowledge in White and Chipewayan Cultures." Ethnohistory 38 (2): 149–73.

Sharp, Lauriston. 1990. "Steel Axes for Stone-Age Australians." Pp. 410–24 in Conformity and Conflict, 7th ed., edited by James P. Spradley and David W. McCurdy. Glenview IL: Scott Foresman.

Shaw, Clifford R., and Henry D. McKay. 1929. Delinquency Areas. Chicago: University of Chicago Press.

Shaw, Susan M., and Janet Lee. 2005. Women's Voices, Feminist Visions: Classic and Contemporary Readings. 3rd ed. Boston: McGraw-Hill.

Sheehy, Gail. 1995. New Passages: Mapping Your Life across Time. New York: Dutton.

Shepherd, William R. 1964. Historical Atlas. 9th ed. New York: Barnes & Noble.

Sherif, Muzafer, and Carolyn Sherif. 1953. Groups in Harmony and Tension. New York: Harper & Row.

Sherkat, Darren E., and Christopher G. Ellison. 1999. "Recent Developments and Current Controversies in the Sociology of Religion." Annual Review of Sociology 25:363–94.

Shorter, Edward. 1991. Women's Bodies: A Social History of Women's Encounter with Health, Ill-Health and Medicine. Brunswick, NJ: Transaction Publishers.

Showalter, Shari. 2002. "Culture and Pain." College of Nursing, University of Iowa. Retrieved March 19, 2003 (www.nursing.uiowa.edu).

Shu, Xiaoling. 2004. "Education and Gender Egalitarianism: The Case of China." Sociology of Education 77 (4): 311–36.

Shupe, Anson, and Jeffrey K. Hadden. 1989. "Is There Such a Thing as Global Fundamentalism?" Pp. 109–122 in Secularization and Fundamentalism Reconsidered, edited by Jeffrey K. Hadden and Anson Shupe. New York: Paragon.

Siegel, Larry J. 2000. Criminology. 7th ed. St. Paul, MN: West.

Siegel, Larry J. 2006. Criminology. 9th ed. Belmont, CA: Wadsworth.

Simmel, Georg. [1902–17] 1950. The Sociology of Georg Simmel. Translated by Kurt Wolff. Glencoe, IL: The Free Press.

Simmel, Georg. 1955. Conflict and the Web of Group Affiliation. Translated by Kurt H. Wolff. New York: The Free Press.

Simon, David R. 2006. Elite Deviance. 8th ed. Boston: Allyn & Bacon.

Sizer, Theodore R. 1984. Horace's Compromise: The Dilemma of the American High School. Boston: Houghton Mifflin.

Sjoberg, Gideon. 1960. The Preindustrial City: Past and Present. Glencoe, IL: The Free Press.

Sjoberg, Gideon. 1965. "The Origin and Evolution of Cities." Scientific American 213 (September): 56–57.

Slomczynski, Kazimierz, and Tadeusz K. Krauze. 1987. "Cross-National Similarity in Social Mobility Patterns: A Direct Test of the Featherman—Jones-Hauser Hypothesis." American Sociological Review 52 (October): 598–611.

"Small Fortunes: Microcredit and the Future of Poverty." 2005. PBS, October 27, 2005. Retrieved August 25, 2006 (www.pbs.org/kbyu/small fortunes).

Smelser, Neil J. 1963. *Theory of Collective Behavior.* New York: The Free Press.

Smelser, Neil J. 1988. "Social Structure." Pp. 103–29 in *Handbook of Sociology,* edited by Neil J. Smelser. Newbury Park, CA: Sage.

Smerdon, Becky A. 2002. "Students' Perceptions of Membership in their High Schools." *Sociology of Education* 75 (4): 287–305.

Smith, Barbara Ellen. 1999. "The Social Relations of Southern Women." Pp. 13–31 in *Neither Separate Nor Equal,* edited by B. E. Smith. Philadelphia: Temple University Press.

Smith, Brent L. 1994. *Terrorism in America: Pipe Bombs and Pipe Dreams.* New York: State University of New York Press.

Smith, Christian, and Robert Faris. 2005. "Socioeconomic Inequality in the American Religious System: An Update and Assessment." *Journal for the Scientific Study of Religion* 44 (1): 95–104.

Smith, David M., and Gary J. Gates. 2001. "Gay and Lesbian Families in the United States: Same Sex Unmarried Partner Households: A Preliminary Analysis of 2000 United States Census Data." Washington, DC: Human Rights Campaign. Retrieved August 22, 2006 (www.hrc.org).

Smith, Michael Peter, and Joe R. Feagin, eds. 1995. *The Bubbling Cauldron: Race, Ethnicity, and the Urban Crisis.* Minneapolis: University of Minnesota Press.

Smith, Russell. 2005. "How Many Have Died in Darfur?" *BBC News,* February 16. Retrieved February 16, 2005 (http://news.bbc.co.uk/2/hi/africa/4268733.stm).

Snarr, Michael T., and D. Neil Snarr, eds. 2002. *Introducing Global Issues.* 2nd ed. Boulder, CO: Lynne Rienner.

Snow, David A., and L. Anderson 1993. *Down on Their Luck: A Study of Homeless Street People.* Berkeley: University of California Press.

Snow, David A., Louis A. Zurcher, Jr., and Sheldon Ekland-Olson. 1980. "Social Networks and Social Movements: A Microstructural Approach to Differential Recruitment." *American Sociological Review* 45 (5): 787–801.

Snyder, Benson R. 1971. *The Hidden Curriculum.* New York: Alfred A. Knopf.

Solow, Robert M. 2000. *Growth Theory: An Exposition.* 2nd ed. New York: Oxford University Press.

Sommerfeld, Julia. 2002. "U.S. Lags behind in Cutting Teen Births." MSNBC News. Retrieved January 10, 2002 (www.msnbc.com/news/664476.asp?0si).

Sommerville, C. John. 2002. "Stark's Age of Faith Argument and the Secularization of Things: A Commentary." *Review of Religious Research* (Fall): 361–72.

Son, Young-ho. 1992. "Korean Response to the 'Yellow Peril' and Search for Racial Accommodation in the United States." *Korean Journal* 32 (2): 58–74.

Southerland, Anne. 1986. *Gypsies: The Hidden Americans.* Prospect Heights, IL: Waveland.

Sowell, Thomas. 1994. *Race and Culture: A World View.* New York: Basic Books.

Spade, Joan Z. 2004. "Gender in Education in the United States." Pp. 287–95 in *Schools and Society: A Sociological Approach to Education,* 2nd ed., edited by Jeanne H. Ballantine and Joan Z. Spade. Belmont, CA: Wadsworth.

Spade, Joan Z., Lynn Columba, and Beth E. Vanfossen. 1997. "Tracking in Mathematics and Science: Courses and Course Selection Procedures." *Sociology of Education* 70 (2): 108–27.

Sperling, Gene B. 2005. "The Case for Universal Basic Education for the World's Poorest Boys and Girls." *Phi Delta Kappan* November: 213–16.

Sperling, Gene, and Barbara Herz. 2004. *What Works in Girls' Education: Evidence and Policies from the Developing World.* Washington, DC: Council on Foreign Relations.

Stack, Carol. 1998. *All Our Kin: Strategies for Survival in a Black Community.* New York: Harper & Row.

Stallings, Jane A. 1995. "Ensuring Teaching and Learning in the 21st Century." *Educational Researcher* 24 (6): 4.

Stanback, Thomas M. 1991. *The New Suburbanization: Challenge to the Central City.* Boulder, CO: Westview.

Stanford University Webpage. 2006. *The History of Apartheid in South Africa.* Retrieved July 5, 2006 (www-cs-students.stanford.edu/~cale/cs201/apartheid.hist.html).

Staples, Brent. 1992. "Black Men and Public Space." Pp. 29–32 in *Life Studies,* edited by D. Cavitch. Boston: Bedford.

Staples, Robert. 1999. *The Black Family: Essays and Studies.* 6th ed. Belmont, CA: Wadsworth.

Stark, Rodney. 1985. "Church and Sect." Pp. x-x in *The Sacred in a Secular Age,* edited by P. Hammond. Berkeley: University of California Press.

Stark, Rodney. 2000. "Secularization, R.P.I." Pp. 41–66 in *The Secularization Debate,* edited by William H. Swatos, Jr., and Daniel V. A. Olson. Lanham, MD: Rowman and Littlefield.

Stark, Rodney, and William Sims Bainbridge. 1985. *The Future of Religion: Secularization, Revival, and Cult Formation.* Berkeley: University of California Press.

Stark, Rodney, Daniel P. Doyle, and Jesse Lynn Rushing. 1983. "Beyond Durkheim: Religion and Suicide." *Journal for the Scientific Study of Religion* 22 (March): 120–31.

Starnes, Bobby Ann. 2006. "What We Don't Know *Can* Hurt Them: White Teachers, Indian Children." *Phi Delta Kappan* January: 384–92.

Starr, Paul D. 1982. *The Social Transformation of American Medicine.* New York: Basic Books.

State of Alaska, Workplace Alaska. 2006. *How to Apply.* Retrieved July 5, 2006 (http://notes3.state.ak.us/WA/MainEntry.nsf/WebData/HTMLHow+to+Apply/?open).

Steele, Stephen F., and Jammie Price. 2004 *Applied Sociology: Terms, Topics, Tools, and Tasks.* Belmont, CA: Wadsworth.

Steele, Tracey, and Norma Wilcox. 2003. "A View from the Inside: The Role of Redemption, Deterrence, and Masculinity on Inmate Support for the Death Penalty." *Crime and Delinquency* 49 (2): 285–313.

Stein, Nicholas. 2006. "No Way Out." Pp. 293–99 in *Globalization: The Transformation of Social Worlds,* edited by D. Stanley Eitzen and Maxine Baca Zinn. Belmont, CA: Wadsworth.

Stern, Jessica. 2003. *Terror in the Name of God: Why Religious Militants Kill.* New York: HarperCollins.

Stevens, Daphne, Gary Kiger, and Pamela J. Riley. 2001. "Working Hard and Hardly Working: Domestic Labor and Marital Satisfaction among Dual-Earner Families." *Journal of Marriage and the Family* 63 (May): 514–26.

Stevenson, Mark 2003. "Mexico Finishes Repaying Restructuring Debt." *Laredo Morning Times,* June 13, 14A.

Stewart, Vivien. 2005. "A World Transformed: How Other Countries Are Preparing Students for the Interconnected World of the 21st Century." *Phi Delta Kappan* November: 229–32.

Stoltenberg, John. 1993. *The End of Manhood: A Book for Men of Conscience.* New York: Dutton.

Stolzenberg, Ross M., Mary Blair-Loy, and Linda J. Waite. 1995. "Religious Participation in Early Adulthood: Age and Family Life Cycle Effects on Church Membership." *American Sociological Review* 60 (February): 84–103.

Stone, Norman, ed. 1991. *The Times Atlas of World History.* 3rd ed. Maplewood, NJ: Hammond.

Straus, Murray, and Richard J. Gelles. 1990. *Physical Violence in American Families.* New Brunswick, NJ: Transaction Publishers.

Stringer, Donna M. 2006. "Let Me Count the Ways: African American/European American Marriages." Pp. 170–76 in *Intercultural Communication: A Reader,* edited by Larry A. Samovar, Richard E. Porter, and Edwin R. McDaniel. Belmont, CA: Wadsworth.

Stryker, Sheldon. 1980. *Symbolic Interactionism: A Social Structural Version.* Menlo Park, CA: Benjamin Cummings.

Stryker, Sheldon. 2000. "Identity Competition: Key to Differential Social Involvement." Pp. 21–40 in *Identity, Self, and Social Movements,* edited by Sheldon Styker, Timothy Owens, and Robert White. Minneapolis: University of Minnesota Press.

Stryker, Sheldon, and Anne Stratham. 1985. "Symbolic Interaction and Role Theory." Pp. 311–78 in *Handbook of Social Psychology,* edited by Gardiner Lindsey and Eliot Aronson. New York: Random House.

Suarez-Orozco, Marcelo M. 2005. "Rethinking Education in the Global Era." *Phi Delta Kappan* November: 209–12.

Sun, Yongmin. 2001. "Family Environment and Adolescents' Well-Being before and after Parents' Disruption: A Longitudinal Analysis." *Journal of Marriage and the Family* 63 (August): 697–713.

Sutherland, Edwin H., Donald R. Cressey, and David Luckenbil. 1992. *Criminology.* Dix Hills, NY: General Hall.

Swatos, William H., Jr., and Luftur Reimur Gissurarson. 1997. *Icelandic Spiritualism: Mediumship and Modernity in Iceland.* New Brunswick, NJ: Transaction.

Sway, Marlene. 1988. *Familiar Strangers: Gypsy Life in America.* Urbana: University of Illinois Press.

Szymanski, Linda A., Ann Sloan Devlin, Joan C. Chrisler, and Stuart A. Vyse. 1993. "Gender Role and Attitude toward Rape in Male and Female College Students." *Sex Roles* 29: 37–55.

Tapscott, Don. 1998. *Growing Up Digital: The Rise of the Net Generation.* New York: McGraw-Hill.

Taub, Diane E., and Penelope A. McLorg. 2007. "Influences of Gender Socialization and Athletic Involvement on the Occurrence of Eating Disorders." Pp. 81–90 in *Sociological Footprints,* 10th ed., edited by Leonard Cargan and Jeanne Ballantine. Belmont, CA: Wadsworth.

Tavris, Carol, and Carol Wade. 1984. *The Longest War.* 2nd ed. San Diego: Harcourt Brace Jovanovich.

Taylor, Craig Harrison. 1990. The Age-Gender Controversy in Cross-Cultural Studies. Paper presented at Southern Sociological Society meetings, March 24 Louisville, KY.

Taylor, Humphrey. 2002. "Scientists, Doctors, Teachers, and Military Officers Top the List of Prestigious Occupations." *The Harris Poll,* October 16, 5A. Retrieved August 22, 2006 (Harrisinteractive.com/harris_poll/index.asp?Pollyear=2002).

Thiagaraj, Henry, ed. 1994. "Dalits of India." Pp. x-x in *The Wounded Society: A Review.* Madras: Human Rights Education Movement of India.

Thomas, Charles B. 1985. "Clergy in Racial Controversy: A Replication of the Campbell and Pettigrew Study." *Review of Religious Research* June: 379–90.

Thomas, V. J., and F. D. Rose. 1991. "Ethnic Differences in the Experience of Pain." *Social Science and Medicine* 32 (9): 1063–66.

Thorne, Barrie. 1993. *Gender Play: Girls and Boys in School.* New Brunswick, NJ: Rutgers University Press.

Tichenor, Veronica Jaris. 1999. "Status and Income as Gendered Resources: The Case of Marital Power." *Journal of Marriage and the Family* 61 (August): 638–50.

Tipton, Steven M. 1990. "The Social Organization of Zen Practice: Constructing Transcultural Reality." *American Journal of Sociology* 96 (2): 488–90.

Tjaden, Patricia, and Nancy Thoennes. 2000. "Full Report of the Prevalence, Incidence and Consequences of Violence against Women: Findings from the National Violence against Women Survey." Washington, DC: National Institute of Justice.

Toffler, Alvin, and Heidi Toffler. 1980. *The Third Wave.* New York: Morrow.

Tonnies, Ferdinand. [1887] 1963. *Community and Society.* New York: Harper & Row.

Torche, Florencia. 2005. "Privatization Reform and Inequality of Educational Opportunity: The Case of Chile." *Sociology of Education* 78 (4): 316–43.

Toynbee, Arnold, and D. C. Somervell. [1934–61] 1988. *The Study of History.* Oxford, UK: Oxford University Press.

Transparency International. 2003. "Corruption Perceptions Index, 2003." Retrieved August 4, 2006 (http://www.transparencyinternational.org).

Travers, Jeffrey, and Stanley Milgram. 1969. "An Experimental Study of the Small World Problem." *Sociometry* 32: 425–43.

Treiman, Donald J. 1977. *Occupational Prestige in Comparative Perspective.* New York: Academic Press.

Tuchman, Gaye. 1993. "Realism and Romance: A Study of Media Effects" *Journal of Communication* 43 (4): 36–41.

Tuchman, Gaye. 1996. "Women's Depiction by the Mass Media." Pp. x-x in *Turning It On: A Reader on Women and Media,* edited by Helen Baehr and Ann Gray. London: Arnold.

Tumin, Melvin M. 1953. "Some Principles of Social Stratification: A Critical Analysis." *American Sociological Review* 18 (August): 387–94.

Turnbull, Colin M. 1962. *The Forest People.* New York: Simon & Schuster.

Turner, Bryan S. 1991a. "Politics and Culture in Islamic Globalism." Pp. 161–81 in *Religion and Global Order,* edited by Roland Robertson and William R. Garrett. New York: Paragon.

Turner, Bryan S. 1991b. *Religion and Social Theory.* London: Sage.

Turner, Jonathan H. 2003. *The Structure of Sociological Theory.* 7th ed. Belmont, CA: Wadsworth.

Turner, Ralph H., and Lewis M. Killian. 1993. "The Field of Collective Behavior." Pp. 5–20 in *Collective Behavior and Social Movements,* edited by Russell L. Curtis, Jr., and Benigno E. Aguirre. Boston: Allyn & Bacon.

Tyler, Sir Edward B. [1871] 1958. *Primitive Culture: Researches into the Development of Mythology, Philosophy, Religion, Art and Custom.* Vol. 1. London: John Murray.

U.S. Bureau of Justice Statistics. 2001. *National Crime Victimization Survey Report.* Washington, DC: U.S. Department of Justice.

U.S. Bureau of Justice Statistics. 2002, 2003, 2004, 2005. *Sourcebook of Criminal Justice Statistics.* Washington, DC: U.S. Department of Justice.

U.S. Census Bureau. 2000. "Money Income in the United States 2000." *Current Population Reports.* Issued September 2001.

U.S. Census Bureau. 2001a. *Current Population Survey, 2001.* Washington, DC: U.S. Government Printing Office.

U.S. Census Bureau. 2001b. "9-in-10 School-Age Children Have Computer Access; Internet Use Pervasive Census Bureau Reports." Retrieved July 20, 2006 (http://www.census.gov/Press-Release/www/2001/cb01-147.html).

U.S. Census Bureau. 2003a. "2001 Annual Report: The Status of Equal Employment Opportunity and Affirmative Action in Alaska State Government." *Alaska Fact Sheet.* State of Alaska, Office of the Governor, Office of Equal Employment Opportunity. Retrieved September 29, 2006 (http://factfinder.census.gov/servlet/ACSSAFFFacts?_event=&geo_id=04000US02&_geoContext=01000US%7C04000US02&_street=&_county=&_cityTown=&_state=04000US02&_zip=&_lang=en&_sse=on&ActiveGeoDiv=&_useEV=&pctxt=fph&pgsl=040).

U.S. Census Bureau. 2003b. Population Division, International Programs Center. "International Database." Retrieved August 26, 2006 (www.census.gov/ipc/www/idbnew.html).

U.S. Census Bureau. 2003c. "Statistical Abstract of the United States: 2003." Retrieved August 23, 2006 (www.census.gov/prod/2004pubs/03statab/vitstat.pdf).

U.S. Census Bureau. 2004. "Geographical Mobility: 2002–2003." *Current Population Reports.* Retrieved September 29, 2006 (www.census.gov/prod/2004pubs/p20-549.pdf).

U.S. Census Bureau. 2005a. "America's Families and Living Arrangements 2005." Retrieved August 22, 2006 (http://www.census.gov/population/www/socdemo/hh-fam/cps2005.html).

U.S. Census Bureau. 2005b. "Annual Demographic Supplements." *Current Population Survey 2005.* Washington, DC.

U.S. Census Bureau. 2005c. "Computer and Internet Use in the United States: 2003." *Current Population Reports.* Issued October.

U.S. Census Bureau. 2005d. "Educational Attainment in the United States: 2004." *Current Population Survey.*

U.S. Census Bureau. 2005e. "Housing Vacancies and Housing Ownership." *Annual Statistics 2005.* Retrieved September 15, 2006 (http://www.census.gov/hhes/www/housing/hvs/annua105/ann05def.html).

U.S. Census Bureau. 2005f. "Income, Poverty, and Health Insurance Coverage in the United States: 2004." *Current Population Reports.*

U.S. Census Bureau. 2005g. "National Population Estimates: Characteristics." Retrieved August 22, 2006 (http://www.census.gov/popest/national/asrh/NC-EST2005-srh.html).

U.S. Census Bureau. 2005h. "Number of Uninsured Americans." Retrieved August 26, 2006 (www.census.gov/Press-Release/www/2005).

U.S. Census Bureau. 2005i. *Statistical Abstracts of the United States: 2004–2005*. 124th ed. Washington, DC: U.S. Government Printing Office. Retrieved August 26, 2006 (www.census.gov/Press-Release/www/releases/archives/labor_table597.pdf).

U.S. Census Bureau. 2006a. "Census Bureau Factfinder." Retrieved June 22, 2006. (http://factfinder.census.gov).

U.S. Census Bureau. 2006b. *International Database*. Population Division, International Programs Center. Retrieved September 29, 2006 (www.census.gov/ipc/www/idbnew.html).

U.S. Census Bureau. 2006c. *International Database Population Pyramids*. Retrieved September 29, 2006 (www.census.gov/ipc/www/idbpyr.html).

U.S. Census Bureau. 2006d. "Poverty Thresholds." Retrieved August 22, 2006 (www.census.gov/hhes/www/poverty/threshld).

U.S. Census Bureau. 2006e. "Statistical Abstracts of the United States, 2006." Washington, DC: U.S. Census Bureau, Department of Commerce. Retrieved August 30, 2006 (www.census.gov/prod/2005pubs/06statab/health.pdf).

U.S. Census Bureau. 2006f. "The 2006 Statistical Abstract, The National Data Book, Table 18." Retrieved August 6, 2006 (http://www.census.gov/compendia/statab/education/educational_attainment/).

U.S. Census Bureau News. 2005. *U.S. Citizens over 65*. Washington, DC: U.S. Department of Commerce.

U.S. Department of Agriculture. 2002. "Economic Research Service: Data set of United States Farm and Farm-Related Employment, 2002." Washington, DC.

U.S. Department of Agriculture. 2005a. "Characteristics of Food Stamp Households: Fiscal Year 2004 Summary." Washington, DC. September.

U.S. Department of Agriculture. 2005b. "Household Food Security in the United States, 2004." *Economic Report* Vol. 11. Washington, DC. October.

U.S. Department of Education. 2006. National Library of Education. Retrieved July 14, 2006 (www.ed.gov/offices/UESE/esea/index).

U.S. Department of Energy. 2006. "Energy Consumption: Energy Kids Page" at www.eia.doe.gov/kids/energyfacts/saving/efficiency/savingenergy_secondary.html. Retrieved November 8, 2006.

U.S. Department of Health and Human Services. 2005. Table 46. Hyattsville, MD: Centers for Disease Control and Prevention.

U.S. Department of Interior, Office of Education. 1930. *Availability of Public School Education in Rural Communities*. Bulletin No. 34. Edited by Walter H. Gaummitz. Washington, DC: Government Printing Office.

U.S. Department of Justice. 2002. National Crime Victimization Survey. Washington, DC: U.S. Department of Justice.

U.S. Department of Justice. 2004. "2004 National Crime Victimization Survey." Washington, DC: Bureau of Justice Statistics.

U.S. Department of Labor. 2005. "Current Population Survey." Washington, DC: Bureau of Labor Statistics. Retrieved August 9, 2006 (http://www.bls.gov/cps).

U.S. Department of State. 2001. "Patterns of Global Terrorism 2001 Report." Retrieved September 29, 2006 (http://www.state.gov/s/ct/rls/pgtrpt/2001.pdf).

U.S. Federal Bureau of Investigation. 2005a. "Crime in the United States in 2004." *Uniform Crime Reports*. Washington, DC: U.S. Department of Justice. Retrieved August 4, 2005 (http://www.fbi.gov/ucr/cius_01/01crime1.pdf).

U.S. Federal Bureau of Investigation. 2005b. "Fact Sheet for Hate Crime Statistics, 2004." *Uniform Crime Reports*.

U.S. General Accounting Office. 2003. "Defense of Marriage Act—Update to Prior Report." Retrieved August 18, 2006 (www.gao.gov/new.items/d04353r.pdf).

U.S. Trade Representative. 2003. "North American Free Trade Agreement: Overview." Retrieved September 29, 2006 (www.ustr.gov/regions/whemisphere/overview.shtml).

UNAIDS–Joint United Nations Programme on HIV/AIDS. "Fact Sheet 2006: Sub-Saharan Africa." Retrieved <date> (http://data.unaids.org/pub/GlobalReport/2006/200605-FS_Sub SaharanAfrica_en.pdf).

UNESCO. 2005. *Education for All Global Monitoring Report 2005: The Quality Imperative*. Paris: UNESCO.

UNESCO. 2006. *Education for All Global Monitoring Report 2006: The Quality Imperative*. Paris: UNESCO.

UNESCO, Institute for Statistics. 2003. "Pupil-Teacher Ratio: Primary." New York: United Nations. Retrieved August 26, 2006 (http://education/en/ev.phb-URL_ID=13602&URL).

UNESCO, Institute for Statistics. 2005. "Fact Sheet International Literacy Day 2005." New York: United Nations.

UNESCO, Institute for Statistics. 2006. "Global Education Digest 2006: Comparing Education Statistics across the World." Retrieved July 28, 2006 (www.uis.unesco.org/TEMPLATE/pdf/ged/2006/GED2006.pdf).

UNHCR. 2006. "2005 Global Refugee Trends: Statistical Overview of Populations of Refugees, Asylum-Seekers, Internally Displaced Persons, Stateless Persons, and Other Persons of Concern to UNHCR." Retrieved August 15, 2006 (http://www.unhcr.org/cgi-bin/texis/vtx/statistics).

UNICEF. 2004. *Progress for Children: A Child Survival Report Card, No. 1*. New York: UNICEF.

United Nations. 2002. World Urbanization Prospects, 2001 Revision. New York: United Nations Population Division. Retrieved September 29, 2006 (www.unpopulation.org).

United Nations. 2003. *Demographic Yearbook: 2003*. Retrieved August 22, 2006 (http://unstats.un.org/unsd/demographic/products/dyb/dyb2.htm).

United Nations Department of Economic and Social Affairs, Population Division. 2005. "World Population Prospects: The 2004 Revision. Vol. 3: Analytical Report."

United Nations Development Programme. 2005a. "Human Development Indicators." Human Development Report. Retrieved September 20, 2006 (http://hdr.undp.org/reports/global/2005).

United Nations Development Programme. 2005b. United Nations Office on Drugs and Crime. 2005. *World Drug Report 2005*. Retrieved August 4, 2006 (http://www.unodc.org/unodc/world_drug_report.html).

United Nations International Telecommunication Union. 2004. "Internet Indicators by Country for 2004." Retrieved August 9, 2006 (http://www.itu.int/ITU-D/ict/statistics/at_glance/Internet04.pdf).

United Nations Office on Drugs and Crime. 2003. "Global Illicit Drug Trends 2003." New York: United Nations.

United Nations Office on Drugs and Crime. 2006a. "Annual Reports Questionnaire Data/DELTA." Retrieved September 20, 2006 (www.unodc.org/pdf/WDR_2006/wdr2006_ex_summary.pdf).

United Nations Office on Drugs and Crime. 2006b. "World Drug Report 2006, Volume 1." Retrieved September 20, 2006 (http://www.unodc.org/pdf/WDR_2006/wdr2006_volume1.pdf).

United Nations Population Division. 2001. "World Urbanization Prospects: The 2001 Revision." New York: United Nations Population Division.

United Nations Population Division. 2003. "World Urbanization Prospects: The 2003 Revision." New York: United Nations Population Division Revision. Retrieved September 29, 2006 (www.un.org/esa/population/publications/wup2003/WUP2003Report.pdf).

United Nations Population Division. 2005. *World Urbanization Prospects: The 2005 Revision*. Retrieved September 29, 2006 (http://esa.un.org/unup).

United Nations Population Fund. 2005. *State of the World Population 2005*. Retrieved September 29, 2006 (www.unfpa.org/swp/2005/pdf/en_swp05.pdf).

University of Michigan. 2002. Demographic Transition: An Historical Sociological Perspective. Online. Ann Arbor: University of Michigan.

University of Michigan Documents Center. 2003. *Documents in the News—1997/2003.* Retrieved June 29, 2006 (www.lib.umich.edu/govdocs/affirm.html).

Vandell, Deborah Lowe, and Sheri E. Hembree. 1994. "Peer Social Status and Friendship: Independent Contributors to Children's Social and Academic Adjustment." *Merrill-Palmer Quarterly* 40 (4): 461–75.

Vandenburgh, Henry. 2001. "Emerging Trends in the Provision and Consumption of Health Services." *Sociological Spectrum* 21 (3): 279–92.

Von Holzen, Roger. 2005. "The Emergence of a Learning Society." *The Futurist* 39 (January-February): 24–25.

Waite, Linda J., and Maggie Gallagher. 2000. *The Case for Marriage: Why Married People Are Happier, Healthier, and Better off Financially.* New York: Doubleday.

Waitzkin, Howard. 2000. "Changing Patient-Physician Relationships in the Changing Health-Policy Environment." Pp. 271–83 in *Handbook of Medical Sociology.* 5th ed., edited by C. Bird, P. Conrad, and A. Fremont. Englewood Cliffs, NJ: Prentice Hall.

Walby, Sylvia. 1990. "The Historical Roots of Materialist Feminism." Paper presented at the International Sociological Association, Madrid, Spain.

Walker, Henry A., and Jennifer A. Karas 1993. "The Declining Significance of Color: Race, Color and Status Attainment." Paper presented at the annual meeting of the American Sociological Association, Miami, FL.

Wallenstein, Peter. 2002. *Tell the Court I Love My Wife: Race, Marriage, and Law—An American History.* New York: Macmillan.

Waller, Willard. [1932] 1965. *Sociology of Teaching.* New York: Russell & Russell.

Wallerstein, Immanuel. 1974. *The Modern World System.* New York: Academic Press.

Wallerstein, Immanual. 2004. *World Systems Analysis: An Introduction.* Durham, NC: Duke University Press.

Wallerstein, Immanuel. 2005. "Render Unto Caesar? The Dilemmas of a Multicultural World." *Sociology of Religion* 66 (2): 121–33.

Wallerstein, Judith. 1996. *Surviving the Breakup: How Children and Parents Cope with Divorce.* New York: Basic Books.

Wallerstein, Judith S., and Sarah Blakeslee. 1996. *The Good Marriage: How and Why Love Lasts.* New York: Warner Books.

Wallerstein, Judith S., and Sandra Blakeslee. 2004. *Second Chances: Men, Women and Children a Decade after Divorce.* 15th ed. Boston: Houghton Mifflin.

Walsh, Edward J., and Rex H. Warland. 1983. "Social Movement Involvement in the Wake of a Nuclear Accident: Activists and Free Riders in the IMI Area." *American Sociological Review* 48 (December): 764–80.

Walsh, Mark. 1991. "Students at Private Schools for Blacks Post Above-Average Scores, Study Finds." *Education Week,* October 16.

Walters, Suzanna Danuta. 1999. "Sex, Text, and Context: (In) Between Feminism and Cultural Studies." Pp. 222–57 in *Revisioning Gender,* edited by Myra Marx Ferree, Judith Lorber, and Beth B. Hess. Walnut Creek, CA: AltaMira.

Walum, Laurel Richardson. 1974. "The Changing Door Ceremony: Some Notes on the Operation of Sex Roles in Everyday Life." *Urban Life and Culture* 2 (4): 506–15.

Ward, Martha C. 1996. *A World Full of Women.* Boston: Allyn & Bacon.

Ward, Martha C., and Monica Edelstein. 2006. *A World Full of Women.* 4th ed. Boston: Allyn & Bacon.

Warner, R. Stephen. 1993. "Work in Progress toward a New Paradigm for the Sociological Study of Religion in the United States." *American Journal of Sociology* 98 (5): 1044–93.

Warr, Mark, and Mark Stafford. 1991. "The Influence of Delinquent Peers: What They Think and What They Do. *Criminology* 29 (November): 851–66.

Warren, Jenifer. 1990. "Schoolbook Furor Rends Rural Town." *Los Angeles Times,* August 20, A3.

Waters, Melissa S., Will Carrington Heath, and John Keith Watson. 1995. "A Positive Model of the Determination of Religious Affiliation." *Social Science Quarterly* 76 (1): 105–23.

Weber, B. J., and L. M. Omotani. 1994. "The Power of Believing." *The Executive Educator* 19 (September): 35–38.

Weber, David. 2003. "25 Health Care Trends: What's Hot, What's Not, and What Does the Future Hold." *Physician Executive* 29 (1): 6–14.

Weber, Max. [1904–1905] 1958. *The Protestant Ethic and the Spirit of Capitalism.* Translated by Talcott Parsons. New York: Scribner.

Weber, Max. 1946. *From Max Weber: Essays in Sociology.* Translated and edited by Hans H. Gerth and C. Wright Mills. New York: Oxford University Press.

Weber, Max. 1947. *The Theory of Social and Economic Organization.* Translated and edited by A. M. Henderson and Talcott Parsons. New York: Oxford University Press.

Weber, Max. 1964. *The Theory of Social and Economic Organization.* Translated and edited by A. M. Henderson and Talcott Parsons. New York: Oxford University Press.

Weeks, John R. 1999. *Population: An Introduction to Concepts and Issues.* 7th ed. Belmont, CA: Wadsworth.

Weeks, John R. 2005. *Population: An Introduction to Concepts and Issues.* 9th ed. Belmont, CA: Wadsworth.

Weidenbaum, Murray. 2006. "Globalization: Wonderland or Waste Land?" Pp. 53–60 in *Globalization: The Transformation of Social Worlds,* edited by D. Stanley Eitzen and Maxine Baca Zinn. Belmont, CA: Wadsworth.

Weiss, Gregory L., and Lynne E. Lonnquist. 2006. *The Sociology of Health, Healing, and Illness.* 3rd ed. Englewood Cliffs, NJ: Prentice Hall.

Weitz, Rose. 1995. "What Price Independence? Social Reactions to Lesbians, Spinsters, Widows and Nuns." Pp. 448–57 in *Women: A Feminist Perspective,* edited by Jo Freeman. Mountain View, CA: Mayfield.

Weitzman, Lenore J., Deborah Eifler, Elizabeth Hokada, and Catherine Ross. 1972. "Sex-role Socialization in Picture Books for Preschool Children." *American Journal of Sociology* 77 (May): 1125–150.

Welch, Michael. 1996. *Corrections: A Critical Approach.* St. Louis, MO: McGraw-Hill.

Weller, Christian E., and Adam Hersh. 2006. "Free Markets and Poverty." Pp. 69–73 in *Globalization: The Transformation of Social Worlds,* edited by D. Stanley Eitzen and Maxine Baca Zinn. Belmont, CA: Wadsworth.

Wells, Amy Stuart, and Jeannie Oakes. 1996. "Potential Pitfalls of Systemic Reform: Early Lessons from Research on Detracking" *Sociology of Education* 69 (Extra Issue): 135–43.

Wenglinsky, Harold. 1997. "How Money Matters: The Effect of School District Spending on Academic Achievement." *Sociology of Education* 70 (3): 221–37.

Werner International Management Consultants. 2005. *Primary Textiles Labor Cost Comparisons.* Herndon, VA: Werner International. Retrieved August 18, 2006 (www.wernertex.com).

Werth, James L., Dean Blevins, Karine L. Toussaint, and Martha R. Durham. 2002. "The Influence of Cultural Diversity on End-of-Life Care and Decisions." *American Behavioral Scientist* 46 (2): 204–19.

Wessinger, Catherine. 2000. *How the Millennium Comes Violently: From Jonestown to Heaven's Gate.* New York: Seven Bridges.

West, Candace, and Don H. Zimmerman. 1987. "Doing Gender." *Gender and Society* 1 (2): 125–51.

Westermann, Ted D., and James W. Burfeind. 1991. *Crime and Justice in Two Societies: Japan and the United States.* Pacific Grove, CA.: Brooks/Cole.

Westheimer, Joel. 2006. "Patriotism and Education: An Introduction." *Phi Delta Kappan* 87 (8): 569–72.

Wheeler, David L. 1995. "A Growing Number of Scientists Reject the Concept of Race." *The Chronicle of Higher Education,* February 17, A15.

White, Kevin. 2002. *An Introduction to the Sociology of Health and Illness.* London: Sage.

White, Merry I. 1987. *The Japanese Educational Challenge: A Commitment to Children*. New York: The Free Press.

Whorf, Benjamin Lee. 1956. *Language, Thought, and Reality*. New York: John Wiley.

"Why Comprehensive Health System Reform Failed." 1994. Editorial. *American Family Physician* 50 (5): 919–20.

Whyte, William H. 1956. *The Organization Man*. New York: Simon and Schuster.

Wilcox, Norma, and Tracey Steele. 2003. "Just the Facts: A Descriptive Analysis of Inmate Attitudes toward Capital Punishment." *The Prison Journal* 83 (4): 464–82.

Williams, Brian K., Stacey C. Sawyer, and Carl M. Wahlstrom. 2006. *Marriages, Families, and Intimate Relationships*. Boston: Allyn & Bacon.

Williams, Catrina. 2000. "Internet Access in U.S. Public Schools and Classrooms 1994–1999." Washington, DC: National Center for Education Statistics.

Williams, Christine L. 1992. "The Glass Escalator: Hidden Advantages for Men in the 'Female' Professions" *Social Problems* 39 (3): 253–66.

Williams, D. R., and C. Collins. 1995. "U.S. Socioeconomic and Racial Differences in Health: Patterns and Explanations." *Annual Review of Sociology* 21: 349–86.

Williams, Gregory H. 1996. *Life on the Color Line: The True Story of a White Boy Who Discovered He Was Black*. New York: Dutton.

Williams, J. Allen, Joetta Vernon, Martha Williams, and Karen Malecha. 1987. "Sex Role Socialization in Picture Books: An Update." *Social Science Quarterly* 68 (1): 148–56.

Williams, Robin Murphy, Jr. 1970. *American Society: A Sociological Interpretation*. 3rd ed. New York: Alfred Knopf.

Williams, Terry, and William Kornblum. 1985. *Growing Up Poor*. Lexington, MA: Lexington.

Willie, Charles Vert. 2003. *A New Look at Black Families*. 5th ed. Walnut Creek, CA: AltaMira.

Willis, Paul. 1979. *Learning to Labor: How Working Class Kids Get Working Class Jobs*. Aldershot, Hampshire, England: Saxon House.

Wilmore, Gayraud S. 1973. *Black Religion and Black Radicalism*. Garden City, NY: Doubleday.

Wilson, Bryan. 1982. *Religion in Sociological Perspective*. Oxford, UK: Oxford University Press.

Wilson, Edward O. 1980. *Sociobiology*. Cambridge, MA: Belknap.

Wilson, Edward O. 1987. *The Coevolution of Biology and Culture*. Cambridge, MA: Harvard University Press.

Wilson, Edward O., Michael S. Gregory, Anita Silvers, and Diane Sutch. 1978. "What Is Sociobiology?" *Society* 15 (6): 1–12.

Wilson, K. 1993. *Dialectics of Consciousness: Problems of Development, the Indian Reality*. Madras: Oneworld Educational Trust.

Wilson, Mary E. 2006. "Infectious Concerns: Modern Factors in the Spread of Disease." Pp. 313–19 in *Globalization: The Transformation of Social Worlds,* edited by D. Stanley Eitzen and Maxine Baca Zinn. Belmont, CA: Wadsworth.

Wilson, Warren H. 1924. "What the Automobile Has Done to and for the Country Church." *Annals of the American Academy of Poetical and Social Science* 116 (November): 85–86.

Wilson, William Julius. 1978. *The Declining Significance of Race: Blacks and Changing American Institutions*. Chicago: University of Chicago Press.

Wilson, William Julius. 1984. "The Black Underclass." *The Wilson Quarterly* (Spring): 88–89.

Wilson, William Julius. 1987. *The Truly Disadvantaged: The Inner City, the Underclass, and Public Policy*. Chicago: University of Chicago Press.

Wilson, William Julius. 1993a. *The Ghetto Underclass: Social Science Perspectives*. Newbury Park, CA: Sage.

Wilson, William Julius. 1993b. "The New Urban Poverty and the Problem of Race." *The Tanner Lecture on Human Values,* October 22 (printed in *Michigan Quarterly Review,* 247–73).

Wilson, William Julius. 1996. *When Work Disappears*. New York: Alfred A. Knopf.

Winders, Bill. 2004. "Changing Racial Inequality: The Rise and Fall of Systems of Racial Inequality in the U.S." Paper Presented at the Annual Meeting of the American Sociological Association, San Francisco.

Winkler, Karen J. 1991. "Revisiting the Nature vs. Nurture Debate: Historian Looks Anew at Influence of Biology on Behavior." *Chronicle of Higher Education,* May 22, A5, 8.

Wirth, Louis. 1964. "Urbanism as a Way of Life." *American Journal of Sociology* 44 (1): 1–24.

Witte, John F., and Christopher A. Thorn. 1996. "Who Chooses? Voucher and Interdistrict Choice Programs in Milwaukee." *American Journal of Education* 104 (May): 186–217.

Witzig, Ritchie. 1996. "The Medicalization of Race: Scientific Legitimation of a Flawed Social Construct." *Annals of Internal Medicine: American College of Physicians* 125 (8): 675–76.

Wong, Sandra L. 1991. "Evaluating the Content of Textbooks: Public Interests and Professional Authority" *Sociology of Education* 64 (January): 11–18.

Wood, Julia T. 2003. *Gendered Lives: Communication, Gender, and Culture*. 5th ed. Belmont, CA: Wadsworth.

Wood, Julia T. 2005. *Gendered Lives: Communication, Gender, and Culture*. 6th ed. Belmont, CA: Wadsworth.

Wood, Julia T., and Nina M. Reich. 2006. "Gendered Communication Styles." Pp. 177–86 in *Intercultural Communication,* 11th ed., edited by Larry A. Samovar, Richard E. Porter, and Edwin R. McDaniel. Belmont, CA: Wadsworth.

Woodberry, Robert D., and Christian S. Smith. 1998. "Fundamentalism et al: Conservative Protestants in America." *Annual Review of Sociology* 24: 25–26.

Woolhandler, Steffie, Terry Campbell, and David U. Himmelstein. 2004. "Health Care Administration in the United States and Canada: Micromanagement, Macro Costs." *International Journal of Health Services* 34 (1): 65–78.

Working Group on Assisted Suicide and End-of-Life Decisions. May 1, 2000. Retrieved September 29, 2006 (www.apa.org/pi/aseol .html).

World Almanac Education Group. 2001. *The World Almanac and Book of Facts 2001*. Mahwah, NJ: World Almanac Books.

World Bank Organization. 2006. *World Development Indicators*. Database. Retrieved August 9, 2006 (http://www.worldbank.org/data).

World Development Indicators. 2006. World Bank. World Development Indicators, online. Retrieved August 19, 2006 (http://goddard40. clarku.edu:2251/dataonline).

World Fact Book. 2005. Retrieved August 9, 2006 (www.worldfactbook .com).

World Fact Book. 2006. Retrieved September 29, 2006 (https://www .cia.gov/cia/publications/factbook/index.html).

World Health Organization. 2002. "The World Health Report: Reducing Risks, Promoting Healthy Life." *The World Health Report 2002*. Retrieved September 29, 2006 (www.who.int/whr/2002/en/whr 02_en.pdf).

World Health Organization. 2003. "SARS: Status of the Outbreak and Lessons for the Immediate Future." Retrieved September 29, 2006 (www.who.int/csr/media/sars_who.pdf).

World Health Organization. 2006a. "The Current State of Global Health." Pp. 356–63 in *Beyond Borders: Thinking Critically about Global Issues,* edited by Paula S. Rothenberg. New York: Worth.

World Health Organization. 2006b. "World Health Statistics 2006" and "The World Health Report, 2006 Edition." Retrieved August 14, 2006 (http://www.who.int/statistics/en/).

World Health Organization/UNAIDS. 2006. "HIV and AIDS Estimates and Data, 2005 and 2003." *2006 Report on the Global AIDS Epidemic*. Retrieved August 14, 2006 (http://www.unaids.org/en/HIV_data/2006 GlobalReport/default.asp).

World Resources Institute. 2003. "Coalition of Twelve Major U.S. Corporations and WRI Announce Largest Corporate Green Power

Purchases in U.S." Retrieved September 17, 2006 (www.thegreen-powergroup.org/groupevents.html).

Wright, Erik Olin. 2000. *Class Counts: Comparative Studies in Class Analysis.* Student ed. Cambridge, MA: Cambridge University Press.

Wright, Stuart A. 1995. *Armageddon in Waco: Critical Perspectives on the Branch Davidian Conflict.* Chicago: University of Chicago Press.

Wuthnow, Robert, ed. 1994. *"I Come away Stronger:" How Small Groups are Shaping American Religion.* Grand Rapids, MI: William B. Eerdmans.

Yablonski, Lewis. 1959. "The Gang as a Near-Group." *Social Problems* 7 (Fall): 108–17.

Yamane, David. 1997. "Secularization on Trial: In Defense of a Neosecularization Paradigm." *Journal for the Scientific Study of Religion* 36 (1): 109–22.

Yinger, J. Milton. 1960. "Contraculture and Subculture." *American Sociological Review* 25 (October): 625–35.

Yinger, J. Milton. 1970. *The Scientific Study of Religion.* New York: Macmillan.

Yoon, Mi Yung. 2001. "Democratization and Women's Legislative Representation in Sub-Saharan Africa." *Democratization* 8 (2): 169–90.

Yoon, Mi Yung. 2004. "Explaining Women's Legislative Representation in Sub-Saharan Africa." *Legislative Studies Quarterly* 29 (3): 447–68.

Yung, Judith. 1995. *Unbound Feet: From China to San Francisco's Chinatown.* Berkeley: University of California Press.

Zborowski, Mark. 1952. "Cultural Components in Response to Pain." *Journal of Social Issues* 8 (4): 16–30.

Zhao, Yong. 2005. "Increasing Math and Science Achievement: The Best and Worst of the East and West." *Phi Delta Kappan* November: 219–22.

Zigler, Edward, Sally J. Styfco, and Elizabeth Gilman. 1993. *Headstart and Beyond.* New Haven, CT: Yale University Press.

Zimbardo, Philip C. 2004. "Power Turns Good Soldiers Into 'Bad Apples.'" *Boston Globe,* May 9.

Zimbardo, Philip C. 2007. "You Can't Be a Sweet Cucumber in a Vinegar Barrel." Pp. 122–25 in *Sociological Footprints,* edited by Leonard Cargan and Jeanne Ballantine. Belmont, CA: Wadsworth.

Zimbardo, Philip C., Craig Haney, Curtis Banks, and David Jaffe. 1973. "The Mind Is a Formidable Jailer: A Pirandellian Prison." *The New York Times,* April 8, 38–60.

Zimolzak, Chester E., and Charles A. Stansfield, Jr. 1983. *Human Landscape.* 2nd ed. Columbus, OH: Merrill.

Chapter 1: Globe: Istockphoto.com; UN in Geneva: Markus Seidel/Istockphoto.com; Oxford University: Istockphoto.com; Parliament in Ottawa: David Raboin/Istockphoto.com; Dominican Republic: Juan Collado/Istockphoto.com; happy couple: Kevin Russ/Istockphoto.com; sailboat: Judy Foldetta/Istockphoto.com.

Chapter 2: Microscope: Viktor Pryymachuk; Space walk: NASA; egg & injection: Andrei Tahernov/Istockphoto.com; archae-ological dig: Istockphoto.com; archaeologist: Mike Murley/Istockphoto.com; science student: Laurence Gough/Istockphoto.com.

Chapter 3: Computer board: Simon Smith/Istockphoto.com; American Native dancer: Piotr Przeszlo/Istockphoto.com; Japanese drummers: Radu Razuaa/Istockphoto.com; Burmese fish-erman: Pavel Pospisil/Istockphoto.com; African street football: Peeter Viisimaa.

Chapter 4: Children in uniforms: Yang Liu/Corbis; baseball players: Corbis; making cookies: Sean Locke/Istockphoto.com; working on the computer: Istockphoto.com; classroom: J.B. Russell/Corbis Sygma; playing doctor: Don Mason/Corbis.

Chapter 5: Paper cut-outs: Mike Bentley/Istockphoto.com; crowded street: Aaron Kohr/Istockphoto.com; business meeting: Sean Locke/Istockphoto.com; band: Tim Pannell/Corbis; huddle: Istockphoto.com.

Chapter 6: Time-out: Corbis; handcuffed: Corbis; shoplifting: Corbis; behind bars: Istockphoto.com; piercing: Jose Fuste Raga; graffiti: Peter Chen/Istockphoto.com.

Chapter 7: Money: Skip O'Donnell/Istockphoto.com; cocktail party: Claire Artman/zefa/Corbis; yacht: Bob Thomas/Corbis; homeless man: Gideon Mendel/Corbis; children: Juan Collado/Istockphoto.com; poor housing: Istockphoto.com; house: Bob Ainsworth/Istockphoto.com.

Chapter 8: From top to bottom: Peter Viisimaa/Istockphoto.com, Heidi Breeze-Harris/Istockphoto.com, Ryan K.C. Wong/Istock photo.com, Kevin Russ/Istockphoto.com, Bradley L.Marlow/Istockphoto.com, Anna Bryukhanova/Istockphoto.com, Matthew Cole/Istockphoto.com, Jason Stitt/Istockphoto.com, HeidiTuller/Istockphoto.com, Jon Horton/Istockphoto.com, Istockphoto.com.

Chapter 9: Mom carrying babies: Kazuyoshi Nomachi/Corbis; Business women: Anna Bryuhanova/Istockphoto.com; National League for Democracy: David Van Der Veen/epa/Corbis; Condoleeza Rice: Liu Weibing/China Features/Corbis; harvest: Paul Souders/Corbis; factory: Chris Sattleberger/Corbis; fishing: epa/Corbis; market: Jeanne Ballantine.

Chapter 10: Broken window: Akram Salen/Reuters/Corbis; lesbian moms: Noah K. Murray/Star Ledger/Corbis; Shinto wed-ding: Radu Razuan/Istockphoto.com; argument: Fred Palmieri/Istockphoto.com; African dad: Peeter Viisimaa; new mom: Sheli Biggs; wedding: Nancy Louie/Istockphoto.com.

Chapter 11: Chalkboard: Istockphoto.com; outdoor classroom: Viviane Moos/Corbis; temporary classroom: Anders Ryman/Corbis; secret: Michael Prince/Corbis; building: Keren Su/Corbis; University of Cape Town: Louise Gubb/Corbis Saba.

Chapter 12: Jerusalem: Steven Allen/Istockphoto.com; baptism: Terry Healy/Istockphoto.com; Bar Mitzvah: Nancy Louie/Istockphoto.com; Buddhist: Robert Ahrens/Istockphoto.com; Muslim: Istockphoto.com.

Chapter 13: Pills: Andrzej Tokarski/Istockphoto.com; offerings: Macduff Everton/Corbis; Sudan: Silvia Morara/Corbis; makeshift hospital: Luis Enrique Ascui/Reuters/Corbis; open heart surgery: Tony Arruza/Corbis.

Chapter 14: Earth: NASA; satellite image of Europe: NASA.

Chapter 15: Constitution: Lara Solt/Dallas Morning News/Corbis; Gap protest: Najlah Feanny/Corbis Saba; Lebanese rally: Damir Sagolj/Reuters/Corbis; A Day Without Immigrants: Fred Greaves/Reuters/Corbis; Islam: Istockphoto.com.

Note: An *f* following a page number denotes a figure on that page; an *m* after a page number denotes a map on that page; a *t* following a page number denotes a table on that page.

Folkways, 80–81*t*

Foot binding, 300

Force-field analysis, 495

Formal agents Mechanisms by which the self learns the values, beliefs, and behaviors of the culture. Formal agents usually have some official or legal responsibility for instructing individuals; socialization is the stated goal. Families, school, teachers, and religious training are examples, 104, **110**, 112

Formal education Schooling that takes place in a formal setting with the goal of teaching a predetermined curriculum, 8, 11, 37, 104, **325**–326, 328–329, 344, 425

Formal organizations Modern rational organizations comprised of complex secondary groups deliberately formed to pursue and achieve certain goals, 125, **142**–143, 344, 414

Formal rules/regulations, in bureaucracy, 146

Formal sanctions Rewards or punishments conferred by recognized officials to enforce the most important norms, **81**–82, 162

Formal statuses, 135

Free choice marriage, 303–304

Front stage behavior, 132

Frustration-aggression theory, 233–234

Functional theory (structural-functional perspective) A theory that assumes that all parts of the social structure, culture, and social processes work together to make the whole society run smoothly and harmoniously, 87

    latent functions and, 50–51, 330–331

    manifest functions and, 51–52

    on deviance, 159, 167–172

    on dominant minority-group contact, 243–244

    on education, 328–331, 339

    on family, 297–299

    on health/illness, 403–404

    on religion, 382, 384–386

    on social change, 496

    on stratification, **49**–51, 196–197, 243–244, 276–277

Functions, 87, 297

Fundamentalism, religious, 151, 393–394

G-7, 509

G-8, 509, 510, 511*m*, 512, 514

G-77, 510, 511*m*

Gag rule, for birth control access, 449

Gaje (non-Gypsy), 369

Game stage In the process of developing a social self, the role-taking stage in which a child learns to take the role of multiple others concurrently, **102**

Gangs, in schools, 332

Geeks, 332

Gemeinschaft German term meaning "small traditional community," **461**

Gender digital divide, 274

Gender identity A society's notions of masculinity and femininity—socially constructed meanings associated with male or female—and how individuals construct their identity in terms of gender within these constraints, **258**, 264

Gender issues

    in education, 332–334, 335, 340, 341, 342, 354–355, 356

    in health/illness, 406

    one-child policy, 449

    social mobility, 204

Gender pattern as factor in health care, 409

Gender patterns as factor in health care, 409, 410*f*

Gender roles The rigidly assigned tasks or expected behaviors of individuals because of their sex category, 10, 13, 54, 94, 150, 170, 256, **258**–259, 264, 364, 391, 440

    in children's book, 266–267

    See also Gender stratification

Gender stratification

    at institutional level, 259–260

    at national/global level, 260–264

    at personal level, 259

    boy code and, 265

    changing stratification/policy considerations, 284–287

    childhood, gender socialization during, 264

    conflict theory on, 277

    corporation role in, 266–268*t*

    costs/consequences of, 282–284

    educational system role in, 269–270

    feminist theory on, 277–279

    gender differences in Internet use, 274

    gender identity/gender role/sexuality, differences among, 258–259

    gender/minority group status and, 280–282

    gendered organization role in, 272

    government positions and, 260, 261*m*, 262*t*–263*t*

    infancy, gender socialization during, 264

    institution role in, 272–274

    mass media role in, 268–269

    micro credits, effect on women empowerment, 261

    psychological/social consequences of, 283–284

    religious belief role in, 260, 270–272, 386

    socialization and, 264–272

    structural-functional theory on, 276–277

    symbolic interactionism on, 275–276

    theory on, 274–280

    See also Sex

Generalized others A composite of societal expectations, **102**–103

Genocide The systematic effort of a dominant group to destroy a minority group, 10, 71, 73, 155, 221, 239–**240**, 242, 247

Gentrification Refers to members of the middle and upper class, mostly young white professionals, buying and renovating rundown properties in central-city locations, 463, **468**–469, 470

Geographic mobility The process of changing the place of residence, **453**

Gerontology, 457

Gesellschaft German term meaning "large impersonal urban areas," **461**

Glass ceiling Barriers that keep females and other minority groups from reaching high levels of management in organizations, **147**, 272, 284

Glass escalator, 272

Global 8 (G-8), 509–510

Global crimes, 180–181

Global culture Behavioral standards symbols values and material objects that have become common across the globe, 59, **78**

Peer group, 141
People's Republic of China, health care in, 425–426
Peripheral country, 497–498
Permanent underclass, 474–475
Personal distance, 129
Personal space, 128–129
Physicians, 404, 406, 407, 414, 418–420
    per 1,000 people, 418m
Play stage   In the process of developing a social self, the role-taking stage that involves a kind of play-acting in which the child is actually "playing at" a role, **102**–103
Plea-bargain, 175
Pluralism   Occurs when each ethnic or racial group in a country maintains its own culture and separate set of institutions, 76, 240–**241**, 242, 373, 386, 388, 390, 393
Pluralist theory, 210–211
Political science, 13–14
Pollution, 486–487
Polyandry   A wife having more than one husband, 307, **308**
Polygamy, 307
Polygyny   A husband having more than one wife, **307**–308
Pop culture, 68
Population
    antinatalist policy, 449
    baby boom, 452, 456–457
    baby bust, 452, 456–457
    community needs services and, 459
    composition of, 447
    conflict theory, 446
    demographic transition theory, 444–446
    dependency ratio, 440
    distribution of, 447
    fertility rate factors, 446–451f
    growth effects, 437–438
    growth over time, 438–439f
    illegal immigration, 454–454
    institutional affects on change in, 447–460
    internal migration, 454, 455–456, 458–459
    international migration, 454–455
    Malthus's theory of population, 442–444
    micro-level population patterns, 456–460
    migration, 447, 453–456, 458–459
    mortality rates, 447, 451t, 453
    population momentum, 438
    predictors of growth, 439–442
    projected, urban/rural, 447f
    projected, U.S., 457f
    pronatalist policy, 449
    retirement issues, 437–438
    social change and, 488, 490
    World Population Clock, 436t
    world population growth patterns, 438–447
    world population growth rate, 439f
    See also **Urbanization**
Population pyramids   Pyramidal diagrams that illustrate sex ratios and dependency ratios, **441**–442f, 459
Population transfer   The removal often forced of a minority group from a region or country, 240–**241**

Populations   all permanent societies states communities adherents of a common religious faith, racial or ethnic groups, kinship or clan groups, professions, and other identifiable categories of people, **438**
Positive sanctions, 81, 112, 162
Postindustrial cities, 467–469
Postindustrial/information societies, 66–68
Postindustrial technology, 513
Poverty
    absolute, 212–213
    eliminating, 214–215
    family and, 309t–310
    feminization of, 213
    functions of, 215
    Growing Up Poor study, 213
    relative, 213
    worldwide, 474–475
Power elite, 210
Predatory/street crimes, 172–173
Predestination, 376
Preference policies, 249, 250–251
Preferred Provider Organization (PPO), 419, 422
Prejudice   Refers to attitudes that prejudge a group usually negatively and not based on facts, **231**
    See also **Discrimination**
Present-time orientation, 309–310
Primary deviance   A violation of a norm that may be an isolated act, **164**
Primary groups   Groups characterized by close contacts and lasting personal relationships, **139**, 140t–141
Prisons/jails, 182–188
    alternatives to, 186–188
    functions/effectiveness of, 183–186
    privatization of, 187
Private sphere, 277
Private *vs.* public schools, 353–354
Proactive social movements, 508
Probation, 186
Process of change *See* **Social change**
Process (social dynamics), 31
Progress *vs.* change, 483
Proletariat, 52, 496
Promise Keepers, 374
Props, 131
Protestantism, membership in, 388
Psychology, 13
Public distance, 129
Public issues, 10
Public order crimes (victimless crimes)   Acts committed by or between consenting adults, **173**
Public sphere, 277
Public *vs.* private schools, 353–354
Purdah, 271
Purposeful discrimination, 237
Push-pull theory, 453

Quackery, 430
Qualitative research, 39

Reproduction of class   Occurs when the socioeconomic positions of one generation pass on to the next generation, **331**

Resistance or regressive movements   These movements try to protect an existing system or part of a system when societal change is seen as a threat to values or practices. The goal of these movements is to either maintain the status quo or return to a former status by reversing the change process, **508**, 509–510

Resocialization   The process of shedding one or more positions and taking on others; it involves changing from established patterns learned earlier in life to new ones suitable to the newly acquired status, 106, **108**–109

Revolutionary movements   Attempt to transform society to bring about a total change in society by overthrowing existing power structures and replacing them with new ones. These movements often resort to violent means to achieve goals, **508**

Riots   An outbreak of enraged violence against random or shifting targets committed by individuals expressing frustration or anger against people, property, or both; often occur due to conditions such as deprivation or an unresponsive or unfair judicial system, 228, 246, 250, 465, 494, 498–**500**, 501f

Rituals   Group activities in which myths are reinforced with music, dancing, kneeling, praying, chanting, storytelling, and other symbolic acts, 68, 75, 260, 292, 301, 340, 365–366, **371**–373, 375, 384, 486

Role conflict   Conflict between the roles of two or more social statuses, **135**–136, 310

Role strain   Tension between roles within one of the social statuses, 135–137, 254, 336, 338

Role-taking   George Herbert Mead explained this process by which individuals take others into account by imagining themselves in the position of the other, 54, **99**, 102–103

Roles   The expected behaviors, rights, and obligations of a social status, **133**–135

Romantic love   Love based on romance and free choice of mates, 303–304

Rumors   A form of mass behavior in which unsupported or unproven reports about a problem, issue, or concern circulate widely throughout the public, 334, **500**–501, 502

Sample   In research involving a survey or field observation, a small or more manageable group of people, systematically chosen to represent a much larger group. The objective of sampling is to select a group that accurately represents the characteristics of the entire group (or population) being studied, 36, **40**–41, 306, 320, 350, 387, 389, 391

Sanctions   Reinforce norms through rewards and penalties, **81**, 114